ISBN 978-1-333-78085-2
PIBN 10312647

1 MONTH OF
FREE
READING

at
www.ForgottenBooks.com

By purchasing this book you are eligible for one month membership to ForgottenBooks.com, giving you unlimited access to our entire collection of over 700,000 titles via our web site and mobile apps.

To claim your free month visit:
www.forgottenbooks.com/free312647

Counties of England

EDITED BY WILLIAM PAGE, F.S.A.

A HISTORY OF

LANCASHIRE

VOLUME IV

THE

OF THE COUNTIES
OF ENGLAND

LANCASHIRE

CONSTABLE AND COMPANY LIMITED

This History is issued to Subscribers
By Constable '& Company
and printed by Eyre & Spottiswoode Limited
H.M. Printers   London

INSCRIBED
TO THE MEMORY OF
HER LATE MAJESTY
QUEEN VICTORIA
WHO GRACIOUSLY GAVE
THE TITLE TO AND
ACCEPTED THE
DEDICATION OF
THIS HISTORY

Old Dock and Custom House, Liverpool 1721

THE COUNTY OF

AN

EDITED BY

WILLIAM FARRER, D.Litt., and J. BROWNBILL, M.A.

VOLUME FOUR

LONDON

CONSTABLE AND COMPANY LIMITED

1911

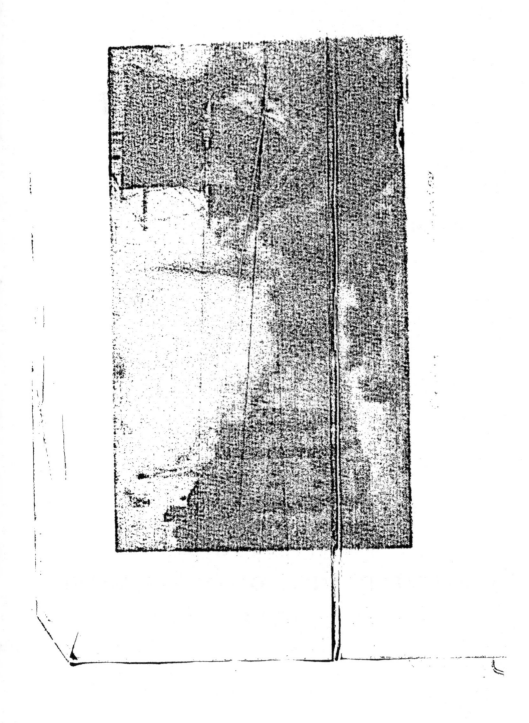

THE
VICTORIA HISTORY
OF THE COUNTY OF

EDITED BY

WILLIAM FARRER, D.Litt., and J. BROWNBILL, M.A.

VOLUME FOUR

CONSTABLE AND COMPANY LIMITED
1911

CONTENTS OF VOLUME FOUR

INDEX OF PARISHES, TOWNSHIPS, AND MANORS

In the following list (m) indicates manor, (p) parish, and (t) township

INDEX OF PARISHES, TOWNSHIPS, AND MANORS

288

LIST OF ILLUSTRATIONS

xiii

LIST OF ILLUSTRATIONS

LIST OF MAPS

xiv

EDITORIAL NOTE

THE Editors are desirous of expressing their thanks to Mr. C. W. Sutton, M.A., Mr. Ernest Axon, and Mr. H. T. Crofton, for their assistance with regard to the history of Manchester and in many other ways ; and in addition to those whose help has been acknowledged in previous volumes they desire to record their obligations to the following : The Earl of Wilton, the Earl of Ellesmere, Sir Humphrey de Trafford, bart., Mr. T. H. Davies-Colley, Mr. H. T. Folkard, F.S.A., Mr. S. Mills, Mr. J. J. Phelps, and the Town Clerks and Librarians of Eccles and Salford.

For the use of plans and for information regarding the architecture of the county, the Editors are indebted to the late Mr. Alfred Darbyshire, F.S.A., Mr. John Douglas, Mr. Harold Gibbons, Mr. A. Corbett and the Manchester Society of Architects, Mr. Frank Oakley, Mr. George Pearson, Mr. R. Basnett Preston, and Mr. Henry Taylor, F.S.A.

For the use of photographs for illustrations the Editors desire to express their obligations to Mr. Fletcher Moss, J.P., and Mr. James Watts for permission to reproduce those of Chetham's Hospital in Mr. Moss's 'Pilgrimages to Old Homes,' to Mr. A. E. H. Blackburn, and also to the Editor of the *Manchester City News* for the block of Platt Hall.

Owing to unforeseen circumstances the publication of this volume has been delayed, and although an attempt has been made to bring the information up to the date of finally going to press, it has been impossible to do so in every instance.

It should be noted that the class of documents at the British Museum here cited as 'Norris Deeds' has been re-named 'Aston Hall Charters.' The Towneley Manuscripts denominated G G and R R are in the British Museum ; C C is in the Chetham Library.

A HISTORY OF
LANCASHIRE

TOPOGRAPHY

THE HUNDRED OF WEST DERBY

(*Continuation*)

LIVERPOOL

Liuerpul (1207); Leuerepul (1229); Liuerpol (1266); Lyuerpole (1346); Leuerpoll (1393); Lytherpole (1445); Letherpole (1545); Litherpoole otherwise Liverpoole (1752). The form in *th* is found mainly in the 15th and 16th centuries.

The city of Liverpool extends for 6 miles along the eastern margin of the Mersey estuary, covering the western and part of the eastern slope of a ridge which runs from north to south, roughly parallel with the river, and varying in height from 100 ft. to 200 ft. In the southern part of the city this ridge rises by gradual stages from the water's edge ; in the northern part it is more abrupt, and stands back at some distance from the river, leaving a broad margin of comparatively flat ground. The modern city (1906) includes not only the ancient township of Liverpool, but also the townships of Kirkdale, Walton, part of Fazakerley, Everton, West Derby, Wavertree, the Toxteths and Garston, as well as Smeddon or Smithdown, the *Esmedun* of Domesday. These areas have been added by successive enlargements in 1835, 1894, and 1902. The continuous house-covered or urban area economically dependent upon Liverpool includes also the townships of Bootle, Litherland, and Great Crosby. The history of these townships is separately treated elsewhere in this work, and the original township of Liverpool is all that has to be considered here.

There are few cities whose modern development has more profoundly modified the original topographical features of its site. The water-line has been pushed out for a considerable distance by the erection of a continuous line of 6 miles of docks. The first of these docks, opened in 1715,[1] was made out of the mouth of a tidal creek re-entering from the estuary, the upper reaches of which were at the same time filled in. This creek, known as the Pool, curved inland in a north-easterly direction along the line of the modern Paradise Street, Whitechapel, and the Old Haymarket for a distance of nearly half a mile.[2] It was fed by two streamlets, one coming from Everton at the northern end of the ridge, while the other ran a more rapid course from a marshy expanse, called the Mosslake, which lay half-

[1] See below. [2] See map.
[3] The evidence for these and other topographical details is to be found mainly in the numerous local deeds of land-transfer preserved by the Moore and Crosse families. [4] See below.

Street to the west, and Dale Street and Moor Street to the east. All these streets are known to have existed in the 14th century,[5] and no others were added until the 17th.

The geography of the fields of early Liverpool forms a very obscure and difficult subject. The chief authorities for them are the numerous deeds of transfer of lands from the 13th century onwards, which were preserved in the muniments of the Moore and Crosse families ; but it has not yet been possible to construct a detailed map of the mediaeval field system. Many field-names are given in the deeds, the chief being the Old Fields (Great and Little), the Heathy Lands (Nether and Over), the Brecks, the Dalefield, the Wallfield, the Milnefield, the Sheriffacres, the Castle field, the Whiteacres, the Wetearth.[6] Some of these doubtless represent approvements from the waste ; but only one of these approvements can be definitely dated. This was the Salthouse Moor, of which 45 acres were inclosed between 1296 and 1323,[7] and 19 more between 1327 and 1346.[8] The Salthouse Moor probably lay at the north-west of the township by the Mersey shore, but it is not possible to be certain.[9]

Next to nothing is known of LIVER-MANOR POOL before the creation of the borough in 1207. In Domesday it is almost certainly one of the six unnamed berewicks attached to the manor of West Derby.[10] What degree of dependence upon the parent manor was involved in the berewick period cannot be determined ; but probably the Liverpool tenants did suit at the West Derby balmote, as the tenants of the other berewicks long continued to do.[11] At some date between 1166 and 1189 Liverpool was granted by Henry II to Warine de Lancaster, along with other lands, and this may have involved separation from West Derby and the institution of a distinct court. The deed of grant does not survive, but is referred to in an undated confirmation[12] granted to Henry son of Warine by John Count of Mortain, after his succession to the honour. But Liverpool was not long permitted to remain in the hands of a mesne lord. On 23 August 1207 John reacquired it,[13] giving the township of English Lea near Preston in exchange. Five days later the so-called 'charter'[14] was issued which turned the vill into a borough. Henceforward the descent of the lordship of the borough follows the descent of the honour of which it formed a part ; except during the brief interval, 1315–22, when it was held by Robert de Holand under grant from Thomas Earl of Lancaster.[15]

BOROUGH Liverpool is distinguished from most other boroughs by the fact that it owes its foundation absolutely to an exercise of the royal will ; there is no evidence that the place was a centre of any trade before the date when John fixed upon its sheltered Pool as a convenient place of embarkation for men and supplies from his Lancashire lands for his Irish campaigns. He may have visited the place in February 1206, on the way from Lancaster to Chester ;[16] and probably the creation of the borough should be regarded as part of the preparation for the great expedition of 1209. Some part of the new population which was necessary may have been found by a transplantation from West Derby, which is described in 1208 as having been remota usque ad Liverpul ;[17] others doubtless came in response to the 'charter,' which may more accurately be described as a proclamation of invitation ; and the original tenants of the township appear all to have been enfranchised. For the reception of the new population John had set apart a number of burgages facing on the seven main streets of the borough. The number of the original burgages it is impossible to determine. There were 168 in 1296,[18] and thereafter the number remained fixed. But it is probable that there were fewer to begin with. Nor is it possible to be precise about the area of the burgage proper, i.e. the building lot. It was big enough to be divisible into minute fractions, as small as $\frac{1}{34}$ or $\frac{1}{48}$.[19] Probably each burgage was a selion. In 1346 the commonest holding was half a burgage, and it is likely that the burgages were divisible from the outset. At the same date large holdings are found of 2, 3, 4, 5, and even 8 burgages. To each burgage proper was attached one Cheshire acre in the town-fields, usually consisting of two strips in different fields.[20] The rent for burgage and field-holdings together was 12d. per annum,[21] payable half-yearly, a figure which suggests the influence of Norman parallels. Or, rather, it would be more accurate to say that the rent was chargeable for the burgage, but 'acquitted' also the corre-

LIVERPOOL. *Argent a cormorant sable beaked and legged gules holding in his beak a branch of seaweed called laver inverted vert.*

---

[5] Moore and Crosse deeds, passim.

[6] The positions of these lands (in some cases conjectural) are indicated in the map. The names of most frequent occurrence are the Oldfields, the Heathy Lands, and the Dalefield, and it is probably in these that we should look for the original town-fields. It may be conjectured that the Dalefield formed originally a part of the Little Oldfield, which, lying round the village, was naturally broken up by the streets ; that the two Oldfields thus reconstructed formed the lands of the township on a two-field system before the constitution of the borough ; and that the Heathy Lands (as the name itself suggests) were an approvement from the waste on the north between Liverpool and Kirkdale, made at an early date, probably to meet the requirements of the new population whom King John

introduced at the creation of the borough. Other field-names may represent either the original demesne (e.g. Castlefield), or distinct portions of the older fields (e.g. Milnefield, part of one of the Oldfields), or more recent approvements (e.g. Wetearth).

[7] See Muir in *Trans. Hist. Soc.* (new ser.) xxi, 16, 17. Cf. *Inq. p.m.* 25 Edw. I, no. 51, with L.T.R. Enr. Accts. Misc. 14, m. 76 d.

[8] Ibid. and Add. MS. 32103, fol. 140.

[9] The name seems to have been an official one, not popularly adopted, for it does not appear in the Moore or Crosse deeds.

[10] *V.C.H. Lancs.* i, 283.

[11] See *Lancs. Ct. R.* (Rec. Soc. of Lancs. and Ches. xli), passim.

[12] Original at Hoghton Tower. Printed in Farrer, *Lancs. Pipe R.* 432.

[13] *Chart. R.* (Rec. Com.), 171b. In the Charter Rolls the date is given as Aug. xxviii ; but this is a mistake for xxiii. The deed is dated from Worcester, where John was on the 23rd (Itin. of John) ; on the 28th he was at Winchester.

[14] Orig. in Liv. Munic. Archives. Printed in *Hist. Munic. Govt. in Liv.* 153.

[15] *Inq. p.m.* 1 Edw. III, m. 88.

[16] Itin. of John prefixed to Pipe R. of John.

[17] Pipe R. of 1207–9 in *Lancs. Pipe R.* 220, 228, 234 ; where an allowance of £9 8s. is made to the sheriff 'in defalta de West Derbei quae est remota usque ad Liverpul, per breve Regis.'

[18] *Inq. p.m.* 25 Edw. I, no. 51.

[19] Moore and Crosse deeds. Also Add. MS. 32103 (extent of 1346).

[20] Moore deeds, passim.

[21] Add. MS. 32103.

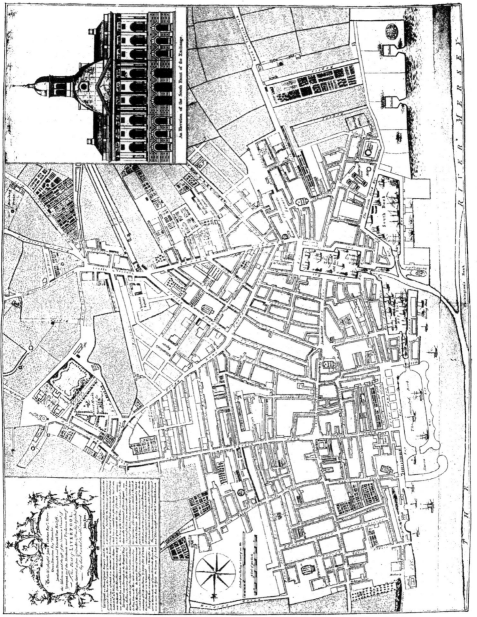

An Elevation of the South Front of the Exchange.

RIVER MERSEY

PLAN OF LIVERPOOL, 1765

sponding holdings in the fields ; for, as the Moore and Crosse deeds abundantly show, these could be separately sold or let by the tenant, still being 'acquitted' so far as the lord was concerned by the burgage to which they were originally attached. The 12d. rent, together with suit at the borough court, constituted the whole of the 'service' due from the tenants.[22] There is no evidence for the payment of a heriot, such as was exacted in Salford.[23]

The privileges which John promised to the occupants of the burgages are included under the general phrase 'all the liberties and free customs which any free borough on the sea has in our land.' This, if taken literally, would place Liverpool from the outset at the same level of burghal liberties as Bristol and Southampton ; but probably nothing of the sort was intended,[24] and the phrase is to be taken merely as securing to the burgesses personal liberty, freedom from service, free tenure of land, and exemption from the payment of tolls within the limits of the borough, though seemingly not beyond them. The grants of John are essentially promises to individuals, not formal concessions of powers to an organized community. During the next twenty-two years the borough was doubtless governed by a royal bailiff or steward, and the burgesses were represented, as in the rural period, by a reeve.[25] Probably, however, 1207 saw also the establishment of a weekly market and an annual fair, the erection of a mill,[26] and perhaps of a chapel.[27]

The gradual progress of the new borough is best illustrated by the history of its yield to the royal exchequer. From 1211 to 1219 the profits of Liverpool seem to have been included in those of West Derby, from which it may be inferred that the borough was administered in these years by the steward of the neighbouring manor. In 1222 and the following years[28] an assized rent of £9 was charged on the borough, being answered for by William de Ferrers as sheriff of Lancaster. How much was covered by this rent it is not easy to determine,[29] but if it included mills, ferry, and courts as well as the burgage rents the borough must have been poor enough, or the sheriff have made a substantial profit. Possibly the burgesses may themselves have paid the assized rent, but more probably the borough was farmed for this sum by the sheriff. The tallages assessed on the borough during the early years of Henry III show, however, a steady advance. In 1219[30] Liverpool paid half a mark, West Derby a mark, Preston 10

marks. In 1222[31] Liverpool paid 5 marks, West Derby 1 mark, Preston 15 marks. In 1227[32] Liverpool paid 11 marks 7s. 8d., West Derby 7 marks 4s. 4d., Preston 15 marks 6d. In these years the parent manor of West Derby had been completely outstripped, while the new borough was rapidly overtaking Preston.

A very important step forward was taken when on 24 March 1229 Henry III granted a charter[33] to Liverpool, the burgesses paying for it 10 marks. The payment shows that they had learnt to take common action ; perhaps they had formed an illicit gild. The charter of Henry III is of the first importance, as it remained the governing charter of the borough down to 1626, all the intervening charters being merely confirmations with or without modifications. The charter is on the most ample scale. It opens by conceding that Liverpool should be a free borough (*liber burgus*), for ever ; but this, though it secured, probably did not extend the privileges already conferred by John. In the second place it grants independent jurisdiction to the borough court in the regular formula of sac and soc, thol and theam, and infangenethef, and exempts the burgesses from suit at shire and hundred-courts for their holdings in the borough. In regard to trade, the exemption from tolls in the Liverpool market granted by King John was now extended to all markets within the king's dominions, and the Liverpool traders were thus placed on a level with the burgesses of the most favoured boroughs. But the most important concession of the charter was the right to have 'a gild merchant with a hansa and all the liberties and free customs pertaining to that gild' ; the privileges of trade, previously confined to holders of burgages, being now limited to members of the gild, while in future no one might be permitted to trade in the borough without licence of the gild. No evidence whatsoever survives as to the mode of organization of the gild thus granted, or its relation to the ordinary governmental machinery of the borough. Doubtless all holders of burgages were entitled to membership.[34]

During the first century of the borough's existence it is as difficult to say anything definite about the borough government as about the gild. With regard to officers, in 1246 the 'vill' was represented at the eyre of the justices by twelve jurors, including 'Ranulf de Moore, *reeve* of the vill,'[35] but this seems to be the only mention of a reeve ; probably he was

[22] Add. MS. 32103 ; Reg. St. Werburgh Hall MS. 1965, fol. xviiib.

[23] For discussion of this, see *Hist. Munic. Govt. in Liv.* 13 n. 3.

[24] Ibid. 15-17.

[25] A reeve is mentioned in 1246 ; Assize R. 1404, m. 16.

[26] The mills certainly existed from 1256, and probably from 1229.

[27] The small chapel of St. Mary del Key was in existence before 1257 ; see below.

[28] Pipe R. 10 Hen. III ; *Hist. Munic. Govt. in Liv.* 295.

[29] *Trans. Hist. Soc.* (new ser.), xxi, 6, 7.

[30] Pipe R. 3 Hen. III, m. 12 d.

[31] Ibid. 6 Hen. III, m. 5 d.

[32] Ibid. 11 Hen. III, m. 1.

[33] Orig. in Liv. Munic. Archives ; Chart. R. 13 Hen. III, m. 9 ; *Hist. Munic. Govt. in Liv.* 155.

[34] In the 16th century it had become the practice to admit to the freedom of the gild all sons and apprentices of free-

men (Munic. Rec. *passim*) on payment of a small fixed fee, whether they held burgages or not ; and as early as 1525 non-resident merchants were admitted in large numbers ; Duchy of Lanc. Misc. vol. 95, fol. 36b ; *Hist. Munic. Govt. in Liv.* 402. Whether or no this practice existed from the beginning it is impossible to say ; but in any case the grant of gild-powers rendered possible the admission to trading privileges of persons other than burgage holders, and thus prevented the limitation of these privileges to a narrow landholding oligarchy. But the non-burgess members of the gild, in so small a borough, must always have been few ; and there can have been little distinction between the burgess body proper and the gild. Hence it is probable that, as in other cases (Gross, *Gild Merchant*, i, chap. v.), a single assembly and a single set of officers served for both.

There is, indeed, throughout the Middle

replaced by a bailiff. In 1292 [36] the burgesses asserted that they 'had been accustomed to have' a bailiff 'of themselves,' i.e. elected by themselves; numerous local deeds,[37] the earliest dating from 1309, show, however, that there were two bailiffs. The probability is that the burgesses normally elected one, and that the lord appointed the other to look after his dues. When the burgesses held the farm of the town they may have elected both bailiffs. In the only roll [38] of the borough court [38] of Liverpool which survives from the mediaeval period, the lord's steward presides; but this may be because the burgesses did not then hold the farm of the town.[39]

The great advance marked by the charter of Henry III was completed by the concession to the burgesses on the following day, 25 March 1229, of a lease of the farm of the borough [40] at a rent of £10. The lease is in the most general terms, but it is clear from the items included in the same rent in 1256 [41] that it comprised the burgage rents, the market tolls, and the profits of two water-mills and a windmill.[42] If at this date the burgages at all approximated to their ultimate number of 168 the burgesses must have made a substantial profit on this lease. But the lease was only for four years, expiring in 1233. While it lasted, the lease freed the burgesses from the intervention of royal agents.

The burghal system of Liverpool had no sooner been completed by these deeds than the borough passed from royal to baronial control, as a result of the grant of the borough, along with the rest of the Lancashire lands of the Crown, to Ranulf, Earl of Chester.[43] During Ranulf's occupancy, which lasted for three years only, and that of the three Ferrers, Earls of Derby, whose tenure extended (with the interval of the minority of Robert de Ferrers, 1254–62 (?)) until 1266, the material for the history of the borough is singularly scanty. But the Ferrers family appear to have respected the burghal liberties, and to have renewed the lease of the farm (which fell in

in 1233) regularly at the same rental throughout the period of their control.[44] In 1266, just before his last rebellion and confiscation, Robert de Ferrers confirmed the charters [45] of Liverpool; probably as a means of raising money.

The most important event of the period *CASTLE* was the erection of the Liverpool Castle, which had taken place before 1235 and may safely be attributed to the first William de Ferrers.[46] There had long been a castle at West Derby; it was in ruins in 1296,[47] but it had been in existence in 1232,[48] when the first Ferrers took possession; when his son succeeded him, Liverpool Castle had been built; [49] probably the one was intended to take the place of the other. No record of its erection survives, nor any account of the fabric before a late date. It was demolished in 1720, and no satisfactory views or plans of it survive.[50] It stood at the top of the modern Lord Street;

FERRERS, Earl of Derby. *Vairy or and gules.*

that is, on the highest point of land in the town, immediately overlooking the entrance to the Pool. Occupying an artificially created plateau, almost exactly 50 yds. square, it was surrounded by a moat some 20 yds. wide, cut out of the solid rock.[51] The main fabric consisted of (1) a great gatehouse surmounted by two small towers, which stood at the north-eastern corner, and looked down Castle Street; (2) three circular towers at the three other corners; one of these, probably that at the south-east corner, was built later than the rest of the fabric, in 1442; the south-western tower seems to have been regarded as the keep of the fortress; (3) curtain walls connected the four main towers; on the eastern side the wall rose from the edge of the rock-plateau; on the north and

[36] *Plac. de Quo War.* (Rec. Com.), 381.

[37] Moore D. *passim.*

[38] Roll of 1324; *Lanc. Ct. R.* (Rec. Soc. xli), 77–88.

[39] As to lesser burghal officers there is no evidence before the 16th century, when we get the titles (*Munic. Rec.* i, 2a) of a hayward, two burleymen, two moss-reeves, two ale-founders, all of whom must have had mediaeval predecessors; and two water-bailiffs, four merchant prysors, and two leve-lookers, who were probably officials required by the gild powers obtained under the charter of Henry III (Gross, *Gild Merchant*); the 16th century also shows us in existence a body of jurats like those of Leicester (Bateson, *Rec. Leic.*), Ipswich (Little Domesday of Ipswich), and other towns. They numbered twelve or twenty-four, and made regulations for the better government of the town, besides making presentments in the portmoot. Their decrees were at that date disregarded, but they were considered to be the representatives of an institution which had once been powerful (Picton, *Liv. Munic. Rec.* i, 52). It is likely, therefore, that in mediaeval Liverpool, as in Leicester, Ipswich, 'and all the other boroughs of England' (Little Domesday of Ipswich), there was a standing body of jurats who exercised a general control over the adminis-

tration carried on by the bailiff and other elected officers.

In the 16th century all the officers were elected at an assembly of all freemen held on St. Luke's Day, 18 October. Other assemblies were summoned for special business as occasion required. There were also two solemn courts, or portmoots, in each year; the great port-moot being held a few days after the electoral assembly. In the mediaeval period the only general bodies of which there is mention (Add. MS. 32103; Court Roll of 1324, *Lanc. Ct. R.* 77–88) were two great courts, corresponding to the portmoots of the 16th century, at which all burgesses were bound to be present, and a lesser court held theoretically every three weeks, but in practice at irregular intervals. Thus in 1324 twelve courts were held, at intervals varying from a week to three months.

It is likely that the 16th century differentiation between the portmoots for legal business and the assemblies for general business did not exist in the early days of the borough; but that the single governing organ of the borough was the portmoot, at which all burgesses were entitled to be present, and, on two solemn occasions a year, required to be present. For a fuller discussion of the burghal constitution under the charter of Hen. III see *Hist. Munic. Govt. in Liv.* 20–36.

[40] *Pat.* 13 Hen. III, m. 9; *Hist. Munic. Govt. in Liv.* 296.

[41] *Trans. Hist. Soc.* (new ser.), xxi, 8.

[42] On the history of the mills and milling soke of Liverpool, see Bennett and Elton, *Hist. of Corn-milling,* iv, chap. iv, where the facts are fully marshalled.

[43] *Cal. Close,* 1227–31, p. 221; Chart. R. 13 Hen. III, pt. i, m. 2.

[44] This is a fair inference from the fact that in 1256, during the minority of Robert and the occupancy of his lands by the king's son Edward, Edward's bailiff renders account for the farm of the vill of Liverpool at the old rent; Duchy of Lanc. Mins. Accts. bdle. 1094, no. 11; *Hist. Munic. Govt. in Liv.* 39, 296.

[45] *Hist. Munic. Govt.* 156. Original in Liv. Munic. Archives.

[46] *Cal. Pat.* 1232–47, p. 89.

[47] *Inq. p.m.* 25 Edw. I, no. 51.

[48] *Cal. Close,* 1231–4, p. 169.

[49] *Fine Roll,* 32 Hen. III, pt. i, m. 14.

[50] The best discussion and reconstruction of the castle is by E. W. Cox, *Trans. Hist. Soc.* (new ser.), vi.

[51] Mr. Cox has been followed in inferring these main features of the castle from (1) the Extent of 1346; (2) detailed instructions for repairs in 1476 (Duchy of Lanc. Bk. of Orders, etc. Edw. IV, fol. 140); (3) report of commissioners on demolition of the castle, 1706, Okill MSS. iv, 337.

LIVERPOOL : OLD HAYMARKET, 1850

(From a Water-colour Drawing)

south it was recessed so as to be commanded from the towers ; on the west it formed an obtuse angle, the angle touching the edge of the rock ; (4) the hall and a chapel probably lay respectively along the western and southern walls, and were connected with the south-western tower ; (5) there were also a brew-house and a bakehouse, the sites of which cannot be determined ; they may have been in the north-west angle, near which a postern gate led to an under-ground passage from the moat to the edge of the river.[51] The courtyard seems to have been divided by a wall running from north to south. A survey of 2 October 1559[51a] gives further interesting details of the building. It was at the time 'in utter ruin and decay,' there having been no lead on any of the buildings within the memory of man. The great tower, probably that at the south-west, had a slated roof, and the commissioners suggested that it should be repaired and used for the keeping of the 'Quenes Majesties Courtes for Her Graces Wappentacke of West Derbyshyre, being a very greate soken,' and for the storage of the court rolls. The 'ringe walle' or curtain and the masonry of the towers seem to have been fairly sound, and only needed protection from the weather, and the com-missioners strongly advised the putting of the castle into substantial repair at a cost of about £100, ' otherwaies it were a grate defacement unto the said towne of Litherpole.' No mention is made of any moat in the report, and there is some tradition that none existed till the Civil Wars, but no proof of this is obtainable.

There was a dovecot under the castle wall, and an orchard ran down the slope to the Pool on the east. Out of this orchard Lord Street was cut in the 17th century. Thus the first period of baronial suzerainty had resulted in the overawing of the burgesses by a formidable fortress.

On the rebellion and forfeiture of Robert de Ferrers Liverpool, with other possessions between Ribble and Mersey, passed to the hands of the Crown. Henry III at once granted them with the honour of Lancaster to his second son, Edmund ; to whose representatives Mary de Ferrers, wife of the forfeited earl and niece of the king, was ordered to surrender the castle of Liverpool in July 1266.[53] This begins the second part of the baronial period of Liverpool history, extending over the earldoms of Edmund and Thomas of Lancaster, 1266–1322. Both of these earls seem to have treated the borough with some harshness. In the first place the lease of the farm was not renewed. Earl Edmund took the administration of the town into his own hands,[54] or at least broke up the farm into several parts ; and the total yield under the new system in place of the old rent of £10 amounted to £25 10s. in the latter years of Earl Edmund and about £30 by the end of

the reign of Earl Thomas ; the tolls of market and fair alone brought in as much as the old rent ; but there seems reason for believing that a farm of these tolls was held by the burgesses.[55]

The greatly increased yield of the town affords evidence, however, that the earl was doing his best to develop its resources, and the beginning of a period of prosperity may perhaps be attributed to this time. In addition to the suppression of the lease of the farm, Edmund overrode the chartered rights of the burgesses. In 1292 the bailiffs and community of Liverpool were summoned on a quo warranto[56] plea to Lancaster. No bailiffs came ; but several men came for the com-munity, and, producing the charters of John and Henry III, stated that they had been a free borough with a gild, &c. ; but that Earl Edmund suffered them not to have a free borough, or to elect a bailiff ' of themselves ' ; wherefore they did not claim these liberties at present. The further hearing of the case was adjourned, but there is no record of the decision. Whatever the decision, the burgesses did not regain their rights till the beginning of the reign of Edward III.

During this period the growing importance of the town (or the power of its masters) is recognized in the summons of burgesses from Liverpool to the Parliament of 1295, and again to that of 1307.[57] The first Liverpool members of Parliament were Adam son of Richard, and Robert Pinklowe. After 1307 the borough did not again return members to Westminster until the middle of the 16th century.

During the earldom of Thomas of Lancaster the steady progress of Liverpool appears to have continued. It is to this period that we must attribute the inclosure of Salthouse Moor, of which no mention is made in 1296, but which was in occupation and yielding rent in 1322.[58] This is the only large approvement from the waste of which there is any trace, before the 17th century. The area first in-closed amounted to 45 acres ; which were in 1346[59] divided among 51 free tenants and 47 tenants-at-will, and in 1322–7 yielded 40s. of rent. Most of the tenants in these new lands already held burgages in the borough, but 32 of them were not included in the burgess roll, and this involved that they were a new class of tenants, not sharing in the liberties, but directly under the control of the lord. He could hold a distinct court for them if he wished ; and though this does not seem to have been done at this period, that was only because the lord's steward was presiding over the borough-court. At a later date questions of the first

THOMAS, Earl of Lan-caster. ENGLAND with a label of FRANCE.

[51] A rock-cut passage still runs under James Street, from somewhere near the position of the castle, towards the river. It was entered and examined in May 1862 by Mr. P. M. Coogan (Rep. in vol. 2, p. 132 of the Misc. Rep. in the City En-gineer's Office), and a plan and sections were made, showing that it varied in height and width, averaging about 8 ft. in height, and has in its floor on the south side a channel, which, when lately sounded on the suggestion of Mr. Robert Glad-stone, junr., has proved to be as much as

7 ft. 6 in. deep. It was again examined by the city engineer in 1908, and a new plan made. That it had some connexion with the ditch of the castle seems pos-sible, and its depth is said to be sufficient to allow the river water to reach the ditch at high water.

[51a] Duchy of Lanc. Special Commis-sions, no. 9.

[52] Pat. 50 Hen. III.

[53] Inq. p.m. 25 Edw. I, no. 51 ; L.T.R. Enr. Accts. Misc. no. 14, m. 77. Perhaps this may have been the result of

his visit to Liverpool in 1283 ; Whalley Coucher, 507.

[55] Trans. Hist. Soc. (new ser.), xxi, 11.

[56] Plac. de Quo War. (Rec. Com.), 381b. ; Hist. Munic. Govt. in Liv. 41, and 397.

[57] Parl. Writs, i, 39 (18).

[58] L. T. R. Enr. Accts. Misc. no. 14, m. 77.

[59] Extent of 1346, Add. MS. 32103, to which a full list of burgesses and tenants in Salthouse Moor is appended.

importance were to arise from the existence of this group of tenants.

This was not the only new use made of the waste by Thomas of Lancaster. In the year 1310, on a visit to the borough, the earl granted to the burgesses[60] 6 Cheshire acres of moss 'adjoining the mill-pool of the vill of Liverpool' at a rental of one silver penny per annum. This was in exchange for the right which they had previously possessed of digging peat in Toxteth Park. Important as being the first piece of corporate property owned by the burgesses, this patch of moss lay at the upper end and on the eastern side of the Pool, and formed part of the Mosslake. The rent of it appears among the revenues of the town during the remainder of the 14th century; in the 15th it disappeared, being merged in that general control over the whole of the waste which the burgesses of that period quietly usurped. But in spite of this gift the earl does not seem to have attached much value to the borough, for in 1315 he granted both castle and borough to Robert de Holand. But no charter was sealed, nor did the tenants do homage;[61] in consequence of which Holand's son, after the death of Thomas of Lancaster, failed to obtain restitution of the estate, though he petitioned Parliament and obtained a favourable report from the treasurer and the barons of the exchequer.[62]

The confusion produced by the turbulence of Thomas of Lancaster and the weak government of Edward II was felt at Liverpool as elsewhere. In 1315 Adam Banastre, Henry de Lea, and William de Bradshagh raised a rebellion against the earl; and marching from their rendezvous at Charnock by way of Wigan, under the standard of Adam Banastre, made an assault upon Liverpool Castle.[63] They were driven back, and then fell upon West Derby. This is the only occasion on which the castle is known to have been attacked before the Civil War.

On the attainder and execution of Thomes of Lancaster royal agents reappeared in the borough. The very full accounts[64] which they rendered from 1322 to 1327 supply some of the most valuable material for ascertaining the condition of the town; and it is to this time that the single court roll for the mediaeval period —that for the year 1324—belongs. In 1323 King Edward II himself visited Liverpool, staying for a week in the castle between 24 and 30 October. In preparation for him the castle was thoroughly repaired and victualled;[65] and the sum of 1s. 8d. in particular was expended in mending the roof of the hall.[66] During the last troubled years of Edward II, the bailiffs of Liverpool were kept busy carrying out feverish orders: such as to hold ready for the king's service all ships of sufficient burthen to carry 40 tuns of wine, to make returns of such ships, to warn mariners to beware of pirates,[67] to proclaim kindly usage for Flemings.[68] When, in 1326, the situation became really critical, the bailiffs were ordered to send all ships of 50 tons and upwards to Portsmouth;[69] to search all persons entering or leaving the port, and to

seize letters prejudicial to the king;[70] and to prevent the export of horses, armour, or money.[71] So, amid feverish feeble strife, the reign of Edward II came to an end. With it ended an epoch for Liverpool. The century from 1229 to 1327 had seen a serious diminution of burghal liberties, but it had also witnessed a substantial expansion of the borough's resources. In the next age this expansion continues, and is accompanied by a remarkable revival of the privileges of the burgesses, which attained their highest point at the end of the century.

The disorders which had marked the later years of Edward II continued to disturb Liverpool in the early years of his successor, and their echoes are audible in the trials of the period of which record remains. In 1332 Robert son of Thomas de Hale slew Henry de Walton at Liverpool, in the church before the altar; a few days later Simon son of William de Walton struck and wounded Henry Ithell, and on the next day his brother Richard struck and wounded Robert the Harper.[72] In 1335 Sir William Blount, sheriff of the county, was murdered in Liverpool while engaged in the execution of his office,[73] and four years later five men, in consideration of their having 'gone beyond the seas' in the king's service,[74] were pardoned for this crime and also for the murder of Henry Baret and Roger Wildgoose. As late as St. Valentine's Day 1345 there was a serious disturbance of the peace in Liverpool:[75] a body of lawless men having entered the town in arms, with banners unfurled as in war, forced their way into the court where the king's justices were in session, and after hurling 'insulting and contumacious words,' 'did wickedly kill, mutilate, and plunder of their goods, and wound very many persons there assembled, and further did prevent the justices from showing justice . . . according to the tenour of their commission.' Three weeks later special justices were appointed to deal with the offenders, and in July a large number of persons, many of them being men of position in the county, were pardoned at the request of the Earl of Lancaster, on condition that they went at their own charges for one year to do service to the king in Gascony.

A condition of society such as is indicated by these events could scarcely be favourable to the growth of peaceful trade; nevertheless, the growth of Liverpool continued. In 1338 the earl appears to have made an addition to the approved lands in Salthouse Moor, and enfeoffed a number of tenants at fines of 5 marks to the acre;[76] and the details of the assessment for the levy of a ninth in 1340 show a number of substantial persons to have been resident in the town.[77] We now obtain the first clear indications of the extent and nature of the trade of the town, of which something will be said later; it would appear that Liverpool had become one of the most considerable ports of the west coast. As such, during the Scottish wars of the early years of Edward III, and during the Irish wars of the later years of his reign, it proved very useful as

[60] Original in Liv. Munic. Archives.
[61] Inq. p.m. 1 Edw. III, m. 88. The manor of West Derby was granted to Holand 3 Feb. 1320. The charter was inspected and the grant confirmed by the king 22 Feb. 1320. Cal. Pat. 1317-21, p. 431.
[62] Rot. Parl. ii, 18.
[63] Coram Rege R. 254, m. 52.

[64] L.T.R. Enr. Accts. Misc. no. 14.
[65] The walls, towers, houses, and gates of the castle were ordered to be repaired and the castle victualled 7 Feb. 1323. Cal. Close, 1318-23, p. 627.
[66] L.T.R. Enr. Accts. loc. cit.
[67] Cal. Close, 1323-7, p. 183.
[68] Ibid. pp. 367, 378.
[69] Ibid. p. 641.

[70] Ibid. p. 537.   [71] Ibid. p. 546.
[72] Assize R. no. 1411, m. 2.
[73] Cal. Pat. 1334-8, p. 580.
[74] Ibid. 1338-40, pp. 217, 229, 232, 235.
[75] Ibid. 1343-5, pp. 495-9; Coram Rege R. 344, m. 8.
[76] Add. MS. 32105, GG. 2901.
[77] Exch. Lay Subs. bdle. 130, no. 15.

a port of embarkation ; and it is probably to the attention thus directed to it that we must attribute the revival of the town's political fortunes.

In 1327 the constable of Liverpool Castle was ordered [78] to receive within the castle men fleeing from the invading Scots. Next year the bailiffs of Liverpool were ordered to have all vessels in the port of 40 tons burthen in readiness to resist the king's enemies from Normandy and Poitou. [79] In 1333 the bailiffs were commanded to retain all vessels of burthen sufficient for 50 tuns of wine, and to prepare them hastily with double equipment for the defence of the kingdom against the Scots, [80] and the mandate was repeated in the next year, a royal commissioner being told off to supervise the preparations. [81] In 1335 a clerk of the Exchequer was told off to provide two ships of war fully manned and armed, to sail from Liverpool in pursuit of a great ship loaded with wine and arms, coming from abroad, and destined for the aid of the king's enemies in the castle of Dumbarton. [82] These ships seem also to have been used to carry supplies for the royal army to Skymburnesse, at the mouth of the Solway. [83] In the same year six of the largest ships to be found on the west coast between Liverpool and Skymburnesse were ordered to be manned and armed and sent against the Scottish ships. [84]

In the French wars of the middle part of the reign Liverpool naturally took less share ; [85] but the insecurity of English waters which marked the first part of the war is indicated by the receipt of an order to the Liverpool bailiffs not to permit vessels to leave the port for foreign parts save in great fleets and under escort, [86] while on more than one occasion Liverpool ships were summoned to southern ports to help in dealing with threatened French attacks. [87]

In the later part of the reign of Edward III, and during the reigns of Richard II and Henry IV, Liverpool was still more actively engaged in connexion with the Irish than she had been at the commencement of the period with the Scottish wars. In 1361 'the whole navy of the land, competently armed,' was brought to transport Lionel of Clarence and his army to Ireland from Liverpool and Chester ; [88] in 1372 all ships between 20 tons and 200 tons burthen between Bristol and Liverpool were ordered to be collected at Liverpool for the transport [89] of William de Windsor, 'governor . . . of our realm of Ireland, and of the men at arms and others about to depart in our service in the retinue of the said William.' In the next year all ships between Southampton and Furness were ordered to be brought to Liverpool for a similar purpose. [90] The port was constantly utilized for the embarkation of troops, and the Patent Rolls contain frequent notices of the assemblage of

ships and considerable forces of men in the town on the way to Ireland. [91]

This frequent use of the port for royal purposes, which doubtless brought with it an expansion of trade to both Scotland and Ireland, is beyond question the main reason for the favour now shown to Liverpool both by the king and by the earl. [92] The first sign of this is the grant of the right to collect certain dues for paving the town, first made in 1328 for a period of three years, and renewed several times during the century. [93] The collection of these dues and the spending of them represent a new kind of corporate action on the part of the burgesses, and therefore mark a stage in the development of municipal government. The money does not seem always to have been used for the purpose for which the grant was made, for in 1341 a commission of investigation had to be sent to Liverpool, as the king was informed that much of the money collected had been misappropriated. [94] In 1333 a still more valuable favour was received from the king in the grant of a new charter. [95] The charter contains no new grant, being merely a confirmation of its predecessors. But we have seen that such a confirmation was highly necessary, and we may assume that from this date the free exercise of chartered liberties, prevented since the accession of Edmund of Lancaster, recommenced.

Still more important than the charter, the lease of the farm of the borough is gradually regained during this period. [96] At the beginning of the reign of Edward III the burgesses seem to have held a lease only of the tolls of the market and fair. [97] The first great advance is marked by the extent of the lands of the second Henry of Lancaster, made in 1346 after his succession to the earldom. In this deed there is a combined farm of the mills, tolls, and ferry for £24 per annum, which has been held for some years by an unnamed farmer, almost certainly representing the burgesses, and which is henceforward to be raised to £26. [98] In 1357 there comes a highly important new lease of the farm, [99] at a rent of £33, which was granted to eight leading burgesses on behalf of the community. This lease included the burgage rents and the profits of courts, in addition to the rights covered by the previous lease. [100] From this lease, however, the rents of the new inclosures in Salthouse Moor seem to be omitted, and it would appear that while the burgesses resumed control of their own borough-court, a separate court was now instituted for these tenants. Apart from this, the sole reservations were the castle with its purlieus, forfeitures of lands, and (probably) escheats. By 1357, therefore, the burgesses had again attained to all but the highest degree of municipal liberties. The 1357 lease appears to have been continued

[78] *Rot. Scot.* i, 209.
[79] *Cal. Close,* 1327–30, p. 307.
[80] *Rot. Scot.* i, 248, 258.
[81] Ibid. 306, 309.
[82] *Cal. Close,* 1333–7, p. 414 ; *Rot. Scot.* i, 321. [83] Pipe R. 9 Edw. III.
[84] *Cal. Rot. Scot.* i, 355.
[85] It has long been supposed that one Liverpool ship took part in the siege of Calais ; Baines, *Liverpool,* 152 ; Kaye's *Stranger in Liv.* (1825 ed.), 15. It is clear, however, that this vessel hailed from Mersea in Essex, and not from the River Mersey, as pointed out by Mr. Robert Gladstone, jun. See the *Liverpool Courier,* 26 Dec. 1905.

[86] *Rot. Scot.* i, 467.
[88] Pat. 35 Edw. III, pt. 2, m. 24.
[89] Ibid. 47 Edw. III. Printed in Baines, *Liv.* 165–6, from Okill's transcripts.
[90] Ibid. 48 Edw. III ; Baines, op. cit. 166.
[91] *Cal. Pat.* 1377–81, p. 385 ; 1385–9, p. 163 ; 1388–92, pp. 134. 405, 385 ; 1399–1401, p. 164, &c.
[92] Ibid.
[93] Ibid. 1327–30, p. 231 ; 1330–4, p. 396 ; 1334–8, p. 223 ; 1381–5, p. 130.
[94] Ibid. 1340–3, p. 313.
[95] Original in Liv. Munic. Archives. *Hist. Munic. Govt. in Liv.* 158.
[96] The steps in this process are analysed

[87] Ibid.

in detail in *Trans. Hist. Soc.* (new. ser.), xxi, 1–27.
[97] Ibid. 13 ; L. T. R. Enr. Accts. Misc. no. 14, m. 77.
[98] Ibid. 19 ; Add. MS. 32103 ; *Hist. Munic. Govt. in Liv.* 299.
[99] Duchy of Lanc. Chan. R. no. 2 ; *Hist. Munic. Govt. in Liv.* 302 and 47. See also *Trans. Hist. Soc.* loc. cit. 23.
[100] In view of these additions the rent is extremely moderate, for the burgage rents of £8 more than make up the difference between the old rent of £26 and the new rent of £33. Possibly the reason for this moderation was that the town suffered severely from the Black Death.

regularly until 1393,[101] when it was replaced by a still more extensive lease granted by John of Gaunt, which represents the highest point attained by the municipal liberties of Liverpool during the Middle Ages.[102] The rent was raised to £38, but the lease included a grant of control over the whole of the waste, a power which the burgesses were never to lose, though it is not mentioned in later leases; it included all the lord's jurisdictional rights (embracing, apparently, the right of holding a court for the Salthouse Moor tenants, which brought these tenants under the control of the borough courts and officers); and it included the right of taking escheats and forfeitures. In brief, the effect of this lease was to extrude the feudal power entirely from the borough, except within the walls of the castle. The lease was for seventeen years, and expired in 1410. It thus extended well into the new period which began when, by the accession of the House of Lancaster to the throne, the borough was once more brought into direct relation with the Crown.

The extension of municipal powers represented by these leases was accompanied by a development of the burghal system of government. In 1351 there is the first mention of a mayor of Liverpool.[103] No royal or ducal grant of the right to elect such an officer survives, and the probability is that his appearance is the result of the re-acquisition of the lease of the farm, and perhaps dates from 1346, or even earlier. Up to that time it seems probable that the burgesses had only elected one bailiff,[104] the other being nominated by the lord; and as the functions performed by the latter (collection of dues and presidency of the court) were much the more important, he would be very definitely *major ballivus*. When these functions pass into the hands of the burgesses, they elect their own *major ballivus*. It was as *major ballivus* that the mayor began,[105] but later he nominated a bailiff of his own. It is instructive to find that this second bailiff was always regarded as representing the Crown (i.e. the lord) as well as the mayor.[106]

It is possible that the same period also saw the institution of another element in burghal government —the Court of Aldermen.[107] Each of the leases from 1357 was granted to a group of leading citizens, most of whom repeatedly occupied the mayoral chair, and who were probably selected as substantial men, able to stand surety for the payment of the rent. In the lease of 1393 they were formally empowered to hold the borough courts. Both in its functions and in its personnel, this group closely resembles the Court of Aldermen as it is found in the 16th century, when records begin to be abundant.

Thus the 14th century, in spite of the disorders of its first half, and the distresses caused by plague and war in its second half, witnessed firstly a steady growth of the town and a steady expansion of its prosperity; and secondly a striking revival and development of its municipal liberties. One exception to this statement,

however, must be made. Though there is no trace of it in the records, it would appear that the influence of the Peasants' Revolt extended to Liverpool. One of the demands made by the rebels was the withdrawal of the monopoly enjoyed by the privileged burgesses in towns; and it is probably to some such demand that we must attribute the grant of the charter of Richard II in 1382, the year after the rising.[108] The only distinctive feature of this charter is its revocation of the power of prohibiting trade by non-members of the gild which had been contained in the earlier charters, and it is inconceivable that the burgesses can have applied for this. But in spite of this charter, clearly the little borough was thriving; and it is possible, through the greater abundance of material, to get some notion of its life and working at this, the moment of its greatest prosperity.

The burgess roll appended to the extent of 1346 shows that there were 196 householders in Liverpool paying rent to the lord. On the usual basis of calculation, this would give a population of just under 1,000. But as the more substantial burgesses, who held large holdings in the fields or engaged largely in trade, must have had dependants not included in this estimate, the population may perhaps be put down at something like 1,200. It probably did not increase—it may have decreased—during the second half of the century, for Liverpool suffered severely from the Black Death; in 1360 the deaths were so numerous that the dead could not be buried in Walton Churchyard, and a licence was obtained from the Bishop of Lichfield for burials in St. Nicholas's Churchyard.[109]

This population must be regarded as being still, for the most part, except on market days, engaged in agriculture. Every burgess had holdings in the fields. The commonest holding was half a burgage, with about 1 acre in the fields, but some of the leading townsmen held much larger allotments. The will of William de Liverpool,[110] the leading burgess in the second half of the 13th century, survives, and an inventory of his property attached to it shows that his wealth was almost purely agricultural in character. He has grain in his barn worth £6 13s. 4½d., and 24 selions of growing wheat in the fields, worth £7. He has nine oxen and cows worth about 10s. apiece, six horses worth about 7s. each, and eighteen pigs valued at 1s. 6d. each. His domestic furniture is valued at £7 6s. 8d. But no merchandise is included in the inventory. As we shall see, William de Liverpool derived most of his wealth from milling.

The trade of the borough was probably mainly local in character. The weekly market, held every Saturday, and the annual fair on St. Martin's Day, probably mainly dealt in agricultural produce from the neighbouring parts of Lancashire and Cheshire. The ferries over the Mersey were of first-rate importance for this purpose; of these there seem to have been three. There seem to have been two ferries included in

[101] *Trans. Hist. Soc.* loc. cit. 26–7; *Hist. Munic. Govt. in. Liv.* 47–54, 304–6.

[102] The original of this is lost. A copy is printed in Gregson's *Fragments*, 352; there is another copy among Okill's manuscripts in the municipal archives. Printed in *Hist. Munic. Govt. in Liv.* 306.

[103] Elton, 'Early Recorded Mayors of Liv.' *Trans. Hist. Soc.* (new ser.), xviii,

119 ff. gives a catalogue of the early mayors, taken from the witnesses to the deeds in the Moore and Crosse collections.

[104] They only claim *one* bailiff in the Quo Warranto Plea of 1292.

[105] Willielmo filio Ade tunc maiore de Lyverpull, Roberto filio Mathaei *tunc altero ballivorum ibidem*; Add. MS. 32105, GG. 219.

[106] Thus in 1647 Richard Williamson

nominatus et electus est Ballivus *pro domino rege* et majore burgi predicti; Johannes Sturzaker nominatus et electus est Ballivus pro villa et burgo predicto.

[107] On this see *Hist. Munic. Govt. in Liv.* 51.

[108] Original in Liv. Munic. Archives; *Hist. Munic. Govt. in Liv.* 52 and 159.

[109] Lich. Epis. Reg. v, 44–5.

[110] Crosse Deeds, 77.

the Liverpool farm,[111] one to Runcorn, the other (probably) to Birkenhead. In addition, the prior of the Benedictine monastery in Birkenhead enjoyed, from 1330 at the latest,[111a] the right of ferry from Birkenhead to Liverpool. In 1317[112] Edward II granted to the prior the right of building houses of entertainment for the use of the 'great numbers of persons wishing to cross there,' who were 'often hindered,' by reason of 'contrariety of weather and frequent storms.' From the record of a *Quo Warranto* inquiry, to which the prior was summoned in 1354,[113] we learn that the ferry tolls from the Birkenhead side were : for a

BIRKENHEAD PRIORY.
Quarterly gules and or, over all a crozier erect proper, in the first quarter a lion of England.

man on foot, ¼d. ; for man and horse, 2d. On Liverpool market days a man on foot was charged ½d., and if carrying baggage 1d. Probably the fares on the Liverpool ferry were the same. The connexion of the Birkenhead monastery with Liverpool was intimate. The prior held in Water Street a house and barn for the storage of corn waiting for the market.[114] There is no evidence as to the nature of the tolls charged in the Liverpool market and fair. They yielded in all never less than £10 a year during the 14th century.

With regard to the sea-going trade of Liverpool the evidence is equally scanty.[115] The appointment by the Crown of the mayor as deputy steward for the prisage of wines in the Port of Liverpool in 1364[116] seems to indicate that there was some importation of wines from Gascony, and this is borne out by other notices. Probably the sea-going trade of Liverpool at this period, as in the 16th century, was mainly with Ireland, and consisted of an exchange of rough manufactured goods and iron, against cattle and hides. The fact that down to the 18th century Bristol, Waterford, and Wexford were the only ports[117] in which Liverpool merchants claimed, and to whose traders the Liverpool burgesses habitually conceded, that right of exemption from dues which the charters granted in universal terms, seems to show that it was the Irish trade which was alone developed to any considerable extent.[118] In 1350 we get a glimpse of the nature of a Liverpool merchant's goods from a suit in which William de Longwro sued Adam de Longwro, his bailiff, for an account of his stewardship during the previous year, and his use of twenty entire woollen cloths (pieces), 10 quarters of barley, 40 quarters of oats, and iron worth £100, and of 100s., which he had received to trade with.[119] Lancashire and Yorkshire woollen goods, iron from Furness, and corn seem to be the staples of export trade. Perhaps salt from Cheshire may be added.

Nor can much be said about the industries of the

borough. There is no trace of the existence of craft gilds in the mediaeval period. Two such gilds are recorded to have come into existence in the 16th century, but they were then novelties ;[120] probably the number of craftsmen was too small—a few weavers and smiths may have exhausted the list. Two goldsmiths are named in the burgess roll of 1346. But the industries were doubtless merely the normal industries of a rural market-town. Brewing seems to have been carried on very actively. In the single year 1324[121] there were thirty-five prosecutions for breaches of the assize of ale, and this involves that many more were brewing and selling ale on legal terms. Not only the demands of market days, but especially the healthy thirst of the soldiers who were constantly encamped in Liverpool during this period, makes it natural to imagine almost every burgess as making some profit in this way.

The mills play an important part in the life of the borough.[122] In 1256[123] there had been three mills, two water-mills and a windmill, probably all at or near the same place, on the stream which ran into the upper end of the Pool, where a mill-dam remained long after the mills had vanished. By 1296 one of the water-mills had disappeared ;[124] by 1323 the second had been replaced by a horse-mill,[125] probably in Castle Street. The single windmill was that of Eastham, on the rising ground south-east of the Pool, behind the modern art gallery. By 1348[126] a second windmill had been added. This was the Townsend Mill, which stood close to the Eastham Mill, near the site of the Wellington monument. The horse-mill still survived, and the three mills were included in the leases held by the burgess body from (at the latest) 1348 ; each of them being separately sub leased to a working miller. At one or another of these mills all inhabitants of Liverpool were bound to grind, and they may also have been used by some of the neighbouring townships.[127] Much the most important of the mills was that of Eastham, for which, in the next century, twice as much rent was paid as for the Townsend Mill.[128] In 1375 it was leased to William son of Adam de Liverpool, the most important burgess of the period.[129] The lessors were Richard Nunn, the parson, and John Heathorn, who may have acted on behalf of the burgess body. The Townsend Mill, and perhaps the horse-mill, may have been held by the Moore family, who held them both at a later date ; Sir Edward Moore, in the 17th century, claimed that his ancestors had built the Townsend Mill.[130] Thus the mills of the borough were probably in the hands of its two chief families.

It would be possible to give, from the Moore and Crosse deeds, the assessments for subsidies, and the burgess roll of 1346, an account of a number of principal families in the town. Some of these were branches of important county families, or landholders in neighbouring townships. Such were the Waltons, lords of the manor of Walton, who held the serjeanty

[111] Duchy of Lanc. Mins. Accts. bdle. 103. no. 1821.
[111a] Harl. MSS. 2101, fol. 208.
[112] Pat. 11 Edw. II, pt. 1, m. 14.
[113] Chester Pleas, 27 Edw. III.
[114] Moore D. 280 (20), 297 (38), 309 (50), &c.
[115] The pavage grants give long lists of commodities upon which dues may be charged, but in all probability these were conventional lists, and cannot be taken as

representing the actual commodities dealt in. [116] Close, 40 Edw. III, m. 22.
[117] Picton, *Munic. Rec.* i, 77. [118] Ibid.
[119] Duchy of Lanc. Assize R. no. 2. pt. 2, m. 4 d. [120] Picton, *Munic. Rec.* i, 74.
[121] *Lanc. Ct. R.* (Rec. Soc. Lancs. and Ches. xli), 77.
[122] Bennett and Elton, op. cit. iv, 125-210.
[123] Duchy of Lanc. Mins. Accts. bdle. 1094, no. 11.

[124] Inq. p.m. 25 Edw. I, no. 51.
[125] L.T.R. Enr. Accts. loc. cit.
[126] Duchy of Lanc. Accts. various, bdle. 32, no. 17.
[127] Everton, e.g. which had no mill of its own.
[128] Duchy of Lanc. Mins. Accts. bdle. 101, no. 1800.
[129] Moore D. no. 450.
[130] *Moore Rental* (ed. W. F. Irvine), 63 ff. 87.

of the wapentake of West Derby,[131] and provided at least one constable for the Castle of Liverpool ;[132] in 1346 Richard de Walton held four burgages in Liverpool;[133] or the Fazakerleys, or the Irelands of Hale, or the Bootles of Kirkdale, or the herediaty reeves of West Derby, all of whom held lands in Liverpool. Among the more purely burghal families something might be said of the Barons, the Corvesors, the Longwrens, the Mariotsons, the Tippups. But two families stand out in such marked prominence as to deserve special mention. The first of these was the family of Liverpool, which from the mere fact that it habitually used the place-name as its surname may be supposed to have been settled in the borough from a very early date. In 1346 the various members of the family seem to hold among them something like fifteen burgages,[134] and the Moore and Crosse deeds show them making constant acquisitions. The earliest notice of a member of this family, Richard de Liverpool, occurs between 1212 and 1226 ;[135] and it may be his son, or grandson, who, as Adam son of Richard, is recorded as one of the first Liverpool members of Parliament. From the beginning of the 14th century their genealogy can be traced in detail.[136] Adam de Liverpool, who in 1346 held five and five-eighths burgages, had in 1332 paid a larger sum towards the subsidy on goods than any other person in Liverpool ;[137]

WALTON or Walton. *Sable three swans argent.*

and he was one of the jurors in the Inquisition into the earl's lands in 1346. His father, his uncle, his brother, and his nephews, each in their generation appear in more or less prominent positions. But the most distinguished member of the family was William son of Adam, whose will has been already referred to. He lived through the period of the revival of burghal liberties, dying

LIVERPOOL. *Quarterly gules and or a cross formy argent.*

in 1383, and he played a principal part in securing this remarkable advance. He was the first recorded mayor of Liverpool in 1351, and though the list of mayors is

far from complete, he is known to have held the office eleven times.[138] As mayor he received, and probably took a large part in obtaining, the writ for the erection of the chapel of St. Nicholas in 1356.[139] In 1357 he is named first among the lessees of the great lease of the farm of the borough which forms so remarkable a landmark in the history of burghal liberties.[140] In 1361 he was rewarded by Duke Henry, for 'the good and free service' which he had done, by the grant of a pension of 20s. for life from the profits of a West Derby manor.[141] We have already seen him a tenant of the principal mill of Liverpool. In addition he owned a bakery in Castle Street,[142] and seems to have controlled a fishery, probably leasing from the duke the weir which he had erected near Toxteth Park.[143] In short, he is at once the wealthiest and the most public-spirited Liverpool burgess of his day.[144]

William de Liverpool left two sons, by different wives, both named John, one of whom founded the chantry of St. John in the Liverpool Chapel,[145] perhaps in memory of his father ; but his lands and his mill presently passed into the hands of Richard de Crosse, a son of his wife by another marriage.[146] With him begins the connexion with Liverpool of the Crosse family, who are to play an exceedingly prominent part in the affairs of the borough during the next century.[147] The other branches of the Liverpool family seem to have adopted various surnames, especially Williamson[148] and Richardson, and to have become indistinguishably merged in the mass of burgesses.

The other principal Liverpool family of whom mention must be made was that of the Moores, for whom their descendant Sir Edward Moore claims that they were established in Liverpool from the earliest date.[149] This claim is probably not without justification if, as seems likely, they took their name[150] from the moorish piece of ground which lay to the north of the upper end of the Pool, at the end of Moor Street or Tithebarn Street ; and we

MOORE or MORE Hall. *Argent three greyhounds courant in pale sable collared or.*

may regard them as the rivals of the Liverpool family throughout the first three centuries of the borough's history. Their seat, More Hall, lay at the northern end of the house-covered area, and its gardens ran down to the estuary. When in

131 See *V.C.H. Lancs.* iii, 3.
132 Lanc. Exch. R. 20 Edw. I.
133 Extent of 1346 already quoted.
134 From the burgess roll appended to the Extent of 1346. But owing to the dropping of the surname, it is not possible to be certain in the allocation of their lands.
135 Margaret, relict of Adam de Garston, married Richard de Liverpool between 1212 and 1226 ; *Lancs. Inq. and Extents* (Rec. Soc.), i, 128 ; *Whalley Coucher,* 579.
136 Mr. Elton has given an account of some of the principal members of the family in his paper on 'William the son of Adam,' *Trans. Hist. Soc.* (new ser.) xix–xx, 133.
137 Exch. Lay Subsidies.
138 Elton, 'Early Recorded Mayors of Liv.' *Trans. Hist. Soc.* (new ser.), xviii.

139 Pat. 29 Edw. III ; see Okill, iv, 415.
140 Duchy of Lanc. Chan. R. no. 2.
141 Close R. of Duke Henry, 52.
142 Moore D. no. 257.
143 Ibid. 'Quoddam gurgitum vocatum le ffisheyard juxta parcum de Toxtath' is mentioned in the Extent of 1346 (but in no other document) as yielding 6s. per annum.
144 His will contains one of the few personal notes surviving from the mediaeval period. 'I bequeath my soul to God and the blessed Virgin and all saints and my body to be buried in the Chapel of Liverpool before the face of the image of the Virgin, where is my appointed place of burial. I leave to be distributed in bread on the day of my burial three quarters of wheat. I leave six pounds of wax to be used about my body. I leave to every priest in the chapel of Liverpool fourpence.

I leave the rest of my goods to Katherine my wife and our children born of her' ; Crosse D. no. 77.
145 Raines, *Lancs. Chantries* (Chet. Soc. lix), 82.
146 Add. MS. 32105, GG. 2301, 2840.
147 Perhaps their mansion of Crosse Hall, with its croft sloping down to the Pool near the town's end on the south side of Dale Street, may represent the original home of William son of Adam.
148 In 1668 Sir E. Moore writes of Richard Williamson and his relations. 'There is a great faction of them . . . They have always been enemies of me and all your predecessors time out of the memory of man' ; *Moore Rental* (ed. W. F. Irvine), 58 and note.
149 *Moore Rental* (ed. W. F. Irvine), 8, 111.
150 Moore D. 377 (120) *et passim.*

the 15th century they acquired a large amount of land in Kirkdale,[151] and built a new mansion, Bank Hall, there, the More Hall came to be called the Old Hall ; and has given its name to a modern street. They appear in prominent parts in the borough affairs, contemporary with the Liverpools. In 1246 Ranulf de More appears as reeve of Liverpool,[152] and in 1292 John de la Mor, along with Richard de Liverpool, represented the burgesses at the *Quo Warranto* plea already referred to.[153] Down to the middle of the 14th century they are frequently found acting as bailiffs.[154] The younger members of the family seem often to have acted as clerks, and in that capacity to have written and preserved many deeds of land-transfer ; [155] hence the archives of the family included numerous deeds not relating to their own lands. In 1346 the holdings of the family in Liverpool included sixteen and one-eighth burgages,[156] so that they slightly surpassed the Liverpools. In 1348 it was John del Mor who held, probably on behalf of the burgesses, the farm of the tolls, market, and mills.[157] But after that date the leadership of the borough seems to have been wrested from them by the Liverpools. While William son of Adam held the mayoralty at least eleven times, and his intimate friend and ally, Richard de Aynsargh, nine times, the name of Moore is conspicuously absent from the roll of mayors until 1382,[158] when William de Liverpool had practically retired. Thereafter the Moores in their turn have almost a monopoly of the mayoralty.[159] There seems here to be indicated a keen rivalry between these two leading houses, which would doubtless be accentuated if, as has been suggested above, both were rival millers. This rivalry found vent in the law courts when in 1374 Thomas del More sued William de Liverpool for having dispossessed him of the Castle Street bakery, the fishery and some turbary.[160] The matter was compromised by William's remaining in possession, but paying More an annual rent of 3s. These are the dim echoes of what was probably a pretty lively feud.

Outside of the liberties of the borough, but constantly affecting its fortunes, was the castle. It was ruled by a constable, receiving an annual salary of £6 6s. 8d. ; [161] the constable was generally, if not always, also keeper of Toxteth Park, and sometimes also of Croxteth and Simonswood Parks,[162] for which he received a further salary of £2. The connexion of Toxteth Park in particular with Liverpool was so intimate that in the next century the Crown found it necessary to make a special statement in the farm leases reserving it from the farm.[163] The names of several constables survive ; [164] the office at this period being not yet hereditary, as it became in the next century. The constable did not usually reside in the castle, but in a house just outside of its gate.[165] In normal times there was no standing garrison in the castle, and the permanent paid staff seems to have consisted of a watchman and a doorkeeper, each of whom was paid 1½d. per diem.[166] There were, however, several houses within the castle,[167] where there may have been permanent rent-paying residents, though they may have been reserved for the use of the officers of the forces, which constantly passed through the town. A detailed list of the castle plenishment survives ; [168] it includes 186 pallets, 107 spears, 39 lances, 15 *ballistae*, 2 engines, 7 'acketouns, old and weak,' 1 large vat for brewing, and a considerable amount of domestic furniture.

The 15th century, for many English trading ports a period of advance, was for Liverpool a period of retrogression—in population, prosperity, and political freedom. The process of decay does not perhaps become evident until the reign of Henry VI ; but already, before that date, the causes which were to contribute to it were making their appearance : namely, the weakness of the Crown, and the turbulence of the uncontrolled nobility. In 1406[169] Sir John Stanley obtained licence to fortify a house in Liverpool. This was the Tower, at the bottom of Water Street, which remained in the possession of the house of Stanley until the Commonwealth. This is the first appearance in the borough of a family which from that time onward was to play a mightily important part in its history. The reason for it was that, having acquired the Isle of Man as a result of the forfeiture of the Percies after the battle of Shrewsbury, Stanley needed a base for communications with his new dominion. The Tower seems to have been, at any rate occasionally, used as a residence by the family ; it was frequently occupied by troops. Thus the town was burdened by the presence of a second feudal fortress, only a bowshot from the original castle.

By the accession of Henry IV, which united the duchy of Lancaster to the Crown, Liverpool again came under direct royal control. It might have been expected that this would redound to the advantage of the borough, but the reverse was the case. The lease of the farm of the borough of 1393 was, it is true, confirmed by Henry IV ; [170] but only for the remainder of its term, which expired in 1410. Immediately on its expiration serious trouble began. From an interesting memorandum inscribed on the back of the confirmation[171] it appears that the burgesses had resolved to apply not only for a renewal, but also for a supplementary charter, conveying to them new powers, in particular the right to hold courts under the Statute of Merchants and the right to make arrests for debt. Henry V did actually grant a charter[172] in the first year of his reign, probably as a result of this application ; but it was merely a confirmation of the previous charters, and its sole advantage was that by disregarding the charter of Richard II it restored to the burgess body the right of prohibiting non-members of the gild to trade in the town. But it was over the renewal of the lease that the chief difficulties arose.

151 See under Bootle and Kirkdale for the lands of the Moores outside of Liverpool.
152 Assize R. 1404, m. 16.
153 *Plac. de Quo War.* (Rec. Com.), 381.
154 Moore D. *passim.*   155 Ibid.
156 Extent of 1346, loc. cit.
157 Duchy of Lanc. Accts. various, bdle. 32, no. 17.
158 Elton, loc. cit. ; Moore D. 255.
159 Ibid. Thomas del More held the

mayoralty at least 16 times—more often than any other Liverpool man has ever done.
160 Moore D. 190, 230, 231, 257.
161 e.g. Harl. Cod. 433, fol. 317a.
162 e.g. Reg. Duc. Lanc. 46 Edw. III, fol. 50, 232 ; 14 Hen. IV, fol. 29.
163 Duchy of Lanc. Mins. Accts. bdle. 117, no. 1934.
164 A partial list is given in Gregson's *Fragments.*

165 Moore D. 452 (1694).
166 L.T.R. Enr. Accts. Misc. 14, m. 77.
167 Duchy of Lanc. Book of Orders, &c. Edw. IV, 140.
168 L.T.R. Enr. Accts. loc. cit.
169 Pat. 7 Hen. IV, pt. ii, m. 14.
170 *Hist. Munic. Govt. in Liv.* 308.
171 Original lost ; printed in Gregson's *Fragments,* 352 ; *Hist. Munic. Govt. in Liv.* 309.
172 Ibid. 161.

It appears from the memorandum already referred to that the mayor and leading burgesses had to face opposition on the part of a section of the inhabitants described as 'those that hold of the king in Liverpool,' and, in order to frighten these recusants into line, thought of obtaining a privy seal ordering them all to appear before the king's council in London, unless they came to an agreement with the mayor. 'Those that held land of the king' can only have been the tenants in the recent inclosure in Salthouse Moor. It has already been suggested that these tenants had been separately governed up till 1393, when the great lease put them under the control of the burgess body. If they had been since that date forced to pay 'scot and lot,' to bear their share of burgess burdens without being admitted to burgess privileges, it is easy to understand why they should object to a renewal of the lease, and should prefer to return to the state of things before 1393. It is probably due to their opposition that the lease was not renewed in all its amplitude. No lease at all, indeed, survives for the period 1411–21. But such evidence as exists goes to show that the burgesses obtained a partial farm consisting of the market tolls, ferry and burgage-rents; the perquisites of courts and the mills, together with other miscellaneous rights, being reserved by the Crown and administered by royal agents, who now reappeared in the borough for the first time since 1393, or perhaps since 1357. The rent paid by the burgesses seems to have been £22 17s. 6d.[173]

But trouble at once resulted from this arrangement. In 1413[174] the royal agents do not appear to have been able to collect any money at all; and in the following years they got only £25 to £26, including the burgesses' payments, in place of the £38 paid under the old lease. There is no entry at all in their accounts for perquisites of courts; the only moneys they were able to get over and above the 'rent and farms' which represent the burgesses' payment was a payment for mills, generally largely swallowed up in repairs. The explanation of this curious state of affairs is to be found in an interesting petition sent by the burgesses to the House of Commons in 1415,[175] in which they ask for protection against the 'officers and servants' of the king, who, 'since the confirmation (of 1413) and not before . . . have come, usurped and held certain courts' in the borough, in defiance of the terms of all the burghal charters, and of the king's own confirmation. By right of the grant of sac and soc contained in these charters, the burgesses claimed to 'have at all times had and continued a court' and to 'have taken and received the perquisites of the said court with all the profits belonging thereto.' The assertion that the king had no claim to the profits of burghal justice is directly contradicted by the whole preceding history of the borough: it was only since 1357 that the burgesses had taken these profits, and then only in virtue of a special grant in the lease. But the episode is a striking illustration of the difficulty of regaining rights once conveyed by lease. One right included in the lease of 1393 was not even claimed by the Crown,

being forgotten on both sides. This was the control of the waste, which from this time remained burghal property.

It is not known what was the result of the petition to Parliament, which was referred to the king's council. But the burgesses continued to resist the royal agents, and to hold the courts themselves; and apparently they also quarrelled with the Crown over some question of tolls—possibly customs duties such as the prisage on wine, which in later leases the Crown is careful to define as not being covered by the lease. At length in 1420[176] the steward of West Derby Hundred was ordered to summon all the mayors and bailiffs of Liverpool for the preceding seven years to appear before the Exchequer Court of the duchy at Lancaster 'to render us account for the time they have held our courts at Liverpool . . . and for the tolls and other profits levied by them in the meantime.' This summons, however, had no better result. In the next year (1421) Henry V found it necessary to grant a lease[177] of the whole farm, without limitation, for a year, pending an inquiry into the terms on which it ought to be held. The rent paid was £23; that is, 2s. 6d. more than the burgesses had been paying for their partial farm, and £15 less than they had paid up till 1410. Before this inquiry could be completed Henry V had died, and during the minority of his son it was not to be expected that rights would be enforced which the vigorous father had failed to defend. The burgesses continued to hold a lease, at the slightly increased figure of £23 6s. 8d., until 1449.[178] Thus the conflict with the Crown had ended in a burghal victory; the burgesses were left in possession of several royal rights, above all the control of the waste and the supremacy of the Borough Court over all the inhabitants.

In the meanwhile, however, the disorder and turbulence of the district had been increasing. In 1424 a violent feud broke out between Thomas Stanley and Sir Richard Molyneux.[179] Ralph Radcliffe and James Holt, justices of the peace for Lancashire, were sent by the sheriff to keep order. They found Stanley entrenched in his father's tower in Liverpool, with about 2,000 men, waiting for the attack of Sir Richard Molyneux, who was advancing from West Derby with 1,000 men or more in battle array. The two protagonists were both arrested by the sheriff, and forced to withdraw, Stanley to Kenilworth, and Molyneux to Windsor. Record of this episode, which nearly made the streets of the borough the scene of a pitched battle, survives because the period of full anarchy was not yet begun. The episodes of the age of the war are left unrecorded.[180]

In February 1421–2 Sir Richard Molyneux obtained a grant of the constableship of Liverpool Castle, together with the stewardship of West Derby and Salford, and the forestership of Toxteth, Croxteth, and Simonswood.[181] In 1440–1 the offices were renewed for the lives of Sir Richard and his son, and five years later they were made hereditary.[182] In 1442 the castle was further fortified by the erection

---

[173] Duchy of Lanc. Mins. Accts. bdle. 731, no. 12021a; Hist. Munic. Govt. in Liv. 56 n. 4, and 58 n. 1.

[174] Mins. Accts. B 731, 12017, 12019a, 12027.

[175] Rot. Parl. iv, 55; Hist. Munic. Govt. in Liv. 399.

[176] Duchy of Lanc. Misc. vol. 17, fol. 87.

[177] Ibid. fol. 100.

[178] Mins. Accts. bdles. 117, 732, 733; Hist. Munic. Govt. in Liv. 312, 313.

[179] Dods. MSS. 87, 89.

[180] The outrage at Bewsey in 1437 in which the leader, Poole, is described as a Liverpool man, is another significant episode.

[181] Reg. Duc. Lanc. Bk. 17, fol. 75.

[182] Ibid.; Com. Hen. VI, fol. 57b; Okill Transcripts, iv, 275.

of the south-east tower.[183] The cost of the addition was £46 13s. 10¼d. The stone was obtained from Toxteth Park, the wood from the royal forest, now controlled by Molyneux, and the money from the Duchy Exchequer. Throughout the period the expenditure in repairs of the castle was large and constant.[184] The effect of the establishment of the Stanleys in the tower, and of the Molyneuxes in the castle, was to leave the borough very much at the mercy of the two great noble houses entrenched

MOLYNEUX. *Azure a cross moline or.*

STANLEY. *Argent on a bend azure three harts' heads caboshed or.*

in their midst, especially at a period when the Crown was perfectly incapable of maintaining order. Simultaneously, the prosperity of the borough steadily diminished,[185] and it was not till the beginning of the 17th century that it again stood on the level to which it had attained at the beginning of the 15th, either in population or in trade.

The decay is most strikingly demonstrated in the history of the lease. The last of the continuous series of burgess leases which followed the quarrel with the Crown expired in 1449, and apparently the burgesses found themselves unable to offer to continue it. A royal agent, Edmund Crosse,[186] of the local family already noticed, appears; but could only collect a little less than £19 in 1450, and £15 14s. in 1452, as compared with even the reduced rent of £23 6s. 8d. long paid by the burgesses. The most striking decline is in the market-tolls, which in 1450 yield only £2, though in 1327 they had yielded £10, and in 1346 much more. The failure of Crosse to produce increased revenues enabled the burgesses to get a new farm in 1454[187] at the low rent of £17 6s. 8d., but they were 5s. in arrears on the first year, though they had never been in arrears when they had to pay £38. In 1461 Edmund Crosse again rendered account[188]: the town was at farm, whether held by himself or by the burgess body it is not possible to say. But it was a 'new farm,' and the rent was only £14. Dur-

CROSSE. *Quarterly gules and or a cross potent argent in the first and fourth quarters.*

ing the period of this lease the Crown, disregarding its terms, made a special grant of one of the mills[189] and of one of the two ferry-rights,[190] apparently with the desire of increasing the yield. The burgesses held a lease at £14 from 1466 to 1471 ; but for the last two years of the period no account was rendered. The civil war had broken out afresh after Warwick's insurrection, and the burgesses were either suffering from its effects, or seized the opportunity to withhold payment. When Edward IV was again safely established on his throne, he did his best to exact arrears for these two years ; but never succeeded in getting from the poverty-stricken burgesses more than £9 of the £28 due from them.[191] He did not renew their tenure, but granted a lease, this time unquestionably a personal lease, to Edmund Crosse (1472) at £14 2s.[192] The burgesses never regained the lease. But even Crosse was unable to pay so modest a figure. Three years later (1475) his son, on having the lease renewed,[193] got the extra 2s. knocked off again, and obtained also a concession of the two rural mills of Ackers and Wavertree, in addition to the burghal mills. But this was not enough. In the next year (1476) he obtained a revised lease,[194] by which the rent was reduced to £11. This represents probably the lowest ebb of Liverpool prosperity. When, in 1488, the lease passed out of the hands of the Crosses and was granted to David Griffith,[195] the rent was raised to £14 ; this was increased to £14 6s. 8d. in 1528,[196] and at that figure it remained. Evidence is lacking as to the trade of the port during this period ; but its absence is in itself significant. And indeed it is needless to ask for more striking evidence of the decay of the borough than that afforded by the leases of the farm. At the same time the very misery of the place, removing it from all envy, saved to it some valuable privileges.[197] The control of the burgess body over the waste, their right to conduct their own courts, and the extension of their governmental authority over the non-burgess inhabitants, should probably be regarded as having been established by usage in this period of helplessness and poverty.

It is with the Tudor period that the material for Liverpool history begins to be abundant. To the regular records of the borough, which begin in 1555, there is prefixed a collection of 'elder precedences,' some of them dating from 1525 ; and in addition, the national or duchy muniments provide ampler material than before. But the reign of Henry VII, the period of transition, is still very scantily supplied. Substantially all that is known of this period is that in 1488 Henry VII gave a lease of the farm to David Griffith,[198] in whose family it remained till 1537[199] at the increased rent of £14 ; that in 1492 he empowered Thomas Fazakerley[200] to form a fishing station on the shore of the waste, between Toxteth Park and the Pool ; that in 1498 the burgesses were summoned to a *Quo Warranto*[201] plea which does not seem to have been heard ; and that in 1486 he made to one Richard Cook[202] a grant of ferry at £3 per

[183] Okill Transcripts, iv, 208 ; Cox, 'Liv. Castle,' *Trans. Hist. Soc.* (new ser.) vi, 195 ff.
[184] Okill, iv, 208, has summarized these expenditures from the Mins. Accts.
[185] A like decline is observable in the prosperity of Preston at this period, though the circumstances, apart from the weakness of the Crown and the distress caused by the war, were different from those of Liverpool.

[186] Duchy of Lancs. Mins. Accts. bdle. 101, no. 1800; 117, no. 1941.
[187] Ibid. 101, no. 1804.
[188] Ibid. 102, no. 1820.
[189] Duchy of Lanc. Chan. R. 3 Edw. IV, no. 54 ; *Hist. Munic. Govt. in Liv.* 318.
[190] Chan. R. 8 ; *Hist. Munic. Govt.* 319.
[191] Duchy of Lanc. Mins. Accts. bdle. 102, no. 1818.
[192] Duchy of Lanc. Chan. R. no. 55 ; *Hist. Munic. Govt.* 321.

[193] Chan. R. 55 ; *Hist. Munic. Govt.* 324.
[194] Chan. R. 57 ; *Hist. Munic. Govt.* 325.
[195] Duchy of Lanc. Misc. no. 21.
[196] Croxteth Mun. (Liv. box 10, R 2, no. 2).
[197] On this see *Hist. Munic. Govt.* 62-6.
[198] *Hist. Munic. Govt.* 328.
[199] Ibid. 329, 330, 331.
[200] Duchy of Lanc. Reg. Bk.
[201] *Hist. Munic. Govt.* 401.
[202] Ibid. 327.

annum, and for seven years, in place of a grant for life and without rent, which had been made two years before by Richard III.[203]

In the first half of the 16th century Liverpool seems to have begun slowly to emerge from the profound depression of the previous period, though even in the second half she is still described as a 'decayed town.' Perhaps the revival was partly due to the renewed use of the port, under Henry VIII, for transport to Ireland. Skeffington's army in 1534 shipped from Chester and Liverpool;[204] and a memorial of 1537 for the instruction of the king states that the army in Ireland 'must be vitelid with bere, biskett, flowre, butter, chease, and fleshe out of Chestre, Lirpole, Northwales and Southwales and Bristow.'[205] Some of the bullion required by the Irish army was also exported through Liverpool.[206] Probably the Irish trade of the port revived as a consequence. Leland, in a brief note on Liverpool,[207] says that 'Irish merchants come much thither, as to a good haven . . . At Liverpool is small custom paid that causeth merchants to resort. Good merchandize at Liverpool; and much Irish yarn, that Manchester men do buy there.' Thus already Liverpool was importing raw material for the nascent industries of Lancashire, and exporting the finished product.[208] We hear of one Liverpool merchant[209] trading with Drogheda, who in 1538 had for sale 12 lb. of London silks, and 12 pieces of kerseys, white, green and blue; three of the latter sold for £15 12s. But the trade of the reviving port extended beyond home waters. Edmund Gee of Chester and Liverpool, who is spoken of as the 'chief man and head merchant' of Liverpool,[210] persuaded a Spaniard, Lope de Rivera, to import into Liverpool large quantities of wine;[211] in 1534 the deputy-butler for Lancashire complains that William Collinges has imported 18 tuns of wine into Liverpool without paying prisage;[212] while in 1545 we hear of a Biscayan ship 'stayed at Liverpoole.'[213] When the embitterment of the Reformation struggle led English traders to prey upon Spanish ships, Liverpool sailors seem to have taken some part in these piratical adventures: in 1555 Inigo de Baldram, a Spaniard, complained to the Privy Council that he had been robbed by 'pirates of Lierpole and Chester.'[214] But the Spanish trade can only have been of the smallest proportions; even that with Ireland, the staple of Liverpool traffic, was humble enough.

Within the borough a modest development can be traced. In 1516 Oldhall Street was, by agreement with William Moore of the Oldhall, made an open road to the fields.[215] From 1524 a deed survives[216] in which the burgesses granted to Sir William Molyneux at a rental of 6s. a few roods of waste land beside the Moor Green, for the erection of a tithe-

barn to hold the tithes of Walton Church, which belonged to the Molyneux family. Moor Street now becomes Tithebarn Street. The importance of this deed is that it shows the burgesses acting as owners of the waste; and this is still more clearly exhibited in a borough rental of 1523,[217] prefixed to the Municipal Records, in which eight tenants pay among them 7s. 5d. for patches of common. A rental of the king's lands in Liverpool[218] dating from 1539 yields further interesting particulars. The total value was £10 1s. 4d., which was, of course, included in the lease of the farm. It is significant that only 3¾ burgages are enumerated; which appears to indicate that the burgage as a distinctive holding was passing out of use. Twenty-six burgages were included among the endowments of the four chantries in 1546.[219]

The early years of the century saw the establishment of the last of the chantries, that of the priest John Crosse, who provided that the chaplain should also teach a school.[220] His will contains also a bequest to the 'mayor and his brethren with the burgesses' of the 'new [house] called our Ladie house to kepe their courtes and such busynes as they shall thynke most expedient.' Thus by one act the borough became possessed of a school and a town hall.

The period, however, witnessed a number of disputes between the burgesses and the Crown or the lessees of the farm. In 1514 (David Griffith with his wife and son being then the lessees)[221] a commission[222] was appointed by the Crown 'on the behalf of our farmer of our toll within our said town of Liverpool' to inquire whether 'the Mayor and Burgesses . . . for their own singular lucre and advantage now of late have made many and divers foreign men not resident nor abiding in the said town to be burgesses of the same town to the intent to defraud us and our right of toll there.' The result of this inquiry (which was probably due to dissatisfaction with the yield of the farm) is not known. But it shows the burgesses trying to recoup themselves for the loss of the farm by taking payments for the admission of non-burgesses to that exemption from dues which was their chartered privilege. In 1528[223] another commission was appointed to 'survey search and examine the concealments and subtraction of all and every such tolls customs and forfeitures as to us rightfully should belong . . . of any goods . . . conveyed to or from our port of Liverpool.' In the next year a new cause of quarrel appears. Thirteen men had been working a ferry from Liverpool to Runcorn. This ferry-right was covered by the farm; and as a result of his complaint to the Crown, the mayor was ordered[224] to put an end to this illegal ferry. The order seems to have been neglected, for

[203] Hist. Munic. Govt. 326. As a ferry-right was also included in the farm lease, this grant is only explicable on the assumption that there were two ferries. The probability is that Cook's ferry plied between Liverpool and Runcorn.

[204] State Papers, Hen. VIII, ii, 205.

[205] Ibid. ii, 415.

[206] Acts of P.C. 1552-4, p. 104.

[207] Leland, Itin. vii, fol. 50, 44.

[208] See Duchy Plead. v, m. 2 (19 Hen. VIII).

[209] Duchy Plead. (Rec. Soc. Lancs. and Ches. xxxv), ii, 119.

[210] In the judgement in the case of Molyneux v. Corporation of Liv.; Hist. Munic. Govt. 411.

[211] Duchy Plead. ix, c. 10, p. 47.

[212] Duchy Plead. (Rec. Soc. Lancs. and Ches. xxxv), ii, 50.

[213] Acts of P.C. 1542-7, p. 248.

[214] Ibid. 1554-6, p. 236.

[215] Okill Transcripts, xiv, 118.

[216] In the Municipal archives.

[217] Munic. Rec. i, 5.

[218] Printed in Gregson, Fragments, App. lxv.

[219] Raines, Lancs. Chant. (Chet. Soc. lix), 82-93.

[220] Duchy of Lanc. Depositions, P. & M. v, m. 3; Inventories of Ch. Gds. (Chet. Soc. cxiii), 97-8.

[221] Duchy of Lanc. Misc. 21; Hist. Munic. Govt. in Liv. 329.

[222] Duchy of Lanc. Misc. 95, 366; Hist. Munic. Govt. in Liv. 402.

[223] Duchy of Lanc. Misc. 22; Hist. Munic. Govt. in Liv. 403.

[224] Duchy of Lanc. Misc. 95, fol. 104 b; Hist. Munic. Govt. in Liv. 403.

LIVERPOOL : OLD TITHE BARN

(From a Water-colour Drawing, c. 1800)

LIVERPOOL : ST. JOHN'S LANE, 1865

in the next year Ackers petitioned the Chancellor of the Duchy for redress.[225] The dispute was settled by the lessee granting a sub-lease[226] to the burgess body, whereby they undertook to collect all the customs, tolls, and ferry-dues, and pay half of the total proceeds and £10. The royal rents of £10 and the mills (separately leased at 50s.)[227] were excluded from this sub-lease ; and as the sub-lease must have yielded to the lessor at least £20, his income from the town must have amounted to over £32, yielding him a handsome profit after he had paid his £14 6s. 8d. to the Crown. Incidentally these figures show that the town was regaining much of its prosperity, and approximating to the conditions of 1394, when the rent was £38 ; though it should be remembered that the value of money had in the meantime materially declined.

Of the effects of the first stages of the Reformation there is little to record. The only monastic property connected with the borough was the house and barn in Water Street and the ferry-right over the Mersey, which belonged to the Priors of Birkenhead, and passed with the manor of Birkenhead to Ralph Worsley. But the later confiscation of the chantries affected Liverpool deeply. There were now four chantries in the chapel of St. Nicholas ; their lands in 1546 had been worth £21 11s. 3d.,[228] paying in chief rents to the king 10s. 3d.[229]

WORSLEY. *Argent a cheveron sable between three falcons of the last beaked legged and belled or.*

The lands of two of these chantries—those of the High Altar and of St. John—were sold, though the priests attached to them seem to have remained resident in the town.[230] Among the purchasers[231] were many of the burgesses of Liverpool, who were thus to some extent committed to support of the Reformation. The lands of the chantries of St. Nicholas and St. Katherine remained in the hands of the Crown, and their revenues were respectively devoted to the maintenance of a priest for the Liverpool chapel and of a schoolmaster for the parish of Walton,[232] the pre-suppression chantry priests remaining to perform these functions.[233] In 1565 the administration of these lands seems to have been transferred from the Duchy officers to the mayor and burgesses,[234] who added further revenues raised among themselves,[235] and henceforth controlled the appointment both of the priest and of the schoolmaster of the town.

Difference of opinion on the religious question may

have helped to precipitate a serious quarrel between the borough and the lessee of the farm. This had been since 1537 in the hands of Sir William Molyneux[236] and his son Sir Richard, who however had continued the arrangement of their predecessors whereby the burgesses administered the various powers and collected the dues,[237] retaining half of them on payment of £10 per annum. In 1552 a mysterious lease was issued by Edward VI to one James Bedyll.[238] It never took effect, but it may have been intended as an attack by the Protestant court upon the Roman Catholic Molyneuxes. If we suppose the burgesses to have been concerned in obtaining this lease, the quarrel with Molyneux which broke out immediately on the accession of Mary is easier to understand. Molyneux obtained a renewal[239] of his lease, though his previous lease was still unexpired, and, the sub-lease to the burgesses having expired,[240] he put in his own officers to collect the dues and hold the portmoot. The burgesses on their side obtained a confirmation of their charters,[241] though, having apparently overlooked the charter of Henry V,[242] it was the less favourable charter of Richard II of which they obtained a renewal. They seem to have trusted to this to justify their claim to collect the dues and hold the portmoot, which they proceeded to do in spite of the lessee, even throwing his agents into prison.[243] The question was tried before the Chancery Court of the Duchy[244] which gave its award on every point in favour of the lessees, awarding them ' all and singular tolls and other profits in any wise appertaining to the said town,' whether paid by freemen or by strangers, and also definitely declaring that the lessee had the right to ' keep courts within the said town . . after such sort . . . as the courts . . have been used to be kept,' and that suit at these courts must be rendered by all inhabitants.[245] This was a serious blow to the burgesses ; and, while space does not permit of an examination of the question, it seems clear that the burgesses were deprived of some rights which justly belonged to them.[246] Two years later, on the intercession of Lord Strange and the attorney of the Duchy court, the quarrel was compromised by the renewal to the burgesses of the old sub-lease, which seems to have been continued throughout the remainder of the century.[247]

The municipal records from 1555 enable a clear account to be given of the mode of government to which the burgesses had now attained. At an assembly of burgesses held on St. Luke's Day, 18 October, a mayor and one bailiff were elected, a second bailiff being nominated by the new mayor at the same meeting.[248] Other assemblies were held as occasion

---

[225] Duchy of Lanc. Judic. Proc., Pleadings, iv ; *Hist. Munic. Govt. in Liv.* 404 ; *Lanc. Pleadings* (Rec. Soc. Lancs. and Ches. xxxii), i, 186.

Probably the ferry in dispute was not the farm-ferry, but a continuance of that district ferry-right granted by Henry VII to Richard Cook.

[226] Croxteth Mun. Liv. Box 10. R 2, no. 7 ; *Hist. Munic. Govt.* 335.

[227] Croxteth Mun. loc. cit. no. 3 ; *Hist. Munic. Govt.* 333.

[228] Raines, *Lancs. Chant.* (Chet. Soc. ix), 82–93.

[229] Rental of Hen. VIII, loc. cit.

[230] Munic. Rec. *passim.*

[231] The list of purchasers is printed in Gregson's *Fragments,* lxiv.

[232] In the list of official payments of the Duchy printed in Gregson's *Fragments,* 31, ' the stipend of a clerk to serve in the chapel at Litherpoole £4 17s. 5d. and the fee of a clerk and schoole mr. of Walton £5 13s. 4d.'

[233] Munic. Rec. i, 13b and 39a.

[234] Ibid. 39.

[235] Ibid. 13b.

[236] The details of the history of the farm during this period, and copies of the leases, will be found in *Hist. Munic. Govt. in Liv.,* 70–7 and 336–53.

[237] Ibid. 338.

[238] Ibid. 345 and 71 n.

[239] Ibid. 349.

[240] The previous sub-lease had been for 15 years.

15

demanded.[249] Attendance was compulsory on all burgesses on penalty of a fine of 1s.[250] The assembly elected freemen,[251] and occasionally expelled them from the liberties.[252] Distinct from the assembly was the Portmoot and Great Leet, held twice yearly. The Great Portmoot immediately followed the annual assembly, and elected all the minor officers, among whom may be named the serjeant at mace, two churchwardens, two leve-lookers, two moss-reeves, four mise-cessors and prysors, two stewards of the common-hall, a water-bailiff, a hayward, two ale-testers.[253] The portmoot was the lineal descendant of the old manorial court, and as such the right to hold it was claimed by the lessee of the farm. When this right was exercised, as in 1555, portmoot and assembly were at war,[254] but normally almost all business was indifferently transacted at either. At the portmoot presentments of breaches of burghal custom were made by a jury of twenty-four or twelve burgesses impanelled by the bailiffs; they also 'appointed and set down' all sorts of orders or by-laws, indistinguishable in character from those passed by the assembly of burgesses, and including many affairs not properly coming within the sphere of a manorial court, but rather belonging to the sphere of the gild-merchant.

The mayor exercised supreme control over the whole executive business of the borough, the bailiffs and other officers being under his orders. He was always either a leading merchant, or a country gentleman of the neighbourhood. He presided over the ordinary sessions of the borough court, now called the mayor's court, which does not seem to have been claimed by the lessees. With him acted 'the Mayor's Brethren' or aldermen, who were not popularly elected, but seem to have consisted of the ex-mayors. It is clear that this system of government was breaking down; and it was to undergo great changes in the next period.

In the second half of the century it becomes possible to trace in more detail the movement of population and the development of trade. In 1565 there were 144 names on the burgess rolls,[255] but some of these were non-resident, and the number of resident burgesses was probably about 120. In the same year the number of householders is given as 138.[256] In 1572,[257] of 159 names in the burgess roll about 130 may have been resident, while in 1589[258] there were 190 names on the roll, of whom over 150 were resident. The number of houses rated for a subsidy in 1581 was 202.[259] Including therefore resident burgesses and other non-burgess inhabitants, we may estimate the population at about 700 or 800 in the middle of the century, increasing slowly to about 1,000 or 1,200 at its close. In other words, the 16th century only succeeded in bringing the population back to the figure it had already attained in 1346. The explanation of this slow growth is to be found largely in the ravages of the plague which repeatedly attacked Liverpool during the period. The visitation of 1558 was so virulent that the fair was dropped in that year, no markets were held for three months, and over 240 persons, or one-fourth of the population, are said to have died.[260]

The progress of shipping was equally unsatisfactory. A return of 1557[261] shows that there were in the port one ship of 100 tons and one of 50 tons,[262] together with seven smaller vessels, while four vessels of between 10 and 30 tons were at sea; there were 200 sailors connected with the port. In 1565[263] there were fifteen vessels, three of which belonged to Wallasey; the largest was of 40 tons burthen, and the number of seamen was about eighty. In 1586[264] sixteen vessels can be counted in the entrances and clearances for a single month; probably the list is not exhaustive. The character of the port's trade continued unchanged. Manchester, Bolton, and Blackburn men frequented the market to buy Irish yarns,[265] and sell 'Manchester cottons' (coatings);[266] the outgoing trade was mainly to Ireland, and consisted of mixed cargoes of coals, woollens, Sheffield knives, leather goods, and small wares. The return cargoes from Dublin, Drogheda, and Carlingford were invariably of yarns, hides, and sheep skins or fells. The foreign trade was of small proportions, and seems mainly to have been conducted by foreigners. But we hear of a Lancashire family sending to Liverpool to buy '44 quarts of sack, 85 quarts of claret, 4 cwt. of iron, 4 lb. of pitch.'[267] French and Spanish ships were sometimes brought as prizes into Liverpool, but not by Liverpool captains.[268] Piracy was rampant, and government had much ado to keep it in check even in the Irish Sea.[269] There were, it is true, one or two merchants in Liverpool who traded with Spain;[270] one of these spent twelve months in a Spanish prison in 1585-6, and on returning was the first to give details of the preparation of the Armada.[271] But the trade with Spain was on so small a scale that when the monopolist Spanish trading company was established in 1578,[272] the Liverpool merchants were contemptuously excused from submission to its regulations on the ground that they were only engaged in small retail trade. Even from the payment of tonnage and poundage duties Liverpool was exempt until the reign of Elizabeth,[273] no doubt because the yield would be so small as not to be worth the cost of collection.

It was probably for this reason that during the reign of Elizabeth the central government treated Liverpool as part of a large customs district which included the ports of North Wales, and had its centre at Chester. Orders of various sorts were frequently transmitted to the Mayor of Liverpool through the Mayor of Chester;[274] in one writ Liverpool and Chester were treated as a single port,[275] while in another Liverpool was actually catalogued with Chester

[249] Mun. Rec. i, passim.
[250] e.g. Ibid. i, 12b, 13b.
[251] Ibid. i, 6a, 7b.
[252] Ibid. i, 12b.
[253] See especially the elections of 1551 and 1558; Munic. Rec. i, 3a, and 39a.
[254] Munic. Rec. i, 12a, 13b.
[255] Ibid. i, 131a.
[256] Ibid. i, 32b.   [257] Ibid. ii, 21.
[258] Ibid. ii, 375.
[259] Ibid. ii, 210.
[260] Ibid. i, 39a.

[261] Ibid. i, 32a.
[262] These may have come from other ports, as there is no mention of ships of this size in Liverpool later in the century.
[263] Munic. Rec. i, 144.
[264] This list of clearances is printed from the Munic. Rec. by Baines, Liverpool, 242 ff.
[265] Picton, Munic. Rec. i, 76.
[266] Acts of P.C. 1558-70, p. 308; Picton, Munic. Rec. i, 88.

[267] Stewards Accts. of the Shuttleworths (Chet. Soc. xxxv), 18.
[268] Acts of P.C. 1558-70, pp. 271, 305; 1580-1, p. 212.
[269] Ibid. 1558-70, pp. 278, 288.
[270] Picton, Munic. Rec. i, 39.
[271] Hist. MSS. Com. Rep. v, App. i, 578.
[272] Picton, Munic. Rec. i, 44.
[273] Munic. Rec. i, 156a.
[274] e.g. Acts of P.C. 1580-1, p. 214.
[275] Acts of P.C. 1589-90, p. 298.

and 'Ilbrye' as one of the ports of Cheshire.[276] This was made the basis of a claim on the part of Chester to superiority over Liverpool. This was not merely due to the claim of the Mayor of Chester to be vice-admiral of Lancashire and Cheshire ;[277] Chester claimed that Liverpool was only 'a creek within its port,' and that all ships entering the Mersey should pay dues through Chester. This claim, first formally advanced in 1565,[278] was, in spite of backing from London, entirely repudiated by the Liverpool burgesses.[279] They petitioned the Crown for protection; and eventually a commission sent down to investigate reported in Liverpool's favour.[280] When Chester in 1578 made the more limited claim of supremacy over the Cheshire shore of the Mersey,[281] equal vigour was shown in repudiation. The question was not settled during this century; it reappeared in the early part of the 17th century,[282] and was not disposed of till in 1658[283] an award was given in favour of Liverpool by the Surveyor-General of Customs—an award which was later confirmed by the first Restoration Surveyor-General in 1660.[284]

The administrative arrangement which gave to Chester the pretext for this claim had been dictated largely by convenience in organizing the transport of troops to Ireland, which went on with great vigour throughout the period. In 1573 Essex and part of his army were transported from Liverpool,[285] and substantial forces also left the port in 1565,[286] 1574,[287] 1579,[288] 1588,[289] 1595,[290] and 1596.[291] The transport of these troops was not unprofitable ; 2s. a head was allowed for food during the passage,[292] and the cost of transport was more than £1 a head,[293] while during the stay of the troops in Liverpool, which lasted sometimes for a long period,[294] 3d. a head was allowed for each meal, and 4d. a day for a horse's fodder.[295] But the visits of the troops were troublesome. Quarters and food had to be compulsorily provided. Even when they were promptly paid for, it must have been difficult for a town of less than 200 houses to provide for large forces ; but the payment was often long delayed.[296] Moreover the troops were often riotous. The town records give a vivid account of an affray which broke out among Lord Essex' men in 1573,[297] and which brought out all the burgesses in battle array on the heath, while in 1581 there was a formidable mutiny[298] which was only suppressed after sharp and exemplary punishment. A third inconvenience arose from the fact that the shipping of the port was often withdrawn from trade and detained for long periods in harbour, waiting for troops which never came. In 1593 it was only the intercession of Lord Derby[299] for 'the poor masters and owners of vessels stayed at Liverpool' which obtained their release, though no troops were nearly ready.

This was by no means the only occasion on which Lord Derby came to the aid of the burgesses. He was almost officially described by Walsingham as the 'patron of the poor town of Liverpool,'[300] and was appealed to on every occasion. One of the seats in Parliament (to which Liverpool had resumed the right of election in 1545),[301] was always reserved for his nominee ; the other was usually placed at the disposal of the Chancellor of the Duchy, from whom, in all probability, Francis Bacon received the nomination which made him member for Liverpool in the session of 1588–9.[302] When in 1562[303] the burgesses celebrated their reconciliation with Sir Richard Molyneux by nominating him to the seat usually reserved for the Chancellor, that official was so angry that he made a separate return, so that two sets of Liverpool members appear in the lists for that year,[304] and it was only the protection of Lord Derby that reassured the town against his direful threats. Nothing can exceed the pitiful submissiveness of the burgesses when they have the misfortune to offend Lord Derby,[305] nor the lavish enthusiasm with which they welcomed him in his visits to the town.[306] He was their one protector against aggressive lessees, greedy rival towns, crushing monopolist companies or angry chancellors.

It follows from the use they made of their Parliamentary privilege that the burgesses took small interest in the progress of national affairs. They lit bonfires on the Queen's birthdays,[307] but the only reflection of the excitement of 1588 which their records contain is the note of the erection of one gun on the Nabbe at the entrance to the Pool.[308] Even the change of religious opinion is but faintly reflected in the records. As time went on they became more and more Protestant ; their patron, the fourth Earl of Derby, was one of the keenest of Protestants by profession, offering the use of the Tower for the safe-keeping of recusants.[309] Towards the end of the century we find the burgesses ordering the closing of all ale-houses on the 'Sabbath' day, demanding a sermon or homily every Sunday, and engaging, in addition to the 'minister,' a zealous and faithful preacher at £4 per annum.[310]

For the burgesses indeed, the development of their own institutions (which now entered on a striking new phase) was more vital than political or religious events. Probably it was the series of disputes into which they had been drawn, and which had so seriously threatened their liberties, that led to the development of an executive committee within the assembly of burgesses, hitherto supreme.[311] The assembly was unsuited to carry on these struggles,[312] and after several experiments with councils elected for a limited period, which all failed through the jealousy of the burgess body, in 1580 a permanent self-renewing council of twenty-four ordinary members with

[276] Acts of P.C. 1558–70, p. 288.
[277] Cal. S.P. Dom. 1625–6, p. 430.
[278] Munic. Rec. i, 143b.
[279] Ibid. i, 159a ; ii, 31.
[280] Ibid. i, 156a.
[281] Picton, Munic. Rec. i, 37.
[282] Cal. S.P. Dom. 1619–23, pp. 24, 34, 43.
[283] Picton, Munic. Rec. i, 153.
[284] Ibid. 306. The award is printed in full by Baines, Hist. Liv. 242 n.
[285] Acts of P.C. 1571–5, p. 113.
[286] Ibid. 1558–70, p. 264.
[287] Ibid. 1571–5, p. 279.
[288] Ibid. 1578–80, p. 223.

[289] Ibid. 1588, p. 331.
[290] Ibid. 1595–6, pp. 280, 314, 422.
[291] Ibid. 1596–7, pp. 165, 478.
[292] Harl. MS. 1926, Art. 10, fol. 29.
[293] Acts of P.C. 1588, p. 331.
[294] Ibid. 1578–80, p. 296 ; 1571–5, p. 279.
[295] Ibid. p. 296.
[296] Ibid. 1571–5, p. 279.
[297] Picton, Munic. Rec. i, 109.
[298] Acts of P.C. 1580–1, pp. 64, 96.
[299] Ibid. 1592–3, p. 439.
[300] Picton, Munic. Rec. i, 44.
[301] Pink and Beavan, Parly. Rep. of

[304]

[309]

twelve aldermen was appointed.[313] Though it was to go through some vicissitudes, this body remained in control of the borough till 1835.

The records of this period present a very vivid picture of the social condition and customs of the borough. Space does not permit of any summary of these, but something must be said on the methods of conducting trade.[314] The regulation of trade was in the hands of the mayor and aldermen, acting under by-laws laid down by the portmoot or the assembly of burgesses. In the weekly market for local traffic no outsider was allowed to purchase corn until the wants of the burgesses had been satisfied. Forestalling and regrating were severely punished. Ingate and out-gate dues were charged for goods brought to or from the market; from these the burgesses and also the inhabitants of Altcar and Prescot were free. The masters of ships bringing cargoes into the Mersey, after paying anchorage dues, had to obtain permission from the mayor before offering their goods for sale. First the mayor determined whether he should offer to take the whole cargo as a 'town's bargain.' If he decided to do this, a sum was offered which had been estimated by the merchant prysors. If the importer refused this offer he must either leave the port or agree with the mayor as to the sum he must pay to 'make his best market,' i.e. to offer his goods for sale in open market. It was a system of high protection for the burgesses and minute regulation, so vexatious and hampering to trade that it was already breaking down by the end of the century.

The first three decades of the 17th century saw the prosperity and the burghal liberties of Liverpool safely re-established. The port was largely used for transport to Ireland during the reigns of James I and Charles I[315]—more largely now than Chester. In 1625 five transports containing 550 men were wrecked on the coast of Holyhead on the way to Carrickfergus, and less than two hundred men were saved.[316] The loss of five vessels was a serious blow to a small port, and the mayor feared that 'unless the king compassionates the town, it will be the utter overthrow of that corporation.' Pirates, too, still haunted the Irish seas; frequent levies of money had to be raised for dealing with them,[317] and even under the firm rule of Wentworth in Ireland a 'Biscayan Spanish rogue' took up his station off Dublin Bay, 'outbraved the two kingdoms,' and captured two Liverpool vessels, one of which had cargo to the value of £3,000, while another bore ' a trunk of damask' belonging to the lord-lieutenant himself.[318] Nevertheless the prosperity of the port steadily increased, and gained especially from the development of Irish industries under Wentworth. In 1618 the number of vessels in the port[319] was twenty-four, with a total tonnage of 462. In the next year Chester had to represent to the Crown that it possessed no ships, trading only in small barks.[320] The superior rival of the previous century had been distanced; and this being so, it is not surprising that Liverpool should have repudiated, with even greater vigour than in 1565, the claim of Chester to supremacy, which was revived in 1619.[321] To retain a share of the trade in Irish yarn, Chester had to make special treaties with Irish exporters; [322] but even then Liverpool more than held its own.[323] Foreign trade as well as Irish trade was increasing,[324] especially with Spain; a part of the salt of Cheshire, hitherto almost monopolized by Chester, came to supply outgoing cargoes; malt was brought from Tewkesbury to Liverpool by the Severn and the sea; [325] and there is even a record of one cargo of tobacco[326] brought direct from the Indies—the beginning of Liverpool's American trade.

This growing prosperity is reflected in a growth of population, despite a visitation of the plague in 1609.[327] The number of freemen rose from 190 in 1589 to 256 in 1620 and to 450 in 1645.[328] Though some of these were non-resident, there was also a considerable non-freeman population in the borough, and the population on the eve of the Civil War may, perhaps, be estimated at 2,000 or 2,500. At the same time the corporate revenue undergoes a remarkable expansion. In 1603 it was £55; in 1650 it had risen to £273.[329]

The borough was comparatively little troubled during the early years of the century by the difficulties by which it had been faced in the preceding age. In 1617 the copyholders of West Derby, instigated by Sir Richard Molyneux, raised a claim to a part of the Liverpool waste,[330] now administered by the borough; but the mayor and bailiffs were instructed to 'make known unto them . . . that time out of mind the liberties which we claim have belonged to our town, and that we have evidence to maintain the same,' and the question was not pressed. In 1620 there was an obscure dispute with Sir Richard over the levying of prisage duties on wine,[331] the issue of which is unknown. Several times during the period the borough authorities came in conflict with the Duchy courts on the question of the competence of the borough courts to try all cases arising within the liberties,[332] a right which was vigorously and successfully maintained. But the questions which occupy most space in the records are internal disputes, especially concerning the powers and duties of the burghal officers. From 1633 to 1637 a fierce controversy raged with the town-clerk,[333] Robert Dobson, who, having paid £70 for his office, considered himself irremovable, and bore himself with intolerable insolence towards the mayor and bailiffs. This controversy eventually led to a dispute with the Chancery Court of the Duchy, to which Dobson tried to remove his case. There were disputes also with the bailiffs. The bailiffs of 1626[334] were imprisoned in the Common Hall for refusing to carry out the instructions of the Town Council; the bailiffs of 1629[335] brought an action against the corporation in the King's Bench, for which one of them was deprived of the freedom.

[313] Picton, *Munic. Rec.* i, 52; and *Hist. Munic. Govt.* 85.

[314] Munic. Rec. *passim*; the detailed regulations of trade occupy perhaps a larger amount of space in the records than any other single subject.

[315] Liv. Munic. Rec. *passim*; Hist. MSS. Com. Rep. viii, App. i, 380*b*–6*b*; ibid. iv, 2, 3, 6; ibid. v, 350; Cal. S.P. Dom. 1625-6, p. 40, &c.

[316] Cal. S.P. Dom. 1625-6, pp. 5, 6, 8.

[317] Ibid. 1619-23, pp. 24, 43.

[318] Hist. MSS. Com. Rep. xii, App. ii, 10.

[319] S.P. Dom. Jas. I, cix, 9 (1).

[320] Cal. S.P. Dom. 1619-23, p. 24.

[321] Ibid. pp. 34, 104.

[322] Hist. MSS. Com. Rep. viii, App. i, 381*b*.

[323] Ibid. 399*a*.

[324] Liv. Munic. Rec. *passim.*

[325] Picton, *Liv. Munic. Rec.* i, 181.

[326] Ibid.

[327] *Shuttleworth Accounts* (Chet. Soc. xxxv), 186; *Hist. MSS. Com. Rep. x,* App. iv, 62.

[328] Picton, *Liv. Munic. Rec.* i, 124.

[329] Ibid. 174.

[330] Ibid. 169.

[331] Ibid. 274.

[332] Ibid. 136, 131, 165, 171.

[333] Ibid. 161 ff.

[334] Ibid. 126.   [335] Ibid.

Probably the cause of these disputes was the control exercised by the new Town Council over officials, who, before its establishment, had been accustomed to uncontrolled authority. During this period the Town Council seems to have remained on good terms with the body of burgesses ; [336] partly because its meetings were open ; partly because it appears to have been the practice for the bailiffs, elected on the annual election day, to become thereafter members of the council for life.[337] This gave to the burgess-body some control over the membership of the council, and probably left few places to be filled up by the council itself.

But the most striking sign of the growing independence of the borough is to be seen in the use made of its privilege of electing to Parliament. Lord Derby still occasionally nominated one member, but the Chancellor of the Duchy lost his right ; always one, and sometimes both, of the members were now genuinely elected by the borough, wages were paid to them, and care was taken that they earned them. In the elections all freemen took part, and, probably because the Town Council was so recently established and because national politics were beginning to be interesting, this power was never usurped from the freemen by the council. An illustration of the mode of treatment of their members by the burgesses may be quoted. In 1611 Mr. Brook [338] sent in a bill for £28 10s. for the wages of his attendance during the previous session. Of this he had already 'received in allowance and payments £14 5s. 7d., and so rested due to him £14 4s. 5d., which 4s. 5d. was deducted in regard of his stay in Chester about his own business four days, and so he was allowed £14 absolutely, provided he delivered first the New Charter.'

Mr. Brook did not produce a charter, and we are left to infer that his wages were not paid. This is one of a series of applications for a charter which occur at frequent intervals in the later years of the 16th century and the first quarter of the 17th, inspired by the sense of insecurity in their privileges to which the controversies of the previous fifty years had given rise. There survives a memorandum,[339] dating from about 1580, in which the Recorder gives it as his opinion that the borough had never in any of its charters been incorporated in express words, and that all its privileges must remain insecure until this was rectified. Applications in 1603,[340] 1611,[341] and 1617[342] were unsuccessful ; but at length in 1626[343] a new charter was purchased from Charles I, then embarrassed by the war with Spain and by the quarrel with Parliament.

The charter of Charles I is the most important of the series, after that of Henry III. It definitely incorporated the borough ; confirmed it in all the powers it exercised, whether enjoyed by grant or by usurpation ; vested in the burgess body full powers of legislation not only for themselves but for all inhabitants of the borough ; and granted, probably for

the first time,[344] the right to hold a court under the Statute of Merchants. The charter did not even name the town council, which was thus left at the mercy of the burgess body ; but in the next year the existing council was re-elected, and as there is no trace of any discussion of the question until the second half of the century, it would seem that no attack on the powers of the council was intended. The existence of the bench of aldermen is only incidentally recognized by the appointment of the senior alderman for the time being as a justice of the peace. The charter thus gave ground for a good deal of dispute, though none seems to have arisen. But it was an invaluable grant, for it secured the burgesses in the possession of all the vague rights which they had usurped since 1394, but which had been threatened since the Molyneuxes obtained possession of the lease of the farm ; particularly the ownership of the waste and the sovereignty of the borough officers over the whole population of the borough. It left unsettled, however, several questions at issue between the borough and the lessees of the farm which had remained dormant since 1555.

It was fortunate that the charter had been obtained before 1628, for in that year Charles I sold Liverpool,[345] with some three hundred other manors, to trustees on behalf of the citizens of London, in acquittance of a number of loans. So long as the Molyneux lease lasted the Londoners' ownership of the lordship meant nothing beyond the right of receiving the £14 6s. 8d. of farm rent, which had to be at once paid over to the Crown, the sale having been made subject to an annual rent-charge of this amount. The lordship was therefore worthless to the Londoners ; it was valuable only to Sir Richard Molyneux, who by buying it from them for £400 in 1636 [346] obtained in perpetuity and in freehold the rights he had previously enjoyed by lease, as well as any other rights that might be construed as coming under the lordship. This placed the burgesses more fully than ever at his mercy. In 1638 he commenced an action in the Court of Wards [347] to prohibit the burgesses from working an illicit ferry and mill which had somehow got into their possession. The burgesses, resisting, petitioned the Crown for a grant of the lease of the farm to themselves ; [348] but this, although the king 'made a most gracious answer,' was obviously out of his power since the sale, and they found it necessary to come to an agreement,[349] whereby they were to pay Molyneux £20 per annum without prejudice to their rights. Before the question could be raised again, and before Molyneux could attempt to press home other claims, the Civil War had broken out, and the later stages of the dispute were postponed until after the Restoration.

The side which Liverpool was likely to take in the great struggle would not have been easy to predict from its action during the preceding years. On the whole the temper of the burgesses, in religious matters,

---

[336] It is impossible to tell whether the assembly had in this period been wholly superseded, the word 'Assembly' being used for both types of meetings. There is some evidence that council meetings were open to freemen ; *Liv. Munic. Rec.* i, 127.

[337] *Hist. Munic. Govt. in Liv.* 88 and note.

[338] Picton, *Liv. Munic. Rec.* i, 157.

[339] *Hist. Munic. Govt. in Liv.*, 90.

[340] *Norris Papers* (Chet. Soc. ix), 8.

[341] Picton, *Munic. Rec.* i, 157.

[342] Ibid. 156.

[343] Orig. in Liv. Mun. Archives ; *Hist. Munic. Govt.* 165–89. An analysis of the charter is given in the same work, 91–4.

[344] The docquet of the charter speaks of it as 'a confirmation . . . of ancient liberties *with an addition* of a clause for

the acknowledgment of statute merchant ;' ibid. 166.

[345] The deed of sale is printed in *Hist. Munic. Govt. in Liv.* 362–81.

[346] Deed of sale at Croxteth (Liv. box 10, bdle. R, No. 6), *Hist. Munic. Govt. in Liv.* 381.

[347] Picton, *Liv. Munic. Rec.* i, 132.

[348] Ibid.

[349] Ibid. 133.

seems to have been Puritan. Thus it was found necessary to have, in addition to the incumbent of the chapel, a 'preacher of the Word of God,'[350] who received £20 or £30 per annum together with 'a reasonable milk cow,' which was to be 'changed at the discretion of the Council;' and in 1629 the mayor petitioned the Bishop of Chester, Bridgeman, for permission to arrange 'once a month two sermons upon a week-day.'[351] The list of preachers arranged for the following year in accordance with the licence then obtained, is significant. It includes Kay, Vicar of Walton, who later became a Presbyterian, and Richard Mather, minister of the Ancient Chapel of Toxteth Park, who was driven to America by Laud in 1636. Probably the presence in Toxteth of a little group of Puritan farmers, planted there by Sir Richard Molyneux when the park was brought under cultivation in 1604,[352] had considerable influence upon the Puritan temper of the borough.

On the other hand, the influence of the surrounding gentry was exercised almost entirely on the Royalist side. The Royalism of West Derby Hundred was even stronger than the Parliamentarianism of Salford Hundred, and the centre and support of it was the special patron of Liverpool, Lord Strange, who during the incapacity of his father, until he succeeded to the title in 1642, represented the house of Stanley. The only considerable family in the district which took the Parliamentarian side was that of the Moores, of Liverpool,[353] and, local as they were, they could not balance the Derby influence. Thus torn asunder, the borough followed an extremely vacillating course. To the Parliament of 1623 two Royalist members were returned.[354] In that of 1625 the Puritan, Edward Moore, was balanced by Lord Strange.[355] In the Petition of Right Parliament there were again two strong Royalist members.[356] Thus in the first period of the national controversy, the influence of the neighbouring gentry was able to outweigh the Puritan tendencies of the borough. But during the eleven years of personal government, the tide of opinion turned. On the first levy of ship-money in 1634, Liverpool was required to pay £15 as its share of the cost of a ship of 400 tons, to be raised by the maritime counties of Wales, by Cheshire, Lancashire, and Cumberland;[357] the same sum was assessed by a committee of mayors and sheriffs upon Carlisle, while Chester had to pay £100. The burden was a light enough one for a town which a little later raised without difficulty £160 to fight a single law-suit;[358] but there was keen opposition,[359] several burgesses declined to pay, and threatened the bailiffs with actions at law if they should attempt distraints; the Town Council had to resolve that the costs of such actions should be borne at the town's expense, but there were two members of the council itself who protested against this. In the next year John Moore, the regicide, was elected mayor, and on the second levy of ship-money there were similar difficulties.[359a]

When the meeting of the Short Parliament ended

the period of personal government, both of the Liverpool members were in the opposition;[360] while to the Long Parliament Liverpool returned the acrid Puritan, John Moore, along with Sir Richard Wynne,[361] who, though he had accompanied Charles I on his journey to Spain, was by no means a staunch Royalist: he voted against the attainder of Strafford, but he was a member of the deputation to present the Grand Remonstrance to the king.[362] It is tolerably clear that had the burgesses been left to themselves, without the influence of Lord Derby and others, Liverpool, like other ports, would have been enrolled on the Parliamentarian side.

When, on the outbreak of war, the Parliamentarian party in Lancashire began to organize their resistance against the vigorous action of Lord Strange, John Moore of Liverpool was the only gentleman of West Derby Hundred whom they could find to include in their list of deputy-lieutenants. Even he was apparently helpless in Liverpool, for he is found with the other Parliamentarian leaders at Manchester in the middle of 1642.[363] Liverpool, controlled by the Molyneux Castle and the Stanley Tower, was defenceless against the Royalist party. Lord Strange was able to seize the large stock of powder which lay in the town,[364] and to garrison both castle and tower. He was actively supported by the mayor, John Walker,[365] who received a royal letter of commendation for his action; but the presence of a considerable Parliamentarian party in the town is indicated by the note that the mayor had been threatened, perhaps by John Moore, with imprisonment and transportation from the country.[366] Colonel Edward Norris, of Speke, became governor,[367] and thirty barrels of gunpowder were sent into the town from Warrington.[368] Nothing, however, seems to have been done to strengthen the defence of the town. It remained under Royalist control so long as Lord Derby's strength was sufficient to hold the western half of the county. When, in the early months of 1643, his main force was called off for service in the midlands, the Parliamentarian forces from Manchester rapidly overran the western half of the county, and by May, Lathom House and Liverpool were the only Royalist strongholds left. Colonel Tyldesley, with the remnant of the Royalist forces, fell back upon Liverpool;[369] but he was hotly followed by Assheton with the Manchester Parliamentarians,[370] while a Parliamentarian ship entering the Mersey cut off retreat in that direction.[371] After two days' fighting Assheton had captured the whole line of Dale Street and also the chapel of St. Nicholas, in the tower of which guns were mounted which commanded the town. Tyldesley was forced to treat, asking for a free retreat to Wigan with arms and artillery. These terms were refused, and an assault completely routed the Royalists, who lost eighty dead and 300 prisoners, while the loss of the attacking force was only seven killed.[372] the date of this first siege is unknown, but it was probably at the end of May 1643.

The Parliamentarians, now masters of Liverpool,

[350] Picton, *Liv. Munic. Rec.* i, 197.
[351] Ibid. 200.
[352] *V.C.H. Lancs.* iii, 42.
[353] The Irelands of Hale were a little too far away.
[354] *Ret. of Memb. of Parl.*
[355] Ibid.   [356] Ibid.
[357] *Hist. MSS. Com. Rep.* viii, App. i, 383a; *Cal. S.P. Dom.* 1634–5, p. 568.
[358] Picton, *Liv. Munic. Rec.* i, 133.

[359] Ibid. 220. The money was, however, duly paid; *Cal. S.P. Dom.* 1634–5, p. 569.
[359a] *Cal. S.P. Dom.* 1636–7, pp. 205–6.
[360] *Ret. of Memb. of Parl.*
[361] Ibid.
[362] *Commons' Journ.* sub die.
[363] *Hist. MSS. Com. Rep.* v, 32a.
[364] Ibid. ix, App. iii, 391b. It amounted to 3,000 cwt. of powder in 1637 and 1638;

Cal. S.P. Dom. 1637, p. 507; 1638–9, p. 387.
[365] Picton, *Liv. Munic. Rec.* i, 137.
[366] Ibid.   [367] Ibid. 138.
[368] Ibid. 137.
[369] 'Exceeding joyful News,' &c. printed in Ormerod, *Lanc. Civil War Tracts* (Chet. Soc. ii), 104.
[370] Ibid.   [371] Ibid. and 138.
[372] Ormerod, loc. cit. 105.

proceeded to make very effective use of their capture. Lieut.-Col. Venables was appointed governor,[373] with martial powers overriding the town council. On his recall, early in 1644, he was succeeded, as a result of a petition from the burgesses, by Colonel John Moore,[374] who remained in command until the town fell before Rupert. The German engineer Rosworm was brought from Manchester to reconstruct the fortifications,[375] which were, however, not very skilfully laid out. A ditch 36 ft. wide and 9 ft. deep was cut from the river,[376] north of the Old Hall, to the Pool. Behind it ran a high earthen rampart, which was broken by gates where it was crossed by Oldhall Street, Tithebarn Street, and Dale Street, each gate being protected by cannon. Earthworks with batteries guarded the line of the Pool, and a strong battery of eight guns was placed at the angle of the Pool, below the castle. In addition, a number of guns were placed on the castle. A regular garrison, consisting of a regiment of foot and a troop of horse,[377] was kept in the town; but in addition military service was required of the burgesses, for whose use 100 muskets, 100 bandoliers, and 100 rests were delivered to the mayor and aldermen,[378] a fine of 1s. being imposed on any burgess who failed to turn out for duty 'at the beating of the drum.'[379] During the period of military occupation the authority of the governor overrode that of the town council. He was present at its meetings,[380] and most of his officers were admitted to the freedom. John Moore seems to have been far from successful as a governor. Adam Martindale, who served as his chaplain,[381] gives a terrible picture of the governor's entourage, though he praises[382] the 'religious officers of the company' with whom he 'enjoyed sweet communion,' as they met 'every night at one another's quarters, by turnes, to read scriptures, to confer of good things, and to pray together.'

The functions which Liverpool had to perform were threefold. On land, the garrison had to hold a Royalist district in check, and to take part in the siege of Lathom House. In addition it had to keep in touch with the Parliamentarian forces in Cheshire, and be prepared to deal with movements of the Royalist garrison of Chester. On the sea the function of Liverpool was still more important. It was the 'only haven'[383] of the Parliamentarians on the west coast, and it therefore became the base of naval movements intended to prevent communication between Ormond, in Ireland, and the English Royalists.[383] For this purpose part of the fleet was stationed here as early as June 1643,[384] and five months later this force amounted to six men-of-war,[385] and Colonel Moore, Governor of Liverpool, became Vice-Admiral for Lancashire and Westmorland.[386] It was under the command of one Captain Danks or Dansk,[387] and though the prevalent north-west winds sometimes shut him into the Mersey, he was able very seriously to harass the Royalists, intercepting supplies[388] upon which the Irish Royalists were

dependent, and preventing the transport of troops. Royalist vessels from Bristol, indeed, disputed with the Liverpool ships the command of the Irish Sea,[389] but not very effectively; the Puritan sailors of Bristol were half-hearted in the service, and one Bristol ship laden with arms and supplies for Chester deserted and sailed into the Mersey.[390] Ormond felt the position to be so serious for himself that he wrote to the Royalist forces in Cheshire,[391] 'earnestly recommending' them to attack Liverpool 'as soon as they possibly can,' and urging that 'no service to my apprehension can at once so much advantage this place (Dublin) and Chester, and make them so useful to each other.' The same urgent advice was given by Archbishop Williams,[391] in command at Conway. The capture of Liverpool was one of the immediate objectives of Byron's force of 3,000 Irish, which landed in Cheshire in November 1643, and on its arrival supplies were sent in to Liverpool,[392] and forces called up to its aid.[394] The defeat of Byron in January 1644 left the Liverpool garrison free to press the siege of Lathom[395] in conjunction with Assheton's forces from Bolton. But the straits of Lathom formed an additional reason for a vigorous blow from the Royalist side. Lord Derby was urgent[396] upon Prince Rupert to relieve Lathom, and to seize Liverpool, 'which your highness took notice of in the map the last evening I was with you, for there is not at this time fifty men in the garrison.'

Urged by these motives, the capture of Liverpool was one of the tasks which Rupert set himself on his northward march, in May and June, to the relief of Newcastle in York. His approach caused Moore to retreat hastily to Liverpool, while the garrison was reinforced by 400 men sent from Manchester;[397] the ships in the Mersey were drawn up in the port to assist in repelling the attack;[398] women, children, and suspects were removed from the town,[399] and all who remained 'were resolute to defend' the place.

It was on 9 June that Rupert, fresh from a brilliant success over the Parliamentarians, came down over the hill which overlooked and commanded the little town. 'A mere crow's nest,' he is said to have called it, 'which a parcel of boys might take.'[400] But two furious assaults of the kind which had carried all before them at Bolton were alike unsuccessful,[401] the loss to the besieging force being stated at 1,500. Rupert had then to throw up earthworks[402] and bring up his artillery, which during several days' cannonade cost 'a hundred barrels of munition, which,' says a correspondent of Lord Ormond, 'makes Prince Rupert march ill-provided.'[403] At length a night attack was led by Caryll, brother of Lord Molyneux,[404] whose local knowledge brought the surprise party through the fields on the north to the outhouses of the Old Hall, the family mansion of the governor of the town, which they reached at three o'clock in the morning. They found the ramparts deserted by the regular garrison, which had been drawn off by Colonel

[373] Hist. MSS. Com. Rep. x, App. iv, 66.
[374] Ibid.
[375] 'Rosworm's good service,' &c. in Ormerod, loc. cit. 229.
[376] Seacome, Hist. of the House of Stanley.
[377] Martindale, Autobiog. (Chet. Soc. iv), 36-7.
[378] Picton, Liv. Munic. Rec. i, 138.
[379] Ibid. 139.   [380] Ibid.
[381] Martindale, Autobiog. 36-7.
[382] Ibid. 37-8.

[382a] Hist. MSS. Com. Rep. xiii, App. i, 157.
[383] Ibid. 713.   [385] Ibid. 157.
[386] Ibid. x, App. iv, 67.
[387] Carte, Life of Ormond, iii, 190.
[388] Hist. MSS. Com. Rep. xiii, App. i, 133.
[389] Ibid. 153.
[390] Ormerod, op. cit. 154.
[391] Carte, Life of Ormond, iii, 229.
[392] Ibid. 212.
[393] Hist. MSS. Com. Rep. x, App. iv, 68.

[394] Ibid.
[395] Ormerod, op. cit. 162, 173, 185.
[396] Warburton, Rupert, 364.
[397] Merc. Brit. in Ormerod, op. cit. 199.
[398] Seacome, House of Stanley, 117.
[399] Ibid.
[400] Ibid.
[401] Ormerod, op. cit. 199.
[402] Seacome, loc. cit.
[403] Ormond MSS. ii, 319.
[404] Moore Rental (ed. W. F. Irvine), 16.

Moore during the night, and embarked with the military stores on the shipping in the Pool.[405] About 400 men of the garrison, however, still remained, and these offered a vigorous resistance. Street fighting went on for several hours ; though there seems to have been some sort of surrender, 'Prince Rupert's men did slay almost all they met with, to the number of 360, and among others . . . some that had ne er borne arms, . . . yea, one poor blind man ' ;[406] Caryll Molyneux, according to Sir Edward Moore, the runaway Colonel's son, killing 'seven or eight poor men with his own hands.' [407] The remainder of the garrison surrendered at the High Cross. They were imprisoned in the tower and the chapel, while Rupert took up his quarters in the castle, and the town was given over to sack. The number of the killed is indicated by the fact that six months later every household had to provide a man to aid in 'better covering the dead bodies of our murthered neighbours' of the 'great company of our inhabitants murthered and slain by Prince Rupert's forces.' [408]

The capture of the town probably took place on 14 or 15 June ; it is mentioned in the *Mercurius Britannicus* of 17 June.[409] Rupert remained in the castle till the 19th,[410] when he marched for Lathom. The intervening days were probably spent in drawing up proposals for the refortification of the town, which was intrusted to a Spanish engineer, de Gomme. His excellent plan survives, but was never carried out.

The defeat of Rupert at Marston Moor probably gave pause to these elaborate schemes. On his retreat he was expected to call at Liverpool,[411] but does not seem to have done so. Liverpool was now again, except Lathom, the only Royalist stronghold in Lancashire.[412] To garrison it Sir Robert Byron had been left with a large force of English and Irish troops ;[413] there was also a considerable number of cattle within the walls,[414] while guns had been mounted on 'Worrall side' (probably near the modern New Brighton) to prevent the approach of Parliamentary ships.[415] To deal with Liverpool and Lathom 1,000 horse were detached by Lord Fairfax from the main army on 8 August to join the Lancashire Parliamentarian levies,[416] and the whole force was placed under the command of Sir John Meldrum. During August the Royalists were strong enough to keep the field, and there was a good deal of fighting between Liverpool and Lathom. But after 20 August, when the Royalists were severely defeated at Ormskirk,[417] it is probable that the formal siege of Liverpool began. Meldrum did not waste men on assaults, but sat down before the town and drew formal lines of entrenchment.[418] He was assisted by a fleet in the river under Colonel Moore,[419] probably the same with which he had escaped in June ; and 'the sad inhabitants from both sides are deeply distressed.' The Royalist forces in the neighbourhood strained every nerve to effect a relief ; a new force raised by Lord Derby had to be beaten back on

10 September ;[420] the Chester garrison had to be strictly blockaded to prevent its sending relief ; and on 17 September a force of 4,000 men was met by the Parliamentarians at Oswestry [421] marching to the relief of Liverpool. It was doubtless the value of Liverpool as a point of contact between Ireland and the northern Royalists which accounted for the importance attached to it. Well provisioned and strongly garrisoned, the town held out for nearly two months. In the last days of October fifty of the English soldiers in the garrison, fearing to share the fate threatened to the Irish, deserted,[422] driving with them into Meldrum's camp the greater part of the cattle in the town. On 1 November the remainder of the garrison mutinied, imprisoned their officers, and surrendered the town at discretion.[423] An attempt to imitate Moore's example by shipping supplies and ammunition in some vessels in the river was checked by the commander of the besieging force, who sent out rowing-boats to capture the ships.

During the remainder of the war Liverpool remained at peace, but for some years seems to have been used as one of the principal places of arms in the county.[423a] Colonel Moore for a time resumed command ; but his prestige was ruined by his behaviour during Rupert's siege ; and though Meldrum exonerated him from blame,[424] the townsmen themselves felt that the town had been needlessly abandoned, and petitioned Parliament to inquire as to whose was the 'neglect or default.' [425] Moore left for Ireland, and was replaced by another governor. His family never recovered from the discredit into which he had brought it, or from the financial difficulties in which he involved himself. As a recompense for its services and sufferings the town obtained several important grants from the Commonwealth government ; money for the relief of widows and orphans,[426] licence to cut timber from the Molyneux and Derby estates for the rebuilding of the town,[427] the abolition of the Molyneux tenancy of the lease,[428] and a grant of £10,000 worth of land, at first assigned from the estates of 'malignants,' in Galway,[429] which, however, turned out to be entirely illusory. At the same time the Tower passed from the possession of the house of Stanley, being sequestrated, and on 19 September 1646 sold by the Committee for Compounding.[430] The period of the Civil War thus saw the borough released from the feudal superiority which had so long oppressed it ; and though this came back at the Restoration it was less patiently endured, and lasted but a short time. The period also saw the division of the burgesses into two acrimonious political and religious parties, whose strife was to give a new character to the political development of the next epoch.

In the second half of the 17th century the development of Liverpool, which had begun in the first half of the century and been checked by the Civil Wars, received a remarkable impetus ; so that in 1699 the

---

[405] Ormerod, op. cit. 199.
[406] Martindale, *Autobiog.* (Chet. Soc. iv), 41.
[407] *Moore Rental* (ed. W. F. Irvine), 16.
[408] Picton, *Liv. Munic. Rec.* i, 140.
[409] Ormerod, op. cit. 199.
[410] *Hist. MSS. Com. Rep.* xiii, App. i, 179.
[411] Ibid. iv, App. 275b.
[412] *London Post*, 30 Sept. 1644, in Ormerod, op. cit. 206.
[413] Vicars, *Parl. Chron.* iv, 62.
[414] Ormerod, op. cit. 207.

[415] *Hist. MSS. Com. Rep.* iv, App. 270b.
[416] Ormerod, op. cit. 206.
[417] Ibid.
[418] *London Post*, in Ormerod, op. cit. 206.
[419] Ibid.   [420] Ibid. 207.
[421] Ibid. 206.
[422] *Perfect Diurnall*, in Ormerod, op. cit. 207.
[423] *Hist. MSS. Com. Rep.* vii, App. i, 449a.
[423a] See *Cal. S.P. Dom.* 1649–54, where there are numerous references.

[424] *Hist. MSS. Com. Rep.* x, App. iv, 73.
[425] Picton, *Liv. Munic. Rec.* i, 226.
[426] Ibid. 144.
[427] Ibid. 145.
[428] Ibid.   [429] Ibid. 147 ff.
[430] *Cal. of Com. for Compounding*, ii, 118. The purchaser was one Alexander Greene, who was still in possession in 1663 ; *Trans. Hist. Soc.* (new ser.), xvi, 136. These points have been brought out by Mr. Peet, *Liv. in Reign of Queen Anne*, 55 and note.

LIVERPOOL: LORD STREET, ABOUT 1798

(From a Water-colour Drawing)

borough could claim [431] that 'from scarce paying the salary of the officers of the Customs, it is now the third port of the trade of England, and pays upwards of £50,000 per annum to the king.' In 1673 the topographer Blome [432] found that it contained 'divers eminent merchants and tradesmen, whose trade and traffic, especially unto the West Indies, make it famous.' When in 1689 the Commissioners of Customs were asked to report as to the ports which could best supply shipping for transport to Ireland, they stated [433] that while Chester had 'not above 20 sail of small burden from 25 to 60 tons,' Liverpool had '60 to 70 good ships of from 50 to 200 ton burden, but because they drive a universal foreign trade to the Plantations and elsewhere,' it was impossible to tell how many of them would be available.

The port continued to control the larger share of the Irish trade. It still maintained a considerable traffic to France and Spain, and also to Denmark and Norway. [434] But, as the statements above quoted show, it was the opening out of a lucrative trade with 'the plantations,' especially the West Indies and Virginia, in sugar, tobacco, and cotton, which made this period mark the beginning of Liverpool's greatness. Several causes conspired to assist this development. The industries of Manchester were undergoing a rapid development, so that, in the words of Blome, [435] the situation of Liverpool 'afforded in greater plenty and at reasonabler rates than most places in England, such exported commodities proper for the West Indies.' The plague and fire of London had caused 'several ingenious men' to settle in Liverpool, 'which caused them to trade to the plantations,' [436] while when the French wars began in 1689 London traders found that 'their vessels might come safer north about Ireland, unload their effects at Liverpool, and be at charge of land-carriage from thence to London than run the hazard of having their ships taken by the enemy,' [437] and Liverpool profited accordingly. As early as 1668 a 'Mr. Smith, a great sugar-baker at London,' was bargaining with Sir Edward Moore [438] for land on which to build 'a sugar-baker's house . . . forty feet square and four stories high'; and Sir Edward Moore expected this to 'bring a trade of at least £40,000 a year from the Barbadoes, which formerly this town never knew.' Even more important than the establishment of a sugar-refining industry was the tobacco trade, which grew to large dimensions in these years. In 1701 it was asserted [439] that a threatened interference with the tobacco trade would 'destroy half the shipping in Liverpool'; [440] it was 'one of the chiefest trades in England,' and 'we are sadly envyed, God knows, especially the tobacco trade, at home and abroad.' [441] All the tobacco of Scotland, Ireland, and the north of England was supposed to come to Liverpool. [442] The result of this growing trade was a remarkably rapid increase of shipping ; in the twelve years between 1689 and 1701 the number of vessels in the port had grown from '60 or 70' to 102, which compares not unfavourably with the 165 vessels owned by Bristol in the same year. Shipping brought with it several new industries, and in particular rope-walks began to be a feature of the town, and remained so for more than a century to come. Many new families of importance begin to appear ; the Claytons, the Clevelands, the Cunliffes, the Earles, the Rathbones, the Tarletons, and the Johnsons, [443] win the superiority in municipal affairs from the Moores and the Crosses ; 'many gentlemen's sons of Lancashire, Yorkshire, Derbyshire, Staffordshire, Cheshire, and North Wales are put apprentices in the town,' [444] and a new set of names appears in the records. The population was steadily increasing. The ravages of the war, together with outbreaks of plague in 1647 and 1650, [445] had kept it down, so that in 1673 only 252 householders were assessed for the hearth tax, [446] giving a total population (allowing for exemptions) of about 1,500 ; but by the beginning of the 18th century the number was well over 5,000. [447] And now, for the first time, new streets began to be made in addition to the original seven : Moor Street, Fenwick Street, Fenwick Alley, and Bridge's Alley [448] having been cut by Sir Edward Moore out of his own lands, while Lord Street was cut by Lord Molyneux in 1668 through the castle orchard to the Pool, and Preeson's Row, Pool Lane (South Castle Street), and several other thoroughfares were being built upon. [449] Public improvements on a large scale began to be carried out or talked of. In 1673 a new town hall was built, 'placed on pillars and arches of hewn stone, and underneath the public exchange for the merchants.' [450] This building replaced the old thatched common hall with which the burgesses had been content since it was bequeathed to them by John Crosse ; it stood immediately in front of the modern town hall. The difficulty of accommodating the growing shipping of the port was already felt, and among the modes suggested for relieving the pressure was the deepening of the Pool, [451] a scheme which, in a modified form, ultimately led to the creation of the first dock. Proposals for improving the navigation of the Weaver [452] to facilitate the Cheshire trade, and for erecting lighthouses [453] on the coast, met indeed with keen opposition at first from the burgesses, who feared to see trade carried past their wharves ; but they were to be converted to both of these schemes before half a century had passed. In the meantime an improvement in the navigation of the Mersey below Warrington, carried out by Mr. Thomas Patten, [454] of the latter place, led to a material increase of Liverpool's trade, and was the first of a

[431] In the case for the establishment of a separate parish, printed in Picton, *Liv. Munic. Rec.* i, 325.

[432] Blome, *Britannia*, 134.

[433] *Hist. MSS. Com. Rep.* xii, App. vi, 169.

[434] Picton, *Liv. Munic. Rec.* i, 309 and *passim.*

[435] Loc. cit.

[436] Case for the new parish, loc. cit.

[437] *Hist. MSS. Com. Rep.* xiv, App. iv, 430. In 1694 we hear of no less than 32 ships sent from Liverpool to the West Indies ; *Cal. S.P. Dom.* 1694-5, p. 237.

[438] *Moore Rental* (ed. W. F. Irvine), 99. Apparently he did not complete his bargain ; but a sugar-house was built by his firm in Redcross Street ; Peet, *Liv. in the Reign of Queen Anne*, 32 n.

[439] *Norris Papers* (Chet. Soc.), 81.

[440] Ibid. 110.   [441] Ibid. 114.

[442] Ibid. 89.

[443] Mun. Rec. *passim* ; Peet, *Liv. in the Reign of Queen Anne*, 6 and *passim.*

[444] Case for the new parish, loc. cit.

[445] Picton, *Liv. Munic. Rec.* i, 192, 194.

[446] *Trans. Hist. Soc.* (new ser.), xvi, 136.

[447] Mr. Peet, on the basis of the poor-rate assessment of 1708, estimates the population in that year at a little under 7,000 ; *Liv. in the Reign of Queen Anne*, 16.

[448] *Moore Rental, passim.*

[449] *Moore Rental, passim* ; also Picton, *Munic. Rec.* i, 314 ff.

[450] Blome, loc. cit. ; Picton, *Munic. Rec.* i, 286.

[451] *Moore Rental* (ed. W. F. Irvine), 79 ff, 101, 102, 104.

[452] *Hist. MSS. Com. Rep.* viii, App. i, 396a.   [453] Ibid. 395b.

[454] *Norris Papers*, 38.

series of such improvements which were pushed forward during the next period.

The rapid growth of the town, and the influx of a new and thriving population unused to the influences by which the town had been so long dominated, reflects itself in a rapid shaking-off of old connexions, which had already been seriously weakened by the Civil War and its consequences. This is perhaps clearest in the case of the Moores, so long the leading family of the town ; for Sir Edward Moore, son of the regicide and runagate Colonel John Moore, has left, in the form of instructions to his son, an elaborate description [455] of his own properties in the town and of his relations to its leaders which is invaluable as an elucidation of this period of transition. Deeply embarrassed by the debts incurred by his father, his estates had only been saved from confiscation by the fact that his wife, Dorothy Fenwick, was the daughter of a noted Royalist ; he suffered also, doubtless, from the shadow which hung over his father's name since his desertion in the siege of 1644. Soured by his misfortunes, he was on the worst of terms with the burgess-body, whose records are full of quarrels with him.[456] Moore had a clear prevision of the growth of the port, and hoped by its means to rehabilitate the fortunes of his house ; but the Town Council checked more than one of his schemes. Worse than this, the burgesses refused to elect him either to the mayoralty or as a representative of the borough in Parliament, and this he regarded as ingratitude to his family, as well as a direct injury to his fortunes. His Rental is full of bitterness on this score. 'They have deceived me twice, even to the ruin of my name and family, had not God in mercy saved me ; though there was none at the same time could profess more kindness to me than they did, and acknowledge in their very own memories what great patrons my father and grandfather were to the town . . . . Have a care you never trust them . . . for such a nest of rogues was never educated in one town of that bigness.'[457] He exhausts an extensive vocabulary for epithets to characterize those who were 'against him,' 'either for parliament man or mayor.' One of his greatest troubles was the difficulty which he experienced in enforcing the use of his mill. The ancient feudal milling rights had now quite broken down, and it was only by inserting a special clause in his leases that Moore, though lessee of two of the principal mills, could enforce the use of them even upon his own tenants.[458] Sir Edward Moore died in 1678, a worn-out old man at the age of forty-four. His son, Sir Cleave Moore, a 'useless spark,'[459] was the last representative of the family in Liverpool ; in 1712 he allowed a foreclosure to be made on his heavily mortgaged Liverpool lands and retired to estates in the south of England which he had got by marriage.[460] The departure of the Moores was the breach of one of the last links with the past of a town rapidly reshaping itself.

The same period which saw the departure of the Moores saw also the final settlement of the long feud with the Molyneuxes. At the Restoration the confiscation of their lordship during the Commonwealth was of course annulled. Immediately on taking possession, Caryll Lord Molyneux renewed the action [461] which his father had brought against the burgesses for invasion of his rights as lord of the manor. The burgesses, knowing that the case would go against them, made an accommodation similar to that which they had made in 1639, whereby they paid £20 per annum for a lease of all the lordship rights. But this did not settle the dispute. Lord Molyneux claimed that the burgesses were bound to pay the rent-charge of £14 6s. 8d. due from him to the Crown over and above the £20 ; they, on their side, contended that this sum was included in the £20. This dispute presently merged in another.[462] In 1668 Lord Molyneux had made a thoroughfare through the castle orchard to the Pool. Wishing to continue it, he consulted counsel, who advised him that as lord of the manor he was owner of the waste and had a right to make a thoroughfare over it. He therefore erected a bridge, thus raising the whole question of the ownership of the waste. The mayor and burgesses pulled down the bridge ; Molyneux replied with a whole series of actions at law, concerning 'the interests and title of the Corporation of Liverpool as to their claim in the waste grounds of Liverpool,' and also raising anew the old questions of tolls and dues. Had the question been fought out (as the burgesses were prepared to fight it) they would probably have won ; for the charter of Charles I, antedating the sale of the lordship, with its grant of all lands, &c. which they then held, however obtained, certainly covered the waste. After two years' fighting, however, a compromise was arranged, by which Molyneux was allowed to build his bridge on payment of a nominal rent of 2d. per annum in recognition of the borough's ownership of the waste ; while on the other hand he granted to the borough a lease of all the rights of lordship except the ferry and the burgage-rents (which he still had to pay to the Crown) for 1,000 years at £30 per annum.[463] In 1777 the lease was bought up from the then Lord Sefton, and this purchase included ferry and burgage-rents, which the Molyneuxes had previously purchased from the Crown.[464] Thus the ancient connexion of this family with the government of the borough came to an end ; and with it feudal superiority vanished from the borough.

Molyneux, indeed, remained hereditary constable of the castle,[465] which was still outside the liberties of the borough, and received the tithes payable to the parochial church of Walton. But both of these powers also vanished during this period. The castle had been partially dismantled between 1660 and 1678,[466] and it was now mainly used by a number of poor tenants who were allowed to remain within its walls,[467] beyond the control of the borough authorities. But when in 1688 and 1689 Lord Molyneux, actively supporting James II, made use of the castle for stores and arms,[468] and when in 1694 he was suspected of

---

[455] The Moore Rental, already quoted, has been published by W. F. Irvine, under the title of *Liverpool in King Charles II's Time* ; also by the Chetham Society (vol. iv).

[456] Picton, *Liv. Munic. Rec.* i, 154 ff.

[457] *Moore Rental* (ed. W. F. Irvine), 10, 11.

[458] Ibid. 64 and *passim*.

[459] *Hist. MSS. Com. Rep.* xiv, App. iv, 284.

[460] *Moore Rental* (ed. W. F. Irvine), xxx.

[461] Picton, *Liv. Munic. Rec.* i, 34.

[462] Ibid. i, 275-81.

[463] These documents are printed in *Hist. Munic. Govt. in Liv.* 391 ff.

[464] Ibid. 395, 227.

[465] Picton, *Liv. Munic. Rec.* ii, 37 ff.

[466] Ibid. ; Cox, *Liv. Castle.*

[467] Picton, *Liv. Munic. Rec.* ii, 40.

[468] *Hist. MSS. Com. Rep.* xiv, App. iv, 234, 235.

being concerned in the organization of a Jacobite rising,[469] he was confiscated, and the constableship passed out of his hands.[470] In 1699 the burgesses obtained a lease of the castle for a year,[471] thus for the first time bringing its precincts under their control. In 1704 they obtained from the Crown a lease[472] of the castle and its site for fifty years with power to demolish its ruins. Disputes with Lord Molyneux, who still claimed the hereditary constableship, delayed the settlement, and it was not until 1726 that the last relics, the wall at the top of Lord Street, disappeared.[473] The acquisition of the lordship and of the castle by the burgesses marks the conclusion of the period of struggle with feudal superiors which has hitherto been the staple of burghal history; and, no less than the great development of trade, makes this period the real beginning of modern Liverpool.

The establishment of Liverpool as a separate parish is another sign of the same tendency. The arrangement whereby the tithes paid by Liverpool to Lord Molyneux had during the Commonwealth period been devoted to the provision of a minister for the new parish of Liverpool had, of course, with other Commonwealth arrangements, been suppressed at the Restoration. But the rapid growth of the town made some readjustment inevitable. In 1673 Blome noted[474] that the chapel of St. Nicholas, though large, was too small to hold the inhabitants of the town, and this inadequacy became accentuated as the influx of population continued. In 1699, in response to a petition from the Corporation,[475] Liverpool was cut off from the parish of Walton, and created into a separate parish with two rectors appointed and paid by the Corporation. Compensation to the rector of Walton and to Lord Molyneux was also paid by the Corporation.[476] The borough thus became ecclesiastically as well as administratively independent. Under the same Act which constituted the parish, a new church, that of St. Peter, was erected on the continuation of Lord Molyneux's road across the waste, henceforth to be known as Church Street. But the creation of the parish involved the institution of the vestry as a separate poor-law authority, levying its own rates;[477] and this marks the beginning of a subdivision of administrative authority which was to be greatly extended during the next century.

The new temper of the burgesses, induced by their prosperity, is further exhibited in the use they made during the period of their Parliamentary franchise. Contested elections had been rare before the Restora-

tion, but almost every election after 1660 was acrimoniously contested. Lord Derby, who had once regularly nominated to one of the seats, was still influential, and his support often sufficed to turn the scale; but he was now only one of a group of magnates who wrote to use their influence at elections,[478] and after the Revolution his preferences were entirely disregarded. The wealthy merchants who now controlled Liverpool were not to be dictated to. Party feeling had run high, and influence in elections now mainly took the form of bribery, which became rampant in this period.

The bitter feud of two organized parties is indeed the chief feature of municipal history during these years. Since the fever of the Civil War the great issues which divided the nation affected the town as they had never done before; and under the stress of strife between Puritans and Cavaliers, or Whigs and Tories, the forms of borough government underwent a series of remarkable changes, always influenced by the synchronous events in national history. The rising port had emerged from its backwater into the full stream of national life.

Puritanism had been strong in Liverpool, and continued to be strong under Charles II. The Act of Uniformity drove forth two of the ministers of Walton and Liverpool; but there remained a substantial number of Nonconformists.[478a] No less than five aldermen and seven councilmen, together with the town clerk, refused to take the oaths in 1662–3,[479] being almost one in three of the council; though many who were Puritan in sympathy, like Colonel Birch,[480] who had been governor of the town under the Commonwealth, made no difficulty about accepting the oaths. Wandering Nonconformist preachers like Thomas Jolly[481] found 'many opportunities' and 'much comfort' when they came to Liverpool; and on the issue of the Declaration of Indulgence a licence was obtained for a Presbyterian conventicle in 'the house of Thomas Christian,' as well as for two chapels in Toxteth Park.[481a] The rector of Walton writes in 1693 of the presence in Liverpool of 'a number of fanatics from whom a churchman can expect little justice.'[482]

The presence of this substantial element of declared Nonconformists, backed by a number of Conformists who were Puritan in their sympathies in both political and religious affairs, brought it about that Liverpool was the scene of acute and acrimonious party strife down to, and even after, the Revolution. In 1662 a

---

[469] *Hist. MSS. Com. Rep.* xiv. App. iv, 292 ff. 302. He received a commission from the exiled monarch giving him 'instructions for the care and government of Liverpool.'

[470] There was much competition among the local nobility to obtain the succession. *Hist. MSS. Com. Rep.* i, 20, 21; iii, 270b.

[471] Picton, *Liv. Munic. Rec.* i, 292 ff.

[472] A full abstract of the lease is given by Picton, *Liv. Munic. Rec.* ii, 33 ff. The condition was at first imposed that part of the castle should be used as an armoury for the local militia; but in 1709 Lord Derby as lord lieutenant empowered the removal of these arms to the custody of the mayor. Ibid. 41.

[473] Picton, *Liv. Munic. Rec.* ii, 61.

[474] Loc. cit.

[475] Picton, *Liv. Munic. Rec.* i, 325.

[476] Ibid.

[477] It would appear, however, that Liverpool had acted as a poor-law authority for some time before it became a separate parish, no doubt under the terms of 13 & 14 Chas. II, cap. 13, which provided that in certain counties of the north of England populous townships should have overseers of their own, distinct from those of the large parishes of which they formed parts. From 1682, when the records begin, a poor-rate was levied and administered by elected 'overseers of the poor.' The amount raised rose from £40 in 1682 to £100 in 1698, the year before the Act constituting the parish was passed. There is no marked change either in the amount raised or in the mode of administration after the Act. Vestry Minutes, i.

[478] *Ormond MSS.* (Hist. MSS. Com. new ser.), iii, 367.

[478a] In 1669 the Bishop of Chester reported to Archbishop Sheldon that at 'Leverpoole was held a frequent conventicle of about 30 or 40 Anabaptists, mostly rich people,' while 'two conventicles of Independents' were held in Toxteth Park, 'the usual number of each is between 100 and 200, some of them husbandmen, others merchants with severall sorts of tradesmen'; Lambeth MSS. 639, quoted Bate, *Declaration of Indulgence*, App. viii.

[479] Picton, *Liv. Munic. Rec.* i, 238, 240. Cf. for presence of 'fanatics' in Liverpool, Cal. S.P. Dom. 1665–6, p. 243.

[480] Ibid.

[481] *Notebook of T. Jolly* (Chet. Soc. new ser. xxxiii), 60.

[481a] Bate, op. cit. App. lxx and xxxii.

[482] *Hist. MSS. Com. Rep.* xiv, App. iv, 279.

batch of thirty-eight new freemen were admitted,[483] nearly all powerful local landowners, and presumably good church and king men, and the object of this was doubtless to modify the Puritan complexion of the borough. But in spite of this it seems clear that the Puritans (or, as it will be more convenient and more accurate to call them, the Whigs) remained in a standing majority in the burgess body, throughout the period, and for a time held their own even in the carefully purified council.[484] This is especially indicated in the mayoral elections, the only function now left by the council to the burgess body at large. In 1669 a mayor was elected who had refused to take the oaths in 1662 ;[485] and when a petition against his election was sent to the Privy Council, a majority of the Town Council voted in favour of paying the costs of resistance. From this it would appear that in 1669 the Whigs were still strong in the council. So long as the bailiffs continued to be elected, under the terms of the Charter of Charles I, by the burgess body, and to become thereafter life members of the council, it seemed impossible for Tory predominance to be established.

Applications for a new charter were made in 1664[486] and 1667 ;[487] and as the influence of Lord Derby, that sound Cavalier, was enlisted in favour of these applications, it is reasonable to suppose that their object was to obtain a revision in a sense favourable to the Tories. The non-success of these applications may be attributed to the fact that Charles II, until the secession of Shaftesbury in 1672, hoped for Puritan support in his monarchic aims, and was unwilling therefore to weaken Puritan power.

In 1672 the Tories, now in a majority in the council though not in the assembly, and led by a Tory mayor, took the law into their own hands. They appear to have assumed the right of nominating the bailiffs ; and when a protest was made, it was condemned as 'very scandalous and of bad consequence,' and a resolution was passed deposing any of the (Whig) members of council who should be proved to have been concerned in it.[488] At the next electoral assembly the outgoing mayor, having declared his successor duly elected, adjourned the meeting seemingly without proceeding to the election of bailiffs.[489] A number of the burgesses, however, refused to be adjourned, and forcing the mayor to continue in the chair, transacted business for two hours, until the mayor was relieved by force. There is no record of their proceedings, which were regarded as illegal. They may have held that the result of the mayoral election was not truly declared ; they may have demanded an election of bailiffs ; and they may also have insisted upon exercising their chartered right of passing by-laws. For this riotous conduct twenty-six men were deprived of the freedom. In 1676, however, there was again a Whig mayor ;[490] who in conjunction with three Whig aldermen, proceeded to admit a number of new freemen without consulting the council, doubtless for the purpose of affecting the next elections. The council refused to recognize these freemen ; and when in 1677

another Whig mayor was elected, declared his election void on the ground that he had been struck off the commission of the peace for the county.[491] It is worth noting that these events occurred at the time when the Crown was engaged in its death-grapple with Shaftesbury.

On 18 July 1677 the council at last succeeded in obtaining from Charles II a new charter.[492] In the charter of William III, by which its main provisions were repealed, this charter is described as having been obtained ' by a few of the burgesses by a combination among themselves, and without a surrender of the previous charter or any judgement of *quo warranto* or otherwise given against the same.'[493] This doubtless means that the application was made by the Tory majority of the council, without confirmation by the assembly, to which under the charter of Charles I full governing powers belonged. The main purpose of the new charter was to secure the predominance of the council, unmentioned in the Charles I charter, and its control over the whole borough government. The number of the council was raised from forty to sixty in order to permit of the inclusion of ' fifteen . . . burgesses of the said town *dwelling without that town*,' i.e. fifteen good Tory country gentlemen who would secure the Tory majority. The charter also transferred from the assembly to the council the right of electing both the mayor and the bailiffs, as well as the nomination of freemen. As the election of the mayor and bailiffs was the sole municipal power remaining in the hands of the body of burgesses, this provision deprived them of any shadow of power over the government of the town. Their only remaining function was that of electing members of Parliament, and the right of nominating freemen gave control even over these elections ultimately into the hands of the council. Thus the result of this charter was to place the absolute control of the borough in the hands of a small self-electing Tory oligarchy.

The action of the council in the restless strife of the later years of Charles II was what might have been predicted. They passed vigorous loyal addresses against the Exclusion Bill[494] and in condemnation of the Rye-house Plot ;[495] the latter address contains an interesting allusion to Dryden's *Absalom and Achitophel*, which shows how keenly the movement of national affairs was now followed in the borough. But there is visible in the addresses also an undercurrent of nervousness ; their fear of ' Popish contrivances,' and their ' adherence to the true Protestant religion ' is a little too loudly insisted upon. This may explain why it was thought necessary to include Liverpool in the list of general revisions of municipal charters at the end of the reign of Charles II and the beginning of that of James II. Issued in the first year of James II, the new charter[496] simply confirmed its predecessor, but it contained also two new clauses, one reserving to the Crown the right of removing any member of the council or any borough official : the other conveying the power of exacting from any

[483] Picton, *Liv. Munic. Rec.* i, 240.
[484] On this point see *Hist. Munic. Govt. in Liv.* 102, 103.
[485] Picton, *Liv. Munic. Rec.* i, 245.
[486] Munic. Rec. iii, 779. A ' ley ' of £80 was raised for the purpose.
[487] Ibid. 837, 847.
[488] Picton, *Liv. Munic. Rec.* i, 246.
[489] Ibid. 247 ; and *Hist. Munic. Govt. in Liv.* 102–3, where this curious episode is discussed.
[490] Picton, *Liv. Munic. Rec.* i, 248.
[491] Ibid.
[492] *Hist. Munic. Govt. in Liv.* 191 ff.
[493] Ibid. 237. The only allusion to the episode in the Council minutes is a resolution on 1 Nov. 1676 authorizing the mayor ' to take care about renewing of our charter, taking to his assistance such as he shall think meet at the charge of this Corporation.' Munic. Rec. iv, 137. Clearly the assembly of burgesses had not been consulted.
[494] Picton, *Liv. Munic. Rec.* i, 251.
[495] Ibid. 253.
[496] *Hist. Munic. Govt. in Liv.* 207 ff.

LIVERPOOL IN 1680

From an Engraving of a Painting now in the Liverpool Museum

freeman the oaths hitherto required only from councillors, and thus rendering possible a further purification of the burgess body, still predominantly Whig.

Under the terms of this charter, the deputy-mayor and the senior alderman (both Tories) were removed[497] by the Crown for persisting in prosecuting two Catholics, a surgeon and a schoolmistress, for pursuing their professions, in spite of a licence issued by the Crown. This indicates that in Liverpool, as elsewhere, the loyalty of the Tories to the Crown was limited by their loyalty to the Church. Tory as it was, the council never willingly accepted this charter, which indeed would appear never to have had legal force.[498] The increasing restiveness of the council is still more clearly shown in the answer given[499] to commissioners who were in 1687 sent round to obtain promises of aid in securing a Parliament favourable to the repeal of the Test Act. The mayor answered 'that what is required by his Majesty is a very weighty and new thing; and that he was not prepared to give any answer but this : when it shall please the King to call a new Parliament, he proposed to vote for such persons as he hoped would serve the just interests both of his Majesty and the nation.' Only 'four or five customs officers' were ready to promise their votes.[500]

The borough as a whole was thus ready to welcome, and even the ruling oligarchy was ready to accept, the Revolution. A small force of royal troops were for a time in Liverpool,[501] and Lord Molyneux, Constable of the castle, took a vigorous part for James as Lord Lieutenant of the county ;[502] but the attitude of Lord Derby, who, Tory as he was, after some wavering, threw himself on the side of the Prince of Orange,[503] had more to do with determining the attitude of the town ; and one of the things he protested against was the 'extravagant methods practised by the new magistrates in the ancient loyal corporations' of Wigan, Liverpool, and Preston, into which he urged that inquiry should be made.[504] Though some of the townsmen made some difficulty about accepting the oaths to the new monarchs,[505] on the whole the Revolution was most enthusiastically received in Liverpool ; and during 1689 the port was very actively employed in the transport of troops for the Irish campaign,[506] General Kirke being for a time in command in the town,[507] while Schomberg passed through it[508] on his way to embark at Hoylake. So great was the demand for shipping that the merchants complained that they were being ruined.[509]

The Revolution brought about a temporary reconciliation between the two parties in the town. Not only the Tory magistrates removed by the Crown,[510] but some of the Whigs who had declined the oaths in 1678,[511] returned to the council. The charter of James II was dropped by common consent, if it had

ever come into force, and in 1690 an inspeximus and confirmation[512] of the charter of Charles II was obtained from William and Mary. In the first Parliament of the Revolution Liverpool was represented[513] by Lord Colchester, son-in-law of Lord Derby and a sound Tory, and by Thomas Norris, a strong Whig.

But it was inevitable that the Whigs, in a majority in the burgess-body, should desire power in the town government, and the reconciliation did not last long. In 1694, Lord Colchester being called up to the House of Peers, a Whig was elected in his place by 400 votes against 15 cast for his Tory opponent,[514] in spite of the support given by Lord Derby to the latter. The Tory mayor went so far as to declare the defeated candidate elected,[515] for which he was reprimanded by the House of Commons. This election was regarded as a triumph for the party which was anxious to overturn the charter of Charles II ; and the two members, Jasper Maudit and Thomas Norris, worked actively[516] to obtain a new charter. The Town Council voted funds for the defence of the Charles II charter,[517] and appealed to Roger Kenyon, member for Clitheroe, and to Lord Derby, to fight their case for them at Westminster.[518] In 1605, however, a new charter[519] was granted, which first declared the Charles II charter invalid on the grounds already noted, then recited and confirmed the Charles I charter, and went on to reduce the number of the Town Council to forty. This charter remained the governing charter of the borough until 1835. Its general principle (in consonance with the conservative character of the whole revolution of which it was a part) was to restore the system of government as it was supposed to have been before the recent changes. But it was badly drafted ; and left open several vital questions over which there was much discussion during the next century—notably the question whether it was within the power of the burgess body at its pleasure to override the powers of the Town Council.[520]

The Whigs were now in power in the council as well as in the assembly ; and though the Tories refused to accept the new charter,[521] and the ex-mayor (deposed from the council) refused to yield up the town plate,[522] they were powerless ; and the Whig predominance remained unshaken until the middle of the 18th century. An attempt to obtain the revocation of the William III charter, made by the Tories during the period of Tory ascendancy in national councils in 1710, was unsuccessful ;[523] as were also sundry attacks in a different form upon the dominant Whigs, to which we shall have to allude in the next section. The Liverpool members of Parliament during this period were also steadily Whig.

[497] Picton, *Liv. Munic. Rec.* i, 257.
[498] Against the docquet of the charter are written the words 'never past,' *Hist. Munic. Govt. in Liv.* 206. In a list of charters in the House of Lords MSS. it is entered with a note '(did not pass),' *Hist. MSS. Com. Rep.* xii, App. vi, 299.
[499] Picton, *Liv. Munic. Rec.* i, 257–8.
[500] *Hist. MSS. Com. Rep.* xii, App. vii, 206.
[501] Ibid. *Rep.* xiv, App. iv, 201–2.
[502] Ibid. *Rep.* xii, App. vii, 205 ff.
[503] Ibid. *Rep.* xiv, App. iv, 198 ff.
[504] Ibid. 198.
[505] Ibid. 223.

[506] Ibid. *Rep.* xii, App. vi, 170, 174, 175, 183, 187 ; App. vii, 237, 244, 248, 250.
[507] *Abbott's Journ.* (Chet. Soc. lxi), 2.
[508] *Hist. MSS. Com. Rep.* xii, App. vii, 250.
[509] Ibid. *Rep.* xiv, App. iv, 263.
[510] Picton, *Liv. Munic. Rec.* i, 260.
[511] Ibid. 281.
[512] *Hist. Munic. Govt. in Liv.* 233.
[513] *Ret. of Memb. of Parl. ; Norris Papers* (Chet. Soc. ix), 21.
[514] *Hist. MSS. Com. Rep.* xiv, App. iv, 321 ; Picton, *Liv. Munic. Rec.* i, 261.
[515] Ibid.

[516] *Norris Papers* (Chet. Soc. ix), 25–30.
[517] Picton, *Liv. Munic. Rec.* i, 262.
[518] *Hist. MSS. Com. Rep.* xiv, App. iv, 378.
[519] *Hist. Munic. Govt. in Liv.* 110–14, and 236 ff.
[520] For an analysis in detail of these points see *Hist. Munic. Govt. in Liv.* 110–14.
[521] Picton, *Liv. Munic. Rec.* i, 263–4.
[522] Ibid.
[523] Ibid. ii, 4–7 ; *Hist. Munic. Govt. in Liv.* 114, 115 ; *Hist. MSS. Com. Rep.* xiv, App. iv, 673.

The chief of them, Sir Thomas Johnson, sat for Liverpool from 1701 to 1727,[524] and all attacks upon his seat were unsuccessful.[525] He and his father had been the leaders in the struggle against the Tory supremacy. A representative of the new class of Liverpool merchants, he was assiduous in his attentions to the interests of the town,[526] and deserves to be regarded as one of the principal fosterers of its new prosperity. He died a poor man after a laborious life, and his memory now survives only in the name of Sir Thomas Street.[527]

Fairly launched on its upward career by 1700, Liverpool was to enjoy during the course of the 18th century a rapidly increasing prosperity, the course of which it will be impossible to follow in any detail. Staunchly loyal to the Protestant succession, the town enjoyed the favour of the Whig party. Its Whiggism may be illustrated by the fact that in 1714 it forwarded an address to the Crown, asking for the punishment of the Tory ministers of Anne, who had endeavoured to restore the exiled Stuarts;[528] by the fact that in 1709 it was the only provincial town to offer hospitality to the exiled 'Palatines,' of whom it took 130 families;[529] and above all by the fact that in the rebellion of 1715, during which it was the single stronghold of Whiggism in Lancashire, it threw itself vigorously into a state of defence.[530] When the rebellion was crushed it was not unnaturally chosen as the venue for many of the trials;[531] two of the unfortunate prisoners were executed on the gallows in London Road, while many hundreds were transported, to the no small profit of the Liverpool traders who took them out. The later rebellion of 1745 found Liverpool equally loyal; a regiment of foot was raised and equipped by public subscription,[532] and after having a brush with the Highlanders near Warrington, it played a useful part in garrisoning Carlisle, during the Duke of Cumberland's northward advance, its conduct earning warm praise.[533] When the rising was over, the party feeling of the town burst forth in mob riots, in the course of which the only Roman Catholic chapel was burnt.[534] As might be expected in a town so vigorously Whig, the ascendancy of the Whig party remained almost unshaken both in municipal politics and in the Parliamentary elections. Liverpool was generally regarded as a safe Whig borough,[535] and the power of electing new freemen, hitherto pretty generously exercised, now began to be used by the Town Council for the purpose of securing party ascendancy.[536] Under these circumstances the Tory party, extruded from power, made themselves the advocates of the rights of the burgess body as against the Town Council—rights of which they had formerly been the principal opponents. The election of Sir Thomas

Bootle as one of the members for the borough from 1727 to 1734[537] represents the partial triumph of this interest. During the same period, and largely under Bootle's influence, a vigorous attack was made on the ascendancy of the Town Council,[538] which was for some years quite overridden, the government of the town being assumed, in accordance with the popular interpretation of a clause in the William III charter, by a succession of popular mayors acting through the assembly of burgesses. In 1734 Lord Derby was elected mayor, and under his powerful direction, an attempt was made to regularize the position of the assembly, and to establish its right of passing by-laws and electing freemen. Lord Derby died before the end of his year of office; and after his death the agitation quietly and completely died out. There was a partial revival of the controversy in 1757, when Mr. Joseph Clegg,[539] one of the aldermen who had been mayor in 1748, led a renewed attack upon the council. But though the council tried in vain to obtain a new charter[540] establishing beyond question its control of borough government Clegg's attack came to nothing, and the challenge of the council's authority was not again renewed until the time of the French Revolution. The chief interest of this struggle is the demonstration which it affords that the ascendancy of the Whigs was as narrowly oligarchic as that of the Tories had been after the Restoration. Indeed, it was even more so; for it is to this period that we must attribute an increasing chariness in granting the freedom of the borough to new-comers.[541] Up to the beginning of the 18th century it would appear that almost all residents obtained the freedom without difficulty. By the middle of the century it was rarely granted to new-comers except for the purpose of influencing elections; and finally in 1777 the rule was laid down[542] that none but apprentices and sons of freemen should be admitted to the freedom. Thus in the second half of the century a minority of the principal merchants of the town exercised political rights in it. This increasing restriction was peculiarly unfortunate at a period when, owing to the rapid growth of trade, the population was increasing with unheard-of rapidity. But it is probably to be attributed to the very fact of this increase of trade, the town council being unwilling to sacrifice the large revenue which they derived from the dues paid by non-freemen. These dues were now for the first time becoming very valuable; and hence arose a new series of struggles, due to the attempt of boroughs such as London, Bristol and Lancaster, to obtain exemption from the payment of dues in Liverpool under the mediaeval charters which freed them from the payment of dues throughout the kingdom. One such question had

[524] *Ret. of Memb. of Parl.*

[525] Even in 1710, when the Tory reaction was at its height; *Hist. MSS. Com. Rep.* xiv, App. iv, 579.

[526] See *Norris Papers* (Chet. Soc. ix), *passim.*

[527] The facts of Johnson's life have been summarized by E. M. Platt, *Trans. Hist. Soc.* (new ser.), xvi, 147.

[528] *Lancs. in 1715* (Chet. Soc. v), 4.

[529] *Hist. MSS. Com. Rep.* viii, App. i, 47a. The reception of the 'Palatines' was a very definite party issue; cf. for example, Swift's attacks on it, *Examiner*, nos. 41, 45.

[530] Picton, *Liv. Munic. Rec.* ii, 78; Ware, *Lancs. in 1715, passim.*

[531] Ware, *Lancs. in 1715*, 190–202; Picton, *Liv. Munic. Rec.* ii, 79; *Stuart MSS.* (Hist. MSS. Com.), ii, 232; *Milne-Home MSS.* (Hist. MSS. Com.), 112.

[532] Picton, *Liv. Munic. Rec.* ii, 105 ff.

[533] Walpole, *Letters* (ed. Toynbee), ii, 165.

[534] Picton, *Liv. Munic. Rec.* ii, 109; *Hist. MSS. Com. Rep.* xv, App. vii, 334.

[535] *Hist. MSS. Com. Rep.* xiv, App. iv, 579; *Rep.* xv, App. vii, 121–2 *et passim.*

[536] Ibid. *Rep.* xv, App. vii, 122–3.

[537] Picton, *Liv. Munic. Rec.* ii, 99.

already been raised by the London cheesemongers in 1690 ;[543] it was revived at intervals during the century,[544] both on behalf of the freemen of London, and on behalf of those of other towns, and was not finally determined till 1799,[545] when after a long trial, it was laid down that only 'freemen residing within the liberties' of the borough which put forward the claim were entitled to the exemption.

All these disputes were in themselves evidences of the growing wealth to which they were due. The secret of this rising prosperity was that Liverpool was in this period obtaining an increasingly large share of the trade which was then the richest in the world— that with the West Indies, whence almost all the sugar, tobacco, and other 'colonial produce' consumed by Europe was derived. In comparison with the West India trade, the trade with the American colonies was of very small importance, and as late as 1752 only one Liverpool vessel is said to have plied to New York.[546] Not only was there the direct trade with the British West Indies, but, even more lucrative, a large irregular smuggling trade with Spanish America was carried on, in spite of the prohibition of the Spanish government. In this traffic, the southern ports of Bristol and London possessed at the end of the 17th century a very great advantage. During the early years of the 18th century Liverpool rapidly gained at their expense. For this two reasons are alleged. The first is that her ships were largely manned with apprentices who received next to no wages until they reached the age of twenty-one, and that the customary rate of pay for the captains and officers was lower than the rate which held in the southern ports.[547] More important was the second cause : namely, that the coarse stuffs of mixed linen and cotton, or linen and woollen (linsey woolsey) which were produced by the looms of Manchester were in great request in the West Indian markets, and were produced more cheaply than the corresponding German goods with which the southern traders endeavoured to supply the market.[548] Thus, as always, the growth of Liverpool trade was concurrent with the growth of Manchester industry. The smuggling trade with the Spanish colonies, and the frequent conflicts with Spanish *guarda costas* to which it gave rise, ultimately led to the Spanish war of 1739, and was almost brought to an end by an Act of Parliament of 1747, which forbade foreign vessels to frequent British West India ports.[549] But while it was at its height (about 1730) this branch of trade alone is said to have brought into Liverpool an annual profit of £250,000 and to have consumed over £500,000 worth of Manchester goods.[550]

The legitimate and illegitimate trade of the West Indies and South America equally led on the traders who engaged in it to the still more lucrative African trade which could be worked in combination with it.

It was in this period that Liverpool first entered upon the slave trade, out of which she was to draw, during the century, fabulous riches ; and which was to earn for her a highly unsavoury reputation. At the end of the century the greatness of Liverpool was generally attributed—by her own citizens as well as by others [551] —entirely to the slave trade. Yet it was not until the fourth decade of the century, when Liverpool was already rapidly overtaking Bristol, that this line of trade began to be seriously developed ; and she had long been preceded in it by the two great southern ports. Up to 1698 the monopoly of the African trade had been held by the Assiento Company of London. In that year its formal monopoly was abolished,[552] though it still retained the sole right of importing slaves into the Spanish dominions. In the early years of the eighteenth century Bristol began to compete with London—led on, as Liverpool was later to be, from the West Indies to the source of their labour supply. Indeed the Bristol merchants seem to have been driven to the African trade largely by the successful competition of Liverpool in the Spanish smuggling trade.[553] In 1709 one Liverpool vessel of 30 tons burthen was dispatched to Africa ; [554] but the venture does not seem to have been successful, probably owing to the jealousy of the Bristol and London men, for it was not repeated for twenty years. In 1730 an Act of Parliament for the regulation of the African trade [555] established an open company to which any person trading to Africa might belong on payment of 40s. The money was to be used for the up-keep of factories on the African coast ; and the administration of these was entrusted to a committee of nine, consisting of three members elected by the merchants of each of the three ports, London, Bristol, and Liverpool. At once, under the new system, Liverpool threw herself energetically into the trade. In the same year, 1730, fifteen vessels of 1,111 tons were dispatched to Africa.[556] In 1752 the number had risen to eighty-eight vessels accommodating nearly 25,000 slaves,[557] though it had sunk by 1760 to seventy-four vessels of 8,178 tons.[558] In 1751 a separate Liverpool company was established [559] by Act of Parliament. The Act states that there were 101 African merchants in Liverpool, but though there were 135 in London and 157 in Bristol, 'their trade to Africa is not so extensive as the merchants of Liverpool.' The methods and development of this trade cannot here be described. The materials for its history have been fully marshalled by Mr. Gomer Williams, to whose valuable book [560] the reader who is inquisitive on this subject may be referred. But it should be noted that the immensely lucrative character of this traffic is to be attributed to the fact that a treble profit was made on every voyage. The cheap guns, ornaments, and stuffs which formed the outward cargo were exchanged for

---

[543] Picton, *Liv. Munic. Rec.* i, 265, 301 ff.

[544] Ibid. ii, 21 ff. *et passim.*

[545] Ibid. 212.

[546] Smithers, *Liverpool*, 112. A useful general description of Liverpool trade in the 18th and early 19th centuries, with statistics, is contained in this book, and indeed, forms its best feature. See also, Kaye, *Stranger in Liverpool* (1825 ed.).

[547] Wallace, *General Descr.* 216. Derrick (*Letters from Liv.* &c. 1767) attributes the success of Liverpool to the

slaves at an average cost of about £15 ; the slaves were then shipped to Virginia or (more often) to Kingston, Jamaica (where the Liverpool merchants combined to maintain permanent agents) and sold at a price which varied from £60 upwards ; the ships were then loaded with sugar, tobacco, and other highly saleable West Indian produce for the homeward voyage. Comparatively few slaves were brought home to England, though occasional advertisements in the Liverpool papers show that a few were imported before 1772, when the Somerset case made such importations illegal. This 'great triangle' of trade was probably the most lucrative in the history of commerce, for its profits were not only very large but rapid. Thus vast fortunes were made, and a vast capital accumulated in Liverpool, much of which went to develop other lines of trade, or to aid those works, now beginning to be undertaken, for the improvement of the equipment of the port and its communications with inland markets.

Of these activities the most important was the creation of the first dock. The idea of deepening the Pool which curved round the town and turning it into a more effective harbour had long been entertained by some of the more enterprising townsmen ; it is alluded to by Sir Edward Moore as early as 1668.[561] But in the first years of the 18th century the necessity of some such provision for the increasing shipping became obvious. The first project, put forward in 1708 by a Mr. Henry Hun of Derby,[562] was one for simply deepening and walling in the whole length of the Pool. But in the next year Mr. Thomas Steers, an engineer brought from London by Sir Thomas Johnson, proposed the alternative scheme of making a square dock with gates in the mouth of the Pool. This proposal was accepted, and an Act of Parliament obtained to empower the Town Council to borrow the necessary funds and to raise dock dues for the payment of the interest thereon.[563] The construction of the dock was begun in 1710 under the direction of Steers. It took longer, and cost more to build, than had been anticipated ; it was opened for use on 31 August 1715, but was not then completed, and a second Act had to be obtained in 1716[564] to empower the council to raise additional funds for the completion of the works. A 'dry dock' or basin was added two years later.[565] From the first the dock (whose site is now represented by the Custom House) was fully used, but it was not until 1734[566] that the creation of a new dock, known as the South or Salthouse Dock, was begun. This, as there was no natural inlet to facilitate the work, took nineteen years to build, and was not opened until 1753.[567]

The beginning of the dock estate marks an epoch in the history of the town ; it is the beginning of modern Liverpool. The Pool, the characteristic feature of mediaeval Liverpool, now vanishes from the maps, leaving as its sole trace the irregularity of

the directions of the streets that had been compressed into the triangle between it and the river. But the creation of docks was not the only enterprise of this period for the improvement of the port's trading facilities. The channel of the river was buoyed and charted ;[568] lighthouses were erected,[569] the first good carriage roads out of the town were made with the aid of the Town Council ;[570] the streams running into the Mersey estuary were deepened so as to make them navigable : the Weaver (not without opposition) in 1720,[571] the Mersey and the Irwell also in 1720,[572] and the Sankey Brook in 1755 ;[573] while the deepening of the Douglas from Wigan to the Ribble[574] cheapened the transport of coal. The Sankey navigation, carried out seemingly by a Liverpool engineer, and largely financed by Liverpool men,[575] departed frankly from the line of the original brook, and so foreshadowed the era of canals.

The increment of trade which produced all these activities may be indicated by the single fact that during the first half of the 18th century the shipping of the port rose from seventy ships with 800 men (in 1700) to 220 ships with 3,319 men in 1751.[577] In the same period the population rose from 5,000 (est.) in 1700 to 18,000 (est.) in 1750.[578] New local industries were also created or greatly developed in this period : shipbuilding, sugar refining, rope-making, iron-working, watch-making, and pottery, all flourished.[579] In pottery, in particular, Liverpool enjoyed in this age a brief eminence. By the middle of the 18th century, therefore, the town was already vigorous and thriving ; rejoicing especially in its recently acquired mastery of the most lucrative trade in the world.

In the second half of the 18th century the commercial triumph of Liverpool was secured. This was due to several causes, the first of which was the effect of the wars which almost filled this age.

In the Spanish War of 1739 and the War of the Austrian Succession into which it merged, Liverpool seems to have taken comparatively little part, though she had shared so largely in the irregular traffic of the South Seas from which it sprang. Four or five privateers are known to have plied from the town, and they made a number of valuable captures ;[580] but the non-existence of local newspapers during this period makes it difficult to discover the exact extent of these privateering activities. On the other hand 103 Liverpool vessels are known to have been captured by the enemy.[581] Nevertheless the port profited exceedingly from the war, owing to the comparative security of the route through the Irish Sea. A local observer writes in 1753 that the war had brought such wealth that if it had lasted 'seven years longer it would have enlarged the size and riches of the town to a prodigious degree . . . Trade since the late peace has not been so brisk as formerly.'[582] War therefore was welcomed in Liverpool.

From the Seven Years' War the town derived even

[561] Moore, *Rental* (ed. W. F. Irvine), 104 *et passim*.
[562] Picton, *Liv. Munic. Rec.* ii, 47.
[563] 8 Anne, cap. 12 ; Picton, *Liv. Munic. Rec.* ii, 48. [564] 3 Geo. I, cap. 1.
[565] Picton, *Liv. Munic. Rec.* ii, 141.
[566] Ibid. 133, 143.
[567] Ibid. [568] Ibid. 49.
[569] *Hist. MSS. Com. Rep.* viii, App. i, 395b.

[570] Picton, *Liv. Munic. Rec.* ii, 63 ; Acts of 12 Geo. I, cap. 21 ; 19 Geo. II, cap. 19 ; 26 Geo. II, cap. 65.
[571] *Hist. MSS. Com. Rep.* viii, App. i, 396a ; 7 Geo. I, cap. 10 ; 7 Geo. II, cap. 28.
[572] 7 Geo. I, cap. 15.
[573] 28 Geo. II, cap. 8 ; 2 Geo. III, cap. 56.
[574] 6 Geo. I, cap. 28.

[575] Picton, *Liv. Munic. Rec.* ii, 144 ; Brooke, *Liv. in the xviii Cent.* 105–6.
[577] Smithers, *Liv.* 185. [578] Ibid. 195–6.
[579] Williamson, *Liv. Memorandum Bk.* (1753).
[580] Williams, *Hist. of Liv. Privateers*, 39, 40.
[581] Ibid. App. i, p. 659.
[582] Williamson, *Liv. Memorandum Bk.* 1753.

greater advantages. Though Thurot,[583] a brilliant French privateer, found his way into the Irish Sea, and in 1758 and 1759 caused much alarm in the Mersey, rendering necessary the fortification of the port,[584] and though ninety-eight Liverpool vessels were during the course of the war captured by the French,[585] the activity of the Liverpool traders in privateering was vastly greater than it had ever been before, and their captures were on the whole exceedingly valuable. It is not possible to state the exact number of ships employed ;[586] but it was very large, and these years in particular were distinguished by the activity of William Hutchinson, perhaps the boldest and most successful of Liverpool privateers.[587] The result of the war was practically to sweep French commerce from Atlantic waters, and to establish English ascendancy in the West Indies almost as completely as on the North American continent. In the commercial gains which thus accrued Liverpool had the lion's share.

In the War of the American Revolution the port suffered very seriously. Not only was trade with the revolted colonies practically stopped, but American privateers made West Indian waters unsafe, and under Paul Jones even ravaged the coasts of Britain,[588] while the commerce of the Americans themselves was of such negligible amount as to make privateering useless.[589] 'Our once extensive trade with Africa is at a stand ; all commerce with America is at an end,' and the 'gallant ships' were 'laid up and useless' in the docks.[590] During the war the population actually decreased, and the shipping of the port diminished from 84,792 to 79,450 tons.[591] The distress thus caused led to grave riots, the most serious of which broke out in 1775, when 3,000 unemployed sailors laid siege to the Town Hall, and terrorized the town for a week.[592] The regular troops of the garrison had to be distributed through the town.[593] Nevertheless the town took a vigorous and patriotic part in the war. A large fort with barracks was erected on the north shore, where the Prince's Dock now is ;[594] a regiment of regular troops known as the Liverpool Blues was raised, mainly at the cost of the Corporation—it was employed in the garrisoning of Jamaica ;[595] a corps of local volunteers was also raised in 1782 ;[596] while the pressgang found a field in Liverpool for its unpopular activity.[597] When in 1778 France and later Spain and Holland joined in the war, privateering once more became a profitable pursuit, and provided employment for idle ships ; no less than 120 privateers,[598] of 31,000 tons, were plying from Liverpool within a

year of the French declaration of war, and nearly 9,000 sailors thus found employment.[599] The years from 1778 to 1782 were the period of Liverpool's greatest activity in privateering ;[600] 'the merchants of Liverpool,' we are told, 'have entered more into the spirit of arming ships than any others in England' ;[601] and many brilliant feats are recorded, of which no account can here be given. Some hundreds of French prisoners occupied during these years the old tower and the powder magazine in Brownlow Hill.[602]

The profits of privateering, however, great as they were, were a poor consolation for the almost complete destruction of trade. The declaration of peace was immediately followed by a great revival, and the decade, 1783–93, was an era of amazingly rapid advance.[603] The French Revolutionary War did not at first interrupt this advance, but rather accentuated it. Though it at first caused a commercial panic, which rendered necessary the issue of Corporation notes under Parliamentary powers,[604] this was temporary only ; and the port gained far more by the destruction of French trade than it lost by the dislocation of its commerce caused by the war. At the outset of the war privateering was again actively undertaken ;[605] but it never attained the same dimensions as during the American War, because there were not so many idle vessels to welcome this mode of employment ; and after a few years privateering almost ceased, for the very satisfactory reason that there were so few ships belonging to France and her allies on the seas as to make it an unprofitable enterprise.[606] French privateers made the seas dangerous, and trading vessels had to be prepared to fight unless they sailed in large convoys ;[607] many hundreds, perhaps thousands, of Liverpool sailors were captured by the enemy and peopled French prisons, from which they sometimes made daring escapes.[608] On the other hand French prisoners in large numbers (4,009 in 1799) were immured in the gaol in Great Howard Street, and formed a feature of Liverpool life.[609]

Deprived to a large extent of the excitement of privateering, the military enthusiasm of the turbulent Liverpool population found other vents. The pressgang was a continual terror, and its ravages frequently passed all reasonable bounds.[610] The fort was strengthened and armed with fifty guns, while batteries were erected at the mouths of the docks.[611] Large forces of volunteers and yeomanry were raised ;[612] in 1804 180 officers and 3,686 men were reviewed.[613] A

583 Williams, op. cit. 172 and passim.
584 Picton, Liv. Munic. Rec. ii, 120 ; Derrick, Letters from Liv. &c.
585 Williams, op. cit. App. iii, 665.
586 Mr. Williams has collected a large amount of material bearing upon this period, op. cit. 79–178.
587 Williams, op. cit. 127 ff.
588 Brooke, Liv. in the last quarter of the xviii Cent. 365–6 ; Williams, op. cit. 223, 262 ; Mahan, Infl. of Sea-power.
589 Nevertheless, it was carried on not without success; cf. Hist. MSS. Com. Rep. xv, App. vi, 371.
590 Liv. General Advertiser, 29 Sept. 1775.
591 Williams, op. cit. 181.
592 Brooke, Liv. in the last quarter of the xviii Cent. 328 ff.
593 Hist. MSS. Com. Rep. xv, App. v, 152.

594 Picton, Rec. ii, 181–3 ; Brooke, op. cit. 371.
595 Brooke, Liv. in the last quarter of the xviii Cent. 339, 379 ; Amer. MS. in Royal Inst. (Hist. MSS. Com.), i, 178.
596 Brooke, op. cit. 372 ; Williams, op. cit. 319.
597 Williams, op. cit. 189–302, collects many examples from contemporary newspapers and other sources.
598 Ibid. 183.
599 Ibid. 20.
600 Ibid. 183.
601 St. Vincent Gazette, 7 Mar. 1778, apud Williams, 215.
602 Brooke, op. cit. 135.
603 Thus the number of ships engaged in the slave trade, which had sunk as low as 11 (tonnage 1,205) in 1779, rose at

once to 85 (12,294) in 1783, and to 132 (22,402) in 1792.
604 33 Geo. III, cap. 31 ; Picton, Liv. Munic. Rec. ii, 251–2 ; Hughes, Liv. Banks and Bankers, 144–58.
605 Williams, op. cit. 315.
606 Ibid. 316.
607 Williams, op. cit. 306 ; Picton, Liv. Munic. Rec. ii, 189.
608 Seacome Ellison, Prison Scenes, gives a typical narrative of such an escape.
609 Brooke, op. cit. 489 ; Troughton, Hist. Liv. 226.
610 Williams, op. cit. passim ; for a peculiarly flagrant episode, see Liv. Advertiser, 19 May 1794.
611 Picton, Liv. Munic. Rec. ii, 254, 287.
612 Brooke, op. cit. 434.
613 Liv. Advertiser, 11 Jan. 1804.

regiment of regulars was, after the peace of Amiens, enlisted in the town at the expense of Mr. John Bolton,[614] a wealthy merchant; and the Duke of Gloucester[615] took up his quarters at San Domingo House, Everton, to command all these forces.

The first part of the war unquestionably told heavily in favour of Liverpool trade, in spite of the commercial insecurity caused by the ever-present risk of capture. In the second period Napoleon's continental system inflicted grave hardship, especially severely felt by the poor of the town;[616] and its result, the American War of 1812, which produced a swarm of dangerous American privateers,[617] was disastrous in its effects: the number of ships entering the port declining from 6,729 in 1810 to 4,599 in 1812.[618] Yet even this struggle ultimately tended to the increase of Liverpool's trade, by driving finally all rival shipping from the seas; at the end of the period of war in 1815, Liverpool found herself practically absolute mistress of the trade between America and Europe.

While the wars were securing to Liverpool the dominance of the Atlantic trade, the other main source of her wealth, the industries of Lancashire, were being transformed. The amazing story of the great inventions and the great development of roads and canals of this period concern Lancashire at large and the whole of England. But it should be noted that no town more directly profited by these developments than Liverpool, for almost the whole of the districts most affected by the new inventions lay within a hundred miles of her harbour; while the canals and roads made communication with them easy, and for the first time overcame that geographical isolation which had been the main obstacle to her progress. For this reason the merchants at Liverpool took an immense part in devising and carrying through these enterprises, and much of the capital for the new canals was supplied by the wealth earned in the slave trade or the trade with America.

Concurrently with these movements, the same period saw a remarkable development of foreign markets. The great expansion of the United States into the Middle West[619] began in the last years of the 18th century, and was much stimulated by the Louisiana purchase; emigration on a large scale, caused by the distress which accompanied the Industrial Revolution, helped to fill up these lands; they provided new sources of raw materials, and it was in this period, in particular, that the supply of raw cotton began to be derived mainly from the Southern States; as late as 1784 it was so exclusively drawn from the West Indies that a custom-house officer is said to have seized a small consignment brought in by an American vessel on the ground that its importation was an infringement of the Navigation Acts.[620] At the end of the period (in 1813) the trade with the East Indies, hitherto confined to the East India Company, was thrown open, and in 1814 the first Liverpool ships rounded the Cape of Good Hope.[621] In a few years

India had become one of the principal markets for the goods exported from Liverpool. The period of the Revolutionary wars also saw Spanish America thrown open to trade. When Napoleon took possession of Spain the Spanish colonies declined to accept his rule, threw off the close restrictions which the mother-country had imposed upon their trade; and, on the restoration of peace, declined to return to their allegiance, mainly because they were unwilling to sacrifice their newly-acquired commercial freedom. From the first Liverpool controlled the bulk of this rapidly expanding South American trade,[622] which she has held ever since; and it is more than a coincidence that Canning, the minister responsible for the British recognition from the Spanish-American colonies in 1825, had himself been member for Liverpool for ten years (1812–22). Thus during the years when the commerce of rival nations was being driven from the Atlantic mainly to the advantage of Liverpool, the unexampled development of the industrial and mineral advantages of Lancashire and the northern midlands was supplying the Liverpool merchants with an inexhaustible supply of goods for export, and the expansion of America and the opening of trade to India and South America were providing enormous new markets. It is not surprising that the trade of the port advanced with a rapidity hitherto unknown in English history, and that the population of the port grew concurrently.

The growth of trade during this period is indicated by the fact that the gross tonnage owned in the port, 19,175 in 1751, had risen to 72,730 in 1787, to 129,470 in 1801. Other figures tell the same tale. During the period 1756–1815 four new docks and two tidal basins were opened. The dock area of the port, less than 30 acres in 1756, had risen to over 50 acres in 1815. Still more rapid was the expansion of the next period, as the table on p. 42 will show. During the same period several local industries rose to their highest prosperity, and then decayed and vanished—destroyed mainly by that localization of industrial functions and that growing ease of communication which were the principal causes of Liverpool's commercial ascendancy. Thus shipbuilding was at its height in the last quarter of the 18th century;[623] it decayed thereafter. The Greenland fishery,[624] which began for Liverpool in 1764, and in 1788 employed 21 ships, had almost vanished by 1815, as had the oil-refining industry to which it gave birth. The curing-houses for herring,[625] which carried on a large export trade with the Mediterranean, were at their height about 1770, but had almost vanished by 1815. Two or three iron foundries existed in the town in the same period;[626] they were driven out of work by the competition of the coalfield towns. The pottery industry also came to an end during these years.[627]

The destruction of productive industries is indeed a feature of this period. It did not interfere with the growth of the town's wealth or population, but it left

[614] Picton, *Mem.* i, 301; *Liv. Advertiser*, 30 May, 1803.

[615] Picton, *Liv. Munic. Rec.* ii, 289–90.

[616] Ibid. ii, 311; *Liv. Courier*, 1 Feb. 1809; *Liv. Advertiser*, 25 Nov. 1811 *et passim.*

[617] Williams, op. cit. 442–9.

[618] Ibid. 407. For the general effects on prices and trade in Liverpool see Ewart, Rutson's trade circular, quoted in

Baines' *Liverpool*, 738–41. For insurance rates, *Mercury*, 13 May 1813.

[619] For a fuller summary of these causes of development, see Muir, *Hist. of Liv.* chap. xiv.

[620] Smithers, *Liverpool*, 124.

[621] Ibid. 160. Within seven years the port possessed one-seventh of the total British trade with India. Ibid. 161.

[622] Ibid. 163.

[623] Smithers, *Commerce of Liv.* 190; [Wallace], *General Descr.* 180 ff.

[624] Brooke, op. cit. 241; Smithers, *Commerce of Liv.* 97–8.

[625] Smithers, *Commerce of Liv.* 95; [Wallace], *General Descr.* (1795), 26.

[626] [Wallace] and Smithers, loc. cit.

[627] Brooke, op. cit. 248; J. Mayer, *Liv. Pottery.*

it entirely dependent upon sea-borne commerce, and imposed upon it the specific social characteristics involved in that fact.

The growth of population in this period was very rapid. About 20,000 in 1751, it was 60,000 in 1791, 77,000 in 1801, 94,000 in 1811, 118,000 in 1821. The last two figures do not fully represent the actual growth, for the town had by this time overpassed the limits of the old township, especially on the south and on the north-east, and very populous suburbs had been created in Toxteth and Everton, which contained in 1831 a population of 40,000.

The great inrush of new inhabitants represented by these figures came from all parts of the United Kingdom. A writer of 1795 notes 'the great influx of Irish and Welsh, of whom the majority of the inhabitants at present consists.' [628] There were also many Scots, especially among the captains of ships and the heads of great trading-houses. Irish immigration became still more vigorous after the rising of 1798, though it was not to reach its height until the potato-famine of 1846. Though the town was expanding geographically with great rapidity, building did not go on fast enough to accommodate the numerous immigrants. They were crowded together in the most horrible way in the older part of the town ; in 1790 it was calculated [629] that over one-ninth of the population lived in cellars, at the rate of four persons to each cellar.[630] In the new quarters built for the reception of these immigrants the building was so shoddy that a storm in 1823 blew many of the houses down ; [631] there were no building regulations, and the houses were erected back to back, without adequate provision for air and light, and almost without any sanitary arrangements ; it is with these slum areas that the government of the city has been struggling ever since. Most of the streets were unsewered. The water supply was exceedingly scanty ; before 1800 water was sold from carts ; [632] after the institution of the two water companies in 1799 [633] and 1802,[634] the supply, being conducted for a commercial profit, was naturally inadequate in the poorer quarters. Public-houses were extraordinarily numerous ; as early as 1772 the Town Council had to urge the magistrates to reduce the number,[635] and in 1795 it was calculated that one house in every seven was licensed for the sale of strong drink.[636]

Overcrowded, unhealthy, dirty and drunken, the population of the town was also very turbulent, as might be expected from the influence upon them of the slave traders and the privateers-men. The police arrangements were quite inadequate. Under an Act of 1748,[637] which established a commission, independent of the Town Council, for the watching, lighting, and cleansing of the town, the police force consisted of sixty night watchmen ; the number was increased under the Act of 1788,[638] but no day police was provided until 1811, when the Town Council divided the borough into seven districts and allotted three constables to each.[639]

Thus the evils which had followed the sudden growth of wealth and population seemed to outweigh its advantages. This was in part due to the fact that the system of borough government had been in no way adapted to the new conditions.[640] The self-elected Town Council still continued in absolute control of the corporate estate, including the docks, and still possessed the power of regulating the trade of the port. It regarded itself merely as the trustee of the body of freemen, which now formed only a small part, and by no means the most important part, of the population. Even the freemen's privileges, however, were limited to the right of voting in the election of mayor, bailiffs, and members of Parliament, and to exemption from the payment of town dues. They were admitted to no further share in the government of the borough, and hence arose, under the influence of the French Revolution, a new challenge to the authority of the council, and a new attempt to establish that of the assembly of burgesses. Begun in 1791,[641] it was brought into the law courts, where a verdict was three times given in favour of the claims of the assembly. The council, however, was always able to claim a new trial on technical grounds, and in the end the attack on their position was abandoned, partly because private resources were unable to stand the conflict with public funds, partly because the reaction against the French Revolution distracted support from this quasi-democratic movement. Liverpool had, indeed, by this time become very firmly Tory, and the change in its politics from the Whiggism of the previous age is one of the most curious features of the period. It seems to have begun in the early years of George III, when the Town Council took the side of the king in the Wilkes struggle, sending up addresses of support.[642] The body of burgesses still, however, remained predominantly Whig, as is shown by the continual election of Sir William Meredith as member until 1780. At the outset of the American struggle addresses of protest against the policy of government were sent from Liverpool,[643] but the Town Council and the mass of the burgesses loyally supported the war,[644] and in spite of the distress which it caused, its progress only made the town more Tory.[645] The first

[628] [Wallace], General Descr. 267.
[629] Ibid.
[630] Ibid. 69.
[631] Smithers, Commerce of Liv. 227 ; Picton, Liv. Munic. Rec. ii.
[632] [Wallace], General Descr. 88.
[633] Bootle Company, instituted by 39 Geo. III, cap. 36, under the title of the Company of Proprietors of the Liverpool Waterworks, powers enlarged by 50 Geo. III, cap. 165, and 53 Geo. III, cap. 122 ; Brooke, Liv. in last Quarter of the xviii Cent. 387.
[634] The Corporation obtained power to contract for the supply of water by 26 Geo. III, cap. 12. A company was formed to carry out the work, which was incorporated as the Liverpool Corporation

events of the French Revolution revived Whiggism for a time,[646] but the reaction after the September massacres completed the Tory victory; and the group of leading Whigs who surrounded Roscoe had to withdraw from public life.[647] In the first years of the new century Whiggism held up its head again. Roscoe was returned to Parliament in 1806,[648] but mainly on the ground of his local popularity, and the votes which he cast against the slave trade and for Catholic emancipation earned him an unpopularity which expressed itself in riots on his return to Liverpool.[649] During the struggle on the slave trade question, indeed, Liverpool had been absolutely committed to the support of the party from which alone it had any prospect of the maintenance of its most lucrative traffic,[650] while the inrush of Catholic Irish, having produced already the characteristic Orangeism of the Protestant population, formed another motive to Toryism. Not even the unpopularity of the Orders in Council sufficed to enable Brougham (who had been mainly identified with the opposition to them) to defeat Canning in the fiercely-fought election of 1812,[651] and Liverpool remained steadily Tory down to the eve of the Reform Act.

Alongside of its more unpleasant developments, this period witnessed the rise of many promising movements. The administration of the Poor Law[652] was undertaken with exceptional vigour and enlightenment, and while in other suddenly-grown industrial and commercial towns the old administrative fabric of the annual Easter vestry and the elected overseers broke down completely, in Liverpool there was gradually developed a system of government through an annually elected committee, which regulated extralegally the work of the overseers with such success that Liverpool has been described as the model urban poor-law district of this period. The chief credit for the successful establishment of this system, which had assumed its final form by 1775, belongs to Mr. Joseph Brooks, who as unpaid treasurer from 1768 to 1788 exercised almost absolute authority over the affairs of the parish. It was under his direction that in 1770 the new workhouse in Brownlow Hill was erected ;[653] it was on the whole so well administered that the poor rates—in a town where poverty was more widespread than in most others—never rose beyond 3s. 9d.[654] in the £ even in the height of the Revolutionary war. The committee, that is to say, kept itself free from the extravagant and mischievous methods of indiscriminate relief which were general throughout England from 1795 onwards. This remarkable success is mainly to be attributed to the work of a group of public-spirited citizens, among whom may be named Dr. Currie, the friend of Roscoe.[655]

The Evangelical revival affected Liverpool deeply. Wesley visited the town several times,[656] with considerable effect, and within the Church of England the Evangelical party became dominant in the town.[657] This was a period of great activity in church building, as will be seen later. It was also a period of considerable activity in the provision of schools for the poor,[658] a movement which was carried on in Liverpool in the last twenty years of the century with a concerted activity greater than was displayed in most other towns. An eager charity, too, was born,[659] the expression of that new humanitarian spirit, born of the Evangelical revival, of which another expression was to be found in the movement for the abolition of the slave trade. In Roscoe, William Rathbone, Currie, Rushton, and others, Liverpool provided some of the most vigorous apostles of this reform ; their courage is the more noteworthy because the popular feeling of the town was, naturally, intensely strong on the other side.

The period witnessed also a remarkable intellectual revival. This showed itself in the wit and humour of the numerous squibs issued during parliamentary elections,[660] many of which still retain some of their salt ; it showed itself in that keen interest in the history and antiquities of the borough which produced no less than four Histories of Liverpool between 1770 and 1823,[661] and was still more profitably displayed in the learning of Henry Brown[662] the attorney, which illuminates the trials on the powers of the Town Council in 1791, in the researches of Matthew Gregson, whose *Portfolio of Fragments* was published in 1819, and above all in the monumental collections made by Charles Okill, which are still preserved in the municipal archives and have formed the basis of all later work on the history of the borough. But above all these newborn intellectual interests were fostered by the circle of *illuminati* which surrounded William Roscoe, and of which no detailed account can here be given.[663] Roscoe himself wrote lives of Lorenzo de' Medici and of Leo X which were hailed with delight throughout Europe ; he produced also a great monograph on the Monandrian plants, a good deal of verse, and a large number of pamphlets, including some very enlightened speculations on Penal Jurisprudence ; he took a profound interest in the fine arts, and himself did some etching ; he threw himself into the movement for agricultural improvements ; he corresponded with many of the leading men of his day ; he formed a noble library and a fine collection of pictures. His friend William Shepherd,[664] Unitarian minister of Gateacre, wrote a life of Poggio Bracciolini which is still valuable. Dr. James Currie,[665] besides taking up poor-law admini-

[646] *Life of W. Roscoe*, i, 99 ff. ; *Life of J. Currie*, passim.

[647] Ibid.

[648] Poll-book and squibs of the election.

[649] *Life of W. Roscoe*, i, 392 ff.

[650] Cf. the addresses of the corporation, on, and grants of freedom for, energy in this cause—the defence of the slave trade; Picton, *Liv. Munic. Rec.* ii, 220, 347, &c.

[651] Poll-books and squibs of the election ; Creevey Papers.

[652] The administration of the Poor Law in Liverpool is the theme of an admirable chapter by S. and B. Webb, *Hist. Local Govt.* i, 130 ff. An edition of full extracts

from the Vestry Minutes, with introduction by W. L. Blease, is in preparation.

[653] Picton, *Liv. Munic. Rec.* ii, 160 ; Vestry Minutes s.d. ; Brooke, *Liv. in the last Quarter of the xviii Cent.* 69, 70. This building replaced one in College Lane dating from 1732.

[654] Vestry Minutes, April 1802 and passim.

[655] W. W. Currie, *Life of James Currie*, passim.

[656] Tyerman, *Life of Wesley*, ii, 196, 274, 328, 566, &c. ; *Wesley's Journal*.

[657] See Morley's *Life of Gladstone*, i, chaps. i, ii.

[658] Picton, *Liv. Munic. Rec.* ii, 284 ;

LIVERPOOL : NORTH SHORE MILL

(From a Water-colour Drawing c. 1860)

stration, was the friend and biographer of Burns. Others also might be named if space allowed.[666] Under the encouragement of this group of friends Liverpool became for a time a centre of fine printing and of exquisite bookbinding ; [667] Roscoe had his own books printed in his own town. From this intellectual revival proceeded a remarkable group of public institutions. The Liverpool Library, founded as early as 1758,[668] became a thriving institution.[669] The Athenaeum was founded in 1798 [670] as a library for scholars, and was later enriched by many of Roscoe's books. The Botanic Gardens were instituted in 1803.[671] The Medical Library came to birth in 1775.[672] Finally, the Royal Institution, meant to be the focus for every kind of intellectual interest, was projected in 1813 and opened in 1817.[673] These promising beginnings did not lead to any very striking results ; partly, no doubt, because they were not spontaneous ; but were due to the accidental presence in uncongenial surroundings of a group of fine spirits; partly because they were swamped by the flood of growing wealth ; partly because the coming of the railway imposed, during the greater part of the 19th century, the intellectual dominance of the metropolis upon the provincial towns.

The twenty years which followed the great war saw a steady expansion of foreign trade—less swift, indeed, than had been expected ; but more steady in Liverpool than in England at large. The course of this expansion may be best indicated by the figures of entrances and clearances [674] of vessels engaged in the foreign trade :—

Year	Entrances		Clearances		Total	
	Ships	Tonnage	Ships	Tonnage	Ships	Tonnage
1816 . .	1,340	300,673	1,606	341,390	2,946	642,063
1821 . .	1,770	391,473	1,913	403,626	3,683	795,159
1826 . .	2,067	480,944	2,132	479,409	4,199	960,353
1831 . .	2,840	678,965	3,037	718,987	5,877	1,397,952
1835 . .	2,978	787,009	3,065	796,766	6,043	1,583,775

But the principal interest of these years is to be found rather in the signs of coming political change which they exhibited, and which resulted from the expansion of the earlier period, than in the proof that the earlier causes of prosperity were still at work. Though Liverpool remained predominantly

Tory in sentiment until the eve of the Reform Bill, the twenty years which followed the war saw many movements towards change, and an increasingly clear realization of the necessity of recasting the traditional system of administration. It was, indeed, with the left or progressive wing of the Tory party that the town was associated ; as is shown by the election of Canning by large majorities from 1812 to 1822 and of Huskisson from 1822 to 1830—beyond comparison the most distinguished politicians who have ever represented Liverpool.[674a] The steady growth of the population of the town, which, with its suburbs, had reached the figure of 205,000 in 1831, and the expansion of trade, which has been already summarized, made the earlier system of administration impossible. These years witnessed an awakening on the part of the Town Council to a keener sense of its responsibilities, as is shown by the large schemes of public improvements for which parliamentary authority was obtained ; [675] by the establishment in 1826 of two elementary schools in the north and south of the borough,[676] at the expense of the corporation, as a sort of compensation for the old grammar school which had been suppressed in 1802 ; [677] by the purchase of lands on a large scale in Birkenhead [678] with a view to preventing the creation of a rival port, and providing for the possible future requirements of Liverpool in the extension of the docks, which were increased between 1815 and 1835 from 50 acres to 80 acres of area. The rise of a demand for change is perhaps most clearly seen in the discussions on the administration of the Dock Estate, hitherto under the absolute control of the corporation, which led in 1825 to the addition to the Dock Committee of representatives of ratepayers using the docks.[679] The same kind of discontent was shown in the attempt of a number of non-freemen ratepayers to escape from the payment of town dues, which led to long litigation extending from 1830 to 1833.[680] But the most serious aspect of the situation was the fact that the council, regarding itself simply as the trustee for the property of the body of freemen, had allowed many of the main functions of urban government to slip, wholly or partially, out of its hands. Thus the control of the watching, lighting, and cleansing of the streets had been since 1748 under the control of a separate commission [681] consisting partly of the mayor and some of the borough magistrates, partly of representatives of the ratepayers elected at the annual Easter vestry ; while the control of sewerage, except in the 'old streets,' had recently been vested in another commission.[682]

The corporation had since the 17th century ceased to raise rates, and all public functions which necessitated the raising of rates were performed by

[666] About 150 volumes printed or published in Liverpool between 1770 and 1800 are catalogued in the admirable *Cat. of the Collection of Liv. Prints and Documents* issued by the City Library, 1908. These include nineteen volumes of poems, fifteen of history and biography, an edition of Burns in four volumes, many volumes on politics, &c., &c.

[667] Ibid. J. McCreery's printing in this period has not since been surpassed.

[668] Brooke, op. cit. 89–92 ; papers in *Trans. Hist. Soc.* ix, xxii. This library claims to be the oldest circulating library in England.

[669] [Wallace] *General Descr.*, 171.

[670] Shaw, *Hist. of the Athenaeum, Liv.* (1898).

[671] *Life of Roscoe*, i, 253 ff.; Smithers, op. cit. 367.

[672] Smithers, op. cit. 366 ; Bickerton, *Hist. of the Liv. Medical Inst.*

[673] *Life of Roscoe*, ii, 151 ff.

[674] Compiled from the Reports on Trade and Navigation laid before the Houses of Parliament, 1847. The figures for the coasting trade which are omitted would, of course, enormously increase these totals ; but it is the foreign trade that forms the best barometer of Liverpool's prosperity.

[674a] The poll-books and squibs, espe-

cially for the hard-fought elections of 1812, 1818, 1820, provide excellent illustrations of the sentiments of the borough.

[675] 1 Geo. IV, cap. 13, and 7 Geo. IV, cap. 57.

[676] Picton, *Liv. Munic. Rec.* ii, 395.

[677] Ibid. 394.   [678] Ibid. 343, 345.

[679] 26 Geo. IV, cap. 43. For discussions see *Munic. Corp. Com. : Rep. of Proc. in Liv.*, passim.

[680] Report of the resistance of payment of town dues in Liverpool by Bolton and others, 1835.

[681] Under 21 Geo. II, cap. 24.

[682] Under a special local Act, 1 Will. IV, cap. 15.

other public bodies of limited powers, so that there was no single body responsible for the general oversight of the health and well-being of the town. The corporation, while, as we have seen, it retained control of public improvements and of the dock estate, had to perform these functions out of the revenue from its estate and from the town dues and other traditional payments, and as these were inadequate to the purpose these functions had not been fully performed, while their partial performance had formed so grave a strain upon the resources of the corporation that the value of the borough estate had been seriously diminished.[683] But for this condition of things the borough might very well have been the owner of the greater part of the land on which it was built ; as it was, a large part of the corporate estate, secured originally by the burgesses' usurpation of the waste in the 15th century, had been sold to meet the corporate debt.[684] Finally, the exclusive political privileges of the freemen and their exemption from the payment of town dues had become an anomaly and an injustice, because the body of freemen, which since 1777 had not been increased except by the customary modes of inheritance or service, no longer at all represented the community. There were in 1833 only 3,000 freemen[685] out of a population of 165,000, and many of the 3,000 were non-resident. This number included few of the principal merchants, and only seven out of the 200 doctors practising in the town.[686] It was composed principally of artisans, to whom their privileges were chiefly valuable for the money to be made out of them in bribes at elections. Hence Liverpool had become so notorious for its political corruption that in 1830 a bill for the disfranchisement of the borough was only prevented by the prorogation of Parliament from passing into law.[687]

The unsatisfactoriness of the old institutions was shown also in the sphere of poor-law administration, which had been perhaps the most efficient department of borough government. The committee which had for so long controlled the administration of the Poor Law was not recognized by law, and was liable at any time to be overridden by the overseers, if they chose to disregard its orders. In 1814 the committee tried in vain to persuade the open vestry to make an application for a private Act legalizing their position ;[688] after two years' discussion the proposal was rejected,[689] and in 1817 a Mr. Dennison, being elected overseer, justified these fears by paying no attention to the committee, and launching upon lavish expenditure.[690] The Sturges-Bourne Act of 1819[691] came in the nick of time to prevent the breakdown of the system, for its adoption legalized the position of the committee by turning it into a select vestry, and for some years it was able to do admirable work.[692] But in the excitement of the agitation for the Reform Act party feeling crept in here also and showed itself by constant appeals to the open vestry and to polls of the whole body of ratepayers on the smallest points.[693] The survival of the open

vestry in so large a population was a nuisance and a danger.

Liverpool was thus ready for the Reform movement, and it is not surprising that in the reforming Parliament of 1830 and in its successor the Tory town was for the nonce represented by Whig members. The Reform Act of 1832 itself began the process of local reconstitution. Not only did it enfranchise the ratepayers, placing them on a level, for the purposes of parliamentary elections, with the freemen, but, for the same purpose, it enlarged the borough's boundaries, including within them the populous suburbs of Everton and Kirkdale, the northern half of Toxteth, and part of West Derby,[694] and thus foreshadowing the full absorption of these districts for municipal purposes also.

But the legislation which followed the Reform Act was of far greater local import. The two great commissions—that on the Poor Laws and that on the Municipal Corporations—which the Reformed Parliament sent out to investigate the condition of local government both reported not unfavourably on Liverpool : the Poor Law Commission found the town, indeed, to be among the best administered in England,[695] while the Municipal Corporations Commission, though it disclosed many grave defects, found no evidence of serious maladministration.[696] But the changes introduced by the two great Acts were of such a character as to mark the beginning of a new epoch. The terms of the new Poor Law did not, indeed, involve any such wide change in Liverpool as in other places ; it established finally the authority of the popularly elected select vestry, and put an end to the defects and uncertainties of the Sturges-Bourne Act ; but the authority of this body was still confined to the limits of the old township and parish, the new and populous outlying districts being left to the administration of the Toxteth Board of Guardians or the West Derby Union. The Municipal Reform Act was far more serious in its results. It made the Town Council for the first time in its history a popularly elected body. It placed the election in the hands of the body of ratepayers, to whose level the freemen were now in practice reduced. It empowered the council to take over the functions of the Watching, Lighting, and Cleansing Board ; that is to say, it turned it from being the mere administrator of the estate of a privileged minority into a body responsible for the health and general well-being of the whole community, and thus rendered possible, and indeed suggested, an indefinite enlargement of municipal functions. Finally, in one of its schedules, it enlarged the boundaries of the municipal borough so as to correspond with those of the parliamentary borough as fixed in 1832.

The history of Liverpool since 1835 has been one of rapid and steady development on all sides, unmarked by outstanding or conspicuous episodes. It is impossible to follow its course in detail ; and it will be most convenient to summarize it under headings, in a more or less tabular form.

[683] Picton, *Liv. Munic. Rec.* ii, 224–6.
[684] Ibid. ii, 338–9.
[685] *Munic. Corp. Com.: Rep. of Inquiry in Liv.* 50.
[686] Ibid. 325.
[687] Walpole, *Hist. Engl.* i, 125 ; Picton, *Liv. Munic. Rec.* ii, 333.
[688] 'Address to all who are assessed to

the Poor-rates . . . by the Parish Committee, 1814.'
[689] Vestry Minutes, 6 Aug. 1816.
[690] Ibid. 1818 and 1819 ; Picton, *Memorials*, i, 391–2.
[691] S. and B. Webb, *Hist. Local Gov.* i, 159.
[692] Vestry Minutes, *passim.*

[693] *Liv. Chron.* April and July 1832 ; Vestry Minutes, April 1833.
[694] The area was increased from 1,860 to 5,210 acres.
[695] *Poor Law Com. Rep.*
[696] *Munic. Corp. Com. Rep.* (Liv.), 295, 400.

The following table shows the growth of the foreign trade of the port, as measured by the entrances and clearances of vessels from or to foreign or colonial ports [697] at intervals of five years : —

GROWTH OF TRADE

FOREIGN TRADE : ENTRANCES AND CLEARANCES, 1835–1906

Year	Entrances		Clearances		Total	
	Ships	Tonnage	Ships	Tonnage	Ships	Tonnage
1835 .	2,978	787,009	3,065	796,766	6,043	1,583,775
1840 .	3,492	1,042,232	3,808	1,103,955	7,300	2,146,187
1845 .	4,045	1,406,541	4,197	1,412,473	8,242	2,819,014
1850 .	4,531	1,605,315	4,807	1,656,938	9,338	3,262,253
1855 .	4,197	2,074,168	4,483	2,223,044	8,680	4,297,212
1860 .	4,902	2,773,439	5,358	2,899,474	10,260	5,672,913
1865 .	4,827	2,644,821	4,425	2,631,827	9,252	5,276,648
1870 .	5,058	3,416,933	4,778	3,356,138	9,836	6,773,071
1875 .	5,440	4,388,952	4,640	3,996,288	10,080	8,385,240
1880 .	5,263	4,913,324	4,878	4,746,489	10,141	9,659,813
1885 .	4,668	5,173,330	4,246	4,822,021	8,914	9,995,351
1890 .	4,646	5,782,351	4,030	5,159,450	8,676	10,941,801
1895 .	3,716	5,598,341	3,168	4,883,199	6,884	10,481,540
1900[698]	3,516	6,050,526	3,140	5,678,114	6,656	11,728,640
1905 .	3,523	7,806,844	2,890	6,932,687	6,413	14,739,531
1906 .	3,487	8,145,441	2,870	7,125,417	6,357	15,270,858

Two periods only show an actual decline in this table. The first is the quinquennium 1860–65, the period of the American Civil War, when the blockade of the southern ports caused the Lancashire cotton famine and for a brief time brought about a revival, in blockade-running expeditions, of the adventurous spirit of the age of privateering.[699] The other is the quinquennium 1890–95, a period of general bad trade. The periods of most rapid growth are those from 1850 to 1860, from 1865 to 1880, and again from 1900 onwards. The period from 1880 to 1900 is one in which Liverpool was feeling for the first time seriously the competition of the European nations which from 1815 to 1870 had left to England almost a monopoly of oversea trade. This competition may be said to have begun about 1870, and though the gross increase since that date has been twice as great as the increase in the preceding period of the same length, its effects have been shown in a tendency to more violent fluctuation, which will perhaps better be illustrated by the value of imports and exports than by the record of the actual sailings of vessels that might be either full or empty.

TABLE OF IMPORTS AND EXPORTS, 1875–1906

Year	Value of Imports	Value of Exports	Total
1875 . .	105,095,188	79,460,771	184,155,959
1880 . .	107,460,187	84,029,651	191,489,838
1885 . .	94,912,069	89,954,372	184,866,441
1890 . .	108,476,672	117,741,836	226,218,508
1895 . .	95,630,489	90,620,396	186,250,885
1900 . .	124,713,436	102,572,890	227,286,326
1905 . .	139,295,487	138,285,465	277,580,952
1906 . .	146,701,650	150,348,511	297,050,161

Space does not permit of any detailed analysis of the character and direction of Liverpool trade during this period, but some idea of its principal features may be derived from the following summary of the ten leading articles of import and the ten leading articles of export, with their approximate value, as in the year 1906 :—

Imports	Value in Millions	Exports	Value in Millions
	£		£
Raw Cotton . .	42·56		46·24
Dead Meat . . .	17·15		13·98
Corn and Cereals .	14·65		
India-rubber . .	8·42		8·87
Wool . . .	5·74		8·68
Live Animals . .	4·84		3·88
Copper . . .	4·23	. .	3·61
Timber	3·78		3·43
Tobacco	3·18		2·86
Sugar	3·16		1·54
		. . .	1·02

A further striking feature of the first table above, which indicates a characteristic of Liverpool's development, is the fact that, especially from 1850 onwards, the number of vessels employed tends to increase slowly, or even to diminish, while the tonnage rapidly grows. Thus in 1906 almost the same number of vessels entered and cleared as in 1835, but their tonnage is ten times as great. This remarkable increase of the tonnage of vessels is due above all to the replacement of sailing vessels by steamships, and to the increasing employment of large ' liners ' sailing at regular intervals in place of the irregular sailings of an earlier period. The first regular liners begin with the institution of the Cunard line in 1842. The figures of the shipping registered in the port of Liverpool since 1850 bring out this point still more clearly.

SHIPPING REGISTERED IN LIVERPOOL

Year	Sailing		Steam		Total	
	No. of Ships	Tonnage	No. of Ships	Tonnage	No. of Ships	Tonnage
1850 .	1,750	503,224	93	11,411	1,843	514,635
1860 .	2,228	933,723	223	67,885	2,451	1,001,608
1870 .	2,155	1,156,566	456	280,807	2,611	1,437,373
1880 .	1,824	999,809	667	555,062	2,491	1,554,871
1890 .	1,352	916,726	967	1,006,713	2,319	1,923,439
1900 .	1,018	614,968	1,073	1,713,506	2,091	2,328,474
1906 .	914	410,251	1,305	2,401,432	2,219	2,811,683

Though steamboats had appeared in the Mersey as early as 1815, they were for long used purely for

---

[697] The figures for coasting trade are omitted. This table is compiled from the Annual Reports on Trade and on Shipping and Navigation laid before the Houses of Parliament.

[698] Including transports for the South African War.

[699] Running the Blockade.

river or at most coasting traffic;[700] it was not until the forties that they began to be employed for the ocean trade in which Liverpool is mainly concerned. But as soon as this happened, the size of the vessels in the port rose with great rapidity, from an average of 280 tons in 1850 to an average of 1,270 tons in 1906. Liverpool has indeed become peculiarly the home of large vessels. While the number of her vessels is only two-thirds of that of London, their total tonnage is one-third greater;[701] that is to say, the average Liverpool ship is twice as big as the average London ship. Of 271 British vessels which in 1906 measured over 4,000 tons, no less than 146 belonged to Liverpool; and while in number Liverpool possesses not much more than one-tenth of the British mercantile marine, in tonnage she possesses considerably more than one-fifth.

In regard to the position of Liverpool among the ports of the world, the following comparative statement of the value of the trade of the first six ports of the world may be quoted.[702] In 1905 the trade of London was estimated to be worth £261,000,000; of Liverpool, £237,000,000; of New York, £221,000,000; of Hamburg, £196,000,000; of Antwerp, £147,000,000; of Marseilles, £86,000,000.

GROWTH OF POPULATION

The following are the census returns during the period, including for the earlier dates the suburban districts later added to the town :—

1841	.	286,487
1851	.	376,065
1861	. .	462,749
1871	. . . .	493,405
1881	. . . .	611,075
1891	. . .	617,032
1901	. . . .	684,947
1907 [703]	.	746,144 [704]

These figures, however, do not adequately represent the growth which has taken place, since they omit notice of the growth of Bootle, of the northern suburbs of Seaforth, Waterloo, and Crosby and other outlying districts outside of the municipal boundary, as well as of the population of about 200,000 in Wirral, which almost wholly depends economically upon Liverpool. The whole of this population has been created during the period under notice, and the urban population dependent upon Liverpool now exceeds 1,000,000.

It should be noticed that the Irish population of Liverpool, always large, was enormously increased by the inrush of immigrants after the Potato Famine of 1845–6; over 90,000 entered the town in the first three months of 1846, and nearly 300,000 in the twelve months following July 1847. Most of these subsequently emigrated to America, but many thousands, unable to find the passage money, remained to swell the misery of the Liverpool slums.

GEOGRAPHICAL GROWTH

No account can here be given of the rapid expansion of the street-covered area, but it is necessary to note the stages of the expansion of municipal control over this area.

After the enlargement of the boundaries in 1835 nearly sixty years passed without any further enlargement; in the meantime the borough of Bootle, which was essentially an expansion of Liverpool, had grown up and obtained its incorporation without opposition in 1869; beyond it the populous areas of Seaforth and Crosby lay separated from the town; the borough of Birkenhead was similarly incorporated in 1877. At the end of the century, however, the city awoke to the danger of allowing the wealthy residential suburbs which derived their prosperity from the city to escape from their share of the costs of government. In 1895 the township of Walton, a second large section of the extensive township of West Derby, the township of Wavertree, and the remaining southern half of the township of Toxteth, were added to the city.[705] In 1901 the township of Garston, on the eve of applying for an incorporation which would have shut in the city on the south as it was inclosed by Bootle on the north, was also taken in. In 1903 an attempt was made to incorporate Bootle in the city; but though the approval of the Local Government Board was obtained, the vigorous opposition of Bootle prevented the passage of the bill through Parliament. In 1904 the township of Fazakerley was incorporated. The increase of the city's area involved in these successive enlargements may be briefly shown :—

1830	. . . .	1,860 acres
1835	. . . . . .	5,210 „
1894	. . . . .	13,236 „
1900	. . . . . .	14,909 „
1907	. . .	16,619 „

DEVELOPMENT OF MUNICIPAL GOVERNMENT

After the Municipal Reform Act the Whig party for a brief period enjoyed control of the borough government. At the outset they possessed an overwhelming majority, but by 1842 this majority had disappeared. The main cause of this was the unpopularity of the Whig attempt to abandon compulsory Anglican religious teaching in the two corporation schools, which was advocated on the ground that the population served by these schools was mainly Roman Catholic; but the proposal aroused a fierce opposition. The Whigs, however, also initiated a series of elaborate inquiries into the various departments of borough government, reconstituted the corporation service and effected large economies by reductions of salaries, and commenced a vigorous progressive policy in regard to the regulation of buildings and the safeguarding of the health of the town. In these respects the transference of power to the Tory party led to little change; and the years from 1835 to 1870 witnessed a vigorous, sustained, and not unsuccessful campaign for the amelioration of the conditions of the borough. The powers of the Watching, Lighting, and Cleansing Board had been taken over by the corporation under the Act of 1835, and were administered by a special Watch Committee; they were now enlarged by a new local Act,[706] under which the council took powers to impose numerous penalties for

---

[700] Smithers, Liverpool, 186.

[701] In 1906 London had 3,300 vessels of 2,100,000 tons; Liverpool 2,200 vessels of 2,800,000 tons.

[702] Annual statement of the Chairman of the Dock Board, quoting American official estimates.

[703] From the Medical Officer's Report (estimated).

[704] The birth-rate, which shows a slow but steady decline throughout the later half of the period, was in 1907 estimated at 31·7 per 1,000, as compared with 26·3 per 1,000 for England and Wales. On the other hand the death-rate has sunk from an average of 32·5 per 1,000 in 1861–70 to 20·4 in 1901–7.

[705] 59 Vict. cap. 7.

[706] 1 Vict. cap. 98.

neglect of civic duties. In regard to the regulation of buildings the new régime was especially vigorous. The council obtained powers by an Act of 1839[707] to appoint building surveyors who should be required to certify before any new building was permitted to be occupied that it fulfilled the numerous requirements laid down in the Act. These regulations were made still more exacting by the important Act of 1842,[708] which forbade the erection of inadequately lighted courts ; the same Act also empowered the magistrates to order the cleansing at the owner's expense of any 'filthy or unwholesome' house. The most important clause of this epoch-making Act was that which decreed the appointment of a Health Committee to carry out its terms. Another Act of the same year,[709] while providing for the widening of certain main streets, provided (section 107) that on the presentment of the grand jury or the complaint of four or more householders the council might demolish a ruinous house. Meanwhile the Commissioners for Paving and Sewerage had continued to perform their duties independently, being expressly safeguarded from any interference by the growing activity of the council ;[710] but in 1842 it was provided that half of them should be elected by the council.[711] Their authority extended only over the old township, and in the same year a separate commission was created for Toxteth Park.[712]

The new Health Committee found its work hampered by the existence of these independent and unrelated authorities. Moreover, in 1843 a very powerful pamphlet[713] published by Dr. Duncan, then a lecturer in the Royal Infirmary School of Medicine, awoke the town to a new sense of the horrors of its slums. He showed that nearly half of the working-class population lived in cellar-dwellings ; that most of the poorer streets were quite unprovided with sewers ; that the water supply was such as to render impossible even ordinary personal cleanliness ; in short, that the condition of the poorer quarters of the town was such as not only to degrade their inhabitants, but also to form a grave menace to other residents. This powerful statement came at a moment when the corporation was already awakening to the difficulty of the problem, and the ineffectiveness of its weapons for coping with it. The immediate result was that a new Act was obtained in 1846,[714] which was of the most far-reaching importance. It provided for the first time for the appointment of a Medical Officer of Health—an office to which, with singular appropriateness, Duncan was the first to be appointed. It transferred the powers and properties of the Liverpool and Toxteth Paving and Sewerage Boards to the Health Committee of the Town Council, on which it imposed the obligation to pave and sewer every street and house.[715] It also imposed upon the council a totally new obligation, namely that of laying down pipes and supplying water throughout the borough ; for which purpose the Green Lane Waterworks were transferred to the corporation.

Under Duncan's guidance the council now began a systematic campaign against cellar-dwellings ; in 1847 over 5,000 such dwellings were declared unfit for human habitation, and absolutely closed, while over 10,000 more were measured, registered, and in some cases cleansed at the owners' expense.[716] But the powers possessed by the council for carrying out such reforms were as yet slight. By the Sanitary Amendment Act of 1864[717] these powers were very largely increased ; so much so that under the terms of this Act the facilities for the demolition of insanitary property are in some respects more useful than any conferred by the later national Acts for this purpose.

Even more important than the demolition of insanitary property was the provision of an adequate water supply. The supply of water had hitherto been in the hands of two companies—the Company of Proprietors, and the Liverpool and Harrington Company, founded respectively in 1799 and 1802 ; both drew their supply from wells, some of which are still in use. These were now taken over ;[718] but in addition the corporation took powers to construct a series of reservoirs on the Rivington moors, north of Bolton.[719] The scheme produced much discussion, being one of the first of its kind, and several additional Acts[720] were passed before it had been finally settled. The Rivington Waterworks were not completed till 1857 ; their completion for the first time rendered possible a continuous supply of water throughout the city. As population grew, it in turn became inadequate ; and in 1879 the Vyrnwy scheme was entered upon. This involved the acquisition of the valley of the River Vyrnwy in Merionethshire, with its drainage area of 22,742 acres ; the construction across the mouth of the valley of a masonry dam 1,172 ft. long, 161 ft. high, and 127 ft. thick, thus creating a lake 4¾ miles long, capable of yielding a supply of forty million gallons of water per diem ; and the construction of an aqueduct 68 miles long, including tunnels of 4½ miles, one of which passes under the Manchester Ship Canal and the Mersey. The supply was first brought to Liverpool in 1891, after eleven years' work. The value to the community of this magnificent achievement cannot be exaggerated.[721]

Meanwhile the town had not been altogether neglectful of the amenities. St. George's Hall,[722] designed to serve the double purpose of a public hall and assize courts, had been projected by private citizens in 1835, and was begun in 1838, and completed by the corporation in 1854 at a cost of £238,000. The design was by a young architect, H. L. Elmes, who died before his work was completed, and much of the interior was carried out by R. P. Cockerell. The design was much criticized, but it is now agreed that the building is one of the noblest modern classic buildings in the world. It is enriched by a fine pediment by Alfred Stevens at the south end and by a series of external bas-relief panels ; it contains one of the best organs in England, long played by W. T. Best ;

[707] 2 & 3 Vict. cap. 92.
[708] 5 Vict. cap. 44.
[709] 5 & 6 Vict. cap. 106.
[710] 1 Vict. cap. 98 ; 2 & 3 Vict. cap. 92.
[711] 5 Vict. cap. 26.
[712] 5 & 6 Vict. cap. 105.
[713] Read before the Lit. and Phil. Soc. in 1843.
[714] 9 & 10 Vict. cap. 127.
[715] An excellent account of the sanitary administration of the city is given in Hdbk. of Congress of Roy. Inst. of Pub. Health, 1903.
[716] Gore's Annals, 1847.
[717] 27 & 28 Vict. cap. 73.
[718] Under powers conferred by 39 Geo. III, cap. 36 ; 9 Vict. cap. 35 ; and 10 & 11 Vict. cap. 261.
[719] 10 & 11 Vict. cap. 261.
[720] 13 & 14 Vict. cap. 80 ; 15 Vict. cap. 47 ; 18 Vict. cap. 66 ; 19 Vict. cap. 5.
[721] On the history of the water supply in general, Hist. and Descr. Account of the Liv. Water Supply (Water Engineer's Rep. 1899) ; article in Hdbk. of Congress of Roy. Inst. of Pub. Health, 1903.
[722] R. P. Jones, 'H. L. Elmes,' Archit. Rev. 1904 ; H. L. Elmes, Corresp. relative to St. George's Hall, &c.

and both the great hall and the plateau without are used for the display of statuary.

Another fruitful new enterprise was begun in 1852. As early as 1849—before the Free Libraries Act— the establishment of a public library had been projected. In 1851 the thirteenth Earl of Derby had bequeathed his large natural-history collection to the town. At the same time the Liverpool Academy, founded in 1810, had succeeded in stimulating artistic interests in the town by its annual exhibitions. In order to meet this triple need a private Act[733] was obtained empowering the council to establish and maintain a public library and museum with a gallery of arts, to provide lecture rooms and arrange lectures. With this were at first linked the Botanic Gardens, originally started as a private organization by Roscoe, but taken over by the corporation in 1846.[734] A fine classic building for the library and museum was provided by Sir William Brown, replacing the rather ragged houses at the north of Shaw's Brow, and facing St. George's Hall. Thus began a noble group of buildings devoted to knowledge and the arts, gradually extended by the erection of the Picton Reading Room, a fine rotunda, in 1872, the Walker Art Gallery (the gift of Sir A. B. Walker)

BROWN of Astrop, Bart. *Gules a cheveron or between two bears' paws erased in chief argent and four hands conjoined in saltire of the second in base, on a chief engrailed gold an eagle displayed sable.*

WALKER of Osmaston, Bart. *Or three pallets gules surmounted by a saltire argent charged with a hart's head erased proper, on a chief azure a garb between two stars of the first.*

in 1877, and the Museum Extension and Technical School in 1902; a proud adornment to the city, later made still more attractive by the laying out of gardens with statues in the centre of the great place. The development of these institutions during the last half-century can only be briefly summarized. The Central Library, opened in 1852 with 8,296 volumes, now contains close on 150,000 volumes; it is most strongly equipped on local history and topography, natural history, and the fine arts; the last-named section has been greatly strengthened by the bequest of the Hornby Library, now housed in a beautiful additional room. There are also nine lending libraries in various parts of the city, having among them nearly 140,000 volumes.[735] The Museums fall into two sections— the Museum of Natural History, which has been built

up round the nucleus bequeathed by Lord Derby in 1852, and is now of great range, probably unsurpassed out of London ; and the Museum of Antiquities and Anthropology, which includes some very valuable collections mainly provided by bequest of Mr. Joseph Mayer in 1867. The large extension of the buildings effected in 1902 for the first time gives adequate room for the display of these collections.[736] In the Art Gallery a large permanent collection has been accumulated by gift and purchase. It includes some modern paintings of wide fame, also the Roscoe collection of Early Italian art, formerly housed at the Royal Institution. The controlling committee has wisely set itself to obtain as full a representation as possible of the remarkable group of Liverpool painters who flourished in the middle of the 19th century. An exhibition of contemporary art has been held annually since 1871, and many special exhibitions have also been organized.[737]

The increasing attention to the amenities which the council were now showing was exhibited especially in 1868. Up to that date the town had possessed no public parks, except the small public gardens in St. James's Mount; for though as early as 1848 the Newsham estate had been purchased, no use had been made of it. In 1868 powers were obtained[738] for the creation of three parks—Sefton Park, Newsham Park, and Stanley Park—at a cost of £670,000. The expenditure thus begun has been continued without intermission, and supplemented by private munificence, to which the city owes Wavertree Playground and Bowring Park. The total area of parks and gardens laid out in various parts of the city amounts to almost 1,100 acres.

The last twenty-five years of the 19th century were largely engaged in a renewed attack on the problem of the housing of the poor. In the earlier period the council had been content with the demolition of insanitary property, a work in which it had been a pioneer ; it now began to undertake the replacement of the demolished property by model dwellings. The first block of cottages to be thus erected was in 1869.[739] In 1885 a large group of dwellings was erected, known as Victoria Square. By 1900 accommodation had been provided for over 700 families. More recently this work has been pushed on with such vigour that in February 1907 over 2,200 dwellings were either in occupation or almost completed. The total cost has been more than £1,000,000, the interest on which is almost met by the rents paid. The elaborate and efficient tramway service, taken over by the corporation in 1897, has also tended to facilitate the solution of the housing problem.

Of other municipal activities no account can here be given. But enough has been said to show that the seventy years since the Municipal Reform Act have been marked by a systematic attempt at the reorganization and reconstruction of the city. In the last part of the period the establishment of the separate diocese of Liverpool in 1880, the more recent

[733] 15 Vict. cap. 3.

[734] 8 & 9 Vict. cap. 43. The library of the Botanic Gardens, founded by Roscoe, was transferred to the City Library in 1907.

[735] Cowell, *Liv. Public Libraries, a history of fifty years* (1903).

[736] Forbes, descriptive account of the Liverpool Museums in *Hdbk. of the Con-*

gress of Roy. Inst. of Pub. Health, 1903; annual reports.

[737] *Annual Reports,* 1872–1907. On the Liverpool painters, Marillier, *The Liv. School of Painters,* 1904.

[738] 28 Vict. cap. 20.

[739] The following facts are from information supplied by the Medical Officer of Health. It may be noted that the Royal

Com. on the Housing of the Working Classes reported in 1885 that housing reform was more urgently needed in Liverpool than in any other Lancashire town. A good account of housing work in Liverpool may be found in the *Hdbk. of the Congress of Roy. Inst. of Pub. Health,* 1903.

commencement of the erection of a cathedral, and the foundation of a university, have added the dignities of a cathedral, episcopal, and university city to those of a great port. The advance thus made was re-cognized by the first charter of Queen Victoria in 1880,[730] whereby the title of 'City' became the official designation of Liverpool, and by the queen's second charter in 1893,[731] whereby the chief magis-trate of the city was empowered to assume the style of Lord Mayor of Liverpool.

DOCKS Under the first Dock Act, 1708,[732] the mayor, aldermen, bailiffs, and Common Council became the trustees of the proposed dock, and were empowered to construct the dock and to levy dues. They were not incorporated, but used the corporation seal; managing the first and successive docks through committees, which were as completely under their control as any other council committees. By an Act of 1811,[733] however, they were separately in-corporated and given a seal of their own; the finances of the docks were separately administered from those of the corporation, by a statutory committee of twenty-one members appointed by the trustees (i.e. the Town Council), but the Town Council still claimed and exercised the right of voting sums from the dock funds, and of overriding the actions of the com-mittee. The control of the docks by a close corpora-tion, which was in no way representative of the rate-payers or of those who used the docks, led to much discontent and discussion, and in the end produced a new Act, that of 1825,[734] whereby, though the trust remained unaltered, the committee was changed by the inclusion of eight members elected by dock ratepayers. The council still retained a majority, thirteen of the committee being councillors, while the chairman was also selected from among the members of the committee by the council. The Act also provided that the proceedings of the dock committee could only be overridden by a majority of two-thirds of the council, and only at the meeting of the council immediately following that of the committee. By an Act of 1851[735] the number of the committee was raised to twenty-four, half of whom were to be dock ratepayers, while the chair-man was to be elected by the committee itself. But the power of revision still remained with the Town Council. Outside of both council and committee there had been from the first an independent body of auditors, numbering nine under the Act of 1708,[736] and appointed in equal groups by the corporation, the justices of the county of Lancaster, and the jus-tices of the county of Chester. An Act of 1734[736a] raised the number to twelve, four nominated by the council, eight by the dock ratepayers. By an Act of 1841[737] the mayor, the chairman of the dock committee, and the senior borough magistrate, were appointed revisers of rates.

Even with these safeguards, however, and even though the council was now a representative elected body, dissatisfaction was felt with this system of ad-ministration, which identified the interests of the

dock estate with those of the municipality. This ex-pressed itself in controversies on the rating of the dock estate, and in the agitation for the Act of 1851, which was originally an attempt to alter the consti-tution of the dock committee so as to leave the council only the mere shadow of control, but which was amended to the effect already described. It also lowered the voting franchise for dock ratepayers. But the strongest opposition came from the merchants of Manchester and the railway companies, which re-sented the traditional charges for town dues; this went so far that a society was founded in Manchester called 'The Society to secure the right appropriation of the Liverpool Town Dues.' In 1857 they pro-moted a Bill, based upon the recommendations of the Commissioners of the Board of Trade, who had in 1853 reported in favour of the appointment of in-dependent bodies of conservators for the regulation of public harbours, and of the transference to them of all dues levied by municipal corporations. The Town Council fought the Bill with all its power, especially objecting to the confiscation of its tradi-tional town dues; but eventually withdrew its opposi-tion in consideration of a payment of £1,500,000 for the loss of the town dues, and of certain other modifications. By the Act thus passed[737a] the Mersey Docks and Harbour Board was constituted, and took over the control both of the Liverpool and of the Birkenhead Docks, and the right of collecting not only dock dues but also the ancient traditional town dues. The board has continued to collect the town dues, despite the fact that opposition to these dues was one of the principal causes of its establishment. The board consists of twenty-eight members, four of whom are nominated by the Mersey Conservancy Com-missioners (the First Lord of the Admiralty, the Presi-dent of the Board of Trade, and the Chancellor of the Duchy of Lancaster); while the other twenty-four are elected by all persons paying rates on ships or goods to the amount of not less than £10 per annum. Members of the board must be resident within 10 miles of the boundary of the borough or port of Liverpool, and must have paid rates on ships or goods to the amount of not less than £25 per annum. The office of Chairman of the Dock Board is commonly regarded as the most honourable at the disposal of Liverpool citizens.

The history of the actual dock estate may be conveniently divided into three periods,[737b] corre-sponding to the periods in the history of its governing body :—

I. Between 1709 and 1825, when the docks were under the direct control of the corporation, the fol-lowing wet docks were opened :—

1. Old Dock, opened 31 August 1715; closed 31 August 1826.

2. Salthouse Dock, opened 1753; altered 1842; en-larged 1855.

3. George's Dock, opened 1771; enlarged 1825; closed 1900.

---

[730] Printed in *Hist. Munic. Govt. in Liv.* 290.   [731] Ibid. 292.

[732] 8 Anne, cap. 12. On the whole history of the administration of the docks, see the Town Clerk's Report on the Pos-sibility and Expediency of obtaining re-presentation of the Corporation on the Dock Board (1907).

[733] 51 Geo. III, cap. 43.

[734] 26 Geo. IV, cap. 43. For the de-fects of this system, see *Munic. Corp. Com. Rep. of Liv. Inquiry, passim.*

[735] 14 & 15 Vict. cap. 64.

[736] 8 Anne, cap. 12.

[736a] 7 Geo. II, cap. 29.

[737] 4 & 5 Vict. cap. 30.

[737a] 20 & 21 Vict. cap. 162.

[737b] Figures taken from Memorandum Bk. of the Mersey Docks and Harbour Board, 1908. Smithers, *Liv.* 169 ff. and 452, describes the condition of the docks in 1824; Baines, *Liv.* App. describes them in 1852.

4. King's Dock, opened 1788 ; closed 1906, the name being preserved for two new branches of the Wapping Dock.
5. Queen's Dock, opened 1796 ; enlarged 1816 ; deepened and half-tide dock added 1856, and closed 1905 ; enlarged 1901 ; branches added 1901, 1905 ; altered 1906.
6. Union Dock, opened 1816 ; **thrown into Coburg** Dock 1858.
7. Prince's Dock, opened 1821 ; half-tide dock added 1868.

The total area of wet docks in 1825 amounted to 46 acres 3,179 sq. yds. ; **the lineal quayage to a** little over 2 miles. The dock dues paid in the same year amounted to £130,911. It may be noted that the first London Dock was not opened until 1802.

II. Between 1825 and 1857, when the docks were under the control of the Dock Committee, the Old Dock was closed (1826), and the following new docks were opened :—

1. Canning Dock, opened 1829 ; previously a basin known as the Dry Dock, opened 1753 ; enlarged 1842.
2. Clarence Docks, &c., opened 1830 ; enlarged 1853.
3. Brunswick Docks, opened 1832 ; enlarged 1848, 1858, 1889 ; branch dock added 1878 ; altered 1900.
4. Waterloo Dock, opened 1834 ; reconstructed as E. and W. Waterloo Docks, 1868.
5. Victoria Dock, opened 1836 ; altered 1848.
6. Trafalgar Dock, opened 1836.
7. Coburg Dock, opened 1840 ; altered from Brunswick Basin ; enlarged 1858 ; altered 1900.
8. Toxteth Dock, opened 1842 ; closed to make way for new works, 1884.
9. Canning Half-tide Dock, opened 1844.
10. Harrington Dock (bought), opened 1844 ; closed to make way for new works 1879.
11. Albert Dock, opened 1845.
12. Salisbury Dock, opened 1848.
13. Collingwood Dock, opened 1848.
14. Stanley Dock, opened 1848 ; partly filled in 1897.
15. Nelson Dock, opened 1848.
16. Bramley Moore Dock, opened 1848.
17. Wellington Docks, opened 1850 ; half-tide dock closed 1901.
18. Sandon Dock, opened 1851 ; half-tide dock added 1901 ; altered 1906.
19. Manchester Dock (bought), opened 1851.
20. Huskisson Dock, opened 1852 ; branch docks added 1861, 1872, 1902 ; altered 1896, 1897; enlarged 1900.
21. Wapping Dock and Basin, opened 1855 ; two King's Dock branches added 1906.

The water area in 1857 amounted to 192 acres 129 sq. yds., or an increase of over 82 acres in twenty-five years ; the lineal quayage was about 15 miles ; and the river-wall, when the Dock Board came into existence, already extended for just over 5 miles. At the same time the Dock Committee and the Corporation had acquired the Birkenhead Docks, which do not fall within the purview of this work. It is clear that the old Dock Committee did not lack energy. For the ten years preceding the establishment of the Dock Board the dock dues averaged nearly £250,000. It was on the security of these that the capital for the construction of the docks was raised ; and no profits were used for purposes other than the service of the port.

III. During the fifty years of the Mersey Docks and Harbour Board more time and money have been spent on the enlargement and reconstruction of the existing system than on the creation of new docks. The new docks of this period are :—

---

788 These are names of old docks, given to new docks in the same region.

788a See table of entrances and clearances, p. 37 above.

utilized for the magnificent domed building in which the offices of the Dock Board are now housed ; two of the main shoreward thoroughfares were continued across the site of the dock direct to the pier-head ; and the main entrance to the city has thus been materially improved and dignified.

The total water area of the docks (excluding those on the Cheshire side of the river) now (1908) amounts to 418 acres 320 yds., and the lineal quayage to 26 miles 1,083 yds. The continuous dock-wall fronts the river for a distance of 7¼ miles.

In addition to the docks controlled by the Dock Board, the London and North-Western Railway has three docks at Garston, now within the limits of the city, which have a water area of 14 acres 2,494 yds.

As the period of the Dock Board's administration has been the period of the rapid development in the size of ships, which is in no port more marked than in Liverpool, a large part of the Board's work has consisted in maintaining a clear channel in the river. The task of dredging the bar which impedes the entrance to the river was seriously begun about 1890. Carried on by dredgers of unusual magnitude and power, it has cost not far short of half a million of money during the last fifteen years, but the result has been to provide a clear deep-water passage, lacking which Liverpool might have found it impossible to maintain her control over ocean trade under the new conditions. No account can here be given of the other works of the Board, of its vast warehouses, of its appliances for the disembarkation of cargo, or of the immense floating stage, 2,478 ft. long, whereby the landing of passengers at all times is rendered possible despite the very great rise and fall of the tides in the Mersey.

CHURCHES   The erection of a chapel at Liverpool was probably contemporaneous with the foundation of the borough ; burgages 'next to the chapel' are mentioned in a charter of the middle of the 13th century.[789] The building is identified with the chapel of St. Mary del Key (or Quay) which was standing, 'a great piece of antiquity,' used as the free school, in 1673.[740] It was a chapel of ease to Walton, and without any permanent endowment.

In or before 1356 there was built, perhaps at the cost of the town, the larger chapel of Our Lady and St. Nicholas, which then became the chapel of Liverpool. In the year named the king allowed the mayor and commonalty to devote lands of the value of £10 a year to the maintenance of divine service in the chapel according to an agreement they had made with Henry, Duke of Lancaster,[741] who himself gave an allowance of 12s. a year to the chapel.[742]

In September 1361 the Bishop of Lichfield granted a licence for burials in the churchyard, during a visitation of plague ;[743] and in the following February he gave permission for the chapel and cemetery of St. Nicholas of Liverpool to be consecrated 'by any Catholic bishop having the grace of the Apostolic See and faculties for his office.'[744] Shortly afterwards William de Liverpool gave a rent of 6s. 8d. towards the stipend of the chaplain, as long as the chantry should continue.[745] The chantry referred to was probably that at the altar of St. John, founded by John de Liverpool to celebrate for the souls of his ancestors, the priest of which was nominated by the mayor and burgesses.[746] Another ancient chantry was that of St. Mary at the high altar,[747] founded by Henry, Duke of Lancaster ;[748] while the succeeding duke, John of Gaunt, founded one at the altar of St. Nicholas.[749] There were thus three priests in residence serving the chantries from the latter part of the 14th century down to the Reformation.

Further endowments were acquired from time to time ;[750] and in 1459 the Bishop of Lichfield granted an indulgence of forty days on the usual conditions to contributors to the restoration of the old chapel of St. Mary del Key and to the maintenance of a chaplain there and of its ornaments, or to those who should devoutly pray before her image.[751] This

---

[789] Most of the information relating to this ancient chapel is derived from an essay by Mr. John Elton in *Trans. Hist. Soc.* (new ser.), xviii, 73–118, and the documents there printed.

Randle del Moore of Liverpool, who occurs from 1246 onwards, granted to Margery his daughter and John Gernet half a burgage next to the chapel ; Moore D. no. 264 (1). In the same deeds 'the Chapel street' is mentioned in 1318 (ibid. no. 331 [71]), in a grant by John son of Alan de Liverpool, to which John del Moore was a witness.

Liverpool was named as a chapelry in 1327 at the ordination of the vicarage of Walton ; Gastrell, *Notitia Cestr.* (Chet. Soc.), ii, 191.

[740] Blome, *Britannia* (quoted by Picton).

[741] Elton, op. cit. 80, quoting Pat. 29 Edw. III. The rents were to be paid 'to certain chaplains to celebrate divine service every day, for the souls of all the faithful departed, in the chapel of Blessed Mary and St. Nicholas of Liverpool, according to the order of the mayor and commonalty.' The sum of £10 may include the endowments of the two chantries of John de Liverpool and Henry Duke of Lancaster.

[742] Elton, op. cit. 79, quoting a rent roll of 1395.

[743] Ibid. 83, from Lich. Epis. Reg. v, fol. 44.

[744] Ibid. 82, from Lich. Epis. Reg. v, fol. 45. Facsimiles of this and the preceding entry are given.

[745] Elton, op. cit. 86, from Moore D. no. 466 (183), dated 6 Sept. 1361.

[746] William de Liverpool's phrase, 'as may be ordained by the mayor and commonalty,' agrees with the above-quoted licence of Edward III, and with the condition of the chantry in 1548 ; Raines, *Chantries* (Chet. Soc.), 82. At this date the priest (John Hurdes) did 'sing and celebrate there according to the statutes of his foundation' ; the plate and ornaments were scanty ; the rents, derived, as were those of the remaining chantries, from burgages, houses, and lands in Liverpool, amounted to 105s. 1d. In 1534 the cantarist was Thomas Rowley, and the net revenue was 73s. 4d.; the founders' names were recorded as John de Liverpool and John del Moore ; *Valor Eccl.* (Rec. Com.), v, 221.

It was the duty of the priest of the altar of St. John to say mass daily between five and six in the morning, so that all labourers and well-disposed people

might come to hear it ; Picton, *Munic. Rec.* i, 31.

[747] Raines, op. cit. 86. Ralph Howorth was the incumbent in 1548, 'celebrating accordingly,' 'with the chalice and other ornaments pertaining to the inhabitants of the same town' ; the gross income was 115s. 11d., a chief rent of 2s. 3d. being paid to the king's bailiff of West Derby. Richard Frodsham was cantarist in 1534, when the revenue was £4 7s. 11d.; *Valor Eccl.* (Rec. Com.), loc. cit.

[748] Duchy of Lanc. Auditors' Accts. bdle. 728, no. 11987.

[749] Raines, op. cit. 89. Richard Frodsham was in 1548 'the priest remaining and celebrating there according to his foundation' ; there were chalice, two sets of vestments, and missal, and an endowment of 114s. 5d. Ralph Howorth was cantarist in 1534, when the income was 75s. 11d., the foundation being ascribed to Henry and John, Dukes of Lancaster ; *Valor Eccl.* loc. cit. Probably there has been some transposition of the names of the incumbents of these chantries.

[750] See Elton, op. cit. 86, 88.

[751] Lich. Epis. Reg. xii, fol. 124h. It is described as 'the chapel of Blessed Mary within the cemetery of the chapel of the town of Liverpool.'

ancient chapel continued in use until the Reformation, for John Crosse in 1515 made a bequest to 'the priest that sings afore our Lady of the Key.'[752] The same benefactor established the chantry of St. Katherine, the priest of which was also to 'teach and keep a grammar school.'[753] By this means the endowed staff was raised to four priests. A house was provided for them, with a garden adjoining.[754] The church, consisting of a nave and a chancel of about equal lengths, with a tower at the west end, a south porch, and an aisle on the north side,[755] had four or five altars—the high altar, St. Nicholas's (perhaps the same), St. John's, St. Katherine's, and the Rood altar.[756] The chapel of St. Mary of the Key, which was a separate building standing on the river bank, a little to the west of St. Nicholas's, also had its altar.[757] There is no means of deciding how many priests and clerks were employed, but the size of the chancel indicates a considerable staff.

The suppression of the chantries and the change of religion made a great difference. St. Nicholas's chapel continued to be used, and one of the old chantry priests, John Hurdes, was placed in charge in 1548; he appeared at the visitation in 1554, but not in 1562.[758] At the abolition of the ancient services in 1559 it is uncertain what took place at Liverpool ;[759] Vane Thomasson was curate in 1563,[760] and next year the Crown allowed the old stipend of one of the chantry priests for the payment of a minister to be nominated by the burgesses.[761] In 1590 the minister was 'a preacher,'[762] and the corporation afterwards took pains to secure a preacher or an additional lecturer.[763]

In 1650 the Commonwealth surveyors found that the Committee of Plundered Ministers had assigned to the curate of Liverpool all the tithes of the township and £10 from the rectory of Walton ; the duchy rent of £4 15s. was also paid to him ; the curate had, on the other hand, by the committee's order, to pay £11 10s. to the wife of Dr. Clare, the ejected rector of Walton.[764] Shortly afterwards, in 1658, Liverpool was made an independent parish,[765]

---

[752] Church Goods, 1552 (Chet. Soc.), 98.

[753] Raines, Chantries, 84 ; Valor Eccl. (Rec. Com.), v, 221. Humphrey Crosse was the incumbent in 1534 and 1548, celebrating for the souls of his founder and heirs, with a yearly obit at which 3s. 4d. was distributed to the poor, and teaching the grammar school. The endowment amounted to £4 15s. 10d. For a dispute concerning this foundation see Duchy Plead. (Rec. Soc. Lancs. and Ches.), i, 156. John Crosse's will is printed in full in Church Goods, 97, 98.

[754] Raines, op. cit. 85.

An account of the chantry lands after the confiscation is given by Elton, op. cit. 97, 98 ; see also Trans. Hist. Soc. (new ser.), iii, 165 ; and Gregson, Fragments (ed. Harland), 348–50.

The ornaments of the chapel in 1552 are detailed in Church Goods, 96.

[755] A south elevation is given in Enfield's Liverpool. The spire and the upper story of the tower were additions to the original building. Perry's plan of 1769 shows that there were then two aisles on the north side, but one of these had been built in 1697, with an addition in 1718 ; Picton, Memorials, ii, 58. The principal changes were : A west-end gallery, erected in 1681 ; an organ, provided in 1684 ; the boarded ceiling, painted and starred in 1688 ; the churchyard wall on the east and south, built in 1690 ; a spire, built in 1745 ; the churchyard extended in 1749 ; a new organ procured in 1764 ; and in 1774 the whole body of the church was rebuilt in its present form, the interior, which must have been very irregular, being entirely transformed, and the exterior walls being made uniform ; ibid. ii, 57–9. The following is Enfield's description of the old building : 'In its structure there is no appearance of magnificence or elegance. The body of the church within is dark and low ; it is irregularly though. decently pewed ; it has lately been ornamented with an organ. The walls have been repaired and supported by large buttresses of different colours and forms, and a spire has been added to the tower' ; Liverpool, 41.

The Corporation arranged the order of precedence in the pews ; Munic. Rec. i, 103, 210, 329.

The old peal having been reduced to a single bell, three more were ordered in 1628, but were not satisfactory, and

changes were made in 1636 and 1649; Munic. Rec. i, 211, 212. A new peal was procured in 1725, the number being increased to six. Their ringing brought about the ruin of the tower. The present peal consists of twelve bells, cast in 1813 ; an account of them will be found in Mr. Henry Peet's Inventory of the Parish Churches of Liverpool. Mr. Peet has kindly given other information respecting the churches.

A clock was set up in 1622, on the motion of the curate ; Munic. Rec. i, 212.

Notes of the arms in the windows, taken in 1590, have been printed in Trans. Hist. Soc. xxxii, 253, with an account of Captain Ackers, by Mr. J. P. Rylands.

After the fall of the tower and spire on 11 Feb. 1810, the present tower with its open lantern-spire was built. It stands at the centre of the west end, instead of at the south-west corner like the former one. The church now retains no traces of antiquity, being in a dull modern Gothic style, and is chiefly interesting for the many monuments of 18th and 19th-century date. The spire is, however, a creditable piece of work for its date.

[756] St. Katherine's altar is mentioned in 1464 ; Munic. Rec. i, 23.

[757] This building, ceasing to be used for divine worship, was purchased by the corporation, apparently for 20s. ; it became the town's warehouse, but later was used as the schoolhouse, and so continued until the 18th century, when it was demolished ; Elton, op. cit. 103, 112–18.

At the west end of this chapel was an image of St. Nicholas, 'to whom seafaring men paid offerings and vows ' ; see Blome, op. cit. and Pal. Note-book, iii, 119.

[758] The corporation seem to have continued to hold and regulate the chapel ; Elton, op. cit. 99–104. Many details will be found in Picton's Munic. Rec.

The clerk, Sir John Janson, in 1551 went away to Spain ; one Nicholas Smith was clerk in 1555 ; Elton, op. cit. 100, 104.

[759] The priest in charge, Evan Nicholson, appointed in or before 1555, was still there in 1559, but does not appear in the Visitation List of 1562 ; Munic. Rec. i, 97.

[760] Visitation List. It is possible that Vane (Vanus) Thomasson was the Evan Nicholson of 1555.

In 1564 Master Vane Thomasson, curate of Liverpool, and one of the wardens appeared before the Bishop of Chester, and

were enjoined to 'charge the people that they use no beads' ; the curate was to minister the sacrament and sacramentals according to the Book of Common Prayer ; Erasmus's Paraphrase must be procured ; and ' all manner of idolatry and superstition' was to be immediately 'abolished and utterly extirpated' ; Raines, op. cit. 92, quoting the Liber Correct. at Chester.

[761] Elton, op. cit. 104. The amount allowed was £4 17s. 5d. a year.

[762] Lydiate Hall, 249; quoting S.P. Dom. Eliz. ccxxxv, 4.

[763] In 1591 the mayor and burgesses paid £4 to 'Mr. Carter the preacher,' in consideration of 'his great good zeal and pains' in his 'often diligent preaching of God's word amongst us more than he is bound to do, but only of his mere good will' ; Picton, Munic. Rec. i, 102. In 1621 a stipend of £30 a year was promised to 'Mr. Swift to be a preacher here' ; in 1622 James Hyatt, afterwards vicar of Childwall and Croston, was appointed ; and in 1629 an arrangement was made with clergy of the neighbourhood to preach week-day sermons ; ibid. i, 197, 198, 200.

The authorities were in the 17th century inclined to the stricter Puritan side, as this insistence on preaching suggests ; but in 1602 the portmoot inquest presented the curate 'for not wearing his surplice according to the King's injunctions' ; and in 1610 it was 'agreed' that he should wear it 'every Sabbath and every holiday at the time of Divine service.' The clerk also was to wear one ; ibid. i, 102, 196.

Laud's reforms apparently did not reach Liverpool. In 1623 it was ordered by the corporation that, as the place where read was 'more convenient for the reading of Common Prayer than the place in the chancel where it hath formerly been read, in respect the same place is in the middle of the same church and in full audience and view of the whole congregation,' the whole service should be read there ; ibid. i, 198. In 1687 Bishop Cartwright had to command the churchwardens to 'set the communion table altarwise against the wall' ; Pal. Note-book, iii, 124.

[764] Commonwealth Church Survey (Rec. Soc. Lancs. and Ches., 84 ; Plund. Mins. Accts. (Rec. Soc. Lancs. and Ches.), i, 1.

[765] Plund. Mins. Accts. ii, 215, 224.

LIVERPOOL : SHAW'S BROW, c. 1850

(From a Water-colour Drawing)

St Nicholas's Church

(From Enfield's History of Liverpool, 1774)

but on the Restoration this Act was adjudged to be null, and St. Nicholas's became once more a chapel under Walton. The following is a list of the curates :—

c. 1563	Vane Thomasson [766]
oc. 1577	James Seddon [767]
1585	James Martindale [768]
oc. 1590	Hugh Janion [769]
1596	— Bentley [770]
1598	Thomas Wainwright [771]
? 1625	Edwin Lappage [772]
c. 1634	Henry Shaw [773]
1643	Joseph Thompson [774]
1645	John Fogg [775]
1662	John Leigh [776]
1670	Robert Hunter [777]
1688 {	William Atherton [779]
	Robert Stythe

Liverpool had by this time become so important that the governing body thought they might claim full parochial rights for the township.[778] After negotiations with the rector and vicar of Walton, and the patron, Lord Molyneux, an Act of Parliament was procured 'to enable the town of Liverpool to build a church and endow the same, and for making the same town and liberties thereof a parish of itself, distinct from Walton.'[780] Two joint rectors were appointed, the first being the two curates then ministering, and it was directed that £110 should be levied from the parishioners for each of them.[781] The church built under this Act was St. Peter's in Church Street, consecrated in 1704, which has since been regarded as the principal church of the parish, and was therefore appointed the pro-cathedral in 1880. It is a plain building with wide round-headed windows, consisting of a chancel with vestries, nave, and west tower. Its chief merit lies in the woodwork, and it preserves its galleries on three sides of the nave, the general arrangement of the seating having been but little altered since its first building.[782] It is to be demolished as soon as part of the new cathedral is in use.

The patronage was vested in the mayor and aldermen, such as had been aldermen or bailiffs' peers, and the common council. In 1836 the reformed corporation sold the patronage to John Stewart, and about the same time provision was made for the union of the two rectories.[783] From the Stewarts the patronage was purchased in 1890 by the late W. E. Gladstone, whose son, the Rev. Stephen E. Gladstone, now holds it.[784] There is no rectory-house, but the gross value of the benefice is stated as £1,600 a year, largely derived from fees.[785]

GLADSTONE. *Argent a savage's head wreathed with holly and distilling drops of blood proper within a flowered orle gules all with an orle of martlets sable.*

[766] Visitation Lists of 1563, 1564; name crossed out in 1565.

[767] Picton, *Munic. Rec.* i, 97.

[768] Ibid. 98.

[769] Ibid. He was also vicar of St. John's, Chester. He died in 1596; p. 97.

[770] Ibid. 97, 98. He could not endure the interference of the mayor and council, and only remained two years. He is called 'Mr.,' and was therefore a graduate of some university.

[771] Ibid. 98. He was also appointed schoolmaster, 'until God send us some sufficient learned man.' He was only a 'reading minister,' as might be inferred from this; *Hist. MSS. Com. Rep.* xiv, App. iv, 13. Accordingly in 1616 the mayor and burgesses considered 'the providing of a preacher to live within the town'; *Munic. Rec.* i, 196. He contributed £1 to the clerical subsidy of 1622; *Misc.* (Rec. Soc. Lancs. and Ches.), i, 65.

In 1609 he appears to have had an assistant named Webster; Raines MSS. (Chet. Lib.), xxii, 298.

The will of Thomas Wainwright, dated 26 June 1625, and proved in the following October, shows that he had a small library, including commentaries, Perkins on the Creed, and *Synopsis Papismi ;* these two books he left to Thomas son of his half-brother Godfrey Wainwright. To Mr. Hyatt he left Fulke upon the Rhemish Testament, on condition that he preached the funeral sermon. To John Moore of Bank Hall he left his watch. He also mentions his sisters, Ellen Okell and Cecily Blinston, and other relatives. He desired to be buried 'within the chapel of Our Lady and St. Nicholas under the Communion table there.'

[772] *Munic. Rec.* i, 199. He is described as 'minister and preacher.'

[778] He

The following is a list of the rectors :—

I

1699	Robert Stythe, B.A.[786]	1699
1714–17	vacant, owing to a dispute.[786a]	1706
1717	Thomas Bell, M.A.[787]	1721
1726	John Stanley, D.D.[788]	1753
1750	Robert Brereton	1772
1784	George Hodson, M.A.[789]	1783
1794	Samuel Renshaw, M.A.[790]	1796
1829	Jonathan Brooks, M.A.[791]	1829

1870	Alexander Stewart, M.A.[800]	
1904	John Augustine Kempthorne, M.A.[803]	

St. George's Church, for which an Act of Parliament was obtained in 1715,[802] was begun in 1726 on the site of the castle; it was completed in 1734. 'It had originally an elegant terrace, supported by rustic arches, on one side; these arches the frequenters of Red Cross market used to occupy.'[803] The church was re-built piecemeal between 1819 and 1825, and its new spire was reduced in height in 1833; in its time it was regarded as 'one of the handsomest in the kingdom.' It was the property of the corporation and maintained by them, the mayor and the judges of assize at one time attending it. On Mr. Charles Mozley, who was a Jew, being elected mayor in 1863, the incumbent preached a sermon denouncing the choice, and from that time the mayor and corporation ceased to attend St. George's. The building having long failed to attract a congregation was closed in 1897 and then demolished, the site being acquired by the corporation.[804]

St. Thomas's, Park Lane, was built in 1750 under the provisions of an Act of Parliament.[805] 'The land was given by Mr. John Skill, who, however, afterwards charged three times the value of the ground for the churchyard when it was required.'[806] A very tall and slender spire was a feature of the exterior; after various accidents it was taken down in 1822, and the present miniature dome replaced it. A large part of the churchyard was acquired by the corporation about 1885 for a new thoroughfare.[807]

St. Paul's, one of the corporation churches, was begun in 1763 in accordance with an Act obtained the previous year,[808] and opened in 1769. Its chief

[786] Educated at Brasenose College, Oxford; B.A. 1680; ordained deacon and priest by the Bishop of Chester in 1680 and 1682; master of the Free School at Liverpool, 1684. Held the rectory of Garstang for twelve months (1697–8), apparently as a 'warming pan.' He is regarded as co-founder, with Bryan Blundell, of the Blue-coat School, Liverpool. He died in Dec. 1713. See H. Fishwick, Garstang (Chet. Soc.), 185.

[786a] Picton, Munic. Rec. ii, 63.

[787] Educated at Pembroke College, Oxford; M.A. 1698; Foster, Alumni.

[788] Son of Sir Edward Stanley of Bickerstaffe; Fellow of Sidney-Sussex College, Cambridge; rector of Winwick 1740 to 1742, and 1764 to 1781; also rector of Bury 1743 to 1778.

[789] Son of the Rev. George Hodson, curate of West Kirby; educated at Brasenose College, Oxford; M.A. 1763; died 14 Apr. 1794; Foster, Alumni; Manchester School Reg. i, 53.

[790] Son of John Renshaw of Liverpool; educated at Brasenose College, Oxford; M.A. 1775; died 19 Oct. 1829, nine days after the other rector, Mr. Roughsedge; Foster, Alumni. He published a volume of sermons in 1792.

[791] He belonged to a mercantile family in Liverpool, being son of Joseph Brooks, Everton. He was educated at Trinity College, Cambridge; M.A. 1802; Archdeacon of Liverpool, 1848. He died 29 Sept. 1855. 'Few men have enjoyed in their day and generation more general respect than fell to the lot of Archdeacon Brooks. Of a dignified and noble presence, his manners were genial, courteous, and, with perfect truth it may be said, those of a gentleman. When presiding at vestry meetings in the stormy times of contested Church rates, when occasionally very strong language was indulged in, a and his son Thomas were successively

Memoirs.

and council.

[799] Also vicar of Childwall, 1824–70.

[800] Educated at Clare College, Cambridge; M.A. 1852. Vicar of Cogges, Oxfordshire, 1868–70; Hon. Canon of Liverpool, 1880.

[803] Educated at Trinity College, Cambridge; M.A. 1890. Vicar of St. Mary's, Rochdale, 1895; of St. Thomas's, Sunderland, 1900; Rector of Gateshead, 1901; Hon. Canon of Liverpool, 1905.

[802] 1 Geo. I, cap. 21.

[808] Stranger in Liverpool. From this guide, of which there were many editions, much of the information in the text is derived.

At one end of the 'terrace' was the office of the clerk of the market; at the other that of the night watch. There was a vault beneath the church for interments. The interior fittings were good. The east window had a picture of the Crucifixion, inserted in 1832. There were originally two ministers, the chaplain and the lecturer, and the appointment was usually a stepping-stone to the rectory; D. Thom in Trans. Hist. Soc. iv, 161. This essay on the changes and migrations of churches was continued in vol. v, and illustrated with views of the older buildings.

[804] An effort was made to retain the spire. There is an account of this church and St. John's by Mr. Henry Peet in Trans. Hist. Soc. (new ser.), xv, 27–44.

[805] 1 Geo. II, cap. 24.

[806] Stranger in Liverpool.

[807] The Bishop of Liverpool's commission in 1902 recommended that the incumbency be extinguished at the next vacancy, the district to be annexed to St. Michael's, Pitt Street.

[808] 2 Geo. III, cap. 68; the same Act authorised St. John's Church. There were formerly two incumbents at St. Paul's.

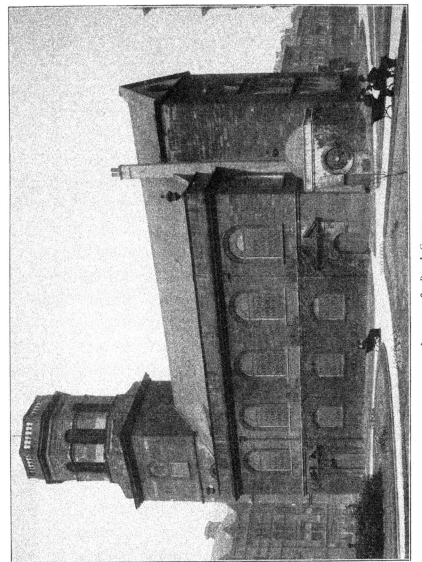

LIVERPOOL   ST. PETER'S CHURCH

feature is a dome ; internally this had the result of rendering the minister's voice inaudible. In time this defect was remedied, but changes in the neighbourhood deprived the church of its congregation, and falling into a dangerous condition, it was closed by the corporation in 1900.[809]

St. Anne's, also erected under the authority of Parliament,[810] was built by two private gentlemen in 1772 ; it was ' chiefly in the Gothic style.' The first minister, the Rev. Claudius Crigan, was appointed to the see of Sodor and Man in 1783, in the expectation, as it was said, that he would live only a short time, until the son of the Duchess of Atholl, sovereign of the Isle, should be old enough ; he lived thirty years longer, surviving his intended successor.[811] The old church was removed a little eastward to enable Cazneau Street to go through to St. Anne Street, the corporation replacing it by the present church, consecrated in 1871.

In 1776 a Nonconformist chapel in Temple Court was purchased by the rector of Aughton and opened in connexion with the Established Church. In 1820, some time after his death, it was purchased by the corporation and demolished.[812] In 1776 also another Nonconformist chapel, in Harrington Street, was opened as St. Mary's in connexion with the Established Church ; the congregation is supposed to have acquired St. Matthew's, in Key Street, in 1795, after which St. Mary's was demolished.[813]

St. John's, like St. Paul's, was built under the auspices of the corporation, and consecrated in 1785 : the style was the spurious Gothic of the time. There was a large public burial ground attached, consecrated in 1767. Becoming unserviceable as a church, there being but a scanty congregation, it was closed in 1898, demolished, and the site sold to the corporation.[814]

Trinity Church, St. Anne Street, was erected by private subscription in 1792.[815] In the same year a Baptist Chapel in Byrom Street was purchased and opened as St. Stephen's Church.[816] This was taken down in 1871 in order to allow the street to be widened, the corporation building the present church further north. In 1795 the English Presbyterian

or Unitarian Chapel in Key Street was purchased for the Established worship, being named St. Matthew's. It was consecrated in 1798. The site being required in 1848 for the Exchange railway station, the Lancashire and Yorkshire Company purchased a Scotch Presbyterian Chapel in Scotland Road, which was thereupon consecrated as St. Matthew's.[817] In 1798 a tennis court in Grosvenor Street was converted into a place of worship and licensed for service as All Saints' Church. It continued in use until the present church of All Saints', Great Nelson Street, was built in 1848.[818]

Christ Church, Hunter Street, was built in 1797 by John Houghton.[819] It was intended to use an amended version of the Book of Common Prayer, but the design proving a failure, the church was 'put on the establishment,' and consecrated in 1800.[820] Originally there was a second or upper gallery, close to the roof, but this was taken away about 1865.

St. Mark's was built by subscription in 1803, and consecrated in 1815, becoming established by an Act of Parliament ;[821] the projector was the Rev. Thomas Jones, of Bolton, who died suddenly on a journey to London before the opening. St. Andrew's, Renshaw Street, was erected by Sir John Gladstone in 1815 ;[822] the site being required for the enlargement of the Central Station, a new St. Andrew's was built in Toxteth in 1893. St. Philip's, Hardman Street, was one of the 'iron churches' of the time ; it was opened in 1816 and afterwards regulated by an Act of Parliament.[824] It was sold in 1882, the Salvation Army acquiring it, and a new St. Philip's built in Sheil Road.[825]

More costly churches were about the same time designed and slowly carried out by the public authorities. St. Luke's, Bold Street, was begun in 1811, but not completed and opened till 1831 ;[826] it is a florid specimen of perpendicular Gothic, the chancel being a copy of the Beauchamp Chapel, Warwick.[827] St. Michael's, Pitt Street, in the Corinthian style, but with a lofty spire, was begun in 1816 under Acts of Parliament,[828] and opened in 1826. There is a large graveyard around it.

The chapel of the Blind Asylum was built in 1819

---

[809] It is proposed to abolish the incumbency and sell the site.

[810] 12 Geo. III, cap. 36. The church was remarkable for being placed north and south. It stood on the line of Cazneau Street between Rose Place and Great Richmond Street. A part of the ground remains open.

A district was assigned to it under St. Martin's Church Act, 10 Geo. IV, cap. 11.

[811] *Church Congress Guide,* 1904. This contains much information as to the present condition of the churches, of which use has been made.

[812] *Trans. Hist. Soc.* iv, 139. It had been called the Octagon. It is mentioned in Brooke's *Liverpool as it was.*

[813] *Trans. Hist. Soc.* iv, 157. Other ' private adventure ' chapels were tried with greater or less success. A Rev. Thomas Pearson opened the Cockspur Street Chapel from 1807 to 1812, calling it St. Andrew's ; then he went to Salem Chapel in Russell Street, which he renamed St. Clement's, until 1817. The curious history of the latter building is given in the essay in *Trans. Hist. Soc.* v, 33.

[814] An effort was made in 1885 to secure the site for a cathedral for the newly erected Anglican diocese ; but it failed, although an Act of Parliament (48 & 49 Vict. cap. 51) was obtained authorizing the scheme. See *Trans. Hist. Soc.* (new ser.), xv, 27–44.

[815] 32 Geo. III, cap. 76.

[816] *Trans. Hist. Soc.* iv, 178. A district was assigned to it under St. Martin's Church Act, 10 Geo. IV.

[817] Ibid. iv, 143. The old building was demolished in 1849. A district was assigned under St. Martin's Church Act.

[818] Ibid. iv, 166. The incumbent and sole proprietor, the Rev. Robert Bannister, was the most popular minister of the time locally ; he died in 1829. Some singular occurrences in the church's history are related in the essay referred to. It does not seem to have been licensed until 1833.

[819] A small burial ground was attached, and a vault was constructed below the church. The endowment was £105 a year, derived from the rents of twentyfour pews. The upper gallery was free, for the poor. The view from the cupola was in 1812 recommended to the *Stranger in Liverpool.*

in Hotham Street in imitation of the Temple of Jupiter at Ægina. The site being required for Lime Street Station, the building was taken down and carefully re-erected in its present position in Hardman Street in 1850.[829] It is the Liverpool home of Broad Church doctrine.

St. David's, for Welsh-speaking Anglicans, was built in 1827.[830] As far back as 1793 Welsh services had been authorized in St. Paul's Church.[831] Another special church was the Mariners' Church, an old sloop-of-war moored in George's Dock. It was used from 1827, but ultimately sank at its moorings in 1872.[832]

St. Martin's in the Fields, a Gothic building with a western spire, was erected out of a Parliamentary grant in 1829, the land being a gift by Edward Houghton.[833] It was the first Liverpool church to be affected by the Tractarian movement.[834]

St. Catherine's, Abercromby Square, was consecrated in January 1831,[835] a fortnight after St. Bride's.[836] The first church of St. Matthias was built in 1833–4 in Love Lane, but the site being required by the railway company, the present church in Great Howard Street was built in 1848 ; the old one was accidentally destroyed by fire.[837] St. Saviour's, Falkner Square, was built by subscription in 1839 ; it was burnt down in 1900 and rebuilt in 1901 on the old plan.[838] In 1841 a congregation which had for some five years met in the chapel in Sir Thomas's Buildings, which they called St. Simon's, acquired a chapel previously used by Presbyterians and Independents, and this was consecrated as St. Simon's.[839] The site being required for Lime Street Station, a new church was in 1848 built close by,[840] and this was taken down and rebuilt in its present position in 1866–72, on an enlargement of the station.

A building in Hope Street, erected about fifteen years earlier for the meetings of the 'Christian Society,' and in 1838 occupied by the Rev. Robert Aitken, an Anglican minister who adopted 'revivalist' methods, was in 1841 acquired for the Established Church and called St. John the Evangelist's.[841] It was abandoned in 1853, but under the name of Hope Hall is still used for religious and other meetings. In 1841 also the churches of St. Bartholomew and St. Silas were opened.[842] St. Alban's, Bevington, dates from 1849–50.

In 1854 Holy Innocents' in Myrtle Street, primarily the chapel of the adjoining orphan asylums, was opened. All Souls', begun in the same year, had as first incumbent Dr. Abraham Hume, one of the founders of the Lancashire and Cheshire Historic Society.[843] 'As the population of this parish is mostly Roman Catholic' it is proposed to abandon the building.[844] A Wesleyan chapel was acquired and in 1858 consecrated as St. Columba's ; soon afterwards St. Mary Magdalene's was erected for an object indicated by its dedication ;[845] and more recently St. James the Less'[846] and St. Titus'[847] have been built, the former serving to perpetuate the High Church tradition of St. Martin's when this had resumed its old ways.[848]

The new cathedral is being erected within the township. The Church House in Lord Street provides a central meeting-place and offices for the different societies and committees ; it contains a library also.

Scottish Presbyterianism was first represented by the Oldham Street Church, opened in 1793 ;[849] St. Andrew's in Rodney Street in 1824 ;[850] and Mount Pleasant in 1827.[851] Others arose about twenty years later : St. George's, Myrtle Street, in 1845 ;[852] Canning Street[853] and Islington in 1846,[854] and St. Peter's, Silvester Street, in 1849.[855] Another was

[829] *Trans. Hist. Soc.* iv, 153 ; 10 Geo. IV, cap. 15.

[830] 7 Geo. IV, cap. 51.

[831] This was supposed to be the first instance of the kind in England ; the corporation allowed an additional £60 salary on account of it ; *Stranger in Liverpool*. The services were still held in 1852.

[832] The vessel was the *Tees*, and was presented by the government to the Mariners' Church Society, formed in 1826.

[833] Out of two millions voted £20,000 was spent on this church. The Act 10 Geo. IV, cap. 11, vested it in the mayor and burgesses, and made provision for the division of the parish into districts.

[834] *Church Congress Guide.*

[835] It exhibited 'the Grecian style in its purity and perfection,' according to the opinion of the time. A district was given by a special local Act, 10 Geo. IV, cap. 51.

[836] A district was assigned to it under St. Martin's Church Act. For its endowment an Act was passed, 1 & 2 Will. IV, cap. 49.

[837] *Trans. Hist. Soc.* iv, 159.

[838] A district was assigned to it under St. Martin's Act, and it was consecrated in 1854. One of the incumbents, the Rev. John Wareing Bardsley, was promoted to the bishopric of Sodor and Man in 1887 and of Carlisle in 1892 ; he died in 1904.

[839] *Trans. Hist. Soc.* iv, 155. The site was above the centre of the present Lime Street Station.

[840] In St. Vincent's Street.

[841] *Trans. Hist. Soc.* iv, 182.

[842] They were consecrated in 1841 and 1843 respectively.

[843] Dr. Hume considered that only an endowed church could minister to the needs of the poorer districts, and pointed to the regular migration of Nonconformist chapels from the poorer to the richer districts, i.e. the building followed the congregation. All Souls' appears to have been built to illustrate his theories. He remained its incumbent until his death in 1884. See *Dict. Nat. Biog.*

[844] *Church Congress Guide.*

[845] Districts were assigned under St. Martin's Church Act, 10 Geo. IV. St. Mary Magdalene's was built in 1859 and consecrated in 1862.

[846] Opened January 1863 ; consecrated, 1873.

[847] Built in 1864 and consecrated in 1865. It is proposed to extinguish the incumbency and dispose of the site.

[848] The patronage of many of the new churches is in the hands of trustees. The Crown and the Bishop of Liverpool present alternately to All Saints', All Souls', St. Alban's, and St. Simon's ; the Bishop alone to Holy Innocents' ; the Bishop, Archdeacon, and Rector of Liverpool jointly to St. Mary Magdalene's ; the Archdeacon and Rector of Liverpool and the Rector of Walton to St. Titus's ; the Rector of Liverpool to St. Matthew's, St. Matthias's, and St. Stephen's. Mr. H. D. Horsfall has the patronage of St. Paul's. The incumbent of St. David's, the Welsh church, is appointed by trustees jointly with the communicants.

[849] Previously, it is said, they worshipped with the Unitarians, who still retained their old title of Presbyterians in consequence of the legal penalties attaching to a denial of the Trinity. Oldham Street Church was built by a combination of shareholders or proprietors, among them being (Sir) John Gladstone.

In 1792 the Scotch Presbyterians used Cockspur Street Chapel, previously the Liverpool cockpit ; *Trans. Hist. Soc.* v, 38, where an account of the many uses of the building may be seen.

[850] A full account of the Scottish churches in Liverpool, by Dr. David Thom, may be seen in *Trans. Hist. Soc.* ii, 69, 229.

[851] This was built by the Scotch Seceders, afterwards the United Presbyterians ; it replaced a smaller chapel in Gloucester Street, built in 1807—afterwards St. Simon's. The United Presbyterians used a meeting room in Gill Street about 1868.

[852] The congregation were seceders from St. Andrew's, Rodney Street, under the influence of the Free Church movement.

[853] A secession, under the same influence, from Oldham Street Church.

[854] This was connected with the Irish Presbyterians. It is now a Jewish Synagogue.

[855] An earlier St. Peter's, built in 1841, in Scotland Road, had to be abandoned owing to the Free Church controversy breaking up the congregation ; it is now St. Matthew's ; *Trans. Hist. Soc.* iv, 148.

built in Vauxhall Road in 1867. Except the first two, which remain connected with the Established Church of Scotland, they are now associated with the Presbyterian Church of England. The formal union which constituted this organization out of many differing ones took place at Liverpool in 1876.[857]

The German Evangelical Church occupies Newington Chapel, formerly Congregational. It seems to have originated in a body of converted Jews speaking German, who met for worship in the chapel in Sir Thomas' Buildings from about 1831, and were considered as attached to the Established Church.[856]

Wesleyan Methodism made itself felt by the middle of the 18th century. Pitt Street chapel was built in 1750,[859] enlarged 1765, rebuilt in 1803, and altered in 1875; John Wesley preached here for a week in 1758. A second chapel within the township was built in 1790,[860] and Cranmer Chapel at the north end in 1857.[861] These are now all connected with the Wesleyan Mission, formed in 1875, which has also acquired the old Baptist Chapel in Soho Street, now Wesley Hall, and a mission room near.[862] Leeds Street Chapel, of some note in its day, was opened about 1798 and pulled down in 1840.[863] Formerly, from 1811 to 1864, the chapel in Benn's Gardens was also used by Welsh-speaking Wesleyans.[864] Trinity Chapel, Grove Street, erected in 1859, is the head of a regular circuit; the conference was held here in 1881. The Wesleyans have also mission rooms.

The Wesleyan Methodist Association, later the United Methodist Free Church, had a chapel in Pleasant Street before 1844, St. Columba's; it was replaced in 1852 by Salem Chapel or St. Clement's Church, in Russell Street,[865] recently given up, the Pupil Teachers' College now occupying the site. Another chapel in Scotland Road, built in 1843, is still used, as also one in Grove Street, built in

1873.[867] The Welsh-speaking members used a chapel in Gill Street from 1845 to 1867.[868]

The Methodist New Connexion, who appeared as early as 1799, had Zion Chapel, Maguire Street, by St. John's Market, before 1813; they removed to Bethesda in Hotham Street about 1833, after which the old building was converted into a fish hall.[869] They had also a chapel in Bevington Hill. Both have long been given up.[870] The Primitive Methodists also had formerly meeting-places in Liverpool.[871]

At the Bishop of Chester's visitations in 1665 and later years Anabaptists were presented, and it was said that conventicles were held. The Baptists, who had from 1707, if not earlier, met in Everton, opened a chapel in Byrom Street in 1722.[872] A much larger chapel was erected in 1789 in the same street, and the old one sold to the Established Church. The later building is still in use as Byrom Hall.[873] Myrtle Street Chapel, the successor of one in Lime Street, built in 1803, was opened in 1844 and enlarged in 1859.[874] In 1819 a chapel was built in Great Crosshall Street.[875] Soho Street Chapel, begun for 'Bishop West,' was used by Baptists from 1837 to 1889, when Jubilee Drive Chapel replaced it.[876] The Welsh-speaking Baptists had a chapel in Ormond Street, dating from 1799, but it has been given up, one in Everton succeeding it.[877]

The Sandemanians or Glassites long had a meeting-place in the town.[878]

Newington Chapel was in 1776 erected by Congregationalists dissatisfied with the Unitarianism of the Toxteth Chapel, and wishing to have a place of worship nearer to Liverpool.[879] It was given up in 1872, and is now the German Church. A youthful preacher, Thomas Spencer, attracting great congregations, a new chapel was begun for him in 1811 in Great George Street; he was drowned before it was finished,[880] and Dr. Thomas Raffles, who was its

[857] The Reformed Presbyterian Church or Covenanters had a meeting-place in Uunter Street in 1852, afterwards moving to Shaw Street, Everton; see *Trans. Hist. Soc.* ii, 73, 230.

[858] Ibid. iv, 174; v, 49.

[859] Ibid. v, 46.

[860] In Mount Pleasant; afterwards called the Central Hall.

[861] Less permanent meeting-places were in Edmund Street, used in 1852, and Benledi Street, in 1863. For the former see *Trans. Hist. Soc.* v, 49.

[862] The head of this mission for many years was the late Rev. Charles Garrett, one of the notable figures in local Methodism. He died in 1900. The site of the Unitarian church in Renshaw Street has been acquired for the Charles Garrett Hall, in connexion with the work he organized.

[863] *Trans. Hist. Soc.* v, 47. The chapel in Great Homer Street, Everton, replaced it.

[864] Ibid. v, 51. The chapel in Shaw Street, Everton, took its place. Another meeting-place of Welsh Wesleyans was in Burroughs Garden, which seems to have been replaced by a chapel in Boundary Street East about 1870. Services have also been held in Great Crosshall Street (1871–84) and Hackins Hey (1896).

[865] For the history of this building, occupied by preaching adventurers and different denominations, including the Swedenborgians, see *Trans. Hist. Soc.* v, 33–7.

[867] The same body has a preaching place in Bostock Street. In 1852 it had one in Bispham Street.

[868] *Trans. Hist. Soc.* (new ser.), vii, 322.

[869] *Trans. Hist. Soc.* v, 50. They had previously had Maguire Street, Cockspur Street, and other places, 43, 40.

[870] Bethesda was given up about 1866; it is represented by a chapel in Everton. The old building was for some time used as a dancing room. Bevington Hill was given up about the same time.

[871] *Trans. Hist. Soc.* v, 42, 44. One in Rathbone Street was maintained until about 1885. It seems to have belonged to the Independent Methodists.

[872] *Trans. Hist. Soc.* iv, 178. The first minister, J. Johnson, offended some of his congregation by his doctrines, and a chapel in Stanley Street was in 1747 built for him, where he preached till his death. This congregation migrated to a new chapel in Comus Street in 1800; ibid. v, 51.

[873] Ibid. v, 23; services were discontinued from 1846 to 1850 on account of its purchase by the London and North Western Railway Company.

[874] Ibid. v, 26; the stricter Calvinists separated about 1800 from the Byrom Street congregation.

[875] Ibid. v, 49; the Particular Baptists, who had had Stanley Street Chapel from 1800, succeeded the first congregation, and moved in 1847 to Shaw Street. The Welsh Baptists had it in 1853 and 1864. The building has ceased to be used for worship.

Other places are known to have been used at various times by Baptist congregations; ibid. v, 33, 48, 49. Two, in Oil Street and Comus Street, existed in 1824; the latter was still in use in 1870, and seems to have been replaced in 1888 by one at Mile End, now abandoned.

[876] Ibid iv, 177. This congregation had sprung from a split in the Byrom Street one in 1826, and had had places of worship in Oil Street and Cockspur Street. A somewhat earlier division (1821) resulted in the Sidney Place Chapel, Edge Hill.

[877] This was perhaps the Edmund Street Chapel mentioned in the *Directory* of 1825; later were the chapels in Great Crosshall Street (already named) and Great Howard Street. The last-named, begun in 1835, was removed to Kirkdale in 1876. A later congregation (1869) met in St. Paul's Square for some years.

[878] For details see *Trans. Hist. Soc.* (new ser.), vii, 321. The places were Matthew Street, and then Gill Street to about 1845.

[879] For the history of these buildings see *Trans. Hist. Soc.* v, 3–9; and Nightingale's *Lancs. Nonconformity*, vi, 120 on.

[880] See his *Life* by Dr. Raffles (Liverpool, 1813). Thomas Spencer was born at Hertford 21 Jan. 1791; commenced preaching when fifteen years of age; was called to Newington Chapel in Aug. 1810, and after a remarkably successful ministry there, was drowned while bathing at the Dingle, 5 Aug. 1811.

minister for nearly fifty years, became one of the most influential men in Liverpool.[851] This chapel was burnt down in 1840, and the present building erected. Seceders from All Saints' Church in 1800 met for worship in Maguire Street and Cockspur Street, and in 1803 built Bethesda Chapel in Hotham Street ; from this they moved in 1837 to Everton Crescent.[882]

Burlington Street Chapel was bought as an extension by the Crescent congregation in 1859 ; about 1890 it was weakened by a division, most of the congregation assembling in Albert Hall for worship ; this is now recognized as a Congregational meeting, but Burlington Street was worked for a time as a mission by the Huyton Church.[883]

The Welsh Congregationalists have a chapel in Grove Street, in place of Salem Chapel, Brownlow Hill,[884] given up in 1868. Formerly they had one in Great Crosshall Street, built in 1817, but the congregation has migrated to Kirkdale and Everton.

In Elizabeth Street is a United Free Gospel Church, built in 1871 to replace one of 1845 as an Independent Methodist Church.

The Calvinistic Methodists, the most powerful church in Wales, are naturally represented in Liverpool, where Welshmen are very numerous. The first chapel was built in Pall Mall in 1787, and rebuilt in 1816, but demolished to make way for the enlargement of Exchange Station in 1878, a new one in Crosshall Street taking its place.[886] There are others in Chatham Street and Catherine Street built in 1861 and 1872 respectively ; at the latter the services are in English.

The Society of Friends had a meeting-place in Hackins Hey as early as 1706, by Quakers' Alley ; this remained standing until 1863. The place of meeting was removed to Hunter Street in 1790 ; this continues in use.[887]

The Moravians held services ' for many years ' in the Religious Tract Society's rooms.

The Berean Universalist Church was opened in 1851 in Crown Street, but had only a short existence.[868]

The Bethel Union, an undenominational evangelistic association for the benefit of sailors, maintains several places of worship near the docks.[889]

The Young Men's Christian Association has a large institute in Mount Pleasant, opened in 1877.

It has been shown above that Nonconformity was strong in the town after 1662. A chapel was built in Castle Hey, and the minister of Toxteth Park is said to have preached there on alternate Sundays from 1689.[890] This was replaced by Benn's Gardens Chapel in 1727, from which the congregation, which had become Unitarian, moved in Renshaw Street in 1811, and from this recently to Ullet Road, Toxteth. Another Protestant Nonconformist chapel was built in Key Street in 1707 ; in this case also the congregation became Unitarian.[891] A new chapel in Paradise Street replaced it in 1791, and a removal to Hope Street was made in 1849, the abandoned building being turned by its new owners into a theatre. The Octagon Chapel in Temple Court was used from 1762 to 1776 to meet a desire for liturgical services, the organ being used ; but it proved a failure and was sold to the Rev. W. Plumbe, Rector of Aughton, who preached in it as St. Catherine's. The Unitarians have a mission room in Bond Street.[892]

The Christadelphians formerly (1868–78) had a meeting-place in Gill Street.

The Catholic Apostolic Church (Irvingite) was built in 1856. The choir is a rich specimen of flamboyant Gothic.

The ancient religion appears to have been stamped out very quickly in Liverpool, which became a decidedly Protestant town, and there is scarcely even an incidental allusion to its existence[894] until the beginning of the 18th century. Spellow and Aigburth were the nearest places at which mass could occasionally be heard in secret. Fr. William Gilli-

[851] His biography was written by his son, Thomas Stamford Raffles, who was for many years the stipendiary magistrate of Liverpool ; see also Dict. Nat. Biog. Dr. Raffles was born in London in 1788, educated at Homerton College, LL.D. Aberdeen 1820, died 18 Aug. 1863, and was buried in the Necropolis.

[882] Salem Chapel in Russell Street was used from 1808 to 1812 by seceders from Bethesda.

[883] Gloucester Street Chapel was occupied by Congregationalists from 1827 to 1840, when it became St. Simon's Church.

[884] Salem Chapel in Brownlow Hill was bought in 1868 by the Crescent congregation, and occupied until 1892. It is now a furniture store.

[886] In 1825 they had two chapels, in Pall Mall and Great Crosshall Street ; in 1852 they had four, in Prussia Street (i.e. Pall Mall), Rose Place (built 1826), Burlington Street, and Mulberry Street (built 1841). The last-named, having been replaced by the Chatham Street Chapel, was utilized as Turkish baths. Burlington Street seems to have been removed to Cranmer Street, built in 1860, now disused. The Rose Place Chapel was at the corner of Comus Street ; it seems to have been disused about 1866, a new one in Fitzclarence Street taking its place.

[887] The old meeting-house had a burial ground attached. The building was used

as a school from 1796 to 1863, when it was sold and pulled down.

[888] Its minister was Dr. David Thom, whose essay on the migration of churches has been frequently quoted in these notes. He had been minister of the Scotch Church in Rodney Street, but seceded ; in 1843 he had a congregation in a chapel in Bold Street.

[889] The society had a floating mission vessel, the William, in the Salthouse Dock in 1821. Afterwards three buildings on shore were substituted, in Wapping, Bath Street, and Norfolk Street.

[890] Hist. MSS. Com. Rep. xiv, App. iv, 231 ; the 'new chapel in the Castle Hey in Liverpool ' and Toxteth Park Chapel were licensed ' for Samuel Angier and his congregation.' See also Peet, Liverpool in the Reign of Queen Anne, 100. Castle Hey is now called Harrington Street.

[891] For the Unitarian churches see Trans. Hist. Soc. v, 9–23, 51 ; Nightingale, op. cit. vi, 110.

[892] Ibid.

[894] In the catalogue of burials at the Harkirk in Little Crosby is the following : ' 1615, May 20. Anne the wife of George Webster of Liverpool (tenant of Mr. Crosse) died a Catholic, and being denied burial at the chapel of Liverpool by the curate there, by the Mayor, and by Mr. Moore, was buried ' ; Crosby Rec. (Chet. Soc.), 72. The Crosse family did not change their religious profession at

once, for in 1628 John Crosse of Liverpool, as a convicted recusant, paid double to the subsidy ; Norris D. (B.M.).

John Sinnot, an Irishman, who died at his house in Liverpool, had been refused burial on account of his religion in 1613 ; Crosby Rec. 70.

The recusant roll of 1641 contains only five names, four being those of women ; Trans. Hist. Soc. (new ser.), xiv, 238.

In 1669 four 'papist recusants' were presented at the Bishop of Chester's visitation, viz. :—Breres gent., Mary wife of George Brettargh, and William Fazakerley and his wife.

In 1683 there were thirty-five persons, including Richard Lathom, presented for being absent from church, and in the following year thirty-nine ; Picton's Munic. Rec. i, 330. The revival of presentations was no doubt due to the Protestant and Whig agitation of the time. James II endeavoured to mitigate the effects of it ; in 1686, being 'informed that Richard Lathom of Liverpool, chirurgeon, and Judith his wife, who keeps also a boarding-school for the education of youth at Liverpool,' had been presented for 'their exercising the said several vocations without licence, by reason of their religion (being Roman Catholics),' and being assured of their loyalty, he authorized them to continue, remitted penalties incurred, and forbade further interference ; ibid. i, 256.

brand, S.J., who then lived at Little Crosby, in 1701 received £3 from Mr. Eccleston 'for helping at Liverpool.' [895] The first resident missioner known was Fr. Francis Mannock, S.J., who was living here in 1710 ; and the work continued in the hands of the Jesuits until the suppression of the order. The next priest, Fr. John Tempest, better known by his *alias* of Hardesty, built a house for himself near the Oldhall Street corner of Edmund Street, in which was a room for a chapel. [896] In 1746, after the retreat of the Young Pretender, the populace, relieved of its fears, went to this little chapel, made a bonfire of the benches and woodwork, and pulled the house down. [897] Henry Pippard, a merchant of the town, who married Miss Blundell, the heiress of Little Crosby, treated with the mayor and corporation about rebuilding the chapel. This, of course, they could not allow, the law prohibiting the ancient worship under severe penalties, whereupon he said that no one could prevent his building a warehouse. This he did, the upper room being the chapel. [898] It was wrecked during a serious riot in 1759, but was enlarged in 1797 and continued to be used until St. Mary's, from the designs of A. W. Pugin, was built on the same site and consecrated in 1845. In consequence of the enlargement of Exchange Station it was taken down, but rebuilt in Highfield Street on the same plan and with the same material, being reconsecrated 7 July 1885. The baptismal register commences in 1741. After the suppression of the Jesuit order in 1773 the two priests then in charge continued their labours for ten years, when the Benedictines took charge, and still retain it. [899]

They at once sought to obtain an additional site at what was then the south end of the town, and in 1788 St. Peter's, Seel Street, was opened. It was enlarged in 1843, and is still served by the same order. [900] The school in connexion with it was opened in 1817.

About the same time Fr. John Price, an ex-Jesuit, was ministering at his house in Chorley Street (1777), and by and by (1788) built the chapel in Sir Thomas's buildings, which was used till his death in 1813. [901] It was then closed, as St. Nicholas' was ready, work having been commenced in 1808, and the church opened in 1812. [902] Since 1850 it has been used as the cathedral. At the north end of the town St. Anthony's had been established in 1804 ; the present church, on an adjacent site, dates from 1833, and has a burial ground. [903] St. Joseph's in Grosvenor Street was opened in 1846, a new building being completed in 1878. [904]

These buildings [905] sufficed till the great immigration of poor Irish peasants, driven from home by the famine of 1847. St. Vincent de Paul's mission had been begun in a room over a stable in 1843, but after interruption by the fever of 1847 a larger room in Norfolk Street was secured in 1848, and served until in 1857 the present church was erected. Holy Cross was begun in 1848 in a room over a cowhouse in Standish Street, and in 1850 was given to the care of the Oblates of Mary Immaculate, who are still in charge. The church was built in 1860, and the chancel opened in 1875. St. Augustine's, Great Howard Street, was an offshoot in 1849 from St. Mary's, and is still in charge of the Benedictines.

---

[895] Foley's *Rec. S. J.* v, 320. It may be inferred that some attempt was made to provide regular services, and, of course, that there was a congregation.

[896] 'While I lived in the foresaid town I received, one year with another, from the people about one or two and twenty pounds a year, by way of contribution towards my maintenance, and no other subscription was ever made for me or for the buildings. From friends in other places I had part of the money I had built with, but much the greatest part was what I spared, living frugally and as not many would have been content to live. . . . Nor do I regret having spent the best years of my life in serving the poor Catholics of Liverpool ;' Letter of Fr. Hardesty in Foley, op. cit. v, 364. Edmund Street at that time was on the very edge of the town. On Palm Sunday 1727 there were 256 palms distributed here ; N. Blundell's *Diary*, 224.

[897] Picton's *Liverpool*, i, 180. An account by Thomas Green, written in 1833, is preserved at St. Francis Xavier's College ; his mother witnessed the scene. It was printed in the *Xaverian* of Feb. 1887, and states : 'The incumbents, the Revs. H. Carpenter and T. Stanley, met the mob, which behaved with the greatest respect to the priests and several of the principal Roman Catholic inhabitants attending there—among the rest, Miss Elizabeth Clifton (afterwards Mrs. Green) —and without noise or violence opened a clear passage for the Rev. Mr. Carpenter to go up to the altar and take the ciborium out of the tabernacle and carry it by the same passage out of the chapel.'

[898] Subscriptions were collected for it. The site was at the upper end of Edmund

...

Later came St. Philip Neri's Oratory near Mount Pleasant, 1853. All Souls', in Collingwood Street, was erected in 1870 by the efforts of a Protestant merchant, who was anxious to provide a remedy for the horrible scenes at wakes ; the middle aisle of the church was for the bodies of the departed to lie in previous to interment, and was quite cut off from the aisles where the congregation assembled, by glass partitions. This has recently been changed. St. Bridget's, Bevington Hill, was also opened in 1870, and rebuilt in 1894. St. Sylvester's in Silvester Street began with schools in 1872 ; at the beginning of 1875 a wooden building was erected adjacent, continuing in use until 1889, when the present permanent church was opened.

There are two convents : Notre Dame, at the training college, Mount Pleasant, 1856 ; and St. Catherine, Eldon Place, 1896.

The followers of Emmanuel Swedenborg have long had a place of meeting in Liverpool, where they had been known from 1795.[906] The present building, New Jerusalem, in Bedford Street, was opened in 1857.

The Mormons have an institute.[907]

The Jews have had a recognized meeting-place since about 1750. The earliest known was at the foot of Matthew Street ; it had a burial place attached ; afterwards Turton Court, near the Custom House, and Frederick Street were places of Jewish worship.[908] The synagogue in Seel Street was built in 1807, the congregation migrating to Princes Road in 1874. A disused Presbyterian church in Islington has recently (1908) been purchased and reopened as the Central Synagogue. The Hope Place Synagogue of the New Hebrew Congregation was built in 1856.[703]

The establishment of the diocese *CATHEDRAL* of Liverpool[910] immediately gave rise to the demand for the erection of a cathedral ; the parish church of St. Peter, which had been assigned as pro-cathedral by an Order in Council of 1880, being manifestly inadequate, being indeed the most modest church to which that dignity has been allotted in any English diocese. A committee was formed in 1881, and a lively discussion as to sites was carried on,[911] the St. John's churchyard site (west of St. George's Hall) being eventually decided on. In 1885 an Act was obtained empowering the erection of a cathedral, and a competition was held for designs,[912] and the premium was awarded to Mr. William Emerton. The problem of raising funds, however, was found too great, and in 1888 the project was abandoned. Under Bishop Ryle the main strength of the diocese was devoted to the urgently-needed provision of new churches and the augmentation of poorer livings. At the beginning of 1901, however, the project was revived[913] by Bishop Chavasse, who appointed a committee to discuss the question of sites. Amid much public discussion,

St. James's Mount, in the south-central district of the city, was decided upon—a rocky plateau occupied in part by public gardens and overlooking an ancient quarry, now used as a cemetery. The site presented a clear open space of 22 acres ; the steep side of the plateau, clothed with trees, gives it something of the picturesqueness of Durham, while the deep hollow of the cemetery will serve to isolate the cathedral and give to its architecture its full effect. Over 150 ft. above sea-level, the site will enable the cathedral to dominate the city and the estuary. The drawbacks of the site were two : its shape forbade a proper orientation, and made it necessary to put the 'east' end of the cathedral to the south, while the fact that the southern part of the plateau was made ground involved a large expenditure for foundations.

The scheme was formally initiated and committees appointed[914] at a town hall meeting on 17 June 1901, and on 2 August 1902 an Act was obtained authorizing the purchase from the corporation of the St. James's Mount site. After a preliminary competition, competitive designs were submitted by five selected candidates on 30 April 1903 ; the assessors, Mr. G. F. Bodley and Mr. Norman Shaw, selected the design of Mr. G. Gilbert Scott, who was accordingly appointed architect in conjunction with Mr. Bodley. On 19 July 1904 the foundation stone was laid by His Majesty the King. The general character of the design is Gothic, but it is not a reproduction of the style of any particular period. The main qualities aimed at are simplicity and massiveness. The most striking features will be the twin central towers and a third tower at the north end, respectively rising 415 and 355 ft. above sea-level ; the vast height of the nave and choir, and the six high transepts, which are carried to the full roof height, and will produce unusual light effects. Both in height and in area the dimensions considerably exceed those of any other English cathedral. The principal dimensions are as follows :—

Total external length (including Lady chapel)	584 ft.
Length of nave, without narthex	192 „
Width of nave between centres of pillars . .	53½ „
Width across transepts .	198 „
Width of north façade . . .	196 „
Height of arches in nave and choir	65 „
Height of barrel-vaulting in nave and choir	116 „
Height of vaulting in high transepts	140 „
Height of vaulting under towers	161 „
Height of central towers . . .	260 „
Height of northern tower . .	200 „
Superficial area	90,000 sq. ft.

[906] They occupied Key Street Chapel from 1791 to 1795. In 1795 Maguire Street Chapel was built for them, but the donor became bankrupt and the place was sold. From 1815 to 1819 the Swedenborgians used Cockspur Street Chapel, from 1819 to 1823 they shared Maguire Street with the Primitive Methodists, and from 1838 to 1852 they occupied Salem Chapel in Russell Street, removing to the Concert Room in Lord Nelson Street until the Bedford Street Church was ready ; *Trans. Hist. Soc.* v, 33, 38, 43.

[907] In 1863 their meeting-place was at the corner of Crown Street and Brownlow Hill ; later in Islington, and Bittern Street.

[908] For fuller accounts see *Trans. Hist. Soc.* v, 53, and (new ser.), xv, 45–84. There were burial places at Frederick Street and at the corner of Oake and Crown Streets.

One of the results of the Jewish settlement in Liverpool was a series of three letters addressed to it by J. Willme of Martinscroft near Warrington, printed in 1756.

It is estimated that the cost of erecting the whole cathedral will be at least £750,000 ; of the Lady Chapel, choir, and twin towers, which are being first built, about £350,000. Towards this sum over £300,000 has been already contributed, including over £70,000 for special purposes, among which may be named the Lady Chapel, to be erected by the Earle and Langton families, the chapter-house, to be erected by the Masonic Lodges of the West Lancashire province, as well as several windows, the organ, the font, &c., which have been already given by various donors.

UNIVERSITY The first attempt to establish in Liverpool an institution for higher education was the foundation of the Royal Institution, opened in 1817 ; it maintained collections of scientific objects and paintings, it also organized series of lectures in its early years.[915] But, though highly valuable as a nucleus for the meetings of various learned societies, it never developed, as its founders had hoped, into a great teaching institution. In 1857 an attempt was made to develop, in connexion with the Mechanics' Institute (now the Liverpool Institute), a system of courses of instruction in preparation for London degrees.[916] This organization was called Queen's College ; but, based upon the fundamentally false idea that instruction of this type could be made to pay its own expenses, it never attained any success, and being merely a drain upon the resources of the flourishing schools to which it was attached, it was finally suppressed in 1879.

Meanwhile, in 1834, the physicians and surgeons of the Royal Infirmary had organized a Medical School, which attained considerable success, though quite unendowed. This school was to be the real nucleus of the university. It was from the teachers in this school—all leading medical men in the city, among whom should be especially named the late Sir W. M. Banks and Dr. R. Caton—that the main demand came for the foundation of a college, during the seventies, when such institutions were springing up in most large English towns.[917] They received warm support from a few of the most enlightened citizens, especially from the Rev. Charles Beard, whose influence in the early history of the university can scarcely be overvalued ; and the proposal to found a university college was formally initiated at a town's meeting in 1878. But the merchants of the city were found to be hard to convert to any interest in the scheme. It took a year to collect £10,000 ; and it was not until Mr. William Rathbone,[918] relieved from Parliamentary duties by a defeat at the election of 1880, took up the cause that money came in freely. In a few months, mainly by his personal efforts, £80,000 were collected. In October 1881 a charter of incorporation was obtained, based on the lines laid down in London, Manchester, and elsewhere ; in January 1882 the institution, under the name of University College, Liverpool, commenced its work in a disused lunatic asylum on a site beside the Royal Infirmary and the Medical School, provided by the corporation. At the outset there were six chairs and two lectureships.

The next stage in the history of the university was marked by its admission in 1884 as a member of the federal Victoria University, in association with Owens College, Manchester, and (after 1887) Yorkshire College, Leeds. In order to obtain this admission an additional endowment of £30,000 was raised by public subscription, out of which two new chairs were founded ; while the old Medical School was formally incorporated with the college as its medical faculty. The association with the Victoria University lasted for nineteen years, and was in many ways advantageous. The progress of the college in equipment and teaching strength during this period was both rapid and steady. A series of admirably equipped buildings was erected ; a spacious chemical laboratory (opened 1886, enlarged 1896) ; a large engineering laboratory (the gift of Sir A. B. Walker, 1889) ; the main Victoria building, including a fine library presented by Sir Henry Tate, and the clock tower erected from the civic subscription to commemorate the jubilee of 1887 (opened 1892) ; magnificent laboratories of physiology and pathology, given by Rev. S. A. Thompson Yates (opened 1895) ; and a handsome botanical laboratory given by Mr. W. P. Hartley (1902). During the same period eight additional chairs were endowed, and many lectureships and scholarships were founded. Throughout the early history of the college it had rested mainly on the support of a comparatively small group of friends ; among those whose munificence rendered possible the rapid development of the college, special mention should be made, in addition to those already named, of the fifteenth and sixteenth Earls of Derby, successive presidents of the college, both of whom founded chairs ; of Mr. George Holt, most princely of the early benefactors ; of Sir John Brunner, Mr. Holbrook Gaskell, and Mr. Thomas Harrison, all of whom founded chairs ; and of Mr. E. K. Muspratt, Mr. John Rankin, Mr. J. W. Alsop, Mr. A. F. Warr, Mr. C. W. Jones, Sir Edward Lawrence, and others. But the chief feature of the later part of this period was the gradual acquisition of the confidence and respect of the city at large. This came slowly ; but it was due especially to the demonstration of the utility of the institution which was afforded by the creation of a remarkable series of special schools, due in large measure to the vigour and inventiveness of the teaching body, among whom may be especially named Professor (now Sir Rubert) Boyce and Professor J. M. Mackay. A training college for teachers, a school of architecture and the applied arts, the first of its kind in England, a school of commerce, a school of law, a school of public health, and, most remarkable of all, the now world-famous school of tropical medicine, were successively organized. These organizations brought the college into intimate contact with the most important intellectual professions of the city, demonstrated to the community the direct value of higher studies, and earned the growing support both of the public and of the city council, which co-operated in the organization of most of them. They also gave to the college a distinctive character of its own, and rendered its continued association with other colleges, developing along different lines, more and more inappropriate.

The establishment of an independent university in

---

[915] Life of W. Roscoe, ii, 151 ff.; Rep. of the R.I.

[916] Rep. of the Liverpool Institute and of Queen's College.

[917] J. Campbell Brown, First Chap. in the Hist. of Univ. Coll. ; R. Caton, article on The Making of the Univ. (1907); Univ.

Coll. and the Univ. of Liv. : a Retrospect (1907).

[918] E. Rathbone, Life of W. Rathbone.

Birmingham sharpened this feeling, and in 1901 a movement began for the securing of a separate university charter. This demand, which involved the dissolution of the Victoria University, met with keen opposition. But it also aroused a quite remarkable and unexpected popular interest in the city. An endowment fund of £180,000 was raised in a few months; the city council unanimously supported the application, and later voted an annual grant of £10,000; and in 1903, after a searching inquiry by the Privy Council, a royal charter was granted establishing the University of Liverpool. It began its career distinguished among British universities by the intimate relations in which it stands to the city which is its seat, an intimacy which time increasingly accentuates.

Since the grant of the charter, the growth of the university has been remarkable; despite the large subscription of 1903, each year since that date has brought gifts of the average value of £30,000. A series of new buildings, including the George Holt Physical Laboratory, the William Johnston Laboratory of Medical Research, a new medical school building, laboratories of zoology and electrical engineering, and the first British laboratory of physical chemistry, built by Mr. E. K. Muspratt, have been erected. Thirteen new chairs have been endowed, besides numerous lectureships, fellowships, and scholarships. The number of students has grown rapidly, from 581 in 1901 to 1,007 in 1907. But perhaps the most striking feature of these years has been that while the more utilitarian studies, to which some hostile critics expected the whole strength of the new university to be devoted, have by no means been starved, the greatest developments have been in the field of advanced research in pure arts and science. Several chairs exist exclusively for the encouragement of research. Perhaps the most astonishing result of the establishment of the university has been the institution, in a trading town, of the most powerfully-organized school of archaeology in Britain, a school which possesses three endowed chairs, has got together admirable teaching collections, and has organized expeditions for the excavation of sites in Egypt, Central America, and Asia Minor.

The university is governed by the king as visitor, by a chancellor, two pro-chancellors, a vice-chancellor and a treasurer, by a court of over 300 members representing donors and public bodies, a council of 32 members, a senate of 42 members, a convocation of graduates, and five faculties. Its capital amounted in 1907 to £735,000,[919] entirely provided by private gifts, and its annual income to £61,000, derived in part from interest in endowments (£17,000), in part from government grants (over £12,000), in part from municipal grants (over £14,000, of which the largest item is £11,750 per annum from the Corporation of Liverpool), and in part from students' fees (£15,000). The university is divided into five Faculties—Arts, Science, Medicine, Law, and Engineering. Of these the Faculty of Arts is the largest, both in the number of students and in the number of its endowed chairs; the University of Liverpool having been from its initiation distinguished among modern English universities by the prominence which it has given to arts studies. All the principal hospitals of the city are connected for clinical pur-

poses with the Faculty of Medicine, while St. Aidan's College, Birkenhead, Edge Hill Training College, and the Liverpool Training College are affiliated to it.

Elementary education began in Liver-
SCHOOLS pool with the provision of a number of
Sunday-schools for the poor, founded as the result of a town's meeting in 1784.[920] These were rapidly followed by the institution of day-schools, provided either by various denominations or by endowment. The earliest of these schools were the Old Church School in Moorfields (1789), the Unitarian Schools in Mount Pleasant (1790) and Manesty Lane (1792), and the Wesleyan Brunswick School (1790). In 1823 there were thirty-two day-schools 'for the education of the poor'[921] educating 7,441 children, of which 14 were Church Schools with 2,914 pupils, 2 Roman Catholic with 440 pupils, and 18 Nonconformist with 4,087 pupils. The number of schools largely increased between 1823 and 1870, so that there was no very serious deficiency of school places when, in 1870, education became universal and compulsory. When the school board began its work in Liverpool in 1871 there were already two public elementary schools, founded by the corporation in 1826, and transferred to the administration of the board; and the provision of school places in voluntary schools was above the average for England; but many new places had to be gradually provided by the erection of board schools. The following table shows the state of elementary education in 1871, and the progress made up to 1902 :—[922]

ELEMENTARY SCHOOLS

Type of School	1871		1902	
	No. of Schools	School Places	No. of Schools	School Places
Church of England . . .	47	25,773	66	43,180
Roman Catholic	16	12,145	37	32,614
Undenominational and Wesleyan	16	8,084	10	6,519
Board	—	—	49	49,765
Total	79	46,002	162	132,078

No detailed account can be given of the work of the board during the thirty years of its work, but two or three features deserve note. In a city which beyond most others is torn asunder by religious strife, the intrusion of this strife was throughout avoided, owing to the wise policy initiated in the early years, largely by Mr. S. G. Rathbone and Mr. Christopher Bushell. The school board was distinguished almost from the beginning by the attention which it gave to the training of teachers. As early as 1875 a Pupil Teachers' College was established in two houses in Shaw Street, the rent of which was provided by Mr. S. G. Rathbone. In 1898 the college entered upon its handsome premises in Clarence Street, and in 1906 it became the Oulton Secondary School. It was largely also through the zeal of members of the school board that the Edge Hill Training College for women teachers was founded in 1884. A further striking feature of the work of the board was its intimate association with the Liverpool Council of Education, founded in 1873, which in the days before any public authority was empowered to undertake such work provided a scholarship ladder

[919] R. Muir, *The Univ. of Liv. : in present state,* 1907.

[920] Picton's *Liv. Munic. Rec.* ii, 284.
[921] Smithers, *Liverpool,* 264.

[922] Information supplied by the Education Office.

LIVERPOOL   THE OLD BLUECOAT SCHOOL
(*From an old Print*)

LIVERPOOL : GOREE BUILDINGS, 1828
(*From an Engraving*)

from the elementary schools to the secondary schools of the city, by which many poor boys have climbed to the universities and thence to important positions in the world. The Council of Education still exists. It administers a scholarship trust fund of over £20,000, as well as the Waterworth Scholarship fund, the income of which is over £300 per annum. Its scholarships are now merged in the scholarship system instituted by the City Education Committee.

The elementary schools now controlled by the City Education Committee are as follows ;—[923]

—	No.	Depts.	Teachers			Pupils	Average per School	Pupils per Teacher [923a]
			Head	Asst.	P.T.			
Council Schools	50	134	162	1,361	315	57,011	1,140	37½
Church of England	64	155	154	899	101	37,631	588	36
Roman Catholic	36	102	102	689	193	32,466	902	41
Wesleyan	7	17	16	106	7	4,040	577	33
Undenominational	4	8	7	48	4	1,543	386	28
Totals .	161	416	441	3,103	620	132,691	824	37⅞

There are also five day industrial schools, to which children from drunken homes are committed on a magistrate's order, and receive food as well as instruction ; ten ordinary certified industrial schools, a reformatory ship, the *Akbar*, five schools for physically and mentally defective children, and one truants' industrial school. The total cost of the elementary system in 1906–7 was £625,623.

During the last few years the Education Committee has been engaged in providing facilities for higher education, in which, thanks to the failure to develop the ancient grammar school,[924] Liverpool was behind most other English cities. Of the older secondary schools some account has been already given.[925] Of these schools three—the Liverpool Institute, Blackburne House, and the Liverpool Collegiate School (formerly Liverpool College Middle and Commercial Schools)—have passed under the direct control of the Education Committee. The Pupil Teachers' College in Clarence Street has been turned into the Oulton Secondary School, with 873 pupils ; one of the most highly developed of the elementary schools has been turned into a secondary school (Holt Secondary School), and a large secondary school for girls has been built. Eight city scholarships, tenable at the University of Liverpool, are thrown open to the competition of pupils of these and other secondary schools in the city. Outside of the system controlled by the Education Committee, there are, in addition to the schools enumerated in *V.C.H. Lancs.* ii, 595, four denominational pupil teacher centres, two of which,

St. Edmund's College (Church of England) and the Catholic Institute, have been transformed into secondary schools. Note should also be made of the school-ship *Conway*, moored in the Mersey, which trains boys to be officers in the mercantile marine, and for Dartmouth.

The Technical Instruction Committee conducts classes in the Central Technical School, Byrom Street ; it has three branch schools in other parts of the city, and conducts regular evening classes also in ten other institutions. There are also a nautical college, a school for cookery, and a school of domestic economy. The City School of Art is largely attended, and has now incorporated the School of Applied Arts, formerly associated with the University School of Architecture.

The city also contains two training colleges for teachers, the Liverpool Training College, Mount Pleasant, founded in 1856, and conducted by the sisters of the Notre Dame, and the Edge Hill Training College (undenominational) founded in 1884. Both are for women, and both are affiliated to the university. For the training of Roman Catholic priests there is St. Edward's College, in Everton.

CHARITIES The earliest Liverpool charities, apart from the grammar school,[926] were the almshouses.[927] In 1684 twelve almshouses were built by David Poole near the bottom of Dale Street ; in 1692 Dr. Silvester Richmond founded a small group of almshouses for sailors' widows in Shaw's Brow ; in 1706 Richard Warbrick established another small group, also for sailors' widows, in Hanover Street. Successive small gifts during the 18th century, amounting in all to over £2,500, increased the endowment. In 1786 the almshouses were consolidated and removed to their present site in Arrad Street (Hope Street). They are administered in part by the corporation, in part by the rector, in part by trustees.

In 1708 the Bluecoat Hospital was founded by the Rev. R. Styth, one of the rectors, and by Bryan Blundell, master mariner, as a day school for fifty poor boys, on a site granted by the corporation in School Lane.[928] Blundell, by liberal gifts and assiduous collection, raised sufficient funds for the erection of a permanent building where they could be housed. The graceful and dignified building, still standing, was begun in 1714 and completed in 1718. The number of inmates has been successively increased ; there are now 250 boys and 100 girls. In 1905 the school was removed to a spacious and handsome new building on open ground in Wavertree. The Bluecoat Hospital ranks as the premier charity of the city, and has always received the warm support of Liverpool merchants.

One hundred and twenty-eight distinct charitable institutions now in existence are enumerated by the Charity Organization Society.[929] They cannot all be enumerated, and it will be convenient to group them.

i. *Medical Charities.*—The *Royal Infirmary*, which is the second oldest medical charity in the north of England, was instituted in 1745. Its first building

---

[923] Rep. for 1907.

[923a] Omitting Pupil Teachers.

[924] *V.C.H. Lancs.* ii, 593.

[925] Ibid. 595.

[926] For the grammar school, see *V.C.H. Lancs.* ii, 593.

[927] See Digest of Lancs. Charities (House of Commons Papers, 1869). The annual income at that date was £2,037. This was mainly derived from the interest on the Molyneux foundation, which was wisely invested in lands in the township of Liverpool (the Rector's Fields, formerly part of the Moss Lake). When leases fall in the charity will be very rich.

[928] *Trans. Hist. Soc.*, papers in vols. xi, xiii, xvi, xxxi.

[929] On charities, *Liv. Charities* (annual) ; Burdett, *Hosp. and Charities* ; reports of the individual charities.

was on the site of St. George's Hall, and was opened in 1749. In 1824 it was removed to Pembroke Place, and it was again rebuilt in 1890. From 1792 to 1879 a lunatic asylum was connected with it ; it also maintained a lock hospital ; and in 1860 it instituted, under the guidance of William Rathbone,[930] a nurses' home which formed the basis of the first English experiment in district nursing. In 1834 a medical school was established at the infirmary ; it has since developed into the medical faculty of the university. The other general hospitals are the Northern, instituted in 1834, rebuilt by aid of a grant from the David Lewis fund in 1896-7, whence it is now known as the David Lewis Northern Hospital ; the Royal Southern Hospital, instituted in 1814 and rebuilt in 1872, which provides clinical teaching for the Liverpool School of Tropical Medicine ; and the Stanley Hospital, established in 1867. These three hospitals, together with some of the special hospitals, unite to form the United Hospitals Clinical School in connexion with the medical faculty of the university. There is also a homeopathic hospital, opened in 1887. In 1778 a dispensary was opened in John Street,[931] eight years after the opening of the first English dispensary in London. There are now three dispensaries, for the north, south, and east of the city. The special hospitals, in the order of their foundation, are :—the Ladies' Charity (founded in 1796 ; Lying-in Hospital opened 1841) ; the Eye and Ear Infirmary[932] (Eye 1820, Ear 1839) ; the St. George's Skin Hospital (1842) ; the Children's Infirmary (instituted in 1851, rebuilt in 1905-7) ; the Dental Hospital (1860) ; the Cancer Hospital (1862) ; the Consumption Hospital (1863, rebuilt 1904), to which is attached a fine sanatorium in Delamere Forest, founded in 1901 ; the Liverpool Convalescent Institution at Woolton (1873) ; the Hospital for Women (1883) ; the Hospital for Diseases of the Throat, Nose, and Ear (1884) ; the Home for Epileptics (1887) ; the County Hospital for Children ; the Home for Female Incurables ; and the Vergmont Institution for Female Inebriates. To the same group belongs the District Nursing Association, in Prince's Road, founded by Mr. William Rathbone in 1862, the first of its kind in England. The income of these charities from endowments and subscriptions amounted in 1906 to more than £80,000. But in addition to these voluntary hospitals the corporation maintains six hospitals for infectious diseases, with 881 beds ; and the select vestry not only maintains a workhouse infirmary, but also, in conjunction with the Toxteth and West Derby Guardians, a consumption hospital at Heswall on the Dee. The total number of beds available in all the Liverpool hospitals is over 4,000.

For the blind, deaf, and dumb, there are :—The School for the Indigent Blind (founded 1791), the oldest institution of its kind, with 210 inmates ; the School for the Deaf and Dumb (1825) with 110 pupils ; the Catholic Blind Asylum (1841) with 199 inmates ; the Workshops and Home Teaching Society for the Outdoor Blind (1859) ; the Adult Deaf and Dumb Benevolent Society (1864) ; and the Home for Blind Children (1874).

ii. *Homes, Orphanages, &c., for Children.*—In addition to the Bluecoat Hospital, already described, the following institutions exist for the rescue of children :—Female Orphan Asylum (1840), Orphan Asylum for boys (1850), Infant Orphan Asylum (1858), each accommodating 150 inmates ; the Sheltering Homes for Destitute Children (1872) annually train and send out to Canada 250 children ; the Seamen's Orphan Institution, which is comparatively well endowed, maintains 350 children ; the *Indefatigable* training ship (1865), with which is connected a sailing brigantine, prepares about 250 boys for the mercantile marine ; the Lancashire Navy League Sea-training Home does similar work ; the Children's Friend Society (1866) maintains a Boys' Home ; the Newsboys' Home takes in sixty-five street boys ; and there is a group of homes for training poor girls, chiefly for domestic service, including the Magdalen Institution (1855) for fifty girls ; the Mission to Friendless Girls (1862) ; the Preventive Homes (1865) for forty-four girls ; the Training Home for Girls (1894) for thirty-two girls ; and the Bencke Home ; while the Ladies' Association for the Care and Training of Girls maintains four distinct homes. There also exist a Children's Aid Society for clothing poor children attending elementary schools, and a Police-aided Clothing Association, which provides clothes for children engaged in street-trading (who are in Liverpool required to be registered) and with the aid of the police prevents parents from selling the clothes. The Liverpool Society for the Prevention of Cruelty to Children has been at work for a longer time than the National Society.

iii. *Penitentiary Charities.*—The Lancashire Female Refuge (1823) maintains a home for women coming out of prison, and is the oldest charity of its kind. The Discharged Prisoners' Aid Society does the same work on a more general plan. For fallen women there are the Female Penitentiary (1811), the Benevolent Institution and Rescue Home (1839), the Home of the Midnight Mission (1875), and the Home of the Liverpool Rescue Society (1890).

iv. *Homes for the Aged.*—These include the Widows' Home (1871) ; the Homes for Aged Mariners (1882), including a large central building founded by Mr. William Cliff, and seventeen detached cottages in the grounds in which married couples may live ; and the Andrew Gibson Home for the widows of seamen (1905).

v. *Pension Charities.*—These are numerous. The Aged Merchant Seamen and Widows' Fund (1870) gave 166 small pensions in 1906 ; the Governesses Benevolent Institution (1849) distributes £900 per annum in pensions ; the Seamen's Pension Fund was founded by Mr. T. H. Ismay in 1887 with a capital of £20,000, to which Mrs. Ismay later added £10,000 for seamen's widows ; the Shipbrokers' Benevolent Society (1894) distributes annuities of not more than £30 to old employees ; and the Merchant Guild administers ten distinct pension funds, chiefly for the relief of distressed persons of the middle and upper classes ; it awarded 179 pensions in 1906, the largest being of £42.

vi. *Of Miscellaneous Charities* there are too many to

---

[930] *Life of W. Rathbone.*
[931] Now North John Street. It was in 1781 removed to Church Street.
[932] Originally Ophthalmic Infirmary. In 1820 was also founded the Liverpool Institute for Curing Diseases of the Eye, now defunct.

be enumerated, but mention should be made of the Sailors' Home, founded in 1852, which provides cheap lodging and help for sailors when they are paid off. And it should be noted that its continuous existence, since in 1809 it was founded as the Society for Preventing Wanton Cruelty to Brute Animals, makes the local branch of the R.S.P.C.A. an older body than the national institution. The David Lewis Club and Hostel is an immense Rowton House with a very handsome club in relation with it.

WIGAN

WIGAN	BILLINGE HIGHER	UPHOLLAND	ABRAM
PEMBERTON	END	DALTON	HAIGH
BILLINGE CHAPEL	WINSTANLEY	INCE	ASPULL
END	ORRELL	HINDLEY	

This large parish was at the time of the Conquest included within the hundred of Newton, with the exception of its western townships, Upholland and Dalton, which were within West Derby, and perhaps also of Haigh and Aspull in the north-east. The parish with the same exceptions became part of the fee or barony of Makerfield. Aspull was either then or later placed in the hundred of Salford, in which it has remained till the present. Except in the township of Abram the geological formation consists entirely of the Coal Measures. Coal was discovered and used in the 15th century, or earlier ; the mines were extended, and during the last century became the predominant feature of the district. Other industries have also grown up.

Though Wigan was the meeting place of Roman roads which traversed the parish, but few remains of the Roman period have been discovered, and these

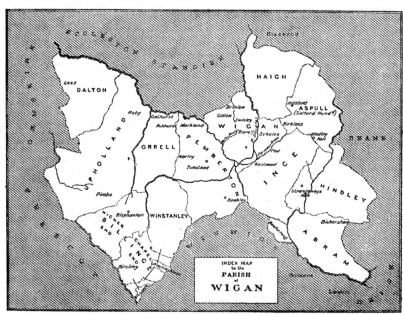

£10 ; Richard Ashton, £15 ; Aspull, Ralph Haughton, £6 13s. 4d. ; Billinge, Edmund Bispham, £3 ; Birchley, Roger Anderton, £21 12s. 4d. ; Dalton, Thomas Bank, £2 ; John Reskow, £2 ; Haigh, William Bradshaw, £3 6s. 8d. ; Hindley, Abraham Langton of Lowe, £10 ; Ince, Thomas Gerard, £40 ; Thomas Ince, £8 ; Pemberton, Edmund Winstanley, £2 10s.[1]

The Civil War found the district as a whole loyal to the king ; but the Ashhursts and some other families were Parliamentarians. There was fighting at Wigan in 1644 and 1651, and much confiscation by the Commonwealth authorities. The Restoration appears to have been generally welcomed. At the Revolution there was much more division, but no open opposition was made, and the Jacobite rising of 1715 does not seem to have had any adherents in the parish. The march of the Young Pretender through Wigan, Ince, and Hindley in 1745 brought in no recruits. The more recent history has, as in the north of England generally, been that of the growth of manufactures and commerce.

The total area of the parish is 29,033¼ acres. Of this at present 12,938 acres are arable, 7,179 permanent grass, and 854 woods and plantations. The population in 1901 numbered 157,915. The county lay of 1624 was arranged so that the parish counted as six townships and a half, Wigan itself answering for two. The other groups were—Pemberton and Ince, Hindley and Abram, Holland and Dalton, Orrell, Billinge and Winstanley ; Haigh was the half township. Aspull, being in Salford Hundred, was grouped with Blackrod. When the hundred paid £100 Wigan parish, excluding Aspull, paid £12 10s. The ancient fifteenth was more irregularly levied thus : Wigan £3, Haigh 7s., Hindley 16s. 8d., Ince 9s., Dalton 19s., Abram 11s. 8d., Upholland £1 7s. 8d., Billinge cum Winstanley 17s., Orrell 6s., Pemberton 18s. 4d., or £9 12s. 4d. when the hundred paid £106 9s. 6d. Aspull paid 7s. 8d. in Salford.

The church of ALL SAINTS[2] has a

CHURCH   chancel of two bays with north and south chapels, the Legh chapel on the north and the Bradshagh or Bradshaw chapel on the south, a nave of six bays with aisles, and a tower at the north-east angle of the north aisle of the nave, with the Gerard (now Walmesley) chapel adjoining it on the west. East of the tower is a modern vestry.

Though the plan of the church is ancient, the building has undergone even more than the general amount of renewal which has been the lot of so many of the neighbouring churches. The chancel is recorded to have been rebuilt in 1620 by Bishop Bridgeman, and was again rebuilt in 1845. The Bradshagh and Legh chapels, which had been repaired if not rebuilt in 1620, were also rebuilt in 1845, and the nave taken down and rebuilt from the foundations in 1850, much of the old material being however used. The Gerard chapel, rebuilt about 1620, escaped the general fate. The tower and the lowest parts of the stair turrets at the west end of the

chancel were not rebuilt, and contain the oldest work now existing. With such a history, any definite idea of the development of the plan is out of the question. The tower is at least as old as the 13th century, and in the course of rebuilding some 12th-century stones are said to have been found.

The nave arcades, as noted by Sir Stephen Glynne,[3] have somewhat the appearance of 14th-century work, with moulded arches and piers of four engaged shafts of good proportion. All the old stone has been re-tooled at the rebuilding of 1850, and the capitals are entirely of that date, so that it is impossible to deduce the former details of the work. A clearstory runs for the whole length of the nave and chancel, and the nave roof retains a good deal of old work, being divided into panels by moulded beams. The figures of angels on the roof corbels are terra-cotta substitutes for old oak figures. All the windows of the church before 1850, except the east and west windows, were like those still remaining in the Gerard chapel, with uncusped tracery and four-centred heads. The tower opens to the north aisle by a pointed arch, with half-octagon responds, and its ground story is lighted by a two-light window on the north, and a three-light window on the west. The latter was built up, perhaps when the Gerard chapel was added, and was opened out again in 1850 ; it is of three lights, apparently of the second half of the 13th century, though much repaired. In the sill of the north window is set an effigy of which only the face can be seen, the rest being entirely plastered over. It is said to be that of an ecclesiastic, wearing a mitre, and was found under the tower. In the east jamb of the same window is set a panelled stone with two scrolls on the top, locally believed to be part of a Roman altar. It is impossible to examine it satisfactorily in its present condition. The tower has been heightened to make room for a clock, and has pairs of windows on each face of the belfry stage, and an embattled parapet with angle pinnacles. In its upper stages no ancient detail remains, but it seems probable that all above the first stage was rebuilt in the 15th century. Of the ancient fittings of the church nothing remains. The turret stairs at the west end of the chancel doubtless led to the rood-loft, and before 1850 a gallery spanned the entrance to the chancel, carrying an organ given to the church in 1708, and afterwards moved into the Legh chapel. At the west end of the nave was a gallery with seats for the mayor and corporation, and a 'three-decker' pulpit and desk stood against the fourth pillar of the nave arcade. The altar-table is of the 17th century, of oak with a black marble slab. A piece of tapestry with the story of Ananias and Sapphira, formerly hung as a reredos to the altar, is now above the south doorway of the nave. A font dating from c. 1710, removed from the church in 1850, is now in St. George's church, and the present font is modern.[4] Two 14th-century gravestones with floriated crosses are built into the walls of the tower, and near them lies a slab with a plain cross and the inscription, 'o ▸ 1585.' In the Bradshagh chapel is an altar-tomb with two effigies,

[1] From the list in Lucas's 'Warton' (MS).

[2] By an inquisition in 1370 it was found that Roger Hancockson of Hindley had, without the king's licence, bequeathed a rent of 40d. to the church of Blessed Mary of Wigan. Possibly the gift was to the Bradshagh chantry, which had this dedication. See Q. R. Mem. R. 160 of Mich. 6 Ric. II. The All Saints' fair dates from 1258. For burial places in the church in 1691, see Genealogist (new ser.), i, 282. Arms in the church ; Trans. Hist. Soc. xxxiii, 248.

[3] Chs. of Lancs. (Chet. Soc. xxvii), 58.

[4] The octagonal bowl of a 14th-century font, used successively as a water trough and flower pot, lies in the garden of Wigan Hall ; Trans. Hist. Soc. (new ser.), xvii, 68.

WIGAN CHURCH, FROM THE NORTH-WEST, SHOWING TOWER

UPHOLLAND PRIORY CHURCH : INTERIOR, LOOKING EAST

said to be those of Sir William de Bradshagh and his wife Mabel, the effigy of the lady alone being old. Sir William's effigy was much damaged, and a new figure has taken its place, the remains of the old effigy being put inside the altar-tomb. Against the south wall of the chapel is the monument of Sir Roger Bradshagh, 1684, and there are several 19th-century Balcarres monuments.[5]

There are eight bells; the first seven of 1732, by Abraham Rudhall of Gloucester, and the tenor of 1876, by Taylor of Loughborough. There is also a priest's bell of 1732, by Rudhall.

The church plate was for the most part given by Richard Wells in 1706, but was remade about 1850, the former inscriptions recording the gift being preserved. One large paten is, however, old, having an embossed centre with the Adoration of the Magi. There are three sets of large silver-gilt communion plate, and a smaller set, also silver-gilt. Of plain silver are three flagons and three cruets, and two almsdishes, the last dating from 1724. There are also seven brass almsdishes of various dates, two pewter dishes of 1825, and twelve of 1840.

The registers begin in 1580, and are contained in over seventy volumes,[6] and the churchwardens' account books are complete from 1651. The sexton's day book has much detailed information about the burials in the church.

ADVOWSON In 1066 'the church of the manor' of Newton had one ploughland exempt from all dues.[7] It may be assumed that the lord of Newton, who at that time was the King, was patron. When the Makerfield barony was formed the patronage of this church naturally went with it, although owing to frequent minorities the kings very often presented.[8] This led to disputes. On a vacancy in 1281 the patronage was claimed by Edward I, but judgement was recorded for Robert Banastre.[9] At the following vacancy, 1303, William son of Jordan de Standish claimed the right to present, but failed to justify it.[10] The value of the benefice in 1291 had been estimated at 50 marks a year.[11] The value of the ninth of sheaves, wool, &c., was only £24 2*s.* in 1341, but Wigan borough was not included.[12]

In 1349 the crown revived its claim to the patronage and this time obtained a verdict.[13] It was certainly an erroneous decision, and the Bishop of Lichfield seems to have been unwilling to accept the royal nominee,[14] John de Winwick. It is to the credit of this rector that some time before resigning in 1359 he persuaded the king to restore the advowson to the Langtons.[15] The Standish family afterwards revived their claim to the patronage, and the matter appears to have been closed only in 1446 by a verdict for James de Langton, then rector.[16]

In the 16th century the Langtons began to sell the next presentations,[17] and in 1598 Sir Thomas Langton appears to have mortgaged or sold 'the parsonage of Wigan' to the trustees of John Lacy, citizen of London; the latter in 1605 sold it to a Mr. Pearshall, probably a trustee for Richard Fleetwood, of Calwich, the heir of the Langtons.[18] Bishop Bridgeman, then rector, agreed about 1638 to purchase the advowson for £1,000 from Sir Richard Fleetwood, but Sir Richard Murray, D.D., warden of Manchester, offering £10 more, secured it, and then tried to sell it to the crown for £4,000.[19] Charles I not being

[5] The monuments are fully described in Canon Bridgeman's *Wigan Ch.* (Chet. Soc.), 689–715.

[6] The first volume, 1580–1625, has been printed by the Lancashire Parish Register Society. The volume for 1676–83 is among Lord Kenyon's family deeds; *Hist. MSS. Com. Rep.* xiv, App. iv, 102.

[7] See *V.C.H. Lancs.* i, 286*a*.

[8] This, it will be found, was the case in the earliest recorded presentation, 1205. About ten years later Thurstan Banastre granted the patronage to the canons of Cockersand, but this gift does not appear to have had effect; *Cockersand Chart.* (Chet. Soc.), ii, 676. The Wigan charter of 1246 was witnessed by Robert Banastre, lord of Makerfield, as 'true patron' of the church.

[9] *Abbrev. Plac.* (Rec. Com.). 201; *Dep. Keeper's Rep.* l, App. 262. A few years earlier there had been a dispute as to the patronage, but the particulars are not recorded; De Banco R. 7, m. 39.

[10] William de Standish alleged that his ancestor Ralph, living in the time of King Richard, had presented his own clerk, Ulf by name, to the chapel of Wigan; and that Ulf was instituted and received the tithes, oblations, and dues, 'amounting to half a mark and more.' Nothing otherwise is known of this Ulf. Although it is unlikely that such a claim would have been put forward by the Standishes against great personages like the lords of Makerfield unless there was justification for it, the description as a 'chapel' and the very small amount of dues received raises a doubt. The distinction of 'church' and 'chapel' was at once seized upon by the defence; 'We cannot yield up what plaintiff demands, for we hold the advowson of a *church*, and at present we do not know if he demands the advowson of a *chapel* in that church, as we have seen in other cases, or if he means to say that there is another *chapel*.' See the late Canon Bridgeman's *Hist. of the Ch. of Wigan* (Chet. Soc.), quoting *Year Bk. of Edw. I* (Rolls Ser.), 358. The information in the present notes is largely drawn from his work, in which documents quoted are usually printed in full. Many of them are from the family records. The Standish claim was still pending in 1312; Bridgeman, op. cit. 797. The following references to the suit may be added: De Banco R. 153, m. 98 d—an extent of the chapel of Wigan; R. 161, m. 11—the chapel extended at £9 a year, but the case adjourned because Robert de Langton was setting out for Scotland on the king's service. Thomas de Langtree released his claim to the advowson of the church or chapel of Wigan in favour of Standish; Coram Reg. R. 297, m. 20.

[11] *Pope Nich. Tax.* (Rec. Com.), 249. In the claim made by the rector against John del Crosse in 1329 it was alleged that the gross value was about £200 a year.

[12] *Inq. Non.* (Rec. Com.), 41. The values were: Haigh 47*s.* 8½*d.*; Aspull 47*s.* 8¼*d.*; Hindley 64*s.* 5½*d.*; Abram 32*s.* 2½*d.*; Ince 32*s.* 2¼*d.*; Pemberton 64*s.* 5½*d.*; Billinge 64*s.* 5½*d.*; Orrell 32*s.* 2¼*d.*; Holland 64*s.* 5½*d.*; Dalton 32*s.* 2¼*d.* The value of the ninth of the movable goods of the men living in the borough of Wigan was 109*s.* 4*d.*

[13] De Banco R. 358, m. 50. The king alleged in support of his claim that Ralph

able to afford this, Sir John Hotham became the purchaser shortly afterwards ;[90] and his trustees about 1661 sold it to Sir Orlando Bridgeman,[21] son of the bishop, in whose family it has since descended, the Earl of Bradford being the patron.

Sir Orlando and his son adopted a 'self-denying ordinance,' and formed a body of trustees to exercise the patronage,[22] and thus it happened that for nearly half a century the Bishops of Chester were presented to the rectory.[23]

Meanwhile the value had very greatly increased. In the 16th century, and perhaps earlier, the system of farming the tithes prevented the rectors receiving the full revenue,[24] and in 1535 the gross value was set down as £110 16s. 8d., from which had to be deducted a pension of £20, anciently paid to the cathedral of Lichfield, and other fees and dues,[25] so that the net value was reported as £80 13s. 4d. In the first half of the next century Bishop Bridgeman found that the clear yearly value was £570 on an average.[26] Bishop Gastrell, about 1717, recorded it to be 'above £300 clear, all curates paid.'[27] In 1802 the receipts from tithes amounted to £1,306 8s.,[28] and afterwards receipts from the coal mining under the glebe were added. The value is now estimated at £1,500.[29] The rector of Wigan pays a considerable sum from his income to the incumbents of various churches built in the parish.

The following is a list of the rectors and lords of the manor of Wigan :—

Instituted	Name	Presented by	Cause of Vacancy
oc. 1199	Randle [30]	——	——
23 April 1205 .	Robert de Durham [31]	The King	res. of Randle
2 Nov. 1226 .	Ralph de Leicester [32]	,,	——
oc. 1241 . . .	John Maunsel [33]		——

[90] Bridgeman, op. cit. 483 ; quoting the Wigan 'Leger,' in which Sir John Hotham is in 1641 called 'the new patron.' At Michaelmas 1638 an agreement seems to have been arrived at between Charles Hotham and others and the Bishop of London and others as to the advowson ; Com. Pleas, Recov. R. Mich. 14 Chas. I, m. 3. In a fine of Mar. 1642 relating to the advowson, John Murray, esq., and Marian his wife were deforciants ; Pal. of Lanc. Feet of F. bdle. 140, no. 15.

[21] Bridgeman, op. cit. 484. In a fine of 1659 Charles Hotham and Elizabeth his wife were deforciants ; Pal. of Lanc. Feet of F. bdle. 164, no. 16. See also Com. Pleas, D. Enr. Mich. 1662, m. 95 d.

[22] Bridgeman, op. cit. 484 ; 'bearing in mind the corrupt practices of former patrons, who had turned the advowson into a means of private gain,' and wishing to avoid such abuses, Sir Orlando associated with himself as trustees the then Archbishop of Canterbury and others.

[23] Ibid. 601. In 1713 the Bishop of Chester made inquiries as to the conditions of the trust, supposing that some preference was to be given to the Bishops of Chester ; ibid. 613.

[24] See the Kitchin lease described under Rector Kighley. Apart from disadvantageous leases it was not always easy to secure the tithe ; see Duchy Plead. (Rec. Soc. Lancs. and Ches.), ii, 111 ; and the complaint of Rector Smith in 1553, quoted by Canon Bridgeman, op. cit. 123–7, 130 ; see also 158, 159. The difficulties of the rectors concerning their tithes were quite independent of those they had with the corporation of Wigan as lords of the manor.

Besides disadvantageous leases and open violence the rectors lost through prescription, by which a modus or composition in lieu of tithes was established. Thus the Earls of Derby had long held the tithes of the townships of Dalton and Upholland at a low rent ; and about 1600 William, the sixth earl, claimed an absolute right to the tithes, paying only £12 13s. 4d. a year to the rector. Rector Fleetwood tried to defeat this claim, and Bishop Bridgeman made a still more vigorous effort, but in vain ; and the same modus is still paid by the Earl of Derby's

assigns in lieu of the tithes ; Bridgeman, op. cit. 161–3, 254–9, 647–50. Prescription was likewise established in the case of Ince, £4 being paid by the Gerards and their successors ; ibid. 190, 655.

[25] Valor Eccl. (Rec. Com.), v, 220. The gross value was made up of the rents of tenants, free and at will, £25 ; rent of two water-mills 66s. 8d.; tithes of corn, hay, wool, &c., £61 3s. 4d. ; oblations, small tithes, and roll, £18 ; perquisites and profits of the markets, 66s. 8d. Robert Langton as chief steward had a fee of £4.

[26] Bridgeman, op. cit. 417. A statement of his receipts and payments for his first year of occupation ending at Christmas 1616 is printed 188–203 ; many curious details are given. A later account of the profits of the rectory will be found on pp. 307–19. Bishop Bridgeman compiled his 'Leger,' extant in a copy made by Rector Finch in 1708, recording all the lands and rights belonging to the rector and the endeavours he had made to recover and preserve them. In 1619 he compiled a terrier of the demesne lands of the rectory ; op. cit. 244–6. The names of the fields include Parson's Meadow, Diglache or Diglake, the Mesnes, Conygrew, Rycroft, Carreslache, Parsnip Yard, and Cuckstool Croft. Potters used to come for clay to the parson's wastes, undertaking to make the land level again ; 268. Another terrier was compiled in 1814, and is printed ibid. 651–8.

[27] Notitia Cestr. (Chet. Soc.), ii, 242. The rector was instituted to 'Wigan with the chapel of Holland.' There were two wardens and eighteen assistants, serving jointly for the whole parish ; seven of the assistants were for the town.

[28] Bridgeman, op. cit. 642. 'The tithes were valued by two competent persons and offered to the farmers at their separate valuations, which they all accepted, and paid their respective shares on the first Monday after Christmas, which is the day usually appointed for payment.' The tithes of Wigan itself were gathered in kind. The mode of tithing is thus described : 'The corn in this parish is bound up in sheaves. Eight sheaves set up together make one shock, and every tenth shock is the rector's property, and

Instituted	Name	Presented by	Cause of Vacancy
1265 . . .	Mr. Richard de Marklan [34] .	Robert Banastre . . .	d. of J. Maunsel
? 1281 . . .	Mr. Adam de Walton [35]	——	
22 Sept. 1303 .	Mr. Robert de Clitheroe [36] .	John de Langton . . .	
15 June 1334 .	Ivo (John) de Langton [37]	Sir Robert de Langton .	d. of Rob. de Clitheroe
13 Nov. 1344 .	John de Craven [38]	,,	——
26 Dec. 1344 .	Mr. John de Craven [39]		——
oc. 1347 . . .	Henry de Dale, M.A. [40]	——	——
12 Mar. 1349–50 } 3 May 1350 . }	John de Winwick [41] . . .	The King	——
10 July 1359 .	Richard de Langton [42] . .	Sir Rob. de Langton . .	
4 Sept. 1359 .	Robert de Lostock [43] . .	,,	res. R. de Langton
2 Jan. 1361–2 .	Walter de Campden [44] . .	John Earl of Lancaster .	res. R. de Lostock

Lancs. Inq. and Extents, i, 147. In local history he is notable as procuring the first borough charter. He died abroad in great poverty at the end of 1264 or beginning of 1265.

There are numerous references to him in *Cal. of Papal Letters*. Alexander IV, in 1259, approved the dispensation granted, at the king's request, by Pope Innocent, allowing Maunsel to be ordained and promoted although his mother married his father, a man of noble birth, not knowing that he was a deacon; his father repenting, resumed his orders, and a divorce was declared; the dispensation should hold good, even though the mother's plea of ignorance and the reputation of a lawful marriage could not be sustained; ibid. i, 362. Many documents refer to his superabundance of benefices; see specially ibid. 378.

[34] He in July 1265 joined with the patron, Sir Robert Banastre, in assigning an annual pension of 30 marks to the mother church of Lichfield. Canon Bridgeman states: 'A sum of £16 is now (1887) paid annually by the rector of Wigan to the sacristan of Lichfield Cathedral.'

Master Richard was still living in 1278; Assize R. 1238, m. 33 d. His surname shows that he was a local man. He had a son Nicholas, who in 1292 was summoned to warrant William, rector of Donington, in the possession of a messuage in Wigan claimed by Robert Sperling and Sabina his wife; Assize R. 408, m. 35 d.

[35] This rector was probably appointed at the vacancy in 1281, when the king, as stated in the text, claimed the patronage. Adam was the rector summoned in 1292 to show his title to manorial rights in Wigan; *Plac. de Quo War.* (Rec. Com.), 371. He was chancellor of Lichfield Cathedral from 1276 till 1292, when he was made precentor, retaining the latter office till his death in August 1303; Le Neve, *Fast.* i, 579. His executors were Adam de Walton, rector of Mitton, Adam de Walton, junior, and Richard de Fulshaw; De Banc. R. 164, m. 300 d.

[36] Lichfield Epis. Reg. i, fol. 9b. He was not ordained priest till he became rector; ibid. i, fol. 98b. John de Langton, afterwards Bishop of Chichester, presented as guardian of Alice Banastre, heiress of the barony of Newton.

The new rector was a king's clerk and held several public appointments; *Parl. Writs*, ii (3), 685–6. Leave of absence was granted by the bishop in September 1322; Lich. Epis. Reg. ii, fol. 7. He sided with Thomas, Earl of Lancaster, and in 1323 was called upon to answer for the part he had taken in the rising of 1321. By the jury of the wapentake of West Derby it was pres Cl'th r , re o o thirty years been chancery and for so side of Trent, had two men at arms t one of them being Clitherow, accompa foot, all p operly a certain solemn d church at W'g n b had told them that to the earl and m cau g · h k cause ; q his hearers j ined once den'ed that h swell the earl' f said in church was to pray for the kin for the peace of the ever, convicted, and kin b fi P

Instituted	Name	Presented by	Cause of Vacancy
24 Aug. 1370	James de Langton [45]	Ralph de Langton	d. W. de Campden
oc. 1415–31	William de Langton [46]	———	———
oc. 1432–47	James de Langton [47]	———	———
oc. 1451	Oliver de Langton [48]	———	———
oc. 1485	John Langton [49]	———	———
9 Aug. 1504	Thomas Langton [50]	Langton feoffees	d. J. Langton
16 Aug. 1506	Richard Wyot, D.D. [51]	The King	d. T. Langton
10 Oct. 1519	Thomas Linacre, M.D [52]	Thos. Langton	res. R. Wyot
oc. 1528–32	Nicholas Towneley [53]	———	———
oc. 1532–3	Richard Langton [54]	———	———
24 Mar 1534–5	Richard Kighley [55]	Sir T. Langton	d. R. Langton
8 Aug. 1543	John Herbert [56]	Thos. White	d. R. Kighley
? March 1550	John Standish, D.D. [57]	The King	———
1550	Richard Smith [58]	,,	———
2 Mar. 1554–5	Richard Gerard [59]	Earl of Derby, &c.	d. R. Smith
10 Aug. 1558	Thomas Stanley [60]	{ John Fleetwood . Peter Farington .	d. R. Gerard

[45] Lich. Epis. Reg. iv, fol. 85b; v, fol. 28b, 30. He had received only the tonsure, but was made priest 11 April 1371; ibid. v, fol. 100b.

James de Langton is mentioned as rector down to 1414, about the end of which year he died; *Dep. Keeper's Rep.* xxxiii, App. 12, 'late rector.' He was one of the feoffees of Richard de Molyneux of Sefton in 1394; *Lancs. Inq. p.m.* (Chet. Soc.), i, 70; ibid. 103.

[46] William de Langton is mentioned as rector a number of times from 1417 to 1430; *Dep. Keeper's Rep.* xxxiii, 13, &c. In 1431–2 he was 'late rector'; ibid. 32.

[47] In a plea of 1441 mention is made of William de Langton as rector before 10 Hen. VI, and James de Langton as rector in the same year; a note is added, recording a pardon to the latter, dated 1446–7; Pal. of Lanc. Plea R. 3, m. 31b.

In 1436 James de Langton, rector of Wigan, was proceeding to France in the retinue of the Duke of York; *Dep. Keeper's Rep.* xlviii, App. 310.

He appears to have been a violent and lawless man, and his name frequently occurs in the plea rolls. In 1442 the sheriff was ordered to arrest Christopher, Edward, Edmund, and Oliver de Langton, sons of James de Langton, the rector; also Margaret Holerobyn of Wigan, the rector's mistress; Pal. of Lanc. Plea R. 4 (quoted by Canon Bridgeman).

[48] Oliver Langton in 1451 covenanted to pay the £20 yearly to Lichfield; Bridgeman, op. cit. 69. He was still living in 1462; ibid. 70.

In 1457 the Bishop of Lichfield issued a commission to Dr. Duckworth, vicar of Prescot, and others to inquire as to the pollution of the churchyard of Wigan by bloodshed, forbidding it to be used for interments until it should be reconciled; Lich. Epis. Reg. xi, fol. 91b.

[49] John Langton, rector of Wigan, occurs in July 1485; *Local Glean. Lancs. and Ches.* i, 266. In 1498 he was called upon to show by what title he claimed various manorial rights in Wigan; Pal. of Lanc. Writs, Lent, 13 Hen. VII.

[50] Lich. Epis. Reg. xiii–xiv, fol. 53; the patrons were James Anderton, William Banastre, Thomas Langton (brother of Gilbert Langton of Lowe), and William Woodcock, feoffees of Ralph Langton, deceased.

[51] Lich. Epis. Reg. xiii–xiv, fol. 54b; Act Bks. at Chester; the king presented on account of the minority of Thomas Langton. Dr. Wyot was a man of some university distinction, being at one time

master of Christ and he held several nae Cantab. i, 26.

[52] Lich. Epis. Reg. b ography of this dis be read in Dr. J. N him; also in the D Canon Bridgeman, appear to h e e h ship of York Minst W g n, y t office on 13 Novemb Fasti, iii, 156. It w years that Linacre, t Mersham in 1509, theology, and he was until 22 December

Instituted	Name	Presented by	Cause of Vacancy
Apl. 1569 .	William Blackleach, B.A.[61] . . .	John Fleetwood . . .	d. Bp. Stanley
8 Feb. 1570–1 .	Edward Fleetwood[62]	The Queen	res. W. Blackleach
9 Oct. 1604 .	Gerard Massie, D.D.[63]	The King	d. E. Fleetwood
21 Jan. 1615–16.	John Bridgeman, D.D.[64] . . .	„ . .	d. G. Massie
c. 1643	James Bradshaw, M.A.[65] . . .	Parliamentary Comm'rs. .	——
1653 . .	Charles Hotham, M.A.[66] . . .	[Hotham Trustees] . .	[d. Bp. Bridgeman]
1662 . . .	George Hall, D.D.[67]	Sir O. Bridgeman . . .	ejec. C. Hotham
1668 . . .	John Wilkins, D.D.[68]	Bridgeman Trustees . .	d. Bp. Hall
1673 . . .	John Pearson, D.D.[69]	„ „ . .	d. Bp. Wilkins

[61] Church P. at Chester. First-fruits paid 22 June 1569.

[62] Ches. Reg. (quoted by Canon Bridgeman) ; first-fruits paid 12 Feb. The queen presented by reason of the minority of Thomas Langton, and opportunity was taken to place in this important rectory a staunch adherent of the newly-established religious system. Edward Fleetwood was a younger son of Thomas Fleetwood of the Vache, Buckinghamshire. He was but a young man, and established a good example by residing in his rectory ; he was 'the first beginner' of monthly communions at Wigan ; Bridgeman, op. cit. 235. He also caused forms to be placed in the nave ; they were made from the timber of the rood-loft ; ibid. 272. He instituted various suits for the recovery of the revenues and rights of his church ; Bridgeman, op. cit. 143–63.

He took part in the persecution of 'Popish recusants,' and it is clear from the letter printed in Bridgeman, 166–71, as from his not wearing the surplice in 1589 (Visit. Bks.), and his joining in the petition to Convocation in 1604, that he was a Puritan ; he was indeed charged with 'neglect and contempt' in not observing the forms of the Book of Common Prayer, op. cit. 160 ; also Hist. MSS. Com. Rep. xiv, App. iv, 597. A sympathizer with the victims of his zeal 'could not stay his pen from writing unto him to commend him to leave off blaspheming against this our Catholic faith or else he would drink of Judas' sop,' and threw the protest into the rector's pew ; Bridgeman, op. cit. 174. For some of the presentments made by Rector Fleetwood against parishioners alleged to have received priests, see Gibson, Lydiate Hall, 239, 240.

[63] On 21 June 1604 the benefice was sequestered to preserve the fruits for the next incumbent ; on 6 Oct. Brian Vincent, B.D., was presented by John Sweeting and William Hobbes, acting by demise of Sir Thomas Langton ; but this grant not being satisfactory, the Bishop of Chester referred the matter to the king, who had presented Gerard Massie, B.D., as early as 17 July ; Bridgeman, op. cit. 179. The first-fruits were paid 23 Feb. 1604–5. See also Pal. of Lanc. Plea R. 296, m. 5, where it is stated that the advowson was held by the fifth part of a knight's fee.

The new rector was son of William Massie of Chester and Grafton, near Malpas ; Ormerod, Ches. (ed. Helsby), ii, 706. He was educated at Brasenose College, Oxford ; B.A. 1592 ; D.D. 1609 ; Foster, Alumni Oxon. In 1615 he was nominated to the bishopric of Chester, but died in London, 16 Jan. 1615–16, before consecration ; Bridgeman, op. cit. 180.

[64] Bridgeman, op. cit. 181–455, the whole of pt. ii. The following is a brief outline :—John son of Thomas Bridgeman

was born at Exeter Oriel College, Oxf Cambridge being el lene in the latter u also took degrees Cambridge, 1612. ferment, and marri the attention of Jam rapid (pp. 181 6). many rights of the ch increased the rector 262). In 1619 he of Chester, retain rectory of Wigan held at Exeter an He comp led the va caused the chur h t the erection of an o the Commonwealth in the body of the c out interfering with sitting places, 'he the best in the high on the one side o other side their wi seclude children and with h

s.

Instituted	Name	Presented by	Cause of Vacancy
1686 . . .	Thomas Cartwright, D.D.[70] . . .	Bridgeman Trustees . .	d. Bp. Pearson
1689 . . .	Nicholas Stratford, D.D [71] . . .	„ „ . .	d. Bp. Cartwright
Mar. 1706–7 .	Hon. Edward Finch, M.A.[72] . .	„ „ . .	d. Bp. Stratford
30 April 1714 .	Samuel Aldersey, M.A.[73] . . .	„ „ . .	res. E. Finch
12 May 1741 .	Roger Bridgeman, D.D.[74] . . .	„ „ . .	d. S. Aldersey
(3 July) 1750 .	Shirley Cotes, M.A.[75] . . .	Wm. Lord Digby . . .	d. R. Bridgeman
27 Feb. 1776 .	Guy Fairfax, M.A.[76]	Sir H. Bridgeman . . .	d. S. Cotes
30 July 1790 .	George Bridgeman[77]	Sir H. Bridgeman, &c. .	d. G. Fairfax
4 Jan. 1833 .	Sir Henry John Gunning, M.A.[78] .	Earl of Bradford . .	d. G. Bridgeman
17 Oct. 1864 .	Hon. George Thomas Orlando Bridgeman, M.A.[79]	Bishop of Chester . . .	res. Sir H. Gunning
24 Feb. 1896 .	Roland George Matthew, M.A.[80] .	Earl of Bradford . .	d G. T. O. Bridgeman

The earlier rectors of Wigan, when presented by the kings, were busy public officials, who probably never saw the church from which they drew a small addition to their incomes ; and when presented by the hereditary patrons were, with few exceptions, men of no distinction, whose only recommendation was their family connexion.

The *Valor* of 1535 does not record any chapelries or chantries nor mention any clergy except the rector and the Bradshagh chantry priest, but Upholland

[70] Thomas Cartwright was a grandson of his namesake the famous Puritan of Queen Elizabeth's days. His parents were Presbyterians, and he was educated at Queen's College, Oxford, while it was under Puritan rule ; M.A. 1655. This makes it the more noteworthy that he ignored the laws in force and was ordained in the year just mentioned according to the Anglican form by Dr. Skinner, who had been Bishop of Oxford, but was then living in retirement. He took a benefice under the existing rule, but as might be expected, at once conformed on the Restoration, and received various preferments. He also secured the firm friendship of the Duke of York, and was one of the very few who thoroughly devoted themselves to his cause when he became king. He was made Bishop of Chester and also rector of Wigan in 1686, and retired to Ireland with the king, dying in Dublin 15 Apr. 1689. His diary, printed by the Camden Society, contains many particulars of local interest.

See Bridgeman, op. cit. 564–78 ; Foster, *Alumni Oxon.*; *Dict. Nat. Biog.*; *Chester Arch. Soc. Trans.* (new ser.), iv, 1–33.

[71] He was the son of a tradesman at Hemel Hempstead ; educated at Trinity College, Oxford ; M.A. and fellow 1656 ; D.D. 1673 ; warden of Manchester 1667–84 ; dean of St. Asaph 1674 ; noted for his tolerance of Dissenters ; Bishop of Chester and rector of Wigan, 1689, being one of the first bishops nominated by William III. He resided at Wigan occasionally, and rebuilt the parsonage house in 1695. See Bridgeman, op. cit. 578–601 ; Foster, *Alumni Oxon.*; *Dict. Nat. Biog.*

[72] The bishopric of Chester was at this time kept vacant for a year, while the rectory of Wigan was filled by the appointment of the Hon. Edward Finch, a son of the first Earl of Nottingham, and a brother of Henry Finch, dean of York and rector of Winwick. He was educated at Christ's College, Cambridge, of which he was a fellow ; M.A. 1679. He represented his university in the Parliament of 1690 ; Le Neve, *Fasti*, iii, 650. The patrons were Sir John Bridgeman, the Bishop of London, Lord Digby, and John and Orlando Bridgeman. The old organ, situated in a gallery in or near the arch between the nave and chancel—'between the two hollow pillars which divide the new and old chancel,' was the phrase used—had been pulled down in the Commonwealth period, and in its place the mayor and corporation had in 1680 made themselves a pew. This was pulled down in 1709 and a new organ erected, the rector being himself a musician ; while the rents from the west end gallery, originally intended for the singers, were appropriated to the organist's salary. Members of the corporation did not take kindly to this ejection from their gallery, and it was probably owing to the ill-feeling and disputes thus engendered that Rector Finch resigned in 1713, apparently before the new organ had been brought into use. He died at York, where he had a canonry, in 1738. See Bridgeman, op. cit. 601–13 ; *Hist. MSS. Com. Rep.* xiv, App. iv, 447 ; *Dict. Nat. Biog.*; Le Neve, *Fasti*, iii, 223 ; i, 48.

[73] He was the second son and eventual heir of Thomas Aldersey of Aldersey ; was born in 1673, educated at Brasenose College, Oxford ; M.A. 1700. He no doubt owed this promotion to his marriage with Henrietta, daughter of Dean Bridgeman of Chester ; Ormerod, *Ches.* (ed. Helsby), ii, 740. He appears to have resided at Wigan. Among the improvements in the church during his incumbency were the recasting of the bells, including 'the little bell called the Catherine bell,' a new clock, 'repairing the curtains at the altar,' a new gallery, &c. At other times (e.g. p. 658) 'a small bell called the Ting-tang' is named. The dispute as to the corporation seat was settled by assigning them the western gallery. See Bridgeman, op. cit. 614–28 ; Foster, *Alumni Oxon.*

[74] He was a son of Sir John Bridgeman ; educated at Oriel College, Oxford, of which he became fellow ; M.A. 1725 ; D.D. 1736. He held several benefices, and was appointed vicar of Bolton in 1737. He appears to have resided at Wigan from time to time. He died unmarried in June 1750. See Bridgeman, op. cit. 628–34 ; Foster, *Alumni Oxon.*

[75] Lord Digby was the only surviving trustee.

The new rector was a son of John Cotes of Woodcote in Shropshire, &c. ; educated at Magdalen Hall, Oxford ; M.A. 1737. He appears to have resided at Wigan until the last years of his life. He died at Woodcote, 11 Dec. 1775. His eldest son John was member for Wigan

Priory was still in existence.[81] The *Clergy List* of 1541-2 [82] shows that there were four priests within the parish, apart from rector and cantarist ; one of these was the curate, Ralph Scott ; two were paid by Robert Langton and Thomas Gerard ; the maintenance of the other is not recorded.

In the Visitation List in 1548 is left a blank for the rector's name ; then follow eight names, one being that of the chantry priest ; but two of the clergy seem to have been absent. In 1554 Master Richard Smith, rector ; the curate, and three others appeared, including the former chantry priest. No improvement took place under the episcopate of Bishop Scott, though he had a personal interest in the parish. In 1562 the Bishop of Sodor and Man did not appear, being 'excused by the Bishop of Chester.' Ralph Scott appeared and exhibited his subscription, so that he was prepared to accept the Elizabethan order, as he had accepted all the previous changes ; two other names also appear in the list, one of an old priest, the other a fresh name. In 1565 only three names are shown in the list—Bishop Stanley, who 'did not exhibit,' his curate Ralph Scott, and Thomas Baron or Barow, who had appeared in each list from 1548, and who perhaps had no ministerial office.[83] Thus it appears that by this time the working clergy had been reduced to one, the curate of the parish church.[84]

The short incumbency of William Blackleach, of whom nothing is known, was followed by that of a decided Protestant, Edward Fleetwood. He was one of the two 'preachers' in 1590 at the parish church ; there were no preachers at the two chapelries, Uphol-

land and Billinge.[85] The Puritan rector and his curate in 1592 were reported to 'wear no surplice,' nor did they catechise the youth, and were admonished accordingly ; it is also stated that 'they want a chancel.' [86] In 1610 there was 'a preacher' at the parish church, but none at either of the chapels.[87]

The Commonwealth surveyors of 1650 recommended the subdivision of the parish ; Holland Chapel had already been cut off by an Act of 1646, and the committee of Plundered Ministers had made several increments in the stipends of the incumbents of the chapelries out of Bishop Bridgeman's sequestered tithes.[88] After the Restoration both the rector and a large number of the Protestants remained firm in their attachment to the Presbyterian discipline, while the rectory was till 1706 held by the Bishops of Chester, among them the learned Pearson. Here, as in other parishes, the great increase in population during the 19th century has led to the erection of many new churches and the subdivision of the ancient parish, there being now twenty parochial churches in connexion with the Establishment, besides licensed churches and mission rooms.[89]

There was only one endowed chantry ; it was founded in 1338 by Mabel, widow of Sir William de Bradshagh, who endowed it with a messuage in Wigan and tenements at Haigh.[90] In 1548 the chantry priest was celebrating at the altar of our Lady in the church according to his foundation.[91]

CHARITIES

The charities of Wigan [92] comprise a large number of separate benefactions, mostly for the poor in general, but some especially for clothing or apprenticing boys.[93]

[81] *Valor Eccl.* (Rec. Com.), v, 220.

[82] Printed by the Rec. Soc. of Lancs. and Ches. p. 14.

[83] A Thomas Baron, perhaps the same, had been chantry priest in 1534 ; *Valor Eccl.* v, 220.

[84] These details are taken from the Visitation Lists preserved in the Diocesan Registry at Chester. A communion table had replaced the altar by 1561 ; Bridgeman, op. cit. 136.

[85] Gibson, *Lydiate Hall*, 248, quoting S.P. Dom. Eliz. ccxxxv, 4. The second preacher at the parish church was paid by the lord of Newton, apparently in continuation of the old custom.

[86] *Trans. Hist. Soc.* (new ser.), x, 192. Bishop Bridgeman gives a full account of the 'old chancel' as it was in 1620. Rector Fleetwood had removed the 'goodly, fair choir seats' formerly there and allowed 'plain, rude seats' to be placed instead. The communion table stood in the middle of it ; the bishop as rector was placed at the west end, his 'wife, &c.,' at the east end, on the south side ; the 'minister's box' was on the north side, where also the clerks had a seat. In the old rood-loft the bishop had lately placed an organ ; and he built up a 'new chancel,' at the east end of the old one. See Bridgeman, op. cit. 263, 264. This new chancel was several steps higher than the old, and contained the altar, 271.

[87] *Hist. MSS. Com. Rep.* xiv, App. iv, 13.

[88] *Commonwealth Ch. Surv.* (Rec. Soc. Lancs. and Ches.), 59-64 ; *Plund. Mins. Accts.* (Rec. Soc. Lancs. and Ches.), i, 25, 41 ; ii, 129.

A list of the modern curates is given by Canon Bridgeman, op. cit. 723-9.

[89] An account of the sale of a pew in

the parish church in 1796 is given in *Lancs. and Ches. Antiq. Notes*, i, 128.

[90] Kuerden MSS. ii, fol. 213, no. 16-21; *Cal. Pat.* 1334-8, p. 468. The chaplain was to celebrate at the altar of St. Mary in Wigan Church for the souls of Edward II, Sir William de Bradshagh, Mabel his wife, and others.

Very few names of the chantry priests have been preserved ; Raines, *Lancs. Chant.* (Chet. Soc.) i, 66 :—

1338. John de Sutton, presented by Dame Mabel de Bradshagh. Richard Fletcher.

1488. William Holden, presented by James Bradshagh, on the death of R. Fletcher.

oc. 1521. Geoffrey Coppull, vicar of Mountnessing and chantry priest of our Blessed Lady at Wigan, aged 56, gave evidence in a plea of 1521-2 ; *Duchy Plead.* i, 102.

oc. 1534. Thomas Baron.

1535. Vacant.

1544. Hugh Cookson. In 1541 he was paid by Thomas Gerard, and soon afterwards appointed to this chantry. In 1553 he had a pension of 60s. 3d., and was fifty-one years of age. He was not summoned to the visitation of 1562, so that probably he had died before that time.

[91] *Lancs. Chant.* loc. cit. His duty was 'to celebrate for the souls of the founders and to sing mass with note twice a week.' There was no plate, as he used the ornaments of the church. The total rental was 66s. 10d., but 1s. was paid to the rector as chief rent, perhaps for a burgage in Wigan.

[92] There was an inquiry at Wigan in the time of Jas. I concerning £100 given in 1616 by Hugh Bullock the elder, citizen and haberdasher of London, for setting the poor of the borough to work 'in spinning of cotton, wool, hemp, flax, and making of fustians, and other stuffs ;' it was alleged that the fund was misapplied ; and an order was made, 3 Mar. 1624-5, to rectify it ; Harl. MS. 2176, fol. 32b, 34.

[93] The particulars hereafter given are taken from the *Char. Com. Rep.* xxi (1829), 271-319. An inquiry into the endowed charities of the parish, except the township of Wigan, was made in 1899.

For Wigan township Hugh Bullock of London, as recorded in the previous note, and Henry Mason, rector of St. Andrew Undershaft, London, each gave £100, the latter adding £140 later, which in 1632 and 1639 were conveyed to the corporation ; and a farm in Rainford, and lands called Bangs in Wigan, and Hall Meadow in Pemberton, were purchased. In 1828 these were underlet at rents amounting to £60 a year, of which only part was received by the charity. This was used in binding apprentices. In a feoffment of 1665 lands at Angerton Moss, Broughton in Furness, are described as the gift of Oliver Markland, citizen and innholder of London ; this land was sold in 1706, and with the proceeds, £25, a rent-charge of 20s. a year on premises in Standishgate, Wigan, was purchased ; but in 1828 no payment had been received for many years, and it was not known upon what premises the charge was made.

John Guest, by will in 1653, charged £3 15s. upon premises in Abram called Bolton House, for cloth to the poor, to be

Some have been lost.[94] The most important used to be the Edmund Molyneux bread charity, being the profits of his estate at Canewdon in Essex.[95]

In the following notes the *Report* of the 1899 inquiry has been used ; in it is reprinted the *Report* of 1829.

distributed by the minister of the parish church ; in 1828 £3 10s. was divided among Wigan and the other townships in the parish.

Robert Sixsmith, by his will dated 1688, gave two closes in Wigan and one in Ince, for the needy people of the town, half the rents being applicable to schools. In 1828 the nominal income was about £30 ; the usual practice was to give to each poor person in the districts into which the town was divided for distribution, so that from 2d. to 1s. was all that each received. Gilbert Ford, in 1705, left the moiety of a close at Wigan called the Bannycroft ; in 1828 the half-rent amounted to £3, which was spent in linen or flannel garments.

In 1707 Ellen Wells left £100 for the poor, and Richard Wells, her husband, £200 for apprenticing boys ; Edward Holt in 1704 bequeathed £150 and £75 for oat bread or other sort for a Sunday distribution of bread ; these sums and other charitable funds were in 1768 used in building a workhouse, and in 1828 £27 6s. 3d. was paid to the churchwardens out of the poor-rate as interest, which was to be laid out according to the wishes of the donors in linen, apprenticing boys, doles of bread, and school fees. An inquiry respecting the Wells charity is printed in *Local Gleam. Lancs. and Ches.* ii, 143.

John Baldwin in 1720 left closes called Barker's Croft and Pilly Toft, charged with the payment of £100, which had been entrusted to him by Orlando Bridgeman for apprenticing two boys each year ; £3 a year was still paid in 1828. William Brown in 1724 augmented a bread charity founded by his uncle George Brown ; and £2 a year was paid by the owner of a farm in Poolstock as interest, and laid out in bread.

Ellen Willis, widow, by her will of 1726 left a bond for £100 to her sons Thomas and Daniel Willis, as trustees, and added another £100 ; Margaret Diggles, widow, gave £100 also ; and in 1737, Daniel Willis, the surviving son, and William Hulton, conveyed to trustees closes called the Page fields in Frog Lane, Wigan ; two-thirds of the interest was to be spent in clothing for poor persons 'frequenting the communion of the Lord's Supper in the parish church of Wigan,' while the other third might be used for apprenticing boys. In 1828 the rental amounted to about £42, which was distributed with the Sixsmith and Guest charities.

Thomas Mort of Damhouse, in 1729 gave money for the Throstle Nests or Baron's fields, near Gidlow Lane, the interest to be spent in binding children as apprentices. The rent in 1828 was £16, but the trustee being in difficulties, a considerable sum was in arrears. John Hardman in 1742 left £200 to found a clothing charity, and £9 10s. a year was available in 1828, being spent on woollen coats and cloaks distributed by the curate of Wigan.

James Molyneux, by his will of 1706, left his lands of inheritance, as also a leasehold messuage in the Wiend, until £100 should accrue from the rents to

found a charity fo prent cing boys. paid, but in 1757 executor of Lord given a bond for will, gave Hought burgage in Wigan fulfil the trust. for 1000 years, br £11 5s. ; but th inc uding the Wo over £100 a ye Pennington in 17 two charities, one the other for appr dishgate ; this see in 1828.

In 1899 the f reported in some John Guest's charge on Bolton deemed, and £14 income required fo Holt's Charity ing been sold £ conso s as the sha income was prac recently been app for poor boys in t

[94] John Bullock a year on prem's the East, and St poration of Wigan

Abram has certain lands, the rents of which are devoted to charitable uses, and some minor benefactions.[96] Pemberton also had some small charities.[97] At Ince, linen, oatmeal, and gifts of money were provided,[98] but part of the fund is lost ; while at Aspull of the two charities one survives.[99] At

Haigh Dame Dorothy Bradshagh about 1775 erected a building called the Receptacle, being an almshouse for twenty poor persons ;[100] there were also a poor's stock and some minor charities, most of which have been lost.[101] Hindley has linen or flannel charities and one or two others.[102]

For the Billinge townships the principal foundation is that of John Eddleston, who in 1672 bequeathed his house and lands here for charitable uses ;[103] there were several other benefactions.[104] At Winstanley are two charities founded by James and William Bankes, with incomes of about £20 and £17, used to provide cloth and blankets.[105] In Orrell, out of a number of gifts, about £6 a year is still distributed in doles of calico.[106] Pimbo Lane House and other tenements in Upholland were given by Henry Bispham in 1720 and 1728 for the benefit of that and neighbouring townships ;[107] there are

---

[100] The Receptacle in 1828 contained ten dwellings, each having a sitting-room and pantry below and a chamber above, with a little garden attached. The townships of Haigh, Wigan, Aspull, and Blackrod were to benefit. The donor's charitable bequest of £3,000 was void by the Statutes of Mortmain, but the Earl and Countess of Balcarres decided to give effect to her charitable designs. The income in 1828 was about £110, of which £80 was given to the almspeople, £10 to the chaplain, and £12 on an average to the apothecary.

In 1899 the annual income was found to be £139. Some of the rules—as that against the use of Bohea or green teas—are now inapplicable ; but preference is still given to Haigh people who have worked in the mines ; applicants must be over fifty, and adherents of the Established Church.

[101] Ellen Kindsley charged an estate in Whittington Lane with £1 a year, which was usually distributed with other charities. Ralph Greaves in 1696 gave £20 for apprenticing children or for the poor ; James Monk £20 in 1723 for cloth or apprenticing ; William Higham in 1729 a similar sum for linen or woollen ; and Sir Roger and Lady Bradshagh in 1767 each gave £20 to augment the fund ; it appears to have been lost before 1828 by the practical bankruptcy of the person to whom it had been lent. A poor's stock of £68 5s. existed in 1744, but no information could be obtained in 1828. James Grimshaw in 1822 left £40 for the poor.

For Kindsley's charity in 1899 the rent-charge of £1 on Hilton Farm was found to be paid by the Wigan Coal and Iron Company ; the money is distributed in doles of flannel. All the other charities have been lost.

[102] Frances Dukinfield in 1662 left four closes in Mobberley for the minister of Hindley Chapel, 'So as he should be elected or approved by the trustees for the time being, by any two or more godly ministers, and by the greater number of the householders and masters of families in Hindley,' and for other charitable purposes ; in 1828 £4 was given for the poor of Hindley and Abram from this source, being £2 8s. for the former and £1 12s. for the latter, and laid out in linen cloth. Randle and Mary Collier also left £60 for linen cloth and a further £10 ; and Edward Green and Robert Cooper £30 for the poor ; all was in practice used for gifts of linen.

In 1899 it was found that £7 10s. was paid out of land at Mobberley in respect of the Dukinfield charity ; under a scheme sanctioned in 1890 £2 10s. was paid to the vicar of All Saints', Hindley, £1 to the grammar school, £1 12s. to the trustees of the Abram United Charities, leaving £2 8s. for distribution in Hindley. The other charities have a capital of £151 consols, the interest being spent on flannel, which is distributed on New Year's Day.

Richard Mathe tain lands to tru school and for b the school has bee scheme was in Thomas Winnard the benefit of t Peter s, Hindley the library are als

[103] The estate c about 14 acres of leyhurst es te, called Gr ndlesto ject to a fee-farm Blackburn and hi Gerard in 1828 was for the maint orthodox min ste for the school, an In practice the occupied by the in and the profits of a year n 1828, poor of the two The gross income of which £1 gr Lord Gerard. Th stands on this pro becoming

here also other charities of considerable value, though several gifts have been lost.[108] Dalton has nothing for itself.[109]

WIGAN

Wigan, 1199 ; Wygayn, 1240 ; Wygan, common. Pronounced Wiggin (g hard).

The River Douglas, in its unrestricted days, flowed down from the north and turned to the west round the hill upon which Wigan Church stands, thence running north-westward and northward to the Ribble. The township of Wigan consists of the triangular area inclosed by the river and a line drawn across in a north-easterly direction from one part of the river's course to the other ; in addition there are the district called Scholes on the eastern side, inclosed between the Douglas and a brook once called the Lorington, and now the Clarington,[1] which formerly joined it near the southernmost point of its course ; and a small area to the south of the river. It is curious that Wigan is cut off by the river from the rest of the parish and hundred, and has on the north no marked physical separation from Standish, in a different parish and hundred. The area is 2,188 acres, including 47 of inland water. The population in 1901 numbered 60,764.

The church stands on the crest of the hill, which slopes away rapidly to the south and more gently to the north. To the north-west is the hall or rectory, with Hallgate leading to it, and beyond this again the Mesnes—part of it now a public park—or rectory demesne lands. Further away in the same direction lie the districts known as Gidlow and Brimelow,[2] the latter on the Standish boundary ; while to the west is Woodhouses, near the river.

On the eastern side of the church is a street representing the ancient Roman road to the north, opening out just at that point into the irregular area in which the market was formerly held, and from which Market Street goes off to the north-west. As the main road goes northward it is called in succession Standishgate and Wigan Lane, with Mab's Cross as dividing mark, and has Swinley and Whitley on the

west and Coppull on the east. The ground once again rises as the northern limit is neared, attaining about 250 ft.

The same road, descending south from the church and turning to the west through the more level ground running nearly parallel to the Douglas, is there called Wallgate. The border district to the south of Wallgate is called Poolstock.

Another road, called Millgate, begins at the old Market-place, and proceeding south-east, crosses the Douglas by a bridge,[3] near which was formerly the principal corn-mill of the town, and then goes north-east through the Scholes and Whelley. There is an easterly branch called Hardy Butts, starting near the river and proceeding through Hindley towards Manchester, probably on the line of another ancient Roman road.

Around the church and along the main roads mentioned the town of Wigan grew up. As the head of a great coal-mining district, the Douglas navigation scheme of 1720,[4] and the Leeds and Liverpool Canal, opened in 1774, have been of great service ; the Lancaster Canal followed in 1794, and a branch to Leigh connected the town with the Worsley Canal. The railway companies have also contributed to the progress of the place ; the London & North Western Company's main line from London to Scotland passes through the place,[5] having a station in Wallgate, to the south of the church. The Lancashire and Yorkshire Company's Liverpool and Bury line, opened in 1848, has a station (1860) in Wallgate, near to the church ; the company's Wigan and Southport branch (1855) turns in here. More recently the Great Central Railway has found access to the town, having a station near Millgate, opened in 1892.

Wigan is identified with the Coccium of the Antonine Itinerary ; it stands at the point where the Roman road, north and south, was joined by another important road from Manchester. Its position on a hilltop, surrounded on two sides of its triangular area by a rapid stream, suggests that it had been a British fort. Various Roman remains have been found.[6]

The town continued to grow and prosper throughout the mediaeval period, and Leland thus describes

[108] Henry Prescot in 1638 gave £20 for poor householders ; Richard Walthew in 1643 gave £130 ; James Fairclough, £250, and others smaller sums ; the 1829 information concerning the total sum of £446 13s. 4d. was that in 1771 £376 had been placed out on private security. James Fairclough also gave £100 to establish a bread charity, and in 1828 £5 a year was received from the rents of the Moss estate, and added to the share of Edmund Molyneux's benefaction. Thomas Barton in 1674 gave to the poor of Upholland £3 6s. 8d. charged on an estate there, and paid in 1828 ; Thomas Mawdesley, by his will of 1728, devised his copyhold lands—the Little, Rushy, and Meadow Baryards—to the use of the poor as an addition to 'Barton's dole' ; in 1828 £17 10s. was received, and, with the preceding gift, divided among the poor in sums of 2s. or 2s. 6d. The Rev. Thomas Holme in 1803 left £100 for a gift of blankets ; it was in operation in 1828.

Of the above the Fairclough charity has benefited by the working of mines, and now has an income of £40 from the Moss estate and £124 from consols aris-

its appearance about 1536 : 'Wigan paved ; as big as Warrington and better builded. There is one parish church amid the town. Some merchants, some artificers, some farmers.'[7]

Apart from its internal growth, the history of Wigan is interesting on account of the part taken in the Civil War. The townspeople were Royalist,[8] and the Earl of Derby appeared to make it his head quarters, its central position rendering it very fit for the purpose. He placed a garrison there,[9] but on 1 April 1643, the town was captured by the Parliamentary forces under Colonel Holland, after only two hours' resistance. Many prisoners were taken, and the soldiers were allowed to plunder and carry away what they could.[10] The Earl of Derby, who was 12 miles away, marched to its relief, but hearing that the town had surrendered, and that the Parliamentary forces had retired after breaking down some of the defensive works, he desisted and went to Lathom.[11] A second assault and capture took place three weeks later.[12] In 1648 Duke Hamilton's forces occupied Wigan after their defeat by Cromwell near Preston, but after plundering the people 'almost to their skins,' retired to Warrington, pursued by Cromwell.[13] A pestilence followed.[14]

When, in August 1651, the Earl of Derby was raising a force for Charles II, he again tried to secure Wigan. On 26 August a hot fight took place in Wigan Lane between his forces and those of Colonel Lilburne. At first the former were victorious, but a reserve of horse coming to Lilburne's assistance, put the Royalists to flight. Lord Derby took refuge in Wigan for a brief time, and after his wounds had been dressed, he went south to join Charles at Worcester. Sir Thomas Tyldesley and other notable Royalists were killed in the battle.[15]

The Restoration and Revolution do not appear to have affected Wigan much.[16] Some of those condemned for participation in the rising of 1715 were executed here.[17] The Young Pretender with his Highland army passed through the town on 28 November 1745, on his way to Manchester, and again on 10–11 December on his retreat northward. The inhabitants were not molested, but no recruits joined the force.[18]

At present the whole of the district is thickly populated, the industrial town of Wigan occupying the greater part of the township, whilst its collieries, factories, &c., fill the atmosphere with smoke. There is, however, a fringe of open country beyond the town itself, on the north, and here are arable and pasture lands, the crops raised being chiefly potatoes and oats. The soil is clayey and sandy. The woodlands of Haigh in the adjoining township make an agreeable background. The Douglas, turning many a factory wheel on its way, winds erratically across the district. The south-westerly part of the township lies very low, and is almost always flooded, the result of frequent subsidences of the ground.

The worthies of the town include Ralph Brooke or Brooksmouth, York Herald in the time of Elizabeth ;[19] Henry Mason, divine and benefactor, 1573 to 1647 ;[20] John Leland, nonconformist divine and apologist for Christianity, who died 1766 ;[21] Anthony Wilson, alias Henry Bromley, publisher of catalogues of Engraved British Portraits, 1793 ;[22] John Fairclough, a minor Jesuit writer, 1787 to 1832 ;[23] John Roby, author of the romances entitled Traditions of Lancashire, 1795 to 1850 ;[24] John Howard Marsden, antiquary, 1803 to 1891 ;[25] John C. Prince, minor poet, 1808 to 1866 ;[26] and John Fitchett Marsh, antiquary, 1818 to 1880.[27]

A number of tokens were issued by local tradesmen in the 17th century.[28]

The printing press is said to have been introduced into Wigan about 1760 ; books dated in 1780 and later years are known.[29] There are three newspapers, two published three times a week and the other weekly.[30]

---

7 Itin. vii, 47.

8 'Wigan was better manned with soldiers than Preston, it being the next garrison to the earl's house and the most malignant town in all the county ; for there were (for anything that was heard) not many in it that favoured the Parliament ;' Lancs. War (Chet. Soc.), 16. Wigan, however, had joined in the Protestation of 1642 ; Pal. Note Bk. i, 81.

9 The Wigan garrison, 'full of desperate cavaliers,' had made several assaults upon Bolton ; Lancs. War, 32 ; Civil War Tracts (Chet. Soc.), 63, 81–3.

10 Lancs. War, 36 ; also Stanley Papers, (Chet. Soc.), iii, p. lxxxvi, where a facsimile of the Countess of Derby's letter, announcing its fall, is given. See also Civil War Tracts, 93, 225–7.

11 Lancs. War, loc. cit.

12 Civil War Tracts, 98.

13 Ibid. 263 ; 'a great and poor town, and very malignant,' is Cromwell's description of the place ; see Carlyle, Cromwell Let. i, 286, &c., for the details.

14 Civil War Tracts, 278 ; there were 'two thousand poor, who for three months and upwards had been restrained, no relief to be had for them in the ordinary course of law, there being none at present (April 1649) to act as justices of the peace.' The Wigan registers contain many entries referring to the deaths from plague, the last burial being on 23 July 1649.

A petition by the mayor and others in 1660, addressed to Charles II, states that the people of the town had garrisoned it at their own charge for the king ; that it had been seven times plundered, burdened with free quarters, &c., by the Parliament army ; and that many estates had been sequestered ; Cal. S.P. Dom. 1660–1, p. 119.

15 Stanley Papers (Chet. Soc.), clxxxiv–ix. For the monument to Sir T. Tyldesley near the spot where he fell, see cccxxxiii ; Lancs. and Ches. Hist. and Geneal. Notes, iii, 62.

A graphic account of the battle is given in Lancs. War, 74–6.

16 Ogilby, writing about 1670, called it 'a well-built town, governed by a mayor, recorder and twelve aldermen, &c., and electing Parliament men.' It had two markets, on Monday and Friday, but the former was discontinued, and three fairs. It was noted for its pit coal, ironworks, and other manufactures. A somewhat later description, by Dr. Kuerden, giving many details, may be read in Local Glean. Lancs. and Ches. i, 209, 211, 212, 214.

Bishop Cartwright procured an address to James II from the mayor and corporation in 1687 ; Bridgeman, op. cit. 570. Their action was not popular ; Hist. MSS. Com. Rep. xiv, App. iv, 189.

Several persons went to Chester in 1687 to be touched by the king for the evil ; their names are given in Trans. Hist. Soc. i, 26.

17 See Lancs. and Ches. Antiq. Soc. iii,

70. James Blundell, James Finch, John Macilliwray, William Whalley, and James Burn, who had been tried and sentenced at Preston, were executed at Wigan 10 Feb. 1716 ; see Pal. Note Bk. iv, 93.

18 The town was then famous for its manufactures of coverlets, rugs, blankets, and other sorts of bedding, brass, copper, &c., as well as for the adjacent Cannel coal mines ; Ray, Hist. of Rebellion, 154.

There is a brief notice of the place as it appeared in 1791 in Pal. Note Bk. iii, 275, and a description written in 1825 in Baines, Lancs. Dir. ii, 610.

19 Pal. Note Bk. iii, 33.

20 Dict. Nat. Biog.   21 Ibid.   22 Ibid.

23 Gillow, Bibl. Dict. of Engl. Cath. ii, 218.

24 Dict. Nat. Biog. For a note on the Rev. James Clayton of Wigan, the inventor of gas, see Local Glean. Lancs. and Ches. i, 140, 248.

25 Dict. Nat. Biog.   26 Ibid.   27 Ibid.

28 Lancs. and Ches. Antiq. Soc. v, 93, 94.

29 See Local Glean. Lancs. and Ches. i, ii. The 1780 book was a translation of Gessner's Death of Abel, printed by R. Ferguson, ii, 57. The 'Local Catalogue' issued from the Wigan Free Library gives a list of nineteen books printed at Wigan between 1780 and 1796. At the end is a list of printers.

30 The offices of the Examiner were formerly the Public Hall or Mechanics' Institute.

Coal-mining is the characteristic trade of the place, but there are large cotton mills also; ginghams, &c., are made. Forges, iron and brass foundries, wagon, screw and nail, oil and grease works, and breweries are also in operation. The ancient walk-mills show that cloth was made here from early times. A goldsmith was killed at Wigan in 1341.[31] The potters' right to dig clay on the wastes was vindicated in 1619.[32] 'Digging and delving mines for coals' was common in 1595.[33] Bell-founding is a lost trade; it was formerly in the hands of the Scott and Ashton families.[34]

In 1624 Bishop Bridgeman notified his objection to the 'barbarous and beastly game of bear baiting' at the wakes; but on the mayor's request he allowed the baiting to take place on the market hill after the market was over and the people had packed up their wares.[35]

An old Wigan nursery rhyme is printed in Harland and Wilkinson's *Legends.*[36]

The stocks were formerly near the main entrance to the churchyard from Wallgate. There was a cross in the market place, where proclamations were made, and the base of Mab's Cross, already mentioned, is in Standishgate.[36a]

There was formerly a spa in Scholes.[36b]

The curfew bell, anciently rung at eight o'clock, was in 1881 rung at half-past ten.[37]

A body of volunteers, called the Wigan Rifles, was raised in 1804.[38] The present volunteer force consists of five companies of the 6th battalion of the Manchester Regiment.

MANOR In Domesday Book *WIGAN* is not named; it was only 'the church of the manor' of Newton,[39] and a century later it is the church that brings it forward once more, a resident vicar being appointed.[40] The rectors were thus from before the Conquest until recently lords of the manor of Wigan under the lords of Newton, and the rectory was the hall. From the account of them already given it will be seen that a large number were non-resident, and exercised their authority by deputies.

Among the rights which gave most trouble to the rectors were those over the mills. Rector Fleetwood in the first year of his incumbency (1571) had insti-

tuted a suit against Hugh, Gilbert, and James Langshaw to recover seisin of two ancient water-mills, described as walk mills.[41] The dispute went on for many years.[42] Bishop Bridgeman, thirty years later, complained that William Langshaw was endeavouring to deprive the rector of his ownership of the mill.[43] The mills were situated at Coppull and a little lower down the river by the school; in 1627 they paid a rent of £4 a year to the rector.[44]

The corn mills, of which in the year just named there were five, also caused trouble. The principal was that on the Douglas in Millgate, of which Miles Leatherbarrow was the tenant in 1617.[45] In Rector Fleetwood's time a new water corn-mill was erected by Miles Gerard of Ince upon Lorington or Clarington Brook, the boundary of the manors of Wigan and Ince, and the water-course was diverted to feed it. The rectors complained of the injustice done to them, but Dr. Bridgeman allowed the mill to stand on condition that 20s. a year should be paid for tithe.[46]

In his first year Dr. Bridgeman received £16 13s. 2d. as manor rents,[47] and 10s. each for seven mortuaries.[48]

BOROUGH It is an indication that there was a strong community existing around the church to find one of the absentee rectors, the busy official John Maunsel, procuring from the king a charter creating a borough. This was granted on 26 August 1246 to John Maunsel; the town of Wigan was to be a borough and a free borough for ever; the burgesses should have a gild merchant, with a hanse and all the liberties and free customs pertaining to such a gild; and no one but a member of the gild should do any business in the borough except by consent of the burgesses. Further, to the burgesses and their heirs the king conceded that they should have soke, sac, toll, theam, and attachment within the borough, infangenthef, utfangenthef; that they should throughout the country and sea ports be free of toll, lastage, pontage, passage, and stallage; that they should do no suit to county or wapentake for tenements within the borough; also that traders, even foreigners, provided they entered England peaceably and with the king's leave, should be allowed to pass in safety to and from the borough with their merchandise upon paying the usual dues.[49]

[31] Assize R. 430, m. 12 d.

[32] Bridgeman, *Wigan Ch.* 222.

[33] Ibid. 161; see also 242. *The Industries of Wigan*, by H. T. Folkard, R. Betley, and C. M. Percy, published in 1889, gives an account of the development of coal-mining and other trades.

[34] J. P. Earwaker, *Trans. Hist. Soc.* (new ser.), vi, 170; *N. and Q.* (Ser. 10), v, 257. The will of John Scott was proved in 1648, and that of Jeffrey Scott in 1665. William Scott occurs 1670–1700; R. Ashton 1703–17, and Luke Ashton 1723–50.

[35] Bridgeman, op. cit. 286.

[36] Op. cit. 182.

[36a] *Lancs. and Ches. Antiq. Soc.* xix, 228, 232.

[36b] Ibid. 234; quoting from *England Described*, 1788. It had been ruined by 1824; Baines, *Lancs. Dir.* ii, 612.

[37] *Lancs. and Ches. Hist. and Geneal. Notes*, ii, 33.

[38] *Local Glean. Lancs. and Ches.* ii, 182, 217. The Earl of Balcarres was colonel; there were eight companies, and 552 men.

[39] *V.C.H. Lancs.* i, 286.

[40] Farrer, *Lancs. Pipe R.* 436. See also *Engl. Hist. Rev.* v, 395.

[41] Bridgeman, op cit. 130. In 1316 Edmund de Standish granted to Aymory the Fuller land adjoining a narrow lane leading towards the Coppedhull mill; Crosse D. (Trans. Hist. Soc.), n. 27.

[42] Bridgeman, op. cit. 144–6.

[43] Ibid. 225. The defendant relied upon the charter of John Maunsel; he was a burgess of Wigan, and had by descent from his ancestors divers burgages in the said borough; and those ancestors had enjoyed his share in the mills as parcel of their own inheritance, paying the accustomed rent for the same. The rector's right to the mills, as part of his glebe, was affirmed by a decree of June 1618; ibid. 227, 229.

[44] Ibid. 309.

[45] Ibid. 220, 231. Miles seems to have claimed ownership. He died early in 1628, and his widow Alice begged that either she or her son Orlando might be admitted as tenant. The bishop told her to take comfort, as he had never dealt unkindly with his tenants; but as his

right to this mill had been questioned he had determined to take it into his own hands for a time that there might be no possibility of dispute in future. On receiving this answer the widow refused to give up possession, and Lord and Lady Strange took up her cause. The bishop promised them that the widow should have the mill after a while; but as she still remained obstinate, the matter came before the quarter sessions. It was not till the end of March 1630 that she finally submitted, gave up the key, and allowed the bishop to take possession. She retained it for three weeks, and then admitted her as tenant; ibid. 320–8.

[46] Ibid. 240, 241. Two horse-mills were allowed to stand, rent being paid to the lord; ibid. 240, 243.

[47] Ibid. 189.   [48] Ibid. 192.

[49] This charter is known by its recital in that of Edw. II; see Bridgeman, op. cit. 9, 32. The charters are printed in Sinclair's *Hist. of Wigan*. See Chart. R. 7 Edw. II, m. 4, 3; 24 Edw. III, 145, m. 2, 4; m. 3, 7. The charter of 1314 is still preserved at Wigan.

The rector's concomitant charter grants that the burgesses of Wigan and their heirs and assigns should have their free town, with all rights, customs, and liberties as stated in the king's charter ; that each burgess should have to his burgage 5 roods of land ; that they should grind at the rector's mill to the twentieth measure without payment, should have from his wood sufficient for building and burning, quittance of pannage and other easements ; and that they should have their pleas in portmote once in three weeks, with verdict of twelve men and amercements by the same ; paying annually to the rector 12d. a year for each burgage for all services. Robert Banastre, lord of Makerfield and patron of the church, added his confirmation ; as did also Roger, Bishop of Lichfield.[50]

The burgesses,[51] regarded as equals, thus became the free tenants of the rector, as lord of the manor, with the usual liberties, and the special privilege of a portmote. The royal charter looks on the place as a trading centre and gives internal and external privileges accordingly ; these last, which the rector could not give, were doubtless the reason for invoking the king's help. A later charter, 1257–8, granted that the rectors should have a market at their borough of Wigan on Monday in every week, and two fairs there of three days each, viz., on the vigil, day and morrow of the Ascension and of All Saints.[52]

In 1292 Adam de Walton, then rector, was called upon to show by what warrant he claimed certain liberties ; it was asserted that Master Adam and his bailiffs had exceeded the terms of the charters by trying persons accused of felonies beyond their jurisdiction, when those persons had placed themselves on a jury of their country. In reply to particular charges the community of the vill appeared by twelve men of the vill. As to the court and liberty of the vill they said that these belonged to the rector, and they were suitors there. The jury decided that soke and sac and other liberties had been granted to the burgesses, who did not claim them, and not to the rector, who did ; let them therefore be taken into the king's hands. As to the taking of emends of the assize of bread and beer on the market and fair days the rector's claim was allowed ; but as he had punished some frequent transgressors at his discretion and not judicially, he was at the king's mercy.[53] The

liberties claimed by the rectors were afterwards restored, on the application of the guardian of Robert Banastre's heiress.[54]

The commonalty of Wigan were sued for a debt in 1304.[55]

In 1314 Robert de Clitheroe obtained from the king a confirmation of the charter of 1246.[56]

About 1328 the rector complained that the burgesses, his tenants, every day held a market among themselves, and with strangers, in divers goods, although these be ill-gotten or stolen ; taking toll for such merchandise and appropriating it to themselves. They also made assay of bread and tasting of beer every day except Monday, taking amercements and profits by force and power ; all to the prejudice of the rector's market.[57] Possibly it was on this account that the charter was confirmed in 1329.[58]

A further confirmation was granted in 1350 ;[59] with a special indemnity to the rector and the burgesses for any abuse or non-claim of the liberties and acquittances of former charters. The king also granted a view of frankpledge, freedom from the sheriff's tourn, cognizance by the bailiffs of the rector of all pleas concerning lands, tenures, contracts, &c., within the borough ; with many similar and complementary liberties. 'Moreover, whereas there has been a frequent concourse at the said borough, as well of merchants and others, for the sake of trading and otherwise,' the rectors, as lords of the borough, might for ever 'have a certain seal, by us to be ordained, of two pieces, as is of custom to be used, for recognisances of debts there according to the form of the statutes published for merchants ; and that the greater part of the seal aforesaid may remain in the custody of the mayor or keeper of the borough aforesaid for the time being, or other private person of the greater or more discreet men of the borough to be chosen for this purpose (with the assent of the rector) if there shall not be a mayor or keeper there.'[60]

As a result of this charter suits by Wigan people were frequently stopped in the assize court by the bailiffs of the rector appearing to claim the case as one for the local court.[61] Another result was probably the regular election of a mayor, the language of the charter implying that the burgesses had not hitherto had such a generally recognized head. There are numerous instances of 'statutes merchant' before

[50] Bridgeman, op. cit. 9, 10. Not many years later William de Occleshaw granted to Simon son of Payn de Warrington and Emma his wife a burgage and an acre of land in Wigan, rendering to the rector of Wigan 12d. yearly, and to the grantor a peppercorn. In 1284 Simon Payn, son of the said Simon (son of) Payn, claimed the land ; Assize R. 1268, m. 11. Simon Payn and Amabil his wife were engaged in suits in 1292 ; Assize R. 408, m. 77d. 60. Simon Payn of Wigan obtained a house and land here in 1336 ; Final Conc. (Rec. Soc. Lancs. and Ches.), ii, 101.

[51] There does not seem to be any means of ascertaining the number of burgages. The earliest poll-book, 1627, shows that there were then about a hundred in-burgesses, but does not state their qualifications ; Sinclair, Wigan, i, 197.

[52] Bridgeman, op. cit. 33. A charter for a fair at All Saints and a market on Monday had been secured in 1245 ; Cal. Chart. R. 1226–57, p. 284. In 1314 the

All Saints' fair was changed to the vigil, day, and morrow of St. Wilfrid the Bishop ; Chart. R. 7 Edw. II, m. 4, 4 d. ; but in 1329 reverted to the old day ; ibid. 3 Edw. III, m. 6, 14. The autumn fair was afterwards held on the vigil, feast, and morrow of St. Luke ; Wm. Smith, Descr. of Engl. 1588 ; Hist. MSS. Com. Rep. xiv, App. iv, 4.

[53] Bridgeman, op. cit. 31–6, from Plac. de Quo War. (Rec. Com.), 371, 372. The rector stated that he did not claim utfangenthef, though named in the charter.

[54] Bridgeman, op. cit. 37. There exists a petition by the people of Wigan for the restoration of their franchises made after the death of Edmund, Earl of Lancaster, 1296 ; Anct. Petitions, P.R.O. 316, E 225.

[55] De Banco R. 151, m. 112. In 1307 there were complaints that Welshmen, returning probably from the Scottish wars, had been maltreated and killed at Wigan ; Assize R. 422, m. 4 d.

[56] Bridgeman, op. cit. 41.

the mayor of Wigan commencing about 1370.[62] From a petition of Rector Wyot (1506–19) it appears that, 'for a long time past,' the custom had been that on a vacancy in the mayoralty the burgesses elected three of their number and presented them to the rector, who chose one to act for the ensuing year.[63]

The rectors in the time of Henry VIII, and probably much earlier, exercised their authority as lords of the borough through a steward and a bailiff, with an under-steward who was clerk of the court.[64]

About 1560 Bishop Stanley began to assert his rights as lord of the manor, and he challenged the claim to hold markets,[65] fairs, and courts leet put forward and exercised by the mayor and burgesses. Those accused of withdrawing 'did not know' whether suit was due to the rector's law-day or leet, or to his three weeks court, though 'most of them had done so, until now of late'; and they endeavoured to draw attention from this aspect of the question by an allegation of outrage upon the mayor by one of the bishop's servants. Nothing seems to have been done, except that the bishop confirmed Maunsel's charter to the burgesses.[66] He yielded 'upon fear and for a fine of money received,' according to Dr. Bridgeman.[67]

Under Rector Fleetwood the struggle was more determined. The corporation about 1583 laid claim to the lordship of the manor, as lords improving the wastes and commons, and letting the houses built thereupon; also digging for coal within the demesnes of the manor, and in many other ways usurping the rector's rights. They stated that a mayor, two bailiffs, and sundry burgesses were annually elected for the town and borough of Wigan, which had also five aldermen, the Earl of Derby being one; that Maunsel's charter gave the burgesses all the liberties in dispute; and that the moot-hall was their inheritance. They had kept courts, taken waifs and strays, &c., in accordance with their right. The rector's reply traversed all this, alleging in particular that the burgesses had no grant enabling them to elect a mayor to be head of the corporation, though they had done so 'for divers years' by usurpation, and that the appointment of aldermen was a recent usage, 'without due rite.'[68] A charter was granted about this time, viz. in 1585.[69]

A decree in the nature of a compromise was made in 1596 by the Chancellor of the Duchy. It was ordered that the corporation should keep such courts as they had usually kept, except the leets, and take the profits to their own uses; that, as to the leets,

the rector should appoint a steward to sit with the mayor and burgesses or their steward and take half the profits. Clay and stone might be dug as customary, but the ways must be mended as quickly as possible, and any damage done to the moat round the rectory must be repaired. As to the fairs and markets and the profits arising from them, the corporation should have them as before, but the rector's tenants must not be required to pay any increase upon the customary tolls. The rents claimed by the rector must be paid, with arrears. The question as to the improvement of the wastes does not seem to have been decided.[70]

The corporation were then left at peace for twenty years. Dr. Massie seems to have been very yielding.[71] Bishop Bridgeman, however, an able man and strong in the royal favour, upon being appointed to the rectory made a vigorous and fairly successful effort to recover certain of his manorial rights as against the corporation.[72] The ownership of the markets and fairs, with the tolls belonging to them, had been held by the town for upwards of fifty years. On 17 October 1617, being the eve of the fair, the rector sent his man to the mayor, entreating him not to deal or meddle with the fair until the controversy as to all these matters had been decided, and inviting the mayor and aldermen, &c., to meet him at the pentice chamber next morning. At this conference the rector desired them to allow him the rights his predecessors had enjoyed, without any lawsuits; they answered that he had what his predecessors had, and ought not to ask more. The mayor was bold enough to challenge the rector's right to the manor, but met no support from the burgesses, who acknowledged their obligation to pay 12d. for each burgage plot. On matters of land-ownership no opposition was made; but when the rector claimed the fairs, markets, courts leet, courts of pleas, and courts baron and other privileges, the burgesses' reply seems to have been firm and unanimous: 'They had a right to them and hoped so to prove in law.' No compromise was possible, the answer being that they were 'all sworn to maintain the privileges of the town.'[73]

A special tribunal was appointed, and at the beginning of 1619 a decision was given: the rector was lord of the manor, with a right to the wastes and court baron and suit and service of the freeholders and inhabitants; the moot-hall to be common to the rector and corporation for the keeping of their courts, of which the pentice plea and court of pleas should be the corporation's, the leets at Easter and Michaelmas being adjudged, the former to the rector and the latter to the corporation; the Ascension-day fair and

[62] Early in 1406 Adam de Birkhead, mayor of Wigan, and William de Medewall, clerk, for taking recognizances of debts at Wigan, certified that in March, 1372-3, Sir William de Atherton came before Thomas de Heywood, then mayor, and Thomas Clerk, then clerk, and acknowledged that he owed his brother, Nicholas de Atherton, £100 sterling; which he ought to have paid at the Christmas next following, but had not done so; Pal. of Lanc. Chan. Misc. bdle. i, file 9, m. 38.

[63] Bridgeman, op. cit. 72.

[64] Ibid. 101. Sir Thomas Langton, who, as lord of Newton, was chief lord of the manor, about this time laboured hard to secure appointment as the rector's

steward, and though rejected he took it upon himself to act, making himself very obnoxious to the corporation. In 1539 the mayor and burgesses complained that whereas it had been their custom to elect a mayor on the Saturday after Michaelmas Day, Sir Thomas with a number of associates had disturbed the election, and declared that he would not take Adam Bankes for mayor, though he had been duly chosen. A few weeks afterwards there was an invasion of the town by the Langton faction, which necessitated an inquiry by the Crown. It then appeared that the disturbers asserted the election of mayor to belong to the rector of Wigan or his steward; ibid. 108-11.

[65] A book of tolls 1561-7 is among

Lord Kenyon's deeds; Hist. MSS. Com. Rep. xiv, App. iv, 4.

[66] Bridgeman, op. cit. 133-8.

[67] Ibid. 213.

[68] Ibid. 147-57.

[69] A contemporary paper copy is extant at Wigan. In Pal. of Lanc. Plea R. 253, m. 26, are copies of the earlier charters.

[70] Bridgeman, op. cit. 157, 158.

[71] Ibid. 213. Dr. Bridgeman affirmed that 'none of his predecessors, except Dr. Massie, were without the use and possession of all those things which he claimed; or did at least claim and sue for them as Mr. Fleetwood did.' Dr. Massie was rector from 1605 to 1615.

[72] Ibid. 205. [73] Ibid. 213-15.

the Monday market to be the rector's, but St. Luke's fair and the Friday market to be the corporation's.[71]

In October 1620 the mayor of Wigan appeared in the moot-hall where the justices were sitting at quarter-sessions, and, 'putting on his hat before them,' claimed the ordering of the alehouses in Wigan, as belonging to his leet. The justices objected to his manners, and as he refused to find sureties for good behaviour sent him to prison; but their action was annulled, though the mayor's action for false imprisonment also failed.[75]

Bishop Bridgeman in 1622 claimed the pentice chamber in the moot-hall as built upon his waste within living memory, and appears to have succeeded.[76] His next correction of the assumptions of the corporation was provoked by the latter; they refused liberty to one William Brown to sell his goods, on the ground that he was not a burgess. The bishop pointed out that they had no right to elect burgesses; the true burgesses were those who paid the lord of the manor 12d. rent for a burgage, and he had made William Brown a burgess by selling to him a burgage house recently bought of Thomas Gerard of Ince. The mayor and burgesses were by this time convinced that it was useless to contend with their lord; they made no demur, and asked him to appoint his son Orlando as one of their aldermen; he, however, did not judge it well to do so.[77]

From this time, 1624, till after the Restoration there appears to be no record of any dispute between rector and corporation. It can scarcely be doubted that the Commonwealth period would be favourable to the latter, and when in 1662 Sir Orlando Bridgeman was selected as arbitrator in a fresh misunderstanding, he ruled that though the rector was lord of the manor and must keep a court baron, yet in view of the municipal court of pleas it was of little importance except for inquiring into the chief rents due to the rector, and preventing encroachments on the waste. Hence the court baron was to be held once in two years only, in the moot-hall; no pleas were to be held between party and party; and the mayor and such aldermen as had been mayors should be exempt from attending. The streets and wastes were to be regulated as to encroachments by the rector and mayor. Sir Orlando's father had, by his advice, leased the rector's Ascensiontide fair and weekly market to the corporation; and the arbitrator recommended the continuance of this system as 'a great means to continue peace and goodwill' between the parties, a lease, renewable, for 21 years being granted at a rent of five marks a year. The lease included the yearly fair, weekly market, and court leet, and all tolls, courts, piccage, stallages, profits, commodities, and emoluments belonging to them.[78]

Forty years ago the corporation purchased the manorial rights, an agreement being made 9 July 1860 between the rector and patron on the one side, and the mayor, aldermen, and burgesses on the other. The rights transferred were the summer fair, the Monday market, and various tolls; quit rents and manorial rights in slips of waste lying uninclosed adjoining streets in the borough and in mines under these slips; rights in Bottling Wood and the wastes; and the ancient quit rents amounting to £45 3s. 4d. The price paid was £2,800. The conveyance was signed by the rector on 2 September 1861.[79]

The charter of 1662, under which the borough was governed down to the Municipal Corporations Act of 1835, confirmed to the mayor, bailiffs, and burgesses of Wigan all their ancient liberties, and ordained that the corporation should consist of a mayor and eleven other aldermen, a recorder, two bailiffs, and a common clerk. The mayor was to be not only a magistrate for the borough, but also for the county, but this privilege was not maintained.[80] A supplementary charter was granted by James II in 1685,[81] providing in particular that eighteen burgesses might be chosen to act as 'assistants,' so that there should be a common council of thirty-two in all. The mayor was to be chosen yearly 'on the Sabbath day next after the feast of St. Michael.' The corporation, like others of the time, was a close or self-electing one, the townsmen being able to make their wishes known only through the jury and court leet. The mayor was coroner *ex officio*.[82]

The election of burgesses was in the jury and court leet. The corporation had the power of admitting non-resident and honorary burgesses to vote at elections without limitation; in 1802 they made a hundred burgesses in order to rid themselves of the Duke of Portland's 'patronage.'[83]

Under the Act of 1835 Wigan was classed with other boroughs having a commission of the peace; it was divided into five wards, to each of which were assigned two aldermen and six councillors.[84] In 1888 it

---

[74] Bridgeman, op. cit. 221, 222. The bishop, accordingly, as rector, held his first court leet and court baron for the manor of Wigan just after Easter 1619, and at Ascension-tide his first fair. The matter was of great importance as preserving the lord's rights, but the profits of the courts were barely sufficient to pay the fees of the officers; ibid. 237.

The following year he discharged one William Brown from his service because though no burgess he had served in the mayor's court, 'as they call it,' upon the jury. He did so because in former times the corporation had claimed the courts as their own on finding that servants of the rector had sued or served in them; ibid. 270, 271.

[75] Ibid. 265, 266.

[76] Ibid. 268, 274. On Christmas-eve in the same year, 'and properly no market day,' he prohibited the serjeants and bailiffs of the town from receiving toll, 'because the wastes and streets are the parson's'; and the jury were instructed to find that the town officers had wronged the lord of the manor by receiving such tolls on the Saturday before the wake day. The jury demurred to the contention that the streets were part of the wastes, but gave way, and the tolls collected that day were given to the rector; ibid. 274.

[77] Bridgeman, op. cit. 287. The dispute marks another step in the growth of the rights of the community; first was the election of mayor; next, the appointment of aldermen; and thirdly, the co-option of burgesses. The last was important, because the burgage plots had a tendency to become the possession of a very few persons.

[78] Bridgeman, op. cit. 486-91. See also *Hist. MSS. Com. Rep.* xiv, App. iv, 441, for a declaration in this sense by the corporation in 1708.

In 1743 Dr. Roger Bridgeman refused to renew the lease, and a lawsuit followed which lasted for many years; 'the result

became a county borough, and in the following year a rearrangement of the wards was authorized ; the borough was divided into ten wards, each with one alderman and three councillors, the membership of the council being thus unchanged in number.[85] The inclusion of Pemberton in 1904 has caused the increase of the council to fifty-six members, chosen from fourteen wards.

The old town hall, rebuilt in 1720 at the expense of the members for the borough, stood at the western side of the market-place. It was pulled down and rebuilt in the first half of last century. It stood on pillars, the space underneath being subsequently filled with shops. The moot-hall, a stone building in Wallgate, with meeting-room above and shops below, was demolished in 1869, and 'the new town hall' in 1882, the present town hall and borough courts having been finished in 1867. A new council chamber was opened in 1890. The county police courts date from 1888. The Fish-stones, which were at the northern side of the market place, were removed in 1866. The new market hall was opened in 1877 ; there is a separate fish market. The ancient cloth hall was superseded by a commercial hall in the market-place, erected in 1816.

The Public Libraries Act was adopted in 1876, and two years later there was opened the new free library building, presented to the town by Thomas Taylor, who died in 1892. A Powell Boys' Reading-room, presented by the member for the borough, was added in 1895. A school board was created in 1872. The mining college was founded in 1858 ; in 1903 the present mining and technical building was opened.

The corporation have acquired or inaugurated a number of works and institutions for the health and convenience of the people. The first Wigan Water Act was passed in 1764 ; the waterworks were purchased by the corporation in 1855 ; the gasworks, established in 1822, were acquired in 1875 ; and the tramways, opened in 1880, in 1902. An electric-power station was erected in 1900, and the following year the corporation electric tramways started running. The Mesnes Park was opened in 1878, the sewerage works in 1881, public baths in 1882, and a sanatorium in 1889. Victoria Hall was built in 1902. The cemetery was established in 1856.

A dispensary was started in 1798, and a building in King Street provided in 1801, now the Savings Bank. The Royal Albert Edward Infirmary was opened by the King, then Prince of Wales, in 1873.

A court of quarter-sessions was granted to the borough in 1886.

Impressions of the borough seal of the 15th century are known.[86] The device upon it—the moot-hall—is used as a coat of arms for the borough.

As a borough Wigan sent two burgesses to the Parliaments of 1295 and 1306, but not again until 1547. From this year the borough regularly returned two members until 1885, except during the Commonwealth, when owing to its royalist tendencies it was disfranchised by Cromwell.[87] In the 17th century the burgesses were of two classes—in and out ; the latter were principally neighbouring gentry, and do not seem to have availed themselves to any great extent of the privilege of voting. On the other hand a large number of the townsmen made strenuous efforts to obtain a vote, and in 1639 the mayor, bailiffs, and burgesses prepared a memorial to Parliament on the subject. This stated that they were 'an ancient corporation by prescription, and that all such persons as are or have been burgesses of that corporation have always been received into that corporation by election made by the burgesses for the time present of that corporation, and have been afterwards sworn and enrolled as burgesses in the burgess roll,' and that from time immemorial only such enrolled burgesses had voted for the burgesses who served in the Parliament ; but at the recent election, after the choice had been made—but apparently before a formal declaration— 'divers inferior persons, labourers, and handicraftsmen, being free only to trade within the said town and not enrolled burgesses,' demanded voices. The mayor and bailiffs had replied asking them 'to make it to appear that they or any others of their condition had any time formerly any voices in election of the burgesses for the Parliament' ; they could not prove anything of the sort, and so their votes were not allowed ; but the mayor and bailiffs, at the instance of the elected burgesses, judged it right to inform the Parliament concerning the matter.[88] By the Redistribution Act of 1885 Wigan was allowed but one member instead of two as previously.

A number of families come into prominence from time to time in the records. One of the early ones took a surname from Wigan itself,[89] another from Scholes.[90] Other surnames were Jew,[91] Botling,[92]

[85] The central ward is called All Saints ; to the north is Swinley ward, and to the west of both St. Andrew's ward. The small but populous district in the south has three wards, Victoria and St. Thomas, on the west and east, being divided by Wallgate ; and Poolstock, to the south of the Douglas. Scholes has four wards : St. George and St. Patrick the innermost, divided by the street called Scholes ; and Lindsay and St. Catherine outside, divided by Whelley.

[86] *Lancs. and Ches. Hist. and Geneal. Notes,* iii, 100 ; an impression of it occurs among the De Trafford deeds.

[87] Pink and Beaven, *Parl. Rep. of Lancs.* 217, where an account of the members will be found.

[88] Sinclair, *Wigan,* i, 222.

[89] In 1292 in various suits appear Quenilda widow of Nigel de Wigan, Thurstan de Wigan, Henry son of Hugh de Wigan, and others ; Assize R. 408, m. 54 d, 97, &c.

Birkhead,[93] Duxbury,[94] Preston,[95] Ford,[96] and Scott.[97] The Crosse family, afterwards of Liverpool and Chorley, were long closely connected with

CROSSE. *Quarterly gules and or a cross potent argent in the first and fourth quarters.*

Wigan : Adam del Crosse[98] appears in 1277, his son John in the first half of the 14th century.[99] John's son Thurstan[100] was followed by Hugh del Crosse his son,[101] after whose death the property went to Richard del Crosse of Wigan and Liverpool. He may have

[93] This family held a good position in the town, and furnished several of the mayors. There is a quaint note concerning the Birkheads in Leland's *Itinerary*, vi, 14 ; he suggests a relationship with the Windermere Birkheads or Birketts.
In 1308–9 John de Birkhead, son of Ralph, granted a burgage to Richard del Stanistreet ; Kuerden MSS. ii, fol. 253. John de Birkhead attested various local charters down to 1324 ; Adam de Birkhead others from 1377 to 1417 ; in the last-named year his son and grandson, Henry and John, also attested ; Crosse D. nos. 41, 72, 126. John Birkhead was living in 1434 ; Towneley MS. OO, no. 1301. In 1471 Richard was son and heir of Henry Birkhead ; ibid. no. 148. John Birkhead appears in 1504 ; ibid. no. 165.
In 1338 Hugh son of Robert de Birkhead claimed from Richard de Birkhead, litster, various tenements in Wigan, but did not prosecute his claim ; Assize R. 1425, m. 2. Thurstan de Birkhead and John his brother were defendants in 1356 ; Duchy of Lanc. Assize R. 5, m. 26 ; and Matthew son of Thurstan de Birkhead, in 1376 ; De Banco R. 461, m. 276 d. Adam de Birkhead and Joan his wife were plaintiffs in 1374 ; De Banco R. 456, m. 10 d. ; 460, m. 364. Euphemia daughter of William son of Richard de Birkhead, litster or tinctor, demanded in 1357 20 acres in Wigan from Sir Robert de Langton, Robert his son and others ; Pal. of Lanc. Misc. 1–8, m. 3, 4, 5 ; Duchy of Lanc. Assize R. 6, m. 3. The younger Robert defended, saying the land had been granted to himself and Margaret his wife and their issue.
An undated petition, addressed to the Archbishop of Canterbury, as Chancellor, complained that John Birkhead, feoffee of Richard Birkhead, had refused to make over an estate in the latter's land to William Marsh, the cousin and heir ; Early Chan. Proc. 16–528.
Richard Birkhead, who died in or before 1512, held land in Rivington and a burgage in Wigan ; Joan, his sister and heir, was four years of age ; Duchy of Lanc. Inq. p.m. iv, no. 26. A later inquisition shows that they were the children of Hugh, son of Richard, son of Henry 'Birkenhead' of Wigan. The last-named Henry, who had another son John, had granted nine burgages in Wigan and other lands there, held of the rector by a rent of 43s. 4d., to feoffees who had granted five burgages to Maud, the widow of Richard Birkhead for her life, and four burgages to Elizabeth, widow of Hugh Birkhead, who died 16 Jan. 1510-11, ibid. v, no. 23. Joan, the heiress, married Thomas, son and heir of Thomas Tyldesley of Wardley ; *Visit.* of 1567 (Chet. Soc.), 44.
[94] Thomas de Duxbury was mayor of Wigan in 1402-3 ; he or another of the name was outlawed in 1420 ; Crosse D. (*Trans. Hist. Soc.*), no. 95, 127. John de Duxbury also occurs ; ibid. no. 116, 130.
[95] In 1277 Maud widow of Orm de Wigan claimed burgages and land in Wigan against William son of William de Preston, and Eleanor his wife and others ; De Banco R. 21, m. 62 d. About the same

time Adam del Crosse obtained from the same William and Eleanor a messuage and 14 acres of land in Wigan ; *Final Conc.* (Rec. Soc. Lancs. and Ches.), i, 153.
From one of the Crosse D. (no. 19), dated 1310, it appears that Eleanor de Preston was a daughter of Nicholas de Wigan, clerk ; this charter concerns land in Henhurst Meadow, Hitchfield, Lorrimer's Acre, Loamy Half-acre, Hengande Half-acre, &c. ; the Stonygate is mentioned.
Adam Russell of Preston had land here in 1307 ; De Banco R. 163, m. 214 d. For Henry Russell see *Lancs. Inq. and Extents* (Rec. Soc. Lancs. and Ches.), i, 275.
[96] There were two families of this name, of Swinley and of Scholes ; see Bridgeman, *Wigan Ch.* 259. They supplied many mayors. In Oct. 1864 representatives of James Horrocks of Spennymoor, claiming to be the heir of Robert Ford who died in 1772, took possession of the 'Manor House' in Scholes and were besieged for some days, to the excitement of the town.
[97] 'Roger Scott's land' is mentioned in 1323 ; Towneley MS. GG, no. 2561. Roger son of Roger Scott of Wigan in 1345 complained that Robert del Mourihilles had been wasting lands 'held by the law of England' ; De Banco R. 345, m. 95 d. Further particulars of the family will be found in the account of Pemberton.
[98] About seven hundred of the family deeds are contained in Towneley's MS. GG (Add. MS. 32107), no. 2196-905. Some of these and others are printed in the *Trans. Hist. Soc.* (new ser.), v-ix, Crosse D. no. 1-224.
The first of the family of whom any particulars can be stated is the Adam del Crosse, 1277, mentioned in a preceding note. Two grants to him are known, one being of land in Holywell Carr ; Crosse D. no. 7 ; Towneley's GG, no. 2535. To his daughter Ellen he gave land in the Rye Field and Holywell Carr ; Crosse D. no. 13. She was living in 1292 ; Assize R. 408, m. 32 d. Adam del Crosse was also living in 1292 ; ibid. m. 32. The Adam son of Richard del Crosse of 1311 (Crosse D. no. 20), was probably a different person. The *de Cruce* of Latin deeds also appears as 'de la Croyz,' 'atte Crosse,' and 'del Crosse.' The family seems to have come from Lathom ; Crosse D. no. 5.
In 1277 Richard, rector of Wigan, had a dispute with William del Crosse as to whether the latter's toft belonged to the church of Wigan or to a lay fee ; De Banco R. 18, m. 54.
[99] John son of Adam del Crosse was defendant, with others, in a plea of mort d'ancestor in 1295 ; Assize R. 1306, m. 20 d. Later he had various disputes with Alan son of Walter the Fuller, husband of his sister Ellen. As early as 1299 he released all his right in the lands his father had given Ellen on her marriage, and in 1315 a final agreement was made ;

been a descendant of Aymory the Walker, who appears to have been a Crosse also.[102] The Marklands were prominent up to the beginning of the 18th century.[103] A number of deeds concerning the Marsh family have been preserved by Kuerden.[104] Other surnames were derived from various trades carried on here.[105] In few cases can any connected account be given of them.

By an inquisition taken in 1323 it was found that one William de Marclan had held two messuages and two acres of land and half an acre of meadow in Wigan of the rector by the service of 12 d. yearly, and other lands in Shevington of Margaret Banastre. He granted them to feoffees, who in turn granted a moiety to Robert de Holand. The last-named at Christmas 1317 assigned an annual rent of 29 s. 6 d. out of his

life) ; to Imayne daughter of Hugh and Katherine ; to William and to Gilbert, brothers of Hugh ; ibid. GG, no. 2356. These are not heard of again.

From all this it appears that Katherine, who was a daughter of Adam son of Matthew de Kenyon (Crosse D. no. 56), was four times married : (1) to John son of Aymory, about 1366 ; (2) to William, son of Adam de Liverpool, who died in 1383 (ibid. no. 77) ; (3) to Hugh del Crosse, who died about 1392 ; and (4) to Thomas de Hough, of Thornton Hough in Wirral, who died in 1409 ; see Ormerod, *Ches.* (ed. Helsby), ii, 549, 550 (from p. 576 it appears that Thomas had a previous wife, also named Katherine). She had issue by the three earlier marriages. She was still living in 1417 ; Crosse D. no. 126. The pedigree recorded in 1567 *Visit.* (Chet. Soc. 107) gives her yet another husband, William de Houghton, the first of all ; but this may be an error.

[102] Adam del Crosse, who heads the pedigree, had another son William, who may have been the William del Crosse already mentioned in 1277. In 1292 William son of William the Tailor of Wigan claimed a tenement from William son of Adam del Crosse on a plea of mort d'ancestor ; Assize R. 408, m. 46 d. This William married Emma daughter of Thomas de Ince. The widow in 1316 released to John del Crosse all her right in her husband's lands in Ormskirk ; Towneley MS. GG, no. 2384.

There seems, however, to have been another of the name, for in 1331 Isolda widow of William de Cros complained that she had been deprived of 40 s. rent from a messuage and 60 acres in Wigan ; Assize R. 1404, m. 18 d.

In 1329 Aymory the Walker, son of William del Crosse, granted to feoffees all his lands in Wigan ; these were regranted forty years later, with remainders to William, John, Henry, and Thurstan, sons of Aymory ; Towneley MS. GG, no. 2513, 2556.

An Aymory the Walker appears as early as 1309, when William the Frere granted him half a burgage next to the half-burgage he already held ; ibid. GG, no. 2588. In 1316 he had a grant from Richard de Ince ; ibid. GG, no. 2654. In 1345 Lora widow of Robert de Leyland granted to Aymory the Walker land called the Souracre ('Sowrykarr') in Wigan ; ibid. GG, no. 2544 ; and in the same year he is named in De Banco R. 344, m. 432.

Before 1347 John son of Aymory had acquired land near Standishgate from Adam son of John Dickson, whose divorced wife in that year released all claim to it ; Towneley MS. GG, no. 2568. A little later he purchased land in Liverpool from Adam son of Richard de Liverpool ; ibid. GG, no. 2576. In 1347 William son of Aymory granted to Thomas son of Henry Fairwood a toft lying in the Wirchinbank ; ibid. GG, no. 2604. In July 1359 William son of Aymory the Walker and

Isobel his wife were non-suited in a claim against Agnes, widow of Aymory ; Duchy of Lanc. Assize R. 7, m. 3 d. William had a son Aymory, who about 1380 made a feoffment of his lands in Wigan ; ibid. GG, no. 2567, 2534. In 1388 Aymory the Walker leased the Priestsacre in Botlingfield to Richard de Longshaw ; Crosse D. no. 96.

John son of the elder Aymory in or about 1366 married the above-named Katherine daughter of Adam de Kenyon ; Crosse D. no. 56 ; see also Towneley MS. GG, no. 2550. He died in 1369, leaving three sons by her, Richard, Nicholas, and Thurstan ; Crosse D. no. 66. In 1377 Robert de Picton, cousin and heir of Robert Barret of Liverpool, released to William son of Adam de Liverpool, Katherine his wife, and Richard son of John Aymoryson of Wigan, all actions ; Towneley MS. GG, no. 2713.

It is uncertain whether the Richard del Crosse who followed Hugh was the latter's son or the Richard son of John Aymoryson and Katherine born about 1367. The latter is the statement in the *Visit.* of 1567, and has probabilities in its favour. The charters state Richard del Crosse to have been the son of Katherine, but do not name his father, and he is not named in the remainders to Hugh's feoffment of 1395. Richard del Crosse first occurs in the charters in 1400-1 (when, if he were son of Hugh, he could not have been of full age) ; Towneley MS. GG, no. 2526 ; Crosse D. no. 96. On the other hand, in a writ excusing him from serving on juries, dated 1445, he is said to be over sixty years of age, while Richard the son of John and Katherine would have been nearly eighty years of age ; Towneley MS. GG, no. 2286. In 1423-4 Richard Aymory son of Henry Aymoryson (i.e. son of Aymory son of William) released to his 'cousin' Richard del Crosse all his right in land which had belonged to Aymory the Walker, son of William, son of Aymory de Wigan ; Towneley MS. GG, no. 2511.

Richard del Crosse prospered. He was receiver for Lady Lovell (ibid. GG, no. 2199) ; and acquired lands in Liverpool and Chorley at the beginning of the 15th century. Settling in the former town he and his successors had little further direct connexion with Wigan. A schedule of lands in Wigan included in the marriage settlement of John Crosse and Alice Moore in 1566 is printed in Crosse D. no. 224. Some of these were sold in 1591 and later years ; Pal. of Lanc. Feet of F. bdle. 53, m. 13, &c. For a complaint by John Crosse regarding trespass on his lands at Wigan see *Local Glean. Lancs. and Ches.* ii, 203.

[106] A pedigree was recorded at the *Visit.* of 1664 (Chet. Soc.), 193. A descendant acquired Foxholes in Rochdale by marriage with an Entwisle heiress ; Fishwick, *Rochdale*, 411. The surname is derived from Markland in Pemberton. Adam son of Richard de Marklan(d) attested

a charter dated about 1280 ; Matthew and Henry one in 1323 ; Crosse D. no. 13, 34.

John and Matthew Markland occur in the time of Richard II, and John son of Matthew Markland in 1413 ; Kuerden MSS. ii, fol. 253. John Markland of Wigan, mercer, occurs in 1443 and 1445 ; Pal. of Lanc. Plea R. 5, m. 1 ; 7, m. 2, 6 d. Alexander son of Matthew Markland was one of the receivers of the persecuted priests in 1586 ; Bridgeman, *Wigan Ch.* 166, quoting Harl. MS. 360. Ralph Markland, as a landowner, contributed to the subsidy in 1628 ; Norris D. (B.M.).

Captain Gerard Markland had served in a regiment of horse raised for the Parliament, but disbanded in 1648, after which he applied for arrears of pay. He may be the alderman Gerard Markland who left £5 to the poor of Wigan ; *Cal. of Com. for Compounding*, i, 173 ; Bridgeman, *Wigan Ch.* 716. A short letter of his is printed in *Hist. MSS. Com. Rep.* xiv, App. iv, 62.

[104] Kuerden MSS. ii, fol. 253. Grants of land were made to Roger del Marsh by Richard son of Adam son of Orm de Wigan and by Adam son of Roger son of Orm de Wigan in 1322 and 1336. In 1323-4 John son of Robert del Marsh granted his inheritance to John del Marsh and Roger his brother.

John son of Roger del Marsh gave land in Scholefield to Robert de Laithwaite and Anabel his wife.

In 1398-9 Adam del Marsh received from the feoffees the lands he had granted them with remainders to Roger his son by his first wife ; this seems to have been upon the occasion of his latter marriage with Joan, daughter of Hugh de Winstanley.

Deeds of the time of Hen. VI show the succession ; Roger—s. William, who married Isabel—s. Robert, whose wife was Margaret.

In the time of Hen. VIII the lands of this family appear to have been sold to Thomas Hesketh.

[105] The following occur in the 14th and 15th centuries : Baxter, Bowwright, Carpenter, Ironmonger, Litster, Lorimer, Potter, Skinner, Tanner, Teinturer, Walker, and Wright.

Three minor families occur in the Visitations. The Rigbys of Wigan and Peel in Little Hulton recorded a pedigree in 1613 ; *Visit.* (Chet. Soc.), 65. In 1664 Colonel William Daniell of Wigan recorded a pedigree ; Dugdale, *Visit.* (Chet. Soc.), 95. Also the Pennington family ; ibid. 232. David de Pennington and Margery his wife occur in pleas of 1374 ; De Banco R. 455, m. 424 d. ; 457, m. 341. Margery afterwards married Richard del Ford, and in 1384 a settlement by fine was made between them and John de Swinley and Alice his wife concerning the latter's inheritance ; Pal. of Lanc. Feet of F. bdle. 2, m. 27.

For the Baldwins of Wigan see *Pal. Note Bk.* i, 54.

share to Aline the recluse of Wigan for her maintenance. This payment ceased when Sir Robert's lands were forfeited ; whereupon the recluse petitioned for its restoration, and inquiry was made.[105a]

William Ford and the widows of James Houghton and Nicholas Standish contributed to a subsidy of Mary's reign as landowners.[106] The following were returned as freeholders in 1600 : Gilbert Barrow, Peter Marsh, Oliver Markland, William Foster, Hamlet Green, Charles Leigh, William Burgess, Edward Challenor, John Tarleton, Gilbert Bank, Ralph Markland of Meadows ; Thomas Molyneux and E lward Laithwaite of Wigan Woodhouses ; Alexander Ford of Swinley, William and Hugh Langshaw, and William Bankes of Scholes.[107] William Ford contributed to the subsidy of 1628 as a landowner.[108]

Wigan people generally were royalists, but William Pilkington was in 1650 singled out as a 'grand delinquent' ; he escaped with a fine of £29 5s.[109] Minor offenders against the Parliament were Robert Baron, William Brown, and William Tempest.[110] The following 'papists' registered estates at Wigan in 1717 : Nicholas Mather of Abram, Richard Tootell, Thomas Naylor of Orrell, Gilbert Thornton, Thomas Scott, gent., John Thornton, Dr. Thomas Worthington, and Anne Laithwaite of Borwick.[111]

The parish church has been described above. The first additional church in the township in connexion with the Establishment was St. George's, between Standishgate and the Douglas, consecrated in 1781. A district was assigned to it in 1843, and this became a parish in 1864, on the resignation of Sir Henry Gunning, rector, as did the two following : [112] St. Catherine's, Scholes, consecrated in 1841, had a separate district assigned in 1843.[113] There is a small graveyard attached. St. Thomas's, consecrated in 1851, had in the following year a district assigned to it.[114] The rector of Wigan is patron of the above churches. St. James's, Poolstock, was consecrated in 1866, for a district formed in 1863. The patronage is vested in Mr. J. C. Eckersley.[115] St. Andrew's, Woodhouse Lane, consecrated in 1882, had a district assigned to it in 1871.[116] The church of St. Michael and All Angels, Swinley, was consecrated in 1878 as a chapel of ease to the parish church, and became parochial in 1881.[117] The patronage of these two churches is vested in the rector of Wigan.

The various bodies of Methodists have in all eight churches and mission-rooms, the Wesleyans having two, the Primitive Methodists three, the Independents two, and the United Free Church one. The Wesleyans have also built the Queen's Hall, a large structure opened in 1908.

A Particular or Calvinistic Baptist congregation was formed in 1795 by seceders from the Countess of Huntingdon's Connexion (St. Paul's) ; [118] the chapel in King Street was opened in 1854. There is another chapel in Platt Lane.

What provision was made by those who became Nonconformists by the Act of 1662 does not appear. In 1689 William Laithwaite's barn was certified as a meeting-place of the Wigan Dissenters,[119] and two years later Roger Kenyon knew of two meeting-places, one held by Mr. Green, the supporter of Presbyterianism in Hindley, and the other by 'dissenters who do furiously dissent from each other.' [120] An 'old English Presbyterian congregation' is mentioned in 1773, and a little later William Davenport, also minister at Hindley, was in charge. He was probably a Unitarian, but after his death the chapel was about 1797 secured for the Scottish Presbyterians, who have retained possession to the present time. Trinity Presbyterian Church was built upon the old site in 1877.[121]

The Congregationalists formed a church about 1777, probably as a protest against the Unitarianism taught at the existing chapel ; in 1785 they opened a chapel, now St. Paul's Congregational Church. For some time it belonged to the Countess of Huntingdon's Connexion. Becoming 'unhealthy' in 1839, it was dissolved and reformed.[122] A new Gothic church replaced the old building in 1902. A new minister coming to Wigan in 1812 drew a congregation from dissatisfied Nonconformists, and a chapel was opened in 1818. Hope Congregational Church, opened in 1889, is a short distance from this older chapel, and continues its work.[123] Silverwell Congregational chapel originated in a secession from St. Paul's in 1867 and continued till 1888, when it was bought by the Manchester, Sheffield and Lincolnshire Railway Company.[124] There is a chapel in Gidlow Lane.

The Welsh Presbyterians have a place of worship ; the Christian Brethren have two ; and the Catholic

---

[105a] Inq. a.q.d. 17 Edw. II, no. 137 ; Anct. Petitions, P.R.O. 150–7470.

[106] Mascy of Rixton D.

[107] Misc. (Rec. Soc. Lancs. and Ches.), i, 239–43. Richard Molyneux of Wigan Woodhouses was trustee for lands in Orrell in 1522 ; Pal. of Lanc. Feet of F. bdle. 11, m. 192. Thomas Molyneux was buried at Wigan, 18 Nov. 1611. John Molyneux of the same place followed ; Lancs. Inq. p.m. (Rec. Soc. Lancs. and Ches.), i, 279. In the same work (ii, 154) is the inquisition taken after the death of John Lowe of Aspull, who died in 1619, holding lands in Wigan.

[108] Norris D. (B.M.).

[109] Cal. of Com. for Compounding, iii, 2175. 'It was by his aid that the Earl of Derby got into Wigan ; he helped in its defence, assisted Prince Rupert with hay and money, and told the Earl of Derby that all the Wiganers would go with the Prince to York or Liverpool and turn out the Roundheads ; and when others refused, he went himself.' He

had an estate of great value, which he had gone to London to undertake.

[110] Ibid. iv, 2913 ; iii, 1804, 2011.

[111] Engl. Cath. Nonjurors, 97, 124, 125, 136, 144. At the time of the Oates Plot Dr. Worthington of Wigan and his son Thomas fled into Yorkshire for fear of an indictment ; Lydiate Hall, 125, 126. 'Old Dr. Worthington' in 1682 entreated Roger Kenyon to withdraw the warrant out against him ; Hist. MSS. Com. Rep. xiv, App. iv, 139 ; Dr. Thomas Worthington was with other suspected persons imprisoned in 1689 ; ibid. 314.

[112] Bridgeman, op. cit. 783 ; Lond. Gaz. 1 Aug. 1843 ; 28 July 1863. Under an Act obtained in 1904, St. George's will be removed to the east side of the Douglas. The Rev. Benjamin Powell, incumbent from 1821 to 1860, was the father of Sir Francis Sharp Powell, bart., M.P. for Wigan from 1885 to the present.

[113] Bridgeman, op. cit. 786 ; Lond. Gaz. 1 Aug. 1843 ; 14 June 1864 ; 14 Jan. 1868. There is a mission church in Whelley.

Apostolic Church has a meeting-room. There are two unsectarian mission-rooms.

The Swedenborgians have a meeting-place called New Jerusalem.

Something has already been recorded of the loyalty of a large number of the people of Wigan to the ancient faith at the Reformation.[125] In 1681 there were ninety-one 'convicted recusants' in Wigan, and an attempt to levy a fine for recusancy—a result of the Protestant agitation of the time—led to a riot.[126] The Jesuits were in charge of the mission. In the time of James II they had a flourishing school and well-frequented chapel, but at the Revolution the excited mob destroyed the buildings and the work was stopped for a short time.[127] The Society of Jesus, however, still possesses the ancient property. Fr. James Canell is known to have been there in 1696, and died at Wigan 1722.[128] Fr. Charles Brockholes built a house about 1740, the upper room being designed as a chapel.[129] Near this a chapel was built in 1785, and enlargement being necessary it was replaced by the present church of St. John in 1819. It is still served by the Jesuits.[130] The other churches, served by secular clergy, are St. Mary's,

Standishgate, built in 1818;[130a] St. Patrick's, Scholes, founded in 1847 and rebuilt in 1880; St. Joseph's, 1870; and the Sacred Heart, Springfield, 1903. A convent of Sisters of Notre Dame is served from St. John's.[131]

The grammar school was founded before 1596.

PEMBERTON

Pemberton, 1212.

Pemberton is cut off from Wigan on the north-east by the River Douglas, and from Ince on the east by another brook running into that stream. Through the township runs eastward the brook dividing Orrell from Winstanley. Going north from this brook on the eastern side are found Hindley Hall, Worsley Hall, Newtown, Laithwaite House, Marsh Green, Walthew House, and Markland[1]; and on the western side Tunstead, and Lamberhead Green, Norley, Kit Green, and Orrell City. To the south, on the eastern side lie Smithy Brook, Worsley Mesnes, Goose Green, Hawkley,[2] and Wheatlees. The lowest ground is that in the Douglas valley; the surface rises to the south-west, where a height of

[125] E.g. in the account of Rector Fleetwood. In 1580 the sons of Ford of Swinley and Markland were being educated beyond the seas, 'where they were accustomed and nourished in papistry'; Gibson, *Lydiate Hall*, 218, 226, 240. For Alexander Markland see Foley, *Rec. Soc. Jesus*, vi, 147; *Douay Diaries*, 12, 321, &c. For James Ford, ibid. 12, 202, &c.

In 1583 the Bishop of Chester described the 'papists' about Preston, Wigan, and Prescot, as 'most obstinate and contemptuous,' and desired the Privy Council to arrange 'to deal severely and roundly' with them; ibid. 222 (from S.P. Dom. Eliz. clxiii, 84).

The story told by John Laithwaite, born at Wigan in 1585, gives a picture from the other side. He was the son of Henry Laithwaite by his wife Jane Bolton, and he and three brothers became Jesuits and two of them laboured in England. He stated, on entering the English college at Rome in 1603, 'I made my rudiments at Blackrod under a Protestant schoolmaster, with two of my brothers; but being a Catholic, our parents removed us and we received instruction at home from a Catholic neighbour for about half a year. At length it was arranged for our attending schools at Wigan until we were older, and that I did for four years or more. My father's family is descended from the Laithwaites, a wealthy family of the middle class.

'For his faithful adherence to the Catholic religion my father was driven away by the Protestants, and compelled to abandon all his property and possessions, and seek an asylum in another county, until at length, by favour of Henry Earl of Derby, he was reinstated in his property, but rather in the condition of a serf, totally dependent upon the pleasure and ambition of the earl, who had the power of committing or discharging him at will. He was thus enabled to live quietly and securely at home, protected by the earl from the insults of the heretics, for the space of two years; after which, at the earl's pleasure, he was thrown into Lancaster Gaol, but was liberated after two months, on account of corporal infi[rmity?]... home with health c... died a fortnight after

'My mother, wh... the ancie[n]t stock... severing in the Cath... years after my f[ather's?] t... loss of her whole... at length released h[er?]... bulation

. . . .

245 ft. is attained. The area is 2,894 acres.[3] The population in 1901 was 21,664, including Goose Green, Highfield, Little Lane, and other hamlets. The whole district is unpicturesque, bare and open, occupied for the most part by collieries, mine shafts, and pit banks. There are, however, fields where some crops are raised, potatoes and oats surviving the smoke of the environs. Pastures are scattered about also. The soil is clay and loam, over Coal Measures and stone.

There are several important roads. That from Ormskirk to Wigan enters the township at Lamberhead Green and passes through Newtown, where it is joined by the road from St. Helens through Billinge, and by that from Warrington to Wigan, through Goose Green. This last road has a branch to Wigan through Worsley Mesnes. The principal railway is the Lancashire and Yorkshire Company's line from Liverpool to Wigan, which has a station called Pemberton; a loop line, avoiding Wigan, goes east to join the Wigan and Bolton line. The same company's Wigan and Southport railway crosses the northern corner of the township. There are minor lines for the service of the collieries.

The Local Government Act of 1858 was adopted by the township in 1872.[4] The board was changed to an urban district council of fifteen members by the Act of 1894. It has now been dissolved and the township added to the borough of Wigan, with four wards each returning three councillors and having an alderman.

A hospital was erected in 1886 by the local board. A public park was given by Colonel B. H. Blundell in 1903; and a Carnegie library has been opened.

Coal-mining is the principal industry. There are stone quarries, boiler works, iron foundry, cotton mill, and brick-making. The soil is loam and clay, with subsoil of clay, stone, and coal; potatoes and oats are grown, and there is some pasturage.

The pedestal and portion of a cross exist at Goose Green.[5]

There was formerly a burning well at Hawkley.[6]

At Lamberhead Green in 1775 was born William Atherton, a Wesleyan divine, president of the Conference in 1846. He died in 1850.[7]

Before the Conquest, as afterwards, *MANOR PEMBERTON* seems to have formed one of the berewicks or members of the manor of Newton.[8] It is so regarded in the inquisitions.[9]

During the 12th century it was held in thegnage by a certain Alan,[10] whose son Alan, settling at Windle, was known as Alan de Windle. At the Survey of 1212 the latter was holding Pemberton, assessed as two plough-lands, by the rent of 20s. and the service of finding a judge for the court of Newton.[11] Like other Windle properties this mesne lordship may have descended to the Burnhulls[12] and Gerards[13]; no record of it occurs in their inquisitions, but Sir Thomas Gerard, who died in 1621, held certain lands in the township 'of the lords of Pemberton.'[14] It seems, however, to have been alienated to the Walton family,[15] and so to have descended with Northlegh or *NORLEY* to Legh of Lyme.[16]

PEMBERTON. *Argent a cheveron between three buckets sable with hoops and handles or.*

The first Alan de Pemberton had created a subordinate manor for a younger son, known as Adam de Pemberton.[17] He in 1212 was holding it of Alan de Windle, and had granted out a quarter of it to Henry son of Lawrence, who in turn had granted an oxgang, i.e. a quarter of his share, to Alan son of Aldith.[18] Adam de Pemberton made grants to the Hospitallers[19] and to Cockersand Abbey.[20] He was

---

[3] 2,895, including 15 acres of inland water; Census of 1901.

[4] *Lond. Gaz.* 20 Aug. 1872.

[5] *Lancs. and Ches. Antiq. Soc.* xiv, 235.

[6] Baines, *Lancs.* (ed. 1836), iii, 563, quoting Bowen's *Geog.* Roger Lowe records that on 1 June 1665 he went to see the burning well at Pemberton, 'and we had two eggs which was so done by no material fire'; *Local Glean. Lancs. and Ches.* i, 180.

[7] *Dict. Nat. Biog.*

[8] *V.C.H. Lancs.* i, 286.

[9] See for example *Lancs. Inq. p.m.* (Chet. Soc.), i, 138; ibid. (Rec. Soc. Lancs. and Ches.), i, 105.

[10] In the Pipe Roll of 1200–1 the sheriff rendered account of 10 marks from Alan son of Alan for having seisin of the land of Pemberton and for his relief; also for a writ of right against Nicholas le Boteler, formerly deputy sheriff, concerning 40s. already paid; Farrer, *Lancs. Pipe R.* 132, 141. In 1202 Edusa, widow of Alan de Windle, claimed dower in Pemberton from Alan son of Alan; *Final Conc.* (Rec. Soc. Lancs. and Ches.), i, 37.

[11] *Inq. and Extents* (Rec. Soc. Lancs. and Ches.), i, 75.

[12] See the case cited below.

[13] In the inquisition made in 1447 after the death of Sir Peter Gerard it was found that he had held messuages, lands, and tenements, rents, and services in

Pemberton, but the jurors did not know of whom they were held; Towneley MS. DD, no. 1465.

[14] *Lancs. Inq. p.m.* (Rec. Soc. Lancs. and Ches.), ii, 300.

[15] Alan de Windle granted to Master Adam de Walton the homage of Adam son of William de Pemberton, and this being transferred to Adam de Walton, lord of Walton le Dale, was by him granted to Thurstan de Northlegh in 1316; Raines MSS. (Chet. Lib.), xxxviii, 509. In 1292 Adam de Pemberton was nonsuited in a claim against Adam de Northlegh; Assize R. 408, m. 43. In 1305 Adam de Pemberton disseised estovers as against Thurstan de Northlegh and Maud, the widow of Adam de Northlegh, and his claim was allowed; *Abbrev. Plac.* (Rec. Com.), 258b. Adam de Pemberton acknowledged that Thurstan and Maud had a right to housebote and haybote without view of the forester, but they had cut down their wood beyond due measure, 93 oaks having been removed; Coram Rege R. 184, m. 53. By a fine of 1321 7 messuages, 2 oxgangs and 37 acres of land and 5 acres of meadow in Pemberton were settled upon Thurstan de Northlegh and Margery his wife; *Final Conc.* ii, 40; see also ii, 33, 43. Margery, widow of Thurstan de Northlegh, occurs in 1346; Assize R. 1435, m. 31.

[16] Robert de Legh of Adlington and

still living in 1246.[21] His descendant William died about 1292,[22] leaving a son Adam,[23] who in 1331 made a settlement of the manor, his son William, who had married Eleanor, being the heir.[24]

In or before 1362 William died, leaving Eleanor a widow,[25] with six children. Thurstan, the heir, was a minor, and his wardship was in 1367 claimed by Robert de Legh and William son of Robert de Radcliffe, in right of their wives.[26] Thurstan died soon afterwards and his five sisters were his heirs. One of these died young; the other four each had a share, and it is easy to trace the descent of two: that

of Emma, who married Robert de Hindley of Aspull;[27] and of Katherine, who married Alexander de Worsley.[28] The family of Molyneux of Rainhill had Hawkley in Pemberton, and in 1578 acquired a fourth part of the manor.[29] As late as 1415, however, the lord of the manor was said to be Henry de Pemberton.[30]

But few particulars can be given of the descent of the various portions of the manor. *HINDLEY HALL* became the property of Meyrick Bankes of Winstanley, and is held by his trustees.[31] The Worsleys of *WORSLEY MESNES*[32] were succeeded by the Downes

---

between Stephen's assart and the charcoalman's assart, and by the syke to the Douglas. He also granted an assart which Randle de Pemberton had held, and another called White's cross. Henry son of Lawrence released his share of these lands to the canons.

The abbot shortly afterwards (before 1235) gave them to William son of Richard White of Wigan, who had married Hawise, daughter of Adam de Pemberton, at a yearly rent of 12d.; ibid. 671. About 1268 John the Smith held these lands by the same rent and a payment of ½ a mark at the death of wife or heir; ibid. 668. For the inquisitions after the death of Edmund the Smith of Pemberton in 1408, see *Lancs. Inq. p.m.* (Chet. Soc.), i, 92.

[21] Assize R. 404, m. 9. Adam de Pemberton sued Peter de Burnhull for 200 acres in Pemberton, of which Alan, the plaintiff's father, was seised in the time of Henry II, i.e. before July 1189. The decision was committed to the hazard of a duel, and Adam's man Philip being defeated, Peter de Burnhull was allowed to hold the land in peace. The sureties for Philip were Alan de Windle, William and James de Pemberton, and John del Marsh. See also Assize R. 454, m. 25.

At the same time Adam de Pemberton was summoned to answer Robert son of Hugh, who complained that the lord of Newton compelled him to do service to the three-weeks court at Newton, which Adam as mesne tenant should perform. Robert's tenement was 17 acres, for which he paid a rent of 7d.; Assize R. 404, m. 12.

Adam and William his son, together with James de Pemberton, were charged with having disseised William White, John del Marsh, and Adam his brother of their common of pasture in Pemberton; ibid. m. 2. Peter de Burnhull also claimed 6 acres in Ince from Adam de Pemberton, William his son, and James son of Henry; ibid. m. 12 d. The last may be the James de Pemberton of the preceding case; then the father may be the Henry son of Lawrence of 1212.

[22] The exact relationship is uncertain. A case in 1254, in which an Adam son of William was defendant, alludes to William de Pemberton as if he were then dead; Cur. Reg. R. 154, m. 20. In 1292 William son of Roger de Ince acquired a messuage and two oxgangs in Pemberton from William son of Adam de Pemberton and Mary his wife; *Final Conc.* i, 176. Two years later Mary, widow of William, did not prosecute the claim she made against Adam son of William son of Adam de Pemberton; Assize R. 1299, m. 14 d. John son of William de Pemberton was of full age in 1292; Assize R. 468, m. 27 d.

[23] Adam de Pemberton was both

plaintiff and defen R. 408, m. 58 d. 4 de Pemberton were *Inq. and Extents,* i, berton, enfeoffed b (probably the g seisin of a messua Adam de Pemberto Assize R. 1306, m (*Final Conc.* i, 203 agreement between

[24] Ibid. ii, 79.

William son of is mentioned in 1 m. 26

Hugh de Pembe was about this tim of disputes and sett possibly he was the mentioned in 133 de Pemberton and Henry de Pember his son, Edmund a berton, and severa victed o having di

of Wardley,[33] and their estates are now held by the Earl of Ellesmere.[34] The Molyneuxes of *HAWK-LET* continued in possession until the death of Bryan William Molyneux in 1805.[35] By his will the Rev. William Hockenhull of Lymm in Cheshire succeeded, and assumed the surname of Molyneux.[36]

Hawkley, however, was afterwards sold, and is now the property of the trustees of Meyrick Bankes.[37]

The estate called *TUNSTEAD* was in the possession of a branch of the Pembertons during the whole of the 15th century.[38] One of the daughters and co-heirs of George Pemberton then carried it by mar-

---

with James Winstanley and Thomas Taylor respecting lands abutting on Saltersford Brook ; *Ducatus Lanc.* (Rec. Com.), ii, 403. (It may be stated by the way, that an Adam the Salter and his wife Juliana had a tenement in Pemberton in 1292 ; Assize R. 408, m. 44.) James Worsley died in September 1590, holding the capital messuage or manor house called the hall of Worsley, and other houses and lands, of Thomas Langton by a rent of 5s. ; Duchy of Lanc. Inq. p.m. xv, no. 29.

His brother Ralph succeeded. He was one of the 'comers to church but no communicants' in 1590 ; *Lydiate Hall*, 246. He had spent some time in Salford gaol for religion in 1582 ; *Engl. Martyrs* (Cath. Rec. Soc.), 23–5. Dying in 1610 it was found that he had held the 'hall of Worsley ' in Pemberton with messuages, lands, and rents there, and in Parr, Winstanley, Wigan, and Hindley. The Pemberton lands were held of Richard Fleetwood in socage, by a rent of 5s. but part had belonged to Upholland Priory, and was held of the king by the two-hundredth part of a knight's fee and 2s. rent. His widow Ellen was in possession in 1611, and his heirs were his sister Alice, aged sixty years, and Roger Downes of Wardley, son of another sister, Elizabeth ; *Lancs. Inq. p.m.* (Rec. Soc. Lancs. and Ches.), i, 171–3.

An account of the sinking of a coal pit on his estate in 1600 is printed in *Lancs. and Ches. Antiq. Soc.* vii, 49–53.

[33] Roger Downes represented Wigan in the Parliaments of 1601 and 1620 ; Pink and Beaven, *Parl. Rep. of Lancs.* 223, 224. He was buried at Wigan 6 July 1638. A monument to his grandson Roger, who died in 1676, is in Wigan Church. See the pedigree in Dugdale, *Visit.* (Chet. Soc.), 100, and the account of Worsley.

[34] In a fine concerning the Wardley estates in 1741 George Lewis Scott was plaintiff and James Cholmondeley and Penelope his wife were deforciants ; Pal. of Lanc. Feet of F. bdle. 327, m. 80. Lady Penelope sold them to the Duke of Bridgewater in 1760.

[35] Some particulars as to this family will be found in the accounts of Rainhill and Whiston.

The *Visit.* of 1567 suggests that their coming to Pemberton was due to marriage with the heiress of the Ince family. Gilbert de Ince of Hawkley occurs in 1374 ; Inq. a.q.d. 48 Edw. III, no. 19 ; see also Coram Rege R. 426. John Molyneux of Hawkley occurs in 1469 and 1490–1 ; Kuerden MSS. ii, fol. 245, no. 1012 ; Towneley MS. GG, no. 2537.

An agreement was made in 1512 between Richard Molyneux of Hawkley or Hawcliffe and Thomas Gerard of Ince for the marriage of the former's son Richard (? Roger) with the latter's daughter Elizabeth ; Chet. P.

In 1543 Thomas Molyneux, son of Roger and the last-named Elizabeth, and Elizabeth his wife had a dispute with Roger Molyneux concerning Hitchcock carr ; *Ducatus Lanc.* (Rec. Com.), i,

174. A settlement of lands in Pemberton and Hawkley was made by fine in 1546 between Roger Molyneux and Thomas, his son and heir apparent, and Elizabeth his wife ; Pal. of Lanc. Feet of F. bdle. 12, m. 193. Roger was living in 1547 ; ibid. bdle. 12, m. 250.

Hawkley Hall is mentioned in a dispute between John Kitchen and Isabel his daughter and Thomas Molyneux, the owner, in 1561 ; *Ducatus Lanc.* (Rec. Com.), ii, 228. Thomas Molyneux and his second wife Sibyl occur in various fines concerning lands in Pemberton and Markland from 1572 ; Pal. of Lanc. Feet of F., bdles. 34, m. 39, &c. 'Thomas Molyneux of Hawkley, gent., in lands £40 and in goods £100,' was a recusant in 1577; *Lydiate Hall*, 215, quoting S.P. Dom. Eliz. cxviii, 45. He was buried at Wigan 16 May 1586 ; and soon afterwards disputes arose between his son and heir Richard and Sibyl the widow. In the pleadings the descent is thus given : Richard Molyneux–s. and h. Roger–s. and h. Thomas–s. and h. Richard. The estate is described as a capital messuage called Hawkley, containing demesne lands in Hawkley and Pemberton, and various lands in Aughton and Upfitherland of very good yearly value ; Duchy of Lanc. Plead. Eliz. cliv, M. 11 ; Decrees and Orders, Eliz. xx, fol. 37.

Richard Molyneux of Hawkley was in 1590 among the 'comers to church, but no communicants,' but he and his family appear to have soon afterwards conformed to the Established religion ; *Lydiate Hall*, 246 (quoting S.P. Dom. Eliz. ccxxxv, 4). Pedigrees were recorded in 1567 and 1664 ; *Visit.* (Chet. Soc.), 108, 200.

Richard Molyneux and Thomas his son and heir-apparent made a settlement of the manor of Pemberton in 1607 ; Pal. of Lanc. Feet of F. bdle. 71, no. 25. Richard paid £10 in 1631 on refusing knighthood ; *Misc.* (Rec. Soc. Lancs. and Ches.), i, 213. He was still living in 1664, but Thomas was dead, and his son Richard, aged forty at the Visitation in that year, soon afterwards succeeded to the estate. Early in 1681 he made a settlement of the manor and various lands in Pemberton, as also in Wigan, Ince, Standish, and Croft, Anne his wife, and Hugh his son and heir-apparent being joined as deforciants ; ibid. bdle. 206, m. 91. Richard Molyneux was buried at Wigan 31 Oct. 1681 ; Hugh succeeded, but appears to have had no issue, and administration of his estate was granted at Chester in 1687.

William Molyneux succeeded his brother Hugh ; he was buried at Warrington in 1698 and there is an inscription in the churchyard commemorating him ; *Local Glean. Lancs. and Ches.* i, 216. His son William was succeeded by an uncle, Reginald, brother of the preceding William and Hugh ; and in turn was succeeded by his sons William (buried at Wigan 4 Nov. 1740) and Richard (buried at Warrington in 1748). In a settlement made in 1721, William Molyneux, gentleman, being in possession, their part of the manor is described as 'the

---

4   81

riage to Robert Molyneux of Melling,[39] and it descended with the other lands of this family [40] until they were sold in the middle of the 18th century.

MARKLAND was the property of the Hollands,[41] and in 1360 was granted to the Priory of Upholland. On the suppression it was acquired by John Holcroft.[42]

Alexander Worsley, Thomas and John Molyneux, Gilbert Scott, and Robert Higginson, contributed to a subsidy of Mary's reign as landowners.[43] The freeholders in 1600 [44] were : Ralph Worsley, — Downes,[45] Richard Molyneux of Hawkley, Robert Arrowsmith, Thomas Laithwaite,[46] Richard Pemberton,[47] Hugh Scott,[48] William Walthew,[49] Thomas

---

granted the estate to Juliana daughter of John Gillibrand, for life, with remainders to her sons, Thurstan and Adam, and then to the plaintiff Simon, apparently a brother. Adam died before Thurstan without issue ; Thurstan died at Oxford ; and Simon, who was then in Scotland, returned to Wigan to take possession, but found Robert's men in the tenement. At Pemberton, Adam de Pemberton, as lord, had entered, and held until Simon appeared to claim ; Simon had married a daughter of his. The lands in Wigan were held of Robert de Holland by the service of a barbed arrow ; Assize R. 408, m. 16 d.

Nothing further is known of its history for a century. Richard de Pemberton died in possession of it in 1415, as also of other lands called the Marsh, &c. ; his son Thomas being dead the heir was his grandson Hugh ; Lancs. Inq. p.m. (Chet. Soc.), i, 103. In the same year William, another son of Richard, as trustee granted Tunstead to Alice, the widow of Richard, for life, with remainders to Hugh son of Thomas de Pemberton, and then to Hugh and Thurstan, sons of Richard ; Towneley MS. GG, no. 2626, 2655.

Hugh de Pemberton by his wife Douce had a son John, whose son George was the last of the direct male line of the family. For Hugh's marriage see ibid. GG, no. 2596, 2597, dated 1435. He died in or before 1466, when Douce was a widow, and the son John in possession ; ibid. GG, no. 2650, 2671, and Crosse D. no. 146.

[39] Beatrice, Elizabeth, Ellen, and Alice were the daughters and co-heirs of George son of John Pemberton ; Towneley MS. GG, no. 2362, 2890, 2405, dated 1512 and 1514 ; and Crosse D. no. 172. Beatrice Pemberton and others in 1512 claimed the wardship of Elizabeth Birkenhead ; Ducatus Lanc. (Rec. Com.), i, 127.

The third of the daughters, Ellen, married Robert Molyneux of Melling (Visit. of 1567, p. 100), and in the inquisition taken after the death of their son and heir John Molyneux in 1582, the estate, comprising Tunstead Hall and various lands, is fully described ; among the fields were Bridgeley and Mabcroft ; it was held of the heirs of the lords of Pemberton, James Worsley and Robert Hindley, in socage by rents of 4s. 8d. and 7d. respectively ; Duchy of Lanc. Inq. p.m. xiv, no. 73.

[40] See Lancs. Inq. p.m. (Rec. Soc. Lancs. and Ches.), i, 43 ; Pal. of Lanc. Feet of F. bdle. 94, no. 15.

[41] In 1241 Robert de Holland quitclaimed to Adam de Pemberton all his title to twelve oxgangs in Pemberton in return for the homage and service of Thomas de Sifrethley ; Final Conc. i, 82. In 1292 Robert de Holland and Robert his son had an estate in Pemberton and Orrell ; ibid. i, 173.

In 1348 Maud, widow of Robert de Holland, had claimed dower in the 'manor of Markland,' described as three plough-lands ; De Banco R. 355, m. 307.

Inquiry was made at Prescot on 25

Jan. 1346-7 as to would be to the king' a mill, 60 acres of la dow, and 6 acres of w and the reversion o for a term by Adam d las h's son, should be and convent of Uph were held of Ralph d and rendering a rose were of the annual v answer of the jury w the king had alread lands to the value after this land had be de Holland had the worth 100 marks a discharge his liabiliti others ; Inq. p.m. nos.), no. 12.

In 1535 the clear at £8 10s. a year, and the various rents amount ; Dugdale, M

[42] Pat. 37 Hen. V in th g lg t Markland was soon Worsley of Booths, purchasing part from Pal. of Lanc. Feet 111, 147 ; 35, m. 41

Whalley,[50] Humphrey Winstanley, and John Worthington. The landowners who contributed to the
subsidy of 1628 were Roger Downes, for Worsley's
lands ; Richard Molyneux, and the heirs of Richard
Pemberton.[51] Several 'delinquents' compounded for
their estates under the rule of the Commonwealth.[52]
The following 'papists' registered estates here in
1717 : Barbara and Margaret Green, George Unsworth, and William Winstanley.[53] The land tax
returns of 1787 show the chief owners to have been
the Duke of Bridgewater, the heirs of T. Barton,
Mrs. Percival, W. B. Molyneux, and John Markland.

During the last century a number of places of worship have been erected in Pemberton. In connexion
with the Established Church St. John's was
consecrated in 1832 as a chapel of ease to the parish
church; a burial ground was attached to it. The
rector of Wigan is the patron.[54] The church of St.
Matthew, Highfield, built in 1894, serves as a chapel
of ease. St. Mark's, Newtown, was built in 1891.
The patronage is vested in trustees. There is a
licensed chapel at Worsley Mesnes.

The Methodist denominations are well represented,
the Wesleyan, Primitive, Independent, and United
Free Methodists having places of worship. There are
also Free Gospel and Congregational chapels.

The Roman Catholic church of St. Cuthbert
dates from 1872 ; it was enlarged in 1887.[55]

A schoolhouse was built at Goose Green by Thomas
Molyneux ; but no endowment was provided.[56]

BILLINGE

Bulling, 1212 and commonly in xiv cent. ; Billinge,
1284 ; Bollynge, 1292 ; Bullynth, 1292.

This township, which originally included Winstanley, has long been divided into two halves regarded as
separate townships and known as Chapel End and
Higher End. They form the south-west corner of
the parish.

The position of Chapel End township—the eastern
one—is bleak and open, and the country bare except in the south, where there are more trees and
green fields about the neighbourhood of Carr Mill
Dam, a fairly large sheet of water. In the middle of
this lake the boundaries of three townships meet. In the
north there are sandstone quarries on the highest
point of the hill. There are fields where potatoes,
wheat, and oats are grown, besides pastures nearer the
base of the hillside. The soil is sandy, over a sub-
stratum of gravel and sandstone rock. The chapel
lies near the centre of the boundary between Chapel
End and Winstanley on the north. The village,

with its long straggling street and stone houses, spreads
from it along the road from Wigan to St. Helens,
which is the principal thoroughfare. About the
middle of the township it is crossed by another road
which runs eastward from the chapel to Ashton
in Makerfield. The south-western boundary is formed
by Black Brook, near which lies Birchley ; and the
south-eastern by the Goyt, its affluent, on which
is Chadwick Green. Two detached portions of Winstanley lie on this side. The surface rises from
the two streams, a height of nearly 600 ft. being
attained at the northern border. Here stands Billinge
Beacon,[1] from which fine views can be obtained. The
area of Chapel End is 1,161 acres,[2] and the population
in 1901 numbered 2,068.

Billinge Higher End, on the north-west side of
the former township, has an area of 1,571 acres.[3]
The population in 1901 numbered 1,600.[4] Near
the centre, by Brownlow, a height of 560 ft. is
attained, the surface falling away somewhat quickly
to the south-west boundary, which is formed
by Black Brook, and also to the west and north. This
ridge of high ground, known as Billinge Hill, is visible
for miles around. There are extensive quarries of sandstone and a gritstone used for making mill-stones.
In the north of the district there are one or two
unimportant coal-mines. In this part the hill is not
entirely bare in spite of its exposed situation, for there
are plantations of small pine trees and some larger
deciduous trees. The west side of the township is
occupied by cultivated fields where wheat, oats, and
potatoes are grown in a rich sandy soil. On the west
lies Billinge Hall ; to the north are Bispham Hall,
Gautley, and the Great Moss. On the east a brook
divides the township from Winstanley ; Longshaw lies
here, with the village adjacent, on the road from
Billinge chapel to Upholland. The main roads are
macadamized ; others set with square blocks of native
sandstone ; they are protected by walls in the upper
parts and hedges in the lower parts of the township.

A local board for Billinge was formed in 1872,[5] the
district including both the townships and also part of
Winstanley. This was succeeded in 1894 by an urban
district council of twelve members.

The present townships of *BILLINGE
MANOR* (Higher End and Chapel End) and *WIN-
STANLEY* were originally but one manor,
rated as half a plough-land, and probably forming one
of the berewicks of Newton before the Conquest, just
as they constituted members of the Newton barony
after it.[6] The inquest of 1212 shows that this extensive manor had long been divided into three portions, almost equal. The lord was Adam de Billinge,

old ; *Lancs. Inq. p.m.* (Rec. Soc. Lancs.
and Ches.), i, 80.

Robert Walthew of Pemberton was
charged with delinquency by the Parliament in 1650, and his estate was in
danger of sequestration ; *Cal. of Com. for
Compounding*, iii, 2333. In 1667 he built
the school at Upholland ; his daughter and
heir Elizabeth married Ralph Markland
of the Meadows ; Gastrell, *Notitia Cestr.*
ii, 259, 260, with a reference to Nichol,
Lit. Anec. iv, 657.

[50] John Whalley of Pemberton, yeoman,
died in 1587, holding lands of the queen
in Orrell and Pemberton by a rent of
2s. 4d. ; Thomas his son and heir was
twenty-eight years of age ; Duchy of
Lanc. Inq. p.m. xiv, no. 36. A later

holding of 'ancient feoffment' by the service of 10s. rent and the finding of a judge at the Newton court.[7] The two subordinate manors were held by Simon and by Roger de Winstanley ; each was considered an oxgang and a third, but the services due are not recorded. Roger's share soon became independent. Yet another tenant, Uctred Leute, held a ridding, and paid 16d. rent.[8] Adam had made grants to Cockersand Abbey and to the Hospital of Chester.[9]

No satisfactory account can be given of the descent of these manors, through lack of evidence. Adam de

Knowsley had lands here in 1246 ; [10] and six years later he and his wife Godith seem to have had the lordship.[11] Henry de Huyton, the son of Adam, was in 1292 lord of two-thirds of the manor, the other third being Winstanley.[12] Billinge, however, did not descend with Huyton ; Robert, son of Henry, becoming lord of it, either by special grant or in right of his mother. His daughters were his heirs.[13] In 1374 the manor is found to have been divided into four parts, which seem to have been held by Eves, Heaton, Billinge and Winstanley.[14] The Eves share

[7] Lancs. Inq. and Extents (Rec. Soc. Lancs. and Ches.), i, 76. Adam de Billinge contributed half a mark to the scutage in 1201 and later years ; Farrer, Lancs. Pipe R. 152, 179, 205.

[8] Inq. and Extents, loc. cit. Uctred Leute's holding may have been in Crookhurst, a family taking its name from this place. Richard son of Richard de Crookhurst was a defendant in 1302 ; Assize R. 418, m. 10 d.

[9] To Cockersand Abbey Adam de Billinge gave all Falling and Ruhlow, the boundaries beginning at Kidsay Brook, going to Blackley, to Walley Clough, by this to Wetcroft Lache, and so by Little Ruhlow to the starting point. Further he gave half of Crookhurst, the bounds being from Swinepit Clough to Birchley Brook and Blackley Brook, and so to the start ; Cockersand Chart. (Chet. Soc.), ii, 665, 666. William son of Simon de Bulling granted the same abbey a part of his land called Leyerich Ridding, within the carr and Hennecroft ; also his portion of Crookhurst, the bounds being named with great minuteness ; 'the ford next the house of Thomas Cert which was burnt' is among them ; ibid. ii, 667. From the charter last quoted 'the Hospital' is identified as that outside the north gate of Chester.

The Abbey's lands in Crookhurst were in 1461 held by Henry Atherton of Bickerstaffe, and descended with this estate ; ibid. ii, 668 ; Duchy of Lanc. Inq. p.m. iv, no. 68. The rent paid was 18d. William de Falling, probably the tenant of the Abbot of Cockersand, in 1308 held lands under the lord of Winstanley ; Assize R. 423, m. 2. A later bearer of the name forfeited his lands for felony, but those he held of Cockersand were given up to the abbot in 1384 ; Dep. Keeper's Rep. xxxii, 356, 357. The Cockersand lands here, as in other places, were granted to Thomas Holt ; Ducatus Lanc. (Rec. Com.), ii, 288.

[10] Christiana widow of Henry son of Quenilda sued Hugh de Crookhurst for dower in 12 acres ; it was found that Adam de Knowsley held the land ; Assize R. 404, m. 13. Crookhurst was the subject of an agreement in 1256 between William son of Hugh and Emma his wife, and Adam son of Hugh and Agnes his wife ; Final Conc. (Rec. Soc. Lancs. and Ches.), i, 127. William son of Hugh is called William de Rainford in a suit of 1292 ; Assize R. 408, m. 61.

[11] Final Conc. i, 114.

[12] In 1278 William de Billinge complained that Henry de Huyton had destroyed one of his ditches in Billinge ; Assize R. 1238, m. 35. Six or seven years later Adam de Billinge complained that Henry de Huyton and another had disseised him of his free tenement in Billinge ; Assize R. 1268, m. 19 d.

In 1290 it was Henry de Huyton who was plaintiff, regarding two-thirds of certain wood and moor, and iron mineral ; Assize R. 1288, m. 12, 13. The defendants were Roger de Winstanley and Henry son of Ralph de Billinge ; they made an exchange of lands in 1283, to which Hugh son of Ralph de Billinge was one of the witnesses ; Cockersand Chart. ii, 659. Richard de Crookhurst in 1292 complained that Henry de Huyton, Adam de Billinge, and Roger de Winstanley had deprived him of estovers in 100 acres of wood for housebote and haybote—i.e. for burning, fencing, and building—pannage for his pigs, &c. Henry, in reply, said he was chief lord of two-thirds of the vill, and Roger of one-third ; as chief lords they had approved from the waste, and the complainant, who was Henry's tenant, had sufficient estovers outside the approvement. He was non-suited ; Assize R. 408, m. 12 d. Adam de Billinge's right in the manor is not here defined ; it appears that he was the representative, and no doubt descendant, of the Simon of 1212. He should, therefore, have had a moiety of Henry de Huyton's two-thirds, and from another suit of 1292 it appears that he claimed the moiety of 50 acres of moor and wood from Henry de Huyton, here called de Rycroft, and others ; ibid. m. 25. Nine years later the suit, or a similar one, appears in the rolls, Adam claiming the moiety of 60 acres of wood and waste. Henry de Huyton, the principal defendant—the others were William Bird and Alan son of Eva de Billinge—replied that he was lord of the two-thirds of Billinge and Adam of one-third ; and they had agreed that the 60 acres should pertain to Henry, and another portion of the waste, called Catshurst, should belong to Adam. The jury found that Catshurst was only 12 acres, and that Henry had approved 40 acres, a share of which should be given to Adam ; Assize R. 1321, m. 5 d. In the following year Adam de Billinge and Henry de Huyton were chief lords, the complainants being William de Huyton and Robert his brother ; Assize R. 418, m. 10 d. A possible solution is that Winstanley, having become detached, paid 3s. 6d. rent to the lord of Newton ; that the remaining 6s. 6d. was shared between Henry de Huyton and Adam de Billinge in the ratio of two to one, while they divided the land equally.

[13] Robert and William de Huyton were among the defendants in a suit of 1309 affecting the boundaries of Billinge and Winstanley, Henry de Huyton and Adam de Billinge being also joined ; Assize R. 423, m. 2. Four years later Robert de Huyton recovered from Henry de Huyton the manor of Billinge ; Assize R. 424, m. 1 d.

In 1321 William son of Robert de Huyton settled messuages and lands upon Robert de Huyton the elder for his life ; Final Conc. ii, 41. The pedigree of the Huyton family is not clear ; but Robert de Huyton the elder was probably a brother of Henry. Robert son of William brother of Henry de Huyton and Robert son of Henry de Huyton were last in the remainders of a settlement made by Ellen de Torbock in 1332 ; Croxteth D. Z, i, 4. In the same year Robert de Huyton and William de Billinge contributed to the subsidy ; Exch. Lay Subs. (Rec. Soc. Lancs. and Ches.), 26. Six years later Robert de Huyton of Billinge acquired some land in Ashton ; Final Conc. ii, 108. Robert de Huyton of Billinge, probably a descendant, complained in 1348 of the damage which William Dawson of Billinge had done to property while he had it on lease ; he had pulled down a hall worth £10, and two chambers worth £5 each, and cut down twenty apple-trees worth 20s. each, &c. ; De Banco R. 355, m. 21 ; 356, m. 234 d. Four years later certain lands were held jointly by Alan the clerk of Rainford, whose wife was Agnes, and Robert son of Matthew de Huyton ; Duchy of Lanc. Assize R. 2 (Pent.), m. 2. Another defendant in the case was Isolda, widow of Roger de Winstanley and daughter of Roger (? Robert) de Huyton. Richard de Huyton appears in 1357 ; ibid. R. 6, m. 5.

[14] By charter of June 1331 Robert de Huyton and Mary his wife granted an estate in Billinge to trustees, with remainders successively to their children, Henry, Richard, Isolda, Agnes and Avice. By 1363 Robert and Mary were dead, and Henry and Richard had died without issue ; Isolda was the wife of William the clerk of Wigan, and her estate having been taken into the king's hands for some default of Eustace de Cottesbech, for whom her father had been a surety, she petitioned for restoration ; L.T.R. Memo. R.128, m. 5. Isolda seems to have been the widow of Roger de Winstanley ; in 1363 Hugh de Winstanley sued William the clerk of Wigan and Isolda his wife for waste ; De Banco R. 416, m. 299 d. It appears from the following that there was another daughter who shared the inheritance. From a plea of 1372 it is clear that the manor of Billinge, i.e. the Huyton half as previously explained, had become divided among four co-heirs and their issue ; for Geoffrey de Wrightington and Ellen his wife, executors of the will of Robert de Winstanley (Ellen being the widow), in that year claimed dower from Henry de Scarisbrick as guardian of the land and heir of Robert de Billinge, from Richard de Heaton and Isolda his wife ; and from Alan the Barker and Agnes his wife, each of the defendant parties holding a fourth part of the manor ; De Banco R. 447, m. 184 d. ; 454, m. 141. Alan the Barker may have succeeded

BILLINGE BISPHAM HALL

ABRAM BAMFURLONG HALL

descended to the Lathoms of Mossborough;[15] and one of the parts was later held by the Bispham family.

The Heatons also held *BIRCHLEY* in Chapel End, the service to the lord of Newton being 3s. 2d. rent.[16] This manor of Birchley was acquired in the 16th century by the Andertons of Lostock, a younger son settling here.[17] It is now owned by Lord Gerard.[18]

Higher End contains Bispham Hall and Billinge Hall, named after the lords of other portions of the manor. The share of the Bispham family[19] was described as a fourth part even in the 18th century, when it passed by marriage to Thomas Owen of

Upholland,[20] and then by his two daughters to Holt and Edward Leigh.[21] From Holt Leigh it has

ANDERTON of Lostock.
Sable three shackbolts argent.

GERARD, Lord Gerard.
Argent a saltire gules.

Alan de Rainford, who, with Agnes his wife, had a quarter of a moiety of the manor in 1366, when it was settled upon them for their lives, with remainder to Robert del Eves and his heirs; *Final Conc.* ii, 172. It may be conjectured that this Robert was the son of Agnes by a former marriage. Thus the four co-heirs were in 1374 represented by Winstanley, Billinge, Heaton and Eves, and each quarter would pay a rent of 1s. 1d. to the lord of Newton.

Some further light on the descent is given by claims for debt made by the executors of the will of Sir John de Dalton in the next year against Geoffrey de Wrightington and Ellen his wife, executrix of the will of Robert de Winstanley; Geoffrey de Urmston, executor of the will of Joan, who had been wife and executrix of Robert de Billinge; Alan the Barker of Billinge, executor of the will of Margery, who was the wife and executrix of Robert de Staverley; and Robert de Huyton, executor of the will of Agnes, who was the wife of Alan de Rainford; De Banco R. 457, n. 186. 341 d.

[15] Agnes de Rainford being dead, as appears in the last note, Robert del Eves came into possession, and was defendant in 1375; De Banco R. 459, m. 162. He died in or before 1398; having held Galfhey (? Gautley) in Billinge of Ralph de Langton, baron of Newton, in socage by the rent of 13d.; Nicholas, his son and heir, was twenty-four years of age; *Lancs. Inq. p.m.* (Chet. Soc.), i, 68. The heiress of this family married a Lathom of Mossborough; *Visit.* of 1613 (Chet. Soc.), 106; and in 1620 Henry Lathom died, holding messuages and lands in Billinge of the barony of Newton by a rent of 13d.; *Lancs. Inq. p.m.* (Rec. Soc.), ii, 205; see also Duchy of Lanc. Inq. p.m. x, no. 2.

[16] The rent appears to be made up of 2s. 2d. due by the heir of Adam de Billinge, and 1s. due from the quarter of the manor inherited from the Huyton family. In a later inquisition the rent is given as 3s. 3d.; Duchy of Lanc. Inq. p.m. xxx, no. 7.

What is known of the Billinge family has been stated in previous notes. A member of the family married one of the Huyton co-heirs, while the heiress of the main branch appears to have married William de Heaton, son of the Richard de Heaton who held another quarter of the Huyton share. In 1398 a dispensation was granted for the marriage of Joan de Billinge with William de Heaton; Raines MSS. (Chet. Lib.) xxxvii, B, 61; Dods. MSS. vii, fol. 326. In 1422 a settlement was made of the manor of Birchley and messuages and lands in Billinge, &c., the holders being William de Heaton and

Joan his wife; Pal. of Lanc. Feet of F. bdle. 5, m. 9. In 1530 Richard Heaton gave the manor of Billinge, and his messuages, mills, and lands there and in Birchley to trustees, for the benefit of his son William; Pal. of Lanc. Plea R. 151, m. 8.

[17] In a fine of 1581 relating to Birchley and a quarter of the manor, James and Thurstan Anderton, sons of Christopher, were plaintiffs, and William Heaton and his sons Ralph and Richard, deforciants; Pal. of Lanc. Feet of F. bdle. 43, m. 133. Previously, e.g., in 1542, the manor of Birchley had been included in the Heaton settlements; ibid. bdle. 12, m. 66, &c. James Anderton, of Lostock, died in 1613, seised among other properties of the capital messuage called Birchley Hall, and of various houses and lands in Billinge, held of the Baron of Newton, in socage, by a rent of 3s. 2d.; *Lancs. Inq. p.m.* (Rec. Soc.), ii, 26, 27. Roger, his younger brother, had Birchley by arrangement with his brother Christopher, of Lostock; Pal. of Lanc. Feet of F. bdle. 94, m. 3, and note of Mr. Ince Anderton. In 1631 he paid £10 on refusing knighthood; *Misc.* (Rec. Soc. Lancs. and Ches.), i, 213. He was buried at Wigan, 1 Oct. 1640, and Anne, his widow, on 14 Sept. 1646.

His son, James Anderton, of Gray's Inn, took arms for the king in the Civil War, and joined in the attack on Bolton. Though comprised within the articles of Ludlow he forebore to compound within the time fixed, being a recusant, though not convicted. In 1649 he petitioned to be allowed to compound. His estates were, however, confiscated, and included in the third act of sale, 1652; *Index of Royalists* (Index Soc.), 41; and Thomas Wharton purchased Birchley in the following year. Soon afterwards, however, a composition was arranged, the fine of £800 being reduced to £650 3s. 4d., and further afterwards; *Royalist Comp. Papers* i, 75–81. Captain Thurstan Anderton, another of the family, was wounded at the battle of Newbury, and died at Oxford, in Sept. 1643 : Castlemain, *Cath. Apology.* Early in 1654, in a fine concerning the 'manor of Billinge,' James Anderton, Thomas Wharton, and Joseph Rigby were deforciants; Pal. of Lanc. Feet of F. bdle. 153, m. 81. James Anderton died in 1673; *Cavalier's Note Bk.* 305. His only child was a daughter Elizabeth, who married John Cansfield of Cantsfield. A pedigree was recorded in 1664; Dugdale, *Visit.* 5.

[18] Mary, the daughter and heir of the above John Cansfield, married Sir William Gerard, and in 1692 her lands were settled as the manors of Robert Hall and Cantsfield, and a fourth part of the manor of Billinge, with messuages and lands in

these places, including Birchley; Pal. of Lanc. Feet of F. bdle. 229, m. 109.

[19] No pedigree was recorded. The earliest of this family known is Thomas Bispham, who in 1552 was one of various persons charged with destroying timber in Gaitly Wood, and who early in 1558 made a settlement of three messuages, and other lands in Billinge and Rainford; *Ducatus*, i, 242; Pal. of Lanc. Feet of F. bdle. 20, m. 112. Henry and Thomas, jun., appear in a fine of 1571; ibid, bdle. 33, m. 39. Two years later, Thomas Bispham (probably the younger, on succeeding), made a settlement of 4 messuages and lands in Billinge and Rainford; ibid. bdle. 35, m. 19. In 1600 he was among the freeholders of the township.

William Bispham, who appears in 1628, on refusing knighthood paid £20 in 1631 : *Misc.* (Rec. Soc. Lancs. and Ches.), i, 212. He died 10 Oct. 1639, holding lands in Orrell and Billinge, the latter of the Baron of Newton by a rent of 13d., the regular rent for a fourth part of the manor; his son and heir, Samuel, was of full age; Duchy of Lanc. Inq. p.m. xxx, no. 97. William Bispham of Billinge married a niece of Bishop Bridgeman's; *Wigan Ch.* 348. See also *Fun. Certs.* (Rec. Soc. Lancs. and Ches.), 198, for further particulars of the family; Samuel Bispham was one of King Charles's physicians in ordinary, and had a son and heir, Thomas, aged 18 months at his grandfather's death.

In 1641 the manors of Orrell and Billinge, and messuages, windmill, and lands there were the subject of a settlement by Samuel Bispham, esq.; Pal. of Lanc. Feet of F. bdle. 139, n. 32. Thomas Bispham died 22 Sept. 1677, aged 40; *Wigan Ch.* 746; and another of the same name followed, for Frances Bispham, widow of Thomas, and Thomas Bispham were vouchees in a recovery of the manors in 1703; Pal. of Lanc. Plea R. 477, m. 6. Frances died at the end of the same year; *Wigan Ch.* loc. cit.

[20] Thomas Bispham had an only daughter and heir Margaret, who about 1731 married Thomas Owen; Pal. of Lanc. Plea R. 532, m. 7; Feet of F. bdle. 307, m. 8; *Wigan Ch.* 746.

[21] Pal. of Lanc. Feet of F. bdles. 368, m. 64; 371, m. 137; Plea R. 599, m. 12; the 'manor or lordship of Orrell, a fourth part of the manor or lordship of Billinge, with lands, &c., in Orrell, Billinge, Upholland, Rainford, and Wigan.'

Holt Leigh died 11 March 1785, aged 55, and was buried at St. Clement Danes, London; his widow Mary died 28 Nov. 1794, aged 53; *Wigan Ch.* 745, 746. Bispham Hall was about 1850 the property of John Holt; Raines, in Gastrell's *Notitia*, ii, 254.

descended like Orrell to Mr. Roger Leigh, of Hindley Hall, Aspull.

The shares of the Billinge[32] and Winstanley[33] families cannot be traced satisfactorily.

One of the quarters of the manor was acquired by the family of Bankes of Winstanley.[34]

Thomas and John Winstanley and Thomas Bispham,[35] as landowners of Billinge and Winstanley, contributed to a subsidy levied about 1556. The freeholders in 1600 were: Anderton of Birchley, Thomas Bispham, Richard Billinge, William Atherton, and John Wood.[36] In 1628 the landowners, contributing to the subsidy were: Roger Anderton, William Bispham, William Blackburn, Edmund Wood, and Edmund Bispham. The first and last of these, as convicted recusants, paid double.[37] Those who contributed for lands to the subsidy of 1663 were James Anderton of Birchley, Thomas Bispham, Peter Parr, Geoffrey Birchall, and Alexander Leigh.[38] In 1717 the following, as 'papists,' registered estates here: John Gerard of Ashton, John Howard, Richard Mather, and Robert Rothwell of Winstanley.[39] The principal landowners in 1787, according to the land tax returns, were William Bankes, Edward Leigh, and Sir Robert Gerard, contributing together about half of the sum total raised.

LEIGH. *Gules a cross engrailed argent between four louenges ermine, a canton or.*

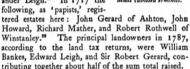

BISPHAM. *Sable a saltire between four harts' heads cabossed erminois.*

The Inclosure Award, with plan, is preserved in the County Council offices at Preston.

A chapel of ease was built here in the CHURCH time of Henry VIII at the cost of the inhabitants, who also paid the priest's wages.[30] At the beginning of Mary's reign James Winstanley of Winstanley, 'minding utterly to destroy the same chapel for ever, out of very malice and hate that he had and bore towards the service of God, which he perceived the Queen's majesty was minded to advance and set forwards,' assembled a band of twenty 'evil-disposed persons,' and forcibly carried off the chalice and paten and other ornaments, broke the windows, turned out forms and chairs and the like furniture, and made it a barn, keeping his hay and corn there by force.[31] There was 'no preacher' at Billinge in 1590.[32] Eight years later the building was found to be out of repair; there were no books but a Bible, the curate was 'no minister, but one licensed to read.' No attempt had been made to collect the 1s. a week fine for absence from the legal services, nor were there any collections for the poor. Very few came to the communion thrice yearly; the parishioners could not say the Catechism, and many did not know the Creed, the Lord's Prayer, and commandments.[33]

The Commonwealth surveyors recommended that the chapel should be made a separate parish church, but this does not seem to have been carried out.[34] The minister in charge was ejected in 1662.[35] The old building was demolished and rebuilt in 1717-18.[36] The church has been of late considerably enlarged under the direction of Mr. T. G. Jackson, R.A. The oldest part of the building dates only from 1717, and before the additions was a plain rectangle in plan, 57 ft. by 37 ft., with a small eastern apse. The elevations are very plain, divided on north and south into four bays by shallow pilasters, with a round-

---

[32] A pedigree, imperfect, was recorded in 1665; Dugdale, *Visit.* (Chet. Soc.), 30.

John Billinge was in 1590 reported as 'soundly affected in religion' *Lydiate Hall*, 246. He was a trustee in 1573, and Richard Billinge was a freeholder in 1600. His grandson, another Richard, recorded the pedigree, being then 52 years of age. As a 'papist' two-thirds of his estate fell into the hands of the Parliamentary authorities, and in 1652 the whole was sequestered; on inquiry it was found that his estate in Wigan parish had been sequestered for recusancy, and that in Ormskirk parish for recusancy and delinquency. Afterwards he petitioned to be allowed to compound; *Royalist Comp. Papers,* i, 173; *Cal. of. Com. for Compounding,* iv, 3102. His son John was aged 17 in 1665, and in 1691 Frances Bispham, widow, purchased from John Billinge and Margaret his wife, and Margery Billinge, widow, the fi.th part of the manor of Billinge, with houses, windmill, dovecote, and lands in Billinge and Rainford; Pal. of Lanc. Feet of F. bdle. 226, m. 44. This 'fifth part' of the manor is named in a later fine, Holt Leigh being possessor; ibid. bdle. 368, m. 64.

[36] This family may be the Winstanleys of Blackley Hurst, a detached part of the township of Winstanley.

[34] In a recovery of the fourth part of the manor of Billinge in 1729 Hugh Holme was vouchee; this was before his marriage with the Bankes heiress; Pal.

headed window in each bay, each window subdivided by mullions into three lights. The walls are crowned with an embattled parapet, with urns at intervals on the parapet, and in the west front is the doorway, with a window of semi-Gothic style over it. All the work is very good of its kind, of wrought stone without, and the fittings of oak, while a fine brass chandelier hangs from the ceiling. Galleries put up in 1823 have now been taken away. It has lately been dedicated to St. Aidan. In 1765 the patronage was disputed, but the rector of Wigan established his right, and is the present patron.[37] The church became parochial in 1882.[38]

The curates in charge and vicars have been as follows [39] :

1609	Richard Bolton [40]
1625	Edward Tempest
1626	Peter Travers
1646	John Wright [41]
c. 1686	Nathan Golborne [42]
1699	Edward Sedgwick
1704	John Horobin
1708	Humphrey Whalley
1749	Edward Parr
1763	Thomas Withnell
1776	Richard Carr
1813	Samuel Hall,[43] M.A. (St. John's Coll. Camb.)
1833	John Bromilow
1853	Howard St. George, M.A. (T.C.D.)
1898	Francis Broughton Anson Miller, M.A. (Trinity Coll. Camb.)

There is a Wesleyan Methodist chapel at Higher End, built in 1845, and a Primitive Methodist one in Chapel End.

If Billinge has afforded some evidence, though questionable, of the existence of a vigorous Protestantism in this part of the county as early as 1550, it also affords evidence of the vitality of the ancient faith, the Andertons of Birchley sheltering the missionary priests. One of the earliest to labour here was the Jesuit Roger Anderton, who served from 1645 until his death fifty years later.[44] The present church of St. Mary was built in 1828. A manuscript preserved in the presbytery contains the *Forma Vivendi* of Richard Rolle of Hampole.[45]

WINSTANLEY

Winstaneslege, 1212 ; Wynstanesleigh, 1252 ; Wynstanlegh, 1292 ; Winstanislegh, 1293.

Winstanley is situated on the eastern lower slopes of Billinge Hill, 440 ft. above sea level being reached, on the edge of an extensive colliery district, several coal-mines being found in the township itself. The principal object in the landscape is the mass of trees surrounding Winstanley Hall, the grounds of which occupy nearly one-third of the whole area of the township. The rest of the country is divided into fields, usually separated by thin hedges, and sometimes by low stone walls. The arable fields produce crops of potatoes, oats, and wheat, whilst there are pastures and meadows, with isolated plantations. The surface soil is sandy, mixed with clay in places, with sandstone rock not far from the surface.

The park is bounded on two sides by the roads from Billinge to Wigan and from Haydock to Upholland, which cross at its southern point. The Lancashire and Yorkshire Company's Liverpool and Wigan Railway passes through near the northern boundary. A colliery railway goes south-west through the township.

Withington lies in the north-west corner, and Longshaw on the western boundary ; south of this is Moss Vale. Two detached portions of the township lie within Billinge Chapel End ; one of these is called Blackley Hurst.

The township has an area of 1,859 acres,[1] and in 1901 the population numbered 564.

Thomas Winstanley, an Oxford scholar of some distinction, was born in the township in 1749. He became Camden Professor of History in 1790 and held other university and college appointments. He died in 1823.[1a] James Cropper, 1773 to 1840, philanthropist, was also a native of Winstanley,[2] and Henry Fothergill Chorley, 1808 to 1872, musical critic and general writer, of Blackley Hurst.[3]

MANOR The earlier stages of the history of the manor have been described in the account of Billinge.[4] There are no materials at present available for tracing the descent in the family of Winstanley, which continued in possession until the end of the 16th century.[5] Early in 1596 Edmund Winstanley and Alice his wife sold the manor

[37] *Wigan Ch.* 755.

[38] Ibid. 756 ; *Lond. Gaz.* 8 Dec, 1882.

[39] *Wigan Ch.* 756, 757. The first who was formally licensed to the cure was Humphrey Whalley, in 1708. Most of the earlier ones, therefore, except during the Commonwealth, were probably curates of Wigan who read the service at Billinge on Sundays.

[40] He was merely a 'reader' in 1609 (Raines MSS. xxii, 298), but contributed to the subsidy of 1622 as curate ; *Misc.* (Rec. Soc. Lancs. and Ches.), i, 65.

[41] He was a 'very honest, godly minister, and of good life and conversation, but kept not the fast day appointed by Act of Parliament' ; *Commonw. Ch. Surv.* 63.

[42] There is probably some error in Canon Bridgeman's list at this point, as Humphrey Tudor's name does not appear in Bishop Stratford's visitation list of 1691. In 1689 Nathan Golborne was 'minister' at Billinge, and was 'conformable' ; *Hist. MSS. Com. Rep.* xiv, App. iv, 228. In Stratford's list he is described as curate of Wigan, ordained in 1686. He is probably the Goulburn of

of Winstanley, with the coal mines and view of frank-pledge, to James Bankes.[6] The purchaser, who belonged to a Wigan family,[7] died 4 August 1617,

WINSTANLEY. *Or two bars azure and in chief three crosses formy gules.*

BANKES. *Sable a cross or between four fleurs de lis argent, a canton of the second.*

leaving a widow Susannah, and a son and heir William, then twenty-four years of age. The manor was held of Sir Richard Fleetwood, baron of Newton, in socage by a rent of 3s. 6d.; the other possessions of James Bankes included the manor of Houghton in

Winwick, and lands in Winstanley and adjacent town-ships.[8] William Bankes, the heir, represented Liverpool in Parliament in 1675;[9] his son, another William, represented Newton in Makerfield in 1660;[10] the latter's son, also William, represented Wigan in 1679.[11] The last William Bankes dying in 1689, the manors passed to his brother Thomas's son and grandson.[12] Thomas had also a daughter Anne, who married Hugh Holme of Upholland in 1732, and their descendants, assuming the name of Bankes,[13] ultimately acquired possession, retaining it until the death of Meyrick Bankes in 1881. His daughter, Mrs. Murray, was left a life interest in the estate, and it was entailed in tail male on her sons. She resumed her maiden name and died December 1907, when her only surviving son George Bankes came into the property.[14]

Another branch of the Winstanley family[15] is found at Blackley Hurst, a detached portion of the township. Their lands were sold to Richard or William Blackburne in 1617,[16] and Blackley Hurst was later acquired by the Gerards, owners of the adjacent Birchley.

408, m. 44 d.; and in the same year Henry son of Roger de Winstanley and Adam son of William de Winstanley were defendants; ibid. m. 36 d.

In 1305 Roger son of Roger de Winstanley recovered messuages and lands from Richard son of William the Lewed, Alice his wife, and Amota daughter of Alice. Alice, it appeared, was the real defendant; her title came from a grant by Robert de Huyton and William de Winstanley; Assize R. 1306, m. 19. In 1332 Roger de Winstanley contributed to the subsidy; Exch. Lay Subs. (Rec. Soc. Lancs. and Ches.), 26. Roger son of Roger de Winstanley and Isolda his father's widow had disputes in 1352; Assize R. 435, m. 29. Particulars of various suits will be found in the account of Billinge.

Hugh de Winstanley contributed to the poll tax in 1381; Exch. Lay Subs. bdle. 130, no. 24. In 1388 he had licence for an oratory for two years; Lich. Epis. Reg. Scrope, vi, fol. 124. Henry de Winstanley and Malin his wife made a grant of land in Houghton in Winwick in 1400–1; Towneley MS. GG, no. 1007.

At the end of 1433 James de Winstanley the elder granted to trustees all his lands, &c., in Wigan, Winstanley, Pemberton, and Billinge; these in the following year were regranted to him with remainder to his son James and Agnes his wife; ibid. no. 2857, 2224. In 1490–1 Gilbert Langton (of Lowe in Hindley), as trustee enfeoffed Gilbert Langtree, James Molyneux, rector of Sefton, and Robert Langton, son of the grantor, of his manor of Winstanley and all his lands in Winstanley, Wigan, Orrell, and Billinge, then occupied by Agnes mother of Edmund Winstanley, and by Randle and Robert Winstanley. After Edmund's death the manor and lands were to descend to James the son and heir of Edmund, with remainder to James's brother Humphrey; ibid. no. 2537. Edmund Winstanley was tenant of the Cockersand lands in 1501; *Rentale de Cockersand* (Chet. Soc.), 5. Richard Crosse of Liverpool in 1493 agreed to marry Elizabeth daughter of Edmund Winstanley; Towneley MS. GG. no. 2250; *Visit.* of 1567 (Chet. Soc.), 107.

Humphrey Winst among the gentry 1512. A marriage h'm and Evan Hay Towneley MS. GG. child marriage of H and Alice sister of F. J. Furnivall's *Ch* Engl. Text Soc.), 2.

[6] Pal. of Lanc. F m. 348. The rema

In 1600 the freeholders were James Bankes, Edmund Atherton, and James Winstanley of Blackley Hurst.[17] William Bankes and William Blackburne contributed to the subsidy of 1628.[18] William Bankes, Thomas Blackburne of Blackley Hurst, clerk, and the heirs of James Winstanley of Hough Wood, contributed in 1663.[19] A number of Winstanley Quakers were in 1670 convicted as ' Popish recusants,' two-thirds of their properties being sequestrated.[20] Thomas Marsh, John Buller, William Jameson, and Thomas Appleton, as 'papists,' registered estates here in 1717.[21]

ORRELL

Horul, 1212 ; Orel, 1292 ; Orhull, 1294 ; Orul, 1307.

This township, sometimes called Orrell in Makerfield, to distinguish it from Orrell in Sefton parish, has an area of 1,617½ acres.[1] It is divided from Upholland on the west by Dean Brook, flowing through a pleasantly-wooded dingle to join the Douglas, which forms the northern boundary. It is situated on the eastern slope of the ridge of high ground stretching north from Billinge to Dalton. The country is open and varied, and consists of pasture land and fields, where the crops are chiefly potatoes, wheat, and oats. Towards the south the country is even more bare and treeless as it merges into the colliery district. The soil is clay with a mixture of sand, over a foundation of hard stone. The town of Upholland is partly situated in this township, and the Abbey Lake, a small sheet of water, is the rendezvous of picnic parties and excursions from the larger towns in the neighbourhood, such a lake being attractive on account of the scarcity of water in the district.

The principal road is that from Ormskirk to Wigan, which passes through the township from west to east, and is crossed by a road leading northwards from St. Helens to Standish. Orrell Mount, over 300 ft., and Orrell Post are to the east of the point where the roads cross ; to the south-west is Far Moor, and to the north Ackhurst. Lamberhead Green lies on the eastern edge, partly in Pemberton. The Lancashire and Yorkshire Company's Liverpool and Wigan line crosses the southern corner of the township, having a station there called Orrell ; the same company's Wigan and Southport line passes through the northern portion, close to the Douglas, with a station called Gathurst.

The population in 1901 numbered 5,436.

Nail-making is carried on, and there is a cotton mill. Roburite is made at Gathurst. In 1787 there were coal mines working under five different ownerships.[2]

A local board was formed in 1872.[3] The township is now governed by an urban district council of twelve members.

Before the Conquest, as afterwards, *MANOR ORRELL* was the extreme north-west berewick of the manor or fee of Newton in Makerfield,[4] and it remained a member of it until the 17th century.[5] The available materials for its history are but scanty. At the survey of 1212 it was held in thegnage by Richard de Orrell as half a ploughland, by the service of 10s. rent and finding a judge ; this was an arrangement 'of ancient time.'[6] There was an ancient subordinate holding, William holding half an oxgang after giving Thomas de Orrell two oxgangs in free marriage in the time of King Richard. Richard de Orrell himself had recently given one oxgang to his brother John, and previously 4 acres to the Hospitallers.[7] Soon afterwards grants were made to Cockersand Abbey by Richard de Orrell and John his son.[8]

Gent. Mag. 1785, ii, 747. She died in 1803 without issue.

The following members of the family matriculated at Oxford, Brasenose College: William son of William Blackburne of Billinge, plebeian, 1626, aged 17 (afterwards vicar of Chartbury) ; Richard son of William, 1633, aged 21 ; Thomas son of William, of Blackley Hurst, 1639, aged 18 (B.D. 1661) ; John son of William, of Billinge, 1640, aged 18 (B.D. 1662) ; Foster's *Alumni*.

William son of Thomas Blackburne occurs in 1673 in the account of Newton in Makerfield.

William Blackburne, of Blackley Hurst, John his son and heir apparent, and William the son of John, are all mentioned in a lease enrolled in 1718 ; Piccope MSS. (Chet. Lib.), iii, fol. 200, from 2nd R. of George I at Preston.

A Roger Rigby of Blackley Hurst, brother of Edward Rigby of Burgh, was in 1590 reported as ' evil given in religion '; *Lydiate Hall*, 250.

[17] *Misc.* (Rec. Soc. Lancs. and Ches.), i, 239, 242. Edward Winstanley and Humphrey Atherton had a dispute concerning lands in Winstanley in 1593 ; *Ducatus Lanc.* (Rec. Com.), iii, 291, 319. A settlement of lands in Billinge was made in 1596, Humphrey Atherton and Alice his wife, and Edmund, the son and heir, being deforciants ; Pal. of Lanc. Feet of F. bdle. 59, m. 21.

Edmund Atherton of Winstanley died in 1613 holding land in Billinge of the Baron of Newton ; Humphrey his son and heir was four years old ; *Lancs. Inq. p.m.* (Rec. Soc. Lancs. and Ches.), i, 277.

From deeds in the possession of W. Farrer it appears that Romeshaw House was part of the Atherton estate.

[18] Norris D. (B.M.).

[19] Schedule in possession of W. Farrer. A William Blackburne of Blackley Hurst is also named.

[20] *Local Glean. Lancs. and Ches.* i, 234, where lists referring to this and neighbouring townships are printed.

[21] *Engl. Cath. Nonjurors*, 97, 125, 135, 151. Appleton's house was called The Riddings.

[1] Including 7 acres of inland water ; Census of 1901.

[2] Land tax returns at Preston. The owners were William German, Blundell & Co., Hardcastle & Co., Rev. Thomas Holme, and Richard Culshaw & Co.

[3] *Lond. Gaz.* 21 June 1872.

[4] *V.C.H. Lancs.* i, 286.

[5] See the various inquisitions of the Langtons ; e.g. *Lancs. Inq. p.m.* (Chet. Soc.), i, 138 ; ii, 99 ; ibid. (Rec. Soc. Lancs. and Ches.), i, 105.

[6] *Lancs. Inq. and Extents* (Rec. Soc. Lancs. and Ches.), i, 76. Richard de Orrell occurs from 1201 in the Pipe R. (*Lancs. Pipe R.* 152, 179, &c.), but it appears from the Survey that he had been in possession in the time of Henry II.

[7] *Lancs. Inq. and Extents*, loc. cit.

Before the end of the century, in what way does not appear, the manor was acquired by the Holands of Upholland,[9] from whom it descended, like their other manors, to the Lovels,[10] and, after forfeiture, to the Earls of Derby.[11]

William, the sixth earl, sold it to William Orrell of Turton,[12] and the latter soon after sold to the Bisphams, lords of part of the adjacent manor of Billinge ;[13] then by marriage it descended to Thomas Owen,[14] and to Holt Leigh of Wigan.[15] His son, Sir Roger Holt Leigh, of Hindley Hall in Aspull, left it to his cousin, afterwards Lord Kingsdown, for life, and then to the present owner, Mr. Roger Leigh of Aspull.[16]

The Orrell family had numerous offshoots, but the relationships cannot be traced. The survey of 1212, quoted above, shows that there were then two subordinate holdings of one-eighth and a quarter of the manor. The former may have descended to the Orrells of Turton,[17] and the latter may be the holding of Alexander Orrell of Orrell Post, whose land in 1607 was held by a rent of 3s.[18]

The freeholders in 1600 were the Alexander Orrell just named, William Prescott, and Thomas Tipping.[19] James Bankes of Winstanley also held lands here in 1618.[20]

About the same time another family, the Leighs of Ackhurst, are mentioned, continuing down to the

---

[9] Robert de Holand was lord in 1292 ; Assize R. 408, m. 37 ; *Final Conc.* (Rec. Soc. Lancs. and Ches.), i, 173.

In 1307 Robert de Holand desiring to give a plough-land in Orrell to the chaplain of Upholland, inquiry was made on behalf of the king ; the manor of Orrell was found to be held of John de Langton and Alice his wife by the service of 10s. 6d.—an increase of 6d.—and doing suit at the court of Newton in Makerfield from three weeks to three weeks ; *Lancs. Inq. and Extents,* i, 322.

At a later inquiry in 1324 the same statement was made as to the tenure ; the value of the manor was £6 6s. 3¾d. ; Inq. a.q.d. 18 Edw. II, no. 68. See also Inq. p.m. 47 Edw. III (1st nos.), no. 19.

[10] *Lancs. Inq. p.m.* (Chet. Soc.), ii, 2.

[11] Pat. 4 Hen. VII, 25 Feb. ; Duchy of Lanc. Inq. p.m. v, no. 68. In 1597 the deforciants of the manors of Orrell and Dalton were William, Earl of Derby, and Edward Stanley ; Pal. of Lanc. Feet of F. bdle. 58, m. 254.

[12] Bridgeman, *Wigan Ch.* (Chet. Soc.), 257 ; see further below.

[13] See *Lancs. Inq. p.m.* (Rec. Soc.), i, 200, in 1607. William Bispham died in 1639 holding the manor of Orrell of the king as of his manor of East Greenwich ; Duchy of Lanc. Inq. p.m. xxx, no. 97.

[14] See the account of Billinge.

[15] See the account of Aspull.

[16] Burke, *Landed Gentry.*

[17] In 1292 Adam son of William de Orrell, asserting that he was lord of an eighth part of the vill, complained that Robert de Holland and Robert his son had disseised him of his free tenement in Orrell. Some of the waste had been improved by the elder Robert, and it was shown that sufficient pasture had been reserved for the commoners ; thus Adam lost his case ; Assize R. 408, m. 37.

In 1334 William Hert and Emma his wife, Roger Hert and Agnes his wife—the wives being granddaughters (or daughters) and heirs of Adam de Orrell—claimed lands in Orrell against Henry de Orrell and the brothers Roger and William de Orrell, Henry alleging a grant by Adam ; Coram Rege R. 297, m. 103.

[18] In 1530 there was a recovery of the manor of Orrell by William Orrell, sen., against William Orrell, jun.; Pal. of Lanc. Plea R. 151, m. 1. William Orrell of Orrell claimed against John Orrell of Turton in 1551 a messuage and lands in Orrell, as heir of a certain Robert Orrell, giving his pedigree thus : Robert —s. John—s. Peter—bro. Henry—s. William ; ibid. R. 191, m. 12.

In disputes which arose in the time of Elizabeth are numerous details regarding this manor.

It was stated tha Orrell was sei ed o called the Hall of O mill, and lands in Or his ancestors. Abou the estate to Hugh it passed to Richard Inn, and then to Sir gave it to his son R Robert, at the desir assured the premises ton of Gray's Inn, w to Francis Sheriogto wife. Two years l was charged with for possession, his son pl ce, and ' they wer hooting arrows at th her servants' ; Duc Eli lxx ii', S. 8

From another docu Sir   W

...

...

middle of the 18th century.[31] They were recusants and incurred the usual penalties. Emma, or Emerentia, Leigh, widow, Margaret and Catherine Leigh, spinsters, and their sister, Anne Sandford, widow, registered their estates in 1717.[32] Thomas Duxon and William Tarleton were the other 'papists' who did the same.[33]

Orrell was formerly considered part of the chapelry of Upholland. Recently, in connexion with the Established Church, St. Luke's Chapel-of-ease has been erected.

The Wesleyans and Primitive Methodists have chapels in the township, as also have the Welsh Calvinistic Methodists.

Salem Chapel, built in 1824, belongs to the Congregationalists, who formed a church here about 1805 and erected a temporary chapel about 1810. The building is still called John Holgate's Chapel, from the name of one of the early ministers, 1820–50. A later minister conformed to the Established religion, an occurrence which almost ruined the Congregational interest.[34]

The Roman Catholic mission was founded at Crossbrook in 1699 and removed to the present site at Far Moor in 1805; the church of St. James was enlarged in 1841, and a bell-tower erected in 1882. There is a burial-ground attached.[35] Anne Sandford in 1740 gave £100 to the mission with an obligation to say mass for herself, her mother, and two sisters.[36] A convent of French Benedictine nuns, driven out of their country by the Revolution, in the first half of last century occupied the house at Orrell Mount, but afterwards removed to Princethorpe, Warwickshire.

UPHOLLAND

Hoiland, Dom. Bk.; Hollande, 1202; Holand, 1224 and common; Holande, 1279; Upholond, 1292; Upholland, xvi cent.

This township, distinguished by the prefix from Downholland near Halsall, is the largest in the parish, having an area of 4,685 acres.[1] The population in 1901 numbered 4,773.[2] From the northern and eastern boundaries, formed by the River Douglas and its affluent the Dean Brook, the surface rises rapidly to a point near the middle of the western boundary, where a height of about 550 ft. is attained. From this a ridge extends southerly, the ground to the south-

west falling away continuously to the boundary, which is formed by Raw Moss and Holland Moss. The southerly aspect of the township is open and bare; on the north there are more trees as the land dips down to the romantic valley of the Douglas. The arable fields, many divided by stone walls, are sown with oats and wheat, and potatoes are very extensively grown. On the south and west there are collieries and fire-brick works, whilst stone quarries give work to a section of the inhabitants. The soil appears to be chiefly sandy, clayey in places, a shaley rock appearing now and again on the surface, but the solid base is sandstone.

The 17th-century registers name many 'coalers' and 'delf men'; there were also nailers, linen-weavers, glovers, watchmakers, and other craftsmen, whose names are found in the township.

Upholland village, where the priory formerly stood, lies on the eastern slope of the ridge, near the Orrell boundary. Through it pass from east to west the road from Wigan to Ormskirk, and from north to south that from Chorley to St. Helens. The village has a steep main street, with the church at the south end, overlooking a wide open space of churchyard on the north and east. Immediately south of the church is the site of the claustral buildings, but their remains, with a single exception, are buried in the ground and have never been explored. The houses of Upholland are from an architectural point of view of little interest, except one, an early 17th or late 16th-century house on the south side of the main street, with mullioned windows and a panel with the Stanley crest. To the north lie Walthew Green, Roby Mill, and Holland Lees; to the west are Holland Moor, Birch Green, Digmoor, and Tawd Bridge, the River Tawd forming a portion of the boundary at this point, and being joined by Grimshaw Brook; to the south and southwest are Tontine, Pimbo, and Crawford. The Lancashire and Yorkshire Company's railway from Liverpool to Wigan passes through the southern part of the township, with a station at Pimbo Lane now called Upholland.

Edward II stayed at Upholland for a fortnight in October 1323, on his way from the north to Liverpool.[3]

The Local Government Act of 1858 was adopted by the township in 1872.[4] The local board was, in 1894, replaced by a district council of fifteen members.

[31] The inheritance of this family was derived from Edmund Molyneux, mercer of London, lord of Vange in Essex, who died 31 Jan. 1615–16, seised of lands in Orrell and Upholland, held of Richard Fleetwood and of the king respectively. His heir was James Leigh, son of his sister Agnes, aged forty in 1618; *Lancs. Inq. p.m.* (Rec. Soc. Lancs. and Ches.), ii, 99. He was a benefactor of Wigan and Upholland. His will is printed in Gisborne Molineux's *Molineux Family,* 143; it shows that he was related to the Molyneuxes of Hawkley. An Edmund Molyneux and his wife Agnes had lands in Orrell (apparently in the latter's right) in 1532; Pal. of Lanc. Feet of F. bdle. 11, m. 192.

James Leigh and Margaret his wife, with their daughters Alice, Jane, and Ellen, were fined for recusancy in 1616.

A figure, probably of Cupid, dating from Roman times was found here.[5]

A fair, for pigs only, is held on Easter Monday. There was formerly a market on Wednesday.[6] There were several crosses which have now disappeared.[7]

In 1066 the manor of *HOLLAND* or *MANOR* Upholland was held by Steinulf; it was assessed as two plough-lands and worth 64d.[8] Nothing further is known of its tenure until 1212, when it together with Melling was held in thegnage by Henry de Melling; of him Matthew and Alan held the two plough-lands in Upholland by a rent of 12s. a year.[9] Ten years earlier Matthew de Holland—or Holand, as the name was usually spelt—held fourteen oxgangs here, to which Uctred de Church quitclaimed all his right.[10] Nothing further seems to be known of Alan, the joint tenant with Matthew. The latter was a benefactor of Cockersand Abbey.[11]

In 1224 Simon de Halsall quitclaimed to Robert de Holland all his right in the two plough-lands in Upholland.[12] The relationship of this Robert to his predecessor Matthew does not appear in the records. He was the ancestor of the great Holand family. His last appearance was to answer a charge of setting fire to one of the rector's houses in Wigan in 1241; he and his son Thurstan were lodged in prison, but released till the trial.[13]

Thurstan is said to have married a daughter of Adam de Kellet; eventually the lordship of Nether Kellet descended to his heirs by this wife.[14] He also acquired lands in Hale, and large grants in Makerfield.[15] Sir Robert de Holland, the son of Thurstan, who succeeded about 1276, married Elizabeth daughter and co-heir of Sir William de Samlesbury.[16]

Robert's son and namesake, Sir Robert de Holland, became one of the leading men in the county, being a favourite official of Thomas, Earl of Lancaster, from whom he secured an alteration in the tenure of Upholland, which does not seem to have been permanent.[17] He extended his possessions by a marriage with Maud, daughter and co-heir of Alan de la Zouch,[18] and had many grants from his patron the earl;[19] some of these were held to be invalid. He was summoned to Parliament as Lord Holland from 1314 to 1321. He took part in the earl's rebellion, and all his lands were forfeited;[20] he himself was murdered in October 1328, it is said by followers of the earl who regarded him either as a coward or a traitor.[21] Among his other acts was the foundation of the priory at Upholland in 1310 to 1317.[22] This was practically the conclusion of the family's active interest in the manor.

The forfeiture of the estates was in 1328 reversed by Edward III,[23] and Holland descended regularly to Sir Robert's son, Robert, who distinguished himself

---

[5] Watkin, *Roman Lancs.* 230.

[6] It had long been discontinued in 1836; Baines, *Lancs.* (1st ed.), iii, 561.

[7] *Lancs. and Ches. Antiq. Soc.* xix, 237.

[8] *V.C.H. Lancs.* i, 284b.

[9] *Lancs. Inq. and Extents* (Rec. Soc. Lancs. and Ches.), i, 15.

[10] *Final Conc.* (Rec. Soc. Lancs. and Ches.), i, 14. The two oxgangs not accounted for may have been Alan's portion.

[11] *Cockersand Chart.* (Chet. Soc.), ii, 610. The boundaries of his donation began at the head of the Ridge on the division between Holland and Dalton, followed this division as far as Black lache, and by Black lache, Rutand Clough, Green lache, Pool lache, to the syke between St. Mary's land and the assart of Outi; then by the carr beyond the Ridge to the starting point. He added an assart called Lithehurst, lying between Philip's boundary and Hawk's Nest Clough. The easements included oak mast and shealings (*scalingis*). The 'St. Mary's land' mentioned was perhaps the abbey's land in Dalton.

[12] *Final Conc.* i, 47.

[13] Cur. Reg. R. 121, m. 25 d., 26 d., 32. The result is not given. Robert de Holland granted to Cockersand Abbey all the land which Hugh and Wronow held of him in Bothams, on the boundary of Dalton, and apparently adjoining that granted by Matthew de Holland; *Chart.* ii, 611.

[14] See *Final Conc.* ii, 118. Thurstan de Holland was one of the jurors as to those liable to contribute to the Gascon scutage in 1242–3; *Lancs. Inq. and Extents*, i, 146.

In 1246 Thurstan de Holland was acquitted of having disseised Amice, wife of Thomas de Pendlebury, of 16 acres in Upholland; Assize R. 404, m. 1.

In 1268 Thurstan de Holland, his brothers Matthew, Richard, Robert, and

William, and his s moned to answer a Cur Reg

in the French wars, and died 16 March 1372–3 ;[24] and to the latter's granddaughter Maud, who married John Lovel, fifth Lord Lovel of Titchmarsh.[25] She

HOLLAND. *Azure semée de lis a lion rampant guardant argent.*

LOVEL. *Barry nebulée of six or and gules.*

survived her husband, and died 4 May 1423, holding the manor of Upholland of the king as Duke of Lancaster in socage by the ancient rent of 12s. ; also the manors of Halewood, Walton in West Derby, Nether Kellet, half of Samlesbury, Orrell, and a quarter of Dalton, burgages in Wigan and Lancaster, and lands in Aughton, Cuerdley, and Ditton. The other estates had descended to her father Robert's brother John, as heir male, and he was succeeded by Henry Holland, Duke of Exeter.[26]

Lady Lovel's son John having died in 1414 Upholland was inherited by her grandson William, seventh Lord Lovel and fourth Lord Holland. It descended on his death in 1455 to his son John, Lord Lovel, who died ten years later, and then to the latter's son and heir Francis, created Viscount Lovel in 1483. Adhering to the cause of Richard III he had many offices and honours bestowed upon him ; but was attainted by Henry VII in 1485 and his honours and lands were forfeited. Two years later he fought on the Yorkist side at the battle of Stoke, and was either killed there or died soon afterwards.[27]

Upholland and the other forfeited manors were

retained by the Crown until 25 February 1488–9, when they were granted to Thomas, Earl of Derby, with the lands and manors of other Yorkists.[28] It continued to descend with Lathom and Knowsley until 1717, when it was sold by Lady Ashburnham, as heir of William, the ninth earl, to Thomas Ashhurst of Ashhurst in Dalton.[29] In 1751 Henry Ashhurst sold it to Sir Thomas Bootle of Lathom,[30] and it has since descended with his manors, the Earl of Lathom being the present lord.[31]

After the foundation of the monastery the prior' were the chief residents within the manor. As i:· the case of most other religious houses the externa: history was uneventful.[32] After the suppression of the house by Henry VIII in 1536 the site and all the lands were granted to John Holcroft,[33] who soon transferred them to Sir Robert Worsley of Booths.[34] Seventy years later the site was owned by Edmund

BOOTLE. *Gules on a cheveron engrailed between three combs argent as many crosses formy fitchy of the field.*

WILBRAHAM. *Argent three bendlets wavy gules.*

Molyneux of London,[35] who bequeathed it to his nephew, Richard Leigh.[36] It is said to have been acquired by the Bisphams of Billinge, and descended with their estates to the Leighs of Orrell and Aspull.[37]

[24] G.E.C. loc. cit. Robert was sixteen years old in 1328 ; *Cal. Close*, 1327–30, p. 348. From the fine above quoted (*Final Conc.* ii, 193) it will be seen that Sir Robert had three sons—Alan, Robert, and Thomas. Of Alan nothing further is known, and it is supposed that he died before the restoration of the honours. Thomas married Joan daughter of Edmund, Earl of Kent, and granddaughter of Edward I ; he was summoned to Parliament as Lord Holland in 1353 and as Earl of Kent in 1360 ; G.E.C. op. cit. iv, 237, 351, 352.

The inquiry made in June 1349, after the death of Maud, widow of Robert de Holland, showed that she had held the manor of Upholland for her life, with reversion to her son Robert and his heirs, in socage by a rent of 12s. ; and doing suit to county and wapentake ; also the manors of Hale, &c. ; Inq. p.m. 23 Edw. III, pt. 1, no. 58. She died outside the county ; Sir Robert, her son, was of full age.

A similar return was made after the death of Sir Robert in 1373. The heir to Upholland and other manors was his granddaughter Maud (daughter of his deceased son Robert), wife of John Lovel, and seventeen years of age. The heir to the moiety of the manor of Haydock, &c., was his son John, aged twenty-four and upwards ; Inq. p.m. 47 Edw. III (1st

nos.), no. 19. See also *Surv.* of 1346 (Chet. Soc.), 42.

Sir Robert in 1367 increased the endowment of Upholland by a grant of Markland in Pemberton and other lands ; Inq. p.m. 41 Edw. III (2nd nos.), no. 12.

[25] G.E.C. op. cit. iv, 236 ; v, 164–6, from which this account of the Lovels is derived.

[26] *Lancs. Inq. p.m.* (Chet. Soc.), ii, 1–3. For the Exeter family see G.E.C. op. cit. iii, 296.

[27] *Dict. Nat. Biog.*

[28] Pat. 4 Hen. VII. There is a later grant of this and other manors to James Lord Strange ; Pat. 13 Chas. I, pt. 27, 3 July.

In the inquisition taken after the death of Ferdinando, fifth earl, in 1595, it was found that Upholland was still held by the rent of 12s. ; Add. MS. 32104,· fol. 425.

[29] James, Earl of Derby, seems to have released his right in the manors sold, in Sept. 1715 ; Pal. of Lanc. Feet of F. bdle. 276, m. 52.

Thomas Ashhurst and Diana his wife were in possession in 1721; Pal. of Lanc. Plea R. 512, m. 8.

Baines (ed. 1836) gives the date 1717, apparently from the *Lathom* D. ; iii, 559.

[30] Pal. of Lanc. Feet of F. bdle. 347, m. 26.

[31] See the account of Lathom.

Little can be said of the remains of the monastic buildings. They were on the south of the church, but did not, as it seems, join it except as regards the western range of the claustral buildings. Part of the west wall of this range is standing, enough to show that it was of two stories with a row of narrow windows on the west side. In the deed of grant to John Holcroft in 1546 a chamber at the west end of the church is mentioned, which may be that on the south face of the tower, the roof corbels of which still remain.

Sir John de Dalton and his accomplices, after carrying off Margery de la Beche in 1347, took refuge for a time in Dame Maud de Holland's manor at Upholland, which was then vacant; but fled north on the arrival of the king's writ for his arrest.[38]

Among the landowners in the township may be named Hesketh,[39] Orrell,[40] Standish,[41] Crosse,[42] and Fairclough.[43] In 1600 the only freeholder recorded was Robert Smallshaw.[44] In 1628 William Whalley, Roger Brownlow, and Richard Smallshaw, as land-owners, contributed to the subsidy.[45] A family

named Holme were also settled here. Hugh Holme of Upholland House in 1732 married Anne daughter of Thomas Bankes of Winstanley, and her descend-ants ultimately succeeded to the manors and lands of the Bankes family.[46] Pimbo was held of the Earl of Derby.[47] Though the Recusant Roll of 1641 con-tains but few names of residents here [48] the Ven. John Thewlis, a priest, executed for religion at Lancaster in 1617, was a native of this township.[48a]

CHURCH The earliest record of a church of any kind is that concerning Sir Robert de Holland's endowment of his chapel in 1307.[49] This was succeeded by the priory church, which, after the destruction of the monastery, was preserved for the use of the people, as a chapel of ease to Wigan.[50] It appears to have been well fitted, but the church goods were seized by the Crown, as part of the priory,[51] and in 1552 it was but poorly furnished.[52]

The church of ST. THOMAS THE MARTYR stands at the south-east end of the village on sloping ground, the churchyard, which lies on the north and

---

88 Chan. Inq. p.m. 21 Edw. III, no. 63.

89 The Heskeths of Rufford held various properties in this and neighbouring town-ships; see Duchy of Lanc. Inq. p.m. v, no. 16. In 1555 Richard Hey acquired a messuage and lands from Sir Thomas Hesketh and Alice his wife; this property seems to have been secured in 1578 by Robert Hey from James, the bastard son of Richard; Pal. of Lanc. Feet of F. bdles. 16, m. 137; 40, m. 167. See also *Ducatus Lanc.* (Rec. Com.), iii, 145.

40 The families of this name make frequent appearances. Henry Orrell was a defendant in a suit respecting Dean riddings in 1516; *Ducatus*, i, 127. Wil-liam Orrell and Thomas his son were deforciants in 1561 and 1562; Pal. of Lanc. Feet of F. bdles. 23, m. 193; 24, m. 256. Lewis Orrell and Ellen his wife in 1566; ibid. bdle. 28, m. 102.

41 George Standish of Sutton held land in Upholland of the Earl of Derby by the 100th part of a knight's fee; Duchy of Lanc. Inq. p.m. ix, no. 3 (6 Edw. VI). William Standish, the grandson and heir of George, had secured to him in 1561 the reversion of a tenement of Robert son of Thomas Topping; Pal. of Lanc. Feet of F. bdle. 23, m. 153. William Standish and Margaret his wife made a settlement in 1573; ibid. bdle. 35, m. 56. John, William's son and heir-apparent, was joined with them in 1597; ibid. bdle. 58, m. 26.

42 Roger Crosse of the Liverpool family, in the time of Henry VIII, had copyhold lands in Upholland of the Earl of Derby at a rent of 17s.; Duchy of Lanc. Inq. p.m. vi, no. 18; also x, no. 20. See Crosse D. *Trans. Hist. Soc.* no. 165.

48 Oliver Fairclough purchased lands from James Worsley and Beatrice his wife in 1584; Pal. of Lanc. Feet of F. bdle. 46, m. 10. Arthur Fairclough oc-curs in 1613; *Lancs. Inq. p.m.* (Rec. Soc.), i, 276.

Thomas Winstanley, clerk, and Thomas Fairclough were in 1588 defendants in a suit regarding Dean Mill in Upholland and Orrell; *Ducatus* (Rec. Com.), iii, 199.

Dr. James Fairclough, 1636, and his son James were benefactors; *Notitia Cestr.* ii, 260.

44 *Misc.* (Rec. Soc. Lancs. and Ches.),

i, 241. William an occur in fines of El of Lanc. Feet of F. The name takes Smoshay

Thomas Chisnall holland in 1549 and Feet of F. bdles 13 They appear to hav ward Chisnall or Duchy of Lanc. Inq

45 Norris D. (B

east sides, falling rapidly from west to east and allowing the introduction of the vestry under the east end.
The building consists of chancel 32 ft. 6 in. by
22 ft. 6 in., nave 80 ft. by 22 ft. 3 in., with north and
south aisles 11 ft. wide, and west tower 14 ft. by 16 ft.,
all these measurements being internal. With the
exception of the chancel and the tower the building
is of 14th-century date, the original structure having
been planned as a T-shaped church with large
central western tower and transepts, the present nave
forming the chancel. Whether this plan was ever
carried out is extremely doubtful, and only excavation
on the west end could determine the extent of the
original building, if it were ever greater than at present. It is probable, however, that the building
came to a standstill somewhere about the middle of the
14th century, perhaps during the Great Pestilence,
and that in this unfinished state it remained till late
in the 15th century, when the present west tower was
added in the rather clumsy manner now apparent.
In this form the church continued till late in the last
century, the sanctuary being formed in the easternmost
bay, inclosed on the north and south by low walls,
the evidence for which may still be seen in the
arcades ; but in 1882 (when a drastic restoration was
commenced), a new chancel was begun to the east,
and the building was brought to its present condition.

It may be assumed that the original chapel founded
here in 1307 was a small building, and that it stood
for some years after the foundation of the priory
twelve years later. There is no record, indeed, of
the erection of a church by the convent, but probably
a larger and more important building would be
thought necessary, and the present structure begun
towards the middle of the first half of the 14th
century. The conditions of the site, which rises
steeply at the west end, preclude the idea that the
building was ever intended to extend much further
in that direction, and the evidence of the masonry at
the west end of the nave and aisles makes a transeptal
T-shaped plan the only likely one.

The walls are constructed of rough sandstone,
finishing with a plain parapet, and the nave and aisles
are roofed in one rather low span, which detracts
somewhat from the external dignity of the building.
This roof, which is covered with stone slates, is
however not the original one, the line of which may
still be seen on the exterior of the east face of the
tower. The old pitch is only slightly more acute
than the present one, and it may be assumed that the
original aspect was not very different from that which
now exists, the height of the aisle walls precluding
the idea of there having ever been a clearstory.

There seems to have been a restoration in the
middle of the 18th century, the present roof dating
from 1752 according to a date roughly cut on it,
with the initials P T on one of the principals, and
T W on another. The tower also appears to have
been repaired at this time, and many of the bench-ends
put in during the previous century renewed. Galleries
were also inserted, and in 1799 a vestry was built on
the north side at the east end of the aisle, a door being
cut through the wall in the north-east angle of the
aisle. The galleries, which were on the north,
south, and west sides, projected in front of the nave
piers, which were much damaged in being cut away
to receive them. The interior remained in this state,
with square pews and no chancel, down to the

time of the restoration of 1882–6. In this restoration, in addition to the erection of the new chancel,
the tracery of all the old windows which had not
been already restored was renewed. A plan of the
church with the seating as it existed in 1850 now
hangs in the vestry.

The chancel is built in 14th-century style, and is
lit by a large five-light traceried window at the east
and two windows on the north and on the south.
On the north side a stone circular staircase leads
down to the vestry beneath, access to which is
gained on the outside by two doors at the east end.
To obtain room for the vestry the chancel is raised
four steps above the level of the nave, which makes
it dominate the interior rather aggressively. The
chancel arch is modern, of three moulded orders,
and takes the place of a very poor east window,
inserted in 1840, after a former 14th-century
window had been blown out. The older window
is shown in Buck's drawing of 1727.

The nave is of four bays with north and south
arcades of pointed arches springing from piers, and
responds composed of four rounded shafts with
hollows between, with moulded capitals and bases.
The arches are of two orders with the characteristic
14th-century wave-moulding. There is no clearstory,
and the nave roof is ceiled with a flat plaster
ceiling at the level of the crown of the arches, the
aisles having plaster ceilings following the line of the
roof. The 18th-century king-post roof above is of
a very plain description, and not intended to be
exposed. At the west end of the aisles are pointed
arches springing from responds composed of three
shafts, the moulded capitals of which range with those
of the nave piers, and were designed to open to the
transepts on each side of the tower. The arches are
now filled in with modern windows, apparently
reproducing early 16th-century work. The responds,
both to nave and aisles, form on each side of the tower
part of the great eastern piers of the crossing, the
lofty clustered shafts of which, facing west, are now
partly exposed on the outside of the building in the
internal angles of the tower and aisle walls, and
partly hidden by the later masonry.

The north aisle has four three-light pointed windows on its north side with net tracery, all modern
copies of the original 14th-century work, and one
similar window at the east end ; the later window,
already mentioned, on the west end is of four lights
with poor tracery, and all the windows have external
labels. The south aisle is similarly lighted except in
the west bay, where there is a deeply-splayed window
placed high in the wall. Originally the wall of this
bay appears to have been pierced for an opening about
12 ft. wide which gave access to the western range of
the priory buildings, which abutted here. The
straight joints in the masonry on the outside wall
show distinctly the extent of the former opening, and
the present window must be a late insertion after the
opening had been built up. At the east end of the
south aisle is a good double 14th-century piscina, in
the usual position, with trefoiled head, and on the
corresponding side of the north aisle a square hole
in the wall, probably an aumbry. Under the
windows at a height of 6 ft. there is a moulded
string, which is cut away for some distance on each
wall on the west end. Below the string the walls
have been cemented, but above it are of rough

masonry. The capitals and upper parts of the western responds have also been much cut away at the time when the galleries were inserted.

The west tower is narrower than that originally designed, built of very friable sandstone, and having apparently been untouched since the 18th century is in a very bad state of repair. Some refacing appears to have been done on the west front on the north side of the doorway and at the belfry stage, and a scheme of restoration which it is proposed shortly to carry out will include the refacing of the tower. It has little architectural merit, being of low proportion and little in keeping with the rest of the building. Externally on the west face it is of four stages, with rather weak diagonal buttresses of nine stages at the north and south-west angles. On the north and south sides the walls are quite plain up to the string under the belfry windows. The west doorway, now much decayed, consists of a pointed arch with moulded head and jambs, with a series of hollows filled with carvings, and so weathered as to be unrecognizable. Between the buttresses a moulded string-course forms the lower member of the sill of a large three-light west window similar to those of the nave, with net tracery and external hood-mould. The tracery is modern, but the jambs appear to be old, and the window must have been moved here when the tower was built. Above this again is a string ornamented with four-leaved flowers which goes round the tower, breaking round the buttresses at the level of the belfry window-sills. The belfry windows, which are of similar detail on all three sides (north, west, and south) are of two lights under a pointed traceried head, and appear to be of 14th-century date. They seem to have been originally intended for glass, as the jambs and mullions are grooved, and probably belong to some part of the monastery building either destroyed or in decay when the tower was erected. They have now stone louvres. Above the belfry stage there is a single-light narrow window on the north, south, and west sides, and on the east side one of two lights, but these are now hidden by the clock face. The present clock was given in 1907, replacing an older one. The tower ends in an embattled parapet with 18th-century angle pinnacles, one only of which is perfect. The roof is apparently of the same date, being in the form of a stone-slated gable running east and west. There is a door also on the north side of the tower in the east angle, and on the south side below the string underneath the belfry window are three corbels, showing that a building was set against it at this point. On the face of the north buttress is a niche now much decayed, with a trefoiled head. There is no vice in the tower, the first floor being gained by a wooden staircase, and the others by ladders, but at the belfry stage in the south-east corner is a stone staircase in the thickness of the wall, descending to a door which is now blocked. This must have been the original means of access to

the upper part of the tower, and from this stage a stair in the south-east angle of the tower leads up to the roof. The tower was evidently meant to be open to the church up to 35 ft. from the ground, and at this level a chamfered string, with four-leaved flowers cut on it, shows on the inner face of the walls, marking the position of the original floor here.

The tower arch is of two moulded orders springing from a 15th-century impost moulding, and is filled in at the ringing-chamber stage with modern glazed wooden tracery, and below with a modern wooden door screen to the porch under the tower.

The fittings are mostly modern, the pulpit and font, both of wood, dating from 1882. In the north and south aisles are the 17th-century bench-ends already mentioned, carved with initials, names, and dates, the majority belonging to the year 1635,[63] and at the west end of the nave is a good oak churchwardens' pew with the names of the wardens and the date 1679. There is a good 18th-century brass chandelier in the middle of the nave, suspended by a long ornamental iron rod. In the tower porch above the north door is the board with the royal arms, dated 1755; and on the opposite wall is an oak cupboard with doors inscribed with the churchwardens' names, Scripture texts, and the date 1720.

There were formerly fragments of ancient stained glass in various parts of the church, but these were collected and brought together in the middle window of the south aisle in 1883.

There is a ring of six bells cast by John Warner & Sons, London, 1877.

The church plate consists of a chalice 1706, a paten 1720, another paten 1738, inscribed 'The gift of Thomas Henry Ashhurst Esqr. to the Chappel of Upholland in Lancashire 1739'; two flagons of the same date; one with a similar inscription, but the other without, and a chalice 1817, with the inscription 'The gift of Meyrick Bankes Esqre. to the Chapel of Upholland 1817.'

The registers of marriages begin in 1600, those of baptisms in 1607, and those of burials in 1619. The first volume (1600–1735) has been printed.[63a]

During the time of Elizabeth, and probably later, only a reading minister was provided;[54] but an improvement took place under Bishop Bridgeman,[55] and in 1643 Upholland was made a parish, the district including also the townships of Dalton and Orrell, and parts of Billinge and Winstanley.[56] The Act was treated as null at the Restoration, and Upholland remained a chapelry until 1882, when by Order in Council it was made a parish.[57]

The income of the minister appears to have been about £60 in 1650.[58] The principal tithes were owned by the Earls of Derby, who paid a small composition to the rectors of Wigan[59]; the lands of the monastery were tithe-free.[60] In 1724 Bishop Gastrell found the curate's income about £40, of

---

[53] Many have been recut and a late 18th-century date added.

[53a] Transcribed and edited by Alice Brierley. Lanc. Par. Reg. Soc. xxiii, 1905.

[54] Gibson, *Lydiate Hall*, 248; *Hist. MSS. Com. Rep.* xiv, App. iv, 13. In 1598 there was no curate, but Mr. Moss, unlicensed, had done service for a time; *Wigan Ch.* 744.

[55] It appears from the Act of 1643 that

Lancs. and Ches.), 60, 62. There was no residence.

[59] *Wigan Ch.* 254–59. The tithes of Upholland were sold by Edward, the twelfth earl, in 1782 to John Morris, and those of Dalton to — Prescott. The rector of Wigan still receives £8 8s. 10½d. and £4 4s. 5½d. or 19 marks in all, as composition for the tithes of the townships.

[60] Ibid. 258.

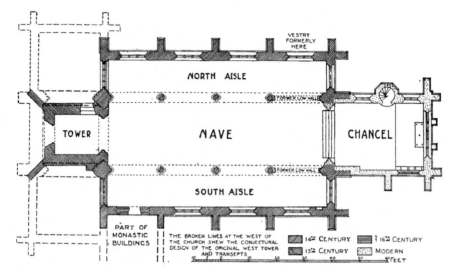

NORTH AISLE

VESTRY
FORMERLY
HERE

FORMER LOW WALL

TOWER

NAVE

CHANCEL

SOUTH AISLE

PART OF
MONASTIC
BUILDINGS

THE BROKEN LINES AT THE WEST OF
THE CHURCH SHEW THE CONJECTURAL
DESIGN OF THE ORIGINAL WEST TOWER
AND TRANSEPTS

14ᵀᴴ CENTURY   ? 16ᵀᴴ CENTURY

15ᵀᴴ CENTURY   MODERN

0   10   20   30   40   50   60 FEET

PLAN OF UPHOLLAND CHURCH

which half was paid by the rector.[61] Various grants and benefactions have since been added, and the gross income is now about £300.[62] The rector of Wigan is patron.

The following is a list of the curates and vicars :[63]

1598	William Moss
1609	Edward Tempest
1626	William Lever
1628	William Lewes [64]
1634	Richard Eaton
1636	Richard Whitfield [65]
1646	Henry Shaw [66]
1650	Richard Baldwin [67]
1653	Samuel Boden [68]
bef. 1671	Gerard Brown
occ. 1681	John Leigh
1683	Roger Bolton, M.A.[69]
1694	William Birchall
1719	John Allen, M.A.[70]
1726	Adam Bankes, M.A.
1728	William (Simon) Warren
1746	Thomas Winstanley, B.A.[71]
1747	John Baldwin
1758	Thomas Holme [72]
1767	Richard Prescott
1798	John Fawel
1802	Thomas Merrick, B.A.
1821	John Bird, B.A.
1844	Charles Bisset, B.D. (Clare Coll. Camb.)
1881	Frederick D'Austini Cremer, M.A. (Wadham Coll. Oxf.) [72a]
1888	George Frederick Wills.

There is a licensed mission-room.

There are Wesleyan, Primitive, and United Free Methodist chapels.

The grammar school was founded in 1668 by Peter or Robert Walthew.[73]

At Walthew Park, in the north-east part of the township, is situated St. Joseph's College, the seminary for the Catholic diocese of Liverpool. After collecting a sufficient sum the foundation was laid in April 1880, and in 1883 the building was open to receive students preparing for the priesthood. The museum contains a rich collection of ancient furniture, china, &c.[74]

[61] *Notitia Cestr.* ii, 258. There were two wardens.

[62] *Liverpool Dioc. Cal.* For particulars of the grants see *Wigan Ch.* 744, 745.

[63] This list is taken, with a few additions from Visitation lists, &c., from that compiled by Canon Bridgeman; *Wigan Ch.* 748. It is not continuous until 1719.

[64] Perhaps the same as 'Lever.'

[65] In 1639 Richard Whitfield, curate, paid 10s. to the clerical subsidy; *Misc.* (Rec. Soc. Lancs. and Ches.), i, 122. He was in charge when the Act of 1643 was passed.

[66] He was a member of the classis in 1646; Baines, *Lancs.* (ed. 1870), i, 227.

[67] 'A very able minister, a man of honest life and conversation,' but he had not kept the last fast day ; *Commonw.*

Ch. Surv. 61. The name is spelt Bowden on p. 63.

[68] Paid first-fruits 9 April 1653 ; *Lancs. and Ches. Rec.* ii, 414. Probably a Baldwin also. He had recently been in trouble with the authorities, it being alleged that he had taken part with the Earl of Derby in his recent attempt to raise forces for Charles II ; *Cal. of Com. for Compounding*, iv, 2955 ; v, 3266. He is mentioned in 1658 ; *Plund. Mini. Accts.* (Rec. Soc. Lancs. and Ches.), ii, 214.

[69] Bishop Stratford's Visitation List. He was 'conformable' in 1689; *Hist. MSS. Com. Rep.* xiv, App. iv, 229.

[70] At this time the church papers at Chest. Dioc. Reg. begin.

[71] It is possible that a James Miller (inserted between Winstanley and Baldwin by Canon Bridgeman) was assistant curate for a time.

For Thomas Winstanley see Foster, *Alumni Oxon.*

[72] He succeeded his cousin, William Bankes, at Winstanley in 1800 ; died 17 Aug. 1803.

[72a] Now vicar of Eccles.

[73] *End. Char. Rep.* 1899.

[74] *Liverpool Cath. Ann.* 1886.

[1] 2,102, including five of inland water ; Census Rep. of 1901.

[2] *V.C.H. Lancs.* i, 284b.

[3] *Lancs. Inq. and Extents* (Rec. Soc. Lancs. and Ches.), i, 55.

[4] Ibid. 154 (Dalton probably included with Parbold) and 248. For claims by Lord La Warr see *Ducatus Lanc.* (Rec. Com.), i, 264 ; ii, 74. From the *Manchester Ct. Leet Rec.* (ed. Earwaker) it appears that constables for Dalton and Parbold were summoned to the court leet down to 1733, though they did not appear ; vii, 25.

The descent of the mesne lordship it is not possible to trace clearly. The descendants of Orm were the Kirkbys of Kirkby Ireleth, who long retained an interest in part of the fee of Dalton, Parbold, and Wrightington. Dalton and Parbold as half a knight's fee seem very early to have been granted to the Lathom family,[5] and Parbold and part at least of Dalton were in turn granted to younger sons. In the 13th century Dalton was held by Richard de Orrell, Richard le Waleys of Aughton, and Henry de Torbock, but how their interests had arisen there is nothing to show, though the Torbocks no doubt held their quarter of the manor by a grant from the Lathoms.

The Orrell portion, called a fourth part of the manor,[6] was like Orrell itself acquired by the Holland family,[7] and descended in the same way to the Lovels,[8] and, on forfeiture, to the Earls of Derby.[9] The latter sold it about 1600 to the Orrells of Turton,[10] who soon afterwards sold all their rights to the Ashhursts.[11] The Dalton family, who took their name from this township, but who are better known as lords of Bispham in Leyland and afterwards of Thurnham, probably held under the Hollands and their successors.[12]

The Waleys portion was divided, half being given to a younger branch of the family. Richard le Waleys had a brother Randle, whose son Richerit was a benefactor of Cockersand Abbey.[13] Adam the son of Richerit sold his quarter share to Robert, lord of Lathom, who granted it to the priory of Burscough.[14]

The priory continued to hold this quarter of the manor to the Suppression, after which its fate has not been ascertained; but all or most was probably

---

[5] *Inq. and Extents*, i, 55; see also *Final Conc.* (Rec. Soc. Lancs. and Ches.), i, 18. Robert de Lathom was holding the knight's fee in Parbold and Wrightington in 1242 (p. 154). Robert de Lathom was one of the tenants in 1282, but Thomas de Ashton did suit; *Mamecestre* (Chet. Soc.), i, 136. The Lathom tenure was remembered in 1349; ibid. 443; and even in the Feodary of 1483 it is stated that 'Lord Stanley holds Allerton and Dalton of Lord la Warre'; see also *Feud. Aids*, iii, 94.

[6] In the grants to Burscough for a quarter of the vill John de Orrell has the position of a superior lord, confirming the grant; Burscough Priory Reg. fol. 31b. The same John granted to Burscough land held of him by Robert son of Henry the Smith of Lees; ibid.

He and his father Richard were benefactors of Cockersand Abbey. One of the father's grants was the half of Lithurst, the other half of which seems to have belonged to Richard le Waleys, with lands of Burscough Priory adjacent. John de Orrell made grants of Nelescroft and Fernyhurst and of a piece of land, the bounds of which cause the naming of Full clough, Mickle clough, the Hill, Edwin's ridding, Barn lache, the Dyke, the carr, Lithurst and Buke side; acquittance of pannage for thirty pigs in Dalton Wood was allowed with other easements; *Cockersand Chart.* (Chet. Soc.), ii, 621-5.

[7] See the account of Orrell.

In 1320 Sir Robert de Holland was the principal mesne tenant, Richard le Waleys, the Prior of Burscough and Ellen de Torbock following; Dalton and Parbold are joined, but the tenant of the latter is omitted; the service was 3s. for sake fee and 5s. for ward of the castle of Lancaster. From the later statement of rents it is evident that half of this was due from Dalton, and the other half from Parbold; thus each of the four quarters of the former should pay 1s.

In 1341 and again in 1349 it was found that Maud de Holland held the fourth part of Dalton of the lord of Manchester in socage by a rent of 13d. and the lord of Manchester of the Earl of Lancaster by the same service; Inq. p.m. 15 Edw. III (2nd nos.), no. 30; 23 Edw. III, pt. i, no. 58. In the latter year it was worth, in all issues, 53s. 4d.

[8] *Lancs. Inq. p.m.* (Chet. Soc.), ii, 2. The rent is this time stated as 6d., so that half had been alienated, probably to the Daltons.

A Manchester ren division of the mano Prior of Burscough, jun (of Turton) 12d of Uplither and, 12d smith of Warrington 6d.; — Dalton, 6d. (de Lathom (of Parbo the 8s. paid for sake as in 1320; *Ma   e*

[9] Pat 4 Hen. VII

[11] Bridgeman, *Wig* 257. Bishop Brid division of the mano of whom the Prior one; and says—'A called themselves lor

DALTON : SCOTTS FOLD, DOUGLAS VALLEY

DALTON : STANE HOUSE, DOUGLAS VALLEY

acquired by the Earls of Derby,[15] and remained with this family till the sale of Lady Ashburnham's estates.[16]

The fourth part retained by the Waleys family descended like Uplitherland to the Bradshaghs,[17] and was sold in 1546 to Matthew Clifton,[18] and then apparently to the Ashhursts, who before that seem to have been the tenants under Waleys and Bradshagh.

The remaining quarter, that of the Torbocks, descended for some time with the principal manor of Tarbock; but this portion of Dalton became, like Turton, the share of the Orrell family.[19] The estate was often called the manor of Walton Lees. A family named Lascelles, of long continuance in this township

ORRELL. *Argent three torteaux between two bendlets gules, a chief sable.*

and Upholland, appear to have been the immediate holders.[20]

In 1598 William Orrell of Turton was called lord of 'three-fourths' of the manor, holding his hereditary share and that of the Holland family; and William Ashhurst lord of 'one-fourth,' i.e. probably the Waleys share.[21] The Burscough quarter does not seem to be accounted for. Shortly afterwards, as stated above, the Ashhursts acquired the Orrells' lands and rights, and became sole lords of the manor. In 1751 they sold it to Sir Thomas Bootle, and it has since descended with Lathom, the Earl of Lathom being lord of the manor.

In the absence of records it is not possible to give a satisfactory account of the Ashhurst family.[22] The earliest known is Simon de Ashhurst, who about the end of the reign of Henry III granted to his son Robert all his land in Dalton, and to his son John all his land in Ashhurst.[23] Robert son of Simon next occurs;[24] and in 1300 Richard son of Robert de Ashhurst made

[15] A grant of Burscough lands, including Dalton, was made to the Earl of Derby in 1603; Pat. 1 Jas. I, pt. v, 21 July.

William Rigby of Lathom, who died just before this date, held land in Dalton of the Earl of Derby, as parcel of the possessions of the dissolved monastery of Burscough; *Lancs. Inq. p.m.* (Rec. Soc. Lancs. and Ches.), i, 20; see also i, 30, and ii, 185.

Part of the Burscough lands was later granted to Robert Hesketh; Pat. 12 Jas. I, pt. 5.

[16] Lands in Dalton were included in a fine concerning the Derby manors, &c., in 1708, John Earl of Anglesey and Henrietta Maria his wife, being deforciants; Pal. of Lanc. Feet of F. bdle. 260, m. 53. They were sold under a decree of 14 July 1719 to Thomas Franke; *Cal. Exch. of Pleas,* D. 3; see the account of Lathom.

[17] John le Waleys acquired land in Dalton in 1283; *Final Conc.* i, 161. Richard le Waleys in 1322 held a fourth part of the manor of Dalton; ibid. ii, 46. This was in possession of Eleanor wife of Thomas de Formby in 1372; ibid. ii, 183.

[18] Pal. of Lanc. Feet of F. bdle. 12, m. 173; William and Edward Bradshagh were the vendors. About a year afterwards Matthew Clifton had a dispute with John Orrell and others regarding a coalmine in Dalton; *Ducatus,* i, 222. William Clifton was hanged at Lancaster 28 Aug. 1562 for participation in the murder of William Huyton of Blackrod; he had lands in Dalton held of William, Lord La Warr, by knight's service and the rent of 12d.; also lands in Mawdesley and Ormskirk; Duchy of Lanc. Inq. p.m. xi, no. 40.

[19] For the descent see the account of Tarbock. See also *Final Conc.* ii, 183. Maud widow of Richard de Torbock granted her annuity from Walton Lees to Gilbert de Haydock in 1340; Raines MSS. (Chet. Lib.), xxxviii, 45; also 247, &c., for other arrangements, in one of which John the son of Maud is named; he is not otherwise known. In the endorsement of one deed Maud is called 'de Standish.' Walton Lees and Turton were early secured by the Orrells, according to the award of the arbitrators in 1425; Croxteth D. Z. i, 21. Ralph Orrell, who died in or before 1535, held messuages and lands in Dalton of the Earl of Derby by a rent of 14d. and of

Lord La Warr by a of Lanc. Inq. p.m v to be held of the Ea haps in Upholland o

In 1543 f mal between Lord La W of Turton, setting held his lands, &c. of Manchester by rent of 12d, and co rt of ma year; Manchester *Lanc* (Rec. Com) or confirmation o D

a release of lands in Pemberton.[25] This Richard acquired lands about the same time from Henry the Miller of Skelmersdale, whose daughter Alice afterwards released her right in the same.[26] Richard's son Adam was the most distinguished member of the family until the Commonwealth period. He fought in the French wars under Edward III and was knighted, receiving also a grant of lands in Essex and Hertfordshire.[27] He was succeeded by his son John, who married Margery, daughter of Henry de Orrell,[28] and had a son Roger. This Roger about 1385 married Maud,[29] daughter of Henry de Ince, leaving a son Robert, whose son John de Ashhurst about 1437 married a daughter of Roger de Dalton.[30] From this date there is an absence of documentary evidence until the middle of the 16th century,[31] about which time, as already stated, William Ashhurst acquired, probably from the Bradshaghs of Aughton, a quarter of the manor, and afterwards acquired the remainder from William Orrell.

This William Ashhurst was in 1590 reported to be 'soundly affected in religion' ;[32] and the family continued Protestant, adopting Puritan and Presbyterian tenets. William Ashhurst died in 1618,[33] and was succeeded by his son Henry, who married Cassandra Bradshaw,[34] and had several children, including Henry, the draper and alderman of London, a wealthy man and a consistent Puritan.[35] The eldest son William

was a member of the Long Parliament, and also of Cromwell's Parliament of 1654.[36] He died in January 1656–7, and was succeeded by his eldest son and heir Thomas, who recorded a pedigree in 1664. John Ashhurst, the brother of William and Henry, took an active part in the Civil War on the Parliamentary side, having a commission as captain and major. He engaged in the second siege of Lathom, and was present at the surrender in December 1645 ; he was subsequently governor of Liverpool.[37]

ASHHURST. *Gules a cross between four fleurs-de-lis argent.*

Thomas Ashhurst, aged twenty-five in 1664,[38] was succeeded in 1700 by his son Thomas Henry, who made a settlement of the manor of Dalton in 1706,[39] and about thirty years later succeeded also to the manor of Waterstock in Oxfordshire, which had been bought by the above-named Alderman Henry Ashhurst. In 1751 the manors of Dalton, Upholland, and Skelmersdale, with various lands, were sold to Sir Thomas Bootle by Henry Ashhurst, son of Thomas Henry,[40] and apparently an elder brother of Sir William Henry Ashhurst, the judge.

Families named Arrowsmith,[41] Prescott,[42] and Hol-

[25] Harl. MS. 2112.
[26] Ibid. ; *Visit.* of 1613. Richard and Adam de Ashhurst contributed to the subsidy of 1322, the former paying 5s. out of a total of 16s. ; *Exch. Lay Subs.* (Rec. Soc. Lancs. and Ches.), 8.
[27] *Staff. Hist. Coll.* (W. Salt Soc.), xviii, 38, 85, &c. Pardons were granted at his request in 1347 ; ibid. 277. His retinue consisted of four esquires and two archers; ibid. 200.

In 1336, already a knight, he received a grant of land in Dalton from John the Harper of Dalton ; *Visit.* of 1613. Three years after he had a protection from the king, dated at Brussels, as being in the royal service in parts across the seas ; Harl. MS. 2112. There are also references to him in the *Cal. Pat.*

In 1341 he acquired land in Dalton from Richard son of Adam de Huyton and Alice his wife ; *Final Conc.* ii, 114 ; see also De Banco R. 328, m. 155 d. He was still living in 1366, when he granted his lands to his son John ; Harl. MS. 2112.
[28] *Visit.* of 1613 ; Harl. MS. 2112.
[29] *Visit.* of 1613.
[30] Ibid. A John Ashhurst of Dalton in 1481 granted to William Bolland, Abbot of Cockersand, a rent of 12d. and 6s. 8d. at death as an obit ; Towneley MS. DD, no. 1553.
[31] About 1540 William Ashhurst was tenant of the Hospitallers' land in Dalton, at a rent of 12d. ; Kuerden MSS. v, fol. 84. The rent suggests an alternative origin for the 'fourth part of the manor' subsequently claimed for this family. In 1559 a settlement was made of lands in Dalton by William Ashhurst and Cecily his wife, who according to the pedigree of 1613 were the parents of the William Ashhurst of 1590 ; Pal. of Lanc. Feet of F. bdle. 21, m. 143.
[32] Gibson, *Lydiate Hall*, 246 ; quoting S.P. Dom. Eliz. ccxxxv, 4.
[33] *Manchester Ct. Leet Rec.* iii, 19 ; 'his will dated 6 February 1615–16 was proved at Chester 9 April 1618. He mentions his wife Margaret ; his son

Henry Ashhurst, and Elston and Robert, Henry, Anne, and Ma the latter. Henry his mother £40 a yea she was to have all t

land [43] also held lands in Dalton. In 1600 William Ashhurst and William Moss were the only freeholders recorded.[44]

The Knights Hospitallers had land.[45]

In the 13th century an estate called Sifredlea is recorded ; it disappeared later.[46]

About 1400, 2 acres of land in Dalton, granted without royal licence for the repair of Douglas Bridge, were confiscated, but restored.[47]

For the adherents of the Established Church John Prescott of the Grange, owner of the great tithes of the township, turned the tithe barn into a place of worship ; a district was assigned to it in 1870,[48] and it was consecrated in 1872 ; but five years later the present church of St. Michael and All Angels was built on an adjoining site, and the old one destroyed. The patronage is in the hands of Mrs. Prescott.[49]

INCE

Ines, 1212 ; Ins, 1292 ; Ince, xvi cent.

Ince, called Ince in Makerfield to distinguish it from Ince Blundell in the same hundred, lies immediately to the east of Wigan, of which it is a suburb, and from which it is separated by a small brook, the Clarenden or Clarington. A large part of the boundary on the south-west and eastern sides is formed by mosslands. Ambers or Ambrose Wood lies on the eastern edge. The ground rises slightly from south-west to north-east, a height of over 200 ft. being attained on the latter boundary. The area is 2,320 acres.[1] The population in 1901 was 21,262, including Platt Bridge.

Two great roads cross it, starting from Wigan ; the more northerly is the ancient road to Hindley and Manchester, while the other goes through Abram to Warrington. A cross road joining these is, like them, lined with dwellings. The portion of the township to the north-west of it is called Higher Ince. Numerous railway lines traverse the township, as well

as minor lines for the service of the collieries. The Lancashire and Yorkshire Company's line from Wigan to Bolton and Manchester crosses the centre from west to east, and has a station called Ince ; it is joined near the eastern boundary by the loop line through Pemberton. The London and North - Western Company's main line goes through from south to north, and has junctions with the lines from Manchester and St. Helens, as also with the Joint Companies' railway through Hindley and Haigh. The Great Central Company's line from Manchester to Wigan also crosses the township, with a station called Lower Ince. The Lancaster Canal traverses it near the Wigan boundary, and the Leigh branch of the Leeds and Liverpool Canal near the western and southern boundaries.

The general aspect is unpleasing, it being a typical black country in the heart of the coal-mining area. The flat surface, covered with a complete network of railways, has scarcely a green tree to relieve the monotony of the bare wide expanses of apparently waste land, much of it covered with shallow 'flashes' of water, the result of the gradual subsidence of the ground as it is mined beneath. A good deal of the ground appears to be unreclaimed mossland. Needless to say no crops are cultivated. All the energies of the populace are employed in the underground mineral wealth of the district, Ince being famous for cannel and other coal.

The northern part of the township merges into the town of Wigan, the principal features being huge cotton mills and warehouses, crowding the banks of the canals and River Douglas, which here degenerates into a grimy ditch, with never a bush or tree to shade its muddy banks.

The soil is clay, with a mixture of sand and gravel lying over coal. There are iron works, forges, and railway wagon works ; cotton goods also are manufactured.

The Local Government Act of 1858 was adopted by the township in 1866.[2] The local board was

for Dalton Hey and Gorstilow. Alice and Edward Prescott were among the defendants in a case regarding these lands in 1548 ; *Duchy Plead.* (Rec. Soc. Lancs. and Ches.), iii, 51. Richard Prescott and Ellen his wife occur in 1560 ; Pal. of Lanc. Feet of F. bdle. 22, m. 108. He seems to have been a lessee of the Orrells for their manor of Walton Lees, and his children were orphans in 1596 ; *Ducatus,* iii, 206, &c.

The Recusant Roll of 1641 includes two Prescotts, also Crosses, Holland, &c. ; *Trans. Hist. Soc.* (new ser.), xiv, 239. The Earls of Derby owned the tithes of Dalton, and about 1782 sold their right to Mr. Prescott, in whose family it remains ; Bridgeman, *Wigan Ch.* 258.

[48] In 1554 Lewis Orrell had a dispute with Robert, Ralph, Hugh, and Agnes Holland respecting a close in Dalton called the Barn Hey ; Duchy of Lanc. Plead. Edw. VI, x, O. 1. In 1560 Richard Holland and Margaret his wife had land at Dalton ; Pal. of Lanc. Feet of F. bdle. 22, m. 102.

In a fine of 1572 concerning land in Dalton in which Richard Holland, Ralph Crosse, Philip Moss, and Edward Prescott were plaintiffs, and Richard Chisnall and Thomas Lathom deforciants, the latter warranted Richard Holland and his heirs against Lord La Warr, the heirs of

William Bradshagh, deceased, James Howorth, and Margaret his wife, and Margaret's heirs, and John Parbold and Margery his wife ; ibid. bdle. 34, m. 16.

Richard Holland died 29 Apr. 1587 holding lands in Dalton, Parbold, and Ormskirk, which by his will he left to his wife Margaret for life and then to his son and heir James ; the latter was sixty-eight years of age ; Duchy of Lanc. Inq. p.m. xiv, no. 20. James Holland, perhaps a son of the last-named James, died in 1605, leaving a son and heir Richard, eleven years old ; *Lancs. Inq. p.m.* (Rec. Soc. Lancs. and Ches.), i, 30.

In 1717 Ellen Holland, daughter of James Holland, as a 'papist' registered an estate at Dalton for the life of her sister Mary ; *Engl. Cath. Nonjurors,* 131.

[44] *Misc.* (Rec. Soc. Lancs. and Ches.), i, 239, 241. In 1653 Edward Moss of Dalton, two-thirds of whose estate had been sequestered for recusancy, asked leave to contract for the same ; *Royalist Comp. Papers* (Rec. Soc. Lancs. and Ches.), iv, 199.

[45] *Plac. de Quo War.* (Rec. Com.), 375 ; see also a preceding note.

[46] The name has a great variety of spellings.

In 1202 Syfrethelegh was part of the tenement of Alan de Windle (or de Pemberton) in which Edusa his widow claimed dower ; *Final Conc.* i, 38. In

changed into an urban district council by the Act of 1894 ; it consists of fifteen members.

The manor of INCE appears to have been a member of the royal manor of Newton before the Conquest,[3] and to have been included in the fee of Makerfield from its formation.[4] In 1212 Alfred de Ince held this in the thegnage with Haydock,[5] in succession to his father, Orm de Haydock, whose name occurs as early as 1168.[6] The whole of Haydock had been granted out, and half of Ince was held of Alfred by Richard de Perpoint.[7]

Some forty or fifty years later Henry de Sefton began to acquire a share in the manor. In 1261 he held the Perpoint moiety by grant of Thomas de Perpoint,[8] and seems to have acquired the remainder, with the mesne lordship, from Henry son of John de

Ince.[9] He was still living in 1288,[10] but in 1291 his son, styled Richard de Ince, was in possession.[11] Richard de Ince occurs as late as 1333 ;[12] he was succeeded by his son Gilbert, living in 1347.[13] At this time Gilbert had a son Ivo living ; but in 1382 the manors of Aspull and Ince were granted to feoffees by Richard son of Robert de Ince, whose relationship to Gilbert is not known.[14] The manor went with Ellen, daughter of probably the same Richard de Ince, who married John Gerard, a younger son of Peter Gerard of Brynn.[15]

From their son William the manor descended regularly to Thomas Gerard of Ince, who in 1514 had a dispute with Sir Thomas Gerard of Brynn, as to the possession of Turneshea Moss, on the boundary of Ince and Ashton.[16] At his death in 1545 it was

---

[3] V.C.H. Lancs. i, 286.

[4] Ibid. 366, note 8. For later notices see Lancs. Inq. p.m. (Chet. Soc.), i, 138; ii, 99 ; ibid. (Rec. Soc. Lancs. and Ches.), i, 105.

[5] Lancs. Inq. and Extents (Rec. Soc. Lancs. and Ches.), i, 74. The separate assessment of Ince appears to have been one plough-land : and its share of the thegnage rent was probably 10s. ; one of the judges being also supplied by it. In 1544 the Gerards' rent was stated to be 5s. only ; possibly this was a moiety of the manor, the other moiety being held by the Ince family.

[6] Farrer, Lancs. Pipe R. 12. Orm de Haydock gave to Cockersand Abbey a portion of land in Ince, between two brooks, as marked out by the canons' crosses ; Cockersand Chart. (Chet. Soc.), ii, 673. Robert Anderton held this in 1501 at a rent of 10d. ; Cockersand Rental (Chet. Soc.), 5.

[7] Lancs. Inq. and Extents, i, 74 ; the half plough-land was held 'of ancient feoffment.'

Richard de (or le) Perpoint was a benefactor of Cockersand, his grant being thus bounded : The great brook up the Thele lache, down the lache between Beric-acre and Wolveley to the syke between Hardacre and Bircacre, to the great brook ; Cockersand Chart. ii, 672. He seems to have been succeeded by Robert son of Adam de Perpoint, who released to the canons the lands he had held of them in Ince, and whose daughter Godith did the same ; ibid. 673, 674. For Alfred de Ince see Lancs. Pipe R. 152, &c.

[8] Cur. Reg. R. 171, m. 28 ; Henry de Sefton called Thomas de Perpoint to warrant him as to 4 oxgangs in Ince. He may be the Henry de Seveton who with his wife Alice was taken into confraternity with the Knights Hospitallers in 1256 ; Final Conc. (Rec. Soc. Lancs. and Ches.), i, 128.

[9] Assize R. 408, m. 21 d. John de Ince was witness to an Abram charter about 1240 ; Cockersand Chart. ii, 664.

[10] Assize R. 408, m. 73. It is possible that there is an error in the date.

[11] Assize R. 407, m. 3 d. Gilbert de Southworth claimed in right of the dower of his wife Emma, who seems to have been the widow of Henry de Sefton ; but this would not have been so if Henry de Sefton was living in 1288.

About this time there was a long suit between John son of Richard Maunsel of Heaton and Richard son of Emma de Marhalgh as to messuages, mill, &c., and 6 oxgangs of land in Ince and Aspull.

Richard is described as son and heir of Henry de Wigan, a brother of Richard Maunsel ; Assize R. 1265, m. 22 d. ; R. 1321, m. 13 d. ; R. 418, m. 2, 11. As in one of the pleadings in 1284 (Assize R. 1268, m. 11) Gilbert de Southworth and Emma his wife were joined in the defence with Richard son of Emma de Marhalgh, it might seem that Henry de Wigan was the same as Henry de Sefton, but there is probably some other explanation.

[12] In 1292 he was defendant in a number of suits concerning his father's acquisitions.

Henry de Litherland claimed 4 oxgangs less 12 acres ; he had in 1288 released his right in them to Henry de Sefton, but now said he was a minor at the time ; Assize R. 408, m. 73. It is possible that the plaintiff was the Henry son of Thomas de Ince who at the same assizes claimed 6 acres of land, &c., from Robert son of Fulk Banastre, Hugh de Hindley, Alan son of Peter, Adam de Urmston and Isabel his wife, and Richard de Molyneux and Beatrice his wife ; ibid. m. 68. Agnes widow of Thomas de Ince was also a claimant in respect of dower ; 2 oxgangs of land are named ; ibid. m. 3, 13 d., 64 d. Henry son of Thomas de Ince held 12 acres claimed by William, brother and heir of Robert de Wytonelake, who asserted that Thomas had demised to Henry de Sefton, who had disseised Robert ; ibid. m. 51. Robert de Abram and Emma his wife, in right of the latter, claimed the moiety of an oxgang of land, &c., from Richard son of Henry de Sefton of Ince, and from Gilbert de Southworth and Emma his wife. The latter pair said they had only Emma's dower out of Richard's inheritance. The plaintiffs said that Henry de Ince gave the tenements to Adam son of Wido and Margery his wife ; the latter being, it would seem, a daughter of Henry; and that Emma was their daughter and heir ; Robert was the son of John de Abram, who had married the said Margery. Richard de Ince's reply was that Margery had granted the lands to his father while she was a widow and free to do so ; but the jury decided for the plaintiffs, believing a grant was made after she had married John de Abram. Gilbert and Emma were also to have nothing from the land, 'because the seisin of the latter's first husband was unjust' ; ibid. m. 26 d. The last sentence seems to prove that this Emma was widow of Henry de Sefton.

In the same year, 1292, Richard de Ince and Alice his wife, 'put in their

claim' in a fine concerning the manor of Haydock ; Final Conc. i, 174.

Late in 1334 Richard son of Henry de Ince granted Gilbert de Culcheth leave to carry turves from Hindley to Wigan through Ince ; Lancs. and Ches. Hist. and Gen. Notes, i, 52.

[13] In 1323–4 Gilbert son of Richard de Ince remitted to Gilbert de Haydock a rent of 13s. 4d. ; Raines MSS. (Chet. Lib.), xxxviii, 33. Gilbert de Ince was witness in 1334 ; Crosse D. no. 45. Ten years later John de Tyldesley made a claim against Gilbert son of Richard de Ince and others concerning land ; Assize R.1435, m. 47. A little later, 1347, William son of John Donning de Ince sued Gilbert son of Richard de Ince for a messuage in Ince. Gilbert claimed by a grant from Elias Donning and Margery his wife, parents of John Donning ; in the defence there were associated with him his brothers Richard, Thomas, and John ; also his son Ivo ; ibid. m. 41 d. Gilbert de Ince at Easter 1354 was convicted of disseising John son of Thomas Jew of a rent of 13s. 4d. in Ince ; and Hugh, Gilbert's brother, cut off John's arm ; Duchy of Lanc. Assize R. 3, m. 3. Henry, another brother, occurs in 1347 ; Cal. Close, 1346–9, p. 49. Gilbert de Ince attested a charter in 1358 ; Standish D. no. 46.

[14] Pal. of Lanc. Feet of F. bdle. 2, m. 36 ; a list of the tenants is given.

Robert was perhaps yet another brother of Gilbert's, for a Robert son of Richard de Ince was plaintiff in 1353 against Roger de Leigh, and others ; Assize R. 435, m. 20.

Richard and Thomas de Ince contributed to the poll tax of 1381 ; Lay Subs. Lanc. bdle. 130, no. 24.

[15] Ormerod, Ches. (ed. Helsby), ii, 131, where it is stated that a dispensation was granted for the marriage. John Gerard of Ince occurs in 1425 ; Lancs. Inq. p.m. (Chet. Soc.), ii, 13.

In 1420 John Gerard of Ince and Ellen his wife arranged for the succession of the manor of Ince, with fifteen messuages, 140 acres of land, &c., in Warrington, Wigan, and Aspull ; Pal. of Lanc. Feet of F. bdle. 5, m. 18. At the inquisition after his death, taken in 1434–5, his son and heir William was said to be aged twenty-three ; Ormerod, loc. cit.

[16] Duchy Plead. (Rec. Soc. Lancs. and Ches.), i, 3–7; the date should be 6 Hen. VIII. The plaintiff's pedigree is given : 'The said moss . . . is the freehold and inheritance of plaintiff as parcel of his manor of Ince, whereof William Gerard his great-grandfather, Thomas

found that he had held the manor of Ince of Sir Thomas Langton in socage by a rent of 5*s.*; also the manor of Aspull, a burgage in Wigan, and lands in Abram and Hindley. Miles Gerard his son and heir was thirty years of age.[17] Miles died in August 1558,[18] leaving a son William,[19] who in turn was succeeded by his son, another Miles Gerard.[20] The family adhered to the ancient faith, and Miles Gerard in 1590 was reported to be 'in some degree of conformity, yet in general note of evil affection in religion.'[31]

Miles Gerard was still living in 1613, when a pedigree was recorded, showing Thomas his son and heir to be twenty-two

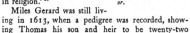

GERARD. *Azure a lion rampant ermine crowned or.*

years of age.[77] Thomas was a convicted recusant in 1628,[33] and his estates were in 1643 sequestered 'for his recusancy and supposed delinquency.'[34] The documents relating to the matter give a number of interesting particulars as to the mining of cannel and the charges upon the lands ;[35] they also show that Thomas Gerard, his son, had fought against the Parliament, and had been taken prisoner at Naseby in 1645 ; afterwards he took the National Covenant and compounded for his part of the estate.[76]

It appears to have been Anne, the daughter and heir of the younger Thomas, who carried the manors of Ince and Aspull to her husband John Gerard, a younger son of Sir William Gerard, third baronet ; and the manors were afterwards sold to Richard Gerard, uncle of John.[77] Richard's son and heir Thomas and his wife, Mary Wright, were in possession in 1683.[78] His son Richard Gerard of Highfield

his grandfather, and William his father, and many others of his ancestors were time out of mind peaceably seised.'
In 1448 Thomas Gerard son of William Gerard, Roger Gerard, and Cecily wife of William Gerard, were accused of causing the death of Robert Gidlow, but were acquitted ; Pal. of Lanc. Plea R. 12, m. 25 ; see also R. 11, m. 15, 16.
In that year a dispensation was granted by Nicholas V for the marriage of Thomas son and heir of William Gerard of Ince, and Elizabeth a daughter of William Norris of Speke, the parties being related in the third degree ; Norris D. (B.M.), no. 643. Ten years later an indenture was executed, reciting the fact of this marriage, and stating that lands in Aspull and Hindley had been assigned to them ; William Gerard, the father, 'had not made and would not make any alienation of the manor of Ince or of any messuage, lands, and tenements that were Ellen's that was wife to John Gerard mother to the said William Gerard,' but such as should determine at his death. William's brothers, Robert, John, Hugh, and Richard are named, as also his younger sons, Roger, Edmund, Lawrence, and Seth; ibid. no. 644.
To Thomas Gerard, the son, a pardon was granted in 1479 ; Towneley MS. RR, no. 1430. In this year Thomas Gerard of Ince and William his son, with Roger and Seth his brothers, were parties to an engagement to keep the peace with Alexander Standish and others ; Standish D. nos. 160, 161.
In 1490 the marriage of Thomas son and heir apparent of William Gerard, and Maud daughter of Sir Henry Bold, was agreed upon ; Dods. MSS. cxlii, fol. 210, nos. 118, 119.
[17] Duchy of Lanc. Inq. p.m. vii, no. 27. The burgage in Wigan was held by the rent of a pair of gloves.
[18] Ibid. xi, no. 12 ; he held the manors of Ince and Aspull, with various messuages and lands, &c. ; including a windmill and a water-mill in Ince, and the same in Aspull ; sixty burgages, &c., in Wigan, and various lands there, held by a rent of 57*s.* 1*d.* ; also lands in Pemberton, Abram, and Hindley. William his son and heir was twenty-three years of age.
[19] William was a plaintiff against Sir Thomas Gerard in 1549 ; *Ducatus Lanc.* (Rec. Com.), ii, 101.
In 1567 a pedigree was recorded ; *Visit.*

(Chet. Soc.), 101. William Gerard was buried at Wigan, 29 Nov. 1583 ; Reg.
[20] A settlement of the manors of Aspull and Ince was made by fine in 1586 ; Miles Gerard and Grace his wife being deforciants ; Pal. of Lanc. Feet of F. bdle. 48, m. 299 ; there was a later one in 1612 ; ibid. bdle. 82, m. 51. Several other fines relate to dealings with their properties ; ibid. bdle. 47, m. 57, &c.
In 1599, as lord of the manor, he complained that Ralph Houghton and others were withholding suit ; *Ducatus Lanc.* (Rec. Com.), iii, 336, 399.
[21] Gibson, *Lydiate Hall,* 245, quoting S.P. Dom. Eliz. ccxxxv, 4. He and his wife had been accused in 1586 of sheltering one Worthington, a persecuted priest ; and his own brother, Alexander Gerard, was another priest in the neighbourhood ; ibid. 239, 240. Thomas and Alexander Gerard, aged eighteen and seventeen respectively, entered Brasenose College, Oxf. in 1578 ; Foster, *Alumni.* In spite of a discrepancy in the dates—it being recorded that Alexander left Rheims for England in 1587—it seems certain that Miles's brothers were the Thomas and Alexander Gerard imprisoned for religion in Wisbech Castle, where Thomas died ; their brother Gilbert, born in 1569, and therefore not recorded in the Visitation pedigree, entered the English College, Rome, in 1587, and became a Jesuit ; Foley, *Rec. S.J.* vi, 175 ; vii, 293.
In September 1590 Miles Gerard was indicted for fourteen months' absence from church, but for most part of the time he had been 'so extreme sick' that his life had only been preserved by the use of goat's milk ; before that he said he had been a regular attendant at church ; *Hist. MSS. Com. Rep.* xiv, App. iv, 597. See also *Local Glean. Lancs. and Ches.* ii, 252.
Miles Gerard, a Douay priest, executed at Rochester in 1590 for his priesthood, is supposed to have been of this family ; Gillow, *Bibl. Dict. of Engl. Cath.* ii, 430-2. He does not occur in the pedigree, but Miles seems to have been a favourite Christian name in this branch.
[22] *Visit.* of 1613 (Chet. Soc.), 25. 'Miles Gerard of Ince, esquire, was buried at Wigan, 1615, in his own chancel, the 28th day of September' ; Reg.
Thomas son and heir of Miles Gerard of Ince entered St. Mary Hall, Oxf. in 1607, aged seventeen ; he was afterwards of Gray's Inn ; Foster, *Alumni Oxon.*
[28] Norris D. (B.M.). For a settlement

in 1641 see Pal. of Lanc. Feet of F. bdle. 138, m. 38. He paid £13 6*s.* 8*d.* on refusing knighthood in 1632 ; *Misc.* (Rec. Soc. Lancs. and Ches.), i, 222.
[34] *Royalist Comp. Papers* (Rec. Soc. Lancs. and Ches.), iii, 34 ; petition of his wife and daughters.
[25] Ibid. iii, 34–51. Thomas Gerard had a mine of cannel in Aspull, for which he needed a trench through lands of James Gorsuch, paying him £20 for leave. Owing to neglect in the various sequestrations the trench was filled up, and the mine was 'totally drowned up' ; the fault being that of the agents of the sequestrators. He asked for compensation or assistance to put the mine in order.
The rents of the confiscated two-thirds of the estates amounted in 1653–4 to £111 17*s.* 6*d.* ; it consisted of the demesne lands at Ince, a mill, tenants' rents, tithe corn, rents in Aspull, and a cannel mine in Aspull farmed to his son Thomas Gerard ; ibid. 47.
Ince Hall was the subject of suits between Thomas Gerard and Roger Stoughton in 1663 ; *Exch. Dcpos.* (Rec. Soc. Lancs. and Ches.), 37, 48.
In 1667 an inquiry was made touching an annuity granted by Thomas Gerard to John Biddulph ; *Lancs. and Ches. Reci.* (Rec. Soc. Lancs. and Ches.), ii, 343.
[26] *Royalist Comp. Papers,* iii, 40–43. It being alleged that the younger Thomas was 'a delinquent papist and not to be admitted to composition, notwithstanding his conformity,' his friends moved that he might be allowed to give the committee further satisfaction by taking the oath of abjuration.
[27] For Richard Gerard see *Dict. Nat. Biog.*

succeeded, but dying without issue the manor of Ince went by the provisions of his will [28] to his wife Margaret for life and then to his heir, his cousin Richard Gerard's son William.[29] William's heirs were his sisters, Mary and Elizabeth ; but as the latter died unmarried, the whole devolved on the former, the wife of John Walmesley, a relation of the Showley family.[31] They settled at West-wood House in Ince, and the manor has descended regularly to the present lord, Mr. Humphrey Jeffreys Walmesley, of Ince and Hungerford.[32] The Hall of Ince was sold by Richard Gerard in 1716 to John Walmesley of Wigan, whose descendant Mr. John Walmesley of Lucknam and Ince is the present owner.[33]

Ince formerly possessed three halls, each bearing the name of the township ; two of them, very much modernized, still stand. The first of these, now known as above mentioned as Hall of Ince, stands in Warrington Road, near the cemetery, and was restored about ten years ago, the old timber work at the back, which was then visible, being removed, and the wall rebuilt in brick.[33a] The whole of the exterior of the building, which was formerly timber framed, is now stuccoed and otherwise modernized, but the roofs retain their old stone slates. The building is now divided into three houses.

Another branch of the Gerard family also resided in Ince from about 1600 ; their house was called the New Hall.[34]

The house now known as Ince Hall, which is situated off Manchester Road, near Rose Bridge, was originally surrounded by a moat and approached by a fine avenue of elms. It was a good specimen of timber and plaster building erected about the reign of James I, with a picturesque black and white front of five gables.[34a] The entrance hall is described as being spacious and with a richly ornamented plaster ceiling and wainscoted walls. Three other rooms also were stated to have been panelled in oak, and the drawing-room ceiling was ornamented with 'carved work representing birds, shells, fruit, and flowers. There were two chimney-pieces of fine Italian marble. The staircase was of oak and 6 ft. wide, the ceiling much ornamented with stucco. The best bedrooms were covered with tapestry.'[34b] In 1854 the house was so seriously damaged by fire as to necessitate a practical rebuilding. The ancient timber front has therefore given place to a brick elevation of no architectural pretension, and the house is internally wholly modernized. The line of avenue still remains, but the trees have disappeared, and the opening of coal pits in the immediate vicinity about thirty years ago has destroyed any sense of picturesqueness that the rebuilt structure might have possessed.[35]

A family using the local surname came into note in the 16th century.[35a] Thomas Ince, who died in April 1573, held a capital messuage and other messuages with lands and wood at Ince of Thomas Langton in

Aspull. As a 'papist' he registered his estate in 1717, the value being given as £345 17s. 4d. ; Richard Gerard, of High-field, who registered an annuity of £150 out of the manor of Aspull, was no doubt his son ; Engl. Cath. Nonjurors, 128, 153; he also owned the hall of Southworth ; Piccope, op. cit. Two of his sisters were nuns.

In 1694 an inquiry was made as to the suspected devotion of the Hall of Ince to religious uses ; Exch. Depos. 84.
[29] Richard Gerard of Highfield died without issue in 1743. In 1721 he was in the remainders to the Bryan estate. By his will dated 1 Feb. 1734-5, he gave the manor of Ince to his wife Margaret, who was daughter of John Baldwin of Wigan, for life, with remainder to his right heirs ; his manors of Southworth and Croft to his brother Thomas ; Piccope, op. cit. This Thomas and another brother Caryll were priests ; for the latter see Foley, Rec. S.J. vi, 468.
[30] Richard Gerard, a younger brother of Thomas, was an apothecary in Wigan. He and his son Richard registered as 'papists' in 1717 ; Engl. Cath. Non-jurors, 107, 148. They mortgaged a messuage in the Market-place in 1731. The son, who died in 1743, married Isa-bella, another daughter of John Baldwin of Wigan ; and their son William, de-scribed as an apothecary in 1744, was the heir to Ince. Aspull is not mentioned, having probably been sold. In 1751-2 William Gerard was deforciant of the manor in a fine, which included lands in Ince, Abram, Hindley, Newton in Maker-field, and Wigan ; also 'one chapel open to the north side and adjoining the parish church of Wigan' ; Pal. of Lanc. Feet of F. bdle. 346, m. 108.
[31] In 1773 John Walmesley and Mary his wife, Elizabeth Gerard, spinster,

William Moss and and Richard B

estate was sequestrated about the end of 1651 by the Parliamentary authorities ; as ' son and heir of Miles Gerard, late of Ince,' he was admitted to Gray's Inn, 1646 ; Royalist Comp. Papers, iii, 21 ; iv, 34.

In 1671, on a complaint by Henry Backer and his wife Jane against Ellen Gerard, depositions were taken as to the marriage of John Davies of Manby in Cheshire, with Alice eldest daughter of Miles Gerard, late of Peel Ditch in Ince, and moneys agreed to be paid to Jane and Margaret, daughters of Miles ; and touching a sum of £400 lent to Thomas Gerard of Ince ; Exch. Depos. 49.

socage by a rent of 5s.[85b] The residence was known as Ince Hall, or the New Hall. They also adhered to the ancient faith,[36] and John Ince's estate was sequestered by the Parliamentary authorities during the Commonwealth,[37] but not confiscated outright. It descended from him to his great-great-granddaughter Frances Sobieski, daughter of Christopher Ince, and wife of William Anderton of Euxton. She died in 1816, when the family ceased to reside here.[38]

Ince. *Argent three torteaux between two bendlets gules.*

The third hall, the residence of the family of Ince, stood on a site a short distance from the junction of Ince Green Lane and Warrington Road, part of which is occupied by a building apparently erected some sixty years since from the materials of the former house. Two date stones, now on a rockery in front of the house, are said to belong respectively to the old barn and a stable now pulled down. One bears the date 1578 and the initials G^IM, and the other the inscription referring to the above-named William Anderton and Frances his wife. There is also part of a stone sundial, dated G M. The hall is said to have been built about 1721.

Property here was acquired by a family named Brown,[39] in which it descended for about a century and a half.[40] Henry Brown, by his will in 1726, left it to his grand-nephew Edward, son of Robert Holt of Wigan; by two daughters and co-heiresses it became the property of General Clegg and Thomas Case of Liverpool.[41]

Miles and Peter Gerard, Thomas Ince, and Ralph Brown were the landowners recorded about 1556.[42] Richard Pennington was a freeholder in 1600.[43] The four halls of Ince were duly noted by Kuerden

---

[85b] Duchy of Lanc. Inq. p.m. xiii, no. 6. Miles Ince was his son and heir, and of the age of twenty-five years. The rent payable seems to prove that this was a moiety of the manor. Mr. H. Ince Anderton gives the descent as: Thomas Ince (15 Edw. IV) —s. Henry (20 Hen. VII) —s. Arthur —s. Thomas; from Harl. MS. 1987, fol. 88b.

The father of Thomas was Arthur Ince, who in 1546 and later had a dispute with Ralph Brown over the marriage between the latter's daughter Ellen and Thomas Ince, son and heir apparent of Arthur; *Duchy Plead.* ii, 211. In 1569 Miles Ince, as grandson of Ralph Brown, put in a claim to lands in Ince, Aspull, and Wigan; *Ducatus Lanc.* (Rec. Com.), ii, 378, 360.

[86] Miles Ince was one of the 'comers to church but no communicants' in 1590; *Lydiate Hall,* 246 (quoting S.P. Dom. Eliz. ccxxxv, 4). He was buried at Wigan 7 Apr. 1593; Reg.; and was succeeded by John Ince, probably his son, returned as a freeholder in 1600; *Misc.* (Rec. Soc. Lancs. and Ches.), i, 241. With him begins the pedigree recorded in 1664; Dugdale, *Visit.* (Chet. Soc.), 163. In 1628 he paid double to the subsidy as a convicted recusant; Norris D. (B.M.); and died the following year, being buried at Wigan.

[87] In 1643 two-thirds was sequestered for Thomas Ince's religion only, and so remained till his death in Feb. 1653–4; it does not appear that he took arms for the king. John Ince was the only son and heir, thirty-four years of age, and in 1654 had a wife and four small children depending on him. He mortgaged his property in order to pay his father's debts and provide for his wife Margaret and his children Thomas, Hugh, &c.; *Royalist Comp. Papers,* iv, 1–13.

[88] Dugdale's pedigree is supplemented by that of Piccope (MS. Pedigrees, ii, 291), who consulted the Roman Catholic deeds enrolled in the House of Correction, Preston. It appears that Thomas, the eldest son of John, mentioned in the preceding note, had no issue, and the estate descended to Christopher Ince, a younger brother, who in 1717 as a 'papist' registered his estate, being described as 'of Aughton;' *Engl. Cath. Nonjurors,* 112. His four sisters, Dorothy, Anne, Ellen (wife of James Twiss), and Elizabeth also registered; ibid. 124.

Christopher was executor of his brother Thomas's will (dated 1703), and by his own will, dated 12 Dec. 1728, he left Ince Hall to his grandson Christopher; John, the son, to have 'the profits of part of Brook House,' if he behaved himself to the satisfaction of the trustees. Thomas, a younger brother of John, had lands in Aughton and Billinge, divided between his sons Thomas and James; Piccope, op. cit.

Mr. Ince Anderton adds that papers in Chest. Dioc. Reg. show that Christopher Ince died in 1735, leaving two sons, John and Thomas; and that administration of the goods of John Ince of Ince was granted on 14 Jan. 1739–40.

Christopher Ince, son of John, accordingly succeeded to Ince; in 1740 he married Mary Catherine Parry of Holywell; and their daughter and heir, Frances Sobieski Ince, married in 1769 William Anderton of Euxton; Piccope.

[89] In a suit in 1609 respecting a place called Rundiefield in Ince, the following pedigree was adduced:—Roger le Brown, to whom the rent of 4s. from the land had been granted by William de Ince —s. Rowland —s. William —s. Ralph. Ralph in 1545 granted the rent to William Brown, whose son Roger was defendant in 1609; Pal. of Lanc. Plea R. 303, m. 16

---

about 1696.[44] In 1717 John Clarkson and Richard Richardson, as 'papists,' registered estates here.[45]

Ambrewood inclosure award may be seen at Preston.

The Established Church has two places of worship in the township; Christ Church, consecrated in 1864, the district assigned being the whole township;[46] and St. Mary's, Lower Ince, consecrated 1887.[47] The patronage of both is vested in Simeon's trustees.

The Wesleyan Methodist chapel was built in 1866; the Primitive Methodist one in 1885. The Congregationalists also have a place of worship.

The adherents of the ancient religion found assistance in the constancy of the families of Gerard and Ince. The chapel at New Hall was built in 1760; this was closed in 1818. There was a private chapel at Westwood House, and in 1873 the church of St. William was opened. Twenty years later the Church of the Holy Family at Platt Bridge was added.[48]

HINDLEY

Hindele, 1212; Hindelegh, 1260 (common); Hindeley, 1292.

Hindley lies in the centre of the great Lancashire coalfield, and consists of a level-surfaced country dotted over with collieries and black pit-banks. A close network of tramways and railways covers the face of a singularly dreary stretch of country, where the pastures are scanty and blackened. Frequent pools of water lie between the collieries, indicating subsidences of the earth caused by mining. What trees remain standing appear as dead stumps, with leafless branches reflected weirdly in the 'flashes' of water. In the more favoured parts of the township, wheat, oats, and potatoes manage to find an existence. There is some pasturage also. The area is 2,610½ acres,[1] and the population in 1901 was 23,504.

The ancient road from Manchester to Wigan goes west-north-west through the township. The town of Hindley lies to the north of this road. At this point is a cross road leading north-eastward from Platt Bridge and Lowe Green to Westhoughton, having a branch north to Aspull. Through the town, adjacent to this cross road, runs a brook known here as the Borden. Near the eastern boundary is the

village of Hindley Green; from this a road leads south to Leigh. The London and North-Western Company's Manchester and Wigan Railway passes through the township from east to west, with stations at Hindley Green and Platt Bridge. The Lancashire and Yorkshire Company's line from Wigan to Manchester also crosses the northern corner, where there is a station; and the two companies' joint railway runs north through the western part of the township, being there joined by a connecting line from the North-Western main line. The Great Central Railway's line to Wigan crosses the western end, and has a station called Hindley and Platt Bridge.

There were formerly two 'burning wells' here, one in Derby Lane, the other near Dog Pool, now called Grange Brook.[2]

The great business is coal-mining; there is also an iron foundry, and cotton manufacturing is carried on extensively. The first factory is said to have been erected near the end of the 18th century by Richard Battersby at Lowe mill, formerly a water corn-mill. A little later hand-loom weaving was one of the chief industries, each cottage having a weaving shop attached.[3]

The Local Government Act of 1858 was adopted by the township in 1867.[4] Under the Act of 1894 an urban district council of fifteen members has been constituted. New council offices were opened in 1904.

A fair is held on the first Thursday in August.

A sundial, dated 1699, formerly stood at Castle Hill.[5]

HINDLEY was no doubt one of the
MANOR fifteen berewicks of the royal manor of Newton before the Conquest.[6] After the Conquest it continued to form part of the fee of Makerfield,[7] and in 1212 one part was held in thegnage, in conjunction with Ashton, by Thomas de Burnhull.[8] The remainder was held by local families.

Swain son of Leofwin held the Burnhull share, and gave it to a certain Gospatric in free marriage; in 1212 Roger the son of Gospatric held this portion of Thomas de Burnhull. Two oxgangs were at the same time held by Adam de Hindley 'of ancient feoffment,' i.e. by a title going back to the time of Henry I at least. Another half plough-land was held by Richard de Hindley, son of Robert; portions of this had been given to the Hospitallers and to Cockersand Abbey. Some portion was perhaps still held in demesne.[9]

[44] *Local Glean. Lancs. and Ches.* i, 209-14. He states that the Browns had the Cockersand lands.

[45] *Engl. Cath. Nonjurors*, 125, 152.

[46] Bridgeman, *Wigan Ch.* 787; a district had been assigned in 1862; *Lond. Gaz.* 4 Nov.

[47] Bridgeman, loc. cit.

[48] *Liverpool Cath. Ann.* 1901.

[1] 2,612, including 30 of inland water; Census Rep. of 1901.

[2] Leyland, *Hindley*, 7. Baines quotes an account from the *Life of Lord Guildford*, of a visit to the burning well in 1676; *Lancs.* (ed. 1836), iii, 555.

[3] Leyland, op. cit. 96, 104. An interesting account is given, pp. 105-8, of the former customs of the place; the pace-eggers and their drama, the Eastertide lifting, maypole on the green, rush-bearing, &c.

[4] *Lond. Gaz.* 2 July 1867.

[5] *Lancs. and Ches. Antiq. Notes*, i, 165.

[6] *V.C.H. Lancs.* i, 286. The ancient assessment appears to have been a plough-land or a plough-land and a half.

[7] See e.g. *Lancs. Inq. p.m.* (Chet. Soc.), i, 138; ii, 99; ibid. (Rec. Soc. Lancs. and Ches.), i, 105.

[8] *Lancs. Inq. and Extents* (Rec. Soc. Lancs. and Ches.), i, 74. He had half a plough-land in Hindley.

[9] Ibid. 75. The Hospitallers' holding is named in the *Plac. de Quo War.* (Rec. Com.), 375; see also *Lancs. and Ches. Hist. and Gen. Notes*, i, 35. In the rental of their lands compiled about 1540, the following particulars are given: John Atherton, a messuage, 11. 4d., and a close 21. 8d.; Robert Lee, a messuage, 6d.; Jonathan (?) Bate for Crockholes, 6d.; Peter Langton, a messuage, 6d.; Gilbert

Hindley, a messuage, 6d.; 61. in all; Kuerden MSS. v, fol. 84. John Leigh of Westhoughton in 1619 held lands formerly belonging to the Hospitallers by a rent of 6d.; *Lancs. Inq. p.m.* (Rec. Soc. Lancs. and Ches.), ii, 133.

The *Cockersand Chart.* (Chet. Soc.), ii, 642-51, contains particulars of the grants made to this abbey. Robert de Hindley gave 6 acres, partly in Twiss Car by Lanulache and partly by Aspenhead, with pasture for as many animals as the man might have who held the land from the canons; he also gave an acre on the northern side of Bickershaw. Richard his son confirmed these charters, and gave further parcels in Berlets-housted and Osbern meadow, and a third with his body. Adam de Hindley also was a benefactor, 10 acres and a messuage on the north of Stony street, 4 at Ferny-

The mesne lordship of the Burnhulls appears to have been surrendered, and the lords of Makerfield had the various Hindley families as immediate tenants. It appears, however, down to 1330, and the Pemberton holding was part of it.[10] Gospatric's immediate successors seem to have been the Waleys or Walsh family.[11]

The two oxgangs of Adam de Hindley may have been joined to that half plough-land or to the half plough-land of Richard de Hindley to form the moiety of the manor held by a family bearing the local name. Gilbert de Culcheth was overlord of this in 1300. In November 1302 Adam de Hindley complained that a number of persons had joined in disseising him of a free tenement in Hindley, a messuage with an acre of land, and an acre of meadow, which he had had from one Adam de Plumpton, who had purchased from Hugh de Hindley. Gilbert de Culcheth replied as chief lord; he had taken possession fearing that the feoffment made by Adam de Plumpton was contrary to the statute.[12] Some settlement was made, and the claim was not prosecuted.

This moiety was divided into four parts, the descent of which can be traced for some time.[13]

In 1308 half of the manor was claimed by Robert son of Fulk Banastre.[13a] This was afterwards recovered by Robert de Langton, baron of Newton, from Jordan de Worsley,[14] and about 1330 the lordship of the whole manor, together with lands in it,

---

halgh, and a land called Crokeland, one head of which lay towards Platt and the other towards Thuresclough, and another portion bounded in part by the Lanulache. These grants conveyed the usual easements, including quittance of pannage for pigs in Hindley Wood. Godith daughter of Adam de Hindley gave Tunkercroft by Glazebrook, lying north of the Hospitallers' land. Robert Banastre gave land in Fernyhalgh, and Robert his son confirmed the preceding and other gifts to the abbey. Thurstan Banastre gave all his portion of the water called Glazebrook from Marefalford to the ditch of Henry the Hosteller of Hindley. In 1501 the heirs of Thomas Turton (6d.) and Gilbert Langton (6d.) held these lands; *Cockersand Rental* (Chet. Soc.), 4.

[10] Katherine wife of Hugh de Venables, as widow of Peter de Burnhull, in 1331 claimed dower in two-thirds of an eighth part of the manor of Hindley; De Banco R. 284, m. 119; 287, m. 185 d. Peter's sisters and heirs, then minors, were called to warrant; ibid. R. 286, m. 170. William son of Adam de Pemberton was the tenant.

[11] Gospatric also had a grant of land in Lathom, supposed to be represented by the Cross Hall estates, of which in the 13th century the tenants were named Waleys (i.e. Welsh). In Hindley Richard le Waleys and Eleanor his wife held lands, of which a portion was given in arms to Cockersand Abbey; *Cockersand Chart.* ii, 648.

[12] Assize R. 418, m. 3, 13. The defendants were: John de Langton and Alice his wife, as chief lords of the fee; Gilbert de Culcheth and Gilbert his son, as lords of Hindley; Henry de Atherton; Richard de Molyneux of Crosby and Beatrice his wife; Alan de Windle; Robert son of Fulk Banastre; Adam de Bradshagh; Adam de Urmston and Isabel his wife; Robert Bulgut; Henry son of Roger de Ince; Hugh de Hindley; John son of Henry le Suur of Hindley; and Richard son of William Hert.

[13] Some tenants occur in the last note. In 1306 and 1307 Beatrice widow of Hugh de Hindley claimed dower from Hugh son of Roger de Ashton and others. Hugh de Ashton called to warrant him Adam son of Hugh de Hindley; Adam de Bradshagh and Margaret his wife also called Adam de Hindley and John de Broadash; Thomas son of John son of Maud called William son of Simon de Warrington and Emma his wife; John Gillibrand called Hugh and Gilbert sons of Richard de Culcheth; De Banco R. 161, m. 132; 164, m. 212. Henry de Atherton and Beatrice his wife in 1330

claimed 25 acres Ince from Cecily the son of Rob appeared that B demised them to title was therefo 1411, m. 12 d.

In the followi ton the elder an not prosecute a c and Hindley; H younger was one R. 1404, m. 18. William, John, a R 297, m. 103.

The younger daughter and hei of Richard de M Beatr ce his wif 12 d., *Final C* Agnes were conce

was granted to Robert de Langton, a younger son of the Robert just named, from whom descended the Langtons of *LOWE* in Hindley,[15] the last of the line being Edward Langton, who died in 1733. The descent is stated in cross-suits by Peter Langton and Ellen widow of John Langton in 1444. The former said that Henry son of Adam de Manchester, chaplain, holding (as trustee) the manor of Hindley, granted it to Robert de Langton and Margaret his wife and their heirs.[16] In virtue of this their son and heir Robert succeeded them, and was followed by his son John, who married Amice daughter of Roger de Bradshagh of Westleigh. John lived to a great age, dying in July 1443 ; his son Gilbert died before him, leaving as heir his son, the above-named Peter ; John's second wife Ellen was the other party to the suits.[17] Peter Langton died at sea in May 1450, leaving a son and heir Gilbert, seven years of age.[18]

In 1528 there was a dispute between Robert Langton of the Lowe and others as to the title to waste lands and the right to dig coal. The plaintiff, son of Gilbert Langton, asserted that he was sole lord and owner of the manor of Hindley, and he had built some cottages on the waste, assigning to each a plot of ground ; this was on account of 'the increase and

LANGTON.   *Argent three cheverons gules.*

multiplying of the people in those parts,' and sufficient pasture had been left for the other free tenants. Gilbert Culcheth, however, held a manor described as 'half the manor,' and a dwelling called Hindley Hall ; and Hugh Hindley of Aspull, whose ancestors had from time immemorial been seised of nine messuages and 80 acres in this moiety of the manor, took the law into his own hand, disregarded the inclosure, and dug and got coal and turf as accustomed, and this 'with strong hand, by the aid of certain his masters, gentlemen.' It appeared that about 1475 permission to get coal had been asked by 'old Hugh Hindley's wife,' and had been granted by Gilbert Langton, then chief lord of Hindley. Inclosures being then a general grievance, the Chancellor of the Duchy and his council ordered seven of the cottages to be pulled down and various parcels of land to be restored to the common, from thenceforth 'not to be kept in severalty by any pretending to be lords of the said waste.' Others they allowed to stand. The tenants were to have the right to take turf and dig coals, which, 'within late years,' had been found on the waste ; but to prevent abuses Robert Langton and his heirs were to nominate three charter-holding tenants and Gilbert Culcheth one, to 'appoint the places where coal and turbary should be digged and taken for fuel' of the general body of tenants.[19]

Peter Langton at his death in January 1572–3 held the manor of Hindley of the heirs of Thomas Langton of Makerfield in socage by fealty only.[20] The heir was his son Robert, then twenty-six years of

grant to Fulk had been in fee and not to his issue, but seems to have withdrawn, and the case went against him for default ; De Banco R. 216, m. 56 ; 257, m. 72 d. ; 264, m. 264. In 1319 there was also a claim for the third part of the moiety against Adam de Bradshagh and Isabel his wife, widow of Fulk Banastre ; De Banco R. 229, m. 129.

Jordan de Worsley left a daughter and heir Margaret, who married Thurstan de Tyldesley, and they at Michaelmas 1352 claimed the manor of Hindley against Sir Robert de Langton. The jury, however, did not allow it ; Duchy of Lanc. Assize R. 2, m. 2 d.

Edward Tyldesley of Morleys in 1621 held his lands in Hindley of Philip Langton ; *Lancs. Inq. p.m.* (Rec. Soc. Lancs. and Ches.), ii, 260.

[15] *Lancs. Inq. p.m.* (Chet. Soc.), ii, 95. There is a difficulty in having a younger Robert de Langton so early as 1330, but the pleadings seem to require it. It should be noticed that Robert de Langton, the husband of Margaret, is usually identified with the baron of Newton ; see *Lancs. Inq. p.m.* (Chet. Soc.), i, 98, and *Visit.* of 1533 (Chet. Soc.), 24, 25.

[16] *Final Conc.* ii, 194. The whole grant comprised a third part of the manor of Langton in Leicestershire, a messuage and plough-land in Hendon, a messuage and 38½ acres in Walton le Dale, the manor of Hindley, and half the manor of Golborne.

A number of Hindley deeds are among the additional charters in the B.M. including :—

No. 17670. Grant by Robert son of Sir John de Langton to Henry de Milnegate, chaplain, of the manor of Hindley ; 1325.

No. 17674. Grant by Robert son of Langton to Henry (son of Adam) de Man-

chester, chaplain, of the manor of Hindley and half the manor of Golborne ; 1334.

No. 17683. Quitclaim by Ralph son and heir of Sir John de Langton to Robert son of Sir Robert de Langton of the manors of . Hindley, Langton, and Hendon ; 1361.

No. 17687. Quitclaim by Henry son and heir of Ralph de Langton to John son and heir of Robert de Langton, junior, of the manor of Hindley, &c. ; 1395.

No. 17690. Refeoffment to John de Langton of Hindley and Agnes his wife of tenements in Hindley ; 1419.

No. 17694. Settlement by John de Langton of Hindley in favour of his wife Ellen de Radcliffe ; 1429.

No. 17698. Grant in tail by Peter de Langton, chaplain, to John de Langton his brother ; 1432.

No. 17699. Grant to William son of John de Langton ; 1433.

[17] Pal. of Lanc. Plea R. 6, m. 15, 16. In the former of these suits Peter claimed from Ellen a box of charters, containing among others the final concord and marriage covenant referred to and an exemplification of the said fine granted by Richard II in 1391 at the request of John de Langton. In the second Ellen claimed damages from Peter Langton, Robert Gerard, and many others, for trespass on her close at Hindley and destruction of her corn and grass. Ellen claimed a life interest in the manor by grant from her late husband ; but as she did not appear when summoned judgement was given for the accused.

In a later case William son of John Langton is mentioned ; ibid. R. 8, m. 1, 37b.

The inquisition taken after the death of John Langton in 1443 confirms the statements in the text ; Peter the grandson and heir was then twenty-four years

of age. It recites a grant made in 1413 by the deceased to Gilbert his son and his wife Elizabeth daughter of Sir Thomas Gerard, who afterwards married William Gernet. The manor was held of Henry Langton, lord of Makerfield, but by what service the jury were ignorant ; it was worth, including the Hollinhey, £10 a year ; Towneley MS. DD, no. 1471.

[18] Early Chan. Proc. 22–137, and 26–611 ; petitions by William Langton, to whom his 'cousin' Peter had bequeathed Gilbert's wardship.

[19] *Duchy Plead.* (Rec. Soc. Lancs. and Ches.), i, 160–71. The hall was tenanted by James Strangeways, and came to be known as Strangeways Hall.

The Gilbert Langton, father of Robert, had a brother Thomas, to whom in 1485 certain tenements in Hindley were granted for his life ; Agecroft D. no. 348. By an indenture of the same date Robert son and heir of Gilbert Langton of the Lowe confirmed a grant by Ralph Langley, warden of Manchester, to Peter Langton, son of the said Gilbert, for life ; B.M. Add. Chart. 17707.

Gilbert Langton of Lowe, 'squyer,' was one of the gentry of the hundred in 1512. Robert his son and heir apparent occurs in 1505 ; Towneley MS. GG, no. 1534. In 1512 Gilbert Langton made a grant of certain lands in Hindley to Robert his son and heir apparent ; B.M. Add. Chart. no. 17715. In Aug. and Sept. 1555 Sir Thomas Hesketh of Rufford and others made grants of lands in Hindley to Gilbert son of Peter Langton of Hindley, deceased ; ibid. 17719–20.

[20] Duchy of Lanc. Inq. p.m. xii, no. 14. Peter Langton was in possession of the manor in 1549, when he made an exchange of lands with Gilbert Culcheth ; *Local Glean. Lancs. and Ches.* ii, 1. It is with him that the recorded pedigree begins.

age. The tenure is stated 'as in free socage, by a rent of three pepper-corns' in the inquisition after the death (1595) of Robert Langton, who was succeeded by his son Philip, then aged twenty-six.[21] Robert Langton of the Lowe, a justice of the peace but of 'mean living,' was in 1590 reported to be 'well affected in religion'; he had spoiled his estate and used 'bad company.'[22] At the same time Edward Langton of Hindley, one of the 'gentlemen of the better sort,' and perhaps a brother of Robert, was a 'recusant and thereof indicted.'[23] The head of the family, however, soon reverted to the ancient religion,[23a] and Abraham Langton, son and heir of Philip, in 1628, as a convicted recusant, paid double to the subsidy.[24]

This Abraham Langton, as a 'papist delinquent,' had his estates sold for treason by the Parliament in 1652;[25] but appears to have recovered at least a portion of them. He was living, sixty-six years of age, in 1664, when he recorded a pedigree at the Visitation.[25a] His son Philip, then aged thirty-six, succeeded him, and was tried in 1694 for participation in the Lancashire Plot.[26] Very shortly afterwards he was succeeded by his son Edward Langton,[27] who as a 'papist' registered his estate in 1717.[28] Edward died without issue in 1733, leaving his property to Catherine his wife for life and to nephews and nieces named Pugh. William Pugh had Hindley, and his nephew and heir, Edward Philip Pugh of Coetmor in Carnarvonshire, sold the manor of Hindley and the Lowe Hall estate to the Duke of Bridgewater, the Earl of Ellesmere being the present owner.[29]

The Culcheth moiety of the manor descended to Thomas Culcheth, who died about 1744; by his will it passed to the Traffords of Croston.[30]

EGERTON, Earl of Ellesmere. *Argent a lion rampant gules between three pheons sable.*

Among the other early families of the place may be named Nightegale,[31] Barker,[32] and Harper.[33]

---

[21] Duchy of Lanc. Inq. p.m. xvi, no. 12. Philip Langton and Mary his wife were deforciants of tenements in Hindley in 1597; Pal. of Lanc. Feet of F. bdle. 58, m. 324; and of the manor and estate in 1612–13; ibid. bdle. 81, m. 52.

[22] Gibson, *Lydiate Hall*, 244, quoting S.P. Dom. Eliz. ccxxxv, 4.

[23] Gibson, op. cit. 246.

[23a] In 1607 lands of Philip Langton, recusant, were farmed out to Sir Arthur Aston; Pat. 5 Jas. I, pt. 22, 25 July.

He died at Lowe 22 Jan. 1625–6; the manor was held of Sir Richard Fleetwood and the heir was Abraham Langton son of Philip, then aged twenty-nine years and more; *Local Glean. Lancs. and Ches.* ii, 2. The heir's christian name was derived from his mother's surname, she being one of the coheirs of Thomas Abram or Abraham of Abram.

[24] Norris D. (B.M.). Elizabeth his wife occurs in the Recusant Roll of 1641; *Trans. Hist. Soc.* (new ser.), xiv, 239. Abraham Langton in 1631 paid £10 as a composition on declining knighthood; *Misc.* (Rec. Soc. Lancs. and Ches.), i, 213.

[25] *Index of Royalists* (Index Soc.), 43. He afterwards petitioned to be allowed to compound; and on the petition of 'divers well-affected persons,' his tenants, he was informed that it was 'just and reasonable' to request him to allow his tenants liberty of pre-emption or a renewal of their leases at the ancient rents. Later, in Dec. 1653, Major John Wildman, who had contracted to purchase, received an order to take possession; *Royalist Comp. Papers* (Rec. Soc. Lancs. and Ches.), iv, 56–9.

[25a] Dugdale, *Visit.* (Chet. Soc.), 174.

[26] *Hist. MSS. Com. Rep.* xiv, App. iv, 303, &c.; on p. 362 is an account of his arrest at Wepre in Flintshire, where he was attending the burial of his sister-in-law; he had married a daughter of Edward Pennant of Bagillt. In Jan. 1688–9 he broke an innkeeper's head with his cane, for proposing the health of the Earl of Derby—a sufficient indication of his politics; see the amusing anecdote on p. 214. He had been indicted for recusancy in 1678; ibid. 109.

[27] In Aug. 1687 a fine was made concerning the manor of Hindley, seventy

messuages, a water-mill, dovecote, gardens, lands, wood, furze and heath, turbary, moor and moss and 80s. rent in Hindley and Westleigh; the deforciants were Philip Langton and Elizabeth his wife, Edward Langton son and heir of Philip and Katherine his wife, and George Langton; George Pennant was one of the plaintiffs; Pal. of Lanc. Feet of F. bdle. 219, m. 64.

[28] *Engl. Cath. Nonjurors*, 123. The value of the estate was £69 1s. 2d. For a mortgage by him see *Local Glean. Lancs. and Ches.* i, 272. Edward Langton of Lowe in 1728 granted to John Rigby of Hindley a messuage and land there; B.M. Add. Chart. 17733.

[29] Baines, *Lancs.* (ed. 1870), ii, 191; from information 'supplied by Mr. William Langton.' In Piccope's MS. Pedigrees in the Chet. Lib. (ii, 234) it is stated that Edward Langton's sister Elizabeth married — Pugh; their son William is described as 'of Lowe, jeweller.' Their other children were Philip Pugh of Pemerhyn or Penwryn, Carnarvonshire (whose son Edward was the vendor), Joseph, Winifred, Anne, and Frances. The references are to Piccope MSS. (Chet. Lib.), iii, 178, 234, 254, 258, 270, from the Roman Catholic D. enrolled at Preston.

In Aug. 1758, by fine, Edward Philip Pugh and Mary his wife remitted to William Carghey messuages and lands in Hindley; the manor is not named; Pal. of Lanc. Feet of F. bdle. 361, m. 132.

[30] Cal. Exch. of Pleas, Lancs. C. 301, where the will of Thomas Culcheth is given. In 1771 Humphrey and John Trafford were vouchees of the manor of Croston and various other lordships, including a fourth part of the manor of Hindley, with the hall known as Hindley Hall or Strangeways Hall; Pal. of Lanc. Plea R. 613, m. 10; also at Aug. Assizes, 1797, R. 11.

In 1364 Gilbert de Culcheth, a minor, by his guardian John de Blackburn, demanded against Cecily, widow of Gilbert de Culcheth the elder, messuages and land in Hindley which the elder Gilbert gave to Gilbert his son and Joan his wife, and which should now descend to the plaintiff as son and heir. Cecily claimed

Philip Langton of Lowe, Robert Pinnington, and Peter Harrison of Hindley, occur among the freeholders of 1600.[34] In 1628 Abraham Langton and Christopher Stananought were the freeholders contributing to the subsidy.[35] Nicholas Ranicars of Hindley had his estate sequestered by the Parliament in 1650 ' for delinquency in the late wars,' and was allowed to compound.[36] A family named Marsh resided here.[37]

A decree concerning the boundaries between Hindley and Ince, and the division of the wastes, was made in the time of Charles I.[38]

Before the Reformation there was a chapel at Lowe in Hindley ; but the Langtons probably claimed it as private property, and then allowed it to decay.[39]

The next church in Hindley was erected in 1641 on land given by George Green,[40] subscriptions being collected for the building from the inhabitants. It was built with the approbation of the rector of Wigan, then Bishop Bridgeman ; there was a chancel at the east end, and the Established services were adhered to, one of the Wigan curates officiating.[41] The place was, as early as 1643, regarded as Puritan,[41a] and its first regular minister, Thomas Tonge, conformed readily to the Presbyterian discipline established a few years later.[42] He was succeeded by William Williamson,[43] and he by James Bradshaw, ejected in 1662 for nonconformity.[44] The chapel seems to have remained unused for six years, and

then a succession of curates followed ; some of the feoffees were Nonconformists or sympathizers, and thus conforming ministers had probably an uneasy time.[45] In 1690 a determined attempt was made to secure the chapel for the Dissenters, their worship now being tolerated, by the appointment of Thomas Whalley, an open Nonconformist.[46] The matter was finally taken into the Duchy Court ; after a long trial the chapel was secured for the Establishment and consecrated in 1698 on All Saints' Day.[47] It was rebuilt in 1766,[48] and with some alterations remains in use. It is now known as All Saints' Church. The church property is still in the hands of trustees, but the curates and vicars since 1708 have been appointed by the rectors of Wigan.[49] There is a mission chapel called St. Augustine's.

St. Peter's, Hindley, was consecrated in 1866, the patronage being vested in trustees.[50] To the recent churches of St. Nathaniel, Platt Bridge (1905), and St. John the Evangelist, Hindley Green (1903), the Bishop of Liverpool collates.[51]

The Wesleyan Methodists acquired land in 1846, and built a chapel in 1851. Another chapel was built in 1869 in Walthew Lane, Platt Bridge.[52] The United Methodist Free Church have two chapels at Hindley Green—Brunswick Chapel, built in 1855, and another in 1866.[53] The Primitive Methodists have one at Castle Hill, built in 1856, and another at

1462 ; *Trans. Hist. Soc.* (new ser.), iv, 161 ; the purchaser had a son Richard, who in 1430 made a settlement of his lands ; OO, no. 1459. The ancestor of this branch of the Hindley family was perhaps the Richard son of Beatrice who had a grant from Robert Banastre, lord of Makerfield ; the rent was to be 4*s.* a year ; no. 1471.

A grant of Burghurst in Hindley by Hugh de Thursaker is printed in *Pal. Note Bk.* iv, 150.

[34] *Misc.* (Rec. Soc. Lancs. and Ches.), i, 238, 243, 251.

In the *Hindley D.* printed in *Local Glean. Lancs. and Ches.* ii, 167, are some referring to the Harrisons of Hindley ; Peter Harrison, living in 1637 and 1651, had a son and heir John, who in the latter year was rector of Ashton under Lyne, and has found a place in *Dict. Nat. Biog.*

Peter Harrison, 'late solicitor to the County Committee,' had in 1651 joined the Earl of Derby, but being angry with him for plundering, recalled his two sons ; *Cal. of Com. for Compounding,* iv, 2955. These sons are called Captain Jeremiah and Lieutenant Nathaniel Harrison in 1652 ; *Cal. of Com. for Advancing Money,* iii, 1445.

Richard Wood of Hindley died 12 Jan. 1612–13 seised of a messuage and lands in Hindley held of the king, as of his manor of Enfield by a rent of 3*s.* 4*d.* ; *Lancs. Inq. p.m.* (Rec. Soc. Lancs. and Ches.), i, 262.

[35] Norris D. (B.M.). Christopher Stananought was son and heir of William, living in 1602 ; Hindley D. no. 10.

[36] *Cal. of Com. for Compounding,* iv, 2519. John Ranicars was not allowed to compound for a messuage and lands purchased from Nicholas.

[37] Wills of John and James Marsh, of 1670 and 1687 respectively, are printed in *Lancs. and Ches. Hist. and Gen. Notes,* ii, 44, 80. See also Gillow, *Bibl. Dict. of Engl. Cath.* iv, 467–70.

[50] *Lond. Gaz.* 14 May 1867, 26 Mar. 1875, &c. See Bridgeman, op. cit. 780 ; Leyland, *Hindley,* 57, 58.

[51] Leyland, op. cit. 75–7 ; Nightingale, *Lancs. Nonconf.* iv, 13.

[52] Leyland, op. cit. 78, 79 ; Nightingale, op. cit. iv, 21. The chapel was practically unused from 1862–82.

[53] Leyland, op. cit. 79.

Platt Bridge, built in 1854.[54] The Independent Methodists have one at Lowe Green, built in 1867.[55]

The Particular Baptists built Ebenezer Chapel in Mill Lane in 1854.[56]

The Congregationalists made a first effort in 1794, but no church was formed until 1812 ; St. Paul's Chapel was built in 1815, meetings for worship having been held some years earlier in cottages. Certain differences between the minister, the Rev. William Turner, and the majority of the congregation caused him to resign in 1830 ; his friends opened a temporary building in the Bridge Croft, and built a church in 1838, where he officiated till 1862.[57]

The ejected Presbyterians of 1698 built another place of worship for themselves ; it has been continuously used, the present congregation being Unitarian in doctrine.[58]

Nothing is known of the permanence of the ancient religion during the 17th century, but mass was probably said at Lowe Hall as opportunity was afforded. Dom John Placid Acton, a Benedictine, was stationed at this place in 1699, and died there in 1727 ; succeeding priests, who till 1758 resided chiefly at Park Hall in Charnock Richard, or at Standish Hall, moved the chapel to Strangeways and then to Hindley village ; this change was made in 1789. From 1758 there has been a resident Benedictine priest in charge ; and the present church of St. Benedict in Market Street was built in 1869.[59]

ABRAM

Edburgham, 1212 ; Adburgham, 1246, and common ; Abraham, xvi cent. ; Abram, xviii cent. Pronounced Abbram.

Abram is situated in the centre of a coal-mining district ; the surface of the country is flat except in the south, where it is very slightly undulating. The surroundings are characteristic of a coal-producing district, distinctly unpicturesque, dingy grass-fields alternating with collieries, pit-banks, and railway lines. Some fields are arable and produce crops of wheat and oats. There is much pasture land. Trees are in the minority, and stunted and blackened with smoke. The hawthorn hedges which divide the fields are low and spare. The soil is a stiff clay which holds a quantity of water on its surface, for besides occasional 'flashes' caused by mining, the fields appear to be slightly flooded at most seasons of the year. It is a district of sett-laid roads and cinder-paths. In the northern part of the township the geological forma-

tion consists of the Coal Measures. At some distance from the southern boundary this formation dips under the New Red Sandstone and the intervening Permian Beds.

The area is 1,982 acres,[1] and in 1901 the population numbered 6,306. Part of the western and nearly all of the southern boundary is formed by a brook running through Hindley, and called successively Eye Brook and Glazebrook ; by it Bamfurlong,[2] in the extreme west, is cut off from the main portion of the township.

Abram village lies in the north-western corner, where the road from Wigan to Warrington by Golborne crosses the township, meeting at the village other roads from Ashton on the south-west, and from Leigh on the east. Bickershaw [3] lies by the last-named road, near the eastern boundary. Plank Lane is a hamlet in the south-eastern corner, situate on the road from Leigh to Newton. Dover is a hamlet on the south-west border.

The London and North Western Company's railway from Warrington to Wigan crosses the western corner of the township, with a station called Bamfurlong ; a branch of its Wigan and Manchester line has a station at Plank Lane ; the Great Central Company's Manchester and Wigan line passes north through the middle of the township, with two stations called Westleigh and Bedford, and Bickershaw and Abram. The Leigh branch of the Leeds and Liverpool Canal passes through near the southern border.

Coal-mining began about sixty years since.

A local board was formed in 1880. The township is now governed by an urban district council of twelve members, elected by four wards.

Before the Conquest, as after, ABRAM MANOR appears to have been a member of the manor and fee of Newton.[4] Henry II gave it to Warine son of Godfrey, and his descendants, assuming the local name, held it to the 17th century. This Warine confirmed a grant by his nephew, William de Occleshaw, to Cockersand Abbey, for the souls of King Henry and others.[5] His son Richard was a benefactor to the same house, granting Bernegrenes, on the south of Walter's Pool, with other lands and liberties.[6] Richard de Abram was in possession in 1212, holding the manor as 4 oxgangs by a rent of 4s. ; a third part had been given in alms.[7] John son of Richard confirmed the previous grants to Cockersand and added a ridding by Glazebrook.[8] Warine Banastre granted an oxgang of his demesne to the same canons,[9] and Robert son of Robert Banastre gave a general confirmation about 1250.[10]

[54] Leyland, op. cit. 79.

[55] Ibid. 79.

[56] Ibid. 78.

[57] Ibid. 75–7; Nightingale, op. cit. iv,13.

[58] Leyland, Hindley, 64–75. The chapel was built in 1700 by Richard Crook of Abram and conveyed to trustees in 1717, James Green of Abram being one. Owing, it is said, to an attempt by William Davenport, minister in 1777, to carry the endowment to the Presbyterian chapel at Wigan, he became unpopular, was assaulted and finally resigned. He is said to have been Arian in doctrine. Unitarianism prevailed here by the end of the 18th century, but from the account of a disturbance in the chapel in 1833 it would seem that some Trinitarians then remained in the congregation. Particulars of the endow-

ment, now considerable, on account of coal mining on the land, are given in the Report of the End. Char. of Wigan, 1899, pp. 90–7.

[59] Mr. Gillow in Trans. Hist. Soc. (new ser.), xiii, 153, 154, where it is stated that Bishop Matthew Gibson confirmed fifty-nine at Strangeways in 1784 ; there were 259 communicants ; Liverpool Cath. Ann. 1901. See further in Leyland, Hindley, 62, 63, for reminiscences of Dom Anselm Appleton, 1808–36.

[1] 1,984, including 26 of inland water ; Census of 1901.

[2] Banforthlang, 1448.

[3] Bykershagh, 1365.

[4] V.C.H. Lancs. i, 286.

[5] Cockersand Chart. (Chet. Soc.), ii, 661.

[6] Ibid. 663.

names ' the deep lache which was the boundary between Abram and Occleshaw.'

[7] Lancs. Inq. and Extents (Rec. Soc. Lancs. and Ches.), i, 77. How King Henry came to have Abram in his hands is unknown. The third part in alms probably refers to the Occleshaw and other gifts recorded in the text.

[8] Cockersand Chart. ii, 664. In 1246 John de Abram quitclaimed his right in 200 acres of land to Peter de Burnhull ; Final Conc. (Rec.Soc. Lancs.and Ches.),i, 98.

[9] Cockersand Chart. ii, 660.

[10] Ibid. ii, 643. The following were the abbey tenants in 1501 : John Ashton, 12d. ; William Culcheth, 12d. ; Richard Atherton and Robert Bolton, in Bickershaw, each 6d. ; Cockersand Rental (Chet. Soc.), 4.

The family pedigree cannot be traced satisfactorily.[11] A Gilbert Abram died about 1470 leaving two daughters as heirs; Constance married Henry Byrom and Isabel married James Holt,[12] and the later holdings of these families probably represent the inheritance of the daughters.[13] The manor, however, continued in the male line[13a] to Thomas Abram, who died in 1606, also leaving two daughters to divide the property.[14] The elder, Susan, married Henry Lance,

ABRAM. *Azure a sun in splendour or.*

of a Cornish family,[15] and the manor was assigned to her; the younger daughter, Mary, married Philip Langton of the Lowe in Hindley.[16] All adhered to the ancient religion, and suffered accordingly under the persecuting laws in force.[17] In 1652, however, Abraham Lance, the son and heir of Henry and Susan, being 'conformable,' petitioned for the removal of the sequestration of his mother's lands, and on condition that he abjured his religion they were allowed to him.[18] It does not appear whether he actually regained possession or not, but the ruin of the family, several members of which fell in the Civil War fighting as Royalists, could not be averted.[19]

Shortly afterwards William Gerard and Anne his

---

[11] Adam de Abram occurs in 1246; Assize R. 404, m. 13 d. In 1270-1 Robert de Abram and Robert and Adam his sons were defendants; Curia Regis R. 201, m. 15 d. From one of these may descend the John son of Richard son of Robert de Abram mentioned in 1342; Towneley MS. GG, no. 2670.

Richard de Abram, probably the head of the family, was a juror in 1288; *Inq. and Extents*, i, 273. John son of Richard de Abram was a defendant in 1301; Simon de Holland was plaintiff; Assize R. 419, m. 4 d.; 418, m. 2. John de Abram seems to have died soon after his father, for in 1305 the defendants in a case concerning land were Richard son of John de Adburgham, Agnes widow of John, Maud widow of Richard (probably the grandfather), Henry de Huyton, William and Roger de Bradshagh, Simon de Holland, John Gillibrand, and William son of Roger de Ashton; the plaintiff was Richard son of Adam del Lache. This list probably includes all or most of the freeholders; Assize R. 420, m. 8. Many years later, in 1324-5, Richard del Lache claimed common of pasture from Richard de Abram; Assize R. 426, m. 9. In 1324 an agreement was made between Adam de Kenyon and Richard de Abram that the latter should marry Adam's daughter Godith, her portion being £40; Harl. MS. 2112, fol. 159-95.

William de Abram was a juror in 1387; *Lancs. Inq. p.m.* (Chet. Soc.), i, 25. Soon afterwards there are several references to Gilbert de Abram, who was a juror in 1416; ibid. i, 116. In 1419 a proclamation was issued forbidding armed men to go about to the peril of the king's peace, with special reference to Gilbert de Abram and his sons John and William, who had entered the lands of Richard del Lache at Abram; *Dep. Keeper's Rep.* xxxiii, App. 17.

John de Abram, probably the son of Gilbert just mentioned, appears to have died about the beginning of 1446, when the writ *Diem clausit extremum* was issued; *Dep. Keeper's Rep.* xxxix, App. 533. William de Abram, gentleman, and Joan daughter of John de Abram, occur in suits of 1445; Pal. of Lanc. Plea R. 8, m. 1, 6.

[12] In the time of Edward IV there was made a settlement of his estate, or part of it, in favour of his two daughters; Towneley MS. CC, no. 651. It is described as seven messuages, 124 acres of land, &c. John Abram was the deforciant. Possibly he was the heir male; in which case Gilbert must have been dead at that time. In the Visitations the father's name is given as John.

About 1500 James Holt with Isabel his wife and Constance Byrom a widow, as

cousins and heirs o daughters and heirs claimed a right of tol the Mersey between wall; *Duchy Plead. Ches.*), i, 39-41. In Helsby), i, 596, it one of the sisters an Boydell, was marrie early as 1405; Gilb heir; a few years l of Nicholas Langto Margaret, married also p. ' i, 723

[13] Duchy of Lanc Thomas Holt of Gri quisition taken after Byrom in 1613, it w held lands in Abram Newton, but the ser *Lancs Inq p m.* (R Ches) i 273; i'

wife were in possession,[20] and sold the manor to Richard Hilton,[21] with whose daughter Abigail it descended to her children by her husband Thomas Crook.[22]

The new owner it appears was a zealous Protestant, and his son Richard Crook was the builder of the Nonconformist chapel at Hindley, after the existing one had been recovered by the Bishop of Chester.[23] Richard died without issue in November 1727, and the inheritance, which, besides Abram, included lands in Walton le Dale and elsewhere in the county,[24] passed to his five sisters as co-heirs.[25] The manor of Abram seems to have been the portion of the second sister, Anne, who married John Darbyshire of Warrington, and her only child, Abigail, married Thomas Clayton, M.D., of Little Harwood.[26] Their grandson,

Thomas Clayton, in 1785 sold the manor to Peter Arrowsmith of Astley, who in 1828 sold it to John Whitley, and his son Henry Jackson Whitley, of Biggleswade, succeeded.[27] His son, Mr. John Henry Arthur Whitley, of Bourton, Salop, is the present owner ; but no manorial rights are claimed.[28]

The portion called *OCCLESHAW*, as has been seen, was granted to Cockersand Abbey,[29] and was occupied by the Urmston family ;[30] after the Dissolution it came into the possession of the Earl of Derby.[31] The Occleshaw family long continued to hold an estate in the township ;[32] this eventually passed into the hands of Abigail Crook, and became part of her Abram estate.[33]

BAMFURLONG was the possession of the Ashton family for a long period[34] ; it then passed to a junior

---

[20] In 1649 Abraham Lance appointed William Gerard of Garswood, son and heir apparent of Sir William Gerard of Brynn, receiver for behoof of Abraham Lance and his wife and their heirs, with remainder to the use of the said William Gerard ; a bond, signed by William Gerard in 1667, mentions that Abraham Lance had died about seven years before without male issue. See J. Leyland's *Abram*, 12, for fuller abstracts of these and other deeds.

Fines relating to the above are Pal. of Lanc. Feet of F. bdles. 146, m. 111 ; 180, m. 17.

[21] On 16 Sept. 1667 the estate was conveyed to Richard Hilton of Westleigh, yeoman, for £1,505 ; it included two pews in Wigan Church ; also the following fee-farm rents : 'William Leyland, 5s. ; John Anderton, 3s. 4d. ; late Frances Dukinfield, 11d. ; Richard Occleshaw, 13d. ; James Wreast, 3s. 5d.; Thomas Holland, 1s. 6d. ; Roger Culcheth, 2d. ; John Lithgoe, 1d. ;' see Leyland, op. cit. 12, 13. Richard Hilton died at the beginning of 1690.

[22] Ibid. 14. Thomas Crook is described as of Hoole, Lancashire. He was the founder of numerous charities, and left money 'to the preaching Protestant minister of Hindley chapel.' He expressed a desire to be buried with his mother (Margaret Green) and brother in Standish parish church ; Leyland, op. cit. 14, 118–21 ; also *Local Glean. Lancs. and Ches.* i, 147. An accusation of coin clipping, probably false, was made against William Crook and Thomas his brother in 1684 ; *Hist. MSS. Com. Rep.* xiv, App. iv, 173, 175.

[23] Leyland, *Hindley*, 65.

[24] The will of Thomas Crook already quoted mentions estates at Bretherton, Much Hoole, Mawdesley, Walton le Dale, Billinge, Euxton, Ulnes Walton, Leyland, Farington, Alston, and Whittingham.

Richard had an elder brother Caleb, who also died without issue.

Abigail Crook, the widow, died about 1705 ; an abstract of her will is printed in *Local Glean.* ii, 231, in which volume is much information as to the Crook family. Several documents about their properties are in the possession of W. Farrer.

[25] Ibid. ii, 231, 237. The eldest sister, Lydia, married Thomas Yates of Whitchurch ; the second, Anne, married John Darbyshire of Warrington ; the third, Abigail, married in 1707 John Andrews of Bolton le Moors ; the fourth, Margaret, married (1) John Percival of Liverpool and Allerton, and (2) Thomas Summers of Liverpool ; the fifth, Isabel, married (1) —Danvers, and (2) Rev. Thomas Heys of Rainhill.

[26] In 1734 all t lease of the manor o mas Yates and Lyd Clayton and Abigail drews and Abigail h mers and Margare Heys and Isabel h account of the Clayt *Blackburn*, 556–61.

[27] Leyland, *Abram*

[28] Informat on o Mr. William Valian

[29] 'The whole lan granted by William canons of Cockersa the 12th century. given : 'From wh down from Bageley Glazebrook, up this brook, to Rushy lac

---

branch of the Gerards, described as ' of Brindle '[35] ; and probably by sale to the later Gerards of Ince, and has descended with the Westwood property.[36]

Nothing definite can be stated about the descent of *BICKERSHAW*, formerly called a manor.[37] In the 16th century it was owned by the Holcrofts, and sold by them to Richard Ashton in 1599.[38] Ralph Ashton about thirty years later sold it to Frances widow of Robert Dukinfield of Dukinfield near Stockport.[39] It descended in this family until 1760, when it was sold to Richard Clayton of Adlington ; and it was again sold in 1790 to Edward Ackers of Newton, surgeon. The trustees of Abraham Ackers, who died in 1864, are the owners ; it is leased to the Abram Coal Company.[40]

A branch of the Culcheths were long seated in Abram.[41] The inquisition taken after the death of John Culcheth in 1586 shows that he had held lands in Abram of Thomas Abram by a rent of 1*d*., and in

Hindley of John Culcheth of Culcheth by a rent of 6*d*.[42] A pedigree was recorded in 1664,[43] but the family afterwards migrated to Warwickshire, and in 1750 sold the property.[44]

Adam Bolton,[44] John Occleshaw, John Southworth, Roger Culcheth, Cecily Ashton, and Nicholas Huyton, were the landowners contributing to a subsidy collected about 1556.[45] The Corless,[47] Lithgoe,[48] and Leyland[49] families were long resident here.

A plot of land in Park Lane,

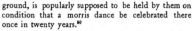

CULCHETH. *Argent an eagle sable preying upon a child swaddled gules.*

known as the Morris Dancers' ground, is popularly supposed to be held by them on condition that a morris dance be celebrated there once in twenty years.[50]

---

true heir ; ibid. iii, 124, 125. At the same time John Ashton and Richard his son alleged their title to Bamfurlong against Richard, Cecily, and Anne Ashton, Roger Anderton, Gilbert Lee, Gilbert Houghton, and Ralph Anderton ; *Ducatus Lanc.* (Rec. Com.), ii, 114.

John Ashton of Bamfurlong, senior, and his son and heir were in 1590 among the ' comers to church but no communicants'; Gibson, *Lydiate Hall*, 246, quoting S.P. Dom.Eliz.ccxxxv, 4. In 1598 as an avowed recusant he was called upon to pay £10 for ' her Majesty's service in Ireland ' ; ibid. 262, from S.P. Dom. Eliz. cclxvi, 80.

John Ashton, claiming by inheritance from Richard Ashton, deceased, demanded in 1594 an estate in Bamfurlong, &c., from Adam Hawarden, Margaret Ashton, and Lawrence Bispham ; *Duchy Plead.* iii, 293. In that year Richard Ashton of Bamfurlong had after holding nothing, as the inquest found, and leaving a son Richard who was but sixteen in 1609 ; *Lancs. Inq. p.m.* (Rec. Soc. Lancs. and Ches.), i, 130. At the *Visitation* in 1613 (Chet. Soc. 17) Richard was said to be twenty years of age ; his father Richard was son of John Ashton of Bamfurlong. John Ashton had died in 1603, being buried on 30 July at Wigan ; Reg. Richard Ashton, being a convicted recusant, paid double to the subsidy in 1628 ; Norris D.(B.M.).

[35] This family recorded a pedigree in 1664, in which they are already described as ' of Bamfurlong' ; Dugdale, *Visit.* (Chet. Soc.), 118. It is not clear how they obtained possession. In 1684 John Ashton called for an inquiry as to the title of Henry Gerard, son of Henry Gerard, a solicitor, deceased, to the hall of Bamfurlong, a water corn-mill, and various lands, formerly the property of Richard Ashton and his daughter Mary, deceased ; *Exch. Depos.* (Rec. Soc.), 65. There is a charge of ' dishonest contrivances ' against the elder Henry.

[36] See Gillow, *Bibl. Dict. of Engl. Cath.* ii, 431 ; Leyland, *Abram*, 18, 19. From the latter it seems that Henry Gerard the son in 1681 married Cecily West, who in 1717 (now Cecily Howett) as ' a papist ' registered an annuity of £80 derived from her first husband ; *Engl. Cath. Nonjurors*, 128. Henry's brother Ralph, a priest, served the domestic chapel at Bamfurlong.

[37] Sir Thomas Holcroft held Bickershaw manor of James Browne by a rent of 6*d*. in 1558 ; Duchy of Lanc. Inq. p.m. x, no. 13. There was a large amount of dis-

puting about it at the time, as will be seen by a reference to the *Ducatus Lanc.* (Rec. Com.), i, 145, 150 ; ii, 56, 194. Hugh Bradshaw and Constance his wife were in possession in 1535, but Thomas Holcroft's title was allowed.

[38] William Holcroft and Elizabeth his wife were vendors ; Pal. of Lanc. Feet of F. bdle. 61, m. 139.

[39] It was purchased from Edward Bolton in 1671, according to the statement in Leyland's *Abram*, 20 ; but was acquired by Frances Dukinfield in 1633 or 1634 from Ralph Ashton and Katherine his wife ; Pal. of Lanc. Feet of F. bdle. 124, m. 18. The later succession is described in Leyland, 21–8. See also Pal. of Lanc. Feet of F. bdle. 362, m. 129.

[40] Leyland, op. cit. 23, 24 ; and information of the secretary to the company. Nothing of the old house remains.

[41] Some deeds concerning the family have been preserved by Towneley, Add. MS. 32105, no. 906–23. The other information is given in the Culcheth papers published in *Lancs. and Ches. Hist. and Gen. Notes.*
In 1392 John son of Thomas de Culcheth had lands in Abram and Hindley ; his son Roger had married Ellen daughter of Henry son of Robert de Blackrod ; Add. MS. 32105, no. 915.
William Culshaw in 1531 arranged for the marriage of Roger, his son and heir, with Janet daughter of John Richardson ; his own wife was named Margery ; ibid. no. 911, 912, 919. The lands in Hindley were called Occleshull and Taleor, and in Abram, Longfield.

[42] Ibid. no. 909. The holding in Abram was two messuages, two tofts, two gardens, two orchards, 40 acres of land, 20 acres of meadow, and 20 acres of pasture. Roger Culcheth was his son and heir, and six years of age.

[43] Dugdale, *Visit.* (Chet. Soc.), 92. Roger Culcheth was still living, aged eighty-four ; his son George recorded the pedigree. His two eldest sons had been slain at Newbury, and a younger son in Wirral in the Civil Wars ; Thomas, the third son, aged forty-four, was the heir.

[44] See *Lancs. and Ches. Hist. and Gen. Notes*, ii, 228, for a continuation of the pedigree by Mr. J. P. Rylands. Roger Culcheth of Wottenbury in Warwickshire, by his will of 1701, left his estate in the parish of Wigan to his brother Thomas of Studley in Warwickshire, tanner ; ibid. p. 120. This Thomas left a son William, who seems to have been the

last of the family connected with Abram; ibid. i, 275, 276. See also Payne's *Engl. Cath. Rec.* 26. Part of their land is now the property of the trustees of Abigail Crook's charities.
Roger Culcheth of Abram, as a ' papist,' registered his estate in 1717, the value was £64 15*s*. 4*d*. ; *Engl. Cath. Nonjurors*, 124. The name of the family had constantly appeared on the Recusant Rolls ; Gillow's *Bibl. Dict. Engl. Cath.* i, 608.

[45] Adam, son and heir-apparent of Robert Bolton, was a surety for William Culcheth in 1531 ; Add. MS. 32105, no. 912. The father and son were engaged in numerous disputes as to their property, called Blackfields, Mossheys, Lower House, New Earth, etc. ; see *Ducatus Lanc.* (Rec. Com.), i, 166, &c. It appears that Robert Bolton died in 1552 or 1553 ; his wife's name was Elizabeth Holden. Another Robert Bolton is mentioned in 1583 (ibid. iii, 149), and the inquisition after the death of Edward Bolton in 1587 is in Duchy of Lanc. Inq. p.m. xv, no. 48. The tenure is not recorded ; Edward's heir was his son William, twenty-three years of age.
William Bolton was a freeholder in 1600 and Edward Bolton in 1628 ; *Misc.* (Rec. Soc. Lancs. and Ches.), i, 239 ; Norris D. (B.M.). This is perhaps the Edward Bolton who sold Bickershaw Hall in 1671. Deeds relating to Bolton House in Abram and other properties of the family are printed in *Lancs. and Ches. Hist. and Gen. Notes*, ii, 39, 47.

[46] Masey of Rixton D.

[47] Richard Corless as a landowner contributed to the subsidy of 1628 ; Norris D. (B.M.).

[48] Nicholas Huyton of Blackrod in 1528 held lands in Abram of the heirs of John Abram by a rent of 5*s*. ; Duchy of Lanc. Inq. p.m. vi, no. 53. In 1628 John Lithgoe contributed to the subsidy for Huyton's lands ' ; Norris D. (B.M.).

[49] William Leyland was a trustee in 1626 ; Add. MS. 32105, no. 906. Their connexion with the township ceased about 1780 ; but John Leyland of Cheetham House (afterwards called the Grange) in Hindley represented them down to his death in 1883 ; his accounts of Hindley and Abram, published in 1873 and 1881, have been used in these notes. A grant of arms was made to him in 1863 ; *Lancs. and Ches. Hist. and Gen. Notes*, iii, 34.

[50] Leyland, op. cit. 114 ; the custom was observed in 1880. Mr. William Valiant informs us that this is still kept up.

The church of St. John was erected in 1838 for the accommodation of members of the Established Church.[61] The rector of Wigan is patron of this, but trustees present to the new church of St. James and St. Elizabeth, Bickershaw.

A Congregational chapel was built in 1897.

A school was founded at Lowe in 1632 by Mrs. Mary Abram.[52]

HAIGH

Hage, 1193 ; Hagh, 1298, and common, with Haghe ; Ha, Haw, xvi cent. ; also Haigh.

This township forms the north-eastern corner of the parish. On the west it is bounded by the Douglas, and on the north a small brook running into the Douglas divides it from Blackrod. The ground rises towards the east and north, and the village of Haigh, near the middle of the Aspull boundary and 2½ miles north-east of Wigan, is one of its highest points, about 520 ft. above sea level. The Hall is on the slope of the hill to the west of the village. The area is 2,135½ acres.[1] The population in 1901 was 1,164.[2]

Roads lead from the village, north to Blackrod, west to Standish, and south to Wigan and Aspull. The London and North Western and Lancashire and Yorkshire Companies' joint railway passes through the township on the western side, where it is joined by a short connecting line from the Wigan and Preston Railway ; there is a station called Red Rock. The Lancaster Canal also winds through the western part of the township, near the Douglas.

The woods and grounds of Haigh Hall, occupying 500 acres, clothe the south-western slopes with pleasant scenery in contrast with the surrounding collieries of a black country. It is a common sight to see the gaunt and black coal-shafts rising from the midst of corn fields and plantations. For Haigh has its agriculture, as well as mining and manufacturing industries, wheat, oats, and potatoes being grown in spite of an exposed situation and smoke from neighbouring factories &c., the soil being clay upon a shaley rock. The Hall itself commands a fine panorama of the district around Wigan. Haigh has long been celebrated for its cannel coal ;[3] this is almost exhausted, but coal-mining is the great industry of the place. There are also a brewery, and dyeing and bleaching works.

The township is governed by a parish council.

William Roby, 1766 to 1830, a Congregational divine of note, was a native of Haigh.[4]

The early history of the manor of *MANOR HAIGH* cannot be traced. About 1220–1230 it belonged to the Marsey fee, sold to Ranulf, Earl of Chester.[5] A Hugh de Haigh, most probably Hugh le Norreys, to whom the adjacent Blackrod was granted, paid 3 marks in 1193–4 for having the king's good will.[6] Richard de Orrell granted to Cockersand Abbey land in Haigh, adjacent to Hugh's ridding, about 1220 ;[7] and as a century later Sir Robert de Holland held it of the Earl of Lancaster,[8] together with other manors which had belonged to Richard de Orrell, it might be supposed that Haigh was part of the Orrell family's holding.[9] In 1282, however, Hugh son of Alan le Norreys was lord of Haigh.[10]

In 1298 William son of Richard de Bradshagh and Mabel his wife were in possession of the manors of Haigh and Blackrod,[11] which were Mabel's right as heir of the last-named Hugh le Norreys. Her husband from his name is supposed to have been a descendant of the Bradshaghs of Bradshaw, near Turton.

In 1302 William de Bradshagh held the twelfth part of a knight's fee in Haigh of the Earl of Lancaster ;[12] ten years later the title of William and

[51] Leyland, *Abram*, 29–35. The tenures of the second and third of the incumbents appear to have been shortened by their parishioners' objection to what was called 'ritualism.' The district chapelry was formed in 1843 ; *Lond. Gaz.* 1 Aug. and 3 Oct. 1843.

[52] Gastrell, *Notitia*, ii, 256.

[1] 2,130 acres, including 68 acres of inland water ; Census Rep. of 1901.

[2] Including Willoughby's.

[3] See the account by Roger North in 1676, quoted in Baines, *Lancs.* (ed. 1836), from the *Life of Lord Guildford*, iii, 554 ; see also Baines, *Lancs. Dir.* 1825, ii, 613. There is a notice of a cannel mine being on fire in 1737 in *Lancs. and Ches. Hist. and Gen. Notes*, iii, 106.

[4] *Dict. Nat. Biog.*

[5] Ormerod, *Ches.* (ed. Helsby), i, 37, from the Duchy Coucher. The Marsey fee is only imperfectly described in the survey of 1212.

[6] Farrer, *Lancs. Pipe R.* 78 ; after the rebellion of John, Count of Mortain, afterwards king. If Hugh le Norreys be rightly identified with Hugh de Haigh it may indicate that he had been settled in Haigh before Blackrod was granted to him; *Lancs. Inq. and Extents* (Rec Soc. Lancs. and Ches.), i, 68, where he is called Hugh de Blackrod.

[7] *Cockersand Chart.* (Chet. Soc.), ii, 612. The boundaries began at 'the road to the church,' and went up to the head

Mabel was assured by a fine.[13] For his share in Adam Banastre's rebellion in 1315 and the death of Henry de Bury,[14] Sir William de Bradshagh was outlawed for felony and by 1317 his manors of Haigh and Blackrod had been taken into the king's hands and demised to Peter de Limesey, but Mabel de Haigh intruded herself.[15] Sir William was living in 1328,[16] and appears to have been killed at Winwick in August 1333.[17]

Mabel's title to the Norreys lands must have been recognized, for in 1336 and 1337, when a widow and childless, she arranged for the succession to the manors as absolute owner, granting them to her husband's nephews; Haigh to William, a son of John de Bradshagh, and Blackrod to Roger son of Richard, who was another son.[18] In 1338 she founded a chantry in Wigan Church for her husband's soul and her own, as also for the soul of Edward II.[19] In 1346 Mabel de Bradshagh, heir of Hugh le Norreys, held the manor of Haigh for the twelfth part of a knight's fee and by the service of 10d. yearly.[20] She was living two years later.[21]

Early in 1365 Roger de Bradshagh of Westleigh demanded the manor of Haigh from William de Bradshagh and Sir Henry de Trafford, in virtue of the settlement of 1312.[22] There may have been two Williams in succession, for William de Bradshagh, who died in 1380 seised of the manor of Haigh, left a son and heir Thomas only twelve years of age.[23] Thomas de Bradshagh took part in the Percy rising of 1403 and was present at the battle of Shrewsbury; afterwards he received a pardon from Henry IV.[24] He was living in 1425.[25]

His son and heir was James Bradshagh,[26] who, with many others, was accused of the death of John Tailor; he appears to have been released from attendance at the trial, but died in the summer of 1442 before it came to an end.[27] He had held lands in Wigan called Rudgatehurst of the rector, and the manor of Haigh of the king, as Duke of Lancaster, for the twelfth part of a knight's fee and by the service of 10d. yearly. His son and heir was William Bradshagh, aged twenty-three.[28]

William Bradshagh was accuser and accused in various pleas of the next succeeding years.[29] He had several children, but the manor descended to his son James,[30] who died in May 1491, leaving as heir his son Roger, then twenty-three years of age and more. There were also two younger sons, Ralph and William, and a daughter Constance.[31] Roger, who was made a knight, had no children, and died in December 1537, the heir being his brother Ralph, then about

[13] *Final Conc.* ii, 9. The remainder was to 'the heirs of William,' which occasioned a lawsuit later. Also Kuerden, loc. cit. no. 3.

[14] Coram Rege R. 254, m. 52.

[15] Inq. a.q.d. 11 Edw. II, no. 4. The inquiry was made at Haigh in June 1318, when the manors had been in the king's hands a year and a day. It may be added that in 1319 Mabel asserted that her husband was dead; Assize R. 424, m. 8 d.

These facts are utilized in the well-known legend of Sir William and his wife; see Bridgeman, *Wigan Ch.* 695-9; also Harland and Wilkinson, *Lancs. Legends*, 45; *Topog. and Gen.* ii, 365-9. That there is some basis for the legend may be gathered from entries in the Close R., Mabel being called wife of Peter de Limesey in 1318 (unless there is an error in the record) and 'Mabel de Haigh' simply in the following year; *Cal. Close*, 1313-18, p. 554; 1318-23, p. 8.

[16] De Banco R. 273, m. 121 d.; Sir William de Bradshagh charged Adam de Hindley and others with having forcibly carried off his goods at Haigh and Blackrod.

[17] Coram Rege R. 297, Rex, m. 23 d.

[18] *Final Conc.* ii, 101, 107. The former of these was a grant of the manor of Haigh to William de Bradshagh for his life. The latter was a settlement of the succession after Mabel's death; to William son of John de Bradshagh, with remainders to the sons of Richard de Bradshagh his brother, and a further remainder to Henry son of Robert le Norreys. Alan son of Henry de Eltonhead, another Norreys, put in his claim. Also Kuerden, loc. cit. nos. 11, 13.

As Mabel de Haigh she made a grant of two plough-lands (probably the manor) in Worthington in 1318; *Final Conc.* ii, 28.

[19] See the account of Wigan Church; Kuerden, loc. cit. no. 16-21.

[20] *Surv.* of 1346 (Chet. Soc. 36). In the same year Dame Mabel accused

William son of John de Bradshagh of breaking down her close and doing other damage; De Banco R. 348, m. 338.

[21] The sheriff accounted for 10d. from Mabel de Bradshagh for the manor of Haigh for ward of Lancaster Castle; Duchy of Lanc. Var. Accts. 32117, fol. 7b.

[22] De Banco R. 419, m. 180 d.; 425, m. 363 d.; 429, m. 68. The descent is clearly stated; Sir William de Bradshagh died without issue, and the claimant, as son of Richard son of John de Bradshagh, brother of Sir William, was the heir entitled to the manor. For the Trafford feoffment see Kuerden, loc. cit. nos. 35-8.

[23] *Lancs. Inq. p.m.* (Chet. Soc.), i, 9; *Dep. Keeper's Rep.* xxxii, App. 354.

In the aid collected in 1355 William de Bradshagh contributed for the twelfth part of a knight's fee formerly held by Hugh le Norreys; *Feud. Aids*, iii, 91.

In 1397-8 Isabel, widow and executrix of William de Bradshagh, was called upon to account for the issues of a house at Haigh; L.T.R. Mem. R. 163, m. xiii, 167, m. x.

[24] Add. MS. 32108, nos. 1491, 1495, 1507.

[25] He was juror from 1397 to 1425; *Lancs. Inq.* (Chet. Soc.), i, 65 &c. In 1399 his feoffees regranted the manor to him with remainder to James his son and heir; Kuerden, loc. cit. no. 39.

William de Bradshagh seems to have been in possession of Haigh at the time of Thomas's outlawry; Duchy of Lanc. Knts. Fees, 1/20, fol. 8b. Edward was there in 1429; *Lancs. Inq.* (Chet. Soc.), ii, 35.

[26] Croston's Baines, iv, 292; his mother was Margaret, daughter of Robert de Highfield. It was an earlier Robert de Highfield who granted lands in Rudgatehurst to William de Bradshagh and Mabel his wife; Kuerden, loc. cit. no. 10, 12.

[27] Lettice, widow of John Tailor, summoned a large number of people in

sixty years of age.[32] Ralph died early in 1554, his heir being his brother William's son Roger, aged about thirty-six.[33]

. Roger Bradshaw of Haigh died 20 February 1598–9.[34] To the religious system established by Elizabeth he showed 'some degree of conformity,' but was of 'general note of evil affection in religion, and a non-communicant.'[35] In temporal matters the time was one of prosperity for the family, the cannel-coal of Haigh being famous already, and bringing wealth to the lord of the manor.[36]

BRADSHAW OF HAIGH.
Argent two bendlets between three martlets sable.

His son James having died before him he was succeeded by his grandson Roger, twenty-one years of age in 1599.[37] He also, after some wavering, adhered to the ancient religion,[38] but died in May 1641, before the outbreak of the Civil War.[39] His grandson and heir Roger, being then only thirteen years of age, took no part in the war, and the estates escaped the sequestration and forfeiture which would no doubt have overtaken them under the Commonwealth.[40] The minority, however, involved the placing of the heir under a Protestant guardian ; he changed his religion and conformed to that established by law.[41] In 1679 he was made a baronet[42] ; he was knight of the shire in 1660,[43] showing himself an opponent of the Presbyterians[44] and also of the adherents of Monmouth.[45] He died in 1684, and his son Roger three years later,[46] when the third Sir Roger Bradshaw, his son, succeeded.[47]

[32] Duchy of Lanc. Inq. p.m. vii, no. 16 ; the fine of 1477 and other settlements are recited. Roger Bradshagh was 'not at home' when the herald came in 1533, so that only his arms were recorded ; *Visit.* (Chet. Soc.), 174. His will is in P.C.C.

Sir Roger's widow Anne married Nicholas Butler of Rawcliffe and various disputes followed ; *Ducatus Lanc.* (Rec. Com.), ii, 70. She died at Hoole 22 Aug. 1554 ; *Duchy Plead.* (Rec. Soc. Lancs. and Ches.), iii, 182.

Henry Bradshagh of Halton, Buckinghamshire, attorney-general of the king, seems to have been concerned in the manor ; Close, 37 Hen. VIII, pt. ii, no. 46 ; pt. iv, no. 37.

[33] Duchy of Lanc. Inq. p.m. x, no. 41. William Bradshaw is named in various suits of the time ; *Ducatus* (Rec. Com.), ii, 32.

[34] Duchy of Lanc. Inq. p.m. xvii, no. 59 ; the tenure was unchanged. A pedigree was recorded in 1567 ; *Visit.* (Chet. Soc.), 88.

[35] Gibson, *Lydiate Hall,* 245, quoting S.P. Dom. Eliz. ccxxxv, 4. His son Thomas was a serjeant-at-arms to the queen ; *Ducatus* (Rec. Com.), iii, 295.

[36] Leland, writing about 1536, noted that 'Mr. Bradshaw hath a place called Haigh a mile from Wigan. He hath found much cannel like sea coal in his ground, very profitable to him' ; *Itin.* vii, 47. These mines led to various law suits ; see *Ducatus* (Rec. Com.), ii, 179, &c.

In 1554 Roger Bradshaw said that he was owner of the demesne lands of the manor of Haigh, within which there had always been certain mines or pits of a kind of fuel called cannel, wherein the tenants within the lordship had been accustomed to dig and get cannel to be 'spent and brent' in their tenements, for which they had paid by boons, presents, and averages ; *Duchy Plead.* iii, 182.

[37] James son and heir of Roger Bradshaw married, in or before 1567, Jane the daughter and heir of Thomas Hoghton of Hoghton ; Dods. MSS. cxlii, fol. 44.

[38] Richard son of Roger Bradshaw of Haigh was baptized at Wigan, 28 Dec. 1601 ; *Reg.* 51. In 1623, on entering the English College at Rome under the name of Barton, he gave the following particulars : 'My true name is Richard Bradshaw. I am in my twenty-second year, was born in Lancashire, and for the most part brought up there. My parents are Roger Bradshaw of Haigh . . . and Anne his wife. The former, who had been brought up in the Catholic religion,

left it in his youth ; by the goodness of G ago, he again embrac I hope will perseve My mother, brought parents [Anderton o professed any othe seven brothers and s are Cathol'cs. I r schooling until my fi gave myself up to h youthful sports , b being sent to St. applied myself to h was always a Catho joined the Society 1655 to 1660 was Province ; Foley,

2   h

His son Sir Roger, the last baronet, died in 1787 without issue,[48] the heir to the manor and estates being his sister Elizabeth.[49]

She married John son of Sir Humphrey Edwin,[50] and her daughter and heir, Elizabeth, married Charles Dalrymple of North Berwick, whose daughter and heir, Elizabeth Bradshaigh,[51] married Alexander Lindsay, sixth Earl of Balcarres. He thus became lord of the manor of Haigh,[52] which has descended regularly [53] with the title to James Ludovic Lindsay, Earl of Crawford and Balcarres, who succeeded in 1880.[54] His son, Lord Balcarres, is the member of Parliament for the Chorley division of the county. At the Hall is a valuable library, including a Mazarin Bible among the printed books.[55]

LINDSAY, Earl of Crawford and Balcarres. *Quarterly, 1 and 4 : Gules a fesse checky argent and azure for LINDSAY; 2 and 3 : Or a lion rampant gules debruised by a ribbon sable, for ABERNETHY.*

Apart from the Bradshaw family there do not seem to have been any important landowners [56] in the township, though in 1600 Ralph Charnock was also returned as a freeholder.[57]

A poor man named John Rycroft was in trouble with the Commonwealth authorities during the Civil War ; he explained that he had assembled with the king's men on Westhoughton Common but had not joined them later.[58]

In connexion with the Established Church St. David's, Haigh, was consecrated in 1833 as a chapel of ease to Wigan ; a district was assigned five years later. The rector of Wigan is patron.[59] At New Springs, St. John Baptist's, an iron church, was licensed in 1871 ; and rebuilt in brick in 1897.

A school was founded here about 1660 by the township.[60]

[48] Little seems to be known of the last Sir Roger, or of the male descendants of the previous baronets.
[49] These and the subsequent particulars are from the pedigree in Baines, *Lancs.* (ed. Croston), iv, 294–296.
[50] See the note in G.E.C., *Complete Peerage*, ii, 419 ; *Herald and Gen.* vi, 62 ; viii, 186, 187.
[51] She died 10 Aug. 1816. There is a monument to her in Wigan Church ; Bridgeman, op. cit. 703. There was a recovery of the manor in 1804 ; Aug. Assize, 44 Geo. III, R. 5.
[52] The Earl of Balcarres resided at Haigh, which has since remained the principal seat of the family. He became *de jure* 23rd Earl of Crawford in 1808, but did not assume the title. He died in 1825, and was buried at Wigan ; see *Dict. Nat. Biog.*
[53] See G.E.C. loc. cit. James, son of the sixth earl by Elizabeth Dalrymple, was member for Wigan 1820 to 1825, and was created Baron Wigan of Haigh Hall in 1826. In 1848 the House of Lords decided that he had justified his claim to the earldom of Crawford. He died 15 Dec. 1869. For his younger son Colin, see *Dict. Nat. Biog.*
The eldest son and heir, Alexander William Crawford Lindsay, Earl of Crawford and Balcarres, author of *Hist. of Christian Art*, &c., died 13 Dec. 1880 ; see *Dict. Nat. Biog.* He was succeeded by his son, the present lord of Haigh.

ASPULL

Aspul, 1212 ; 1292 ; Hasphull, 1277 ; Haspehull, 1292; Aspehill, 1292 ; Aspell, 1301; Asphull, 1304, common ; Aspull, 1356, common. Aspden and Aspshaw occur in the district.

This township, though in the parish of Wigan, is in the hundred of Salford. It is separated from Westhoughton by a brook running through Borden or Borsdane Wood, but has no marked physical separation from the other neighbouring townships, which, like itself, are in Wigan parish. The ground rises from south to north, reaching 400 ft. The area is 1,905 acres.[1] The population in 1901 was 8,388.[2]

The principal road leads north from Hindley to Haigh, passing through Pennington Green, which lies 2¼ miles east-north-east of Wigan Church. To the south-west of this lies Hindley Hall, and a road branches off to the north-west, going through New Springs to Wigan. The Lancaster Canal passes through the northern corner of the township. Aspull Moor lies in the northern half of the township.

Cannel coal was found in Aspull. There are several large collieries, also malt kilns and a cotton mill. Wheat, oats, and potatoes are grown.

A local board was formed in 1876. This has been succeeded by an urban district council of nine members.

The earliest notice of *ASPULL* is that contained in the survey of 1212, when, as one plough-land, it formed part of the Childwall fee held by Richard son of Robert de Lathom, under the lord of Manchester.[3] Immediately after this lands in Aspull are found among the possessions of William de Notton, being described as the right of Cecily his wife, daughter of Edith, lady of Barton-on-Irwell.[4] The Lathom mesne manor was commonly ignored [5] ; thus, in 1302 Richard de Ince, as son and heir of Henry de Sefton, and Adam de Hindley, were

MANOR

found to hold Aspull, as the eighth part of a knight's fee, directly of Thomas Grelley.[6] From this time the lordship has been held with the adjacent Ince by the families of Ince and Gerard in succession; until Aspull was sold to the Earl of Crawford and Balcarres, lord of Haigh.[7]

The Hindley family appear to have had a quarter of the manor by grant of William son of Richard son of Enot de Aspull. The succession can be traced from Adam son of Hugh de Hindley, living in 1292,[8] until the 17th century,[9] when Roger Hindley suc-

---

[6] *Lancs. Inq. and Extents*, i, 314. Richard de Ince and Robert de Hindley held the same in 1322; *Mamecestre* (Chet. Soc.), 579.

Towneley (GG, no. 1604), preserves an agreement between Henry de Sefton and the free tenants of Aspull, including those of the Hospitallers, their names being given. These granted to Henry as their lord all the land bounded by a line starting at Haigh on the west, going to the Quintacres, Terneshaw Brook, Brinshope Bridge, and so to Quintacres; also land in Faldworthing shaw. Henry on his part granted them certain liberties.

[7] See the account of Ince above.

John son of Peter Gerard and Ellen his wife made a settlement of the manor of Aspull in 1421; Pal. of Lanc. Feet of F. bdle. 5, m. 12.

Thomas Gerard, in 1473, held the lordship of Aspull of the lord of Manchester by a rent of 8d. and the same sum for ward of the castle of Lancaster; *Mamecestre*, 481.

Miles Gerard, in 1558, held the manor, &c., of Lord La Warre in socage by a rent of 18d.; Duchy of Lanc. Inq. p.m. xi, no. 12.

Aspull descended with Ince until the early years of the 18th century, when Richard son of Thomas Gerard of Highfield appears to have sold it to the Gerards of Brynn. The manor of Aspull was Sir William Gerard's in 1796, as appears from R. 12 of the Lent Assizes, 1796 (Pal. of Lanc. Plea R.). It was sold to the Earl of Crawford and Balcarres before 1825; Baines, *Lancs.* (ed. 1836), iii, 553.

[8] A plea of 1292 gives an account of the acquisition. Adam de Hindley alleged that Robert de Lathom, Richard de Ince, Gilbert de Southworth, Emma his wife, and others had disseised him of a messuage and 12 acres of moor and pasture in Aspull. Gilbert, however, claimed nothing but common of pasture. Robert de Lathom claimed lordship only. Richard de Ince, as tenant, asserted that Adam had no right beyond common of pasture, but had inclosed the disputed land by night, his fence being promptly thrown down the next day.

The jury, however, found that Adam's title was derived from William son of Richard son of Enot de Aspull, who had delivered seisin of all his lands to Adam de Hindley; that Henry de Sefton and Richard son of Enot had been lords of the waste in common, and had divided an approvement, Henry taking three parts and Richard the other part, amounting to 7 acres; that after they had lain uncultivated Adam inclosed them, at the same time adding 5 acres more without the assent of Richard de Ince, and he and his man dwelt there some time; that Richard ejected him *vi et armis*; and that the 7 acres should be restored to Adam, and the 5 remain waste as formerly; Assize R. 408, m. 6.

The Hindleys had several branches, one by marriage acquiring Culcheth. The Hindleys of Aspull continued to hold land in Hindley also. Hugh de Hindley, father of Adam, is mentioned in 1258–9; Originalia, 43 Hen. III, m. 3. Hugh de

Hindley was livi 408, m. 12; and de Hindley—per claimed dower 1 161, m. 132; L *Gen. Notes*, i, 27.

Adam son of Robert his son, w concerning a mar and Ince in 129 407, m 3 d.; a s through a house, who gave wife Alice; she John N ghtega e, Henry son of he the tent of 13*s.* seems to have se fused to pay the half a mark to th

Then Cecily, Adam de Woodho lands in Hindle son of Hugh de wife; they asser dead, but living a m. 55 Adam d tiff or defendant i R. 419, m. 12 ·

[12 d] There w Richard de Hin m. 9 d

[9] A pedigree w

ceeded.[10] *HINDLEY HALL*, as the residence of the Hindleys was called, became the property of James, a younger son of Robert Dukin-field of Cheshire.[11] In the 18th century it was acquired by the Leighs of Whitley Hall, Wigan, and Sir Robert Holt Leigh lived here till his death in 1843.[12] His estates then passed for life to his cousin Thomas Pemberton, who took the name of Leigh, and made Hindley Hall his residence; he was raised to the peerage as Baron Kingsdown in 1858.[13] After his death in 1867 it passed by the will of

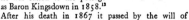

HINDLEY. *Azure a hart lodged argent.*

Sir R. H. Leigh to Mr. Roger Leigh, the present owner.[14]

The Knights Hospitallers held lands here from an early period.[15]

One of the ancient families here was that of Occleshaw. In 1246 Richard son of William recovered 8 acres in Aspull from Gilbert de Barton, Henry de Occleshaw, and Hugh his brother.[16] Thirty years later the prior of St. John of Jerusalem was claimant against John de Occleshaw and another;[17] and John de Occleshaw and Henry his brother occur in 1291.[18] Afterwards Occleshaw was acquired by the Ince family.[19]

Yet another early family was that of Gidlow, whose residence was long known as *GIDLOW HALL*. In 1291 Robert de Gidlow was a freeholder in Aspull,[20] and the name occurs frequently down to the 17th century,[21]

---

son Robert, then about twenty-four years of age, appearing and renouncing his title; *Duchy Plead.* iii, 69.

Roger's son Robert, one of the 'gentle-men of the better sort' who were 'soundly affected in religion' in 1590 (Gibson, *Lydiate Hall*, 246), was living at the *Visitation* of 1613 (p. 118), and his will was proved in 1620. Roger Hindley was assessed to the subsidy in 1622, and refusing knighthood compounded in 1631; *Misc. Rec. Soc. Lancs. and Ches.*), i, 162, 216.

[10] It appears from the Wigan Registers that he had several children; his wife Alice died in Jan. 1624–5; Roger Hind-ley himself was buried at Wigan, 15 Nov. 1651. Robert son of Roger Hindley was baptized at Winwick in 1607.

Margaret, a 'daughter and co-heir of Roger Hindley of Hindley,' is said by Dugdale, *Visit.* (54), to have married Roger Bradshaw of Aspull; it appears from the registers that the marriage took place in 1596, a daughter Elizabeth was born in 1597, and in the following year the wife died.

[11] Ibid. p. 100; Ormerod, *Ches.* (ed. Helsby), iii, 817. Old Mrs. Dukinfield and her son James are mentioned in Roger Lowe's *Diary*, 1663; *Loc. Glean. Lancs. and Ches.* i, 170, 171, 189. The mother left money to the chapel and school of Hindley.

[12] Alexander Leigh, the grandfather, procured the Act of 1720 for making the Douglas navigable from Wigan to Preston; for an anecdote of him see *Hist. MSS. Com. Rep.* xiv, App. iv, 458. Holt Leigh, the father, of Hindley Hall, Aspull, and Whit-ley Hall, Wigan, married Mary daughter and co-heir of Thomas Owen, of Uphol-land; acquiring the manors of Orrell and Billinge. Robert Holt Leigh was born at Wigan in 1762. He was educated at Manchester School, and Christ Church, Oxford, but though he passed the examina-tions he did not graduate till 1837. He was made a baronet in 1815, at the in-stance of Canning, and represented Wigan in Parliament from 1802 to 1820; he is described as 'a high Tory and firm Church-man, but strenuous Protestant.' He had a high reputation as a scholar, linguist, and man of culture, but 'over the latter years of his life it is better that a veil should be drawn. It is very sad to record folly and profligacy in the mature years of a life in which, otherwise, there is much to admire;' *Manchester School Reg.* (Chet. Soc.). He died at Hindley Hall, 21 Jan. 1843.

His brother, Roger Holt Leigh, of Leeds, died 13 May 1831 from injuries received during election disturbances.

[13] *Dict. Nat. Bi Peerage*, iv, 401.

[14] Burke, *Landed*

[15] *Plac. de Quo W* The rental compil that there were fou total rent of 4s., v by Thomas Gorsu by Alexa der Catter House, by John messuage by Will Kuerden MSS. v, f

[16] Assize R. 404,

[17] De Banco R.

[18] Assize R. 129

[19] By her charte John de Occleshaw born son John all from her father i Occleshaw was a

when a short pedigree was recorded.[22] In 1584 and 1586 rights of way were investigated, Thomas Gidlow claiming a footpath from Gidlow Hall westward across Roger Hindley's meadows called Longer Hey to the highway between

GIDLOW. *Azure a chevron argent between two leopard's heads in chief and a cross formy fitchy in base or.*

Aspull Moor and Pennington Green, and so to Wigan.[23]

The Houghtons of *KIRKLEES* long continued in possession ;[24] Ralph Houghton in 1653 renounced his faith in order to secure his lands.[25] The Bradshaghs, already mentioned,[26] the Lathoms of Wolfall,[27] and the Lowes[28] also held lands here. Later families were the Rigbys[29] and Penningtons.[30]

&c., for the use of Anne Shakerley, widow, for her life. Robert asserted that he was of full age, and not sixteen only, when the former inquisition was taken ; also that the premises in Aspull were held of Thomas Gerard of Ince and not of Lord La Warre. The messuage in Langtree had been the property of one John Perlebarn, whose heirs were Ralph Gidlow, Roger Haydock, and James Aspenall, descendants of his daughters Joan, Katherine, and Margaret. Joan had married a Gidlow (obviously the John Gidlow, senior, of a previous paragraph), and her son was Ralph father of John father of the Ralph Gidlow of 1531 ; Duchy of Lanc. Inq. p.m. iii, no. 6.

On Robert's coming of age Lord La Warre remitted all actions, &c. ; GG, no. 1610 ; and soon afterwards, in 1541, Robert made a settlement of his lands, the remainder being to Thomas his son and heir ; Kuerden MSS. loc. cit. no. 20. In 1552 a further settlement seems to have been made by Robert Gidlow and Ellen his wife ; Pal. of Lanc. Feet of F. bdle. 14, m. 106 ; and another including the capital messuage called Gidlow, Hindley House, Bank House, &c., three years later, perhaps on the marriage of his son Thomas with Elizabeth daughter of William Kenyon of Pilkington ; GG, no. 1601, 1609, 1611. A release was made to Thomas in 1584 by John son of William Kenyon ; GG, no. 1606. Two years later Thomas Gidlow was elected coroner ; GG, no. 1608. He died 28 Oct. 1606, holding various lands and the Lee in Aspull of Miles Gerard of Ince, by a rent of 14s. and 12d. ; also 12 acres and the water-mill of the king, as of the late Hospital of St. John of Jerusalem. Thomas his son and heir was aged thirty-three years ; Lancs. Inq. p.m. (Rec. Soc. Lancs. and Ches.), i, 73.

William Kenyon, who died in 1557, held part of the old Hospitallers' lands in Aspull by the gift of Robert Gidlow ; John his son and heir was sixty years of age in 1586 ; Duchy of Lanc. Inq. p.m. xiv, no. 27.

[22] *Visit.* of 1613 (Chet. Soc.), 50. The last-named Thomas Gidlow recorded it ; his son and heir, another Thomas, being then twenty years of age.

The elder Thomas died about 1618-19, but the age of his son Thomas is given as only twenty-two years ; Kuerden, loc. cit. no. 23. Thomas Gidlow contributed to the subsidy in 1622 ; *Misc.* (Rec. Soc. Lancs. and Ches.), i, 162.

[23] Towneley, GG, no. 1613-15. Risley Hey and a stile called the Merrel are mentioned ; also a lane called 'a certain lisle lane' which led to Aynscough Lane, going north to Aspull Moor.

[24] John son of Thomas de Halghton, or Houghton, of the Westhoughton family, had two messuages and land in Aspull in 1317 ; *Final Conc.* ii, 25. John son of Thomas de Houghton was defendant in a claim for dower in 1351 and 1352 ; Duchy of Lanc. Assize R. 1, m. v d. and R. 2, m. 2.

A Ralph Houghton of Kirklees married Margery daughter of Richard Molyneux

of Hawkley ; *Visit.* of 1567 (Chet. Soc.), 109. For a plea of 1554-5 by Roger Heigham claiming against Ralph Houghton lands called Smyrrels and Gromerscroft in Aspull see *Ducatus Lanc.* (Rec. Com.), ii, 184.

Richard Houghton acquired lands in Aspull, Ince, and Wigan from Christopher Kenyon and Margery his wife in 1572, and made a settlement in 1577 ; *Lancs. and Ches. Rec.* (Rec. Soc. Lancs. and Ches.), ii, 255 ; Pal. of Lanc. Feet of F. bdle. 34, m. 138 ; bdle. 39, m. 13. Ralph Houghton was a purchaser in 1593 ; ibid. bdle. 55, m. 200. He was one of the 'comers to church but no communicants' in 1590 ; Gibson, *Lydiate Hall*, 246.

Richard Houghton of Kirklees in 1616 married Bridget daughter of Adam Mort ; Dugdale, *Visit.* (Chet. Soc.), 211. Richard son and heir apparent of Ralph Houghton of Kirklees in Aspull was a trustee for William Heaton in 1619 ; *Lancs. Inq. p.m.* (Rec. Soc. Lancs. and Ches.), ii, 160. The succession of the various Richards and Ralphs is not quite clear ; for Clemence Simpson, formerly wife of Ralph Houghton, in 1604-5 claimed an interest in the Great Scraps in Aspull ; she had formerly had a writ of dower against Richard Houghton, uncle to Ralph, Thomas, and Anne Aspull, Christopher and Margaret Kenyon ; Duchy of Lanc. Plead. Hil. 2 Jas. I, bdle. 221.

A 'Mr. Ralph Houghton of Kirklees' was buried at Wigan 12 Aug. 1643.

[25] 'By some omission or mistake' his estate was in 1653 ordered to be sequestered ; he had never 'acted against the State,' had subscribed the engagement, but was also required to take the oath of abjuration. He was conformable, but being infirm asked for more time ; and afterwards took the oath. The sequestration was discharged in 1654 ; *Royalist Comp. Papers* (Rec. Soc. Lancs. and Ches.), iii, 293 ; *Cal. of Com. for Compounding*, iv, 3124.

[26] In 1343 John de Ince, John son of Henry de Tyldesley, and Robert son of Robert de Bradshagh were charged with having overthrown the house of William son of Adam de Bradshagh at Aspull, and shot at him ; Assize R. 430, m. 18 d. 20 d. 26.

In 1473 Henry Bradshagh held a messuage of the lord of Manchester, by rent of 2d. and 2d. for ward of the castle ; *Mamecestre*, 480. The name of William Bradshagh of Aspull occurs in a list of the local gentry compiled about 1512. William Bradshagh contributed to the subsidy of 1541, 'for £20 in goods' ; *Misc.* (Rec. Soc. Lancs. and Ches.), i, 143. For his will see *Lancs. and Ches. Wills* (Rec. Soc. Lancs. and Ches.), 187.

James Bradshagh in 1568 was deforciant of fourteen messuages in Aspull, Wigan, Hindley, and other places ; Humphrey Bradshagh was one of the plaintiffs ; Pal. of Lanc. Feet of F. bdle. 30, m. 75. Roger Bradshagh was a purchaser or feoffee in 1583 ; ibid. bdle. 45, m. 122. He was reported as 'soundly affected in religion' in 1590 ; Gibson, *Lydiate Hall*, 246.

Margaret Bradshagh, daughter of Roger Hindley, was in 1598 found to have held lands in Aspull called the Several or Inland of Miles Gerard by the hundredth part of a knight's fee ; and other lands of Roger Hindley. Elizabeth Bradshagh, her daughter and heir, was only a year old ; Duchy of Lanc. Inq. p.m. xvii, no. 43.

Roger Bradshagh was a freeholder in 1600 ; *Misc.* (Rec. Soc.), i, 247. The same or a later Roger contributed to the subsidy of 1622 as a landowner ; ibid. 162. He died 17 June 1625, holding three messuages and cottages and lands in Aspull of Edward Mosley, as of the manor of Manchester, by the tenth part of the eighth part of a knight's fee ; also other messuages and lands in Hindley ; William and John were his sons by his first wife, living in 1619, and Edward by his second wife Ellen ; Duchy of Lanc. Inq. p.m. xxvi, no. 52.

There is a short pedigree of these Bradshaghs in Dugdale, *Visit.* 54.

About the end of the 17th century Nathaniel Molyneux had lands in the Hall of Bradshaw in Aspull, Westhoughton, &c.

[27] The Atherton family may have derived their holding here as also in Hindley from a grant by Adam de Hindley. In each township it seems to have descended to the Lathoms of Wolfall. The evidence, however, is defective.

In 1420 Thomas de Atherton and Margery his wife were deforciants of eight messuages in Aspull, &c. ; Pal. of Lanc. Feet of F. bdle. 5, m. 16. In 1473 Thomas Lathom of Knowsley held of the lord of Manchester a messuage in Aspull, in right of his wife, daughter and heir of Henry Atherton of Prescot, by the rent of 3d. with 3d. for ward of the castle ; *Mamecestre*, 481.

The Lathoms, as the inquisitions show, held the lands here till the end of the 16th century, when Thomas Lathom and Frances his wife disposed of them ; Pal. of Lanc. Feet of F. bdle. 36, m. 158, 250.

[28] Robert Law or Lowe in 1473 held a messuage of the lord of Manchester, by a rent of 3d. and 3d. for castle ward ; *Mamecestre*, 481.

[29] Alexander Rigby of Middleton in Goosnargh, who died in 1621, held land in Aspull of Thomas Gerard by a rent of 10s. 8d. ; *Lancs. Inq. p.m.* (Rec. Soc. Lancs. and Ches.), iii, 456, 458. His son, Joseph Rigby 'of Aspull,' Parliamentarian officer, to whom it had been bequeathed, is named in the pedigree in Dugdale, *Visit.* 245 ; *Dict. Nat. Biog.* Joseph and Alexander Rigby were clerks of the peace under the Commonwealth ; *Pal. Note Bk.* iv, 144-5. The father, Major Joseph Rigby was, however, accused of 'impeding profits,' by trying by threats to secure the lands of 'papists and delinquents' for himself under value ; *Cal. of Com. for Compounding* i, 371. The son, Alexander, was said to have joined Lord Derby in 1651 ; *Cal. Com. Advancing Money*, iii, 1455.

[30] In addition to those already named Robert Pennington, Robert Gorton, Roger Rycroft, and John Ainscough were free-

In 1626 the landowners contributing to the subsidy were Roger Hindley, the heirs of Roger Bradshaw, Thomas Gidlow, and Ralph Houghton. The two last-named, as convicted recusants, paid double.[31]

The hearth tax roll of 1666 shows that 135 hearths were charged. The most considerable houses were those of Richard Green, nine hearths; Peter Orrell and James Dukinfield, eight each; Major Rigby and Thomas Molyneux, seven each; and Edward Gleast, six.[32]

John Roscow of Aspull compounded for his estate under the Commonwealth.[33] Besides Thomas and Richard Gerard of Highfield, the following 'papists' registered estates here in 1717:—James and Roger Leigh, Thomas Cooke, and Robert Taylor.[34]

The land tax returns of 1797 show the landowners

to have been Robert Holt Leigh, Sir Richard Clayton, and others.[35]

In connexion with the Established Church St. Elizabeth's was built in 1882 by Mr. Roger Leigh. The patronage is vested in trustees.[36] There is also a licensed chapel known as Hindley Hall chapel.

There are Wesleyan, Primitive Methodist, and Independent Methodist churches.

The adherents of the ancient faith were formerly indebted to the lords of the manor for the mission established at Highfield; the Jesuits were serving it in 1701.[37] In 1858 the permanent church of Our Lady of the Immaculate Conception was erected[38]; and more recently services have been commenced at New Springs.

WINWICK

NEWTON	GOLBORNE	HOUGHTON, MIDDLETON,
HAYDOCK	LOWTON	AND ARBURY
WINWICK WITH HULME	KENYON	SOUTHWORTH WITH
ASHTON	CULCHETH	CROFT

The ancient parish of Winwick lies between Sankey Brook on the south-west and Glazebrook and a tributary on the north and east, the distance between these brooks being 4½ or 5 miles. The extreme length of the parish is nearly 10 miles, and its area 26,502 acres.

The highest ground is on the extreme north-west border, about 350 ft.; most of the surface is above the 100 ft. level, but slopes down on three sides to the boundaries, 25 ft. being reached in Hulme in the south. The geological formation consists of the Coal Measures in the northern and western parts of the parish, and of the Bunter series of the New Red Sandstone in the remainder. Except Culcheth, which belonged to the fee of Warrington, the whole was

holders in 1600; *Misc.* (Rec. Soc. Lancs. and Ches.), i, 249, 251.

Robert Pennington contributed to the subsidy in 1622; ibid. 162. Pennington Hall is still marked on the map.

Robert Gorton purchased a messuage &c. in 1581; Pal. of Lanc. Feet of F. bdle. 43, m. 129. He died 10 Dec. 1624, holding a messuage and lands in Aspull of Edward Mosley, lord of Manchester, by the twentieth part of the eighth part of a knight's fee; James, his son and heir, was aged forty and more; Duchy of Lanc. Inq. p.m. xxvi, no. 48. James died soon afterwards; ibid. xxvi, no. 11.

Roger Rycroft seems to have purchased part of the Lathom holding; Pal. of Lanc. Feet of F. bdle. 36, m. 250. He died 15 Dec. 1612 holding of Miles Gerard, as of the manor of Aspull; his eldest son William having died before him he was succeeded by his grandson, Roger Rycroft the younger, son of William; *Lancs. Inq. p.m.* (Rec. Soc. Lancs. and Ches.), iii, 314.

Thomas Shaw and Alice his wife, and John Ainscough and Ellen his wife, were deforciants of a messuage and lands in Aspull in 1392; Pal. of Lanc. Feet of F. bdle. 54, m. 67. Miles Ainscough of Aspull was a juror in 1619; *Lancs. Inq. p.m.* (Rec. Soc. Lancs. and Ches.), ii, 127.

One of the great roads from south to north has from the earliest times led through Winwick, Newton, and Ashton, and there are several tumuli and other ancient remains.

The Domesday Survey shows that a large part of the surface consisted of woodland, and Garswood in Ashton preserves the name of part of it. In the Civil War two battles were fought near Winwick. In more modern times coal mines have been worked and manufactures introduced, and Earlestown has grown up around the wagon-building works of the London and North-Western Railway Company.

The agricultural land in the parish is utilized as follows :—Arable land, 16,258 acres ; permanent grass, 4,820 acres ; woods and plantations, 653 acres. The following are details :—

	Arable	Grass	Woods, &c.
Winwick	2,192	247	25
Southworth and Croft	1,596	130	
Newton in Makerfield	1,614	423	17
Lowton	960	570	
Haydock	1,244	411	72
Golborne	951	448	16
Ashton in Makerfield . .	3,228	1,210	433
Culcheth and Kenyon	4,473	1,381	90

Newton has given the title of baron to the lord of the manor, who has, however, no residence in the parish ; Lord Gerard of Brynn has his principal seat at Garswood.

Dr. Kuerden thus describes a journey through the parish made about 1695 :—'Entering a little hamlet called the Hulme you leave on the left a deep and fair stone quarry fit for building. You meet with another crossway on the right. A mile farther stands

a fair-built church called Winwick church, a remarkable fabric. . . . Leaving the church on the right about a quarter of a mile westwards stands a princely building, equal to the revenue, called the parsonage of Winwick ; and near the church on the right hand stands a fair-built schoolhouse. By the east end of the church is another road, but less used, to the borough of Wigan.

'Having passed the school about half a mile you come to a sandy place called the Red Bank, where Hamilton and his army were beaten. Here, leaving Bradley park, and a good seat belonging to Mr. Brotherton of Hey (a member of Parliament for the borough of Newton) on the left hand, and Newton park on the right, you have a little stone bridge over Newton Brook, three miles from Warrington. On the left hand close by a water mill appear the ruins of the site of the ancient barony of Newton, where formerly was the baron's castle.

'Having passed the bridge you ascend a rock, where is a penfold cut out of the same, and upon the top of the rock was lately built a court house for the manor, and near to it a fair re-edified chapel of stone built by Richard Legh, deceased, father to Mr. Legh, the present titular baron of Newton. There stands a stately cross, near the chapel well, adorned with the arms belonging to the present baron. Having passed the town of Newton you leave a cross-road on the left going to Liverpool by St. Helen's chapel. You pass in winter through a miry lane for half a mile ; you leave another lane on the left passing by Billinge. . .

'Then passing on a sandy lane you leave Haydock park, and (close by the road) Haydock lodge, belonging to Mr. Legh, and going on half a mile you pass

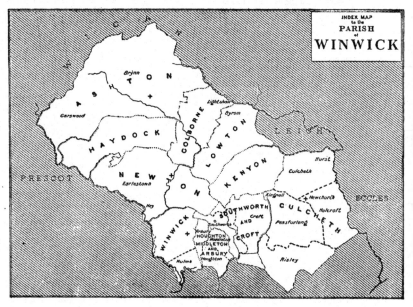

by the chapel and through the town of Ashton, standing upon a rocky ground, which belongeth to Sir William Gerard, bart., of Brynn, who resides at Garswood, about a mile to the east (*sic*). Having passed the stone bridge take the left hand way, which though something fouler is more used. You then pass by Whitledge Green, a place much resorted to in summer by the neighbouring gentry for bowling. Shortly after, you meet with the other way from Ashton bridge by J. Naylor's, a herald painter and an excellent stainer of glass for pictures or coats of arms. Through a more open coach-way passing on upon the right leave the Brynn gate, a private way leading to the ancient hall of Brynn, and upon the left another road by Garswood to the hall of Parr, a seat belonging to the Byroms, and to St. Helen's chapel ; and thence past Hawkley to Wigan.' [2]

Among the worthies of the parish may here be noted Thomas Legh Claughton, born at Haydock Lodge in 1808, who became Bishop of Rochester in 1867, resigning in 1890, and died in 1892 ; [3] also Thomas Risley, a Nonconformist divine, 1630 to 1716. [4]

The following in 1630–3 compounded by annual fines for the two-thirds of their estates liable to be sequestered for their recusancy : Ashton, Sir William Gerard of Brynn, £106 13s. 4d. ; Jane Gerard ; Culcheth, Richard Urmston, £6 ; Lowton, Peter and Roger Haughton, £3 ; Southworth, Christopher Bow of Croft, £2 10s. [5]

The church of ST. OSWALD has a
CHURCH chancel [6] with north vestry, nave with aisles and south porch, and west tower and spire. It is built of a very inferior local sandstone, with the result that its history has been much obscured by repairs and rebuildings, and cannot be taken back beyond the 14th century ; though the dedication and the fragment of an early cross, now set up outside the chancel, both point to an early occupation of the site.

The chancel was entirely rebuilt in 1847–8 in 14th-century style, the elder Pugin being the architect, and is a fine and well-designed work with a high-pitched leaded roof, a four-light east window, and three-light windows on north and south. There are three canopied sedilia and a piscina, and the arched ceiling is panelled, with gilt bosses at the intersection of the ribs, and a stone cornice with carved paterae.

The nave is of six bays, with a north arcade having pointed arches of two orders with sunk quarter-round mouldings, and curious clustered piers considerably too thick for the arches they carry, and projecting in front of the wall-face towards the nave. The general outline is octagonal with a hollow between two quarter-rounds on each cardinal face, and a deep V-shaped sinking on the alternate faces. The abacus of the capitals is octagonal, but the necking follows the outline of the piers, and pairs of trefoiled leaves rise from the hollows on the cardinal faces. The bases, of very rough work, are panelled on the cardinal faces, with engaged shafts 6 in. high, while on the diagonal faces are badly-cut mitred heads.

There is a curious suggestion of 14th-century detail in the arcade, in spite of its clumsiness, but the

actual date is probably within a few years of 1600. The clearstory above has three windows set over the alternate arches, of four lights with uncusped tracery and low four-centred heads.

The south arcade, ' from the first pillar eastward to the fifth west,' was taken down and rebuilt from the foundations in 1836. It has clustered piers of quatrefoil section, and simply moulded bell capitals with octagonal abaci, the arches being of two chamfered orders with labels ending in pairs of human heads at the springing. The original work belonged to the beginning of the 14th century. The clearstory on this side has six windows, of four uncusped lights without tracery, under a four-centred head, all the stonework being modern.

At the east end of the north aisle is the Gerard Chapel, inclosed with an iron screen, which about 1848 replaced a wooden screen dated 'in the yere of our Lord MCCCCLXXXI.' There is a three-light east window and two four-light windows on the north, all with 16th-century uncusped tracery. In the aisle west of the chapel are three four-light north windows with embattled transoms and uncusped tracery, and a north doorway with a square-headed window over it, of four uncusped lights. The tracery, except part in the Gerard Chapel, has been lately renewed, the original date of the windows being perhaps c. 1530–50. On the external faces of the transoms is carved the IHS monogram. The two east bays of the south aisle are taken up by the Legh Chapel, and separated by an arch at the west from the rest of the aisle. This western portion was rebuilt in 1530, being dated by an inscription running round the external cornice, and the Legh Chapel is somewhat earlier in date, perhaps c. 1500. The chapel has a small doorway on the south, a three-light window on the east, and two on the south, all with uncusped tracery, the stonework being mutilated, and in the aisle are three four-light windows on the south, with embattled transoms and tracery uncusped except in the upper middle lights, and one window at the west, also of four lights, but of different design. On the external faces of the transoms are carved roses, all the stonework being modern. The aisle has a vice at the south-west angle. The south porch is low, and the inscribed cornice of the aisle runs above it without a break. The porch has been completely refaced, and opens to the south aisle by a four-centred doorway with continuous mouldings. Both aisles and clearstory have embattled parapets and leaded roofs of low pitch. The inscription round the south aisle is in leonine hexameters, running from west to east, and is as follows :—

Hic locus Oswalde quondam placuit tibi valde ;
Nortanhumbrorum fueras rex, nuncque polorum
Regna tenes, prato passus Marcelde vocato.
Poscimus hinc a te nostri memor esto beate.
Anno milleno quingentenoque triceno
Sclater post Christum murum renovaverat istum ;
Henricus Johnson curatus erat simul hic tunc.

The tower retains much of its old facing, though the surface is much decayed. It has a vice at the

---

[2] *Local Gleanings Lancs. and Ches.* i, 209. On p. 214 is his note of the other road from Winwick to Wigan as follows : 'Leaving the church on the left hand, half a mile from thence you have a fair built house formerly belonging to Charles

Herle, parson of Winwick. . . . You leave Lowton township, passing over Lowton Cop, leaving Byrom not far on the right and the New Church, being a parochial chapel to Winwick.'
[3] *Dict. Nat. Biog.*

[4] *Ibid.* ; see also the account of Culcheth. [5] Lucas, 'Warton' (MS.).
[6] For the former chancel see Sir S. Glynne's account, *Ch. of Lancs.* (Chet. Soc.) 27, 91 ; also generally the Rev. W. A. Wickham in *Trans. Hist. Soc.* 1908.

WINWICK CHURCH, FROM THE SOUTH

WINWICK CHURCH : NORTH ARCADE OF NAVE

south-east angle, which ends with a flat top at the level of an embattled parapet at the base of the spire. The spire is of stone, and has two rows of spire lights, and the belfry windows are of two trefoiled lights with quatrefoils in the head. All the work belongs to the first half of the 14th century, and in the ground story is a three-light west window with modern net tracery, flanked by two empty niches, with below it a four-centred doorway with continuous wave-mouldings. The tower arch is of three continuous wave-moulded orders. On the west face of the tower, to the south of the niche flanking the west window on the south, is a small and very weathered carving of a pig with a bell round his neck, known as the Winwick pig. His story is that, like other supernatural agencies under similar circumstances elsewhere, he insisted on bringing all the stones with which the church was being built on another and lower site to the present site, removing each night the preceding day's work.[7]

The roof of the Gerard Chapel is modern, but that of the Legh Chapel has heavily-moulded timbers, ceiled between with plaster panels having moulded ribs and four-leaved flowers at the centres. Below the beams, at the wall plates, are angels holding shields with heraldry.[8]

The roofs of the aisles have cambered tie-beams and braces, with panels between the beams divided into four by wood ribs. Neither roof is set out to space with the arcades or windows, the south aisle roof being of seven bays, that in the north aisle of six; they belong probably to c. 1530.

In the vestry is a very fine and elaborate 15th-century carved beam, found used up in a cottage. It has eleven projecting brackets for images, that in the middle being larger than the others, and may have been the front beam of the rood-loft. It is 15 ft. long. An altar table dated 1725 is inlaid with mahogany, with a 'glory' in the middle and initials at the corners, and a monogram A T.

In the Gerard Chapel is the fine brass of Piers Gerard, son of Sir Thomas Gerard of the Brynn, 1485, and in the Legh Chapel is a second brass, now set against the east wall, with the figures of Sir Peter Legh, 1527, and his wife Ellen (Savage), 1491. Sir Peter was ordained priest after his wife's death, and is shown on his brass tonsured and with mass vestments over his armour. Below are figures of children. There is a brass plate in the chancel pavement to Richard Sherlock, rector, 1689.

Later monuments in the Legh Chapel are those of Sir Peter Legh, 1635, and Richard Legh and his wife, 1687. On the south side of the chapel some alabaster panels with strapwork and heraldry, from a destroyed Jacobean monument, are built into the wall.[9]

There are six bells, re-cast in 1711.

The church possesses two chalices, patens, and flagons of 1786; two chalices, four patens, and two flagons of 1795; and a sifter and tray of the same date. Also a pewter flagon and basin, two large copper flagons, red enamelled, with gold flower painting of Japanese style, a gilded brass almsdish and two plates, designed by Pugin, and an ebony staff with a plated head, the gift of Geoffrey Hornby, rector, 1781-1812.

In the chancel hangs a brass chandelier, given by the Society of Friends of Warrington.

The registers begin in 1563, the paper book not being extant. The first volume contains the years 1563-1642, the entries to 1598 being copies. The next volumes in order are 1630-77, 1676-95, 1696-1717, 1716-33.

The octagonal bowl of a 14th-century font found in 1877 beneath the floor of the church now lies outside the east end of the chancel, in company with the piece of an early cross-head described in a previous volume.[10] It is much worn, but has had four-leaved flowers on each face, with raised centres, and must have been a good piece of work when perfect.[11]

ADVOWSON
'St. Oswald had two plough-lands exempt from all taxation' in 1066, so that the parish church has been well endowed from ancient times.[12] Possibly the dedication suggested to Roger of Poitou the propriety of granting it to St. Oswald's Priory, Nostell,[13] a grant which appears to have been renewed or confirmed by Stephen, Count of Mortain, between 1114 and 1121.[14] In 1123 Henry I wrote to the Bishop of Chester, directing that full justice should be done to the prior and canons of Nostell, whose clerks in Makerfield were depriving them of their dues.[15] From this time the prior and canons presented to the church, receiving certain dues or a fixed pension; but beyond the statement in the survey of 1212 [16] nothing is known until 1252, when Alexander, Bishop of Lichfield, having been appealed to by the prior and the canons, decreed that on the next vacancy they should present 'a priest of honest conversation and competent learning' as vicar, who should receive the whole of the fruits of the church, paying to Lichfield Cathedral and to Nostell Priory a sum of money as might be fixed by the bishop. In the meantime the annual pension of 50s. then paid to Nostell from the church of Winwick was to be divided equally, half being paid to the church of Lichfield.[17] A century

NOSTELL PRIORY.
Gules a cross between four lions rampant or.

[7] *Lancs. and Ches. Antiq. Soc.* xxiii, 213. The niche may have held an image of St. Anthony.

[8] These shields have been repainted, and it is evident that this has been done incorrectly. They seem, however, to be intended for the arms of the following families:—Butler of Merton, Croft of Dalton, Legh of Lyme, Boydell, Boydell and Haydock.

[9] The inscriptions on the various monuments are given in Beamont, *Winwick*, 119-25; see also Thornely, *Brasses*, 61, 169. Notes of the arms, &c. found in the church in the 16th and 17th centuries

later it appears that a pension of 24 marks was due from the vicarage to the monastery.[18]

In 1291 the annual value was estimated as £26 13s. 4d.,[19] while in 1341 the ninth of the corn, wool, &c. was valued at 50 marks.[20]

The first dispute as to the patronage seems to have occurred in 1307, when John de Langton claimed it in right of his wife Alice, heiress of the lords of Makerfield. The priors of Nostell, however, were able to show a clear title, and the claim was defeated.[21] About fifty years later the patronage was acquired by the Duke of Lancaster.[22] In 1381 the king was patron,[23] and the Crown retained the right until Henry VI granted it to Sir John de Stanley, reserving to the prior an annual pension of 100s.[24] From this time it has descended with the main portion of the Stanley properties, the Earl of Derby being patron.

In 1534 the net value was returned as £102 9s. 8d.,[25] but in 1650 the income was estimated at over £660,[26] and Bishop Gastrell reckoned it at about £800 after the curates had been paid.[27] At the beginning of last century, before the division of the endowment, the benefice was considered the richest in the kingdom,[28] and its gross value is still put at £1,600.[29]

The following have been rectors :—

Instituted	Name	Presented by	Cause of Vacancy
oc. 1191	Hugh [30]	——	——
oc. 1212	Richard [31]	——	——
oc. 1232	Robert [32]	——	——
c. 1250	N [33]	——	——
—— ——	Alexander de Tamworth [34]	Priory of Nostell	——
—— ——	Augustine de Darington [35]	,,	——
oc. 1287	John de Mosley [36]	,,	——
8 Feb. 1306–7	John de Bamburgh [37]	,,	——
—— —— 1325	John de Chisenhale [38]	Bishop of Lichfield	d. of J. de Bamburgh

[18] Lich. Epis. Reg. ii, 125b.

[19] Pope Nich. Tax. (Rec. Com.), 249.

[20] Inq. Non. (Rec. Com.), 40. The separate townships stood thus :—Ashton, £8 6s. 8d.; Haydock, 31s. 8d.; Newton, £4 3s. 4d.; Golborne, £3 1s. 8d.; Lowton and Kenyon, £4; Middleton and Houghton, £1; Culcheth, £5 16s. 8d.; Croft and Southworth, £2 6s. 8d.; Winwick and Hulme, £3.

[21] De Banco R. 162, m. 4. The canons had presented on the three preceding vacancies, viz., Alexander de Tamworth, Augustine de Darington in the time of Henry III, and John de Mosley. These were probably all that had been appointed since the termination of the old arrangement.

Again in 1325, on the death of John de Bamburgh, the Prior of Nostell had to defend his right, the Bishop of Lichfield claiming on the ground that the prior having appointed an unfit person (Roger de Atherton, Canon of Nostell) the right had devolved on himself as ordinary, and he had conferred the vicarage on one John de Chisenhale. The prior vindicated his right, but the bishop's presentee retained possession; De Banco R. 258, m. 4 d.

In 1349 it was agreed that a canon of Nostell should thenceforward be appointed to the vicarage; Cal. Pat. 1348–50, p. 423.

[22] In 1360, and later, the king and John de Gaunt claimed the advowson, the church being then vacant; De Banco R. 404, m. 3; 406, m. 252; 409, m. 18 d. All charters relating to Winwick have been omitted from the Nostell chartulary.

[23] See the appointments in 1384 and later years. One of those nominated was a Boteler, as if the claim of Sir William Boteler had been recognized in some way.

At this time, however, the prior of Nostell sold to Robert de Morton an annuity of 8 marks for £240, which sum the prior was to employ in procuring the appropriation of Winwick; he misspent the money and involved the house in a debt of 1,200 marks; Beamont, Winwick, 12, quoting Batty, Nostell Priory, 20.

[24] Close, 12 Hen. VI, m. 13 d. which records a grant (undated) of the advowson made by John, Prior of Nostell, to Sir John

1277 as having made a grant of land; De Banco R. 19, m. 54 d. In 1271 Robert son of the rector of Winwick, and Amaria and Juliana his sisters accused Henry de Sefton of taking their goods and chattels; Cur. Reg. R. 204, m. 11 d. He was a son of Robert the rector; see Beamont, Winwick, 16. William son of Robert the rector also occurs; Towneley MS. HH, no. 1699.

[33] 'N. rector of Winwick' attested a deed made about 1250; Dods. MSS. liii, fol. 17b.

[34] De Banco R. 162, m. 4.

[35] Ibid.; appointed in the time of Henry III, and vicar for thirty years. He appears as plaintiff in the early years of Edward I down to 1279, and is sometimes called Augustine de Winwick; De Banco R. 18, m. 15; 23, m. 21.

[36] De Banco R. 162, m. 4; his death was the occasion of a dispute as to the patronage early in 1307. He was vicar as early as 1287 and in 1292; Harl. MS. 2112, fol. 158b–194b; Assize R. 408, m. 58 d.

In a plea of 1352 it was asserted that 'John de Warnefield, vicar of the church of Winwick,' granted the lands in dispute in the time of Edward II; Duchy of Lanc. Assize R. 2, m. 6 (Mich.). Beamont, however, states that his name occurs in 1292 (Winwick, 17); in which case he must be identical either with John de Mosley, who died a short time before the accession of Edward II, or with John de Bamburgh.

[37] Lich. Epis. Reg. Langton, i, fol. 10b; he was ordered to reside in the parish. Nothing further is known of him except that he was defendant in a case in 1307; De Banco R. 164, m. 324.

[38] For the circumstances of his presentation see a preceding note. He gave a bond to the prior of Nostell for £316; Nostell Reg. fol. 23 (B.M. Cott. Vesp. E. xix). He occurs as vicar in 1332 as defendant in a suit concerning land in Culcheth: De Banco R. 290, m. 3; and Final Conc. (Rec. Soc. Lancs. and Ches.), ii, 86, and in later cases, e.g. Coram Rege R. 297, m. 6 d. (where he is called 'parson').

Instituted	Name	Presented by	Cause of Vacancy
12 Dec. 1349	Geoffrey de Burgh [39]	Priory of Nostell	d. J. de Chisenhale
— —	William de Blackburn [40]	—	—
oc. 1384–5	John de Harwood [41]		
23 Jan. 1384–5	Thomas le Boteler [42]	The King	—
— 1386	Walter de Thornholme [43]		—
— — 1388	Robert le King [44]		—
6 May 1389	William Daas [45]	{ Th { Th	—
3 April 1423	Mr. Richard Stanley [46]		—
11 Mar. 1432–3	Thomas Bourchier [47]		d. R. Stanley
oc. 1436	George Radcliffe, D.Decr. [48]	—	—
19 June 1453	Edward Stanley [49]		d. G. Radcliffe
22 Nov. 1462	James Stanley [50]		d. E. Stanley
25 Aug. 1485	Robert Cliff [51]		d. J. Stanley
27 Feb. 1493–4	Mr. James Stanley, D.Can.L. [57]		res. R. Cliff
21 June 1515	Mr. Thomas Larke [53]	”	d. Bp. of Ely
— 1525	Thomas Winter [54]	The King	res. T. Larke
23 Dec. 1529	William Boleyne [55]	”	res. T. Winter
10 April 1552	Thomas Stanley [56]	Earl of Derby	d. W. Boleyne

[39] Lich. Epis. Reg. Northburgh, ii, fol. 125b. He was a canon of Nostell. His institution was confirmed eight years later, viz., 28 Nov. 1357; ibid. ii, fol. 126. In the following year he was described as 'lately vicar'; Raines MSS. (Chet. Lib.), xxxviii, 425. The church was vacant in 1360; De Banco R. 404, m. 3.

[40] Dep. Keeper's Rep. xl, App. 523. It is not known whether Blackburn and his immediate successors were ever instituted.

[41] Ibid. A protection for John de Harwood, vicar of Winwick, against William de Blackburn, late usurper of the benefice; dated 22 Jan. 1384–5.

[42] Cal. Pat. 1381–5, p. 528. It will be noticed that he was presented the day after the protection to John de Harwood was granted.

[43] Ibid. 1385–9, p. 127; this was only a 'ratification of his estate.' He was to have accompanied John of Gaunt into Aquitaine in 1388, but stayed behind in London; ibid. pp. 497, 518.

[44] Robert le King is named as 'perpetual vicar' of Winwick, in July 1388; Towneley MS. OO, no. 1539.

[45] Cal. Pat. 1388–92, pp. 32, 363. After the disputes and unsettlement indicated by these rapid changes came a time of rest, this rector remaining for about thirty years.

It was the pope who presented William Daas to the rectory, the advowson being in his hands; but the Statute of Provisors causing difficulty the king presented the same clerk, and afterwards ratified his title. These facts appear from a petition by the rector, about 1398, complaining that a certain Robert de Hallam had informed the king that the church was vacant, and procured a presentation for himself; P.R.O. Anct. Pet. file 220, no. 10099.

William Daas had licence for an oratory in 1393; Lich. Epis. Reg. Scrope, vi, fol. 129b. From this and other evidences he appears to have been resident. A complaint was made by him in 1393 that having closed a path through one of his glebe fields, Sir John le Boteler and others had forcibly broken through. The verdict was in his favour; Pal. of Lanc. Misc. bdle. 1, file 8, m. 6, 7. He is also mentioned in 1404 and 1405; ibid. file 9, m. 71, 68. In 1407 he purchased from Sir William Boteler the right

to make a weir or attachment for capturing fish in Sankey water; Beamont, Winwick, 19 (quoting Butler Deeds). He with Thomas de Longley (late Archdeacon of Norfolk), Eustace Daas, and John Drewe, gave fine for a writ in 1411–12; Dep. Keeper's Rep. xxxvii, App. i, 173.

[46] Lich. Epis. Reg. Heyworth, ix, fol. 112b. As the bishop collated, the 'vicarage,' as it is still called, must have been vacant for some time, but the reason is not given. Master Richard Stanley was appointed archdeacon of Chester in 1426; Le Neve, Fasti, i, 567.

[47] Lich. Epis. Reg. Heyworth, ix, 121b. The new 'rector' probably held the benefice till his consecration as Bishop of Worcester in 1435; he became Archbishop of Canterbury; Dict. Nat. Biog.

[48] Dr. George Radcliffe, son of Sir Ralph Radcliffe of Smithills, was Archdeacon of Chester in 1449; Le Neve, op. cit. He held a canonry in St. John's, Chester, till his death; Ormerod, Ches. (ed. Helsby), i, 310. He is mentioned as rector in 1436; Kuerden MSS. iii, W. 6, no. 79. He had been rector of Wilmslow and Longford in succession; Earwaker, East Cheshire, i, 88. For pedigree see Whitaker, Whalley (ed. Nichols), ii, 319.

[49] Lich. Epis. Reg. Boulers, xi, fol. 37b. He was also appointed Archdeacon of Chester; Le Neve, loc. sup. cit.

[50] Lich. Epis. Reg. Hales, xii, fol. 100b. Henry Byrom was patron for this turn. James Stanley was a son of the first Lord Stanley; Archdeacon of Chester 1478, Warden of Manchester 1481, and Rector of Warrington 1482, holding all these till his death; see Le Neve.

[51] Lich. Epis. Reg. Hales, xii, fol. 120; he engaged to pay a pension of 24 marks a year to the dean and chapter of Lichfield. One Robert Cliffe was priest of a chantry in St. John's, Chester, from 1478 to 1516; Ormerod, op. cit. i, 313.

[52] Lich. Epis. Reg. Smith, xii, fol. 157b. He was son of the patron, and had succeeded his uncle as Warden of Manchester in 1485. He became Bishop of Ely in 1506, retaining Winwick till his death. An account of him will be found in Dict. Nat. Biog.

[53] Lich. Epis. Reg. Blyth, xiii–xiv, fol. 59. He held various benefices, being one of Cardinal Wolsey's chaplains, and his confessor. He continued faithful to Wolsey on his fall and died just before him in 1530; see L. and P. Hen. VIII, iv, 2936,

Instituted	Name	Presented by	Cause of Vacancy
19 Mar. 1568–9	Christopher Thompson, M.A. [57]	Thomas Handford	d. Bp. Stanley
7 Jan. 1575–6	John Caldwell, M.A. [58]	Earl of Derby	{depr. or removal of Chr. Thompson
18 Feb. 1596–7	John Ryder, M.A. [59]		
27 Mar. 1616	Josiah Horne [60]	The King	prom. Bp. Ryder
27 June 1626	Charles Herle, M.A. [61]	Sir Edward Stanley	d. J. Horne
—	Thomas Jessop [62]		
19 Oct. 1660	Richard Sherlock, D.D. [63]	Earl of Derby	
24 July 1689	Thomas Bennet, B.D. [64]	John Bennet	d. R. Sherlock
30 July 1692	Hon. Henry Finch, M.A. [65]	Earl of Derby	d. T. Bennet
9 Sept. 1725	Francis Annesley, LL.D. [66]	Trustees	res. H. Finch
13 Sept. 1740	Hon. John Stanley, M.A. [67]	Charles Stanley	d. F. Annesley
18 May 1742	Thomas Stanley, LL.D. [68]	Earl of Derby	res. J. Stanley
24 Aug. 1764	Hon. John Stanley, M.A. [69]	,,	d. T. Stanley

compromise the hall and manor were given to the rector, but the remainder continued to be held by the Earl of Worcester, Sir John and Dame Frances Fortescue, and Petronilla Stanley, representatives of Sir Thomas Stanley, whose son, Sir Edward, had left four daughters as co-heirs. It continued to give trouble until its expiry in 1662. See Beamont, *Winwick*, 32, 37, 41, 56; also references in *Lancs. and Ches. Recs.* ii, 263, 346.

[57] Church Papers at Chester Dioc. Reg. Thomas Handford presented by grant of the Earl of Derby. The new rector paid his first-fruits 31 March 1569; *Lancs. and Ches. Recs.* ii, 409. He afterwards renounced Protestantism, went to Douay, and being ordained priest, was sent on the English mission in 1577; Knox, *Douay Diaries*, 8, 25, 276. He was very soon apprehended by the Earl of Derby 'as a vagrant person and one suspected of some lewd practices by reason of his passing to and fro over the seas'; *Acts of Privy C.* 1577–8, p. 309. After suffering seven years' imprisonment in the Marshalsea and Tower he was sent into exile in 1585; *Misc.* (Cath. Rec. Soc.), i, 70; ii, 228; Knox, op. cit. 288.

[58] Raines MSS. (Chet. Lib.), xxii, 52. It appears that the Bishop of Chester claimed the presentation, perhaps by lapse, John Shireburne, B.D., being nominated by him (see Brindle). The Earl of Derby's nomination prevailed, and Caldwell paid his first-fruits on 20 Feb. 1575–6; *Lancs. and Ches. Recs.* ii, 410. He was also rector of Mobberley; Ormerod, *Ches.* (ed. Helsby), i, 412, 428. He was one of the earl's chaplains, and a favourite preacher; *Derby Household Bks.* (Chet. Soc.), 132, 133.

[59] *Lancs. and Ches. Recs.* ii, 411. He was born at Carrington in Cheshire, and educated at Jesus Coll. Oxf.; M.A. 1583. He had a number of preferments in England and Ireland, and does not seem to have resided at Winwick. On being made Bishop of Killaloe in 1613 he was allowed to hold Winwick 'in commendam'; but resigned it in 1615; Foster, *Alumni Oxon.*; *Dict. Nat. Biog.*

John Andrews, M.A., was presented by the Earl of Worcester in 1609; Act Bks. at Ches.

[60] *Lancs. and Ches. Recs.* ii, 412; Pat. 13 Jas. I, pt. xxiii. The king presented on the ground that the previous rector had been appointed to a bishopric; but the claim was challenged, and Thomas Bold, M.A., was presented by the Earl of Worcester; later still John Mere, a prebendary of Chester, was presented. Horne, however, retained the rectory till his death in 1626. There was a lecturer

at Winwick, Mr. Golty, who paid £1 to a subsidy in 1622: *Misc.* (Rec. Soc. Lancs. and Ches.), i, 53, 65.

[61] From this point the dates of institution have been taken from those in the Inst. Bks. P.R.O. printed in *Lancs. and Ches. Antiq. Notes*. Herle paid his first-fruits 1 July 1628; *Lancs. and Ches. Recs.* ii, 412. This, the most distinguished of the modern rectors of Winwick, was born at Prideaux Herle, in Cornwall; educated at Exeter Coll. Oxf.; M.A. 1618; had various preferments, and was chaplain to the Countess of Derby; was a zealous Puritan, and became president of the Westminster Assembly, 1643. He was not resident at Winwick during the war, but returned in 1650, and was buried at Winwick in 1659. See *Dict. Nat. Biog.*; Fuller, *Worthies*; Foster, *Alumni Oxon.* For his conduct in 1651 see *Royalist Comp. Papers* (Rec. Soc. Lancs. and Ches.), iii, 175.

[62] As early as 20 June 1660 Dr. Sherlock petitioned for admission to the rectory, stating that he had been presented by the true patron, whereas Mr. Jessop had only 'an illegal grant from the commissioners of the pretended Great Seal, after the interruption of the late Parliament so called;' *Hist. MSS. Com. Rep.* vii, App. 500. Mr. Jessop conformed, and in Oct. 1662 became vicar of Coggeshall in Essex; Baines, *Lancs.* (ed. Croston), iv, 359.

[63] Dr. Sherlock was a kinsman of Richard Sherlock, rector of Woodchurch, Cheshire; educated at Trinity Coll., Dublin; M.A. 1633; he was a zealous adherent of the royalist party during the Civil War, and employed by the Earl of Derby in the Isle of Man. He published various works, including *Mercurius Christianus; the Practical Christian*, in 1673; *Dict. Nat. Biog.* The 6th edition of *the Practical Christian*, printed in 1713, contains a portrait of Sherlock and a memoir by Bishop Wilson. He did not obtain full possession of Winwick for some time, owing to the disputes with his predecessor. He received a presentation or confirmation of the rectory from the king in 1663; Pat. 15 Chas. II, pt. iv, no. 27. He constantly resided on his benefice and employed three curates; Beamont, *Winwick*, 61. His will is printed in *Wills* (Chet. Soc. new ser.), i, 173. The inventory shows a library valued at £64. The funeral sermon, preached by his curate Thomas Crane (see Newburgh in Lathom), was printed; *N. and Q.* (2nd Ser.), ii, 233.

[64] He was the son of John Bennet of Abingdon, Cambridgeshire; educated at University Coll. Oxf.; M.A. 1681; B.D.

1689. He became master of the college in 1690, and died there 12 May 1692; Foster, *Alumni Oxon.* The patron for this turn was probably the John Bennet of Abingdon, who was one of the members for Newton from 1691 to 1695, and afterwards a master in Chancery; Pink and Beaven, *Lancs. Parl. Representation*, 284.

[65] A son of Sir Heneage Finch, Earl of Nottingham. He was educated at Christ's Coll. Camb., of which he was fellow; M.A. 1682. His brother Edward was for a time rector of Wigan. Henry was in 1702 made Dean of York, but held Winwick also until 1725; Le Neve, *Fasti*, iii, 127.

[66] The patrons were the Earl of Anglesey and Francis Annesley, trustees of the Hon. Henrietta Ashburnham, granddaughter and heir of William, ninth Earl of Derby. Annesley was educated at Trinity Coll. Dublin; LL.D. 1725; married Elizabeth Sutton, divorced 1725; and secondly, Anne, daughter and co-heir of Sir Robert Gayer, by whom he had a son Arthur, ancestor of the present Viscount Valentia; Baines, op. cit. iv, 361.

[67] The patron exercised his right according to the wish of James, Earl of Derby. The earl's will reads; 'To the same Charles Stanley (eldest son of Thomas Stanley, of Cross Hall, deceased), the first and next turn of presentation and right of nomination to the rectory of the parish church of Winwick, whensoever vacant; providing he instituted the said Thomas Stanley (younger brother of Charles) if of age and ordained; if not, then to appoint some other clerk who should give security to resign the said rectory when the said Thomas was of age, if then ordained.'

The new rector was a younger son of Sir Edward Stanley of Bickerstaffe, who became Earl of Derby in 1735; educated at Sidney-Sussex Coll. Camb. of which he became a fellow; M.A. 1717. He held many benefices—Liverpool, 1726 to 1740; Winwick, 1740 to 1742, and 1764 to 1781; Bury, 1743 to 1778; Halsall, 1750 to 1757. For his character see Beamont, op. cit. 67. He took Winwick till his successor was ready.

[68] Of Trinity Hall, Camb.; LL.B. 1744; LL.D. 1757. Second son of Thomas Stanley of Cross Hall, Lathom; from his son James descends the present owner. This was the relation the late earl had wished to appoint, but in 1735 he was at Cambridge, and had not been ordained when Dr. Annesley died; Gregson, *Fragments* (ed. Harland), 285.

[69] He died 16 May 1781, and there is a tablet to his memory in Winwick Church.

Instituted		Name	Presented by		Cause of Vacancy
7 June 1781	.	Geoffrey Hornby [70]	Earl of Derby		d. J. Stanley
19 Dec. 1812	.	James John Hornby, M.A. [71] . .	„		d. G. Hornby
— Nov. 1855	.	Frank George Hopwood, M.A. [72] .	„		d. J. J. Hornby
29 April 1890	.	Oswald Henry Leycester Penrhyn, M.A. [73]	„		d. F. G. Hopwood

As in the case of other benefices the earlier rectors were probably married 'clerks,' enjoying the principal part of the revenues of the church, and paying a priest to minister in the parish. Two sons of Robert, rector in 1232, are known. After the patronage had been transferred to the Stanleys the rectory became a 'family living,' in the later sense.

In the Valor of 1535 the only ecclesiastics mentioned are the rector, two chantry priests at Winwick, and a third at Newton.[74] The *Clergy List* of 1541–2 [75] shows three others as residing in this large parish, including the curate, Henry Johnson, paid by Gowther Legh, the rector's steward. The list is probably incomplete, for at the visitation of 1548 the names of fourteen were recorded—the rector, his curate, Hugh Bulling, who had replaced Henry Johnson; the three chantry priests and two others just named, and seven more. By 1554 these had been reduced to six—the rector, his curate, Richard Smith, two of the chantry priests still living there, but only two of the others who had appeared six years earlier. In 1562 a further reduction is manifest. The rector, Bishop Stanley, was excused from attendance at the bishop; three others appeared, one being a surviving chantry priest, but the fifth named was absent. In the following year the rector was again absent; the curate of Newton, the former chantry priest, did not appear; but the curates of Ashton and Culcheth were present, and another is named. The improvement was only apparent, for in 1565 the rector, though present, *non exhibuit*, and only two other names are given in the Visitation List, and they are crossed out and two others written over them. It seems, therefore, that the working staff had been reduced to two—Andrew Rider and Thomas Collier.[76]

How the Reformation changes affected the parish does not appear, except from these fluctuations and reductions in the staff of clergy. The rector was not interfered with on the accession of Elizabeth; his

dignity and age, as well as his family connexions, probably saved him from any compliance beyond employing a curate who would use the new services. His successor became a Douay missionary priest, suffering imprisonment and exile. Though the rector in 1590 was 'a preacher' he lived in Cheshire, and his curate was 'no preacher'; nor were the two chapels at Newton and Ashton any better provided.[77] The list drawn up about 1610 shows that though the rector, an Irish dignitary, was 'a preacher,' the resident curate was not; while at the three chapels there were 'seldom curates.'[78]

The Commonwealth surveyors of 1650 were not quite satisfied with Mr. Herle, for though he was 'an orthodox, godly, preaching minister,' and one of the most prominent Presbyterians in England, he had not observed the day of humiliation recently appointed by the Parliament. They recommended the creation of four new parishes—the three ancient chapelries, and a new one at Lowton.[79] After the Restoration two or three meetings of Nonconformists seem to have been established.[80] In 1778 each of the four chapelries in the parish was served by a resident curate, paid chiefly by the rector, except Newton, paid by Mr. Legh.[81]

The great changes brought about by the coal mining and other industries in the neighbourhood have ecclesiastically, as in other respects, produced a revolution; and by the munificence of Rector J. J. Hornby—a just munificence, but rare—the modern parishes into which Winwick has been divided are well endowed.

There were two chantries in the parish church. The older of them was founded in the chapel of the Holy Trinity in 1330 by Gilbert de Haydock, for a fit and honest chaplain, who was to pray for the founder by name in every mass, and say the commendation with *Placebo* and *Dirige*, every day except on double feasts of nine lessons. The right of pre-

[70] Eldest son of Edmund Hornby of Poulton and Scale Hall. He is said to have served in the Navy in his early years; in 1774 he was sheriff of Lancashire; P.R.O. *List*, 74. Afterwards he was ordained, and having married a sister of the Earl of Derby was presented to Winwick. He died in 1812, and was buried at Winwick. One of his curates, the Rev. Giles Chippendale, who had lost an arm in the naval service, was said to have been with him in the same ship; Beamont, op. cit. 68.

His son Sir Phipps Hornby had a distinguished career in the Navy.

[71] Second son of the preceding rector. Educated at Trinity Coll. Camb.; M.A. 1802.

An attractive sketch of his character is given by Mr. Beamont (op. cit. 71–80). As rector, his most conspicuous act was the procuring, in conjunction with the Earl of Derby as patron, of the Winwick Church Acts of 1841 and 1845, by which Croft, Newton, Culcheth (Newchurch), Lowton, Golborne, and Ashton

sentation was vested in the founder and his heirs, but after a three months' vacancy it would lapse to the bishop.[82] A few of the names of the priests of this foundation occur in the Lichfield Registers, and others have been collected by Mr. Beamont from the Legh deeds.[83] In 1534 the income was 66s. 8d., and it remained the same till the confiscation in 1548.[84]

The second chantry, known as the Stanley chantry, was founded by the ancestors of the Earl of Derby. It was in the rector's chapel, and endowed with burgages in Lichfield and Chester, bringing in a rent of 66s. 8d.[85]

A grammar school, once of some note, was founded by Gowther Legh in the time of Henry VIII, and refounded in 1619 by Sir Peter Legh.[86]

CHARITIES The charities of this parish are numerous and valuable. As in other cases, some are general, others applicable to particular objects or townships.

For the whole parish are the ancient bread charities and other gifts to the poor,[87] the Bible charity founded by Dean Finch,[88] and the modern educational funds.[89]

For Winwick-with-Hulme are gifts of linen, &c., for the poor,[90] and funds for binding apprentices,[91] and buying school books.[92] At Houghton, Middleton, and Arbury are poor's cottages.[93] Golborne and Lowton together share in William Leadbeater's benefaction.[94] The townships separately have some minor charities,[95] including poor's cot-

---

[82] Lich. Epis. Reg. Northburgh, iii, fol. 76b, and Beamont, *Winwick*, 82. The original endowment consisted of eight messuages, seven tofts, 41¾ acres of land, with appurtenances in Newton in Makerfield, with the reversion of others held for life by Adam de Walton. Chalices, books, vestments, and other ornaments were provided by the founder. Should the chaplain be unable through infirmity to attend to his duties he was to receive a portion of the fruits sufficient to support him decently. See *Final Conc.* ii, 81.

[83] Beamont, 83–6. The list (omitting the first names and making one or two other corrections) is as follows :—

1334. Peter de Winwick, nominated by the founder, Gilbert de Haydock; Lich. Epis. Reg. Northburgh, ii, fol. 109b.
oc. 1343. William de Rokeden.
1358. Richard de Heton, presented by John de Haydock, on the death of W. de Rokeden; Lich. Epis. Reg. Northburgh, ii, fol. 134b.
1361. Ralph de Tabley, presented by John de Haydock, on the resignation of Richard de Heton; ibid. Stretton. iv, fol. 78b.
oc. 1370. William de Wigan, by the same patron.
Matthew de Haydock by the guardian of P. Legh.
oc. 1478. Matthew Fowler, by Peter Legh.
oc. 1478. William Gam, by Sir Peter Legh.
1505. Christopher Houghton, by the same.
Robert Garnet ; by the same.
1532. Lawrence Pennington ; by the same. He was celebrating according to his foundation up to the suppression ; Raines, *Lancs. Chant.* (Chet. Soc.), i, 69. He was then aged 48, and lame ; ibid. i, 72 n. He appeared in the Visitation of 1554, but not later.

[84] *Valor Eccl.* (Rec. Com.), v, 220. In 1478 a further endowment was made by Sir Peter Legh the patron ; Raines MSS. xxxviii, 523.
The endowment in 1548 is given in detail in *Lancs. Chant.* i, 71–4 ; it was derived from a number of tenements in Newton in Makerfield, the principal tenant being James Greenforth, who paid a rent of 14s. A chalice and two old vestments belonged to it.

[85] *Valor Eccl.* v, 220 ; *Lancs. Chant.* i,

67–9. There was no plate. The chantry priest in 1534 was Roger Gillibrand, and in 1548 William Stanley ; the latter was fifty-six years of age. He was living in 1553, but did not appear at the Visitation of 1554. The lands of the Stanley chantry were given by Queen Mary to the Savoy Hospital when she refounded it, and were leased by the Master to Christopher Anderton ; Anderton of Lostock D. no. 8, 10, 15 ; Duchy of Lanc. Misc. Bks. xxiii, 168.

[86] *End. Char. Rep.*
The Rev. Robert Wright, master of the school from 1717 to 1735, published tables of longitude ; *Local Glean. Lancs. and Ches.* i, 177, 226.

[87] The particulars in the following notes are taken from the *Winwick Endowed Charities Report* of 1901, which includes a reprint of that of 1828.
Dr. Richard Sherlock, rector, by his will in 1689 directed £300 to be invested for the use of the poor ; it was employed in buying chief rents from premises in Croft, amounting in 1824 to £11 8s. 5d., distributed in bread at the parish church and four chapels-of-ease. In 1900 the rent-charges amounted to £9 13s. 3d., others having been redeemed and the money invested in consols. The sum available is divided in a customary proportion among the different ecclesiastical districts, and is spent chiefly in bread for the poor.
Adam Mather in 1818 left money for bread for poor persons who were also communicants ; the latter condition is how not insisted upon.
Rector Stanley in 1772 left £1,000 for the poor, and £50 interest was in 1828 given in various ways—doles or blankets, &c. The capital, invested in the Warrington and Wigan Turnpike, was in great part lost on the termination of the Turnpike Act ; £400 was recovered and invested in consols, producing £11 17s. 4d. yearly ; this is distributed by the rector and other clergy at their discretion.

[88] He died in 1728 and left £200 to the rector and churchwardens for Bibles, prayer books, and instruction in the Church of England catechism. In 1828 the income was £9 15s. 9d., given usually in books, but sometimes applied to the Sunday schools. The income is now £6 14s. 8d., and is distributed by the rector every three years, being chiefly devoted to the Sunday schools.

[89] These are partly derived from the endowments of the older schools, and partly by gifts by George McCorquodale, of about £600 in all, for prizes at the Endowed School and St. Peter's School, Newton.

[90] In 1685 a poor's fund had accumu-

lated by the gifts of sundry benefactors, and Dr. Sherlock, the rector, added £89 ; other gifts were made in subsequent years, and in 1828 the interest amounted to £7 2s., spent on gifts of linen, &c., to poor cottagers. The capital has to a great extent been lost, and the yearly income is now £1 13s. 8d., distributed in gifts of calico.

[91] Thomas March and Henry Low about 1720 left money for binding apprentices, but by 1828 half the original capital, £52, had been lost, and the interest was added to the linen charity ; this erroneous use continued down to 1900.

[92] John Bankes, sometime schoolmaster at Winwick (died 1775), left a small sum for books for the children attending the school in Winwick churchyard. This in 1828 had been wrongly united to the linen charity, and so continued in 1900.

[93] The poor's money appears to have been invested in two cottages, but the rents, £11, were applied to the poor rate in 1828. A rent of 12s. from Delph House in Middleton had then ceased. In 1840 the rent had increased to £14, but £3 was and is payable to the highway authority : the rest is given by the rector of Winwick in clothing.

[94] The testator gave an estate in Lowton and Golborne to the poor, and by his will in 1685 gave £40 to erect at his house at Lowton two good bays of building, and £10 more to raise up the bay called 'the shop' the height of the afore. said bays, &c. ; a large stone was to be laid upon his burial place inscribed so that people might learn of his benefaction. In 1828 the rents amounted to £55, equally distributed in linen or flannel for the poor of the two townships. Various changes have since occurred ; part of the land has been sold to the Wigan Junction Railway, 1877 ; another part has been let on a building lease of 999 years ; and the coal under another has been mined. The rental is now £119 17s. 6d., of which £23 is derived from the founder's house in Church Lane, Lowton, and is distributed by the trustees appointed under a scheme made in 1892.

[95] For Golborne John Mather left a charge of 10s. for the poor, to be added to Leadbeater's Charity ; and Hannah Hooper left £20, the interest, £1, being paid in 1828. These have been added to the Golborne share of the Leadbeater Charity under the scheme of 1892, and the amount is applied in subscriptions to dispensaries, nurses, clothes, &c., or temporary relief in money.
Miss Frances Moon, by her will in 1873 bequeathed £1,000 for the sick and aged poor ; but only about £420 was realized.

tages at Lowton.[96] Newton had an ancient poor's stock, spent in providing linen, and other benefactions.[97] A legacy by James Berry in 1836 has failed.[98]

For the township of Culcheth as a whole, most of the ancient charities have been united;[99] the Blue Boy Charity continues.[100] For Newchurch with Ken-

yon are funds for the poor, &c.;[101] at Risley the almshouse has failed,[102] but John Ashton's Charity, founded in 1831, produces £31 10s. a year, distributed in money doles.[103]

At Southworth-with-Croft a calico dole is maintained.[104] Ashton in Makerfield has charities for linen, woollen, apprenticing boys, &c.[105] At Hay-

[96] For Lowton Richard France left £5 to the poor, and in 1828 5s. was paid as interest by the overseer of Lowton. Nicholas Turner, by his will of 1712, charged the Little Meadow in Golborne with 20s. for linen for the poor; this also was still paid in 1828; and like the previous sum was added to the Lowton half of Leadbeater's Charity. So also was £2 10s. derived from tenements purchased with a bequest of Elizabeth Byrom, widow, in 1738. The overseers in 1828 had £22 10s. derived from the rents of two cottages, which sum had been devoted to the poor, but was then applied to the debt incurred in rebuilding the cottages.

In 1900 these charities had been united with the Lowton share of the Leadbeater Charity, and were administered under the scheme of 1892, the objects permissible being almost the same as those in Golborne. The payment of 5s. out of the rates had been disallowed by the auditor in 1846, and thus France's Charity has lapsed.

[97] James Low in 1634 and others subsequently contributed various sums, which together amounted to £273 by 1733; sixty years later the total was £288, laid out upon the workhouse, and the interest was spent on linen for the poor. In 1825, interest having fallen into arrear, it was agreed that the capital should be considered £400, and in 1827 £20 was paid as interest. Robert Bankes in 1747 left £40 for the poor, and the interest in 1828 was added to the foregoing charity. — Brotherton left £50 to found a bread charity; and Mrs. Legh left £100, which with £50 (probably the last-mentioned sum) was in 1800 in the hands of Thomas Claughton, trustee of Thomas Legh of Lyme during minority, by whose bankruptcy the capital was endangered. A sum of £5 had been paid out of the estate of William Brown Brotherton to the eldest poor widow in Newton; the estate having been sold about 1821 to Thomas Legh, the payment has been since discontinued.

The workhouse was sold in 1856, when £288 was invested in consols, this being held to be all that was legally chargeable. The income, £8 5s. 8d., is distributed in tickets for clothing. The Bankes Charity was still continued in 1900 by Mrs. Bankes of Winstanley Hall, and distributed with the foregoing. The other charities had been lost, no dividend apparently having been paid out of Thomas Claughton's estate.

[98] This was a bequest of £50 for the benefit of poor communicants at Newton Chapel. The executors paid interest for some time, but the residuary legatee, on coming of age, refused to pay.

[99] The amalgamation took place under a scheme of the Charity Commissioners in 1898. There were six different foundations :—

i. Twiss Green School, founded by John Guest of Abram, Adam Shaw and Christopher Bordman assisting. A lease of 1808 stated that the purpose of the school was instruction in the English language and in the precepts of the Christian religion.

ii. Th
iii John
iv. Willia
Culcheth ca
Bate, the in
to the poor
called Shack
v. Ambro
tenements a
Henry and
the poor
was in 1828
Bate of M
Henry Bate
vi Mrs
poor, and Th
Culcheth H
official trust
The yearl
Charity in
Clare, owne
to the officia
of the Yates
£500; in e
vested in co
By the ne
are adminis
the Twiss G
Church of E
and the dol
various ways,

dock there are an ancient poor's stock and a clothing endowment.[106]

NEWTON IN MAKERFIELD

Neweton, Dom. Bk.
Makeresfeld, 1205, 1351; Makefeld, 1206; Makerefeld, 1213; Makerfeld, 1242; the last is the prevailing form.[1]

This township is usually called Newton in Makerfield or Newton le Willows, to distinguish it from other places of the name. It has an area of 3,103 acres,[2] and the population in 1901 numbered 16,699. Sankey Brook and its tributary Newton Brook form the greater part of the southern boundary; the latter is joined by the Millingford Brook, which crosses the township from north to south.

The surface of the country is generally flat, only slightly undulating in the south and west, where the ground is 142 ft. above sea level. The pebble beds of the Bunter series of the New Red Sandstone underlie the greater part of the township. The Coal Measures fringe the western and north-western borders. The town of Newton is pleasantly situated; by it is a large lake surrounded by willows.

Earlestown has the less pleasant surroundings of bare open country and few trees. The open country consists of arable fields and pasture land, the former yielding crops of potatoes and corn, with occasional turnip fields. In the west there are still a few patches of mossland, gradually becoming invaded by factories and railways.

The northern road through Warrington and Wigan, here somewhat to the east of the ancient Roman road, passes through the village. From this point roads lead eastward to Leigh and westward to St. Helens and Haydock. The St. Helens Canal goes by the side of the Sankey Brook. The Liverpool and Manchester line of the London and North Western Railway crosses the centre of the township, having stations at Earlestown and Newton.[3] The same company's main line from London to the North also passes through the township, and has a junction with the former line.

Newton, from its position on a great road, half way between Warrington and Wigan, and from its feudal dignity as the head of a hundred and then of the fee of Makerfield, has long been a place of importance. A borough was formed and a market and fairs were granted. Leland thus describes its condition

about 1536: 'Newton on a brook; a little poor market, whereof Mr. Langton hath the name of his barony.'[4] Soon afterwards it returned two members to Parliament.

The borough returned two members to Parliament in the 17th century.[5]

A gathering of the gentry at Newton in 1748, ostensibly for hunting, was regarded by the populace as a Jacobite meeting, and considerable rioting ensued.[6]

In 1824 the market had fallen into disuse; but the court baron and court leet were still held in April, May, and October by the steward of the borough and the bailiff of the manor. A race-course and cockpit existed, but the sports had been discontinued; the race-meeting was revived and is still held. The fairs were held on 17 and 18 May and 11 and 12 August. There were daily coaches to Liverpool and Bolton, and a market coach from Wigan to Warrington passed through on Wednesdays.[7]

Manufactures sprang up, cotton-spinning, crown glass, iron founding, and vitriol works existing in 1840. A large iron foundry and printing and stationery works are among the chief industries at present; there are also paper mills, glass works, and collieries.

In addition to these EARLESTOWN has grown up in recent years around the great wagon works of the London and North Western Railway Company at the Sankey Viaduct; it has also engineering works and a sugar refinery. A market is held on Friday. Two newspapers are published weekly. The railway company have erected a mechanics' institute. The Vulcan Foundry has given its name to the village which has grown up round it. Wargrave is another village in the same part of the township, and Hey, by the Sankey, is near.

A local board was established in 1863.[8] Newton is now governed by an urban district council of fifteen members, the township being divided into five wards.

There is an ancient barrow called Castle Hill about half a mile north of the village. There is another at the western end of the township. St. Oswald's Well is near the junction of the boundaries of Newton, Winwick, and Southworth.[9]

There is a town hall in High Street. The Liverpool Farm Reformatory School was established in 1859.[10] The old market cross was taken down in 1819.[11] The stone uprights of the stocks remain

Land producing £4 5s. a year had been given by Gerard Ashton in 1759, but nothing was known of it in 1828.

The apprenticing system having become obsolete the fund was in 1836 added to the grammar school estates. The property belonging to the other stocks now brings in £92 2s. 1d. annually, but from various causes the charity was in debt in 1899 to the extent of £260, so that the amount of clothing distributed had had to be curtailed.

Something appears to have been recovered from the Burn bequest, for in 1832 £6 15s. was deposited on its account in the Wigan Savings Bank. This has been allowed to accumulate, the fund now being over £43. To the trustees of the Abram charities 6s. 6d. a year is paid.

Lord Gerard pays 10s. to the incumbent for a sermon on St. John's Day for Catherine Wallis's charity.

[106] In 1706 the poor's fund amounted to £18 10s., and £80 more was added by later benefactors; the capital was invested in the workhouse at Newton, and in 1828 £6 to £7 was paid out of the township rates as interest. This was laid out by the overseer in the purchase of linen. On the sale of the workhouse in 1856 £99 10s. was paid to the official trustees, and the interest, £2 17s. 4d., is distributed with the Haydock Clothing Endowment—a capital of £327 11s. 8d. subscribed in 1863, principally by Mr. William John Legh and the Messrs. Evans. Blankets, flannel, and linsey are given.

[1] The phrase 'Two Makerfields' as the name of a piece of land occurs in an Ashton document; End. Char. Rep.

[2] 3,105, including 55 of inland water; census of 1901.

[3] It was at Parkside, to the east of Newton, that William Huskisson, M.P.,

was killed at the opening of the line in 1830. The Sankey Viaduct is near.

[4] Itin. vii, 47; the words 'on a brook called Golforden' (? Golborne) seem to belong to this sentence.

[5] Ret. of Memb. of Parl. 1213–1702, p. 536.

[6] Lancs. and Ches. Antiq. Notes, ii, 157.

[7] Baines, Lancs. Dir. 1825, ii, 433–5. Fairs in May and Aug. were held in 1836; others had fallen into oblivion; Baines, Lancs. (ed. 1836), iii, 647.

[8] Lond. Gaz. 8 Dec. 1863; 18 June 1869. [9] See V.C.H. Lancs. i, 366 n.

[10] Lond. Gaz. 12 Apr. 1859.

[11] Baines, Lancs. (ed. 1836), iii, 647; a handsome cross, the shaft on the model of Cleopatra's Needle, was in the cemetery; ibid.

Newton Cross was the scene of an interview between a Haydock man, who had been to the smith at Hulme with

outside the churchyard. The village wake was falling into disuse in 1836,[12] and no wakes have been held in the district for the last half-century.

Among the place names in 1824 were Pepper Alley, Wagry Moss, and Ruff House.

Before the Conquest *NEWTON HUNDRED* was the head of a hundred assessed at five hides. One of the hides, including Newton itself, was held in demesne by Edward the Confessor, as lord of the manor. In 1086 the demesne was valued at £4.[13]

Afterwards the *BARONY* fee or barony of *MAKERFIELD* was formed, embracing much the same area as the older hundred, and Newton became the head of the barony. The story of this fee and its successive lords—Banastre, Langton, Fleetwood, and Legh—has been told elsewhere.[14]

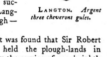

LANGTON. *Argent three cheverons gules.*

In 1346 it was found that Sir Robert *MANOR* de Langton held the plough-lands in *NEWTON* by the service of one knight's fee, paying 10s. for ward of Lancaster Castle, and doing suit at the wapentake court at West Derby

every three weeks.[15] The manor of Newton, with its members, Lowton, Kenyon, Arbury, a moiety of Golborne, and the advowson of Wigan Church, was so held; the other manors of Newton fee —Southworth, Wigan, Ince, Hindley, Abram, Ashton, Pemberton, Billinge, Winstanley, Haydock, Orrell, Winwickwith-Hulme, Woolston, Poulton, Middleton, Houghton, and the other moiety of Golborne—were held by fealty only.[16] At Newton a three-weeks court was kept for the barony.[17] A grant of free warren was obtained by Robert Banastre in 1257,[18] and licence to crenellate his mansion by Robert de Langton in 1341.[19] Manorial rights are still claimed, but no court has been held for many years.

BANASTRE. *Argent a cross patonce sable.*

A number of grants by the Banastres and Langtons[20] have been preserved.

A resident family or families took the local name; one of them in the time of Edward III was known as Richard the Receiver, from the office he held under the lord of the fee.[21] Another also had an official name—Serjeant; the family remained here down to the end of the 17th century.[22] Among the other

---

some plough irons, and the spirit of his departed mistress, who begged him to have masses said for her in her torment; from a *Narracio de celebracione Misse* by Mr. Ric. Puttes, 1372, in Trin. Coll. Oxf. MS. vij, fol. 49, kindly transcribed by the Rev. H. E. D. Blakiston, B.D., fellow and tutor.

[12] Baines, *Lancs.* loc. cit.

[13] *V.C.H. Lancs.* i, 286. About 1141 Randle Gernons, Earl of Chester, confirmed a grant of the demesne tithes of Newton to the abbey of Shrewsbury, which appears to have been first made by Roger of Poitou; Farrer, *Lancs. Pipe R.* 277.

[14] *V.C.H. Lancs.* i, 366–75. For a manumission of villeins by Robert Banastre in 1256 see *Final Conc.* (Rec. Soc. Lancs. and Ches.), i, 125. A deed of sale of the barony of Newton in 1594, Thomas Langton being vendor and Thomas Fleetwood purchaser, is printed in *Local Glean. Lancs. and Ches.* ii, 184.

[15] *Surv.* of 1346 (Chet. Soc.), 36.

[16] *Dep. Keeper's Rep.* xxxiii, App. 6, 17; also *Lancs. Inq. p.m.* (Chet. Soc.), ii, 99.

[17] Assize R. 404, m. 412. The 15th-century description of the tenure does not agree with the survey of 1212, by which the lords of Lowton and Golborne were found to be charged with the knight's service of the fee; *Lancs. Inq. and Extents* (Rec. Soc. Lancs. and Ches.), i, 73, 74. In 1201 Adam de Lawton and Thomas de Golborne had rendered account for 2 marks due for the fee of one knight; *Lancs. Pipe R.* 133. About the middle of the 13th century the Golborne plough-lands appear to have reverted to the lord of Newton, who granted them to Thurstan de Holland in socage; see the account of Golborne.

[18] *Cal. Chart. R.* 1226–57, p. 458. There was a second grant for the demesne lands of Newton, Golborne, and Lowton in 1301; Chart. R. 29 Edw. I, m. 12.

[19] *Cal. Pat.* 1340–3, p. 304.

[20] Robert lord of Makerfield granted a part of his land to William Payvant, Plattclough being part of the boundary; Raines MSS. (Chet. Lib.), xxxviii, 113. Robert Banastre, lord of Makerfield, granted to Henry son of William Curtis a number of pieces of land in the vill; 'the outlane to the wood of Burton' is named; ibid. 117.

A grant by Robert Banastre to Matthew son of Gilbert de Haydock in 1289 gives the bounds thus: From the old ditch on the east, by Roger the Carpenter's lands, so to a 'spertgore' in the south, by the ditches westward to John de Orrell's land, and then across to the commencement. Matthew was also to be toll free and hopper free in all the mills of Newton; ibid. 125. It was perhaps this grant which occasioned a lawsuit in 1347, Gilbert de Haydock as son and heir of Matthew complaining that he had been disseised of his common of pasture in 300 acres of wood; Sir Robert de Langton and others were defendants, including Hugh de Laye, 'hermit'; Assize R. 1435, m. 9.

In 1334 Robert de Langton, lord of Makerfield, granted Gilbert de Haydock ten acres, including the Rushy Field on the west of the highway; the Gunk by the Longmarsh; and a piece next to Pimcock's Acre; Raines, loc. cit. 141. The names and services of many tenants in Newton lordship in 1502 are given in Duchy of Lanc. Inq. p.m. iii, no. 101.

[21] Richard Banastre gave to Paulinus son of Richard de Newton land lying between Rece-riding and Cockshaw Head; Raines, loc. cit. 113. Roger son of Paulinus is named in another deed; ibid. In 1334 John de Langton authorized Richard de Newton, his receiver, to give seisin of two acres of the waste to Gilbert de Haydock; ibid. 143. The seal of Richard the Receiver is attached to several deeds; ibid. 139, 143.

Richard the Receiver of Newton in

families were those of Bingley[33] and Pierpoint.[34] Neighbouring lords, as those of Haydock,[35] also acquired lands in Newton ; the Leghs, besides inheriting the Haydock estate, went on adding to it, so that in 1660, when Richard Legh purchased the barony, he already owned a large part of the township.[36]

The Blackburnes, afterwards of Orford and Hale, acquired lands here in the latter part of the 16th century.[37] Their house, known more recently as Newton Hall, was built by Thomas Blackburne in 1634.[38] About a century ago John Blackburne, M.P., sold it to the Leghs.[39]

Newton le Willows Hall is a small H-shaped house standing north and south, with hall between living rooms and kitchen. The front is towards the east, the entrance being by a two-story timber porch opening to a lobby between the hall and kitchen. The hall is also of timber construction, with a line of windows on the east, and has a large fireplace at the north end with the royal arms of Elizabeth. The staircase starts from the middle of the west side of the hall, and a panel above it. There are rooms over the hall, it has a flat plaster ceiling, with simply moulded beams. The north wing, containing the kitchen with a large fireplace adjoining that of the hall, is of brick, with low mullioned windows and plain round-headed lights. The heads and mullions are of brick plastered, ornamented with raised lozenges and fleurs-de-lys. The wall surfaces are relieved with raised patterns in brick-work of a simple character. The south wing has similar details, but is modernized.

The little estate of HEY, sometimes called a manor, appears to have been held by a family so surnamed,[30] who were succeeded by the Brethertons or Brothertons, the tenants from the 16th century to the beginning of the 19th.[31] A pedigree was

BRETHERTON of the Hey. *Argent a cross patonce raguled sable.*

---

roffe meadow, lying by the Sankey ; Raines, loc. cit. 173. The Woodrows or Woodroffes were known in the 13th century.

Henry Serjeant, outlawed for felony in 1528, held eight messuages, 200 acres of land, &c., in Newton of Thomas Langton; Duchy of Lanc. Inq. p.m. vi, no. 61.

William Serjeant next appears ; he contributed to the subsidy in Mary's reign ; Mascy of Rixton D. At the end of 1556 he confirmed his father John's lease to Peter Legh, junior, of his capital messuage called Crow-lane Hall, dated 1534 ; Raines, loc. cit. 173 ; *Ducatus Lanc.* (Rec. Com.), i, 302, 304. In the will of Gowther Legh of Winwick he directs 'Mine executors to take yearly the whole profits of Serjeant's lands to the bringing up and finding to school of William Serjeant, now heir apparent to John Serjeant, and to the relieving of his brethren and sisters'; Raines, *Chantries* (Chet. Soc.), 73. William Serjeant had also an interest in the Pembertons' estates in Sutton and Bedford.

Peter Serjeant was in 1592 found to have held lands in Newton of the queen ; also in Bedford ; Thomas, his son and heir, was nine years of age ; Duchy of Lanc. Inq. p.m. xv, no. 16.

In 1660 a free rent of £1 13s. was due to the lord of Newton from the free rent of Peter Serjeant ; abstract of title in possession of W. Farrer. Margaret, daughter of Henry Ashhurst of Dalton, married Peter Serjeant of Newton ; Dugdale, *Visit.* (Chet. Soc.), 9. Administration was in 1673 granted to the estate of Thomas Serjeant of Newton.

Crow-lane House, perhaps the hall above mentioned, was in 1673 sold by William Blackburne, son of Thomas of Blackley Hurst, to John Stirrup of Newton ; and about forty years later was purchased by Peter Legh of Lyme. There was a rent-charge of £3 upon it for the benefit of the free school ; abstract of title.

[30] Adam son of Hugh de Booth claimed lands from John de Bingley and Katherine his wife in 1329 ; De Banco R. 279, m. 183 d.; 280, m. 127. Three years later Adam de Booth released his claim in favour of Katherine and her son Peter ; part of the road leading from his house to Bradley Bridge was included ; Raines MSS. xxxviii, 143. Katherine de Bingley and Richard her son and heir granted part of their land to Henry de Haydock in 1343 ; ibid. 145.

In 1364 John son of John de Bingley gave seisin of land near the Sankey to Sibyl his sister and Cecily de Haydock, her daughter ; ibid. 147. Five years later Richard de Bingley, senior, granted the reversion of certain lands to John, the son of Henry de Haydock by Sibyl his wife, the sister of Richard ; ibid. 148 ; also 159.

[34] Some account is given of this family under Golborne. The seal of (John son of) Richard le Pierpoint in 1350 showed barry of six ; ibid. 153.

[36] Some acquisitions of the family have been recorded in previous notes.

The Orrells also had lands in Newton. Robert de Holland granted to John de Orrell and his heirs land which Robert Banastre had given to his father Thurstan de Holland ; the bounds began at Eyolfs Brook by the Heuese in the north, went south to Trastans Clough, thence by a ditch to Haydock boundary, along this to Eyolfs Brook, and so back to the starting point ; half a pound of cummin was to be rendered to the chief lord ; Raines, loc. cit. 115. John son of Adam de Orrell of Hardshaw in 1318 granted to Henry de Orrell land in Newton which Richard the Baker had held ; and two years later Henry son of John de Orrell made a grant to Richard ; Add. MS. 32106, no. 1185, 1634.

Richard Bradshagh was in 1528 found to have held lands in Newton of Thomas Langton by a rent of 5s. 9d. ; Charles Bradshagh was his heir ; Duchy of Lanc. Inq. p.m. vi, no. 54.

The Southworths also had lands in Newton ; ibid. vii, no. 23 ; *Ducatus Lanc.* (Rec. Com.), i, 201, 281.

[36] The abstract of title already quoted shows that in 1660 the Leghs' free rents, payable to the lord of Makerfield, amounted to £6 13s. 4d. The other free rents, payable by Peter Serjeant and John Bretherton, amounted to no more than £2 9s.

In 1687 Peter Legh purchased from John Derbyshire two closes called the 'Ring Wines,' formerly the holding of Matthew Eden (1647) and William Baxter (1682). By an early deed Hugh Wait and Cecily his wife made a grant of lands, part of which lay in 'Ring Winit' ; Raines, loc. cit. 117.

NEWTON IN MAKERFIELD   NEWTON-LE-WILLOWS HALL

NEWTON IN MAKERFIELD : VILLAGE STREET, LOOKING TOWARDS CHURCH

recorded in 1664.[31a] The landowners contributing to the subsidy about 1556 were William Bretherton, John Maddock, William Serjeant, and Richard Wood.[32] In 1600 the resident freeholders were given as William Green, John Maddock, Philip Mainwaring, George Sorocold, John Tunstall, and Roger Wood.[33] The landowning contributors to the subsidy of 1628 were John Bretherton, the wife of James Eden, William Morris, James Maddock, and Thomas Serjeant.[34] To the land tax in 1787 the chief contributors were Peter Legh, — Brotherton, William Bankes, and — Blackburne.

Some of the inhabitants had their estates sequestered by the Commonwealth authorities.[35]

Among various place-names occurring in the charters may be recorded Apshaw, Heald, Kirkacre, and Pipersfield.

BOROUGH At an early date a borough was created, but the charter does not seem to have been preserved. The typical burgage consisted of a house with its toft, and an acre of land; a small rent was payable.[36] From 1559 to 1832 it returned two members of Parliament; the electors, according to a decision in 1797, were the freemen or burgesses, that is any persons 'seised of a corporeal estate of freehold in any house, building or lands within the borough of the value of 40*s.* a year and upwards'; in the case of a joint tenancy only one person could vote.[37] In practice Newton was a close borough, the members being nominees of the lord of the manor.

A market and two fairs were in 1301 granted by Edward I to John de Langton; the market was to be held every Saturday, and the fairs on the eve, day, and morrow of St. John *ante Portam Latinam* (6 May) and of St. Germain (31 July).[38]

CHURCH Although in 1066 'the church of the manor' was at Wigan, about 6 miles to the north, there may have been also a domestic chapel at the royal manor house. In the early part of the reign of Edward I, Robert Banastre, lord

---

his son William, twenty-five years of age; Duchy of Lanc. Inq. p.m. xvi, no. 27. This William is said to have died about 1640; *Visit.*

His son John succeeded. He was over seventy years of age in 1664, and married in 1620 Isabel daughter of Roger Nowell of Read and widow of John Byrom; Grappenhall Reg. Their son John was baptized at Winwick 30 Jan. 1622–3. At the beginning of the Civil War, John Bretherton, 'to free himself from the assaults and troubles put upon him by the Earl of Derby and his agents, left Lancashire and retired into Wales—then the king's quarters; for which his estate was sequestrated.' He wished to go to London to protest against this, but was advised to compound, and this he did in 1646 at a rental of £50. Afterwards the Commonwealth authorities were told that he had greatly undervalued his estate for the composition, and a new sequestration was ordered. He had taken the negative oath and the National covenant; *Royalist Comp. Papers,* i, 237–9. He made a settlement of the manor of Hey, and lands in Newton, Westhoughton, and Hindley, in 1654; Pal. of Lanc. Feet of F. bdle. 156, m. 142. He was buried 7 Sept. 1671, at Winwick, and his eldest son having died in the previous May, the heir was the grandson John, aged eleven in 1664. John the grandfather had a son Edward, who resided in Newton, and was buried in 1711; the baptisms of several children were recorded in the Winwick registers.

John Bretherton, the heir, died in 1679 and was buried at Winwick, the estate passing to his brother Thomas, aged seven in 1664. Thomas, who seems to have changed the spelling of the surname to Brotherton, was a barrister of Gray's Inn; and in 1693 at Gray's Inn Chapel he married Margaret Gunter of Aldbourne, Wilts.; *Mge. Alleg. Abp. Cant.* (Harl. Soc.), 259. In a fine concerning Hey in Aug. 1693, Thomas Brotherton, esq. was deforciant, and Thomas Gunter, esq. was plaintiff; Pal. of Lanc. Feet of F. bdle. 231, m. 62. Thomas Brotherton was one of the Tory members for Newton, from 1695 till 1701. He died in London 11 Jan. 1701–2, and was buried at Winwick; Pink and Beaven, *Parl. Repre. of Lancs.* 285; Winwick Reg. There is a monument to him in the church.

His successor was Thomas Brotherton, no doubt his so aged sixty, and 1 Sept. 1757. recovery of the m Pal. of Lanc. P seems to have scribed as 'of t whose son Will entered Chris C at the age of sev W. B. Brotherto of Hey, but was Charity inquiry liam Brotherton in possession in

of Makerfield, granted a rent of 12d. a year for the maintenance of the lamp of St. Mary in Winwick Church, as an acknowledgement of the permission he had received to endow a chantry in his chapel of Rokeden. This permission was granted by the prior and canons of Nostell, as patrons of Winwick, in 1285; the usual stipulation was made—that nothing should be done to the injury of the parish church.[39] Licence was granted or renewed by the Bishop of Lichfield in 1405 for service in the chapel at Rokeden.[40] In 1534 John Dunster was chaplain.[41] He was in 1548 celebrating for the souls of his founders.[42]

After the suppression of the chantry Dunster was allowed a pension and continued to reside. He appears to have conformed in 1562, but next year was absent from the visitation;[43] he was buried at Winwick in 1571. Ten years later there was a curate at Newton of scandalous character;[44] in 1590 the curate was 'no preacher,'[45] and two years afterwards there was no surplice for the minister.[46] About 1610 it was stated that there was seldom a curate, the stipend being but small.[47] It is probable that here, as in other chapelries, the legal services were more or less regularly conducted by a 'reading minister.'[48]

An improvement took place in the 17th century. A regular curate seems to have been appointed; the Commonwealth Surveyors in 1650 found that Richard Blackburne had given £20 a year for a 'preaching minister,' and recommended that Newton should be made a separate parish; the tithes of the township, worth £60 a year, had been appropriated to the minister's use.[49] This arrangement would cease at the Restoration; but Bishop Gastrell in 1718 found the curate's income to be over £38.[50] The chapel, now called St. Peter's, was rebuilt in 1684, consecrated in 1735, and enlarged in 1819 and 1835. The township became a separate rectory in 1841, the Earl of Derby being patron; but Emmanuel Church, War-

grave, built in that year, was made the parish church instead of the old chapel.[51] The latter had a district assigned to it in 1845 ;[52] Lord Newton is patron.

ST. PETER'S CHURCH stands at the east end of the long and wide village street, and is a modern building with chancel, north and south chapels and north vestry, nave and aisles with porches at the west ends of the aisles, and a west tower. A few mural tablets from the old church are preserved, and the wrought-iron altar-rails are of 18th-century style, but otherwise, all the fittings, oak screens and seats and alabaster pulpit, &c., are modern.

The following is a list of curates and vicars :—

oc. 1622	— Gee [53]
? 1635	William Thompson [54]
oc. 1645	Thomas Norman [55]
oc. 1650	Thomas Blackburne [56]
oc. 1684	Samuel Needham, B.A.[57] (St. John's Coll. Camb.)
1686	Edward Allanson, M.A.[58] (Magdalene Coll. Camb.)
1735	Philip Naylor, B.A.[59] (Trinity Coll. Camb.)
—	Ashburnham Legh, M.A.[60] (Brasenose Coll. and All Souls, Oxf.)
1775	John Garton, M.A. (Brasenose Coll. Oxf.)
oc. 1806–13	Francis Bryan [61]
—	Robert Barlow
1823	Peter Legh, B.A.[62] (Trinity Coll. Camb.)
1864	Thomas Whitley, M.A. (Emman. Coll. Camb.)
1871	Herbert Monk, M.A. (Trin. Coll. Camb.)
1898	James Ryder

The church of St. John the Baptist at Earlestown was built in 1878, and had a district assigned to it in 1879.[63] The rector of Newton is patron.

A school, called Dean School, was built in 1646 by John Stirrup.[64]

---

[39] Reg. St. Oswald of Nostell (B.M.). Thomas Gentle was 'chaplain' in 1312; Raines, loc. cit. 127.

[40] Raines, Lancs. Chant. (Chet. Soc.), i, 75 n. Licence for an oratory at Newton had been granted to Ralph de Langton in 1374; Lich. Epis. Reg. Stretton, v, fol. 30.

[41] Valor Eccl. (Rec. Com.), v, 220.

[42] Lancs. Chant. i, 74; the foundation is erroneously ascribed to 'Sir Thomas Langton, knight.' The clear income was 68s. 3d. derived chiefly from Walton-le-Dale and Preston. A chalice and two sets of vestments belonged to it.

[43] Visit. Lists at Chester.

[44] Articles were exhibited in 1581 against Robert Bradshaw, clerk, curate of Newton, to the effect that he had become 'infamous' among his parishioners and a 'slander to the ministry,' being a 'common drunkard and a common gamner or player at tables and other unlawful games'; further he had solemnized 'divers unlawful marriages,' in one of which a sister of the squire of Risley was a party; Ches. Consistory Ct. P.

[45] Lydiate Hall, 248; quoting S.P. Dom. Eliz. ccxxxv, 4.

[46] Trans. Hist. Soc. (new ser.), x, 190.

[47] Hist. MSS. Com. Rep. xiv, App. iv, 13.

[48] Richard Pickering was 'reader' in 1609; Raines MSS. (Chet. Lib.), xxii, 298.

[49] Commonwealth Ch. Surv. (Rec. Soc. Lancs. and Ches.), 47.

[50] Notitia Cestr. (Chet. Soc.), ii, 271.

A pension out of the duchy had been settled by Edward VI, viz. £3 1s. 7d., the old chantry rent, less the tenth retained by the Crown; £25 came from an inclosure of common, and £10 was allowed by the rector of Winwick.

[51] Notitia Cestr. ii, 273 n.

[52] Lond. Gaz. 11 Feb. 1845.

[53] Visit. List at Chester. Bishop Gastrell says that a curate or 'perpetual preacher' was licensed in 1620; Notitia Cestr. ii, 272.

[54] In 1635 the ship-money collectors conceived his stipend to be insufficient to maintain him and his wife and children, and therefore forbore to lay any tax upon him; Misc. (Rec. Soc. Lancs. and Ches.), i, 110.

[55] Plundered Mins. Accts. (Rec. Soc. Lancs. and Ches.), i, 6. He signed the 'Harmonious Consent.' His will was proved in 1649.

[56] He 'came into the place' by the general consent of the chapelry, and was a 'godly preaching minister, supplying the cure diligently upon the Lord's day,' but he had not observed the recent day of humiliation appointed by Parliament; Commonwealth Ch. Surv. 48. Roger Low heard him preach at Newton in 1664; he heard Mr. Taylor there in the following year. It is possible that these were Nonconformists; Local Glean. Lancs. and Ches. i, 178, 180.

[57] Mentioned in the Winwick registers in 1684 and 1685. Also rector of Claughton for a time. He was master of

Stockport School 1674 to 1683; afterwards he had a school at West Bradenham, Norfolk; Earwaker, East Ches. i, 417.

[58] Stratford's Visitation List at Chester. He was buried at Winwick in 1731; will proved 1733. He was also rector of Grappenhall as a 'warming-pan' from 1708 to 1722; Lancs. and Ches. Antiq. Notes, ii, 60.

[59] The church papers at Chester begin at this time, when the sentence of consecration was given.

[60] Also rector of Davenham, 1745–75.

[61] The following was his story : 'Parson Brien [Bryon], an apostate Jesuit, was [Dec. 1806] curate of Newton. Went at college by the name of Francis Plowden out of gratitude to Lady Goring, whose coachman his father was, and who sent him to college. Came over to mission in Lancashire in 1751; 'Ghented,' 1755; taught 'little figures' for some time and at petition of Squire Dicconson allowed to come over to be his chaplain 1758. Company of Colonel Legh, &c., completed his ruin. He read his recantation 1761 and obtained curacy of Newton'; Misc. (Cath. Rec. Soc.), iv, 258; Foley, Rec. S.J. vii, 100. He was buried at Winwick in 1813 aged eighty-eight.

[62] He was one of the illegitimate sons of Thomas Peter Legh of Lyme; Ormerod, Ches. (ed. Helsby), iii, 678.

[63] Lond. Gaz. 17 May 1879.

[64] Notitia Cestr. ii, 273; End. Char. Rep.

The Wesleyan Methodists have a church, Brunswick, at Earlestown ; and the Primitive Methodists also have one there. The Welsh Calvinistic Methodists have a place of worship at Earlestown ; as also have the Welsh Baptists. The English Baptists have a chapel in Newton, where there is also a Free Gospel mission room.

Occasional preaching by Congregational ministers began in 1806, the steps of the town cross being the pulpit till the constable interfered, but there was no chapel till 1842. A new church was built in 1878, largely through the benefactions of the family of Richard Evans, the great colliery proprietors.[65] In the churchyard is a fine monument of Mr. Evans erected by his workpeople.

The Roman Catholic church of St. Mary and St. John, built in 1864, originated about three years earlier.[66]

Ashton in Makerfield lie upon the Bunter series of the New Red Sandstone.

The principal road, all along lined with dwellings, is that from St. Helens, passing east and north-east through Blackbrook and Haydock village to meet the great north and south road from Wigan to Warrington. The Liverpool, St. Helens and South Lancashire Railway, worked by the Great Central Company, passes through the township, and has a station at Haydock ; and two others, called Ashton in Makerfield and Haydock Park, on the boundary of Ashton. An electric tramway service connects it with St. Helens. The St. Helens Canal goes by the side of Sankey Brook.

Coal-mining is the great industry of the place.

A local board was formed in 1872,[2] and in 1894 became an urban district council of twelve members.

Haydock Lodge is now a lunatic asylum. A cottage hospital was opened in 1886. A stone celt was found here.[3]

HAYDOCK

Hedoc, 1169 ; Heddoch, 1170 ; Haidoc, 1212. The local pronunciation is Haddock.

This township has an area of 2,409 acres.[1] From its situation between Newton and Ashton it seems to have been cut off from the former township. Clipsley Brook separates it from Garswood in Ashton, and Sankey Brook forms the south-west boundary. The population in 1901 numbered 8,575.

Haydock is varied in its natural features, sometimes undulating, sometimes flat. On the west the surroundings are unpicturesque but typical of a colliery country, scattered over with pit-banks and shafts of mines. On the east the country is pleasanter, with fields and plantations, and in this part is the locally celebrated race-course of Haydock Park. Crops of oats, wheat, potatoes, and cabbages seem to be the principal produce of the clayey soil. The geological formation consists largely of the Coal Measures, but the old Haydock Park and a small area to the west of the main road leading from Newton to

HAYDOCK of Haydock. *Argent a cross with a fleur-de-lis sable in the first quarter*

---

[65] Nightingale, *Lancs. Nonconf.* iv, 144. Richard Evans of Haydock died in 1864 ; his sons Josiah and Joseph in 1873 and 1889. One of the daughters married Richard Pilkington of Windle ; the other, Ruth, built the memorial churches at Rainhill and Haydock.

[66] The ancient religion appears to have died out very quickly in this township. Thomas Langton, Baron of Newton, was in 1590 'in general note of evil affection in religion,' though 'in some degree of conformity'; his wife was a 'recusant and indicted thereof.' Peter Legh of Lyme, who had just succeeded his grandfather, had married a daughter of Sir Gilbert Gerard, Master of the Rolls, a decided Protestant, and was 'of great good hope ;' *Lydiate Hall,* 243, 244, 247 ; for the Langton family see further, pp. 258, 260. The recusant roll of 1641 gives only one name in Newton ; *Trans. Hist. Soc.* (new ser.), xiv, 244.

Roger Ashton of Newton in 1653 petitioned to be allowed to contract for his estate, two-thirds having been sequestered for recusancy ; *Royalist Comp. Papers,* i, 112.

[1] 2,411, including 30 of inland water ; Census of 1901.

[3] *Lond. Gaz.* 16 July 1872.

Thurstan and his son Sir Robert, and lapsed to the Crown by the forfeiture of Henry, Duke of Exeter, in 1461.[11]

It is unlikely that the Hugh de Haydock of 1212 was the Hugh acting on inquests of 1242 and 1265 ;[12] more probably the latter was a son. Hugh de Haydock had a son Gilbert, who married Alice daughter of Matthew de Bold, and received lands in Bold with her.[18] Their son and heir was named Matthew, and in 1286 ten messuages, eight oxgangs and 4 acres of land in Haydock and Bold were settled on Matthew by his father,[14] and the moiety of the manor of

Haydock was granted in 1292.[15] Some other acts of Gilbert's are known ;[16] he seems to have died about 1300.[17]

Matthew de Haydock lived till about 1322 ;[18] a number of his charters are extant,[19] showing that he acquired fresh properties ; one of these, in Walton le Dale, he gave to his son Hugh.[20] His son Gilbert succeeded. He had a grant of free warren in Haydock and Bradley in 1344 ; also leave to make a park in Haydock.[21] By his wife Emma[22] there was a numerous offspring, but elder sons, named Matthew and Gilbert, seem to have died young,[23] and the

---

[11] Maud, widow of Robert de Holland, died seised of the manor of Haydock, held of Robert de Langton in socage by a service of 6s. 8d. and suit to Newton ; Inq. p.m. 23 Edw. III (1st nos.), no. 58. See also Lancs. Inq. p.m. (Chet. Soc.), ii, 3.
In September, 1458, Henry Duke of Exeter, and Anne his wife (sister of Edw. IV), leased their manors of Haydock, Newton, Breightmet, Harwood, and Over Darwen to John Dutton and Hugh Dawne for thirty-nine years at the rent of £19 6s. 8d., of which £15 was allowed to John and Hugh ; Raines, loc. cit. 65.
In 1465 Edw. IV granted to his sister Anne and her heirs by her husband Henry late Duke of Exeter the manors of Newton and Haydock ; and three (?) years later, the duchess having died and the remainder to Anne daughter of the said duchess having failed through her death childless, Edw. IV granted these manors to his consort Elizabeth, the queen ; Add. MS. 32107, fol. 171, referring to Pat. 5 Edw. IV, pt. ii, m. 3, and 8 Edw. IV, pt. iii, m. 3. There is some error in the latter reference, as Anne, Duchess of Exeter, did not die until 1476 ; G.E.C. Complete Peerage, iii, 298.
At an inquiry made in 1506 at the instance of Peter Legh it was found that half the manor was his, as heir of the Haydock family, and the other half was the Crown's, by the forfeiture of Henry, Duke of Exeter, and the failure of issue ; Raines, loc. cit. 499–503 ; Duchy of Lanc. Misc. Bks. xxi, 7, 7a. The Holland mesne lordship over the whole of Haydock was ignored, and in 1541 Peter Legh was stated to have held his half of the manor at a rent of 6s. 8d. directly of the lord of Newton ; Duchy of Lanc. Inq. p.m. viii, no. 10.
[12] Lancs. Inq. and Extents, i, 74, 146, 232. The Hugh of 1212 had married a daughter of Adam de Lawton ; ibid. 73.
Hugh de Haydock granted to William de Coldcotes, in free marriage with Amice his daughter, land in Haydock which Henry Roebuck formerly held in Fathercroft ; Raines, loc. cit. 221. The grantee afterwards restored it to Gilbert son of Hugh, for '100s. given in his great need ' ; ibid.
[18] Ibid. 277 ; Cronshaw, Timberhead, and Blacklache are named among the bounds. Hugh and Robert, rectors of Standish and Winwick, were among the witnesses.
Gilbert de Haydock, with the consent of Alice his wife, made a grant of land in Bold to Alan de Penketh ; Dods. MSS. cxlii, fol. 217b, no. 168.
[14] Final Conc. (Rec. Soc. Lancs. and Ches.), i, 164.
[15] Ibid. i, 174. Richard de Ince and Alice his wife put in their claim. This seems to be the latest notice of the Ince family's claim on the manor.
Matthew was probably not the eldest

son, for in 1260 Gilbert de Southworth granted all his lands in Warrington to Hugh son of Gilbert de Haydock in marriage with his daughter Agnes ; Raines, loc. cit. 75.
[16] In 1299 he gave Matthew his son lands in Haydock and Bold, the natives with their sequel, &c. ; Raines, loc. cit. 235. At another time he gave his son four oxgangs of land—three once held by Ralph, Orme, and Moses, and one called ' Waltheuronys oxegeng,' with Dicherys croft, and other lands ; the son to perform the services due to the chief lord of the fee, ' my lord Robert de Holland,' and his heirs, and suit of a judge of the court of Newton for the mediety of the manor of Haydock ; ibid. 223 ; also 229. Probably in connexion with one of these grants Gilbert wrote in 1285 to ' his beloved and faithful man ' William son of Richard le Roter of Cayley, telling him that he had granted his service to his son Matthew, to whom in future the accustomed homage and service must be rendered ; ibid. 227.
From William son of Richard de Orrell he purchased in 1273 an acre in Ladymarsh, in a field called the Halgh ; ibid. 123.
[17] In 1304 William son of Richard de Haydock released to his ' chief lord' Matthew de Haydock all claim on lands which should have descended to him on the death of Hugh his brother ; apparently this was two oxgangs ; ibid. 237.
[18] His son Gilbert appears to have been in full possession in 1323 ; among other acts he granted Richard de Ince a rent of 13s. 4d. from his lands in Haydock, Bold, and Golborne ; ibid. 33.
In 1329 are named the executors of the will of Matthew de Haydock, viz. Gilbert de Haydock, Peter de Winwick, chaplain, and Hugh de Hulme ; De Banco R. 279, m. 300 d.
[19] The earliest which has a date (1284–5) is by Robert Banastre, lord of Makerfield, to Matthew son of Gilbert de Haydock, granting land in Newton called Galpesch—Waterfall Clough and Kulne Clough are named in the boundaries ; also in Bentfurlong ; the rent was 11s. ; Raines, loc. cit. 123.
In 1304 William son of Richard de Haydock released to his chief lord, Matthew son of Gilbert de Haydock, all his claim in two oxgangs in Haydock, and all he had by hereditary right after the death of Hugh his brother ; ibid. 237.
Eleanor, the daughter of Matthew de Haydock, married Simon son of William de Walton, and in 1340 had sons Henry and Gilbert ; ibid. 253. Gilbert de Haydock had grants of lands in Spellow and Newsham from his brother-in-law ; ibid.
[20] Ibid. 245 ; dated at Haydock, 6 Aug. 1321.
[21] Chart. R. 18 Edw. III, m. 5, no. 24 ; Raines, loc. cit. 505.

[22] Gilbert de Haydock and Emma his wife had a grant in Burtonwood in 1332 ; ibid. 531.
Sir Gilbert de Haydock was knight of the shire in 1320, 1321, and 1324 ; Pink and Beaven, Parl. Repre. of Lancs. 19, 20. He is not described as knight in later deeds. In the return of 1324 the name of Thomas de Lathom was substituted for his.
[28] In 1336 William le Boteler of Warrington granted to Gilbert de Haydock and Matthew his son land in Burtonwood ; Raines, loc. cit. 293. It is possible that he was the Matthew de Haydock who accompanied Lord Stafford to Guienne in 1345 ; Rymer, Foedera (ed. Cayley), iii, 36. In 1347 Sir Matthew de Haydock was concerned in the abduction of Margery de la Beche ; Cal. Pat. 1345–8, p. 310. Gilbert de Haydock was also charged, but pardoned soon afterwards on the king being assured that he was ' wholly guiltless;' ibid. 319, 345, &c.
Gilbert was described as ' son and heir' in 1325 in a grant by William son of Richard de Orrell of land in Newton ; Raines, loc. cit. 35. He is not further mentioned as son and heir ; but a Gilbert son of Gilbert de Haydock was living in 1343, when he had a grant in Newton from John son of Richard le Perpont ; ibid. 145.
A settlement of the moiety of the manor of Haydock and lands in Haydock, Bold, Newton, and other townships was made in 1332 ; the children of Gilbert are thus named : Matthew, John, Richard, Peter, Leonard, Nicholas, Anabel, Eleanor, and Katherine ; Final Conc. ii, 82 ; Raines, loc. cit. 329.
In another deed of the same year the remainders to the children of Gilbert son of Matthew de Haydock are thus given : Matthew, Peter, Richard, John, Anabel, and Eleanor ; ibid. 236. The two daughters are named as late as 1368 ; ibid. 165. In the remainders in a provision for the younger children made in 1335 the order is John, Richard, Katherine, Anabel, and Eleanor ; with final remainder to Matthew ; ibid. 43.
Gilbert de Haydock was living in 1354, when he received a grant of lands in Newton from Sir Robert de Langton ; ibid. 157.
At Christmas 1361, Gilbert le Norreys, administrator of the goods of Gilbert de Haydock, arranged for certain payments to be made according to the will of the deceased : £4 to Geoffrey de Worsley, 33s. 4d. each to the churches of Winwick and Warrington, and £5 7s. 6d. to certain chaplains singing divine service for his soul ; ibid. 53.
A contemporary, Henry de Haydock, was knight of the shire from 1328 to 1337 ; Pink and Beaven, op. cit. 22. One of the name, brother of Gilbert de Haydock, is named in 1347 ; Raines, loc. cit. 421.

heir to the manor was John de Haydock, who was in possession by 1358.[24]

He married Joan, daughter of Sir Thomas de Dutton,[25] and died 12 December 1387, holding the moiety of the manor of Haydock and lands there of Sir John de Holland of Thorpe Watervill in socage by a rent of 17s.; holding also various lands in Newton, Golborne, and Bold. His son and heir Gilbert was thirty years of age.[26] Of Sir Gilbert's children the heir was his daughter Joan, who carried this and other manors to the family of her first husband, Peter de Legh of Lyme in Cheshire.[27] She afterwards married Sir Richard de Molyneux of Sefton, and her tomb is in Sefton Church.[28] The manor has since remained a part of the Legh inheri-

tance,[29] Lord Newton being the present lord as well as chief landowner.[30]

Numerous other branches of the Haydock family [31] and minor holders existed in the 13th and 14th centuries.[32] No resident freeholders are named in the lists of 1556, 1600, and 1628.

The Ven. Edmund Arrowsmith, S.J., executed for his priesthood at Lancaster in 1628, was born in Haydock.[33] Katherine Arrowsmith, a leaseholder under Sir Peter Legh, had two-thirds of her tenement sequestered by the Commonwealth authorities for her recusancy; Thurstan her son, 'a Protestant and conformable,' claimed it in 1652, and it was allowed him on his taking the oath of abjuration.[34] Thurstan Callan and Mary his mother, widow of William

---

[24] He had a grant from Sir Robert de Langton in that year; Raines, loc. cit. 157. He had earlier, in 1350, purchased lands in Newton from William son of John son of John the Piper, Emma, widow of the younger John, assenting; ibid. 155. Piperfield in Newton was the subject of a grant by him in 1373; ibid. 146.

[25] John son of Gilbert de Haydock and Joan his wife occur in 1353; Assize R. 435, m. 32; she was the widow of Richard le Boteler, with whom she had a third of the Boteler lands; these she took to her second husband, whose heirs retained them, an act which led to disputes between the families not settled till the 16th century; see Raines, loc. cit. 73, 79, 80.

In 1368 a number of family arrangements were made. William de Wigan, chaplain, regranted to John de Haydock and Joan his wife, daughter of Sir Thomas de Dutton, various lands in Newton, with remainders to the children of John and Joan, and then to Sir Lawrence de Dutton, and Anabel and Eleanor, sisters of John de Haydock; Raines, loc. cit. 165. A grant by John son of Sir Robert de Langton names the children of John and Joan thus: Gilbert, Matthew, and Nicholas, Ellen, Emma, Agnes, and Philippa; ibid. 167. Four years later Talpeshaw in Newton was granted with remainders (after the children) to Sir Lawrence de Dutton (brother of Joan), Sir Geoffrey de Worsley, and Sir John Mascy of Tatton and his wife Alice daughter of Geoffrey de Worsley; ibid. 238. The reason for the Worsley remainder is that Geoffrey, the father of Sir Geoffrey and Alice, had married Anabel daughter of Gilbert de Haydock; ibid. 421.

In 1352 John and Richard sons of Gilbert de Haydock were acquitted of the murder of Adam son of William del Moore; Assize R. 434, m. 2. Provision for Richard was made in 1348; Final Conc. ii, 127. Richard died before July 1361, when his lands reverted to his brother John; Raines, loc. cit. 53.

[26] Lancs. Inq. p.m. (Chet. Soc.), i, 31. John de Haydock had been summoned to the Scrope-Grosvenor trial in 1386, being then sixty-four years of age; Roll (ed. Nicolas), 290.

[27] In Sept. 1394, Gilbert son and heir of John de Haydock enfeoffed Richard de Carleton, rector of Warrington, and others of his manors of Haydock and Bradley, and various lands in Haydock, Newton, Golborne, and Bold; Raines, loc. cit. 57. A year later Henry de Haydock released to the trustees all his claim in the manors; ibid. 59; and shortly

afterwards Sir John de Holland of Thorpe Watervill leased to Sir Gilbert de Haydock the park in Haydock; ibid.

In 1420 Sir Gilbert de Haydock, Sir Peter de Legh and Joan his wife received from the trustee, Reginald del Downes, mayor of Macclesfield, who had married Sir Gilbert's daughter Alice, a release of his interest in their manors in Lancashire; ibid. 63. The marriage covenant is given on p. 525; Gilbert de Haydock, kt., and Sibyl his wife, and Peter de Legh, esq., were parties; the date is illegible, but that it was in or before 1414 is shown by another deed; ibid. 393. The son and heir, Peter de Legh, was born in June 1415.

The Bishop of Lichfield granted Gilbert de Haydock licence for his oratories at Haydock and Bradley in Dec. 1387; Lich. Epis. Reg. Scrope, v, fol. 123b.

Sir Gilbert de Haydock had from Ric. II a protection from serving as escheator, &c., and this was confirmed by Hen. IV in 1403; Pal. of Lanc. Ch. Misc. 1–9, m. 15. He is last named in 1425; Lancs. Inq. p.m. (Chet. Soc.), ii, 12.

[28] See the account of Sefton. She died in Jan. 1439–40.

[29] Duchy of Lanc. Inq. p.m. vi, no. 63; viii, no. 10; xxviii, no. 32; xxix, no. 16. Accounts of the Legh family are in Earwaker, East Ches. ii, 293–306, and Ormerod, Ches. (ed. Helsby), iii, 673–8.

[30] In 1787 Peter Legh contributed £42 out of the £43 levied as land tax.

[31] Some of these have been noticed in the account of the parent family, to which most of the minor properties appear to have returned by purchase or inheritance.

William son of Hugh son of Hugh de Haydock granted to Matthew son of Gilbert de Haydock land by Matthew's orchard in Oldfield, to be held of his chief lord, Sir Robert de Holland; Raines, loc. cit. 229. Henry son of William de Haydock granted land in Oldfield (or Heldfield), abutting on Taylor's Marsh, to his chief lord, Matthew de Haydock; ibid. 227. William son of Richard son of Hugh de Haydock gave to the same Matthew four selions in Aldenather, Crooked Beancroft, and Hengrave; ibid. 235. The seal shows a lion rampant reguardant.

[32] Hawise daughter of Henry de Hargrave in 1335 made a grant to Gilbert son of Matthew de Haydock; ibid. 41. Richard son of Stephen del Edge confirmed this charter; ibid. 43. The same or another Hawise was in 1327 the wife of Thomas son of Agnes del Shaw; ibid. 37. Robert son of Laysig sold for 100s.

Callan, in 1717 as 'papists' registered their estate in the house called Blackbrook.[35]

The Hospitallers' estate at *CAYLEY* was held by Guy Holland about 1540.[36] The Holland family had other estates in the same part of Haydock.[37]

In connexion with the Established Church St. James's was built in 1866;[38] there is a mission chapel called St. Mark's. The rector of Ashton in Makerfield is the patron.

A Wesleyan Methodist chapel was built in 1846; and a Primitive Methodist one in 1875. The Baptists have a place of worship, erected in 1876. A Congregational church was built in 1892 by Miss Ruth Evans, in memory of her brother Joseph, one of the colliery owners of the district.[39]

The Roman Catholic school-chapel of the English Martyrs was opened in 1879; it was at first served from Blackbrook, St. Helens, but a resident priest was appointed in 1887.[40]

WINWICK WITH HULME

Winequic, 1170; Winewich, 1204; Wynewyc, Wynequic, 1212; Wynequick, 1277. The suffix -quick or -whick long survived.

Hulm, 1276; Holum, xiii cent.; Holm, 1279.

Winwick consists of open country, and is chiefly celebrated for the beautiful parish church in the village, which stands slightly elevated above the surrounding country. There are many picturesque old houses, some with thatched roofs. Some little distance north of the town is St. Oswald's Well, a shallow depression in a field, and easily overlooked on account of its insignificant appearance. There are still some fine beech trees around the village, which are particularly

noticeable in a country where timber has dwindled to apologies for trees. The outlying land is composed of arable and pasture land. Crops of potatoes, oats, and wheat flourish in the loamy soil, with clay in places, over a solid sandstone rock. There is some marshy mossland, bare of trees, on the south-west. The geological formation consists wholly of the Bunter series of the New Red Sandstone; to the south-west of Winwick and south of Hulme of the Upper Mottled Sandstone of that series, elsewhere of the Pebble Beds.

This township, which has an area of 1,440 acres,[1] lies on the east side of the Sankey; Newton Brook bounds it on the north, while another small brook on the south cuts it off from Orford and Warrington. The southern end is called Hulme; there is no defined boundary between it and Winwick proper. The township was enlarged in 1894 by the addition of Orford from Warrington;[1a] and it has been divided into three wards—Winwick, Hulme, and Orford—for the election of its parish council.

The principal road leads north from Warrington to Wigan; it is to the east of the old Roman road. At the church it divides; one branch goes by Newton and Ashton, and the other by Golborne and Ince, to Wigan.

The London and North-Western Company's main line to the north passes through the township, with a junction for Earlestown near the northern boundary. The Sankey Canal passes along the western boundary.

A great lunatic asylum has been erected by the County Council on the lands of the former rectory.

Two encounters took place here in the Civil War; in 1643 Colonel Assheton routed the Cavaliers,[2] and in 1648 Cromwell overtook and defeated the Duke of Hamilton and his Scottish force.[3] This battle took

---

[35] *Engl. Cath. Non-jurors*, 114.

[36] Kuerden MSS. v, fol. 84; the rent was 12d. In 1546 Sir Peter Legh acquired Guy Holland's lands in Haydock; Pal. of Lanc. Feet of F. bdle. 12, m. 196.

[37] Sir Thurstan de Holland granted to William his son all his part of Cayley in Haydock, the bounds beginning where Kemesley Clough fell into the Sankey and going across outside the hedge of Cayley to Clippesley Brook and Blackbrook, then up Sankey to the starting point. He further gave him three oxgangs in the Butterscrofts under the wood of Haydock, with the usual easements and common rights. A rent of a mark was to be paid yearly to Sir Thurstan during his life, and nothing afterwards; but the rent of 12d. due to the Hospitallers was to be paid by William de Holland and his heirs; Raines, loc. cit. 229. He also granted Barley Metes to William; ibid. 225. Matthew son of Gilbert de Haydock granted William son of Thurstan de Holland land in Cayley in the Blackridding (or in Warrington Cliff), in exchange for another piece on Ewittinges Hedge, abutting upon Hengrave; ibid. 231, 233. In 1307 William son of Sir Thurstan demised to his lord William son of Sir Robert de Holland two oxgangs in Haydock for a term of sixteen years at a rent of 11s. Seven years later Sir William de Holland gave land near the Blackridding to Richard son of William de Holland of Cayley, in exchange for the two oxgangs Sir William had on lease; ibid. 31, 33. William son of Richard de Holland of Cayley is mentioned in 1339; ibid. 45.

Margaret widow of William de Holland of Cayley in 1347 leased to Gilbert de Haydock and John his son for six years lands in Cayley, which she held by reason of the minority of her son Richard, at a rent of 40s.; ibid. 47. The son may be the Richard de Cayley to whom in the following year John son of Gilbert de Haydock gave all his lands and buildings in Haydock; ibid. 49. Another William de Holland of Cayley occurs in 1383; ibid. 57.

[38] A district was assigned in 1864; *Lond. Gaz.* 30 Aug.

[39] Nightingale, *Lancs. Nonconf.* iv, 166; preaching had begun a few years earlier.

[40] *Liverpool Cath. Ann.* 1901.

[1] Including 1,091 in Winwick and 349 in Hulme. The census of 1901 gives 2,081, but this includes Orford. The population, 1,253, also includes Orford.

[1a] Local Govt. Bd. Order 31665.

[2] 23 May 1643. 'Whilst the duty (of prayer and fasting) was in performing tidings came of the taking of Winwick Church and steeple, they on the steeple standing on terms till God sent a deadly messenger out of a fowling piece to one of them; also a strong hall [the rectory] possessed by professed Roman Catholics and stored with provision, as if it had been purposely laid in both for our supply and ease'; *Civil War Tracts* (Chet. Soc.), 138.

For a counter attack on the parsonage in 1650, and its tragic results, see the account of Rixton.

[3] Cromwell wrote: 'We could not engage the enemy until we came within

three miles of Warrington, and then the enemy made a stand at a pass near Winwick. We held them in some dispute till our army came up, they maintaining the pass with great resolution for many hours, ours and theirs coming to push of pike and very close charges, and forced us to give ground; but our men, by the blessing of God, quickly recovered it, and charging very home upon them, beat them from their standing, where we killed about a thousand of them and took (as we believe) about two thousand prisoners, and prosecuted them home to Warrington town'; *Civil War Tracts*, 264. It is stated that the 'foot threw down their arms and ran into Winwick Church,' where they were kept under guard; ibid. This fight took place 19 Aug. 1648.

Another account states: 'The greatest stand they (the Scots) made was between Newton and Winwick, in a strait passage in that lane that they made very strong and forcible, so that Cromwell's men could not fight them. But by the information of the people thereabouts and by their direction they went so into the fields that they came about so that they drove them up to that little green place of ground short of Winwick church and there they made a great slaughter of them, and then pursued them to Warrington'; *Lancs. War* (Chet. Soc.), 66. In the notes (p. 145) is an extract from Heath's *Chron.* (323): 'The Scots at Red Bank fight were commanded by a little spark in a blue bonnet who performed the part of an excellent commander and was killed on the spot.'

place at Red Bank, near the border of Newton; and Gallows Croft, on the Newton side, is said to mark the place where many of the prisoners captured were hanged.[4]

Winwick Wake ceased in 1828.[4]

MANOR The rector of *WINWICK* having been from before the Conquest lord of the manor and owner of almost all the land, the story of the place is the story of the rectors above related. The lords of Makerfield enumerated Winwick as a member of their fee,[5] but the only lay owners appear to have been the Southworth family, holding a little land directly of the lord of Makerfield.[6] Under an Act of Parliament passed in 1884 the Ecclesiastical Commissioners became lords of the manor in 1890, and the hall was sold to the County Council.

In 1086 the church of St. Oswald held two ploughlands exempt from all taxation,[7] and was given by Roger of Poitou to the canons of St. Oswald, Nostell. Under them in 1212 Richard, the rector of Winwick, held two-thirds of the land, and Robert de Walton the remainder.[8] Robert had granted out his portion—three oxgangs—to Alfred de Ince and three to Hugh de Haydock.[9] If Robert's interest were

merely temporary his grants would probably expire at his death; but similar grants were made by the rectors, and a few particulars of them have been preserved. All the land seems to have been recovered by the rectors by the beginning of the 14th century.[10]

But few incidents are recorded of the township.

The lease of the rectory from time to time by absentee parsons resulted in the hall being occupied by the lessee or steward. One of these, Gowther Legh, founded the grammar school. A later one, Sir Thomas Stanley, son of Edward, Earl of Derby, made the rectory his residence. His son, Sir Edward Stanley, was in 1590 in 'some degree of conformity' to the established religion, but 'in general note of evil affection' towards it.[11] From the beginning of the 17th century the rectors seem to have been usually resident, and as they had complete authority it is not to be supposed that expressions of nonconformity were numerous.[12] Their rule appears to have been mild and readily acquiesced in by the people.[13]

John Launder paid to the subsidy of 1628 as holding lands.[14] Under the Commonwealth, Thomas Goulden, member of a recusant family of long continuance in the district, petitioned to be admitted as tenant of the sequestered two-thirds of his estate.[15]

---

[4] Baines, *Lancs.* (ed. 1836), iii, 647.

[5] *Lancs. Inq. p.m.* (Chet. Soc.), ii, 99, &c.

Winwick seems to have been at one time appropriated to the church and rectory, Hulme having been the township name.

[6] This seems to have begun in a grant by William de Sankey about 1260 of land in Hulme held by a charter of Henry de Ince; Towneley MS. HH, no. 1654. In the inquisition after the death of Thomas Southworth, taken in 1547, the tenement in Hulme is grouped with the others 'held of Sir Thomas Langton in socage'; Duchy of Lanc. Inq. p.m. vii, no. 23.

Thurstan Southworth, as a landowner, paid to a subsidy in Queen Mary's time; Mascy of Rixton D.

[7] *V.C.H. Lancs.* i, 286a.

[8] *Lancs. Inq. and Extents* (Rec. Soc. Lancs. and Ches.), i, 72.

[9] Ibid.

[10] Two charters relating to the township are contained among the Legh of Lyme deeds in Raines' MSS. (Chet. Lib.), xxxviii, 393: (1) Robert de Winwick released to Gilbert de Haydock all his claim to four oxgangs in Hulme, being a fourth part of the vill, which Hugh de Haydock had formerly purchased from him, the said Gilbert having given Robert 40s. 'in his great need.' (2) John the clerk of Hulme granted to Hugh son of John de Haydock, in free marriage with Margery his daughter, two messuages in Hulme and a croft called Flaxhalgh.

Henry de Hulme granted a house for a rent of 4d. payable at Halton Fair; Towneley MS. GG, no. 997. William son of John de Hulme granted to Robert, 'called Robin,' land between that of Robert de Holland and Hugh de Hulme.

In 1276 Simon the Messer, of Warrington, claimed four oxgangs of land in Hulme against Richard de Haydock, and other messuages, &c. against Robert the Smith, Austin vicar of Winwick, Richard de Houghton, Hugh son of John de Haydock, and others; De Banco R. 15, m. 15 d.; 17, m. 84 d.

At the same time the vicar (rector) of Winwick had leave to withdraw his plea against Thurstan de Holland and other tenants in Hulme; Assize R. 405. He proceeded against William son of John and others respecting three oxgangs of land of which he alleged his predecessor Robert was seised in the time of Henry III, Henry de Sefton having taken possession after Robert's death on the allegation that they were a lay fee; De Banco R. 18, m. 15; 19, m. 54 d. William son of John called the Prior of Nostell to warrant him.

Margery, widow of Robert de Kinknall, who claimed dower in two oxgangs in Golborne against Robert Banastre, also claimed lands in Hulme against Peter the chaplain and others—including Austin the vicar—in respect of four oxgangs of land; De Banco R. 20, m. 15 d, 26 d.

Austin the vicar prosecuted his claim against Robert de Holland respecting three oxgangs in Hulme, and William de Aintree, on being called to warrant, averred that his father Henry died seised, and the charter to Thurstan, father of Robert de Holland, never having been executed; De Banco R. 23, m. 21; 28, m. 41; 30, m. 33.

In 1292 John son of Hugh de Hulme claimed an oxgang in Hulme from John the vicar of Winwick, but did not prosecute it; Assize R. 408, m. 21. In 1313 John de Bamburgh, then rector, claimed six messuages and three oxgangs in Winwick from John son of Hugh de Hulme, who called John, Prior of Nostell, to warrant him, alleging that he held by charter of Henry de Aberford, a former prior; De Banco R. 199, m. 37 d.; 207, m. 108; 212, m. 431 d.

It should be remembered that Henry de Sefton represented the Alfred de Ince of 1212, and that William de Aintree was a Haydock. John de Chisenhale, rector of Winwick, asserted in 1334 that William le Boteler of Warrington and others had disseised him of a mill and certain lands in Winwick. In reply it was urged that John was 'vicar,' not 'parson,' of Winwick, but in general the jury sustained his

claim. William le Boteler, grandfather of the defendant, had purchased from Richard son of Hugh de Hulme an acre of land in Winwick, from olden time arable; Coram Rege R. 297, m. 6 d.

[11] *Lydiate Hall*, 244; quoting S.P. Dom. Eliz. ccxxxv, 4. He was 'of great living.' His wife, Lady Lucy, was an indicted recusant. Sir John Fortescue, who married Sir Edward Stanley's daughter and enjoyed the rectory, was also a recusant; *Cal. of Com. for Compounding*, iv, 2539.

[12] In Beamont, *Winwick*, 41, 42, may be seen presentments made at the visitations of the chancellor and archdeacon of Chester in 1632 and 1634. 'Roger Burchall was presented as a depraver of religion as established in the Church of England and a negligent comer to church, and as having reported that my lord suffered seminary priests to walk hand in hand and did not so much as point at them.' 'My lord' was perhaps the Bishop of Chester, or the Earl of Derby. Another was presented for having a candle on the bier, and others had 'sent for the blesser to bless cattle that were sick at Winwick.' John Norman was presented in 1669 for saying that 'this Church of England is not a true church, and that the worship therein is odious to God and hateful to man'; Visit. books at Chester.

[13] See Baines, *Lancs. Directory* of 1825, for the methods used by Rector Hornby to promote good conduct; ii, 717.

[14] Norris D. (B.M.); Elizabeth Lunt (or Williamson) and Thomas Goulden, as convicted recusants, paid double on goods; for these see *Trans. Hist. Soc.* (new ser.), xiv, 244. The Launder family acquired an estate in Ashton in Makerfield.

[15] *Cal. of Com. for Compounding*, iv, 3160. Thomas and John Goulden, in Elizabeth's time, had fallen under suspicion because they were recusants and had been known to resort to the seminary priest at Samlesbury; Baines, *Lancs.* (ed. 1870), i, 180 (from Harl. MS. 360, fol. 32b). The family occurs in Southworth, Pendleton, and St. Helens; see J. Gillow, *Bibl. Dict. of Engl. Cath.* ii, 324.

For Fortescue Goulding, born at Win-

Among the miscellaneous deeds preserved by Towneley is an agreement made in 1546 concerning Pagefield, lying between Winwick and Southworth.[16]

ASHTON

Eston, 1212; Ayston, 1246; Ashton, 1254; Assheton, 1292.

Grateswode, 1367; Garteswood, xvi cent.

This township, called Ashton in Makerfield or Ashton-le-Willows for distinction, has an area of 6,249½ acres.[1] The highest ground, 350 ft., lies near the boundary of Billinge; the lowest, about 90 ft., is at the eastern corner, where Glazebrook forms part of the boundary. Sankey Brook is the south-west boundary, and two of its tributaries separate Ashton from Billinge and Haydock. Millingford Brook runs through the centre of the township from north-west to south-east. Ashton village lies on its northern bank; on the same side are Stubshaw Cross, Heybridge, Brynn, Whitley Green, and Brocksteads. The southern side of the brook contains Garswood, with Seneley Green, Leyland Green, and Downall Green. The population in 1901 was 18,687.

The place-names Soughers lane, Skitter farm, and Cramberley occur in 1825.

The surface is sometimes undulating, mostly flat, the soil being clay, sand, and stone. There are occasional patches of old moss-land, but the greater part of the country is cultivated, where possible, and good crops of potatoes, turnips, wheat, and oats are produced. In the south there are fine plantations, including the grounds of Garswood Park, which make a refreshing clump of greenery. But in the northern parts the majority of the trees are reduced to blackened stumps, standing leafless and gaunt, until they fall from sheer decay. As in other mining districts collections of water lie in many places, indicating the subsidence of the ground, as the result of mining.

A narrow strip of the Permian rocks extends from Abram to Edge Green, separating the Coal Measures from the New Red Sandstone, and the latter formation covers the former in the immediate vicinity of the town of Ashton. Elsewhere the Coal Measures alone are in evidence.

The principal road, that from Wigan to Warrington, roughly agreeing with the old Roman road, passes north and south through the township and village; at this point it is crossed by the road from St. Helens to Hindley. The road from Ashton to Billinge is crossed at Leyland Green by one from St. Helens to Winstanley. The Lancashire Union line of the London and North Western Railway from St. Helens to Wigan has stations at Garswood and Brynn. The Liverpool, St. Helens, and South Lancashire Railway of the Great Central system touches the southern border.

Traces of the Roman road have been discovered, and a coin of Trajan was found.

In 1825 Ashton was a 'large and populous village,' 'the centre of a brisk manufacturing district where the poor are industrious and their employers prosperous.'[2] It had in 1840 cotton-spinning establishments and fustian manufactures, and was noted for hinges and locks. The making of tools, screws, and locks continues; large collieries are also worked.

Stubshaw Cross, Ashton Cross, and Four-footed Cross, once marked on the map, have quite disappeared,[3] but the first has given a name to a hamlet.

A lazaretto for those suffering from an epidemic of the sweating sickness in the time of Elizabeth is said to have been built on Ashton Common.[4]

A fair of two days' duration was held on 22 and 23 September, principally for toys and amusements.[5]

A local board was established in 1872,[6] but has become an urban district council of fifteen members with five wards under the Local Government Act of 1894. The council owns the water and gas works.

MANORS Before the Conquest *ASHTON* was no doubt one of the fifteen berewicks or dependent manors of the royal manor of Newton.[7] Later it was a member of the fee of Makerfield, which had Newton for its head.[8] At the survey of 1212 it was found to be held by Thomas de Burnhull or Brindle, being three plough-lands of the three and a half held by him in thegnage for 35s., and providing a judge and a half at the court of Newton.[9] Two plough-lands he had in his own hands, embracing, it would appear, Ashton proper, or Brynn, north of the Millingford Brook; the third plough-land, probably Garswood, was held of him by Henry de Ashton, 'of ancient feoffment,'[10] and under this Henry appears to have been held by Henry son of Roger, 'of ancient marriage.' Henry de Ashton had also granted 20 acres to the Hospitallers.[11]

Thomas de Burnhull was followed by a son Peter,[12] who married Avice, the heiress of Windle and other manors.[13] In 1254 he obtained the right to erect a mill in Ashton.[14] The son of Peter and Avice was Peter, who dying about 1295[15] was succeeded by his brother Alan. Alan, who was living in 1315,[16] left

wick Hall, and educated at St. Omers and Valladolid, see *Pal. Note-book*, iii, 103.

The will of John Goulden of Southworth, dated 1701 and proved 1715, in the Ches. Reg. mentions his wife Katherine, his son Thomas, and his nephew Richard Hitchmough. The testator had property in Southworth, Croft, Poulton, Woolston, Fearnhead, and Moscroft.

[16] Towneley MS. GG, no. 1069.

[1] 6,251, including 6¾ of inland water, according to the census of 1901.

[2] Baines, *Lancs. Dir.* ii, 717.

[3] *Lancs. and Ches. Antiq. Soc.* xix, 235, 23.

[4] Baines, *Lancs.* (ed. 1836), iii, 628; no reference is given.

[5] Ibid. 639.

[6] *Lond. Gaz.* 14 June, 1872.

[7] *V.C.H. Lancs.* i, 286.

[8] Ibid. 366 n. It is regularly entered among the members of Newton fee in the inquisitions; see *Lancs. Inq. p.m.* (Chet. Soc.), ii, 99.

[9] *Lancs. Inq. and Extents* (Rec. Soc. Lancs. and Ches.), i, 74, 75.

[10] i.e. reaching back to the time of Henry I.

[11] Ibid. The grant to the Hospitallers does not appear again.

[12] *Whalley Coucher* (Chet. Soc.), iii, 852; Thomas de Burnhull and his son Peter attested a charter. Peter de Burnhull was in possession of Ashton by 1246; *Final Conc.* (Rec. Soc. Lancs. and Ches.), i, 98.

[13] See the account of Windle; her manors were Windle, Skelmersdale, and half of Rainhill.

[14] *Final Conc.* i, 116. By this Robert Banastre also released to Peter de Burnhull all right to any suit of mill from Peter and his heirs and the men of his fee in Ashton; for the grant and quit-

a son Peter, and two daughters, Joan and Agnes. The son died before 1330, and his sisters became heirs of the property.[17]

Joan married William Gerard, son of William Gerard, lord of a moiety of the manor of Kingsley, near Frodsham;[18] and Agnes married David Egerton of Egerton, near Malpas, but probably died without issue, as nothing is known of any claim to the Burnhull manors by her descendants.[19] The heiresses and their husbands were children at the time of their marriage, William Gerard being but thirty years of age in 1352, when his father died.[20] Two years later he made a settlement of the manor of Ashton, the remainders being to his son Peter, and then to the heirs of Joan daughter of Alan de Burnhull.[21]

Little is known of the son, except that he became a knight.[22] Sir Peter Gerard died in 1380, and was succeeded by his son Sir Thomas Gerard, who like others of the family is traditionally said to have been engaged in the wars of the time.[23] At his death in 1416 he was found to have held the two-thirds of the manor of Ashton of Henry de Langton, baron of Newton, in socage by the service of 20s. a year, besides many other manors and lands in Lancashire.[24] His son and heir John, aged thirty at his father's death, succeeded. He died 6 November 1431, leaving a son and heir Peter, then twenty-four years of age.[25] This son, afterwards Sir Peter Gerard, had a comparatively short life, dying on 26 March 1447, when the manors devolved on

a minor, his son Thomas being but sixteen years of age.[26]

Sir Thomas Gerard, who came of age in 1452,[27] was married in childhood to Douce daughter of Sir Thomas Ashton; afterwards he married Cecily, daughter of Sir Robert Foulshurst, by whom he had a son and heir Peter, and other children.[28] He died on 27 March 1490;[29] his widow Cecily afterwards made a vow of chastity.[30] The son Peter, aged thirty at his father's death, married Margery daughter of Sir Thomas Stanley of Hooton, and granddaughter and coheir of Sir John Bromley, by

BROMLEY. *Quarterly per fesse indented gules and or.*

GERARD of Brynn. *Azure a lion rampant ermine crowned or.*

whom the estate of Gerard's Bromley came to this family. Peter Gerard died four years after his father,[31] leaving as heir his son Thomas, only six years of age. He was made a knight, but showed himself a turbu-

---

[17] Assize R. 424, m. 2; De Banco R. 284, m. 119.

[18] It will be seen from the account of Kirkby that William Gerard, the father, had a share of the manors of Kirkby and Melling in right of his wife.

An account of the Gerards of Kingsley is given in Ormerod, *Ches.* (ed. Helsby), ii, 96, and 131, 132. Abstracts of inquisitions and family deeds are there printed.

[19] Ibid. ii, 628. In 1346 inquiry was made as to why William Gerard, jun., and David de Egerton had not been made knights: a list of their possessions was made; Q.T. Mem. R. 122, m. 123 d.

[20] Ormerod, op. cit. ii, 96. William and Joan were in possession of Ashton in 1338, when they made a sale of land; *Final Conc.* ii, 108.

[21] Ibid. ii, 143, 144.

[22] The Bishop of Lichfield granted to Sir Peter Gerard a licence for his oratory at Brynn for two years from 7 Oct. 1379; Lich. Epis. Reg. Scrope, v, fol. 33. The writ of *Diem cl. extr.* after his death was issued 20 Feb. 1380–1; *Dep. Keeper's Rep.* xxxii, App. 353.

[23] Ormerod, ii, 96. Thomas Gerard was knight of the shire in 1384, 1388, and 1394; Pink and Beaven, *Parl. Repre. of Lancs.* 40, 43, 44. In 1393 Thomas Gerard received the royal pardon for having entered into certain estates during his minority and for having married, when he should have been in ward to the king; *Dep. Keeper's Rep.* xxxvi, App. 195. In 1402 he made provision for the marriage of his son John with Alice daughter of Sir John Boteler; ibid. 196.

[24] *Lancs. Inq. p.m.* (Chet. Soc.), i, 123; the clear value was 100 marks. His name does not occur in Sir Harris Nicolas's account of the Agincourt campaign.

[25] Ormerod, loc. cit. The writ of

Diem cl. extr. was issued 10 Dec. 1431, and writ of livery 14 Mar. 1431–2; *Dep. Keeper's Rep.* xxxvii, App. 301. The writ of *Diem cl. extr.* on the death of Alice, widow of John Gerard, was issued 27 Feb. 1441–2; ibid.

[26] Ormerod, loc. cit. The Lancashire inquisition taken after his death is preserved in Towneley MS. DD, no. 1465. This recites among other deeds, that John Gerard, the father, had in 1428 granted lands in Rainhill, with Smalley, Lawfield, and other parcels in Ashton to his son Peter and Isabel his wife. It also appears that Peter was 'esquire' in 1440, when various lands were settled on Douce, daughter of Sir Thomas Ashton, in view of her marriage with Thomas Gerard, son of Peter. The said Peter died seised of 'the manor of Ashton, otherwise called the manor or capital messuage of the Brynn,' but the jury did not know by what rent it was held of the chief lord, Henry Langton. The custody of the lands of the heir was granted to Thomas Danyell, and afterwards to John Ashton; Isabel, widow of Sir Peter, had dower; *Dep. Keeper's Rep.* xxxvii, App. 302.

[27] Proof of age was given at St. Mary's Church, Chester, on 2 Aug. 1452. John Leicester said that Thomas was of age on 15 July; he remembered being at Winwick Church on pilgrimage to St. Rhadegund on the day of the baptism. John Abram remembered Sir Peter Gerard asking Sir Thomas Stanley to be godfather to his son; Richard Clive remembered the same, and held a lighted candle at the baptism. Others were at Winwick Church attending a funeral, when they heard of Thomas's birth, and others heard of it while staying at Ashton for a 'love day' between Sir William Atherton and Henry Kighley; Ormerod, loc. cit.

A pension of £20 to Sir Thomas Gerard granted by Edward IV was excepted from the Act of Resumption in 1464; *Parl. R.* v, 546.

[28] This appears from the later inquisitions, in which Peter is called the son of Cecily. Other sons were Robert, mentioned in the will of Thomas Gerard, and John, a clerk, to whom the Cheshire manors were granted for life by his father; Ormerod, loc. cit.; *Dep. Keeper's Rep.* xxxix, App. 132.

[29] Duchy of Lanc. Inq. p.m. iii, no. 21: the inquisition was not taken until 1508.

[30] Lich. Epis. Reg. Hales, xiii, fol. 1216; commission to receive the vow and give the widow's veil, ring and mantle, dated 22 May 1491. She died 24 May 1502, having a life interest in the Gerard lands which had been assigned to her as dower by her son Peter; Duchy of Lanc. Inq. p.m. iii, no. 95.

[31] Duchy of Lanc. Inq. p.m. ii, no. 21, where the date is given as 20 June 1494. This does not agree with that on the memorial brass in Winwick Church, which sets forth the lineage of his wife. In 1502, after the death of Dame Cecily, the manors were granted to Margary, widow of Peter, during the minority of the heir; Duchy of Lanc. Misc. Bks. xxi, 32a. Cecily Gerard's Inq. p.m. states that the Bromley lands were in Bromley, Whittington, Beddill, Chadkilne, Ridges, Podmore, Kaunton, Milwich, Woolsall, and Selfort, with a moiety of the manor of Hextell, in Staffordshire.

Margery, the widow of Peter Gerard, requested that as various lands had been assigned to feoffees on the marriage of Sir Thomas Gerard with Cecily daughter of Sir Robert Foulshurst, which Cecily was still living, she should have the rule of Thomas her son during his minority; Duchy of Lanc. Inq. p.m. ii, no. 112.

lent and lawless man,[32] and died at Berwick in 1523, during an expedition against the Scots.[33] His son, another Sir Thomas, was only eleven years of age at his father's death ; but little is known of him. He died between 1550 and 1560.[34]

His son Sir Thomas Gerard sold his interest in the Kingsley estates of the family,[35] and purchased the other third part of the manor of Ashton from John Atherton, thus becoming sole lord.[36] His wife was the heiress of Sir John Port of Etwall in Derbyshire, and this manor-house became a favourite residence of the family.[37] After a brief period of compliance he became conspicuous for his resistance to the religion established by Elizabeth, and suffered accordingly. He was sent to the Tower in 1571, perhaps being suspected of a share in the rising of the previous year or for sympathy with Mary Queen of Scots ; his release is said to have been purchased by the surrender of Bromley to Sir Gilbert Gerard, Master of the Rolls.[38] He was again committed to the Tower in 1586, but liberated about three years later, having been induced to give evidence against Philip Earl of Arundel, then in the Tower also, to the effect that he had prayed for the success of the Spaniards.[39] In 1590 he was reported as having 'made show of conformity' while in Lancashire, but was 'in general note of evil affection' in religion.[40] His younger son John became a Jesuit, and laboured in England until the storm aroused by the Gunpowder Plot, when he escaped to Belgium, and became the chief agent in the foundation of the English College at Liège.[41]

Sir Thomas Gerard is said to have died in September 1601.[42] His son Thomas, made a knight in 1603, and a baronet in 1611, succeeded him.[43] Like his father, he was in 1590 reported as ' of evil affec-

---

[32] In *Duchy Plead.* (Rec. Soc. Lancs. and Ches.), i, 61-7, is an account (wrongly dated) of a cock fight at Winwick in 14 Apr. 1515, attended by Thomas Boteler of Bewsey, son of Sir Thomas, and others of the neighbouring gentry ; James Stanley, Bishop of Ely, though he had arranged to come, does not seem to have been present. The meeting was disturbed by the appearance of Sir Thomas Gerard and a number of retainers, all fully armed, and determined to wreak vengeance on some obnoxious members of the party. His quarrel with Thomas Gerard of Ince occurred a little earlier ; ibid. 3-7. Roger Platt of Ince complained that Sir Thomas Gerard of Ashton, 'of his own rigorous and malicious mind,' had seized his cattle and carried them off to the Brynn, where he detained them, and out of 'further rancour' set in the stocks one Lawrence Charnock, who had taken fodder for the cattle ; ibid. 75.

A settlement of various manors was made in 1511, Thomas Gerard and Margery his wife being in possession ; Pal. of Lanc. Feet of F. bdle. 11, m. 246.

[33] *Duchy Plead.* ii, 234. He died 7 Nov. 1523 seised of the manors of Brynn, Windle, and Brindle, and wide lands in the district. In his will, dated a year before his death, he recited the provision made for his wife Margery daughter of Sir Edmund Trafford; his son and heir Thomas and his wife Joan ; Peter and other younger sons; Katherine, Elizabeth, and Anne, his daughters. The last appears to have been already married to Richard Ashton of Middleton. The remainders were to Robert Gerard, his uncle, and to the issue of his grandfather, Sir Thomas Gerard ; Duchy of Lanc. Inq. p.m. viii, no. 13.

Margery, the widow, afterwards married Sir John Port, and died 10 May 1540, when the son, Thomas Gerard, was thirty-eight years of age ; ibid.

[34] In 1533 he 'would not be spoken with' by the herald ; *Visit.* (Chet. Soc.), 182. He was made a knight in 1544 during the invasion of Scotland ; Metcalfe, *Bk. of Knights*, 78. In 1536 Thomas Gerard of Brynn was expected to bring a contingent of 450 men to serve against the Pilgrimage of Grace ; *L. and P. Hen. VIII*, xi, 511. He was sheriff of the county in 1548 and 1553 ; P.R.O. *List*, 73. In 1552 he was claiming exemptions for the suppressed chantry of Windle ; *Ducatus Lanc.* (Rec. Com.), i,

254. He appears to have had several illegitimate children, of whom one, Thomas, was employed as trustee. Another Thomas Gerard, contemporary with these, was the natural son of William Gerard.

Sir Thomas married Jane, a daughter of Sir Peter Legh of Lyme, from whom he was separated ; Raines MSS. (Chet. Lib.), xxii, 170 ; Ormerod, *Ches.* (ed. Helsby), iii, 677. Her will, in which she is described as Dame Jane Gerard of Bromley, is printed from the Lyme deeds in *Wills* (Rec. Soc. Lancs. and Ches.), 78; she makes bequests to her son, Sir Thomas Gerard and his wife Elizabeth, and to her brother Sir P. Legh.

[35] Ormerod, op. cit. ii, 96.

[36] See below.

[37] With this Sir Thomas and his wife the pedigree recorded in 1665 begins ; Dugdale, *Visit.* (Chet. Soc.), 116. His sons on matriculating at Oxford in 1575 were said to be 'of Derbyshire' ; and ten years later Sir Thomas was described as 'lurking' in his house at Etwall ; Morris, *Life of John Gerard*, 6 (quoting Clifford, *S.P. of Sir R. Sadler*, ii, 525).

Sir Thomas Gerard was sheriff in 1557 (P.R.O. *List*, 73), and knight of the shire in 1562 ; Pink and Beaven, op. cit. 5.

[38] Morris, op. cit. 5, quoting Murdin, *Coll. of S.P.* 771, 35. Those committed to the Tower with him were Sir Thomas Stanley, probably of Winwick Rectory, and Francis Rolleston ; 'they were reconciled to the pope according to the late bull.' The story as to Bromley is quoted in Gregson, *Fragments* (ed. Harland), 237, from Wotton, *Baronetage*, 55. John Gerard says simply that his father 'obtained his release by the payment of a large sum' ; Morris, loc. cit.

[39] The story that he abandoned his religion and adopted a licentious course of life is discredited by Gillow, *Bibl. Dict. of Engl. Catholics*, ii, 426.

[40] *Lydiate Hall*, 244 ; quoting S.P. Dom. Eliz. ccxxxv, 4. Another Thomas Gerard, perhaps the bastard, was 'soundly affected in religion' ; ibid. 246.

[41] His adventurous life is told, mainly from his autobiography, in the work of Fr. Morris already cited ; see also *Dict. Nat. Biog.* and Gillow. The confusion created by the mistakes he made as to his age at entering Oxford, &c. is cleared by the record in Foster, *Alumni Oxon.* showing that he and his elder brother Thomas entered Exeter College, Oxford, in Dec.

1575, at the ages of thirteen and fifteen. When admitted to the English College at Rome in 1587 as a scholar—he had already lived there seven months—his age was recorded as 'in his twenty-third year' ; Foley, *Rec. S.J.* vi, 173. He is said to have been born 4 Oct. 1564. His country upbringing stood him in good stead in his later life, suspicion on one occasion being averted 'as he spoke of hunting and falconry with all the details that none but a practised person could command' ; Morris, op. cit. 43.

[42] A number of settlements were made during the reign of Elizabeth, of which the fines give evidence. In 1573 Sir Thomas claimed from Thomas Gerard, base son of Sir Thomas Gerard deceased, the manors of Ashton in Makerfield, Brindle, Windle, and Skelmersdale, with messuages and wide lands, twelve watermills, twelve windmills, two fulling-mills, two horse-mills, six dovecotes, &c.; Pal. of Lanc. Feet of F. bdle. 35, m. 3. This would be just after Sir Thomas's release from the Tower. A settlement apparently on behalf of his wife Elizabeth was made in the following spring ; ibid. bdle. 36, m. 230. Shortly afterwards he purchased Lord Mounteagle's lands in Ashton ; ibid. bdle. 36, m. 102. '

In 1582 a settlement or mortgage was made by Sir Thomas Gerard, Elizabeth his wife, and Thomas his son and heir apparent ; ibid. bdle. 44, m. 226.

Four years later a large number of settlements were made, separate properties being dealt with. In some the remainders after the death of Sir Thomas and Elizabeth were to Thomas the son and heir and Cecily his wife, and then to John Gerard, second son of Sir Thomas. In many others the further remainder was to Sir Gilbert Gerard, Master of the Rolls, and then to the male issue of William Gerard, late of Harrow, Henry Gerard of Rainhill, and William Gerard, late of Ince ; ibid. bdle. 48, m. 118-198, 262, 305. A number of similar feoffments were made in 1598 ; ibid. bdle. 60, m. 4-22, 43, 47.

[43] Feoffments were made by Thomas Gerard in 1587, his father being then in the Tower ; Pal. of Lanc. Feet of F. bdle. 49, m. 271-9. He had gone up to Oxford in 1575, as above stated ; but he and his brother John soon left, finding that 'at Easter the heretics sought to force them to attend their worship, and to partake of their counterfeit sacrament' —so John Gerard in Morris, op. cit. 14.

tion in religion'; his wife Cecily was then a 'recusant and indicted thereof.'[44] He died at the beginning of 1621, holding the manors of Ashton and Windle in Lancashire, and Etwall and Hardwick in Derbyshire; the tenure of Ashton was stated to be 'in free socage, by fealty only.' His heir was his son Thomas, aged thirty-six and more.[45] This Sir Thomas, second baronet, was succeeded in 1630[46] by his son Sir William Gerard, who warmly espoused the king's cause at the outbreak of the Civil War,[47] and was appointed governor of Denbigh Castle; he sold the Derbyshire estates to provide money for the campaign.[48]

Charles II lodged at Brynn 15 August 1651, on his way from Scotland to Worcester.[49] Sir William's estate was of course sequestered by the Parliament, and being a convicted recusant he was not at first allowed to compound even for the third part retained by recusants who were not 'delinquents' also. The estates were sold under the confiscation Act of 1652, the purchaser being John Wildman.[50] All or most was recovered in some way, probably by composition with the new owner, and Sir William Gerard of the

Brynn recorded a pedigree at the Visitation of 1665.[51] He was buried at Winwick in 1681.

His son Sir William, aged twenty-seven in 1665, succeeded. The family had been greatly impoverished by their fidelity to their religion and to the cause of Charles I, and it is said that even the stipends of the priests serving the domestic chapels at Ashton could not be paid.[52] Sir William's son, another William, married about 1696 the heiress of the Cansfield family, and this probably helped to restore the fortunes of the Gerards.[53] Sir William died in 1702; his son as 'a papist' registered his estate in 1717, and died four years later.[54] For the succeeding century there is but little to record of the family. They were shut out of public employments by the legal proscription of the ancient religion, and do not seem to have produced any distinguished ecclesiastics.

The development of the coal mines in Ashton during the 19th century brought great wealth to the family.

The Sir William Gerard last mentioned was succeeded by his son and grandson, each named William.[55]

Their tutor, Edward Lewknor, followed them, 'being resolved to live as a Catholic in very deed, and not merely in desire.'

For the knighthood see Metcalfe, op. cit. 140; and for the baronetcy G.E.C. Complete Baronetage, i, 21. The fee of £1,000 is said to have been remitted in consideration of the father's services to the king's mother. He represented Liverpool in the Parliament of 1597, and Wigan in that of 1621; Pink and Beaven, op. cit. 184, 224.

In 1612 a settlement was made by Sir Thomas Gerard of the manors of Ashton, Garswood, and Windle—the other Lancashire manors having been disposed of—and lands in Ashton and neighbouring townships; Pal. of Lanc. Feet of F. bdle. 81, no. 26.

[44] Lydiate Hall, loc. cit. In 1592 Thomas Gerard of High Carr was reported to have had a 'notorious recusant' as his schoolmaster for some years; ibid. 258 (quoting S.P. Dom. Eliz. ccxv, 19). His sister Dorothy and her husband Ralph Layton of the Brynn were in like case.

Dame Anne Gerard, widow of Sir Gilbert Gerard, was in 1590 living at Highley Carr, indicted of recusancy; ibid.

[45] Lancs. Inq. p.m. (Rec. Soc. Lancs. and Ches.), iii, 297–301. The fine above cited is given, as also another relating to the Derbyshire manors. The remainders were to Thomas, eldest son of Sir Thomas, and his sons by Frances his wife; in default to John, the second son, &c.

[46] Duchy of Lanc. Inq. p.m. xxvi, no. 57; funeral certificate (with coat of twenty quarters) in Lancs. and Ches. Fun. Cert. (Rec. Soc. Lancs. and Ches.), 203.

Sir Thomas had been made a knight in 1615; Metcalfe, op. cit. 165. He was member for Liverpool in 1624; Pink and Beavan, op. cit. 186. As a convicted recusant he paid double to the subsidy of 1628; Norris D. (B.M.). Gilbert, one of his sons, became a Jesuit priest, and died of a disease contracted while acting as chaplain to some English troops in Belgium in 1645; Foley, Rec. S.J. vi, 337; vii, 294.

Richard, another son, cup-bearer to Queen Henrietta Maria, acquired the manor of Ince in Makerfield.

[47] Sir William Gerard, Sir Cecil Trafford, and four other convicted recusants, joined in a petition to Charles I that their

arms might be restored to them 'in this time of actual war,' for the security of the king's person as well as of their own district and families, 'who are not only in danger of the common disturbance, but menaced by unruly people to be robbed.' The king writing from Chester, 27 Sept. 1642, very readily granted the permission; War in Lancs. (Chet. Soc.), 12–14.

[48] Etwall is said to have been sold to secure the barony of Newton, but the money was spent in providing funds for the campaign of 1651; see Visit. of 1533 (Chet. Soc.), 184.

[49] 'The last night this king lodged at Brynn, six miles from Warrington, being Sir William Gerard's house, who is a subtle jesuited Papist'; letter dated Stockton Heath, 16 Aug. in Civil War Tracts (Chet. Soc.), 288.

[50] G.E.C. op. cit. and Royalist Comp. Papers (Rec. Soc. Lancs. and Ches.), iii, 51–71, where details are given of a settlement made in 1632; see also Pal. of Lanc. Feet of F. bdle. 122, no. 5. It appeared that in 1632 Sir William had compounded with the king for a lease of two-thirds of his Lancashire lands sequestered for recusancy, he having been in ward to the king until April of that year; Royalist Comp. Papers, iii, 62. 'Getting coals' is named among the disbursements; 66. A survey of the lands in Ashton, taken in 1652, is printed on p. 68; it gives the names, areas, and values of the fields. Tootell, Leachfield, Tunstall Heads, Coalpit Banks, Mill Hill and Pingotts appear among the field names.

For the sale see ibid. 70; Index of Royalists (Index Soc.), 42.

[51] Dugdale, Visit. 116. Sir William Gerard and William his son were recusants in 1678; Hist. MSS. Com. Rep. xiv, App. iv, 109. Two of the younger sons went to the English College in Rome—Thomas who entered in 1660, and became a Jesuit, and died in Yorkshire in 1682, while attending victims of an epidemic; and Cuthbert who entered in 1662, and left for England two years later; Foley, op. cit. vi, 401, 404; vii, 296. Thomas, on entering, gave details of his parentage, stating that 'his parents and himself had suffered much for the Catholic religion'; he had been baptized by Fr. Howard in 1641.

[52] Foley, op. cit. v, 361; the time re-

ferred to seems to be early in the 18th century.

An anecdote of Sir William Gerard is given in Hist. MSS. Com. Rep. xiv, App. iv, 142. He remained loyal to James II, and was carried off to Preston a prisoner in 1689, and accused of a part in the 'Lancashire Plot' of 1694; ibid. 294, 359, &c.; inquiry was also made as to whether Garswood Hall was not devoted to 'superstitious uses'; Exch. Dep. (Rec. Soc. Lancs. and Ches.), 84. His son William was also among the accused. A number of the baptisms of Sir William's children are recorded in the Winwick registers.

[53] See the account of Cansfield of Robert Hall.

[54] Estcourt and Payne, Engl. Cath. Nonjurors, 114. The estate was the 'manor of Ashton, &c., entailed with remainders successively to sons by Mary his wife, to John his brother, to Thomas Gerard of Ince, and to Richard Gerard of Wigan; subject to £100 per annum to Dame Mary Gerard of Birchley. Also the rectory of Childwall, for lives of his wife Mary, the granddaughter of James Anderton, and of his daughters Anne and Elizabeth—£1,272 11s. 8d.'

The brother, John Gerard of Garswood, registered an annuity of £80; and the father's widow, Dame Mary of Birchley, also registered; ibid. 99, 97.

[55] The brief summary of the descent here given is quoted from G.E.C. Complete Baronetage, loc. cit. The following references to Pal. of Lanc. Plea R. may be useful: Lent 1693—Recovery of the manors of Ashton and Windle, &c., Sir William Gerard and William Gerard vouchees; R. 457, m. 9. Aug. 1703—King's Silver, manor of Windle, &c., Sir William Gerard and Mary his wife, John, Thomas, and Richard Gerard; R. 478, m. 8. Lent 1721—Recovery of manor of Ashton, Sir William Gerard and William Gerard vouchees; R. 512, m. 6. Aug. 1745—Recovery of manors of Ashton and Windle and a fourth part of Billinge, Sir Thomas Gerard vouchee; R. 563, m. 4. Lent 1796—Recovery of manors of Ashton, Windle, and Aspull, and parcels in Aspull, Billinge, Ince, Golborne, Parr, Winstanley, Prescot, Wigan, Hindley, Hale, Halewood, and Halebank; Lent Assizes 1796, R. 12.

The last was followed by his brothers Thomas and Robert Cansfield; the latter, who died in 1784, had sons, Robert Clifton,[56] and William who succeeded; a younger son John, drowned at Southport in 1822,[57] was father of Sir John Gerard, who succeeded his uncle William in 1826, and held the manors of Ashton and Windle for nearly twenty-eight years. His heir was his brother, Robert Tolver, created Baron Gerard of Brynn in 1876. He has been followed by his son William Cansfield and his grandson Frederick John, second and third lords. The latter, who succeeded to the title and estates in 1902, on the death of his father, came of age in 1904.

In 1836 courts leet and baron were held twice a year;[58] but they seem to have been discontinued.

A description of Brynn Hall, as it existed near the end of the 18th century, is given in Baines's *Lancashire*.[59]

The third part of the manor held in 1212 by Henry son of Roger cannot be traced for some time. It became the possession of the Athertons of Atherton,[60] who held it down to the middle of the 16th century, when it was sold to the Gerards of Brynn[61] as above stated.

The only landowner contributing to the subsidy in Mary's reign was Sir Thomas Gerard;[62] but the following freeholders were recorded in 1600: Sir Thomas Gerard of Brynn, Thomas Gerard of Garswood, James Ashton, Edward Knowles, James Richardson, William Slynehead, and William Stanley;[63] some other names occur.[64]

[56] A short notice of him is printed in *Pal. Note Bk.* iv, 57.

[57] He was described as of Windle Hall. For an account of the accident see Bland, *Ann. of Southport*, 79.

[58] Baines, *Lancs.* (ed. 1836), iii, 639.

[59] Ibid. iii, 637; it is by Barritt, the Manchester antiquary.

[60] The earliest record is in 1302, when Hugh de Atherton claimed reasonable estovers in Ashton, with heybote, housebote, &c., against Alan son of Peter de Burnhull, William de Atherton, and Jordan the Woodward. Thus William de Atherton appears to have been then the lord of a third; Assize R. 418, m. 4. Alan de Burnhull in 1313 claimed William and Hugh de Atherton, Hugh Spark, Henry Tootell and others as suitors at his mill; De Banco R. 199, m. 134 d.

Hugh de Atherton was a brother of William's; Culcheth D. nos. 35, 44 (in *Lancs. and Ches. Hist. and Gen. Notes*, i). Hugh had a son Henry who may be the Henry de Atherton of Aintree in 1332; his daughter Joan married Robert de Nevill of Hornby, who in 1346 claimed Hugh de Atherton's lands in Ashton and elsewhere; De Banco R. 345, m. 393 d.; 346, m. 349. The claim was no doubt successful as lands were held here by Lord Mounteagle in the time of Henry VIII as of the inheritance of James Harrington; Duchy of Lanc. Inq. p.m. v, no. 64, xi, no. 1. They were sold, as already stated, to Sir Thomas Gerard in 1574. The Molyneux lands in Ashton may have been part of the inheritance; ibid. xiii, no. 35.

Various suits are on record involving the principal Atherton family. In 1332 Hugh de Atherton claimed common of pasture in Ashton against Henry son of William de Atherton and others; Hugh de Atherton the younger and Henry his brother were sureties; Assize R. 1411, m. 12 d. At the same time Hugh de Atherton charged Alexander de Atherton with carrying off his goods; De Banco R. 292, m. 231 d. In 1346 Henry son of William de Atherton made a claim for waste against Alexander de Atherton; Agnes de Atherton was the lessee; De Banco R. 348, m. 427 d. She may be the Agnes, widow of Henry de Atherton, who contributed to the subsidy of 1332; *Exch. Lay Subs.* (Rec. Soc. Lancs. and Ches.), 18. Hugh de Atherton in 1347 succeeded in a claim against Adam son of William de Atherton; Assize R. 1435, m. 41 d. This Adam de Atherton who was a chaplain, was in 1352 and 1353 a

plaintiff; Duchy of Lanc. Assize R. 2, m. 4 d.; R. 435, m. 28 d. (where a long list of tenants is given).

In 1367 Ralph de Langton claimed from Sir William de Atherton a certain rent in Ashton in Makerfield due to the lord of Newton, from a third part of the wood and pasture called Garswood within the demesne of the manor of Newton. This rent had been granted in 1331 by Henry son of William de Atherton, and father of the defendant. The latter said that William his grandfather had held the third part, and so settled it that Henry, when the charter was made, had nothing except fee tail only; De Banco R. 438, m. 337.

A later Sir William de Atherton died in 1414 seised, among other estates, of a third part of the manor of Ashton, held of Henry de Langton by fealty and the service of 2 marks a year; its clear value was 40 marks; *Lancs. Inq. p.m.* (Chet. Soc.), i, 107. The increase of the rent from 10s. to 26s. 8d. may be accounted for by the statements in the preceding case.

The manor is named in 1443 in a settlement by William son of Sir William Atherton on marrying Isabel daughter of Richard Balderston; Towneley MS. C. 8, 5 (Chet. Lib.), Hen. VI, no. 43. Isabel was a widow in 1479; ibid. Edw. IV, no. 14.

John Atherton of Atherton, who died in 1488, made various provisions for his illegitimate children from his manor of Garswood and lands in Ashton; at the inquisition taken in 1507 it was stated that the manor was held by fealty only, and the lands by a rent of 26s. 8d.; Duchy of Lanc. Inq. p.m. iii, no. 39. For the settlements alluded to see also Dods. MSS. lviii, fol. 164b, no. 9; Pal. of Lanc. Plea R. 33, m. 7, 7 d., where it is stated that Thomas Harrington of Hornby, Thomas Totehill, and John Standish had paid rents to Sir William Atherton. A similar statement as to the tenure of the manor of Garswood and the lands in Ashton is made in the inquisition taken in 1518 after the death of George Atherton, son of John; Duchy of Lanc. Inq. p.m. v, no. 12.

Thomas Hesketh of Rufford, who died in 1523, held lands of John Atherton, son of George, by fealty and a rent of 20d.; ibid. v, no. 16. Peter Gerard of Aughton, who died in 1528, held lands in Ashton of the same John Atherton in socage by the rent of 13s.; ibid. vi, no. 58.

Under the Commonwealth the Gerard estates, as above related, were confiscated; the properties of Hugh Orrell[65] and Elizabeth Rogerson, widow,[66] were also sequestered for recusancy. In 1717 John Darbyshire, Thomas Naylor, Elizabeth Aray of Chorley, John Taylor of Lydiate, Edward Unsworth, John Boardman, and Andrew Moore registered estates as 'papists.'[67]

The family of Lander of New Hall appears during the 17th century.[68] This estate was acquired by the Gerards about 1796, and became their principal residence.[69]

The Sorocold family were seated at Eyebridge in the 17th century.[70]

A troop of yeomanry cavalry, commanded by Sir William Gerard, existed in 1804, when two companies of infantry volunteers were raised for the protection of the country from invasion.[71]

LANDER of New Hall.
Sable three mullets in bend argent between two bendlets indented or.

CHURCH There is no record of the origin of St. Thomas's Chapel at Ashton, which is first named in the pleadings in 1515 respecting the dispute about Turnshea Moss between Sir Thomas Gerard and his namesake of Ince; it was then deposed that the priest at Ashton Chapel had given public notice that Sir Thomas intended to make a straight ditch through the moss that his turf-rooms might be the drier.[72] Little is known of it for a century after this;[73] but the new services were certainly used there, Sir Thomas Gerard about 1562 forcibly carrying to it his relation Nicholas Gerard as a too obstinate adherent of the old.[74] The ministrations were probably irregular; in 1590 there was 'no preacher' there,[75] and more than twenty years later 'seldom a curate,' there being, it would seem, no income except what the rector allowed.[76] The

Commonwealth Surveyors of 1650 found everything in order, and recommended it to be made a parish church; to the minister had been assigned the sequestered tithes of the township, worth £120 a year.[77]

At the Restoration the curate, proving a Nonconformist, was ejected.[78] In 1718 Bishop Gastrell found the certified stipend only £1 12s.; the rector, however, gave £50, 'being obliged to provide for it;' and other inhabitants subscribed £7 a year on condition that the curate resided and read prayers on Wednesdays, Fridays, and holy-days.[79] The chapel was rebuilt in 1706 on Sir William Gerard's ground, and he leased out the chapel yard.[80] It was enlarged in 1784 and 1815; and in 1845, on the division of the rectory of Winwick, was made a parish church, being endowed with the tithes of Haydock.[81] There is a licensed mission of St. Luke's.

The incumbent has the title of vicar, and is appointed by the rector of Ashton. The following have been in charge :—[82]

oc. 1609	John Janion[83]
1645–62	James Woods[84]
oc. 1663	— Maddock
oc. 1668	— Atkinson[85]
1690	Thomas Wareing[86]
oc. 1710	— Smith[87]
oc. 1736	— Pierce[88]
—	— Shuttleworth
1742	Richard Bevan[89]
1779	Edward Edwards, B.A.
1796	Giles Chippindall
1804	John Woodrow
1809	Edmund Sibson[90]
1848	Edward Pigot, M.A. (Brasenose Coll.)
1857	Frederick Kenney, M.A. (Christ Church, Oxford)
1870	William Page Oldham, M.A. (Christ's Coll., Camb.)
1871	Henry Siddall, B.A. (Clare Coll., Camb.)

[65] *Royalist Comp. Papers*, iv, 236.

[66] *Cal. of Com. for Compounding*, v, 3186; her husband Richard was living in 1641.
 Roger Lowe's Diary (published in *Local Glean. Lancs. and Ches.* i) contains many particulars of local interest about the Restoration period, the writer having been a resident.

[67] *Engl. Cath. Nonjurors*, 97, 98, 99, 110, 124, 127, 153. For John Darbyshire see Payne, *Engl. Cath. Rec.* 25.

[68] Thomas son of Mr. John Gerard of New Hall was baptized at Winwick, 10 Dec. 1608.
 The Launder or Lander family afterwards acquired the property, and were described as 'of New hall' in 1687. An account of them is given in *Local Glean. Lancs. and Ches.* i, 216; ii, 95, from G. S. Master, *Family of Master.* John Launder of New Hall was a benefactor to the poor of Ashton; he died in 1692 and was succeeded by his son Thomas, who died in 1695, and whose daughter Margaret carried the New Hall estate to the Master family. See also pedigree in Burke, *Landed Gentry* (Master of Barrow Green House).

[69] Baines, *Lancs.* (ed. 1836), iii, 639.

[70] George Sorocold of Ashton is mentioned in 1651; *Cal. of Com. for Compounding*, iv, 2787. See further in the account of Leigh.

[71] *Local Glean. Lancs. and Ches.* ii, 205, 206.

[72] *Duchy Plead.* i, 5.

[73] Humphrey Winstanley and Alice Worsley were married in 1559 'in a chapel within the house of Sir Thomas Gerard, by one Oswald Key, chaplain singing at Ashton Chapel;' Furnivall, *Child Marriages* (Early Engl. Text Soc.), 3. The domestic and public chapels were thus quite distinct.
 Oswald Key appeared at the first visitation in Queen Elizabeth's reign.

[74] Foley, *Rec. S. J.* ii, 26. Nicholas, who was gouty and unable to move, sang psalms in Latin as loud as he could, and was taken out again.

[75] *Lydiate Hall*, 248.

[76] *Hist. MSS. Com. Rep.* xiv, App. iv, 13.

[77] *Commonwealth Ch. Surv.* (Rec. Soc. Lancs. and Ches.), 48. The order as to the tithes was made in 1645 upon the petition of the inhabitants; *Plund. Mins. Accts.* (Rec. Soc. Lancs. and Ches.), i, 6.

[78] Nightingale, *Lancs. Nonconformity*, iv, 44.

[79] *Notitia Cestr.* (Chet. Soc.), ii, 267. Even the £1 12s. was not ancient, consisting of £1 for an anniversary sermon and 12s. interest on sums left at various times. To have a resident curate was obviously a recent innovation.

[80] The site was conveyed in 1745, and the chapel was consecrated in 1746; Church Papers at Ches. Dioc. Reg. An article on the church appeared in the *Liverpool Dioc. Gaz.* Nov. 1904.

[81] *Notitia*, 268; note by Canon Raines. See also *Lond. Gaz.* 8 Aug. 1873.

[82] From information in part supplied by the present vicar, the Rev. H. Siddall.

[83] Raines MSS. (Chet. Lib.), xxii, 298.

[84] He 'came in by free election of the whole town;' he was 'a very godly preacher, a man of good life and conversation,' but had not kept the fast day appointed by Parliament; *Commonwealth Ch. Surv.* 48. He was in charge as early as Aug. 1645; *Plund. Mins. Accts.* i, 6. From the Winwick registers it seems that Thomas Potter, afterwards of Culcheth, was assisting in 1656.
 Woods continued to preach for about a year after his ejection, and then removed into Cheshire; Roger Lowe's Diary in *Local Glean. Lancs. and Ches.* i, 170, 173.

[85] Ibid. 186; Roger Lowe, being rebuked by Mr. Atkinson for not standing up at the reading of the gospel, 'told him his mind to the full.'

[86] Stratford, Visitation Bk. at Ches. Dioc. Reg. He seems to have lived at Newton. Vicar of Garstang, 1712.

[87] This name occurs in the Winwick registers. [88] See preceding note.

[89] The church papers at Chester begin here.

[90] He contributed an account of the Roman roads to Baines' *Lancs.* (ed. 1836), iii, 573. There is a eulogy of him in Beamont, *Warrington in 1465* (Chet. Soc.), p. lxxviii.

By the same Act of 1845 Holy Trinity Church, Downall Green, built in 1837, was made the principal church, its incumbent having the title of rector of Ashton, and being endowed with the tithes of the township, from which £50 a year was to be paid to the vicar of St. Thomas's.[91] The rector is presented by the Earl of Derby. At Stubshaw Cross is St. Luke's Mission Church.

A school was founded in 1588.[92]

A Wesleyan Methodist chapel was built here as early as 1821. There are now also places of worship of the Primitive Methodists, the Independent Methodists, and the Welsh Wesleyans.

The Congregational church at Ashton appears to have originated in the occasional preaching visits of the Rev. W. Alexander of Prescot, in 1802 and later. A church was formed in 1824 and a chapel built in 1829. It did not prosper, and from 1846 to 1866 the condition of affairs was 'very low.' The present church was built in 1867 by Richard Evans and his family; the old building was used as a school.[93]

The Society of Friends had a small meeting here from about 1717 to 1835. The place was on the north-west boundary of the township.[94]

On the restoration of the Prayer Book services in 1662 the objectors under the ministry of the ejected curate, James Woods, worshipped in a farm-house.[95] A chapel was built at Park Lane in 1697, which still exists, having been altered in 1871. The congregation, as in other cases, gradually became Unitarian. Some of the ministers were of note in their time.[96]

The dominant family and a large number of the inhabitants adhered to the ancient religion[97] at the Reformation, but nothing is positively known as to the secret provision for worship until the middle of the 17th century, when the Jesuits had charge of the Brynn mission.[98] Later there was another chapel in Garswood; and in 1822 the church of St. Oswald was built in the village; it is in charge of secular priests. Here is preserved the 'Holy Hand' of the Ven. Edmund Arrowsmith, of which many miraculous stories are related.[99] Thomas Penswick, Bishop of Europum and vicar apostolic of the northern district from 1831 till his death in 1836, was born at Ashton manor-house, where also he died.[100]

GOLBORNE

Goldeburn, 1187; Goldburc, 1201; Goseburn (? Goleburn), 1202; Goldburn, 1212; Golburne, 1242. The d seems to have dropped out finally in the 15th century; Golborne, Gowborne, xvi cent.

This township stretches northwards for about 2½ miles from the boundary of Newton to the Glazebrook. Millingford Brook, coming from Ashton, crosses the township and afterwards forms part of the eastern and southern boundaries. The area is 1,679 acres.[1] The surface is highest near the centre, reaching about 150 ft. The population in 1901 numbered 6,789.

There is land sufficiently fertile to produce potato and wheat crops, whilst in the south there are clumps of woodland about Golborne Park, continuing all along the western boundary, so that from these quarters Golborne appears to be bowered in foliage. In the north, however, the country presents the characteristic bareness of the other coal-mining districts of the hundred. The Pebble Beds of the Bunter series of the New Red Sandstone cover the entire surface of the township.

The village of Golborne is near the centre of the township, on the north side of the brook. A road from Warrington to Wigan passes through it, and is there joined by another from Newton; there are also cross-roads between Ashton and Lowton. The London and North Western Company's main line from London to the north passes through the township, and has a station at Golborne; at the southern end is a junction with the loop-line connecting with the Liverpool and Manchester Railway. The St. Helens and South Lancashire Railway (Great Central) crosses the northern part of the township, and has a station called Golborne.

Lightshaw is at the northern extremity; Edge Green on the Ashton boundary, and Golborne Park, a seat of the Legh family, at the southern end.

Cotton-spinning and fustian-making were carried on early last century. There are now cotton-mills, a paper-staining factory and a colliery. A 'glass man' named Hugh Wright appears on the Recusant Roll of 1626.[2]

Some interesting field-names occur in a suit of 1553, e.g. Pillocroft, Bromburhey, Pennybutts, and Parpount hey.[3]

Golborne is now governed by an urban district council of twelve members.

MANORS   At the inquest of 1212 it appears that GOLBORNE was held of the baron of Makerfield in moieties; one half was held by the lord of Lowton, the other by a family using the local surname.[4] As in the case of Lowton itself the former moiety reverted to the lords of Makerfield, and no one else claimed any manor there.[5] In the latter moiety there may have been a failure of

[91] Gastrell, Notitia, loc. cit.

[92] Ibid.

[93] Nightingale, op cit. iv, 52–60.

[94] Information of Mr. J. Spence Hodgson.

[95] John Hasleden's house and his barn in Park Lane were licensed in 1689; Hist. MSS. Com. Rep. xiv, App. iv, 232.

[96] Nightingale, op. cit. iv, 44–52.

[97] See the Recusant Roll of 1641 in Trans. Hist. Soc. (new ser.), xiv, 245.

[98] Foley, Rec. S.J. v, 360–1. Fr. Thomas Tootell was resident at Garswood in 1663. At Brynn Fr. Waldegrave was serving in 1680. In 1701 both Garswood and Brynn are named; ibid. 321. In 1784 ninety-three persons were confirmed at Brynn, where the Easter communicants numbered 180; the corresponding numbers at Garswood were 39 and 100; ibid. 324.

Fr. Cuthbert Clifton probably served Brynn and Garswood as early as 1642; he died there in 1675, being regarded by his brethren as 'a pious man, who laboured with fruit for many years in the Lord's vineyard,' and by Roger Lowe, the Puritan undertaker, as 'the great and profane monster of Jesuitical impiety'; Foley, vii, 139; Local Glean. Lancs. and Ches. i, 196. Some further particulars as to the priests here may be gathered from Lowe's Diary.

[99] Liverpool Cath. Ann. 1901. For E. Arrowsmith see the account of Haydock. The Holy Hand was preserved at Brynn and Garswood till the erection of St. Oswald's; Harland and Wilkinson, Lancs. Legends, 41.

heirs, and a new grant in socage to the Hollands ; but one heiress of the Golbornes[6] appears to have sold her right to Thurstan de Holland,[7] whose descendants continued to be regarded as its lords.[8]

Thurstan, however, granted all or most of his moiety to his son Simon,[9] whose descendant Amice carried the manor of *LIGHTSHAW* in marriage to Nicholas de Tyldesley.[10] From this family by another heiress, it passed to the Kighleys of Inskip,[11] and from these again at the end of the 16th century, to William Cavendish, first Earl of Devonshire, and Thomas Worsley, in right of their wives, the Kighley co-heirs.[12] The former of these secured it, and it descended in the Cavendish family for over a century,[13] but there is no further mention of Lightshaw as a manor. The estate was purchased by Peter Legh of Lyme in 1738 from the Duke of Devonshire, and is now the property of Lord Newton.[14]

The Hospitallers had lands here.[15] Cockersand

Abbey had a tenement called Medewall,[16] for which the free tenants, a family named Langton, paid a rent of 2s. 6d.[17]

The Hoghtons of Hoghton were landowners in Golborne from an early date,[18] and the Haydocks

KIGHLEY of Inskip. *Argent a fesse sable.*

CAVENDISH, Duke of Devonshire. *Sable three bucks' heads cabossed argent.*

In 1599 Thomas Langton, baron of Newton, took action against certain tenants of Golborne for encroachments on the waste and withholding suit and service at the courts ; *Ducatus Lanc.* (Rec. Com.), iii, 402.

[6] The Golborne family held the third part of a knight's fee of the lords of Makerfield. This consisted of the three ploughlands necessary to make up the nine and a half in the knight's fee ; two of these appear to have been in Golborne (Lightshaw), and one in Lowton (Byrom), probably that held by Richard de Winwick in 1212. The earliest member of the family recorded is Augustine de Golborne, who gave three oxgangs to William son of Hamon in the time of Henry II ; *Inq. and Extents,* i, 74. His son Thomas paid 33s. 4d. as relief in 1186 on succeeding, and contributed to the scutage in 1206 ; Farrer, *Lancs. Pipe R.* 64, 216. As already stated, he was in possession in 1212. His son may have been the Ralph de Golborne whose daughter Levota sold her right to Thurstan de Holland. That there was a new grant by the lord of Newton to Thurstan de Holland seems proved by the change of tenure ; see note below.

Though the principal family thus early disappeared, others bearing the local surname appear from time to time. Adam de Golborne had a messuage and an oxgang and a half of land in 1374, but being outlawed for felony the king took possession ; Inq. a.q.d. 48 Edw. III, no. 19.

[7] In 1292 Hugh son of Richard de Woolston, and Quenilda his wife, sought against Simon son of Thurstan de Holland certain lands in Golborne asserted to be the right of Quenilda, to whom they should have descended from her grandmother Levota, the daughter of Ralph de Golborne. Levota had a son and heir Richard, whose son Henry dying without issue, Quenilda his sister succeeded. It was, however, proved that Levota had released all her right to Thurstan, father of Sir Robert de Holland, and that Thurstan had granted the disputed land to Simon de Holland the defendant ; Assize R. 408, m. 38 ; see also m. 25.

[8] There is but little to show the connexion of the Holland family with Golborne.

In 1278 Juliana daughter of John Gillibrand, mother of the Simon de Holland of the last note, complained that Robert de Holland and others had disseised her of a messuage, croft, seven oxgangs of land, and

half the site of the mill ; Assize R. 1238, m. 31 ; 1239, m. 39 ; also R. 408, m. 70 d. 77 d.

After the death of Simon de Holland an inquisition was taken in 1325, when it was found that he had held nothing of the Crown, but had held a certain tenement in Golborne as of the manor of Holland (in the king's hands) by the service of a pound of cummin. There were a messuage worth 12d. a year ; 20 acres of arable land worth 9s., &c. He had also held an alder-grove in Abram, of Richard de Abram, by the service of 2s. 3d. and a wood called Brookhurst in Pennington. His son Simon, then twenty-four years of age, was the heir ; Inq. p.m. 18 Edw. II, no. 33. Twelve oxgangs were in dispute in 1345 ; De Banco R. 342, m. 89 d. In the inquisition taken after the death of Maud widow of Sir Robert de Holland it was described as half the manor of Golborne, held of Robert de Langton in socage by a service of 6d.; Inq. p.m. 23 Edw. III, pt. i, no. 58. Thus the moiety of the manor was held by the Hollands of Upholland by a service of 6d. ; and of them was held by Simon de Holland and his heirs by the service of a pound of cummin.

[9] See the previous notes. The descent of Simon de Holland's manors has not been clearly ascertained ; see the account of Byrom in Lowton.

[10] At Pentecost 1352 Alice widow of Simon de Holland claimed dower in twelve messuages, windmill, water-mill, &c., in Golborne, from Nicholas de Tyldesley and Amice his wife, the latter being the heiress; Duchy of Lanc. Assize R. 2, m. 3 d. ; also (July) m. 1 d. She claimed dower in the manor of Lightshaw from Joan widow of Hugh de Tyldesley ; m. 2 d. This Simon was probably the Simon son and heir of Simon, 1325.

Amice appears to have married, secondly, William son of Roger de Bradshagh ; her sister and co-heir Joan married Henry de Bradshagh, and in 1367 they claimed from Thurstan son of Sir William de Holland, and Richard son of William de Holland, six messuages, mill, and land in Golborne by virtue of the grant of Thurstan de Holland to Juliana Gillibrand ; De Banco R. 429, m. 99.

[11] See the account of Tyldesley and Inskip.

An agreement was made in 1396 between Richard son of Henry de Kighley and Nicholas Blundell of Little Crosby, who married a daughter of Nicholas de

also,[19] with other of the neighbouring families.[20] Elizabeth Kighley and Ralph Haselhurst were the landowners contributing to the subsidy in Mary's reign ;[21] Edward Bankes was the only freeholder recorded in 1600.[22] The Pierpoint family occur in Golborne and the neighbourhood from an early time.[23] Henry Pierpoint died in or before 1642 holding land here ;[24] and another of the same name in 1654 petitioned the Parliamentary Commissioners for the discharge of the two-thirds of his inheritance sequestered in 1643 for the recusancy of his father Richard, deceased ; he himself was 'conformable.'[25]

The Inclosure Award for Golborne Heath, with plan, is preserved at the County Council Offices, Preston.

For the Established Church St. Thomas's was built in 1850 ; the benefice is a rectory, in the patronage of the Earl of Derby.

The Primitive Methodists have a chapel. The Baptists began a meeting in 1894.

The Congregationalists have a church originating in occasional visits from preachers in 1821 onwards ;

a chapel, still existing in part, was built in 1830, replaced by the present one in 1860.[26] The Welsh Congregationalists also had a place of worship.

For Roman Catholic worship[27] the church of All Saints was erected in 1863.[28]

LOWTON

Laitton (? Lauton), 1201 ; Lauton, 1202.

Lowton is situated in flat uninteresting country, covered for the most part with bricks and mortar, for the very scattered town of Lowton spreads itself in every direction, leaving spaces only for pastures between the streets or groups of dwellings. Lowton is a residential suburban retreat, easily reached by electric car from the industrial town of Leigh. Such a description is enough to indicate that what natural features once existed have long ago been superseded. In the extreme south a little patch of unreclaimed ground, known as Highfield Moss, represents the last relic of undisturbed nature. The Pebble Beds of the

[19] Robert Banastre, lord of Makerfield, in the latter part of the 13th century granted to Richard de Halghton or Houghton and Robert his son land, the bounds of which began in the north by Meurickys Ford and passed by Herniys Croft to the brook ; also another plat by the land of Elias son of Robert, the rent to be 3s. 4½d. ; Raines MSS. (Chet. Lib.), xxxviii, 395.

Robert de Halghton afterwards gave them to his brother Elias, who was to pay a rent of 12d. for one portion and of 26d. for the other to the lord of Newton ; ibid. The latter of these was given by Elcock son of Richard de Halghton to his son Roger, and this Roger in 1333 sold the whole to Gilbert de Haydock ; ibid. 395, 397. Roger afterwards claimed land from William son of Cecily de Haydock, and Robert son of William ; De Banco R. 292, m. 28 d. This may have been a continuation of Roger's suit in 1315 against Maud and Cecily, daughters of his brother Richard ; De Banco R. 212, m. 342.

Richard de Haighton and Hawise his wife did not prosecute the suit they brought against Thurstan de Holland in 1276 ; Assize R. 405, m. 1.

Matthew de Haydock, father of Gilbert, had in 1296 purchased land in Golborne from Elias son of Thurstan de Holland and others ; Raines, loc. cit. 395, 397. Elias son of Thurstan had been enfeoffed by Thomas Clynkard, whose son John afterwards tried to recover, but failed ; Assize R. 408, m. 23 d. and Raines, loc. cit. 395, where are given the grants by Thomas Clinkard and the release by his widow Mabel. William son of William Clinkard of Golborne occurs in 1356 ; Duchy of Lanc. Assize R. 5, m. 4 d.

The Feodary in Dods. MSS. cxxxi, fol. 34b, has some entries partly explained by the foregoing : Roger son of Robert holds [in Lightshaw] a messuage and land by the service of 16d. ; Roger de Snythull a messuage and land by 6d. ; Elias son of Richard a messuage and land by 27d. (22d.).

Another son of Richard de Halghton, named William, had land in Golborne—an oxgang and a half. Being very ill, and wishing to benefit his nephew Roger son

of William son of Hugh de Haydock, he granted him the tenement, putting him in seisin by delivering to Roger the door of the house by the hasp. William died next day, and his niece Eva, daughter of his brother Henry, claimed in 1294, but was defeated ; Assize R. 1299, m. 16 d.

[20] Margery widow of Robert de Kinknall claimed dower in Lowton and Golborne in 1277 against Elias de Golborne and various others ; the estate was two oxgangs, &c. ; De Banco R. 20, m. 15 d., 26, 26 d. Later she claimed against Robert de Holland and others, the estate being now called three oxgangs and five oxgangs ; ibid. R. 21, m. 44 d. 51 d. Robert de Holland called Henry de Sefton to warrant him, probably as bailiff of Makerfield ; ibid. R. 23, m. 51.

In 1350 a dispute between members of the Clayton family shows that John de Clayton and his wife Agnes held a messuage and lands in Golborne. He gave them to his son John, and on the latter's death without issue his three sisters became tenants—Agnes wife of John son of Simon Alotson ; Alice widow of Robert Wilkeson, and Ellen. The elder John married a second wife Cecily and had a son Richard, who made a successful claim to the estate ; Assize R. 1444, m. 6 d.

Anthony Green, who had lands also in Turton, purchased cottages and land in 1562 from Thomas Houghton ; Pal. of Lanc. Feet of F. bdle. 24, m. 57 ; also bdle. 31, m. 91. This was no doubt the origin of the estate of Ralph Green of Turton, held of the heirs of Richard Fleetwood in 1611 ; Lancs. Inq. p.m. (Rec. Soc. Lancs. and Ches.), i, 193.

The Crosses of Liverpool held lands of the lord of Newton by a rent of 3s. 8d. ; Duchy of Lanc. Inq. p.m. vi, no. 18 ; see also Pal. of Lanc. Feet of F. bdle. 57, m. 120.

Nicholas Huyton of Blackrod died in 1527 holding a tenement in Golborne of Thomas Langton by a rent of 6s. 3⅜d. ; Duchy of Lanc. Inq. p.m. vi, no. 53.

[21] Mascy of Rixton D. Ralph Haselhurst was one of the free tenants of Richard Langton in 1502, paying a rent of 2s. ; Duchy of Lanc. Inq. p.m. iii, no. 101.

[22] Misc. (Rec. Soc. Lancs. and Ches.), i, 241.

Henry Bankes and James his son had lands in Golborne and Charnock Richard in 1548 ; Pal. of Lanc. Feet of F. bdle. 13, m. 130. Other fines relate to the estate of Henry Bankes and Katherine his wife between 1562 and 1570 ; ibid. bdle. 24, m. 37, &c.

[23] See e.g. the account of Ince in Makerfield. In the Legh deeds in Raines MSS. xxxviii the family is often mentioned, chiefly in Newton, where Richard le Perpont had a grant of land about the end of the 13th century ; loc. cit. 117. He occurs as witness in 1316 ; ibid. 129. Contemporary with him was William son of Robert le Perpount of Newton ; Add. MS. 32106, no. 1550.

John son of Richard le Pierpoint follows in the time of Edward III ; Raines, loc. cit. 145 ; and Simon le Pierpoint in that of Henry VII ; ibid. 167, 169, 401. In Jan. 1430–1 Clemency daughter of Simon le Pierpoint was contracted to marry Thomas son and heir of William de Houghton in Winwick ; Towneley MS. HH, no. 1565.

An account of the family in Lancs. and Ches. Hist. and Gen. Notes, iii, 15, 20, 36, gives the succession of the Golborne Pierpoints from 1550 to 1700, when their estate was sold to John Johnson of Westhoughton, whose son John in 1710 sold it to Peter Legh of Lyme. The descent seems to have been—Richard, Henry the elder, Henry the younger, Richard, Henry, Richard.

[24] Duchy of Lanc. Inq. p.m. xxix, no. 47. This would be the 'Henry the younger' of the last note ; Richard his son and heir was of full age. Richard Pierpoint, Elizabeth his wife, Henry Pierpoint and Anne his wife, were among the recusants in 1641 ; Trans. Hist. Soc. (new ser.), xiv, 245.

[25] Cal. of Com. for Compounding, v, 3201.

[26] Nightingale, Lancs. Nonconformity, iv, 61–7.

[27] The Ven. James Bell, priest, was early in 1584 'condemned according to the statute for saying mass in Golborne upon St. John's Day in Christmas last' ; Foley, Rec. S.J. ii, 136, quoting S.P. Dom. Eliz. clxvii, 40. He suffered at Lancaster in April.

[28] Liverpool Cath. Ann. 1901.

New Red Sandstone (Bunter Series) cover the entire township. The area is 1,830 [1] acres. The population in 1901 was 2,964.

The principal road is that from Newton to Leigh; entering at the south-west corner, and keeping near to the eastern boundary, it passes through the hamlets known as the town of Lowton, Lane Head, Lowton St. Mary's, and Lowton Common. Another road to Leigh branches off from it, keeping near the western boundary, and passing through Lowton village, Byrom, and Mossley. A cross road, lined with dwellings, passes through Lowton village and Lane Head. The London and North-Western Company's Liverpool and Manchester line crosses the southern end of the township, where it is joined by a loop line connecting with the same company's main line to the north; there is a station called Lowton. The Great Central Company's line from Manchester to Wigan passes through the northern half of the township, and at Lowton Common is joined by the line from St. Helens (Liverpool, St. Helens, and South Lancashire Railway); a station at this point is called Lowton St. Mary's.

Cotton-spinning and fustian-making were formerly carried on here.[2] Some silk-weaving is done as a cottage industry. Glue is made.

On 27 November 1642 Lord Derby's levies were routed on Lowton Common by the people of the district.[3]

A stone cross formerly stood at Four Lane Ends, near the present parish church.[4]

There is a parish council.

Before the Conquest *LOWTON*, which **MANOR** then no doubt included Kenyon, was one of the berewicks of the royal manor of Newton; and in later times it formed one of the members of the fee or barony of Makerfield.[5] In 1212 William de Lawton held a manor assessed at 6½ plough-lands, and comprising not only two-thirds of Lowton and the whole of Kenyon, but half of Golborne and the small manor of Arbury.[6] His father Adam, who was living in 1200,[7] had made a number of infeudations,[8] and William himself granted Kenyon to a younger son.[9] Robert de Lawton succeeded him about 1260.[10] From this time, however, though the local surname frequently appears,[11] it does not seem that anyone claimed the lordship of the manor except the barons of Makerfield.[12] It is probable, therefore, that direct heirs failed, the manor reverting to the chief lord. It has since descended in the same way as Newton.[13]

The manor of *BYROM* in the northern portion of Lowton may reasonably be identified as the whole or chief part of the plough-land held in 1212 by Richard de Winwick of Thomas de Golborne.[14]

About 1270 Robert Banastre, lord of Newton, granted the Golborne lands to Thurstan de Holland.[15] The descent is not clear, but Byrom came by inheri-

---

[1] Including 9 of inland water.

[2] Baines, *Dir.* 1825, ii, 718.

[3] Report quoted in Baines's *Lancs.* (ed. 1836), ii, 17.

[4] *Lancs. and Ches. Hist. and Gen. Notes,* i, 203–5.

[5] *V.C.H. Lancs.* i, 366 n. The total assessment of Lowton seems to have been three plough-lands.

[6] *Lancs. Inq. and Extents* (Rec. Soc. Lancs. and Ches.), i, 73. The manor was held by knight's service, 'where 9½ plough-lands make the fee of one knight.'

[7] Farrer, *Lancs. Pipe R.* 133. He was the son of Pain de Lawton; Kuerden, fol. MS. 363, R.

[8] *Inq. and Extents,* loc. cit. They were: 4 oxgangs (in Golborne) to Hugh de Haydock; 2 oxgangs to Robert son of Siward; half a plough-land (in Arbury) to Geoffrey Gernet; 2 oxgangs to Orm de Middleton, and the same to Robert de Kenyon; also Flitcroft to the Knights Hospitallers. The three grants of two oxgangs each may be those subsequently held by Robert de Winwick, Ellen daughter of Aldusa, and William de Sankey.

[9] See the account of Kenyon. William gave Witherscroft, lying by Byrom Brook, to Alan de Rixton at farm for 12d.; *Inq. and Extents,* loc. cit. William de Lawton was still in possession in 1242; ibid. 148. Alice his widow, daughter of Hugh de Winwick, released to Jordan de Kenyon all her dower in Kenyon; Kuerden, loc. cit.

Alan de Rixton gave his lands in Byrom to Henry son of Richard de Glazebrook. In 1303 a marriage was agreed upon between Henry son of Henry de Glazebrook and Isabel daughter of Alan de Rixton; Kuerden, fol. MS. 364; see also *Trans. Hist. Soc.* (new ser.), iv, 159 (W. 14). Alan son of Alan de Rixton claimed common of pasture in Lowton in 1292; Assize R. 408, m. 63 d. The lands de-

scended to the Byr Rixton Deeds, R 63

[10] As

tance to Alice, who married Henry son of Henry son of Richard de Glazebrook, whereupon he obtained the surname of Byrom.[16] The family improved its position by later marriages, and about 1420 Henry de Byrom married Lucy a daughter and co-heir of Henry son of John de Parr.[17] His grandson Henry married Constance daughter and co-heir of Gilbert Abram, and one of the heirs of the Boydells of Grappenhall ; by this considerable lands in Cheshire were acquired, together with the advowson of Grappenhall.[18]

The family continued to prosper. Henry Byrom, living in 1553,[19] married successively daughters of Ralph Langton and Sir Richard Bold, and his eldest son Thomas[20] married a daughter of Sir Thomas Langton, but dying without issue the manor of Byrom passed to his younger brother John, who about 1559 married Margaret widow of Thomas Parr.[21] He

acquired much of the Parr inheritance, and Parr Hall became the chief seat of the Byroms.

John Byrom was in 1590 among the ' more usual comers to church,' but not a communicant ; " Mary the wife of his son and heir Henry was at the same time a ' recusant and indicted thereof.' [23]

John Byrom died in 1592 or 1593, holding the manor of Byrom and various lands, windmills, &c., in Lowton, Golborne, and Abram, of Thomas Langton, in socage, by a rent of 4s. 7½d. ; he also held the manor of Parr, and lands there and in other town-

BYROM of Byrom.
Argent a cheveron between three hedgehogs sable.

[16] An account of the Byrom families by Canon Raines will be found in the Chetham Society's edition of John Byrom's *Correspondence* (old ser. xliv) ; and supplementary matter in *Lancs. and Ches. Antiq. Notes*, ii, 26, 91, 154.

The descendants of Thurstan de Holland are not clearly ascertained. He appears to have had three sons by Juliana daughter of John Gillibrand—Thurstan, Adam, and Simon. He is not usually called their father, but made grants to them ; Assize R. 408, m. 16 d. In a suit of 1292 Simon is called son of Thurstan ; ibid. m. 25. In a claim of the same date made by Alan son of Alan de Rixton against Simon son of Thurstan de Holland, Byrom was said to be ' neither town, borough, nor hamlet ' ; ibid.

Simon the youngest son succeeded ; in 1303 he claimed land from Henry de Glazebrook, but the jury found that it was really in Newton and not in Lowton or Golborne ; Assize R. 420, m. 2 d. Alice the wife of Henry de Byrom was perhaps Simon's granddaughter by an elder son, for a son Simon is afterwards described as ' son and heir,' Alice's parentage not being recorded, though she claimed in her own right. Henry's parentage is shown by the Mascy of Rixton Deeds already quoted ; R. 63, W. 14. It appears that Alan de Rixton's grant of lands in Lowton to Henry son of Richard de Glazebrook was absolute, and that the marriage of Henry's son with Isabel de Rixton did not take place, this son Henry, whose wardship was claimed in 1306 by Alan de Rixton, being the Henry de Byrom of 1335.

Henry de Byrom first occurs in 1325 as witness to a local charter ; Raines MSS. xxxviii, 397. Three years later, by fine, Thurstan son of Simon de Holland settled lands in Byrom, Newton, Lowton, and Golborne upon Henry de Byrom and Alice his wife ; *Final Conc.* (Rec. Soc. Lancs. and Ches.), ii, 70. The remainder was to the right heirs of Henry.

In 1344–5 Henry de Byrom and Alice his wife recovered certain lands in Lowton from Robert son of Sir Robert de Langton and others ; Assize R. 1435, m. 34, 36 d.

In the next years Simon son of Simon son and heir of Simon de Holland, who had a grant from Thurstan de Holland, who in turn had received from Robert Banastre, claimed and recovered common of pasture in Lowton against Henry de Byrom and Adam his brother, Alice wife of Henry (claiming in her own right), and

John, Simon, and William, sons of Henry. The recognitors found that an agreement had been made between Henry and Simon de Holland, the grandfather, as to an inclosure and division of the wood, but this was not carried out ; Assize R. 1435, m. 9 d.

At the same time other claims were made against the Byroms respecting land called Medewale in Lowton. Adam son of Adam son of Robert de Medewale claimed by grant of William, lord of Lowton, to one Roger de Pennington, father of Robert de Medewale ; and Roger de Flitcroft, as cousin and heir of Roger son of Richard de Wirral, to whom Robert de Lawton had made a grant, claimed another portion of the same land ; ibid. m. 16, 17. William son of Adam son and heir of William de Hesketh was another claimant ; ibid. m. 19.

Simon de Byrom, possibly the younger son of Henry already mentioned, occurs in various ways down to 1400 ; Raines, *Byrom Pedigrees* (Chet. Soc.), 5. He was defendant in a suit in 1356 ; Duchy of Lanc. Assize R. 5, m. 17. In a Subsidy Roll of about 1380 he is described as a ' franklin ' ; Lay Subs. Lanc. bdle. 130, no. 24.

Simon was perhaps the father of Thurstan de Byrom, who before 1398 had married Cecily daughter and co-heir of Richard de Lawton. Alice the other daughter married Thurstan son of Richard de Tyldesley ; Harl. MS. 2112, fol. 151/ 187. In 1391–2 Richard de Tyldesley of Lowton had become bound to Simon de Byrom ; Kuerden MSS. vi, fol. 86, no. 236. Cecily does not seem to have had any children, but Alice had several daughters, and Agnes daughter of George Hartley was her representative in 1547 ; Harl. MS. 2112, fol. 152*b*/188*b*, 159/ 195. Thomas de Byrom is named in 1411 (Towneley MS. RR. no. 1533) and was witness to charters in 1414 and 1423; Raines, loc. cit. 6.

[17] See the account of Parr. The marriage took place in or before 1422 ; Pal. of Lanc. Feet of F. bdle. 5, m. 10.

John Byrom, apparently the son of Henry, who received £20 on the marriage, espoused Margaret daughter of William de Lever of Great Lever in 1437 ; Add. MS. 32103 ; Lever D. no. 126, 127. Margaret is called the widow of John Byrom in 1473 (Kuerden MSS. vi, fol. 84, no. 207), but John seems to have been living in 1476 ; Culcheth D. no. 257, 259.

[18] The marriage probably took place in

or before 1466, when Henry Byrom, senior, John Byrom, and Thomas Byrom, priest, no doubt as trustees for the younger Henry and his wife, presented to the rectory of Grappenhall ; Ormerod, *Ches.* (ed. Helsby), i, 600.

Among the deeds at West Hall, High Legh, Cheshire, is one dated 1486, referring to the appointment of arbitrators to decide the disputes between Henry Byrom of Lowton and Constance his daughter, and Thomas Legh of High Legh.

In 1487–8 Henry Byrom and Constance his wife and James Holt and Isabel his wife received from the trustees the manor of Handley near Chester, and lands there and in Latchford, Ringey (Hale), Stockport, and Stoke ; ibid. ii, 723. For an interesting claim to tolls on the passage across the Mersey see *Duchy Plead.* (Rec. Soc. Lancs. and Ches.), i, 39–41. For other notices see Dep. Keeper's *Rep.* xxxvii, App. 111. In 1502 Henry Byrom paid 4s. 7½d. annual rent to the lord of Makerfield ; Duchy of Lanc. Inq. p.m. iii, no. 101. He died before his wife.

John son and heir of Henry Byrom occurs with his four sisters in a grant by the father dated 1506 ; Raines, loc. cit. 7. He was forty years of age in 1512 when the inquisition after his mother's death was taken ; Dep. Keeper's *Rep.* xxxix, App. 45.

Thomas Byrom, dead in 1526, is supposed to have been the son of John and father of Henry Byrom ; Raines, loc. cit.; Piccope, *Wills* (Chet. Soc.), i, 20 ; Dep. *Keeper's Rep.* ut sup.

[19] In this year he made a settlement of the manor of Byrom, lands in Lowton, &c. ; Pal. of Lanc. Feet of F. bdle. 14, m. 7.

[20] In a Subsidy Roll of Mary's reign he and Elizabeth Byrom (widow of Henry) were the only landowners contributing in Lowton and Kenyon ; Mascy of Rixton D. By his will, dated 1559, Thomas Byrom gave his soul to St. Mary and all the saints, and his body to be buried in the churchyard at Winwick, ' near to the place where my father lieth buried, whose soul God pardon ' ; he left 5s. to the repair of the church ; Raines, loc. cit. 8.

Mary his widow was in 1560 a plaintiff against John Byrom and others ; *Ducatus Lanc.* (Rec. Com.), ii, 221.

[21] Ibid. See also the account of Parr.

[22] Gibson, *Lydiate Hall*, 245 ; quoting S.P. Dom. Eliz. ccxxxv, 4.

[23] Ibid. 247.

ships.[24] Henry Byrom of Parr, his son and heir, who was then thirty years of age, died in 1613, holding Byrom by a rent of 3s. 7½d. His son John had died in 1611, and the heir was John's eldest son Henry Byrom, born in 1608.[25] He espoused the royal side in the Civil War, and is said to have been killed at the battle of Edgehill in 1642.[26] He had seven children, the eventual heir being the fifth son, Samuel, born in 1634.[27] His son John succeeded him in infancy, and died in 1696,[28] the heir (his son Samuel) being once again a minor. In 1706, having attained his majority, he came to an agreement with his sisters, mother, and grandmother, and obtained possession of the manors and lands.[29] He was, however, a spendthrift, and four years later was negotiating the sale of 'the royalty, manor, and demesne of Byrom.'[30] The purchaser was Joseph Byrom, a wealthy Manchester mercer.[31] His daughter Elizabeth carried it by marriage to her cousin, the celebrated John Byrom of Kersal, and it descended to their great-granddaughter Eleonora Atherton of Byrom and Kersal, who died in 1870, having bequeathed this and most of her estate to Mr. Edward Fox, her godson. He took the name and arms of Byrom.[32]

The Hospitallers had land here by the grant of Pain and Adam de Kenyon.[33]

The Mathers of Lowton are said to have been the parent stock of a celebrated Puritan family.[34]

In 1600 James Lowe was a freeholder.[35] The heirs of John Byrom, John Lowe, and the heirs of John Baxter contributed as landowners to the subsidy of 1628.[36] John Widdows of Lowton compounded for his 'delinquency' in 1649; as he had not 'engaged in the latter war' he had possibly joined the king's forces at the opening of the conflict.[37] Richard Holcroft, as a recusant, asked leave to compound for the sequestered two-thirds of his estate in 1653.[38]

An Inclosure Award was made in 1765.[39]

The Commonwealth surveyors in 1650 recom-

---

[24] Duchy of Lanc. Inq. p.m. xvi, no. 37. The pedigree recorded at the visitation of 1664 begins with him; Dugdale, Visit. (Chet. Soc.), 66. His will is printed in Piccope's Wills, ii, 116. It names his wife Mildred, his son Henry, and grandson John; 6s. 8d. or 5s. each was granted to serving men, maids, &c., and twenty windles of barley were to be distributed among his poor neighbours; the sum total of the inventory was £259 18s. 9d. The will of his brother, Richard Byrom of Middleton, is also given (p. 117).

[25] Lancs. Inq. p.m. (Rec. Soc. Lancs. and Ches.), i, 271, 274; ii, 11.

Henry Byrom in 1594 acquired a considerable property in Lowton from Thomas Langton and Thomas Fleetwood; Pal. of Lanc. Feet of F. bdle. 59, m. 371. His will is among the Mascy of Rixton Deeds; Trans. Hist. Soc. (new ser.), iv, 175. Lands in Lowton were to be sold to pay debts; there were no religious or charitable bequests.

The inquisitions show that John Byrom was twice married—to Ellen Lister of Thornton in 1604, and in 1607 to Isabel Nowell of Read, who survived her husband. The heir was clearly the issue of the later marriage.

[26] Dugdale, Visit. loc. cit. He was a major in the regiment of foot raised by Lord Molyneux.

Immediately after his grandfather's death he had been betrothed to Margaret, the nine-year-old daughter of Sir Thomas Ireland of Bewsey, but the contract was afterwards annulled; Raines, loc. cit. 10.

[27] Two of the elder sons were lunatics, and two died young. Samuel had a younger brother Edward, who recorded the family pedigree at the visitation of 1664. The heirs being minors and the family Protestant, the estates were not interfered with by the Commonwealth authorities. Three of the sons—Adam, Samuel, and Edward—were admitted to Gonville and Caius College, Cambridge, in 1646 and 1650; Venn, Admissions, 221, 231.

Samuel Byrom of Byrom was buried at Winwick 26 Jan. 1665-6. Allegations concerning his will, dated 1668, are preserved in the Diocesan Registry at Chester; see Index (Rec. Soc. Lancs. and Ches.), ii, 20; also Lancs. and Ches. Antiq. Notes, ii, 154. Entries in the Wilmslow registers are printed in Local Glean. Lancs. and Ches. i, 12.

[28] John Byrom was born 24 June 1659, as appears by an entry in the Rostherne registers. He was admitted to Gray's Inn, 1676, and about 1683 married Elizabeth daughter of Sir John Otway; she afterwards married Robert Hedges and — Hamilton; Raines, loc. cit. 10. At the beginning of 1694 he was chosen at a bye-election to represent Wigan in Parliament; Pink and Beaven, Parl. Repre. of Lancs. 230; Hist. MSS. Com. Rep. xiv, App. iv, 282, 283. He was buried at Winwick 3 Mar. 1695-6, the register describing him as 'of Parr.' The monumental inscription describes him as 'a hearty champion of the Church of England, vigorously resisting the sacrilegious usurpations of the schismatics at his own charges'; as for instance in his recovery of St. Helen's Chapel for the Established Church; Hist. MSS. Com. Rep. xiv, App. iv, 246.

[29] Raines, loc. cit. 12.

Early in 1707 in a fine concerning the manors of Byrom and Parr, and various houses, mills, and lands in Lowton, Parr, Westleigh, Abram, Hindley, Sutton, Windle, and Golborne, the deforciants were Samuel Byrom, John Robinson, Lady Elizabeth Otway, widow, Robert Hedges and Elizabeth his wife, and Elizabeth Byrom, spinster (Samuel's sister); Pal. of Lanc. Feet of F. bdle. 258, m. 33.

[30] He was known as 'the Beau.' An account of his pamphlet, written in the Fleet Prison in 1729, will be found in Canon Raines's book, 13, 14. He states in it that 'he had a competent estate in Lancashire, but by being ill-introduced to the world, and soon falling into the hands of sharpers and gamesters (the very bane and ruin of many young gentlemen when they first come from the University), his estate was diminished, and, what was more valuable, his reputation was lost.' He was still living in destitution in London in 1739.

[31] An account of this family is given in Canon Raines's work already cited. See further under Kersal.

[32] Baines, Lancs. (ed. Croston), iv, 372.

[33] Pain de Lawton gave Flitcroft to the Hospital and Adam his son regranted or confirmed it. Afterwards the Hospitallers granted part to Jordan de Kenyon; the land appears to have been in two places, one in Lowton and the other in Kenyon; Kuerden, fol. MS. 363, R.

mended that a church should be built in the township, but nothing was done.[40]

St. Luke's Church was erected for the worship of the Established Church in 1732. By the Winwick Rectory Act of 1845 it became a parish church, the incumbent being rector; the Earl of Derby is patron.[41] St. Mary's Church was built in 1861; the benefice is a perpetual curacy in the gift of Mrs. Leach.[42]

A Methodist chapel is said to have been erected in 1788;[43] there are now Primitive and Independent Methodist chapels.

KENYON

Kenien, 1212; Kenian, 1258; Keynan, 1259. Kenylow is at the border of Kenyon and Croft.

This township has an area of 1,685[1] acres and stretches north-west from the boundary of Newton to the Carr Brook, a distance of 2½ miles. The geological formation consists mainly of the Bunter series of the New Red Sandstone. To the north-east of Twist Green the Pebble Beds give place to the Upper Mottled Sandstone of this series. The surface of the country is level, with an upper soil of clay, beneath which a stiffer red clay lies. Meadow lands alternate with fields of potatoes and corn, and a fair number of trees are sprinkled about the country. Hedges appear well-grown and trimly kept. The district is deficient in water-courses. The population numbered 329 in 1901.

The principal road is that from Lowton to Cul-cheth, a branch of it passing south through Kenyon village. The Liverpool and Manchester Railway of the London and North Western Company crosses the township and has a station at Kenyon Junction, whence a branch goes off to Leigh. The Great Central Company's Manchester and Wigan line also passes through the township.

Pocket Nook, Diggle Green, and Broseley occupy the north-east corner, Sandy Brow the south-west.

Bricks are manufactured.

The bronze tongue of a Roman fibula was found here.[2] There is a Bronze-age barrow.[3]

MANOR KENYON was originally part of Lowton, but about the end of the reign of Henry III William de Lawton granted to his son Jordan 'the whole vill of Kenyon,' at the rent of 1d. a year or a pair of white gloves.[4] This was confirmed shortly afterwards by Robert, lord of Lowton, son of William.[5] Jordan de Kenyon lived on until about 1300,[6] when he was succeeded by his son Adam.[7] This Adam, who was living in 1330, was followed regularly by a son[8] and grandson of the same name. The third Adam de Kenyon came into his inheritance about 1346, when a number of settlements were made.[9] Three years later his son John was contracted in marriage to Joan daughter of Gilbert de Southworth,[10] but probably died soon afterwards, as the manor descended with Adam's daughter Amery, who in 1358 was married to Richard son of Thurstan de Holland of Denton.[11] Subsequently it descended,[12] like Denton, Heaton, and

---

[40] *Commonwealth Cb. Surv.* (Rec. Soc. Lancs. and Ches.), 49.

[41] Raines in *Notitia Cestr.* (Chet. Soc.), ii, 262.

[42] A district was assigned in 1862; *Lond. Gaz.* 7 Jan. 1862.

[43] Baines, *Lancs.* (ed. 1836), iii, 635.

[1] 1,686, including 4 of inland water; Census Rep. 1901.

[2] *Lancs. and Ches. Antiq. Soc.* x, 250.

[3] Ibid. xxi, 120.

[4] Harl. MS. 2112, fol. 145/181, &c., contains a collection of the Holland of Denton family deeds. The charter referred to is on fol. 146b/182b; 'R. rector of Winwick' was one of the witnesses.

[5] Ibid. fol. 147/183.

[6] In 1256 Jordan de Kenyon gave half a mark for an assize taken before P. de Percy; Orig. 42 Hen. III, m. 11. He was therefore in possession of Kenyon by that time. Two years later he and Robert de Lawton and Hugh de Hindley were defendants in a suit by Roger de Twiss, who complained that they had destroyed his chattels in Kenyon and Culcheth; Cur. Reg. R. 160, m. 6; 162, m. 6 d.

In 1276 Agnes widow of Henry de Hindley claimed common of pasture in Kenyon from Jordan de Kenyon and from William de Sankey and Robert his son, an approvement from the waste having been made; but the jury found she had sufficient; Assize R. 405, m. 1 d.

In 1287 Jordan de Kenyon came to an agreement with Gilbert de Southworth respecting the bounds of the waste between Kenyon and Croft; Harl. MS. 2112, fol. 158b/194b. In 1292 he was plaintiff in several cases (Assize R. 408, m. 42, 26 d. 36), and defendant in 1295; Assize R. 1306, m. 15.

To Richard his son and his heirs he granted a piece of land in Kenyon, together with another piece formerly held by another son, Hugh, and the rent of Robert de Woodhouse; Harl. MS. 2112, fol. 158b/194b and fol. 160/196. John de Mosley, rector of Winwick, was one of the witnesses, so that the grant was before 1306. This Richard, mentioned with his father in the plea of 1295, was probably the father of the Jordan son of Richard de Kenyon of later deeds—1324 and 1347; ibid. fol. 157b/193b, 155/191; also Assize R. 425, m. 4.

Hugh and Roger sons of Jordan de Kenyon occur among witnesses to charters about 1300; Towneley MS. GG, no. 998, 1119.

[7] Adam de Kenyon received a grant of land in Lowton in the time of his father Jordan; Harl. MS. 2112, fol. 151/187. He married Godith daughter of Richard son of Stephen de Lawton; Culcheth D. (*Lancs. and Ches. Hist. and Gen. Notes*, i), no. 3, 15. Her father had a grant of lands in Lowton from Robert Banastre; Harl. MS. 2112, fol. 147/183. Adam occurs in various ways down to 1330, when as lord of Kenyon he granted a rent-charge of £40 sterling to Adam the son of his son Adam and heirs by Maud daughter of Robert de Hesketh; ibid. fol. 155/191. Jordan his son is named in the deed and in Assize R. 1435, m. 47. His daughter Godith married Richard de Abram in 1324; Harl. MS. 2112, fol. 159/195; 151/187.

[8] In 1344 Gilbert de Culcheth senior received from Adam de Kenyon senior, Adam son and heir of Adam de Kenyon senior, Jordan de Kenyon, and others, £10 in part payment of £100; ibid. fol. 153/189. A similar receipt in 1346 names only one Adam de Kenyon; ibid. fol. 151b/187b.

[9] Margery widow of Adam de Kenyon in 1346 gave to Adam her son two-thirds of the manor of Kenyon; ibid. fol. 151/187. In the following year Adam de Kenyon granted to trustees the manor of Kenyon with wards, reliefs, and escheats; also the reversion of the lands held by his mother Margaret in dower, and by Jordan de Kenyon for life; ibid. fol. 155/191.

Margaret widow of Adam de Kenyon was in 1356 summoned to answer the younger Adam concerning waste he alleged she had caused or allowed in her dower lands in Kenyon and Lowton. She had pulled down a hall and sold the timber to the value of 100l.; two chambers each worth 40s., &c.; had made pits and taken marl and clay, and sold it to the value of 60s.; had cut down eight oaks in the wood, each worth half a mark, and apple trees and pear trees in the gardens worth 2s. each. Margaret denied the accusation, and said that a grange and ox-house had fallen down through old age, and she had taken an oak for repairs; Duchy of Lanc. Assize R. 5, m. 7 d.

In 1347 also John, Jordan, and Hugh, sons of Adam de Kenyon senior, recovered their annuities from Adam de Kenyon, Maud his wife, and their son John; Assize R. 1435, m. 14, 14 d, 16. The first of these claimants, John, was a priest, and in the pleas just cited is called 'son and heir' of the elder Adam (m. 14); he was afterwards trustee for his brother; Harl. MS. 2112, fol. 150b/186b. Jordan de Kenyon and his wife Amery, Hugh de Kenyon and his wife Alice, are mentioned in 1353; Assize R. 435, m. 18 d; 20.

[10] Harl. MS. 2112, fol. 155/191.

[11] Ibid. fol. 147b/183b, 151/187.

[12] Richard de Holland died in 1402 seised of the manor of Kenyon as of the right of Amery his wife; it was held of the lord of Makerfield by knight's service and a rent of 4s.; Thurstan his son and heir was over thirty years of age; Towneley MS. DD, no. 2461. In later inquisitions the tenure is described as socage,

the other estates of the family, to the Earl of Wilton. Lord Grey de Wilton in 1787 contributed £23 to the land tax of £29.

William son of Henry de Sankey had a grant of

KENYON. *Sable a cheveron engrailed between three crosses patonce or.*

EGERTON, Earl of Wilton. *Argent a lion rampant gules between three pheons sable.*

Windycroft and Snapecroft in Kenyon from William de Lawton ;[13] he had sons William and Robert. The former died before his father, leaving a daughter

Margery, who married successively Robert de Risley and William Gillibrand.[14] The Risleys appear to have secured most or all of the inheritance, but William de Sankey endowed his younger son Robert with a portion.[15]

In the 14th and 15th centuries a minor Kenyon family had lands in this and the neighbouring parishes. Katherine daughter of Adam son of Matthew de Kenyon was in 1366 the wife of John Amoryson of Wigan.[16] A Matthew de Kenyon left three children, William, who died early ; Agnes, who married John Eccleston ; and Ellen, who married Oliver Anderton. The two daughters divided the inheritance.[17]

The Hospitallers had lands in Kenyon.[18]

A family named Woodhouse was seated here in the 14th century.[19] The Morleys of Billington long held lands here.[20]

Richard Thompson petitioned in 1653 to be allowed to compound for the two-thirds of his estate sequestered for recusancy.[21] Robert son of Richard Speakman in 1717 registered an estate as a 'papist.'[22]

---

without rent ; Duchy of Lanc. Inq. p.m. iv, no. 36, 58. Richard Holland died in 1619 holding the manors of Kenyon and Lowton of the lord of Newton in socage, by a yearly rent of 18*s.* ; *Lancs. Inq. p.m.* (Rec. Soc. Lancs. and Ches.), ii, 145.

[13] Hale D. ; William de Sankey also acquired lands in Kenyon from Jordan de Kenyon and in Lowton from Robert Banastre, in Croft from Gilbert de Southworth, in Culcheth from Robert de Kinknall, and in Dallam and Penketh from Roger son of Jordan, whose right seems to have been derived from Jordan son of Roger, grantee of Robert Banastre and William de Penketh ; ibid. Henry de Sankey, father of William, had had a burgage in Warrington from William le Boteler.

[14] Assize R. 1306, m. 15 ; a suit in 1295 as to whether Jordan de Kenyon, Adam and Richard his sons, and others had disseised Robert de Risley and Margery his wife of their common of pasture in 13 acres of wood and 60 acres of moor in Kenyon ; also of mast for their pigs in 50 acres of wood, and wood for housebote, heybote, and burning. It was alleged, among other things, that Robert, the younger son, when his father was lying on his deathbed, went to Jordan, chief lord of the town of Kenyon, and promised him that if he would help him to procure seisin of his father's tenements he would let him have a writing sealed with his father's seal ; and that Jordan accordingly drew up a charter, then proffered in court, which Robert sealed with his brother William's seal. The jury did not pronounce on this point, but their decision was generally in favour of the claimants.

Margery had been a plaintiff in 1284, when her guardianship had been unsuccessfully claimed by Jordan de Kenyon ; Robert de Hindley (or Risley) was her guardian ; Assize R. 1265, m. 5.

See also *Abbrev. Plac.* (Rec. Com.), 237*b* ; the service was that of two oxgangs of land where 9½ plough-lands made a knight's fee. From this it appears probable that the Sankey estate was two oxgangs, which Adam de Lawton gave to Robert de Sankey to acquit himself of the office of judge ; *Lancs. Inq. and Extents* (Rec. Soc. Lancs. and Ches.), i, 73. There was, however, another estate of two ox-

James Anderton was in 1552 found to have held lands in Kenyon of Edward Holland in socage, by a rent of 21. 4½*d.* ; Duchy of Lanc. Inq. p.m. ix, no. 14. His son Hugh Anderton and Alice his wife sold them to John Urmston in 1556 ; Pal. of Lanc. Feet of F. bdle. 17, m. 100.

[18] *Plac. de Quo War.* (Rec. Com.), 375. In 1332 the prior of St. John claimed a messuage and land in Kenyon from Peter de Risley ; De Banco R. 292, m. 354 d.

[19] John son of Adam del Woodhouse (or Woodhouses) was defendant in 1292 respecting land in Kenyon, and lost the case by default ; Assize R. 408, m. 18 d. Robert del Woodhouse was a defendant in 1295 ; ibid. 1306, m. 15. Henry son of Robert del Woodhouses in 1309 had a release of their claim on lands in the Woodhouses granted by John son of Adam son of Henry to his sister Ellen, wife of Henry Nightegale ; Lord Wilton's D. ; *Final Conc.* ii, 6. A grant to John son of Adam del Woodhouses is in Harl. MS. 2112, fol. 147*b*/183*b*. Henry del Woodhouses, Agnes his mother, and Richard his son occur in deeds up to 1347 ; ibid. fol. 147/183 ; 156/192. In 1421 Nicholas son of Ivo del Woodhouses was contracted to marry Katherine daughter of John son of Robert de Worsley ; ibid. fol. 147/183. William Leyland in 1467 seems to have bought the lands from Otwell Woodhouse and Margaret his wife ; Pal. of Lanc. Feet of F. bdle. 6, m. 2.

[20] *Final Conc.* ii, 176. Richard and Nicholas, sons of Richard Morley, had lands in Billington, Dinkley, and Kenyon in 1448–9 ; Towneley MS. DD, no. 1923. In 1528 it was found that Ughtred Morley had held a messuage and lands in Kenyon of the lord of Newton by the rent of a grain of corn ; Duchy of Lanc. Inq. p.m. vi, no. 67. His son Robert Morley held them in 1586 ; Pal. of Lanc. Feet of F. bdle. 48, m. 58.

[21] *Cal. of Com. for Compounding,* iv, 2176. He and his wife appear on the Recusant Roll of 1641 ; *Trans. Hist. Soc.* (new ser.), xiv, 245.

[22] Estcourt and Payne, *Engl. Cath. Non-jurors,* 117.

CULCHETH

Culchet, 1201; Kulchit, 1242; Culchith, Kil-chiche, Kylchiz, 1292. The usual spelling is Cul-cheth or Culchith; the local pronunciation is shown by the surnames Culshaw and Kilshaw, derived from it.

Peasfurlong, Holcroft, and Risley: there has been no material change in the spellings.

This large township, with an area of 5,369[1] acres, has long been divided into four quarters, though the boundaries are not always clearly defined, viz.: Culcheth proper in the north; Holcroft and Peas-furlong, the eastern and western parts of the centre; and Risley in the south. The eastern and northern boundaries are formed by the Glazebrook and its tributary the Carr Brook; another brook on the west divides Peasfurlong from Croft. The southern boundary appears to be drawn chiefly through moss-land.

The surface of the country is flat, the highest elevation at Twiss Green being but 107 ft. above sea level. In the north is agricultural country, fairly well timbered. In the south the land is but sparsely inhabited, and consists of reclaimed moss-land; some patches still exist where peat is cut for fuel and moss litter.

The characteristic vegetation of the moss-land is still in evidence here and there, where birch and bracken and nodding cotton sedges flourish. Potatoes and corn, more particularly oats, thrive in a clayey soil, where the land has been cleared of the bulk of the peat. The geological formation is represented by the Bunter series of the New Red Sandstone, and consists mainly of the Upper Mottled Sandstone of that series. Between Risley and Holcroft Mosses the pebble beds extending from the north-west almost touch an area of the Lower Keuper Basement Beds, which juts into this county from south of the Mersey.

The population in 1901 numbered 2,294.

Cotton is manufactured, and bricks and tiles are made. In the 17th and 18th centuries many of the inhabitants followed the occupation of linen weaving.

Culcheth proper has Carr, Hurst, Fowley and Twiss Green in the north-west, north-east, south-east, and south-west corners; the village of Glaze-bury[2] has sprung up in the last thirty years by Hurst, on the banks of the Glazebrook. The hall is to the east of Twiss Green. The area measures 1,310½ acres.

Holcroft Hall is near the Glazebrook; to the north is Eshot Lane, and a mile to the south Schole-field. The chapel was built in this division, at the corner where the boundaries of Holcroft, Peasfurlong, and Culcheth meet. The area of this quarter is 1,206½ acres.

Peasfurlong, which measures 1,296 acres, has Kingnall, or Kinknall, and Wigshaw in the north-west corner and Flitcroft near the centre.

Risley Old Hall is near the northern boundary of the quarter; the area is 1,556 acres. In Risley Moss pre-Roman and Roman remains have been dis-covered.

The principal road is that leading north and north-east from Warrington to Leigh. It is joined near the church by the road from Winwick through Croft. The Wigan Junction Railway of the Great Central system crosses the township, having a station (Culcheth) near Kinknall.

Culcheth Wake ceased in 1822.[3]

The township is governed by a parish council, and has been divided into three wards: Newchurch, Glazebury, and Risley.

MANORS The first notice by name of the manor of *CULCHETH* is that in the survey of 1212, when it was within the fee or barony of Warrington.[4] It so continued with some modification of tenure[5] until 1601, when Thomas Ireland of Bewsey, in consideration of 100 marks, released all his rights in the tenures, suits and services, ward, homage and reliefs in Culcheth held of the barony of Warrington.[6]

In 1212 Hugh son of Gilbert held the manor, by knight's service, of William le Boteler, as four plough-lands paying 4 marks a year. A certain Reynold had held it of Pain de Vilers, and as nothing is said as to the origin of his tenure, he may have been in posses-sion when the Warrington fee was granted to Pain.[7]

Gilbert de Culcheth, probably a son or grandson of Hugh son of Gilbert, held the manor in 1242.[8] He was killed in 1246 by unknown malefactors, and the township was fined because it made no pursuit.[9] He left four infant daughters as co-heirs, Margery, Elizabeth, Ellen, and Joan, who became wards of the lord of Warrington; and in course of time William le Boteler granted their marriage to Hugh de Hindley. Hugh married them to his own four sons, and Cul-cheth was divided among them,[11] its four quarters becoming the manors of Richard de Culcheth, who took the name of Culcheth; Adam, called de Peas-furlong, and later de Hindley; Robert, called de Risley; and Thomas, called de Holcroft.

I.—Margery, the wife of Richard de Culcheth, was dead in 1276 when Richard son of John de Haydock complained that he had been disseised of his common of pasture in *CULCHETH*. Richard de Culcheth replied that the land had been divided, and that the

---

[1] 5,373 according to the census of 1901, including 9 acres of inland water.

[2] The old name was Bury Lane; see *Lancs. and Ches. Antiq. Notes*, i, 2.

[3] Baines, *Lancs.* (ed. 1836), iii, 647.

[4] *Lancs. Inq. and Extents* (Rec. Soc. Lancs. and Ches.), i, 9.

[5] In 1548 four rents each of 2s. 2½d. were payable to Sir Thomas Boteler from Culcheth, Peasfurlong, Holcroft, and Ris-ley, the tenants being Gilbert Culcheth, Sir John Holcroft (two), and John Risley; Pal. of Lanc. Feet of F. bdle. 13, m. 142. The total rent of 8s. 10d. shows a great reduction from the 4 marks of 1212, being one-sixth only.

[10] Culcheth D. no. 20; it would appear from no. 2 that 40 marks was paid by Hugh.

This Hugh was lord of the manor of Hindley, or a moiety of it, which de-scended with Culcheth. There were others of the name.

[11] This appears from various suits re-ferred to, and from the deeds preserved by Dodsworth, cxlii, fol. 113; by one, Richard's approvements in the Little Twiss, Blind Hurst, Kinknall, and the mill houses were allowed. Richard and Margery's acknowledgement of the justice of the partition is no. 22 of the Cul-cheth D.

tenement for which common rights were claimed was in his late wife's portion, and Thomas, their son, should have been joined as defendant.[12] Thomas probably died soon after, for he is not mentioned again, later suits involving either Richard or Gilbert, sons of Richard and Margery.[13] Gilbert seems to have been the elder, and in 1291, that is, no doubt, as soon as he came of age, he brought a suit against his father respecting houses and land in Culcheth, which had been exchanged by his mother Margery with her mother Cecily.[14] In the following year he had entered into possession of his share of the dower of his grandmother Cecily, who was then dead.[15] Richard his father was still living in 1292, he and his

son Richard being involved in several suits with the other parceners, as also with tenants and others.[16] The father, however, died in or before 1298,[17] and Gilbert seems to have been lord of Culcheth until about 1342.[18]

He was succeeded by his son Gilbert,[19] who, by his first wife, had a son and heir Gilbert, married in 1345 to Joan daughter of Adam de Kenyon,[20] their son Gilbert being born about a year afterwards.[21] There were thus four Gilberts in succession, lords of Culcheth.[22] The last of them, who died between 1393 and 1402, had several children. His eldest son Thurstan dying about 1430 without male issue,[23] a younger son, Thomas, succeeded,[24] and had four sons, Gilbert,[25] Nicholas, Oliver, and George. Gilbert's two sons,

[12] Assize R. 405, m. 2. The defendants were Richard de Culcheth, Thomas de Holcroft, and Joan his wife, Robert de Hindley and Ellen his wife, Adam de Hindley and Isabel his wife, also Roger del Twiss, this last being a tenant of Richard's. In the following year Richard and his son Richard, together with Adam and Elizabeth, Thomas and Joan, were summoned to answer Hugh de Hulme, who charged them with taking his goods ; De Banco R. 21, m. 53 d.

In 1278 John de Haydock continued his suit against Richard del Twiss, Adam and Thomas and their wives being joined, also Roger del Twiss and Henry son of Robert de Paris ; but Richard, 'chief lord of Culcheth,' was not named ; Assize R. 1238, m. 34 d. ; 1239, m. 39 d. ; also 1268, m. 11.

[13] Richard son of Richard has been mentioned in the preceding note. Gilbert occurs in a plea by Cecily de Layton in 1284 ; Assize R. 1265, m. 22 ; he must at this time have been regarded as the heir.

[14] Assize R. 1294, m. 8.

[15] Ibid. 408, m. 50 d. Gilbert de Culcheth and Robert de Risley and Ellen his wife and others were at the same time plaintiffs against the Abbot of Cockersand, regarding a tenement in Hutton in Leyland, probably Dame Cecily's ; ibid. m. 58 d.

[16] Ibid. m. 27, 57, &c. ; Richard the son ; m. 32. In Aug. 1294 William le Boteler, lord of Warrington, agreed with Richard de Culcheth not to distrain the demesne of Culcheth for services during the life of Richard, the latter being allowed to distrain his men for them as if he were their immediate lord ; Culcheth D. no. 27. In 1300 William le Boteler agreed that in future Gilbert de Culcheth should find only one bedell for the court of Warrington ; Hale D.

[17] In this year Gilbert son of Richard de Culcheth granted to Hugh de Hindley all his manor of Culcheth for life, with remainder as to one half to his wife Beatrice for life should she survive him ; Culcheth D. no. 28. This was regranted in 1307 ; ibid. no. 33. See also no. 29, 31.

[18] The name of Gilbert de Culcheth occurs constantly in the charters of the time. In 1330 he 'put in his claim' in a settlement of the Risley portion of the manor ; Final Conc. (Rec. Soc. Lancs. and Ches.), ii, 74.

The most probable date for his death is that named in the text. In 1338 Gilbert de Culcheth granted to Gilbert his son his mills in Hindley and all his part in the water of Glazebrook and Ballisdene in Hindley ; Culcheth D. no.

48. In later deeds is named ; no. 49, Gilbert de Culcheth were the first witnes no. 51. Two yea Culcheth, no longe therefore probably th going deeds, agreed Warburton a to t son and heir Gilbe to marry by Sir Ge no. 52.

[19] Mentioned in His first wife is sai daughter of Sir Ge his second was Ceci ard de Bradshagh ; sh Hugh de Worseley 57, 63, &c. See a m. 3 d. ; 441, m. 5 Assize R. 7, m. 2 d.

[20] Cu

John[36] and Randle,[37] successively held the manor, which, on failure of male issue, reverted about 1495 to their uncle Nicholas, rector of East Bridgeford,[38] whose youngest brother Oliver thus became heir. In the year named he married Douce daughter of Gilbert Langton of Hindley,[39] but died in or before 1512, leaving Gilbert his heir, born in 1496, a minor.[30] Gilbert died in 1559[31] leaving several children by his wife Margaret daughter of John Holcroft.[32]

John, the eldest of these, married Cecily daughter of Thomas Southworth, and died in 1593.[33] He adhered in heart to the ancient faith, and in 1590 was reckoned among the 'more usual comers to church,'

though not a communicant.[34] His son John succeeded him,[35] and was followed by another son also named John in 1626. The latter died in 1640, just before the outbreak of the Civil War.[36] His eldest son, John, a 'papist delinquent,' had his estates sequestered by the Parliamentary authorities,[37] and died without issue in 1647, soon after attaining his majority, of wounds received in fighting for the king.[38] His brother Thomas,[39] admitting recusancy, petitioned the Commonwealth authorities to be allowed a third of his estate ; he was also admitted as lessee of the sequestered two-thirds, agreeing to pay £86 a year for it.[40] His two brothers became Jesuit priests.[41] He married

---

[36] John son and heir of Gilbert Culcheth was in 1462 contracted to marry Parnell daughter of Hamlet Mascy of Rixton, deceased, and Joan his wife ; Gilbert was dead, his widow Agnes being the wife of Ralph Langton ; Alice, the widow of Thomas Culcheth, was still living ; Culcheth D. no. 112.

John Culcheth occurs again ten years later ; no. 113. He left two daughters, Agnes and Isabel, living in 1500 ; no. 121-3.

[37] In 1483 Thurstan Anderton released to Randle Culcheth his right in Culcheth Carrs, inherited from his grandfather Oliver Anderton and Ellen his wife, to whom it had been given by Thomas Culcheth in 1448 ; no. 114, 106. Three years later arbitrators were appointed in a dispute between Robert Rixton and his wife Parnell, formerly wife of John Culcheth, and Randle Culcheth, brother and heir of John; no. 116.

In July 1491 Randle did homage for Culcheth to Thomas Boteler of Warrington, and paid 10s. 10d. relief ; Misc. (Rec. Soc. Lancs. and Ches.), i, 13, 14.

[38] Culcheth D. no. 124, dated 1502.

[39] Ibid. no. 120. Master Nicholas made an estate to her of lands in Hindley of the value of 8 marks a year for her life. At the same time he declared he had not encumbered the lands of Thomas his father, or Gilbert his brother, or of John and Randle Culcheth his 'cousins,' except certain lands granted for life to Agnes, late the wife of Gilbert but then of Ralph Langton, and to Parnell, later the wife of John. Nicholas was living in 1499 ; B.M. Add. Chart. 17700.

Oliver Culcheth did homage in 1503-4, paying 10s. 10d. relief ; Misc. (Rec. Soc.), i, 16, 22. In 1505 he made a feoffment of his manor of Culcheth and his lands there and in Hindley ; Culcheth D. no. 126.

[30] Ibid. no. 128 ; an assignment of dower to Douce widow of Oliver Culcheth, with a proviso that when Oliver's son Gilbert came of age it should not prejudice her claim to a reasonable part of the lands in Hindley held for the use of George Culcheth, brother of Gilbert.

In 1515 Sir Thomas Boteler sold the wardship and marriage of Gilbert Culcheth to Thomas Langley, rector of Prestwich, and others, for 80 marks ; ibid. no. 130. In the same year bond was given to perform the covenants of marriage in an indenture between Gilbert Culcheth and Sir William Leyland ; ibid. no. 131. This marriage appears to have been with Jane, daughter and heir of Guy Green of Naburn, Yorkshire, for in 1533 Gilbert was holding her lands as tenant by courtesy ; ibid. no. 147.

Gilbert was of full age in 1517, when he covenanted to pay his mother Douce, then wife of James Strangeways, an annuity of

£6 10s. as her dower, in the chapel at Lowe in Hindley ; no. 132, 133. George Culcheth also had an annuity ; no. 141.

By 1526 he had married Margaret daughter of John Holcroft ; and in the following year his father's trustees released to him the manor of Culcheth ; no. 138, 140.

[31] Manch. Ct. Leet Rec. (ed. Earwaker), i, 51.

[32] A pedigree wa Visit. (Chet. Soc.), Oliver Culcheth.

[33] Culcheth D. no these (no 165) John covenanted with Sir levy a fine of his lan self for life, with rem John, Thomas, and deed (no. 269) h s and his daughter Ma in 1595 ; no. 182

For his death see ii 76

Anne daughter of James Bradshaw of Haigh, and by her had a numerous offspring ; [41] two of his three sons

CULCHETH of Culcheth. *Argent an eagle sable preying on an infant swaddled gules banded or.*

TRAFFORD. *Argent a griffon segreant gules.*

became Jesuits, one being a priest, and four of his six daughters were nuns. [42] The descendants of the other daughters, Anne and Catherine, ultimately inherited the manor. He died in 1683, [44] and was succeeded by his grandson Thomas, whose father had died a year or two previously. [45]

Thomas Culcheth, the last of the male line, died childless in 1747, [46] and in accordance with his dispositions the manor passed to his cousin Thomas Stanley

of Eccleston in the Fylde, son of Richard Stanley by his wife Anne Culcheth. [47] Thomas Stanley enjoyed the estate only two years ; [48] his son Richard was declared a lunatic, and on the death of the daughter Meliora, wife of William Dicconson, [49] the manor went in 1794 to John Trafford of Trafford, grandson of John Trafford of Croston, who had married Catherine Culcheth. [50] The new possessor died in 1815, and about ten years later the manor and lands were sold, Peter Withington being the purchaser ; from him the estate has descended to his grandson, the present owner, Mr. Thomas Ellames Withington. [51]

II.—To Elizabeth, the second daughter of Gilbert de Culcheth, was assigned *PEAS-FURLONG.* [52] By her husband, Adam de Peasfurlong, she had two daughters, Margery [53] and Beatrice, [54] the former of whom carried this quarter of Culcheth to her husband, William son of Richard de Radcliffe of Radcliffe. [55] It descended regularly in this family until

RADCLIFFE of Radcliffe. *Argent a bend engrailed sable.*

[42] In 1677 a settlement was made of the manors and lands by Thomas Culcheth and Anne his wife ; Pal. of Lanc. Feet of F. bdle. 198, m. 65.

[43] From a pedigree in Foley, op. cit. vi, 690, said to be taken from one compiled in 1692. Thomas Culcheth *alias* Parker mostly resided at Liège, where he died in 1730, aged 76 ; he served the London mission for a short time. James Culcheth died at Liège during his period of study, in 1692, aged 27 ; ibid. vii, 188.

[44] He was buried in linen at Winwick 20 Dec. 1683.

[45] John, the son of Thomas Culcheth, was buried at Winwick, 4 Feb. 1681–2.

[46] He was buried at Winwick 8 Oct. 1747 ; his wife Anne had been buried 16 July previously.
Thomas Culcheth was vouchee in a recovery of the manor in 1710 ; Pal. of Lanc. Plea R. 492, m. 4.
As a 'papist' he in 1717 registered his entailed estate, with remainder to sons by Anne his wife, charged with annuities to his mother Mary and his brother John, who also registered their estates. It included the capital messuage called Culcheth Hall, with 170 acres of land ; the tithes of Culcheth, out of which £10 was payable to the rector of Winwick, &c. ; there was a mortgage of £1,000 ; *Engl. Cath. Nonjurors,* 115–16 ; *Lancs. and Ches. Hist. and Gen. Notes,* i, 274. In the latter place are printed some other deeds of the period. The brother John is said to have been a lawyer of Gray's Inn.

[47] Ibid. i, 276. The disposition of the estates is recited in the Cal. of the Exch. of Pleas, C, 301 ; Culcheth Hall went in the manner described in the text ; Hindley Hall, otherwise Strangeways Hall, with the fourth part of the manor, was granted to John Trafford of Croston.

[48] He was buried at Winwick 21 July 1749. His brother Henry, a Jesuit priest, was buried there four years later.

[49] William Dicconson and Meliora his wife were vouchees in a recovery of the manor in 1783 ; Pal. of Lanc. Plea R. 637, m. 7, 10.

[50] See the accounts of Stretford and Croston.

[51] Burke, *Landed Gentry.*

[52] The agreement for partition assigned to Adam de Peasfurlong all the waste between the Southwood and Westwood, and between Peasfurlong and Croft, which could be ploughed and sown ; the remainder of the waste to be held in common, a right of way being allowed to Robert and the other brothers and their men. Adam was also to hold all the land and wood which he had inclosed between his house and Southwood, with part of Halghus carr ; and his grant to Robert son of William de Sankey was ratified ; Dods. MSS. cxlii, fol. 113.

From the suits already cited it appears that Isabel or Elizabeth died between 1278 and 1284 ; Assize R. 1238, m. 34 d. ; 1265, m. 22.

Another family had taken a name from the place, for John son of Thomas de Peasfurlong in 1278 released to his lord, Richard son of Hugh de Hindley, all the land in Culcheth which he claimed to hold by right of inheritance ; Dods. MSS. xxxix, fol. 125*b.*

[53] Adam de Hindley and Margery his daughter were defendants in 1284 and 1285. In the latter year Agnes widow of John de Haydock claimed common of pasture in 25 acres of moor in Culcheth. Adam replied that it was the inheritance of Elizabeth, formerly his wife, and that they, with Robert de Risley and Ellen his wife and Thomas de Hindley and Joan his wife, were chief lords of the said town ; Assize R. 1268, m. 11.

Adam son of Hugh de Hindley was defendant in several Culcheth cases in 1292 ; Assize R. 408, m. 32, &c.

He appears also in the Culcheth Deeds as witness and as releasing his right in the water of Glazebrook to Richard de Hindley ; no. 9. In 1280 he had a grant from his brother Richard of land at Wigshaw head next the land of William de Sankey, up to an oak tree marked with a cross ; no. 24. In this he is called Adam de Peasfurlong, a surname he appears to have relinquished after his wife's death.

the time of Henry VIII,[56] when on a failure of male issue it passed to a junior branch represented by Robert Radcliffe, Lord FitzWalter, created Earl of Sussex in 1529.[57] This and other Lancashire estates were sold to provide his daughters' dowries. Sir John Holcroft purchased it,[58] and it descended to a younger son Hamlet,[59] whose son, John Holcroft, sold it in 1605 to Ralph Calveley.[60] It appears afterwards to have reverted to the Holcroft family[61] and to have descended with their principal manor, until the division of their estates, when it was assigned to the Standishes.

III.—HOLCROFT was the share of Joan, the daughter of Gilbert de Culcheth who married Thomas de Hindley.[62] William le Boteler conceded

to them that they should in future provide puture for one bedell instead of two, when doing the services pertaining to the court and fee of Warrington; he also acquitted them of 'bode and witness.'[63] From Thomas the manor descended to his son Adam,[64] after whom no satisfactory account can be given till the beginning of the 16th century,[65] when Sir John Holcroft was lord of it.[66] He was elder brother of Sir Thomas Holcroft, who shared largely in the plunder of

HOLCROFT of Holcroft. *Argent a cross and a bordure both engrailed sable.*

[56] *Lancs. Inq. p.m.* (Chet. Soc.), i, 94—James the elder Radcliffe, 1409, with a son and heir Richard, who died about 1441; ii, 121. John Radcliffe, 1485; ii, 148, 152. In 1483 a dispute about lands in Culcheth between Sir Christopher Southworth and John son and heir of James Radcliffe was decided in the latter's favour by John Hawarden of Chester; Towneley MS. HH, no. 2139. Richard Radcliffe, who died in 1502, held the fourth part of the manor of Culcheth of Sir Thomas Boteler by knight's service and a rent of 3s. 6d.; Duchy of Lanc. Inq. p.m. iii, no. 98. His brother and heir John died about 1513, holding the same part of the manor by a rent of 3s. 4d.; ibid. iv, no. 7.

[57] In the will of John Radcliffe, recited in the inquisition above referred to, it is said, 'Provided always that inasmuch as the manor of Culcheth came to my ancestors by marriage with a gentlewoman, therefore according to the entail thereof I will the said manor shall descend as it ought to have done before the making of this my will.' Lord FitzWalter, however, obtained the manor, and Ralph Eccleston in 1523 was found to have held lands in Culcheth of him; ibid. v, no. 46.

[58] Sir John Holcroft was in possession by 1549; the rent payable to the lord of Warrington was 3s. 6d.; Pal. of Lanc. Feet of F. bdle. 13, m. 77.

[59] By a settlement in 1574 it went to Hamlet, the brother of Sir John Holcroft the younger, who had no sons; the estate included two water-mills, two dovecotes, and a free fishery in the Glazebrook; Pal. of Lanc. Feet of F. bdle. 36, m. 13. For Hamlet Holcroft see also *Ducatus* (Rec. Com.), iii, 96, 188. He and his wife were returned as recusants in 1575.

[60] Pal. of Lanc. Feet of F. bdle. 68, no. 6; the sale (or mortgage) included the manor of Peasfurlong and lands, &c., 100 acres being 'covered with water,' in all four quarters of the township; there was added a clause of warranty against Hamlet Holcroft, the father of John. Another fine was made in 1622–3, John Calveley being plaintiff, and John Holcroft, junior, son and heir of John Holcroft, deforciant, with a clause of warranty against Anne mother of the younger John; ibid. bdle. 96, no. 1. The sale was alleged to be fraudulent; *Hist. MSS. Com. Rep.* iii, App. 57. In 1634 Edward Calveley was in possession of Great and Little Woolden in Barton, Holcroft, Peasfurlong, and Wigshaw in Culcheth; Dods. MSS. cxlii, fol. 113.

[61] In Sept. 1642 the deforciants of the manors of Holcroft and Peasfurlong were Sampson Erdwick and Anne Erdwick,

widow; and there was a warranty against the heirs of Richard Erdwick, father of the former; Pal. of Lanc. Feet of F. bdle. 141, no. 30. Anne Erdwick seems to have been the widow of John Holcroft previously mentioned.

[62] Their share of the inheritance was Holcroft and Mill Houses, with the lands which Orm and Adam his son and Wyon had formerly held; the woods of Southwood, Westwood, and Ings were to be common to all the coparceners; Dods. MSS. cxlii, fol. 114b.

[63] Ibid. fol. 115b. An account of the Holcroft family by Mr. J. Paul Rylands, originally printed in the *Leigh Chron.*, has been utilized; *Local Glean. Lancs. and Ches.* ii.

[64] *Final Conc.* ii, 18. Adam's name occurs in the deeds down to 1347. In 1334 he was commanded to join the king in Scotland with horse and arms; and eight years later he was one of the commissioners for assessing the ninths; *Rot. Scot.* (Rec. Com.), i, 307; *Inq. Non.* (Rec. Com.), 40.

In 1330 Adam de Holcroft arranged for the succession of his part of the manor of Culcheth, except three messuages and certain lands. It was to descend to his son Hugh and heirs male; in default successively to John, Thomas, Richard, and Robert, his other sons. William the son of Adam de Holcroft by his second wife Margery put in his claim; *Final Conc.* ii, 74.

In 1331 John son of John de Woolden agreed with Adam son of Thomas de Holcroft concerning the latter's mill and mill pool upon Glazebrook, the embankment stretching across the stream; Dods. MSS. cxlii, fol. 116.

The male issue of the eldest son Hugh appears to have failed, but he may have had a daughter, for in 1353 William son of Thomas de Sale alleged he was the heir of Adam son of Thomas de Holcroft, in a claim for lands in Bedford brought by William de Holcroft son of Adam and Margery; Assize R. 435, m. 30d.

John de Holcroft, the second son, is probably the man of that name acquitted of killing John son of Simon de Holland at Culcheth in 1343; Assize R. 430, m. 32d.; he was himself killed in 1352; Assize R. 433. Possibly it was on account of his character that Adam de Holcroft in 1347 settled the estate upon Thomas son of John de Holcroft; Dods. MSS. cxlii, fol. 116b. The bounds are thus recorded: Beginning in the centre of Lynbrook where it falls into Glazebrook, up the former brook to the boundary of Kenyon, then by the bounds of Croft, Woolston, and Flixton to Glazebrook, and so back to the starting point; i.e. all his

lands within Culcheth, Blacklow excepted.

[65] As there were two families of the same surname in the township—of Holcroft and of Hurst—it is difficult to trace the descent of either, in the absence of documentary evidence. There is a pedigree in Harl. MS. 1925, fol. 59, showing the double line; also in Piccope, MS. Pedigrees (Chet. Lib.), i, 227.

John de Holcroft occurs at various times from 1373 onwards. He is probably the heir of Thomas son of John de Holcroft from whose guardian (Simon son of Henry de Byrom) Goditha widow of William de Holcroft claimed dower in Aug. 1355; Duchy of Lanc. Assize R. 4, m. 18; 5, m. 24d. See Culcheth D. no. 78, 79.

In 1382 his daughter Elizabeth was engaged to marry Thurstan de Culcheth; ibid. no. 80, 81; Pal. of Lanc. Feet of F. bdle. 2, m. 35. He was plaintiff in later fines (from 1386 to 1394) regarding properties in Culcheth and Kenyon; ibid. bdles. 2, m. 4, 5; 3, m. 19. In 1394 he was escheator; *Lancs. Inq. p.m.* (Chet. Soc.), i, 49.

Thomas de Holcroft was serving beyond the seas in 1417 in the retinue of Thomas, Duke of Exeter; Towneley MS. CC, no. 510. He occurs as witness in 1400 and 1408; Towneley MS. GG, no. 2674, 2415; and John de Holcroft in various ways about forty years later (Culcheth D. no. 107, 108) as arbitrator in a dispute between Thomas Culcheth and Oliver Anderton in 1448; also no. 112. He was 'in mercy for defaults' in 1444; Pal. of Lanc. Plea R. 6, m. 11; 7, m. 4. In 1492 John Holcroft did homage and service to the lord of Warrington and paid 10s. 10d. for relief; *Misc.* (Rec. Soc. Lancs. and Ches.), i, 14. It was probably his son John who in 1505 did homage and service for lands in Culcheth and Pennington, paid relief, and three years later did fealty in the court leet; ibid. 18, 22. Margaret daughter of John Holcroft senior was in 1525 married to Gilbert Culcheth; her brother, John Holcroft, afterwards knighted, being the principal agent; Culcheth D. no. 137–9. In a plea regarding land in 1514 the descent of John Holcroft was thus alleged: John —s. Thomas —s. John —s. Thomas —s. John —s. John (plaintiff); Pal. of Lanc. Plea R. 118, m. 13.

A pedigree was recorded in 1567, giving a few steps; *Visit.* (Chet. Soc.), 117.

[66] In 1536 John Holcroft had fifty-three men for service under the Earl of Derby against the Northern Rising; *L. and P. Hen. VIII,* xi, 511. He was sheriff of Cheshire in 1541–2; ibid. xvi, 644. He was made a knight at the coronation of

the religious houses,[67] and Sir John himself had a grant of Upholland Monastery and its lands.[68] His son, another Sir John, succeeded him,[69] and left an only daughter Alice as heir, who married Sir Edward Fitton of Gawsworth.[70] Shortly afterwards Holcroft came into the hands of Ralph Calveley of Saighton, Cheshire.[71] In 1642, as previously stated, the manors of Holcroft and Peasfurlong were in the possession of Sampson Erdwick and Anne Erdwick,[72] widow. Ten years later John Holcroft and Margaret his wife were in possession.[73] Of his son Thomas's children two daughters became coheirs ;[74] Eleanor married Thomas Tyldesley of Myerscough and Morleys, and Margaret married Sir Richard Standish of Duxbury,[75] and afterwards Sir

Thomas Stanley of Bickerstaffe. The manors were divided ; Peasfurlong went to the Standish family and Holcroft descended with the Tyldesleys until 1761, after which there is no trace of them in the records.[76]

IV.—To Ellen, the remaining daughter of Gilbert de Culcheth, and her husband was assigned RISLEY,[77] and the family descended from de Culcheth, and her husband them retained possession until the 18th century. Robert de Risley and Ellen his wife were among the defendants

TYLDESLEY. *Argent three mole-hills vert.*

Edward VI ; Metcalfe, *Book of Knights,* 90.

From Sir Thomas Butler in 1549 he procured the enfranchisement of his manors of Holcroft and Peasfurlong, with the lands there and in Pennington. The manor of Holcroft, with messuages, lands, and two water-mills, had been held by homage, fealty, uncertain scutage, and a rent of 3s. 6d. with suit to the court of the manor of Warrington ; thenceforward it was to be held by fealty only for all services, customs, exactions, and demands ; Pal. of Lanc. Feet of F. bdle. 13, m. 77. Sir John died in 1560 and was buried in Newchurch in Culcheth ; Dods. MSS. cliii, fol. 46. His will with the inventory is printed in Piccope, *Wills* (Chet. Soc.), i, 148–57.

[67] Thomas Holcroft first appears in the records as a gentleman servitor at the coronation of Anne Boleyn in 1533 ; L. and P. Hen. *VIII,* vi, 246. He had a place at court and was trusted by the king and Cromwell with various missions, including the visitation of the monasteries. He procured grants of the friaries at Warrington, Preston, and Lancaster ; a portion of the Whalley lands, and Cartmel Priory; also Vale Royal Abbey in Cheshire; see L. and P. Hen. *VIII* ; also Ormerod, *Cheshire* (ed. Helsby), ii, 153, 154. He was knighted during the Scottish expedition in 1544 ; Metcalfe, *Knights,* 74. His family very soon died out. His son Thomas in 1590 was 'professed in religion, but not so forward in the public actions for religion as was meet' ; Gibson, *Lydiate Hall,* 243.

[68] See the account of Upholland. In 1539 he also procured a grant of the tithes of Culcheth for ever, paying a rent of £10 to the rector ; *Lancs. and Ches. Recs.* (Rec. Soc. Lancs. and Ches.), ii, 302 ; Lichfield Epis. Reg. xiii–xiv, fol. 24.

[69] An agreement between John Holcroft and Margaret widow of Sir Richard Bold, on the marriage of the former's son John with Dorothy Bold, is in Dods. MSS. xxxix, fol. 107. A fine as to the manor of Peasfurlong was made in 1553 between Sir John Holcroft senior and Sir John Holcroft junior ; Pal. of Lanc. Feet of F. bdle. 14, m. 4. Sir John Holcroft was the plaintiff in a right-of-way case in 1565, the disputed road leading from Hollinfare through Culcheth to Leigh ; *Ducatus Lanc.* (Rec. Com.), ii, 285.

[70] In 1589 a settlement of the tithes of Culcheth was made by Sir Edward Fitton and Alice his wife ; Pal. of Lanc. Feet of F. bdle. 51, m. 148. In 1590 it was reported that he resided but little in Lancashire ; he was 'of good conformity' to the religion established by law, but 'not much commended for any forwardness in

the cause' thereo (quoting S.P. Dom was returned in 16 was also a justice Lancs and Ches.),

The male line Fittons quickly die tance passed to fem of the third Sir Ed see Ormerod, *Che* 553.

[71] Ralph Calvele holding Holcroft mills, free fishery i messuages and lan he had purchased o and others, probab tons ; the hall was Fitton, who reside *p.m.* (Rec Soc Lan 61

in pleas already cited of the time of Edward I.[78] The next steps in the descent are not quite certain,[79] but in 1324 Robert de Risley and Isabel his wife made a settlement of their fourth part of the manor of Culcheth, three daughters only being mentioned.[80] Robert was still living in 1365,[81] and had a son Henry,[82] whose sons were William and Nicholas. William in 1397 released to his brother and his heirs all his right to his father's lands in Risley, Culcheth, Kenyon, Croft, Lowton, Warrington, and Penketh, except a messuage and 20 acres ; and his daughter Katherine in 1422 gave a similar release.[83]

Nicholas Risley remained in possession till the year 1454 or later.[84] He had a dispute with Richard de Radcliffe concerning a certain moor and moss which had been reclaimed and on which a dwelling-house had been built. The evidence adduced contains one of the rare allusions to the ' foreign death ' or plague of 1348.[85] He was succeeded by his son Gilbert,[86] his grandson Richard,[87] and his great-grandson Henry. The last-named did homage for his lands to the lord of Warrington in 1492.[88] He had a son Robert,[89] who succeeded about 1509, and died in 1516, leaving a son and heir, Richard, then eighteen years of age.[90] The guardianship was granted to Sir John Ireland, who married the ward to his daughter

Southwood. The bounds are carefully recited, Hollinhurst and Stockley Wood being named. A road for Robert and his tenants was allowed through Peasfurlong to the common of Westwood, then following the Haigh Field to Holcroft ; by the Brook House to the mills at Culcheth and further to Fastonbrook. In compensation for the ' waste and desert ' character of much of Risley, Robert and Ellen received Gilbert de Culcheth's lands in Lowton. This deed may be dated about 1270.

[78] From these it appears that Robert and Ellen de Risley were living in 1292 ; Assize R. 408, m. 44 d. Ellen in or before 1303 married John Gillibrand, and was living in 1314, when she and her husband ' put in their claim ' in a settlement regarding Holcroft ; Final Conc. i, 200 ; ii, 18. She had a portion of Longton in Leyland Hundred, which descended to Peter and Gilbert de Risley, younger sons ; ibid. i, 200 ; ii, 63 ; Harl. MS. 2042, fol. 100b, &c.

[79] Robert and Ellen appear to have had sons, Robert and Richard ; as also the Peter and Gilbert named in the last note.

Robert son of Robert de Risley, and Margery his wife, claimed various lands in Kenyon, Lowton, Culcheth, Warrington, and Pemberton, from Robert son of William de Sankey ; Harl. MS. 2112, fol. 151-87 (undated). Margery was the daughter and heir of William, elder son of William de Sankey, and in 1295 claimed her grandfather's lands in Kenyon, &c. Her father had died before the elder William, and she had been given in ward to Robert de Risley, who had married her to his son Robert ; Assize R. 1306, m. 15. Margery seems to have married before 1321 William son of the John Gillibrand named in the previous note ; Final Conc. ii, 44.

The Robert de Risley who had the reversion would be the grandson of the first Robert de Risley, and this settlement may have been made on his coming of age or marriage. ' John Gillibrand and William his son ' occur in 1299 ; Towneley MS. OO, no. 1465 ; William had married Margery by 1311 ; Harl. MS. 2112, fol. 151-87 ; Final Conc. ii, 7. In 1347, in a grant to the next Robert de Risley, his mother ' Margaret ' is named as then living ; from the deeds at Hale Hall, near Liverpool, among which are a large number relating to Risley.

It would thus appear that the first Robert de Risley died before 1303, and the second (his son) before 1311.

Adam son of Hugh de Hindley granted lands near Westwood in Culcheth, which he had acquired from John de Haydock, to Giles de Penketh. Giles was to render the following services to

the chief lords : T Ellen his wife and Robert de Risley, 1 son of Robert R at Christmas ; to G de Cu cheth, 1 lb rent ; Kuerden M 48 ; Towneley MS

Richard de Ris son of the elder Ro tion of his estate cliffe and Margery liii, fol. 27. I Richard de Ris ey Holcroft all his cla lache, between boundary of Croft

[80] Final Conc. 1 garet, Margery, an Robert must ther about 1300 Ada Holcroft his mot clifie and Margery their son put in t

Alice. The union was not permanent, for in 1536 Alice sought a divorce on the ground that her previous husband, Thomas Stanley, was still living, and her plea being successful, her son Thomas Risley was declared illegitimate, and the manor of Risley and other estates were in 1543 adjudged to be the right of John, the younger brother of Richard.[91]

John Risley and his descendants held the manor from this time.[92] His son John[93] had 'conformed' to the established religion before 1590, and was then reported to be 'soundly affected' in the matter.[94] The family do not

RISLEY of Risley. *Argent three antique drinking-horns with legs azure.*

appear to have taken any prominent part in public affairs,[95] and Captain John Risley, who died in 1702, without issue,[96] was succeeded by his uncle Thomas, and he by his sister Elizabeth, wife of Hamlet Woods of Risley. She died in 1736; the manor was acquired by the Blackburnes and descended with Orford and Hale until about 1850, when it was sold to Richard Watson Marshall Dewhurst, at whose death it was sold to — Ainscough.

An agreement for inclosing and dividing the commons and waste grounds in Culcheth was made in 1749 and confirmed next year by a private Act of Parliament.[97] The lords of the manors were Richard Stanley of Culcheth, Sir Thomas Standish of Peasfurlong, John Blackburne of Risley, and James Tyldesley of Holcroft.[98]

The estate of *HURST*, sometimes called a manor, was for a long period held by a branch of the Holcroft family.[99] Geoffrey Holcroft in 1577 made a settlement of his 'manor' called Hurst and lands in Culcheth.[100] He died in or before 1591, holding Hurst and other lands of John Culcheth by a rent of 2s. His son and heir was Geoffrey.[101] A settlement of the 'manor' was made by Geoffrey Holcroft in 1613.[102] Thomas Holcroft son of Geoffrey died 31 March 1637, holding the Hurst, a water-mill, and lands in Culcheth of John Culcheth; also lands in Bedford, Pennington, and Kenyon; Geoffrey his son and heir was twenty-three years of age.[103]

KINGNALL or Kinknall was another quasi-manorial estate, which in the 16th and 17th centuries was the seat of an Urmston family. William Urmston died in 1600, holding the capital messuage and lands of John Culcheth by the hundredth part of a knight's fee. Richard his son and heir was ten years old.[104]

Some minor families occur in early times, deriving

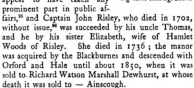

pute between him and John Ashton as to the lands in Penketh had been settled in 1513 by an agreement to pay the free rent of 12d., all arrears being released; Hale D.

[91] Hale D.; *Ducatus Lanc.* (Rec. Com.), ii, 67. The dispossessed Thomas may be the Thomas Risley who in 1566 claimed lands in Culcheth by grant of Richard Risley; *Ducatus* (Rec. Com.), ii, 331.

[92] He made a feoffment of his estates in 1556, expressing a wish that his son and heir John should marry Magdalen daughter of John Grimsditch; Hale D.

[93] John, the son and heir of John Risley, was in possession of the manor in 1567, when he had a dispute with Richard Byrom and Margaret his wife, widow of John Risley; *Ducatus* (Rec. Com.). ii, 351; iii, 47. In 1588 he charged John Culcheth and Gilbert Unsworth with encroachments on the waste grounds called Southwood, Westwood, Twiss Green, Shaw Moss, Riggs and Fowley; ibid. iii, 513.

He died 24 April 1616, his son and heir Richard being then forty years of age. Besides Risley Hall he had lands and burgages in Culcheth, Warrington, Penketh, Lowton, Kenyon, and Croft; also an acre in the Twiss or Lockers meadow in Bruch. In 1593 he had settled his lands with remainders to his eldest son Richard and heirs by Anne his wife, and to his younger sons Henry and George, and then to his brother Richard. From the Inq. p.m. among the Hale D.

[94] *Lydiate Hall*, 245; quoting S.P.Dom. Eliz. ccxxxv, 4.

[95] A pedigree was recorded in 1665 at Dugdale's *Visitation* (Chet. Soc. p. 246). There is a full one by Mr. J. P. Rylands, in *Misc. Gen. and Herald.* (new ser.), ii, 273.

Richard Risley in 1631 paid £10 on refusing knighthood; *Misc.* (Rec. Soc. Lancs. and Ches.), i, 213.

[96] His monument (a brass) was formerly in Winwick Church, and being found among the Risley deeds was restored to

the church by the Blackburne about *Winwick*, 123 T Zachary Tay *Lancs. and Ches* i, 1 at Christ's Co

their surnames from the Twiss,[105] the Hurst,[106] the Shaw,[107] and Kinknall.[108]

In 1600 the freeholders not already named were William Lewis and Thomas Richardson.[109] Those who paid to the subsidy in 1628 were John Calveley, John Culcheth, Geoffrey Holcroft, Richard Risley, Richard Thomasson, and Richard Urmston; of these the last, as a convicted recusant, paid double.[110] Besides Thomas Culcheth, Robert Guest of Culcheth in 1653 petitioned to compound for two-thirds of his estate, sequestered for recusancy.[111] In addition to the Culcheths, a considerable number of persons, as 'papists,' registered estates in 1717.[112]

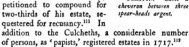

URMSTON. *Sable a cheveron between three spear-heads argent.*

A number of extracts from the Culcheth town books of the 17th and 18th centuries have been printed.[113]

The land-tax returns of 1787 show the principal proprietors at that date to have been John Blackburne, Sir Frank Standish, John Trafford, and Samuel Pool, these contributing about two-thirds of the total sum levied.[114]

CHURCH

Before the Reformation there was at Culcheth a chapel of ease known as Trinity Church.[115] It was perhaps not then very old, and the name NEWCHURCH has remained attached to it till the present time. After the changes of the reigns of Edward VI and Mary, the building probably ceased to be used for a time at Culcheth on Elizabeth's revival of the Edwardine services.[116] Sir John Holcroft by his will of 1559 left his chain of gold or £10 towards the payment of a priest and clerk if the other inhabitants of the township could be induced to subscribe.[117] The service was probably read occasionally, but in 1592 there was neither surplice nor 'table cloth.'[118] In 1612 this chapel had 'seldom a curate,'[119] but ten years later there was one who contributed £1 to the subsidy.[120]

The Commonwealth Surveyors in 1650 recommended that Newchurch should be made into a parish; the endowment was less than £4 a year, but £10 was added by the rector of Winwick, and £40 out of the sequestered property of Royalists.[121] After the Restoration, with some exceptions, there was no

---

[105] Roger del Twiss complained of trespasses on his lands at Culcheth by Hugh de Hindley and others in 1258; Cur. Reg. R. 160, m. 6. Richard and Roger del Twiss have been mentioned already as concerned in the suits of 1277–8; the former held his land under Richard de Culcheth; Assize R. 1238, m. 34 d.

Hugh del Twiss in 1314 secured three messuages and land from Thomas de Holcroft and Joan his wife; *Final Conc.* ii, 19.

Gilbert de Culcheth in 1339 leased to Richard del Twiss and his daughters Margery and Godith a plat of land near the boundary of Kenyon; Harl. MS. 2112, fol. 158b/194b. Alan son of Richard del Twiss in 1338 released all his lands in Turnours carr to Gilbert de Culcheth the elder; Culcheth D. no. 49. These deeds contain many other references to the family. Matthew son of Gilbert del Twiss in 1361 claimed certain lands which had been taken into the Duke of Lancaster's hands because his father's widow, Godith, had granted them to Adam de Tyldesley, who had been outlawed for felony; Gilbert was son of Alan son of Richard del Twiss, who had formerly held the lands; *Dep. Keeper's Rep.* xxxii, App. 347.

John Culcheth, who died in 1640, bought the Twiss from Thomas Holcroft of Hurst; *Lancs. and Ches. Hist. and Gen. Notes,* i, 374.

The Paris family also occurs in the Culcheth Deeds, no. 15, 16; Robert de Paris and Henry his eldest son. Thomas son of Robert de Paris was a plaintiff in 1294; Assize R. 1299, m. 16; also R. 408, m. 11, which shows that Robert was still living in 1292.

[106] In 1275 Roger son of Richard del Hurst granted to Robert de Hindley a rent of 2s. formerly paid by Norman son of Robert de North Meols; and at the same time Gilbert the Tailor, son of Thurstan del Hurst, granted to Robert de Hindley the rent of 3d., which Richard son of Richard de Martinscroft formerly paid for land of Norman son of Robert

de North Meols, in The rent of 2s. nam st'll paid for Hurst ı
Mabe 'd f A
H t ght d r
408, m. 27. R'char
Hur h d g t
Culcheth D n

curate [122] specially appointed to Newchurch until 1749, when a grant was about to be made from Queen Anne's Bounty. The church was rebuilt in 1743, a plain brick structure. This was burnt down in April 1903, and has been rebuilt in the Norman style. A communion cup is believed to be an old chalice altered.[123] The registers 1599–1812 have been printed by the Lancashire Parish Register Society, 1905.

In 1845, under the Winwick Rectory Act, a separate parish was created for Culcheth and Kenyon, the incumbent being styled rector of Newchurch and receiving the tithes.[124] The Earl of Derby is patron.

The following is a list of the curates in charge—the most noteworthy being Thomas Wilson, afterwards Bishop of Sodor and Man—and the rectors :—[125]

oc. 1563	Henry Abram
oc. 1599	William Pennington [126]
oc. 1611	Richard Mallory
oc. 1617	James Whitworth
oc. 1622	— Hopwood
oc. 1627	John Burtonwood [127]
oc. 1630	H. Atherton
oc. 1635	Thomas Hall, 'incumbent'
oc. 1636	Richard Wilson, 'curate of New-church'
oc. 1639–40	Robert Gee [128]
oc. 1645–54	William Leigh [129]
oc. 1654	John Bird
Jan. 1657–8	Thomas Potter [130]
Feb. 1686–7	Thomas Wilson, B.A. (T.C.D.)[131]

PERPETUAL CURATES

Jan. 1748–9	John Hilton, B.A. (Brasenose College, Oxford) [132]
Aug. 1772	Hugh Grimshaw
Apr. 1783	Robert Barker
Feb. 1785	Thomas Heyes, M.A. (Oxford)[133]

Aug. 1816	Joseph Jones, M.A.
June 1841	John Healy
Apr. 1842	Joseph Wilding Twist, B.A. (Queen's College, Oxford)

RECTORS

Feb. 1845	Frederick Augustus Bartlett[133a]
Sept. 1855	Wm. Henry Strong, B.A. (T.C.D.)
June 1862	Robert William Burton, M.A.
Mar. 1864	Wm. Faussett Black, D.D. (T.C.D.)
May 1897	Eugene Walter Whittenbury Kaye

The church of All Saints, Glazebury, was erected in 1851, and had a district assigned to it in 1878.[134] The Earl of Derby is the patron.

There are Wesleyan and Primitive Methodist chapels at Glazebury, and an Independent Methodist one at Twiss Green.

After 1662 those who were attached to the Presbyterian worship[135] were ministered to by one Thomas Risley, of the local family. He was fellow of Pembroke College, Oxford, and though he was, on the Restoration, ordained according to the Anglican rite, he refused to conform further, and was ejected in 1662. A chapel was built by him at Risley in 1707,[136] and has continued in use to the present time. As in most other cases, Unitarian tenets prevailed in the latter part of the 18th century; but in 1836, after appeal to the Court of Chancery, the Unitarian minister and congregation were ejected, building a new chapel for themselves at Croft, and Risley was given to the Scottish Presbyterians, who still use it.[137]

After the Elizabethan settlement of religion a large number of the people remained steadfast to the ancient faith,[138] and with the connivance and assistance of the Culcheths and Urmstons it is probable that the missionary priests were able to minister here from time to time, but no records exist until 1670, when Fr. John Penketh, S.J., was resident.[139] The succession

---

[122] Bishop Gastrell about 1720 found that nothing belonged to the church but the interest of £50, given by some one unknown ; £50 a year was allowed by the rector ; *Notitia Cestr.* (Chet. Soc.), ii, 269.

[123] *Lancs. and Ches. Antiq. Soc.* xxi, 172 (with plate).

[124] *Notitia Cestr.* ii, 270 n.

[125] This list, compiled from the parish registers and documents at Chester, is mainly due to Mr. J. Paul Rylands. See also *Local Glean. Lancs. and Ches.* i, 180, and introduction to printed Registers.

[126] Raines MSS. xxii, 64.

[127] Previously at St. Helens.

[128] For the Gee family see *Local Glean.* ii, 301.

[129] 'A very godly minister, of good life and conversation,' though he had not observed the day of humiliation appointed by Parliament in June 1650 ; *Commonwealth Ch. Surv.* loc. cit. He seems to have been in charge in 1645 ; *Plund. Mins. Accts.* (Rec. Soc. Lancs. and Ches.), i, 6 ('Mr. Lee') ; and in 1648 he signed the 'Harmonious Consent.' He was transferred to Gorton in 1657 ; ibid. ii, 183.

[130] Ibid. ii, 214. He had been minister at Ashton. He continued as curate of Winwick after the Restoration, and was buried there 12 Nov. 1671.

[131] Bishop Stratford's Visitation List, 1691. He was 'conformable' in 1689 ; *Hist. MSS. Com. Rep.* xiv, App. iv, 229.

[132] He was the first of the perpetual curates of Newchurch ; but had been licensed to the curacy of Winwick in 1742. The church papers at Chester Dioc. Reg. begin at this point ; among them the following is preserved : (13 Jan. 1748–9)—'Whereas the curacy of New-church in the parish of Winwick is shortly intended to be augmented by the Governors of the Bounty of Queen Anne, I do hereby nominate John Hilton, clerk (the person employed by me in serving the said cure), to be curate of the said chapel of Newchurch, and do allow him £50 per annum.—Thos. Stanley.'

[133] In 1804 he gave the following account of Newchurch : '340 houses, without any village or hamlet or any family of distinction. About 155 Papists of the lower class with a public place of worship and a resident priest at Culcheth Hall of the name of Barry. About 70 Presbyterians of the lower rank of people, having a licensed meeting-house and a teacher of the name of Aspinal qualified according to law, without any school for religious instruction, and whose number I believe to be upon the decline.' Heyes was curate of Westhoughton also, and resided there, Newchurch having no parsonage house. There was a resident curate, with service twice every Sunday and two sermons ; 'sacrament every first Sunday in the month, communicants about 40.' In 1814 a house was built by subscription,

for the minister's residence. These details are from the Bishop's Registry at Chester.

[133a] Afterwards of St. Olave's, York.

[134] *Lond. Gaz.* 29 Nov. 1878.

[135] In 1634 Robert Downing of Risley had been presented 'for receiving the cup standing, and refusing the bread unless out of another man's hands and not the minister's' ; Beamont, *Winwick*, 42. William Leigh, the minister under the Commonwealth, was chosen by the Puritan rector and the people of Culcheth ; *Commonwealth Ch. Surv.* loc. cit.

[136] An account of him is in *Local Glean. Lancs. and Ches.* i, 122.

[137] Ibid. and Nightingale, *Lancs. Nonconformity*, iv, 252–61. The succession of ministers is given.

[138] See the recusant roll in *Trans. Hist. Soc.* (new ser.), xiv, 245.

[139] Foley, *Records S.J.* v, 346. The Jesuits were usually in charge. Edward Scarisbrick was at Culcheth in 1701 with a stipend of £9 ;—Smith in 1721, Thomas Maire about 1750, Thomas Walmesley in 1784, in which year thirty-five were confirmed ; and—Carter in 1793 ; ibid. v, 321–5.

In 1767 it was reported to the Bishop of Chester that two priests were living at Culcheth—(Roger) Leigh, S.J., and William Dicconson; *Trans. Hist. Soc.* (new ser.), xviii, 215 ; Foley, op. cit. vii, 449.

can be traced for over a century, when, owing probably to the failure of the Culcheth line, the hall ceased to have a chapel, Rixton and Croft sufficing.

A schoolhouse on the common was built before 1720.[140]

The Salford Guardians' Cottage Homes for children are built in Culcheth.

HOUGHTON, MIDDLETON, AND ARBURY

Hoghton, 1420; Houghton, 1608. Midelton, 1212. Herbury, 1242; Erthbury, 1246; Erbury, 1420; Arbury, xvi cent.

This township has resulted from the combination of Middleton and Houghton, originally united, with Arbury. This last is a narrow strip of land along the eastern boundary of Winwick; the rest of the area is divided unequally between Middleton on the north, and Houghton on the south, there being no defined boundary between them. The total area is 853½ acres, made up thus: Houghton, 336; Middleton 244½; Arbury, 273½.[1] It is situated on gently sloping ground, rising from south to north to about 100 ft. above sea level. The country is open, portioned out into fields of light sandy loam, with clay in places, producing good potatoes, wheat, oats, clover, and turnips. The land is divided by low hawthorn hedges, and contains a little timber, seldom extending beyond small clumps. The geological formation consists of the Bunter series of the New Red Sandstone, the Pebble Beds in the northern part, the Upper Mottled Sandstone in the southern. Some of the roads are little better than cart-tracks, and badly metalled. Houghton Green is the only village; Middleton has a hall of that name, and Arbury is only a farm-house. In 1901 the population was 214.

A road from Winwick Church leads through Arbury to Croft and Culcheth; it is joined by another from the south, coming from Warrington and Fearnhead through Houghton and Middleton.

In the north of Middleton there is a tumulus, near the Arbury boundary.[2] A spa well is also used.

Blackbrook divides Houghton from Fearnhead.

In 1852 a number of Civil War notices were found concealed in a cavity in an old farm-house at Houghton Green.[3]

The manor of *MIDDLETON*, from which *HOUGHTON* became separate in later times, was included in the fee of Makerfield.[4] It was assessed as a plough-land and a half, and in 1212 was held in thegnage by a total rent of 20s. in four equal shares, each of which appears to have been responsible in turn for providing a judge at the court of Newton.[5] The manor, thus early divided, was further partitioned later, and as the shares are not usually recorded in the deeds, nor the services due to the chief lord, it is impossible to trace the separate parts.[6] The greater part was early acquired by the

---

[140] Gastrell, *Notitia*, ii, 270.

[1] The census report of 1901 gives 855.

[2] This appears to be the Highfield tumulus described by Dr. Robson in *Trans. Hist. Soc.* xii, 189.

[3] *Trans. Hist. Soc.* iv, 18. The occupier of the house about 1640 was Thomas Serjeant, then constable of the township.

[4] *V.C.H. Lancs.* i, 366 n. The manors of Middleton and Houghton, held in socage, and Arbury, held by knight's service, continued to be recognized as parts of Newton fee; see *Lancs. Inq. p.m.* (Chet. Soc.), ii, 99.

[5] *Lancs. Inq. and Extents* (Rec. Soc. Lancs. and Ches.), i, 77. The four tenants were Robert de Middleton, Henry son of Siward, William de Middleton (who is not stated to be responsible for a judge), and Richard son of Henry. Under the first of these John de Middleton held one oxgang and discharged the service due to that quarter, i.e. a rent of 5s. and the fourth part of a judge. There were thus already five tenants.

[6] In a suit of 1334 John son of Geoffrey Henne, John son of John son of Robert de Middleton, Gilbert de Southworth, and Quenilda and Agnes daughters of Thomas Wrych, were stated to be lords of the vill; Coram Rege R. 297, m. 20. This throws some light on the following charters :—

Elias son of Robert de Ainsworth granted to Gilbert de Southworth and his heirs his lordship of a whole fourth part of the vill of Middleton, in return for a mark of silver; Towneley MS. HH, no. 1713. It is curious that Ainsworth is a hamlet of Middleton, near Manchester; Robert de Ainsworth may have been the Robert de Middleton of 1212.

Adam son of Richard de Middleton granted to Adam son of Richard son of Quenilda de Middleton land in

Gilbert de Southworth his claim on land approved by the latter in Cumberhale Carr; ibid. no. 1928. Richard son of William Post granted land in Houghton to his brother Robert in 1345; ibid. no. 1630. Emmota daughter of William Post in 1370 granted to Gilbert son of John de Houghton lands which descended to her on the death of Gilbert son of Richard Post; ibid. no. 1585.

John son of John de Bultham granted to John son of William de Middleton, his uncle and chief lord, half an oxgang in Middleton, which William son of Richard de Middleton granted to Alice his daughter; ibid. no. 1828. The witnesses include John son of Richard de Middleton, William son of Richard de Middleton, Andrew de Middleton, and Peter, vicar of Budworth.

Richard son of Henry de Middleton granted to Richard son of Austin de Middleton half an oxgang in the vill which his mother Margery had held in dower, to be held as the twenty-fourth part of Middleton, by the service of a pair of gloves or ½d.; ibid. no. 1841. He reserved two messuages and the croft in Houghton.

In 1307 William Gillibrand and Margery his wife recovered against Gilbert de Southworth 12 acres of land and ½ an acre of meadow; and as this was owing to the default of Andrew de Middleton, when called to warrant, Roger the son of Andrew granted to Gilbert de Southworth half an oxgang in Middleton and Houghton as compensation; Hultley Hurst in Middleton is named in the charter; ibid. no. 1819.

Roger de Ashton and Alice his wife in 1318 claimed an eighth part of the manor of Middleton, less an oxgang, from Andrew de Middleton, who granted it to them, receiving 20 marks; *Final Conc.* (Rec. Soc. Lancs. and Ches.), ii, 31.

In the same year Thomas son of

Southworth family,[7] and their lordship is the only one appearing in the later records, apart from that of the barons of Makerfield.

Two junior branches of the dominant family were seated at Middleton and at HOUGHTON PEEL. They seem to have descended from Matthew de Southworth,[8] a brother of Gilbert de Southworth, living in the early part of the reign of Edward III.

Their possessions were acquired by the Southworths of Samlesbury in the 16th century.[9] Middleton appears to have been retained with Southworth, and to have descended like it to the present time. Houghton[10] was sold

SOUTHWORTH. *Argent a cheveron between three crosslets sable.*

in 1605 to James Bankes of Winstanley,[11] and descended like Winstanley till the end of the 18th century, when it was sold ;[12] Maire, Claughton, Greenall,[13] and Comber being successively owners.[14]

Henry Brookfield of Longbarrow in Knowsley had some land here in 1530 and 1547.[15]

The manor of *ARBURY* was held in 1212 by the lord of Lowton by knight's service, its rating being half a plough-land. It had been granted by Adam de Lawton to Geoffrey Gernet, who in turn had enfeoffed Thurstan Banastre.[16] Half of it was given by Thurstan to Cockersand Abbey in alms.[17] Afterwards the manor came into the possession of the Southworths,[18] and has descended exactly like Southworth, to the Brooks family. There is practically nothing on record concerning it. John Corless of Arbury as a 'papist' registered his house in 1717.[19]

SOUTHWORTH WITH CROFT

Suthewrthe, 1212 ; Sotheworth, 1293 ; Suthworth, 1306. Croft, 1212.

Croft, the eastern portion of the township, has the larger area, 1,364 acres, and was frequently placed first; but the only hall was in Southworth, which contains 519½ acres. There is now no defined boundary between the two. A brook on the east and south of Croft affords a natural boundary, except that a portion to the south of the brook, reclaimed from the moss, has been added to Croft. The total area is 1,883½[1] acres.

The country is mostly flat, with slight irregularities of surface in places, traversed by fairly good roads and covered with open fields, under mixed cultivation,

alternating with pastures. The crops principally grown are potatoes, oats, and wheat, in a loamy soil. The Pebble Beds of the Bunter Series of the New Red Sandstone are everywhere in evidence.

The population in 1901 was 970. There are many small freeholders.

The principal road is that leading eastward from Winwick to Culcheth.

There is a tumulus in the north-west corner of Southworth.

In the Winwick registers 3 February, 1683–4, is a certificate signed by Dr. Sherlock, rector, for Henry son of Ralph Bate of Croft, 'who had the evil and was touched by his majesty.'

There is a parish council.

A school board was formed in 1875.[2]

The somewhat scattered village of Croft is a favourite resort of picnic parties.

Of the two manors, *SOUTHWORTH MANORS* and *CROFT*, held by different tenures of the lords of Makerfield,[3] the latter appears to have been the more important, as it gave its name to the lord, who in 1212 was Gilbert de Croft. He held it by the service of falconer, and it was held of him in unequal portions by Hugh de Croft and the heir of Randle, the latter of them discharging the service.[4] Gilbert de Croft also held Southworth by a rent of 20s., but in 1212 it was, for some reason unknown, in the king's hands.[5]

Very soon afterwards, before 1219, Gilbert de Croft, who also held the manor of Dalton in Kendal,[6] granted Southworth to Gilbert son of Hugh de Croft, who was probably a near kinsman, and this Gilbert, taking the local surname, was the founder of the Southworth family, which held the manors of South-

---

with remainders to his son Richard and Alice his wife ; no. 2156c. This Richard was living in 1386 ; no. 1804, 1708. The next to occur are Roger 'Jackson' de Houghton in 1382 and 1392 (no. 1506, 1809, 1548) ; and his son John in 1428 ; no. 1911. In 1432 Richard Johnson de Houghton granted lands in Houghton and Middleton to his son John, with remainders to other children—Robert, Margaret, and Joan ; no. 1505, 1808. A settlement of lands in Middleton and Houghton was in 1488 made by John Houghton 'of Middleton,' the remainder being to his son and heir Robert ; no. 1810, 2037.

Seth Houghton died 10 March 1621 holding lands in Middleton, Southworth, and Arbury, his son and heir Henry being thirty years of age ; Towneley MS. C. 8, 13 (Chet. Lib.), 507. A later Seth Houghton died in September 1635, leaving a son Richard, aged three years ; ibid. 502.

[11] Pal. of Lanc. Feet of F. bdle. 67, m. 33 ; Thomas Southworth, Rosamund his wife, and John his son and heir apparent joined in the sale. After the death of James Bankes in 1617 it was found that the manor of Houghton and the lands in Houghton, Arbury, Middleton, and Croft were held of Richard Fleetwood, lord of Newton, in socage by 5s. rent, i.e. the old service for a fourth part of the manor of Middleton ; *Lancs. Inq. p.m.* (Rec. Soc. Lancs. and Ches.), ii, 99.

[12] The manor of Houghton was the subject of a settlement in 1657 by William Bankes, Sarah his wife, and William his son; Pal. of Lanc. Feet of F. bdle. 160, m. 143. It is named in re-

worth and Croft until the beginning of the 17th century. The service to be rendered was a pound of pepper annually.[7] Thurstan Banastre, lord of Makerfield, confirmed this charter, and reduced the annual rent payable to him to 13*s.* 4*d.*[8] The remaining part of Croft was later acquired by the Southworth family ; 1 oxgang of land therein was granted to Gilbert de Southworth by Agnes daughter of Randle de Croft,[9] and 2 oxgangs to Gilbert son of Gilbert.[10] From this time Southworth and Croft have descended together.

By the marriage of Gilbert son of Gilbert de Southworth and Alice daughter of Nicholas de Ewyas in 1325 a moiety of the manor of Samlesbury came to the family,[11] which was thenceforward known as Southworth of Samlesbury, continuing till the latter part of the 17th century. In addition the manors of Middleton, Houghton, and Arbury, adjoining Southworth,

were acquired, and some junior branches of the family settled in them.[12]

As to Southworth itself but little record remains.[13] In 1287 and 1292 there was a settlement of the boundary between Croft and Kenyon by the lords of the manors.[14] An inquisition made in 1325 respecting 'half the manor of Southworth' shows that Sir Robert de Holland had obtained a grant of it.[15] There are a few later charters.[16]

The steadfast adherence of Sir John Southworth to the ancient faith in the time of Elizabeth, with the consequent fines and imprisonments, must have made a serious inroad upon the family resources ; the manors and lands in the Southworth district were mortgaged and sold early in the 17th century.[17] Sir Thomas Ireland of Bewsey purchased Southworth and Croft in 1621.[18] A century later the

---

[7] Dods. MSS. liii, fol. 23, no. 4 ; in a collection of Southworth charters. About five hundred of these deeds are contained in the Towneley MS. HH ; and a number of abstracts are in Kuerden's folio volume (Chet. Lib.).

Gilbert de Croft's charter was made 'with the leave of his heir.' The witnesses included Thurstan Banastre (who died in 1219) and Robert his brother ; also Henry and Roger de Croft. The pound of pepper does not seem to have been demanded, and Southworth was later described as held directly of the lords of Makerfield.

For Gilbert de Croft see *Lancs. Pipe R.* 77, 152, &c.

[8] Dods. MSS. loc. cit. ; Gilbert de Croft is called son of Roger. It is possible that in the charter the 'manor' was Southworth and the 'land' Croft.

Later Robert Banastre released to Gilbert de Southworth his claim on the land outside his park of Lee by the boundary of Southworth, together with all his land outside the park at Edricshull on the east ; Towneley MS. HH, no. 2086.

[9] Agnes released to Gilbert all her share in Aspshaw appertaining to her 3 oxgangs ; the bounds included Aspshaw Brook as far as 'the oak marked with a cross' ; Kuerden fol. MS. 75, no. 313. The name Aspshaw occurs also in Newton.

When a widow she granted 1 oxgang in the vill of Croft, with two messuages formerly held of her by Hugh son of Wion and William son of Henry ; rents of 1*d.* and 5*d.* were payable to her and the chief lord respectively ; ibid. 74, no. 119.

[10] Robert 'Sceryswerz' (? de Erbery or Deresbery) was the grantor ; he had probably acquired them from Agnes daughter of Randle ; Dods. MSS. liii, fol. 17*b.* The date of this charter is about 1250 ; 'N.' rector of Winwick, otherwise unknown, was a witness.

Robert son of Robert Banastre released to Gilbert de Southworth all his right in land called Richard's Croft ; ibid. fol. 21, no. 49.

[11] Towneley MS. HH, no. 1729 ; *Final Conc.* (Rec. Soc. Lancs. and Ches.), ii, 62.

[12] See the account of the township.

[13] All the lords of the manor from 1220 to 1380 seem to have been named Gilbert, so that it is difficult to determine the succession. In the above-cited grant of two oxgangs, Gilbert son of Gilbert was the recipient. Emma wife of Gilbert de Southworth is mentioned in 1290 ; Assize R. 1288, m. 11 d. Gilbert son of Gilbert made a grant in 1294 ; Dods. MSS. liii,

fol. 19, no. 34 ; and the marriage of another Gilbert son of Gilbert was agreed upon, as stated, in 1325.

[14] The land in dispute in 1287 had the following boundaries : Beginning at Strid Lache, where it fell into Kenylaw Lache, up Strid Lache to a ditch in the east, along this southward to Quitslade Lache head, thence to Kenylaw Lache and the starting point. The decision was a compromise, the land to be common to Croft and Kenyon ; Towneley MS. HH, no. 1650.

In 1292 the dispute was concerning land between Kenylaw ends and Southworth Chapel and between Edricshull syke and Kenylaw Lache ; a division of the land was made, a ditch 4 ft. wide being ordered to mark the boundary ; ibid. no. 1697.

[15] The jury decided that it would not be to the king's injury to allow Gilbert de Southworth to enfeoff John de Middleton of the moiety of the manor of Southworth, which he held of the king in chief, in order that the said John might grant it to Gilbert, with remainder to Gilbert his son and Alice his wife and their heirs. The moiety was held in socage of the king (by the forfeiture of Robert de Holland) by fealty and the service of 15*d.* yearly at Christmas, and was worth 43*s.* 4*d.* No other lands remained to Gilbert in the county ; Inq. a.q.d. 19 Edw. II, no. 35 ; see also *Final Conc.* ii, 62. The service of 15*d.* indicates that this 'moiety' of Southworth was the three oxgangs in Croft held in 1212 by the heirs of Randle, for 5*d.* to the chief lord was due from one of the oxgangs.

In 1334 it was declared that Southworth was not a vill, but a hamlet of the vill of Croft ; Coram Rege R. 297, m. 3 d.

[16] Gilbert de Southworth in 1331 granted to Gilbert de Rixton and Denise his wife for life, and their children Richard and Emmota, lands in Croft ; Towneley MS. HH, no. 1534.

Thomas son of Gilbert de Southworth was a plaintiff in 1353 ; Assize R. 435, m. 4. He is probably the Thomas de Southworth of later settlements. In the previous year a feoffee had delivered certain lands, &c., in Arbury, Middleton, Houghton, and Woolston to Geoffrey son of Thomas de Southworth, with remainder to William and other children of Thomas ; Dods. MSS. liii, fol. 27*b.* William de Southworth and Maud his wife appear to have been in possession in 1404 ; ibid.

Southworth is named among the family manors in inquisitions and settlements ; e.g. of Sir John Southworth, who died at Harfleur in 1416 ; *Lancs. Inq. p.m.* (Chet.

---

manor was held by the Gerards of Ince, and bequeathed in 1743 by Richard Gerard to his brother Thomas, a Jesuit priest.[19] This was no doubt a gift to the society to enable it to maintain the local missions, and thus Southworth came into the possession of Stonyhurst College. It was sold about 1820 to Thomas Claughton of Haydock; he failed in 1823,[20] and it was sold to Edward Greenall of Warrington,[21] whose granddaughter Elizabeth, Lady Shiffner, sold it to Samuel Brooks, the banker, after whose death it passed to a younger son Thomas. The latter's sons, Mr. Joseph Raynor Brooks and Mr. Edward Brooks, are the present owners.[22] No manor courts are held, nor are any manorial rights claimed.

Aspshaw anciently gave a surname to the family settled there.[23]

A branch of the Southworths was established in Croft.[24] About 1556 the heirs of Henry Southworth and James Hey contributed to the subsidy as landowners.[25] No freeholders appear in the list of 1600, but in 1628 John Hay contributed to the subsidy.[26] James Bankes of Winstanley held some land in Croft in 1618.[27] Christopher Bate, a recusant, petitioned in 1654 for leave to contract for the sequestrated

two-thirds of his estate in Croft.[28] In 1717 Elizabeth Kay, widow, as a 'papist,' registered a house and 8 acres in the same place.[29]

The 'chapel of Southworth' is mentioned in 1292,[30] but nothing further is known of it ; perhaps it was a domestic chapel.

During the last century several places of worship have been erected. For the Established religion Christ Church was built in 1832. The benefice became a rectory by the Winwick Church Act of 1841 ; the patron is the Earl of Derby.[31] An Independent Methodist chapel was built at Croft in 1817,[32] but has disappeared.

When the Unitarians were ejected from the old Risley Chapel in Culcheth they built for themselves a small chapel in Croft, opened in 1839.[33]

After the suppression of the ancient worship by Elizabeth nothing is known until 1701 of any survival or continuance ; but Gervase Hamerton, a Jesuit, was in that year in charge of the mission of Southworth.[34] The private chapel in the hall continued to be used even after the sale ; but in 1827 the present church of St. Lewis was opened.[35] The mission is now served by the secular clergy.[36]

Lancs. Funeral Certs. (Chet. Soc.), 49–51 ; Duchy of Lanc. Inq. p.m. xxvi, no. 58. George Ireland succeeded him in the Southworth manors and in Pennington ; there is some uncertainty as to his birth, so that he was probably illegitimate. In 1626 he received the manors from his brother Thomas ; Pal. of Lanc. Feet of F. bdle. 110, no. 3 ; and died 6 May, 1632, being buried at Winwick the following day. He left by his wife Helen a daughter and heir Margaret, nearly six years of age ; Duchy of Lanc. Inq. p.m. xxviii, no. 30. He had settled the manors on his heirs male, with reversion to the heirs male of Thomas Ireland of Bewsey and his brothers ; but, as male issue was lacking, Margaret his daughter succeeded. She married in or before 1648 Penistone Whalley, son of Thomas Whalley of Kirton, Notts., and by him had a daughter Elizabeth ; Visit. of Notts. (Harl. Soc.), 118. She was the widow of Cuthbert Clifton of Clifton, but had no issue by him ; Dugdale, Visit. (Chet Soc.), 87. See Pal. of Lanc. Feet of F. bdle. 144, m. 17 ; 148, m. 67 (1650) ; in this Alexander Breres and Anne his wife are joined with Penistone Whalley and Margaret his wife as deforciants ; also bdle. 156, m. 146 (1654).

[19] Piccope, MS. Pedigrees (Chet. Lib.), i, 119, quoting Roman Catholic deeds in the Preston House of Correction ; Thomas Gerard was to divide the profits equally with his brother Caryll (also a priest), and his sisters Anne, Mary, Bridget, and Clare.

There was a recovery of the manor in 1761, Thomas and Caryll Gerard being vouchees ; Pal. of Lanc. Plea R. 593, m. 4.

[20] See the note on the Winwick charities. He married in 1806 Maria sister of Thomas Legh of Lyme, the Eastern traveller ; Earwaker, East. Ches. i, 306. He sat for the borough of Newton from 1818 till his resignation in 1825 ; Pink and Beaven, Parl. Repre. of Lancs. 293. He was the father of Dr. Thomas Legh

Claughton, Bishop o and of St. Albans, 1 Piers Calveley Clau Helena, 1859–62, 1862–71.

[21] Baines, Lancs. Edward Greenall di on John who d

THE HUNDRED OF SALFORD

CONTAINING THE PARISHES OF

MANCHESTER	RADCLIFFE	ROCHDALE (Part)
ASHTON-UNDER-LYNE	PRESTWICH	BOLTON
ECCLES	BURY (Part)	AND THE
DEANE	MIDDLETON	Township of Aspull in Wigan
FLIXTON		

In 1066 King Edward held Salford, with its 3 hides and 12 plough-lands, its forest 3 leagues square with many heys and a hawks' eyry, and a hide in Radcliffe, where a second hide was held as a royal manor. The churches of the manor of Manchester had a plough-land in Manchester. The rest of the 'manor or hundred,' including Rochdale, was divided into twenty-one berewicks, held by as many thegns, assessed as 11½ hides and 10½ plough-lands, with extensive woodlands. The whole manor rendered £37 4s. for farm of the plough-lands. In 1086 the demesne was worth 100s.; there were two ploughs and serfs and villeins with one plough; and by the grant of Roger of Poitou five knights held 3 hides and 7 plough-lands, in which were thegns, villeins, and others, including a priest, having thirty-two ploughs; and the whole was worth £7.[1] The area was probably much the same as that of the existing hundred.[2]

The lordship of the hundred followed the same descent as the district anciently known as 'Between Ribble and Mersey,'[3] and with the honour and Duchy of Lancaster is now vested in the Crown. Nearly a third of the hundred continued to be held in thegnage, as the survey of 1212 shows, the parish of Rochdale being so held of the lord of Clitheroe; the principal military tenant at that time was the baron of Manchester, other prominent holders being the lords of Penwortham and Tottington—whose fees were acquired in the first half of the 13th century by the Lacy family and afterwards incorporated in the honour of Clitheroe—and the lord of Great Bolton.[4] These feudatories did suit to the hundred court of Salford from three weeks to three weeks.[5]

---

[1] *V.C.H. Lancs.* i, 287.

[2] The possible exceptions are the township of Aspull, in Wigan parish; the northern extremity of Bury parish, now in Blackburn Hundred; and Saddleworth in Rochdale, now in Yorkshire.

[3] See the grant to Ranulf, Earl of Chester; *Cal. Close,* 1227–31, p. 221; also the accounts of the honour of Lancaster and the hundred of West Derby in the present work. In 1257, during the minority of Robert son and heir of William de Ferrers, Earl of Derby, the hundred was in the hands of Prince Edward by the king's gift; *Lancs. Inq.* (Rec. Soc. Lancs. and Ches.), i, 205. In 1324 the issues of the hundred or wapentake amounted to £58 per annum; ibid. ii, 203.

[4] *Lancs. Inq. and Extents* (Rec. Soc. Lancs. and Ches.), i, 52–72.

[5] Ibid. 248, 268. Court rolls of the wapentake from 1324 to 1326 are printed in *Lancs. Ct. R.* (Rec. Soc. Lancs. and Ches.), 150–64. The *judices* or doomsmen of Withington, Oldham, Middleton, Barton, Stretford, and Bolton were fined, as were a number of townships (p. 157). Other court rolls (1510 onward), surveys, and ministers' accounts are preserved in the Record Office.

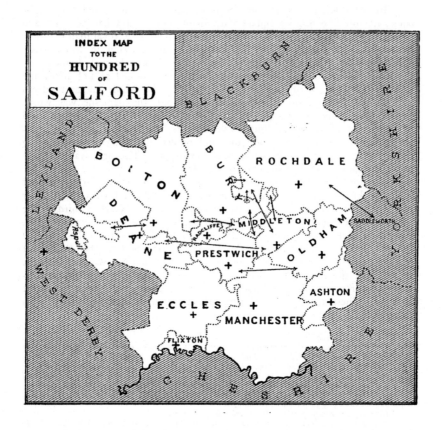

INDEX MAP
TO THE
HUNDRED
OF
SALFORD

SALFORD HUNDRED

The administration was committed to a serjeant or bailiff.[6] In 1436 the king gave Sir Richard Molyneux of Sefton the office of Steward of the Wapentake of Salfordshire, to descend by hereditary right;[7] by virtue of which grant the Earl of Sefton is the present high steward. The courts were formerly held at the Town Hall, Salford,[8] the ancient jurisdiction having been regulated and extended by an Act passed in 1846;[9] but they are now held in Manchester.

In 1237 a subsidy of a thirtieth of movable goods produced £81 7s. 8¼d. for the hundred and £493 9s. 2d. for the whole county.[10] In 1332 the levy of a fifteenth of movable goods yielded £39 4s. for this hundred and £287 13s. 8d. for the whole county. This became the basis of the 'fifteenth,' amounting to £41 14s. 4d. for the hundred and £329 16s. 4d. for the county, which was regularly levied until the imposition of the Land Tax in 1693. Under the provisions for the levying of that tax at the rate of 4s. in the pound on the profits of land and 6 per cent. on personal estate, the valuation of this hundred amounted to £5,438 12s. 10d., that of the whole county being £21,265 16s. 8d.[11]

According to the certificate of a general muster made in 1574 this hundred supplied of furnished men 60 archers and 294 billmen, and of unfurnished men 72 archers and 309 billmen; total 735, out of 4,870 provided by the whole county.

[6] Ellis son of Robert [de Pendlebury] was master serjeant in 1199; Farrer, *Lancs. Pipe R.* 116; but about 1222 Richard de Hulton held the wapentake at the will of the king; *Lancs. Inq. and Extents,* i, 133. Henry son of Wenne was chief bailiff in 1246, and Henry de Lea in 1257; Assize R. 404, m. 16; *Lancs. Inq. and Extents,* i, 205. In 1355 Adam del Hegleghes, bailiff, and his under-bailiffs were indicted for having ridden where they should have gone on foot; Assize R. 436, m. 1.

[7] Croxteth D. W 2. The grant was renewed and confirmed in 1446, and in later times; ibid. W 3, &c.

[8] About 1857 the court leet for the hundred was held twice a year at Salford Town Hall, but has long since ceased.

[9] 9 & 10 Vict. cap. 126; the court was empowered to try actions up to £50. In 1868 a similar Court of Record for the city of Manchester (founded in 1838) was amalgamated with the Salford Court, and the sittings were transferred from Salford Town Hall to Manchester. The Earl of Sefton, as hereditary steward, used to nominate the registrar, but now the City Council nominates him. The judge is appointed by the Crown through the chancellor of the duchy, and he appoints the bailiff.

[10] *Lancs. Lay Sub.* (Rec. Soc. Lancs. and Ches. xxvii), 50. Manchester township paid £5 and Bury parish £6.

[11] Exch. K.R. Accts. of Land and Assessed Taxes, 1693.

MANCHESTER

SALFORD	MOSTON	DROYLSDEN	LEVENSHULME
BROUGHTON	HARPURHEY	OPENSHAW	BURNAGE
MANCHESTER	NEWTON	WITHINGTON	DENTON
CHORLTON - UPON-	FAILSWORTH	DIDSBURY	HAUGHTON
MEDLOCK	BRADFORD	CHORLTON - WITH -	HEATON NORRIS
BLACKLEY	GORTON	HARDY	REDDISH
CHEETHAM	ARDWICK	MOSS SIDE	STRETFORD
CRUMPSALL	BESWICK (Extra-par.)	RUSHOLME	HULME

The ancient parish of Manchester, with an area of 35,152 acres and a population in 1901 of 878,532, has from time immemorial been the most important in the county. The situation of the town from which it derives its name being at the junction of two important roads—from the south to the north-west of the country and from the port of Chester to York— must have attracted. an urban population from very early times,[1] and the convenience of its position beside the Irwell and between two of its tributaries, if not the original reason for a settlement, was a concomitant attraction. The Romans established a fortified station, of which various fragments are known,[2] and from which great roads branched off in five directions.[3] Their English successors also occupied the place, which in the 10th century was included in Northumbria. In 923 King Edward sent a force to the town to repair and man it.[4] History is again silent for a century and a half, and then reveals the existence of an endowed church at Manchester and of a royal manor at Salford, to which not only the parish but the hundred owed service.[5]

By the Norman kings the town of Manchester with the greater part of the parish was granted to the Grelley family, who constituted it the head of their barony ;[6] but Salford, with the adjacent townships of Broughton, Cheetham, Hulme, and Stretford, and the more distant one of Reddish was retained by the king as demesne or bestowed on the great nobleman to whom he entrusted 'the land between Mersey and Ribble' or in later times the honour of Lancaster, the holders of which received the title of earl

[1] For pre-Roman relics see *Lancs. and Ches. Antiq. Soc.* iii, 254 ; v, 327 ; x, 250.
[2] See Thompson Watkin's *Roman Lancs.* 92-124 ; *Lancs. and Ches. Antiq. Soc.* xvii, 87 ; xxiii, 66, 73, 112 ; and the Roman section of the present work. The legend of Sir Tarquin, enemy of King Arthur, who was attacked and slain by Sir Lancelot du Lake, was in the 17th century attached to the old Roman castle. 'Near to the ford in Medlock about Mab house (he) hung a bason on a tree,' on which bason a challenger must strike ; Hollinworth, *Mancuniensis*, 21.
[3] To Chester, Stockport, York, Ribchester, and Wigan.
[4] *Angl.-Sax. Chron.* ; also *V.C.H. Lancs.* ii, 178. Hoards of coins have been found near Alport ; *Lancs. and Ches. Antiq. Soc.* ii, 269 ; *Pal. Note Bk.* iv, 152, 203.
[5] *V.C.H. Lancs.* i, 287.
[6] Ibid. 326.

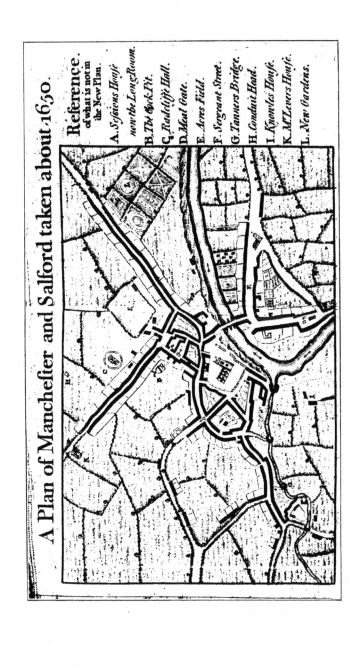

A Plan of Manchester and Salford taken about 1650.

Reference.
of what is not in the New Plan.

A. Sessions House
   now the Long Room.
B. The Oak Pit.
C. Radcliffe Hall.
D. Meal Gate.
E. Acres Field.
F. Serjeant Street.
G. Tanners Bridge.
H. Conduit Head.
I. Knowles House.
K. Mr Levers House.
L. New Gardens.

Thomas del Booth of Barton left money for this bridge.[15] Another, over the Irk, is named in 1381.[16] These rivers were noted for their floods, often very destructive.[17]

About 1536 Leland thus described the place: 'Manchester, on the south side of the Irwell River, standeth in Salfordshire, and is the fairest, best builded, quickest, and most populous town of all Lancashire; yet is in it [but] one parish church, but is a college, and almost throughout double-aisled *ex quadrato lapide durissimo,* whereof a goodly quarry is hard by the town. There be divers stone bridges in the town, but the best, of three arches, is over Irwell. This bridge divideth Manchester from Salford, the which is a large suburb to Manchester. On this bridge is a pretty little chapel. . . . And almost two flight shots

without the town, beneath on the same side of Irwell, yet be seen the dykes and foundations of Old Mancastel in a ground now inclosed. The stones of the ruins of this castle were translated towards making of bridges for the town.'[18] The quarry named was that at Collyhurst.[19]

The privilege of sanctuary which had been allowed to the town[20] was in 1541 transferred to Chester, having proved injurious to good order.[21]

The prosperity of the place was uninterrupted during the religious changes of the 16th century.[21] The endowments of the parish church were confiscated by Edward VI, but restored in great measure by Mary. No resistance was openly offered to any of the changes. The two great families of the parish—the Byrons of Clayton and Radcliffes of Ordsall—though at first

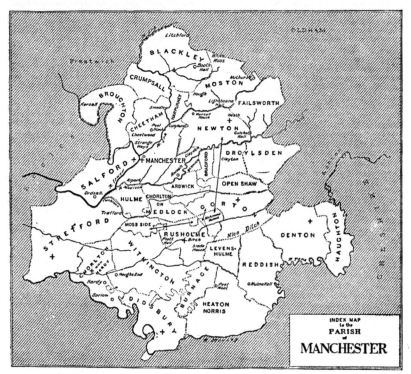

INDEX MAP
to the
PARISH
of

MANCHESTER

[15] His will is printed in Baines's *Lancs.* (1868), i, 283.

[16] Hunt D. no. 52 (Dods. MSS. cxlii, fol. 169); see also *Mamecestre* (Chet. Soc.), iii, 506.

[17] In 1480, in the testimony of the burgesses respecting the highway between Manchester and Collyhurst occurs the statement that 'the water of Irk had worn out' the said highway; Hulme D. no. 22. In 1787 part of Salford Bridge was carried away by a flood of the Irwell.

[18] Leland, *Itin.* v, 94.

[19] *Manch. Court Leet Rec.* iv, 107.

adverse to Protestantism, declined in fortune in the time of Elizabeth, and their estates were early in the 17th century dispersed among the smaller gentry and prosperous traders; the great manor of Manchester itself was about the same time purchased by a wealthy merchant. The smaller gentry, excepting the Barlows, appear as a rule to have gone with the times, often becoming zealous Puritans, while the trading and artisan classes, in Manchester as elsewhere, soon embraced the new doctrines.[23] Thus by the end of Elizabeth's reign the population was almost wholly Protestant, and of the more extreme type. The change was, of course, chiefly due to the clergy of the parish church, the more respected and influential of the ministers serving there and in the dependent chapelries being of the Puritan school.

William Camden visited the place in 1586, and appears to have been pleased with it; he found the notable things to be the woollen manufacture, the market, church, and college.[24] John Taylor, the 'Water Poet,' passed through it about thirty years later.[25]

The Marprelate press was set up in 1588 at Newton Lane near Manchester, but discovered and suppressed soon after starting work.[26]

The number of recognized townships was formerly but small. In the Subsidy Roll of 1541 only seven are named—Salford, Manchester, Cheetham, Reddish, Withington, Heaton Norris, and Stretford—but Moston was taxed with Ashton.[27] The contributions to the ancient tax called the Fifteenth were arranged on the following basis:—When the hundred paid £41 14*s.* 4*d.*, Salford paid £1 2*s.*, Manchester with its members £3, Cheetham 4*s.* 10*d.*, Reddish £1 2*s.*, Withington £3 15*s.*, Heaton Norris 13*s.* 6*d.*, Chorlton 3*s.* 4*d.*, and Stretford £1 1*s.* 8*d.*[28] The county lay, established in 1624, also recognized eight townships:—Manchester paying £9 3*s.* 11½*d.*, Salford £3 1*s.* 3¾*d.*, Stretford £1 4*s.* 6½*d.*, Withington £5 4*s.* 2¾*d.*, Heaton Norris £1 16*s.* 9½*d.*, Chorlton Row 12*s.* 3¾*d.*, Reddish £1 10*s.* 7¾*d.*, and Cheetham 11*s.* 2¾*d.*, or £23 5*s.* in all, when the hundred contributed £100.[29] At this time, however, the 'members' or 'hamlets' of Manchester had separate constables, and were therefore townships.[30]

The geology of the parish of Manchester is represented by the New Red Sandstone, the Permian Beds, and the Carboniferous Rocks. The formation lying on the west side of a line drawn from Reddish through the Manchester Waterworks, Fairfield, Newton Heath, and Blackley, consists almost entirely of the New Red Sandstone, the exception being a long and irregular-shaped patch of the Permian Rocks and, at the widest part to the north-east of Manchester, of the Coal Measures, and lying on the west side of, and brought up by, a fault which extends northward from Heaton Norris, through Kirkmanshulme and Openshaw, trending north-west around Cheetham to Crumpsall. At the widest part this patch of the Coal Measures is 1½ mile in width, tapering out at Crumpsall Hall on the north and at Kirkmanshulme on the south. Further to the east a broad belt of the Permian Rocks, varying in width from ¾ mile to 1½ mile, crops out above the Coal Measures. These occur over the remainder of the parish on the east side of a line drawn from Hyde Hall in Denton through Audenshaw to Failsworth, and from Newton Heath between Blackley and the River Irk to the limits of the parish near Heaton Park.

The principal features of the town of Manchester as it was about 1600 still exist, though changed[31]—the church with the college[32] to the north of it, the bridges over Irk and Irwell adjacent, and the market-place a little distance to the south—originally on the edge of the town. In Salford the small triangle formed by Chapel Street,[33] Gravel Lane,[34] and Greengate[35] was the village or inhabited portion, the dwellings naturally clustering round the bridge over the Irwell.[36] Then, as now, the road through Manchester from this bridge[37] went winding east and north round the church as Cateaton Street,[38] Hanging Ditch,[39]

[23] Ellis Hall, known as 'Elias, the Manchester prophet,' was born in 1502. Probably acted upon by the religious excitement of the period he began to have visions, and in 1562 went to London to see the queen. He was condemned to the pillory and whipped by two ministers; see W. E. A. Axon's *Lancs. Glean.* 312; *Local Glean. Lancs. and Ches.* i, 72, 84. A monstrous birth in 1579 appealed to the superstitious in another way; *Pal. Note Bk.* iii, 269.

[24] Camden, *Brit.* (1695), 746, 747. He mentions the famous quarries of Collyhurst. Saxton's map of the county was published in 1577; he visited the town again in 1596 and made a survey of it, spending several days on the work; Dr. Dee's *Diary* (ed. Bailey), 36–8.

[25] Quoted in Procter's *Manch. Streets*, 218.

[26] *Acts of P.C.* 1589–90, p. 62; also W. Axon in *N. and Q.* IV, iii, 97, quoting Strype's *Annals* (1824), III, ii, 602. Coining was suspected in the same district in 1577; *Acts of P.C.* 1577–8, p. 63.

[27] *Misc.* (Rec. Soc. Lancs. and Ches.), i, 138, &c.

[28] Gregson, *Fragments* (ed. Harland), 18.

[29] Ibid. 22.

[30] There were in 1623 constables for Newton, Droylsden, Ardwick, Bradford, Blackley, Crumpsall, Failsworth, Open-

Toad or Todd Lane,[40] crossing the Irk[41] and mounting Red Bank.[42] Half Street,[43] at the east end of the church, was continued as Millgate,[44] which wound along by the Irk, to reach the lord's mills on that stream. The grammar school, on its original site, and some old timbered houses [44a] still distinguish the street, though the mills have gone. From the northeast corner of the church Fennel Street [45] led eastward past Hyde's Cross,[46] at the corner of Todd Lane, to Withy Grove [47] and Shude Hill.[48]

From the south Deansgate,[49] on the line of the old Roman road from Chester, ran northerly towards the church, but curving to the east near the bridge was continued as Cateaton Street or Hanging Ditch ; at the junction Smithy Door [50] led south to the market-place, which was probably always an open square,

[40] 'Towdlane' is named in 1552; *Court Leet Rec.* i, 6. There was a well in it ; ibid. ii, 268. In 1609 it is called 'Crooked Lane *alias* Tode Lane,' and in 1618 'New Street *alias* Toade Lane' ; ibid. ii, 245 ; iii, 6.

[41] The name Scotland at this point occurs in 1762; Procter, *Manch. Streets*, 45.

[42] Red Bank is named in 1557 and 1573 ; *Court Leet Rec.* i, 40, 159 (a highway). In later times there was bull baiting at Red Bank, at the wakes, with other sports ; Procter, *Manch. Streets*, 43. Knoll Bank, on the east side of the road from Manchester to Cheetham, is mentioned in a deed of 1596 by John Beswick and Elizabeth his wife, as formerly the property of Philip Strangeways ; Chetham Papers, and Raines MSS. (Chet. Lib.), xxvi, 424.

[43] This descriptive name of the present Cathedral Street occurs in 1622 ; *Court Leet Rec.* iii, 59.

[44] Millgate (Mulnegate) is named in deeds from about 1300 ; it gave a surname to resident families ; Manch. Corp. D. undated, 1324, 1343.

[44a] These and other remains are described below.

[45] Fennel Street is named in 1506 ; De Trafford D. no. 71. It was perhaps the same as Middlegate mentioned from 1331 to 1498 ; a burgage in Middlegate stood next to Todd Lane on the west side of it; ibid. no. 6, 29, 68. Middlegate has sometimes been identified with Half Street. In Fennel Street was Barley Cross, where in 1816 the corn market was held ; Aston, *Manch.* 217 ; see also Procter, *Manch. Streets*, 38. The continuation of Fennel Street west to Hunt's Bank was in 1769 used as the apple market and so called ; *Court Leet Rec.* viii, 125. Perhaps it was the Churchyard-side of earlier times.

[46] Hyde's Cross is supposed to have been the place of sanctuary. In 1662 a place was described as in Todd Lane and near Hyde Cross. At that time the swine market was there ; *Court Leet Rec.* v, 62.

[47] The old name was Within-greave ; *Court Leet Rec.* i, 3. The Dove-house Field was in this lane ; ibid. iii, 60. A house known as Within-greave Hall was part of the Hulme trust estate ; see Procter, *Bygone Manch.* 42.

[48] In 1554 James Chetham was ordered to make 'the highway at the Shude Hill as [= which] he hath made, sufficient for carts to come and go' ; *Court Leet Rec.* i, 11.

In later times at least the lord's pinfold was in Shude Hill, at the end of Withy Grove. The pinfold is mentioned in 1535 as 'in the east end' of the town,

and lying wes north by the h the Claypit ;

[49] A burgag the Parsonage Trafford D. no piece of land o Deansgate ; n the Lady Lod The southern Alport Lane ; hi l, supp se in 1564 a clos lord of the m Deansgate see *Soc* xxii, 180.

[50] Smithy name, seems t in 1560, when the Smithy D d

near the Conduit, and that called Olgreave, Culcheth, or Langley Hall in Long Millgate ; further out were Alport Lodge, Garrett, Ancoats, Collyhurst, and one or two others. To the south of Alport was Knott in Mill Hulme ; a licence for the mill-dam was given in 1509.[58] The cockpit lay to the south-east of Old Millgate.[59] There exists a small town plan, of unknown origin but apparently trustworthy, which may be dated about 1650.[59a]

Apart from the streets above mentioned the parish was mainly agricultural, areas of wood,[60] heath,[61] and moss[62] being intermixed with arable and pasture lands; the dwellings were the scattered manor and farm-houses and small villages. The rural population probably then, as later, combined tillage with weaving. The chapels existing in 1650 serve to indicate the chief centres of population—Blackley, Newton, Gorton, Denton, Birch, Didsbury, Chorlton, Stretford, and Salford.[63]

In the Civil War Manchester, as might be expected, took the Parliamentary side.[64] On an outbreak of hostilities becoming imminent, Lord Strange, who soon afterwards succeeded his father as Earl of Derby, fully alive to the disaffection as to the importance of Manchester, endeavoured to secure it for the king. A small quantity of powder was for convenience stored at the College, then Lord Strange's property, and in June 1642, it being expected that the sheriff would endeavour to secure it for the king's use, Mr. Assheton of Middleton managed to obtain possession of it, and removed it to other places in the town.[65] Lord Strange thereupon demanded its return, and on

15 July, after summoning the able men to meet him at Bury in virtue of a commission of array,[66] he came to Manchester, intending to lodge at Sir Alexander Radcliffe's house at Ordsall. The people of Manchester invited him to dine in their town, and he accepted the invitation ; the matter of the powder was discussed and an agreement made.[67] But on the same day the Parliamentary Commissioners had issued their summons to the militia, and the banquet was followed by an encounter between the opposing forces, in which was shed the first blood of the struggle.[68]

The war did not formally begin until September,[69] and Manchester was speedily involved.[70] On Saturday the 24th and the following day Lord Derby assembled his troops against it, and the townsmen summoned assistance from their neighbours.[71] Lord Derby's forces were variously estimated—from 2,600 up to 4,500—and he had some ordnance, which he planted at Alport Lodge and Salford Bridge, thus commanding two of the principal roads into the town.[72] After some skirmishing he proposed terms, but being refused he continued the siege for a week without any success ; on Saturday 1 October he drew off his troops, having been ordered by the king to join him. The success of the townsmen was chiefly due to the skill of a German soldier, Colonel Rosworm, who began on the Wednesday before the siege to set up posts and chains for keeping out horsemen and to barricade and block up street ends with mud walls and other defences.[73] After the raising of the siege he continued his fortifications, and led the 'Man-

---

[58] Procter, *Manch. Streets*, 108. The mill seems to have derived its distinctive name from the miller.

[59] The 'Cockfight Place' is named in 1587, and in 1598 an encroachment on the lord's waste at the cockpit was condemned ; *Court Leet Rec.* ii, 8, 135. It is possible that the cockpit was transferred from one place to another.

[59a] This plan is engraved in a corner of Casson and Berry's plan.

[60] Blackley, Collyhurst, Bradford, and Openshaw were ancient wooded areas, but had probably been cleared by 1600.

[61] Newton Heath, Chorlton Heath, and Barlow Moor indicate some of the greater heaths of old time.

[62] The Great Moss stretched through Withington and Rusholme, giving name to Moss Side ; but there were a great number of other mosses to the north, east, and south of Manchester town.

[63] The trade of the place in 1641 is thus described : ' The town of Manchester buys the linen yarn of the Irish in great quantity, and weaving it returns the same again to Ireland to sell. Neither doth her industry rest here, for they buy cotton wool in London, that comes first from Cyprus and Smyrna, and work the same into fustians, vermilions, dimities, &c., which they return to London, where they are sold ; and from thence not seldom are sent into such foreign parts where the first materials may be more easily had for that manufacture' ; Lewis Roberts, *Merchant's Map of Commerce*, quoted in Reilly's *Manch.* 136.

[64] Though opinion was divided and several influential families, like the Mosleys and Prestwiches, took the king's side, the great body of the people appear to have been zealous for the Parliament. At the report of the array of militia ordered in June 1642, the townsmen, it was

stated, '

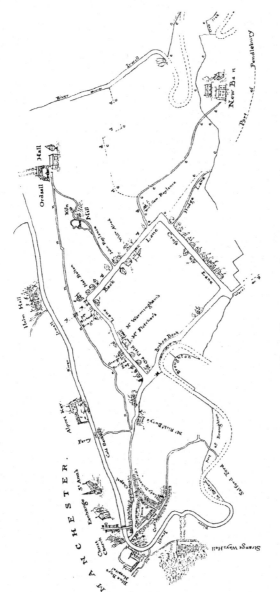

MAP OF MANCHESTER AND SALFORD, 740

chester men' in various excursions to places in South Lancashire, by which the town added to its reputation and the king's forces were harassed or defeated. The remuneration promised him having been refused later, he wrote a bitter complaint of the townsmen ; 'never let an unthankful man and a promise-breaker have another name' than Manchester man.[74] A grant of £1,000 was made for the relief of Manchester out of the sales of 'delinquents'' estates by Parliament in 1645.[75]

The Restoration appears to have been welcomed with hearty loyalty, for the clergy and principal inhabitants were Presbyterians and had in 1659 shown their dissatisfaction with the existing government[76] ; but soon afterwards the religious cleavage between Conformists and Nonconformists[77] was supplemented by the political cleavage between Tories and Whigs. The 'Church and King' riots of 1715,[78] which led to the destruction of Cross Street chapel and other Dissenting meeting-places, showed that the Tories, headed by the collegiate clergy, Sir Oswald Mosley, and others, had a considerable following ; while the Whigs, headed by Lady Bland, included all the Nonconformists and many Churchmen. The composition of the town is shown by the abortive proposal of 1731 that a workhouse should be built, with a board of twenty-four guardians, of whom a third should be High Church, a third Low Church, and a third Nonconformist.[79] The town, not being a borough, had no means of enforcing its political opinions, though public 'town's meetings' were called by the borough

---

Colonel Holland of Denton was in favour of yielding, on the ground that the defenders had neither powder nor match ; but Rosworm counteracted such counsels by sending Mr. Bourne, one of the ministers of the church, an 'aged and grave' man, to encourage the different bodies of defenders ; ibid. 222. Little was done on Thursday ; on Friday there was more cannonading, but the guns were withdrawn in the evening, and the whole attacking force left next day. It is said that their men had been deserting all the time. On the other hand the town's soldiers 'from first to last had prayers and singing of psalms daily at the street ends, most of our soldiers being religious, honest men. . . . The townsmen were kind and respective to the soldiers ; all things were common ; the gentlemen made bullets night and day ; the soldiers were resolute and courageous, and feared nothing so much as a parley' ; ibid. 54-6. In addition to those named above, Captains Robert Bradshaw, Radcliffe, Channell, and Barrington did good service ; Chetham of Nuthurst sent men ; ibid. 46, 52. The thanks of Parliament were at once given to the town ; ibid. 57.

A little later proposals were made on behalf of Lord Derby for the neutrality of the town, but the inhabitants considered that they were able to defend themselves ; ibid. 61.

In July 1643 the Earl of Newcastle called upon the Manchester men to lay down their arms, but he was unable to penetrate into Lancashire ; ibid. 145-7.

[74] For Rosworm's narrative see *Civil War Tracts*, 217-47. He had been promised an annuity of £60 for the lives of himself and his wife ; it was paid for two years only, and he could obtain no redress by law, not being an Englishman. An account of him, with portrait, is given in *Lancs a*

Manchester 'the greatest mere village in England.' Its trade and population had much increased within the previous forty or fifty years; abundance not of houses only but of streets of houses had been provided. It boasted of four extraordinary foundations—a college, a hospital, a free school, and a library, all very well supported. 'I cannot but doubt,' he remarks, 'but this increasing town will some time or other obtain some better face of government and be incorporated, as it very well deserves to be . . . . There is a very firm but ancient stone bridge over the Irwell, which is built exceeding high, because this river, though not great, yet coming from the mountainous part of the country swells sometimes so suddenly that in one night's time they told me the waters would frequently rise four or five yards, and the next day fall as hastily as they rose.' Salford he calls 'the suburb or village on the other side of the bridge.'[85]

The Jacobites in 1745 hoped that Manchester would give them substantial assistance.[86] Mr. Clayton, one of the chaplains of the collegiate church, was an ardent partisan, and the other clergy were sympathizers.[87] One of the nonjuring bishops, Dr. Deacon, lived in the town, ministering to a small congregation. On 28 November a daring sergeant of the Pretender's, having hurried forward, appeared in the town and began to invite recruits.[88] His reception was not cordial, but sufficient supporters were obtained to secure his safety and freedom until the vanguard of the army arrived in the evening. The whole force reached Manchester the following day, the prince himself riding in during the afternoon, when his father was proclaimed king as James III. Mr. Dickinson's house in Market Street was chosen as head quarters and was afterwards known as 'The Palace.'

At night many of the people illuminated their houses, bonfires were made, and the bells were rung. Some three hundred recruits had joined the invaders, and were called 'The Manchester Regiment.' Money due to the government was seized.[89] The army marched south on Monday 1 December, and returned to Manchester in its retreat on the 9th. Out of a contribution of £5,000 then demanded, £2,500 was collected and accepted, and the prince and his forces left the town next day. The Manchester Regiment still accompanied him, and was entrusted with the defence of Carlisle, which surrendered at the end of the month. The officers were tried for high treason in July 1746, and some were executed at Kennington.[90] The heads of two—Thomas Theodorus Deacon and Thomas Siddall—were sent down to Manchester, and fixed on the Exchange.[91] The men of the regiment were tried at Carlisle in August and September, and many of them executed. The successful party had their celebrations, the news of the capture of Carlisle and the victory of Culloden being welcomed by public illuminations and the distribution of liquor.[92] The ill-feeling between the two parties in the town — the Jacobites and the Whigs—continued for many years afterwards.

At this time begins the series of detailed plans of the towns of Manchester and Salford.[93] That of Casson and Berry, 1741-51, shows that the town had expanded considerably, along Deansgate, Market Street, and Shude Hill; a number of new streets had been laid out, but the principal improvement appears to have been the formation of St. Ann's Square on the site of Acresfield about 1720.[94] This drew with it other improvements, as a decent approach had to be formed from Market Street. Several large private houses are figured on the border of the plan of 1750,[95]

Some curious details are given in the diary of Edmund Harrold, wig-maker, 1712–16, printed in *Manch. Collectanea*, i, 172, &c.

Bonfires were lighted to celebrate the king's birthday and accession, as well as the Gunpowder Plot and Restoration of Charles II. Cockthrowing on Shrove Tuesday and 'lifting' at Easter also afforded diversion to the populace. See *Constables' Accounts*, iii, 1, 2, 7, 8, 66, 68.

[85] A Gentleman's *Tour of Great Britain* (ed. 1738), iii, 173–9.
In the *Gent. Mag.* for 1739 (quoted in the *Preston Guardian*) is a statement that 2,000 new houses had been built in the town within twenty years.

[86] The Hanoverians were not idle, but raised a fund for troops; see *Pal. Note Bk.* iii, 235. In the same work will be found a diary of 1745 (iv, 19), and some depositions (iv, 70); see further in *Local Glean. Lancs. and Ches.* i, 89, 153, &c.; and *Lancs. and Ches. Antiq. Soc.* vii, 142; Byrom's *Diary* (Chet. Soc. xl); *Var. Coll.* (Hist. MSS. Com.), ii, 287, 288.

[87] Mr. Clayton openly welcomed the Pretender; another clergyman, Thomas Coppock, a native of Manchester, was appointed chaplain to the Manchester Regiment and promoted to the see of Carlisle, in which city he was executed in 1746; *Local Glean. and Ches.* i, 153, etc.; Procter's *Manch. Streets*, 193.

[88] See Ray's *Hist. of the Rebellion*, 156; Manchester was taken 'by a serjeant, a drum, and a woman.' Chevalier Johnston's account is reprinted in Reilly's *Manch.* 237, 238.

[89] William Fowden, the constable, was brought to trial at Carlisle in 1747 for having executed the orders of Prince Charles Edward; it was proved that he acted under compulsion and he was acquitted. A full account of the matter will be found in Earwaker's edition of the *Manch. Constables' Accts.* iii, 20–28, 354, 355.

[90] The officers were : *Francis Towneley, the colonel; *James Dawson (M), *George Fletcher, John Sanderson, Peter Moss, *Andrew Blood, David Morgan, captains; *Thomas T. Deacon (M), Robert Deacon (M), *Thomas Chadwick, *John Beswick, John Holker (M), Thomas Furnival, *James Bradshaw, lieutenants; Charles Deacon (M), Samuel Maddock, Charles Gaylor, James Wilding, John Hunter, William Brettargh (M), ensigns; and *Thomas Siddall (M), adjutant. Those marked with an asterisk were executed; Moss and Holker escaped; Maddock turned king's evidence; others were transported. Those marked (M) belonged to the parish of Manchester. For James Dawson see Shenstone's ballad; Scott, *Admiss.* to *St. John's Coll. Camb.* iii, 88, 488; *Eagle*, xxviii, 229—last speech (from Raines's MSS. xxv, 370). The last speech of James Bradshaw is in *Pal. Note Bk.* iii, 274. There are notices of Dawson and Bradshaw in *Dict. Nat. Biog.*

[91] A story as to the fate of the heads is told in Procter's *Manch. Streets*, 267.

[92] See *Manch. Constables' Accts.* iii, 28, 32, and notes.

[93] For accounts of the plans of Manchester see Harland's *Manch. Collectanea*, i, 100, &c.; C. Roeder in *Lancs. and Ches. Antiq. Soc.* xxi, 153.

[94] One consequence was that the ancient fair had ultimately to be removed. A man living in 1787 could remember corn and potatoes growing on St. Ann's Square; they had to be carted away the day before the fair as the people had a right to come to hold the fair whether the crops had been removed or not; *Manch. Collectanea*, ii, 188.
The fair continued to be held on 10 Oct. in St. Ann's Square until 1821, when it was removed to Shude Hill. A popular holiday festival, known as Knott Mill Fair, had by that time grown up; it was held on Easter Monday. Acres Fair was transferred to Campfield about 1830. All the fairs were abolished in 1876. See Axon, *Annals*; Baines, *Lancs. Dir.* (1825), ii, 154.

[95] The views are — Christ Church (Cathedral), Trinity (Salford), St. Ann's, the College, the Exchange, the Quay, and St. Ann's Square; the houses of Mr. Floyd near St. Ann's Square, Mr. Marsden and Mr. Dickenson in Market Street Lane, Mr. Croxton in King Street, Mr. Howarth in Millgate, Mr. Touchet in Deansgate, Mr. Johnson, Mr. Miles Bower and his son, Mr. Marriott in Brown's Street, Messrs. Clowes in Hunt's Bank, and Francis Reynolds, esq. (Strangeways Hall). An account of these plans (with a reproduction) will be found in Procter, *Bygone Manch.* 349, &c.
Lists of published views of old Manchester are given in the *Pal. Note Bk.* iii, 53, &c.

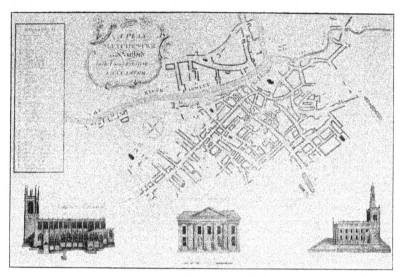

PLAN OF MANCHESTER AND SALFORD IN 1772

SALFORD : BULL'S HEAD INN, GREENGATE

which also gives a bird's-eye view of the town from the Salford side of the river, with a sporting scene in the foreground. Apart from churches and schools the only public building was the Exchange, built in 1729 by Sir O. Mosley, partly for trade and partly for a court-house.[96]

The first newspaper had appeared about 1719,[97] but was discontinued in 1726; four years later another appeared, and had an existence of thirty years. Some others were attempted from time to time, and in 1752 began the *Manchester Mercury*, published down to 1830. The first *Directory* appeared in 1772.[98] The old Subscription Library began in 1757–65 and was followed by others.[99]

From the middle of the 18th century the growth of Manchester was very rapid.[100] The improvement of means of communication was inaugurated in 1721 with the Mersey and Irwell Navigation,[101] and the Duke of Bridgewater's canal system followed in 1758, being imitated by other canals which within fifty years connected Manchester with the principal towns in the manufacturing districts.[102] A long series of

---

[96] There was another Exchange in King Street ; see *Manch. Constables' Accts.* iii, 169.

[97] This was called the *Weekly Journal;* it was printed by Roger Adams, Parsonage, who also issued the Mathematical Lectures of John Jackson, the first known Manchester-printed work ; *Lancs. and Ches. Antiq. Soc.* iv, 13. For Orion Adams, son of Roger, see *Pal. Note Bk.* iii, 48 ; and for notices of the local press, *Local Glean. Lancs. and Ches.* i, 54, 67 ; ii, 6, 142, &c.

An account of the early Manchester booksellers (1600–1700) will be found in *Lancs. and Ches. Antiq. Soc.* vi, 1. For the *Lancs. Journ.* 1738–9, see *Pal. Note Bk.* ii, 205.

Much information about the newspapers is collected in Procter's *Manch. Streets,* 165, &c. There were printers in Manchester as early as 1692.

[98] An account of the earlier Directories will be found in *Manch. Collectanea,* i, 119–66. The dates are—Raffald, 1772, 1773, 1781 ; Holme, 1788 ; Scholes, 1794, 1797 ; Bancks, 1800 ; Dean, 1804, 1808 ; Pigot, 1811. Those of 1772 and 1773 were reprinted in 1889. There is a notice of the Pigots in R. W. Procter's *Bygone Manch.*

[99] See W. E. A. Axon, *Public Libs. of Manch. and Salford* (1877). The books of the Old Subscription Library were sold in 1867. The New (or Exchange) Circulating Library was founded in 1792 ; the Portico in Mosley Street, 1802–6 ; the Law Library in 1820 ; the Medical in 1834 ; the Athenaeum in 1835, the building being opened in 1839 ; while the Free Public Libraries of Salford and Manchester date from 1849–52.

On the Hebrew Roll of the Pentateuch in the Chetham Library see *Lancs. and Ches. Antiq. Soc.* ii, 54 ; on the Black-letter Ballads in the Free Library, and the valuable Owen MSS. in the same, see ibid. ii, 21 ; xvii, 48. A MS. in the Chetham Library (Civil War) is reported in *Hist. MSS. Com. Rep.* ii, App. 156.

The Christie and Bishop Lee collections in the library of the University must also be mentioned.

[100] It is stated in Baines's *Lancs.* (ed. 1836), ii, 306, that an endeavour was made in 1763 to have Manchester made into a borough, but that the same political

and sectarian 1731 defeate Church party a procession known as th been discont Ogden, *Descr*

[101] 7 Geo Geo III, cap the plan of 1 enterprise ; Street

cap. 64.

was paid to beauty by the busy and prosperous traders, it became necessary, in the interests of business itself, to widen the old streets in the heart of the town. In 1775, therefore, an Act was sought for raising money for this purpose,[107] and similar Acts have been obtained frequently since, the result being a great improvement in the appearance of the growing town.[108]

New bridges over the Irwell also became necessary. Blackfriars Bridge was erected in 1761 in a temporary manner by a company of comedians playing in the riding school in Salford, in order to induce Manchester people to patronize them, and was afterwards kept up at the public charge. It was at first a wooden bridge, flagged, for foot passengers only ; the approach from the Manchester side was down twenty-nine steps, to gain the level of Water Street in Salford.[109] In 1817 the old bridge was taken down and replaced by a stone one.[110] In 1783 was laid the foundation of the New Bailey Bridge, opened in 1785 ; it was built by subscription, and a toll was charged until 1803, the capital having by that time been refunded.[111] Regent's Bridge was opened in 1808,[112] about the same time as Broughton Bridge leading from Salford to Broughton.[113] The Strangeways Iron Bridge was built in 1817,[114] and others have followed. Aston's *Picture of Manchester* in 1816 states that there were also seven bridges over the Irk, including Ducie Bridge, completed in 1814 ; nine bridges over the Medlock, and others over Shooter's Brook and various canals.[115]

The same guide book notices the following public buildings in addition to churches and schools : The Infirmary and Asylum in Piccadilly,[116] the Lying-in Hospital in Salford, close to the old bridge,[117] the House of Recovery for infectious diseases, near the Infirmary,[118] the Poor House[119] and House of Correction[120] at Hunt's Bank, the Poor House[121] and New Bailey Prison[122] in Salford, the Exchange, built in 1806–9,[123] somewhat behind the old one, also libraries and theatres.[124-9] The compiler could urge little in favour of the appearance of the town at that time : 'The old part of the town is sprinkled with a motley assemblage of old and new buildings, and the streets, except where they were improved by the Acts of 1775 and 1791, are very narrow. The new streets contain many capital modern houses, but they are more distinguished for their internal than their external elegance.' After noticing Mosley Street and Piccadilly, he proceeds : 'There are few other streets which can claim credit for their being pleasantly situated, attention having been too minutely directed to the value of land to sacrifice much to public convenience or the conservation of health. This, perhaps, has occasioned the present prevalent disposition of so many persons, whose business is carried on in the town, to reside a little way from it, that the pure breath of Heaven may freely blow upon them.'[130]

The agricultural land still remaining in the parish is utilized as follows :—Arable land, 4,835 acres ;

---

[107] 16 Geo. III, cap. 63. **Exchange Street**, leading to St. Ann's Square, was then formed. A deed referring to the improvements of this time is printed in *Local Glean. Lancs. and Ches.* i, 135.

[108] A description of the town as it was in 1783 was reprinted in 1887, with a memoir of the author, James Ogden (1718–1802), a native of the town, by Mr. W. E. A. Axon. It was followed by numerous guide books.
In 1821 an Act (1 & 2 Geo. IV, cap. 126) was obtained for widening Market Street ; the schedule contains a list of the owners and occupiers. The work was not completed till 1834. In 1832 an Act was passed for the improvement of London Road ; 2 Will. IV, cap. 36.

[109] Joseph Aston, *Manch.* (1816), 200. The author afterwards removed to Rochdale and lived at Chadderton Hall, Oldham ; he died in 1844 ; Procter, *Manch. Streets*, 164–74.

[110] 57 Geo. III, cap. 58. The new bridge was opened in 1820, a toll of $\frac{1}{2}$d. was levied on each passenger, the result being that passage by it was avoided. It was made free in 1848.

[111] Aston, *Manch.* 200. It was rebuilt in 1844 and called the Albert Bridge.

[112] Ibid. 202. A toll was levied until 1848.

[113] Ibid. 201. It was built by Samuel Clowes in 1804–6, as an aid to the development of his Broughton estate. His tenants had a free passage, others paid a toll. It was rebuilt in 1869 and made free in 1872.

[114] 56 Geo. III, cap. 62. Lord Ducie's tenants were exempt from the toll.

[115] Op. cit. 202–4. Six of the Irk bridges were low and liable to be overflowed in flood time, but the seventh, the Ducie Bridge (finished in 1816), was lofty.

sall.

[120] Ibid. 192. It is supposed to have

permanent grass, 9,460 ; woods and plantations, 56.[131]

In addition to the older charities mentioned many have since been founded, providing for most of the ills of humanity.[132] A number of scientific and literary societies, beginning with the Literary and Philosophical Society in 1781, have also been established.[133] There are many musical societies and a vast number of religious organizations.

While the development of Greater Manchester in these respects was proceeding steadily the religious and political progress of the people was comparatively peaceful. The Methodist Revival soon affected Manchester, and John Wesley paid the town many visits between 1747 and 1790 ; but perhaps the most singular religious movement was Swedenborgianism. The American Shakers owe their foundation to Ann Lee, a Manchester woman born in Todd Lane in

[131] The details are given thus :—

	A. rable.	Grass	Woods, &c.
	ac.	ac.	ac.
Blackley	167	1,040	—
Broughton	126	185	
Burnage . . .	401	351	—
Cheetham	—	85	—
Clayton	—	167	—
Crumpsall . .	43	258	—
Denton and Haughton	291	1,477	40
Didsbury	311	548	5
Droylsden . . .	3	692	—
Failsworth . .		512	—
Gorton	39	354	—
Levenshulme . . .	2	253	—
Manchester (part) . .	462	452	—
Moston	110	702	—
Newton	19	172	—
Openshaw		6	
Rusholme	10	420	—
Stockport (part) . .	262	658	3
Stretford and Chorlton-with-Hardy . .	1,663	771	
Withington	926	357	8

Salford Royal Hos 1827.
Victoria Dental úp M l k
Deaf a d D b upon-Medlock in Salford.
Homes for Childr
All-night Shelter dilly.
Workshops fo
Home fo Ag d]
Home for Fall] W
St. Mary's Home Rusholme.
Penitentiary, 182
Greenheys, 183
Mrs. Ma

[132] The following is a list of the existing medical and philanthropic charities of the Manchester district, in addition to the endowed charities to be recorded later :

Ancoats Hospital and Ardwick and Ancoats Dispensary, 1841.
Ancoats Dispensary for Women and Children.
Chorlton-upon-Medlock, Rusholme and Moss Side Dispensary, 1831.
Christie Hospital (Cancer Pavilion), Oxford Street.
Ear Hospital, Byrom Street.
Homoeopathic Institution.
Consumption Hospital, near Deansgate with houses at Bowdon and Delamere, 1875.
Hospital for Skin Diseases, Quay Street, 1835.
Hulme Dispensary, 1831.
Lock Hospital, Duke Street, 1819.
Children's Dispensary, Gartside Street.
Jewish Hospital, Cheetham.
Medical Mission Dispensary, Red Bank.
Northern Hospital for Women and Children at Cheetham.
Royal Eye Hospital, founded in 1815, in King Street ; removed to Faulkner Street, 1822 ; to St. John's Street, 1874 ; and to Oxford Road, 1886.
Royal Infirmary, 1752.
St. Mary's Hospital, founded in Salford, 1790.

chester Regiment, was raised in 1777 to serve in the war of American Independence. It took part with distinction in the defence of Gibraltar in 1781–2, and was disbanded in 1783.[137] In 1789 the Dissenters petitioned Parliament for the repeal of the Test and Corporation Acts, and this led to a revival of dissensions. The advocates of reform were stigmatized as Jacobins, and refused admission to public houses.[138] The Government was suspicious, and in 1794 indicted Thomas Walker and others for conspiring to overthrow the constitution and aid the French in case they should invade the kingdom. The charges rested on perjured evidence and were dismissed.[139] The fear of invasion at the same time led to the raising of two regiments of 'Volunteers' in 1794, and others were raised later.[140]

The misgovernment of the town, the disagreements between employers and employed, and occasional periods of famine or bad trade all contributed to quicken the desire for reform both in the town and in the country at large.[141] In 1812 Radical meetings were held, at one of which, in Ancoats, thirty-eight workmen were arrested on charges of sedition ; they were acquitted on trial.[142] The agitation began again in 1816, when meetings were held in St. Peter's Field, on the south side of Peter Street ; they excited alarm and were stopped for a time ; but were resumed in 1819.[143] This resulted in what was denominated the 'Peterloo massacre.' A meeting on 9 August having been prohibited, another was summoned for the 16th, which the magistrates resolved to disperse by arresting Henry Hunt, the leader of the agitation, in the face of the meeting, supposed to number 60,000. There were regular troops at hand, but the duty was assigned to the Manchester Yeomanry, described as 'hot-headed young men who had volunteered into that service from their native hatred of Radicalism.'[144] These drew their swords and dashed into the crowd, while Hunt was speaking, but were unable to effect their purpose, and saw themselves in danger from overwhelming numbers ; whereupon the hussars charged and dispersed the assembly. Some were killed, and about 600 wounded. The magistrates considered they themselves had done well, and received a letter of thanks from the Prince Regent ; but a fierce storm was aroused in Manchester and the whole district.[145] Henry Hunt and four others were brought to trial and condemned for unlawful assembly. For a time

the agitation in this form ceased, but Manchester showed itself clearly on the side of reform in 1832,[146] and was the birth-place of the Anti-Corn Law League of 1838.[147] The Chartist movement of 1848 had adherents in Manchester, and many arrests were made by the police.[148] The rescue of Fenian prisoners in 1867 was a startling incident.[149]

The first royal visit to the district was that of Henry VII in 1495.[150] The next, after a long interval, was that of Queen Victoria in 1851 ; she stayed at Worsley Hall and came through Salford to Manchester.[151] She visited the Art Treasures Exhibition at Old Trafford in 1857, and in 1894 formally opened the Ship Canal. More recently, on 13 July 1905, King Edward VII and Queen Alexandra opened a new dock of the Ship Canal.

The government of the district was greatly altered by the formation of the municipal boroughs of Manchester in 1838 and of Salford in 1844. After several extensions of the former the ancient townships then within its bounds were in 1896 reduced to three —Manchester, North Manchester, and South Manchester ; more recently the borough has been enlarged again. The township of Reddish has been added to the borough of Stockport.

While Manchester has taken a prominent part in English commerce and politics, it has not neglected learning. Its University is a typical modern one.[152] It traces its origin to the bequest of some £97,000 by a local merchant, John Owens, who died in 1846. He desired to found a college for higher studies which should be free from all religious tests, and in 1851 his wish took effect, the Owens College being opened in Quay Street, with a staff of five professors and two other teachers. Its first principal was A. J. Scott, the friend of Edward Irving. After a struggling existence it seemed about to fail, but in 1857, under Dr. J. G. Greenwood as principal, and with (Sir) Henry Roscoe as professor of chemistry, it began to grow. In 1870–1 it was reorganized,[153] and the management was transferred from the founder's trustees to a court of governors, and in 1873 the old site was left for the present one in Oxford Street. Not long afterwards came proposals to raise the college to the position of a degree-giving university. After opposition from other colleges it was agreed with the Yorkshire College at Leeds that the new university should have its seat at Manchester but should not bear

[137] Manch. Guard. N. and Q. no. 303, 720.
[138] Prentice, Manch. 7–9, 419, &c.
[139] Ibid. 10–14.
[140] For the volunteers of 1783, 1798, and 1804, see Local Glean. Lancs. and Ches. i, 73 ; ii, 44 ; i, 25, 14, &c.
[141] The story of the political agitation of the time is told in Archibald Prentice's Recollections of Manch. (1851), referred to above. The author was the son of a Scotch farmer and settled in the town in 1815, starting the Manch. Times, afterwards the Examiner and Times, in the interest of reform. He died at Plymouth Grove, Chorlton-upon-Medlock, in 1857.
[142] Prentice, op. cit. 76–82, and 'Trial at full length of the 38 men,' 1812.
[143] See Prentice, op. cit. 159–71. The attendants at these meetings came from all the factory districts around Manchester, as Oldham, Rochdale, and Middleton.
[144] Prentice, op. cit. 160.

General View of Manchester

1802 from a Painting by W. M. Craig

a local name.[154] Thus Victoria University came to be founded by royal charter in 1880, the Owens College being the first college in it. From the outset attendance at courses of lectures was required from candidates for degrees, the university being a teaching body.[155] University College, Liverpool, was admitted in 1884, and Yorkshire College, Leeds, in 1887. This federal constitution was dissolved in 1903, when Liverpool and Manchester became seats of separate universities, the Owens College being then incorporated with the latter under the name of the Victoria University of Manchester.[156]

The charter defines the constitution. The governing body is the court, consisting of the chancellor, vice-chancellor, and other members, in part representative of local bodies; it appoints the council which acts as an executive committee. The studies are controlled by the senate, which consists of the professors; under it are the boards of the eight separate faculties in which degrees are given: Arts, Science, Law, Music, Commerce, Theology, Technology, and Medicine. The staff comprises forty-four professors and a large body of lecturers. Women are admitted to all degrees. Liberal endowments have been given by Manchester men and others,[157] and the university receives annual grants from the national treasury, the county councils of Lancashire and Cheshire, and Manchester and other local corporations.[158]

The corporations of Manchester and Salford provide great technical and art schools. There is a training school for candidates for the Church of England ministry, and important colleges of several of the chief Nonconformist churches—Wesleyan, Primitive and Free Methodist, Congregational, Baptist, and Unitarian—have long been established on the south side of Manchester for the education of ministers.[159]

Secondary and elementary education is well provided for by the Grammar School, the High School for girls, and a multitude of others.

Of the various social movements of the last century there may be mentioned as originating in Manchester: the Rechabite Society, founded in 1835; the

171

---

154 Thompson, op. cit. 530–42.
155 A supplemental charter for medical degrees was obtained in 1883.
156 The charter of 1903 and the Act of 1904 incorporating Owens College with Manchester University will be found in full in the annual *Calendar*. This volume of over 800 pages gives full information as to courses of study, &c. and an appendix of 500 pages contains the examination papers.
157 Large sums have been raised by subscription. The principal individual benefactors have been Charles Frederick Beyer, Richard Copley Christie, Charles Clifton of Jersey, U.S.A., and the legatees of Sir Joseph Whitworth. The capital amounts to about £1,000,000.
158 The Hulme Trustees give £1,000 a year.
159 There is also a Moravian college at Fairfield to the east.
160 This was a union of the lodges in the Manchester district, effected in 1810; it has extended over a great part of the kingdom, and become one of the greatest of the friendly societies.
161 James Fraser, second Bishop of Manchester, 1870–85; see *Dict. Nat. Biog.* and memoir by Thomas Hughes

4

Benefactors of the town were Oliver Heywood, 1825–92,[176] and Herbert Philips, 1834–1905.[177]

The list of noteworthy natives of the parish is a long one, and, as might be expected, many of the more famous have found their opportunities outside its bounds. The names [178] include Thomas Sorocold, 1591–1617, author of *Supplications of Saints ;* [178a] John Booker, 1601–67, a notorious astrologer ; [179] Samuel Bolton, D.D., 1607–54, a Puritan divine, born in Manchester ; [180] John Worthington, D.D., 1618–71, master of Jesus College, Cambridge, during the Commonwealth period ; [181] John Chorlton, Presbyterian divine, 1666–1705 ; [182] Henry Gore, who died in 1733, a mathematician ; James Heywood, author, 1687–1722 ; [183] Thomas Falkner, S.J., 1706–84, author of an account of Patagonia ; [184] Robert Thyer, born in 1709, was Chetham Librarian from 1732 till his death in 1781 ; [185] Thomas Patten, a divine, 1714–90 ; [186] Samuel Ogden, D.D., 1716–78, Woodwardian professor at Cambridge ; [187] Charles White, M.D., 1728–1813, an eminent surgeon ; [188] John Whitaker, 1735–1808, a fanciful antiquary, who published two volumes of a *History of Manchester ;* [189] Thomas Barritt, 1743–1820, saddler and antiquary ; [190] George Hibbert, merchant and collector, 1757–1837 ; [191] John Hampson, miscellaneous writer, 1760–1817 ; [192] William Green, 1760–1823, the Lake artist ; [193] John Hadden Hindley, oriental scholar, 1765–1827 ; [194] Daniel Orme, portrait painter, c. 1766–1832 ; [195] Joseph Entwisle, the 'boy preacher,' 1767–1841 ; [196] James Crowther, botanist, 1768–1847 ; [197] John Allen, D.D., 1770–1845, Bishop of Ely ; [198] William Ford, bookseller and bibliographer, 1771–1832 ; [199] James Townley, a Wesleyan divine, 1774–1833 ; [200] Charles Hulbert, miscellaneous writer, 1778–1857 ; [201] Jabez Bunting, D.D.,

1779–1858, another celebrated Wesleyan minister ; [202] Samuel Clegg, gas engineer, 1781–1861 ; [203] Samuel Hibbert, M.D., 1782–1848, who wrote a history of the *Manchester Foundations ;* in 1837 he assumed the additional surname of Ware ; [204] Edward Hobson, botanist, 1782–1830 ; [205] George Ormerod, 1785–1873, the historian of Cheshire ; [206] Benjamin Rawlinson Faulkner, portrait painter, 1787–1849 ; [207] Francis Russell Hall, D.D., theological writer, 1788–1866 ; [208] John Briggs, b. 1778, Bishop of Trachis, Vicar Apostolic of the northern district, 1836, and Bishop of Beverley 1850–60, died 1861 ; [209] James Heywood Markland, 1788–1864, antiquary ; [210] Thomas Wright, philanthropist, 1789–1875 ; [211] John Blackwall, zoologist, 1790–1881 ; [212] John Owens, 1790–1846, founder of Owens College ; [213] James Daniel Burton, Methodist preacher, 1791–1817 ; [214] David William Paynter, author of tragedies, 1791–1823 ; [215] William Pearman, vocalist, 1792–1824 (?) ; [216] Sir Thomas Phillipps, baronet, 1792–1872, a great collector of books and manuscripts ; [217] Edward Bury, engineer, 1794–1858 ; [218] Charles H. Timperley, printer and author, 1794–1846 ; [219] Samuel Robinson, Persian scholar, 1794–1884 ; [220] Nathaniel George Philips, artist, 1795–1831 ; [221] Thomas Heywood, 1797–1866, who edited several volumes for the Chetham Society, &c. ; [222] Alfred Ollivant, D.D., 1798–1882, who was appointed to the bishopric of Llandaff in 1847 ; [223] Elijah Hoole, orientalist, 1798–1872 ; [224] Richard Potter, scientific writer, 1799–1886 ; [225] John Stanley Gregson, 1800–37 ; [226] Sir Edwin Chadwick, Poor Law Commissioner and miscellaneous writer, was born at Longsight in 1800, he died in 1890 ; [227] Frank Stone, painter, 1800–59 ; [228] Henry Liverseege, 1803–29, an artist ; [229] Mary Amelia Warner, actress, 1804–54 ; [230] William

---

[176] He was a native of Pendleton. A statue of him has been erected in Albert Square.

[177] He was born at Heybridge, in Staffordshire.

[178] These were nearly all natives of the township as well as of the parish.

[178a] *Dict. Nat. Biog.*

[179] He was son of a John Booker or Bowker ; *Dict. Nat. Biog.* ; Baines, *Lancs.* (ed. 1836), ii, 367.

[180] *Dict. Nat. Biog.* ; *Lancs. and Ches. Antiq. Soc.* vi, 67. He was master of Christ's College, Cambridge, 1651–54.

[181] *Dict. Nat. Biog.* ; *Pal. Note Bk.* i, 128 ; *Local Glean. Lancs. and Ches.* i, 199, 208 ; ii, 5. His *Diary,* &c. have been printed by the Chetham Society. Though deposed from the mastership in 1660, he conformed to the restored ecclesiastical establishment, and was beneficed in Lincolnshire.

[182] *Dict. Nat. Biog.*   [183] Ibid.

[184] Ibid. ; Gillow, *Bibl. Dict. Engl. Cath.* ii, 224. He was a convert, and laboured in the famous Jesuit settlements in Paraguay, being expelled in 1768 by the Spanish government. He joined the English province and died at Plowden in Shropshire.

[185] *Dict. Nat. Biog.*   [186] Ibid.

[187] See *Dict. Nat. Biog.* ; Baines, *Lancs.* i, 408.

[188] *Dict. Nat. Biog.* ; Baines, op. cit. i, 409. He was one of the founders of the Manchester Lying-in Hospital, and effected a revolution in the practice of midwifery. The Town Hall (now the Reference Library) was built on the site of his house.

MANCHESTER CATHEDRAL FROM THE SOUTH-EAST

Harrison Ainsworth, 1805–82, novelist ;[231] Thomas Bellot, surgeon, 1806–57 ;[232] William Harper, minor poet, 1806–57 ;[233] William Knight Keeling, painter, 1807–86 ;[234] James Stephenson, engraver, 1808–86;[235] William Rathbone Greg, 1809–81 ;[236] John Bolton Rogerson, poet, 1809–59 ;[237] Charles Christian Hennell, author, 1809–50 ;[238] Fred Lingard, musician, 1811–47 ;[239] George Aspull, musician, 1813–32 ;[240] Joseph Baxendell, astronomer and meteorologist, 1815–87 ;[241] Thomas Bayley Potter, politician, 1817–98 ;[242] John Cassell, 1817–65, temperance lecturer and publisher ;[243] George John Piccope, 1818–72, an antiquary, whose collections are in the Chetham Library ; Charles Brierley Garside, divine, 1818–76 ;[244] William Hepworth Dixon, 1821–79 ;[245] Isabella Banks, author of *The Manchester Man*, and other works, 1821–97 ;[246] Lydia Ernestine Becker, advocate of women's suffrage, 1827–90 ;[247] Charles Beard, Unitarian minister, 1827–88 ;[248] Shakspere Wood, sculptor, 1827–86 ;[249] James William Whittaker, painter, 1828–76 ;[250] James Croston, editor of Baines' *History of Lancashire*, 1830–93 ;[251] Constantine Alexander Ionides, connoisseur, 1833–1900 ;[252] Henry James Byron, 1834–84, author of 'Our Boys' and other plays ;[253] Walter Bentley Woodbury, 1834–85, inventor of the Woodbury-type process ;[254] Alfred Barrett, philosophical writer, 1844–81 ;[255] John Parsons Earwaker, 1847–95, author of a history of *East Cheshire* and other antiquarian works ;[256] John Hopkinson, optician and engineer, 1849–98.[257]

Of minor matters to be noted there occur the institution of an omnibus in 1825, to run between Market Street and Pendleton ; and the appearance of the cab in 1839. The British Association held its meetings in Manchester in 1842, 1861, and 1887.

Manchester does not seem to have had any rush-bearing of its own, but the rush carts from neighbouring towns and villages were brought to it.[258]

At Hulme Barracks are stationed a battery of the Royal Horse Artillery and an Army Service Corps. There are numerous volunteer corps—the 7th L.V. Artillery, Hyde Road ; 3rd L.R. Engineers ; 2nd, 4th, and 5th V.B. Manchester Regiment, at Stretford Road, Chorlton-upon-Medlock, and Ardwick respec-

[231] See *Dict. Nat. Biog.* ; *Pal. Note Bk.* ii, 38 ; Procter, *Manch. Streets*, 269. There is a presentation portrait of him in the Manchester Free Library.
[232] *Dict. Nat. Biog.*   [233] Ibid.
[234] Ibid.
[235] Ibid.
[236] *Dict. Nat. Biog.* His elder brothers, Robert Hyde Greg, 1795–1875, economist and antiquary, M.P. for Manchester, 1839 ; and Samuel Greg, 1804–76, philanthropist, are also noticed in *Dict. Nat. Biog.*
[237] *Dict. Nat. Biog.*   [238] Ibid.
[239] Ibid.   [240] Ibid.
[241] Ibid.   [242] Ibid.
[243] Ibid. ; *Pal. Note Bk.* iii, 213.
[244] Gillow, op. cit. ii, 397 ; *Dict. Nat. Biog.*
[245] *Dict. Nat. Biog.* He was editor of the *Athenaeum* from 1853 to 1869, and published many historical and geographical works.
[246] *Dict. Nat. Biog.* ; her maiden name was Varley.
[247] Ibid.   [248] Ibid.
[249] Ibid.   [250] Ibid.
[251] The notice in the *Evening News*

stated that he was educated at Manchester Grammar School, and traded as a gingham manufacturer. He took part in the public life of the district in various ways—as a worker in Cotton Famine relief of 1862–3, the City Council (conservative member), and Anglican Church defence ; he also wrote a number of popular works on the history of the district, and in 1873 was elected F.S.A. He added accounts of the parochial clergy in his edition of Baines. He died 1 Sept. 1893, while travelling from Manchester to his home at Prestbury.
[252] *Dict. Nat. Biog.*   [253] Ibid.
[254] Ibid.   [255] Ibid.
[256] *Dict. Nat. Biog.* ; *Lancs. and Ches. Antiq. Soc.* xiii, 143. He edited the *Ct. Leet Rec.* and *Constables' Accts.* for the Manchester Corporation.
[257] *Dict. Nat. Biog.*
[258] Alfred Burton, *Rushbearing*, and the illustration in Procter's *Manch. Streets.*
[259] A full list is given in the Official Red Book.
[260] The publishing office was transferred to London in 1884.
[261] For a description written about

Lady chapel, the lower parts of the walls of which still remain. The old west tower, pulled down 1864, is said to have been in part of 14th-century date, though the recorded evidence is by no means decisive on the point, but during the pulling down of the nave arcades enough re-used material of the former nave was recovered to show that it had aisles and arcades of considerable scale in the 13th century. The oldest worked stone yet found on the site is the relief of an angel holding a scroll with an inscription, perhaps 10th-century work; but with this exception no details earlier than the 13th century have come to light. The traditions of the occupation of this or a neighbouring site in Saxon times by a wooden building, though embellished by a good deal of circumstantial evidence, seem to have no more solid foundation than the similar stories told of so many ancient sites in England. There may well have been a wooden building here as elsewhere in early times, but the attempts of various local historians to identify its remains with beams at Ordsall, Trafford, Stand, &c. need not be taken seriously. A fine 13th-century church certainly existed here, and was perhaps not the first stone building on the site. It had aisles to its nave, and perhaps to its chancel also, but its plan must remain uncertain. In a building of such a scale the possibility of a cruciform plan with a central tower must always be taken into account, and it is tempting to see in the positions of the west walls of the Derby chapel, and what was once the Jesus chapel, evidences of former north and south transepts. It would be also quite in the normal course of development if it could be shown that the building of a west tower in the 14th century marked the destruction of an older central tower about that time, and the conversion of the church from a cruciform to a continuously aisled plan. Unfortunately five centuries of rebuilding and alteration have reduced any such speculations to the level of an academic exercise, and in any case there is ample interest in the architectural history of the building from the 15th century onwards.

John Huntington, first warden of the college, 1422–58, 'built the choir of Manchester Church with the aisles on both sides, being in length thirty yards, and in breadth twenty yards, from the two great pinacles, where the organs stood betwixt, to the east end of the church.' This work seems to have followed the lines of the older building, but very little of it remains in its original position, both arcades of the quire and the north wall of its north aisle having been rebuilt late in the 15th century; so that it is only in the east walls of quire and aisles, and the south wall of the south aisle, that any of Huntington's work can now exist as he left it. The spacing of the two eastern bays of the south wall of the south aisle, 12 ft. 9 in. from centre to centre, is practically that of four of the six bays of the Derby chapel, and if it be assumed that the width of the third bay of the south aisle, containing the entrance to the chapter-house, preserves that of the bay which opened to a chapter-house built at this place by Huntington, there is space between it and the west end of the aisle for three more bays of about 12 ft. 9 in. each. This dimension, then, probably represents the normal width of the bays of Huntington's aisles, and makes it possible that some of the bays of this width in the outer walls of the chapels afterwards added to the aisles may be in part Huntington's work moved outwards and reset.

The main arcades are of six bays, with an average width of 13 ft. 5 in. from centre to centre. At the east end, where they abut on the responds of the 14th-century work, there is a width of 22 ft. across the main span, but at the west of the quire the width is 25 ft. 3 in. This irregularity is evidently due to a desire to get as great a width as possible for the stalls of the collegiate quire, and is, as it seems, the work of James Stanley, the second warden of that name, after 1485. The details of the arcades, however, are of earlier character than would have been the case if they had been built anew at this time, and it must be concluded that the arcades are Huntington's work reset, and adapted to the later arrangements.

Huntington died in 1458, and Ralph Langley, who became warden in 1465, carried on the general scheme of rebuilding. Till his time the nave seems to have been of 13th-century date, and in order to bring it into harmony with the new quire he rebuilt it from the ground, using up a good deal of the old materials. His work has been even more unfortunate than that of his predecessor, the outer walls of his nave-aisles having been entirely removed in later alterations, while the north and south arcades of his nave are now represented by faithful but entirely modern copies, and only the south arcade occupies its original position. The details of the work are evidently inspired by those of Huntington's quire, and are of the same excellent and refined style. When in 1883 both arcades of the nave were taken down, it became evident that the north arcade had been previously taken down and rebuilt, its jointing being much inferior to that of the south arcade. The nave is not on the same axis as the tower, but it is clear from the position of the south arcade that it was so at first, and it was doubtless at the rebuilding of the north arcade that the irregularity came into being, the arcade being set up a little to the north of its former line. The object of this widening was to make the nave symmetrical with the quire after its rearrangement by Stanley, and the rebuilding is no doubt due to him. The panelling on the east wall of the tower must also be part of his work, and it is probable, in spite of a tradition that the tower was in the main the work of George West, warden, about 1518, that Stanley completed this part of the church also.

The general development of the church, up to this point, followed without material difference the scheme common to so many Lancashire churches, which consists of a long clearstoried chancel and nave with north and south aisles, a west tower, and a pair of stair turrets at the junction of chancel and nave. The north stair turret must have been rebuilt when the nave was widened northward, and the chancel-arch must also be of Stanley's work, but the south turret may be of Langley's time. It is to be noted that the diameter of the stair it contains is 4 ft. 6 in., as compared with 5 ft. in the north turret.

In the 15th century the church began to be enlarged by the addition of chantry chapels. The first to be built was that of St. Nicholas, or the Trafford chantry, on the south of the two east bays of the south aisle of the nave; its date seems doubtful, but the original of the present building was probably set up in 1486. Next came the

PLAN OF MANCHESTER CATHEDRAL.

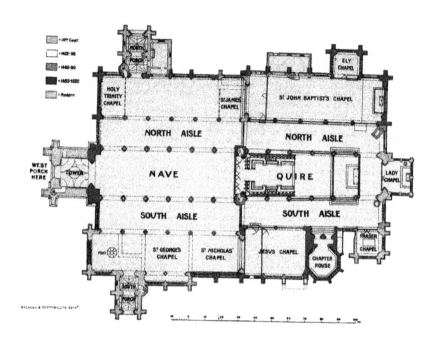

Trinity chapel, built by William Radcliffe of Ordsall, about 1498, at the west of the former north porch of the nave, whose site is now included in the outer north aisle. In 1506 the Jesus chapel, or Byrom chantry, filling the space between the Trafford chapel and the chapter-house, was built by Richard Bexwicke. The small Hulme chapel adjoined it on the south-east. In 1507 St. James's chapel, afterwards called the Strangeways chapel, was built at the north-east of the nave, by one of the Hulmes of Halton, or by one of the Chetham family. In 1508 St. George's chapel was built by William Galey to the west of St. Nicholas's chapel. There appears to be no precise record of the building of the north chapel of the nave, between St. James's chapel and the old north porch. In 1513 the large Derby chapel was finished and dedicated in honour of St. John the Baptist by James Stanley, fifth warden, on the north side of the north aisle of the quire, equal in length to it, and 24 ft. wide. The Ely chapel, opening northward from the second bay of this chapel, was finished in 1515 by Sir John Stanley, son of the warden, who became Bishop of Ely in 1506. The Lady chapel, built early in the 14th century, is said to have been rebuilt in 1518 by George West, warden 1516–28, but this seems doubtful from the slender architectural evidence which remains. The chapel seems to have been again rebuilt in the 18th century, with tracery which was a curious copy of 14th-century work, and all the external stonework has since been renewed.

The college was dissolved in 1547, but re-established in 1553 ; the fabric of the church probably did not suffer any serious damage at this date. Again dissolved in 1646, it was again re-established under Charles II, and through the 17th and 18th centuries underwent a good deal of repair in its external stonework. In 1815 a barbarous work of mutilation, in the name of repair, was begun, all the internal stonework of the nave and clearstory, with the north aisle, chancel-arch, and tower-arch, being hacked over with picks and then covered with a coat of cement, completely destroying the old face of the stonework and seriously weakening the arches. The screens in the nave chapels were also destroyed and the roofs of the aisles hacked about and covered with plaster. Galleries were set up in the nave, and the irregular line of arches separating the southern chapels from the south aisle of the nave was destroyed and replaced by a uniform arcade which when finished was coated like the older work with cement.

A series of repairs undertaken in a very different spirit, but even more far-reaching in the matter of destroying the old work, began in 1863 with a re-building of the west tower, nothing of the former tower beyond part of its east wall being preserved. In 1870 the external masonry of the clearstory, which had been entirely renewed as lately as 1855, was again renewed, and the design altered in several particulars, and in 1872 the main arcades of the nave were taken down and rebuilt in new stone, accurately copying the old. The south porch, which had been rebuilt late in the 17th century by a Manchester merchant named Bibby, was partly reconstructed in 1871, and entirely rebuilt in 1891, while the present north porch dates from 1888, and a baptistery was

---

[961a] A complete list of the repairs between 1638 and 1884 will be found in T. L. Worthington's *Historical Account of the Cathedral Church of Manchester* (pp. 49–51).

details being different on the two sides, and there are carved foliate bosses on the carved arms of the seats, and a very fine series of carved misericordes. Some of these have allusions to the Stanley family, but the majority belong to the type of secular and often humorous subjects common on these carvings. They are of very great merit in some instances, though, unfortunately, a good deal broken. The hare cooking the hunter and his dog, the pilgrim robbed by monkeys, the man who has broken his wife's cooking-pot, two men playing backgammon, &c., are among the best of them.

The quire arcades, which have been already referred to as perhaps being Huntington's work, have panelled spandrels and a line of cresting over the arches. Slender shafts run up from the piers to clustered capitals at the springing of the clearstory windows, which are of five cinquefoiled lights with tracery. From the capitals, on which stand eagles bearing shields, spring the cusped braces of the low-pitched roof, with its rich traceried panels and carved bosses at the intersections of the heavy moulded timbers. Huntington's rebus occurs on the roof, and at the repairs carried out by Mr. Crowther evidence was found that some of the timbers were parts of a differently-arranged roof, re-used by Stanley, and probably belonging to Huntington's quire, which must have had a clearstory of much the same height as at present. It seems to have had in each bay a pair of two-light windows instead of the present arrangement. Two dates, 1638 and 1742, are cut on the roof, marking repairs done in those years.

At the west of the quire is the screen, a fine piece of woodwork which has been a good deal restored, the coved canopy and front of the loft having been added by Scott in 1872. On the loft stands the organ, given in that year, and replacing one made in 1684 by Father Smith, and renewed in 1742.

The Derby chapel, or Chapel of St. John the Baptist, is separated from the north aisle of the quire by an arcade of five bays with four-centred arches, and details which are much plainer than those of the main arcades of the quire. Its north elevation does not correspond to the arcade, being of six unequal bays, each set in a wall arcade of excellent detail, perhaps Huntington's work reused. The first, third, fourth, and fifth bays contain four-light windows flanked on the inside by blank tracery and canopied niches, filling up the remaining spaces within the wall arcades, whose arches also form the heads of the windows. On the outside the blank tracery does not occur, and the windows in consequence have segmental heads. At the west the chapel opens by a wide arch and a flight of four steps to the north chapel of the nave, the site of the former chapel of St. James. The chapel is closed in by contemporary wooden screens, the entrance being from the south-west, where, over the door, are the arms of Sir John Stanley, son of Warden Stanley, impaling the quartered coat of Handforth, with a modern inscription on brass giving the date of its completion as 1513. The Ely chapel, opening from the north-east of the Derby chapel, is entered through a screen of early 16th-century date, moved here from St. James's chapel, and was completed after Warden Stanley's death by Sir John Stanley, being intended to contain his tomb. The tomb now in the chapel is a copy made in 1859 of the original altar-tomb, and on it is fixed the mutilated brass figure of

Stanley in his episcopal dress as Bishop of Ely. The design of the chapel harmonizes with the Derby chapel, but being wider from east to west than the other bays, it has a north window of five lights instead of four. The eastern bay of the south aisle of the quire opens southward to the chapel, built in 1890 in memory of Bishop Fraser and containing his tomb ; while the second bay, with its four-light south window, resembles the north side of the Derby chapel, and probably preserves the old design of Huntington's aisle, though the masonry is for the most part renewed. The third bay contains the entrance to the chapter-house, probably the work of Stanley, and consisting of two deeply-recessed four-centred doorways set in a wide panelled recess. The chapter-house itself is octagonal, with a modern wooden vault, and is lighted by four-light windows in its four outer faces ; its present design is probably due to Stanley, though Huntington seems to have built a chapter-house here, which, according to some evidence quoted in Mr. Worthington's book on the cathedral, was octagonal as at present. The foundations, however, of part of a square building are said to have been found here, and are claimed as Huntington's chapter-house, and it can only be said that, no further investigation being at present possible, the question must be left as a contested point. The remainder of the aisle is taken up by a library, vestry, and passage, occupying the area of the old Jesus chapel. Its use as a library dates from the end of the 16th century, when its then owners, the Pendletons, sold it to the city of Manchester. The small Hulme chapel which opened southward from its east bay, after being rebuilt in 1810, has been pulled down, and no trace of it now exists. A door opens from the library to the chapter-house, which is panelled in oak with seats round the walls, and a chair for the bishop on the south side. From the crown of the vault hangs a fine chandelier.

The nave arcades, the history of which has already been given, are of six bays, and faithfully reproduce Langley's work, which they succeed. In general design they closely resemble the arcades of the quire, having the same traceried spandrels and line of cresting over the arches ; but the detail is simpler, though still very effective. The clearstory windows are of five lights, and before restoration were entirely without cusps ; these have, however, been added in the new work. Externally their effect is richer than that of the clearstory of the eastern arm, as there is tracery in the spandrels over the windows and pairs of angels holding shields at the bases of the pinnacles which mark each bay, neither of which features occurs to the east of the chancel arch. The turrets flanking this arch break the long line of windows very satisfactorily, rising above the parapets and ending in crocketed spirelets, while internally they make a very effective feature, masking the junction between the nave and quire arcades, and by their size and solidity atoning for the rather insignificant chancel-arch. The nave clearstory seems to have had much the same history as that of the quire, and as built by Langley probably had two windows in each bay, an arrangement altered to that which now obtains at Stanley's rebuilding of the north arcade. This was deduced by Mr. Crowther from the evidence of re-used timbers found by him in the nave roof, which had been adapted to the wider span caused by the setting back of the north arcade.

MANCHESTER CATHEDRAL : THE QUIRE

MANCHESTER CATHEDRAL : STALLS IN THE QUIRE

SALFORD

There are practically no remains of old work in the aisles and chapels of the nave. St. James's chapel, at the east end of the outer north aisle, has entirely disappeared. It was built about 1507, before the present Derby chapel, and originally had a five-light east window, and the plinth of its east wall is said to remain beneath the present floor-level. It was afterwards called the Strangeways chapel, and Hollinworth [261b] tells us that there was in it a picture of the Resurrection, and beneath it an inscription reciting a pardon of 26,026 days for all who there said five paters, five aves, and a credo. A piscina was found at the southeast angle of the chapel when it was taken down, and has been replaced near its old position. The chapel was narrower than the outer north aisle, but its north wall has now been carried out to the same line as the rest. The Trinity chapel, at the west end of the aisle, has also left no traces of its arrangements. The north porch, built in 1888 in memory of Mr. James Craven, is a very good piece of modern work, with a stone vault in two bays and an upper story used as a muniment room, and built entirely of stone ; to the east of the porch is a registry office.

On the south side of the nave the south wall of the chapel of St. Nicholas, at the south-east, stands on its original line, but has been entirely renewed, and the south porch and south-west baptistery are modern additions. The old south porch stood opposite the fifth bay of the modern arcade. It was of a single story, built in 1685 by one Bibby, and afterwards rebuilt by the parish ; it seems, however, to have retained some 13th-century detail, and the springers of a vault of that date. The present south porch follows in general design the north porch, being vaulted in two bays with a parvise over.

In St. George's chapel, west of St. Nicholas's chapel, hung an image of St. George, and in Hollinworth's time the chapel was called the Radcliffe chapel ; the arcade on the south side, carrying on the line of the south wall of the chapel of St. Nicholas, is a modern insertion.

The west tower retains nothing of its old masonry except its east arch and the wall in which it is set, ornamented with shallow cinquefoiled stone panelling, which is hacked over to make a key for the cement coat put on it in 1815 and since removed. The old tower stood till 1863, and was of four stages, 124 ft. high, with a panelled parapet and groups of three pinnacles at each angle, and a smaller pinnacle in the middle of each face. The belfry windows were pairs of two-light openings with transoms and tracery, the wall over them being panelled in continuation of the tracery, with recesses for images on either side. The west doorway was two-centred with continuous mouldings, and over it was a fine five-light window with a transom and tracery, the buttresses on either side of the window having canopied niches at this level. The present tower is some 15 ft. higher than its predecessor, 139 ft. as against 124 ft., but is otherwise not unlike it, except in the presence of elaborate clock-faces below the belfry stage. Its outline is good, and forms a welcome contrast to its rather prosaic surroundings, the westward fall of the ground adding

[261b] *Mancuniensis*, 1656.

[262] See a paper by Rev. H. A. Hudson in *Proc. Lancs. and Ches. Antiq. Soc.* xxv (1907).

[262a] For the Radcliffe brasses see *Proc. Lancs. and Ches. Antiq. Soc.* ix, 90.

[263] See *Trans. Hist. Soc.* (new ser.), xiv, 205, for notes taken between 1591 and 1636 ; Thornely, *Lancs. and Ches. Brasses*, 15, 39, 113 ; and *Lancs. and Ches. Antiq. Soc.* xxiii, 172, for the ancient sculpture of St. Michael. There are copies of monumental inscriptions and gravestones in the interior and the graveyard in the Owen MSS.

The present organ in its Gothic case set on the rood-loft succeeds one made by Father Smith about 1684. This, after having been sent to St. Saviour's Church, Chetham, was returned to the cathedral, and set up in the north aisle of the quire.—

The list of cathedral plate includes—

Two chalices, 1584–5, each inscribed, 'This belongs to the Collegiate Church of Manchester.'

Two chalices, 1626, each inscribed, 'Given to the Church of Manchester by Margarett Nugent, Widdowe, 1626.'

Three patens, 1676–7, each inscribed, 'This belongs to the Collegiate Church of Manchester, and was bought at ye parish charge, Anno Dom. 1676.' Almsdish, 1675–6, same inscription as patens, but date-letter a year earlier.

Small flagon, 1697–8, with the mark of Peter Harracke; no inscription.

Pitcher flagon, 1701, inscribed, 'The gift of Mrs. Mary Holbrook to the Collegiate Church of Manchester 1701,' with the mark of John Ruslem.

Four large flagons, 1707–8, 17 in. high, with mark of Nathaniel Lock, each inscribed, 'Deo et ecclesiae Mancuniensi Sacrum anno 1708. Johannes Sandiford D.D.D.' Two patens, same marks and inscriptions.

Almsdish, 1715, inscribed, 'The gift of Mrs. Elizabeth Cartwright, Widdow, to ye Collegiate Church of Manchester, Anno Dom. 1715.'

Chalice, 1875, given in memory of Canon Richson by an unknown donor. Silver gilt.

Four beaker cups made for the Scots church of the Scots Factors at Campvere, Holland, in 1620 (no marks), presented by Earl Egerton of Tatton. They are numbered 1, 2, 3, and 4, and bear Latin and English inscriptions, the latter reading :—

1. According zeal off factors at Campheir
2. Gives us four coups for the Lord's table heir
3. The year of God a thousand with sax hunder
4. And twenty in Janvar, Macduff being minister.

There is a ring of ten bells, five being dated 1706.[264]

The registers begin in 1573.[265]

The endowment of St. Mary's *ADVOWSON* Church at Manchester is recorded in Domesday Book.[266] Rather more than a century later the rector is named.[267] In addition to the parish, there was a deanery of Manchester, and several of the early deans are known ;[268] their position with regard to the parish church, however, is not ascertained ; they may have been the chaplains in charge.[269] The original endowment was the plough-land in Newton referred to above ; to this Albert Grelley the elder added four oxgangs from his demesne, supposed to be the land afterwards called Kirkmanshulme, which, though detached, was considered part of the township of Newton ;[270] the church had also some land between Deansgate and the Irwell, known as the Parsonage land. In 1282 the value of the rectory was estimated as 200 marks,[271] though in the official taxation of nine years later it is given as less than half that sum, viz. £53 6s. 8d.[272] The value of the ninth of the sheaves, wool, &c., was returned as 60 marks in 1341.[273]

The patronage of the church descended with the manor until the confiscation of the college endowments in 1547 ; on the refounding by Mary it was assumed by the Crown.[274]

The church was made collegiate in 1421–2 by Thomas, Lord La Warre, the rector and patron, in honour of St. Mary, St. Denis, and St. George.[275] The tithes were appropriated to its maintenance, and the old manor-house and certain lands were given to increase the endowment, £3,000 being set apart for building a suitable residence on the site of the manor-house.[276] The new foundation consisted of a warden or master, eight fellows or chaplains, four clerks or deacons, and six choristers.[277] In 1534 the revenue from lands was £40 5s. 3d., and from tithes £186 7s. 2d. ; payments of £13 1s. 6d. had

[264] For the bells see *Lancs. and Ches. Antiq. Soc.* xvii, 75–86.

[265] Extracts ranging between 1573 and 1750 have been printed by Mr. John Owen, 1879. The Owen MSS. in the Free Reference Library include two transcripts (one alphabetically arranged) of the 16th to 18th-century portions.

[266] *V.C.H. Lancs.* i, 287. A speculation as to a possible change of site may be read in *Lancs. and Ches. Antiq. Soc.* xxiii, 96–7.

[267] W. Farrer, *Lancs. Pipe R.* 331.

[268] Jordan, Dean of Manchester, occurs in 1177, when he was fined for some offence against the forest laws ; ibid. 38. In 1193–4 he rendered account of £20 'for the service of Count John' ; ibid. 78, 92, 97.

Geoffrey, Dean of Manchester, attested a Grelley deed about 1200 ; *Trans. Hist. Soc.* (new ser.), xvii, 42. G. Dean of Manchester, perhaps the same, occurs about 1240 ; *Whalley Coucher* (Chet. Soc.), ii, 601. See also Booker, *Birch* (Chet. Soc.), 231.

Randle, the dean in 1294, was witness to a grant of land in Ancoats ; Trafford deed quoted by Canon Raines. He was no doubt the same as Randle de Welhum, dean ; Booker, *Prestwich*, 250.

[269] William Knight, archdeacon of Chester, held the deanery in 1534 ; *Valor Eccl.* (Rec. Com.), v, 224. In later times

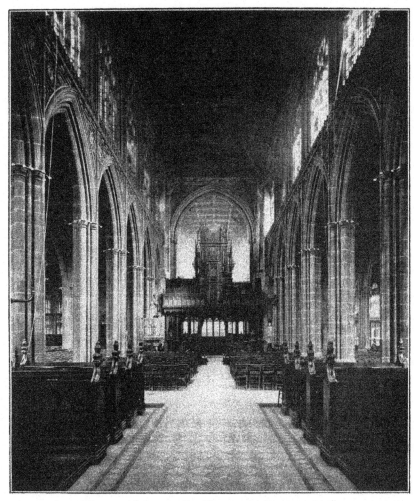

MANCHESTER CATHEDRAL : THE NAVE, SHOWING SCREEN AND ORGAN

to be made, and the clear value therefore was £213 10s. 11d. The warden received £20, and each of the eight fellows or vicars £4, so that a large sum remained for the minor officers and the general expenses of maintenance.[278]

The college was dissolved in 1547 under Edward VI, and its lands were confiscated ;[279] it was, however, refounded on the old lines by Mary in 1557, and parts of its lands in Newton and Kirkmanshulme which still remained in the Crown, as also the rectorial tithes, were given back to it.[280] As Mary's refoundations were again confiscated at the beginning of Elizabeth's reign[281] the position of Manchester College was doubtful ; it was not actually seized by the Crown, though plundered indirectly, and in 1578 was formally refounded by the queen.[282] The name was changed to Christ's College ; the warden and four fellows constituted the foundation, and were to appoint two chaplains or vicars to visit the sick, administer the sacrament and other divine services ; also four laymen and four children skilled in music were to sing, say prayers, read chapters, and continue other divine exercises in the collegiate church. The warden was to receive 4s. for each day he was present and resident ; each fellow 16d. each day he was present ;[283] a chaplain 6¾d. a day, a chorister 4½d., and a singing boy 2¾d. The

The following is a list of the rectors, wardens, and deans :— [289]

RECTORS

Instituted	Name	Patron	Cause of Vacancy
c. 1200 . . .	Albert de Nevill [290]	——	——
oc. 1291 . . .	William de Marchia [291]	——	——
oc. 1295 . . .	Walter de Langton [292]	——	——

[278] Valor Eccl. (Rec. Com.), v, 224. The site of the college was valued at 30s. a year. A rent resolute of 18d. was due to Lord La Warre for certain of the estates in Manchester ; fees of £4 and £5 were paid to the seneschal and bailiff ; and £2, £1, and £1 respectively were paid to the bishop and archdeacon of Chester and to Lichfield Cathedral.

[279] Edward was in this carrying out his father's designs. The college building, now Chetham's Hospital, was granted to the Earl of Derby, and other grants were probably made. The warden and fellows received pensions.

[280] Pat. 3 & 4 Phil. and Mary, pt. 11, 15 July 1557. George Collier was appointed warden or master, John Cuppage and Lawrence Vaux chaplains, and they were to choose the six other priests who were to be their fellow chaplains.

[281] By an Act passed in the first year of her reign.

[282] The charter is printed in Hibbert-Ware's Manch. Foundations, i, 89–99. It recites that the college 'is deemed in the judgment of divers to be quite dissolved and so come into our hands, or else is not so effectually ratified and confirmed in all points as were to be wished.' Mary simply restored the old foundation ; but Elizabeth reduced the staff of fellows and choristers, perhaps on account of the waste of revenues which had gone on. A vacant fellowship was to be filled by the election of the warden and surviving fellows.

A notice of the tithe corn book of 1584 is given in Lancs. and Ches. Antiq. Soc. xxii, 170.

[283] The warden was, however, allowed three months' absence each year, without

4

25

Instituted	Name	Patron	Cause of Vacancy
— 1296 . .	William Sygyn [293]	The King	res. Bp. Langton
18 Nov. 1299	Otho de Grandison [294] . . .	,,	———
12 Apr. 1306 .	Geoffrey de Stokes [295] . . .	Thomas Grelley . . .	———
24 Jan. 1313–4 .	Mr. John de Everdon [296] . .	Sir John La Warre . .	———
28 Sept. 1323 .	Mr. Adam de Southwick [297] .	,,	res. J. de Everdon
24 Aug. 1327 .	John de Claydon [298]	,, . . .	d. A. de Southwick
21 Aug. 1351 .	Thomas de Wyke [299] . .	Joan Dame La Warre . .	d. J. de Claydon
oc. 1390 . . .	Thomas Lord La Warre [300]	———	———

WARDENS

25 Nov. 1422 .	John Huntington, B.Decr. [301] . .	T. La Warre	res. T. La Warre
1459 . . .	Roger Radcliffe, LL.D. [302]	———	———

face VIII at the king's request allowed his clerk Walter de Langton, deacon, papal chaplain, to hold a number of benefices and canonries, resigning some and accepting Manchester among others ; *Cal. of Papal Letters*, i, 559. There is a notice of him in *Dict. Nat. Biog.*

[293] In 1299 W. Bishop of Lichfield and formerly rector of Manchester agreed with William de Gringley, rector of Marnham, and the other farmers of the church of Manchester concerning moneys due to him, amounting to over £40 ; also 6s. which the Dean of Manchester received during the time of vacancy, and 10s. 6d. which the farmer of William Sygyn, rector in 1299, had received ; Lich. Epis. Reg. Langton, i, fol. 4.

The king presented his clerk Master William Segini del God to the rectory in 1296 ; *Cal. Pat.* 1292–1301, p. 190. In 1297 the pope allowed his chaplain Master William Siguin to hold the rectory of Manchester, having resigned a benefice in Agen (France), and having canonries and prebends there and in Wells and Howden ; he had been under age when first beneficed ; *Cal. of Papal Letters*, i, 572.

[294] Lich. Epis. Reg. i, fol. 4b, 8b. ; on the day of his institution he had leave to be absent at the schools for two years, and a few months afterwards (29 Mar. 1300) the time was extended to five years. It is probable, therefore, that he never saw Manchester. Thomas Grelley, the lord of Manchester, was a minor in 1299, so that the king presented, as in the preceding vacancies ; *Cal. Pat.* 1292–1301, p. 440.

In 1301 the pope made provision, at the request of Otho de Grandison, to his nephew Otho of a canonry and prebend of York, notwithstanding that he held canonries and prebends of Lausanne and Autun, the church of Manchester, and two others which he was to resign ; *Cal. of Papal Letters*, i, 594. In the same year Otho was a clerk at Cambridge, and he and his men were the victims of an assault ; *Cal. Pat.* 1292–1301, p. 629. In 1304 he had the king's licence to go beyond the seas (ibid. 1301–7, p. 217), and does not seem to have returned to Manchester.

[295] The custody of the church (in sequestration) was granted on 31 Mar. 1306 to Geoffrey de Stokes, one of the king's clerks, and a fortnight later he was instituted to the rectory ; Lich. Epis. Reg. Langton, i, fol. 10b. The reason for the sequestration is not expressed. Geoffrey de Stokes was rector of Gransden, Cambridge, in 1302, and resigned Wotton for Brightwell in 1304 ; *Cal. Pat.* 1301–7, pp. 63, 304.

[296] Lich. Epis. Reg. Langton, i, fol. 60b ; he was a priest. In the survey of 1322 it is recorded that John de Everdon was rector, and in possession of the endowment, valued at 200 marks a year, consisting of eight burgages in Manchester, the vills of Newton, Kirkmanshulme, and appurtenances ; *Mamecestre* (Chet. Soc.), ii, 378. He held a prebend at St. Paul's and became dean in 1323 ; he died 15 Jan. 1336–7 ; Le Neve, op. cit. ii, 417, 311. He had held other benefices and canonries before coming to Manchester ; *Cal. of Papal Letters*, ii, 23, &c. ; Le Neve, op. cit. i, 586, 418.

[297] Lich. Epis. Reg. Northburgh, ii, fol. 99b ; he was a clerk. He was rector of Rostherne in Cheshire from 1319 to 1323 ; Ormerod, *Ches.* (ed. Helsby), i, 437. He died 31 July 1327.

[298] Lich. Epis. Reg. Northburgh, ii, fol. 102 ; a priest. In June 1344 he had leave of absence for fifteen months ; ibid. ii, fol. 11. He attested several local deeds ; see Raines, *Wardens*, 8. He was rector of Swineshead in 1327 ; Dods. MSS. cxlix, fol. 156b. Probably he resigned it for Manchester. In 1330 John XXII granted him the provision of a canonry at St. Paul's, with reservation of a prebend ; *Cal. of Papal Letters*, ii, 321 ; Le Neve, op. cit. ii, 407. From a plea in the following year it appears he had owed £130 to John son of Roger La Warre ; De Banco R. 286, m. 28d.

[299] Lich. Epis. Reg. Northburgh, ii, fol. 129 ; a chaplain. In the following January, being described as priest, he received leave of absence for study ; ibid. ii, fol. 12b. He obtained leave of absence for a year or two at various later dates—1355, 1361, 1362, 1365, 1371, and 1380 ; ibid. ii, fol. 14b ; v, fol. 7b, 9b, 24b, 33b ; Raines, (op. cit. 10) records a similar licence in 1357, so that Wyke's residence at Manchester was but intermittent. In 1368 he had leave to absolve his parishioners until Easter, and to choose a confessor for two years ; Lich. Epis. Reg. Stretton, ii, fol. 19. He is sometimes called ' the elder ' to distinguish him from Thomas de Wyke the younger, rector of the adjoining parish of Ashton from 1362 to 1371.

[300] The date of his institution has not been discovered, but was probably about 1390 ; he had the bishop's leave of absence for two years, the church being let to farm ; Lich. Epis. Reg. Scrope, vi, fol. 125b. He succeeded to the lordship of Manchester in 1398 on the death of his brother John, being then ' over forty years ' of age ; Inq. p.m. 22 Ric. II, no. 53. In 1363, being ' in his twenty-first year,' he obtained the papal dispensation to be ordained priest and hold a benefice ; *Cal. of Papal Letters*, iv, 31. From 1371 to 1373 he was rector of Ashton-under-Lyne ; he held a canonry at Lincoln from 1376 till his death in 1427, others at York from 1381 to 1397 and 1407 to 1427, at Southwell 1397 ; Le Neve, *Fasti*, ii, 161, 158 ; iii, 191, 209,

MANCHESTER CATHEDRAL   VIEW ACROSS THE NAVE FROM THE SOUTH-WEST

Instituted	Name	Patron
12 Dec. 1459	John Booth [303]	Lord La Warre, &c. . . .
9 Nov. 1465	Ralph Langley [304]	R. Hatfield, &c. . . .
27 July 1481	James Stanley [305]	T. Lord La Warre . .
22 July 1485	James Stanley [306]	,, . .
29 Oct. 1506	Robert Cliffe, LL.B. [307]	The King . . . .
29 July 1516	George West [308]	Sir T. West . .
2 Oct. 1528	George Collier, M.A. [309]	Lord La Warre . .
c. 1558	Lawrence Vaux, B.D. [310]	—
1560	William Birch, M.A. [311] . .	The Queen . . . . .
1562	Thomas Herle, B.D. [312] . . .	,, . . .

writ was issued to allow Sir Richard West to present to the church ; *Dep. Keeper's Rep.* xxxvii, App. 177. Dr. Radcliffe was Canon of York in 1456 and of St. Paul's in 1458, Archdeacon of Sarum in 1465, and Dean of St. Paul's in 1468, holding these dignities till his death in 1471 ; Le Neve, op. cit. iii, 203 ; ii, 383, 625, 313.

[303] Lich. Epis. Reg. Hales, xii, fol. 97, 97*b* ; an exchange was made by which Roger Radcliffe became rector of Adbolton, John Booth resigning. The patrons of Manchester were Sir Richard West Lord La Warre (lord of Manchester), and Thomas Uvedale, John Whittokesmede, Richard Cooke, and Thomas Baille, feoffees of the lordship to the use of Lord La Warre. For the patronage at this time see *Dep. Keeper's Rep.* xxxvii, App. 177. John Booth son of Sir Robert Booth of Dunham, who had been rector of Leigh, held many ecclesiastical dignities, finally becoming Bishop of Exeter, 1465 to 1478; Le Neve, *Fasti*, i, 376, &c.

[304] Lich. Epis. Reg. Hales, xii, fol. 102; the patrons for that turn were Richard Hatfield and Nicholas Statham, by grant of Lord La Warre and the feoffees named in the last note. Ralph Langley was also rector of Prestwich, 1445 to 1493. He is said to have given the first chimes to Manchester Church. He had a dispute with his predecessor in respect of certain goods claimed by the bishop ; Pal. of Lanc. Plea R. 34, m. 30.

[305] Lich Epis. Reg. Hales, xii, fol. 113*b* ; Warden Langley took the prebend in St. Paul's vacated by James Stanley, who had held it since 1458. The new warden was also Archdeacon of Chester, 1478 to 1485, and held the family rectory of Winwick ; see Le Neve, op. cit.

[306] Lich. Epis. Reg. Hales, xii, fol. 120; he was a clerk. He became rector of Winwick in 1493, and was also rector of Walton on the Hill and Rostherne ; he was Dean of St. Martin's le Grand, and Archdeacon of Richmond (1500) ; he became Bishop of Ely in 1506, and died in 1515. In the Stanley family poem he is called ' a proper man,' but regret is expressed that he became a priest instead of a soldier, not having the gift of continence. His illegitimate son, Sir John Stanley of Hanford in Cheshire, was a soldier of distinction, and became a monk at Westminster ; Earwaker, *East. Ches.* i, 245–50. The bishop was fond of cockfighting down to the later years of his life ; *Duchy Plead.* (Rec. Soc. Lancs. and Ches.), i, 63. For a defence of his character see the Rev. E. F. Letts in *Lancs. and Ches. Antiq. Soc.* vi, 161, &c. He died at Manchester and was buried there; his memorial brass remains in the cathedral. There are notices of him in *Dict. Nat. Biog.* and Cooper, *Athen. Cantab.* i, 16.

[307] Lich. Epis. Reg. Blyth, xiii–xiv, fol. 55 ; the king presented because the patron

had not th
Robert Cliff
law at Oxf
years ; *Gra*
He had be
1485 to 14
chester held
see Cooper,
later career.
that the wa
death, but t
letters from
are printed
they are end
bout the
VIII ' and s
ing of Pa
may be erro
meet in 15
king's divor
Cooper, *An*
Burnet's Rec

[308] L'ch.
59*b*. Geor
at his appo
des rihed a

Instituted	Name	Patron	Cause of Vacancy
1578	John Wolton, B.D.[313]	The Queen	———
1579 . . .	William Chadderton, D.D.[314] . .	,,	prom. Bp. Wolton
1595 . . .	John Dee, D.Math.[315]	,, .	trans. Bp. Chadderton
1609 . . .	Richard Murray, D.D [316] . .	The King	d. Dr. Dee
1635 . . .	Richard Heyrick, B.D.[317] .	,,	dep. Dr. Murray

estates of his church for the benefit of those in power or his own family ; a lease made by him to the queen in 1576 was specially mentioned in Elizabeth's charter. Archbishop Parker in 1566 recommended him as 'a grave, priestly man,' for promotion to the bishopric of Bangor. In the same year Herle complained that some of his difficulties in collecting tithes came from the action of Lawrence Vaux—deprived (he said) 'for Papistry and holding of most erroneous opinions against the Catholic faith '—in giving the college deeds into the custody of Alexander Barlow. One result was a 'great hindrance to the true, sincere, and Catholic religion,' because the warden and fellows were not able to pay preachers who might teach the people 'their duties towards God and the Queen's most excellent Majesty' ; Vaux, Catechism (ed. Law), 19, 20 (introd.). Herle had to resign, or was deprived, in order to allow the refounding of the college in 1578. He died nine years later, holding canonries at Worcester and Chester, and the vicarage of Bromsgrove ; Raines, op cit. 75–84, where various particulars of his leases and grants are given.

[313] He was appointed warden under the new charter, and was next year advanced to the bishopric of Exeter, so that his tenure was brief, and he probably did not reside. He was born in Whalley and sent up to Oxford (B.A. 1555), but fled to the Continent to join the Protestant exiles. Returning on the death of Mary, he was made canon of Exeter in 1560 and rector of Spaxton in 1563. As Bishop of Exeter he actively persecuted the adherents of the ancient faith—to whom his own son joined himself—as well as the more extravagant Protestant sects, the Family of Love and others, showing himself a zealous servant of the queen. He died in 1594. He published several works, one of which was reprinted by the Parker Society. See Raines, op. cit. 84–8 ; Wood, Athenae ; Dict. Nat. Biog.; F. O. White, Eliz. Bishops, 259–63.

[314] He was the son of Edmund Chadderton of Nuthurst ; educated at Queens' College, Cambridge, and became fellow of Christ's College, Lady Margaret's Professor of Divinity, and Master of Queens' College. He was a Protestant of the Puritan type, being chaplain to the Earl of Leicester in 1568. In the same year he became Archdeacon of York, and in 1579 was made Bishop of Chester, the wardenship of Manchester being added in commendam. He was a bitter persecutor of the adherents of the ancient religion, and being placed on the Ecclesiastical Commission for the North, resided at Manchester as a convenient centre for directing operations. He actively encouraged the Puritan preaching-exercises in the Manchester district, but on his removal to the see of Lincoln in 1595 he was obliged by the queen to repress them there. He died in 1608. Hollinworth (op. cit. 89) calls him 'a learned man and liberal, given to hospitality, and a more frequent preacher and baptiser than other bishops of his time ; he was resident in Manchester till the daily jarrings between his attendants and some inhabitants

of the town, occasio and stiffness on one casioned him to remo Chester.' See Rain F. O. White, Eliz Foley, Rect. S.J. 11, Biog. ; Cooper, Athen portrait is given in H Foundations, 1, 101

[315] Educated at Cambridge, and Lo great fame as a astronomer. He wa fellows of Trini y C 1546, and received b of Edward VI, prov to the satisfaction of held his benefices fo he was deprived on a as Canon Raines su on them, hi ordin matter of dispute · called 'clerk' on Manchester. He ha was addicte to the s magic, to which h ce ebr ty ; 'n this m upon others, he was luded, as in his up of meta s, and interco Lancashire, says Hol 100), he discou aged lawful exorcism an

SALFORD HUNDRED

Instituted		Name			Patron		
29 Aug. 1667	.	Nicholas Stratford, D.D.[318]	. . .	The King	. .
1 May, 1684	.	Richard Wroe, D.D.[319]	. .	”
1718 . . .	.	Samuel Peploe, B.D.[320]	. .	
25 Oct. 1738	.	Samuel Peploe, D.C.L.[321]	.	”	.
7 March 1782	.	Richard Assheton, D.D.[322]	.	.	”	. .
12 July 1800	.	Thomas Blackburne, D.C.L.[323]	.	”	. .
8 March 1823	.	Thomas Calvert, D.D[324]	. .	”	. .

DEANS

10 July 1840	.	Hon. William Herbert, D.D.[325]	. . .	The Queen	. . .	d. T. Calvert
— July 1847	.	George Hull Bowers, D.D.[326]	. .	”	. . .	d. W. Herbert
7 Dec. 1872	. .	Benjamin Morgan Cowie, D.D.[327]	. .	”	. . .	res. G. H. Bowers
30 April 1884	.	John Oakley, D.D.[328]	. . . . .	”	. . .	prom. B. M. Cowie
28 Oct. 1890	.	Edward Craig Maclure, D.D.[329]	. .	”	. . .	d. J. Oakley
25 July 1906	.	James Edward Cowell Welldon, D.D.[330]	.	The King	. .	d. E. C. Maclure

[318] He was educated at Trinity College, Oxford, of which he became a fellow in the Commonwealth period ; M.A. 1656 ; D.D. 1673. There is a portrait of him in Hibbert-Ware's *Manch. Foundations*, ii, 5. He conformed to episcopacy at the Restoration, and had various benefices and dignities, resigning Manchester on becoming vicar of St. Mary Aldermanbury in London. The strength of the Presbyterians in the Manchester district, and a troublesome lawsuit with the Trafford family regarding the tithes of Stretford, are thought to have influenced him in resigning. He adhered to the Whig party, and on the Revolution was made Bishop of Chester and Rector of Wigan. At Manchester he restored the use of the surplice, antiphonal singing by the choir, and the reception of the communion at the altar rails ; 'he was very laborious and extraordinarily charitable, affable, and humble in his place, and generally beloved.' See Raines, op. cit. 139–47, where there is a list of his works ; *Dict. Nat. Biog.* ; Wood, *Athenae*.

It should be explained that though Heyrick himself did not conform, the surplice was used in the church after the passing of the Act of Uniformity ; see Newcome, *Diary* (Chet. Soc.), 120. The churchwardens' accounts of 1664 record a payment for washing the surplices.

[319] Act Bks. at Chester Dioc. Reg. He was born at Radcliffe ; educated at Jesus College, Cambridge, of which he was elected fellow ; M.A. 1665 ; D.D. 1686. In 1675 he was elected fellow of Manchester, and became exceedingly admired in the district, the epithet 'silver-tongued' distinguishing him. Several of his sermons were published. He had some other church preferment. In politics he was a Whig, and thus was untouched by the Revolution and the Hanoverian succession. He died 6 January 1717–18. See Raines, op. cit. 148–57 ; *Dict. Nat. Biog.* ; also *Pal. Note-Bk.* ii, 1, 33 (with portrait). He lived in Deansgate in 1683 ; *Ct. Leet Rects.* vi, 231.

[320] He was educated at Jesus College, Oxford ; M.A. 1693. There is a portrait in Hibbert-Ware, op. cit. In 1695 he became rector of Kedleston and in 1700 vicar of Preston. He was a latitudinarian in religion and a Whig in politics. His courage in praying for King George in 1715 during the Jacobite occupation of Preston is said to have led to his promotion to Manchester. The appointment was resisted on the ground that the statutes required the B.D. degree in the warden, and that his obtaining

such degree from Canterbury would n chester he was unpo of the collegiate chu Churchmen and Jaco antagon'sm to the b trell). On the bi h Peploe was in 1726 ret ining the warden warden and as visitor popular. He publi See Raines, op. cit. 15

[321] The church pa with this warden. H the king on 'the dea S.T.P., last warden tenure of Bishop P He was the only so educated

J

The cathedral staff consists of the dean, four residentiary canons, who have rectories within the parish, and undertake the duties of the sub-dean, bursar, collector of rents, and registrar; twenty-four honorary canons and two minor canons, assisted by two clerks in orders, of whom one acts as precentor.[331]

Of the fellows and canons no account is given in this place, but as many of them were beneficed in the county, they are not altogether unnoticed.

The earlier rectors were often men of distinction, but pluralists and non-resident. It was to remedy this abuse that the college was founded, and to some extent it met the necessities of the case. The various chantries also helped to maintain an adequate supply of clergy; in particular, the foundation of Richard Bexwick for priests and schoolmaster in the Jesus chapel was made with this intention.[333] The first college possessed a library, which seems to have perished with it;[334] but another was in 1653 founded in the Jesus chapel and maintained by the town.[335] Just before the destruction of the college there appear to have been the warden, five priests, and four deacons on the foundation, 'all resident and observing their statutes'; also two curates, six chantry priests, and a fluctuating number of others—fifteen or more—who had casual offices or served the outlying chapelries. Thus for a population estimated at 6,000 'houseling people,' there were over thirty priests available. The church was decently furnished with plate, vestments, and other ornaments.[336]

The simultaneous abolition of college and chantries and the confiscation of the endowments made a vast difference. It is not exactly known how the Edwardine services were conducted, or what payments were made to the ministers.[337] In the Visitation list of 1548 twenty-two names appeared; ten of them reappeared in 1554, when six new names were added, two being those of the 'curates'—Ralph Birch and Hugh Ormishaw. In 1563 Thomas Herle, the warden, headed the list; he had two curates—Robert Prestwich and Edward Holt; five of the chapels of ease had curates in charge; there were four other names, two of which were soon erased, and another was described as 'decrepit.' The number of clergy therefore had been reduced to twelve, nine being effective. In the list of 1565 only those on the foundation were recorded—the warden, four chaplains, four deacons, and four (lay) choristers. The omission of any notice of the chapels of ease was perhaps a fault of the registrar's clerk; but it seems clear that the Pre-Reformation staff of thirty to thirty-four had been reduced to a dozen or less. Only two of the clergy of 1548 appear in the 1565 list, but some of the chapels of ease, if just then in use, may have retained the former curates.[338]

Though the gentry held, for a time at least, to the old ways, and though such wardens as Collier and Vaux were in life and doctrine an instructive contrast to their successors,[339] the people of the district rapidly accepted Protestantism, and that in its more pro-

---

[331] By an Act of 1850 (13 & 14 Vict. cap. 41) the dean has cure of souls in the fragment of the ancient parish which is still served by the cathedral in its parochial aspect, and has the assistance of the chaplains or minor canons. The residentiary canons are rectors of four parishes, formed out of the old parish—St. Andrew, Manchester; St. Matthew, Manchester; St. George, Hulme; and St. Philip, Salford. While the dean is presented by the Crown the canons are collated by the bishop.

The Act named was preceded and accompanied by a sharp local controversy. An important contribution was one by Thomas Turner, in the form of a letter to the Bishop of Manchester; the second appendix contained translations of the licence of Henry V, the petition of the parishioners, and the charter of the Bishop of Lichfield in 1421; also of the charters of Philip and Mary, Elizabeth, and Charles I; with other documents. He showed that practically the whole endowments (as restored by Queen Mary) were rectorial, and that Lord La Warre's additional gifts were of small extent.

[333] Richard Bexwick's foundation was originally for four priests to do divine service, assist the warden, keep the choir, be present at matins, mass, evensong, &c. as it was found that the parish, with '7000 housling people and more resident,' could not be sufficiently served by the warden and fellows without further help. Richard Bexwick was 'an especial benefactor,' having given a suit of vestments worth £45, and built a chapel and one side of the choir at a cost of 300 or 400 marks; Duchy Plead. (Rec. Soc. Lancs. and Ches.), i, 81–3; ii, 233.

[334] Cardinal Langley in 1437 bequeathed the Flores Bernardi to the college of Manchester; Raines, Chant. (Chet. Soc.), i, 121. A later bequest of books to the college library was made by

Henry Piccope,
[335] M

nounced forms. The preaching of John Bradford may have had something to do with the change, though he was so little satisfied that he warned his audiences that 'because they did not readily embrace the Word of God, the Mass should again be said in that church, and the play of Robin Hood acted there.'[340] His letters and George Marsh's show that there were a certain number of resolute Protestants in the town in Mary's reign,[341] and some are stated to have been imprisoned in the college.[342]

The refoundation of the college by Queen Elizabeth gave the church a respectable body of Calvinistic divines,[343] but the wardenships of Dee and Murray again proved disastrous. One of the fellows, however, William Bourne, acquired a dominating position in the town ; 'This is Mr. Bourne's judgement,' was sufficient for the people.[344] It is not surprising to learn that two of the chaplains in 1591 administered the sacrament without a surplice and that other irregularities were allowed ; many of the people, it seems, preferred the churchyard to the church at sermontime.[345] The growing influence of Puritanism is seen in the stricter Sunday observance.[346] The new foundation of Charles I had no perceptible effect in neutralizing its prevalence.[347]

Under the Presbyterian discipline established in 1646 Manchester became the head of a classis, which included also the adjoining parishes of Ashton, Eccles, Flixton, and Prestwich-with-Oldham.[348] Four years later there seems to have been a regular staff of twelve ministers in the parish, of whom three were at the parish church and the others at the various chapels.[349]

Just before the Restoration Richard Heyrick, Henry Newcome, and Joshua Stopford were in charge.[350]

After 1660 a tone a little more High Church gradually prevailed, so that by the end of the 17th century the clergy were strongly Jacobite, and remained so until after 1745. Bishop Gastrell about 1717 found that the warden and four fellows supplied all the turns of preaching, and the two chaplains read prayers and did all the other duty of the whole parish, receiving the surplice fees ; a 'cathedral service' was performed by the four singing men, four choristers, and organist.[351] At this time and afterwards the building of new churches and the growth of Nonconformist congregations continually diminished the importance of the collegiate clergy ; while the great increase of their wealth rendered a change of its distribution desirable, and this was effected in the least injurious mode by several Acts of Parliament.[352] From 1854 the various district chapelries have become independent parishes, the incumbents having the title of rector.

As might be expected from the importance of the place there were a number of chantry endowments, of which particulars are given in the record of their confiscation in 1547. The curates, i.e. the two fellows or chaplains who served the parish, had in addition to their college stipend the profits of the 'Obit lands,' given at various times by a number of benefactors, being in return bound to celebrate certain obits yearly for the souls of the donors. The rents amounted to 102s. 11¾d.[353]

The chantry of St. James, founded by Ralph

Bishop of Chester refused Hall's pension in 1581 ; *Acts of P.C.* 1581-2, p. 266.

A little later it was stated that the clergy had been beaten and one of their preachers attacked and wounded.

The loss of the old hospitality was a grievance with the tenants ; *Newton Chapelry* (Chet. Soc.), ii, 51.

[340] Hollinworth, *Mancuniensis*, 75.

[341] Foxe, *Acts and Monuments* (ed. Cattley), vii, 196, 204, 60, 66.

[342] Hollinworth, op. cit. 79 ; 'their names, as tradition saith, were Ridlestones, Wharmbies, &c.'

[343] The Elizabethan fellows of 1578 were John Molins, D.D., Alexander Nowell, D.D.—both exiles for religion in Mary's time ; the latter became Dean of St. Paul's—Thomas Williamson, and Oliver Carter, B.D. ; the last-named had been a fellow under Herle's wardenship and is noticed in *Dict. Nat. Biog.*

[344] Hollinworth, op. cit. 105 ; see an earlier note.

[345] W. F. Irvine in *Lancs. and Ches. Antiq. Soc.* xiii, 64–9. It is stated that the surplice was not used in the church for upwards of forty years, i.e. from about 1590 onwards ; *Funeral Certs.* (Chet. Soc.), 77. At the Visitation of 1598 the churchwardens were ordered to provide a surplice and Book of Common Prayer ; they had all eaten flesh in Lent and days forbidden. In 1608 Bourne was presented for not wearing the surplice ; some persons communicated standing. In 1622 Henry Holland of Denton was 'suspected of Brownism.' Many persons refused to stand at the Creed and bow at the name of Jesus. Nevertheless the organ playing is mentioned ; Visit. P. at Chester.

[346] Up to 1578 'Sundays' and holidays were the usual times for practising archery ; *Manch. Ct. Leet Rec.* i, 196. In

1611 dealers in fruit, pedlars, and other street traders were forbidden to sell on 'the Sabbath day' ; ibid. ii, 264. In 1634 four men were paid for 'watching packs' on Whitsunday, to see that none should be brought into the town on that Sabbath day ; *Manch. Constables' Accts.* ii, 7. Perhaps it was due to the same spirit that players were ordered to leave ; ibid. ii, 33, 34, 36. For the state of the church see *Cal. S.P. Dom.* 1633-4, p. 523.

[347] The careers of the new warden and of William Bourne, one of the fellows, have been described above. The other fellows of 1635 were Samuel Boardman, Richard Johnson, and Peter Shaw, first elected in 1629, 1632, and 1633 respectively. Of these Richard Johnson, though a Calvinist in doctrine, was the nearest approach to the 'moderate Churchman' of to-day, and suffered insults and imprisonment for his loyalty to the king during the Civil War ; he lived to hold his fellowship again ; Raines, *Fellows*, 114–15.

Another noteworthy fellow chosen in 1643 was Richard Hollinworth, of Magdalene College, Cambridge, author of the *Mancuniensis* frequently quoted in these notes ; ibid. pp. 138-71 ; *Dict. Nat. Biog.* The Hollinworth family was of old standing in the town. Robert Hollinworth held a burgage and a half in 1473 ; *Mamecestre*, iii, 491. In 1502 James, son of Thomas, son of Thomas, son of John Hollinworth, claimed two messuages as heir of his grandfather ; Pal. of Lanc. Plea R. 92, m. 4 ; also Pal. of Lanc. Writs Proton. 10 Hen. VII. For the parentage of Richard Hollinworth see *Ct. Leet Rec.* iii, 188–9 ; and for his works, C. W. Sutton in *Lancs. and Ches. Antiq. Soc.* vi, 138.

Hulme in 1507 from lands left by the first warden, John Huntington, had a clear income of £6 1s. 8d.[354] The 'new chapel' of St. John Baptist—later known as the Stanley or Derby chapel—begun by James Stanley, Bishop of Ely and formerly warden, and completed by his son Sir John Stanley, had an endowment of £4 2s. 8d.[355] This chapel, which has the small Ely chapel at its north-east corner, was used as the baptistry a century ago. The Trafford chapel or 'closet of St. Nicholas' had a chantry founded, it was believed, by Robert Grelley—possibly the lord of Allerton and Chorlton, living in the 14th century; the clear income was £5 9s. 7d.[356] In the same chapel was another chantry founded by the ancestors of Sir Edmund Trafford, the incumbent being known as 'the Lady priest'; the endowment being very

small, 65s. net, the parishioners contributed a quantity of oats for him.[357] At St. George's altar there were two chantries, both founded by Robert Chetham; at one of them the priest was to celebrate Mass at six o'clock in the morning for the souls of the founder and his ancestors; the net endowment of this chantry was £6 2s. 7d.,[358] and that of the second £5 0s. 8d.[359] Another chantry was that founded by William Radcliffe at the altar of the Trinity, with a net income of £5 3s. 2d.[360]

An important foundation, already mentioned, was that of Richard Bexwick at the Jesus altar. His intentions do not seem to have been carried out fully, but in 1547 two priests, one of them teaching a school, were maintained.[361]

There were gilds associated with the Jesus and

---

[354] Raines, *Chant.* i, 25–8; *Notitia Cestr.* ii, 59–62, notes. The circumstances of the foundation are narrated in the account of Warden Huntington already given. The endowment consisted of 26 acres in Alport and three burgages in the town. The chantry priest in 1534 was John Bexwick (*Valor Eccl.* [Rec. Com.], v, 225), and in 1547 Nicholas Wolstonecroft, who paid his first-fruits in 1543 (*Lancs. and Ches. Rect.* [Rec. Soc.], ii, 408), and is named in the list of clergy at the Visitation of 1554.

In the chapel was an 'Image of Pity,' with the announcement of an indulgence or pardon of 26,000 [years] and twenty-six days on reciting five Paternosters, five Aves, and a Credo; Hollinworth, 55. The lands of this chantry were in 1549 bestowed on the Earl of Derby for a payment of £268 3s. 4d.; Pat. 3 Edw. VI, pt. 11.

[355] *Chant.* 28–31. The lands were at Bollington and Lyme in Cheshire. The chapel possessed a chalice and three old vestments. Thomas Johnson was the priest in 1534 and 1547.

[356] Ibid. 31–5. The endowments consisted of three burgages in Manchester and tenements at Grindlow Cross. The ornaments consisted of a chalice, vestments, and altar cloths.

In 1320, when Robert Grelley was living, one Henry de Salford, chaplain, paid to the lord of Manchester a rent of 20s. for Grindlow, and 2s. 4d. for Blackacres; a note—perhaps of the 16th century—states that these were the lands of St. Mary's chantry; *Mamecestre,* ii, 279.

From deeds printed in Canon Raines' notes it appears that the patronage of the chantry was in 1428 in dispute between Sir Edmund Trafford and Thomas Booth of Barton the elder, it having been the right of 'the heir of Bexwick'; De Trafford D. no. 86; Pal. of Lanc. Plea R. 2, m. 9 d. On the death of Thomas Whitehead, Reynold Hobson became chantry priest in 1506 on the presentation of Sir Edmund Trafford (De Trafford D. no. 70), and was in 1508 succeeded by Henry Ryle, perhaps the same who was serving in 1534, though he seems to have resigned in 1514. On the resignation of Charles Gee, Edmund Trafford presented another Henry Ryle in 1542 (Act Bks. at Chester; *Lancs. and Ches. Rect.* ii, 407), and he was serving in 1547; he was summoned to the visitation in 1554. The chapel was long used as the burial-place of the Trafford family.

For grants of the lands of Trafford's chapel see Pat. 32 Eliz. pt. 13; 4 Jas. I, pt. 25; also *Ducatus Lanc.* (Rec. Com.), iii, 382.

[357] *Chant.* 36–40. From deeds there given the chantry seems to have been founded or refounded early in the 15th century, but there has been preserved a gift to Matthew de Sholver, chaplain, and his successors celebrating the Mass of St. Mary at St. Nicholas' altar, which may be dated about 1300; Norris D. (B.M.), no. 951. In 1429 Thomas son of Thomas del Booth of Barton claimed to present to 'the chantry of the Blessed Mary at the altar of St. Nicholas,' against John de Bamford Henry de Trafford, and Hugh de Scholes, chaplain; Pal. of Lanc. Plea R. 2, m. 9 b; see also the preceding. The endowment was derived from burgages in St. Mary Gate, Todd Lane, and Deansgate; the priest celebrated with the ornaments of the other chantry. John Reddish seems to have been the chaplain in 1431; James Smith in 1498 and 1525, John Dickonson in 1532 and 1535, William Ashton (or 'Hache') in 1547.

[358] *Chant.* 40–5. The endowment was derived from burgages in Market Street Lane, Millgate, and Deansgate; there was no plate. From a deed printed in Raines' notes it appears that the chantries were founded in 1501, the priest to be 'one of the priests of the Guild or Brotherhood of our Blessed Lady and St. George of Manchester, in the College Church of Manchester'; the hour of six o'clock was fixed by the founder. John Brideoak was the cantarist in 1534 and 1547. This chantry was partly endowed by the founder's wife—Isabel daughter of Richard Tetlow—out of her father's estate.

[359] Ibid. 46–8. The endowment included Domville House in Salford, and other burgages and lands in Salford, Worsley, and Spotland. From the will of the founder's widow, it is clear that Hugh Marler was the incumbent in 1523. Robert Byrom was there in 1534 (*Valor Eccl.* [Rec. Com.], v, 226) and Edward Smith in 1547. In addition to making regulations for the two chantries Isabel Chetham by her will left a pair of silver beads to our Lady of Manchester, 5 marks to the repair of the church, and 26s. 8d. to the building of Irk Bridge.

Of the Gild of St. George nothing further seems to be known. The chapel was built by William Galey, who died in 1508, and part of the endowment was left by him, viz. a house in Market Street Lane occupied by Robert Chetham, and no doubt part of the endowment of the former chantry. See Raines, loc. cit. in the notes, and Hollinworth, *Mancuniensis,* 55. For the Galey family see *Mamecestre,* iii, 489; *Duchy Plead.* (Rec. Soc. Lancs.

and Ches.), ii, 162; *Manch. Ct. Leet Rect.* ii, 8, 77.

For disputes as to the chantry lands in the Acres and elsewhere see *Ducatus Lanc.*(Rec. Com.), i, 224, 265; *Duchy Plead.* iii, 30.

[360] *Chant.* 49–54. The income was derived from burgages and shops in Market Street, Hanging Bridge, Smithy Door, Hanging Ditch, and Collyhurst Fold ('foyte'). There was no plate. Hugh Brideoak was priest in 1534 and Roger Ireland in 1547; William Woodall succeeded before 1548. This chantry seems to have been founded by William Radcliffe of Ordsall, who died in 1498. In the following year Elizabeth widow of John Radcliffe of Ordsall bequeathed to the chaplain celebrating at Trinity altar a mass book with cover and clasps, a cruet of silver with I.R. on the cover, two towels, a vestment of green and white velvet with bulls' heads on the orphreys, and 3s. 4d., to buy a sacring-bell; Raines, in the notes. The chapel is now the outermost aisle of the nave on the north Hollinworth (op.cit. 47) describes the 'very rich window' and gives the verses inscribed on it 'in worship of the Trinity.'

[361] Some particulars have been given in a previous note; see also *Chant.* 48–52, where are printed several deeds relating to the foundation; e.g. the licence of James Stanley, as warden, to the Gild of St. Saviour and the Name of Jesus to receive all oblations and emoluments offered to the image of the Saviour in the chapel recently built at the south side of the collegiate church; an agreement of 1509 as to the position of the Bexwick chaplains in the choir and in the college, showing that they were to share in all things, except the stipend; a deed by which Isabel daughter and sole heir of Richard Bexwick and widow of Thomas Beck (to whom the chantry was sometimes attributed) conveyed the Jesus chapel in 1562 to Francis Pendleton and Cecily his wife, daughter of Isabel, and others. A case respecting the endowment of this chantry is given in *Duchy Plead.* ii, 82. The revenue was £4 11s. 4d. in 1534, when James Barlow was chantry priest; at that time 18s. 8d. was by the founder's will distributed at his obit to the clergy and the poor; *Valor Eccl.* (Rec. Com.), v, 225. Robert Prestwich was the cantarist and Edward Pendleton the schoolmaster in 1546, when the revenue was £8 12s. 3d.; *Chant.* 246–7.

The chapel had at the south-east corner a smaller chapel, now destroyed, in which were buried the remains of William Hulme, the founder of the Hulme exhibitions at Oxford.

St. George's chapels ;[362] also a gild of the Blessed Virgin Mary, which may have been associated with the Lady chapel.[363] This chapel was at the east end of the church,[364] and there was an altar of St. Michael, probably at the east end of the south aisle of the quire.[365] The chapel of Salford Bridge does not appear to have had any special chaplain or endowment.

The grammar school, founded by Hugh Oldham in 1515,[365a] and Chetham's Hospital and Library, founded under the will of Humphrey Chetham, who died in 1653, are described elsewhere.

CHARITIES Apart from the grammar school there does not seem to have been any endowed charity for the whole parish, but several of the townships have valuable estates. An inquiry was held in 1904, but it concerned only those portions of the parish which are outside the boroughs of Manchester and Salford, so that the latest detailed official report is that of 1826, in which year the following were the existing charitable endowments, apart from schools,[366] some of the funds having been lost.[367] For Manchester the charities of George Clarke,[368] George Marshall,[369] Ellen Shuttleworth,[370] Thomas Hudson,[371] Henry Dickenson,[372] John Alexander and Joshua Brown,[373] Thomas Percival,[374] Joseph Champion,[375] James Moss,[376] Walter and Margaret

[362] See the preceding notes. In the chapel of St. George was a statue of the saint on horseback ; Hollinworth, op. cit. 47. Later it was known as the Radcliffe chapel.

[363] It held burgages in the town in 1473; *Mamecestre*, iii, 506. For the Gilds see *Lancs. and Ches. Antiq. Soc.* x, 1–24.

[364] Afterwards called the Byron or Chetham Chapel.

[365] St. Michael's altar is named in the will of Henry Turton, cited above ; Piccope, *Wills*, ii, 12. 'The east window of the south aisle had Michael and his angels ; the nine orders of angels, fighting with the Dragon and his angels' ; Hollinworth, op. cit. 46.

[365a] *V.C.H. Lancs.* ii, 578.

[366] The scholastic endowments were for schools at Ardwick, Blackley, Crumpsall, Didsbury, Gorton, Heaton Norris, Levenshulme, and Newton. The benefactions for Crumpsall and Newton are still available.

Anne Hinde in 1723 left lands in Salford and Manchester for the instruction of ten poor children of Manchester and ten of Salford, half boys and half girls. They were to be taught to write and read (up to a chapter in the Bible), and they must learn the Church Catechism. Green clothes were to be provided for them ; hence this was known as the 'Green Gown' Charity. The land in Salford was sold for £1,967 10s., the New Bailey prison being erected on it. In 1838 the houses in Fennel Street were sold to the Corporation of Manchester for £2,600. The income in 1826 was almost £200, which sufficed for the education and clothing of fifty-seven children. The income (from consols) is now only £114 2s. 8d., and is spent on education and clothing by the trustees.

St. Paul's (Turner Street) Charity School was founded in 1777. The present income is £40 2s.

Richard Lichford in 1710 left a rent-charge of £5 on Cooper's tenement in Blackley to pay a schoolmaster in that township. This is still in operation.

Elizabeth Chetham in 1689 gave £20 for the teaching of children in Moston and Newton to read the Bible. The income is now £1.

At Heaton Norris there were in 1826 two charity school foundations—one by John Hollingpriest, 1785, the other by public subscription. The latter has been lost ; the former has an income of £24 2s. 4d., paid to schools in the township.

Margaret Usherwood in 1742 left the residue of her estate for the education and clothing of six poor children of Chorlton-with-Hardy ; this was in 1826 represented

by £160 in the hand who paid £8 as inte now invested in a Ma bond producing £4 for the benefit of chi ship

[367] John Whitwort and William Drink £100 for the relief Chorlton in 1706 left pr nticeship fees ; Clayton in 1772 gav be lent without in been lost before 1826

John Barlow of P charged his estate pprenticeship fees of ley and Manchester 1826 it could not Manchester had ever

William B guley the founding of a ch children in Manch

Nugent,[277] Edward Mayes,[278] Richard Holland and others,[279] **Nicholas Hartley,**[280] **Ellen Hartley,**[281] John Partington,[282] **Robert Sutton,**[283] **Thomas Minshull,**[284] **Humphrey Oldfield,**[285] **Francis Cartwright,**[286] Catherine Richards,[287] Jane Corles,[288] Roger Sedgwick,[289] Elizabeth Scholes,[290] Ann Butterworth and Daniel Bayley,[291] Meriel Mosley and others,[292] Daniel Shelmerdine,[293] Ellen Nicholson,[294] Catherine Fisher,[295] James Clayton,[296]

a housewife's kersey of a sad blue colour, and to be given on Christmas Day morning before prayers in the south porch of parish church of Manchester.' In 1826 this was represented by a rent-charge of £5 5s. on the capital messuage called Hope in Eccles. This sum is still received and spent in clothing by the churchwardens and overseers.

[277] For these benefactors see the account of Moston. Walter Nugent and Margaret Nugent his mother in 1609 settled two chief rents of 20s. each for the buying of turves for the poor. In 1826 one of the rents was found to be charged on property held by Clarke's trustees, and the other on a house, 38, Smithy Door, owned by T. C. Worsley of Platt; on the latter the rent-charge had not been paid for many years, but resumption was promised. The income is now £4; it is added to the Clarke and other charities of the Lord Mayor.

[278] In 1621 he left £120 for the poor, the income to be distributed in money or victuals. Land in Millgate and Miller's Lane was purchased, the present Mayes Street indicating its position, and on it the overseers long afterwards erected buildings called the Almshouses, occupied by six poor women. An Act was passed in 1794 allowing the trustees to sell or lease the land, thus enabling the estate to be improved. The rents in 1826 amounted to nearly £430, subject to a chief rent of 13s. 10d. to William Hulton. The present income is £479, which is distributed by the trustees in food or money. For an account of the almshouses see *Ct. Leet Rec.* vi, 139 n.; and Procter, *Bygone Manch.* 80.

[279] Richard Holland in 1622 gave £100, and others about the same time gave sums amounting to £58 3s.; and these with other moneys were in 1681 laid out in building the Almshouses recorded in the last note. It seems therefore that these sums have been merged in the Mayes Charity.

[280] Nicholas Hartley gave £50 for the poor of Manchester, and his brother and executor John in 1628 gave a house and land in Moston, as representing the £50. John Hartley, grandson of the former John, was a trustee in 1692. In 1826 the land, &c., was tenanted by Samuel Taylor, it lying near his residence, at a rent of £15 15s. The present income is £126, which is distributed by the trustees in money gifts.

[281] Ellen widow of Nicholas Hartley in 1626 gave a burgage in Market Stead Lane for the relief of poor persons dwelling in Manchester. It was sold in 1822, under the Act for widening Market Street, and the purchase-money, £1,370, invested in Government stock. This now produces £45 6s., and the Lord Mayor and deputy-mayor, who act as trustees, distribute the income on Christmas Eve in half-crowns to poor aged people, chiefly on the recommendation of the police superintendents.

Anne Collier in 1848 augmented this charity by a gift producing an additional £17 2s. 9d.

[282] By his will of 1677 he left £100 to be invested in land for the benefit of the poor. Lands called Mythom, Delf Hills, & chased, was ma the £10 by Mat of hi lia undertoo st ll paid Mayor i son Cha

[283] He provide ment to poor and h s , Gorton—o provide Land in cha d, were re The £2 cloth ng

[284] In tenemen and Cat rent of 1 b y , 5 as well with clot but was required is £153 m nor c

[285] Hu £

Sarah Brearcliffe,[397] Thomas Henshaw ;[398] for Blackley —Adam Chetham,[399] Thomas and John Traves ;[400] for Didsbury, &c.—Sir Edward Mosley,[401] Thomas Chorlton,[402] Sergeant Boardman,[403] Ann Bland and Thomas Linney,[404] Edward Hampson ;[405] and for Salford—Humphrey Booth the elder,[406] his grandson Humphrey Booth the younger,[407] Charles Broster,[408] Charles Haworth,[409] Robert Cuthbertson,[410] George Buerdsell,[411] Thomas Dickanson,[412] John Caldwell,[413]

Alexander and Mary Davie,[414] and Samuel Haward.[415] The partial report of 1904 shows that many of the above stocks are still available, and that some new ones have been added ; these were, excluding church[416] and educational and recreative endowments,[417] as follows :—For Didsbury—Sarah Feilden, for the poor ;[418] for Heaton Norris—Sir Ralph Pendlebury, stocks producing £4,722 a year for children of this and some other townships,[419] Rev. Stephen

---

[397] She died in 1803, having in 1792 given £3,000 on trust for the relief of fifteen old housekeepers of Manchester and Salford. The income is now £97 10s., and is distributed by the trustees.

[398] He was a hat-maker at Oldham, and died in 1810, having left £40,000 for a blue-coat school at Oldham, and £20,000 for a blind asylum at Manchester, forbidding the money to be used in the purchase of land. In consequence of this provision nothing had been done in 1826 towards carrying out the testator's object, but the money was accumulating at interest. A blind asylum was in 1837 built at Old Trafford.

[399] In 1625 he gave a messuage and land in Blackley for the minister of the chapel (one-third), and the poor of the township (two-thirds). A poor-house was afterwards built on part of the land. The present income is £23 12s., which is given to the preacher at Blackley and to the poor.

[400] This arose from two sums of £20 each given in 1721 and later, half the interest to be given to the minister of Blackley Chapel and half to the poor. The income, £1 6s. 9d., is now given by the trustees to the poor.

[401] In 1695 he charged his manors of Withington and Heaton Norris with £4 for the poor of the two townships, and £4 for Didsbury School. In 1826 both rent-charges were paid by Robert Feilden out of lands formerly part of the manor of Withington. Colonel Robert Feilden of Bebington, grandson of the preceding, in 1874 disputed his liability, and dying soon afterwards his estate at Didsbury was sold, and the charity was lost.

[402] In 1728 he charged his lands at Grundy Hill in Heaton Norris with the payment of £5 yearly, of which £1 was to go to the schoolmaster at Barlow Moor End, and £4 was to be given in bread to the poor each Sunday in Didsbury Chapel. This is now incorporated with the following.

[403] In 1768 he left £50 for a bread charity similar to the preceding, and the two appear always to have been administered together. The total income, £6 18s. 8d., is given in bread at the churches of St. James, Didsbury ; St. Paul, Withington ; and St. John the Baptist, Heaton Mersey.

[404] Dame Ann Bland and Thomas Linney gave £100 each for the poor of Didsbury and district. Twyford's Warth was purchased, and the rent, £13, was in 1826 distributed according to the founders' wishes. The rent is now £7 10s., of which half is distributed in the township of Didsbury, and half in that of Withington, in accordance with customary practice.

[405] He in 1811 left £400 to pay certain legacies, and to use the interest of the remainder to pay £1 to the preaching minister of Didsbury, £1 to the school-

master, and £1 to th the said remainder hands of Robert Fei nterest. The abo Feilden desired to r this also, but was obl rep esenta i e te evading it.

[406] For an accoun the townships of Salf The income of h foundation now amo year. n 1630 he g from Manchester to at the junction f Street), and three clo Croft (or Mileworth appears, the Tue Fie Grea Bridgewater Street), all in Manc of ' poor, aged, needy of Salford. In 177 ment was obtained to grant building l the money was dis and churchwardens doles, in gifts of line

[407] In 6 h l ft

c.

Hooper,[420] Thomas Thorniley,[421] and Albert Edward Nuttall ;[422] for Stretford—Emma Bate.[423]

Among the more recent endowments[424] for Manchester and Salford are those of William Smith for various hospitals,[425] Isabella Catherine Denby for orphan daughters of tradesmen,[426] the Barnes Samaritan Fund with an income of £2,624 for medical relief and nursing,[427] John and Emma Galloway for relief of the poor of Hulme,[428] George Pilkington £417 a year for bedding and clothing,[429] Thomas Porter, £3,500 a year for outfits of orphans,[430] and the Westwood almshouses.[431] There are some further endowments for education,[432] and some smaller benefactions.[433]

SALFORD

Salford, Dom. Bk. and usually ; Sauford, 1168 ; Shalford, 1238 ; Chelford, 1240.

Ordeshala, 1177 ; Ordeshale, 1240 and common ; Ordesalle, 1292 ; Urdeshale, 1337 ; Ordessale, 1338 ; Hurdeshale, 1354 ; Ordesale, 1358.

The township of Salford lies in a bend of the Irwell, which, except for a few deviations caused probably by changes in the course of the river, still forms its boundary except on the west, where a line, 2 miles long, drawn from one part of the stream to another, divides Salford from Pendleton. The area is 1,329 acres.[1] The surface is comparatively level, rising on the north-west side ; on the south-west is a low-lying tract along the Irwell. The population in 1901 was 105,335.

There are five bridges across the river into Manchester, and a railway bridge ; two into Cheetham,[2] and another railway bridge ; two into Broughton ;[3] a footbridge into Hulme, and a swing bridge into Stretford. Starting from Victoria Bridge, on the site of the ancient bridge connecting Manchester and Salford,[4] and proceeding west along Chapel Street, Trinity Church—formerly Salford Chapel—is seen on the

north side. At this point the street is crossed by the road from Blackfriars Bridge to Broughton, which is afterwards joined by the old road towards Broughton from Victoria Bridge by way of Greengate. Further on, Chapel Street is joined by the road from Albert Bridge and Irwell Bridge. On the north side may be seen the Town Hall, and a little further on the Roman Catholic Cathedral. Then the hospital,[5] in what used to be known as White Cross Bank, is passed, and the Irwell is reached. The land on its bank has been formed into a park (Peel Park[6]), in which stand the museum and technical school. Soon afterwards the boundary is touched. Windsor is the local name for this district.

Turning south by Cross Lane, the Cattle Market is passed on the west side.[7] After passing the railway station and crossing Regent Road, the entrance to the great Salford Docks of the Ship Canal Company is seen. Cross Lane, as Trafford Road, continues as far as the swing bridge over the Irwell, the docks lying on its west side, and Ordsall Park[8] on the east. Part of the dock site was formerly the New Barns racecourse, where the Manchester races were held.

Turning to the east before reaching the bridge, a cross street leads into Ordsall Lane, which takes a winding course to the north-east for over a mile and a half, joining Chapel Street near the Town Hall. On the west side of the lane stands Ordsall Hall, an ancient seat of the Radcliffe family. A little distance to the north, Oldfield Road branches off from Ordsall Lane to join Chapel Street opposite the hospital. There is a recreation-ground between Oldfield Road and Ordsall Lane.

Regent Road, a great east and west thoroughfare already mentioned, begins at Regent Bridge over the Irwell, and after passing Cross Lane is called Eccles New Road ; on the north side is the Salford workhouse.[9]

The Manchester and Bolton Canal crosses Salford between Chapel Street and Regent Road, and joins

---

[420] By his will, dated 1897, he left £50 for the purchase of coal at Christmas for the poor of Heaton Mersey Independent Chapel.

[421] By his will of 1886, proved 1900, he gave £200 for the maintenance of the mausoleum, &c., and the residue for the clothing of poor persons attending St. John's Church, Heaton Mersey.

[422] By his will of 1892 he left £200 for the benefit of the sick poor of Heaton Mersey, and £50 for the provision of a Christmas treat for aged persons of the same place.

[423] In 1838 she bequeathed £300, one-half the interest for the Sunday school at St. Matthew's, Stretford, and the other half for poor persons who were communicants at that church ; this is given in bread.

[424] See the Manchester and Salford Official Handbook.

[425] The benefactions, dating from 1866 to 1874, amount to £110 a year, and are administered by the corporation.

[426] This was founded in 1847 ; the income of £139 19s. is administered by the Lord Mayor and three senior aldermen.

[427] Administered by trustees. The founder was Robert Barnes, a cotton spinner ; born in Manchester in 1800 he died at Fallowfield in 1871, having long devoted himself to works of charity. He was mayor of Manchester in 1851. In religion he was a Wesleyan, his family

having been connected with Great Bridgewater Street Chapel.

[428] This was founded by their children in 1895 ; the income, £28 12s. 10d., is administered by the Overseers of South Manchester. John Galloway was head of a great engineering concern in Hulme.

[429] The churchwardens and minor canons administer this fund, which dates from 1858. For a notice of the benefactor, who died in 1864, see The Old Church Clock (ed. J. Evans), pp. xc, 240.

[430] This was established in 1878 ; a board of governors has the management.

[431] This dates from 1877. It was founded by John Robinson, of the Atlas Works and of Westwood near Leek, in memory of his daughters. The income, £229 10s., is administered by trustees.

[432] Alderman Benjamin Nicholls, who died in 1877, bequeathed £3,400 a year for education. Peter Spence in 1879 left £5 4s. a year for the Manchester Sunday School Union. A. Alsop in 1826 and E. Alsop in 1838 left sums producing £89 for education at Blackley. The Byrom Fund, 1859, gives £120 a year for industrial schools at Ardwick. Elizabeth Place in 1855 left £42 a year for industrial schools.

[433] Admiral Duff in 1858 left £34 15s. a year for ' Protestant Scripture readers . . . members of the Church of England.' The Manchester Charity for the Protection and Reformation of Girls and Wo-

the Irwell by Prince's Bridge. The London & North Western Company's Exchange station, Manchester, lies in Salford, in a bend of the Irwell. From this the line runs south-west, mostly on arches, to Ordsall Lane station, at which point it is joined by lines from Manchester, and then proceeds west by Cross Lane station to Liverpool. There are large goods yards at this part of the line. The Lancashire and Yorkshire Company's line from Manchester to Bolton and Bury runs parallel with the other as far as Salford station,[10] situated to the south of Chapel Street, on the road to Albert Bridge ; it then proceeds west and north to Pendleton, having large goods yards along the south side, as well as a cattle station. There is a branch line to the Ship Canal docks.

Some Roman and other early remains have been discovered at various times.[11] Woden's Ford was 'a paved causeway across the Irwell from Hulme to Salford.'[12]

The oldest part of the town is the triangular area formed by Chapel Street, Gravel Lane, and Greengate ; much of it is occupied by the Exchange station. Greengate was continued north by Springfield Lane. In the centre of Greengate, near the junction with Gravel Lane, stood the Court House, with the cross at the east end. The Hearth Tax return of 1666 records a total of 312 hearths liable. The largest house was Ordsall Hall, then Colonel John Birch's, which had nineteen hearths, and there were a number of other considerable mansions.[13] A plan of the town in 1740 shows a line of houses along the west side of Cross Lane ; also the mill and kiln to the north-west of Ordsall Hall.

The present St. Stephen's Street, which was not then formed, may be taken to represent approximately the western boundary of the town a century ago. The New Bailey prison, built in 1787–90 and taken down in 1871, near the site of the Salford station, was at the edge of the town. The plan of 1832 shows a considerable development to the west of Ordsall Lane, between Chapel Street—then known as White Cross Bank, Bank Parade, and Broken Bank—and Regent Road. Houses also stood by the Irwell, between Adelphi Street and the river. The Town Hall and market had been built ; there were numerous churches and schools, also an infantry barracks, which stood till about ten years ago to the south-west of the junction of Regent Road and Oldfield Road. There is no need to dwell on the later history ; new streets have been opened out and lined with houses and business premises, and a great improvement was effected by opening the straight road above-mentioned from Blackfriars Bridge to Broughton Bridge.

Railways and docks now occupy a considerable share of the area. There are also numerous factories and mills, many large engineering works, breweries, and other very varied industries.

Salford retains very few old buildings of any archi-

tectural interest, the only one necessary to mention here being the Bull's Head Inn in Greengate, a picturesque timber-and-plaster building on a stone base with four gables to the street. It has suffered a good deal from restoration and alterations, however, and the roofs are now covered with modern slates. The south gable is built on crucks, an interesting survival in a wilderness of brick and mortar. The house, once the abode of the Allens, has lost the projecting porch and gable, which formerly gave it an air of distinction, and has fallen on evil days.

The town can boast no public buildings of architectural importance. The Town Hall in Bexley Square, of which the foundation stone was laid by Lord Bexley in August 1825, is a plain building with a rather dignified classic front of the Doric order, erected in 1825–7, but now found entirely inadequate for the purposes of the borough. It was extended in 1847, 1853, and 1860, but in 1908 a proposal for the erection of a new and adequate building was put forward. The Roman Catholic Cathedral of St. John is a good specimen of the decorated Gothic style of the middle of the last century (1855), and contains some fine work by E. W. Pugin. At the west entrance to Peel Park are the handsome wrought-iron gates formerly belonging to Strangeways Hall, and bearing the arms of Lord Ducie. A great number of good well-built early 19th-century brick houses yet remain in the town, many of them with well-designed doorways, but the majority have now been abandoned as town residences, and are occupied as offices and for other business purposes.

Henry Clarke, LL.D., a mathematician, was born at Salford in 1743 ; he became professor in the Military Academy, and died in 1818.[14] William Harrison, a distinguished Manx antiquary, was born at Salford in 1802 ; he died in 1884.[15] Richard Wright Procter, barber and author, who did much to preserve the memories of old Manchester, was born in Salford in 1816, and died in 1881.[16] James Prescott Joule, the eminent physicist who determined the mechanical equivalent of heat, was born at Salford in 1818. He died in 1889.[17] Henry James Holding, artist, was another native, 1833–72.[18] Joseph Kay, economist, was born at Ordsall Cottage in 1821 ; he was judge of the Salford Court of Record from 1862 till his death in 1878.[19] William Thompson Watkin, born at Salford in 1836, became an authority on the Roman remains of the district, publishing *Roman Lancashire* in 1883 and *Roman Cheshire* in 1886. He spent most of his life in Liverpool, where he died in 1888.[20]

Before the Conquest *SALFORD* was *MANOR* the head of a hundred and a royal manor, being held by King Edward in 1066, when it was assessed as 3 hides and 12 plough-lands, waste, and had a forest 3 leagues square, containing heys and eyries of hawks.[21] The manor was thus

[10] This station was the terminus of the line when first formed in 1838 ; the extension to Victoria Station was effected six years later.

[11] Watkin, *Roman Lancs.* 38 ; *Lancs. and Ches. Antiq. Soc.* v, 329 ; x, 251.

[12] Thus Barritt the antiquary, who invented the name. The ford is marked on the plan of 1740. 'Woden's Cave,' in Ordsall, was near the Salford end. See *Manch. Guardian N. and Q.* no. 749 ; Hibbert-Ware, *Manch. Foundations,* i, 5–7.

[13] Subs. R. 250–9. Dr. Chadwick had 12 hearths, Robert Birch and Alexander Davie 10 each, Major John Byrom 9, Richard Pennington and Hugh Johnson 8, William Tassle 7, Joshua Wilson, William Higginbotham, James Johnson, Mr. Hewitt, and Dr. Davenport 6 each ; there were four houses with 5 hearths, ten with 4, and fourteen with 3.

[14] There are notices of him in Baines' *Lancs.* and in *Dict. Nat. Biog.*

[15] There is a notice of him in *Dict. Nat. Biog.*

[16] His works include *Mem. of Manch. Streets* and *Bygone Manch.* To the posthumous edition of his *Barber's Shop* (1883) is prefixed a memoir by Mr. W. E. A. Axon ; see also *Pal. Note Bk.* i, 165, and *Dict. Nat. Biog.*

[17] See *Dict. Nat. Biog.*

[18] Ibid.   [19] Ibid.   [20] Ibid.

[21] *V.C.H. Lancs.* i, 287.

much more extensive than the present township. Since the Conquest Salford proper has always been retained by the lord of the land 'between Ribble and Mersey' as part of his demesne, and has therefore descended with the honour of Lancaster, remaining to the present day a manor of the king as Duke of Lancaster. The headship of the hundred has likewise been retained by it.

DUCHY OF LANCASTER. *England differenced with a label azure.*

The men of Salford in 1168 paid £14 10s. to the aid for marrying the king's daughter.[22] An increase of 4s. for the half-year appears in the rent of the manor of 1201.[23] In 1226 the assized rent of Salford was 23s.,[24] and the vill, with its dependencies—Broughton, Ordsall, and a moiety of Flixton—paid 112s. tallage.[25]

The waste included wide strips along Oldfield Road, the road leading to Pendleton, and others. The inhabitants' pigs used to stray at will on this waste.[26]

The 'town of Salford and the liberties of the same' are frequently referred to in the Court Leet Records. Oldfield Lane seems to have been the most important liberty; in 1601 it had a separate bylaw man.[27]

BOROUGH About the year 1230 Ranulf Blundeville, Earl of Chester, erected his vill of Salford into a free borough, the burgesses dwelling therein being allowed certain privileges.[28] Each burgage had an acre of land annexed to it, and a rent of 12d. had to be paid to the lord at the four terms—Christmas, Mid-Lent, Midsummer,

and Michaelmas. Succession was regulated,[29] and right of sale admitted.[30]

A borough-reeve was to be freely elected by the burgesses, and might be removed at the end of a year. A borough court or portman mote[31] was established, in which various pleas affecting the burgesses were to be decided before the earl's bailiffs by the view of the burgesses.[32] No one within the hundred was to ply his trade as shoemaker, skinner, or the like, unless he were 'in the borough,' the liberties of the barons of Manchester, &c., being reserved. The burgesses were free from toll at markets and fairs within the earl's demesnes, but were obliged to grind at his mills to the twentieth measure and to bake at his ovens; common of pasture and freedom from pannage were allowed them, as also wood for building and burning.

A little earlier, viz. on 4 June 1228, the king had granted a weekly market on Wednesdays and an annual fair on the eve, day, and morrow of the Nativity of St. Mary, at his manor of Salford.[33]

By encouraging the growth of the borough as a trading place the lord derived an increasing rent; in 1257 it amounted to about £12 a year.[34] The extent made in 1346 shows that there were then 129⅓ burgages in addition to 12 acres in the place of another burgage, each rendering the 12d. yearly rent. There were also a number of free tenants paying over £8 10s. for lands in Salford and adjoining it. The profits of the portmote were valued at 12s. a year. The total was therefore nearly £16 a year.[35]

The records of the portmote court from 1597 to 1669 are in the possession of the corporation. The head of the Molyneux of Sefton family, as hereditary steward of the hundred, presided, except during the

---

[22] Farrer, *Lancs. Pipe R.* 12.

[23] Ibid. 131.

[24] *Lancs. Inq. and Extents* (Rec. Soc. Lancs. and Ches.), i, 137. A toft in Salford by the bridge produced an additional 12d.; ibid. 138.

[25] Ibid. 135.

[26] Encroachments on the waste are frequently noticed in the *Ct. Leet Rec.* (Chet. Soc.); e.g. an encroachment in 1634 between the lands of Mr. Prestwich and the highway leading to the Irwell, 9 yds. in breadth and 50 yds. in length; ibid. ii, 15.

[27] Ibid. i, 28. In 1631 it was forbidden to allow swine to 'go abroad in the streets within the liberties of the White Cross bank and Shawfoot stile' (leading to Broughton Ford); ibid. i, 239.

[28] The original charter, with seal appended, is in the possession of Salford Corporation, at Peel Park Museum. It was printed, with notes and translation, by J. E. Bailey in the *Pal. Note Bk.* 1882; and more recently by Professor Tait in his *Mediaeval Manch.* 62, &c., with annotations which have been freely used in the present account of it.

The privilege of immunity from tolls in other fairs and markets of the county was claimed in 1541 against the mayor of Preston; *Duchy Plead.* (Rec. Soc. Lancs. and Ches.), ii, 161.

[29] On the death of a burgess his widow might remain in the house with the heir, so long as she remained unmarried. As relief the heir gave arms—a sword, or bow, or spear.

[30] A burgage might not be sold to religious. In any sale the heir had a right

of pre-emption. A burgess who sold his burgage was free to leave the vill, taking all his goods, on paying 4d. to the lord.

[31] It is called 'Laghemote' in clause 3.

[32] The pleas belonging to the borough included robbery, theft, and assault if no blood was shed. The fines were restricted in amount. For breach of the assize of bread or ale the offender forfeited 12d. to the lord for three offences, but on a fourth he was put in the pillory (*facet assiam ville*). A debtor who failed to appear paid a fine of 12d. to the lord and 4d. to the reeve. If one burgess assaulted another the former might make his peace 'by the view of the burgesses,' i.e. by a composition approved by them; he paid 12d. to the lord.

[33] *Cal. Close*, 1227–31, p. 54. In 1588 the fairs were said to be on Whit Monday and 6 Nov.; *Lancs. and Ches. Hist. and Gen. Notes*, ii, 131.

[34] *Lancs. Inq. and Extents*, i, 205. The receipts for a half year were: Assized rent of the borough, 65s. 3d., and 40d.; toll of the borough, at farm, 40s.; perquisites of courts, 5s. 3d.—113s. 10d.; to which was added 6s. 8d. paid by Agnes, the reeve's widow, for the wardship of her daughter's land.

[35] Add. MS. 32103, fol. 145, &c. The free tenants were:—

Henry de Pilkington, three islands of land by the bank of the Irwell, by charter of William de Ferrers to Robert son of Thomas de Salford, at 6s. 8d. rent.; John Bilby [Bibby], the common oven, with 4 acres, at 4s.; John de Radcliffe, 63 acres approved from the waste in Salford, Pendleton, and Pendlebury, at 31s. 6d.;

Thomas de Strangeways, 15 acres from the waste; John de Leyland, 5 acres, at 2s. 6d.; Robert Walker, John de Stanlow, and Adam Wright, in common 3 acres, at 1s. 6d.; Henry de Bolton, 34 acres, at 17s. 3d.; Roger de Manchester (?), 6⅓ acres, at 3s. 3d.; Henry Marche, 1 acre, at 6d.; Robert de Hur', 2 acres, at 1s.; William Magotson, 1 acre, at 6d.; Thomas de Pilkington, 2 acres, at 12d.; Thomas Geoffreyson, 5 acres, at 7s. 6d.; Henry son of William de Salford, 5½ acres, at 2s. 9d.

All the above tenants were obliged to grind the corn growing on those lands to the twenty-fourth measure, but had rights of pasture and turbary.

Other tenants were Roger Dickeson, Maud Linals, Ellen Shokes, and Henry son of William de Salford. John de Radcliffe and Henry de Pilkington held some other lands; the latter claimed the right to keep the pinfold, but had to provide lodgings at the lord's will in two of his burgages.

Many of the free tenants held burgages also. The most considerable burgageholders, however, were John de Prestwich, with fourteen and a fraction, and Henry de Worsley, with about the same. The other holdings ranged from half a burgage up to five. Among the burgesses were Adam de Pendleton, Alexander de Pilkington, John de Oldfield, James de Byrom and John his brother, and the heir of Geoffrey de Trafford.

The sheriff's compotus of 1348 shows a similar total; it states that John de Radcliffe had the water-mill at a rent of 66s. 8d.

Commonwealth period. The courts were held at Michaelmas and April. The officers appointed in 1597 were borough-reeve, constables, mise layers, mise gatherers, bylaw men, afferers, and ale-founders; in 1656 the following additional ones were elected: scavengers for the Greengate and Gravel Hole, scavengers for the Lower Gate, apprisers, officers for

surprising and robbing of coals, for pinning of swine trespassing, for mastiff dogs, for the pump, and for measuring of cloth.[36]

A number of grants of tenements and tolls in Salford are found in the Duchy Records,[37] and some private charters are accessible;[38] the Plea Rolls have some records of disputes among the inhabitants.[39]

[36] The 1597–1669 records have been printed in full by the Chetham Soc. (new ser. 46–8), the late Alderman Mandley being editor; a few earlier ones are at the Record Office, and that for 1559 was in 1857 in possession of Stephen Heelis, mayor of the borough; Raines MSS. (Chet. Lib.), xxxvii, 389.

The business at the courts was of the usual kind: admitting new tenants, adjudging on assaults, breaches of the laws regulating ale-selling, keeping swine, &c. In 1656 a man was ordered to remove, with his wife and children, or give security to hold the town harmless.

The danger of fire claimed attention in 1615, but it was not till twenty years later that expenditure was incurred on buckets of leather, hooks, and long ladders for use in emergency.

In 1608 the jury found that there was no cuckstool, but 'unreasonable women' might be put in the stocks or the dungeon. A general lay was ordered in 1619 to defray the cost of the cuckstool. The bridle was ordered to be placed on a scold in 1655. In the same year two men were fined for profaning the Sabbath. The laying of stalls upon the Sabbath Day had been forbidden in 1615. Three ingrossers were presented in 1658.

Among other offences it was reported (in 1650) that there was 'great abuse committed by divers persons' who brought coals for sale, 'by gelding and robbing their loads before they come to town.' Milk dealers (in 1646) were warned against selling it except 'by true measures, as quart, pint, and gill.'

The inhabitants were about 1606 annoyed by Manchester people driving their swine into 'the Wastes of Salford, there to depasture,' and officers were appointed to impound such swine.

In 1655 it was ordered that the constables should have 'that little house upon the bridge, formerly called Sentry house,' paying 2d. a year to the lord. 'Madam Byrom of Salford, widow,' in 1696 laid claim to the watch-house at the end of the bridge, which had been built by the Salford burgesses; Peel Park D. no. 4.

A number of place-names occur in the records: Galley Lane, Cross Lane, Garnet Acre in Oldfield Lane, High Lane, the Broad Gate towards Ordsall Hall, White-cross Bank and Sandivall Gate, Back Street, Parker Pits, Clay Acre, Docky Platt, Bird Greatacre, Penny Meadow, Lady Pearl, a spring called the Pirle, Hanging Meadow, Barrow Brook, Barley Croft, and Middlefield. Mrs. Byrom had 'two doles in the Oldfield' in 1621.

The footway to Ordsall (from Pirle Spring along the riverside) occasioned much disputing about 1610. One Richard Knott had stopped up a way 'over Goodsteele,' which, it was asserted, had been open for sixty years. Sir John Radcliffe had more recently opened a way over George Croft, 'for the ease of his children which went to school to William Debdall in Salford.'

William Freeman was in 1634 ordered to gravel the way 'where he makes ropes.'

A logwood mill is the 'great ditch in passed the northern e

It was ordered in 1 holding lands within ford should attend th sending every man a carry the same.

The keeper of the enforced poundage fo to their great grievan themselves protected charter. There are the custody of the ch box with lock and 1655. In 1650 a ren was ord red, an in the charter.

One of the Peel P acknowledgement by der, of London, dated received from the r on behalf of the burge of Salford several wei brass, 'sized and seal measures and standard These ere to be used

[37] In 1337 Alexan (? Pilkington) released Lancaster, his right two burgages, reserving

The township continued to be governed in the same way until 1791, when a Police Act was obtained for Manchester and Salford, and the administration of the town by commissioners appointed under it to a great extent superseded the manorial system.[40] In 1832 the parliamentary borough came into existence, one representative being assigned;[41] and in 1844 the municipal borough was created by charter. The area included the township of Salford, together with that small part of Broughton lying south of the Irwell, and it was divided into four wards, each with two aldermen and six councillors. At the same time a court of record was established, debts up to £20 being recoverable.[42] A coat-of-arms was granted in 1844. The town hall, built in 1825–6,[43] was purchased by the commissioners in 1834. The borough was extended in 1853 to include the adjacent townships of Broughton and Pendleton,[44] from which time the area has remained unchanged, except for some minor adjustments.[45] The borough is now divided into sixteen wards, each with an alderman and three councillors; there are seven wards in Salford proper,[46] three in Broughton and six in Pendleton. In 1891 an Act was obtained to unite the district, so that a uniform rate is levied throughout

BOROUGH OF SALFORD.
Azure semée of bees a shuttle between three garbs or, on a chief of the second a woolpack proper between two mill-rinds sable.

the borough. A separate commission of the peace was granted in 1870 and again in 1886, and quarter sessions were established in 1899.

The council has provided police and fire brigade. The cattle market is the principal one for the district. The gas supply[47] is in the hands of the corporation, which also has electric light works. Water is supplied by the Corporation of Manchester. There are four public baths, two within the township of Salford; a sanatorium, two cemeteries, both outside the township —at Weaste and Agecroft—and sewage disposal works at Mode Wheel, opened in 1883. A school board was formed in 1870. A Tramways Act was obtained in 1875,[48] and the cars are now driven by electricity; the lines extend as far north as Whitefield in Pilkington, and west to Monton. Four parks and a large number of recreation-grounds have been acquired and opened.

The museum and library was established at Peel Park in 1850, a lending department being added in 1854. It claims to be the first free public library. Queen Victoria, as lady of the manor, was patroness; hence the epithet Royal.[49] The natural history exhibits have been removed to Buile Hill, so that the museum at Peel Park is now an art collection. There are seven branch libraries, of which two are in Salford.[49a] There is also a technical institute.

Queen Victoria passed through the town on her visit to Manchester in 1851. The king in 1905 unveiled the memorial to the soldiers who died in the Boer war.

Apart from the Radcliffes of Ordsall the Salford families recording pedigrees at the Heralds' visitations were those of Booth, 1613,[50] Byrom,

wife were plaintiffs against William del Highfield in 1354; Duchy of Lanc. Assize R. 3, m. 5 d.; and in 1357 recovered a tenement in Salford against Joan daughter of Thomas de Pilkington, Cecily his widow, and William del Highfield; ibid. R.6,m. 2 d.

Matthew Newton in 1432 acquired a toft in Salford from Henry Chadwick and Cecily his wife; *Final Conc.* (Rec. Soc. Lancs. and Ches.), iii, 97.

[40] See the account of Manchester. Though the Act was the same, the commissioners for Salford were quite distinct from those for Manchester, and always acted by themselves. The legal separation took place in 1829.

[41] See Pink and Beaven, *Parl. Repre. of Lancs.* 304; the parliamentary borough included the three townships of Salford, Broughton, and Pendleton. The number of representatives was increased to two in 1868, and in 1885 to three, selected by three divisions—North, West, and South.

[42] The charter, dated 16 Apr. 1844, is printed in Reilly, *Hist. of Manch.* 553; it was confirmed by the Act 11 & 12 Vict. cap. 93. The wards were named Blackfriars, roughly the eastern part of the town between Chapel Street and Bolton canal; Crescent, the west and south-west; St. Stephen's, the north-west, and Trinity the north-east.

[43] A market originally adjoined it, but gradually decayed, the site being in 1862 utilized for the enlargement of the town hall. The 'flat-iron market,' a sort of rag fair, is held on Mondays by Salford Church.

[44] 16 & 17 Vict. cap. 32.

[45] Part of Pendlebury was added to Pendleton in 1883; Loc. Govt. Bd. Order 14672. An adjustment of the boundaries between Barton and Pendleton was made by the Salford Corporation Act, 1891.

1613 [51] and 1664,[52] and Davenport, 1664.[53]   Richard
Pennington and Nicholas Hewett were ordered to
attend the last visitation.[53a]

Other land-holders are recorded in the inquisitions [54]
and court leet records ; [55] many Manchester people
also held land in Salford,[56] as did several of the sur-

the surname Booth ; dying unmarried in
1788, he was succeeded by his elder brother, who also assumed the surname of
Booth and became ancestor of the present Gore-Booth family ; Booker, op.
cit. 26.

Robert Booth of Salford in 1726, as
heir-at-law and devisee of his brother Humphrey Booth, which Humphrey was eldest
son and heir of Robert Booth, made a
lease of a dye-house, &c. ; Mr. Earwaker's
notes.

[51] Visit. 35. Some account of this
family, with inquisitions, will be found
under Kersal in Broughton. The following fines refer to them : George Byrom
in 1547 acquired eight burgages, &c., from
Gabriel Gibbons and Katherine his wife ;
Pal. of Lanc. Feet of F. bdle. 13, m. 300.
Adam Byrom in 1552 purchased three
messuages, &c., from John (? Richard)
Gibbonson ; ibid. bdle. 14, m. 115. George
Byrom in 1557 purchased some land from
Ralph Radcliffe ; ibid. bdle. 17, m. 65.
Shortly afterwards Henry Byrom acquired
three messuages, &c., from George Byrom
and Margaret his wife ; ibid. bdle. 17, m.
106.   In the following year Adam Byrom
purchased ten messuages, &c., from Joan
Brereton, widow, and Geoffrey her son ;
George Byrom purchased messuages in
Salford, Manchester, Barton, and Hulme,
from Ralph Brown and Jane his wife,
Adam Holland and Ellen his wife ; and
Henry Byrom acquired land from Ralph
Radcliffe ; ibid. bdle. 19, m. 58, 80, 89.
Adam Byrom, in 1559 purchased a messuage, &c., from Richard Gibbonson,
Lawrence Ward, and Isabel his wife ; ibid.
bdle. 21, m. 102. Two years later he obtained another messuage from Thurstan
Tyldesley ; ibid. bdle. 23, m. 173.   Later
fines refer to the estate of Lawrence Byrom and Mary his wife ; ibid. bdle. 49,
m. 107 ; 50, m. 198 ; 53, m. 268 ; 56,
m. 118.

From a subsequent note it will be seen
that Adam Byrom's house was known as
Salford Hall.   It stood in Serjeant Street,
now Chapel Street, between the old bridge
and the chapel, but on the river side. The
mill was probably near it.   Note by Mr.
H. T. Crofton.

Deeds in the possession of W. Farrer
show that James son and heir of Robert
Walker (afterwards called ' of Withington ') in 1536 leased his burgage in Salford to Ralph Brown, and sold it in 1545 ;
in 1554 the purchaser sold to George Byrom, and the fine of 1557 confirmed the
transfer.

The Worsley family long held lands in
Salford.   In 1343 Henry de Worsley
leased to Robert the Miller 1½ roods upon
Sandywell, a rood in the Whitacre, 1½
acres on Ollerschagh and on Kolleschot,
and 3 roods in the Middlefield between
lands of John de Prestwich and Richard de
Pilkington, chaplain, deceased, at a rent
of 6s. ; Earl of Ellesmere's D. no. 118.
Joan Brereton, widow, of Worsley, was
found in 1511 to have held six burgages,
23 acres of land and 3 acres of meadow in
Salford of the king as of his duchy by the
service of 14d. ; Lancs. Tenures (Towneley) MS., fol. 28b.

[52] Dugdale, Visit. (Chet. Soc.), 68.

[53] Ibid. 96.   Edward Davenport, bachelor of physic, a grandson of Sir William
Davenport of Bramhall, was ' of Salford,'

in right of his second
of Humphrey Booth
[53a] Ibid. v.

[54] William son of
a messuage in Salfo
a rent of 12d.) to h
marr'ed one Roger D
and had a daughter
Bibby whose son   ]
1393-4.   Roger D
the messuage to St
Joan his wife and E
(died s.p.) ; Joan a
to William de Ra
under him being E
before 1359   Ell's
pass, but his bastard
possession and held i
ley MS. DD. no. 14

Possibly it was th
in 1338 the proper
Thoma d S lf d,
ford hall' that of E
Elizabeth his wife,
on heir daughters
life, with remainde
Raines MSS. (Che
In 1540 Andrew Ba
Agnes his wife sold
Byrom ; ibid. 35.
Sm'thills died in 15
&c., n Salford ; th
Duchy of Lanc. Inq

In 1420 a mess
was granted to Th
M   f S lf rd

4

27

...

rounding gentry.[57] The freeholders of 1600 were: John Radcliffe of Ordsall, Adam Pilkington, Edward Bibby, (Ralph) Byrom, Thomas Byrom, and Adam Massey of Oldfield Lane.[58] The following contributed for their lands to the subsidy of 1622: Sir John Radcliffe, Dame Anne Radcliffe, Humphrey Booth, Adam Pilkington, Adam Byrom, Thomas Hartley in right of Margaret his wife, and John Duncalf.[59]

The Protestation of 1641 was agreed to by 341 persons.[60]

The Crown was accustomed to lease out the profits of the market, mills, &c.[61]

ORDSALL, which may then have included Pendleton, appears in the Pipe Roll of 1177 as contributing 2 marks to the aid.[62] The manor of Ordsall was in 1251 granted by William de Ferrers to David de Hulton, together with a moiety of Flixton,[63] in exchange for Pendleton.[64] It descended for some eighty years in the Hulton family,[65] and on the partition of his lands made by Richard de Hulton about 1330 Ordsall was given to one of the Radcliffes, probably as near of kin.[66]

About 1354 John de Radcliffe obtained possession after long disputing.[67] He had many lawsuits,[68] but

[57] Besides those already cited the inquisitions name John Strangeways of Strangeways, Robert Radcliffe of Radcliffe, Ralph Assheton of Great Lever, and Sir Edmund Trafford; *Lancs. Inq. p.m.* (Rec. Soc.), i, 132; ii, 75, 288; iii, 327. Thomas son of Geoffrey de Strangeways in 1335 made an unsuccessful claim for land in Salford against Richard de Hulton and Maud his wife; De Banco R. 303, m. 83 d.; 304, m. 367 d.

In 1338 Cecily daughter of Roger the Barker ('Tannator') granted two burgages in Salford to Geoffrey son of Sir Henry de Trafford, and immediately afterwards Roger the Barker gave his lands to the same Geoffrey; De Trafford D. no. 99–100.

[58] *Misc.* (Rec. Soc. Lancs. and Ches.), i, 246–9.

[59] Ibid. i, 148. It appears that John Duncalf was of Oldfield Lane; *Lancs. Inq. p.m.* (Rec. Soc.), i, 284.

[60] *Pal. Note Bk.* iv, 100.

[61] In 1703–4 the mill, with power to grind corn, grain, and malt, was leased, along with part of the waste, to Edward Byrom, and the lease was renewed in 1733; Duchy of Lanc. Misc. Bks. 27, fol. 54 d.

The tolls of the markets and fairs were leased to John Bennett in 1699 and to John Walmesley in 1739; ibid. 27, fol. 181 d.

[62] Farrer, *Lancs. Pipe R.* 36. A half-year's increment of 4s. from Ordsall appears in the roll of 1200–1; ibid. 131; and the full increment of 8s. in the following years; ibid. 148, 163. It contributed 29s. 8d. to the tallage in 1205–6; ibid. 202.

In 1226 the assized rent of Ordsall was 32s.; *Lancs. Inq. and Extents*, i, 137.

[63] Gregson, *Fragments* (ed. Harland), 347. The two were to be held by the service of 2 marks of silver and the sixth part of a knight's fee. Out of the rent 20s. was charged on Flixton and 6s. 8d. with the knight's service on Ordsall. The Hultons had some earlier connexion with the manor, for in 1240 Robert de Hulton was summoned to answer for asserting common land pertaining to the manors of Salford, Ordsall, and Broughton; he replied that he held by a grant from his brother Richard de Hulton, and called Richard's son (also named Richard), to warrant him, but this son being under age the trial was deferred; Cur. Reg. R. 107, m. 9 d.

[64] See the account of Pendleton.

[65] In 1292 Richard son of David (de Hulton) was non-suited in claims against Edmund the king's brother, and against Adam de Prestwich, for tenements in Ordsall; Assize R. 408, m. 3, 36.

Richard de Hulton for the sixth part of a fee in Ordsall and Flixton contributed 6s. 8d. to the aid of 1302; *Lancs. Inq. and Extents*, i, 314.

Richa of 26s. Reddish, Richard holding court, a Reddish tance; Richard de Radc Ordsall, p. 162. Richa by the fol. 38. Robe a plain Richard his wife inherita Lostock, R. 1424, Robert plaintiff de Hul

. . .

SALFORD : ORDSALL HALL, GENERAL VIEW FROM THE NORTH-EAST, 18﹈5

SALFORD : ORDSALL HALL, BAY WINDOW OF HALL, ETC., 18 5

appears to have prospered, as his son Richard,[68a] who died in 1380, held not only the manor of Ordsall and a portion of Flixton, but also the adjacent estates of Hope and Shoresworth, together with lands in Salford and Tockholes.[69]

John de Radcliffe, the son and heir of Richard, was twenty-seven years of age on succeeding.[70] In 1385 he had the king's protection on his departure for Normandy in the retinue of Thomas de Holand, Earl of Kent and Captain of Cherbourg.[71] His title to Ordsall seems to have been called in question in 1399.[72] He was afterwards made a knight,[73] and died in 1422 holding the manor of Ordsall and the rest of the patrimonial estate, except Shoresworth and Hope, which he had in 1396

RADCLIFFE of Ordsall.
Argent two bendlets engrailed sable and a label gules.

leased to Robert son of Roger de Radcliffe all their right in the manors of Ordsall and Flixton, whereby their claim against John de Radcliffe and Joan his wife should be barred, John having Robert's estate ; Duchy of Lanc. Assize R. 5, m. 25 d. ; see also 6, m. 1 (Mich.). The suits went on with varying fortune, until in 1359 Robert and Maud released their claim, in return for an annuity of 33s. 4d. for Maud's life ; *Final Conc.* (Rec. Soc. Lancs. and Ches.), ii, 162.

In July 1356 John de Radcliffe made a claim against Richard de Langley, Joan his wife, and others, respecting lands in Salford and Pendleton ; Duchy of Lanc. Assize R. 5, m. 17.

Thomas de Goosnargh in 1358 proved his right to an annuity of 13s. 4d. granted from Ordsall by Richard de Hulton ; the defendants were John de Radcliffe the elder, Sir Henry de Trafford, John de Bold of Whittleswick and Katherine his wife ; Assize R. 438, m. 18. In the same year Henry son of Richard de Bolton claimed a tenement in Ordsall against John de Radcliffe the elder ; ibid. m. 9.

In the following year John son of Richard de Radcliffe (or John de Radcliffe the elder) was plaintiff; though he did not proceed against Henry del Wood and Joan his wife, and against Henry de Trafford and others, regarding lands in Salford ; his pledges were : (1) John son of John de Radcliffe, Richard son of John de Radcliffe ; (2) Richard de Windle, John de Radcliffe the younger ; (3) John de Radcliffe the younger and Richard his brother ; Duchy of Lanc. Assize R. 7, m. 7 (Lent, beginning 9 D.H.) ; m. 2 (Mich.) ; m. 4. (Lent).

[68a] John de Radcliffe died in or before 1362, in which year his son and heir Richard claimed part of his inheritance in Ordsall, Livesey, and Tockholes, formerly in the possession of Robert de Radcliffe and Cecily his wife ; L.T.R. Memo. R. 127, m. 8.

[69] *Lancs. Inq. p.m.* (Chet. Soc.), i, 8. Ordsall was held by knight's service and a rent of 6s. 8d. ; there were there a hall with five chambers, kitchen, chapel, two stables, three granges, two shippons, garner (worth nothing), dovecote (worth 2s. a year), orchard (12d.), windmill (6s. 8d.), 80 acres of arable land (£4), and 6 acres of meadow (6s.). In Salford

Richard held, by knight's service and 20s. rent, 40 acres of arable land (20s.). He was also bailiff of Rochdale.

He married Maud daughter and heir of John son of John de Legh, lord (in right of his mother Maud daughter of Sir John de Arderne) of a moiety of Mobberley ; the marriage brought the manor of Sandbach and other lands in the county. The Cheshire inquisitions of the Radcliffes are printed in Ormerod's *Ches.* (ed. Helsby), i, 415, 416 ; see also *Dep. Keeper's Rep.* xxxvii, App. 603–9. His second wife was Sibyl daughter and heir of Robert de Clitheroe of Salesbury ; *Lancs. Inq. p.m.* (Chet. Soc.), i, 149.

[70] The escheator was ordered in Sept. 1380 to deliver the manor of Ordsall and other lands to John son and heir of Richard son of John de Radcliffe ; *Dep. Keeper's Rep.* xxxii, App. 353.

[71] *Dep. Keeper's Rep.* xxix, App. 56. He did not go, and the protection was withdrawn ; *Cal. Pat.* 1385–9, p. 117.

[72] *Dep. Keeper's Rep.* xl, App. 528.

[73] In 1413 Sir John de Radcliffe became bound to abide the award of Ralph son of Ralph de Radcliffe on the matters in dispute between Sir John and his sons John, 'Averey,' Edmund, and Peter ; *Dep. Keeper's Rep.* xxxvii, App. 174.

[74] *Lancs. Inq. p.m.* (Chet. Soc.), i, 147–9 ; *Dep. Keeper's Rep.* xxxiii, App. 21. Ordsall was held by the sixth part of a knight's fee and 6s. 8d. rent ; and 50 acres in Salford were held by knight's service and 54s. rent ; the clear values were £10 and 50s. respectively.

From the Cheshire inquisitions it appears that he left a widow Margaret (who quickly married Robert de Orrell) and three younger sons—Alured, who died in 1462 ; Edmund, who died in 1446, leaving a son of the same name, aged eighteen ; and Peter, who died in 1468.

[76] He held Ordsall by the sixth part of a knight's fee in 1431 ; *Feud. Aids,* iii, 96. For some quarrels among the Radcliffes of Ordsall in 1428–9—John de Radcliffe being summoned for an offence against the sumptuary laws by Alured de Radcliffe—see Pal. of Lanc. Plea R. 2, m. 2b, and *Lancs. and Ches. Antiq. Notes,* ii, 130.

[76] Towneley's MS. DD, no. 1480 ; Joan the widow had had settled upon her lands, &c., in Flixton, Shoresworth, and Tock-

holes. It may be noted that according to the inquisitions after the deaths of his father and uncles, Alexander was thirty in 1442, forty-five in 1446, forty in 1462, and fifty in 1468.

[77] Pink and Beaven, op. cit. 56. Alexander son of Sir John de Radcliffe in 1445–6 held the sixth part of a fee in Ordsall, paying 16s. 8d. as relief ; he held Shoresworth and Flixton jointly with his wife ; Duchy of Lanc. Knights' Fees,2/20. Alexander Radcliffe in 1451 charged Lawrence Hyde of Barton and others with the death of Hugh Radcliffe his brother ; Coram Rege, Mich. 30 Hen. VI, m. 92

Sir William Radcliffe, made a knight in the Scottish expedition of 1544,[83] appears to have added to his patrimony ; he died on 12 October 1568, and was succeeded by his son John, then thirty-two years of age, an elder son Alexander having died before his father.[84] Sir John Radcliffe[85] died on 19 January 1589–90 ; the inquisition describes his lands in the counties of Lancaster, Chester, York, Lincoln, Nottingham, and Derby.[86] He had been knight of the shire in 1571 and 1572.[87] Alexander his son and heir was only twelve years of age. He was knighted at the sacking of Cadiz in June 1596,[88] and died on 5 August 1599 without issue, his brother John, seventeen years of age, succeeding him.[89]

John Radcliffe was made a knight in the following year, during the Irish wars,[90] and thereby freed from wardship.[91] He was knight of the shire in three Parliaments, 1620 to 1625,[92] but in 1627 was killed, or died of his wounds, during the Duke of Buckingham's expedition to the Isle of Rhé.[92] By his wife Alice daughter of Sir John Byron he left a son and heir Alexander, twenty years of age.[94] Though so young, he had been created a Knight of the Bath at the coronation of Charles I.[95] The dispersal of the family estates began about this time ; a moiety of Ordsall was mortgaged in 1634 to Humphrey Chetham.[96] Sir Alexander married the step-daughter of Robert Radcliffe, fifth Earl of Sussex, and had with her by the earl's gift the manor of Attleborough in Norfolk.[97]

At the opening of the Civil War he, in conjunction with Lord Derby, took an active part in favour of the king, and was in 1644 committed by Parliament to the Tower.[98] He afterwards made his peace.[99] He was buried at Manchester on 14 April 1654, leaving several children,[100] of whom a younger son, Robert, became ancestor of the Radclyffes of Foxdenton in Chadderton.[101]. The remainder of the Lancashire estates of the Radcliffes appears to have been disposed of by Sir Alexander or his son.[102]

The Chethams did not secure the whole of Ordsall ;[103] their estate descended to the Clowes

---

[83] Metcalfe, op. cit. 77 ; the arms are given as gules, a bend engrailed argent.

The will and inventory of Dame Anne, wife of Sir William Radcliffe, 1551, are in *Wills* (Chet. Soc. new ser.), i, 17, 226.

[84] Duchy of Lanc. Inq. p.m. xiii, 33. The manor of Ordsall with two water-mills, a fulling-mill, &c., and 20 acres of land, &c., in Shoresworth—which by this time seems to have been merged in the demesne—were held of the queen by the sixth part of a knight's fee and a rent of 69s. 8d. Seventeen burgages in Salford, 100 acres of land there, twenty burgages in Salford and Oldfield, and 30 acres in Salford, all held of the queen in free burgage and socage by a rent of 12s., were included in his possessions ; also manors and lands, &c., in Flixton, Pendleton, Hope, Monton, Newcroft, Moston, Tock-holes, and Livesey, Oakenrod and Spot-land, and Radcliffe. In 1561 he had made provision for his wife Katherine, who survived him and lived at Hope ; also for Richard Radcliffe, his younger son. It appears that Sir William's brothers Alexander and Edmund were still living, the former at Ordsall and the latter at Chenies in Buckinghamshire.

The pedigree of 1567 (referred to above) shows that Alexander Radcliffe, the eldest son, was at that date living.

Sir William's tomb in the cathedral, long ago destroyed, bore the following distich :—

' Sandbach cor retinet, servat Mancestria corpus,
    Caelestem mentem regna superna tenent.'

[85] He was dubbed at Hampton Court in Feb. 1577–8 ; Metcalfe, op. cit. 131.

[86] Duchy of Lanc. Inq. p.m. xv, 45. There is recited his provision for William, a younger son, and Margaret, Jane, and Anne, his daughters, from lands at Normanby, &c. ; John, another son, had lands in Notts. and at Moston. Anne his wife survived him at Ordsall.

In religion he was regarded by the authorities as a 'dangerous temporiser,' i.e. he believed the old religion, but conformed to the legally-established system ; see *Local Glean. Lancs. and Ches.* i, 137–9.

Sir John's will, beginning with the Catholic motto ' Jesus esto mihi, Jesu,' orders his burial in the choir of Manchester. He wished his sons to be well brought up, and to be sent to Oxford or Cambridge when fourteen. One son was to be a lawyer and to be sent abroad to study. The inventory shows live stock and goods valued at £1,468 ; Piccope, *Wills* (Chet. Soc.), ii, 68–72.

[87] Pink and Beaven, op. cit. 66.

[88] This is a statement in a pedigree of 1633. He is called ' esquire ' in the warrant for the livery of his father's lands in 1598 ; *Dep. Keeper's Rep.* xxxix, App. 558.

[89] Duchy of Lanc. Inq. p.m. xvii, 35. His mother, Anne, was living at Tock-holes. He had in 1599 granted to Mary Radcliffe and Thomas Gillibrand the manor of Ashby, with various lands in Lincolnshire and Derbyshire, for 2,000 years. His will, dated 22 Mar. 1598–9, confirms the dispositions he had made in favour of his brothers John, Thomas, and Edmund, and his sisters Margaret (one of the queen's maids of honour), Jane, and Anne ; Mary Radcliffe, his cousin, one of the maids of the queen's bedchamber, was an executor ; Chest. Epis. Reg. ii, 232.

[90] On 24 Sept. 1600 ; Metcalfe, op. cit.

SALFORD : ORDSALL HALL, NORTH FACE OF THE HALL AFTER REMOVAL OF PLASTER

Salford: Ordsall Hall, Window of the 'Star Chamber,' c. 1875

family. The hall was sold in 1662 to John Birch of Ardwick.[104] His issue failing, the manor passed through various hands, and is now the property of Earl Egerton of Tatton.[105]

Ordsall Hall has been in its best days a very fine example of a mediaeval half-timbered house, and is still of unusual interest. Within the last two generations it has suffered greatly from neglect and its gradual envelopment in a wilderness of mean and dirty streets. Leland mentions the beauty of its surroundings, when it stood in a pleasant park through which ran a clear stream, now hardly recognizable in the dirty waters of the modern Irwell, and even as late as sixty years ago Ordsall Lane ran between fields and hedgerows, with no buildings in sight except the Throstle Nest Paper Mills, the Blind Asylum, and some houses in Chester Road. The house stood within a rectangular moated inclosure, among gardens and orchards, and there were a number of detached outbuildings, barns, shippons, &c. The north and east arms of the moat still contained water, but the other two were dry. The entrance was from the north, through an embattled doorway in the brick boundary wall, which dated from 1639, being contemporary with the still existing brick west wing. The house was let in three parts, and much cut up by added partitions, the floor levels altered, and a floor inserted at half-height in the great hall, while all the ornamental timber work was hidden by lath and plaster. Some attempt at freeing the old work from its modern obstructions was made about thirty years since, when it was converted into a club for the workmen employed in a neighbouring cotton mill, the great hall being opened out and other parts of the house fitted up as reading and billiard rooms. In 1898 it became a theological college, and in 1904 a clergy training school; and in 1896–8 it was thoroughly repaired, and in part rebuilt, by Lord Egerton of Tatton, the church of St. Cyprian being built in 1899 on the site of the long-destroyed east wing. The lines of the moat are now represented by streets, and the boundary wall and gateway have vanished, together with the orchards and gardens and everything which once went to form a pleasant setting to the old hall; but a few hundred yards away a farmhouse yet stands, hidden among modern buildings and used as a lodging-house. One of the principal outbuildings was the Great Barn, with a nave and aisles divided by great oak posts, and sharing, with several others in the district, the entirely unfounded

---

Raines and Sutton, op. cit. 115. An account of lays, &c., paid for Ordsall demesne, both in Salford and Shoresworth, is given; ibid. 147, 149; for the goods in 'the new barn' in 1653, see ibid. 273.

[104] In Booker's *Birch*, 106, it is stated that Samuel Birch purchased Ordsall, and went to live there in 1662. From Earl Egerton of Tatton's deeds, however (no. 14–21), it is clear that the purchaser was his son, the celebrated Colonel John Birch, whose daughter Sarah became the heir; Booker, op. cit. 113. She married a relative, John Birch, and in 1699 there was a recovery of the manor of Ordsall and lands, &c., the vouchees being John Birch and Sarah his wife; Pal. of Lanc. Plea R. 469, m. 5.

In 1691 Colonel John Birch had conveyed Ordsall Hall to Leftwich Oldfield;

and in 1699 an indenture between John Birch and Sarah his wife (executrix of her father), Alice widow of Leftwich Oldfield, and others concerning the manor of Ordsall and the chapel of St. George in Manchester Church, sets forth that Leftwich Oldfield died soon after 1691, leaving a son and heir of the same name, a minor, and provides for the completion of the sale; Ordsall D. (Earl Egerton of Tatton), no. 24–28.

The manor next occurs in a fine of 1704, when John Stock was plaintiff and Alice and Leftwich Oldfield were deforciants; Pal. of Lanc. Feet of F. bdle. 253, m. 54; Ordsall D. John Stock, one of the trustees of Cross Street Chapel (Baker, *Memo.* 73), died in Nov. 1732, leaving a son John and a daughter Rose. After the death of the son in 1755 Ordsall

was sold to Samuel Hill, who in the following year sold to Samuel Egerton, a near relative. Samuel Egerton had an only daughter, who died without issue, and the Tatton estates on his death in 1780 went to his sister Hester, widow of William Tatton of Withenshaw. She at once resumed her maiden name of Egerton, and dying in the same year was succeeded by her son William, who died in 1806; Wilbraham, d. 1856; —s. William Tatton, created Lord Egerton of Tatton 1859, died 1883; —s. Wilbraham, created Earl Egerton of Tatton 1897, the present owner. See Ormerod, *Ches.* (ed. Helsby), i, 446. For the Oldfield family see ibid. iii, 273.

[105] See N. G. Philips, *Old Halls*, 15; *Trans. Hist. Soc.* (new ser.), vi, 260.

panels, and has a flat ceiling over the dais at the plate level, replacing a panelled cove.

At the north-east of the hall is the great bay window of unusual character, being in plan seven sides of a decagon, with pairs of square-headed lights on each side, and a transom at half height, carved with a running vine pattern. The wooden framing stands on a stone base, with a band of quatrefoils on the inside below the sill of the window, and over the bay is a rectangular chamber or upper story, apparently contemporary with it, its angles projecting in a somewhat awkward manner over the canted sides of the window. The bay opens to the hall by a four-centred arch of wood, and the room over it is also open for its full width, and is reached by a stair contrived in the north-east angle of the hall, within the lines of the passage at the north end of the dais leading to a north-east doorway on the ground floor. The west wall of the hall is framed in square panels inclosing quatrefoils and has at the plate level a wooden cove, the gable above which is similarly treated. In this wall are now two doorways, but traces of the third, making the triple arrangement of buttery, pantry, and kitchen passage, were discovered in 1896. The heads of the doorways, only one of which now remains, were four-centred, cut from a single piece of wood, and with carved spandrels, and at either end of the passage through the screens were similar but wider doorways, that to the north, which still is preserved, being the most ornate, and having a band of quatrefoils above the spandrels. The external north elevation of the hall, though now much repaired, preserves its original design with little alteration. The wall surface is divided into square panels inclosing quatrefoils filled in with plaster, and a continuous line of narrow lights, six between each pair of uprights, runs along the upper part of the wall forming a sort of clearstory to the hall. The upper story of the bay is similarly panelled, but has lost its original window, if such existed. Its gable is also panelled and sets forward on a cove, and a similar cove existed below the eaves of the hall. The framing of the bay window is warped and leans to one side, but is otherwise sound; small shafts ending in crocketed pinnacles run up the face of the mullions. The south wall of the hall was of the same character as the north, but has been entirely rebuilt in grey brick, with two very unattractive four-light windows in terra cotta.

At either end of the hall are buildings which contain work contemporary with it, those at the east end, which were the principal living rooms, being the more interesting. They are of two stories, the original part being one room thick, and having two rooms on each floor. The rooms on the south front are the principal ones, that on the ground floor being known as the Star chamber, from the gilt lead stars with which its ceiling of moulded oak beams is studded. It is doubtless to be considered as the Great Chamber, with a solar over, the name of chapel which has been given to the upper room being entirely fanciful. Its walls are covered on three sides with plain oak panelling with a cresting of Tudor flowers, and from the arrangement of the panelling it seems that the room has been originally wider from north to south. In the south wall is now a modern rectangular bay containing a window, the successor of a very picturesque and interesting bay window of wood two stories in

height, which survived, though in a mutilated state, till 1896. In plan it formed half of a twelve-sided figure, the alternate sides being treated as projecting semicircular bays with seven tall narrow square-headed lights in each. The plain sides were treated as windows of two lights, that in the middle being pierced in later times as a doorway to the garden. The room on the first floor over the Star chamber is also panelled, but with early 17th-century panelling with a modillion cornice and narrow oblong upper panels, the others being square. Above its canted plaster ceiling the mediaeval roof remains, with cambered tie-beam and arched braces beneath, and it was formerly lighted by a continuation of the bay window, ending under a rectangular projecting gable filled in with wooden studding. This room and the Star chamber have fireplaces on the east side, and the chimney-stack was found in 1896 to show clear signs of having been external, proving that at the time of its building the house extended no further eastward. An interesting theory worked out in some detail by the late E. W. Cox that this chimney belonged to a 14th century house seems to rest on too slight a basis of probability. The north side of this part of the house is now occupied by an entrance hall and stairs, the latter having newel posts of an ornamental baluster type, the lower one dated 1699. These are, however, only the posts of a bedstead, and the stairs are not ancient. The partition between these rooms and the great hall is of timber framing, and apparently modern, replacing a brick wall, which in itself cannot have been mediaeval. Adjoining the Star chamber to the east is a three-story block—or rather one of two stories with a low attic—which seems to be of 16th-century date, having on the first floor a room with panelled walls and a ceiling with a geometrical pattern of moulded ribs. The fireplace is of late Gothic type, and has over it four linen-pattern panels of oak. The ground-floor room beneath has no old features of interest, but in the attic, which seems to be an addition, probably of c. 1620, there is a good plaster panel of Jacobean style over the fireplace with the quarterly shield of Radcliffe between four roses: 1. Two bends engrailed, with a label of three points (Radcliffe); 2. Two bars, and over all a bend (Leigh); 3. Three billets and a chief; 4. A fesse between three garbs (Sandbach).

The block to the north of this shows no traces of antiquity, and the south-east wing already mentioned is also of no interest.

The buildings at the west end of the hall have been completely modernized on the south side, and their outer walls rebuilt in brick, and most of the old partitions on the upper floor removed. They are of two stories like the rest, and on the north, towards the courtyard, have a very picturesque timber-built elevation, with a large two-storied 17th-century bay window set against a Gothic front which is probably of the date of the hall, and has the same quatrefoil panels. The bay window is a half hexagon in plan, with square-headed transomed windows of four lights in each side, and quatrefoil panels below them to match the older work. They end below the springing of the gable, which is also panelled with quatrefoils and set forward on a coved cornice with a moulded and embattled string at its base. West of the bay the ground story has a range of narrow windows like those in the hall, now modernized, and on

RIVER IRWELL.

SALFORD : PLAN OF ORDSALL HALL AND ITS SURROUNDINGS IN 1849

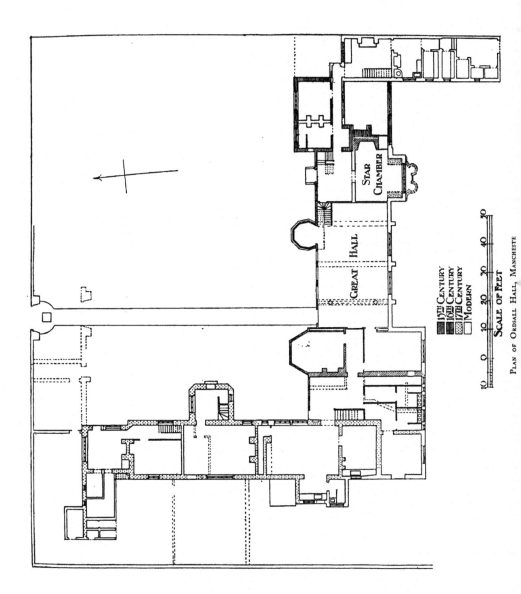

STAR CHAMBER

GREAT HALL

15TH CENTURY
16TH CENTURY
17TH CENTURY
MODERN

SCALE OF FEET

10   0   10   20   30   40   50

PLAN OF ORDSALL HALL, MANCHESTER

the first floor a very pretty six-light window projecting
from the wall, and carried on a coved and embattled
sill with Gothic tracery on the cove and a shield with
the Stanley badge of an eagle's claw. Its gable on
the south front was of half-timber work before its
destruction, and the east side of the gabled wing was
panelled with quatrefoils, which were cut into by the
south wall of the hall. It does not, however, seem
likely that the wing was earlier than the hall. The
interior of this block is unfortunately modernized, and
its original arrangements can only be inferred, as that
the kitchen stood at the south-west, with a lobby or
entry on the north towards the court, and between
these and the hall were the buttery, pantry, and
kitchen passage, while the floor above was divided into
chambers, perhaps five in all. These arrangements
must have been modified when the existing west wing
was added, on the site of an older wing, about 1639.
It is to be noted that the passage into the screens of
the hall is on the axial line of the former courtyard.
being halfway between the 17th-century west wing
and the foundations of the destroyed east wing. The
west wing was designed for the kitchen and servant's
quarters, &c., and the old buttery and pantry were
perhaps at this time converted into living rooms and
the bay window towards the courtyard added. The
wing is of plain character, in red brick, with square-
headed mullioned windows, now to a great extent
renewed in terra cotta, and having towards the court
a projecting bay containing a stair to the first floor,
on which was formerly a panel with the arms and
initials of Sir Alexander Radcliffe, a garter encircling
the arms, and the date 1639. Its place is now taken
by the arms of Lord Egerton of Tatton. The angles of
the bay are cut away below, but corbelled out above to
the square. The roof of this wing preserves its stone
slates, and with its several gables is still very attractive;
one of the original brick chimney stacks remains, with
single bricks set herring-bone fashion between the
shafts, as in other 17th-century work in the district. Near the north end of the wing the east wall
sets back on a line so nearly coinciding with that of a
foundation discovered in 1896, running westward
from the old east wing, that it may be taken as marking the width of an original north wing, and also
suggests that this wing was still in existence when the
17th-century work was begun.

There was formerly a fair amount of old coloured
glass in the windows of the hall and elsewhere, but
much jumbled together ; among other things the coat
of Radcliffe quartered with Fitz Walter in a garter, and
figures of Our Lady and St. Katherine, since removed
to Barlow Hall. Other things, including a lead statue
of Mercury, after John of Bologna, which stood in
the garden, were removed to Tatton.

The land tax in 1787 amounted to £210 [106] ; to
this the principal contributors were Samuel Clowes,

[106] Land tax returns at Preston.

[107] Ibid.

[108] *Picture of Manch.* by Joseph Aston,
1816.

[109] Glynne, *Churches of Lancs.* note of
1892.

[110] The tower seems to have been repaired before this date. Booker, *Hist. of
Blackley Chapel* (1855), 123, says 'the
tower is a square pinnacled one, newly
patched with red sandstones.'

[111] Notes to Glynne, *Lancs. Churches*,
1892, p. 50.

[112] Ibid. The Owen MSS. have copies
of the gravestone inscriptions.

[113] The following licences for this oratory are found in the Lich. Epis. Reg. :—
21 Mar. 1360–1, to John de Radcliffe,
for two years ; v, fol. 5.
7 Mar. 1364–5, to Richard son of John
de Radcliffe, for two years ; v, fol. 10.
19 Dec. 1366, to Richard de Radcliffe,
for two years ; v, fol. 15.
24 Oct. 1383, to John de Radcliffe, for
two years ; v, fol. 36b.

[114] Henry, chaplain of Salford, is named

in 1323 ; Coram Rege R. 254, m. 71b. The
Earl of Lancaster may have had a chapel.

[115] See the account of Humphrey Booth.
Hollinworth states that he built it at his
own cost, except that £200 was contributed by Sir Alexander Radcliffe and
others, and endowed it with £20 in
lands. Then Humphrey Booth, 'being
in great weakness, earnestly desired that
he might live to see the chapel finished,
which he did ; but immediately after the
solemn dedication of it by the Bishop of
Chester he more apparently weakened ;

descended with the Booth estates to Sir J. A. R. Gore-Booth. A district chapelry was assigned to it in 1839.[116] The present income is given as £1,340. The following have been curates and rectors :—[117]

1636	Richard Hollinworth,[118] M.A. (Magdalene Coll., Camb.)
1648	William Meek [119]
1658	Robert Brown,[120] B.A. (Emmanuel Coll., Camb.)
1667	John Hyde, B.A.[120a]
1694	Robert Assheton, M.A. [121] (Magdalene Coll., Camb.)
? 1731	Richard Assheton, M.A. [122] (Brasenose Coll., Oxf.)
1764	Thomas Barker, M.A.
1766	Robert Oldfield, M.A. (Brasenose Coll., Oxf.)
	Robert Kenyon, M.A. [123] (Brasenose Coll., Oxf.)
1787	John Clowes, M.A. [124] (Trinity Coll., Camb.)
1818	Samuel Booth, M.A. (Balliol Coll., Oxf.)
1859	Joseph Nelsey Pocklington, M.A. (St. Catharine's Coll., Camb.)
1861	Edward Allen, M.A. (Oriel Coll., Oxf.)
1876	Capel Wolseley, B.A.
1885	Henry Francis Gore-Booth, M.A. (Corpus Christi Coll., Camb.)
1902	Peter Green, M.A. (St. John's Coll., Camb.)

In recent times, owing to the growth of the town, a number of new churches have been erected, those in connexion with the Establishment being St. Stephen's, near the Town Hall, 1794 ; [125] St. Philip's, more to the west at White Cross Bank, 1825 ; [126] Christ Church, near the Crescent, 1831, enlarged 1847 ; [127] St. Matthias, Broughton Road,[128] and St. Bartholomew's, Oldfield Road,[129] 1842, enlarged in 1863 and 1887 respectively ; St. Simon's, in the extreme north corner of the township, 1849 ; [130] the Stowell Memorial Church, 1869 ; [131] St. Clement's,[132] and St. Cyprian's,

both in Ordsall, 1878 and 1899 ; and St. Ignatius, 1903. All are entitled rectories. The patronage is in most cases in the hands of different bodies of trustees, but to St. Simon's the Crown and the Bishop of Manchester present alternately, while the Dean and canons of Manchester are patrons of St. Philip's and St. Stephen's. There are mission rooms in connexion with nearly every church.

The Wesleyan Methodists had a chapel in Gravel Lane as early as 1790 ; a new one close by has replaced it. The same denomination has other churches in Irwell Street, built in 1827, and now used for the Manchester Mission ; Regent Road, 1870, Ordsall Park, and Bedford Street. The Primitive Methodists have a church in Trafford Road, near the docks ; the United Free Church has two in Salford, and another in Eccles New Road ; the Independent Methodists, who had one near Cook Street in 1807, now have one near the cattle market.[133]

The Baptists have a church in Great George Street, founded in 1833 and rebuilt in 1851.

The Congregationalists appeared in Windsor in 1797, when one John Joule built a chapel there. Another was built in Salford proper in 1819, and is now the Central Mission church. These have been followed by Hope, to the south, in 1837, and Richmond to the north in 1846.[134]

The Welsh Calvinistic Independents had a chapel in Jackson's Square, now under Exchange Station, in 1824, their present one is near Cross Lane. The Welsh Calvinistic Methodists had a chapel called Salem in Rigby Street in 1866, but have removed to Pendleton.

The Presbyterian Church of England has a place of worship in Chapel Street, built in 1847.[135]

The Unitarians built the above-named chapel in Jackson's Square, but had by 1824 removed to an adjacent one in Dawson's Croft ; their present place of worship, known as Pendleton Unitarian Free

---

then he earnestly begged that he might partake of the Lord's Supper there, and then he would not wish to live longer. It pleased God to revive him in such a measure that he was able to go to the chapel constantly till he was partaker of the Supper (which could not be done for some months after the consecration) in the chapel, and was never able to go forth after, nor scarce to get home'; *Mancunien-sis*, 117, 118.

Humphrey Oldfield in 1684 left his divinity books to be placed in the chancel of the chapel. Those left were in 1876 given to the Salford Free Library ; *Old Lancs. Lib.* (Chet. Soc.), 107.

The surveyors of 1650 recommended that it should be made a parish church for the township ; *Commonwealth Ch. Surv.* (Rec. Soc. Lancs. and Ches.), 6. An allowance of £35 10s. was made to the minister in 1655, and was continued to his successor ; *Plund. Mins. Accts.* (Rec. Soc. Lancs. and Ches.), ii, 55, 224, 273.

The certified income in 1717 was £60, including the £20 given by the founder and £40 from seats ; surplice fees and offerings came to about £2. The right of nomination had been given to Mr. Booth and his heirs by the Bishop of Chester, without any mention of the consent of the warden of Manchester. Two wardens were appointed ; Gastrell, *Notitia Cestr.* (Chet Soc.), ii, 92.

[116] The district was reconstituted in

1856 ; *Lond. Gaz.* 29 Mar. 1839, 1 July 1856.

[117] This list is largely due to the late J. P. Earwaker.

[118] See the notes on Manchester Church; Raines, *Fellows of Manch.* (Chet. Soc.), 138 ; *Dict. Nat. Biog.*

[119] He was considered an 'able and sufficient minister' ; *Commonwealth Ch. Surv.* 6 ; *Manch. Classis* (Chet. Soc.), iii, 441. He died in 1658.

[120] He conformed at the Restoration and was presented to Hoole ; *Manch. Classis*, iii, 421.

[120a] He became vicar of Bowdon in

Church, is at the extreme west end of the township, at Windsor.

The Swedenborgians had a New Jerusalem church in 1815 and later, but have removed to Wallness Road. The Bible Christians, a branch of the same denomination founded by the Rev. William Cowherd,[136] worshipped at Christ Church, King Street, from 1809; this about 1869 they abandoned for a new building in Cross Lane. A noteworthy member and minister was Joseph Brotherton, a local cotton spinner, who was the first member of Parliament for Salford, 1832 to 1857. A statue of him was erected in Peel Park in 1858.

The principal Roman Catholic church is St. John's Cathedral. The mission was not begun until 1844; the church, opened in 1848, was consecrated in 1890. The other churches are St. Peter's, begun in 1863, church built 1874; the Patronage of St. Joseph, 1871; Mount Carmel, 1880; and St. Anne's, Adelphi. There is a convent and school of the Faithful Companions of Jesus at Adelphi House.

BROUGHTON

Burton, 1177; Borton, 1257; Burghton, 1332, 1450; Bourghton, 1572; Broughton, Brughton, xvi cent.

Kereshale, Kershal, 1200; Kereshole, 1212.

Tottelawe, Tettelagh, 1302; Tetlawe, 1368.

In the west and south this township is bounded mainly by the winding Irwell. The northern and eastern portions are hilly, the ground sloping west to the river, and also to the south. The old hamlet of Broughton lay on the western side of the township, close to a ford across the Irwell. The higher ground in the north is known as Broughton Park and Higher Broughton; the more level tract to the south as

Lower Broughton, while the north-western arm, in a bend of the Irwell, is Kersal.[1] Almost the whole township is covered with buildings, there being many handsome residences in it.[2] The area is 1,426½ acres.[3] The population numbered 49,048 in 1901.

The principal road is that from Manchester to Bury, joined by another road from Salford, crossing the Irwell by Broughton Bridge.[4] From the Bury Road others branch off to the west, crossing the Irwell into Pendleton by Wallness[5] and Cromwell Bridges.[6] There is no railway in Broughton, but the district is served by the Salford electric tramways. Albert Park, close to Cromwell Bridge, was opened in 1877; there are several recreation grounds.

Some neolithic implements and other pre-Roman remains, as also some Roman coins, have been found.[7] The Roman road from Manchester to Bury passed through the township.[8]

Broughton was incorporated with Salford borough in 1844; there are now three wards—Grosvenor, Albert Park, and Kersal. A branch library was opened in 1890 and a reading-room 1905.[8a]

William Crabtree, the astronomer and friend of Horrocks, lived in the township, at Broughton Spout it is supposed.[9] There were ninety-five hearths paying to the hearth tax in 1666.[10]

The Manchester races were held on Kersal Moor from 1730 till 1847, with a short interruption.[11]

A duel was fought on the moor in 1804.[12] Great reviews were held there in 1831 and 1835, and Chartist meetings in 1838 and 1839.[13]

There were zoological gardens in Higher Broughton from 1838 to 1842.[14]

BROUGHTON was formerly ancient *MANOR* demesne of the honour of Lancaster,[15] being a member of the royal manor of Salford,[16] but was about 1190 granted by John, Count

---

[136] He was born at Carnforth; became curate of St. John's, Manchester, where he adopted the incumbent's Swedenborgian views, but added doctrines of his own, as in abstention from animal food; he died in 1816; W. Axon, *Ann.* 149.

[1] For Kersal generally see Mr. E. Axon in *Bygone Lancs.* A hill in the centre was known as Castle Hill or Cross Hill.

[2] The following from the *Manch. City News* of 20 Jan. 1906 gives a pleasant picture of Broughton as the correspondent saw it seventy years ago : 'At the Strangeways end of Broughton Lane were a few residences, whilst in the near fields was a nest of working men's lock-up gardens, wherein many a rare pink and picotee, and many a swelling stock of celery were nourished with fond and jealous care. The lane was knee-deep in sand, and the resort of numerous red and brown butterflies, till it joined the lower road from Broughton Bridge near the suspension bridge. So by a few cottages to the Griffin Inn, the Cheetham Arms, and its opposite ford —a noted bathing-place for Manchester youths. Round about this locality were several farms, one especially (now covered by Albert Park) lives in our remembrance as the pasture to which was taken each evening, more than a century ago, our ancestor's old mare, the first horse used in Manchester in a gin to turn the mill which perched or straightened the nap on the back of fustian pieces.

'Some little distance beyond the "Griffin," in Lower Broughton Road, opposite Castle Irwell, a clough dipped into the

Stony Knolls, and down it came the rain water and found its way to the Irwell across the road. This watercourse gave the clough the descriptive name of Broughton Spout. From Broughton Bridge, right and left of the new cut, Great Clowes Street, were fields. In the centre of one stood a mansion on an artificially raised mound. Being thus the exceptional house above the floods, it was called Noah's Ark, and was the residence of James Whitlow, solicitor, of St. James's Square, Manchester.'

[3] 1,418 acres, including 32 of inland water ; *Census Rep.* 1901.

[4] Built in 1806–69. Springfield Lane Bridge, to the east, was made in 1850–80.

[5] Opened in 1880. There is a footbridge to the south, from the end of Hough Lane into Pendleton. The suspension bridge, to the north, was opened in 1826 ; it is close to the old Broughton Ford, which was reopened in 1841. A bridge called Littleton Bridge has recently been erected by the Clowes family to develop the Kersal estate.

[6] Opened in 1882.

[7] *Lancs. and Ches. Antiq. Soc.* v, 296, 328, 330 ; x, 250, 251 ; xii, 118 ; ii, 146; viii, 127.

[8] Watkin, *Rom. Lancs.* 52.

[8a] Information of Mr. B. H. Mullen.

[9] *Pal. Note Bk.* ii, 262.

[10] Subs. R. Lancs. 250/9. William Allen's house had 12 hearths, Elizabeth Lever's 9, and George Kenyon's 8.

[11] 'A strange, unheard of race' for women in 1681 is noticed by Oliver Heywood as a sign of the times ; *Diaries*, ii, 284.

The earliest record of horse-racing at Kersal is contained in the following notice in the *Lond. Gaz.* of 2–5 May 1687 : 'On Carsall Moore near Manchester in Lancashire on the 18th instant, a 20l. plate will be run for to carry ten stone, and ride three heats, four miles each heat. And the next day another plate of 40l. will be run for at the same moore, riding the same heats and carrying the same weight. The horses marks are to be given in four days before to Mr. William Swarbrick at the Kings Arms in Manchester.'

The races were interrupted from 1746 to 1759 owing to the opposition of Edward Byrom ; note by Mr. E. Axon ; see further in *Lancs. and Ches. Antiq. Soc.* xxv.

[12] W. Axon, *Manch. Ann.*

[13] Ibid.

[14] *Manch. Guard. N. and Q.* no. 235.

[15] Broughton in 1176–7 paid ⅓ mark to the aid of the vills of the honour ; Farrer, *Lancs. Pipe R.* 36. In 1200 it is found among the other demesne manors paying an increment of 6s. (ibid. 131), which is given as 12s. a year in later rolls ; ibid. 148, 163. It paid 2 marks to the tallage in 1205–6 ; ibid. 202.

[16] In the 17th century Broughton was still regarded as a member or hamlet of Salford, and in 1640, on account of disputes as to the apportionment of taxes laid upon Salford and its members, it was agreed that when the whole paid 20s. Broughton, Kersal, and Tetlow should pay 5s. 5d. as their share of the 20s. ; *Salford Portmote Rec.* ii, 63.

of Mortain, to Iorwerth de Hulton. On becoming king in 1199 John did not confirm this grant, but gave Iorwerth the vill of Pendleton instead of it.[17] Restored to its former position it remained in the hands of the lord of the honour, yielding a varying rent,[18] for perhaps a century longer. About 1324 Broughton proper was held by Katherine daughter of Adam Banastre by a rent of 27s.,[19] and descended to the Harringtons of Farleton [20] and their successors in title, the Stanleys, Lords Mounteagle. In 1578 the manor of Broughton and lands there were sold by William, Lord Mounteagle, to Henry, Earl of Derby,[21] who gave the estate to his illegitimate son Henry Stanley.[22] Ferdinando Stanley, the son and successor of Henry, as a Royalist, had to compound for his estates in 1646.[23] He recorded a pedigree in 1664.[24] Ferdinando and his son Henry having mortgaged the manor and lands to the Chethams of Turton and Smedley, it finally, about 1700, came into the hands of this family.[25]

The manor then descended in the same way as Smedley, and on the partition of the Chetham estates in 1772 became the property of Mary younger sister of Edward Chetham of Nuthurst and Smedley, and wife of Samuel Clowes the younger.[26] She died in 1775, having survived her husband about two years,

and by her will left Broughton and other estates to her eldest son Samuel, who died in 1801, having survived his eldest son Samuel, high sheriff in 1777, and being succeeded by his grandson, also named Samuel. This last died without issue in 1811, and was, in accordance with a settlement he had made, succeeded by his brother the Rev. John Clowes, one of the fellows of Manchester Church, who made Broughton Hall his chief residence till his death there in 1846.[27] A younger brother, Lieut.-Colonel William Legh Clowes, who had served in the Peninsular War, then inherited the estates, and dying in 1862 was followed by his son, Samuel William, who in turn was in 1899 succeeded by his eldest son Captain Henry Arthur Clowes, late of the First Life Guards, born in 1867 ; he resides at Norbury near Ashbourne.

CLOWES. *Azure on a cheveron engrailed between three unicorns' heads erased or as many crescents gules.*

TETLOW was an estate partly in Broughton and partly in Cheetham, held in the 14th century by a family using the local surname,[28] the service due being

---

[17] *Chart. R.* (Rec. Com.), 27.

[18] *Lancs. Inq. and Extents* (Rec. Soc. Lancs. and Ches.), i, 13—in 1226 48s. assized rent. Ibid. 207—in 1257 assized rent of Broughton and Pendleton 78s. 6d., while other rents and profits, including the farm of the mill, and corn and other produce sold, brought the receipts up to £19 4s. 9d.

[19] Dods. MSS. cxxxi, fol. 39. Kersal and Tetlow had been separated from it. The tenure suggests a grant by Thomas, Earl of Lancaster, to Margaret sister of Sir Robert de Holland ; see the next note and the account of Great Bolton, also *Final Conc.* (Rec. Soc. Lancs. and Ches.), ii, 100–1.

[20] In 1346 John de Harrington held Broughton by the sixteenth part of a knight's fee, and Salefield Hey, taken from the waste, by a rent of 27s. 4d.; by charter of Thomas, Earl of Lancaster ; Add. MS. 32103, fol. 146b. To the aid of 1378 Sir Nicholas de Harrington paid 15d. for the sixteenth part of a knight's fee in Broughton ; Harl. MS. 2085, fol. 422. Margaret widow of Sir William de Harrington held it in 1445–6, the relief for it being 6s. 3d. ; Duchy of Lanc. Knights' Fees, 2/20. It is named among the Harrington of Farleton manors as late as 1572 ; Pal. of Lanc. Feet of F. bdle. 34, m. 76, 80.

[21] A settlement of the manor of Broughton and 60 messuages, &c. in Broughton and Hayfield was made in 1574 by Sir William Stanley, Lord Mounteagle ; Pal. of Lanc. Feet of F. bdle. 36, m. 146. The sale in 1578 included the manor and 30 messuages, &c. in Broughton ; ibid. bdle. 40, m. 152.

[22] The grant is recited in the Inq. p.m. of Ferdinando, Earl of Derby, in 1595 ; Add. MS. 32104, fol. 424.

[23] He was taken prisoner by Lord Fairfax at Selby and took the National Covenant on 10 Aug. 1644, being thereupon enlarged ; afterwards he conformed to all the ordinances of the Parliament and took the Negative Oath ; *Cal. of Com. for Compounding,* ii, 1446. The particulars of his estate the dem Jane for £20 5s living. P l nor was

£2,194, and James Chetham, as mortgagee, seems to have taken possession. Henry Stanley agreed in 1696 to sell the manor to George Chetham for £3,600.

The following fines relate to the manor, some being in connexion with the various mortgages : In 1625 Henry Stanley and Joan his wife were deforciants ; Pal. of Lanc. Feet of F. bdle. 108, m. 1. In 1661 George Chetham (as above) secured the manor from Ferdinando Stanley and Ursula his wife ; ibid. bdle. 166, m. 148 ; followed by a similar fine in 1667, James Chetham being the plaintiff and Ferdinando Stanley deforciant ; ibid. bdle. 179, m. 119. In a recovery of the manor in 1700 Henry Stanley was called to vouch ; Pal. of Lanc. Plea R. 471, m. 4 d.

[26] See the account of Smedley in Cheet-

SALFORD

the fortieth (later, the sixteenth) part of a knight's fee
and a rent of 6s. 8d. It
passed by marriage to the
Langleys of Agecroft,[29] and
then descended with Reddish
to the Cokes.[30] The name
Tetlow has long been dis-
used, but is preserved in Tetlow Lane.

KERSAL was in 1142
given to the priory of Lenton,[31] and a small cell called

LENTON PRIORY.
*Quarterly or and azure a
Calvary cross of the first
fimbriated sable standing
on steps of the last.*

Tetlow ; *Lancs. Inq. and Extents,* i, 314.
In 1324 Adam de Tetlow held 10 acres
in Broughton, formerly held by Jordan de
Crompton, by homage and the service of
the sixteenth part of a knight's fee ; Dods.
MSS. cxxxi, fol. 37b. It thus appears
that in Broughton as well as in Crompton Adam succeeded to the inheritance of
others. In 1346 Robert de Tetlow was
tenant, paying a rent of 6s. 8d. ; Add.
MS. 32103, fol. 146b.

[29] See the account of Agecroft in Pendlebury. Several Tetlow families are met
with in the Manchester and Rochdale
district.

In 1346-55 Richard de Langley and
Joan his wife held the fortieth part of a
knight's fee in Crompton and Broughton,
formerly held by Adam de Tetlow of the
Earl of Ferrers ; *Feud. Aids,* iii, 91. In
1358 Richard son of Richard de Tetlow
laid claim to it, alleging that Joan wife
of Richard de Langley was a bastard. It
was, however, decided that Joan was the
lawful daughter of Jordan de Tetlow and
Alice his wife, which Jordan (brother of
Richard de Tetlow, father of the claimant)
had held Tetlow. The mother of Jordan
was named Anabil ; she survived her son ;
Assize R. 438, m. 4 d.

The Langleys seem to have granted it
to the Strangeways family, who held it by
knight's service and the rent of 6s. 8d. ;
Lancs. Inq. p.m. (Chet. Soc.), i, 24, 50.
Afterwards it reverted to the Langleys,
and is named in their inquisitions, though
the tenure is variously described ; e.g. ibid.
ii, 145, where the estate is described as
eight messuages, 40 acres of land, 4 acres
of meadow, and 10 acres of pasture in
Tetlow in the vill of Broughton, held
of the king as duke by the fortieth part
of a knight's fee, and worth 4 marks
yearly. In the time of Henry VIII the
lands in Tetlow and Cheetham were said
to be held in socage by a rent of 1d., but
in 1562 the tenure was again described
as the fortieth part of a knight's fee ;
Duchy of Lanc. Inq. p.m. vi, 7 ; xi, 16.

Margaret wife of Roger Langley in
1445-6 held the sixteenth part of a fee in
Tetlow, the relief for which was 6s. 3d. ;
Duchy of Lanc. Knights' Fees, 2/20.

[30] It is named in fines relating to the
share of John Reddish and his wife in
1567 ; Pal. of Lanc. Feet of F. bdle. 28,
m. 279 ; 29, m. 126. Also in the inquisition after the death of Sarah Coke,
taken in 1630 ; Duchy of Lanc. Inq.
p.m. xxvi, 53. It is included in fines
relating to the Cokes' estate in 1667 and
1685 ; Pal. of Lanc. Feet of F. bdle. 179,
m. 92 ; 217, m. 20.

[31] *Lancs.* Pipe R. 326. The grant of
the 'hermitage of Kersal' was confirmed
by Henry II about thirty years later ;
ibid. 327.

The 'wood (*boscus*) of Kersal' was in-

cluded in the grant of Broughton to Iorwerth de Hulton as above described.

Some notes on the priory are given in
Lancs. and Ches. Antiq. Soc. i, 39.

[31a] *V.C.H. Lancs.* ii, 113.

[32] Pat. 32 Hen. VIII, pt. 8 ; the price
mentioned is £155 6s. 8d.

A settlement was in 1543 made by
Baldwin Willoughby and Joan his wife of
the manor and cell called Kersal, with
twenty messuages, a water-mill, 1,000
acres of land, &c., and 20s. rent ; the
remainder was to Ralph Sacheverell and
Philippa his wife, and the heirs of
Philippa ; Pal. of Lanc. Feet of F. bdle.
12, m. 103. From a later fine it appears
that Philippa was Baldwin's daughter and
heir. Another fine was made in 1548 ;
ibid. bdle. 13, m. 166. In the following
September Ralph Kenyon purchased the
whole ; ibid. bdle. 13, m. 152.

[33] As soon as Kenyon had purchased
Kersal he transferred one-third to James
Chetham of Crumpsall and another third
to Richard Siddall of Withington ; indenture of 10 Sept. 1548, among the Chetham Papers. Each paid Kenyon £132.
From this deed it appears that parts of
the land had been sold to Richard Radcliffe of Langley and Robert Ravald of
Kersal.

[34] The king in November 1548
granted to Sir John Byron the custody
of a third part of the third part of the
manor of Kersal, 6 acres in Manchester,
and 14s. 4d. rent in Ashton, the estate of
Ralph Kenyon deceased, whose son and
heir George was a minor ; George's
wardship and marriage were included ;
Duchy of Lanc. Misc. Bks. xxiii, 60 d.
A settlement of messuages and lands in
Kersal with a third part of the mill, and
4s. 9d. rent in Oakenshaw, was made by
George Kenyon in 1581 ; Pal. of Lanc.
Feet of F. bdle. 53, m. 151. George
Kenyon and Robert Ravald were in 1581
charged by Ralph Byrom and Adam Pilk-
ington with depriving the queen's tenants
of Salford of their common pasture in
Kersal Wood, stated to be 100 acres ;
Pal. of Lanc. Plea R. 270, m. 12, 12 d.

George Kenyon died in 1613 holding
a third part of the manor or cell of Kersal, a third of the mill and wood, and
various messuages and lands ; George his
son and heir was thirty years of age ;
Lancs. Inq. p.m. (Rec. Soc. Lancs. and
Ches.), i, 234. A settlement had been
made in 1590 by the father in favour of
George the son and Ellen his wife,
daughter of Richard Whitworth, with
remainders to Ralph younger son of
George ; to Hugh brother of George the
elder, and his son Ralph ; Earwaker
MSS. The Smethurst fields and Bradshaw meadow are named.

In 1623 George Kenyon sold the
middle Michael meadow and a lane from

purchased by Samuel Clowes in 1775.[39] The Chetham third[40] had already come into the hands of the Clowes family,[41] whose descendants retain their estate in Kersal.

The Kenyon third was about the year 1660 alienated to the Byroms of Manchester,[42] whose line terminated in the death of Miss Eleanora Atherton on 12 September 1870. It had one famous holder — John Byrom of Kersal, Jacobite, hymn-writer, and shorthand inventor ; he was born in 1692, educated at Trinity College, Cambridge, of which

BYROM of Manchester.
Argent a cheveron between three hedgehogs sable, a canton azure.

V

division ; Earwaker MSS. In 1702 Samuel Chetham of Turton and Henry Greenhalgh leased their parts of the mill for 99 years to Edward Byrom of Manchester, linen-draper ; the parties had lately made a brick-kiln ; ibid.

In 1704 land called Dauntesey's Warth was sold by Christopher Dauntesey and others to Henry Greenhalgh ; Piccope's notes. Another piece of this land, called Gooden's Warth, was in 1703 sold by Thomas Gooden of Little Bolton (in Eccles) to Otho Holland of Pendleton ; Manch. Free Lib. D. no. 53. The fields took their name from a ford across the Irwell to Whit Lane in Pendleton.

The Dauntesey interest in Kersal, indicated by the last paragraph, arose from a 21-years' lease in 1539 from Henry VIII to John Wood, one of his 'Oistringers,' of the site of Kersal cell and its lands, including Redstone pasture, Danerode meadow, with sufficient housebote, firehote, &c. to be taken from the king's woods adjacent ; a rent of £11 6s. 8d. was to be paid ; Agecroft D. no. 109. The lease was at once transferred to Robert Langley of Agecroft ; ibid. no. 110. Disputes arose between the lessee and the owners in 1560— James Chetham, Edward Siddall, and George Kenyon—which were submitted to arbitration ; ibid. no. 126.

[39] The Greenhalgh estate in Kersal appears to have come into the hands of the Hopwoods of Hopwood by a foreclosure, and was in 1775 sold as the 'lands, messuages, and tenements late belonging to Anne Greenhalgh' to Joseph Matthews, who at once sold them to Samuel and John Clowes for £4,260, as 'one undivided third part of the manor or lordship of Kersal, and the whole of the capital messuage called Kersal Hall, with the appurtenances belonging,' with third parts of the moor and mill. Samuel Clowes at the same time conveyed a moiety of an undivided third part of the manor to Elizabeth widow of John Byrom, M.A.; Piccope's notes.

[40] See the accounts of Crumpsall and Turton for this family. James Chetham died in 1571, holding a messuage in Kersal, a third part of the water-mill, and various other lands, &c.; also of the third part of a rent of 14s. 4d. from Ashton under Lyne ; and six messuages or burgages in Manchester. A settlement made in 1567 of Kersal Hall, &c., is recited in the inquisition, which states that Kersal and the rent from Ashton were held of the queen by the third part of the fourth part of a knight's fee and a rent of 13s. yearly. Henry the son and heir was twenty-eight years of age ; Duchy of Lanc. Inq. p.m. xiii, 19. For Henry Chetham's inquisition, showing the same estate, see Lancs. Inq. p.m. (Rec. Soc. Lancs. and Ches.), i, 2. He was succeeded by his son James, who from 1613 to 1619 made further purchases in Kersal ; Clowes D.

[41] This was agreed upon by the partition of 1772 between the sisters and coheirs of Edward Chetham of Nuthurst ; Mary the wife of Samuel Clowes re-

ce ved th with Br (Chet. S moiety 1775, as of Kersa

[42] No seen, bu 1668, w Kersal.'

For th with not xliv) 1s Alice will (15 Rober

: cope, Salford d burgages in Li tl chester, Salford duchy in and the exe utor was his George age ; D Adam's (Chet. S sons, Ge

Broughton : Kersal Cell, the South Front

BROUGHTO : KERSAL HALL, THE WEST FRONT

he became a fellow, and died at Manchester in 1763.[43] Like the manor of Byrom it was bequeathed to Mr. Edward Fox, who took the name of Byrom.

The house now called Kersal Cell occupies the site of the old religious house. It is a small two-story building of timber and plaster, much altered from time to time, but probably dating from the middle or end of the 16th century. It stands on low ground near a bend of the River Irwell, facing south, with the heights of Broughton and Kersal Moor immediately to the north and east. In more recent times a large brick addition has been made on the north, and extensions have also been made on the east in a style meant to harmonize with the timber front of the older part. The original house, which possibly is only a fragment of a larger building, has a frontage of about 56 ft. and consists of a centre with a projecting wing at each end. The west wing has a bay window in each floor, but the east wing has an eight-light window and entrance doorway on the ground floor and a slightly projecting bay above. Both wings have gables with barge boards and hip knobs, but the timber construction is only real up to the height of the eaves, the black and white work in the gables being paint on plaster. This is also the case with the east end and the whole of the front of the later extension on the same side. The roofs are covered with modern blue slates, and the west end is faced with rough-cast. The general appearance at a distance is picturesque, but at close view the house is too much modernized to be wholly satisfactory, and it is dominated by the brick building on the north, whose roof stands high above that of the older portion.

In the interior, however, Kersal Cell preserves some interesting features, many of the rooms being panelled in oak and some good plaster-work remaining. The ground floor is now below the level of the garden, the ground apparently having risen something like 3 ft. The plan has been a good deal altered to suit modern requirements, but preserves a centre apartment or hall about 18 ft. long with a seat against its west wall, which is oak-panelled for 6 ft., and has an ornamental plaster frieze. The lower room in the east wing has oak panelling all round to a height of 7 ft., and in one of the upper lights of the window is a circular piece of heraldic glass with the arms and name of AVNESWORTHE. The lower room in the west wing has a bay window 8 ft. 8 in. across and 5 ft. 6 in. deep. The lead lights in this and in other rooms of the house are of good geometrical patterns, and in one of the upper lights of the bay is an interesting glass sundial so fixed that the shadow is visible from the inside. The staircase is of Jacobean date with square oak newels and open twisted balusters, now varnished. It goes up to the top of the house, which in the centre has an attic. The most interesting room, however, is that usually called the chapel, on the first floor at the west end.

It is a small room about 18 ft. long and 13 ft. wide with a five-light window facing west. It occupies the rear portion of the west wing, the room in front with its bay window being sometimes known as the priest's room. What authority there is for these names does not appear, and at present the only indication of the back room having been used for religious purposes is a small square of 17th-century glass in the window depicting the crucifixion. The two side lights of the window are plain, but the three centre ones contain fragments of 16th-century heraldic glass. In the second light is a shield, with the arms of Ainsworth, with helm, crest, and mantling. The centre light has two small diamond quarries in brown stain, over the crucifixion already mentioned. On a beam in front of the window is an elaborate plaster frieze with three shields of arms, somewhat similar to those at Slade Hall, Rusholme. The centre shield bears the royal arms (France quartered with England) with crown and supporters, dexter a lion, sinister a dragon. The left-hand shield is of six quarterings, encircled by a garter, and originally with crest and supporters, but the dexter support and the crest have been cut away, when the plaster panel over the angle fireplace was inserted. The arms are those of Ratcliffe, Earl of Sussex, who quartered FitzWalter, Burnel, Botetourt, Lucy, and Multon of Egremont with his paternal coat.

The right-hand shield has the arms of Stanley, Earl of Derby, encircled by a garter, with crest (eagle and child) and supporters. There is a frieze in the south wall apparently of the same date with Tudor roses and fleurs-de-lys. Over the angle fireplace is a plaster panel of later date, with a shield bearing the arms of Byrom (a cheveron between three hedgehogs) with crest (a hedgehog), and the initials E. B. over. On each side of the shield is a fleur-de-lys, and below is the date 1692. The south and part of the north wall are panelled to the height of 6 ft. in oak, and the door is set across the south-east angle, balancing the fireplace.

There is a tradition that Dr. Byrom wrote 'Christians, Awake' in Kersal Cell, and that it was first sung in front of the house on Christmas Eve 1750, but both events are more likely to have taken place at Byrom's house in Manchester.

North of Kersal Cell, facing west towards the road, is Kersal Hall, a two-story gabled timber building, the front of which has been rebuilt in brick and painted black and white. The back of the house, however, shows the original timber construction above a lower story of brick with stone mullioned windows. The house preserves the central hall type of plan with passage and porch at the north end, and has north and south wings. It is a picturesque building with stone slated roof and brick chimneys. The hall has three windows to the front, and in the lower room of the south wing is some good 17th-century panelling. William Ravald purchased land in Kersal in 1548.[44]

[43] His Diary and other Remains have been published by the Chet. Soc. There is a life in *Dict. Nat. Biog.*

[44] The Ravald family can be traced back in Manchester to the middle of the 15th century. In 1473 William Ravald was tenant of a parcel of land near Irk Bridge at a rent of 4*d.*; *Mamecestre*, iii, 491. This or an adjacent parcel was granted to him by Thomas West, lord of Manchester, by charter in 1474; *Lancs. and Ches. Antiq. Soc.* iii, 109 (from an abstract of title of Sir Watts Horton and others, 1792). William son and heir of John Ravald in 1530 agreed with his brother Robert concerning a burgage in Manchester and a piece of land called the Cockpit at the south end of Irk Bridge; ibid.

In 1548, before the sale of Kersal Manor, William Ravald purchased a messuage, 22 a. of land, &c., in Kersal from Baldwin Willoughby, Joan his wife, Ralph Sacheverell and Philippa his wife (daughter and heir apparent of Baldwin); Pal. of Lanc. Feet of F. bdle. 13, m. 158. He died in April 1560, holding the messuage &c. in Kersal of the queen by

About 1619 this, or part of it, was sold to James Chetham of Crumpsall.[45]

Apart from the families named, little is known of the early landowners.[46] Allen of Broughton recorded a pedigree in 1665.[46a] In 1798 Samuel Clowes paid three-fifths of the land-tax, and a small additional sum in conjunction with Elizabeth Byrom, whose separate estate was but small.[47] The Protestation of 1641 found eighty-three adherents.[48]

In 1836–9 St. John the Evangelist's was built for the worship of the Established Church ;[49] St. Paul's, Kersal Moor, followed in 1852 ;[50] and to these have been added the churches of the Ascension, Lower Broughton, in 1869 ;[51] St. James, Higher Broughton, in 1879 ;[52] and St. Clement, Lower Broughton, in 1881.[53] The residence of the Bishops of Manchester, known as Bishop's Court, was fixed in Broughton by Bishop Fraser.

The Wesleyan Methodists have four churches in Higher and Lower Broughton,[54] the Primitive Methodists one, and the Methodist New Connexion also one, called Salem. The Baptists have a church in Great Clowes Street, 1868 ; and the Congregationalists one in Broughton Park, an offshoot of Richmond Chapel, Salford, in 1874–5.[55] The Presbyterian Church of England has a place of worship in Higher Broughton, founded in 1874.

The Unitarians have a school chapel. The Swedenborgians have a New Jerusalem Church in Bury New Road.

For Roman Catholic worship there are the churches of St. Boniface in Lower Broughton, and St Thomas of Canterbury in Higher Broughton. The latter mission, which includes Cheetham, was founded in 1879 ; the present church dates from 1901.

There is a Greek church in Bury New Road, founded in 1860.[56]

A Jewish synagogue was opened in 1907 in Duncan Street.

MANCHESTER

Mamucium, Mancunium, Anton. Itin. ; Mameceaster, Manigeceaster, A. S. Chron. 923 ; Mamecestre, Dom. Bk. ; this and Mamcestre were the usual spellings till about 1450, when Manchester appears.[1]

The township of Manchester, bounded on three sides—north, west, and south—mainly by the Irk, Irwell, and Medlock, has an area of 1,646 acres, including 27 acres of inland water. Formerly another small brook ran westward to join the Irwell to the south of the church ;[2] and two others, the Tib[3] and Shooter,[4] flowed south-west, the former through the

---

knight's service ; also three burgages &c. and a house called a Cockpit place in Manchester, of Lord La Warre by a rent of 22d. His son and heir William was nineteen years of age ; Duchy of Lanc. Inq. p.m. xi, 53 ; *Court Leet Rec.* i, 52 ; *Dep. Keeper's Rep.* xxxix, App. 558. A settlement of the estate in Kersal and Manchester was made by William Ravald in 1566 ; the remainders were to his wife Katherine for life, to his issue, to his sister Elizabeth wife of Edward Siddall, and to Robert Ravald of Kersal ; Pal. of Lanc. Feet of F. bdle. 28, m. 236.

William Ravald of Kersal died in 1587, holding lands in Kersal and Manchester and leaving a son and heir William, eight years old ; the Kersal lands were held by the hundredth part of a knight's fee ; Duchy of Lanc. Inq. p.m. xiv, no. 23 ; *Court Leet Rec.* ii, 8. The son came of age in 1600 ; ibid. ii, 155. He died in 1623, holding the same estate and leaving a son William, aged sixteen ; ibid. iii, 77 ; Lancs. *Inq. p.m.* (Rec. Soc. Lancs. and Ches.), iii, 409. This son about 1635 sold part of his property in Manchester, and more in 1660 ; *Court Leet Rec.* iii, 223, 228 ; iv, 260.

Robert Ravald of Kersal, mentioned in the remainders of 1566, died in 1578, leaving a son and heir Robert, aged fifteen ; he held a messuage and land in Kersal of the queen by knight's service ; Duchy of Lanc. Inq. p.m. xii, no. 15. His will is printed in Piccope, *Wills*, iii, 43–45. Robert Ravald died in June 1629 holding messuages and land in Kersal by the 200th part of a knight's fee ; Margaret his wife survived him at Kersal ; Robert his son and heir was twenty years of age ; Duchy of Lanc. Inq. p.m. xxvii, 41.

The Protestators of Kersal, 28 Feb. 1641–2, included William Ravald, William Ravald (son), Richard Ravald, Robert Ravald, William Ravald (*Pal. Note Bk.* iv, 125) ; and Mr. J. E. Bailey notes that the first-named William was baptized in 1607, married in 1632 Elizabeth Bale,

and in 1633 (on the of his son George) styled 'gentleman. wa bur'ed 1 Feb. 1 as a yeoman of branch f th f

Hist.

MANCHESTER   THE MARKET PLACE, ABOUT 1825

(From an old Print)

MANCHESTER : CHETHAM'S HOSPITAL, 1797

(From a Drawing by T. Girtin, after a Sketch by W. Orme)

centre and the latter to the east, to join the Medlock;[5] but all have long been covered over. The physical features have been greatly obscured by the buildings which cover the surface, which is in general level, though rising steeply from the Irwell. The portion of the town between Shooter's Brook and the Medlock is called Ancoats. The north-east corner of the township, on the bank of the Irk, is Collyhurst; half-way between this and the cathedral lies Newtown. The population in 1901 numbered 132,316.

In the north-west corner, at the junction of the Irk and the Irwell, stands Chetham's Hospital and Library, with Hunt's Bank to the west. The church, now the cathedral, stands in its cemetery, immediately to the south, the western tower overlooking the Irwell. At its south-west corner lies Victoria Bridge, representing the ancient bridge over the river to Salford. In the open space stands the Cromwell statue, erected in 1875. From the same point start Deansgate, leading south to Alport and Campfield near the Medlock, which river Deansgate crosses at Knott Bridge; and Victoria Street, a new thoroughfare, leading south-east to the Market Place. On the south side of the Market Place another main street of the city runs west to Blackfriars Bridge over the Irwell—being there called St. Mary's Gate and Blackfriars Street—and east and south-east towards Stockport—being called in turn Market Street, Piccadilly, and London Road. The Exchange Building stands in Market Street over against the old Market Place. From its west end may be seen St. Ann's Square, with the church to the south and a statue of Cobden in the centre; its east end stands in Cross Street, which leads past the old Nonconformist chapel and the Free Library to Albert Square, dominated by the new Town Hall. In the square are statues of Prince Albert, Bishop Fraser, W. E. Gladstone, John Bright, and Oliver Heywood. Piccadilly has the site of the infirmary on its southern side; in front are statues of Queen Victoria, Watt, Dalton, Wellington, and Peel.

From the infirmary Mosley Street, in which is the Art Gallery, runs south-west to St. Peter's Square, a little south of the Town Hall, and continues as Lower Mosley Street till it crosses the Medlock into Hulme at Gaythorn. From St. Peter's Square, Peter Street, in which is the Free Trade Hall, goes west to

---

[5] The bed of the Medlock is stated to be 14 ft. higher than its old level; *Manch. Guard. N. and Q.* no. 527.

[6] At the entrance of Oldham Road (formerly Newton Lane) stood New Cross, taken down in 1821. Suicides used to be buried there; ibid. no. 1051.

[6a] Subsidy R. 250/9. Among the larger houses—some of them being inns—were those of Jonas Ridge fifteen hearths, Philip Stampe thirteen, Mrs. Mary Halliwell and John Lightbowne twelve each, Edward Mosley, Mrs. Isabel Mosley, John Holbrook, George Venables, Samuel Dickenson, and Nicholas Mosley, ten each; there were also five houses of nine hearths, seven of eight, nine of seven, twenty-four of six, thirty-four of five, fifty-eight of four, and seventy-five of three.

[6b] Before the change the Irk 'was crossed by a narrow bridge, leading to a street sufficiently wide for only two carts to pass, having tall grimy buildings at the left or College side, and a series of cottages and workshops at the right, with here and there an opening by means of which a glimpse of the Irwell could be obtained. The buildings along the river were continued, and piled step above step from the stream to the churchyard above, and reached quite to the then existing Old Bridge. At the north-west corner of the present churchyard, or a little north of it, a flight of steps gave access to a flagged pathway leading round the churchyard, a portion of which still [1865] exists on the east and south sides; and foot passengers from Broughton could reach the Exchange by this path, either by way of Hanging Ditch and the narrow confined lane called Smithy Door, or by Churchgates, Short Millgate, and the Market Place, both these routes being almost completely blocked up on market days. Carts and coaches from Broughton had then to turn abruptly to the left at the upper end of Hunt's Bank, and to

company's system. The Great Central Company, originally the Manchester and Sheffield Railway, has, since its partial opening in 1841, had a share of London Road Station; the Midland Company has a goods station close by, named Ancoats, opened in 1870. The Great Northern has a goods station at Alport, close by the Central Station, which was opened in 1877 as the terminus of the railway of the Cheshire Lines Committee of the three companies last named; from it lines run to Liverpool and to Stockport.

The Bridgewater Canal has a wharf at Castlefield on the north bank of the Medlock. At the same point begins the Rochdale Canal, which proceeds east and north-east through the township. The Manchester, Ashton, and Stockport Canal begins near London Road Station and goes through Ancoats.

The Corporation Electric Tramways run through most of the principal streets, and on the west side are supplemented by the Salford tramways.

The open spaces in Manchester proper are comparatively few and small, with the exception of Queen's Park in Collyhurst. This was formerly known as the Hendham Hall Estate,[9] and was acquired by the Corporation in 1845. Adjoining is a cemetery, opened in 1837. Near the Irwell is the old St. Mary's Churchyard, called the Parsonage, and there are recreation grounds at Newtown, Collyhurst, Oldham Road, and Holt Town in Ancoats.

Chetham's Hospital, originally the college of Thomas La Warre, stands north of the cathedral on the site of the old hall of the lords of Manchester, at the north-west corner of the inclosure within which the ancient town was contained, and at the junction of the rivers Irk and Irwell. The situation was originally a strongly defensive one, the plateau upon which the buildings stood being upwards of 40 ft. above the ordinary levels of the rivers. Of the baron's hall, the predecessor of the present building, nothing is known, and attempts to prove that parts of the existing structure are earlier than the foundation of the college in 1422 have not been successful, though it is quite possible that some of the old stone and timber may have been used in the new 15th-century building. The hospital as it now stands is, roughly speaking, ⌐ shaped in plan, the longer arm facing north to the River Irk with a frontage of about 250 ft.[9a] The shorter west wing consists of a rectangular block of buildings erected round a small cloistered quadrangle with a frontage to the Irwell on the west side of about 105 ft. The living-rooms were arranged on the north, west, and south sides of the quadrangle, with dormitories over, and the great hall and warden's rooms occupied the east side. The long northern range of buildings contained the kitchen and offices, together with the guest-house, and has a short wing at the end running south-east, with a gatehouse to Long Millgate. The change in the surroundings of the hospital in recent years has been so great that it is now difficult to realize its original aspect, though the structure itself, apart from restoration, has undergone less change than might have been expected. Formerly standing high above the river bank, it presented a very picturesque appearance when approached from the north-west, but the growth of Manchester has surrounded it with tall buildings, altered the configuration of the ground around it by the making of new streets, and robbed it of all its external picturesqueness by the covering over of one river and the hiding of the other. The original character of the site is now no longer discernible, though some idea of the ancient appearance of the north side of the building may yet be gained from the narrow street on that side called Walkers Croft, which preserves in some measure the line of the path on the north side of the Irk. The buildings, which are of two stories, with walls of dressed red sandstone about 3 ft. thick, and roofs covered with stone slates, when seen from the playground on the south side have a low and rather undistinguished appearance, the line of the roofs being unbroken, and the walling having assumed the black hue so characteristic of Manchester. On this side the height of the walls to the eaves is only about 20 ft., but on the north the wall is 35 ft. high, the cellar being well lighted by windows towards the river. Apart from its greater height, however, the north front is architecturally more interesting from the fact of its being well broken up by projecting chimneys[9b] and garderobes, and by a raised platform at the north-west corner with a flight of stairs descending to the river.

The plan of the building would possibly be determined in some measure by that of the formerly-existing baron's hall, the line of which would most likely be fixed by the course of the two rivers. The northern range of buildings follows exactly the course of the Irk, lying rather north-west and south-east and not parallel with the church, which is set accurately east and west. The position of the main building round the quadrangle being once decided on, the length of the north wing would seem to have been determined by the gatehouse, which position was fixed by the street to which it opened—Long Millgate, then the principal thoroughfare from Manchester to the north. In the many changes which have taken place in recent years this street has lost its former importance, and the gatehouse, now overshadowed on both sides by the modern grammar-school buildings, is almost forgotten, the approach to the hospital being always from the south across the playground. Originally approached from the east, the chief entrance to the building proper was by the porch in the angle at the junction of the north and west wings; the door by which visitors now enter the library, if then in existence, being of minor importance.

The architectural evidence is not of itself sufficient to determine precisely the dates of the erection of the different parts of the building, but it is safe to say there is nothing earlier than 1422. How much was completed before the death of Thomas de la Warre in 1426, however (at which time he is recorded to have spent £3,000 on the buildings), it is impossible to say. It is likely that building operations were in progress for many years after this date, probably throughout the second quarter of the 15th century, and that one part was finished before another was begun, thus accounting for what are undoubtedly additions to the original building, but additions which appear to have been carried out within a comparatively short time of the foundation. Un-

[9] For the builder of Hendham Hall (William Dinwiddie, 1789), see *Lancs. and Ches. Antiq. Notes*, i, 24.

[9a] Another description with plan may be seen in *Pal. Note Bk.* iii, 160.

[9b] The great kitchen chimney was entirely rebuilt in 1902.

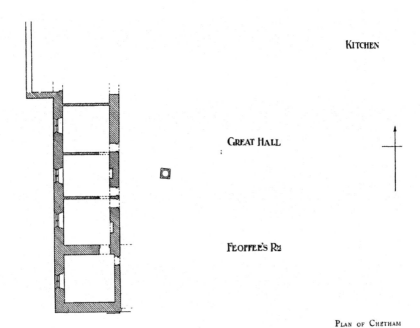

KITCHEN

GREAT HALL

FEOFFEE'S RM

PLAN OF CHETHAM

16ᵀᴴ CENTURY
17ᵀᴴ CENTURY
MODERN

GATE HOUSE

SCALE OF FEET

0   10   20   30   40   50

MANCHESTER.

[James Watts, photo.

MANCHESTER : CHETHAM'S HOSPITAL, THE CLOISTER

[James Watts, photo.

MANCHESTER : CHETHAM'S HOSPITAL, THE GREAT HALL

fortunately many of the documents relating to the early history of the college perished in the Fire of London, and the feoffees' minute-book does not contain any records of alterations of importance during the earlier occupancy of the college as a hospital, though it is clear that considerable reconstruction must have then taken place.

After the dissolution of the collegiate body in 1547 the buildings were used by several members of the family of the Earl of Derby, into whose hands they passed, as a temporary residence, and that work was done at that time is evidenced by the presence of the Stanley badges in different parts ; but after the sequestration of the Derby estates the buildings were allowed to fall into a dilapidated state, and were probably in a more or less ruinous condition when taken over by Humphrey Chetham's executors in 1654. The restoration at that time, however, besides putting the place in repair, involved considerable alterations in adapting the old college to its new use as a hospital and library. The chief of these changes—the staircase in the north-east of the quadrangle and the conversion of the dormitories into a library—are clearly evident. The gateway in Long Millgate was rebuilt in 1816, and in recent years (1883–95) the buildings have been thoroughly restored.

The work done between these latter dates included the restoration of the dining-hall, reading-room, library, kitchen, dormitories, cloister, stairs, house, governor's room, the rebuilding of the ingle-nook in the great hall. The cost was borne by Oliver and Charles James Heywood.

The chief feature of the building is the quadrangle round which the fellows' rooms and the great hall are grouped, which measures 40 ft. in length from north to south. Its width is 20 ft., but was probably in the first instance more, a good many changes having apparently taken place on the east side where the hall is situated. The cloisters themselves have been thought to be an addition, the supposition, however, being chiefly based on a portion of what appears to be an older plinth at the north-east corner, now partly hidden by the 17th-century staircase, which is of different height, and chamfered instead of being moulded. This plinth, but hollow-chamfered, recurs at the south-east corner at the end of the south wall, and is returned as far as the present east wall of the quadrangle, supporting the theory that the stone stairs from the hall to the reading-room are part of the first building. The difficulties of assigning dates to the various parts of the building round the quadrangle, however, are great, and it is, perhaps, safest to assume that the work was more or less continuous, but that changes were made from time to time in the originally-planned arrangement. It is unreasonable to suppose that the doors to the living-rooms were meant to open straight on to the quadrangle, and unless we assume some such proposition the cloister on the north, west, and south sides must have been part of the original intention. The rooms are 16 ft. square, with windows facing outwards, and each with a separate door to the cloister. Those on the north, three in number, are now used as offices or servants' rooms in connexion with the hospital, while the three rooms on the west are in use for various purposes connected with the library. The room in the south-west corner has been altered by the erection in part of it of a new staircase to the library over, this stair-case being that used by visitors to the reading-room. The larger room on the south side is now divided into two, one of which is called the teachers' and the other the muniment room. The cloister walk is 6 ft. 6 in. wide with stone-flagged floor and oak ceiling, and has an upper walk giving access in a similar way to that below to the separate dormitories. If the cloister had been an afterthought, as is sometimes stated, this would mean that the dormitories could have had no separate entrances ; and though this in itself is not unlikely, it at the same time makes the upper doorways of the rooms to be of later date than the wall, of which there is no evidence. It seems reasonable to believe, therefore, that the upper cloister, like the one below, was part of the original plan. On the west side the cloister consists of six bays, each with a three-light window under a plain four-centred arch without a label, the lights having cinquefoiled heads. The windows are separated by buttresses of two stages running up to within 3 ft. of the eaves, and in the upper story there is a window of two trefoiled lights in each alternate bay. The south side of the cloister consists of three similar bays, but on the north the introduction of the staircase has reduced the number to two, the destroyed bay being probably that in which the entrance to the quadrangle was situated. The present entrance is by a modern doorway cut through the second window from the south on the west side. The east side is occupied by the projecting ingle-nook and recess of the great hall with the staircase adjoining, leading over the cloister walls to the warden's rooms. There seem to have been a good many alterations on this side of the court from time to time, and the ingle-nook has been entirely rebuilt in recent years ; but it is not at all certain that the west wall of the hall originally ran right through and that the staircase is a later addition, although the manner in which the buttress of the cloister finishes against it suggests an alteration of some sort. The staircase, however, and the room over it, belong to the days of the college, though they may be considerably later than 1422. The quadrangle with its cobble-stone pavement and old well-head, though small, is a very charming feature of the building, its walls not having been so thoroughly restored as those of other parts, though some portions of the stonework of the windows have been renewed. Some of the old wooden lattices with which the windows were once filled are yet in existence.

The great hall, which is paved with stone flags, is 43 ft. 6 in. long by 24 ft. wide, 22 ft. in height from the floor to the wall-plate, and about 35 ft. to the ridge. The roof is open-timbered and divided into three bays by two principals, between which are solid framed spars, and the walls are of dressed stone their entire height. The screens are at the north end, entered through the porch on the east, with the usual two doorways and buttery and pantry on the north, and at the south end is the dais with a fine panelled and battlemented canopy over. The oak screen is simple in detail, and only 7 ft. in height, of contemporary date with the hall, but with a later embattled cresting. It is a very good early example, consisting of two speres set against the walls, and a movable middle length. There are no remains of a gallery over it, and in the first instance it probably had none. The room is lit by three two-light mullioned and transomed windows on the east side, and has a small dole-window at the end of the high table on the same side. The opposite wall is almost wholly occupied by the ingle-nook, about 11 ft. wide and 12 ft. deep, forming an irregular octagon, curiously twisted to the south, possibly to allow room for the former doorway at the north-east of the quadrangle. The fireplace was originally on the west side, but in the recent rebuilding it has been changed to the north, and the roof of the ingle vaulted in stone. The ingle-nook recess has a deep stone lintel 5 ft. 10 in. high, over which is a relieving arch, and is lit by two small windows to the quadrangle. Above on either side is a two-light pointed window with cinquefoiled heads and wide splays placed high in the west wall, and immediately adjoining it on the south close to the dais is the bay window, 7 ft. wide and 6 ft. deep, forming a kind of alcove between the ingle and the adjoining stone staircase and the warden's room. This staircase leads immediately from the west end of the high table, and is carried on a stone vault over the east end of the south cloister; it has already been mentioned.

South of the great hall, and originally gained from it by a door from the dais, is a room now called the Audit or Feoffees' Room, originally, perhaps, a kind of great chamber or minor hall, or more likely the common room. It is 23 ft. by 24 ft. and 12 ft. high, and has a square bay window on the east side 5 ft. 6 in. wide by 6 ft. deep. The ceiling is crossed each way by two well-moulded beams with carved bosses at the intersections, forming nine panels, having diagonal mouldings, and apparently of 15th-century date. The walls are panelled in oak, 8 ft. high, above which is a deep floriated 17th-century plaster frieze, and the room contains a good deal of interesting furniture.

The arrangement of the kitchen and offices at the north end of the hall follows no accepted type of plan, though the pantry and buttery, opening immediately from the screens, are in their usual place. The exigencies of the site, however, and the determining factors already alluded to, are presumably responsible for the disposition of the kitchen and other offices, which lie almost detached in the north range of buildings with no other way of communication to the hall than through the porch. The position of the kitchen, if it is the original one, and there seems to be no other part of the building where it could have been situated, is certainly unusual, but there is scarcely sufficient warrant to allow of the suggestion sometimes put forward, that it formed an older great hall, or that it was ever put to any other use than at present. It is 29 ft. long by 17 ft. wide, with walls of stone, and is open to the roof, with a wide open fireplace on the north side (now fitted with modern appliances) and lighted by two tiers of windows on the south. High up in the west wall is a hole, apparently for inspection, opening into a room on the upper floor, now the house-governor's bedroom, while at the opposite end in the south-east corner is a series of arches forming the covering to a narrow staircase now blocked up, but which formed the only access to a cellar, and to a small room on the same level as the kitchen beyond it eastward. On the floor of the cellar east of the kitchen is a stone with the outline of a snake cut on it, in memory of an encounter with a formidable serpent, related in the novel, *The Manchester Man*, the scene of which is laid here. Between the pantry and the kitchen a door leads from the porch by a broad flight of stone steps to the cellars, which, as before stated, owing to the fall of the ground are amply lighted along the north side, and whose ceilings are supported by massive oak beams. Beyond the kitchen eastward is a passage through the building, the width of which is here only 23 ft., to a raised platform on the north side, which now forms an approach to a modern addition originally a schoolroom, but now a workshop and gymnasium. The platform, however, which is about 15 ft. above the ground on the north side, appears to belong to the ancient building, and had a flight of steps leading from it down to the river. Beyond this to the east were apparently the hospitium, bakehouse, and wayfarers' and servants' dormitories, rooms now used on the ground floor for various school purposes, and above as the boys' dormitories. The roofs of these latter rooms, which extend the whole length of the eastern range, from the kitchen and the gatehouse, are fine and massive, the arrangement at the skew angle on the north-east being very well contrived by means of an angle principal. Adjoining the gatehouse on the ground floor on the north side is a small porter's-room with a narrow slit window facing the street. The room over the gatehouse, now approached by a later flight of outside steps as well as from the dormitory, may have served as a hospital, but it has been suggested that it may have been a chapel, and the angle at which the room is built being about east and west, lends some likelihood to the supposition.

Before the erection of the staircase in the north-east corner of the quadrangle, the way to the dormitories in the upper floor seems to have been by stairs at the opposite or north-west corner, in the space now forming the west end of the long corridor which runs along the whole length of the main building through the hall screens and the north cloister. The framing of the ceiling beams at this point indicates such an arrangement, and beyond the staircase at the end of the passage a door led on to a garden or small court where the fish-pond was formerly situated. The 17th-century staircase, erected after the building had been acquired by Humphrey Chetham's executors, is a handsome piece of Jacobean work with flat pierced balusters against the walls, lit by windows to the quadrangle, and with one of the upper windows of the great hall on its east side. The upper rooms on the north side of the cloister and hall are now occupied by the house-governor and librarian, the house-governor's room being a charming apartment with two windows facing north and an open timbered roof lately laid bare. From the bedroom beyond a door gives access to a small room over a porch, and on the north side is an old garderobe projection. There is another in front of the librarian's rooms, and at the extreme north-west angle of the building opening from the corner room (now part of the library) is an external door with pointed head leading on to a platform raised some 25 ft. above the river bank, forming the roof of a small north-west wing from which on the ground floor a flight of steps led down to the lake. The dormitories, which originally were separate rooms with divisions stopping short of the roof, which was continuous and open, are now thrown into two long rooms facing respectively west and south, forming the library proper. This consists of a series of reading recesses or compartments formed by

[James Watts, photo.

MANCHESTER: CHETHAM'S HOSPITAL, CORNER OF READING ROOM

[James Watts, photo.

MANCHESTER: CHETHAM'S HOSPITAL, THE SCREENS

MANCHESTER : CHETHAM'S HOSPITAL, THE GATEHOUSE

the bookcases standing at right angles to the external walls, and entered from a corridor on the inside by latticed doors. The bookcases originally stood only about 7 ft. high, or the height of the doors, but were raised in the 18th century. The series of wide square-headed three-light windows which light the library recesses are of late date, but the original open timber roof, similar to that of the hall, remains. At the north end of the west library corridor there is a piece of late 14th-century glass representing St. Martin of Tours and the beggar, in a frame in front of the window, together with a 17th-century fragment, the subject of which is Eutychus falling from the window. The south wing of the library is sometimes styled the chapel of St. Mary, but there seems to be no reason to suppose that it was ever so used in college times, and if a chapel was ever situated there it must have been during the Derby occupancy, or afterwards, when the buildings were put to various uses, including those of a Presbyterian and Independent meeting-house. The east end of the room, however, shows a portion of a 17th-century altar-rail and a bracket in the wall above, which, if they belong to the building at all, would seem to indicate the latter part of the Derby residence. The upper cloister is now used on the west and south side for storing books, and the north side forms a corridor. At the east end of the south cloister is a doorway opening on to the landing at the top of the stone steps from the great hall to the warden's room (now the reading-room of the library), which is situated immediately over the audit-room. There is also a later door to this room from the end of the library corridor adjoining, by which it is now usually entered. The room is the same shape as that below, with a similar square bay window on the east side, but has an open timbered roof of framed spars divided into two bays by a single central principal. During the Derby occupancy the spars were plastered over and a plain elliptical-shaped ceiling inserted, closely following the line of the spandrel over the fireplace at the north end of the room, which is of slightly later date, having been erected in honour of Humphrey Chetham by his executors, probably in the early years of the reign of Charles II. The wall plate, which is about 10 ft. high, is moulded and of oak, and apparently of the time of la Warre's foundation, but it is ornamented with the Derby badge of an eagle's claw and with portcullises, and the panelling which goes all round the room to the wall-plate is of 17th-century date. Over the mantelpiece is a portrait of Humphrey Chetham, and in the plaster spandrel above are displayed his arms with helm and mantling. The bay window has an elaborately vaulted plaster ceiling, with bosses ornamented with the Derby badges, but apparently of comparatively modern date, and the room contains a good deal of 17th-century furniture, and makes, perhaps, the most charming apartment in the whole building. In the bay is a table at which Harrison Ainsworth is said to have written several of his novels ;[9c] the connexion with Sir Walter Raleigh which is claimed for it must unfortunately be ruled

out. A tall clock case with a barometer dated 1695, and given by an old scholar of the hospital, Nicholas Clegg, is a more genuine relic. In the north-west corner a door in the wainscot leads by a second outer door of two thicknesses ($2\frac{1}{4}$ in.), under a four-centred stone arch, through a passage in the thickness of the wall to a small room, about 12 ft. long by 5 ft. wide, built over the stair and bay window of the hall with a range of windows on the west side to the quadrangle. The opposite or east side seems to have been originally open to the hall, a heavy oak beam, with wall posts and curved brackets, being still in position, the posts cut away about 4 ft. from the floor, probably giving the height of a rail or balustrade. At a

POETS' CORNER

later time the opening has been filled in with a narrow stone wall pierced by two quatrefoil openings, but what purpose the gallery or room originally served is not at all clear, and the date of the stone filling is equally a matter of conjecture, but it seems most likely that it was in the first instance a gallery open to the hall and was later turned into a private room, at which time, perhaps, the range of windows to the quadrangle assumed their present aspect. These windows, so noticeable a feature from the outside, preclude the idea that the room was intended as a hiding-place.

In 1878 a new school building was erected on the

[9c] Ainsworth lived and worked in London after 1824.

west side of the open space (playground), south of the hospital buildings, from the design of Mr. Alfred Waterhouse.

The original foundation was for forty boys, but as the endowment became more productive the number was gradually increased till 100 was reached. Lately, however, in consequence of the decline in the value of land and the increased cost of education the foundation boys have numbered only seventy-five.

The growth of the town has caused the destruction of nearly all the old gabled timber-and-plaster houses which were characteristic of Manchester streets at the beginning of the 19th century. Up to 1822, when the first widening took place, Market Street was chiefly composed of houses of this description, erected mostly in the 17th century, with here and there a later 18th-century brick building. One or two of such timber houses still remain, however, notably that in Long Millgate, formerly the Sun Inn, but now known as 'Poets' Corner,' which bears outside the date 1647 and the initials W^AF; and the Seven Stars

have been turned into offices or even common lodging-houses. These houses, plain in detail but of good proportion, generally have well-designed doorways, and often contain fittings belonging to better days.

Of the many handsome buildings which Manchester possesses the majority are either civic or commercial, but as a rule they are seen to less advantage than in most towns of similar size owing in a large measure to a certain lack of plan in the city itself, which is very wanting in wide and open spaces.[11] The atmosphere of the city, also, which turns all stone black in the course of a few years, is antagonistic to architectural work of the best kind.

The older public buildings of modern Manchester belong to the classic style, and are exemplified in the old Town Hall in King Street, now the Free Reference Library (F. Goodwin, architect, 1825), a characteristic specimen of the Greek Ionic of the period ; the Royal Institution, now the City Art Gallery, in Mosley Street (Sir Charles Barry, archi

THE SEVEN STARS INN

Inn, Withy Grove, which preserves its old timber gable to the street. Further up, in Shudehill, the Rover's Return Inn[10] also retains an old gable, but the front has been modernized by the insertion of a large bay window on both floors. In the Market Place, at the corner of the Shambles, is a picturesque old timber house with a gable on each elevation, now completely overshadowed by adjoining buildings.

A fair number of good 18th-century brick houses yet remain, more especially in the district between Deansgate and the River Irwell,[10a] many of them in the vicinity of St. John's Church being little altered and still used as residences, but in other parts less removed from the business centre of the town they

---

[10] The 'Rover's Return' is said to have formed a portion either of Withingreave Hall or of one of its outbuildings.

[10a] There are also some good houses of this description in Marsden Square, Cannon Street, and vicinity, now turned into offices and business premises, and outside the township in Ardwick Square.

[11] Piccadilly is an exception, but no adequate architectural advantage has as yet been taken of it. Albert Square, a new creation to show off the Town Hall, is not large enough for the purpose for which it was designed.

[11a] The original Infirmary building was erected in 1755, and consisted of a central block flanked by two small wings. After several additions and extensions a new front was added in 1832. The dome was a later addition, in 1853.

the open space in which it stood. It was pulled down in 1910.

A new infirmary is now completed in Oxford Road (Chorlton township).

The Free Trade Hall in Peter Street (E. Walters, architect, 1856) is a good example of Renaissance design, now much spoiled by the addition of a glass veranda in front of the open arcade on the ground floor. The front consists of two well-marked stories about 70 ft. high with a heavy cornice, and the interior contains a great hall which has seats for 3,236 persons.

In later years a Gothic tradition was set up by the erection in Strangeways (in Cheetham township) of the new Assize Courts (A. Waterhouse, architect, 1864), a fine building of its kind, standing back from the road on an uncontracted site of which full advantage was taken. The elevation is rather florid, with little of the restraint of the architect's later work, but much of the best work is in the interior, not only in the matter of planning, which is admirable, but of general design and ornamental detail. The City Court House, in Minshull Street (T. Worthington, architect, 1871), is a brick building of a pronouncedly Italian Gothic style, set in a region of tall warehouses at the junction of two narrow streets, but saved from insignificance by the fine tower which rises from the pavement at the outer angle.

The Town Hall (A. Waterhouse, architect, 1868–77), in Albert Square, described as ' one of the very few really satisfactory buildings of modern times,' [12] is purely Gothic in style, but less elaborate and far more dignified than the Assize Courts, being based rather upon early English and French precedents than upon those of Italy. The ashlar facing is of brown sandstone, now black, but in remarkably good condition after thirty-five years' exposure, disposed in blocks varying in size but regularly laid in courses of deep and very narrow stones alternately. The chief external feature of the building is the clock tower, which is carried up over the principal entrance facing Albert Square, and is 280 ft. in height. The plan is an irregular triangle, all three sides facing important thoroughfares, with a truncated angle or short front opposite to the state entrance. The building is widely known and generally admired as a masterly feat of planning, the offices and rooms being arranged round three internal courts, and corridors running in unbroken lines round the building on every floor following the inner sides of the main triangle. The great hall, which occupies the centre of the block on the first floor level, is 100 ft. long by 50 ft. wide, with a hammer-beam roof 58 ft. high, and the lower part of the walls is enriched by a series of twelve paintings by Ford Madox Brown, illustrating events in local history, each painting occupying the width of one bay beneath the windows.[12a]

Albert Square, which is somewhat narrow for its length, shows the Gothic influence in buildings on its south side and in the canopy for the Albert Statue, but it is otherwise architecturally uninteresting. The Royal Exchange (Mills and Murgatroyd, architects, 1871) indicates a return to the classic tradition, the

Corinthian order being used, but it is a building without particular distinction, and is set too near to the pavement on every side to be effectively seen, and has no direct line of approach to its main entrance. The dome, its chief constructional and architectural feature when seen at a distance, is effectually and deliberately concealed by a high blank upper story.

The John Rylands Library, built in memory of her husband by Mrs. Rylands (Basil Champneys, architect, 1890–99), is a fine structure in the Gothic style, built in red sandstone with a boldly original exterior to Deansgate, set back at a peculiar angle to the building line of the street. The library proper is placed on the upper floor, and on the ground floor the whole of the front part of the building is taken up with a spacious vaulted vestibule, and a wide staircase. The library consists of a centre corridor, 125 ft. long and 20 ft. wide, terminating in an apse, and has a groined stone roof 44 ft. high. It is divided into eight bays used as reading recesses, and each with a bay window, and a gallery runs completely round the central space, giving access to other book recesses above. The fittings throughout are of the most lavish character, and the interior is decorated with a series of portrait statues ranged in niches along the gallery front, as well as with carving and stained glass. The library contains over 80,000 volumes, including the famous Althorp Library purchased from Earl Spencer in 1892, and additions are being constantly made. It is particularly rich in early printed books and in Bibles.

The older warehouses were plain structures built in brick, but about the middle of last century a number of such buildings, which, in addition to being ordinary warehouses, were also the head offices of the firm, were erected in the centre of the town, possessing no little architectural merit. Many streets are composed almost entirely of these buildings, which, being constructed of stone, are now black, but their large scale and long frontages give them great dignity, Portland Street in this respect offering a very fine vista of unbroken line. The later warehouse buildings are chiefly constructed in brick and terra cotta, and steel construction has now largely superseded the older methods.

In addition to these and a number of churches and schools, there are many important and useful structures. The Corporation provides libraries, technical schools, markets, and other public buildings. There is a Central Post Office off Market Street ; the Inland Revenue Office is in Deansgate. Besides the infirmary there are numerous hospitals and charitable institutions.[13] The Nonconformists' Memorial Hall in Albert Square, intended to commemorate the steadfastness of various ministers ejected from benefices in 1662, and the Young Men's Christian Association building in Peter Street—about to be rebuilt—may also be mentioned. There are many theatres and music halls.

The woollen and cloth trades and the manufacture of smallwares appear to have been the original staple business of the town. There were also collieries at Ancoats and Collyhurst.[14] An iron foundry was

---

[12] *The Builder*, 7 Nov. 1896, ' The Architecture of our large Provincial Towns ; Manchester.' The writer further states, ' In after years it will probably be accounted one of the most excellent works

which the 19th century has bequeathed to its successors.'
[12a] W. E. A. Axon, *Archit. Descr. of the Town Hall*, 1878.

[13] See the list given in the general account of Manchester.
[14] *Manch. Guardian N. and Q.* no. 173, 217.

established in the 18th century.[15] The first calico printer occurs in 1763.[16] A sugar refinery existed in 1758.[17] There was a silk weaver in the town in 1637.[18] A tobacco-pipe maker in Todd Lane was in 1785 ordered to remove his works, as being a nuisance.[19] Manchester is the centre of the cotton manufacture, with its immense number of factories, bleach and dye works, and calico-printing works; smallwares continue to be an important part of the trade of the district, while iron foundries, engine and machine and tool-making works are numerous and important. Some of these factories and works are within the township of Manchester itself along the rivers and canals and in Ancoats, but the distinguishing feature is the large number of great warehouses for the exhibition and storing of the manifold products of the district.

BARONY The history of the barony of Manchester from its foundation in the early part of the 12th century until its gradual dissolution in the 17th has been related in detail in an earlier portion of the present work.[20]

MANOR Before the Conquest MANCHESTER was one of the dependencies of the royal manor of Salford.[21] Its position in 1086

is not quite clear, but shortly after, as the head of the barony,[22] it came into the possession of the Grelley family.[23] Descending in the male line till 1311, it passed on the death of Thomas Grelley to his sister Joan and her husband John La Warre.[24]

GRELLEY. *Or three bendlets enhanced gules.*

DE LA WARRE. *Gules a lion rampant between eight cross-crosslets fitchy argent.*

For over a century it continued in this family, but in 1426, on the death of Thomas, Lord La Warre, became by his dispositions the property of his nephew Sir Reginald West, son of Thomas's half-sister Joan la Warre by her husband Sir Thomas, third Lord West.[25] The manor and its dependencies

---

[15] Procter, *Manch. Streets*, 44; the proprietor, John Fletcher, died in 1785.
[16] William Jordan; see *Pal. Note Bk.* iv, 140.
[17] *Manch. Constables' Accts.* iii, 92.
[18] *Manch. Ct. Leet Rec.* iii, 260.
[19] Ibid. viii, 247.
[20] *V.C.H. Lancs.* i, 326–34. The court leet records show that as late as 1734 the constables of townships within the ancient barony were summoned to attend at Manchester, but they paid no attention to the summons; *Manch. Ct. Leet Rec.* vii, 25, 27. The practice of summoning the constables appears to have begun about 1625 (ibid. iii, 99), perhaps in consequence of the claims of the Salford Court for the attendance of the constables of Manchester; ibid. iv, 126, and a note below.
[21] In the present account advantage has been taken of Prof. James Tait's study of the barony, manor, and borough in his *Mediaeval Manch.* published in 1904.
[22] The 'manor' in the narrowest sense included the townships of Manchester, Harpurhey, Blackley, Bradford, and Beswick. At Blackley was the lord's deer-park; at Bradford was a wood, and another wood was at Alport (within Manchester). The manor was usually understood in a wider sense, the extent of 1322 mentioning seven or eight hamlets—Ardwick, Openshaw (Gorton), Crumpsall, Moston, Nuthurst, Ancoats, and Gotherswick; *Mamecestre* (Chet. Soc.), ii, 371.
[23] The extent of the manor made in 1282, soon after the death of Robert Grelley, gives an account of the manor-house of Manchester with its orchard, the small park called Aldparc and Litheak, the park of Blakeley with its trees and eyries of sparrowhawks, plats of demesne land at Bradford, Brunhill, Greenlawmon, Openshaw Cross, the Hules, Kepirfield, Millward Croft, Samland, and Kipirclip; rents from Denton and Farnworth, from the water-mill, fulling mill, and oven of Manchester, from the burgages, market, and fair there, from the ploughings near the vill, from Openshaw, the bondsmen of Gorton, the Hall land and mill of the same place, the bondsmen

of Ardw
and th
the fre
castle g
foot ba
co
value o
all these
corn-m

were in 1579 sold for £3,000 by the heir of the Wests to John Lacy, citizen and clothworker of London ;[26] and Lacy in 1596 sold them to. Nicholas Mosley, Lord Mayor of London in 1599.[26a]

The new lord of the manor was knighted in the same year and settled at Withington, acquiring this manor also and building the hall at Hough End.[27]

The manor descended regularly to his great grandson, Sir Edward Mosley, who, dying childless in 1665, bequeathed his manors to a cousin.[28] His widow, however, continued to hold Manchester till her death in 1680,[29] when, as the disposition made by Sir Edward had been set aside owing to litigation, and a division of the estates had been made, the manor went to a cousin Edward, who was succeeded in 1695 by his daughter Lady Bland. After her death in 1734 this manor passed to a second cousin, Sir Oswald

West, Lord La Warre.
Argent a fesse dancetty sable.

went by that highway to the lane to Beswick Bridge as far as Shootersbrook, thence to the head of Dogsfield, and by the boundary as far as the lane from Ancoats to Manchester, and so to Barlow Cross ; Chan. Inq. p.m. 5 Hen. VI, no. 54. The uses for which these and other lands were committed to trustees are not stated. The jury declared John Griffin to be heir general of Thomas La Warre's issue. A number of notices respecting the lands of Thomas La Warre may be seen in *Dep. Keeper's Rep.* xxxii, App. 337-9, 346 ; xxxiii, App. 27-9.

The inquisition after the death of Sir Reginald West in 1450 has some particulars of the manor, which included the hamlets of Withington, Denton, Openshaw, Clayton, Ardwick, Crumpsall, Moston, Nuthurst, Gotherswick, and Ancoats, as well as a borough commonly called Manchester of which each burgess paid 12d. yearly for a whole burgage and in which there was (or ought to be) a common oven at which all the burgesses and residents ought to bake. The fishery of the Irk, Medlock, and Gorebrook was the lord's, as well as the Manchester half of the Irwell. There were two mills, one a fulling-mill, the other for grain ; at the latter all the burgesses and tenants of the borough and hamlets ought by custom to grind to the fifteenth grain. Richard West, the son and heir, was nineteen years of age ; Lancs. Rec. Inq. p.m. no. 41, 42 ; *Dep. Keeper's Rep.* xxxvii, App. 177.

The rental of 1473, printed in *Mamecestre,* iii, 477-91, shows the sums for castle ward and sake fee received from the tenants by knight's service, the chief rents, tolls, and other rents and dues from the whole barony, the net total reaching £131. From Manchester proper the principal receipts were the burgage rents £8 0s. 3d., the fair and market tolls £3 6s. 8d., corn mill £6, fulling mill £2, rents of Over and Nether Alport £4 13s. 4d.

In 1503 the manor with its hamlets was restored by the king to Thomas Lord La Warre for a year ; Duchy of Lanc. Misc. Bks. xxi, p. 32 d. The will of

Thomas (son Ri dated 1505, sp t iv, 382 ; it names W'lliam, and Owen Thom W L 1498 called upon warrant he claimed as a free borough an amends of the assiz fangenthief peace-b

MOSLEY OF MANCHESTER, &c.

(From E. Axon's *Mosley Memoranda*)

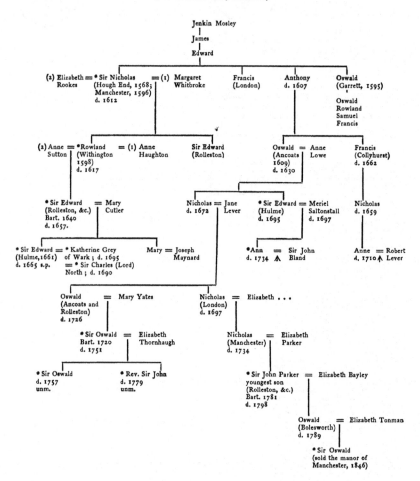

* Lords of Manchester.

borough perhaps arose about the same time, but the earliest charter extant is that of 1301, by which Thomas Grelley granted and confirmed to 'his burgesses of Manchester' certain privileges and liberties. The burgesses were to pay 12d. a year in lieu of all services, but no land in the town fields seems to have been attached to a burgage. From this it may perhaps be inferred that the townsmen were traders and artisans, as in modern times. Provision was made for the sale of a burgess's land, burgage and goods.[35] The heir, on succeeding, was to give the lord some arms as relief. The reeve was to be elected and removed by the burgesses; it was his duty to be a witness of all acquisitions of land within the vill. Certain pleas were to be heard in the borough court, called the portman mote or law mote; but charges of theft were reserved to the lord's court. Suit to the lord's mill was required, and pannage for swine in the lord's woods;[36] the swine were, however, excluded from the park of Blackley. The fines payable to the lord for various offences were limited by the charter, in most cases to small sums; an exception was the fine of 20s. for wounding on Sunday.[37]

Beyond this the town did not advance, no royal confirmation of its position as a borough being obtained. Hence in 1359, after a full inquiry, it was decided that Manchester was a market-town, but not a borough.[38] The duty or privilege of sending a repre-

were exported linen cloth, coals, bakestones and iron. A burgess was by the charter free of tolls, unless he used the stall or shop of a stranger. The profits of the tolls and stallage were £6 13s. 4d.; *Mamecestre*, i, 287.

[35] A burgess might freely sell land which he had not inherited, but his heir had a right of pre-emption; inherited land could, as a rule, be sold only with the heir's consent. A burgess might sell his burgage and buy another, or transfer it to a neighbour; if he sold it, wishing to leave the town altogether, he must give the lord 4d. He could transfer his personal chattels to anyone within the fee without the lord's interference, and in case he had no heir could bequeath his burgage and chattels to anyone.

In 1312 Sir John La Warre, lord of Manchester, granted Thomas Marecall and John Bibby plots of land in the market-place ' for a half-burgage'—*ad dimidium burgagium*—measuring 40 ft. by 20 ft., at rents of 6d. sterling each; Manch. Corp. D. One burgage was called the Kennel; it was opposite the gates of the lord's manor house; ibid. dated 1333,1340, 1345.

[36] The swine were allowed to go into the woods freely during summer time, but not in mast-time.

[37] A small facsimile of the charter is printed as a frontispiece to *Mamecestre*; the text and a translation are printed in the same work, ii, 212–39. Professor Tait has printed the text so as to show its agreement or otherwise with the charters of Salford and Stockport, and has given a commentary and translation, in *Mediaev. Manch.* 62–119.

The borough port mote was in 1320 held four times a year. To its meetings every burgess was bound to come, either in person or by his eldest son or his wife; the burgess, being usually a trader, might often be absent from the town on business. If necessary a law mote might be held between the hall motes for the more speedy ad-

ministration of justice. The profits of the port motes and law motes were estimated at 13s. 4d. a year; *Mamecestre*, ii, 287, 315. The customs of the charter seem to have been in full force.

[38] In 1341 it was declared that there was no city or borough within the wapentake of Salford; *Inq. Non.* (Rec. Com.), 39.

The record of the inquiry of 1359 is printed in *Mamecestre*, iii, 447–50; see also *Dep. Keeper's Rep.* xxxii, App. 339, 346. It appears that the officers of the Duke of Lancaster had fined certain persons in Manchester for breach of the assize of bread and ale, also for breach of the peace; whereupon Sir Roger La Warre put forward his claim to hold the vill of Manchester as 'a borough and market town' with amends of the aforesaid breaches and with various other liberties, particularly those to 'a borough and market-town' appertaining. The jury, after due consideration, reported that Sir Roger did not hold the vill as a 'borough,' nor had his ancestors so held it; but they had, from time without mind, held it as a 'market-town,' enjoying all the liberties claimed by Sir Roger both in the vill and in the manor of Manchester. Afterwards an agreement was come to between the duke and the lord, the latter agreeing to pay 50 marks; but this sum was remitted on 8 Jan. 1359–60, Sir Roger La Warre having justified his claim.

The names of the burgage-holders in 1473 are printed in *Mamecestre*, iii, 487–91. About ninety burgages are accounted for, and the rents, together with the rents for the lands in the town, amounted to £8 0s. 3d. The market tolls were leased for £3 6s. 8d.

[39] Tait, *Mediaev. Manch.* 57.

[40] The usual heading of the record is *Curia cum visu franci plegii*, but in Sept. 1562 it is in English, 'The Portmouthe' &c.; *Manch. Ct. Leet. Rec.* i, 75.

[41] Edited by the late J. P. Earwaker, and published at the expense of the cor-

and caps were used on Sundays and holydays [45] ; but these special officers were not appointed every year.

The juries of the courts leet were constantly occupied with the sanitary conditions of the town.[46] The water supply was regulated.[47] Offensive trades were checked.[48] The streets were kept clear,[49] householders being required to repair the pavements, and encroachments by steps, porches or horsing-stones forbidden.[50] The markets and traders needed constant supervision [51]; regrators and forestallers were punished,[52] standards for weights and measures provided and enforced,[53]

improper qualities of provisions and goods noticed.[54] The morals and amusements of the inhabitants received attention ; [55] rules were made for alehouses,[56] for the residence of unmarried women in the town,[57] for limiting the expenses of wedding-feasts [58] ; for stocks, dungeon, pillory and cucking stools [59] ; also for the public waits,[60] the practice of archery,[61] and the games of tip-cat and football.[62] An endeavour was made to prevent fires by ordering the stock of fuel to be kept at a distance from the dwelling.[63] A special night watch was appointed for the winter.[64] Swine

---

[45] *Ct. Leet Rec.*, i, 199, 200. Butter and suet were forbidden to be put into bread or cakes ; ibid. i, 69, 259. Later, butter and eggs were forbidden in gingerbread ; ibid. iii, 320. Breadmakers in 1639 were ordered to sell to innkeepers and others at thirteen to the dozen, not at sixteen as they had begun to do. Ibid. iii, 289.

[46] In the 16th century, judging from the regulations for dunghills, privies, pigsties and gutters, the town was unsavoury. Casting carrion and other offensive matter into the Irwell and Irk was forbidden ; ibid. i, 67, 80, 122 ; iii, 60.

[47] In 1573 collectors were appointed to gather money for the repair of the conduit, a 'special ornament of the town,' and bring water to it from fresh springs ; ibid. i, 160. The conduit was in 1586 ordered to be unlocked in the winter from 6 a.m. to 9 p.m., and in the summer from 6 a.m. to 9 a.m., and from 3 p.m. to 6 p.m.; this was the revival of an order made in 1536 ; ibid. i, 259. Washing at the conduit was forbidden in 1586 ; ibid. i, 257.

[48] See, for example, the order to a skindresser, ibid. i, 117.

[49] In 1461 it was allowed that each burgage plot should have a clear space of ground from the house front to the middle of the channel ; to this the lord had no claim, but the burgess could not build upon it or close it up, and had to keep it clean ; De Trafford D. no. 49.

[50] The first presentment recorded is 'that Lawrence Langley hath encroached upon the king's highway with building of a house' ; *Ct. Leet Rec.* i, 4 ; see also 118, 185. Erecting a porch in front of a house was a favourite practice, but was often forbidden as obstructing the pathway ; i, 185. Stiles were ordered to be erected at the ends of byways ; ibid. i, 22. Leaving baulks of timber about the streets appears to have been a common offence ; e.g. i, 103.

[51] See the regulations made in 1568 for keeping the market-place clean. Horses were not to be tied there to be fed ; coopers and apple dealers were to pay a small fee to the scavenger ; fish-dealers at Smithy Door must fix their boards over the channel ; ibid. i, 121. The standing place of dealers in turnips, besoms, and straw hats was regulated in 1578 ; ibid. i, 201.

By 1593 a second weekly market had grown up, so that Saturday and Monday were market days ; and ten years later a smallwares market on Friday was forbidden, but had at last to be allowed ; ibid. ii, 78, 189, 295.

[52] The law in this matter was kept in force. In 1582 John Birch *alias* Crook, miller, was forbidden to buy any malt, grain, or corn within the market, and sell it again in the said market ; ibid. i, 232. The offences were guarded against as late

as 1771; *Manch. Constables' Accts.* iii, 206.

[53] An order was made in 1566 that lawful weights of brass should be provided and sealed with the town seal ; *Ct. Leet Rec.* i, 104. The lord of the manor was requested to provide a standard set for use in Manchester ; ibid. i, 126, 154. The market-lookers had charge of them ; ibid. i, 256. In later volumes of the *Records* will be found numerous lists of persons fined for using wrong measures.

[54] See the injunctions to tanners ; ibid. i, 184, &c., and as to wet rug or cotton in the streets ; i, 129.

[55] Thus, an angry woman was punished for calling someone 'no honest man' and 'a recetter (receiver) of thieves.' Two women who had stolen 'chips' from a house 'contrary to honesty and civil order, and to the evil example of all good people,' were sent to condign punishment ; afterwards they were to kneel down and ask mercy from God and the person defrauded. An eaves-dropper was expelled from the town in 1573 ; ibid. i, 24, 70, 155.

[56] The jury in 1573 expressed the opinion that thirty alehouses and inns were enough for Manchester ; ibid. i, 153. In 1588 complaint was made of the number of alehouses and bakers in the town ; *Local Glean. Lancs. and Ches.* i, 127. It had been ordered in 1560 that no one should brew or sell unless he had 'two honest beds' for travellers ; in which case he must hang out a hand as a sign. Those who had a larger number of beds were also to show 'a fair and commendable sign' for the benefit of strangers ; *Ct. Leet Rec.* i, 60. Further regulations were made from time to time ; no drink or food was to be sold, except to passengers, during time of divine service ; drunken men were to be punished by a night in the dungeon ; ibid. i, 151, 161, 185.

[57] Single women were not to be 'at their own hands' and bake, brew or otherwise trade for themselves ; nor might they keep any house or chamber in the town ; ibid. i, 241. 'Inmakes' and strangers were not to be received as lodgers unless they had appeared before the constables of the town and given an account of themselves : this was to prevent the settling of beggars and idle persons ; ibid. i, 226.

[58] No one was to pay more than 4*d.* at a wedding dinner ; ibid. i, 84. This order was frequently renewed.

[59] In 1569 the lord of the manor was requested to make 'a pair of stocks' ; ibid. i, 126.

The dungeon was the old chapel on the bridge. It appears to have had an upper and a lower chamber ; ibid. It remained in use until 1778, when on the bridge being widened it was removed. A cage, or temporary place of confinement, was also in use in 1590 ; ibid. ii, 47. The

were no longer allowed to wander about the streets ; nor were fierce dogs to go unmuzzled.[65] As time went on it became necessary to pay deputy constables to see to the watching of the streets,[66] and in the 18th century a voluntary association existed for police purposes.[67] More trifling matters occasionally amused the jury.[68]

Thus without any great inconvenience or difficulty the government of the town was provided for by the manorial system [69] until the great increase of the population in the latter half of the 18th century made changes necessary. In 1792 a Police Act [70] was obtained for the better lighting, watching, and cleansing of the town ; a rate of 1s. 3d. in the pound upon the rent of houses met the expenses, and the authority was vested in commissioners, including the borough reeve and constables for the time being, the warden and fellows of the collegiate church, and all owners and occupiers of houses of £30 a year value who chose to qualify.[71] Salford was joined with Manchester in this Act, but the meetings for the two townships were held separately. A special Act for the township of Manchester was obtained in 1790 for the better ad-

[65] Those persons who did not send their swine to Collyhurst in charge of the swineherd were ordered to keep them safely in their back premises ; *Ct. Leet. Rec.* i, 15. Pigsties were not to be placed near the street ; ibid. 50.

Mastiffs and great ' ban dogs ' or bitches were not to go abroad unmuzzled ; ibid. 72, 241. This order was frequently renewed.

[66] Ibid. iii, 266 (1638). An earlier payment is recorded in 1613 ; *Manch. Constables' Accts.* i, 9.

[67] A list of the ' Committee for the detection and prosecution of felons, and receivers of stolen or embezzled goods ' is printed in the first Manchester Directory of 1772 ; see also Procter, *Bygone Manch.* 99.

[68] A find of twenty-two ' old Halfaced groats called "crossed groats" ' was recorded in 1575 ; *Ct. Leet Rec.* i, 171. A stray mare having remained in the pound a year and a day became the property of the lord ; three proclamations had been made ; ibid. i, 253.

[69] Dr. Aikin, writing about 1790, thought that Manchester's being an ' open town ' was ' probably to its advantage ' ; *Country round Manch.* 191. The reason was that there were no ' such regulations as are made in corporations, to favour freemen in exclusion to strangers ' ; Ogden, *Description.*

[70] 32 Geo. III, cap. 69. An earlier Act (5 Geo. III, cap. 81) had been obtained for cleansing and lighting the streets.

An abstract of the contract of 1799 for lighting the town is given in the *Directory* for 1800 ; spermaceti and seal oils were to be used ; the lamps were to be lighted for seven months in the year, and twenty dark nights were reckoned in each month.

[71] The Act was several times amended. In 1829 the commissioners for the two townships were definitely separated, and those for Manchester became a limited number elected by the different police districts. The following was the method of government immediately preceding incorporation : The borough reeve and two constables were elected at the court leet by a jury of the most influential inhabitants summoned by the deputy steward of the manor. The duties and precedence

of the borough of the mayor o took cognizan town, having tended the d was u d h sioners, who police hackn scaveng ng all, were elect fourteen distri

number of councillors, there being at present thirty wards with thirty-one aldermen and ninety-three councillors.[80] The mayor was entitled Lord Mayor in 1893. The area governed measures 19,893 acres, nearly two-thirds that of the ancient parish.

The lord's mills had been secured to the grammar school by its founder in 1515,[81] and though the lord of the manor himself tried to break through the monopoly[82] it was maintained until 1758, when an Act of Parliament was passed allowing free corn milling.[83] The malt-grinding monopoly was retained, but the charge was limited to 1s. per load of six bushels ; a sum which, owing to the rise in wages, eventually caused the privilege to be a loss to the school.[84] The tax upon grinding, though small, caused brewers to settle in Salford, Cheetham, and other adjacent townships outside the lordship of Manchester.[85]

The regulation of the markets and the profits of the tolls remained with the lord of the manor until the sale to the corporation. Though Sir Oswald Mosley built an exchange in 1729 with the design, in part, of providing better accommodation for traders, the markets continued in the open spaces accustomed until 1780,[87] when a determined effort was made by two merchants, Thomas Chadwick and Holland Ackers, to overthrow the lord's monopoly. They purchased Pool Court and Hyde Park, collections of poor and old cottages to the south-east of the exchange, and after clearing and preparing the ground, erected and opened a market there, which was at once utilized by the butchers. The lord of the manor, Sir John Parker Mosley, brought a suit, won it, and then compromised the matter with the projectors, as he desired to study the interests of the town.[88] The friction about the markets and other matters[89] which could only be dealt with satisfactorily by the inhabitants was the reason why Sir Oswald Mosley desired to sell his rights.[90] A Market Act obtained by the corporation in 1846 is considered to have abolished the old manorial markets,[91] though there have been attempts to enforce the ancient rights. In 1883 it was decided that the corporation must not charge tolls on goods sold, in addition to rent for stallage.[92] New market buildings have been erected,[93] a foreign animals wharf has been established at Old Trafford, and abattoirs in Water Street and other parts of the city.

A new town hall was begun in 1868 and opened in 1877 ; that of 1822 is now used for the reference library.

The gas,[94] water,[95] and electricity supplies are in

---

ham ; the third, of the old townships of Ardwick, Chorlton-upon-Medlock, Hulme, Rusholme (including parts of Moss Side and Withington), Openshaw and West Gorton. Two of these townships were modern, created in 1894, Clayton having been the western part of Droylsden and West Gorton of Gorton.

[80] The present wards are : Collegiate Church, from the church north-eastwards and south to Lever Street and Piccadilly ; Exchange, south of the former, including the old market-place but not the Exchange building ; New Cross, between Oldham Road and the Medlock, including the eastern part of Ancoats ; St. Michael's, between Oldham Road and the Irk ; St. Clement's, between Piccadilly and Great Ancoats ; Oxford, touching the Medlock, and including Gaythorn ; St. James's, including the Town Hall, Infirmary and Central Station ; St. Ann's, including the church of that name, the Free Library and Exchange building ; St. John's, the corner between the Irwell and Medlock. The above nine are all within the township of Manchester, part of which (Collyhurst) is included with the old township of Harpurhey to form the Harpurhey Ward. Medlock Street and St. George's Wards are the east and west portions of Hulme ; St. Luke's and All Saints' of Chorlton-upon-Medlock. Ardwick coincides with the former township ; Bradford includes Beswick, Bradford and Clayton ; Chorlton with Hardy, Withington, and Didsbury are formed from the townships so named and Burnage, with certain adjustments of boundaries ; Moss Side East and West are the divisions of Moss Side ; Openshaw and Rusholme coincide with those townships ; Longsight is formed from Kirkmanshulme and part of West Gorton, the rest of the latter township being St. Mark's Ward ; Newton Heath and Miles Platting are the east and west portions of Newton; Blackley and Moston includes those townships and part of Prestwich (added in 1903) ; Crumpsall and Cheetham coincide with the old townships.

Each ward has an alderman and three councillors, except six councillors. T man not attached

[81] Hibbert-War iii, 8, &c.

[82] Mosley, Fam. of th h l

the hands of the corporation, which also provides hydraulic power. The great scheme by which water is brought from Thirlmere, 96 miles distant, was started in 1890 ; the first instalment of 10,000,000 gallons daily was opened in 1894 ; the second in 1904, and three more, each of the same quantity, may be added as needed.[96]

A commission of the peace and separate quarter sessions were granted in 1839. The police force and fire brigade, as in other cities, are in charge of the corporation.

The Lord Mayor's charities have an income of over £3,500 and from those under the control of the council another £300 is distributed annually.

Street improvements, begun a century before the charter, have made continual progress. The sewerage of the district has been attended to, and for sewage disposal there are works on the Irlam and Chat Moss estates producing 4,000 tons of concentrated manure annually. The water-carried sewage is dealt with in bacterial beds at Davyhulme. Baths and washhouses have been provided, and the Monsall Fever Hospital in Newton. Two cemeteries, at Chorlton with Hardy and adjoining Philips Park, Newton, are managed by the corporation.

An elaborate and far-extending electric tramway system has been established.[97] The ship canal has

[96] The area now supplied by the corporation includes the old parishes of Manchester (except one or two townships), Eccles, Flixton, and part of Prestwich. Thirlmere water may also be supplied to Wigan, Chorley, Preston, and Lancaster.

[97] The first tramways were opened in 1877.

[98] The first free library was opened in 1852 in a building previously known as the Hall of Science, Campfield, erected in 1839. The reference department was transferred to the old town hall in King Street in 1878. There are in Manchester branch libraries in Deansgate, opened 1882 ; Ancoats, 1857 ; and Livesey Street, 1860 ; also a reading-room at Queen's Park, 1887. A *History* of the libraries by W. R. Credland was issued in 1899. A quarterly *Record* is published.

[99] There is a municipal museum at Queen's Park, Collyhurst, opened in 1884. The Manchester Museum at the University receives an annual grant from the corporation.

[100] The building and contents of the Royal Manchester Institution were in 1881 acquired by the corporation in trust for the public ; there is a permanent collection of pictures and works of art, and yearly exhibitions also are held.

[100a] The school of technology was begun in 1895 and opened in 1902.

[101] In 1282 a 'small park' called Aldeparc and Litheak was valued at 33s. 4d. a year for herbage and pannage ; *Lancs. Inq. and Extents*, i, 244. In 1322 there were at Alport 30 acres of heath, worth 30s. a year ; 2 acres of meadow and 20 acres of pasture, worth 13s. 4d. ; the wood there, a mile in circumference, might be made pasturage at the lord's will, and was worth only 6s. 8d. a year in pannage, honey, eyries of hawks, &c., but the gross value of the timber was £300 ; *Mamecestre*, ii, 363, 367, 368.
There were timber trees in Alport Park in 1597 ; *Ducatus Lanc.* (Rec. Com.), iii, 382.

[102] In 1430 Lord La Warre granted

Over Alport to Ma and Thomas Phillip creasing to 40s. ; H years later he and Nether Alport to H 80. A new feoffm

Adam Smith, the other purchaser, was in 1600 ordered to make a ditch along the nearer Alport field ; *Manch. Ct. Leet Rec.* ii, 156.

In 1620 the jury found that John Gilliam had purchased lands at Alport of Thomas Owen ; ibid. iii, 23.

Robert Neild of Manchester, attorney, whose chief estate was at Warrington, held lands in Deansgate and Alport in Manchester at his death in 1631. He left four infant daughters as co-heirs—Anne, Mary, Ellen, and Katherine ; ibid. iii, 179 ; Duchy of Lanc. Inq. p.m. xxv, 29

17th century, while the other half was held by the Traffords,[109] and sold about 1610 to a Kenyon.[110]

Anthony Mosley, father of the purchaser of Ancoats, was the younger brother of Sir Nicholas, and associated with him in the cloth business, looking after the Manchester trade when the other removed to London. He died in 1607, and is commemorated by a monumental brass in the cathedral.[111] Oswald, his son and heir, the first Mosley of Ancoats, died in 1630 ; he also has a brass in the cathedral.[112] His heir, his eldest son Nicholas, was still under age, but came into court in 1633 to do his suit and service to the lord of the manor.[113] He took the king's side during the Civil War, deserting Manchester for the time. His lands being thereupon sequestered by the Parliament he compounded in 1646 on a fine of £120, his estate in Ancoats, Clayden, and Beswick being of the clear annual value of £60 ; he had taken the National Covenant and the Negative oath.[114] He took a conspicuous part in the Manchester rejoicings at the Restoration,[115] but though an Episcopalian and a justice of the peace he did not join in the subsequent persecution of the Nonconformists.[116] He had three sons ; from Nicholas, the youngest, the present Sir Oswald Mosley descends.

Sir Edward Mosley, who died in 1665, had directed that £7,000 should be invested in land for the benefit of his cousin Nicholas ; but this had not been done in 1672, when Nicholas died, leaving his eldest son Oswald as heir. A division of Sir Edward's estates being agreed upon, Oswald received in lieu of the

£7,000 the reversion of the manors of Rolleston and Manchester, and in 1695, on succeeding to the former on the death of Sir Edward's widow, he went to reside there, and died in 1726.[117] His son and heir, Oswald, was created a baronet in 1720, and in 1734, on the death of Lady Bland, succeeded to the lordship of Manchester. This involved him in many disputes. In 1693, acting for Lady Bland, he had claimed a duty of 2d. per pack on all goods called Manchester wares, but was defeated ; and a later claim to set up a malt mill was defeated by the feoffees of the grammar school.[118] His eldest son Sir Oswald succeeded in 1751, and wished to sell the manor of Manchester, but was unable to do so owing to a settlement he had made.[119] On his death in 1757 the manor, with Ancoats, passed to his brother John, a clergyman of eccentric habits, who died unmarried in 1779, when the baronetcy expired.[120]

In accordance with the dispositions made by the last Sir Oswald the estates then went to a second cousin, John Parker Mosley, created a baronet in 1781. He was the youngest son of Nicholas Mosley, a woollen draper of Manchester, who was son of Nicholas Mosley, an apothecary in London, already mentioned as the youngest son of Nicholas Mosley of Ancoats. The new lord of Manchester, Ancoats, and Rolleston had been established as a hatter in Manchester, but a passion for cockfighting and other dissipations almost ruined him. Steadied by his danger he entered on a new course of life and prospered. He was about forty-seven when he succeeded to the

---

Robert son of Simon de Manchester gave all his land in Ancoats to Henry son of Henry de Trafford (no. 27/244), and Robert son of Robert son of Simon de Manchester made a grant to Alexander the Dyer (no. 82/312). Geoffrey and Joan received other land from Thomas son of Geoffrey son of Simon Cocks of Manchester in 1305 (no. 28/216), and in 1317 Geoffrey de Chadderton of Chadderton granted all his land in Ancoats and Manchester to his son Richard (no. 4/317). This Richard was tenant in 1320, but his rent was only 9d. ; *Mamecestre*, ii, 278. The lord of Ancoats had at that time common of turbary in Openshaw ; ibid. ii, 291.

It does not appear how this portion came to the Byrons, but in 1331 Henry son of Robert de Ancoats leased all his hereditary holding to Sir Richard de Byron, and in the following year sold it outright, together with the reversion of the dower lands held by his mother Agnes ; Byron Chartul. no. 3/238, no. 4/239.

In 1473 John Byron held a moiety of two messuages and two oxgangs in Ancoats in socage by a rent of 3s. 4d.—a moiety of the rent of 1212—and was bound to grind his corn at the Manchester mill ; *Mamecestre*, iii, 482.

Thomas de Hollinworth the elder seems to have been a Byron tenant in 1405, when he made a grant to Hugh his son ; Hugh made a feoffment of his estate in Ancoats in 1433 ; Byron Chartul. no. 3/318, 22/319.

[109] Some grants to the Traffords have been mentioned in the preceding note. Henry de Trafford in 1320 had land in Ancoats, joined with his holding of five oxgangs in Chorlton ; its separate rent appears to have been 9d.; *Mamecestre*, ii, 278. He and Richard de Chadderton

were bound to grind at the mill of Manchester.

In 1373 Sir Henry de Trafford granted in fee to John son of Nicholas de Trafford all the lands, &c., which John then held for life ; and a release was given in 1402 ; De Trafford D. no. 84, 85.

In 1473 Bartin Trafford held messuages, apparently in Ancoats, by a service of 3s. 4d.; *Mamecestre*, iii, 482.

[110] It was found in October 1610 that Ralph Kenyon had purchased of Sir Edward Trafford a messuage within the town of Manchester called The Ancoats, for which an annual service of 3s. 4d. was due to the lord ; *Manch. Ct. Leet Rec.* ii, 256. The purchaser was still living at Ancoats in 1631 ; ibid. iii, 180.

[111] There is an account of the Mosleys of Ancoats in *Mosley Memoranda* (Chet. Soc. New Ser.). For Anthony see also Mosley, *Fam. Mem.* 22, 23 ; and *Manch. Ct. Leet Rec.* ii, 225, where an abstract of his will is given. He several times acted as a constable of the borough. For the Mosley brasses see *Lancs. and Ches. Antiq. Soc.* xi, 82.

[112] Mosley, op. cit. 25. He purchased Ancoats from Sir John Byron in 1609 ; *Mosley Mem.* 16. He acquired lands in Cheshire through his marriage with Anne daughter and co-heir of Ralph Lowe of Mile End near Stockport. A rental of Ancoats in 1608 shows a total of £39 16s. 6d. Adam Smith and John Ashton appear to have had an interest in a fourth part of the fields, which measured 48 acres. The field-names included the Hollin Wood, the Eyes, the Banks, &c. Other surveys, &c., will be found op. cit. 31, &c.

Oswald Mosley was steward of the Court Leet from 1613 until 1618 ; *Manch. Ct. Leet Rec.* ii, 278, &c. The inquisitions taken after his death describe his

estates, and was speedily involved in the disputes as to the markets already described, but established his right. In 1786 he was High Sheriff of Lancashire, and on this occasion was accompanied from his seat at Ancoats by an immense retinue of his friends and neighbours. After this, however, the house was deserted, its owner returning to Staffordshire ;[121] and it was sold to George Murray.

Ancoats Hall is described by Aikin in 1795 as 'a very ancient building of wood and plaster, but in some parts rebuilt in brick and stone.' It stood at the end of Ancoats Lane (now Great Ancoats Street) facing north-west, and at the back of the house the grounds sloped down to the banks of the River Medlock in a series of terraces, from which there was a lovely view over green well-wooded country. The house was of two stories with attics, and the front consisted of three gables with a square tower in the centre, constructed also of timber and plaster, and with a hipped roof. Aikin further remarks that it was the back part of the house that was chiefly rebuilt, but some rebuilding of the west wing had been done before the end of the 18th century. Britton, writing in 1807, speaks of Ancoats Hall as a venerable house, the oldest part of which consisted of timber and plaster, 'the first, disposed of various figures, forms a sort of skeleton, and the latter is employed to fill up the interstices. The upper stories overhang the ground floor, and the great windows project before the face of the building.' The house was built early in the 17th century by Oswald Mosley,[121a] and it stood till the beginning of the last century, when it

---

121 *Fam. Mem.* 54–75. The heir was, as previously stated, his grandson Sir Oswald Mosley, the compiler of the *Memoirs* cited, who sold the manor of Manchester to the corporation. His father Oswald, eldest son of Sir John Parker Mosley, purchased Bolesworth Castle in Cheshire in 1785, where he died in 1789.

121a Axon, *Mosley Mem.* 31.

122 *N. and Q.* (Ser. 5), v. 138.

123 Among the grammar school deeds are the following concerning the family :—

1428, Feoffment by John Oldham of Manchester of a burgage in the Millgate, received from William the Goldsmith of Manchester.

1462, Purchase of various messuages and lands in Ancoats by Roger Oldham from William son and heir of John Dean ; Alice the widow, and Roger (chaplain) and Henry, the other sons of John Dean, released their right, as did John son of John Talbot, esq.

1471, John son and heir of Henry Chadkirk sold a burgage in Millgate to Roger Oldham (endorsed, 'Usher's house ').

1472, Roger Oldham having died intestate, administration was granted to Ellen his widow, Peter and Bernard his sons. (Ellen was no doubt a second wife, for the obits to be kept by the appointment of Bishop Oldham included those of Roger Oldham and *Margery* his wife).

1473, William Dean released to James, son and heir of Roger Oldham, all his right in the Ancoats estate ; in 1477 he gave a similar release to the widow Ellen. (In the rental of 1473 a burgage in Manchester was held by 'the heir of Roger Oldham'; *Mamecestre,* iii, 490.)

239

Edmund Entwisle of Entwisle, who died in 1544, had some land in Ancoats.[127]

GARRETT was formerly the seat of a branch of the Trafford family,[128] and was sold in 1595 to Oswald Mosley, a younger brother of Sir Nicholas and Anthony.[129] His son Samuel sold it, but it can be traced in the records down to 1683.[130] Soon afterwards it was acquired by the Minshulls of Chorlton, and again sold in 1775. A curious story is told of the place.[131]

Garrett Hall stood on the north bank of the River Medlock close to where it is joined by Shooter's Brook. The house was a black and white timber mansion on a stone base, said to have been similar in style to Hulme Hall, and built on four sides of a quadrangle. The principal front faced south towards the Medlock, which here flowed in a series of curves through a large meadow, and is described as 'extremely picturesque with numerous gables and tall chimneys.' The house, whose position was originally one of defence at the junction of two streams, was surrounded by a park through which Shooter's Brook ran on the north side. It appears to have fallen into decay and to have been let in tenements before the end of the 18th century, but is said to have been standing entire in 1824. One wing was in existence forty years later, and a fragment of the house which could till recently be seen at the back of the north side of Granby Row was not demolished till May 1910. Long before the hall disappeared it was closed in by other buildings, and all traces of the park and original surroundings had long been lost.[132]

CLAYDEN appears to represent the four oxgangs of demesne land bestowed about 1160 on Wulfric de Manchester by Albert Grelley senior, at a rent of 5s.[133] In later times it was held by the same rent by a family surnamed Clayden, perhaps descendants of Wulfric.[134] A portion was owned by the Hopwoods

tion of an Adam Oldham living in 1505; he was probably the heir of James Oldham, eldest brother of the bishop. Robert and Hugh Oldham are frequently mentioned in the *Ct. Leet. Rec.* of 1552 and later; Robert died in 1578 or 1579, leaving a son Adam, of full age (ibid. i, 204), no doubt the Adam who heads the recorded pedigree, in which his kinship to the bishop is asserted. He died 22 June 1588, holding a messuage, &c., in Manchester of the queen by the hundredth part of a knight's fee; he left a son and heir Robert, aged four years, and daughters named Elizabeth, Cecily, Ellen, and Margaret; Duchy of Lanc. Inq. p.m. xiv, 31. His will, proved in July 1588, mentions his 'brothers' John and Francis Wirrall, Robert and Hugh Oldham, cousins Robert, Edmund, Roger, and Hugh Oldham, sister Elizabeth Oldham, and mothers-in-law Isabel Oldham and Elizabeth Wirrall (the former would be his stepmother); see *Ct. Leet Rec.* ii, 222.

[127] Duchy of Lanc. Inq. p.m. vii, 30; the tenure is not stated. It was held with lands in Chorlton and Ardwick.

[128] Garrett appears always to have been closely connected with Chorlton-upon-Medlock, as will be seen in the account of Robert and John Grelley's estate in the latter township.

Sir Henry de Trafford, after purchasing the estate just named, appears to have granted part at least to a younger son Thomas; the gift of Gatecote field in 1373 has been preserved; Ct. of Wards and Liveries, box 146D/8; the seal of the grantor shows three bendlets.

Thomas died in 1410 holding lands in Chorlton, probably including Garrett; and leaving a son and heir John, whose wardship and marriage were granted to Sir Ralph de Staveley, in the mistaken belief that the lands were held of the king; *Lancs. Inq. p.m.* (Chet. Soc.), i, 96, 97. Margery, the mother of the heir, was living.

John died in 1412 being only twelve years of age, and his heir was his brother Henry, Henry likewise dying young, another brother, Thomas, became the heir. The estate was (in part at least) six messuages, 100 acres of land, &c., in Chorlton; *Lancs. Inq. p.m.* (Chet. Soc.), ii, 16; see also *Dep. Keeper's Rep.* xxxiii, App. 27, 34. Thomas proved his age in 1433; he was born in 1408; *Lancs. Inq. p.m.* ii, 37. The descent Thomas —s. Thomas —s. Henry (living 1461) is given

'n Ct
13A/FD
Ellen
coats in
Sir Joh
all her l
cxlii, fo
Henry
Trafford
included
cotefield
and 2s.
Leet Rec
The
Oldham,
direction

...

...

of Hopwood, and derived from them the distinguishing name of Hopwood Clayden.[134a] The district was sometimes considered as partly in Newton.[135] The name is perhaps preserved in Gleden Street, Holt Town.

Grants by Albert Grelley to Robert de Bracebridge [136] and by Robert Grelley to Ace the clerk are on record.[137]

The origin of the name Gaythorn is obscure. The place seems to have been owned formerly by the Chethams.[138]

COLLYHURST was part of the waste.[139] The townsmen had various rights of pasturage there,[140] and when the Mosleys acquired the lordship took care to assert them, Rowland Mosley, the son of Sir Nicholas, compounding the disputes by a payment of £10 a year to the poor of Manchester,[141] payment being made till a century ago.[142] Francis Mosley, a younger son of Anthony of Ancoats, was settled on an estate at Collyhurst,[143] which descended on his death in 1662 to his granddaughter Anne, daughter of his son Nicholas, who died in 1659.[144] Both Nicholas and his father had had their estates sequestered for their

and Margaret, nine; ibid. xv, no. 28. A few further details are given in the Ct. Leet Rec. ii, 59, 246, 290; from these it appears that Margaret Clayden married Thomas Holcroft and her share was in 1609 sold to Lawrence Langley.

The whole or a large part of Clayden was about 1640 in the possession of the Mosleys of Ancoats; Great Clayden and Shipponley had been bought of Mr. Charnock; Kilnebank, Green Lee, Copley, Blew Field, and Coal Pit Field were other field names; Axon, Mosley Mem. 34, 39, &c. It was held by a rent of 3s. 6d. with 1s. 6d. more for the portion formerly Charnock's; ibid. 35. Combined these rents amount to 5s., the ancient rent paid by the Clayden family.

[134a] Thomas de Hopwood in 1320 held the place of a kiln (corellus) in Clayden at ½d. rent; Mamecestre, ii, 279. In 1331 John son of Henry de Hulton granted to Adam son of Thomas de Hopwood all his lands in the hamlet of Ancoats, held by demise of Adam son of Robert de Radcliffe; they had belonged to Robert de Gotherswick and Hugh his brother; De Banco R. 290, m. 1 d.

Thomas Beck in 1546 made a settlement of messuages in Manchester, Monshalgh, Salford, and Newton, in favour of his son Robert; Pal. of Lanc. Feet of F. bdle. 12, m. 219, 265. Robert purchased the Hopwoods' estate in Manchester, Clayden, and Newton in 1549; ibid. bdle. 13, m. 29. He died about the end of 1556, leaving a son and heir Thomas, who came of age in 1574; Ct. Leet Rec. i, 32, 168; Piccope, Wills, i, 184. Thomas Beck of Hopwood Clayden was in 1588 succeeded by his son Randle; and the latter in 1599 by his brother Robert, then fifteen years of age. The estate included burgages in Manchester (Broadlache, Marketstead Lane, and Deansgate) and in Salford; see the inquisitions in Duchy of Lanc. Inq. p.m. xiv, 19; xvii, 8; Manch. Ct. Leet Rec. ii, 147, 217. In the Chetham Library are deeds by Robert Beck of Hopwood Clayden dated 1626 and 1636; the latter is a grant to Thomas Beck, his son and heir apparent.

A pedigree was recorded in 1664 (Dugdale, Visit. 29) stating that Robert Beck and Thomas his son, both 'of Hopwood Clayden,' died in 1644; the latter was succeeded by his son Thomas, aged thirty-four in 1664, who had a son John, aged twelve, and other children. Thomas Beck died in 1678, and his son and heir at once sold or mortgaged Hopwood Clayden and other lands to Thomas Minshull; Ct. Leet Rec. vi, 65, and deeds quoted in the note. William Beck, a brother of John, sold lands in 1684; ibid. vi, 214.

The Becks' land in Hopwood Clayden was held by Nicholas Mosley of Ancoats in 1665; Axon, Mosley Mem. 53.

The Hopwood ƒ tate in Manchester (Rec. Soc. Lancs. 207

[135] John son of West Hall in High son of Robert Ma granted to Elizabeth of Richard (son of all his lands in viz. that place ca Ha l D.

[136] Lancs. Inq. a was a grant of two o at a rent of 4s. year B acebridge's name witness to 13th-ce probable that E ayn he d by Thomas Gr same rent, constitut cestre, i, 279, e Liveries, box 13A/F also held Gatecoter ibid All three as an a ot fi d i were granted by hn r

fidelity to Charles I.[145] The heiress carried the estate in marriage to Robert Lever of Alkrington.[146]

Various districts of Manchester are named in the rentals of 1322 and 1473, some of which are now forgotten, e.g. Ashley, Choo, Clements Croft, Dancroft, Hobcroft, Kyperfield, and Riding Brook.[147]

Many of the neighbouring gentry held burgages and lands in the township of Manchester,[148] and there were also a number of the townsmen who acquired wealth and distinction. Some of them are noticed in the accounts of estates they acquired elsewhere ;[149] of the rest may here be named Barlow,[150] Beck,[151] Beswick,[152]

[145] *Royalist Comp. Papers*, iv, 201. Nicholas Mosley and Francis his father, clothiers, had deserted their dwellings and lived for some time in the king's quarters. The son took the National Covenant and Negative Oath in 1646. The statement of his property in Manchester showed it to be worth £40 a year, and that in Collyhurst, 'before the troubles,' £24 ; the £10 to the poor was charged on it ; the father and son were creditors for £1,338 and debtors for £2,490. A fine of £200 was fixed.

[146] Booker, *Prestwich*, 206. Robert Lever was fined 10s. in 1677 for not cleansing his ditch in Collyhurst Lane, by the Long Causeway, and in Wilkin Hills ; *Ct. Leet Rec.* vi, 42. Some of the family resided at Collyhurst, for John Revel Lever, son of John Lever, esq., was born there about 1707 ; Scott, *Admissions to St. John's Coll. Camb.* iii, 50.

[147] *Mamecestre*, ii, 362 ; iii, 482–4. The position of Ashley is indicated by Ashley Lane, leading north from Long Millgate. Choo is believed to have been in Broughton, near the Irwell and on the border of Cheetham ; in Broughton also was Kyperfield, another detached portion of the manor of Manchester ; Information of Mr. Crofton.

For Ashley Henry Boterinde and Robert Rudde in 1320 paid a rent of 18d. ; *Mamecestre*, ii, 279. Alice daughter of Henry Boterinde in 1351 gave her son Robert half a burgage in the Millgate and 5 acres in Ashley ; *Lancs. and Ches. Hist. and Gen. Notes*, i, 54. The land was soon afterwards claimed by Agnes widow of Robert Rudde ; Duchy of Lanc. Assize R. 2 (July), m. 8. The Buldre family, whose heirs were the Hulmes of Manchester and Reddish, next appear in possession ; Thomas son of Thomas Buldre occurs in Manchester in 1338, and Thomas Buldre in 1361 (Hulme D. no. 4, 5), and in 1381 Agnes widow of Henry Dobson granted to William Buldre for her life all her lands and tenements in 'Asshenlegh' and Tuefield near Manchester, formerly her husband's ; ibid. no. 6. In 1421 an agreement was made between Lawrence Hulme and Robert Rudde, who owned 'a field lying in the town of Manchester called Ashley, lying together and in divers parcels,' as to a division of the land and chief rent ; ibid. no. 10. Geoffrey Hulme held Ashley in 1473 at 10d. (or 1d.) rent ; *Mamecestre*, iii, 482, 499. The heir of James Barlow was probably the other tenant (for 'Estley') at a rent of 6d. ; ibid. iii, 483. In 1615 Ralph Hulme of Outwood in Pilkington mortgaged the three closes called Nearer, Middlemost, and Further Ashley, containing by estimation 5 acres of land ; Hulme D. no. 62. In the 17th century it was at least in part owned by the Becks ; *Ct. Leet Rec.* vi, 65, 214.

[148] Among the burgage holders in 1473 (*Mamecestre*, iii, 487) are found the names of many of the neighbouring esquires, the list beginning with Sir John Trafford, who had land near the Booths, on which a shop had recently been built.

The earliest acquisition of the Traffords seems to have been a burgage granted

before 1
de Bolto
Trafford
Manche
burgage
ter's on
the burg
on the w
to Hulm
to the lo
D. no. 3
by Geoff
1333 an
Lists
later yea
Accts. ii
The
among o
lands in
Thom
Duchy o
also *Lan*
Edwa
of Lanc
Inq. p.m
iii, 379.
Willi
Lanc. I
Edwa
no. 20 ;
Ralph
ii, 286.

Bibby,[153] Bowker,[154] Boterind,[155] Gee,[156] Goodyear,[157] Hunt,[158] Laboray,[159] Pendleton,[160] with several note-

[153] This family appears early both in Manchester and Salford. Sir John La Warre in 1313 granted John Bibby two plots of land, and in 1320 the grantee paid 2s. for 2 acres of land on the heath at Manchester; *Mamecestre*, ii, 293, 350.

William Bibby and Cecily his wife in 1348 made a feoffment of their lands; Dods. MSS. cxlii, fol. 198, no. 42. Eleven years later Richard Bibby gave his burgages and lands to William and Robert le Hunt; ibid. no. 45.

John Pouston and Margery his wife in 1361 gave to Robert Bibby all their lands, &c., in Salford; Hopwood D.

William Bibby died in 1577 or 1578, his heir being his brother James; *Ct. Leet Rec.* i, 194, where is printed an elaborate settlement made in 1564.

[154] Edward Bowker died about the end of 1586, leaving a son and heir Geoffrey; *Ct. Leet Rec.* i, 258. The heir was of age in 1589; ibid. ii, 32.

John Pouston and Margery his wife in 1361 gave to Robert Bibby all their lands, &c., in Salford; Hopwood D.

John Bowker, apothecary, in 1623 purchased from Thomas Chadderton of Lees a burgage and smithy in Deansgate; his mother Alice was then living; ibid. iii, 72.

Peter Bowker of Manchester and Adam Bowker of Salford, chapmen, had their estates—tenements in Salford—sequestered by the Parliamentary authorities, they having adhered to and assisted the king's forces. They compounded in 1651; *Royalist Comp. Papers*, i, 214, 215.

[155] Henry Boterind, 1320, has been mentioned. Henry son of Henry de Boterind was one of those killed at Liverpool in 1345 with Adam de Lever; Coram Rege R. 348, m. 22.

Richard son of Henry de Boterind in 1349 made a feoffment of a burgage in the Middlegate by Todd Lane, which he had acquired from Adam son of Robert the Dyer; De Trafford D. no. 14. This burgage had in 1331 been granted by Adam son of Robert de Manchester to Robert the Dyer and Joan his wife, daughter of the grantor; ibid. no. 6. It appears that Richard son of Henry Boterind became a monk; De Banco R. 435, m. 346 d. See also the account of Ashley above.

[156] John Gee appears prominently in the *Ct. Leet Rec.* of the third quarter of the 16th century. In 1559 his mother Elizabeth came into court to confess that he was her eldest son, and that she had granted him all her lands in Manchester and Salford; i, 41. He died at the beginning of 1589, holding lands in Manchester and Salford, and leaving as heir his son John, of full age; ibid. ii, 31; Duchy of Lanc. Inq. p.m xvi, 46. The son also is frequently mentioned; either he or his father was the deputy-receiver for the lord of the manor; *Ct. Leet Rec.* i, 200. The younger John Gee seems to have died in Oct. 1629, leaving son Edmund and Joseph and four daughters; ibid. iii, 168, where an abstract of his will is printed. The inquisition taken after John's death states that Edward was his son and heir, and forty years of age; Towneley MS. C, 8, 13 (Chet. Lib.), p. 463. Joseph Gee died in or before 1655; *Ct. Leet Rec.* iv, 143.

Two members of the family distinguished themselves in the 17th century as controversialists, viz. John Gee, who was probably a Devonshire man by birth, but grandson of Ralph Gee of Manchester (died 1598), brought up a Protestant, reconciled to the Roman Church, reverted to Protestantism, and wrote his experiences in *The Foot out of the Snare* (1624), and died

as Vicar of Tenterden in 1639; also Edward Gee, born in Manchester in 1659, educated at St. John's College, Cambridge, author of the *Jesuit's Memorial*. See *N. and Q.* (Ser. 6), ii, 71; *Local Glean. Lancs. and Ches.* ii, 300; Wood, *Athenae; Dict. Nat. Biog.*

[157] In 1574 Thomas Goodyear was admitted to be burgess in right of Ellen his wife, paying to the lord 8d. a year; *Ct. Leet Rec.* i, 168. He was borough-reeve in 1579–80, and one of the constables in 1580–1; ibid. i, 207, 213. The wife was sister of Ralph Proudlove, who died in 1588; she died in 1591, leaving a son Robert Goodyear as heir; ibid. ii, 21, and note. Thomas Goodyear died in 1599, when this son was not quite of age; ibid. ii, 153; Duchy of Lanc. Inq. p.m. xvii, 38. His lands were in Millgate, Deansgate (part called a dole), Newton Lane (' Gibbs '), and Withy Grove.

Robert Goodyear was borough-reeve in 1606, and died in April 1621, having increased his estate, among the additions being 6 acres called 'Bibby Fields'; he left a widow Elizabeth and a son Thomas, under age; *Ct. Leet Rec.* ii, 211; iii, 36; Duchy of Lanc. Inq. p.m. xxvii, 46. Thomas Goodyear died in 1638, holding the Bibby Fields and a messuage in Millgate; his heir was a posthumous daughter named Anne; ibid. xxx, 25. He sold some of his lands to Robert Neild; *Ct. Leet Rec.* iii, 179 note; and his mother Elizabeth and her daughter Mary in 1639 sold land in Shudehill to Robert Marler; ibid. iii, 286.

Another Thomas Goodyear of Manchester died in 1607, leaving a son Henry, ten years of age; *Lancs. Inq. p.m.* (Rec. Soc.), i, 112. Henry was in 1621 summoned to do his suit and service at the lord's court, and died in 1627, leaving as heir his sister Margaret, wife of Thomas Illingworth; *Ct. Leet Rec.* iii, 36, 136.

Margaret Illingworth died in 1634–5, holding her father's property; Towneley MS. C, 8, 13 (Chet. Lib.), p. 708, reciting Thomas Goodyear's disposition of it. Thomas Illingworth died early in 1639, leaving a son and heir Thomas, under age; *Ct. Leet Rec.* iii, 288; an abstract of his will is printed in the note. The younger Thomas died in 1671; ibid. v, 156.

[158] Abstracts of a number of this family's deeds were made by Dodsworth (MSS. cxlii, fol. 161–72), being in 1635 in the hands of John Holcroft of Marton; they do not suffice to give an exact account of the descent.

The pedigree begins with two brothers, William and Robert le Hunt, to whom in 1359 Richard Bibby granted all his burgages and lands in Manchester; Dods. *ut supra*, no. 65. William son of Geoffrey de Manchester released to them all actions in 1367; ibid. no. 35. Robert le Hunt acquired land in Salford from Thurstan de Prestwich in the following year; and from John le Hare and Alice his wife in Woodfield in Ashton; ibid. no. 37, 49. Alice was no doubt the daughter of John de Whitwood, who had granted Robert her lands in 1358; ibid. no. 57. The brothers William and Robert in 1374 made a feoffment of their lands in Manchester and the Ridge in Ashton; ibid. no. 36.

There was another William le Hunt, a chaplain, distinguished from William the brother of Robert by Agnes widow of the above-named William de Manchester in a grant by which she released to the brothers all her claim in the burgages and lands

which had belonged to William the chaplain; ibid. no 53. About the same time (in Oct. 1381) William and Robert granted to Agnes for her life a garden in Manchester, at the end of Irk Bridge, which had formerly belonged to William the chaplain; ibid. no. 52. The position named suggests that this was the land known as Hunt's Bank.

In 1385 the trustee of the two brothers settled their estate upon Richard son of Robert le Hunt, with remainders to Ralph and William, brothers of Richard; ibid. no. 14. Thirteen years later, Maud widow of William le Hunt of Manchester released to Richard le Hunt her claim on lands in Ashton; ibid. no. 33. Richard in 1402 had a grant of land in Salford from his father's widow Cecily, who had married William Clayton, son of Robert son of Falconer; ibid. no. 32. He seems to have lived at Audenshaw in Ashton; ibid. no. 26, 30. Ralph is not heard of again, but William le Hunt of Manchester occurs in 1421 and 1422 (ibid. no. 27–29, 58); and in 1423–4 Richard le Hunt leased his Manchester burgages, and lands to his brother William at a rent of 21s.; ibid. no. 34.

At this point there arises uncertainty. Richard Hunt, perhaps the same Richard, in 1443 acquired a piece of land in Manchester; ibid. no. 31. Edmund Hunt was a witness, and in 1447 a settlement was made by Richard on the marriage of Edmund's son William with Margaret daughter of Roger Bird (or Brid) of Salford; ibid. no. 38, 59, 39, 22. Edmund Hunt made a feoffment of all his burgages, lands, &c., in Lancashire, in 1460; James Bird being a witness; ibid. no. 3. This James Bird of Salford occurs again in 1467, and his son and heir Roger in 1513; ibid. no. 23, 64.

William Hunt, no doubt the son of Edmund, in 1473 held divers burgages, a grange, and lands in Manchester, and paid 7s. 4d. to the lord; *Mamecestre*, iii, 488.

Richard Hunt was a feoffee of the Oldham family; Hibbert-Ware, *Manch. Foundations*, iii, no. 10. His will was proved in London in 1523; *Manch. Ct. Leet Rec.* i, 158 n.; P.C.C. 15 Bodfelde. In 1524 Agnes Hunt, widow, gave a release to Richard Hunt and James Radcliffe, executors of the will of Richard Hunt, deceased; Dods. *ut supra*, no. 65. Five years later Richard Hunt of Manchester made a settlement in favour of his wife Margaret; ibid. no. 66. It was probably this Richard, or a son of the same name, who died in 1573, leaving as heir a son Richard of full age; *Ct. Leet Rec.* i, 158.

Richard Hunt gave the lord a dagger as heriot; ibid. i, 160. He received a release of all claims on his father's lands from George Birch in 1575; Dods. *ut supra*, no. 67. He died in Dec. 1585, leaving as heir his son John, under age; He held 6 burgages and lands in the town of John Lacy, lord of Manchester; a capital messuage and lands in Middlebrook of the queen; a messuage in Audenshaw; three burgages in Salford and lands in Manchester, of the queen; also the house called the Tollbooth, with the toll and stallage of Manchester, of John Lacy, by a rent of £4; *Ct. Leet Rec.* ii, 19, 20, where the inquisition (Duchy of Lanc. Inq. p.m. xiv, 41) is printed; for his will see Piccope, *Wills*, iii, 116.

John Hunt came of age in 1597, and

worthy offshoots ;[161] Radcliffe[162] — several families, including those of the Conduit[163] and of the

did fealty on admission to his father's land ; *Ct. Leet Rec.* ii, 131. About 1610 he was called upon to defend his title to the Booths, Sir Nicholas Mosley laying claim to it ; but he was able to show that it, with the tolls, &c., had been granted in 1514 to his ancestor Richard Hunt ; ibid. iii, 24, 25, notes. In 1620 the jury ordered him to repair ' the Court-house commonly called the Booths,' and sweep it weekly ; ibid. In 1625 Margaret his daughter and (co-) heir married John Holcroft ; ibid. iii, 76, 352 notes. They appear to have sold their lands ; ibid. iii, 153, 246. For the Holcrofts see *Local Glean. Lancs. and Chs.* ii, 149.

Other branches of the Hunt family occur. Among the De Trafford deeds are grants about 1315 from Ellota Braybon, widow, and William her son of two burgages to Walter le Hunt, Margery his wife, and David and Richard their sons (no. 2, 5) ; and in 1347 Richard son of Walter le Hunt granted land in Manchester to Richard son of Richard Chokes (no. 13). The two burgages, which lay in Deansgate, opposite the Parsonage, had by 1396 passed to Richard del Hulle (no. 23–5). Lawrence, son and heir of John Hunt and grandson and heir of Thomas Barker, held land in St. Mary Gate in 1482 ; ibid. no. 56, 57.

Among the Grammar School deeds is a grant (1337) from Roger son of Richard de Manchester to Richard del Crosseshagh and Dyota his wife of a burgage next the Pirlewallgate ; from the latter Richard to Thomas son of John le Hunt (1357) of goods ; from John son of William del Crosshagh of a burgage in the Millgate (1369) ; bonds to John le Hunt (1361, 1368) ; release to the executors of Richard le Hunt (1385), and from John son of Richard le Hunt to Richard de Worsley (1399) ; the will of Agnes widow of John le Hunt (1390), mentioning Ellen daughter of Richard le Hunt, and leaving the guardianship of John and Richard, sons of Richard le Hunt, to Richard de Worsley and John de Tonwallcliff, her executors ; lease of a burgage in Millgate from Cecily widow of Henry Chadkirk, and Joan le Hunt her daughter, to William Bradford, Richard le Hunt of Audenshaw being a witness.

John le Hunt and Agnes his wife in 1371 sold a messuage to Thomas de Whitley ; *Final Conc.* ii, 180.

[159] Robert Laboray or Laborer, serjeant-at-arms to Henry VII, acquired lands near St. Mary Gate in 1511–2 ; Hulme D. no. 38. He left several daughters as co-heirs, and his widow Isabel in 1544 granted a burgage to their daughter Alice, who had married with Stephen Hulme ; ibid. no. 48. Elizabeth, another daughter, about 1533 married William Hulton of Donnington, Lincolnshire ; a third daughter married Thomas Greenhalgh of Brandlesholme, who was Robert's executor ; and various disputes broke out involving the customs of the county as to the distribution of the goods of a husband or father ; *Ducatus Lanc.* (Rec. Com.), i, 156, &c. ; *Duchy Plead.* (Rec. Soc. Lancs. and Ches.), ii, 136, 152. See also *Manch. Ct. Leet Rec.* i, 26, 180 note. ' Labrey's House ' retained its name in 1586 ; ibid. ii, 6. It was near the present infirmary, and in 1580 was styled ' Laborer's house near the end of Marketstead lane,' in the tenure of Robert Hulme of Newton ; ibid. ii, 111 n. and information of Mr. Crofton, who kindly adds the following pedigree of William Hulton : Roger Hulton of Hulton—younger son William, married Jane Everard of Southcoton, Lincs.—s. Roger, married Katherine Anyas—s. William.

[160] In the account of the chantries it is shown that Richard Bexwick left a daughter Isabel, who married Thomas Beck, and that their daughter Cecily married Francis Pendleton. He was the son of Thomas Pendleton, who died in 1534 and whose will is printed in Piccope, *Wills*, ii, 187. Francis died in 1574, leaving his son Henry as heir ; *Ct. Leet Rec.* i, 164, 167. Henry married Elizabeth daughter and heir of Robert Marler ; ibid. i, 233. He died at the beginning of 1586, leaving a son Francis, a minor ; ibid. i, 257. The inquisition taken after the death of Henry Pendleton states that his father Francis had settled his burgage in Deansgate and other lands with remainders to Henry his son, to Margaret, Isabel, and Ellen his daughters, and to his brother George ; the messuage, &c. in Grundy Lane was held of the queen as of her duchy of Lancaster, by knight's service, and the rest of the queen by a rent of 14d. Robert Marler's lands were held of the queen by the 200th part of a knight's fee. Francis, the son and heir of Henry, was ten years of age ; Duchy of Lanc. Inq. p.m. xiv, 61.

Francis Pendleton was of age in 1596 ; *Ct. Leet Rec.* ii, 115, 166. He was thrice married, and died in 1621, leaving as heir a son, under age ; ibid. iii, 37, where an abstract of his will is given. By his second wife, Anne Holland, he had a son Francis, who died at Manchester in 1626 without a son ; and by his third wife, Sarah Byrestowe, had a son Edward, described as ' son and heir ' in 1627, when he was sixteen years of age ; Duchy of Lanc. Inq. p.m. xxvi, 34. The feoffments and will of Francis the father are fully set out in his inquisition, *Lancs. Inq. p.m.* (Rec. Soc. Lancs. and Ches.), iii, 322–6. The will of Alice widow of George Pendleton of Manchester, dated 1588, is given in Piccope, *Wills*, ii, 218–20 ; they had a daughter and heiress Cecily.

[161] Henry Pendleton, D.D., the most prominent of them, is said to have been a brother of the Thomas who died in 1534. He was of Lancashire birth and educated at Brasenose College, Oxford, M.A. 1544 ; D.D. 1552. He was a Protestant and beneficed in the reign of Edward VI, but in the next reverted to the old religion, having frequent disputations with Bradford and others brought before Bishop Bonner on charges of heresy ; he is said to have been shot at when preaching at St. Paul's Cross. He published some homilies, &c., and died in 1557 ; see *Dict. Nat. Biog.* ; Wood, *Athenae*, and Gillow, *Bibl. Dict. of Engl. Cath.* vi, 256 ; Foxe, *Acts and Monuments* (ed. Cattley), vi, 629 ; vii, 185. His nephew, Edward Pendleton (son of Thomas), became fellow of Manchester and vicar of Eccles. A later Henry Pendleton of Manchester compounded for ' delinquency ' in 1645, having taken part against the Parliament by going into the king's quarters. He returned and submitted, took the National Covenant, Negative oath, and paid a fine of £80 ; *Cal. of Com. for Compounding*, ii, 1270.

[162] Adam de Radcliffe had 4 acres in 1320, paying 4s. rent ; *Mamecestre*, ii, 291. He also had part of Gotherswick. To Adam son of Robert de Radcliffe and Alice his daughter, for life, John La Warre in 1324 granted a place called Osecroft with the Brend-orchard, at a rent of 7s. 6d. ; Manch. Corporation D. See also *Mamecestre*, ii, 412 ; iii, 465. A settlement of Adam's lands was made in 1323 ; *Final Conc.* ii, 55. Alice married John de Hulton of Farnworth ; see Harpurhey.

Margery daughter of Henry Luthare in 1428 granted to her son, Robert Tetlow, two burgages in Manchester ; they lay beside the road from the parish church to Salford bridge, abutting on the Irwell at one end and on the road from the church to the parsonage at the other end ; De Trafford D. no. 34. Robert de Tetlow and Elizabeth his wife made a settlement of the same ; ibid. no. 35, 36 ; but in 1430 sold them to Nicholas son of Sir Ralph de Radcliffe, who acquired land adjoining them ; ibid. no. 38, 39. Five years later a settlement was made, the remainders being to Ralph, Thomas, John, James, William, and Edmund, sons of Nicholas, and then to Sir Ralph de Radcliffe ; ibid. no. 45. Nicholas son and heir of Ralph Radcliffe in 1487 made a lease of a burgage in Deansgate, and in the same year the dowry of Elizabeth his mother was settled ; a chief rent of 21. 2d. was payable to the college ; ibid. no. 62, 63, 61. Margery Leigh, daughter and heir of John Marshall, made a grant to Nicholas Radcliffe in 1490 ; ibid. no. 64. The property had passed to the Traffords by 1548 ; Raines, *Chant.* i, 13.

The rental of 1473 shows that the following held burgages : William Radcliffe, divers burgages and an intake, at a rent of 2s. 4d. ; John Radcliffe, a burgage, 12d. ; and Richard Radcliffe, the same ; *Mamecestre*, iii, 489–91.

Richard Radcliffe, lord of Radcliffe, had lands in Manchester in 1501 ; *Lancs. Inq. p.m.* (Chet. Soc.), ii, 148.

Robert Radcliffe of Radcliffe, who died in 1617, held a burgage, &c., of Richard Holland, by a rent of 12d. ; *Lancs. Inq. p.m.* (Rec. Soc. Lancs. and Ches.), ii, 75.

John Radcliffe, *alias* More, purchased messuages, &c., about 1571 ; Pal. of Lanc. Feet of F. bdle. 33, m. 98 ; 34, m. 66 ; 43, m. 99 ; 46, m. 67.

[163] A pedigree of the Radcliffes of the Conduit was recorded in 1613 ; *Visit.* (Chet. Soc.), 130. In 1511–12 James Radcliffe and Thomas his son granted to Robert Laboray land near the end of St. Mary Gate ; and in 1517–18 Thomas son of James Radcliffe made another grant to the same, as ' my brother-in-law ' ; Hulme D. no. 38, 39. Margaret widow of James (son of Thomas) Radcliffe of Manchester was a defendant in 1535 ; Pal. of Lanc. Plea R. 161, m. 2 d. A William Radcliffe and Elizabeth his wife in 1553 had a dispute with the Hulmes, carried on in violent fashion ; *Duchy Plead.* iii, 143, 193. William Radcliffe, said to be grandson of Thomas, occurs frequently in the *Ct. Leet Rec.*, and served as one of the constables. He was described as ' of the Conduit.' At one time he encroached upon Barkhouse Hill and the Cuckstool Pool, but was in 1598 required to lay the ground open again ; *Ct. Leet Rec.* ii, 6, 145. He died early in 1600, and was succeeded by his son William, then of full age ; ibid. ii, 155. The son died in 1608, and his heir, his son William, was of full

Pool ;[164] Tetlow,[165] Tipping,[166] and Willott.[167] In some other cases the inquisitions have been pre-

served.[168] The only freeholders returned in 1600 were John Marler, Richard Haughton, Lawrence

age ; *Ct. Leet. Rec.* ii, 232. It was he who recorded the pedigree in 1613, having then two sons—Richard (aged six) and William—and a daughter Mary. He took an active part in the town's affairs. He died in 1645, when his son Richard succeeded him ; by his will of 1641 he desired to be buried 'within his chapel at Manchester in the same place where his father was buried' ; ibid. iv, 4 ; *Wills* (Chet. Soc. new ser.), ii, 216. The will of his widow Elizabeth in 1659 (ibid. ii, 79) describes her grandson William as 'of Gray's Inn.'

Richard Radcliffe was an active Parliamentarian, being described as captain and major, and was chosen to represent the borough in Parliament in 1656 ; *Civil War Tracts* (Chet. Soc.), 46, 51, 333 ; Pink and Beaven, *Parl. Repre. of Lancs.* 295 ; *Ct. Leet Rec.* iv, 159. He died in 1657, leaving a son William (named above) then under age ; ibid. iv, 205. This son died in 1670, being succeeded in turn by his brothers John (died 1673) and James. A deed of sale relating to a shop in the Shambles or Fleshboards, made by William Radcliffe in 1668, is printed in *Ct. Leet Rec.* v, 136 n. James Radcliffe was summoned in 1675 to do his suit and service on succeeding ; ibid. vi, 8. He had a son William, probably the William Radcliffe who was steward of the lord's court from 1734 to 1743 ; note by Mr. Earwaker ; *Ct. Leet Rec.* vii, 29, 123.

[164] John Radcliffe died in June 1586, holding various burgages and lands in Marketstead Lane and Deansgate, partly of the queen, partly of John Lacy, and partly of William Radcliffe. Alexander, the son and heir, was twelve years of age ; Duchy of Lanc. Inq. p.m. xiv, 44 ; *Ct. Leet Rec.* ii, 4. Alexander Radcliffe did homage in 1595, on coming of age ; ibid. ii, 92. On 16 Aug. 1606 Mary daughter of Alexander Radcliffe, Manchester, of the Hill in Stretford [probably Coldhill otherwise Colddale or Cowdale near Trafford is meant, see *Hist. of Stretford* (Chet. Soc.), i, 121], was baptized at Manchester, and another daughter, Ellen, was baptized there on 4 Sept. 1608, but Alexander died 24 Mar. 1607-8 (ibid. ii, 193). He left a son John, four years old ; *Ct. Leet Rec.* ii, 233 ; *Lancs. Inq. p.m.* (Rec. Soc. Lancs. and Ches.), i, 133.

John Radcliffe did fealty on coming of age in 1625 ; *Ct. Leet Rec.* iii, 89. He was described as 'of the Pool,' and was buried at the collegiate church 28 June 1645, two sons and three daughters being buried about the same time, having been carried off by the plague ; his widow is mentioned in 1654 ; *Ct. Leet Rec.* iv, 115. In Mr. Earwaker's note is given an account of the descent of the property to John Radcliffe's daughter Sarah, who married John Alexander of Manchester, silversmith, and had a son Radcliffe Alexander, in whose will of 1701 mention is made of his dwelling-place called the Pool. See also ibid. v, 94 and vi, 166 (an order to cleanse the Pool, 1684).

The Didsbury registers record these burials : 2 Oct. 1666 ; Mary the wife of Mr. Alexander Ratlef of Stretford ; 11 Aug. 1703 ; Lidie, the wife of Alexander Ratlef of Stretford ; *Hist. of Stretford*, i, 216.

A large number of extracts from the

Manchester register cliffes were printed Nov. and Dec. 18 count of Pool Fo *Pal. Note Bk.* iii, 26

[165] Richard Tetl burgage formerly Jo *mecestre*, iii, 488.

n 1558 Thomas Thomas Tetlow against Thomas Tr Plea R. 203, m. 9 three messuages a widow ; ibid . 20

John Tetlow in ment in right of his and heir of Edmu *Plead.* ii, 162, 163

[166] Richard Tippin family to appear in cords. In 1561 he ing Ditch close to occupied by R cha Leet Rec i, 67, 92 offices, and prospere linen draper, purcha ibid ii, 9 (where a 1587 is printed). his heirs being h (son of John Tipping h s son Samuel given abstracts of h The will of his w Th m Br wn w printed by Piccope, 149

Richard Tipping

245

Langley, and William Barlow.[169] A pedigree of 'Ridge of Manchester' was recorded in 1665.[170]

The local surname was in use in the 13th and 14th centuries, but no connected history can be given of the family or families using it.[171]

The parish church has been described already and its history related. No other church for the Established worship was erected in the township till the beginning of the 18th century. In 1708 an Act was obtained for building a new church;[172] this was erected on a portion of Acres Field, and the Act provided for the continuance of the fair on part of the ground, while allowing the remainder of the land to be built upon. The rector's income was to be derived from pew-rents, and though baptisms, marriages, and burials were allowed, the fees and the registration pertained to the old church.[173] The Bishop of Chester was to appoint the incumbent; the patronage is now

lord of the manor; he left two young daughters as co-heirs; ibid. i, 112. He had purchased the lands of Henry Ainsworth and John (son of Ralph) Sorocold in 1602; *Ct. Leet Rec.* ii, 177, 84, 239. Alice Edge, one of the daughters, in 1620 sold a moiety of a messuage 'at the end of Salford bridge' to Edward Chetham; ibid. iii, 29.

Robert Hulton, 'whittawer,' died in 1621 holding a messuage, &c., in Manchester of Edward Mosley by a rent of 9*d.*; the heir was his grandson, George, son of George Hulton, twelve years of age; *Lancs. Inq. p.m.* (Rec. Soc.), ii, 244, where the settlement made by Robert Hulton's will is given; *Ct. Leet Rec.* iii, 48.

William Newsome died in 1621, holding a messuage of Edward Mosley; William, his son and heir, was thirty years of age; Towneley MS. C, 8, 13 (Chet. Lib.), 914; *Ct. Leet Rec.* iii, 52. The younger William's executors in 1652 sold lands to Mrs. Elizabeth Lomax; ibid. iv, 74.

Jasper Fox died in 1623 holding burgages, &c., in Marketstead and Deansgate of the king; his son and heir Richard was seven years old; Towneley MS. C, 8, 13, p. 427. Jasper was the son of Richard Fox, who died in 1622 (and who was the son of another Richard Fox, who died in 1587; *Ct. Leet Rec.* ii, 12), holding lands in Deansgate and (Old) Millgate purchased from Shallcross and Byrom; ibid. iii, 51, where his will is given. The family appear to have taken an active part in the town's affairs. Richard, the son of Jasper, came of age in 1637; ibid. iii, 251. He died in or before 1655, leaving two sons, Richard and James; ibid. iv, 240; his will is printed in the note.

Stephen Rodley or Radley, who had an estate in Nottingham, held burgages, &c., in Manchester at his death in 1630, as follows : One in Marketstead, bought of Francis Pendleton; others in Hanging Ditch, Rawlinson's Croft, Withy Grove, and Shudehill Lane; also four messuages in Blackley; William, his son and heir, was twelve years old; Towneley MS. C, 8, 13, p. 1002. The surname frequently occurs in the *Ct. Leet Rec.* from 1552 onwards, and in 1604 it was reported that one Robert Rodley had died, and that his grandson Robert was his heir and of full age; ibid. ii, 198. Stephen Rodley is first named in 1613, when he was appointed a constable; ibid. ii, 281. William his son came of age in 1639; ibid. iii, 285, and see the note. Robert Rodley was of Collyhurst in 1619; *Hist. of Newton Chapelry* (Chet. Soc.), ii, 76; *Manch. Ct. Leet Rec.* iii, 18; also in 1623; *Newton*, ii, 278.

Henry Johnson of Manchester, mercer, held burgages and shops near the Smithy Door, &c., of Edward Mosley by 12*d.* rent, and died in 1637, leaving a son and heir Thomas, sixteen years of age ; Duchy of Lanc probably another in 1653 there is

Willia a messu year old Ct. Leet summary draper.

Willia messuag house w 1639, le —Marga younger Elizabet years of one ; To Leet Rec wife of wills of of his w

Thom ing two

enjoyed by the Bishop of Manchester as his successor.[174] It was called St. Ann's, in compliment to the reigning monarch and to Ann, Lady Bland, lady of the manor, who resided at Hulme Hall, and took an active part in the work.[175] The building was begun in May, 1709, and consecrated on 12 July 1712. A district was assigned to it in 1839.[176] St. Ann's is a good type of the classic town church of its day, rectangular in plan with an apsidal east end and a west tower. It is built of red sandstone which has weathered so badly that the exterior has had to be almost wholly refaced in recent years.[177] Externally the building is of two stories with two tiers of large round-headed windows on each side having moulded sills, architraves, and keystones, but without impost mouldings, the upper windows lighting the galleries, and the wall being divided at half its height by a shallow entablature supported by very flat coupled

ST. ANN'S CHURCH, MANCHESTER

Corinthian pilasters. In the upper stage the pilasters are without capitals and support a cornice only, above which is a square parapet formerly with balusters and ornamented with urns and vases, but now quite plain. There are entrances at the west end of the nave facing north and south, with pediments supported by coupled Corinthian columns, and the apse has fluted pilasters of the same order its full height with an entablature of good proportions the frieze of which is enriched with carved ornament. The tower is of three stages, the upper having a round-headed louvred belfry window flanked by coupled pilasters on each side. Below is a clock. The tower now terminates in a cornice

longing to the 17th century, fourteen to the 18th, and three to the 19th. The earliest is a complete set consisting of two chalices, two cover patens, two credence patens, a large flagon, and an almsdish of 1697, all with the mark of John Bathe. The flagon is inscribed, 'Ex dono Johannis Sandiford,' the cover patens, 'S. Ann's Church, Manchester,' and the almsdish, 'St. Ann's Manchester.' The other pieces are without inscription. The 18th-century plate comprises a tankard of 1701, inscribed 'St. Ann's Ch. M.'; a plate and two tankards of 1716, all inscribed, 'Given to St. Ann's Church by Mr. Edward Mosley, son of Oswald Mosley, Esq., of Ancoats in

174 The patronage of this and other churches held by the Bishop of Chester was transferred to the Bishop of Manchester in 1859.

175 Bardsley, op. cit. 12; the author gives some reasons for supposing that it

was built for the Whigs or Low Churchmen of the town.

176 Lond. Gaz. 29 Mar. 1839.

177 Church 1905, tower 1907.

178 There is a local tradition that Wren or one of his pupils designed the building, St. Andrew's Holborn being the model.

Dr. Byrom wrote to his wife in 1752 from London, 'Mr. Hooper, Clowes, and I went in a coach and light at Holborn and went into St. Andrew's Church. It was the model, I believe, of the new church at Manchester.' There is, however, no evidence to substantiate the tradition.

the parish of Manchester 1714';[178a] a small cup and cover paten of 1743; and a set formerly belonging to St. Mary's Church, consisting of two chalices, two cover patens, a credence paten, two flagons, and an almsdish, of 1756. The almsdish is inscribed 'The gift of Catherine Fisher widow, 1756,' and the credence paten has the following inscription : 'Dei gloriae et honori populi commodo et saluti ecclesia Sanctae Mariae pro lege lata A.D. 1753. Suscepta Festo Sancti Michaelis A.D. 1756 consecrata. Quo die hoc argenteum cum duobus calicibus lagenis et patinis ad eucharistiis perpetuo celebrandum guardiani et Socij Col. Christi in Mancr. jure patronatus gaudentes dederunt.'

There are also three chalices of 1841 made by Elkingtons, inscribed 'St. Ann's Church, Manchester. Rev. H. W. McGrath, M.A., Rector, 1841.'[179] The registers begin in 1736.[179a]

The next church was built under an Act[179b] obtained in 1753 by the warden and fellows of the collegiate church, after the old political animosities had decayed. It stood upon their land called the Parsonage Croft, lying between Deansgate and the Irwell, and was called St. Mary's. It was consecrated in 1756, and the incumbents, styled rectors, were presented by the warden and fellows. It was a plain classic building, with a spire 186 ft. high, which in its time was greatly admired.[180] There was a graveyard round the building. This church was pulled down in 1890, and the site is now an open grass-covered square.[181] The district, assigned in 1839,[182] has been annexed to St. Ann's.

St. Paul's, a plain brick edifice with a stone tower, was built on the eastern border of the town at the corner of Turner Street and Tib Street in 1765;[183] it was in 1878 replaced by the present St. Paul's, New Cross.[184] St. John's (the Evangelist) was built in 1769 in the Gothic of the time by Edward Byrom of Kersal, whose Manchester residence was close by ; a graveyard is attached to it.[185] The tower was finished in May, 1770, and contains a ring of eight bells by Lester and Pack of London, 1768-9. St. James's, behind the Infirmary, was consecrated in 1787; in 1816 its congregation was 'the most numerous of any of the Established churches,' except the old church. This church also had a burial ground.[186] St. Michael's, Angel Street, on the way to Collyhurst, is a plain brick building, with burial ground attached, consecrated in 1787; the church was consecrated two years later.[186a] St. Clement's, Lever Street, has now disappeared; it was opened in 1793 by licence.[186b] St. Peter's, begun in 1788, consecrated in 1794, and demolished in 1907, was a small classic building, near the present town hall.[186c] The patronage of all these churches, except, of course, St. Clement's, is vested in the dean and canons of Manchester.

St. George's Church, formerly distinguished as ' in the Fields,' stood upon part of the site of Oldham Road Station. It was a brick building, opened speculatively in 1798, but not succeeding was transferred to Lady Huntingdon's Connexion ; it was restored to the establishment and consecrated in 1818.[187] In 1877 it was rebuilt in Oldham Road. The Bishop of Manchester has the patronage.

[178a] The inscribed date is two years earlier than the date letter.

[179] Bardsley, *Memorials of St. Ann's Church*, 14 n. The plate formerly belonging to St. Mary's has been transferred to St. Ann's (see inscriptions)

[179a] MS. transcript may be seen at the Reference Library.

[179b] 26 Geo. II, cap. 45.

[180] Aston, *Manch.* 76-8 ; the interior was dark but 'solemnly handsome.' The spire was taken down in 1854.

[181] For an account of the church see *Lancs. and Ches. Antiq. Soc.* viii, 137. The graveyard inscriptions are in the Owen MSS. There is a transcript of the registers in the Reference Library.

[182] *Lond. Gaz.* 29 Mar. 1839.

[183] Aston, *Manch.* 78.

[184] A district was assigned in 1839; *Lond. Gaz.* ut sup.

[185] Aston, op. cit. 79-82. One of the stained-glass windows was brought from a convent at Rouen. The building is of brick, with west tower, and was restored in 1874-8, when the galleries were removed. The patronage was vested in the heirs of the founder for one turn after the first appointment. It was built under a special Act, 9 Geo. III, cap. 60 ; *Pal. Note Bk.* iv, 81.

The church is noteworthy as the scene of the labours of the 'amiable, venerated and respected' John Clowes, M.A., fellow of Trinity Coll. Cambridge. He was from 1773 an ardent disciple of Emmanuel Swedenborg, and devoted his energies and wealth to the propagation of the new doctrines ; it is no doubt through him that Swedenborgianism made great progress in the Manchester district. His zeal did not prevent his receiving offers of preferment in the Established Church. He died in

SALFORD

St. Matthew's, Campfield,[188] and St. Andrew's, Ancoats,[189] were built in 1825 and 1831 respectively, out of the Parliamentary grant for church building; the dean and canons of Manchester are patrons. They also present to All Souls', Ancoats, consecrated in 1840.[190] In this year another church in Ancoats was consecrated—St. Jude's, built in 1821 by the 'Tent Methodists,'[191] and sold by them in 1835;[192] it was rebuilt in 1866. St. Simon and St. Jude's in Granby Row was consecrated in 1842; the Bishop of Manchester was patron of this church,[193] and is still of St. Thomas's, Red Bank, 1844.[194] The other modern churches are:—St. Barnabas, near Oldham Road, consecrated 1844;[195] St. Philip's, Ancoats, 1850;[196] St. Oswald's, Collyhurst, 1855;[197] St. John, the Evangelist's Miles, Platting, 1855—twenty-five years ago famous for a Ritualistic controversy, the incumbent, the Rev. Sidney Faithorne Green, ultimately losing his benefice;[198] patron Sir A. P. Heywood; St. Catherine's, Collyhurst Road, 1859;[199] St. Peter's, Oldham Road, 1860;[200] the Albert Memorial Church, Collyhurst, 1864;[201] St. James the Less, near Great Ancoats, 1870;[202] St. Martin's Ancoats, 1873;[203] St. James's, on the site of Collyhurst Old Hall, 1874,[204] patron the representative of the Rev. C. N. Keeling, first rector, who died in 1907; and St. Saviour's, not yet consecrated, patron the Crown and Bishop of Manchester alternately. Where not otherwise stated the patronage is in the hands of various bodies of trustees. The incumbents are all styled rectors. St. Philip's and the Albert Memorial have mission halls.

From the Revolution down to the end of the 18th century, a non-juring congregation—the True British Catholic Church—existed in Manchester. Dr. Thomas Deacon, who died in 1753, was one of its bishops,[205] and Mr. Kenrick Price, a tea dealer, who died in Liverpool in 1790, was the last.[206]

The Church Congress held its meetings in Manchester in 1863, 1888, and 1908.

---

[188] Sir Charles Barry was the architect. It was one of his first essays in Gothic, and a 'subject for laughter' in his later days; *Life of Sir C. Barry*, 68. The district was assigned in 1828; *Lond. Gaz.* 4 July.

[189] A district was assigned in 1839.

[190] The church was built for Dr. Samuel Warren (father of the novelist), who had been expelled from the Wesleyan Methodist Connexion. A district was assigned to it in 1842; *Lond. Gaz.* 19 July.

[191] For this body see Nightingale, *Lancs. Nonconf.* v, 181, 182.

[192] Axon, *Ann. of Manch.* 195.

[193] The church has been closed; the district is added to St. James's.

[194] A district was formed for it in 1844, and altered in 1856; *Lond. Gaz.* 1 July.

[195] A district was granted in 1844; *Lond. Gaz.* 22 Oct.

[196] For district and endowment, *Lond. Gaz.* 22 Mar. 1850.

[197] A district was assigned in 1856; *Lond. Gaz.* 1 July.

[198] For details of the matter, which lasted from 1879 till 1882, see T. Hughes, *Life of Bishop Fraser*, 254–84.

[199] A district was formed in 1860; *Lond. Gaz.* 16 May.

[200] For district see *Lond. Gaz.* 3 Aug. 1860.

[201] For district, ibid. 10 Jan. 1865.

earlier.[216] The introduction of Unitarian doctrine at Cross Street Chapel is believed to have had much to do with the formation of this separate assembly, which was Trinitarian. In 1762 a new building was erected in Hunter's Croft, Cannon Street; [217] it was soon enlarged, and in 1828 practically rebuilt. By 1856 the congregation had been dispersed in the suburbs, and in 1860 the building was sold, the church in Chorlton Road, Old Trafford, having taken its place. In 1807 a new church had branched off from Cannon Street, though not without friction, and opened a place of worship in Grosvenor Street, near the Infirmary.[217] An earlier secession from Cannon Street, in consequence of a dispute with the minister, led to the formation of a church in Mosley Street in 1788.[218] It was at Mosley Street Chapel that the Lancashire Union of Independent Churches was formed in 1806. This building was abandoned in 1848, being replaced by that in Cavendish Street, Chorlton upon Medlock; Dr. Robert Halley, the historian of Lancashire Puritanism, was minister at that time. Grosvenor Street Church is still in use, and there are five others, at Knott Mill, and between Ancoats and Collyhurst. There is also at Collyhurst a Welsh Congregational church.

The Presbyterian [219] Church of England has a place of worship in Ancoats. It is known as Chalmers Chapel, and was built in 1854.[220]

The Salvation Army has four barracks on the east and north-east fringe of the township.

The Quakers have existed in Manchester since the time of George Fox, who visited the town in 1647, and again in 1657; on the latter occasion the 'rude people' from the country threw at him 'coals, clods, stones and water,' but he remarks that 'the Lord hath since raised up a people to stand for His name and truth in that town.'[221] Their first meeting-house was in Jackson's Row; it was rebuilt in 1732, but quitted in 1795 for a new one in Mount Street; this was rebuilt in 1830.[222] It has a library containing early Quaker books.

The original Nonconformist chapel is that in Cross Street, which was built for Henry Newcome in 1693–4.[223] This celebrated divine had been chaplain of the Collegiate Church for a few years during the Commonwealth, but on the Restoration was not admitted to a fellowship. He then ministered in private as well as he could during the period of proscription from 1662 to 1687. He died the year after the chapel was opened, and was buried there.[224]

The site of the chapel had been known as Plungeon's meadow, from the owner's name.[224a] The place was damaged by the mob in 1715, but was restored with the aid of a grant from Parliament. It was enlarged and rebuilt in 1737. There is a small graveyard.

The following is a list of the ministers of this chapel, some of whom were of more than local eminence [225] :—

Henry Newcome, M.A., 1687–95
John Chorlton, 1687–1705
James Coningham, M.A., 1700–12
Eliezer Birch, 1710–17
Joseph Mottershead, 1717–71
Joshua Jones, 1725–40
John Seddon, M.A., 1741–69
Robert Gore, 1770–79
Ralph Harrison, 1771–1810
Thomas Barnes, D.D., 1780–1810
John Grundy, 1811–24
John Gooch Robberds, 1811–54
John Hugh Worthington, 1825–7
William Gaskell, M.A., 1828–54
James Panton Ham, 1855–59
James Drummond, D.D., 1860–69
Samuel Alfred Steinthal, 1871–93
William Hamilton Drummond, B.A., 1889–93
Edwin Pinder Barrow, M.A., 1893

It was under the joint pastorate of Mottershead and Seddon that the teaching changed from Trinitarian to Unitarian. A secession in 1789 led to the formation of a second Unitarian congregation in Mosley Street, which in 1837 moved to Chorlton upon Medlock.[226] Sunday schools are now maintained in Lower Mosley Street, and there is also a church in Collyhurst. The Academy for training Nonconformist ministers, originally founded at Warrington, was re-established at Manchester in 1786; it was transferred to York in 1803, and afterwards to Chorlton upon Medlock, London, and Oxford, where, as Manchester College, it is still flourishing.[227]

The Swedenborgians had a temple called, as usual, New Jerusalem, built in 1793 in Peter Street.[228] It was sold before 1890, and churches built at Moss Side, Broughton, and Pendleton.

The Bible Christians had Christ Church, built in 1823 in Every Street, and known as the Round Chapel. It came into the possession of the Salvation Army.[228a]

[216] Nightingale, *Lancs. Nonconf.* v, 107–47; from this account the brief summary in the text is derived. For the Ancoats, Oldham Road, Ashley Lane, and Queen's Park churches, see ibid. 180–8, 190.

[217] The *Confession of Faith*, &c., of the Church of Christ in Hunter's Croft, Manchester, was printed in 1764.

[217a] Copies of the inscriptions are in the Owen MSS.

[218] This chapel had a famous minister in Dr. Robert S. McAll, who died in 1838.

[219] The 'Scots Calvinists,' or United Secession Church, built a chapel, called St. Andrew's, in Lloyd Street in 1799; it was removed to Brunswick Street, Chorlton upon Medlock, in 1858, and now belongs to the Presbyterian Church of England. Another Scotch Church, in Mosley Street, was founded in 1831.

Mormon missionaries visited the town in 1840.

The Welsh Calvinistic Methodists formerly had a chapel in Cooper Street, built in 1824.[229]

The Dutch Evangelicals or Lutherans in 1857 had a meeting-place in John Dalton Street.

There exist a City Mission founded in 1837 and supported by what are known as the Evangelical denominations, and a Domestic Mission, which is Unitarian.

The adherents of the ancient faith appear to have disappeared very quickly after the Reformation, and by the end of Elizabeth's reign there were probably few known in the whole parish except the Barlows of Barlow.[230] In 1651 Richard Martinscroft, 'a poor old man, over sixty years of age,' is found to have had two-thirds of his estate 'sequestered for his recusancy only' : he had a large house in Manchester, divided into three dwellings, but lived two or three miles away.[231] The list of 'Papists' supplied to Bishop Gastrell about 1717 records only thirteen in Manchester and three in Salford,[232] but a later list, 1767, gives the number as 373, principally in Manchester, Salford, and Stretford.[233] What attempts were made to provide priests in the first century of the proscription is unknown, but soon after the Restoration one Thomas Weedon had charge of a large district including most of the Salford and Macclesfield Hundreds, and appears to have resided chiefly at Manchester, where he died in 1719.[234] Mass, it is related, was said in secret near the present Blackfriars Bridge, in a room which was used as a warehouse during the week.[235] About 1760 rooms were secured off Church Street in the passage on that account known as Roman Entry. Some fifteen years later a house containing a large room to be used as a church was built in Rook Street.[236] It was known as St. Chad's, and is now represented by St. Chad's, Cheetham Hill Road, erected in 1847. St. Mary's in Mulberry Street was built in 1794,[236a] and rebuilt in 1835 ; the roof fell in soon afterwards, but the church remained in use until 1847, when the present one, on the same confined site, was erected, being dedicated in 1848. To these have been added St. Augustine's, 1820 ;[237] St. Patrick's, 1832 ;[238] St. Anne's, Ancoats, 1847–8 ; St. Michael's, 1859 ; and St. Alban's, Ancoats. St.

William's, Angel Meadow, 1864, is a chapel of ease to St. Chad's ; and the Polish mission of St. Casimir, 1904, to St. Patrick's. The Sisters of Charity have a night refuge in Ancoats.

The Jews had a synagogue, a humble room off Long Millgate, a century ago ; about 1826 they built one in Halliwell Street, which has now disappeared.[239]

Among the distinguishing features of Whit-week in Manchester are the processions of the Sunday School children. They began in 1801.

CHORLTON-UPON-MEDLOCK

Cherleton, 1196 ; Chorleton, Chorelton, 1212 ; Chorlton, 1278. Choleron, perhaps by mistake, xv cent.

This township, formerly known as Chorlton Row,[1] lies on the south side of the Medlock, and has an area of 646½ acres.[2] It has long been urban in character, the plan of 1793 showing that a large number of streets were then being laid out. It was crossed near the centre by Cornbrook, and had Rusholme Brook, a tributary of the former, for its southern boundary. The district called Greenheys lies in the south-west, in the angle between the two brooks. In 1901 there was a population of 57,894.

The principal streets are Oxford Street and Upper Brook Street, going south-east from the centre of Manchester ; the latter has an offshoot called Plymouth Grove, in a more easterly direction, reaching the Stockport Road, which runs along the eastern boundary, near Longsight. There are many public buildings in the township, in addition to churches and schools. On the west of Oxford Street is Grosvenor Square, on one side of which stands the town hall, built in 1831, with police station, dispensary, and school of art adjacent ; the union offices are situated on another side of the square. Further to the south, in the same street, lie the extensive buildings of Owens College, founded in Quay Street in 1851, and transferred to this site in 1873 ; it is now the seat of the Victoria University of Manchester. On the

[229] Baines, Lancs. Dir. ii, 140. They had another in Gartside Street in 1826.

[230] In the whole parish in 1626 there were only four 'convicted recusants and non-communicants' paying specially; Lay Subs. R. 131/312. For presentments of recusants at the beginning of the 17th century see Manch. Constables' Accts. i, 56, 162, 165.

[231] Royalist Comp. Papers (Rec. Soc. Lancs. and Ches.), iv, 122, 123.

[232] Notitia Cestr. ii, 57, &c. Susannah Reddish, widow, in 1717 as a 'papist' registered a small estate in Salford ; Estcourt and Payne, Engl. Cath. Non-jurors, 153. In 1729 the Rev. Will. Huddleston, O.S.B., publicly renounced his religion in the Collegiate Church ; Manch. Guardian N. and Q. no. 1263; Loc. Gleanings, ii, 128.

[233] Trans. Hist. Soc. (New Ser.), xviii, 214. The details of the chapelries were: Manchester, 287 ; Blackley, 1 ; Chorlton, 1 (viz. Mr. Barlow) ; Salford, 64 ; Stretford, 20 (exclusive of Mr. Trafford, who lived mostly at York).

[234] This account is chiefly derived from

a statement prepared by Mr. Joseph Gillow in 1902. Thomas Weedon, a Worcestershire man, was admitted to the English College at Rome in 1658, and was sent on the mission in 1663 ; Foley, Rec. S.J. vi, 395.

[235] Manch. Guardian N. and Q. no. 278. Baines, on the other hand, states that 'in the early part of the last (18th) century the Catholics had a chapel in Smithy Door, in a building now the Grey Horse public-house, behind which there is still a large unoccupied piece of ground, then used as a burial ground' ; Lancs. Dir. ii, 139.

[236] 'At that time toleration was not sufficiently liberal to allow any insulated Catholic chapel, and like all others of that day, the one under consideration is attached to a dwelling-house' ; Aston, Manch. [1816), 93. A description follows.

[236a] The builder was one of the most notable personages in Manchester in his time—Rowland Broomhead, a Yorkshireman, born 1751, educated at the English College, Rome, and ordained priest in 1775. He was sent to Manchester in

1778, and laboured there till his death in 1820, gaining universal respect ; Gillow, Bibl. Dict. of Engl. Cath. i, 316.

[237] This is about to be closed, the site being required for the corporation. It is to be rebuilt in Chorlton-upon-Medlock.

[238] There were stormy scenes at this church in 1846, the priest in charge (Daniel Hearne) having a dispute with the Vicar Apostolic ; Gillow, Bibl. Dict. of Engl. Cath. iii, 232.

[239] Aston, Manch. 105 ; Baines, Lancs. Dir. ii, 141.

[1] This name is found in 1594 ; Ducatus Lanc. (Rec. Com.), iii, 299. It was usual down to the first part of last century. The name may be connected with the Roocroft mentioned in a deed cited below. Row is popularly supposed to have reference to a former avenue of trees from London Road up to Chorlton Hall, but the name is much older than any such row of trees. The epithet was due to a desire to distinguish the township from the other Chorlton, now called Chorlton with Hardy.

[2] 647 acres ; Census Rep. 1901.

border of the township is Whitworth Park, in which is an art gallery. The Royal Manchester College of Music is in Ducie Street. On the east side of Oxford Street is an Eye Hospital, while another hospital lies between Oxford Street and Upper Brook Street. To the east of the latter thoroughfare there is a Free Library, opened in 1866 ;[3] also the Rusholme Road Cemetery, formed in 1823 for the use of Protestant Dissenters. In Plymouth Grove is a large Home for the Aged. There are fire stations on the Stockport Road, and a drill shed at Greenheys. The new Infirmary is within this township.

In 1666 the principal residence in Chorlton Row was that of Ellis Hey, with five hearths liable to the tax ; in the whole township there were forty-nine.[4] Chorlton obtained a Police Act in 1822[4a] and a Lighting Act in 1832.[5] It was included in Manchester borough on incorporation in 1838, and was then divided into two wards, All Saints' and St. Luke's, on the west and east respectively. The township, as such, has now ceased to exist, and forms part of the new township of South Manchester, created in 1896.

Neolithic implements have been found.[6]

Thomas De Quincey, born in Manchester, lived in his youth at Greenheys, which was built by his father about 1791, and has recorded his memories of the place.[7] John Ashton Nicholls, philanthropist, was born in Grosvenor Street in 1823 ; he died in 1859.[8] Mrs. Gaskell resided in the township, and in *Mary Barton* described the district as it

was in 1848. Sir Charles Hallé lived in Greenheys for about forty years.

The manor of *CHORLTON*, which
MANOR once included Beswick, or part of it, was at the beginning of the 13th century held of the king in thegnage by a local family ; it was assessed as two plough-lands, and a rent of 20s. was the annual service.[9] Gospatrick de Chorlton was tenant in 1202, when his son Richard's widow claimed dower,[10] and in 1212, when the great survey was made.[11] He died in or before 1223, when his son Brun received seisin of one plough-land in Chorlton, having paid the king 2 marks as relief.[12] It probably escheated to the Crown soon afterwards, as it became part of the possessions of the Grelleys and La Warres, lords of Manchester, being held as one plough-land by the old service of 20s.[13]

Gospatrick had lost four oxgangs of land to Matthew son of William [de Hathersage] by wager of battle.[14] He had granted a further two oxgangs to his brother Adam, in view of Adam's fighting for him against William son of Wulfric de Withington.[15] Four oxgangs of land also he gave to Henry de Trafford, who held a fifth in 1212.[16]

The Grelleys, on acquiring the lordship, appear to have granted it, without exacting any service, to a junior branch of the family, as one Robert Grelley was in possession in 1278[17] and was succeeded by a son John, who in 1334 alienated his lands in Chorlton to Henry de Trafford.[18] The Traffords thus acquired

[3] The Female Penitentiary, founded in 1836, was formerly on this site.
[4] Subs. R. bdle. 250, no. 9.
[4a] 3 Geo. IV, cap. 14.
[5] 2 & 3 Will. IV, cap. 90.
[6] *Lancs. and Ches. Antiq. Soc.* v, 328.
[7] In *Autobiographic Sketches* and *Confessions of an Opium Eater.*
[8] *Dict. Nat. Biog.*
[9] *Lancs. Inq. and Extents* (Rec. Soc. Lancs. and Ches.), i, 69. This place occurs earlier in the Pipe Rolls, for in 1177–8 account was rendered of the ½ mark of aid due from it ; Farrer, *Lancs. Pipe R.* 36.
  There is much danger of confusion between Chorlton in Manchester and Chorlton (Chollerton) in Withington, as is shown by Booker's *Chorlton Chapel,* &c.
[10] *Final Conc.* (Rec. Soc. Lancs. and Ches.), i, 14 ; Ellen, the widow, received for life one oxgang of land out of two which Austin de Chorlton held ; also four selions—two by Jordan's ditch and two by Jordan's selion—in return for the moiety of the capital messuage belonging to her oxgang.
  Gospatrick de Chorlton occurs about the same time in the Pipe Rolls ; *Lancs. Pipe R.* 152, 205.
[11] *Lancs. Inq. and Extents,* i, 69, 128.
[12] *Fine R. Excerpts* (Rec. Com.), i, 103.
[13] In 1324 John la Warre held it ; Dods. MSS. cxxxi, fol. 38b.
[14] *Lancs. Inq. and Extents,* i, 69. These oxgangs were by Matthew granted to the father of Richard and Jordan le Norreys of Heaton Norris, and became Jordan's by agreement in 1196 ; *Final Conc.* i, 5. Jordan's ditch and selion have been mentioned in a foregoing note.
[15] *Lancs. Inq. and Extents,* i, 70 ; a service of 3s. 4d. was due. Gospatrick's charter is in Harl. MS. 2112, fol. 165 ; and *Stretford* (Chet. Soc.), iii, 232. It referred to ' an eighth part of Chorlton.'

[16] *La* of 6s. 3

practically the whole manor, but part was afterwards held by the Traffords of Garrett.[19] The hall and its demesne lands were in 1590 sold by Sir Edmund Trafford to Ralph Sorocold of Golborne,[20] who sold it to Ellis Hey of Eccles, and in 1644 it was sold by the younger Ellis Hey[21] to Thomas Minshull, apothecary of Manchester.[22] The Minshulls also acquired the adjacent Garrett estate, and Hough Hall in Moston. The whole came by marriage into the possession of Roger Aytoun of Inchdarney in Fife,

township is included, together with the Garrett estate in Ancoats.

John Grelley retained an interest in the lands for his life, and in 1363 complained of waste of houses, &c., in Chorlton by Robert son of Sir Henry de Trafford ; De Banco R. 416, m. 257.

Henry de Trafford in 1389 granted to Sir Ralph de Radcliffe and Margery his wife (widow of Henry's father), for her life, 'two parts of his manor of Chorlton, which lately remained to the said Henry as his right after the death of John Grelley,' at a rent of 4 marks ; De Trafford D. no. 125.

The tenure of this portion of Chorlton seems to be defined in an inquisition of 1410, where Thomas de Trafford's six messuages, 100 acres of land, 20 acres of meadow, and water-mill are stated to be held of the lord of Manchester by rendering a clove gillyflower ; Lancs. Inq. p.m. (Chet. Soc.), i, 96. For other Trafford inquisitions, in which the statements vary, see ibid. i, 128 ; ii, 16. Ellen widow of Thomas de Trafford, in 1448, claimed dower against Henry de Trafford (a minor) in Chorlton and Manchester ; Pal. of Lanc. Plea R. 11, m. 14b.

According to the Manchester Rental of 1473 Henry Trafford held Chorlton by a rent of 6s. ; Mamecestre, iii, 483.

Sir Edmund Trafford, being seised of the manor of Chorlton, with meadow, pasture, and arable land appurtenant, leased the same in 1507 for thirty years to Richard Beswick and Margaret his wife. When left a widow, Margaret was expelled by Edmund Trafford and others in 1523 ; Duchy of Lanc. Plead. Hen. VIII, xvii, B. 5.

Edmund Trafford died in 1563 holding lands in Chorlton of the lord of Manchester by a rent of 12d. only, so that some, probably, had been sold ; Duchy of Lanc. Inq. p.m. xi, 11.

[19] See the account of Garrett in Manchester.

[20] The statement of the descent of the manor is taken from Canon Raines in Notitia Cestr. ii, 83, 84, except where further references are given. It will be seen that it requires some correction.

Sir Edmund Trafford was in 1578 seised of the vill of Chorlton, parcel of the manor of Manchester ; Duchy of Lanc. Plead. cviii, W. 1. He died in 1590, and his son Edmund, who appears to have sold various parts of his inheritance, in Sept. 1590, demised or mortgaged Chorlton Hall and its lands to Ralph Sorocold, and followed this with further leases, including one of the tithes of Stretford (on lease from the warden and fellows of Manchester). He took possession again in 1598 after Ralph's death, alleging payment of his debt ; for the widow Katherine, who had married Thomas Goodyear, made complaint ; Duchy of Lanc. Plead. Eliz. clxxxvi, T. 14. Four years later Edmund Trafford, then high sheriff, complained that Adam Hol-

land of Newton, after agreeing to purchase Chorlton Hall, paying £550 and a ground rent of 20s., had refused to pay, 'to the great inconvenience of the plaintiff, who was in need of the money' ; ibid. ccvii, T. 4.

[21] Some part at least of the Hey lands in Withington and Chorlton was sold to the Mosleys before 1614 ; it was held of the king by the hundredth part of a knight's fee ; Lancs. Inq. p.m. (Rec. Soc. Lancs. and Ches.), ii, 4, 66, 69.

Ellis Hey is described as 'of Chorlton Hall' in 1665, when he recorded a pedigree ; Dugdale, Visit. (Chet. Soc.), 133.

[22] Ibid. 199. The family were near akin to Elizabeth Minshull, Milton's third wife; Earwaker, East. Ches. i, 391. Thomas Minshull is frequently named in the Manch. Ct. Leet Rec. but is not styled 'of Chorlton.' He was the son of Richard Minshull of Wistaston ; he married Anne daughter of James Lightbowne, by whom he had several children, and died in 1698. Thomas, the eldest son, aged twenty-five in 1664, succeeded to Chorlton and died in 1702, the heir being his brother Richard, who died in or about 1722. His son Thomas died in 1749, leaving a son Thomas Samuel Minshull, who died without issue in 1755 ; his daughters and his brother George's daughter also died without issue, and by bequest the estates passed to Barbara Nabb, the widow of Thomas, who married Roger Aytoun in 1769, and died in 1783. This statement is from Piccope's MS. Pedigrees (Chet. Lib.), ii, 296.

The bequest mentioned is recited in a lengthy abstract of the title of William Cooper, Samuel Marsland, Peter Marsland, and George Duckworth to a capital messuage called Chorlton Hall, with the lands, &c., belonging thereto, in Chorlton Row. By his will Richard Minshull of the Inner Temple (1722) devised all his lands to his wife for life, and then to his sons Thomas and George in tail male, and to his right heirs. Thomas the son in 1742–3 suffered a recovery to bar the entail, and by his will of 1744 left his estates to his son Thomas (Samuel), subject to the dower of his wife Barbara, and £1,500, the portion of his daughter Elizabeth, who afterwards married James Rivington, bookseller, of London.

The son by his will of 1754 left Chorlton Hall to his mother for life, charged with an annuity to his grandmother Dorothy Nabb, then to trustees for his sister, his uncle George and daughter, and their issue, with final remainder to his mother (Barbara). In 1769, by the failure of all the heirs named, Barbara became possessed of the Minshull estates, and in 1770 there was a fine concerning Chorlton Hall, Garrett Hall, and other lands, Roger Aytoun and Barbara his wife being deforciants (Pal. of Lanc. Feet of F. bdle. 384, m. 8), quickly followed by various mortgages.

year 1551[17] and probably dispersed soon afterwards.[18]

The Minshulls were thus the first resident owners
of importance, and there are but few references to
Chorlton before the 17th cen-
tury.[19] The land tax returns
of 1784 show that the ownership was much divided ; Roger
Aytoun still had the largest
share, paying about a fifth of
the tax ; then came John Taylor, the Gore-Booths, Mrs.
Piggott, Mr. Melland, Mrs.
Hyde, and John Dickenson.[20]

Chorlton was recognized as
a separate township before
1618, when its constables are
mentioned.[21]

MINSHULL of Chorl-
ton. *Azure a crescent
therefrom issuant an es-
toile argent.*

At one time *GREENLOW HEATH* appears to
have been considered a separate township.[22] About
1320 it was demised to Sir John Byron and his wife
for life at a rent of 100s. a year.[23] A century later
it was in the possession of Thomas la Warre, with
remainder to Sir John Byron, Robert de Langley,
Robert son of John del Booth, and William del
Booth ; it was held of the king as of his duchy, and
was worth 40s. clear per annum.[24]

The township having during the last century become a residential suburb of Manchester, a large
number of places of worship have been built. For
the Established Church St. Luke's was built in 1804 ;
it was consecrated in 1858 and rebuilt in 1865 ;[25]
All Saints', which has a mission church called
St. Matthias', dates from 1820 ;[26] St. Saviour's,

1836 ;[27] St. Stephen's, 1833 ;[28] St. Paul's, 1862 ;[29]
St. Clement's, Greenheys, 1881 ;[30] and St. Ambrose, 1884. The Bishop of Manchester collates
to the last of these ; the dean and canons present
to All Saints' ; the Rev. W. F. Birch, now rector,
to St. Saviour's, and bodies of trustees to the
others. The incumbents are styled rectors. In
connexion with St. Ambrose's is St. David's Welsh
church.

The Wesleyan Methodists have three churches and
the United Free Church one, which superseded an
older one, called the Tabernacle, in 1870. There is
a Welsh Wesleyan chapel at Greenheys.

The Baptists have Union Church in Oxford Road
and two others, one of them belonging to the Particular
Baptists.

The Congregationalists have the Octagon in Stockport Road and five other churches ;[41] and the Welsh
Congregationalists have one.[42]

The Presbyterian Church of England has two
places of worship ;[43] and there was till lately St. Andrew's, Oxford Road.[44]

The Salvation Army has a meeting place, as also
have the Church of United Friends, the Christadelphians, and the Unitarians.

There are places of worship also for the Armenians
(Holy Trinity, Upper Brook Street) and for the
German Protestants (in Greenheys).

The Roman Catholic Church of the Holy Name,
opened in 1871, is served by the Jesuits ;[48] those of the
Holy Family, 1876, and St. Joseph, 1888, by secular
clergy. There are houses of the Little Sisters of the
Poor and others.

The Jews have a synagogue.

[17] Pal. of Lanc. Feet of F. bdle. 14, m.
24-. See also the account of Entwisle.
[18] Edward Tyldesley of Morleys bequeathed ten messuages in Chorlton, Rusholme, and Manchester to William his
third son for life, with remainder to
Edward son and heir of testator's son
Thomas ; they were held of John Lacy
as of his manor of Manchester in socage
by a rent of 18d. ; Duchy of Lancs.
Inq. p.m. xiv, 10. The reduction in
the free rent indicates that much had
been sold.
[19] Humphrey Booth of Salford in 1635
held lands in Chorlton of the lord of
Manchester ; Duchy of Lanc. Inq. p.m.
xxvii, 44. The lands were probably part
of the Garrett estate purchased' rom
Thomas Leigh of High Legh (East Hall)
in 1619 ; *Manch. Ct. Leet Rec.* iii, 17.
Edmund Prestwich of Hulme held lands
in Chorlton at his death in 1629, and
devised them for life to his younger sons ;
the tenure is not stated ; Duchy of Lanc.
Inq. p.m. xxvii, 74 ; *Manch. Ct. Leet Rec.*
iii, 152.
Adam Jepson, of Chorlton Row and
Moston, left his estates to his daughter
Jane, who married the James Lightbowne
whose sister Anne married Thomas Minshull ; Booker, *Blackley*, 191, 172 ; *Manch.
Ct. Leet Rec.* iv, 168.
George Worsley of Blakestake in Chorlton is mentioned in 1677 ; ibid. vi, 36.
The estate of Thomas Stockton was in
dispute in 1701 ; *Exch. Dep.* (Rec. Soc.
Lancs. and Ches.), 99, 101.
[20] Land tax returns at Preston.
[21] *Manch. Constables' Accts.* i, 42 ; also
i, 20, 28, 29 ; see also *Misc.* (Rec. Soc.
Lancs. and Ches.), i, 151 ; the contributor

to the subsidy in 1622 was Ralph Hudson,
'in goods.' He died in 1630, leaving
lands in Chorlton to his son Ralph; *Manch.
Ct. Leet Rec.* iii, 169.
[22] See a deed quoted under Gorton.
The name is often corrupted to Grindlow.
In 1326 the king confirmed a grant of
lands in Greenlow Heath made by John
La Warre to Robert (son of John) Grelley
and Ellen his wife ; *Cal. Pat.* 1324-7, p.
304.
[23] *Mamecestre* (Chet. Soc.), ii, 364. The
land measured 139 acres and was valued
at 8d. an acre rent. It is perhaps the
same as the 'Grenlaw more' of the inquisition of 1282 ; *Lancs. Inq. and Extents,*
i, 244.
[24] Chan. Inq. p.m. 5 Hen. VI, no. 54.
The description reads : 'Three messuages, 140 acres of land, 10 acres of
meadow, and 20 acres of pasture in Greenlow heath, beginning at the Roocroft, and
so following between the Roocroft and
the hedge of Whitaker up to the mete of
Chorlton Edge, thence between Chorlton
Edge and Greenlow heath up to Bal-
shagh field, and so following between the
mete of Rusholme and Greenlow heath
up to the mete of Holt, and so following
between the mete of Holt and Greenlow
heath up to the highway leading from
Stockport to Manchester, and so following
the highway up to Roocroft.'
[25] The district was formed in 1859 ;
Lond. Gaz. 2 Dec. The church adjoins
the old Chorlton Hall, the remaining
part of which is the rectory house. The
inscriptions are in the Owen MSS.
[26] It has had a district chapelry from
1839, reconstituted in 1859 ; *Lond. Gaz.*
29 Mar. 1839 ; 2 Dec. 1859.

Blakeley, Blakelegh, ~~xiii and xiv cents.~~ ; ~~this spelling~~
agrees with ~~the local pronunciation. Blackley,~~
c. 1600.

~~This, the northernmost part of the parish, lies in a~~
~~bend of the Irk,~~ which bounds it on the north-west,
west, and south-west. A ridge over 300 ft. high
projects westward through the northern part of the
township, the greater part of which lies on the
southern slope of the hill. The area is 1,840 acres,
having a breadth of about 2 miles from north to
south, and measuring somewhat more from east to
west. In the southern part a brook runs westward
down Boggart Hole Clough.[1] Barnes Green is on
the border of Harpurhey. The population of Blackley
and Harpurhey together was 24,501 in 1901.

The principal road is that from Manchester to
Middleton, going north. At Blackley village another
road branches off west towards Prestwich, and from
this latter another runs in a zigzag course through
Higher Blackley, formerly known as Crab Lane End,
to Heaton. There are various subsidiary roads, and
the township is becoming a suburb of Manchester,
though most of it remains rural.

To the north of the village is a reformatory.
The soil is sandy, overlying clay.

In 1666 there were four houses with ten hearths
each—those of Mr. Legh, Ralph Bowker, Mr. Bowker, and Edward Dawson—but no other dwelling had
more than five. The total number in the township
was 107.[2] The old water corn-mill was in 1850
used for grinding logwood.[3] The woollen and fustian

1691.[4] Within the township are a match works,
chemical works, a smallware manufactory, and some
minor industries.

Blackley was included in the city of Manchester in
1890, and six years later became part of the new township of North Manchester. There is a free library.

BLACKLEY was anciently a park of
MANOR   the lord of Manchester ; its value in 1282
was £6 13s. 4d., for herbage, dead wood,
pannage, and eyries of sparrow-hawks.[5] Forty years
later its circuit was estimated as seven *leucae*, and
it had two deer leaps ;[6] the pasturage was sufficient
for 240 cattle, in addition to the deer and other wild
animals.[7] Leases and other grants of the land and
pasture were from time to time made by the lords,[8]
and in 1473 John Byron held Blackley village, Blackley field, and Pillingworth fields, with the appurtenances, at a rent of £33 6s. 8d., then recently
increased from £28 1s. a year.[9] On the dispersal of
the Byron estates about the beginning of the 17th
century, Blackley was sold in parcels to a number of
owners.[10] The hall and demesne were acquired by
Sir Richard Assheton of Middleton,[11] and sold to
Francis Legh of Lyme in 1636.[12] They descended
in this family till 1814, when they were sold in
thirty-four lots, William Grant of Ramsbottom purchasing the hall, which was pulled down.[13] It was
haunted by a 'boggart' or ghost, according to the
popular belief.[14]

Among those described as 'of Blackley' in the
inquisitions are Daniel Travis,[15] Francis Nuttall,[16]

---

[1] This name occurs prior to 1700 ; J.
Booker, *Blackley* (Chet. Soc.), 115. The
picturesque clough has been acquired for
a pleasure-ground by the Corporation of
Manchester. The name is sometimes
derived from a deserted house, said to be
haunted, 'Boggart Hall,' but Mr. H. T.
Crofton thinks it a corruption of Bowker
Hall, which stood in Moston at the upper
end of the clough ; see *Manch. Guard. N.*
and Q. no. 401. Oliver Clough, with
Oliver's well in it, joins the main clough
from the north.

[2] Subs. R. bdle. 250, no. 9.

[3] Booker, op. cit. 112.

[4] Ibid. 115. 'Judging by the field
names this mill was either on the stream
coming from Boggart Hole Clough or its
northern tributary coming past Lyon Fold;
most probably the latter, north of which
is a farm called Dam Head.'—Mr. Crofton.

[5] *Lancs. Inq. and Extents* (Rec. Soc.
Lancs. and Ches.), i, 244.

[6] *Mamecestre* (Chet. Soc.), ii, 368 ; the
value was 53s. 4d.

[7] Ibid. ii, 366 ; the value was £6.
The 'fence of Blackley park' is mentioned about 1355 ; *Dep. Keeper's Rep.*
xxxii, App. 344.

[8] See grants to Henry de Smethley in
1343 and to Thurstan de Holland in 1355,
quoted in *Mamecestre*, ii, 439, 445. The
latter grant, at a rent of £5, included the
pasture of the lord's park at Blackley, the
arable land of Bottomley with its meadow,
and an approvement of 10 acres in Ashenhurst.

[9] Ibid. iii, 484. A grant or feoffment
was made in 1430 by Sir Reginald West,
Lord La Warre, at a rent of £26 ; Byron
Chartul. 15/295. After an intermediate
conveyance the estate was transferred to
Sir John Byron in 1433 ; ibid. 19/296,

21/298. See Booker's *Blackley* (Chet.
Soc.), 13–15.

[10] The statements in the text are
mostly taken from the work last quoted.
The 'manor' of Blackley, seventy messuages, two fulling mills, a water-mill,
1,000 acres of land, &c., in Blackley,
Blackley Fields, and Bottomley, were in
1598 sold or mortgaged by Sir John
Byron and John Byron his son and heir
apparent to Richard and William Assheton;
the price named in the fine is £1,000 ;
Pal. of Lanc. Feet of F. bdle. 60, m. 68.
Blackley is, however, mentioned among the
Byron manors in 1608 ; ibid. bdle. 71, m. 2.

[11] In a fine of 1611 respecting the
manor of Blackley, &c., James Assheton
was deforciant, and Sir Peter Legh, Sir
Richard Assheton, John Holt, and Richard Assheton were plaintiffs ; Pal. of
Lanc. Feet of F. bdle. 77, m. 51. In a
later fine the deforciants were Sir John
Byron the elder, Sir John Byron the
younger, Sir Peter Legh, Sir Richard
Assheton, John Holt, and Richard Assheton ; ibid. bdle. 79, m. 34. From the
former it appears that James Assheton of
Chadderton had acquired Blackley, and
sold it to the Asshetons of Middleton.
A feoffment in 1612 by Sir John Byron of
Newstead the elder, his son Sir John Byron
of Royton the younger, Sir Peter Legh of
Lyme, Sir Richard Assheton of Middleton,
John Holt of Stubley, and Richard son of
Sir Richard Assheton, recites a fine levied
of Blackley Manor, surrenders of all free-
holds for lives, and recovery suffered to
the intent that the manor, &c., be sold
for the payment of debts, &c. ; Mr. Crofton's note.
Richard Assheton of Middleton, who
died in 1618, held lands in Blackley of
the king as of the duchy by knight's ser-

vice ; *Lancs. Inq. p.m.* (Rec. Soc. Lancs.
and Ches.), ii, 107.

[12] Booker, op. cit. 17 ; Ralph Assheton
of Middleton, Elizabeth his wife, and
Mary his mother were the vendors, over
£2,000 being paid. The sale included
Blackley Hall, closes called Bottomley,
Hunt Green, Ashenhurst, Hazelbottom,
&c. ; a close called Lidbottom, of 4 acres,
was excluded.

[13] Ibid. 19, where there is a description
of the old building, with a view. There
is also a view in James's series, 1821–5.

[14] 'In the stillness of night it would steal
from room to room and carry off the bed-
clothes from the couches of the sleeping,
but now thoroughly aroused and discom-
fited inmates ' ; Booker, op. cit. 20. An
account is given of the destruction of the
print-shop erected on the site of the hall.

[15] *Lancs. Inq. p.m.* (Rec. Soc. Lancs.
and Ches.), ii, 157. At his death in 1617
Daniel Travis held a messuage, 15 acres
of land, &c., recently purchased from Sir
John Byron and others. The tenement
was held of the king by knight's service.
His will is given. His son and heir, also
named Daniel, was twenty-six years of
age. His wife Anne was the daughter of
Henry Chetham of Crumpsall ; *Manch.
Ct. Leet Rec.* ii, 194.
Of the same family perhaps was John
Travis, whom John Bradford about 1550
styles 'Father Travis.' Some later members of the family were benefactors to the
poor, and concerned in the erection of the
Nonconformist (now Unitarian) chapel.
John Travis, a dealer in fustians, who became bankrupt in 1691, had an estate of
24 acres ; one of the fields was named
the Frith field ; Booker, op. cit. 116.

[16] *Lancs. Inq. p.m.* (Rec. Soc.), ii, 176.
Francis Nuttall died in 1619, holding

Matthew Hopwood,[17] Abraham Carter,[18] John and George Pendleton,[19] Stephen Rodley,[20] Ralph Wardleworth,[21] William Chetham,[22] Patrick Edrington,[23] William and John Cowper,[24] and William Heywood.[25] There were small estates, in most cases resulting from the division of the Byron estate, and held by knight's service.

Humphrey Booth of Salford also had land in the township,[26] and it descended in the family for about a century.[27] *BOOTH HALL* was situated about 4 miles north of Manchester, on high ground a short distance to the east of the old road to Middleton. It is said to have been built during the years 1639–40 by Humphrey Booth for his son, but before demolition, about 1906–7, had undergone many alterations and additions which had robbed it of most of its original architectural features. It was a two-storied house, the oldest portion of which is described as having many gables, and was built of brick, but had been stuccoed and painted over in later years. One addition was made early in the 18th century and another in the first half of the 19th century. On the front of the original part of the house on a wooden beam was carved 'HB : AB : 1640,' the initials of

Humphrey Booth and Ann Booth (born Hough) his wife. In 1855 the old part of the house is described as having suffered much at the hands of recent tenants, most of the original mullioned windows on the ground floor having been built up or replaced by modern casements, and on the first floor nothing but the hood-moulds remained to show that such windows ever existed.[27a] The house was pulled down to make way for the Blackley Hospital, but part of the brick farm-buildings are still standing. The house was acquired by Richard Worthington of Manchester, grocer ; from him it passed to the Diggles family, and by descent to the Bayleys.[28] Amselford or Hoozleforth Gate was the name of a farm in the north-east of the township.

The land tax returns show that the principal proprietors in 1787 were Richard Brown, Thomas Bayley, Richard Taylor, Lord Grey de Wilton, John Hutton, Peter Legh, and Robert Jackson.[29] About 1850 the principal proprietor was the Earl of Wilton, who owned a third of the land, his interest being derived partly by inheritance from the Hollands and Asshetons and partly by purchase.[30]

The most famous personage connected with Blackley

---

ten messuages, 60 acres of land, &c., in Blackley, and land in Harpurhey and Gorton ; the tenure was of the king, by knight's service. John, the son and heir, was twenty-three years of age. The will of Francis Nuttall is given in *Manch. Ct. Leet Rec.* iii, 19, 20, notes.

From deeds of this family in the Manchester Free Library (no. 55–7) it appears that John Nuttall in 1623 leased lands in Blackley to Edward Holland of Heaton for 299 years ; among the field-names are Howgate Meadow, Blackfield, and Gladen Croft.

[17] *Lancs. Inq. p.m.* (Rec. Soc.), ii, 210. Matthew Hopwood had purchased the reversion of a messuage called the 'Deyhouse,' with lands, from the Byrons, held of the king by knight's service. He died in 1613 leaving a daughter Mary about a year old.

[18] Ibid. 235. Abraham Carter, described as 'gentleman,' held a messuage and lands of the king by the hundredth part of a knight's fee, and died in 1621, leaving as heir his son John, nineteen years of age.

[19] John Pendleton died in 1618, holding 20 acres by the three-hundredth part of a knight's fee ; his son John was then nine years old ; *Lancs. Inq. p.m.* (Rec. Soc.), ii, 258.

George Pendleton died in 1633, holding a messuage and lands (including the Warping House and Brerehey Field) of the king by the hundredth part of a knight's fee ; he left a son and heir George ; Duchy of Lanc. Inq. p.m. xxviii, 37.

In 1650 'in Blackley near Manchester, in one John Pendleton's ground, as one was reaping, the corn being cut seemed to bleed ; drops fell out of it like to blood. Multitudes of people went to see it, and the straws thereof, though of a kindly colour without, were within reddish and as it were bloody' ; Hollinworth, *Mancuniensis*, 123.

A John Pendleton of Blackley married Rhoda, daughter and heir of Robert Clough, the son of Thomas Clough of Blackley ; and he and his son John Pendleton in 1676 sold their land to Robert Litchford of Manchester, saddler, a benefactor of the old Baptist chapel at Clough Fold. The house at Blackley, known as

Litchfor
his neph
vised it
in 1783
hester.
it was so
Al
gave it t
George
1835 it

by popular association, if not by birth, is John Bradford, burnt to death at Smithfield on 1 July 1555
for Protestantism.[31] He was born about 1520–5 and
educated at Manchester. Embracing a secular career,
he entered the service of Sir John Harrington, pay-
master of the English forces in France ; a fraud in
his accounts at that time, to the hurt of the king,
afterwards caused him deep sorrow, being greatly
moved to this[32] by Latimer's preaching.[33] He
became a Protestant, and that of the more extreme
type, studied law, and then went to Cambridge,
where he was almost immediately elected fellow of
Pembroke and made Master of Arts.[34] He was urged
to preach, and was ordained deacon by Bishop Ridley,[35]
but does not appear to have advanced further. He
was made prebendary of St. Paul's and chaplain to
the king, and preached in London, Lancashire, and
Cheshire, without undertaking any parochial charge.[36]
Soon after the accession of Mary he was lodged in the
Tower on charges of sedition, preaching without a
licence, and heresy.[37] His first examination took
place in the Tower, and he was again examined on
23 January 1554–5, and later days ; afterwards he was
excommunicated as a heretic.[38] Fresh efforts to con-

CHURCH

There was an oratory at Blackley
as early as 1360,[44] probably the origin
of the chapel existing in 1548.[45] This
was rebuilt in 1736,[46] and again in 1844 ; it is called
St. Peter's.[47] In 1611 the Byrons sold to John
Cudworth, James Chetham, and Edmund Howarth
the chapel and chapel yard, and the chamber and
garden there, for use as a place of worship for the
people of Blackley.[48] The stipend of the minister
was derived from seat rents and offerings. Service
was maintained there during the latter part of Eliza-

---

son John, who died in 1786, and whose
only surviving child, Sarah, married the
Hon. Edward Perceval. The estate was
sold in 1808 to the Earl of Wilton.

Abraham Howarth, described as of
Crumpsall, appears in the *Manch. Ct. Leet
Rec.* in 1684 and 1685 (vi, 214, 235).
'Mr. Howarth's house in [Long] Mill-
gate,' is one of those depicted on Casson
and Berry's Plan.

Some particulars of the Dickenson and
Beswick estates are given by Booker, op.
cit. 47, 48. Several deeds relating to the
Beswicks of Blackley are among the
Raines deeds in the Chetham Library ;
the dates range from 1611 to 1674.

In the Chetham Library also are a few
17th-century deeds of the Sandiforth
family.

[31] For biographies see *Dict. Nat. Biog.* ;
Bradford's *Works* (Parker Soc. 1848),
Foxe, *Acts and Monts.* (ed. Cattley), vii,
143–285 ; Cooper, *Athenae Cantab.* i,
127–9.

Bradford described himself as 'born in
Manchester' (Foxe, op. cit. vii, 204), and
this probably refers to the town rather
than to the parish. The family no doubt
derived its surname from . an adjacent
township, and many members of it occur
from time to time in the records. In
1473 John Bradford held two closes in
Manchester at the will of the lord at 15s.
rent ; *Mamecestre*, iii, 486. Thomas Bradford and Margaret his wife sold land in
Manchester in 1553 ; Pal. of Lanc. Feet
of F. bdle. 15, m. 123. Thomas Bradford of
Failsworth occurs in 1557 ; *Manch. Ct.
Leet Rec.* i, 39 ; see also *Manch. Sessions*
(Rec. Soc. Lancs. and Ches.), 57. There
was a John Bradford at Newton Heath
in 1585 and 1619 ; *Newton Chapelry*
(Chet Soc.), ii, 65, 76.

[32] On this point see *N. and Q.* (Ser. 2),
i, 125. The fraud did not benefit Bradford himself, but his master, who was
quite unaware of it, and he forced Sir
John Harrington to make restitution by
threat of denunciation to the Council.

[33] A fellow student of the Inner Temple,
Thomas Sampson, afterwards the Puritan
dean of Christ Church, Oxford, also had
great influence with him.

[34] M.A. 1549 by
universitie were in
that time, but Brad
dence of study in th
translations from P
Protestant divine) a
with pr f by h'
i, 127, where l'
d

beth's reign,[49] and there exists a plan of the seats made early in the 17th century,[50] from which time can be traced a succession of curates and rectors. In 1650 the Parliamentary surveyors found the chapel provided with a minister's house and an endowment of 17s. 8d. ; the remainder of the stipend came from voluntary contributions.[51] The same thing was reported in 1707,[52] but soon after this benefactors came forward, and about 1720 the income was £27 10s. 8d.[53] The income is now stated to be £500.

A district chapelry was formed in 1839.[54] The registers begin in 1655.[55] The patronage is vested in the Dean and canons of Manchester, and the following is a list of incumbents :—[56]

oc. 1600	Thomas Paget [57]
oc. 1632	William Rathband [58]
oc. 1646	James Hall [59]
1648	James Walton [60]
1652	Samuel Smith, B.A. [61]
1653	Thomas Holland, M.A. (Edin.) [62]
1662	(?) James Booker [63]
oc. 1668	John Brereton [64]
1669	John Dawson, B.A. [65] (Jesus Coll., Camb.)
oc. 1671	William Dunbabin [66]
oc. 1674	Ichabod Furness, B.A. [67]
oc. 1677	William Bray, B.A. [68] (Emmanuel Coll., Camb.)
1683	John Morton [69] (Magdalene Coll., Camb.)
1705	Nathaniel Bann, M.A. [70] (Jesus Coll., Camb.)
1712	William Whitehead, B.A. [71]
1716	Edward Hulton, B.A. [72] (Brasenose Coll., Oxf.)
1763	Peter Haddon, M.A. [73]
1787	John Griffith, M.A. [74]
1809	Richard Alexander Singleton, B.D. [75] (St. John's Coll., Camb.)
1838	William Robert Keeling, B.A. [76] (St. John's Coll., Camb.)
1869	John Leighton Figgins, B.A. [77] (Queens' Coll., Camb.)
1874	William Coghlan [78]

In 1865 St. Andrew's, Higher Blackley, was built,[79] and more recently the district of Holy Trinity has been formed, though a permanent church is wanting.

The first school dates from 1710, when money was left for the purpose by Robert Litchford.[80]

There are six Methodist chapels. The Wesleyans began with a Sunday school in 1801, and built a chapel in 1806.[81] At Crab Lane Head, or Higher Blackley, the New Connexion began meetings in 1815 ; Zion Chapel was built in 1830.[82] The United Free Methodists opened a small chapel in 1836, rebuilt in 1853 ; [83] they have two others. The Primitive Methodists have a chapel at Barnes Green.

The Baptists had a meeting-place in 1880.[84]

The minister of the parochial chapel in 1662, Thomas Holland, was ejected for nonconformity ; many of the people also dissented from the restored services, and as early as 1668 a congregation met at the house of a Mrs. Travis, Thomas Pyke, ejected from Radcliffe, occasionally ministering to them.[84a] A chapel was built in 1697, and was replaced by the present one in 1884. The congregation has been Unitarian since the middle of the 18th century.[85]

[49] The warden and fellows of the collegiate church were responsible for the chapels ; it is said that Oliver Carter, a fellow, officiated at Blackley ; his son Abraham has been mentioned already ; Booker, *Blackley*, 65, 66. In 1581 Joseph Booth was presented for teaching without a licence. In 1598 there was no curate, but the chapel was served by the fellows of the church ; Visit. Presentments at Chest.

[50] Booker (57, 58) prints plans of 1603 and a little later ; the names of the seatholders and the amounts paid are inserted. The pulpit stood near the middle of the north wall ; the communion table was at the east end, but some seats intervened between it and the wall. In 1631 Bishop Bridgeman authorized the allotments of the seats and the payments for them ; ibid. 53.

About 1610 Blackley was returned among the chapels of ease which had ministers supported by the inhabitants ; *Hist. MSS. Com. Rep.* xiv, App. iv, 11.

[51] *Commonwealth Ch. Surv.* (Rec. Soc. Lancs. and Ches.), 9, 10. The 17s. 8d. came from a gift by Adam Chetham in 1625 : in 1838 the income from the same property was £7 ; Booker, op. cit. 82.

[52] See Warden Wroe's account (ibid. 72), which states that George Grimshaw of Manchester had left the interest of £100 and the rent of a house after the death of his servant. The house was in Hunt's Bank, and sold in 1837 for £475, the interest of which is part of the rector's income ; ibid. 82.

[53] Gastrell, *Notitia Cestr.* (Chet. Soc.), ii, 81–3 ; the chief part of this sum was £20 a year charged by Jonathan Dawson on an estate in Salford called Ringspiggot

[83] Ibid. 108.

[68] Ibid.

Roman Catholic worship in recent times began in 1851 in a chapel formed out of two cottages. The church of Our Lady of Mount Carmel, built in 1855,[86] has now (1908) been replaced by a larger one. There is a convent of the Good Shepherd, occupying Litchford Hall.

CHEETHAM

Chetham, 1212 and usually; Chetam, 1276; Cheteham, 1590; Cheetham, xvi cent.

This township, on the western bank of the Irk, has an extreme length of nearly 2 miles, and an area of 919 acres. The high land in the northern part slopes down to the Irk, and more gradually to the south, where the Irwell is the boundary for a short distance. The district called Cheetham Hill is partly in this township and partly in Crumpsall and Broughton; Smedley is to the east of it, near the Irk; Stocks, a name which can be traced back to 1599, is on the border of Manchester, north of Red Bank; and Peel, an old house, formerly moated, is close by.[1] Cheetwood occupies the southern half of the township,[2] in which also lies Strangeways. Alms Hill, or Ormsell, lies to the west of Smedley. The population of Cheetham and Crumpsall was 49,942 in 1901.

The district is now entirely urban, being a suburb of Manchester. The principal roads are those from Manchester to Bury, the older one going northward through the middle of the township, and the newer and more direct one near its south-west border. The latter follows the line of the Roman road from Manchester to Ribchester. The Lancashire and Yorkshire Company's Manchester and Bury line runs near the eastern border, by the Irk, and a branch to Oldham separates from it; Victoria Station, Manchester, the head of the company's system, lies in this township at the junction of the Irk with the Irwell.[3]

Some neolithic implements have been found.[4]

[86] Booker, op. cit. 110.

[1] For the Peel see Procter, *Manch. Streets*, 281–2. By his will in 1806 John Ridings charged his tenement called Stocks and Peel, held of Lord Derby by lease, with £250. These notes are due to Mr. Crofton.

[2] For Miss Beswick of Cheetwood see *N. and Q.* (Ser. 2), xi, 157.

[3] The station was opened in 1844, and the lines from Liverpool and from Leeds connected there. It was enlarged in 1884. The site was previously a cemetery (Walker's Croft), opened in 1815.

[4] *Lancs. and Ches. Antiq. Soc.* x, 251.

[5] Subs. R. bdle. 250, no. 9.

[6] *Lancs. and Ches. Antiq. Soc.* v, 76.

[8] *Dict. Nat. Biog.* [9] Ibid.

[10] *Lancs. Inq. and Extents* (Rec. Soc. Lancs. and Ches.), i, 66.

[11] Roger de Middleton occurs again in 1226; ibid. 137. See a later note, and Dods. MSS. cxxxi, fol. 38.

Henry de Chetham in 1212 also held 4 oxgangs of land in chief; *Lancs. Inq. and Extents*, i, 70. From the accounts of Moston and other townships it will be seen that he inherited or acquired, probably by marriage, a portion of the estates of Orm de Ashton. He attested Audenshaw and Swinton charters; Farrer, *Lancs. Pipe R.* 329; *Whalley Couch.* (Chet. Soc.), 905. In 1227 he went on pilgrimage to Jerusalem; *Cal. Pat.* 1225–32, p. 126.

tenure being altered to knight's service,[15] and on their forfeiture in 1485 it was granted to the Earl of Derby,[16] and descended like Knowsley down to the middle of the 17th century.[17] There does not appear to be any later record of a manor of Cheetham, the estate probably having been dismembered by various sales.[18] Lord Derby, however, is still the chief land-owner.

The principal estate in the township, apart from the manor, was that called STRANGE-WAYS,[19] long held by the family of that name,[20] but sold about the middle of the 17th century to the Hartleys, who retained possession for several

STRANGEWAYS. *Sable two lions passant in pale paly of six argent and gules.*

..

other demesne lands ; *Plac. de Quo War.* (Rec. Com.), 369. His mother Alice (living in 1302) confirmed a grant of lands in Crompton made by him, as if they were part of her inheritance ; Clowes deeds. It is supposed that she was the other sister and co-heir. Geoffrey de Chetham's moiety of Allerton did not descend in the same way, so that it is probable he had no issue by his wife Margery.

By 1312, probably by arrangement be-tween the heirs, the whole of the manor of Cheetham was held by the Pilkingtons; *Final Conc.* ii, 9, 33, 35. In 1313 Geof-frey de Chadderton the elder appeared in an assize of *mort d'ancestor* against Robert de Ashton, Margery his wife ; Alexander, Roger, and William, sons of Roger de Pilkington, and Alice, widow of Alexan-der de Pilkington ; Assize R. 424, m. 4, 10. This may refer to the Crompton estate.

Roger son of Roger de Pilkington in 1357 proceeded against various persons for cutting his trees at Cheetham ; Duchy of Lanc. Assize R. 6, m. 7.

[15] In 1346 Roger de Pilkington held the tenth part of a knight's fee in Cheet-ham, paying 13s. 4d. ; Add. MS. 32103, fol. 146b. From the Book of Reasonable Aid of 1378, it appears that Sir Roger de Pilkington paid 2s. for the tenth part of a knight's fee in Cheetham ; Harl. MS. 2085, fol. 422. So also in the inquisition after the death of Sir Roger de Pilkington in 1407 ; *Lancs. Inq. p.m.* (Chet. Soc.), i, 86, from which it appears that the rent of 13s. 4d. was also paid. In the extent of 1445-6 it is stated that Sir John Pilking-ton held one plough-land in Cheetham for the tenth part of a knight's fee, the relief due being 10s. ; Duchy of Lanc. Knights' Fees, 2/20. Again, in 1483 Sir Thomas Pilkington was found to hold the tenth part of a fee in Cheetham ; Duchy of Lanc. Misc. 130.

[16] Pat. 4 Hen. VII ; styled the manor of Cheetham or lordship of Cheetwood.

[17] Cheetham and Cheetwood are named in 1521 among the manors of Thomas, Earl of Derby, but no particulars are given ; Duchy of Lanc. Inq. p.m. v, 68.

The manor of Cheetham and Cheet-wood, together with lands there and in Harwood and Brightmet, was sold or mortgaged by William, Earl of Derby. about 1596 to Sir Nicholas and Rowland Mosley for £1,600. The purchasers demanded further assurances, and appear to have refused to complete the purchase, according to a complaint by the earl in 1601 ; Duchy of Lanc. Plead. Eliz. ccii, D 10 ; Pal. of Lanc. Feet of F. bdle. 58, m. 291. In 1608 Thomas Goodyer was stated to hold lands in Cheetham of Sir Nicholas Mosley as of his manor of Cheetham ; *Lancs. Inq. p.m.* (Rec. Soc. Lancs. and Ches.), i, 112. The later history shows that Cheetham and Cheet-wood were recovered by the earl, while Brightmet and Harwood were alienated, for in 1653 it was deposed that a chief rent of 13s. 4d. had been paid to

the king for the Ear Cheetham and Cheetw Paper (Rec. Soc L 206. At th time Manchester, and Salf rent' were part o Charlotte, the counte 185. In 1653 she Bird the water corn Mill in Cheetham.

[18] Some of the seve lands were sold to *Royalist Comp. Pape* Com. Pleas Recov. R

[19] It is mentione description of the bo *Mamecestre*, ii, 372. considerably, e.g. Strangewayes, 1349

[20] In 1304 Robert appeared aga'ns Jo Thomas and Geoffr the d ath of his broth Grelley , Coram Re Ellen de Strangewa afterwards charged w John de Strangeways 4. In 1345 Sibyl, w Strangeways, and Th were defendants in

...

generations.[71] In 1711 it was bequeathed by Catherine Richards, widow, to Thomas Reynolds, ancestor of

REYNOLDS. *Or two lions passant gules.*

MORETON, Earl of Ducie. *Argent a cheveron gules between three square buckles sable.*

the Earl of Ducie, the owner in 1850.[72] The present earl owns land in the township.

measuring 4 rods by 2 rods 3 yds.; £20 was paid, and a perpetual rent of 5s. 4d. and 4d. for 'shearing' was due; Earwaker MSS. In 1587 he had stopped an old footway going over the Knolls into the Walkers' Croft, to the annoyance of his neighbours; *Ct. Leet Rec.* ii, 10. He died in 1590, leaving a son and heir John, under age; Strangeways Hall with the appurtenant lands was held of the Earl of Derby as of his manor of Pilkington (i.e. Cheetham) in socage by a rent of four barbed arrows; ibid. ii, 42; *Manch. Coll.* ii, 142.

A contemporary John Strangeways, described as 'of London, mercer,' had land in Salford. He died before October 1598, leaving a son and heir William, about six years old; *Salford Portmote Rec.* (Chet. Soc.), i, 9, 15. The Salford property was sold in 1601 during William's minority to George Holden; ibid. i, 26. Another contemporary, Philip Strangeways, was one of the missionary priests imprisoned at Wisbech at the end of Elizabeth's reign; *Misc.* (Cath. Rec. Soc.), i, 110; ii, 278, &c.

John Strangeways of Strangeways died at the end of 1600, leaving a son John, a minor, as heir; but in 1609 another son Thomas, then seventeen years of age, was found to be the heir; *Manch. Ct. Leet Rec.* ii, 167; *Lancs. Inq. p.m.* (Rec. Soc. Lancs. and Ches.), i, 132. A large part of the estate, as well as property in Salford, had been disposed of, but John Strangeways had held the messuage (i.e. Strangeways Hall), water-mill, 40 acres of land, &c., in Cheetham, the Knolls and other lands in Manchester, Ardwick, Salford, and Withington; the tenure of the Cheetham estate was said to be 'of the king by knight's service.' In October 1601, at the Salford Portmote, it was presented that John Strangeways had died since the last court, and that Thomas his son and heir was about twelve years old; *Salford Portm. Rec.* (Chet. Soc.), i, 27. In 1622 he sold a messuage and garden which he and Ralph Holland owned in Salford to George Cranage the younger, of Salford; ibid. i, 167. Elizabeth, widow of John, recovered her dower in 1603 against Thomas Strangeways, the son and heir; *Pal. of Lanc.* Plea R. 292, m. 10 d. Thomas came of age in 1613, and did his fealty at Manchester Court; *Ct. Leet Rec.* ii, 279. In the same year he recorded a pedigree; *Visit.* (Chet. Soc.), 13. In 1620, as churchwarden, he was interested in the project of a workhouse

for the poor; *Ct. L wa l'ving in 1646, b sold his esta e, being Strangeways.' Dee Guardian.

[71] Richard Hartl Hartley of Manche succeeded his father till age 25s, 323 and note years, leaving as h (ib'd. i'i, 36), the ways. John, who g 40s. towards the rep Conduit (ibid. ii, 2 'of Strangeways' in H d d 6

The Brideoaks of Cheetham Hill [34] produced a Bishop of Chichester.[34a]

The principal contributors to the land tax in 1795 were Lord Ducie, James Hilton, and James Heywood, together paying more than a third.[35]

In connexion with the Established Church St. Mark's was erected in 1794, the first church in the part of Manchester parish lying between the Irwell and Irk ; a district was assigned to it in 1839.[36] It was followed by St. Luke's, 1839 ;[37] St. John the Evangelist's, 1871 ;[38] and St. Albans, Cheetwood, 1874.[39] St. Thomas's, 1863, described as in Lower Crumpsall, is within the township of Cheetham.

The Wesleyan Methodists have three churches ;[40] the Primitive Methodists and the United Free Church one each. The Congregationalists have two churches, one in Bury New Road, usually called 'Broughton Chapel,' and one at Cheetham Hill.[41] The Salvation Army has a meeting place in Hightown.

The Presbyterian Church of England is represented by Trinity Church, Cheetham Hill, built in 1899 ; the cause originated in 1845.[42] The Welsh Calvinistic Methodists also have a chapel. The Unitarians formerly had a chapel at Strangeways.[43]

At Cheetham Hill is the convent of Notre Dame.

The southern end of the township having a large Jewish population, British and foreign, there are nine synagogues, some of the buildings having formerly been used as Nonconformist chapels.[44] A hospital and dispensary have been founded, and there is a Home for Aged Jews. A Talmud Torah school has been opened.

CRUMPSALL

Curmisale, 1282 (copy) ; Curmesalle, Curmeshal, 1320 (copy) ; Curmesale, 1405 ; Cromshall, 1548.

This township lies to the south-west of the Irk, and has an area of 733 acres. The surface is hilly, a ridge which attains 280 ft. over the Ordnance datum occupying the southern side, and sending out numerous spurs towards the Irk. The township has in the main be-

[34] The will of Ralph Bryddocke (Brideoak) of Manchester, clerk, is printed in Piccope, *Wills* (Chet. Soc.), iii, 142. Richard and Geoffrey Brideoak were among the executors.

Richard Brideoak, a tenant of the Earl of Derby in Cheetham, asserted in 1598 a right to common in Crumpsall Moor against Henry Shepherd, bailiff of Alexander Reddish, but his claim was rejected ; Pal. of Lanc. Plea R. 283, m. 14.

[34a] Ralph son of Richard Brideoak of Cheetham Hill was born about 1614, entered Brasenose Coll. Oxford in 1630, and was created M.A. 1636. After various appointments he gained the favour of James, Earl of Derby, and remained loyal to that family during the Civil War and its subsequent misfortunes ; he gained the favour also of Speaker Lenthall, who presented him to the vicarage of Witney in Oxfordshire. He was made D.D. in 1660. He was rector of Standish in 1644, but kept out of his right, which he regained in 1660 and held till his death. In 1667 he was made Dean of Salisbury, and in 1675 Bishop of Chichester, having, it is supposed, bribed the king's mistress, the Duchess of Portsmouth. He died three years later, having (according to Wood) 'spent the chief part of his life in continual agitation for the obtaining of

wealth and settling a family' ; Wood, *Athenae ; Dict. Nat. Biog. ; V.C.H. Lancs.* ii, 585. Another member of the family became rector of Sefton.

[35] Returns at Preston.

[36] For district see *Lond. Gaz.* 29 Mar. 1839, 1 July 1856. Copies of the monumental inscriptions are in the Owen MSS.

[37] *Lond. Gaz.* 1 July 1856 (reciting that a district had been assigned to it in 1840).

[38] For district see *Lond. Gaz.* 14 May

After this the lordship appears to have been granted to the Radcliffes of Radcliffe at a quit-rent of 10s. a year,[11] and they held it down to 1548, when it was sold by the Earl of Sussex to John Reddish.[12] It descended in the Reddish and Coke families[13] until 1789, when Thomas William Coke,[14] afterwards Earl of Leicester, sold the greater part to Lord Grey de Wilton, who added it to his Heaton estate.[15] It has descended to the present Earl of Wilton, who owns about two-thirds of the land.

The remaining portion was sold in 1794 to William Marsden, a Liverpool merchant. After his death this part was again sold in 1819 to several purchasers.[16]

For a long period a branch of the Chetham family held lands in the township,[17] their residence, at least in later times, being known as Crumpsall Hall,[18] famous as the birthplace of Humphrey Chetham, one of the most notable benefactors of Manchester, as founder of the hospital and library bearing his name, and in other ways. Humphrey, the fifth son of Henry Chetham of Crumpsall,[19] was born in 1580,[20] and in 1598 was bound apprentice to Samuel Tipping of Man-

CHETHAM. *Argent a griffon segreant gules within a bordure sable bezanty.*

---

lowed the Irk on the side of Crumpsall as far as the boundary of Chetham, and thence along the boundaries of Cheetham, Broughton, and Prestwich to the starting point. The lands were held of the king as of his duchy of Lancaster, and were worth 66s. 8d. a year. After the death of Lord La Warre, Crumpsall was to remain to Thomas de Langley, clerk, and Henry de Langley his brother; Deeds in possession of Manch. Corp.

[11] It was perhaps purchased from the Langleys. James Radcliffe held Crumpsall at the rent named in 1473; *Mamecestre*, iii, 483.

Lands and rent in Crumpsall are named among the other Radcliffe possessions in 1500 and 1517; *Final Conc.* (Rec. Soc. Lancs. and Ches.), iii, 149; *Lancs. Inq. p.m.* (Chet. Soc.), ii, 148. In the inquisitions the lands in Moston, Crumpsall, and Manchester are all placed together, and said to be held of the lord of Manchester by a rent of 10s., viz. that due for Crumpsall alone; Duchy of Lanc. Inq. p.m. iii, 98; iv, 7.

[12] Pal. of Lanc. Feet of F. bdle. 13, m. 194.

[13] The purchaser, John Reddish, in 1553 granted a messuage to his brother Thomas for life, with reversion to John and his heirs; the rest of Crumpsall descended to a grandson, John Reddish, who died in 1569 holding it (together with lands, &c., in Manchester) of the executors of Lord La Warre in socage by suit of court and a rent of 10s.; Duchy of Lanc. Inq. p.m. xiii, 32.

After the death of Alexander Reddish it was stated that the lands in Crumpsall and Manchester were held of the king by the 200th part of a knight's fee; *Lancs. Inq. p.m.* (Rec. Soc. Lancs. and Ches.), i, 253. In 1606 Crumpsall was sold or mortgaged to Anthony Mosley; Pal. of Lanc. Feet of F. bdle. 70, no. 82.

Sara widow of Clement Coke was one

of the heirs of Alex father-in-law, Sir E seised of var

Henry Chetham died in 1603, holding lands in Kersal, Ashton under Lyne, and Manchester; James his son and heir was over thirty years of age; *Lancs. Inq. p.m.* (Rec. Soc. Lancs. and Ches.), i, 2; *Chetham Gen.* 42; *Ct. Leet Rec.* ii, 194. His will is printed in Piccope's *Wills* (Chet. Soc.), iii, 164–6.

[20] *Life*, 9. [21] Ibid. 10.

    [22] Ibid. 14.

of Turton, Walmsley, and Gorton.[34] There is a portrait of the founder in the Chetham Library ;[35] and in 1853 a statue was erected in the cathedral as a memorial of him,[36] a stained glass window being also placed there.

The Chethams of Crumpsall were leaseholders under the Prestwich family, until in 1622 James Chetham, eldest son of Henry, purchased the holding.[37] His son George ultimately inherited not only the property in Crumpsall, but the Clayton, Turton, and other estates of his uncle Humphrey. These seem to have descended like Turton,[38] until the division in 1770, when Crumpsall was given to Mary wife of Samuel Clowes, and was bequeathed to her grandson John Hilton.[39] It was afterwards sold in parcels.[40]

George Clark, another benefactor of Manchester, was a resident in Crumpsall.[41] A branch of the Oldham family also had an estate.[42] Bishop Oldham is sometimes said to have been born there, but the connexion of his family with the township began very much later than his time.[42a]

In 1655 there were eighteen ratepayers in Crumpsall, including George Chetham, esq., Thomas Percival, 'the wife of Old Oldham,' Thomas Oldham, Robert, Richard, and James Bowker, four Pendletons, &c. The number of houses in 1774 was fifty-seven.[43]

Among the more recent landowners and residents of Crumpsall the Delaunays may be mentioned. Angel Delaunay, from Rouen, in 1788 introduced Turkey red dyeing into Crumpsall and Blackley, and built up a great business. His sons acquired part of William Marsden's estate in 1819, later known as the Cleveland estate. They built a bridge over the Irk for their coach road from Blackley to Cheetham Hill.[44]

A school was built in 1850, and licensed for the worship of the Established Church.[45] In 1859 St. Mary's was built, and rebuilt in 1875.[46] There is a mission church.

The Wesleyan Methodists in 1809 opened a preaching room, which was replaced in 1815 by a more substantial building ; this was followed by a larger one in 1837, repaired and enlarged in 1844. There is a burial-ground attached.[47] Another Wesleyan chapel was built in Lower Crumpsall in 1838.[48] There is also a place of worship belonging to the United Methodist Free church.

MOSTON

Mostun, 1247 ; Moston, 1275.

The township of Moston lies on the north side of the Morris Brook, which flows west to the Irk ; it measures over 2 miles from east to west and has an

---

[34] His will is printed in full; *Life*, 228–62. The private bequests include lands in Bolton by Bowland to his nephew George Chetham [of Turton], to his brother Ralph's children, and £2,000 to his nephew Edward Chetham for the purchase of lands. The inventory of his goods at Clayton, Ordsall, and Turton follows, 263–77 ; a note on his books is appended. The books he recommended for his church libraries were 'such as Calvin's, Preston's, and Perkins' works ; comments or annotations upon the Bible or some parts thereof,' the choice being left to Richard Johnson, Richard Hollinworth (former fellows of Manchester College), and John Tilsley (Deane).

[35] Reproduced as a frontispiece to the *Life*. See also pp. 226, 227 ; *Lancs. and Ches. Antiq. Soc.* xxii, 188, where Bishop Nicolson (1704) says it was 'drawn at a guess.'

[36] Ibid. 224–6 ; a view is given. The Chetham Society may also be regarded as a memorial to him ; it was established in 1843.

[37] *Chetham Gen.* 47 ; it consisted of a messuage and fourteen closes of land.

In 1478 Ellis Prestwich granted to feoffees messuages and lands in Crumpsall held by William Tetlow, Edward Chetham, Hugh Chetham, Henry Siddall, and Adam Pendleton, together with other properties ; De Trafford D. no. 89.

Ralph Prestwich in 1444 had three messuages, 90 acres of land, 12 acres of meadow, and 6 acres of wood in Crumpsall ; *Final Conc.* iii, 111. Another Ralph Prestwich about 1504 complained that certain persons had broken into his close at Crumpsall and stolen three pieces of linen cloth ; *Duchy Plead.* (Rec. Soc. Lancs. and Ches.), i, 41.

James Chetham, who in 1631 compounded for knighthood (*Misc.* Rec. Soc. Lancs. and Ches. i, 215), was twice married and had a numerous offspring ; the principal were his sons George (of Clayton and Turton) and Edward (of Smedley); *Chetham Gen.* 47–9 ; see also *Ct. Leet Rec.*

iv, 134, where there is an abstract of his will.

[38] See the account of Turton.

[39] *Chetham Gen.* 60, 61 ; Booker, *Blackley*, 203. James Hilton, the brother of John, had Nuthurst.

[40] The following is Mr. Booker's account (op. cit. 206): 'About this time [1775] the hall and its adjacent lands had become the property of John Gartside, esquire, who some years later (in 1806) disposed of it by sale to Thomas Blackwall, esquire, of Manchester ; the estate thus transferred being in extent about 60 statute acres. . . . Mr. Hilton still continued to retain the residue of the Crumpsall property devised to him under the will of his grandmother and died seised thereof in the year 1814. By his will, dated 31 May 1814 (proved in the Prerogative Court of Canterbury 19 April 1815), he gives and devises to his nephew Sir John Richard Hilton, knight, a lieutenant in the royal navy, the third son of his brother James, all his estate called Crumpsall. Sir John Richard Hilton was born 27 December, 1785, and is described as of the city of Chester. He appears to have completed the alienation of this portion of his family inheritance by disposing of the remainder of his estate in Crumpsall to Edward Loyd, esquire, and George Faulkner, esquire.'

[41] Booker, op. cit. 211.

George Clark, haberdasher, died 9 Jan. 1637–8, holding six burgages, five shops, &c., in Manchester, and four messuages, 40 acres of land, &c., in Crumpsall. In 1636 he had settled his estate for the relief of the poor of Manchester, one moiety being reserved to his wife Alice for her life. His nearest heir was Henry son and heir of Henry Clark, brother of John father of George ; Towneley MS. C. 8, 13 (Chet. Lib.), 258; see also *Funeral Certs.* (Chet. Soc.). In 1631 he had paid £10 on refusing knighthood ; *Misc.* (Rec. Soc. Lancs. and Ches.), i, 216.

The deed founding his charity is printed and an abstract of the will given in *Manch.*

Ct. Leet Rec. iii, 301–14. Accounts of the estate may be seen in the *Char. Com. Rep.* of 1826 (*Rep.* 16, pp. 138, &c.), and in Booker, 211, 212. About a century ago the land was eligible for building purposes, and 88 acres were disposed of on ground rents amounting to over £1,100. The present income of the charity from lands in Crumpsall and Manchester is £3,129 ; it is administered by the lord mayor of Manchester.

[42] See the account of Ancoats in Manchester. From the *Visit.* of 1664 (p. 224) it appears that Robert Oldham of Manchester, of the family of Bishop Oldham, married Elizabeth daughter of Henry Shepherd of Crumpsall ; he was eighty years old in 1664. His sons Adam and Thomas married daughters of Richard Bowker of Crumpsall, and Thomas is described as 'of Crumpsall.' 'Oldham's tenement' was in the part of the Reddish estates purchased by William Marsden, and in 1854 was in the hands of his executors ; it was also known as the Bongs Farm. A curious wall painting of the time of Elizabeth was discovered in it; and the Oldham arms, with R.O. 1662, were also in the cottage ; see Booker, op. cit. 197–200, where a view is given, and Baker, *Memorials of Oldham's Tenement*, in which are photographs of the paintings. The building was taken down in 1864 to make way for the workhouse.

An Edward Shepherd, 'late of Crumpsall' (1651), had a messuage in Deansgate, Manchester, which descended to his three daughters ; *Ct. Leet Rec.* iv, 60.

[42a] See the deeds quoted under Ancoats in Manchester.

[43] Booker, op. cit. 215.

[44] *Manch. City News*, 1900.

[45] Booker, op. cit. 216 ; the building was in Lower Crumpsall. St. Thomas's Church there is within the boundaries of Cheetham.

[46] The district was assigned in 1860 ; *Lond. Gaz.* 30 Oct.

[47] Booker, op. cit. 214, 215.

[48] Ibid. 215.

area of 1,297 acres.[1] The surface is hilly, a height of 335 ft. being attained near the centre. Moston village lies to the south of this, Nuthurst to the north-east, and Streetfold to the west. On the northern boundary lie White Moss[2] and the district formerly known as Theale Moor, which are partly in Chadderton. The residential hamlet of New Moston is in the extreme east of the township. The population in 1901 numbered 11,897.

Roads from Newton Heath lead north-east and north-west to Moston Church and to Streetfold, to join another road going eastward from Harpurhey to Hollinwood in Oldham. Ashley Lane is in the south-west portion. The Lancashire and Yorkshire Company's railway from Manchester to Rochdale crosses the eastern part of the township and has a station called Moston near the northern boundary.

A Roman pavement was found near Lightbowne Hall.[3]

There are various works, including a wire manufactory. In 1832 the place was 'inhabited by farmers and silk weavers.'[4] There are collieries at Shakerley Green.

In 1666 the hearth tax return shows that there were eighty-nine hearths liable.[5]

The Simpson Memorial Institute stands in Moston Lane. There is a branch library in the building.

Accounts of the people and folk-lore of the place have been issued by Mr. John Ward and others.[5a]

There is a Roman Catholic cemetery in the centre of the township, opened in 1875.

Moston was included in the city of Manchester in 1890 and ceased to be a township in 1896, when it became part of the new township of North Manchester.

MANOR Although in 1320 Moston and Nuthurst are called hamlets of Manchester,[6] the tenants there being obliged to grind at the

---

[1] 1,299 acres, including 7 of inland water ; *Census Rep.* 1901.

[2] An outburst of this moss took place in Jan. 1633–4 ; *Hist. MSS. Com. Rep.* xii, App. ii, 43.

[3] Watkin, *Roman Lancs.* 57.

[4] E. Butterworth, *Chron. Hist. of Manch.* 22.

[5] Subs. R. bdle. 250, no. 9. The chief houses were those of James Lightbowne's executors, with nine hearths; Samuel Sandford, eight, and Francis Chetham, seven.

[5a] Ward, *Moston Characters at Play* ; C. Roeder, 'Moston Folk Lore' in *Lancs. and Ches. Antiq. Soc.* xxv. ; E. Waugh, *Sketches of Lancs. Life.*

[6] *Mamecestre* (Chet. Soc.), ii, 281. The lord of Moston was hopper-free and paid one-twentieth as toll instead of one-sixteenth. The tithes in later times were paid to the college at Manchester.

The lords of Manchester had little to do with Moston, but in 1418 Thomas Lord La Warre granted to his feoffees a messuage and lands in Moston called Brideshagh next Boukerlegh, lately held by Thomas le Bouker ; the bounds began at the south at the gate in the side of the lane leading from the common pasture of Theale Moor to Manchester, passing the holding of Robert Shacklock, and the bounds of Theale Moor and Blackley ; Chan. Inq. p.m. 5 Hen. VI, no. 54. In 1322 Brideshagh seems to be reckoned as part of Crumpsall ; *Mamecestre*, ii, 363.

[7] In charters of 1340 and 1356 quoted below. In 1569–70 an agreement was made between the parish of Ashton and

Pilkington by services unknown.[14] This statement of the tenure is repeated in the inquisitions taken after the deaths of his descendants—John, 1515,[15] Thomas, 1546,[16] John, 1573,[17] Henry, 1577,[18] and James, 1614.[19] In practice the mesne lordship was ignored and the Chethams paid their quit-rent directly to the lord of Manchester.[20]

James Chetham was succeeded by his son Thomas, then a minor. During the Civil War Thomas espoused the Parliamentary side and was a captain of infantry, taking part in the defence of Manchester in 1642 and being appointed a commissioner two years later.[21] He died in 1657. His son Francis[22] quickly mortgaged Nuthurst; dying without issue in 1678, he was succeeded by a younger brother, John Chetham of Linton in Cambridgeshire, who, after encumbering the estate still further, sold it in 1692 to Edward Chetham of

Manchester, son of Edward Chetham of Smedley.[23] The purchaser's son and heir, also named Edward, ultimately inherited not only Nuthurst, but the estates of various branches of the family, and dying unmarried in 1769 his heirs were his sisters—Alice widow of Adam Bland,[24] and Mary wife of Samuel Clowes the younger.[25]

On a division Moston and Nuthurst were part of the latter's portion. She died in 1775. Nuthurst was by her will given to James Hilton, son of her daughter Mary, who married Samuel Hilton of Pennington. The trustees of his son Samuel Chetham Hilton were in possession in 1851.[26]

Roger son of Geoffrey de Chadderton in 1340 settled his lands in Moston upon his son Roger, with remainders to younger sons.[27] The family remained in possession until the beginning of the 17th century,[28]

Thomas de Chadderton; *Lancs. Inq. p.m.* (Chet. Soc.), i, 54–6. His son John was a minor, but obtained livery of his lands in 1404; *Dep. Keeper's Rep.* xxxiii, App. 4. In 1412 John son of Thomas Chetham granted to Ellis son of John Chadderton all his lands in Nuthurst for the term of thirty years at a peppercorn rent; Towneley's MS. DD, 2222. In 1413 John Chetham made a settlement of his lands in Crompton, Ashton, and elsewhere, with remainder to his son James and his issue by Eleanor daughter of Ellis de Buckley; Clowes D. no. 102–3. Charles, another son, was living in 1465; ibid. no. 124. John Chetham was still alive in 1442; ibid. no. 91, 111.

James Chetham, the son of John, married as his second wife, about 1440, Margery daughter of John Langley; ibid. no. 91, 115. James Chetham was living in 1475; ibid. no. 128.

Margery was living a widow in 1480 and 1487; ibid. no. 130, 138. In 1466 a grant was made by William Heaton to Thomas Chetham, son and heir apparent of James, on his marriage with William's daughter Elizabeth; ibid. no. 125. A son Nicholas is mentioned in 1496; ibid. no. 141.

By an agreement between James and Thomas his son in 1468, the latter received Nuthurst and Sidgreaves, paying £4 a year to his father; the father also had 18d., a moiety of the free rent of Moston; ibid. no. 164.

[14] Duchy of Lanc. Inq. p.m. iii, 62. He held a messuage, 34 acres of land, 6 acres of meadow, 200 acres of pasture, and 60 acres of wood in Nuthurst, together with messuages and lands in Butterworth, Middleton, Castleton, and Crompton. John Chetham, the son and heir, was thirty-four years of age.

In 1487 John Chetham married Margery daughter of Ellis Prestwich; Clowes D. no. 138–9.

A Thomas Chetham left a manuscript of the *Gest Hystoriale* to be an heirloom at Nuthurst; see note in *Chetham Gen.* 15; *Lancs. and Ches. Antiq. Soc.* xxiii, 62.

[15] Duchy of Lanc. Inq. p.m. iv, 6. Thomas Chetham, the son and heir of John, was twenty-six years of age.

Thomas married Elizabeth daughter of John Hopwood; Clowes D. A series of rentals from 1520 to 1546 has been preserved. Nuthurst itself seems to have been almost entirely in the hands of the Chethams; there was one under-tenant in 1520 who paid 3s. 4d., and in 1524 a second appears, paying 2s. In 1524 Richard Shacklock, who had made a gar-

den on the waste, ag of leeks to each of th Moss Farm, with a added to the rental in &c.

[16] Duchy of La c. son and heir John w of age. The h ' h *Dep. Keeper's Rep.* xx John Chetham m his lands in 1557; Among the same de 1566 and 1572.

[17] D chy of Lanc By his will he left t mansion house of N appurtenant, and a m towards the bringing and h

producing one noteworthy man, William Chadderton, warden of Manchester and Bishop of Chester in 1579, afterwards translated to Lincoln.[29] In 1623 Edmund Chadderton sold his estate to John Holcroft of Lymehurst,[30] and he, a few years later, sold Little Nuthurst Hall to Nathan and Samuel Jenkinson.[31] The new owners were followed by the Sandfords,[32] who sold their estate to the Chethams, so that Nuthurst was in time united in one ownership.[33]

[29] See the account of Manchester Church.

[30] Clowes D. In a later deed (1625–6) Edmund Chadderton is described as of Wentbridge in Kirk Smeaton, Yorkshire. See also *Manch. Ct. Leet Rec.* iii, 76 ; and *Local Glean. Lancs. and Ches.* ii, 149.

[31] Clowes D. dated 1626–7 ; Edmund Chadderton confirmed the sale in 1629. The purchasers were sons of a Robert Jenkinson *alias* Wilson of Failsworth. In 1631 Nathan and Samuel Jenkinson of Moston, 'gentlemen,'[1] and Thomas Chetham of Nuthurst, gent., refused knighthood, paying £10 composition ; *Misc.* (Rec. Soc. Lancs. and Ches.), i, 215–16. In 1630 Samuel Jenkinson and Elizabeth his wife released their right in Nuthurst to Nathan Jenkinson ; Clowes D. There are also extant a feoffment made by Robert Jenkinson of Nuthurst in 1650, and his will of 1654 ; ibid. From the brief account of the family given by Booker (op. cit. 156–158) it appears that Nathan Jenkinson, who died in 1637, left his estate in Nuthurst and Failsworth to his wife Alice until his son Robert should come of age. The inventory showed goods and chattels worth £557 ; the house had a room called 'the Bishop's chamber.'

[32] See Booker, op. cit. 159–63. A pedigree was recorded in 1664 ; Dugdale, *Visit.* 253. From various deeds it appears that William the son of Robert Jenkinson sold Nuthurst Hall in 1662–3 to Samuel Sandford and that the latter was in possession in 1664 when a fine was made ; Clowes D. The will of Samuel Sandford of Little Nuthurst, made in 1683 and proved in 1684, mentions Ellen his wife, Samuel his son, and Mary his wife, and other sons — Theophilus, Robert, and Daniel ; ibid. Samuel the son sold Nuthurst in 1694 ; Booker, op. cit. 161. Daniel Sandford, of London, silkman, sold or concurred in the sale to George Chetham of Smedley ; Clowes D.

[33] Edward Chetham of Nuthurst was sole owner in 1698 ; *Chet. Gen.* 62.

[34] It has been mentioned (in 1468) in a preceding note.

[34a] Axon, *Chet. Gen.* 28. There are references to it in the Clowes deeds. In 1670 Jonathan Chadwick gave it to James Scholes, and nine years later James Scholes the younger, of Oldham, gave it to Thomas Stevenson ; in 1684 Robert Stevenson of Tetlow gave it to Alexander Davie. It was granted in 1693–4 by John Chetham of Nuthurst and John his son to Mary Davie and others.

[35] Richard de Moston attested the Manchester charter of 1301 ; *Mamecestre*, ii, 216. There is a complaint of his regarding Nuthurst in *Abbrev. Rot. Orig.* (Rec. Com.), i, 124. In 1310 he put in his claim in a settlement of the manors of Manchester and Ashton ; *Final Conc.* (Rec. Soc. Lancs. and Ches.), ii, 5. In 1315 John La Warre granted to Richard de Moston a part of the waste, the bounds beginning at the paling of Blackley, following the stream called

Doddithokes Clough as far down as Moss Brook, then up to the bounds of Moston as far as the paling up to the head of the stream ; together with the Brodeshalgh and 3 acres of waste between it and the hedge of William the Harpur (Harpurhey) ; Manch. Corp. D. Henry de Moston occurs in Ashton in 1332 ; *Exch. Lay Subs.* 32. For some further notes on the family see Booker, op. cit. 142, 143.

In 1325 William de Moston gave to Emmota his sister, daughter of Richard de Moston, land in the township ; and in 1343 another brother, Richard, granted her the manor of Moston ; while three years later the same Emmota granted the manor to John son of Hugh de Moston and Margaret daughter of Richard de Tyldesley, with remainders to Hugh and Robert son of Henry de Tyldesley, and William son of Robert Mascy of Sale ; Clowes D. In the same year (1346) Lucy widow of William de Moston claimed dower in the manor against John son of Hugh de Moston and Margaret his wife ; De Banco R. 347, m. 296 d.

Light is thrown on these grants by suits of a few years later. Emma daughter of Richard de Moston, in Lent, 1352, claimed the manor (except two messuages, one plough-land, and 4 acres of pasture) against William son of Robert de Radcliffe, Robert (son of Roger) de Bolton and Margaret his wife, Alice daughter of Robert de Radcliffe, and James son of Henry de Tyldesley. Robert and Margaret answered as tenants, and stated that Richard, the plaintiff's brother, had enfeoffed her in trust that she would refeoff him with remainders to Adam de Abney and his issue and to John son of Hugh de Moston. Emma at length did enfeoff the last-named, reserving a rent of 5 marks for her life ; Duchy of Lanc. Assize R. 1, m. vi d. It appears later that Margaret was the widow of John de Moston. In 1354 and 1355 Hugh de Toft and Alice his wife, in right of the latter, claimed against Robert de Bolton and Margaret his wife twelve messuages, 200 acres of land, 60 acres of meadow, 80 acres of pasture, and 40 acres of wood in Moston by Ashton. The plaintiffs alleged that Emma de Moston had disseised Robert de Moston, father of Alice and brother and heir of Richard de Moston. It appears that Robert had sons William and Robert ; ibid. R. 3, m. vi ; R. 4, m. 23 d. There is a further statement of the matter in Assize R. 440, m. 1 d.

In 1404 Robert son of Hugh de Toft recovered the manor of Moston against Hugh de Moston and Alice his wife ; the jury found that one Richard de Moston had left issue William, Richard, Robert, Hugh, and Emma ; that William dying without issue, his widow (Lucy de Morley) had a third of the manor from Richard, who gave the other two-thirds to his sister Emma, and the whole afterwards descended to John de Moston and

Shacklock,[38] and another part of the estate to the Bowkers.[39] The Shacklocks held possession of the hall for more than a century; [40] in 1664 it was sold to Edward Chetham.[41] The family name is commemorated by Shacklock or Shakerley Green. The Bowkers' name is preserved in Bowker Hall on the border of Blackley.[42] Another family, the Lightbownes, have a similar memorial; [43] they succeeded the Jepsons.

HOUGH HALL was long the residence of a family named Halgh or Hough; [44] the last of the line, Captain Robert Hough, took the king's side in the Civil War and had his estate sequestered.[45] It was purchased in 1685 by James Lightbowne, and soon afterwards passed to the Minshulls of Chorlton. In or soon after 1774 it was purchased by Samuel Taylor,[46] by whose representative it was sold about

[38] Clowes D. William Radcliffe of Ordsall seems to have released his claim to the Shacklocks; ibid. From the same deeds it appears that the Earl of Sussex had in 1543 made a lease of land in Moston to Adam Shacklock.

There was some family disputing over the acquisition. In 1542 Robert and Thomas Shacklock complained that in the preceding year the Earl of Sussex had made a lease to them, but Richard Shacklock the elder and his sons, Adam, Hugh, and Ellis, had expelled the plaintiffs. The latter seem to have established their case, but in 1544, after the death of Richard Shacklock, they complained that forcible entry had again been made, this time by Margaret widow of Richard, Ellis her son, and others; Duchy of Lanc. Plead. Hen. VIII, xv, S 1, S 12.

[39] Clowes D. To Geoffrey and Oliver Bowker John Reddish sold 26 acres of his purchase, and to Nicholas Bowker he sold 20 acres.

[40] Thomas Shacklock died at the end of 1570, leaving a son and heir Robert, of full age; Manch. Ct. Leet Rec. i, 137; an abstract of his will is printed in the notes.

Robert Shacklock died in 1588, leaving Edward as son and heir, of full age; ibid. ii, 31. For fines referring to his properties see Pal. of Lanc. Feet of F. bdle. 35, m. 158; 49, m. 191.

Edward Shacklock died in 1618, leaving a son and heir John, of full age; Manch. Ct. Leet Rec. iii, 19. The inquisition taken after his death, embodying his will (see Booker, op. cit. 181), is preserved among the Clowes D.; his wife was Alice Cudworth, and his son John was twenty-two years of age. In 1621 an Adam Shacklock and Adam his son and heir appear; ibid.

John Shacklock the elder made a feoffment of Howgate and other lands in 1628, the remainders being to his son and heir John the younger, Edward a younger son, and Daniel brother of John the elder; ibid. John the younger died before 1649, when Edward is described as son and heir apparent; ibid. A further feoffment or mortgage was made in 1655 by John Shacklock, Mary his wife, and Edward then his only son. Daughters Elizabeth and Mary are mentioned; ibid.

Edward Shacklock died in or before 1666, leaving his sister Mary as his heir, ibid.

The will of Thomas Shacklock of Moston, a 'cousin' of the Edward who died in 1618, is printed by Booker (op. cit. 179); he left sons Robert, Oswald, and Henry.

[41] Clowes D. Margaret the widow of Edward Shacklock had a claim for £500 against the estate; but Edward Chetham, the purchaser, refused to discharge it until certain deeds were given up to him. In 1669 the £500 was paid.

[42] Oliver Bowker, 'late of Moston,' died in 1565, leaving a son and heir Edward, of lawful age; Manch. Ct. Leet Rec. i, 93. Edward Bowker purchased

a messuage and la George Bowker in 1 Feet of F. bdle 2 20 Mar. 1585-6, lea then eighteen years o lands in Mo ton wer Manch. Ct. Lee Rec. p.m. in Clowes D.

Nicholas Bowker Jane h s wife in 1 Moston to Robert Sh Pal. of Lanc Feet o

[43] See Booker, o ped gree is given with James Light tradesman of Manch purchased a house Manch. Ct Leet Rec 1621, leaving a son iii, 47, where a full printed The son b Gray s Inn, and rec 1664, arms having and his brother Jame in 1667, when his daughter Elizabeth, Lindley, also of G with the inventory work, 162-8; in law books

.,

1880 to the late Robert Ward, whose widow is the present owner and occupier.

Hough Hall is a picturesque timber and plaster house two stories high standing on the south side of Moston Lane a little way back from the road, and amid a wilderness of modern brick and mortar. The building has been much restored and the interior is wholly modernized, but the outside retains a good deal of its ancient appearance, though all the windows are new and some of its original features have been lost. The house appears to belong to the end of the 16th or beginning of the 17th century, but in the absence of any date or inscription on the building it is impossible to determine the date of its erection. The plan, as far as can be gathered, seems to follow no recognized type, and if the house is now of its original extent is probably of late date. It may, however, be a fragment of a larger building. The principal front faces south and consists of a block about 48 ft. long and 19 ft. deep running east and west, with an eastern wing 18 ft. 6 in. wide projecting 8 ft. 6 in. and with a gable north and south. With the exception of the south part of the east wing the building is constructed entirely of timber on a stone base, but the timbers are severely constructional on the elevations and any decorative fillings, if they ever existed, have entirely disappeared, the spaces having been filled with brick and cemented or plastered over. The old north front had two gables of unequal size side by side at the east end, but a third was added about 1885, when a low lean-to building formerly in the north-west of the house was raised and a room built over it. These three plain gables without barge boards now form the most picturesque feature of the house. On the east side is a large stone and brick chimney originally terminating in diagonally placed brick shafts, but these have given place to a modern stack, and the lower part has been entirely covered with rough-cast. The entrance is in the principal or south front and part of an

original timber porch remains, but a modern front in brick and plaster has been erected in front of it. The south side of the east wing is faced in brick and has a modern bay window on the ground floor. The stone plinth, which on the north side is 3 ft. high, is here very low, the timbers coming almost to the ground. The roofs are covered with stone slates and the whole appearance of the building, which has a garden on the south side, is in somewhat strong contrast to its surroundings. Internally the roof principals show in the divisions between the bedrooms, the wall posts being 17 ft. 9 in. apart, and the roof ceiled at half its height. The entrance hall is centrally placed, and has a flagged floor, but the staircase is entirely modern. The outer door, however, is the ancient one of thick oak, nail studded and with ornamental hinges and ring handle. There is some oak panelling 3 ft. 3 in. high in the dining-room, but otherwise the interior is without interest. A second entrance has been made on the east side, a lobby being taken out of one of the

HOUGH HALL, MOSTON : BACK VIEW

rooms, but this is no part of the original arrangement.[47]

Thomas Greenhalgh of Brandlesholme died in 1576, holding messuages and lands in Moston and 'Blakelowe' of Lord La Warre in socage.[48] Among the old families may be mentioned those of Street,[49] Rodley,[50] and Nugent.[51]

[47] There is an illustration of Hough Hall in Booker's *Hist. of Blackley Chapel* (1855), 187, showing the house as it was before the alterations of twenty-five years ago, with its two gables on the north, and before the entrance was made on the east side.

[48] Duchy of Lanc. Inq. p.m. xii, 10.

[49] Booker, op. cit. 188. Richard Street of Moston died in 1582, his next of kin being William Street, then a minor ; *Ct. Leet Rec.* i, 232. His father was perhaps the Richard Street whose heir was of age in 1597 (ibid. ii, 120), for in 1600 William Street was ordered to come in to do his suit and service ; ibid. ii, 155, 162, 167. In 1624 John Booth purchased a messuage and lands in Moston from William and John Street ; ibid. iii, 86.

George Street of Moston died in 1588 holding a messuage and land, which he

The land tax returns of 1787 show that James Hilton of Pennington was the chief landowner, he paying £22 out of £39 ; smaller owners were Matthias, Boulton, and Wainman.[62] In 1854 there were fifteen landowners in the township.[63]

For about a century there was constant disputing regarding Theale Moor on the border of Moston, Chadderton, and Alkrington. The Chethams were intimately concerned in the matter, not only as owners of Nuthurst but also as farmers of the tithes of Moston. At last, about 1600, a settlement was made and a division arranged.[64]

In 1850 a building society was formed which purchased 57 acres and laid out the land, the district being called New Moston.[65]

For the Established Church St. Mary's was built in 1869 ;[66] a school had been built in 1844.[57] The dean and canons of Manchester present. St. Luke's mission district has been formed at Lightbowne.

The Wesleyan Methodists had a school chapel in 1854.[58] There are also chapels of the Methodist New Connexion and United Free Church.

Mass is said on Sunday in St. Joseph's Chapel in the cemetery. A convent with a chapel stands near the south-west border.

HARPURHEY

Harpouresheie, 1327.

This small township, at one time called Harpurhey with Gotherswick,[1] lies on both sides of the road from Manchester to Middleton, extending westward to the Irk. In 1830 it was described as abounding in pleasant views.[2] It has long been a suburb of Manchester, and almost covered with buildings. The area is 193 acres. In 1901 the population was reckoned with that of Blackley.

The spinning, manufacture, and printing of cotton were carried on in 1833 ;[3] in 1854 there were two print works and a spinning shed. Cotton mills and print and dye works continue to exist.

An ancient stone hammer was found near Turkey Lane.[4]

Harpurhey was included in the Parliamentary borough of Manchester from the first but was not taken into the municipal borough until 1885. It ceased to be a township in 1896, becoming part of the new township of North Manchester.

HARPURHEY may derive its name *MANOR* from the 80 acres demised for life to one William Harpour by Sir John La Warre, lord of Manchester, early in the 14th century, *loco beneficii*.[5] In 1327 the same John La Warre granted 24 acres of land and wood called Harpurshey, lying next to the pale of his park of Blackley, to Adam son of Robert de Radcliffe and Alice his daughter, wife of John son of Henry de Hulton, and the heirs of Alice, at a rent of 26s. 8d.[6] This estate continued to be held by the Hultons of Farnworth until the 16th century,[7] when it passed to the Hultons of Over Hulton.[8] It was sold in 1808–10 by William Hulton to Thomas Andrew and Robert Andrew, the former purchasing Boardman's Tenement and the latter Green Mount and other lands. Thomas Andrew's estate, as Harpurhey Hall, descended to his son Edward, after whose death it was in 1847 sold to John Barratt. Robert Andrew died in 1831, having bequeathed the estate to trustees for his daughter and heir Robina, wife of Captain Conran.[9]

GOTHERSWICK, called a hamlet of Manchester in 1320,[10] was also held by the Hultons of Farnworth [11] and became merged in Harpurhey, the name having long been lost.[12]

The land tax returns of 1797 show that Joseph Barlow, Robert and Thomas Andrew, and Samuel Ogden were the proprietors.[13]

For the Established worship Christ Church, Harpurhey, was built in 1837–8.[14] The patronage is vested in five trustees. St. Stephen's was built in 1901 ; the Crown and the Bishop of Manchester present in turns. There are mission churches. The Wesleyan Methodists have a church. The Salvation Army has a barracks. There is also a Presbyterian Church.[15]

---

in Fennel Street, lately occupied by Richard Nugent, deceased (Chet. Soc. New Ser. xxi, 138, Chet. evidences *penes* Dr. Renaud). For the Nugents see E. Axon in *Lancs. and Ches. Antiq. Soc.* xxi, 127.

[62] Land tax returns at Preston.

[63] Booker, op. cit. 139.

[64] A list of those entitled to get turves on Theale Moor in 1550 is printed in *Manch. Guardian N. and Q.* no. 1273. There are in the *Ducatus Lanc.* (Rec. Com.) many references to those disputes, and numerous documents, with plans, are among the Clowes D. ; see *Chet. Gen.* (Chet. Soc.), 15, 21. The 'Equal' in Nuthurst was also the occasion of a tithe dispute, *Ducatus Lanc.* (Rec. Com.), iii, 401, 487.

[65] Booker, op. cit. 139.

[66] A district was assigned to it in 1870; *Lond. Gaz.* 12 Aug.

[57] Booker, op. cit. 141.

[58] Ibid.

[1] So in 1615 ; *Manch. Constables' Accts.* i, 19.

[2] Clarke, *Lancs. Gazetteer.* The hearth tax return of 1666 shows that the dwellings were small, and the total number of hearths was only twelve ; Subs. R. bdle. 250, no. 9.

[3] Cotton printing was begun here by Thomas Andrew in 1788.

[4] *Lancs. and Ches. Antiq. Soc.* v, 330.

[5] *Mamecestre* (Chet. Soc.), ii, 363 ; the land was valued at 3d. an acre rent.

[6] Hulton D. There was another grant of the same in 1332 ; ibid.

[7] See the account of Farnworth.

John Hulton of Farnworth in 1473 held a messuage near Manchester called Harpurhey in socage, by the rent of 26s. 8d. ; *Mamecestre*, iii, 483. He died in 1487, holding six messuages, 200 acres of land, 40 acres of meadow, 100 acres of pasture and 30 acres of wood called Harpurhey in Manchester, by services unknown ; Duchy of Lanc. Inq. p.m. iii, 26. The estate descended to William Hulton, who died in 1556 ; ibid. x, 32.

[8] Harpurhey passed to Adam Hulton of the Park in Over Hulton by an agreement with the last-named William Hulton. Adam died in 1572 holding Harpurhey of William West Lord La Warre in socage, by the rent of 26s. 8d. ; Duchy of Lanc. Inq. p.m. xiii, 4 ; see also ibid. xvii, 80. In 1613 the tenure was described as 'of

the king, by the two-hundredth part of a knight's fee' ; *Lancs. Inq. p.m.* (Rec. Soc. Lancs. and Ches.), i, 267.

[9] The details are given in Booker's *Blackley* (Chet. Soc.), 124–8.

The Green Mount estate in 1784 consisted of several farms held on lease from the Hultons. Among the field names occur Gutter Twigg, Great Clough, Tough Hey, Bawhouse Field and Pingle ; there was a stream called Moss Brook.

[10] *Mamecestre*, ii, 281 ; the tenants were bound to grind at the lord's mill.

[11] Adam de Radcliffe held Gotherswick in 1320 by a rent of 12d. ; *Mamecestre*, ii, 279. It descended like Harpurhey, and in 1473 John Hulton of Farnworth held it by the old rent of 12d. ; ibid. iii, 483. It is mentioned in the above-cited inquisition of William Hulton (1556).

[12] It is the Gutter Twigg of a preceding note (1784–93).

[13] Returns at Preston. The landowners of 1847 are named by Booker, op. cit. 128.

[14] The district was formed in 1837 and re-formed in 1854 ; *Lond. Gaz.* 16 June.

[15] It was founded in 1882 ; the mission hall, known as Moston St. George's, was built in 1902.

NEWTON

There is no noteworthy variation in the spelling of the name.

This township[1] lies between Moston Brook on the north and the Medlock on the south ; part of the western boundary is formed by two brooks which there unite to flow south-west through Manchester as the now hidden Shootersbrook. The area measures 1,585 acres. The population of Newton, Bradford, and Clayton was 83,501 in 1901.

The principal road is that from Manchester to Oldham, going north-east through the northern half of the township ; in the same direction, but somewhat to the south, goes a fragment of a Roman road. The township is crossed by several portions of the Lancashire and Yorkshire Company's railway ; the line from Manchester to Rochdale crosses the north-west corner, with a station at Miles Platting, where there are extensive goods sidings, and is joined by a branch from the west, another branch going east to Oldham, with a station called Dean Lane ; yet another branch from Miles Platting bends to run along the southern border with stations called Park and Clayton Bridge ; this last line has a junction with one from London Road Station. The Rochdale Canal passes through the centre of the township.

The hearth tax return of 1666 shows that there were 113 hearths liable. The principal houses were those of Mrs. Mary Whitworth, with nine hearths ; William Williamson, with eight, and Thomas Byrom with six.[2]

The district to the north of the canal is quite urban ; the western portion, known as Miles Platting, has long been a suburb of Manchester, and the eastern portion, or Newton Heath, has more recently become one. In the south-east corner of the township stands Culcheth Hall, and the hamlet formerly called Mill Houses (from Clayton Mill) is now Clayton Bridge, from the bridge over the Medlock.[3]

The detached portion of the township called Kirkmanshulme[4] appears to have been taken out of Gorton. It is separated from Newton proper by a distance of 2 miles. In its north-east corner lie the Belle Vue Gardens, formed in 1836 ;[5] the southern portion is known as Crow Croft ; Gore Brook crosses the centre from east to west.

[1] A full description of the ancient and modern topography of the township is contained in H. T. Crofton's *Newton Chapelry* (Chet. Soc. new ser.). See also *Manch. Collectanea* (Chet. Soc.), ii, 184-8.

[2] Subs. R. bdle. 250, no. 9.

[3] Higson, *Droylsden*, 18 ; the mill was in Failsworth.

[4] Kyrdmannesholm, 1292 ; Curmesholme and Kermonsholm are the spellings in the copy of the 1320-22 survey. About 1500-1600 it was frequently called Kerdmanshulme.

[5] Crofton, op. cit. iii, 420.

[6] *Lond. Gaz.* 30 Dec. 1853 ; the district appears to have been in very bad condition ; Crofton, *Newton*, ii, 146.

[7] Act 22 Vict. cap. 31.

[8] Crofton, op. cit. 235.

[9] Ibid. ii, 2 ; the Act was 42 Geo. III, cap. 306.

[10] For some particulars see ibid. i, 213, 204, 236 ; ii, 11 ; i, 151.

[11] Ibid. i, 8, 9, 205.

Gilliams,[31] and by an heiress conveyed to John Greaves of Manchester, apothecary,[32] who was high sheriff in 1733.[33] This family held it for about a century, when it was sold ; the owner in 1862 was named Assheton Bennett.[34]

A family named Holland was long resident in Newton.[35]

MONSALL was an estate which only in part belonged to the warden and fellows. The portion which did not belong to them was about 1872 purchased by the Manchester Infirmary for a fever hospital building, and in 1896 was sold to the corporation.[36]

In 1787 the principal landowner was Edward Greaves, who paid about a sixth part of the land tax. — Hulme, Edmund Taylor, and — Holland were the next contributors.[37]

The chapel, now *ALL SAINTS'* CHURCH *CHURCH*, was built on the heath perhaps not long before the Reformation.[38] In the Visitation list of 1563 Ralph Ridde appeared as curate of Newton.[39] There was no endowment, and the minister in 1610 was paid by voluntary offerings.[30] The Parliamentary Surveyors in 1650 recommended that it be made a parish church ; the minister had a stipend of £40 raised by subscription.[31] In 1717 it was certified that 'nothing belonged to it' except the minister's dwelling ; surplice fees and subscriptions

amounted to about £24. There were two wardens.[32] The chapel was then 'well and uniformly seated' ;[33] it was enlarged in 1738,[34] and rebuilt 1814–16.[35] A separate chapelry was assigned to it in 1839.[36] The rector is presented by the Dean and Canons of Manchester. The following is a list of the curates and rectors :—[37]

oc.	1563	Ralph Ridde
oc.	1598	— Medcalfe
oc.	1609	Randle Bate [38]
oc.	1615	Humphrey Barnett
oc.	1617	George Gee [39]
oc.	1637	Humphrey Bernard [40]
oc.	1642	William Walker [41]
	1649	John Walker [42]
oc.	1670	Thomas Lawton
oc.	1695	James Lawton
	1704	Griffith Swinton [43]
oc.	1729	Thomas Wroe
oc.	1734	William Shrigley
oc.	1735	William Purnell, M.A. (Oriel Coll. Oxf.)
	1764	Richard Millward, LL.B.[44]
	1789	William Jackson, M.A.[45]
	1792	Abraham Ashworth, M.A. (Brasenose Coll. Oxf.) [46]
	1818	Thomas Gaskell

1449 made a settlement of four messuages, 90 acres of moss, &c., in Newton near Manchester and Poulton and Woolston near Warrington ; the remainders were to Richard, Ralph, Katherine, and Ellen, children of Richard, and to the right heirs of Elizabeth ; *Final Conc.* (Rec. Soc. Lancs. and Ches.), iii, 115. A statement of title will be found in Crofton, op. cit. ii, 269.

Ralph Culcheth paid 4s. 6d. free rent for his estate in Newton in 1547 ; Raines, *Chant.* i, 16. He made a settlement of his lands in Newton, Poulton, Woolston, and Fearnhead in 1563 ; Pal. of Lanc. Feet of F. bdle. 25, m. 38. He died a year or two later, holding land in Newton of the warden and fellows of the collegiate church by a rent of 4s. 6d. and a pound of wax ; it was worth £4 a year ; the heir was his daughter Grace, twenty-five years of age ; Duchy of Lanc. Inq. p.m. xi, 34. Immediately William Culcheth *alias* Linaker, bastard son of Ralph, put forward his claim to the estate against Grace, and she admitted it ; Pal. of Lanc. Feet of F. bdle. 27, m. 129. In 1568 John Byron of Newstead acquired a part of the estate from the said William Culcheth ; ibid. bdle. 30, m. 140. Sir John Byron, however, appears to have been in possession of the remaining and greater part of the estate in 1564 ; ibid. bdle. 26, m. 10.

In 1574 William Culcheth granted a lease of land in Culcheth in Newton called the Stormcroft to Adam Holland, for the lives of Adam, Jane his wife, and George their son, at a rent of 20s. ; it was agreed 'that the pits made and to be made within the said Stormcroft should remain only to the use and commodity for fishing to the said William and his heirs,' as had been accustomed ; Raines D. (Chet. Lib.). See further in Crofton, op. cit. i, 209, 210.

[31] There were several families named Gilliam around Manchester ; they took

the Parliamentary Crofton, *Newton,* i, *bury* (Chet. Soc), number of

1834   William Hutchinson, B.D. (Emmanuel Coll. Camb.) [47]

1876   St. Vincent Beechey, M.A. (Caius Coll. Camb)

1885   Ernest Frederick Letts, M.A. (Trin. Coll. Dubl. and Oxf.) [48]

1904   James Andrew Winstanley, M.A. (St. John's Coll. Camb.)

The following more recent churches belong to the Establishment, the Bishop of Manchester collating to the rectories : St. Luke's, Miles Platting, 1875 ; [49] St. Anne's, 1883 ; [50] St. Mark's, 1884, and St. Augustine's, 1888. St. Cyprian's is a temporary iron church at Kirkmanshulme.[51]

A school was founded about 1688.[52]

The Wesleyan Methodists have churches at Newton Heath, Miles Platting, and Monsall.[53] The Methodist New Connexion also have three, the Primitive Methodists two, and the Independent Methodists one, at Miles Platting. The Congregationalists have a school-chapel at Newton Heath, built in 1893.[54] The Salvation Army has a barracks. The Unitarians have a church in Oldham Road.

For Roman Catholic worship St. Edmund's was opened in 1873, and Corpus Christi in 1889–1908 ; both are at Miles Platting. The latter began as a temporary church in a former glass works ; it is served by Premonstratensian canons. The Alexian Brothers have a house at Newton Heath, and the Little Sisters of the Poor have one at Culcheth.

FAILSWORTH

Failesworth, c. 1200.

Failsworth has an area of 1,073 acres.[1] The surface slopes somewhat to the brooks which bound it on the north-west and south-east, and rises slightly towards the east. It had formerly three hamlets : Doblane End, Wrigley Head, and Mill Houses. The population in 1901 was 14,152.

It is traversed near the northern boundary by the road from Manchester to Oldham, which is lined all

---

[47] First rector.

[48] He was greatly interested in the history of Manchester Church and Newton Chapelry ; several essays by him are printed in *Trans. Lancs. and Ches. Antiq. Soc.*

[49] *Lond. Gaz.* 25 July 1876, for district.

[50] Ibid. 11 Sept. 1883, for district.

[51] The Crown and the Bishop of Manchester present alternately.

[52] Gastrell, *Notitia*, ii, 91.

[53] The Wesleyans built a chapel in Oldham Road in 1839 ; Crofton, *Newton*, i, 52.

[54] Nightingale, *Lancs. Nonconf.* vi, 191; services began in 1882.

[1] 1,072 acres, including 15 of inland water ; *Census Rep.* 1901.

[2] Subs. R. bdle. 250, no. 9.

[3] *Lond. Gaz.* 20 Nov. 1863.

[4] A book of local sketches entitled *Failsworth Folk*, by Mr. Percival Percival, was published at Manchester in 1901.

[5] *Dict. Nat. Biog.*

[6] Crofton, *Newton* (Chet. Soc.), ii, 228, 265.

[7] *Lancs. Inq. and Extents* (Rec. Soc. Lancs. and Ches.), i, 67.

The abbey of Cockersand held land in Failsworth by grant of the Byrons.[18]

The land tax return of 1787 shows that Mordecai Greene was then the principal owner, paying nearly a fourth of the tax. George Smith, John Birch, Edward Greaves, and Sir Watts Horton together paid about the same amount.[14]

Accounts of many of the old dwellings, as well as of the families, may be seen in Mr. H. T. Crofton's *Newton Chapelry*.[15] A complete valuation of the township, made in 1794, is printed in the same work.[16]

In connexion with the Established Church St. John's was built in 1846; the rector is presented by the Crown and the Bishop of Manchester alternately.[17] A new district, Holy Trinity, has recently been formed; the patronage is the same, but no church has yet been built.

The old school, built in 1785 by subscription, is now a Free-thought Institute.[18]

The Wesleyans had a chapel at Wrigley Head, built in 1787; it is now a workshop.[19] The Methodist New Connexion, which appeared in 1797, has a chapel called Bethel, built in 1811.[20] The Swedenborgians opened a cottage for services in 1841; the present church, the fifth used, was built in 1889.[21]

In 1662 John Walker was ejected from the chapel of Newton, and he and his successors ministered to the Nonconformists in the neighbourhood. Newton chapel itself seems to have been the usual meeting place, but about 1698 Dob Lane Chapel, on the Failsworth side of the boundary, was erected. It was sacked in 1715 by the 'Church and King' rioters. The present chapel was built in 1878–9 on the site of the old one. The congregation has been Unitarian for more than a century.[22]

The Roman Catholic church of the Immaculate Conception was opened in 1865.[23]

BRADFORD

Bradeford, 1332.

This township,[1] which has an area of 288 acres, lies between the Medlock on the north and Ashton Old Road on the south, and is crossed about the centre by Ashton New Road. It is now almost covered with streets of dwelling-houses. The Manchester and Stockport Canal crosses the northern end. To the north of the canal lies Philips Park, opened in 1846, in which are open-air baths; a recreation ground has been formed near the border of Ardwick. There is a small library, opened in 1887. The population in 1901 was reckoned with that of Newton.

The hearth tax return of 1666 gives a total of twenty-seven hearths; the largest house was that of Edward Charnock with five hearths.[2]

The industries include large ironworks, a mill, and chemical works; the coal-pits have long been worked.[3] There was a water-mill in the 14th and 15th centuries.[4]

Though Bradford was included in the Parliamentary borough of Manchester in 1832 it was left outside the municipal borough in 1838. A local board was formed in 1857,[5] enduring till the township was included in Manchester in 1885. Its existence as a separate township ceased in 1896, when it became part of the new township of North Manchester.

A schoolboard was formed in 1876.[6]

sold to John Hardman of Heywood. John Shacklock of Moston in 1632 sold land to John Hardman; Henry Hardman, who had sons, John and William, sold to Sandford in 1665, and Samuel Sandford soon afterwards sold to Edward Chetham. The Jenkinsons of Nuthurst had land in Failsworth. Some of these families are noticed in the account of Moston.

The Byrons in 1615 sold land to John Dunkerley of Failsworth, including closes called Oldham Field, Brown Knoll, Yarncroft, Little Pingot, &c., with freedom of turbary in a moss room or moss dale on Droylsden Moor. These lands seem to have been acquired by Nathan and Samuel Jenkinson not long afterwards. See Manch. Free Lib. D. no. 59, 64–9.

William Clough died in 1639, holding a messuage, &c., in Failsworth of Edward Mosley as of his manor of Manchester; John, his son and heir, was thirty years of age; Duchy of Lanc. Inq. p.m. xxx, 27.

The following are from the inquisitions in Towneley's MS. C 8. 13 (Chet. Lib.):—

Charles Beswick died in 1631, holding a messuage and land of the lord of Manchester; John his son and heir was thirty years of age in 1638; p. 78.

Hugh Clayton, who died in 1635, had a similar tenement: Richard his son and heir was fifty-two or more; p. 260.

Adam Holland of Newton (d. 1624) had lands in Failsworth also; p. 502.

Nicholas Kempe, who died in 1621, held a messuage and lands of the lord of Manchester; Henry, his son and heir, was fifty-one years of age in 1638; p. 723.

John Thorpe, who died in 1633, held a similar tenement; Ralph, his son and heir, was forty-three years old in 1638; p. 1190.

SALFORD

In 1282 *BRADFORD* and Brunhill *MANOR* formed part of the demesne of the manor of Manchester, and were worth 40s. yearly.[7] A century earlier the Norreys family claimed two oxgangs of land in Bradford, but nothing further is known of their title.[8] The lords of Manchester had in 1322 a wood in Bradford a league in circuit; also meadow and pasture land and heath; a grange and shippon had been built there.[9] Ten years later, at the request of his wife Joan, John La Warre granted his estate in Bradford to John de Salford of Wakerley and Alice his wife for life, £20 being paid down and a rent of £10 being due.[10] In 1357 Roger La Warre granted the manor of Bradford to Thomas de Booth of Barton in Eccles,[11] who at once bought out the Wakerley family,[12] and Bradford descended like Barton until the latter part of the 16th century, when it became the portion of Dorothy, youngest daughter and co-heir of John Booth of Barton.[13] By her first husband, John Molyneux of Sefton, she had a daughter Bridget,[14] who married Thomas Charnock of Astley in Chorley.[15] The manor was still in Bridget Charnock's possession in 1654,[16] and descended to the Brookes of Astley, a branch of the Mere family.[17] On the death of Peter Brooke in 1787 the estates went to his sister Susannah, who married Thomas Townley Parker of Cuerden.[18]

GORTON

Gorton, 1282 (copy), and usually; Goreton, c. 1450.[1]

This township[2] lies to the north and south of Gore or Rush Brook, which flows west to the Mersey.

---

[7] *Lancs. Inq. and Extents* (Rec. Soc. Lancs. and Ches.), i, 244.

[8] *Final Conc.* (Rec. Soc. Lancs. and Ches.), i, 6; the date is 1196. The land no doubt reverted to the chief lord, for Bradford is not named in the survey of 1212, though Heaton Norris is.

[9] *Mamecestre* (Chet. Soc.), ii, 368, 363. The wood, with pannage, honey, and bees was worth 6s., the 'vesture' of the wood, £10; the 2 acres of meadow, 2s., the 54 acres of pasture, 27s., and another 12 acres, which could not be ploughed because within the wood, 4s.; the 70 acres of heath, 33s.

[10] Manch. Corp. D.; the grant was made at Wakerley. See also Dods. MSS. cxlix, fol. 157.

[11] The charter is recited in the Inq. p.m. of Sir John Booth of Barton in 1514; Duchy of Lanc. Inq. p.m. iv, 15. The grant included the manor of Barton, the manor of Bradford, the hamlets of Openshaw and Ardwick, a plot of land in Manchester called Flowerlache, and another plot called Marshal Field; a rent of £10 14s. 2d. was to be paid during Thomas's life, and 1d. afterwards. The manor of Barton was Thomas's patrimony; the remainder was a fresh grant.

Thomas de Booth in 1363 granted Bradford, with its lands and water-mill, to his son John for life; Dods. MSS. cxlix, fol. 160.

[12] A fine between Roger de Wakerley and Margery his wife, plaintiffs, and John de Wakerley and Alice his wife, deforciants, was made in 1355 respecting a messuage, 160 acres of land, and 10 acres of wood 'in Manchester'; *Final Conc.* ii, 146. In 1358 Roger and Margery sold the same lands, described as 'in Bradford and Manchester,' to Thomas de Booth; ibid. ii, 158. Sarah de Wakerley also released her right; ibid. ii, 162; see also Duchy of Lanc. Assize R. 6, m. 2 d.

John de Wakerley was the John de Salford of 1332, and Roger was his son, as appears from Dods. MSS. cxlix, fol.

160 Sarah Wakerley, a de Wakerley lands of Joh Roger La W transfer; ib

The boundary on the west is irregular, Kirkmanshulme, a detached portion of Newton, lying on that side, with a small detached triangle of Gorton to the west of it. There is evidence that the Stockport Road, on the line of the old Roman road from Stockport to Manchester, was not taken as the western boundary till the 17th century, the portions known as Grindlow Marsh and Midway, lying to the north and south of Kirkmanshulme, having been considered as within Rusholme.[3] The southern boundary is defined by the ancient Nico Ditch.[4] Fifty years ago there were four hamlets in the township—Gorton village in the centre, Abbey Hey [5] to the east, Gorton Brook or 'Bottom of Gorton' to the north-west, and Longsight; the last name seems to belong properly to the small detached triangle already mentioned, but is popularly used for the surrounding district.[6] The surface is comparatively level, rising a little towards the east. The area is 1,484½ acres.

The principal road through Gorton is that from Manchester to Hyde; almost the whole township to the north of this has become urban, and there are many streets and cross roads. A branch of the Great Central Railway runs along the northern boundary and has a station called Gorton, 1842–8. A branch line going south-east crosses the western part of the township, with a station called Belle Vue, while another branch passes south through the eastern part and has a station called Hyde Road. The Manchester and Stockport Canal goes south through the centre of the township.

On the south-eastern boundary is a large reservoir of the Manchester Waterworks.

The government of the township was formerly vested in the constables appointed at a town's meeting and confirmed by the Manchester Court Leet.[7] A local board was constituted in 1863.[8] About a fifth of the township was incorporated in the city of Manchester in 1890, under the name of West Gorton; this portion in 1896 became part of the new township of South Manchester. The remainder, known as Gorton,[9] is governed by an urban district council of fifteen members. An agreement has now (1908) been made for its incorporation in Manchester. The population of this part numbered 26,564 in 1901. The place gives a name to one of the county Parliamentary divisions.

In 1666 there were forty-four hearths in all contributing to the tax; none of the houses had as many as six hearths liable.[10] The Maidens' Bridge replaced stepping stones over the brook on the road from Gorton to Denton in 1737.[11] Longsight or Rushford Bridge, over Gore Brook, was built in 1751.[12] The stocks were erected in 1743.[13] Some amusing stories are told of the conduct of the people in 1745.[14] A case of body-snatching occurred in 1831.[15] There were formerly several places reputed haunted.[16] The township was famous for its bull-dogs.[17]

The annual rush-bearing took place on the Friday before the first Sunday in September; the rush cart was accompanied by morris dancers in its tour of the village. The event was usually celebrated by the baiting of bulls, bears, and badgers.[18] Horse-races were established in 1844,[19] but have now ceased.

Bleaching was carried on in the early years of the 18th century.[20] Power-loom weaving was about to be introduced in 1790[21]; the Gorton cotton mills were started in 1824, and after a failure were restarted in 1844.[22] There are now a cotton factory, chemical works, iron works, and tanyard.

There was an old custom, discontinued in 1841, of 'giving an heraldic peal or ring on the bell at the conclusion of divine service.'[23]

Though a manor of GORTON is named in the 17th century the term seems to have been used improperly. In 1282 the place was held in bondage of the lord of Manchester, being assessed as sixteen oxgangs of land and paying 64s. rent; a plat called the Hall land paid 20s. a year; and the mill 26s. 8d.[24] A more detailed account is given in the survey of 1320, according to which Henry the Reeve, a 'native,' held a messuage and an oxgang of land in villeinage, paying 8s. 4d. rent; he ploughed one day for the lord, receiving a meal and 2d. as wages; harrowed one day, receiving a meal and 1d. wages, or for half a day without the meal; reaped one day in the autumn, receiving a meal and 1d.; and carried the lord's corn one day, having a meal and 2d. wages. He and all others owing suit to the mill at Gorton were bound to quarry millstones and take them to the mill, for each pair of stones receiving 4d. for loading them and 3s. for the carriage. He paid a fine on his daughter's marriage, and on his sons being placed at a free handicraft. On his death a third of his goods went to the lord, and the remainder to his widow and son; if either the widow or the son were dead, half went to the lord; if he left neither widow nor son the lord took the whole; a posthumous son or daughter must make a special agreement as to succession. He had to carry as far as Chesterfield. Five other tenants are named.[25]

MANOR

---

[3] See the boundary settlement quoted within.

[4] See *V.C.H. Lancs.* ii, 554.

[5] The origin of this name is unknown; it will be seen that Abbey was a surname in Gorton in 1320.

[6] 'Longsight' may mean the 'long shot' (Mr. Crofton), or a place giving a distant view along the straight road from Manchester to Stockport; *Manch. Guard. N. and Q.* no. 189, 425.

[7] Constables are known to have been appointed in 1623; *Manch. Ct. Leet Rec.* iii, 74.

[8] *Lond. Gaz.* 16 Oct. 1863.

[9] It has an area of 1,147 acres, including 45 of inland water; *Census Rep.* 1901.

[10] *Subs. R.* bdle. 250, no. 9.

[11] Higson, *Gorton Rec.* 87; the bridge was widened in 1810.   [12] Ibid. 95.

By one of the lords of Manchester Gorton seems to have been granted or leased to the Booths, for in 1433 Sir Robert Booth and Douce his wife enfeoffed Sir John Byron and William Booth, clerk, of his lands in the hamlets of Gorton, &c., described in a fine as twenty-four messuages, 500 acres of land, 40 acres of meadow, and 500 acres of pasture, also 2s. 6d. rent, in Manchester.[26] In 1473 John Byron held the vill of Gorton with the appurtenances, paying a rent of £30 11s. to the lord of Manchester.[27] It descended like Clayton till 1612–13, when the manor of Gorton with messuages, lands, water-mill, and horse-mill in Gorton, &c., appears to have been sold by Sir John Byron and the trustees to the tenants.[28] Thirty-three of the purchasers were in 1614 summoned to pay their shares of the rent of £30 11s. due to the lord of Manchester;[29] it was agreed to levy it at the rate of 9d. for each Lancashire acre, the estates called Grindlow Marsh and Midway being exempt.[30]

The township having thus been parted among a large number of proprietors it becomes impossible to give their history in detail.[31] Among the new owners were some bearing the local name.[32] One of the family, Samuel Gorton, went to America in the 17th century and founded a religious sect there, which died out about 1770.[33]

Among the earliest landowners recorded was Adam the Ward of Sharples.[34] An estate called the Forty Acres was long held by one of the Bamford families.[35] Catsknoll was at one time owned by the Levers of Alkrington.[36] The Taylors of Gorton were benefactors.[37]

At *GREENLOW*, or Grindlow, Marsh or Cross appears to have been the land called Withacre or Whitacre, granted by Albert Grelley to the abbey of Swineshead in alms about 1160.[38] In the 16th century it was held by the Strangeways family,[39] and remained an integral part of their estate.[40] There

was by Thomas La Warre given to the college he founded at Manchester; it appears to have been the site of a tithe barn; Higson, *Gorton Recorder*, 48, 218, 219; Hibbert-Ware, *Manch. Foundations*, i, 38.

[26] Byron Chartul. (Towneley MS.), no. 34/281, 28/284.

[27] *Mamecestre*, iii, 484. Lands in Gorton were among those held in 1489 by Sir John Byron by knight's service and a yearly rent; Duchy of Lanc. Inq. p.m. iii, 48.

The rent of £30 11s. appears in the inquisition after the death of Sir Nicholas Mosley as due to him from lands in Gorton and Greenlow or Grindlow Marsh, lately held by Sir John Byron; *Lancs. Inq. p.m.* (Rec. Soc. Lancs. and Ches.), ii, 4.

[28] Pal. of Lanc. Feet of F. bdle. 81, no. 57.

Various documents from the town's chest are printed in Higson's *Gorton Recorder*. In 1581 there was a surrender by forty-nine tenants, whose names are given; op. cit. 213. In 1608 there was another surrender by twenty-seven tenants for lives; ibid. 56, followed by the agreement for the fine above cited, in which the plaintiffs were James Chetham, Oswald Mosley, and Edward Blacklock, perhaps acting for the numerous purchasers.

[29] Ibid. 213, 57, 58. Rowland Mosley of the Hough, as lord of Manchester, was the plaintiff. The tenants again refused to pay in 1650, 1657, 1666, and 1675, but judgement was given in favour of the lord. [30] Ibid. 134.

[31] In the grant of a cottage on Greenlow Marsh in 1708 for the use of the poor the following signed as 'the freeholders, charterers, and proprietors of the waste lands in Gorton': Samuel Worthington, Gerard Jackson, Ralph Shelmerdine, Robert Andrew, James Taylor, John Coffe, John Graver, and Richard Taylor.

Edward Siddall purchased 17 acres in Gorton from John Byron in 1571; Pal. of Lanc. Feet of F. bdle. 33, m. 163. The land was at Longsight; Higson, op. cit. 54, 58.

Nicholas Peake, who died in March 1625–6, held a messuage, &c. in Gorton. He left a widow Isabel, and his heir was his brother John, forty years of age; Duchy of Lanc. Inq. p.m. xxv, 42.

Roger Unsworth, who died in 1638, held land in Gorton of Nicholas Mosley as of his manor of Manchester; Roger

his son and heir wa age; Towneley MS. 1288.

No landowners a Subsidy Roll of 1541 although by the lat become a separate t Soc. Lancs. and C Thomas Pyecroft of holder in 1600; ibi

A family named appear to have held head in the 17th c to the T avis family called the Alderston Chew Redlac

was in 1322 a considerable amount of land in that part of the township in the possession of the lord.[41] It was in 1609 decided that Greenlow Marsh lay in Gorton and not in Chorlton or Greenlow Heath.[42] An ancient chantry endowment was situated at the same place.[43]

From the land tax returns of 1787 [44] it appears that the most considerable owners were :—Richard Gorton, paying about a sixth of the tax, Robert Grimshaw, John Hague's heirs, and Richard Clowes.

The origin of ST. JAMES'S CHAPEL CHURCH is unknown. It existed in 1562, when Ambrose Beswick bequeathed 3s. 4d. to the chapel reeves.[45] It was probably used for service, a lay 'reader' being employed,[46] and one of the fellows of Manchester preaching occasionally. There was no endowment, but the people seem to have contributed according to an assessment.[47] Ministers and people were Puritan, and in 1634 it was stated that the surplice had never been used.[48] The minister had an endowment of 26s. 8d. in 1650, besides the voluntary offerings ; [49] but changes were frequent.[50] The minister in charge in 1662, William Leigh, is said to have been ejected ; but the chapel appears to have been used indifferently by Episcopalians and Presbyterians for some time afterwards.[51] A library was given by Humphrey Chetham.[52] In 1706 the fixed revenue was £8 15s. and the contributions about £18 ; at that time a quarter of the population was avowedly Nonconformist.[53] In 1755 the chapel was rebuilt,[54] and again in 1871. A district chapelry was assigned to it in 1839.[55] The registers date from 1570. The monumental inscriptions are copied in the Owen MSS. The Dean and

[41] Heath land of 223 acres, worth 113s., was held ; 14 acres were let at 8d., and the rest at 6d. Thomas de Chorlton had 7 acres there ; *Mamecestre*, ii, 363.

[42] Note by Mr. Earwaker. Greenlow Heath appears to have been considered a separate township, or at least a conspicuous hamlet of Chorlton. The hamlet of Gorton was at the same time bound to maintain 'one half of the highway in the High Street so far as Gorton and Greenlow Marsh *alias* Greenlow Cross lay to the said High Street, beginning at the bridge near to Edmond Percival's house and so downward to Ardwick, with the one half of the said bridge also.'

[43] *Mamecestre*, iii, 483 ; a rent of 20s. was due to the lord of Manchester. The chantry was that of St. Nicholas, or the Trafford chantry, as will be seen in the account of the parish church.

It was probably in respect of this land that disputes arose among the lessees. Sir Edmund Trafford had had a lease of two tenements there, and in 1588 Thomas Windbank secured from the queen a lease for fifty years from the end of Trafford's term. Roger Kenyon—in another pleading John Kenyon and Robert his son—and Thomas *alias* James Gredlow were occupiers ; and for each tenement 26s. 8d. rent was due to the Crown. Thomas Pyecroft and George Ashton acquired an interest in part of the land about 1600, but their title was questioned; Duchy of Lanc. Plead. Eliz. clxxxi, F. 11; clxxxix, P. 1 ; cxcvi, B. 5. Roger Kenyon and Thomas Greenlow were the tenants of the chantry lands in 1547 ; Raines, *Chant.* (Chet. Soc.), i, 35.

[44] At the County Council Office, Preston.

[45] Higson, op. cit. 52 ; quoting Raines MSS. Pike-house Deeds. The chapel is marked in Saxton's map of 1577.

[46] George Wharmby was licensed as 'reader' in 1576 ; Pennant's Acct. Bk. (Chest. Reg.). He was buried at the collegiate church in 1588 as 'minister at Gorton.'

At the bishop's visitation in 1592 it was found that the curate was unlicensed ; he christened in a basin or dish, there being no font ; he also taught a school. Jewell's *Reply* and *Apology* were wanting ; *Lancs. and Ches. Antiq. Soc.* xiii, 63. As he baptized probably he was ordained.

[47] Thomas Beswick and Mary Beswick, widow, were summoned before the consistory in 1604 for not paying the 'accustomed wages' to the minister ;

Higson, op cit. 55. *Com. Rep* xiv, App.

[48] *Humphrey Chetha*

[49] *Common al* Lancs. and Ches.), £40 out of sequestr 1648 ; *Plund. Min* Lancs. and Ches) i,

[50] Thomas Norm 1619 ; it was report read the whole serv Chester He was ca 1622; *Misc* (Rec So i. 66 , *M n h. Cla* 443. Henry Root been there in 163 curate in 1639, was con M

Canons of Manchester present the incumbents, who are styled rectors. The following is a list :—

1671   Robert Dewhurst [56]
       Joshua Wakefield, [57] M.A. (Queens' College, Cambridge)
1704   John Harpur, B.A. (Brasenose College, Oxford ; Jesus College, Cambridge)
1715   William Burkitt [58]
1764   John Whittingham, B.A. [59] (St. Edmund Hall, Oxford)
1801   John Darby, M.A. [60] (Corpus Christi College, Oxford)
1808   James Gatcliff [61]
1831   Richard Basnett, M.A. (Trinity College, Oxford)
1864   George Philpot, M.A. (Caius College, Cambridge)
1902   John Worsley Cundey, M.A. (Magdalen College, Oxford)

More recently other churches have been added : St. Mark's, 1865 ; [62] and All Saints', West Gorton, 1879 ; [63] the rectors are collated by the Bishop of Manchester. St. George's, Abbey Hey, was consecrated in 1903 ; and the district of St. Philip's has been formed, but no church has yet been built ; the Crown and the Bishop of Manchester present alternately. At Longsight St. Clement's was consecrated in 1876 ; [64] the patronage is vested in trustees.

A school existed in 1716. [65]

Methodism appeared in the township about the end of the 18th century ; a school chapel at Brooke's Green was built in 1809. [66] The Wesleyans now have churches at Gorton, Hyde Road, and Longsight ; the Primitive Methodists two, at Gorton Brook and Belle Vue ; and the United Free Church one.

The Baptists have three churches. The Particular Baptists had a school in Gorton as early as 1828. [67] The Congregationalists have churches at Gorton [68] and Longsight. The latter began as a Sunday school in 1834 ; the present chapel was opened in 1842 on land purchased from Lord Ducie. [69] The Salvation Army has meeting-places at Gorton and Longsight. At Longsight there is also a Presbyterian Church of England, founded in 1871.

The Unitarians have two places of worship at Brookfield, Gorton, and at Longsight. The former represents the old Protestant Dissenters' chapel, built in 1703 ; [69a] and now taken down ; the congregation became Unitarian about a century later. The present church was built in 1871. [70]

The Roman Catholic mission of St. Francis of Assisi, West Gorton, was opened in 1872. It is in charge of the Franciscans, whose monastery adjoins it. The church of the Sacred Heart was opened in 1901. [71]

---

[56] Visitation list of 1671. From Higson's work the names of the incumbents have in general been taken. In Stratford's visitation list, 1691, the date of Dewhurst's licence is given as 1686 ; he had been ordained in 1663. He died in 1697.

[57] Also curate of Didsbury ; Mr. Earwaker's note.

[58] He was called perpetual curate.

[59] He was blind for the last twenty-three years of his life ; Higson, op. cit. 127.

[60] He was what was then called a High Churchman ; ibid. 24.

and ornamented with elegant houses on the border of a canal.'² It was then a fashionable residential district for Manchester merchants.

James Heywood Markland, an antiquary, was born there in 1788; he died in 1828.³ Another native was Martha Darley Mutrie, a flower painter, born in 1824; she died in 1885.⁴ Samuel Reynolds Hole, Dean of Rochester 1887–1904 and famous as a rosegrower, was born at Ardwick in 1820.

In 1825 an Act was obtained for the better government of the township.⁵ On the incorporation of the borough of Manchester in 1838, Ardwick was included; together with Beswick it formed a ward. It was merged in the new township of South Manchester in 1896.

A mock corporation held its meetings from 1764 onwards, a mayor and other officers being elected.

There was, properly speaking, no manor *MANOR* of *ARDWICK*, which was a hamlet in the demesne of Manchester. In 1282 the farm of 10 oxgangs and 9 acres of land in bondage amounted to 43s., and there was a plat of land there called Twantirford, rendering 6s. 8d.⁶ The tenants had turbary on 100 acres of moor in Openshaw, and were obliged to grind at the Irk Mills to the sixteenth measure.⁷ In 1320–2 Richard Akke, a 'native,' held 2 messuages and 2 oxgangs of land in villeinage at a rent of 8s., performing also certain services;⁸ the other land, 8¾ oxgangs, was valued at 45s. 6d.⁹ The hamlet was, with Bradford and other lands, given by Roger La Warre in 1357 to Thomas de Booth of Barton,¹⁰ and descended in this family till the partition at the end of the 16th century, when, like Bradford, it became part of the share of Dorothy, youngest daughter of John Booth. The 'manors of Over and Lower Ardwick,' with messuages, lands, and common rights, were in 1636 sold by Thomas Charnock and others to Samuel Birch.¹¹

A Birch pedigree was recorded in 1664 ¹² in which it is stated that Samuel was the son of Ambrose Birch of Openshaw. He was a friend of Henry Newcome's,¹³ and, dying in 1668–9, left all lands to his son John, of Whitbourne in Herefordshire.¹⁴ John Birch, born in 1616, was a carrier and trader of Bristol; afterwards he entered the army, and was a colonel in 1644, when he was serving for the Parliament against the king,¹⁵ and greatly distinguished himself in the war. He was a Member of Parliament,¹⁶ showing himself a moderate Presbyterian, and being in December 1648 excluded by 'Pride's Purge,' was for a time imprisoned. He was thereafter one of Cromwell's opponents, and took part in the negotiations for the restoration of Charles II.¹⁷ He continued to represent Weobley till his death in 1691. His association with Lancashire is slight; but he acquired Ordsall, which remained in his family for some time.¹⁸

BIRCH of Ardwick.
Azure three fleurs-de-lis argent, a canton or.

Ardwick appears to have been acquired by the colonel's younger brother Samuel, who also took part in the wars and was known as Major Birch.¹⁹ He died in 1693, leaving a son and heir John, who by his will left a messuage and lands in Upper and Lower Ardwick to his wife Elizabeth, with remainder to his son Thomas; a younger son, Samuel, also had lands in Lower Ardwick.²⁰ Thomas Birch, on succeeding in 1728, rebuilt the manor-house, but died without issue in 1753; by his will he divided his estates, Ardwick lands going to his brother George, with remainders to his nephews Samuel and George, sons of his brother Samuel. He left money for a school at Ardwick.²¹

---

² Clarke, *Lancs. Gazetteer.*
³ *Dict. Nat. Biog.* The family occurs in Pemberton and Foxholes near Rochdale.
⁴ Ibid.   ⁵ 6 Geo. IV, cap. 5.
⁶ *Lancs. Inq. and Extents* (Rec. Soc. Lancs. and Ches.), i, 245. The total assessment was probably 10¾ oxgangs.
⁷ *Mamecestre* (Chet. Soc.), ii, 291, 371, from the survey of 1320–22.
⁸ Ibid. ii, 280; his services were the same as those of Henry the Reeve of Gorton, except that he had to carry millstones, not to Gorton Mill, but to that at Manchester, at a gross payment of 4d. for loading and 6s. 8d. for carrying, which he shared with others.
⁹ Ibid. ii, 364; each oxgang was valued at 5s. 6d., except one, worth only 4s. From the total amount it appears that the fraction also was valued at the lower rate. There were eight messuages on the land; ibid. ii, 365.
In 1357 Roger La Warre leased to John son of Adam son of Richard 10 acres in Ardwick which Thomas de Beswick had held for fifteen years past, at a rent of 5s. 5d.; Manch. Corp. D.
¹⁰ See the account of Bradford. From an earlier charter it seems that 'the hamlet of Ardwick' had been leased to Thomas de Booth and John his son in 1352 at a rent of 57s. 11d.; Dods. MSS. cxlix, fol. 160; see also Close R. 42 Edw. III, m. 20 (19). Ardwick is regularly mentioned in the Booth inquisitions, but is not called a 'manor.'

31

Samuel Birch of Lower Ardwick promoted the building of Ardwick Chapel, giving the site in 1740; he was high sheriff in 1747.[22] He died in 1757, leaving three sons—Thomas, who died without issue in 1781; Samuel, who served in the American War and died in 1811; and George, of Ardwick, who died in 1794, leaving issue Thomas and Maria.[23] The manors of Upper and Lower Ardwick were left by the will of Thomas Birch, dated 1780, to his brother, Major-General Samuel Birch, who sold them in 1795 to William Horridge.[24] They changed hands several times, and in 1869 were purchased by Alderman John Marsland Bennett of Ardwick.[25]

A considerable portion of Ardwick was sold by Thomas Charnock to the Mosleys.[26]

Other families formerly had estates in the township—Byrom,[27] Booth,[28] Entwisle,[29] and Strangeways.[30] The land tax return of 1787 shows that the principal contributors were named Birch, Hyde, Ackers, and Tipping.[31]

Ardwick was recognized as a township in 1622, when Richard Hudson contributed to the subsidy for goods.[32]

For the Established Church St. Thomas's, Ardwick Green,[33] was built in 1741, as above-mentioned, and has been enlarged; St. Silas's, a century later, in 1842;[34] St. Matthew's, 1868;[35] and St. Benedict's, 1880.[36] The patronage of the first of these churches is vested in the Dean and Canons of Manchester, of the others in different bodies of trustees. The incumbents are styled rectors. There are mission rooms in connexion with St. Thomas's and St. Matthew's.

The Wesleyan Methodists, the Primitive Methodists, and United Free Methodists, also the Welsh Calvinistic Methodists, have places of worship. The Presbyterians have a preaching station, opened in 1904. The Congregationalists formerly had a chapel in Tipping Street.[37]

The Roman Catholic church of St. Aloysius was opened in 1885; the mission was begun in 1852.

BESWICK

...

---

[22] P.R.O. *List*. 74.

[23] Booker, op. cit. 120.

[24] The estates had become very much encumbered. 'On 9 March, 1795, pursuant to a decree in chancery in a cause Watson *v*. Birch, several freehold estates in the township of Ardwick and a moiety of a limestone quarry, late the property of Thomas Birch, esq., deceased, were offered for sale; a purchaser was found, but disputes having arisen as to the validity of the sale, the estates were directed to be resold, and they finally passed into other hands on 1 February, 1796;' ibid. 120.

[25] The information as to the descent of the manors is derived from Mr. J. Armitage Bennett (1876), who stated : 'William Horridge sold them on 20 August 1803 to Jacob Wood, who by will dated 2 June 1826 left the aforesaid manors to his daughter Elizabeth Wood ; she sold them by indenture of 9 May 1835 to Henry Weech Burgess of Burgess Hill, London,' who sold to Alderman Bennett.

[26] *Mosley Mem.* (Chet. Soc. new ser.), 51 ; the estate comprised 248 acres, and small chief rents were due from Ralph Kenyon, Adam Byrom, and Thomas Smith.

[27] Adam Byrom of Salford (see the account of Kersal) in 1558 held a messuage, &c., in Ardwick of John Booth in socage ; Duchy of Lanc. Inq. p.m. xi, 65. The property is named in later inquisitions of the family, but no further particulars are given.

[28] Humphrey Booth of Salford in 1637

DROYLSDEN

Drilesden, 1502.

This township,[1] on the south side of the Medlock, has an area of 1,621½ acres. The surface is comparatively even, rising towards the eastern boundary, and falling on the north, towards the river. Droylsden proper[2] forms the eastern half of the township, and is parted from Clayton, the western half, by Edge Lane, running south from Newton to Openshaw ; Little Droylsden[3] is a detached area of 2 acres in extent in the extreme east of Openshaw. In the south-east corner of Droylsden lies the hamlet of Fairfield.

The principal road[4] is that called Ashton New Road, leading east from Manchester to Ashton ;[5] another road leads north-east from Openshaw near the eastern boundary of Droylsden ; it is along this road chiefly that the houses are built, though at Clayton there is another group, forming an extension of Bradford. The Lancashire and Yorkshire Company's Manchester and Ashton railway cuts through the northern part of the township, and at Droylsden station[6] has a junction with the London and North Western Company's line from Stockport. The Manchester and Ashton Canal winds along near the southern boundary ; at Clayton it has a junction with the Stockport Canal, coming from the south, and near Fairfield one with the Oldham Canal, from the north.

At Greenside, to the west of the village of Droylsden, is a cemetery.

A stone celt, some Roman coins, and an axe have been found in the mosses at the eastern end.[7]

There were coal-mines at Clayton ; potter's clay has been found on the moss. In 1859 the older people still clung to farming and the hand-loom, and a few to hatting ; oats were the principal crop.[8] Bleaching was introduced as early as the time of James I ;[9] hat-making[10] and linen and cotton weaving[11] were ancient industries ; but the first factory of the modern type was erected in 1785.[12] There are now several cotton mills, print and dye works, chemical works, and a rope walk in Droylsden ; with

similar industries, iron foundries, printing, and brick-making in Clayton.

In 1666 the hearths liable to the tax numbered ninety-three. The largest houses were Clayton Hall (James Chetham), with eighteen hearths, and John Gilliam's with six.[13]

The government of the township was formerly in the hands of the constables elected annually at the town's meeting An Act for lighting Droylsden with gas was passed in 1860.[13a] A local board was formed in 1863 ;[14] but in 1890 the Clayton moiety was taken into the city of Manchester, and became part of the new North Manchester township in 1896. The population of the remaining part, the present Droylsden, was 11,087 in 1901.[15] It is governed by an Urban District Council of twelve members. The institute, built in 1858, is now used as a school and council office.

The wakes, or rush-bearing of the Newton wakes, had a singular custom called Threedy wheel, introduced in 1814.[16] The stocks disappeared long ago. Clayton Hall and other places were supposed to be haunted by ' boggarts.'[17] ' Rocket,' for frock, occurs in the old township accounts.

Although a ' manor ' of DROYLSDEN MANOR is spoken of in the 16th century the word seems to have been used improperly. The only manor in the township was that of CLAYTON, for four centuries the seat of the Byron family.[18] To Robert de Byron the elder Robert Grelley, between 1194 and 1212, granted fourteen oxgangs of his demesne of Manchester to be held by the service of half a knight.[19] The original grant was of Clayton and Barnetby ; this was increased by land in Tunstead and two oxgangs of land in Failsworth, but Tunstead was soon afterwards surrendered.[20]

BYRON. *Argent three bendlets enhanced gules.*

Robert de Byron married Cecily, and had several sons ;[21] in 1212 Robert's heirs were in possession of

---

[1] A valuable account of the township was published in 1859 by John Higson, a resident, under the title of *Droylsden Past and Present*. It contains (p. 57, &c.) an interesting description of the condition of the people in the early part of last century.

[2] This portion fell in 1859 four hamlets—Fairfield, Edge Lane, Greenside, and Castle ; the last name was derived from a dwelling built about 1790, and nick-named Netherlands Castle ; Higson, op. cit. 11, 15. ' The boundary line across the moss [at the east end] before its reclamation and allotment to adjoining estates, was indicated by long oaken poles, fixed upright at distances of from 20 to 30 yards apart' ; ibid. 10. For the tenants' moss rooms see ibid. 160.

[3] The local legend respecting it is given by Higson, op. cit. 12. It was added to Openshaw in 1889.

[4] The condition of the roads in former times is described by Higson (op. cit. 19) ; they were repaired in short sections by the owners of the land, some well, some ill ; ibid. 25.

[5] It was formed under a turnpike Act, 1825–6 ; ibid. 20.

[6] The line was formed in 1846 ; the station was at first called Lum.

[7] Higson, op. cit. 29, 30.

[8] Ibid. 33, 71, &c.

[9] Ibid. 82–5.

[10] Ibid. 86. In 1832 the village was ' chiefly inhabited by hatters ;' E. Butterworth.

[11] Higson, op. cit. 86–8.

[12] Ibid. 89–100.

[13] Subs. R. bdle. 250, no. 9.

[13a] 23 & 24 Vict. cap. 4.

[14] *Lond. Gaz.* 20 Nov. 1863.

[15] The area of this part is 1,010 acres, including 18 of inland water.

[16] Higson, op. cit. 63–6.

[17] Ibid. 66–71.

[18] The name is said to be derived from the village of Buron in Fresnoy le Vieux. Two of the family—Erneis and Ralph de Buron—appear in Domesday Book, holding lands in the counties of York, Lincoln, Derby, and Nottingham. The Byrons of Lancashire, ancestors of the Lords Byron of Newstead, are supposed to have descended from them, but the connexion, if any, is unknown.

In Lancashire documents the prefix varies between *de* and *le*, and is sometimes absent ; the surname has a great variety of spellings—Buron, Burun, Byron, Biroun, Byrun, &c.

his lands ; but one son, Robert, who appears to have
been the eldest, afterwards surrendered all his rights
to his brother Richard,[22] and it was this Richard who
had a grant of the king's moiety of Failsworth.
Richard de Byron's name occurs as early as 1203 ;[23]
several grants by and to him are known.[24]

The next known[24a] in possession of Clayton was John
de Byron, later a knight, who appears all through the
latter part of the 13th century.[25] He was son of
Richard,[26] probably a second bearer of the name.
Sir John married Joan, with whom he had lands

Robert the elder), in 1213 claimed dower
against Gilbert de Notton ; Curia Regis
R. 59, m. 3. There was perhaps some
dispute as to the bounds of their moieties
of Failsworth.

Geoffrey de Byron and his descendants
appear in connexion with Eccles during
the 13th century. In a deed of not much
later than 1200 there appear among the
witnesses Robert de Bur' and Geoffrey his
brother ; Hulme D. no. 1.

Another branch of the family a little
later had an interest in Melling and other
manors in West Derby Hundred.

[22] The Byron Chartulary, usually called
the 'Black Book of Clayton,' was compiled about 1450, and seems to be the
MS. now in the Bodleian Library, Rawlinson B. 460. A transcript of it, re-
arranged by Christopher Towneley in
1665, in the possession of W. Farrer, is
that quoted in the following notes. The
charters preserved in it relate mostly to
Butterworth and other lands in Rochdale.
Robert de Byron released to Richard
his brother his whole right and claim in
Clayton, Failsworth, and Droylsden,
Richard paying 30 marks; Byron Chartul.
no. 3/11. He further released to Richard
'the whole vill of Droylsden, to wit, that
which I hold of him and the homage and
service of Jordan Ruffus,' in return for 22
marks ; ibid. no. 24/4. The said Jordan
Ruffus (le Rous) granted to Richard de
Byron the site of a mill ; ibid. no. 25/5.

A Robert de Byron occurs a little later
in Ashton charters ; possibly he was the
brother of Richard.

[23] Farrer, Lancs. Pipe R. 167.

[24] William de Notton, Alward de
Awnley, and William de Werneth demised
to Richard de Byron their claim to a
parcel of waste near the Redebrook, and
another ; in future there should be free
common up Harestoneshurst syke to the
higher part of Bradley, and up Bradley
syke between Wrigley and Bradley to
Mossbrook ; also in the higher moiety of
Bradley ; Byron Chartul. no. 22/29. The
date is earlier than 1220 ; among the
witnesses were Robert and Geoffrey de
Byron. The land was apparently near
the north-east corner of Failsworth.

A supplementary grant, by Thomas son
of Orm de Ashton, of the moiety of the
land between Red Brook and Stony Brook,
and the bounds of Werneth and the Medlock, provided that part should lie in common between the men of Ashton and
Richard and his men of Failsworth and
Clayton ; ibid. no. 7/19.

About 1220 Richard had some dispute
with Thomas de Ashton respecting waste
and destruction of land ; Curia Regis R.
72, m. 21.

Richard de Byron had the king's protection on going abroad in 1230 with the
Earl of Chester ; Cal. Pat. 1225–32, p. 360.

To Robert Grelley Richard de Byron
surrendered his common pasture right in

the manor of Ma
himself and the me
of pasture w th the
in bounds which se
or parts of Ardwick
From the ford of M
to the head of the h
is set upon Salte
ditch, and brook to
brook to the hedge
the bounds of Bes
Saltersgate · but R
heirs had the right
these bounds ; De
Saltersgate, Mr C
present Mill Street,

[24a] Alice de Byr
had granted Royto
1246 · Assize R 4

[25] He was a juro
and Extents, i, 244
knight in 1270 ; F
Lancs. and Ches.), 1

[26] Richard son a
and heir of Richar
cla m d h

later, left two sons, Sir John [35] and Sir Richard ; and the former, who took part in the battle of Crecy and the siege of Calais,[36] dying without issue, was followed by his brother in 1380.[37]

Sir Richard by his marriage with Joan de Colwick increased the family estates.[38] He died in June 1397, holding the manor of Clayton, and lands in Royton, Butterworth, Woodhouses in Ashton, and others outside Lancashire ; John, the son and heir, was then only ten years of age,[39] and his wardship was granted to Sir John Ashton.[40] A settlement of lands in Droylsden was in 1415 made on the occasion of the marriage of Sir John Byron's daughter Elizabeth with Thomas son of Sir John Ashton.[41] Sir John is stated to have married Margery daughter of Sir John

Booth of Barton, by whom he had three sons and five daughters.[42] He acquired lands in Blackley from Lord La Warre and in Gorton from Sir Robert Booth ; [43] in 1435 he did homage to Nicholas Thorley, one of the feoffees of Lord La Warre ; [44] and in 1440 he made a settlement of his lands in the counties of Lancaster, Lincoln, and Northampton.[45] Two years later he made a grant to John Byron, said to be the son of his younger son Nicholas, who ultimately became heir to the whole of the Byron manors and lands.[46] Sir John was sheriff of the county from 1437 to 1449 ; [47] when he was succeeded by his son Nicholas, a grant of the reversion having been obtained in 1444.[48]

Nicholas Byron remained sheriff till 1460.[49] He

CLAYTON HALL FROM THE SOUTH-WEST

[35] Sir James appears to have been in possession in 1348 ; Byron Chartul. no. 21/189 ; and his son John in 1354 ; ibid. no. 27/10.

Robert the Smith of Ashton in 1353 demanded a messuage and lands in Manchester against Elizabeth widow of Sir James de Byron and against John de Byron ; Assize R. 435, m. 8.

[36] Wrottesley, Crecy and Calais (W. Salt Arch. Soc. xviii), 13, 115. Sir John de Byron had licence for divine service in his oratory at Clayton in 1365 ; Lich. Epis. Reg. Stretton, v, fol. 11b.

[37] The writ of Diem Clausit extr. was issued on 18 July, 1380 ; Dep. Keeper's Rep. xxxii, App. 353.

Sir John de Byron was plaintiff in 1377 respecting lands on the borders of Manchester and Ashton ; Byron Chartul. no. 1/285.

[38] For Colwick see Byron Chartul. no. 32 (1362) ; no. 2/300 (1415) ; no. 5/305 (after 1426). Joan the widow of Sir Richard de Byron died in Dec. 1426 holding various manors and lands ; Chan. Inq. p.m. 5 Hen. VI, no. 41. In

1415 she complained to the Lord Chancellor that her son Sir John Byron had forcibly carried her from Colwick to Lancashire, and made her promise not to alienate her lands ; Early Chan. Proc. bdle. 6, no. 294.

[39] Lancs. Inq. p.m. (Chet. Soc.), i, 65.

[40] Dep. Keeper's Rep. xl, App. 528.

[41] Byron Chartul. no. 1/23 ; no. 8/24. The feoffment included all Sir John Ashton's lands in Droylsden except the Pighill by Lumlache.

[42] The remains of what is believed to be his memorial brass in Manchester Cathedral are described by the Rev. E. F. Letts, in Lancs. and Ches. Antiq. Soc. i, 87.

The Bishop of Lichfield in 1420 granted Sir John Byron and Margery his wife licence for their oratories at Clayton and Begerworth ; Lich. Epis. Reg. ix, fol. 3b.

Sir John was knight of the shire in 1421 and 1429 ; Pink and Beaven, Parl. Repre. of Lancs. 51, 53.

In 1424 there was an arbitration as to the boundary between Droylsden and Ashton ; the limits fixed were—from Lumlache Head, by the moss towards

Audenshaw, by the ditch to Hardhill next Oselache in Droylsden, eastward by the end of Overmost Ditch in Sinderland, across the Little Moss north to the far edge and by the bound of this moss to the starting point ; Byron Chartul. no. 1/286 ; no. 2/287 ; no. 3/288.

In 1429 there was a settlement of the disputes respecting the moorlands in Ashton and Droylsden between Thomas son and heir of Sir John Ashton and Sir John Byron ; ibid. no. 9/289 ; no. 11/291, 13.

In 1439 and 1441 settlements were made by Sir John Byron and Margery his wife of the manor of Clayton, and lands in Clayton, Manchester, Ashton, Withington, Heaton, Oldham, Crompton, Butterworth, Spotland, Edgeworth, and Turton ; Final Conc. iii, 104, 106.

[43] See the accounts of the townships.

[44] Byron Chartul. no. 40/332.

[45] Ibid. no. 39/331.

[46] Recited in the later John Byron's Inq. p.m. (1498).

[47] P.R.O. List, 72.

[48] Dep. Keeper's Rep. xl, App. 538.

[49] P.R.O. List, 72.

was made a knight the year following at the coronation of Edward IV,[50] but died in 1462,[51] when he
was succeeded by Sir John Byron, above mentioned.
Sir John, made a knight by Henry VII as he came
from York in 1486,[52] died 3 January 1488-9, holding
the manor of Clayton of the lord of Manchester in
socage, by 7s. rent, also the manor of Blackley, with
lands there and in Gorton, Royton, Butterworth,
Ogden, and Ashton. His heir was his brother
Nicholas, who in 1498 was stated to be thirty years of
age.[53] Nicholas was made a Knight of the Bath in 1501
at the marriage of Prince Arthur,[54] and died three years
later.[55] It would appear that before this Colwick had
become the principal residence of the family,[56] and
John, son and successor of Sir Nicholas,[57] is usually
described as 'of Colwick'; he was 'not at home' at
the Heralds' Visitation of Lancashire in 1533.[58] In
1540 he procured a grant of Newstead Priory, Nottinghamshire,[59] which afterwards became the chief
seat of the family. He had no issue by his wife, and
his connexion with Lancashire led to his living in
adultery with Elizabeth daughter of John Costerdine
of Blackley and wife of George Haugh. He had
several children by her and afterwards married her.[60]
In 1547 he made a settlement of his estates in favour
of his bastard son John,[61] and died in 1567, expressing penitence in his will,[62] which contained his
open profession of adherence to the old religion, as in
his desire that an honest priest be hired to sing or say
mass for his soul in Colwick Church,[63] and confirmed
the grant of all his manors, lands, leases, &c., to his
'base son' John, whom he appointed executor.

This son, who was made a knight in 1579,[64] died
in 1603, leaving as heir his son, a third Sir John
Byron,[65] who, having many children and being encumbered with debts, sold the Lancashire estates, so
that the connexion of the family with the county
almost ceased. The manor of Clayton, with the
appurtenances in Droylsden and Failsworth, was pur-

[50] Metcalfe, Bk. of Knights, 3.
[51] The writ of Diem Clausit extr. was
issued in 1462; Dep. Keeper's Rep. xxxvii,
App. 176; see also Cal. Inq. p.m. iv, 319
(he held no lands in Nottinghamshire and
and Derbyshire).
[52] Metcalfe, op. cit. 13; the arms are
given.
[53] Duchy of Lanc. Inq. p.m. iii, 48,
61, 70; for livery to Nicholas see Dep.
Keeper's Rep. xl, App. 544. The inscription on Sir John Byron's monument at
Colwick states that he died 3 May 1488;
Collins, Peerage (ed. 1779), vii, 126.
The descent is given in a pleading in
1547, reciting a settlement made by Sir
John Byron about a century before in
favour of his son Nicholas, with remainder
to another son named Ralph; it proceeds :—Sir John–s. Nicholas (who had
a brother Ralph) –s. Sir Nicholas –s. Sir
John (1547); Pal. of Lanc. Plea R.
183, m. 48b.
[54] Metcalfe, op. cit. 35.
[55] Collins, op. cit. vii, 127.
[56] Sir John Byron had a monument in
Colwick Church and his brother Nicholas
put a window in the church, with a
petition for prayers for himself and his wife
Joan ; ibid.
[57] He was a minor in ward to the
king, as appears from a complaint by one
of his tenants at Clayton ; Duchy Plead.
(Rec. Soc. Lancs. and Ches.), i, 31. Described as 'squire of the body' he was in

and P. Hen. VIII, iii

of the 18th century. A licence for an oratory dated 1400 probably gives the date of its erection, and fragments of masonry said to belong to it have been discovered from time to time, and are lying about in front of the present house.

The timber building already referred to consists of two rooms on each floor divided by timber partitions which are not at right angles to its outer walls. This may be accounted for by the supposition that the south wing of the building, which must have abutted near this point, was not set at right angles to the east wing, and that the internal divisions of the east wing followed the lines of those which adjoined them in the south wing. The south wall, however, which is now of brick with a central stone chimney, is at right angles to the outer walls, having superseded a timber end which followed the line of the partitions.

The east front is the most interesting portion of the building with its projecting wooden bays forming an almost continuous line of mullioned and transomed windows. The added corridor on the west front is of timber and plaster on a lower stage of brick, the gable of the staircase being filled in with half-timberwork, while on the roof is a cupola containing a bell.

The newer northern part of the building has

slates, the pitch of the 18th-century building being the flatter of the two. Over the timber building the original roof timbers remain at a fairly steep pitch, and the east slope is still intact. Over the west slope, however, a roof of flatter pitch running over the added corridor was constructed in 1863.

A very thorough restoration of the hall was made in 1900. The south wall on each side of the great chimney was then rebuilt and the 18th-century wing remodelled inside and new windows inserted in the front. The front of the older building was stripped of its coat of plaster and patched in brick, but the general aspect of the house remains unaltered. In front of the entrance is a mounting block with the date 1686 and the initials J. C. (James Chetham).

The bridge, as before mentioned, is built of stone, and is of two arches with a cut-water pier in the centre forming angular recesses above. It has a low parapet, and on the side next the house a tall iron entrance-gate between two well-designed stone piers. The bridge was originally very narrow, but was widened at the beginning of the 19th century, when it assumed its present appearance.

The inside of the house contains nothing of its ancient fittings. The building now belongs to the Manchester Corporation, and the newer portion is used as a caretaker's house. The older part remains unoccupied, but some old stone furniture, said to have belonged to Humphrey Chetham, is kept in the lower rooms, a proposal to use the building as a museum having been at one time put forward.

The bell in the turret over the staircase bears the inscription : 'Je atende meleor,' together with a rose and crown.[74a]

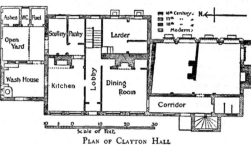

PLAN OF CLAYTON HALL

The old road from Clayton Hall after crossing the bridge ran eastward along the edge of the moat till it joined an old bridle path leading in a south-easterly direction to the Fold, an inclosure of about 4 acres, in which stood three timber buildings. From the Fold a narrow and winding lane led to Manchester. These buildings were designated the wheat barn, the oat barn, and the great barn. The wheat barn was converted into a farm-house (which is still standing) ; the great barn, which is described as having been a picturesque edifice with a steep-pitched thatched roof and with carved oak roof principals, was burnt down in 1852 ; the oat barn, which stood till about the year 1877, was a fine example of a building on crucks, 116 ft. in length and 25 ft. in width. It contained six pairs of crucks internally, but none in the gables, giving a span of a little over 16 ft. to each bay.

Among the ancient families which occur was one that assumed the surname of Droylsden.[75] The

little interest, being built entirely of brick, with a central entrance doorway and windows on each side. At the back (east side) it stands about 8 ft. in front of the older structure, but the length of its frontage is about the same. By reason of the skew in the cross walls already mentioned there is a cavity between the walls of the older and newer parts of the building at their junction, diminishing in width from east to west. There is a door connecting the two houses between the corridor and the parlour of the later house, otherwise the buildings are quite distinct. The dining-room (parlour) of the 18th-century portion has a large projecting fireplace, and in the room above is a large hole behind the chimney-breast. The fireplaces in the older part of the house are of stone, but have been rebuilt.

Both parts of the house are covered with stone

[74a] Tradition says the bell was removed to Clayton from the parish church at Manchester when it was collegiated, and was one of four hung in the chapel till its demolition in the 18th century.
[76] William de Droylsden granted to Alexander son of Richard de Withnell certain land with Ellen his daughter in free marriage ; the bounds began at the

middle of Hustude Clough, went down to the Medlock, up this to Cockshoot Gate, up this to the Hardings, and thence to the starting point, at a rent of 6d. ; Byron Chartul. no. 20/8. The grantor had been free of multure in the mill of the lord of Clayton.

Gilbert son of William de Droylsden made a grant to Thyerit his sister at a

rent of 8d. ; and afterwards sold his lands to Sir John de Byron for £10 ; ibid. no. 4/12 ; no. 5/13.

In 1354 Robert son of Thomas del Snape granted to John son of Sir James de Byron lands in Droylsden which had formerly belonged to Gilbert son of William de Droylsden ; ibid. no. 27/10.

286

Ashtons of Ashton[76] under Lyne had lands, and the Barlows of Clayton are named also.[77]

Much of Droylsden appears to have been by the Byrons sold in small lots to the occupiers.[78] The Halls of Clockhouse were among the principal of these.[79] A few other names can be obtained from the inquisitions and other documents.[80]

The land tax returns of 1783 show that then Mordecai Greene paid nearly a third of the tax; the other considerable landowner was Edward Greaves, about a sixth.[81]

Droylsden was recognized as a township by 1620.[82]

For the Established Church, St. Mary's, Droylsden, was built in 1848;[83] the Crown and the Bishop of Manchester present alternately; while St. Cross's, Clayton, built in 1874, is in the gift of Mr. C. A. R. Hoare.[84]

Methodism made its appearance about 1779, but the first society was not formed till 1806, a cottage being used. A chapel was built in 1825. The Wesleyans have now three churches in the township; and the Primitive Methodists two, the first of them being erected in 1845.[85]

The Congregationalists began with a Sunday school in 1837; a special building was raised ten years afterwards, and a church in 1859.[86]

The earliest and most celebrated religious establishment is that of the Moravians at Fairfield. It was intended to be an industrial village exclusively of their own community, where their special discipline could be freely exercised. The land was acquired in 1783, and the chapel opened two years afterwards.[87]

OPENSHAW

Openshawe, 1276.

This township stretches for over 2 miles along the Ashton Old Road, a long straight road leading east from Manchester to Ashton; it has an area of 579½ acres. The hearth tax return of 1666 shows that the dwellings then were few and small, the total

---

[76] *Ashton Custom R.* (Chet. Soc.), 101.

[77] In 1357 Thomas de Barlow of Clayton was a debtor; Duchy of Lanc. Assize R. 6, m. 3 d. In 1360 Alice widow of John de Whitewood gave to Thomas de Barlow 1½ acre in Clayton in Manchester; Byron Chartul. no. 29/14. In 1372 Sir John de Byron demised to her all the lands in Clayton and Droylsden which he had had from her, being the inheritance of her father Henry de Barlow; she was to pay a rent of 4s., and make two appearances at Sir John's court; ibid. no. 37/25.

James de Barlow in 1400 gave to John del Booth 1½ acre in Clayton, lying between the high street and the Medlock; also another 1½ acre between the Medlock and Cronshaw Brook; and these lands were in 1417 transferred to John de Byron; ibid. no. 1/15; no. 7/16.

[78] Higson, *Droylsden*, 45.

[79] Ibid. 47–48; one John Hall of the Clockhouse in 1712 sold his estate to Miles Nield of Manchester, with whose daughter it descended to the Clowes and Birch families. Another Hall family also ended in an heiress, Anne wife of William Hulton of Hulton Park; she died in 1802.

The list of ratepayers in 1655 is given ibid. 49.

[80] George Blomeley held a messuage, &c., in 'Droylesdale' of Edward Mosley

as of his manor of Manchester; he died in 1640, having bequeathed it to his niece Mary Hulme. He had had four sisters—Jane widow of Robert Hulme, Elizabeth wife of James Swindells, both living, Anne wife of Richard Wood, Ellen wife of John Moore, both deceased, leaving sons Robert Wood and John Moore, under age; Duchy of Lanc. Inq. p.m. xxx, 26.

James Wallwork of Droylsden was in 1665 summoned by the heralds to appear at the visitation; Dugdale, *Visit.* (Chet. Soc.), iv.

[81] Returns at Preston.

[82] E. Axon, *Manch. Sess.* i, 118. Also in 1622; *Misc.* (Rec. Soc. Lancs. and Ches.), i, 150; no landowner is named. The constables are mentioned in 1627; *Manch. Ct. Leet Rec.* iii, 139.

[83] Service was first held in 1840 in a room in the institute; Higson, op. cit. 118, 119. The district was assigned in 1844; *Lond. Gaz.* 22 Oct.

[84] A Sunday school was begun in 1854, and a building was erected in 1857 in which services were held; Higson, op. cit. 124. A district was assigned in 1874; *Lond. Gaz.* 11 Aug.

[85] Higson, op. cit. 129–32.

[86] Ibid. 133; Nightingale, *Lancs. Nonconf.* v, 316–18.

[87] Higson, op. cit. 125–8; the settlement was founded under the direction of

services and customs were those usual in the manor of Manchester.[11] In 1357 Openshaw was included in Roger La Warre's grant of Bradford to Thomas de Booth of Barton, and descended in the same way as Bradford until the division of the Booth estates.[12] It became the portion of Anne, one of the daughters and co-heirs of John Booth,[13] and in 1798 J. G. Legh was the chief landowner.[14] It does not at any time appear to have been considered a manor.

William Hulton of Farnworth had land in Openshaw in 1556,[15] and Thurstan Tyldesley in 1561.[16]

Ambrose Birch of Openshaw was a juror in 1608 ;[17] he was ancestor of the Birches of Ardwick. A Dyson family occurs in 1656.[18]

John Ellor of Openshaw, a life tenant under Sir John Booth, complained in 1506 of wrongs done him by Ralph Holland of Clayton and John Gilliam of Failsworth.[19]

The constables of Openshaw are mentioned in 1616.[20]

For the Established Church St. Barnabas's was consecrated in 1839,[21] and St. Clement's, Higher Openshaw, in 1881 ;[22] in the former there is a monument to Serjeant Brett, killed in Hyde Road at the rescue of the Fenian leaders in 1867. The incumbents, styled rectors, are presented by trustees.

The Wesleyan Methodists and United Free Church have each two places of worship, the New Connexion and Primitive Methodists each one. The Baptists have a church at Higher Openshaw. The Congregationalists have three churches. Preaching began about 1820, but no regular services were held till 1864, when an old chapel was purchased from the Wesleyans.[23] There are two meeting-places for the Salvation Army.

St. Anne's Roman Catholic Church, Higher Openshaw, was opened in 1883 ; the mission was begun in 1849. St. Vincent's followed in 1896.

WITHINGTON

Wythinton, 1212 and usually ; Wythington (copy of) 1282 extent, and common in 14th century ; Whytinton, 1302.

This township has an area of 2,501 acres.[1] The general slope of the surface is downward from east to west, the extremes being 144 ft. and 85 ft. above the Ordnance datum. The population in 1901 was 19,112. A brook which is called Gore Brook in Gorton and Chorlton Brook in Chorlton crosses the middle of Withington from north-east to south-west,

and is joined by the Ley or Cringle Brook coming from the east.

The principal road is that near the eastern border, from Manchester to Northenden in Cheshire, which goes southward through Fallowfield. It is lined with houses all the way, this side of the township being suburban in character, and has a branch towards Didsbury and Cheadle. The north-western portion, adjoining Moss Side, is also suburban and contains Alexandra Park, of 60 acres extent, opened in 1870, and the residential area called Manley Park. The district anciently known as Yeeldhouses, and later as the Healdhouses, lay near the northern border, stretching into Rusholme and Moss Side.

In Withington and its members there were 447 hearths liable to the tax in 1666 ; the largest houses were Barlow Hall in Chorlton and Birch Hall in Rusholme.[2]

A public hall and library were built in 1861.

The Midland Company's railway from Manchester to Stockport crosses the southern end of the township, and from it branches the Great Central Company's line to Guide Bridge, having a station near the centre called Alexandra Park, and another at the eastern border called Fallowfield.

The Manchester Southern Cemetery and Chorlton Union Workhouse are near the southern boundary.

A local board was formed in 1876 ; the area included part of Withington, Chorlton, Burnage, and Didsbury.[3] This was changed into an urban district council in 1894, but in 1904 the whole was incorporated with the city of Manchester. A number of small variations in the township boundaries of Withington, Didsbury, Burnage, and Chorlton with Hardy were made in 1882.

MANOR   At its first appearance in the records the manor or fee of WITHINGTON was held of the lord of Manchester by the service of one knight's fee. It included not only Withington proper, but the adjacent hamlets or townships of Didsbury, Chorlton with Hardy, Levenshulme, Rusholme, and Moss Side ; also the detached portions, Denton and Haughton to the east, and Longworth[4] far to the north, in the parish of Bolton. The manor-house seems to have been built at Hough in Withington, which was frequently reckoned as a separate manor ; thus, after various subordinate manors such as Denton had been separated, the manors of Hough, Withington, and Didsbury were said to be held by the lord of Withington.

[11] Manchester Corporation D.

[12] See the accounts of Bradford and Barton.

[13] From an old abstract of the Legh title (in the possession of W. Farrer) it appears that the partition was made in or before 1587, in which year a settlement was made by George Legh and Anne (Booth) his wife of the old hall of Barton and lands, &c., in Openshaw, Grindlow, Blackstake, and Manchester. See also *Manch. Ct. Leet Rec.* ii, 322. For the pedigree see Ormerod, *Ches.* (ed. Helsby), i, 462.

[14] His contribution to the land tax was £15 out of £21 raised. Other owners were Thomas Nadin, Thomas Tipping, Lord Kenyon, &c.

[15] *Manch. Ct. Leet Rec.* i, 33.

[16] Pal. of Lanc. Feet of F. bdle. 22, m. 39 ; 23, m. 52 ; he sold a messuage,

&c., in Openshaw and Gorton to Thomas Ashton of Shepley. See also *Manch. Ct. Leet Rec.* i, 100.

[17] *Lancs. Inq. p.m.* (Rec. Soc. Lancs. and Ches.), i, 115.

[18] *Manch. Ct. Leet Rec.* iv, 158.

[19] *Duchy Plead.* (Rec. Soc. Lancs. and Ches.), i, 25–7. The defence was that John Ellor had encroached on the moor.

[20] *Manch. Sessions* (Rec. Soc. Lancs. and Ches.), 3.

[21] A district was assigned to it in 1844 ; *Lond. Gaz.* 4 Mar. 1864. There is a mission church.

[22] For the district see *Lond. Gaz.* 2 Sept. 1881.

[23] Nightingale, *Lancs. Nonconf.* v, 62–5. The chapel mentioned in the text was in Lower Openshaw ; it was sold in 1890, and a new school chapel built in 1892.

Work at Higher Openshaw was begun in 1865, where a school chapel was built in 1871. The Central Church was founded in 1889, a building previously used by the Methodist Free Church being purchased.

[1] 2,443 acres, including three of inland water ; *Census Rep.* 1901.

[2] Subsidy R. bdle. 250, no. 9. Mr. Barlow had 16 hearths, Thomas Birch 13, Mrs. Holland 10, Robert Hyde 9, Mr. Worsley 8, Hugh Yannis, John Shelmerdine, and — Angier 7 each. This last would be the celebrated John Angier of Denton Chapel.

[3] 39 & 40 Vict. cap. 161. Small parts of the township of Withington were included in the local board districts of Moss Side and Rusholme.

[4] In a subsidy roll of 1543 (bdle. 130, no. 127) Anglezarke as well as Longworth is described as a hamlet of Withington.

By the inquest of 1212 it was found that Matthew and Roger, sons of William, held of Robert Grelley the fee of one knight 'of ancient time,' and were bound to 'find a judge for the king.'[5] The tenure thus went back to the early years of the 12th century, probably before the creation of the barony of Manchester, when Withington would be held of the king's manor of Salford by the service of finding a judge, which service was still required after the mesne lordship of Manchester had been created.[6]

The lords had the surname of Haversage, from one of their manors[6a] in Derbyshire. Little is known of them,[7] but Matthew de Haversage in 1248–9 procured a charter of free warren for his manors, including Withington and Didsbury.[8] Withington descended

to the Longfords of Longford in Derbyshire, who held it until the end of the 16th century,[9] when Nicholas

HAVERSAGE. *Paly of six argent and gules on a chief azure a bar dancetty or.*

LONGFORD. *Paly of six or and gules a bend argent.*

[5] *Lancs. Inq. and Extents* (Rec. Soc. Lancs. and Ches.), i, 53. Matthew son of William also held four oxgangs in Chorlton; ibid. 69.

In 1282 the fee of Withington owed to the lord of Manchester the ploughing of 15 acres of land, a service valued at 7s. 6d.; it also owed a service of reaping as due from 30 oxgangs of land, worth 2s. 6d. The clear value of the vill of Withington was £31 a year; ibid. 246, 250. From this it appears that Withington was assessed at 30 oxgangs in all.

In the later survey of 1320–2 it was recorded that the lord of Withington was one of the judges of the court of Manchester; *Mamecestre* (Chet. Soc.), ii, 286. Under the title *De consuetudinibus arandi* it was noted that each oxgang of arable land of ancient (not new) assart alike of Nicholas de Longford as of his tenants in Withington, Didsbury, Barlow, Chorlton, Denton, and Haughton, was liable for the ploughing of half an acre in Manchester, wherever assigned, 1d. being paid. There were about 25 oxgangs in all, including one held by Sir Henry de Trafford, called the Constable's oxgang, which was exempt. From the same tenants was due the service of thirty-six reapers for one whole day, the lord providing a meal; while the exempt oxgang was liable for an overseer to see that the services were duly rendered; ibid. ii, 377–8.

[6] A similar tenure was that of Pilkington; *Lancs. Inq. and Extents*, i, 55. Judges were also to be provided by the lords of Kaskenmoor (Oldham) and Stretford, held directly of Salford.

[6a] Now called Hathersage.

[7] William, the father of Matthew and Roger, was probably the William son of Wulfric de Withington whose claim to part of Chorlton was decided by wager of battle; see the account of Chorlton upon Medlock. Matthew son of William occurs in the Pipe Rolls from 1177; Farrer, *Lancs. Pipe R.* 38, 115, &c.

Matthew de Haversage, in the time of King John—no doubt the son of the Matthew of 1212—was according to one story left a minor and in the king's wardship; but according to another was seized by Philip Mark, keeper of Nottingham Castle, and married to his daughter; *Lancs. Inq. and Extents*, i, 260. Matthew son of Matthew de Haversage was a benefactor of Lenton; Dugdale, *Mon. Angl.* v, 112. In 1242 Matthew de Haversage held a knight's fee in Withington of the fee of Thomas Grelley; ibid. 154. The accounts of the succession are not in agreement. From the inquisition already cited (op. cit. i, 260) it would seem that Matthew died without issue, the heir

being his sister Cecily who married a Longford and was grandmother of Oliver de Longford. On the other hand in 1292 (see below) Oliver's son John was called great-grandson of the Matthew of 1248.

Two of Matthew's charters are noted by Booker, *Didsbury Chapelry* (Chet. Soc.), 319. One of them was to Richard son of H. de Handforth; and in 1361 John son of John de Handforth failed to prosecute a claim against Sir Nicholas de Longford; Assize R. 441, m. 5. These and other Handforth deeds are among the Birch charters in Harl. MS. 2112, fol. 178b, &c. In 1572 Robert Chetham purchased from Hugh Handforth and Anne his wife a messuage and lands in 'Chourton' (probably Chorlton with Hardy); Pal. of Lanc. Feet of F. bdle. 34, m. 128. This may be the land granted to Richard de Handforth, but Hugh's name does not appear in the Honford pedigree in Earwaker's *East Ches.* i, 250.

[8] Charter R. 44 (33 Hen. III); *Cal. Chart. R.* 1226–57, p. 345.

[9] John de Byron held Withington for life in 1282; *Lancs. Inq. and Extents*, i, 248. The heir was a minor, being John son of Oliver, grandson of Cecily, the sister of Matthew de Haversage; the Bishop of Chester had the right to his wardship: ibid. 260. Noel (Nigel) de Longford made a grant of land in Didsbury about 1260; Booker, *Birch* (Chet. Soc.), 231. For his ancestry see the account of Goosnargh. The Matthew de Haversage who obtained the charter of free warren was called the *proavus* of John de Longford, who produced it in 1292; at this time also it was stated that Oliver de Longford, father of John, had died seised; *Plac. de Quo War.* (Rec. Com.), 377. John de Longford held the knight's fee in Withington in 1302; *Lancs. Inq. and Extents*, i, 313. Sir John de Longford and Dame Joan, probably his widow, had inclosed part of Burnage before 1320; *Mamecestre*, ii, 283–4.

Another of Matthew de Haversage's sisters married a Gousill; Thoroton, *Notts.* iii, 147. In 1260 there was a partition of estates between Sir Nigel de Longford and Dame Maud de Gousill; Hibbert-Ware, *Manch. Foundations*, iii, 125.

Sir Nicholas, the son of John, was in possession by 1317, as appears by a Trafford deed. He was living in 1347 (Assize R. 1435, m. 33 d) and was knighted at the siege of Calais in that year; Shaw, *Knights*, i, 6. He was probably the Nicholas de Longford returned in 1346–55 as holding the fee in Withington which Matthew de Haversage had

Longford,[10] having no children, sold Withington and left other estates to his sister's heir.[11]

The purchaser of the Withington manor in 1597 was Rowland Mosley.[12] He was the son of Nicholas Mosley, 'cotton man' of Manchester, to whom, in 1568, Hough End House had been leased by Nicholas Longford,[13] the freehold being purchased by Rowland and Francis Mosley in 1588.[14] Rowland was about fifty-three years of age at his father's death ; he served as high sheriff in 1615–16,[15] and died in 1617, leaving a son and heir, Edward, born a few months before the father's death.[16]

Mosley of Hough End. *Sable a cheveron between three pickaxes argent.*

Edward Mosley, in addition to the large paternal estates, also inherited Rolleston in Staffordshire and other lands by the bequest of

his uncle Sir Edward Mosley, attorney-general of the Duchy.[17] By his marriage he acquired yet further property.[18] He was created a baronet in 1640.[19] Adhering zealously to the cause of Charles I he supplied the king with money, and fought in Cheshire, where he was taken prisoner at Middlewich in 1643.[20] His estates were sequestered, but he at last made peace with the Parliament by a fine of £4,874.[21] His own dissipated and extravagant habits further impoverished him.[22] He died at Hough End in 1657, leaving a son and heir, Edward, nineteen years of age.[23]

The second Sir Edward was nominated as sheriff in 1660, but does not appear to have served.[24] He died at Hough End in October 1665. He had married earlier in the year, but had no children, and his next heir was his sister Mary, wife of Joseph Maynard of Ealing.[25] By his will he left all his manors and lands—including his purchase of Hulme—to his cousin Edward Mosley, the second son of Oswald Mosley of Ancoats, but with the obligation

---

heath, moor, a water-mill and 40s. rent, of all which he made a settlement in 1510. The manors were held of Lord La Warre by one knight's fee, and were worth £80 a year. The heir was his grandson Ralph, son of Nicholas and Margery Longford, four years of age, and in the wardship of Sir Thomas Gerard of Bryn ; Duchy of Lanc. Inq. p.m. iv, no. 47. The heir was made a knight in 1529 ; Shaw, op. cit. ii, 47.

There are pedigrees of the Longford family in Booker, *Didsbury*, 113, and Thoroton, *Notts.* iii, 145.

[10] He was son of the last-named Sir Ralph, and in possession in 1544, as appears by the inquisition after the death of Edmund Entwisle, who held land in Withington of the heir of Sir Ralph Longford in socage ; Duchy of Lanc. Inq. p.m. vii, 30.

[11] Among Earl Egerton of Tatton's deeds are a number connected with Nicholas Longford. In 1566 Edward Tyldesley of Morleys conveyed lands, &c. in Withington to Nicholas Longford of Longford. In 1587 Nicholas settled his capital messuage called Hough Hall, with the park and various lands known as Hough Park, Woodhead Meadow, Presefields, Hondirne, Hough Fields, Hough Moss and Moss Green, Willey Leys, Dove Lache Meadow, &c., 'parcels of the demesne lands of the manor of Hough otherwise called the manor of Withington' ; also various messuages, lands, &c. in Hough, Withington, Manchester, Didsbury, Chorlton, Rusholme, Haughton, and Denton, for the jointure of Martha, then his wife. His father Sir Ralph Longford is named. Previous dispositions of the estates were recited, when the remainders were to Richard Longford and William his brother, 'being near cousins to the said Nicholas Longford' ; to Maud his sister, late wife of Sir George Vernon, and then of Francis Hastings ; to Francis Dethick, son of Humphrey Dethick and Elizabeth his wife, another sister of Nicholas, and to the said Elizabeth. The remainders were varied in 1587, and a further change was made in 1588, when Sir Christopher Hatton and his heirs came first in the remainders. The above-named Martha, as 'Martha Southwell, one of the daughters of Sir Robert Southwell, knight, deceased,' also in 1591 released her right to Hatton. In 1595 Sir William Hatton for £2,660

conveyed the mano Hough to Sir Rob Nicholas Longford i selling them the sa 1597 Cecil and th sold the same to Ro

Fines relating t actions are : Pal. bdles. 28, m. 121 · 234, 279 · 53, m

[12] See the preced

[13] a l Eg rto was to b

to invest £7,000 in land for the eldest son, Nicholas, within five years.[26] The obligation was not fulfilled and litigation followed, resulting in a compromise which defeated Sir Edward Mosley's desire to preserve the lands in the male line of the family.[27] Edward Mosley, the beneficiary under the will, was made a knight in 1689 ; he left a daughter and heir, Ann, wife of Sir John Bland,[28] and her son, also Sir John Bland,[29] sold all the Mosley estates that descended to him, including the Withington manors.

The purchaser was William Egerton,[30] from whom they have descended to the present lord, Earl Egerton of Tatton.[31]

Hough End Hall is said to have been built by Sir Nicholas Mosley shortly after he bought the manor of Manchester in 1596, on the site of an older house which is known to have existed in the middle of the 15th century. The house faces

EGERTON, Earl Egerton of Tatton. *Argent a lion rampant gules between three pheons sable.*

south-west and stands about a quarter of a mile to the north-east of Barlow Moor Road, near to Chorlton-with-Hardy. Its back faces the Midland Railway, and Chorlton Brook runs past it on the north side. It is a picturesque brick building of three stories on a stone base 3 ft. high, consisting of a centre portion with a wing at each end. The principal doorway is central, under a porch, opening to a central passage with a door, formerly external, on the north. The total length of the chief or south front is about 94 ft., the central or recessed portion of which measures 42 ft., and the wings project 6 ft. 9 in. On the north face the western half of the space between the projecting wings is filled by a contemporary square staircase, of equal projection with the wings. The detail is rather rough, and the front elevation very plain, but the general effect is extremely good, owing largely, no doubt, to the colour of the bricks and the grey stone slates, which have weathered a beautiful hue, and also to the fact that the house is partly covered with creepers and set off by a well-kept front garden and rural surroundings. The windows are all square-headed and with stone mullions, those to the top floor, however, being built up across the whole length of the front. The wings are gabled and ornamented with balls, and the centre portion is surmounted with a parapet in the form of three smaller

gables with similar finials. The chimneys are square shafts set diagonally on square bases. The bricks are 2¼ in. in thickness, laid in alternate courses of headers and stretchers, and there are no string-courses and no quoins at the angles. A very restful effect has been produced by the simplest means, but principally by the judicious spacing of the windows and a plentiful amount of plain brick walling. The entrance is in the centre of the main front, and was originally through a square-headed door flush with the wall. A projecting porch has since been added. The windows retain their ancient diamond quarries and in the internal angles of the front are two lead rain-water pipes with ornament in relief all down the front of the pipes. The back of the house has been a good deal altered and the windows modernized. It has four gables without copings on the same face, but was originally more broken up and picturesque, a recessed portion or court between the east wing and the staircase having been built upon. The original outer doorway at the back, with the oak nail studded door which opened on to this space, is now inside the house, and a five-light window on the return of the staircase bay is built up and can only be seen from inside. Other additions have been built in later times at the back of the house at both ends. The east wing consists, on the ground floor, of two rooms now used as a toolhouse and blacksmith's shop. A five-light window has been built up on the east side of the front room, and a break in the plinth in another part of the outer wall at the east end, together with a large external cavity which is evidently a former fireplace, suggests considerable alterations at this end of the house. The projection of this now outside fireplace goes up the whole height of the building and finishes in a gable. Lower down, at the level of the first floor, are the marks of a small gable roof, and similar indications are to be seen over what was apparently either a bay window or entrance to the back room. The fireplace may have belonged to a small wing which has been pulled down, or it may have been intended for a purpose to which it was never afterwards put. The interior of the building, which is now used as a farm-house, has few points of interest, having been a good deal modernized and stripped of its old oak, including a handsome staircase at the east end, which was removed by Lord Egerton to Tatton Lodge.

Waltheof de Withington and some others made grants to Cockersand Abbey.[32]

[26] See *Mosley Fam. Mem.* 19–21 ; an earlier will (cancelled) is printed by Booker, *Didsbury*, 158.

[27] *Mosley Fam. Mem.* 40, 41. Another reason of the dispute was that Mary, the sister, was quite disinherited by the later will. The compromise resulted in the Leicestershire property going to Joseph Maynard in right of his wife ; the Staffordshire estates after the death of Lady North (Sir Edward's widow) reverted to Oswald Mosley of Ancoats, to whom the manor of Manchester was also to be bequeathed in default of male issue to Edward Mosley of Hulme ; the remainder of the estates were at the free disposal of the last-named ; Booker, op. cit. 161, 162.

In a fine in 1680 relating to the Mosley manors and lands, including a free fishery in the Mersey and views of frank-

Land in Healdhouses was granted to the Traffords[33] and held by them from the 13th to the 16th century,[34] when part or all was sold to the Mosleys.[35] There are some records also of a Fallowfield family.[36] One or two other small estates appear in the inquisitions.[37] Near Fallowfield was the place called Aldhulme, mentioned in the Cockersand and other grants; it is now represented by fields called Great and Little Oldham, on the south side of Fallowfield Brook.[38] Apart from these alienations, mostly on the outskirts of the township, the land appears to have been re-

tained by the lords of the manor; and in 1784 William Egerton contributed three-fourths of the land tax in Withington and Fallowfield.[39]

About 1567 there were disputes between Edmund Trafford and Nicholas Longford respecting the 'waste grounds, moors or commons called Didsbury Moor, Withington Moor, Moss Green *alias* Moss Side, and Chorlton Moor.'[40]

For the Established Church St. Paul's, Withington, was erected in 1841,[41] and Holy Innocents', Fallowfield, in 1872.[42] The patronage in each case is

---

gerith de Withington gave 8 acres on the south side of the great ditch (Nico Ditch), as marked by crosses; also 4 acres extending from the great ditch along the churchway towards the land of Walter de Withington, &c.; *Cockersand Chart* (Chet. Soc), ii, 729, 731. The Traffords were tenants of these lands in 1451 and later; ibid. iv, 1238. As the charters cited were afterwards among the deeds of Worsley of Platt (Harl. MS. 2112, fols. 46, &c.) this family no doubt acquired the land.

In 1292 the Abbot of Cockersand was called upon to justify his claims in Withington; *Plac. de Quo War.*(Rec.Com.),379.

[38] The de Trafford evidences contain the following : Ellis son of Robert de Pendlebury to Henry son of Robert son of 'Ralph de Trafford all the land of ' Gildehusestide' within bounds beginning at Gooselache, thence to the pool where Matthew son of William raised a dyke to turn the water for his mill ; by another dyke to the moss and so back to Gooselache ; with all the liberties which the freemen of the said Matthew his lord enjoyed, but Matthew would have a road across the land for carrying his hay. A rent of 4s. was payable ; De Trafford D. no. 310.

Another charter concerning the same land (as it seems) reduced the rent to 3s.; no. 311. Roger de Pendlebury afterwards released to a later Henry de Trafford all right to rent for the land in the Gildhouses ; no. 312, 128. At that time Sir Simon de Gousill was the chief lord of the land ; no. 313. Meantime Matthew son of Matthew de Haversage had granted land near Gooselache to Richard de Trafford ; it measured 20 acres by the perch of 22 ft., and the bounds began at the Great Moss, went up Gooselache to the boundary of Platt and thence across to Grenclowlache, with common of pasture of the vill of Withington ; the rent was an iron spur or 3d.; no. 129. The seal shows a coat of five pales with a chief, and part of the legend ⊢— . . . EV : DE : HAVER . . . E.

Simon de Gousill released to Henry de Trafford his claim to the 3s. rent due from the Gildhouses, or rather reduced it to 2s.; and he granted all his part of the land outside Henry's ditch within bounds beginning at the corner of the Twenty Acres (held by Henry of Simon) as far as the ditch called the Hules towards Withington, so that the ditch of the Hules might extend straight across the moss as far as the corner towards Trafford. A rent of 1d. was due ; ibid. no. 131, 132. The charter last quoted is endorsed, ' For the Moss green and boundary of the same,' and the above grants seem to relate to lands partly at least in the later townships of Moss Side and Rusholme.

A further charter from Simon de Gousill remitted the rent above-named, substituting the annual gift of a pair of gloves or 1d.; ibid. no. 133.

Nicholas de Longf ton in 1317, grante Trafford a portion of of Withington within ning at Gooselache t Platt, following the Greenlowlache, down Kemlache, and then ditches) to the 'Yh by t to the startin 17s. was payable , mon of turbary in th was also allowed to S and his tenants ; no Nicholas de Longfo three pales with a bend.

In 1449 some dis between Sir Nichol Edward Trafford re the Moss Green, Yeldehouse Moss gr ferred to the arbitr Ashton and others ,
A dispute as to 20 occurr

WITHINGTON : HOUGH END HALL, SOUTH-WEST FRONT

WITHINGTON : HOUGH END HALL, FROM THE SOUTH-EAST

vested in trustees, and the incumbents are styled rectors.

The Wesleyans and the Primitive Methodists each have churches in the township. The latter body has also a college for candidates for the ministry. A training college for the Congregational ministry, known as the Lancashire Independent College, Whalley Range, was opened in the north-west corner of the township in 1843.[43] The same body has had a church in the village since 1883.[44] The Baptists have a church, founded in 1891. The Presbyterian Church of England is also represented.[45]

The Roman Catholic church of St. Cuthbert was opened in 1881 and completed in 1902.[46] At Alexandra Park is the church of English Martyrs. 1876–96. In the same neighbourhood are St. Bede's College, in a building which was formerly the Manchester Aquarium, and convents of the Ladies of the Retreat and the Franciscan Tertiaries.

The Hulme Trustees have opened a Grammar School near Alexandra Park.

DIDSBURY

Dydesbyre, Dydesbiri, Didsbury, all c. 1280; Dodesbury, 1292.

Didsbury[1] has the Mersey for its southern and western border. Along the river the surface lies open, but the interior is urban in character. The area is 1,552¼ acres.[2] There was a population of 9,234 in 1901.

The principal roads are that on the western side from Manchester to Cheadle, with a modern branch to Northenden and Altrincham, and that through the centre and east from Stockport to Stretford.[3] The Midland Company's railway from Manchester to Stockport crosses the northern part of the township,

[43] Booker, op. cit. 125. It originated in 1810 in Salford; J. Thompson, *The Owens College*, 33. See also *Lancs. and Chet. Antiq. Soc.* iii, 185. The library has some early printed books.

[44] Nightingale, *Lancs. Nonconf.* v, 71; services began in 1881.

[45] The church was built in 1869.

[46] It was preceded by the temporary church of the Holy Ghost and St. Cuthbert in 1877.

[1] Use has been made of Mr. Fletcher Moss's *Didsbury* (1890), a book of 'sketches, reminiscences, and legends.' A description of the village as it formerly was is given by him in the opening chapter. The natural history of the district has a special section.

[2] 1,546 acres, including 24 of inland water; *Census Rep.* 1901.

[3] The first bridge is supposed to have been made by the Highlanders in 1745; it was a rude wooden one. There were also Gatley Ford, Northen Ford and Ferry, Barlow Ford, Jackson's Boat, and another passage across the river; Moss, *Didsbury*, 61, 62.

[4] Ibid. 48, 49; a description of the old wakes. See also A. Burton, *Rushbearing*, 160, where the date is given as 8 to 10 Aug.

[5] The Duke's Hillock on the village green is supposed to have been so named from the Duke of Perth taking his stand there.

[6] *Lancs. and Chet. Antiq. Soc.* x, 250.

[7] In 1323 Margaret widow of Adam de Pendlebury claimed dower in one plough-land in Didsbury against Sir Nicholas de Longford; De Banco R. 248, m. 154 d.

[8] Pal. of Lanc. Feet of F. bdle. 151, m. 152.

[9] Booker, *Didsbury* (Chet. Soc.), 8. The 'daily bullying' of Lady Bland's steward Broome is mentioned in 1720; ibid. 40, 41. William Broome of Didsbury, in or before 1749, married Elizabeth Dawson, and died in 1781; their son William died without issue in 1810. There are monuments in the church; ibid. 29. Richard and William Broome occur in a recovery of land of Sir John Bland's in Withington in 1753; Com. Pleas Recov. R. East. 26 Geo. II, m. 14.

[10] Booker, op. cit. 8. Henry (son of Robert) Feilden by Mary Broome his wife had a son Robert, who married Anne daughter of Sir John Parker Mosley of Ancoats, and died in 1830 aged 69; their son, the. Rev. Robert Mosley Feilden, was rector of Bebington from 1826 to 1862; Burke, *Commoners*, ii, 445; Booker, *Didsbury*, 27.

[11] Ibid. 10. The next considerable landowners were James Heald and H. Ll. Bamford Hesketh.

[12] William de Didsbury claimed common of pasture in Didsbury against John de Byron and Simon de Gousul in 1276 and 1278; the jury, however, found that he had sufficient. John and Simon were at that time sharers of the vill, which, so they pleaded, was neither vill nor borough, but a hamlet of Withington; Assize R. 405, m. 2; 1238, m. 32. William was plaintiff in some other actions about the same time; Assize R. 1235, m. 12;

was in 1576 secured to Thomas Rudd.[16] One Walker of Didsbury was a freeholder in 1600,[17] and the Goodyers and Twyfords also are named about the same time.[18] Richard and Robert Twyford in 1649 compounded for 'delinquency' in adhering to the forces raised against the Parliament, their fines amounting to £44 and £45 respectively.[19]

In 1789 the Broomes and Feildens together paid nearly a third of the land tax; the Reverend Mr. Bayley and William Bamford were the next considerable landowners.[20]

The college of Newark had a small rent from Didsbury, which was in 1549 sold by the Crown to Richard Venables.[21]

The mill of Didsbury is mentioned in a charter, granted about 1260, by which Sir Simon de Gousill released to Henry de Trafford all suit of the mill and liability for the maintenance and repair of the mill pool, and like services.[22]

CHURCH The church of ST. JAMES[23] stands on high ground, to the south-west of the village, the land sloping down on the west side of the site towards the River Mersey. The

of transept or chapel, the outer wall being a continuation of that of the vestries.

Of the original building which stood on the site nothing is known, and so little ancient work remains in the present structure (or what may be ancient is so effectually concealed by modern plaster and paint) that nothing can be said of the development of the plan, and little as to the date of the older parts. The ancient chapel is said to have been entirely rebuilt of stone in 1620, and the building of that date is described as consisting of a chancel 24 ft. square, nave with north and south aisles 45 ft. long by 34 ft. 6 in. wide over all, and west tower.[24] It had two three-light windows on each side of the nave, with entrances north and south opposite to each other at the west end of both aisles. There was also a separate entrance on the south side of the chancel. A gallery was erected at the west end in 1751, and a short one on the south side in 1757. In 1770 the chancel was declared to be 'very old, ruinous, and decayed,' and was taken down and rebuilt on a large scale 'by taking in 8 ft. on the north and also 8 ft. on the south side thereof, so as to make the said intended new chancel of the same breadth or width with the nave

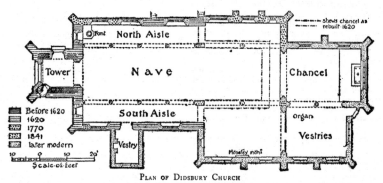

PLAN OF DIDSBURY CHURCH

view from the churchyard on that side, towards Cheshire, is very extensive.

The building consists of a chancel 27 ft. by 19 ft. with south vestry and organ chamber, nave 73 ft. 3 in. by 19 ft., with north and south aisles, and west tower 10 ft. by 11 ft. 3 in., these measurements all being internal. There is also a small building 12 ft. by 8 ft. 9 in., formerly a vestry, at the south-west of the south aisle, and the two eastern bays of the aisle have been extended 11 ft. southwards, so as to form a kind

or body of the said chapel.' Galleries and pews were erected in the new chancel, and at the same time the old pews in the body of the church were taken away and 'handsome and convenient pews or seats all of one decent, regular, and uniform order' put in their place. About twenty years after a north gallery was erected, and the south one extended to the chancel, but there seems to have been nothing done to the structure from this time till 1841, when a faculty was granted to pull down the north and south walls from

[16] Pal. of Lanc. Feet of F. bdle. 38, m. 28; the deforciant was Nicholas Longford, the remainder being to Thomas Rudd. See Ducatus Lanc. (Rec. Com.), iii, 26. Broad Oak stood south or south-east of the church.

[17] Misc. (Rec. Soc. Lancs. and Ches.), i, 249.

[18] Booker, op. cit. 5, 6. For a Goodyer case in 1657 see Exch. Dep. (Rec. Soc. Lancs. and Ches.), 31.

[19] Cal. of Com. for Compounding, iii, 1747, 1950. In 1666 Edward Mosley of Hulme leased a messuage in Didsbury (formerly William Wood's) to Richard

Twyford of Didsbury, gent., then occupier, for the lives of the said Richard, William his son, and Hugh Yannis; Earl Egerton's D. There is a Yannis meadow in the bend of the Mersey west of the church.

[20] Land tax returns at Preston.

[21] Pat. 3 Edw. VI, pt. 9.

[22] De Trafford D. no. 133.

[23] It is supposed to have been dedicated to St. James, the rush-bearing on 5 Aug. corresponding to 25 July Old Style.

[24] Booker, op. cit. 14.

A description of this building is given by Booker (op. cit. 17) from a ground plan

the tower to the chancel, which were 3 ft. 6 in. thick, and rebuild them of a thickness of 2 ft. so as to obtain more room for seats. Only about half the length of the wall, beginning from the west, was thus dealt with, however ; the walls beyond this point are still the original thickness.[25]

In 1855 the building underwent a thorough restoration, in the course of which the outside walls, with the exception of the tower, were cased in stone, new traceried windows inserted, the roof raised over the aisles (north and south galleries), the north and south doors at the west end of the nave done away with and windows substituted, and a large entrance door made through the tower at the west end. By these alterations the building lost any traces that remained of its original appearance, and assumed more or less its present aspect. In 1871 a new chancel was added, the north and south galleries taken down,[26] and a second door opened out in the tower on the north side ; and in 1895 the south aisle was extended and vestries and an organ chamber built on the south side of the chancel.

The walls are built of red sandstone and have plain parapets, the buttresses marking the ends of the old nave, the old chancel, and the present chancel being carried up as pinnacles. The chancel roof is slightly lower than that of the nave, and is separated from it externally by a stone gable surmounted by a cross. The nave roof is continued at a slightly lower pitch over the aisles,[27] and all the roofs are slated. A portion of the exterior walling on the south side between the vestry and the extension shows an old rubble facing, having apparently been left untouched in the restoration of the last century.

The chancel has a five-light window at the east end and two windows of two lights on the north. The south side has two pointed arches opening respectively to the organ chamber and vestry.

The nave consists of six bays, the two easternmost of which formed the 18th-century chancel. These have four-centred arches 13 ft. wide on octagonal piers and responds, which appear to be of later date than 1770.[28] As all the piers, arches, and walling of the nave are stuccoed and painted it is impossible to tell how much of the work belongs to the period of restoration and how much is original. The old chancel walls, however, seem to have been thinned and rebuilt a little in advance of those of the rest of the nave in one of the restorations (probably in 1855). The old nave arcade consists of four semicircular arches 9 ft. wide, resting on circular columns 16 in. in diameter, with square abaci and circular moulded bases, much cut away. The arches and columns have the appearance of 18th-century work, but may possibly belong to the previous century, and be part of the

:—

8ʳ E. M. K : FOUN	E. M. ESQ : 8ᵗ G. B. K.
A. M. WID : DERS	PATRON : BARONET

The inscription on the third stone is partly obliterated . . . 'DOMNI 16/30,' alone being visible.

The initials are those of Sir Edward Mosley, kt., and Ann Mosley (Sutton), second wife of his elder and deceased brother Rowland of Hough End Hall, who are called founders. 'E. M. Esq. Patron' is Edward Mosley, son of Rowland Mosley of Hough End, and afterwards first baronet, and 'Sir G. B. K. Baronet' is supposed to be Sir George Booth, of Dunham Massey (knighted 1595, baronet 1611), but this is uncertain.[31] The stones do not appear to be in their original positions, as when Owen visited the church only the first two are described as on the north side, the dated stone being then 'on the east.' The tower is said generally to have been built in 1620, but more probably an older tower was refaced in stone, as there appear to be traces of older work inside.[32]

---

[25] Other work, however, seems to have been done at this time. John Owen writes (Owen MSS. Manch. Ref. Lib. vol. 13) : 'The east end and the greater part of the body of the church is built of brick with the date 1842.' There is no date to this passage, but Owen's visit was presumably some time before the alterations of 1855.

[26] The west gallery remained till 1895, when the organ was transferred to its present position.

[27] Originally there may have been a low clearstory, but this is not certain. The present roof to the aisles dates from the raising of the outside walls in 1855.

was formerly known as the Barlow Chapel, and here is said to have been found a portion of an early piscina during one of the restorations (article in *Manch. Courier*, 3 June 1907), apparently proving the existence of a stone church prior to the 17th century.

[31] Edward Mosley, the patron, would be an infant at the time ; possibly Sir George Booth was his guardian.

[32] There are remains of two small round-headed openings on the north and south in the ringing chamber, which do not show outside.

The fittings are all modern. There is a chancel screen (1871), and a second screen separating the vestries and organ chamber from the south aisle. The present font, which stands at the west end of the north aisle, dates from 1881, but an older plaster font is preserved at the rectory.[33]

There is no old stained glass.

Between the windows of the south wall of the extension of the south aisle (sometimes called the Mosley Chapel)[34] is a fine marble and alabaster monument to Sir Nicholas Mosley, kt., 1612, sometime Lord Mayor of London, with three lower compartments containing the kneeling figures of his two wives and of three of his sons. Above is his own figure in mayoral robes. Over the figure of Sir Nicholas are his arms (Sable, a cheveron between three pickaxes argent, quartering Or a fesse between three eagles displayed sable), and below on either side over the figures of his wives two shields in oval frames, the first having the arms of Mosley impaling Gules, a chessrook argent, on a chief argent three roses gules, for Elizabeth Rookes, widow of — Hendley, his second wife, who survived him ; the second, Mosley impaling Whitbroke, Argent a lion rampant gules, for Margaret Whitbroke, his first wife. There are four male figures in the lower central compartment, being probably those of Rowland Mosley (died 1616), son and heir of Sir Nicholas, with his eldest son ; Anthony Mosley, and Sir Edward Mosley, the two latter still living when the monument was erected.[35]

At the east end of the north aisle is a mural tablet with good plaster ornament to Ann, Dowager Lady Bland (died 1734), erected by her son 'in memory of one of the best of women' ; with a lozenge over bearing the arms of Bland, Argent on a bend sable three pheons of the field, impaling the quartered arms of Mosley, as on Sir Nicholas Mosley's monument ; on an escutcheon of pretence the Mosley coat is repeated. There is also a mural monument on the west wall of the Mosley Chapel to Sir John Bland (died 1715).[36]

There are six bells all cast by Abraham Rudhall of Gloucester 1727.[36a]

The church plate consists of a small paten (4½ in. diam.) inscribed 'Given to the chappel of Didsbury in the parish of Manchester 1741' ; a small chalice 4 in. high, inscribed 'Belongs to the chapel of Didsbury 1743' ; a paten, 'the gift of Thomas Briarly of Heaton Norris to Didsbury Chapel April 10, 1748' ; a large silver flagon, 'the gift of Joseph Boardman of Manchester to the Church of Didsbury A.D. 1753' ; a chalice marked 'A.M.' with crest, a demi-lion rampant issuing from a coronet (supposed to be the gift of Ann Mosley) ; a chalice, 'the gift of Mrs. Frances Bayley to Didsbury Church 1813' ; an almsdish of 1843, and two breadholders of 1845.

The registers begin in 1561, and have been transcribed (1561–1757) by Mr. H. T. Crofton and Rev. E. Abbey Tindall (vols. 8 and 9 Lancs. Parish Reg. Soc.). The entries from 1561 to 1600 have been apparently copied from previously existing loose sheets.

ADVOWSON A chapel, it is believed, existed at Didsbury from the middle of the 13th century,[37] and the chapel yard was consecrated in 1352 in order to provide for the interment of those who died of the plague.[38] The chapelry, in later times at least, was considered to include Didsbury, Withington, Burnage, and Heaton Norris.

The chapel and its ornaments were confiscated by Edward VI, but the former were acquired by the inhabitants for 13s. 4d.[39] Unlike other chapels in the parish, after the Elizabethan reform it seems to have been served as a rule by a curate of its own.[40] A church library was founded and a few volumes still remain in the vestry.[41] A stock of £48 belonged to the chapel in 1650,[42] and had grown to £104 by 1720,[43]

---

[33] It has been several times taken to the church of late years to be used for adult baptisms, and being by tradition the font in which Barlow was baptized, is still an object of reverence to Roman Catholics.

[34] The Mosley Chapel was originally at the south-east corner of the chancel.

[35] The inscriptions read as follows :— 'This is in memory of Sir Nicholas Mosley, Knight, sometyme Lord Mayor of London, who dyed the 12 day of December 1612 of ye age of 85, and lyeth here interred.'

'Margaret Whitbroke, his 1st wife, by whom he had 6 sonnes and 2 daughters.'

'Elizabeth his second wife, at whose cost this monument was erected, dyed without issue.'

'1. Rowland Mosley, Esq. sonne and heyre of Sr Nicholas, first married Anne Houghton, by whom he had issue a son and daughter.'

'After, the aforesaid Rowland married Anne Sutton, one of the co-heiresses of Sutton, by whom he had issue Edward his son and heyre, and Ann his daughter yet living ; and he dyed 23rd Feby. 1616, and lieth here interred.'

'2. Anthony Mosley his second son yet living. 3. Sir Edward Mosley, Knt. his youngest son, Atty Genl of the Dutchy of Lancaster now living at Rolleston in Staffordshire.'

[36] The inscriptions on these two monu-

ments are given in Booker, op. cit. pp. 25–6.

[36a] The inscriptions on these bells are as follows : (1) 'Let us ring for the Church and the King, 1727' ; (2) 'Prosperity to all our benefactors, 1727' ; (3) 'Lady Ann Bland and St John, her son, bart. Benefactors, 1727' ; (4) 'Robert Twyford, Minister, 1727' ; (5) 'Wm. Twyford and Thos. Whitelegg, Ch. Wardens, 1727' ; (6) 'Abr. Rudhall of Gloucester cast us all, 1727.'

[37] Alexander, chaplain of Didsbury, was a Barlow feoffee about 1300 ; Booker, op. cit. 251. In 1352 the Bishop of Lichfield gave his licence to celebrate divine service in the chapel there ; service had been performed time out of mind, though only seldom of recent years. A chaplain was to be paid by the people. At the same time the cemetery was to be consecrated, the bishop having had testimony of 'their devotion in the time of the late pestilence,' when it was inconvenient to carry the dead all the way to Manchester ; Lich. Epis. Reg. iii, fol. 127.

[38] On 16 Sept. 1361 the Bishop of Lichfield granted licence to the inhabitants of the vill of Didsbury to bury in the cemetery of the chapel there, by reason of the mortality ; Lich. Epis. Reg. Stretton, v, fol. 7.

[39] Raines, Chantries (Chet. Soc.), 277. The chapel had two bells which the people had refused to surrender ; ibid. 274, 259.

The inscriptions are in the Owen MSS.

[40] Robert Lowe was curate of Didsbury in 1563, according to the Visitation list. The following occur in the registers of the chapel :—1580, Ottiwell Baguley ; 1588, — Loydes ; 1589, Richard Massey ; Booker, op. cit. 53, 54.

About 1610 the chapel was described as 'annexed to Manchester the mother church' ; Hist. MSS. Com. Rep. xiv, App. iv, 11.

[41] Christie, Old Lancs. Libraries (Chet. Soc.), 97 ; Moss, Didsbury, 18.

[42] Commonwealth Ch. Surv. (Rec. Soc. Lancs. and Ches.), 13. There was also a leasehold house, worth about £10 a year. It was recommended that a distinct parish should be assigned to the chapel.

The Committee of Sequestrations in 1649–50 ordered £30 a year to be paid to the minister of Didsbury ; Plund. Mins. Accts. (Rec. Soc. Lancs. and Ches.), i, 259. In 1652 the income was only £10 a year, and £40 out of the Manchester tithes was ordered to be added ; ibid. ii, 35. The sum was afterwards reduced to £33 10s. ; ibid. ii, 91.

[43] Gastrell, Notitia (Chet. Soc.), ii, 86, 87. The bishop notes that 'Rowland Mosley, esq., left lands to this chapel worth £20 per annum for 80 years after the death of a person mentioned in the lease ; not known when the person died, but the lands are taken away. There was also a

when the voluntary contributions amounted to £10 a year.[44]

The patronage, which legally belonged to the Warden and Fellows of Manchester College, was conceded to Dame Bland in 1726 on her undertaking to improve the endowment ;[45] it has frequently changed hands,[46] and is now held by Mr. William Norris Heald. A district chapelry was assigned to it in 1839.[47] The incumbents have been styled rectors since 1850. The following is a list of them :[48]

1605	Thomas Rycroft [49]
1612	John Davenport [50]
1639	John Bradshaw
1647	Thomas Clayton,[51] M.A. (St. John's College, Camb.)
1650	Peter Ledsam [52]
1664	No curate
oc. 1671–86	John Walker, M.A. (Magdalene College, Camb.)
1686	Peter Shaw,[53] B.A.
1700	Joshua Wakefield,[54] M.A. (Queens' College, Camb.)
1705	Roger Bolton,[55] M.A. (Jesus College, Camb.)
1709	David Dawson, B.A. (St. John's College, Camb.)
oc. 1716	James Leicester, B.A.[56] (St. John's College, Camb.)
1719	Thomas Wright, B.A.[57]
1721	Francis Hooper, M.A.[58] (Trinity College, Camb.)
1726	Robert Twyford, B.A.[59] (Brasenose College, Oxf.)
1747	William Twyford, B.A.[60] (St. John's College, Camb.)
1795	John Newton, M.A. (Queens' College, Camb.)
1807	John Gatliff, M.A.[61] (Brasenose College, Oxf.)
1840	William John Kidd [62]
1881	Charles Dunlop Smith, M.A.[63] (Wadham College, Oxf.)
1894	Edward Abbey Tindall, M.A. (Caius College, Camb.)

Emmanuel Church, Barlow Moor, was consecrated in 1858 ; the Bishop of Manchester collates to the

CHORLTON-WITH-HARDY

piece of ground called the Ogree meadow, long enjoyed by the curates, but taken away by Sir John Bland.' The correspondence concerning these lost endowments is printed by Booker, op. cit. 36–51, where further particulars of the endowments may be seen.

[44] In 1720 a quarter of the people of the chapelry were Nonconformists (Presbyterians) ; Gastrell, loc. cit. The chapel had two wardens, one chosen by Lady Bland and the other by the people ; ibid.

[45] Booker, *Didsbury*, 52, 53. Bishop Gastrell noted that Joseph Maynard and his wife had claimed the nomination of the curate in 1667, but the warden and fellows nominated in 1704 ; Gastrell, *Notitia*, ii, 87.

[46] Lady Bland, 1726 ; William Broome, 1775 ; John Newton, 1792 ; William Newall, 1829 ; Thomas Darwell, 1840 ; Booker, loc. cit. It was afterwards sold to James Lowe, who sold in 1878.

[47] *Lond. Gaz.* 29 Mar. 1839, and 16 June 1854.

4

MANOR It does not appear that there was ever a separate manor of *CHORLTON*, which was held as part of Withington,[2] but it may have been held in moieties by Trafford and Barlow.[2a] A family bearing the local name is mentioned from time to time,[3] but nothing is known as to its position. The principal family, apart from the lords of Withington and the Barlows, was that of Trafford, but there is nothing to show how the Trafford lands were acquired, apart from the grants quoted in the account of Withington.[4] The lands appear to have been sold about 1590 to Gregory Lovel and others,[5] from whose heirs probably they passed to the Mosleys,[6] and later to the Egertons of Tatton.

HARDY does not occur separately.

The manor of *BARLOW* was long held by a family who adopted that surname.[7] The earliest known member was a Thomas de Barlow to whom about 1200 Sibyl daughter of Uctred and Margaret granted all her lands in Barlow.[8] A later Thomas in 1253 complained that Robert de Reddish and a number of his neighbours had interfered with his stream at Barlow and taken his fish ; it was stated in defence that the fish were caught in Matthew de Haversage's free fishery and Thomas was fined, but excused because he was poor.[9] Alexander son of Albin de Sale gave to Thomas de Barlow all his land and right in the vill of Barlow.[10] Thomas was succeeded by several Rogers.[11] In 1336 Roger de Barlow the elder made a settlement of his manor of Barlow, together with five messuages, 50 acres of land, &c., in Chorlton, and a moiety of the manor in Chorlton.[12] John son of Roger de Barlow was in possession in 1389, and a year or two later a settlement of his lands in Barlow, Chorlton, Hardy, and Withington, was made, with remainders to his son John, Joan his wife, daughter of Richard de Holland, and their issue.[13] The younger John was succeeded by his son Nicholas and his grandson Alexander ;[14] the last-

---

[2] *Mamecestre* (Chet. Soc.), ii, 373, 377. The township is usually distinguishable from Chorlton-upon-Medlock by the spelling of its name—Chollerton instead of Chorleton.

[2a] In 1562 the two principal landowners, Sir Edmund Trafford and Alexander Barlow, claimed to hold the 'manor of Chorlton in Withington,' and made complaint of an encroachment upon the waste ; *Pal. Note Bk.* iv, 210.

[3] Richard and Robert de Cholreton were jurors in 1242 ; *Lancs. Inq. and Extents* (Rec. Soc. Lancs. and Ches.), i, 153. Richard de Cholreton, clerk, appears in 1314 ; *Final Conc.* (Rec. Soc. Lancs. and Ches.), ii, 15. Richard Enotson of Chollerton was defendant in 1347 ; *De Banco R.* 350, m. 201. Robert 'Chorleton' of 'Chollerton' and Joan his wife were defendants in 1448 ; *Pal. of Lanc. Plea R.* 11, m. 10.

[4] See above in the account of Withington. Henry de Trafford and his men of Chorlton were freed from suit to the mill at Didsbury about 1260 ; *De Trafford D.* no. 133. Henry Trafford in 1422 was found to have held part of eight messuages, 100 acres of land, and 20 acres of meadow in Chorlton of Ralph de Longford in socage ; *Towneley MS. DD,* no. 1505. In later inquisitions the whole of the Trafford holding in Withington, including Yeldhouse, Rusholme, Fallowfield, Moss Side, and Chorlton, was regarded as a single tenement ; e.g. Duchy of Lanc. Inq. p.m. xi, 11.

[5] In 1594 Gregory Lovel claimed rights in Chorlton Moor by conveyance from Sir Edmund Trafford ; *Ducatus Lanc.* (Rec. Com.), iii, 306. See also Booker, *Didsbury,* 248, 6.

[6] A capital messuage called Turf Moss, with lands in Stretford and Chorlton, appears in the inquisitions after the death of Rowland Mosley in 1617 ; they were held partly of the heirs of Hamond Mascy, and partly of the king as of his duchy ; *Lancs. Inq. p.m.* (Rec. Soc. Lancs. and Ches.), ii, 66, 69. It does not appear from whom they were purchased ; they may have been acquired directly from the Traffords.

[7] Abstracts of their charters, made in 1653, are in Harl. MS. 2112, fol. 172/208, &c. ; some are printed in Booker's *Didsbury,* 251, 252, and all in *Pal. Note Bk.* iv, 206-9.

[8] Harl. MS. 2112, fol. 172/208. The grantor may have the Hutred de With the Cockersand chart

A Roger son of attested a Withingt part of the reign of op. cit. 319.

[9] *Curia Regis R.* 152, m. 5 d. ; 155 defendants were Ada de Birches, Thoma Hyde, Thomas son of his brother.

The plaintiff seem son of Robert de B

named heads the pedigree recorded in 1567,[15] at which time the lord of the manor was another Alexander Barlow, who was conspicuous among the people of the Manchester district by his steady resistance to the religious changes made by Elizabeth.[16] For this cause he was at last committed to prison, and died in custody on 24 August 1584 leaving a son and heir of the same name, then twenty-six years of age.[17] The son, described in the Douay Records as a 'constant confessor of Christ,'[18] was made a knight on the accession of James I,[19] who at that time showed his inclination towards religious toleration. Sir Alexander died in 1620, holding the manor of Barlow and various lands of Edward Mosley, and other lands in Denton and Haughton ; his son and heir Sir Alexander Barlow was over thirty years of age.[20] Two other sons entered the Benedictine Order,

BARLOW of Barlow.
Sable a double-headed eagle displayed argent, membered or, standing on the limb of a tree raguled and trunked of the second.

Barlow made a feoffment of his manor of Barlow, &c., in 1478 ; Harl. MS. 2112, fol. 174 d./210 d.

William Barlow, a son of Nicholas, claimed certain lands in Withington against Alexander Barlow in 1479 ; Pal. of Lanc. Plea R. 51, m. 3 d.

[15] *Visit.* (Chet. Soc.), 5. The descent is thus given : Alexander –s. Roger –s. Ellis –s. Alexander (living 1567) –s. Alexander.

Writs were issued in 1525 touching Anne Barlow, widow, custodian of the land and heir of Ellis Barlow, and Katherine who was the wife of Roger Barlow ; Pal. of Lanc. Writs Proton. Lent, 16 Hen. VIII. Two years later Edmund Barlow of Hardy, and Katherine Barlow, widow, were executors of the will of Roger son and heir of Alexander Barlow ; ibid. Lent, 18 Hen. VIII ; Pal. of Lanc. Plea R. 142, m. 4.

A settlement of his estates was made by Alexander Barlow in 1555 ; Pal. of Lanc. Feet of F. bdle. 15, m. 43.

[16] Gillow, *Bibl. Dict. of Engl. Cath.* i, 130. It was to him that Lawrence Vaux, warden of Manchester, entrusted some of the college charters ; see *Pal. Note Bk.* iv, 211. He represented Wigan in Parliament from 1547 to 1557 ; Pink and Beaven, *Parl. Rep. of Lancs.* 218–20.

[17] Duchy of Lanc. Inq. p.m. xiv, 7. The manor of Barlow and lands in Barlow, Hardy, Chorlton, and Marshiche were held of Nicholas Longford in socage by a rent of 20d.

[18] As quoted by Challoner. In his will he described himself as 'a true and perfect recusant Catholic.' See also *Manch. Sessions* (Rec. Soc. Lancs. and Ches.), i, 82.

[19] Metcalfe, *Knights*, 149. His son Alexander was made a knight at the same time.

[20] *Lancs. Inq. p.m.* (Rec. Soc. Lancs. and Ches.), ii, 206. The estate comprised the capital messuage called Barlow Hall, a water-mill, and various messuages and lands. The clear value of the whole was declared to be £50. The rent of 20d. for Barlow was unchanged.

An account of the life of this Sir Alexander will be found in *Pal. Note Bk.* iv,

212–14, where also his portrait is engraved, and in Gillow, op. cit. i, 132 ; *Funeral Certs.* (Chet. Soc.). His will is printed in Booker's *Didsbury*, 264–7. He was buried in Manchester Church by torchlight.

[21] His baptismal name was Edward. There are accounts of him in Challoner's *Missionary Priests*, no. 161 ; Gillow, op. cit. i, 134, and *Trans. Hist. Soc.* (new ser.), xiii, 129 (with portrait). He was educated at Douay, where he entered the Benedictine Order in 1615, and was sent on the English mission, where he made himself beloved by 'his great zeal in the conversion of souls and the exemplary piety of his life and conversation.' It is related, as illustrating the devotions of the persecuted recusants, that on the eves of chief festivals 'the Catholics resorted to him from distant places and passed the night after the manner of the primitive Church, in watching, prayer, and spiritual colloquies ; whilst for his part he was employed almost all the night in hearing confessions. On the next day he treated them all to a dinner, where he and some of the more honourable sort of his flock served them that were poor and waited upon them, and then dined off their leavings. When he sent them home he gave each a groat in alms ; and when all had dined he distributed what remained to the poor of the parish.' His name was among those allowed by Leo XIII in 1886 to proceed in the cause of beatification. It has recently been suggested that his is the mysterious skull preserved at Wardley Hall in Worsley. His brother William took the religious name of Rudesind, and became superior of St. Gregory's, Douay. There are notices of both in *Dict. Nat. Biog.*

William Barlow, an Elizabethan divine who became Bishop of Lincoln (1608–13), is said to have been of Lancashire origin, though probably a Londoner by birth ; Baker, *St. John's College, Camb.* i, 256–7 ; Booker, *Didsbury*, 254–64 ; *Dict. Nat. Biog.* There are no Lancashire bequests in his will.

[22] Booker, op. cit. 268–70 ; where his will is printed. He seems to have sold or mortgaged his estate to Edmund Prest-

wich in 1621 ; Pal. of Lanc. Feet of F. bdle. 99, no. 15.

[23] He was high sheriff in 1651, so that he must have professed Protestantism ; P.R.O. *List*, 73. The estates were untouched by the Parliamentarian sequestrations of the time.

[24] Booker, op. cit. 281. A settlement of the manor of Barlow was made by Alexander and Thomas Barlow in 1654 ; Pal. of Lanc. Feet of F. bdle. 156, m. 162. Thomas Barlow and his trustees made a further settlement in 1656 ; ibid. bdle. 159, m. 89, and again in 1683 ; ibid. bdle. 210, m. 62.

[25] Dugdale, *Visit.* (Chet. Soc.), 28.

[26] Booker, loc. cit.

[27] Estcourt and Payne, *Engl. Cath. Nonjurors*, 20, 153 ; the yearly value was returned as £171 9s. for the Barlow Estate, and £7 for one at Northenden. Anthony's will is printed by Booker, op. cit. 282–84. By it the manor of Barlow was given to trustees for the benefit of his sons.

[28] The charge is mentioned in their father's will.

[29] Some depositions are printed by Booker, op. cit. 285–8. A servant deposed that 'she understood that he, Mr. Barlow, was much in debt, in so much that he never or seldom appeared out of doors but on Sundays, and there was but poor housekeeping.' Particulars of the sacred vestments, &c., at the hall are given ; they were 'consecrated goods or ornaments belonging to the Popish chapel at Barlow . . . kept together in a great trunk.'

[30] Indentures of 1760 by Thomas Barlow respecting the manor of Barlow were enrolled in the Common Pleas ; Mich. 1 Geo. III, R. 86, 88. Thomas Barlow's will (printed by Booker, op. cit. 288–91), devised Barlow Hall, &c., to trustees for the discharge of his debts, the payment of his wife's jointure, and various annuities, with remainder to the sons of his brother Humphrey, &c.

[31] The estate was offered for sale by auction on 2 Aug. 1785 ; ibid. 291. A private Act, a copy of which is in the possession of W. Farrer, had been obtained for vesting the estates in trustees.

A house appears to have existed on or near the site of the hall as far back as the reign of Henry VI, but the oldest parts of the present building do not date back further than the first half of the 16th century, and of this original house little or nothing can now be seen, the black and white work now remaining on the outside belonging to a later rebuilding in the same century.

The house stands about a quarter of a mile to the south of Barlow Moor Road between Chorlton-with-Hardy and Withington, on slightly rising ground on the north bank of the River Mersey, the position being originally in a large measure one of natural defence. The building is of two stories, quadrangular in plan, but almost wholly modernized and preserving few

quatrefoil panels in the former porch to the north. The bay window is continued up to the second story in a timber gable, the barge boards of which have been renewed. On the north wall of the quadrangle is a sundial with the date 1574, and the motto *Lumen me regit vos umbra*, marking the work of Alexander Barlow who renovated the Hall in that year. The bay window contains in its six upper lights some good heraldic glass. On one are the heads of a double-headed eagle (the crest of the Barlows), with the motto *Prist en foyt*. Another contains the arms of Holland, and a third those of the third Earl of Derby encircled by a garter, with the date 1574 and initials A.B. below. This appears to have been placed here by Alexander Barlow (whose sister Margaret was the Earl

BARLOW HALL

features of architectural interest. The entrance is by a doorway on the east side of the quadrangle, but it is said to have been formerly on the north side, part of which is described as a porch with gable over, still remaining. The quadrangle is irregular in shape but measures about 40 ft. from north to south, the width varying from 32 ft. on the south end to 38 ft. on the north. The plan of the buildings now surrounding the courtyard preserves very little of the ancient arrangement of the house, which may originally have consisted of the north and west wings, the quadrangle being completed later; but the great hall occupied the west wing, and a bay window in the north-west corner of the courtyard belonged to it. This bay, together with the restored half-timber work on the north side of the quadrangle, is the only picturesque bit of old work now left on the exterior of Barlow Hall, if we except a carved beam and some

of Derby's second wife) two years after his brother-in-law's death.

Booker [81a] gives two more shields, which have now disappeared.

1. Argent a lion rampant gules, collared or, which is the coat of Reddish.

2. A shield of Kendall of seven quarterings : (1) Gules a fesse checky or and azure between three eagles displayed of the second ; (2) Ermine a fesse azure ; (3) Azure a cross or ; (4) Argent three garbs gules ; (5) Argent on a cross azure five fleurs de lys or ; (6) Or a lion rampant guardant azure ; (7) Argent three martlets gules.

A corridor runs all round the house on the inner side next to the courtyard, but in the old west wing it is a modern arrangement, the bay window now lighting its northern end. There is a staircase bay in the north-east angle of the courtyard, and two other

[81a] *Chorlton Chapel*, 293.

staircases in the north-west and south-west interior angles of the building. The kitchen and offices are in the north, and the chief living rooms in the west and south. The internal corridor arrangement is preserved on three sides of the first floor.

By a fire which took place at Barlow Hall in March 1879 the west wing was almost entirely destroyed, and all traces of the original great hall lost. Much damage was also done to other parts of the building. The older part of the house had, however, been greatly modernized before this, and its exterior now presents the appearance of a quite ordinary brick-built house of the middle of the 19th century relieved' from absolute dulness by a covering of ivy on its principal elevation. The roofs are of flat pitch and covered with blue slates, but some later additions on the south-east of the building have higher pitched roofs with gables and are less plain in detail. On the south of the house at the bottom of the terrace is a pond extending the full length of the building, probably a portion of an ancient moat. The fire of 1879 revealed a good deal of the ancient construction. In places where the stucco and lath and plaster had been destroyed the ancient timber framing was exposed, with fillings of 'wattle and daub' and of brick. Much of this work, including the roof of the west wing, which is said to have been built on crucks, probably belonged to the original 16th-century house, but since the rebuilding it is no longer to be seen.[52]

Barlow Hall was in 1784 the birthplace of Thomas Walker, author of 'The Original,' and is now the head quarters of the Chorlton-cum-Hardy Golf Club.

In 1787 the principal landowners in the township were the assigns of Thomas Barlow and William

oc. 1754	Robert Oldfield, M.A.[54]	
1766	Richard Assheton, M.A.[54] (Brasenose Coll. Oxf.)	
1771	John Salter	
1789	Joshua Brookes, M.A.[47] (Brasenose Coll. Oxf.)	
1791	Nicholas Mosley Cheek	
1805	George Hutchinson, M.A.	
1816	Richard Hutchins Whitelock, M.A.[48]	

[52] For the three ghosts of Barlow Hall, see *Lancs. and Ches. Antiq. Soc.* vii, 305.

[53] Land tax returns at Preston.

[54] Booker, op. cit. 296.

[55] Ibid. 298 ; a view is given. There was a sundial over the south door on the wall. On the confiscation by Edward VI the 'ornaments' were sold for 2s. 8d. ; Raines, *Chant.* (Chet. Soc.), 277.

[56] Booker, loc. cit. A brief for a collection in aid was issued in 1774. In the *Manch. Dioc. Cal.* the date of consecration is given as 1782. It was enlarged in 1837.

[57] *Commonwealth Ch. Surv.* (Rec. Soc. Lancs. and Ches.), 13. Sir Nicholas Mosley in 1612 directed that £5 a year for twenty years should be given to a schoolmaster to teach school at Chorlton Chapel, the Mosleys to nominate and discharge the master, who was not to charge any scholar more than 6d. a quarter ; he desired further that the master should read service three times a week in the chapel ; Booker, op. cit. 132.

An addition of £40, afterwards reduced to £35 10s., was made by the Commonwealth authorities from sequestrations and from the Manchester tithes, but this allowance of course ceased at the Restoration ; *Plund. Mins. Accts.* (Rec. Soc. Lancs. and Ches.), i, 264 ; ii, 77.

[58] Gastrell, *Notitia* (Chet. Soc.), ii, 83 ; '£80 was lost by a tradesman in Manchester.' Two wardens were chosen — from Chorlton and from Hardy.

[59] Some details are given by Booker, op. cit. 301.

1833 Peter Hordern, M.A.[49] (Brasenose Coll. Oxf.)
1836 John Morton, B.D.
1843 William Birley, M.A.
1859 John Edmund Booth, M.A.[50] (Brasenose Coll. Oxf.)
1893 Francis Edward Thomas, M.A.[51] (Magdalene Coll. Camb.)

A new church, St. Werburgh's, was consecrated in 1902 ; the Crown and the Bishop of Manchester have the patronage alternately.

Methodism was introduced in 1770. The Wesleyan Methodists opened a chapel in 1805, rebuilt and enlarged it in 1827, and replaced it by another in 1872.[52] They have now two churches in the township, and the Primitive Methodists also have one.

The Baptists, the Congregationalists,[53] and the Presbyterian Church of England[54] each have a place of worship. The Unitarians also have a church, built in 1901.[55]

The Roman Catholic Church of St. Augustine was opened in 1892. It was first known as St. Peter's Priory, of the Gregorian Order, but in 1896 was handed over to the secular clergy.[56]

MOSS SIDE

The principal part of this township[1] lies to the north of Withington ; there are two small detached portions to the east, viz. on the north-west and north-east corners of Rusholme.[2] The total area is 421 acres. The whole is now urban, and forms an indistinguishable part of Manchester. Whalley Range lies on the south-west border.[3] The population in 1901 was 26,677.

A local board was formed in 1856,[4] and became an urban district council in 1894, but the district was taken into the city of Manchester in 1904. The township contains a free library.[5]

Pepper Hill Farm, the scene of the opening chapters of Mrs. Gaskell's *Mary Barton*, stood in the main portion of the township until 1900, when it was taken down. The site forms part of the Westwood Street Recreation Ground.

Several relics of the Stone Age have been found in and near Moss Side.

There was no manor of *MOSS SIDE*, *MANOR* and the development of the township is obscure. Judging from the later ownership the main portion and the nearest of the detached parts were once included in the estates of the Prestwiches of Hulme, for they were, in the latter part of the 18th century, held by the Lloyds. The eastern detached portion, lying near the Stockport Road, may have been the estate formerly known as Holt in Rusholme.[6] Edmund Prestwich, who died in 1577, held messuages and lands in 'Withenshaw' of Nicholas Longford in socage, by a rent of 3s. 4d. ; this is probably the Moss Side estate of the family.[7]

The Traffords and others also held lands in Moss Side,[8] but there seems no way of distinguishing their estate here from other lands held by them of the lords of Withington ; some, or all, of their land in the Yeeldhouses was no doubt in Moss Side, as traces of the name remained till recently.[9]

George Lloyd, representing in his estate the Prestwiches, paid over half the land tax in 1797 ; the other estates in the township were but small.[10]

A large number of places of worship have been built in the township during the last half-century. In connexion with the Established Church are Christ Church, 1850,[11] rebuilt 1899–1904, with a mission room ; St. James's, 1888 ; also, at Whalley Range, St. Margaret's, 1849,[12] and St. Edmund's, 1882.[13] The Bishop of Manchester collates the rector of St. James's ; the other benefices are in the hands of the Simeon and other trustees.

The following also have churches : The Primitive Methodists, Wesleyans (at Whalley Range), Congregationalists, Baptists,[14] Welsh Calvinistic Methodists,[15] Church of United Friends, Salvation Army, and Swedenborgians (New Jerusalem).

The Presbyterian Church of England at Whalley Range dates from 1849 ; the present church was built in 1886.

There is no Roman Catholic church, but the nursing sisters of St. Joseph have a house at Whalley Range.

[49] Also Chetham Librarian.
[50] Previously incumbent of St. Stephen's, Salford.
[51] Previously vicar of Tonge Moor.
[52] Booker, op. cit. 301, 302.
[53] It is called the Macfadyen Memorial Church.
[54] Founded 1904.
[55] The congregation dates from 1891, and therefore has no connexion with 17th-century Nonconformity. In 1689 William Broome's barn in Chorlton was licensed for a dissenting minister, Thomas Kynaston ; *Hist. MSS. Com. Rep.* xiv, App. iv, 232. Kynaston was from about that time minister at Knutsford. In 1718 a quarter of the small population was Presbyterian ; Gastrell, *Notitia*, ii, 83.
[56] Kelly, *Engl. Cath. Missions.*
[1] An exhaustive account of *Old Moss Side* has been compiled by Mr. Henry Thomas Crofton (Manch. 1903). The topography of the township and its immediate surroundings is minutely described, and accounts are given of houses, residents, and incidents occurring in its story.

[2] The north-east portion was joined to the Rusholme Local Board district in 1856 ; the remainder became Moss Side Local Board district.
[3] It was the property of Samuel Brooks, the Manchester banker, who so named it because he was born at Whalley.
[4] 19 & 20 Vict. cap. 26.
[5] It contains special collections relating to Mrs. Gaskell and de Quincey.
[6] See the account of Rusholme.
[7] Duchy of Lanc. Inq. p.m. xii, 4. A similar statement was made in 1598 ; ibid. xvii, 27. From this it would seem that Withenshaw lay on both sides of the Cornbrook.
In 1542 John Birch complained that Robert Hunt and a number of others had taken his beasts at Moss Side in a place called Moss Green ; he stated that Edmund Prestwich, who held six messuages and 200 acres of land in Withenshaw, had common of pasture in Moss Green and in 1540 demised a messuage and land to the plaintiff, who thereupon placed his beasts

SALFORD

RUSHOLME

Russum, 1235 ; Russhum, 1420 ; Rysshulme, 1551; Risholme, 1568.

This township has an area of 974 acres. It is crossed by the Gore, or Rushbrook, the portion to the north of which has now become urban in character, being a residential suburb of Manchester ; part of it, known as Victoria Park, was laid out by a company formed in 1837. On the brook, in the centre of the township, is the district called Birch ; to the west lies Platt, and to the east Slade. The Heald in the north-west is part of a district of the name stretching west into Moss Side. In 1901 the population was counted with Ardwick.

The principal road is that from Manchester through Withington into Cheshire, on the western side of the township. On the eastern border is the ancient road from Manchester to Stockport. There are numerous streets and cross-roads. The Great Central Company's railway crosses the southern end of the township.

A hoard of Roman coins, A.D. 253–73, was found at Birch.[1]

The Green was near the centre of the township, touching Dickenson Road.[2]

A Local Board was formed for Rusholme in 1851;[3] the boundaries were afterwards altered,[4] and the district was taken into the city of Manchester in 1885. The township ceased to have a separate existence in 1896, becoming part of the new township of South Manchester.

A Public Hall and Library was built in 1860 ;

[1] Lancs. Archaeol. Surv. 7.

[2] Manch. Guard. N. and Q. no. 763.

[3] Lond. Gaz. 18 Feb. 1851.

[4] 19 & 20 Vict. cap. 26 ; 45 & 46 Vict. cap. 72. The district was extended to include the detached portion of Moss Side on the north-east corner, and that part of Withington known as Fallowfield.

[5] The land formerly belonged to the Entwisles of Rusholme House, as their residence was called. It had been purchased from the Traffords and the Lloyds. It was acquired in 1888 by the Whitworth legatees, afterwards added to the Whitworth Institute, and in 1904 presented to the corporation of Manchester ; H. T. Crofton, Old Moss Side, 7.

[6] Among the Birch charters are a number which show that one Henry de Rusholme, who lived in the time of Hen. III, owned a large part of the later township. Possibly he had no heirs, and so the lands reverted to the lord of Withington. A number of the charters referred to are printed in full in Booker's Birch Chap. (Chet. Soc.), 183, &c., and abstracts are preserved in Harl. MS. 2112, fols. 178b, &c. Henry de Rusholme granted to Geoffrey son of Luke de Manchester various parcels of land ' within the bounds of Rusholme,' including a messuage by the Out Lane, an acre touching the Menegate, a half-acre touching Gooselache, a selion called the Quickhedge land stretching from Gooselache to the Menegate, 6 acres next Hugh de Haslum's land and stretching from Gooselache to the old ditch, and other lands, the rent being a pair of white gloves ; Booker, op. cit. 183. He further gave Geoffrey his right in 20 acres held by Robert de Hulton ; and released to his lord, Matthew de Haversage, all his own claim to the hom-

age and service of the said Geoffrey son of Luke de Manchester ; ibid. 184.

The Manchester family appear again in grants to Jordan son of William de Fallowfield ; ibid. 185, 186, 231.

[7] See the notices of the Swineshead land and '40 acres' in Gorton.

[8] Booker, op. cit. 189 ; the Worsley charters relating to Platt occupy 189–223. The bounds of the grant were : From the Great Ditch to the lower end of the Little Ditch, up to the cross-marked tree, thence to Gooselache, and so to the path 'Eite' (? Out Lane) between Platt and Rusholme, by this path to Gorebrook as far as the mere (mara) of William de Handforth, and so to the Great Ditch. The land is named among the Hospitallers' estates in 1292 ; Plac. de Quo War. (Rec. Com.), 375.

[9] Booker, op. cit. 189 ; Richard de More was probably identical with the tenant of the Swineshead land in Gorton, which descended to the Strangeways family. This family appear in Rusholme as attesting charters.

[10] Ibid. 190.

[11] Ibid. 191 ; Adam the Clerk had formerly held it. In addition to the rent of 4s. there had to be paid at the death of each holder an 'obit' of the third part of the goods and chattels of the deceased.

[12] A genealogical note dated 1418, on the back of the third deed quoted (Booker, op. cit. 191), was perhaps intended to show the subdivisions. Roger del Platt, son of Cecily, in 1289 granted to Ellen daughter of Henry del Platt (perhaps a half-sister) 2 acres stretching from Thornyditch to Gooselache ; ibid. 192. The Prior of the Hospitallers in 1332 made a claim for services against Robert del Platt ; De Banco R. 292, m. 354 d.

session of the descendants of the grantee, who assumed the name of Platt[13] and retained it, paying the rent of 4s. until 1625. It was then sold to Ralph Worsley,[14] whose descendants and their legatees long retained the estate.[15]

The most prominent member of the family was Major General Charles Worsley, a sincere Puritan, who took an

WORSLEY of Platt.
Argent on a chief gules a mural crown or.

active part in affairs on the Parliamentary side,[16] and had the doubtful honour of dispersing the remnant of the Long Parliament by force in 1653 and taking charge of the 'bauble' which Cromwell ordered to be removed.[17] He was also engaged in the government of Lancashire,[18] confiscating the property of Royalists, filling the gaols with 'Papists,'[19] suppressing horse-races, and otherwise promoting the public good according to his light. Worn out with his labours, he died in June 1656, at the early age of thirty-five.[20] The estate was until recently owned by Mr. Nicholas Tindal-Carill-Worsley, who married

---

[13] The deeds printed by Booker enable the pedigree to be made out fairly well. In 1314 William son of Hugh de Laghokes released to Robert son of Richard de *Farnworth* all his claim to the moiety of Platt ; Booker, op. cit. 192. Laghok, or Laffog, in Parr, also belonged to the Hospitallers. Ten years later Roger del Platt (of the other moiety) agreed with Robert son of Richard del *Platt* as to the division of certain pasture lying between Roger's door and the Geldbrook ; ibid. 193. The above-named Ellen daughter of Henry del Platt in 1343–4 sold her land to the second Platt family ; ibid. 194–7. The remainders were to Richard and John sons of Robert del Platt.

Certain suits between members of the different Platt families may here be noticed. Margery widow of Adam de Farnworth in 1290 appeared against Robert son of Richard de Platt and Geoffrey de Platt for dower in two messuages and 40 acres in Withington ; and against Agnes widow of Richard de Platt for dower in a messuage and 15 acres ; De Banco R. 82, m. 42. Roger del Platt was a plaintiff in 1295 ; ibid. R. 110, m. 12 d. ; 113, m. 137 d.

In 1298 Cecily widow of Henry del Platt claimed 2 acres against Geoffrey del Platt ; ibid. R. 122, m. 195 d. In 1301 Robert del Platt did not prosecute his suit against Robert son of Richard de Faryngworth [Farnworth] ; Assize R. 1321, m. 10. In the same year Ellen daughter of Henry del Platt failed in a claim for a messuage and land in Withington, formerly Geoffrey's, against Cecily del Platt, Roger her son, Agnes de Mascy, and Robert her son ; the plaintiff was excused because she was under age ; ibid. m. 12 d. Geoffrey del Platt did not prosecute his claim against Cecily del Platt, widow of Henry ; Assize R. 419, m. 13. Robert del Platt was in the following year fined for a false claim against Roger son of Henry de 'Bradlow' ; Assize R. 418, m. 3 d. In 1307 he claimed a messuage and land against Adam son of Henry de 'Barlow' ; De Banco R. 164, m. 233 d. ; 171, m. 18.

In 1324 Roger del Platt claimed a messuage and various lands in Withington against Richard de Holland, Hugh de Cheadle, Thomas de Mascy, Robert del Platt, Edith widow of Henry del Platt, Ellen her daughter, and William de Booth. It appeared that the plaintiff had leased the land to John de Byron, and that Hugh and Thomas had wrongfully obtained possession and granted to Richard de Holland, whose possessions were seized by the king for his adherence to Thomas Earl of Lancaster ; Assize R. 426, m. 8 ; 1404, m. 25. It will be seen that there were two men named Henry del Platt. According to the genealogical note above referred to, one of them was son of Geof-

frey del Platt, and married Alexander d Henry was father o

The L ghok fam 1341, cla m ng ag De B nc R 328, following year Will Laghok claimed a land against Rober Farnworth ; ibid. R also R. 335, m

Richard del Plat of a sault by W lli del Booth, who had ibid. R. 344, m. 3 Two ye rs later Ell del Pla cov r in Withington aga d l Booth and Rob Trafford ; Assize R. the same time Will suits against Robert and John his sons and lands in With have had ome succ

,
;

SALFORD

Elizabeth the daughter and heir of Charles Carill-Worsley, and assumed her surname.[21]   Platt Hall and estate is now the property of the Manchester Corporation.

The Hall is a large plain brick house built about the year 1764[22] by John Carill Worsley, in place of the old timber and plaster building which stood not very far away on a site comprised within the area of the present garden.   In an inventory of the contents of the old house taken in 1669, the following rooms and places are mentioned : 'The hall, the great parlor, the buttery, the milk-house, the woman's parlor, the little parlor, the brewhouse, the kitchen

PLATT HALL, RUSHOLME

the name of Carill Worsley.   Deborah had no children by him, and adopted her husband's son by a previous marriage, Thomas Carill Worsley.   This Thomas accordingly came into possession of Platt, and on his death in 1808 was followed by his eldest son Thomas, who died in 1848, and then by his second son Charles.

[21] Burke, *Landed Gentry.*

[22] John Carill Worsley rebuilt 'the old mansion of the Worsleys with brick and stone ornaments in a very handsome style about thirty-five years ago, at the expense, as was then said, of £10,000'; *Gent. Mag.* lxix, 434, May 1799.

[23] Some of the Birch family deeds are printed in Booker's *Birch,* 183, 187, 223 ; others may be seen in Harl. MS. 2112, fol. 142*b*/178*b*, &c.

[24] Booker, *Birch,* 223 ; the date is about 1260.   The next member of the family who appears in the records is Alexander de Birches, who with his wife

the French wars of the 15th century,[25] but its most noteworthy member was Colonel Thomas Birch,[26] a Puritan and Parliamentarian of a somewhat brutal type,[27] who took an active part in the Civil War in Lancashire. He was made Governor of Liverpool on the recapture of the town in 1644, and represented it in Parliament from 1649 to 1658.[28] On the Restoration he retired into private life,[29] and was in 1678 succeeded by his son Thomas Birch the antiquary.[30] Thomas's son died without issue, and his brother, Dr. Peter Birch, a prebendary of Westminster, came into possession.[31] He died in 1710, and his son Humphrey, who took the surname of Wyrley, sold Birch in 1743 to George Croxton of Manchester; by him it was transferred two years later to John Dickenson, another Manchester merchant, who gained some wider notoriety for becoming the host of Prince Charles Edward during his stay in the town.[32] His great-granddaughter Louisa Frances Mary Dickenson, who died in 1837, carried the Birch estate to her husband General Sir William Anson, bart.; it has remained in the possession of their descendants.

BIRCH of Birch. Azure three fleurs de lis argent.

Birch Hall stands· in a pleasant situation to the east of the church, well protected on three sides by trees, and overlooking Birch Fields on the north. The original site would seem to have been determined by a small brook, which still forms the boundary of the grounds of the hall on the south side.[32a] The house was originally a timber and plaster building of considerable extent, to judge from the list of rooms mentioned in an inventory taken in 1678,[33] but the only portion now remaining has been so much modernized and added to that it presents little or nothing of its former appear-

ance. It consists of two wings at right angles facing north and west, the latter of which appears to be part of a 17th-century building. A good deal of the timber construction of the outer walls, and the old roof, still remains, though the walls have been much restored and filled in with brickwork at a later time and new windows inserted. The west elevation and the end gable facing north, however, retain something of their old black and white appearance, though the gable has been mutilated by later work, and portion of the 'half-timber' framing is only plaster and paint. The north wing is of brick with stone quoins, and is probably a rebuilding of a former timber structure. In front of this, at a later time, most likely at the beginning of the 19th century, a new brick front, consisting of two rooms and entrance, has been added, projecting considerably in front of the north wing, and altogether altering the appearance of the house. The building is of two stories with grey stone slated roofs, and all the brickwork is painted yellow. In the west wing are three upper rooms with good 17th-century oak wainscot, but the panelling is not all in its original position, and in one room is painted over. There is a small oak stair to an attic, and one or two old windows remain with diamond quarries. There are portions of 17th-century woodwork in different parts of the house, the fittings of the old building no doubt being treated with little respect in the later alterations. These have been so effective that nothing very definite can be stated as to the original plan or arrangement of the house. There are brick outbuildings on the south side at the end of the west wing.

SLADE, anciently Milkwall Slade, was a composite estate, partly in Rusholme and partly in Gorton,[34] but the mansion-house was in the former district. From about the middle of the 13th century until the reign of Elizabeth it was the property of a branch of the family of Manchester, who adopted the local surname.[35] It was then sold to the Siddalls,[36] Manchester

ter; Booker, op. cit. 72. The will of George Birch, dated 1532, is printed ibid. 74–6. Thomas Birch, his son and heir, in 1548 agreed to marry Elizabeth daughter of Thomas Chetham of Nuthurst, deceased; ibid. 77. In 1551 Thomas Birch bought messuages, &c., in Rusholme from William son and heir apparent of Philip Strangeways; they were held by Robert Davenport and Katherine his wife, for the latter's lifetime; Pal. of Lanc. Feet of F. bdle. 14, m. 226. Thomas's younger son, William Birch, a Protestant divine, was warden of Manchester for a short time. Thomas, who made a settlement of his estate in 1571, died in 1595; Booker, Birch, 78, his will being printed 78–80.

George Birch, the son and heir of Thomas, died at Withington on 31 Jan. 1601–2, holding two messuages called Birch Hall, and other lands, &c., in Birch and Rusholme of Rowland Mosley as of his manor of Withington in socage by a rent of 4s. 2d.; also messuages in Manchester of Sir Nicholas Mosley by the fiftieth part of a knight's fee and a rent of 12d.; Duchy of Lanc. Inq. p.m. xviii, 3. By his marriage with Anne daughter and heir of John Bamford he added considerably to the family estates; she survived him. George, the son and heir, was nineteen years of age at his father's death. He died in 1611, leaving a son

people, whose descendants retain it to the present time. Edward Siddall, who died in 1588, held the capital messuage called Milkwall Slade, with 24 acres in Rusholme and Withington and 20 acres in Gorton, also a burgage in Manchester and a third part of the manor of Kersal in Broughton. The Rusholme part of Slade was held of Nicholas Longford by a rent of 2s. 6d. and the Gorton part of John Lacy then lord of Manchester.[17]

Slade Hall is a timber house on a low stone base built at the end of the 16th century, and still preserving its ancient front. It is of two stories, the upper one projecting on a plaster cove, and has two gables on the principal elevation facing east. The front has been extended northward by an addition, built about 1681, the end of which faces the road, and is now painted to imitate half-timber work. The north end of the house was formerly continued eastward as a projecting wing, but the buildings, which were of brick, and two stories in height, have been pulled down in recent times. The present front of

SLADE HALL : EAST FRONT

the 17th-century addition was rebuilt after the demolition of these buildings in a style harmonizing with the original timber elevation. The length of the principal front is now about 70 ft., but the original building consists only of the middle portion under the two gables and the wing to the south. These stand on three different planes, the main gable being 18 ft. in front of the southern end of the house, and the porch and staircase bay occupying the angle between them. The timber front is composed princi-

&c. in Withington was made by Ralph Slade ; Pal. of Lanc. Feet of F. bdle. 27, m. 24. In 1580 Edward Siddall purchased a messuage, &c. from Thomas Slade, and four years later again from Ralph Slade, Joan his wife, and Thomas his son, this being the final conveyance ; ibid. bdles. 42, m. 6 ; 46, m. 78 ; Booker, op. cit. 128. Edward Siddall had, in 1568, purchased half an acre in Rusholme and Withington from Ralph Aldcroft and William Hardy ; Pal. of Lanc. Feet of F. bdle. 30, m. 44.

Elizabeth. The frieze on the opposite wall has a representation of a stag hunt with a tree in the centre bearing the Stanley crest of the eagle and child. There was formerly a moulded plaster ceiling in this room, but it has been removed.

HOLT, described sometimes as in Withington and sometimes as in Rusholme, seems to have been on the north-east side of the township, and may perhaps be the detached portion of Moss Side.[38] Henry de Rusholme, about 1260, made a grant to Hugh de Haslum, including half an oxgang of land in Rusholme and the Holt, at a rent of 6d.[39] In the 15th century the Holt was in the hands of the Bamfords of Bamford,[40] and descended to John Bamford, who died in 1557 holding the capital messuage called Holt Hall in Rusholme of Nicholas Longford in socage by a rent of 12d.[41] The change of tenure may imply an escheat and re-grant. Anne Bamford, the daughter and heiress, married George Birch of Birch,[42] and Holt has since descended with Birch in the manner above described.

The family of Edge of Birch Hall-houses appears in the 17th century.[43] Captain Oliver Edge, an officer in the Parliamentary army, comes into notice as the captor of the Earl of Derby in his flight after the battle of Worcester. The place of capture was a little south of Nantwich. The earl writes : 'Lord Lauderdale and I, having escaped, hired horses and falling into the enemy's hands were not thought worth killing, but have quarters given us by Captain Edge, a Lancashire man, and one that was so civil to me that I and all that love me are beholden to him.'[44]

The Traffords had land in Rusholme from an early date.[45]

The land tax returns of 1787 show that the land was much divided ; the principal owners then were John Dickenson and John Carill Worsley, who between them owned about half ; William Egerton and John Gartside had smaller estates.[46] The landowners in 1844 numbered a hundred and twenty, of whom

Sir J. W. H. Anson, T. Carill Worsley, and John Siddall represented the ancient owners of Birch, Platt, and Slade; Richard Cobden owned 21 acres.[47]

CHURCH The chapel of Birch, known as St. James's, is supposed to have been built about 1580 by the Birch family.[48] The minister was paid by the scanty and precarious offerings of the people, until in 1640 an attempt was made to establish an endowment fund.[49] Land was purchased, which Colonel Thomas Birch in 1658 settled upon his son Thomas as sole trustee, to the use of 'an orthodox preaching minister of the Gospel, to be constantly resident,' and to perform divine service in the chapel. The neighbours objecting to having a single trustee, a new trust was created in 1672, the income of the land being placed at the disposal of a majority of the trustees. This was probably done with the design of preparing the way for a Presbyterian minister as soon as the persecution of Nonconformists should come to an end.[50] The chapel in fact remained in the hands of the Presbyterians until 1697, when, on the death of Colonel Birch's widow, George Birch seems to have allowed the claims of the Bishop of Chester and other ecclesiastical authorities, and the Presbyterian minister, Henry Finch, was ejected.[51] After two years a Conformist curate was nominated by George Birch, in whose family the patronage seems always to have vested, and the succession remains unbroken to the present. In 1708 the endowment was still only £3 10s. a year, and the contributions of the congregation were about £16 ;[52] but the Dickenson family and others have provided more adequate endowments.[53] The chapel was rebuilt in 1845–6,[54] and a district was assigned to it in 1839.[55] The present patron is Sir W. R. Anson.

The following have been curates and rectors :—[56]

1699 Samuel Taylor, M.A.[57] (Emmanuel College, Camb.)

[38] See the bounds of Greenlow Heath as given in the account of Chorlton-upon-Medlock.

[39] Booker, op. cit. 184.

[40] Ibid. *Didsbury* (Chet. Soc.), 114–20. The Bamford family are several times described as 'of Holt.'

[41] Inq. p.m. printed ibid. 117.

[42] *Lancs. Inq. p.m.* (Rec. Soc. Lancs. and Ches.), ii, 178 ; the capital messuage called Holt Hall and its lands are stated to be 'in Withington,' though the 1557 inquisition described them as 'in Rusholme.'

[43] Booker, *Birch*, 10–12.

[44] *Civil War Tracts*, 311, quoting Seacome.

[45] Richard de Trafford in 1235 released to Robert de Hulton his right in common of pasture in Rusholme in the land between a ditch of Robert's and land formerly held by Hugh de Haslum ; *Final Conc.* i, 65. Matthew the Tailor of Manchester in 1316 gave to Nicholas son of Henry de Trafford all his lands, &c. in Rusholme in the vill of Withington, with various remainders ; De Trafford D. no. 135. The grants in Gildhouses (or Healdhouses) recorded in the account of Withington were perhaps in part or in whole in Rusholme. Lands in Rusholme are named in the later Trafford inquisitions as part of their estate in Withington. Sir Edmund Trafford in 1587 leased to one Anthony Scholefield a messuage and

1707 No curate
1717 Joseph Dale [58]
1720 Thomas Wright, B.A.[59] (Brasenose College, Oxf.)
1721 John Tetlow, B.A.[60]
1742 John Leech, B.A. (St. Catharine's Hall, Camb.)
oc. 1746 Robert Twyford, B.A.[61] (Brasenose College, Oxf.)
1746 William Twyford, B.A.[62] (St. John's College, Camb.)
1752 Thomas Ainscough, M.A.[63] (St. John's College, Camb.)
1762 Miles Lonsdale, M.A.[64] (Brasenose College, Oxf.)
1769 Henry Ainsworth
1795 Rowland Blayney, B.A. (St. Alban Hall, Oxf.)
1838 Francis Philips Hulme, B.A. (St. Alban Hall, Oxf.)
1839 George Gardner Harter, M.A.[65] (Trinity College, Oxf.)
1840 Oliver Ormerod, M.A.[66] (Brasenose College, Oxf.)
1841 George Dugard, M.A.[67] (St. John's College, Camb.)
1846 George Henry Greville Anson, M.A.[68] (Exeter College, Oxf.)
1898 Frederick George Buller, M.A.[69] (Trinity College, Oxf.)

Holy Trinity Church was consecrated in 1846 ; the patron is Mrs. N. Tindal-Carill-Worsley.[70] St. John's, Longsight, was consecrated in the same year ; the patronage is vested in trustees.[71] St. Chrysostom's, Victoria Park, was first consecrated in 1877,[72] and St. Agnes's in 1885 ; the Bishop of Manchester is patron of both. There is a chapel at St. Mary's Home.

An 'English School,' not free, existed at Birch about 1720.[73]

The Wesleyan Methodists, Primitive Methodists, and United Free Methodists have churches, and the last-named denomination has a theological college in Victoria Park. The Congregationalists began services in 1839, and a small chapel built by Baptists was acquired in 1853. After many vicissitudes the present church was built in 1864.[74] The Baptists have a college for students for the ministry,[75] with a chapel attached ; they have another church at Longsight.

On the ejection of Henry Finch from Birch Chapel he continued to minister in the neighbourhood, and in 1700 Platt Chapel was opened for the use of the

LEVENSHULME

Lewenesholm, 1361.

This township is bounded on the north by Nico Ditch, on the east by Pinkbank Lane,[1] and on the south by the Black Brook. The surface is level, sloping down a little towards the west. The area measures 605¼ acres.[2] A house called the Manor House stands near the northern border. There was a population of 11,485 in 1901.

The Stockport Road from Manchester crosses the township in a southerly and south-easterly direction. Adlands Lane and Barlow Lane go eastward through the centre, passing through the hamlet of Back Levenshulme, to the south of which lies Cradock Fold. The London and North-Western Company's railway from Manchester to London passes through the western side of the township, having a station named Levenshulme and Burnage about the centre. The Great Central Company's line from London Road to Central Station, Manchester, crosses the other railway near the southern border, where there is a station called Levenshulme.

The western half of the township has become a residential suburb of Manchester ; the eastern half has print works, bleach works, dye works, and mattress works, also several farms.

A local board was formed in 1865 ;[3] this afterwards became an urban district council of twelve members, but they have recently agreed to incorporation with Manchester. A Carnegie free library was opened in 1904.

John Ellor Taylor, a native of the township, 1837–95, has a place in the *Dictionary of National Biography.*

MANOR The manor of *LEVENSHULME,* a dependency of Withington, was in 1319 in the possession of Sir William de Baguley of Baguley in Cheshire, and by a settlement made in that year it passed to his grandson William Legh of Baguley,[4]

[58] Also of Chorlton Chapel.
[59] Ibid.
[60] Brother-in-law of the patron.
[61] Also curate of Didsbury.
[62] Son of the preceding and curate of Didsbury for a time.
[63] Became one of the fellows of the Collegiate Church ; Raines, *Fellows* (Chet. Soc.), 268.
[64] Afterwards rector of Gawsworth.
[65] He and his two successors were under bond to resign in favour of the patron's grandson.
[66] Afterwards rector of Presteign.
[67] Librarian of the Chetham Library 1834–7 ; incumbent of Barnard Castle, 1847.
[68] Archdeacon of Manchester 1870–90.
[69] Brother-in-law of the patron.

[70] Booker, *Birch,* 159.
[71] Ibid. The district assigned in 1851 was reconstituted in 1854 ; *Lond. Gaz.* 16 June.
[72] For district see *Lond. Gaz.* 21 May 1878. It was rebuilt a few years ago after a fire.
[73] Gastrell, *Notitia,* ii, 80.
[74] Nightingale, *Lancs. Nonconf.* v, 162–5.
[75] It was founded at Chamber Hall near Bury in 1860 and removed to Rusholme in 1874.
[76] Booker, op. cit. 160–70. A plan of the chapel in 1700 is printed on p. 165. See also Nightingale, op. cit. v, 147–58 ; it is stated that 'no doctrinal test is applied either to minister or congregation.'
[1] Pink Pank Lane was the older form of the name ; it was also called the

Old London Road ; see Booker, *Birch Chapel* (Chet. Soc.), 173.
[2] 606 acres, including 7 of inland water ; *Census Rep.* 1901.
[3] *Lond. Gaz.* 2 May 1865.
[4] By the settlement named Sir William de Baguley and his son John arranged that in default of other issue the estate was to go in succession to William, John, and Geoffrey sons of Sir John de Legh of the Booths in Knutsford ; Sir John had married Isabel (or Ellen) daughter of Sir William. On John de Baguley's death William de Legh succeeded accordingly ; Ormerod, *Ches.* (ed. Helsby), i, 550, where an account of the family of Legh of Baguley is given. The date of the deed as given by Sir Peter Leycester appears doubtful in view of the other dates—e.g.

whose descendants continued to hold it down to the 17th century,[4] when the land seems to have been sold

BAGULEY of Baguley.
Or three lozenges azure.

LEGH of Baguley.
Azure two bars argent, over all a bend gules.

to a number of different owners, the manor ceasing to exist.

The township has left scarcely any trace in the records.[5]

The principal owners in 1787 were Edward Greaves of Culcheth in Newton and John Carill-Worsley of Platt, but together they contributed only a sixth part of the land tax.[7] In 1844 there were forty-nine landowners, the chief being Samuel Grimshaw, owning a tenth.[8]

In connexion with the Established Church, St. Peter's was built in 1860 near the centre of the township;[9] the patronage is vested in five trustees. Two new districts, St. Andrew's and St. Mark's, have been defined, but churches have not been built; the patronage is vested in the Crown and the Bishop of Manchester alternately.

The Wesleyans long had a place of worship.[10] The Primitive Methodists, United Free Methodists, and the Congregationalists have churches.

A convent of Poor Clares stands in Alma Park in the south-west corner; the chapel of St. Mary of the Angels and St. Clare was opened in 1853.[11]

A school was built in 1754, but the scheme appears to have failed.[12]

that William de Legh was under age in 1359.

John Savage and Margery his wife in 1359 claimed twenty messuages, &c., in Withington against William son of Sir John de Legh; Duchy of Lanc. Assize R. 7, m. 4 d.

[5] William de Legh of Baguley, who died in Dec. 1435, held ten messuages, 200 acres of land, 40 acres of meadow, and 4 acres of waste in Levenshulme in Withington son and heir of Nicholas Sir Ralph de Longford, by homage, fealty, escuage, and a rent of 4s.; it was recorded that Thomas de Legh, father of William, had done his homage for the lands, &c., to Sir Nicholas de Longford, father of Sir Ralph. The estate was worth 20 marks a year; Edmund, the son and heir of William, was one year old; Towneley MS. DD, no. 1482.

Sir John Legh, son of Edmund, in 1505 settled a tenement in Levenshulme on his illegitimate son John for life; Ormerod, *Ches.* i, 552.

In 1566 Edward Legh made a settlement of the manor of Levenshulme and thirty messuages, lands, &c., there and in Withington; Pal. of Lanc. Feet of F. bdle. 28, m. 263. Ten years later he appears to have made a settlement or mortgage of a portion of the estate; ibid. bdle. 38, m. 15. Shortly afterwards Margaret Vaudrey, claiming by conveyance from Edward Legh, had a dispute with the lessees of William Radcliffe concerning lands in Levenshulme; there were some later suits; *Ducatus Lanc.* (Rec. Com.), iii, 60, 86, 170, 230 (1577 to 1588). She was probably the Margaret daughter of Robert Vawdrey whose 'dis-

honest and unclean living' was censured by her father in his will; Piccope, *Wills* (Chet. Soc.), ii, 84.

Richard Legh, son and heir of Gerard Legh of Baguley, and others in 1604 granted a lease of lands to Thomas Holme of Heaton Norris; note by Mr. E. Axon (quoting T. Holme's will).

The manor and lands were in 1619 in possession of John Gobart (of Coventry) and Lucy his wife; Pal. of Lanc. Feet of F. bdle 95, no. 70. They left three daughters and co-heirs—Frances wife of Sir Thomas Barrington; Anne wife of Thomas Legh of Adlington; and Lucy wife of Calcot Chambrie; *Visit. of Warw.* (Harl. Soc.), 293; Earwaker, *East Ches.* ii, 252.

[6] Levenshulme is named as a dependency of Withington in 1322; *Mamecestre* (Chet. Soc.), ii, 374.

In 1361 Richard son of William de Radcliffe did not prosecute a claim against Sir John de Hyde of Norbury regarding tenements in Levenshulme, Haughton, and Lightshaw; Assize R. 441, m. 1 d. 5. Sir John de Hyde appears to have been the son of Isabel sister and co-heir of John de Baguley (who died in 1356); see Ormerod, *Ches.* iii, 810.

[7] Records at Preston. The Greaves family here as elsewhere succeeded to the estate of the Gilliams, who were at first described as of Levenshulme; Booker, *Didsbury*, 232.

[8] Ibid. 233. The incumbent of Gorton Chapel had 26 acres, purchased in 1734 by a grant from Queen Anne's Bounty augmented by subscription. This land had in 1620 been conveyed by Richard Legh of Baguley and Henry, his son and

36 acres more; these 136 acres, it was considered, might be taken by the lord of Manchester and approved by him, provided enough pasture for the commoners were reserved.[7] Some compromise was no doubt made; the Byrons do not appear again, and John La Warre and Joan his wife afterwards granted to Thomas son of Henry de Trafford 100 acres of moor and pasture in Heaton and Withington, 'namely, that moiety of the place called Burnage lying next to Heaton, which moiety remained to the said John and Joan after a partition of the whole place made between them and Sir Richard de Longford.'[8]

The Longford moiety passed, like Withington, to the Mosleys[9] and Egertons; the Trafford moiety seems to have been sold to a number of small holders. In 1798 William Egerton was the principal contributor to the land tax, paying over a third;[10] and in 1844 Wilbraham Egerton owned about half[11] the land.

Burnage was a township in 1655.[12]

In connexion with the Established Church, St. Margaret's was consecrated in 1875; the Bishop of Manchester is the patron.[13] A temporary district of St. Chad has recently been created at Lady Barn; the patronage is vested in the Crown and the Bishop of Manchester alternately.

The Wesleyan Methodists have a chapel at Lady Barn. The Congregationalists also are represented.

DENTON

Dentun, c. 1220; Denton, 1282, and usually.

This township, lying in the bend of the River Tame, which bounds it on the south, has an area of 1,706 acres, being nearly 2 miles square. It was sometimes called Denton under Donishaw. The highest land, reaching 340 ft., is on the eastern border, dividing Denton from Haughton. The population of the two townships, Denton and Haughton, together numbered 14,934 in 1901.

The principal road is that crossing the township from west to east, leading from Manchester to Hyde and passing through the village of Denton. Crossing it, on and near the eastern border, is the road leading south from Ashton to Stockport, with a bridge over the Tame. The London and North-Western Company's railway from Stockport to Ashton runs through the north-western half of the township, and has a station, called Denton, on the Hyde Road. Part of the Audenshaw reservoir lies in this township.

The place has long been celebrated for its hat manufacture. The trade, after a period of decline has revived.[1] A coal mine is worked.

The village wake used to be held on 10 August.

A local board was formed in 1857.[2] This has become an urban district council of fifteen members. The district includes Haughton also. There is a public library

---

[7] *Mamecestre* ii, 283-4. If the land should be recovered by the lord of Manchester its value would be 34s. (or 3d. an acre) annually.

[8] Charter printed by Booker, op. cit. 173; the grant was made in exchange for 30 acres of pasture in Barton. A rent of 70s. was payable, and 20 acres of other land seem to have been added.

[9] See the will of Sir Nicholas Mosley, ibid. 134.

[10] Returns at Preston.

[11] Booker, op. cit. 175.

[12] Ibid. 174.

[13] A school, used for service, was built about 1857; Booker, *Didsbury*, 176. For the district assigned see *Lond. Gaz.* 29 Oct. 1875.

[1] Booker, *Denton* (Chet. Soc.), 9-13; the trade was almost ruined about 1850 owing to the prevalence of the silk hat, which the Denton hatters had not adopted, and to strikes. A few years later the introduction of new forms of the felt hat led to a revival.

[2] *Lond. Gaz.* 24 Mar. 1857.

[3] Some uncertainty must exist until it can be determined whether or not the two oxgangs of land in Haughton were part of the eight in Denton.

[4] After Withington had been acquired by the lords of Manchester, Denton was reckoned a hamlet of Manchester; e.g. Towneley MS. DD, no. 1511.

[5] Lord Wilton's D. The land was to be held of Matthew de Reddish and his heirs; the first witness was Matthew son of William de Withington.

[6] Ibid. The two oxgangs of land were held of Robert de Reddish; they were occupied separately, one by Jordan, brother of the grantor, who had Richard son of Robert de Hyde as an under-tenant.

[7] Ibid. The date is about 1280. There was a remainder to Geoffrey, brother of William. [8] Ibid.

[9] Ibid. In 1306 William le Norreys of Heaton granted to Alexander, his brother according to the flesh, all the right of succession he might have to land in Denton; and in 1308-9 gave all the lands, &c., in his possession in Denton, 'which is in the fee of Withington,' while another deed of the same year calls the grantee Alexander de Shoresworth. Ro-

manor, being part of their gifts.[11] Thurstan seems to have acquired another fourth part from the heirs of the Moston family.[12] He was living as late as 1376,[13] and his son and heir Richard,[14] who added to his patrimony by a marriage with Amery daughter and heir of Adam de Kenyon,[15] died in 1402 holding 'the manor of Denton' of Sir Nicholas de Longford by knight's service; he also held the manor of Kenyon in right of his wife, a moiety of the manor of Heaton Fallowfield, and land called Mateshead in Claughton in Amounderness.[15a] Thurstan his son and heir was over thirty years of age.[16]

Thurstan,[17] whose widow Agnes was living in 1430 and 1438,[18] left a son of the same name. The younger Thurstan was in 1430 divorced from his first wife, Margaret de Abram,[19] and lived on till about 1461,[20] his widow Ellen being named in 1462.[21] Richard the son and heir held the manors of Denton and Kenyon, and messuages and lands in Heaton, Bolton le Moors, Wardley, Barton, Manchester, Pemberton, and Myerscough. In 1481 he settled part of his lands on himself and Agnes his wife, with life remainders to younger sons. His eldest son Richard succeeded him in 1483, and in 1486 made

provision for Joan daughter of John Arderne, who was to marry his son Thurstan. In the following year and in 1497 he made provision for younger sons, and in 1499 granted messuages and lands in Bolton and Myerscough to his son Thurstan and Joan his wife. Richard Holland was living in 1500, but seems to have died soon afterwards.[22]

Thurstan Holland succeeded, but died in October 1508, leaving a son Robert, who though then but nineteen years of age had in 1500–1 been married to Elizabeth daughter of Sir Richard Assheton of Middleton. The manor of Denton was described as held of Sir Ralph Longford

HOLLAND of Denton. *Azure semée of fleurs de lis and a lion rampant guardant argent, over all a bendlet gules.*

in socage; its clear annual value was £20.[23] Robert died in 1513, leaving his brother Richard as heir, he being twenty years of age; the manor of Denton was held by services unknown, and its value was returned as £11.[24] Richard was afterwards made a

---

[11] Margaret de Shoresworth was twice married—to Henry de Worsley and to Robert de Radcliffe, as will be seen in the accounts of Worsley and Radcliffe. Her connexion with Sir William de Holland is not clearly known; she may have been married to him invalidly. In 1330 Alexander de Shoresworth granted all his lands, &c., in Denton to Margaret daughter of Robert de Shoresworth, and she at once granted to Thurstan her son all her messuages and lands in Denton under Doneshagh in the vill of Withington, with remainders to William son of Robert de Radcliffe, to John brother of Robert, and to Robert son of Henry de Worsley; Lord Wilton's D. Five years later Thurstan regranted the same to his mother; ibid. Margaret de Shoresworth was still living in 1348, when she recovered seisin of her lands in Bolton, Manchester, Pendleton, Wardley, Barton, Myerscough, Heaton, and Denton against Thurstan son of Sir William de Holland and Richard son of Thurstan; Assize R. 1444, m. 7 d.

In 1314–15 land in Pleasington had been settled upon Sir William de Holland and Joan his wife, with remainder in default of issue to Thurstan son of Sir William; Harl. MS. 2112, fol. 158b/194b. Thurstan is described as son of Sir William in other deeds; e.g. ibid. fol. 156/192. In 1355 he was called 'our cousin' by Roger La Warre, in a demise of the park of Blackley; ibid. fol. 160b/196b.

[12] See below in the account of the Moston family.

[13] In that year the feoffee regranted him the manors of Heaton and Denton; ibid. fol. 164b/200b.

Thurstan had a pardon from the king in 1348; Cal. Pat. 1348–50, p. 145.

In 1359 the feoffees regranted to Thurstan de Holland all his messuages, lands, &c., in Denton, Heaton, Manchester, Bolton in Eccles, Barton, Bolton on the Moors, Harwood, Worsley, Myerscough, and Sharples, with homages and services of the free tenants, with remainders to Richard his son and his issue by Amery daughter of Adam de Kenyon; to Robert and John sons of Alice de Cobbeleres;

and to William son of Alice de Pussch; to William son of Robert de Radcliffe; to William son of Robert de Worsley; and to Sir Robert de Holland; ibid.

[14] Richard is named in various grants from 1344 onwards. In that year he had a general grant of Denton and his other manors and lands from his father; Harl. MS. 2112, fol. 164b/200b.

He commissioned his dear and good uncle Robert de Worsley to receive seisin of the same; ibid. fol. 154b/190b.

Richard seems to have been in possession of the manor in 1377, when an agreement was made by him with Richard son of Richard de Hyde respecting the marling of lands in Denton; Lord Wilton's D. He granted a lease of the manor to William de Hulme in 1383 at a yearly rent of 10 marks; ibid.

[15] See a preceding note, and the account of Kenyon. The writ of Diem clausit extr. after the death of Amery was issued on 19 Feb. 1421–2; Dep. Keeper's Rep. xxxiii, App. 20.

[15a] Mateshead is probably the Myerscough estate of preceding deeds.

[16] Towneley MS. DD, no. 1461.

[17] The writ of Diem clausit extr. was issued 12 Mar. 1422–3; Dep. Keeper's Rep. xxxiii, App. 24.

[18] Harl. MS. 2112, fol. 157/193, 159b/195b.

[19] Thurstan son of Richard de Holland, acting with his brothers William and Nicholas, had in 1407 made a settlement of lands in Barton and Harwood on Margaret daughter of Gilbert de Abram, on her marriage with Thurstan the son of Thurstan; ibid. fol. 157/193. The elder Thurstan in 1421 made a further grant to Margaret wife of Thurstan de Holland his son; ibid. fol. 158/194.

A divorce on account of consanguinity was pronounced by the official of the archdeacon of Chester in 1430; ibid. fol. 149b/185b. Margaret thereupon released her jointure lands to Thurstan; ibid. fol. 153b/189b. Thurstan immediately afterwards married Margaret daughter of Sir Lawrence Warren of Poynton, making a feoffment of his manor of Denton and all his lands in Denton and Withington; ibid. fol. 149b/185b; Earwaker, East

Ches. ii, 286. Margaret was his wife in 1439; Lord Wilton's D. Three years later Maud daughter of Sir John Honford was his wife; he settled lands in Denton called Brookwallhursts, Tochetcroft, &c., on her, his son Richard to make a further assurance on coming of age; ibid.

[20] In 1456–7 Thurstan and his son Richard granted two burgages in Manchester, next to the Booths and the Market stead; Harl. MS. 2112, fol. 162/198. They granted another burgage in the Millgate in 1460; ibid. fol. 161, 197.

[21] In that year she became bound to Richard Holland son and heir of Thurstan; ibid. fol. 156b/192b.

[22] These particulars are from the lengthy inquisition after the death of Thurstan Holland, 1510; Duchy of Lanc. Inq. p.m. iv, 36. Closes called Bokulhurst, Newfield, Wheatfield, and the Five Acre in Denton were in 1497 settled on Robert, a younger son. The sons named in the feoffment of 1486 were Thurstan, William, and Thomas; that in 1487 was in favour of William and Thomas.

Lands in Kenyon and Lowton were in 1461 settled on Isabel wife of Richard son of Richard Holland; Harl. MS. 2112, fol. 147b/183b. In 1468 Richard the father acknowledged that he had received 24 marks from Sir William Harrington in part payment of the marriage portion; ibid. fol. 159b/195b.

In 1486 an agreement was made as to the dower of Agnes widow of Richard Holland the elder; ibid. fol. 153b/189b. An agreement as to the bounds of their turbary on the moss called Ashton Moss and Denton Moss was in 1479 made between Sir John Ashton and Richard Holland; Lord Wilton's D.

[23] Duchy of Lanc. Inq. p.m. iv, no. 36, as above.

[24] Ibid. iv, no. 58; many of the feoffments of the previous inquisition are again recited in this. Dower in Denton, &c. was in 1514 assigned to Elizabeth widow of Robert Holland; ibid. iv, no. 52. The wardship of Richard Holland was granted to John Byron; Duchy of Lanc. Misc. Bks. xxii, 37 d.

knight.[25] He died about 1548, and in that year licence of entry, without proof of age, was granted to Edward Holland, his son and heir.[26] Edward, who was sheriff in 1567–8,[27] died in 1570, holding the family estates, probably with some increase, the manor and lands in Denton being held of Nicholas Longford in socage by a rent of 15½d.[28]

His son and heir, Richard Holland, twenty-four years of age, married Margaret one of the daughters and co-heirs of Sir Robert Langley of Agecroft, and appears to have acquired a great addition to his Heaton estates.[29] He built a house at Heaton, and resided there and at Denton.[30] The former place soon became the principal seat of the family, and there Richard Holland died on 2 March 1618–19 holding, among other estates, the manor of Denton and lands, &c., in the township of Edward Mosley in socage by a rent

DENTON HALL FROM THE NORTH-WEST

[25] One Richard Holland was knighted during the Scottish expedition of 1544, but his arms are given as 'per fesse azure and gules, three fleurs de lys'; Metcalfe, *Knights*, 77.

[26] *Dep. Keeper's Rep.* xxxix, App. 554.

[27] P.R.O. *List*, 73.

[28] Duchy of Lanc. Inq. p.m. xiii, 20. He married as his second wife Cecily, widow of Sir Robert Langley of Agecroft, and in 1562 settled on her the Hall of Heaton, with demesne lands, for her life. In 1570 he made provision for his younger sons Edward and John, and granted the capital messuage of Denton Hall with other lands to trustees for his six daughters, until the sum of 1,200 marks had been received. A pedigree was recorded in 1567; *Visit.* (Chet. Soc.), 18.

[29] See the account of Heaton in Prestwich. The additions to the estate may have been made by his father. Richard Holland was sheriff of the county in

he was rector of a mediety of Malpas from 1652 to 1680, when he resigned,[42] dying two years later. His son Edward dying unmarried in 1683 the inheritance went to a daughter Elizabeth, who married Sir John Egerton of Wrinehill, ancestor of the Earl of Wilton, the present lord of Denton.[43]

Of Denton Old Hall only a fragment remains. The original house appears to have been either quadrangular or built round three sides of a courtyard, but of this, however, only a portion of the south or centre wing containing the great hall and the smaller chamber beyond is now standing, together with a detached building, now a barn, on the east side, the timber framing of which seems to indicate that it was originally part of the eastern wing. The Hall is now used as a farmhouse, and the present farm buildings, though modern and built of brick and extending very far westward, preserve to some extent what may have been the original quadrangular aspect of the house. Denton Old Hall was one of a number of houses standing in the valley of the Tame, which here separates Lancashire from Cheshire, and stands about half a mile from the north bank. It was a timber-and-plaster building on a low stone base, built apparently in the 15th century, but has been altered from time

PLAN OF DENTON HALL

to time and faced with brick at the back and ends. The usual arrangement of the great hall, screens, and the rooms at either end could, till recently, be seen, but internal alterations and the destruction of the west wing have rendered them difficult to follow. The front of the central part of the building faced north to the courtyard, and it is a portion of this which still remains. It is a very simple design made up entirely of crosspieces and uprights, with a cove under the eaves, but without any attempt at ornamentation except in the mouldings of the beam under the cove. The timber front now standing is the north wall of the great hall less the passage at the west end. The screens and the whole of the west end of the building were taken down in 1895. This west wing slightly projected in front of the hall and was about 25 ft. in width, and probably contained the kitchen and offices, but they had been much altered on plan by the introduction of a central

through-passage from east to west. The elevation carried on the timber construction of the present front, but with more variety of treatment in its parts. The disappearance of this west wing with its long windows on each story, its overhanging gables and line of quatrefoil panelling, is very much to be regretted. At the east end of the great hall is what was probably the smaller hall, now entirely refaced in brick with a gable north and south. The roofs are covered with stone slates.

The great hall, which was 35 ft. long including the passage and 23 ft. in width, had a massive open timber roof, a canopy at the east over the dais, and a gallery at the west end over the passage. It is now divided into two stories by the introduction of a floor, but some idea of the original appearance may still be gathered by an examination of the roof principals and framing in the bedrooms. There was a square bay at the north-east corner of the hall to the left of the high table, but there seems to have originally been no provision for a fireplace. The room was presumably warmed by a brazier, the coupling of the principals in the centre pointing to there having formerly been a louvre in the roof. The height from the floor to the underside of the tie-beam was about 17 ft. 6 in., and to the ridge 26 ft. The principals are very plain and are disposed in short bays at either end, with a middle one formed by the coupling for the louvre already mentioned, making three small and two large bays in the length of the apartment. The smaller bay at the west end is over the passage, but at the east the space was taken up by the projecting canopy over the high table. The plainness of the roof was only relieved by curved wind braces. At the west end the gallery occupied the space over the passage, but the screen itself was very plain, being constructed of simple chamfered posts and crosspieces on a stone base. The high table was lighted from the bay, and there were two windows at the west end of the north side high up in the wall, one lighting the gallery, the other the hall proper. These windows formed a feature of the north elevation, standing out from the wall on a plaster cove, but only one now remains, the other having been destroyed along with the west wing. The present door in the middle of the apartment is quite modern, having been inserted since the disappearance of the entrance at the west end. There appears also to have been a door at the north-east corner of the hall, now made up, but plainly visible on the outside. From the disposition of the timber framing there does not seem to have been any range of windows on the side of the hall facing the courtyard, the window now on that side, as well as the one on the south, being a modern insertion. At a later time a large fireplace

[42] He appears to have left Malpas finally about 1676, his reasons for non-residence being printed by Booker, op. cit. 18, 19; his will is printed ibid. 21.

[43] Ibid. 20; see also the account of Heaton. 'In 1711 the Denton estate of the Hollands, as appertaining to Sir John Egerton in right of his wife, was under lease to twelve tenants, the annual rental amounting to £162 9s. 8d. Denton Hall

and the demesne was in the occupation of one William Bromiley, who paid for it a rent of £105 6s. 1d. In 1744 the tenantry numbered eighteen, and the rental had increased to £216 2s. 2d. In 1780 the same lands were held by seventeen tenants, and were subject to a rent of £294 6s. 8d. The entire property was held by lease of lives, and the above returns of rentals are exclusive of fines paid on the renewal of

leases. By the terms of their respective leases the tenants were also pledged to the payment of certain rent-boons consisting of a dog and a cock, or at the landlord's option their equivalent in money—for the dog 10s., for the cock 1s.—the landlord thus providing for his amusement in hunting and cock-fighting in a manner least onerous to himself'; ibid. 23.

13 ft. wide inside, with deep ingle nook, has been inserted at the west end, taking up more than half the width of the apartment and entirely destroying the screen and encroaching on the passage way at the back. This seems to have been done before the introduction of the floor, as the upper part of the fireplace is carried up to the roof in an elaborate brickwork composition, with embattled cornices, herringbone panels, and other ornamentation. The upper part of this chimney can still be seen from the bedrooms, but is now covered with whitewash. In the upper part of the bay window, now a bedroom, on the east wall, some of the oak panelling of the hall still remains, together with a plaster frieze on which is a shield of arms bearing Holland impaling Langley.[44] The introduction of the great fireplace and ingle nook into the hall necessitated the partial destruction of the gallery over the passage, and the whole of the original arrangement of the hall at this end suffered a good deal of change. The fireplaces in the destroyed west wing are said to have been of ornamental brickwork corresponding in style with that in the great hall. They were later than' the original arrangement of the kitchen passage, and may have been inserted as late as the beginning of the 17th century, at the time the plaster ornament in the upper part of the bay was put up.

The east end and south side of the house have been entirely rebuilt in brick, and when the west wing was pulled down that end was similarly refaced. The upper part at the east end is approached by a brick and stone staircase on the outside, but this end of the house has no points of interest in it.

In the detached east wing, which is 55 ft. long, are three principals, the tie-beams of which are moulded and ornamented with traceried panels and shields. They are unequally spaced, one being at the south end next the house, and the other two near together at the north. The principals are built from the ground, and have originally had floor beams, the building apparently having always been of two stories, but the lower beam is only retained in the principal at the south end, which on the first floor forms a fully-constructed partition with door on the east side. The other two floor beams have been cut away. The wall

posts and the underside of the lower beam are elaborately moulded, and the beam has a bracket on each side carved with a lion's head and foliage. The two tie-beams at the north end are panelled on both sides, but those at the south on the north side only, being quite plain towards the house. Originally the work has been very rich, but the present disposition of the framing and its incomplete character makes it impossible to state what purpose the wing, which on the outside is entirely refaced with brick, served. Its north gable is of timber patched with brick, with quatrefoil panels but without wing boards.

The other moiety of Matthew de Reddish's estate in Denton was probably Haughton, but may have been the two oxgangs of land which in 1320 were held by the lord of Manchester,[45] Robert de Ashton holding of him at a rent of 13s. 4½d.[46] John de Hulton of Farnworth held the same in 1473.[47] In 1282 Robert Grelley was found to have held two-thirds of an oxgang in Denton ; this land, which is not mentioned again, may have been part of these two oxgangs.[43]

Two other oxgangs of land were in 1320 held of the lord of Manchester by John de Hyde and Adam de Hulton, who rendered 2d. at Christmastide as well as puture.[49] It is not clear whether the former tenant was of Norbury or of Denton.

The Hydes of Hyde and Norbury, who were lords of Haughton by Denton, held lands in the latter township, for Robert de Hyde gave to Alexander his son and his heirs all his lands of Denton, and in confirmation and augmentation of this John de Hyde about 1270 granted all the lands in Denton which he held, also land in Romiley in Cheshire, to his brother Alexander, son of Sir Robert de Hyde.[50] The oxgang of land held in 1320, however, if it were the tenement of the Hydes of Denton immediately, seems to have been acquired in another way from Ellis de Botham.[51] By a settlement of 1331 the

HYDE of Hyde and Norbury. *Azure a cheveron between three lozenges or.*

44 Holland : 1 and 4. Azure semée of fleur de lys a lion rampant argent. 2. A cross engrailed. 3. Argent on a bend sable three lozenges of the field. Over all a bend. Langley of Agecroft : 1 and 4. Argent a cockatrice sable. 2 and 3. A mermaid with comb and mirror. The shield is identified with Richard Holland who died in 1618, having married Margaret daughter and co-heiress of Sir Robert Langley of Agecroft. The initials R. H. were formerly on one of the lights of an upper window. See Booker, op. cit. 23–6.

45 *Mamecestre,* ii, 291 ; the waste of Denton contained 200 acres (by the greater hundred), the lord of Manchester participating in virtue of two oxgangs purchased by Robert Grelley from John the Lord, who had held them of the lord of Withington. The other participators were Alexander de Shoresworth, Alexander de Denton, John de Hyde, Hugh son of Richard de Moston, and Ellis de Botham. Twenty-five acres — one-eighth — might be approved in respect of the two oxgangs.

46 Ibid. ii, 364 ; the tenant held for life.

47 Ibid. iii, 483 ; the rent was 13s. 4d. and the tenure described as socage. John Hulton died in 1487 holding ten messuages, 200 acres of land, 40 acres of meadow, and 200 acres of pasture in Denton of Sir Ralph Longford by services unknown ; Duchy of Lanc. Inq. p.m. iii, 26.

48 *Lancs. Inq. and Extents* (Rec. Soc. Lancs. and Ches.), i, 245. The two parts of an oxgang rendered 4s. 2d. yearly, or nearly the same as 13s. 4d. for two oxgangs. Robert Grelley was the purchaser of the latter, according to the extent of 1320 ; the other one and a third may have been in the lord's hands in 1282.

49 *Mamecestre,* ii, 290.

50 Hyde of Denton Charters in Harl. MS. 2112, fol. 159, 153. Robert son of John de Hyde was in 1292 non-suited in a claim against Thomas Grelley for common of pasture in Withington ; Assize R. 408, m. 29.

51 Stephen de Bredbury about 1270 granted to John the Clerk of Stockport an oxgang of land in Denton, which

lands of John de Hyde in Denton and Romiley were to remain to Richard, the son of John, and Maud his wife, daughter of Roger de Vernon.[52] Richard and Maud in 1366 agreed to make no alienation of the estate,[53] and two years later John, the father, made a grant to Richard, the son of Richard.[54] In 1320 the rent was paid to the lord of Manchester ; but William Hyde, who died in 1560, was stated to hold his messuages and lands in Denton of Robert Hyde of Norbury in socage by the rent of 1d.[55] Richard Hyde, the son and heir of William, having died a month after his father, without issue, was succeeded by his brother Robert, thirty-two years of age.[56] William son of Robert died in 1639 holding the same estate, and leaving as heir his son Robert, thirty-five years of age.[57]

Robert Hyde was a zealous Puritan and took part in the defence of Manchester in 1642.[58] He died in 1684,[59] and his son and heir Robert in 1699, leaving as sole heiress a daughter Mary, who married Sir Ralph Assheton of Middleton, but had no issue. The Denton estate, however, was retained by her husband, and fell to the lot of Katherine, his daughter by a previous marriage ; by her husband, Thomas Lister of Arnoldsbiggin, she had a son Thomas, after whose death in 1761 the Denton estate was sold to William Hulton of Hulton. It was again sold in 1813 to Francis Woodiwiss of Manchester,[60] whose daughter,

Mary Woodiwiss, owned it in 1856.[61] The estate was afterwards acquired by Charles Lowe, whose executors in 1901 sold it to Mr. James Watts of Abney Hall, Cheadle, a descendant (through his mother) of the Hydes.

The situation of Hyde Hall is one of natural defence on rising ground, about a quarter of a mile from the north bank of the River Tame. The front of the house is towards the river, and faces southeast. It is a two-story building of timber and plaster on a stone base originally of the 16th century, but added to and altered in the 17th, when it was partly faced with brick. It appears to have had the usual H type of plan, with central great hall and east and west wings. The east wing, however, has disappeared, and that at the west has been remodelled to suit modern requirements and a new building added on its west side.

The house is entered on the north side through an open porch with stone seats at each side, built in brick with stone dressings, and with the date 1625 and the arms of Hyde on the door head. The porch, which has a segmental opening and moulded jambs, goes up two stories, and has a chamber over lit by a five-light mullioned and transomed window with two lights on each return,[61a] and terminates in a square parapet with moulded coping above a plain string-course. There is a sundial over the window. The whole of the

Gotesbuyth, Milesaundes riddings, Lydiate hursts, Salefield (except in Struyndeley), Brockwalhurst, Dene Evese, Newfield, and 'Stoblade' (except the Dedych dale); also half his waste within and without the bounds of Denton (except in the Dene-croft) ; Lord Wilton's D.

The grantee was no doubt the Adam surnamed 'de Denton,' who gave his lands to Ellis de Botham and Maud his wife (probably daughter of Adam) in 1304; and in 1317 (11 Edw. I appears in the transcript for 11 Edw. II) Ellis granted the same to John son of Alexander de Hyde ; Harl. MS. 2112, fol. 153-4. Maud, as widow of Ellis, released her claim in 1333 ; from her deed it appears that there had been an exchange of lands between Botham and Hyde; ibid.fol.154. The land exchanged may have been the oxgang which Hugh son of Richard de Moston had demised to John son of Alexander de Hyde in 1308-9, and which Richard, the brother and heir of Hugh, appears to have released to John ; ibid. fol. 153.

[52] Ibid. fol. 154.

[53] Ibid. ; the declaration was made in Stockport Church, perhaps on the betrothal of Richard son of Richard.

[54] Ibid. ; the grant was of all his messuages and lands in Denton in the vill of Withington. From the same charters it appears that Richard de Hyde, probably the younger Richard, granted lands in Romiley to his son John and heirs in 1395-6 ; ibid. fol. 154.

There is little notice of the Hydes in the public records. The writ of Diem clausit extr. after the death of Nicholas Hyde of Denton was issued on 20 Nov. 1420 ; Dep. Keeper's Rep. xxxiii, App. 19. In 1429 Robert de Hyde (of Norbury) complained that Geoffrey de Shakerley and Isabel his wife, widow of Nicholas de Hyde, had taken away Ralph, the son and heir of Nicholas, whose marriage belonged to the plaintiff in virtue of a messuage and lands in Denton held by the deceased. The defence was a grant made

by Nicholas ; Pal. of Lanc. Plea R. 2, m. 19.

Ralph son and heir apparent of Nicholas de Hyde in 1428 agreed to marry Margaret daughter of Robert de Dukinfield ; Harl. MS. 2112, fol. 155. This Ralph Hyde of Denton was still living in 1471, when he granted all his goods, &c., to trustees ; but he seems to have died shortly afterwards, and Margaret his widow is named in 1479 ; ibid. fol. 156.

Nicholas son and heir apparent of Ralph was in 1457 contracted to marry Margery daughter of Thurstan Holland, lands in Denton and a rent of 13s. 4d. from Reddish Mill being settled on the bride ; ibid. fol. 156. In 1468 Ralph, the son and heir of Nicholas, was contracted to marry Agnes daughter of John Arderne ; ibid. fol. 154. Ralph probably died, for in 1479 William, the son and heir apparent of Nicholas, was to marry Ellen daughter of Richard Moston ; fol. 154. In 1525 William Hyde of Denton, being over seventy years of age, was excused from attendance on assizes, &c. ; ibid. fol. 155. The age must have been overstated. Two years before this it had been agreed between William Hyde and Alexander Elcock of Heaton Norris, merchant, that the former's 'cousin and heir' (probably grandson) William should marry the latter's daughter Katherine ; lands in Denton of the yearly value of £4 were assigned to Katherine for her life, a similar estate being held by Ellen, wife of the elder William, and by Margaret, then wife of Thomas Browne ; fol. 155. It appears that Margaret was the mother of the younger William ; she was living in 1546, but died before 1552 ; fol. 157.

[55] Duchy of Lanc. Inq. p.m. xi, 51.

[56] Ibid. Pedigrees were recorded in 1567 and 1613 ; Robert was still alive in the latter year ; Visit. (Chet. Soc.), 17 (1567), and 52 (1613). In 1598 a marriage was made between William son and heir apparent of Robert Hyde and Eleanor daughter of John Molyneux of

north side of the house has been rebuilt in brick, probably in the 17th century, and in recent years has been covered with plaster. The south side has been treated in a similar manner, and the plaster lined to represent stone, so that the north and south walls present little or nothing of their ancient appearance, except in the upper windows, which preserve their mullions and transoms, and in the wood and plaster cove under the eaves. The roofs are covered with grey stone slates, and the chimneys are of brick, that from the great hall rising diagonally on plan directly from the roof. The bay window and east wall of the hall, however, retain their timber construction, the bay window forming a picturesque feature at the east end of the south front.

The great hall is similar in plan to that at Denton

HYDE HALL: ENTRANCE FRONT

Hall, and though smaller may have been copied from it. The door is at the north-west corner, opening into a passage which once formed the screens, but is now separated from the hall, as at Denton, by the later insertion of a large fireplace. The passage is still open at both ends, and has the two usual doorways leading from it opposite the hall. Both the north and south walls, which are 1 ft. 9 in. thick, have an external buttress, and there is a third at the north-east angle where the timber and brickwork join. The east wall of the great hall is of timber and plaster, and was no doubt originally the interior wall between the hall and the east wing of the house. The timber construction shows on the outside, but there is no attempt at ornament, the spaces between the timbers being wide and filled with plaster. The

The bay window of the hall is in two stories, as originally designed, built of timber and plaster, but on the ground story the window opening is a modern one of three lights with plaster at both sides and on the returns. In the room above there are ten lights extending the whole length of the front of the bay, but those in the returns are made up. The upper part projects on a plaster cove, and the cove which runs along both sides of the house under the eaves is carried round the top of the bay under the gable, the half-timber work of which is now covered up with plaster, and the barge boards of which have disappeared. The doors at each end of the passage at the end of the hall are the original ones of thick oak, nail studded, and with good hinges, the doorways themselves being of stone with chamfered jambs and four-centred heads.

⁶³ Information from Mr. James Watts, the owner.

The original character of the passage has been altered by the building of the hall chimney and the insertion of a modern staircase.

At the north-east corner of the hall is a small room measuring about 9 ft. by 7 ft. which seems to have been added later, constructed of timber and plaster, and with a window on the south side. It goes up two stories, and has a similar apartment above it opening from the room over the hall.

The plan of the first floor only differs from that of the ground story by the bay window being made into a separate apartment connected with the landing over the passage by a corridor on the south side. The room over the hall is panelled in oak all round, the panelling on the south side, which is made up of odd pieces, forming a partition between the room and the corridor ; it has a six-light wood-mullioned window on the north side, the bottom lights of which are blocked. The room over the bay window extends the width of the corridor over the great hall, and in two upper lights of its window preserves fragments of well-designed lead glazing. In the south wall up-stairs, facing the corridor, is an eight-light stone-mullioned window now built up and invisible from the outside, and the landing is lit by a smaller stone window of four lights, the mullions of which (through the settlement of the building) have fallen out of the perpendicular.

The floor of the room over the porch is now nearly level with the side of the window, the lower lights of which are made up, but was formerly much lower, presumably at the level of the present porch ceiling.[63] It seems to have been raised to the level of the upper floor at the time the present stairs were erected.[64]

There are no features of interest in the west wing. It has been wholly modernized internally, but it pre-serves its 17th-century mullioned windows on the upper floor. The building is now used as a farm-house, but the great hall and rooms over are un-occupied, and after careful restoration are now preserved in something like their original aspect.

To the north of the house are the farm buildings, forming three sides of a large quadrangle, of which the house occupies the fourth side. These were mostly erected about 1839, but a portion of the west side is older, the initials R H M with the date 1687 being carved on a wood beam over the stable door.[65]

The oxgang of land held by Adam de Hulton had been acquired in 1319 by Adam and Avice his wife from Alexander son of Roger de Denton and Cecily his wife.[66] This land, described as the eighth part of the manor,[67] descended in the Hulton family for many centuries[68] and being augmented by the Hulton of Farnworth land,[69] Mr. Hulton's tenants were in 1597 called upon for the second largest contribution to the minister's stipend.[70] This land seems to have been sold with the Hyde estate, as above.

The Denton family's holding it is difficult to trace in the absence of deeds. Roger de Denton in 1309 granted Alexander de

HYDE HALL : SOUTH FRONT

[63] There is now a space between the porch ceiling and the floor of the room above.

[64] What the former staircase arrange-ment was is not very clear, but a portion of what looks like a landing with flat balusters, and the bottom of a newel post, may be seen under the ceiling at the north end of the ground floor passage near the entrance.

[65] Booker gives a view and description of the hall in *Denton*, 35–8.

[66] *Final Conc.* ii, 39. In 1280 Alex-ander de Denton had granted four mar-cates of rent in Denton to Cecily sister of Richard de Hulton ; Lord Wilton's D. These are probably the Alexander and Cecily of the fine. Adam de Hulton and Avice his wife in 1325 failed to prosecute a claim they had made against John de Hyde of Denton, Alina his wife,

Heaton land belonging to two oxgangs in Gotisbucth, and land belonging to one oxgang in Bedecroft, in exchange for land between Thorisbrook and the Merebrook between Denton and Haughton.[71] In 1341 Richard son of Alexander de Denton claimed by right of inheritance a fourth part of the manor of Denton against Adam son of Richard de Hulton and Robert the Tailor of Tatton.[72] The latter defendant was omitted in subsequent suits,[73] and in 1348 Richard continued his claim against Avice widow of Adam de Hulton;[74] four years later he renewed it against Thomas de Booth.[75]

A family surnamed Moston[76] had an estate, once described as a fourth part of the manor, which appears to have been merged in those of the other owners in Denton.[76a]

Among the other landowners of Denton in the 16th and 17th centuries were the Barlow,[77] Hulme,[78] Reddish,[79] and Tyldesley[80] families. In 1597 an agreement as to twenty-four messuages on forty parcels of land reclaimed from the waste of Denton and Haughton was made between Richard Holland, Robert Hyde of Norbury, Alexander Reddish, Alexander Barlow, Adam Hulton, Robert Hyde of Denton, Thomas Ashton of Shepley, and Ralph Haughton on the one part, and Sir Robert Cecil, Hugh Beeston, and Michael Hicks on the other.[81]

From the land tax returns of 1789 it appears that Lord Grey de Wilton and William Hulton paid two-thirds of the tax; the remainder was contributed by a number of owners in small sums.[82]

In 1846 the land was held by twenty-seven proprietors, the principal being the Earl of Wilton, Miss Mary Woodiwiss, and the trustees of Ellis Fletcher, these together holding two-thirds of the total area.[83]

The church of *ST. LAURENCE CHURCH* (formerly St. James, the dedication having been changed about 1800 by the rector)[84] stands on the south side of the town, and

---

[71] Lord Wilton's D. From this it would seem that Roger held three oxgangs.

[72] De Banco R. 326, m. 271.

[73] Ibid. 328, m. 369; 333, m. 92 d.

[74] Ibid. 353, m. 118 d. Richard claimed by a grant made to his father Alexander in the time of Edward II by one William de Tintwisle. Avice replied that what was called a fourth part of the manor was two oxgangs of land in Denton only, and that they had been granted to Adam de Hulton by Alexander son of Roger de Denton, she holding for life with reversion to Roger the son of Adam. The fine above cited (which, however, concerns one oxgang only) was referred to.

[75] Duchy of Lanc. Assize R. 2, m. 2 d. (July). The defence was that Thomas was not in possession.

[76] The Moston family have been mentioned in preceding notes.

In 1256 Richard de Moston made complaint of a ditch overthrown in Denton; Orig. 40 Hen. III, m. 9. In 1278 he appeared as plaintiff in a similar case against Robert Grelley; Assize R. 1238, m. 31; 1239, m. 39. Richard lord of Moston in 1319–20 granted to Richard his son an oxgang in Denton, with the reversion of another then occupied by the grantor's son Hugh; Harl. MS. 2112, fol. 163/199. John son of Hugh de

there was no division between the nave and chancel, a space at the east end being simply railed off for the holy table, but about the year 1800 a small projecting chancel was added. This remained till 1872, when the whole of the present east end of the church, which is faced all round with genuine timber and plaster, was added.

The interior is almost entirely modernized, the division of the bays alone marking the original arrangement. A gallery, which still remains in a modernized form, was set up at the west end in 1728 with a baptistery and churchwardens' pew under. A large family pew was built out at the north-east, but was done away with when the transepts were _dded. The east end of the chancel projects 10 ft. beyond the walls of the transepts, the western part being open on each side to the transepts and fitted with wooden screens, against which the quire seats are set. It is lit by a five-light window at the east and two-light square-headed windows on the north and south.

The nave has three modern square-headed windows of three lights at each side, placed high in the walls, with a five-light window at the west on each side to light the gallery. Under the gallery are two small windows on the north side, and one on the south. The roof is the original one of plain timber restored, with a ceiling at about half its height. The gallery is gained by a staircase on the south of an inner wooden porch, but seems to have been originally approached from the outside by a door which still remains.[64a]

The church was re-seated in 1859,[65] but the two square pews at the west end under the gallery still remain. That on the north side has a good 18th-century stone font on a new shaft, and the church-

wardens' pew on the south side has a portion of a well-shaped 18th-century pew back, which formerly bore the date 1726 on a plate. The seats north of the central passage were originally allotted for the exclusive use of the inhabitants of Denton, and those on the south to Haughton and Hyde.

The fittings are modern, but in the chancel are ten oak panels, of late Gothic style, now much obscured by paint, measuring 2 ft. by 1 ft., let into the front and ends of the modern quire stalls. They are said to have been, in the 18th century, in the front of the gallery, but there is nothing to show whether they were originally made for the church.

In the north and south windows of the chancel, and in the window under the gallery on the south side, are collected fragments of 16th-century glass, and other smaller pieces occur in the middle lights of the transept windows. In 1855[66] these were all in a five-light window at the east of the chancel, but not in their original position. They are evidently parts of a very interesting set, but are too fragmentary to make it possible to discover their original arrangement. The window on the north of the chancel has a shield in each of its lights, one made up of fragments being quarterly, and over all a bend with three escallops (perhaps for Spencer), with helm, mantling, and imperfect crest, while the other has Argent on a cheveron between three lozenges sable, a crescent of the field (probably intended for the arms of Hyde though the tinctures are wrong), and underneath it a female (?) figure in purple with hands uplifted, kneeling before an altar on which is an open book, and with a label bearing the words 'Miserere mei.'

The window on the south side has in its eastern light an angel with a label on which is inscribed 'Ave Maria gratia,' and in the second light the figure

[64a] The outer door, which is now blocked up, at one time gave access to the churchwardens' pew.
[65] There had been a partial renewal of the seats in 1768. A citation was issued on 6 October of that year for repewing the south side, 'the seats, stalls, and forms therein having by length of time become old, ruinous, and decayed.'
[66] Booker, op. cit. 43.

of a saint in a green robe holding in his hands what has been taken to be a gridiron (St. Laurence). Underneath is a portion of a dedicatory inscription, 'Armigi' et Katherine . . . fenestrā fieri feceru . . .' The glass in the window under the gallery is still more fragmentary and confused, showing portions of inscriptions, figures, and shields.

The fragments of inscriptions have been probably brought from other windows and mixed up in an entirely unintelligible manner. In the three lights of the window they appear to be as follows, but are difficult to decipher in places owing to the presence of the leading :—

(1) 'Edward cui Knolis et . . .
    uxis . . . [fi]eri . . . feceru[nt].
(2) . . . et Christian W . . . dñi m'ccccc'x
(3) Jabane uxors sue . . . [Ri]cardi supprt et Rod
    Catherine uxors sue . . . . an hac dau
    Johane uxors sue . . . .

Booker gives three inscriptions on glass in different parts of the building, portions of which bear some resemblance to the fragmentary inscriptions given above, but most of those noted by him appear to have been lost or destroyed. Two of these bore respectively the dates 1531 and 1532, and the names of Hyde and Nicholas and Robert Smith occurred. Judging from the fragments remaining and the records of those that have now disappeared, the 16th-century chapel at Denton seems to have been rich in coloured glass.

The fragments of old glass in the transept windows are very small and include 'I.H.C.' in a circle, the arms of Hyde, part of a figure in red, a head, a shield of arms (Argent a lion rampant gules crowned or), the head of a martyr saint, and a shield with the letter R.

On the west wall of the north transept are two 17th-century monuments, one with a long Latin inscription,[66a] to the memory of Edward Holland (died 1655) and his wife Ann (Warren). The inscription is on a brass plate beneath an entablature supported by columns, and above is a shield with the arms of Holland with a label for difference impaling Warren, Checky or and azure on a canton gules a lion rampant argent : and two crests for Holland (Out of a coronet or a demi-lion rampant holding in the dexter paw a fleur de lis argent), and Warren (On a cap of estate gules turned up ermine a wyvern with knotted tail argent, wings expanded checky or and azure.)

The second monument is a small marble tablet 18 in. square to Eleanor Arden wife of Ralph Arden (or Arderne) and daughter of Sir John Done, from which the inscription is almost effaced, the letters having only been painted. Above on a separate

shaped piece are the arms of Arderne, Gules three crosslets fitchy and a chief or impaling Done, 1 and 6 Azure two bars argent over all on a bend gules three broad arrows of the second. 2, Vert a cross engrailed ermine, over all on an escutcheon argent a bugle sable. 3, Gules a lion rampant argent. 4, illegible. 5, Azure two bars argent ; with the crests of Arderne, Out of a coronet or a plume of five feathers argent, and Done, A hart's head couped at the shoulders proper.

On the corresponding side of the south transept is a good 18th-century monument to Dame Mary Assheton (died 1721), daughter of Robert Hyde of Denton, with the arms and crest of Assheton, and over all a shield of pretence with the arms of Hyde.

During the restorations in the first half of the last century, on the whitewash falling from the walls, several words in an old English lettering were revealed, and eventually the whole history of Dives and Lazarus was laid bare. This was covered up when the walls were newly plastered, but is still in existence.

There is a single bell in the turret, originally cast by Abraham Rudhall in 1715, but recast in 1896.

The plate is modern with the exception of two 17th-century chalices, one inscribed 'The coppe for the Lord's table,' and the other 'A communion cup given to Denton chappel by Mʳⁱˢ Mary Done.'

The registers of burial begin in 1696 (fragments in 1695) and baptisms in 1700. There are marriage registers from 1711 to 1723, after which there is a gap of fifty-five years.

The churchyard surrounds the building, with roads on the east, south, and west, and entrances at the east and south-west. The latter entrance has an ancient timber lych-gate with stone slated roof, probably of the same date as the church. There was formerly a yew tree on the south side, but it was in a very decayed state in 1796,[87] and was cut down four years later. Another tree now marks its position.

The chapel of St. James was *ADVOWSON* built on the waste in 1531-2,[88] and in 1534 an agreement was made by the tenants as to the levy for the payment of the chaplain.[89] Beyond this there was no endowment,[90] but Richard Holland in 1618 left £100 towards the purchase of an annuity of £20 for 'a godly minister to preach the word of God and read divine service,' to be nominated by the Hollands and Hydes or their successors.[91] In 1719 the certified income was £12, to which voluntary contributions of about £10 were added.[92] The right of patronage was disputed in 1677, the warden and fellows of the Collegiate Church claiming to present to this as to the other curacies ; the Hollands, however, succeeded in acquiring or retaining the

[66a] Given in Glynne, notes of 1892.
[87] *Gent. Mag.* 22 Nov. 1796.
[88] Booker, op. cit. 41. A description of the building, which was chiefly of timber, is given ; there was neither chancel nor communion table till about 1800. A small pew was built outside the north wall in 1676 by Robert Hyde, who was deaf ; it had an opening into the church near the pulpit. A double re-christening took place in 1772 ; ibid. 120. There is a view of the building in 1793 in Nightingale's *Lancs. Nonconf.* v, 286.
[89] Harl. MS. 2112, fol. 164/200 ; it was intended to raise £20 by an assess-

ment of 2½d. an acre ; Booker, op. cit. 51.
[90] The chapel was confiscated by Edward VI, the inhabitants acquiring it for 20s. It had a chalice, also confiscated ; Raines, *Chant.* (Chet. Soc.), 278, 270. At the end of Elizabeth's reign it was served by a 'reader' ; there was neither Bible nor surplice ; *Lancs. and Ches. Antiq. Soc.* xiii, 60. There was still 'no surplice' in 1604 ; Visit. Presentments at Chester. About 1610 there was a curate paid by the inhabitants ; *Hist. MSS. Com. Rep.* xiv, App. iv, 11.
[91] Booker, *Denton*, 52. A house on the

chapel yard was afterwards built ; after it ceased to be used by the minister, it was for a time a public house, but was taken down in 1853 ; ibid. 59. In 1650 this house and garden were valued at 16s. a year ; there was also a chapel stock of £5 ; *Commonw. Ch. Surv.* (Rec. Soc. Lancs. and Ches.), 12. An allowance of £50 out of the sequestered tithes of Kirkham was made in 1648 ; *Plund. Mins. Accts.* (Rec. Soc. Lancs. and Ches.), i, 64 ; afterwards £40 was allowed out of the tithes of Manchester ; ibid. ii, 55.
[92] Gastrell, *Notitia* (Chet. Soc.), ii, 84.

patronage, which has descended to the Earl of Wilton. A formal renunciation was made by the warden and fellows in 1750.[95] A district chapelry was assigned in 1839.[94] The following is a list of curates and rectors :—[95]

c. 1611	Humphrey Tylecote [96]
c. 1630	Charles Broxholme [97]
1631	John Angier, B.A.[98] (Emmanuel College, Camb.)
1677	John Ogden [99]
1679	Roger Dale [100]
1691	Joshua Hyde [101]
1695	Noah Kinsey, M.A.[102] (Pembroke College, Camb.)
1696	Daniel Pighells [103]
1707	John Berry, M.A.[104] (Sidney-Sussex College, Camb.)
1709	John Jackson [105]
1720	— Grey [106]
1723	Joseph Dale [107]
1750	William Williams, M.A.[108] (Brasenose College, Oxf.)
1759	William Jackson, B.A.[109] (Brasenose College, Oxf.)
1791	William Parr Greswell [110]
1853	Walter Nicol, M.A. (Glasgow) [111]
1869	Charles James Bowen, B.A.[112] (Trinity College, Camb.)
1881	David Rowe

Christ Church, for which a district was formed [113] in 1846, was consecrated in 1853, the Crown and the Bishop of Manchester having the patronage alternately.[114]

The Wesleyans and Primitive Methodists have churches in Denton.[115] The Congregationalists also have one.[116]

The Roman Catholic school-chapel of St. Mary, with the title of the Seven Dolours, was built about 1870 ; the mission was separated from Ashton in 1889.

---

[96] Booker, op. cit. 62–9.

[94] *Lond. Gaz.* 29 Mar. 1839 ; 16 June 1854.

[95] This list is taken almost entirely from Booker, op. cit. 70–111, where biographies will be found, together with a number of illustrative documents. John Brereton was in 1576 licensed as 'reader' for Denton Chapel; Pennant's Acct. Bk. Chester.

[96] H. T. Crofton, *Stretford* [Chet. Soc.), i, 61.

[97] He was silenced for nonconformity ; Booker, op. cit. 70. Also named Broxopp.

[98] One of the most famous Puritans of Lancashire. He signed the 'Harmonious Consent' of 1648, and was not disturbed in 1662. His life was written by Oliver Heywood ; Booker, op. cit. 71–8 (with pedigree) ; W. A. Shaw in *Manch. Classis,* iii, 406–8 ; *Dict. Nat. Biog.* See also *Royalist Comp. Papers* (Rec. Soc. Lancs. and Ches.), i, 86.

[99] Samuel Angier, nephew of the late minister, was rejected for nonconformity and John Ogden was nominated by the warden and fellows. The people were hostile and he stayed there only a year ; Booker, op. cit. 79–87.

[100] This appointment was made by the landowners—W. Holland and R. Hyde— and agreed to by the warden and fellows. Mr. Dale, 'a great preacher of loyalty and obedience,' exasperated many of the people by 'bringing the surplice, Book of Homilies, &c.' See Booker (op. cit. 88–102) for the attempt to get rid of him in 1685. He took the curacy of Northenden in 1690, and became rector of Radcliffe.

[101] Nominated by the warden and fellows with the consent of Sir John Egerton ; ibid. 103–5.

[102] Ibid. 105 ; nominated by the warden and fellows.

[103] Ibid. 106 ; nominated by the warden and fellows.

[104] Ibid.   [105] Ibid.

[106] Ibid. At this time the Denton people's 'indifference to the Church was so great that a small disobligation would be sufficient to make them join the Dissenters' ; ibid. 107.

[107] Ibid. 107–8 ; nominated by Holland Egerton. He was schoolmaster of Stockport and son of Roger Dale, a former curate ; Earwaker, *East Ches.* i, 418.

[108] Booker, op. cit. 108 ; he was senior fellow of his college. The dispute as to the patronage was settled at this time.

[109] Ibid. 109. He also was master of Stockport School and was curate of Newton in Manchester ; Earwaker, op. cit. i, 418.

[110] Booker, op. cit. 109–11, where a list of his works is given ; five of his sons became fellows of colleges at Oxford, and another was master of the Chetham Hospital.

[111] Afterwards rector of Newton St. Petrock, Devon.

[112] Exchanged with his successor, the latter being rector of Wroot, Lincolnshire.

[113] *Lond. Gaz.* 17 Mar. 1846.

[114] This church owes its existence to the efforts of the Rev. Richard Greswell, of Worcester College, Oxford, a son of the incumbent of the old chapel ; Booker, *Denton,* 124–7.

ton being regarded as an outlying portion of the Cheshire estates.[4]

A branch of the Hyde family had land in Haughton from the time of Edward IV until 1821, when John Hyde of Ardwick sold his estate to John Lowe of Shepley Hall; it afterwards descended to the Sidebothams.[5]

Another family, of unknown origin, took the local surname, and their residence was called Haughton Hall. It was owned afterwards by Booths, Holfords, and Bentleys in succession.[6]

The Barlows and Hultons, who have been noticed under Denton, held lands in this township also.

The principal landowners in 1797 were George Hyde Clarke and Nathan Hyde.[7]

In connexion with the Established Church St. Mary the Virgin's was consecrated in 1876;[8] the Bishop of Manchester collates to the rectory. The patronage of St. Anne's, which was built in 1882, and is also a rectory, is vested in Messrs. J. W. and E. J. Sidebotham.[9]

A Wesleyan chapel was erected as early as 1810;[10] the Primitive Methodists began services in 1840.[11] These bodies still have churches in the township.

HEATON NORRIS

Hetton, 1196; Heton, 1212; Heaton Norreys, 1364; Heyton and Heaton Norres, xvi cent.

This township stretches from Cringle Brook on the north to the Mersey on the south, a distance of 2 miles; it measures about a mile and a half from east to west, and has an area of 2,115½ acres. The highest ground is in the south, with a steep slope to the Mersey and a gentler decline to the north. The south-eastern portion has long been a suburb of Stockport, and was included in the Parliamentary borough in 1832 and in

---

allowed Robert son of John (sic) de Hyde to make a millpool on land in Hyde for the benefit of Haughton Mill, at a rent of a clove gillyflower; Harl. MS. 2112, fol. 165. William lord of Baguley gave a similar but more liberal permission to John de Hyde in free marriage with Isabel his daughter; fol. 162. These were the John and Isabel of the fine above referred to; they occur in an earlier licence of agreement (1306) respecting lands in Haughton; De Banco R. 161, m. 56.

Simon de Gousill gave Thomas de Macclesfield the wardship of the heir of John son of Robert de Hyde in Denton and Haughton; Harl. MS. 2112, fol. 162.

Alexander de Hyde, the brother of John, was ancestor of the Hydes of Denton.

[4] Sir John de Hyde in 1357 made a settlement of his manors, including Haughton, with remainder to Roger son of Margaret daughter of Sir John de Davenport (apparently the first wife of Sir John), and to William, Robert, Ralph, Hugh and Margery, brothers and sisters of Roger; Harl. MS. 2112, fol. 163. Four years later John son of William Hulcockson de Baguley (a feoffee) granted to Sir John de Hyde and Alice his wife the manor of Haughton, with remainder to William de Hyde son of Margaret de Davenport and to Robert, Hugh and Margery as above; fol. 163 d., 163. At this time William the son of Sir John was espoused to Ellen daughter of Richard de Bramhall, and Haughton is named in the settlement; fol. 163 b.

The feoffees of Robert son of John de Hyde restored to him his manor of Haughton in 1377; ibid. fol. 163 b. It thus appears that the elder brothers, Roger and William, had died without issue. Ralph, another brother, was ancestor of the Hydes of Urmston. Robert de Hyde in 1401 made a feoffment of his manors, including Haughton; ibid. fol. 165 d.

A claim for debt was made against John Hyde in 1445; Pal. of Lanc. Plea R. 7, m. 1 b. His grandson John, the son of Hamlet son of John Hyde, was in 1453–4 contracted to marry Margaret daughter of William Booth son of Sir Robert; Harl. MS. 2112, fol. 166. Ten years later (3 Edw. IV) Hamlet Hyde of Norbury made a feoffment of all his manors and lands in Haughton, except certain held by Robert Shepley and others; this was for the benefit of Joan his wife; ibid. fol. 167. In 1478 a remainder to Peter Hyde for life was granted; ibid. fol. 166 d.

Settlements of the manor of Haughton with messuages, lands, &c., there were made by Edward Hyde in 1648, by Edward Hyde and Katherine his wife in 1698, and by the Hon. George Clarke in 1752; Pal. of Lanc. Feet of F. bdle. 144, m. 24; 240, m. 67; 349, m. 68.

[5] Booker, Denton, 137, and information of Mr. E. J. Sidebotham of Erlesdene, Bowdon, the present owner.

[6] Ibid. 136. To Ralph Haughton 22 acres of the wastes of Denton (292 acres) were allotted in 1596; ibid. 5.

The part of the township outside Stockport obtained a local board in 1872 ;[7] this has now become an urban district council, with twelve members. A small portion, 16 acres, was added to Stockport in 1901.

Bennet Woodcroft, F.R.S., inventor and clerk to the Commissioners of Patents, was born at Heaton Norris in 1803 ; he retired from the public service in 1876 and died at South Kensington in 1879.[8] Edward Higginson, born in 1807, was a Unitarian divine of some distinction ; he died in 1880.[9]

MANOR   From the survey of 1212 it appears that *HEATON NORRIS* was a member of the fee or barony of Manchester, and was assessed as two plough-lands. By Albert Grelley the younger it was granted, at a rent of 10s., to William le Norreys, whose heirs held the land in 1212.[10] These heirs were probably the brothers Richard and Jordan le Norreys, who in 1196 made an agreement as to a division of their lands in Heaton, Chorlton, and Bradford, Jordan receiving Heaton.[11] Though the family gave a distinguishing name to the township and though Norris occurs as a surname in it, the manor was, about 1280, surrendered to the lords of Manchester.[12] In 1282 Robert Grelley was found to have held part of it in demesne, and to have farmed 8 oxgangs of land, i.e., half the manor, in bondage. The only free tenant recorded at that time was Adam de Lever, who owed two pairs of gloves yearly. The manor was held of the Earl of Lancaster for the fourth part of a knight's fee.[13]

The manor continued in the Grelley and La Warre families until the 15th century,[14] when it appears to have been granted to Sir James Strangeways,[15] in this way acquiring the alternative name of Heaton Strangeways.[16] In 1569 the manor was in the possession of Leonard and Edward Dacre,[17] and was afterwards ac-

[7] *Lond. Gaz.* 23 Apr. 1872.
[8] *Dict. Nat. Biog.*
[9] Ibid.
[10] *Lancs. Inq. and Extents* (Rec. Soc. Lancs. and Ches.), i, 57.
[11] *Final Conc.* (Rec. Soc. Lancs. and Ches.), i, 6. Jordan granted to Richard that the pigs belonging to his demesne in Chorlton (upon Medlock) should run in Heaton Wood, quit of pannage for ever. Jordan and William le Norreys appear as witnesses to local charters ; Crofton, *Newton* (Chet. Soc.), ii, 119, 300.
[12] All the lands in the fine referred to reverted to the lords of Manchester. A few further particulars of the family may be seen in the accounts of Denton and Chorlton-upon-Medlock.

From a pleading of 1281 it appears that three years earlier William le Norreys had enfeoffed John de Byron of two-thirds of the manor of Heaton, and that John was put in seisin, but was ousted by Robert Grelley after three days ; then John went to Robert's bailiff, claiming nothing except for a term of six years, and on the bailiff's refusal of entry, he went to Manchester to talk with Robert Grelley. He offered to surrender all his claim for 17 marks, and brought William le Norreys, who made a complete surrender of the manor to Robert Grelley, as to the chief lord of the fee. In 1281-2 an agreement was made between Grelley and Byron, the latter surrendered all his claim to two-thirds of the manor, and acknowledged that he owed Robert £200 of silver ; Assize R. 1244, m. 40. The other third was the dower of Cecily de Shoresworth (see Denton), and in 1283 Robert de Shoresworth and Cecily his wife appeared against Amadeus de Savoy and other guardians of the lands and heir of Robert Grelley, respecting her dower in 3½ oxgangs of land, water-mill, &c., in Heaton Norris ; De Banco R. 51, m. 74.

Hawise, widow of Robert Grelley, claimed dower in this part of the manor ; De Banco R. 46, m. 77 ; 112, m. 64 (where it is called Heaton next Wobrythe Bridge).

[13] *Lancs. Inq. and Extents*, i, 246-9. There were 40 acres in demesne, with a chief messuage and garden worth 20s. a year ; a plat called the Mill Ridding and the Sporth was also worth 20s. ; two-thirds of the mill rendered 13s. 4d. ; free tenants paid 3s. 10½d. The 8 oxgangs of land in bondage paid 20s. ; the bondmen also gave twenty-four hens at Christmas worth 2s., and eight score eggs at Easter, worth 6d. wood was valued at

A claim conce Heaton' made in 1 Dav'd de Hulton, th Grelley and Thoma to Heaton Norris m. 79. The Hul an interest in he Reddish.

The surveys o further particulars. at that time were th Cringle Brook, an Cheshire, Reddish, Withington sides road called the Sal

quired by the Mosleys.[18] It descended in the same manner as Hulme until about 1750,[19] when it was sold to William Egerton,[20] who is represented by Earl Egerton of Tatton, the present lord.

The Mosleys also acquired the estate in Heaton of Jane widow of Sir Robert Lovell, whose father, Geoffrey Lovell of Merton, had made purchases from Sir Edmund Trafford.[21]

The Grelleys made grants of land in Heaton to the Byrons and others ;[22] and the Worsleys of Booths,[23] the Hulmes of Reddish,[24] and others are found to have had estates in it,[25] but no clear account can be given of them. The old landowners were non-resident.[26] In 1789 the principal owner was William Egerton, who paid about a third of the land tax ; the remain-

the grant by Sir James Strangeways already recorded, does not seem to have been satisfactory. In 1568 Robert Roos of Ingmanthorpe claimed the manor and lands as next of kin and heir—viz. son of Mary, sister of Thomas, father of Sir James Strangeways — against Leonard Dacre. The defendant pleaded the grant by Sir James, who, he stated, had delivered all his evidences into the hands of William, Lord Dacre ; Duchy of Lanc. Pleadings, Eliz. lxxvii, R 2.

Robert Roos's plea must have been successful, for in 1570 he sold the manor, &c., to Gilbert Gerard, attorney-general ; Pal. of Lanc. Feet of F. bdle. 32, m. 16.

[18] Sir Thomas Gerard sold or mortgaged the manor in 1598 to George Coppin ; ibid. bdle. 60, m. 72 ; the latter, in 1601, in conjunction with Anne his wife, resold to Sir Thomas (ibid. bdle. 63, no. 294), who in the following year transferred it to Sir Arthur Savage ; ibid. bdle. 64, no. 145. This was probably another mortgage, for in 1614 the deforciants in a fine were Sir Thomas Lord Gerard of Gerard's Bromley, Sir Arthur Savage and Joan his wife ; ibid. bdle. 85, m. 1.

The manor had already been sold to Sir Nicholas Mosley, who says in his will (1612) : 'I do hereby give . . . unto my eldest son Rowland Mosley and to the heirs male of his body, &c., the manor or lordship of Heaton Norris . . . which I lately purchased of the Lord Gerard that now is' ; Booker, Didsbury, 135. The manor is not named in Sir Nicholas' inquisition, but his son Rowland died in possession of it in 1617 ; it was said to be held of the king as of his duchy of Lancaster by the twentieth part of a knight's fee ; Lancs. Inq. p.m. (Rec. Soc. Lancs. and Ches.), ii, 66, 69.

[19] Pal of Lanc. Feet of F. bdle. 151, m. 152 ; 204, m. 66. There was a recovery of the manors of Hulme and Heaton Norris in 1746, Sir John Bland being a vouchee ; Pal. of Lanc. Plea R. 562, m. 3.

[20] Mosley Fam. Mem. 29. Wilbraham Egerton was vouchee in a recovery of the manor in 1806 ; Pal. of Lanc. Aug. Assizes, 46 Geo. III, R. 8.

[21] See Ducatus Lanc. iii, 306, 465, 508, for suits in which the family were engaged ; also Booker's Didsbury (Chet. Soc.), 6. The estate, described as twelve messuages, 100 acres of land, &c., in Heaton Norris, Streethouse Lane, and High Street was purchased by Sir Nicholas Mosley, who died in 1612 ; Lancs. Inq. p.m. (Rec. Soc. Lancs. and Ches.), ii, 4, 66.

[22] See the list of free tenants already given.

The Byrons' ho tioned above. In 1 de Heaton (probabl Shoresworth and pl med f a di ch m in Heaton ; Assiz 1238, m 34 d , 12 1292 Mabel daught complained that sh five messuages an Heaton by Stockp and Robert de Sh that he had nothing he and Cecily of the tenement a that Thomas son of the other two thi claim against Thom because he was a king, whom she m A

1865 ;[33] St. Paul's, Heaton Moor, 1877 ;[34] All Saints' Heaton Norris, 1888 ; and St. Martin's, Norris Bank, 1901. To the last-named the Crown and the Bishop of Manchester present alternately ; the bishop alone collates to Christ Church, St. John the Baptist's, and All Saints' ; bodies of trustees present to the others.

The Wesleyans have churches at Heaton Norris, Heaton Moor, and Heaton Mersey.[35] The Primitive Methodists also have one. The Congregationalists have churches in each of the three portions of the township named.[36] In 1857 the Particular Baptists had a chapel in Heaton Lane.[37]

The Unitarians began services at Heaton Moor in 1893 and moved to their present building in 1900.

The Presbyterian Church of England began services at Heaton Chapel in 1899.

St. Mary's Roman Catholic Church was opened in 1897, replacing one used for thirty years.

REDDISH

Redich, 1205, 1212 ; Radich, 1226 ; Rediche, 1262 ; Redditch, 1381 ; Radishe, Reddishe, xvi cent.

This township has a length of 2¼ miles from north to south, and an area of 1,541 acres. The northern boundary is formed by the ancient Nico Ditch ; part of the eastern by the River Tame. The surface is usually level, but slopes away to the river. The hamlets in 1856 were Reddish Green, Sandfold, and Whitehill.[1] The population was in 1901 included in that of Stockport.

The small town of Reddish lies near the centre of the township. From this roads lead away in all directions ; the principal are those to Stockport on the south, passing through the hamlet of South Reddish ; to Heaton Norris on the west ; and to Manchester on the north, passing through Barlow Fold, North Reddish, and Sandfold. The southern end of the township has become a suburb of Stockport. The London and North Western Company's line from this town to Ashton crosses it, with a station called Reddish, near the centre. The Great Central Company's line from Manchester to Stockport touches the northern

end of the township, within which is a station also named Reddish. The same company's loop line from Central Station to London Road, Manchester, crosses the north end. The Manchester and Stockport Canal, 1797, goes through the township from north to south.

In 1666 the principal house was that of Jane Stopford, with ten hearths liable to the tax ; the total number in the township was fifty-six.[2] Though so near Stockport there was in Reddish in 1857 neither post-office, schoolmaster, lawyer, doctor, nor pawnshop. Agriculture was then the chief occupation of the people, but bleaching, hand-loom weaving, and hat-making had at one time been pursued to a slight extent.[3] There are now cotton mills, calico printing works, bleach works, and roperies.

The township was formerly governed by a local board of ten members, constituted in 1881, and more recently by an urban district council. It was added to Stockport in 1901, being divided into two wards.

MANOR In the survey of 1212 it is stated that Roger son of William held a plough-land in REDDISH of the king in thegnage by a rent of 6s., and that Matthew de Reddish held it of him by the same service.[4] The mesne lord was of the Kirkby Ireleth family, and his position was recognized down to the 15th century.[5]

The descendants of Matthew de Reddish[6] cannot be traced, but a family using the local surname, who were apparently connected with the Hultons of Hulton and Ordsall,[7] held Reddish and Heaton in Prestwich down to the 17th century. Richard son of Richard de Reddish was a plaintiff in 1313–14,[8] and ten years later Richard de Reddish held an oxgang of land in Reddish by the service of 6s.[9] Richard son of Richard de Hulton of Reddish in 1331 and later claimed a messuage and lands against Jordan son of John de Reddish, who had them by grant of Richard de Hulton, formerly husband of Ellen de Reddish, the plaintiff being her heir.[10] In 1346 John de Kirkby held Reddish in socage, paying 6s. rent by the hands of Richard de Reddish.[11] This Richard appears in suits for some years afterwards.[12]

A later Richard died in 1404 holding the manor of Reddish of Sir Richard Kirkby in socage by a rent of 6s. ; Ralph, his son and heir, was thirty years of

[33] Lond. Gaz. 30 June 1865.
[34] For district, ibid. 7 May and 9 Aug. 1878.
[35] Teviot Dale Chapel was built in 1824 ; Booker, op. cit. 194.
[36] Hanover Chapel was built in 1821 ; Wycliffe Chapel in 1850 ; ibid. 194.
[37] Ibid. loc. cit.
[1] Booker, Didisbury (Chet. Soc.), 197 ; there were two greens, one by Stockport Road, called Little Reddish Green, and another nearer the centre. Whitehill, at the south end of the township, was so named from a house built about 1820.
[2] Subs. R. bdle. 250, no. 9. Robert Walker's house had seven hearths. No other house had more than three.
[3] Booker, op. cit. 201.
[4] Lancs. Inq. and Extents (Rec. Soc. Lancs. and Ches.), i, 69. William son of Roger de Reddish paid the 6s. rent in 1226 ; ibid. 138.
[5] This is clear from the inquisitions, &c., quoted later.
[6] He held a moiety of Denton, but alienated it. A Matthew de Reddish was

age.[13] Ralph died about five years afterwards,[14] and was probably succeeded by the Richard Reddish who was tenant in 1445–6.[15] Three or four years before this Richard Reddish had settled his lands in view of the marriage of his son John with Elizabeth daughter of Thurstan Holland.[16]

Otes Reddish died 10 Sept. 1521, holding the manors of Reddish and Heaton Fallowfield, with messuages, burgages, water-mill, lands, and rents in those places and in Heaton Norris, Manchester, and Audenshaw. The tenure of Reddish is described as of Sir John Byron in socage, by the yearly rent of one pound of cummin ; its clear annual value was £36 13s. 4d.[17] The change of tenure thus recorded for the first time appears to go back to 1262, when Matthew de Reddish granted a moiety of the manor to Geoffrey de Byron at the rent of one pound of cummin or 2d., and performing to the chief lords of the fee the services due.[18] The inquisitions[19] show the manor to have descended regularly to Sarah daughter and co-heir of Alexander Reddish, who died in 1613.[20] She married Clement youngest son of Sir Edward Coke, the famous chief justice,[21] and the manor descended to her son and grandsons.[22] Then it was bequeathed to another branch of the Coke family,[23] and descended to Thomas William Coke, the celebrated ' Coke of Holkham,' created Earl of Leicester in 1837.[24] He sold it, with his other Lancashire estates, about the end of the 18th century ; the purchaser was James Harrison of Cheadle, whose repre-

sentative in 1808 sold it to Robert Hyde Greg and John Greg of Manchester.[25]

REDDISH of Reddish.
Argent a lion rampant gules collared or.

COKE. *Per pale gules and azure three eagles displayed argent.*

Reddish Hall was situated on the east side of the township, and was taken down about the year 1780. It was a two-storied timber and plaster house, on a stone base, E-shaped on plan, but said to have been originally quadrangular in form, and surrounded by a moat. The principal front, which had three overhanging gables, was entirely covered with quatrefoil panelling, giving the building a very rich appearance. The great hall, as well as several of the other rooms, was wainscoted, the upper panels being carved with the collared lion of Reddish. ' Attached to the hall, and approached by a door to the left under the entrance gateway, was the domestic chapel . . . The apartment over the gateway was known as the priest's chamber.'[26]

[13] *Lancs. Inq. p.m.* (Chet. Soc.), i, 80. (Chet. Soc.)

[14] Add. MS. 32108, no. 1627 ; writ of *Diem clausit extr.* after the death of Ralph Reddish, 10 Hen. IV.

About this time branches off the family of Reddish of Dodleston and Grappenhall in Cheshire ; see Ormerod, *Ches.* (ed. Helsby), ii, 846–8, and many references in the *Dep. Keeper's Rep.* xxxvi and xxxvii.

[15] Duchy of Lanc. Knights' Fees, 2/20; ' Richard Reddish holds Reddish in socage, rendering 6s. yearly ; he says that he holds in mesne of Roger Kirkby, who holds by feoffment.' In a pedigree in Piccope MSS. (Chet. Lib.), ii, 121, Richard is called son of Otes brother of Ralph son of Richard Reddish. Otes Reddish is named in 1420 ; *Dep. Keeper's Rep.* xxxiii, App. 23.

[16] Harl. MS. 2112, fol. 150/186 ; Ellen the mother of Richard was still living.

[17] Duchy of Lanc. Inq. p.m. v, 48.

[18] *Final Conc.* i, 134 ; if Geoffrey should die without issue the land was to revert to Matthew and his heirs. There is nothing to show how the Byrons of Clayton stepped into the place of Matthew de Reddish, while the Reddish family apparently succeeded Geoffrey de Byron, perhaps the same noticed in the account of Eccles. Although it is not mentioned in the later inquisitions, the 6s. rent was paid to the Crown by the Reddish family; thus about the end of Elizabeth's reign Alexander Reddish paid 12s. 8d. for Reddish and Heaton, this sum being made up of 6s. for the former and 6s. 8d. for the latter ; Baines, *Lancs.* (ed. Harland), i, 447.

[19] John Reddish, the son of Otes, was forty-six years of age at his father's death, but lived on until Sept. 1558, when he was succeeded by his grandson John the son of Otes Reddish, then nineteen years of age ; Duchy of Lanc. Inq. p.m. xi, 60. He recorded a pedigree in 1533 ; *Visit.*

The next considerable estate was that of *HULME HALL*. As early as the 13th century a family named Hulme was seated in the township;[27] part at least of their estate was acquired by the Hulmes of Man-chester, a trading family which can be traced back to the early years of the 15th century.[28] Ralph Hulme purchased in 1601,[29] and died in 1623,[30] being suc-ceeded by his eldest son William, who died in 1637.[31]

[27] Jordan in the time of Henry III held a messuage and 50 acres of land in Reddish, which descended to his son Jordan; the latter had a son William, whose son and heir Robert de Hulme in 1343 demanded the same against Richard del Edge; De Banco R. 334, m. 113.

Margaret widow of Robert de Hulme in 1365 claimed dower in a messuage, 38 acres of land, &c., in Reddish against Richard de Reddish; ibid. R. 421, m. 11. William son of Robert de Hulme was a defendant in 1366; ibid. R. 425, m. 504 d.

James Hulme of Reddish, the elder, and Robert his son and heir apparent, were bound to Thurstan Holland and others in 1456; Harl. MS. 2112, fol. 150*b*/186*b*.

Nicholas Hulme in 1523 possessed by inheritance 'manors, lands, &c.' in Red-dish, Hulme, Heaton Norris, and else-where, and settled them upon his heirs male, with remainders to Hugh Hulme, and to Ralph Hulme of Manchester, 'which Ralph is next heir male, after the said Hugh Hulme, to the said lands.' The evidences, in a chest under three locks, kept by John Fitton of Gaws-worth, were not to be delivered to James Hulme, son of Nicholas, until William Davenport of Bramhall, John Reddish of Reddish, and Hugh Hulme of Tottington judged proper; Hulme D. no. 42. Two years later Nicholas made a further settlement of his lands in Lancashire and Cheshire in favour of his son James; Janet, the wife of Nicholas, was to have her dower; ibid. no. 45.

In Aug. 1550 Ambrose Aspenhaugh, perhaps as trustee, obtained from George Hulme, son and heir apparent of James Hulme, a capital messuage and lands in Reddish and Manchester; Pal. of Lanc. Feet of F. bdle. 14, m. 306. In the following spring James Hulme, the father, made a settlement of his estate in Hulme, Denton, Withington, Heaton Norris, and Reddish, comprising twenty messuages, 200 acres of land, &c.; the remainders were to Robert, son and heir apparent of George Hulme, son and heir apparent of James; to Richard, Ralph, Nicholas, John, and Edmund, younger sons of James; ibid. bdle. 14, m. 196. Robert Hulme appears to have succeeded, for in 1568 he and Robert Aspenhaugh (*alias* Asmall) sold or mortgaged some land in Reddish; ibid. bdle. 30, m. 22. He was concerned in some family disputes; *Ducatus Lanc.* (Rec. Com.), ii, 243, iii; 22. Robert Hulme in 1584 suffered a recovery of his messuages and lands in Reddish, Withington, and Heaton, in order that he might dispose of them by his last will or otherwise; Hulme D. no. 54.

Robert Hulme died at Hulme on 7 Mar. 1599–1600 holding a capital mes-suage, &c., in Reddish of Alexander Reddish in socage; also messuages, &c., in Heaton Norris and Withington. He had in the previous year made a settle-ment of his estate, the remainders being to his uncle John (brother of George Hulme), rector of Wickham Bishops in Essex, and then to the heirs of his great-uncle Robert Hulme of the Hudash.

John Hulme, uncle years of age a d o Inq p.m. xviii 10

[28] Their kinship t dish is asserted by deed quoted in the la

Lawrence Hulme chester in 1421, 143 D no. 10, 11–13. tion was made that Lawrence Hulme baron's court of M John Trafford, then after her death all h tenements wer to her son, ibid. no. probably dead, and i Geoffrey Hulme ma estate in Manchester similar deed was exe no. 18. In 1478 Cecily w'fe of Geoff called the Gravers burgage, and a field taining 5 acres, wi heirs of Geoffrey H The year ft d Manchester called th ward Croft, *alias* crofts,' to Elizabeth Beswick the elder, Ralph son of Geoff Lawrence Hulme ·

G

His heir was his son William Hulme, founder of the Hulme exhibitions at Brasenose College, Oxford. He lived at Kearsley, and being left childless, devoted his estates to charitable uses, a life interest to his widow being reserved.[32] She died in 1700, when the trustees came into possession of the whole.[33] Owing to the growth of Manchester the trust estates have increased in value enormously, and several Acts of Parliament have been passed to regulate the uses.[34] Hulme Hall, the residence of the family, was later known as Broadstone Hall.[35]

HULME of Hulme.
Barry of eight or and azure on a canton argent a chaplet gules.

Other families appear from time to time as owning lands in the township, as those of Birches,[36] Bibby,[37] and Stanley.[38] John Reddish was the only landowner contributing to the subsidy of 1541,[39] but in 1622 three are named—Clement Coke, Margaret Hulme, and Thomas Bibby.[40]

In 1788 Thomas Wenman (William) Coke paid £49 out of the total land tax of £68, the next contributor being Brasenose College, Oxford, £9, on account of the Hulme estates.[41] In 1844 John Hyde had an estate of 210 acres in the township, being about a seventh of the land.[42]

For the Established Church St. Elisabeth's was built in 1883 ; Sir W. H. Houldsworth has the patronage of the rectory. In North Reddish is the temporary church of St. Agnes, the Crown and the Bishop of Manchester presenting alternately.

The Wesleyans have a church.

The Roman Catholic Church of St. Joseph was built in 1882.

---

[32] For an account of him see Booker's *Didsbury*, 216–19 ; his will is given in full. A pedigree was recorded in 1664 ; Dugdale, *Visit.* 158.

[33] Booker, op. cit. 219, 220.

[34] Ibid. 220–5. A rental of 1710 is printed in *Manch. Guard. N. and Q.* no. 1263. The Hulme trustees in 1844 owned 225 acres in Reddish ; Booker, op. cit. 201.

[35] Ibid. 225 ; 'Hulme Hall *alias* Broadstone' occurs in 1632.

[36] In 1284 William son of Lycot unsuccessfully claimed a messuage and 8 acres in Reddish against Henry de Trafford, Henry del Birches, and Anabel, daughter of William le Norreys ; Assize R. 1265, m. 5 d. Matthew del Birches in 1323 secured a messuage and lands in Reddish from Hugh son of Richard del Birches and Cecily his wife ; *Final Conc.* ii, 48. A Henry del Wood and Cecily his wife had in 1314 granted a somewhat larger estate to Richard de Chorlton, clerk ; ibid. ii, 15.

[37] James Bibby in 1444 complained that Thurstan Rawlinson of Withington, Robert Chorlton of Chorlton-with-Hardy and Joan his wife, had broken into his closes and houses at Reddish and taken away corn and grass to the value of £10 ; Pal. of Lanc. Plea R. 6, m. 2. James Bibby claimed by a grant from Hugh Bradford and Margaret his wife, she being daughter and heir of Thomas son of Stephen Reddish ; Thomas received the

property from one John Langley. The defendants asserted that one Adam Davy had been the owner, and that Ralph father of Thurstan was his son and heir, which Ralph had wrongfully made a grant to the plaintiff ; ibid. R. 12, m. 8.

In a further suit in 1573 Ralph Bibby, clerk, claimed a messuage and lands against Ralph Dicconson ; it was asserted that the Margaret daughter of Thomas Reddish above mentioned was the mother of James Bibby, and that the succession was : James –s. and h. Henry –s. and h. Thomas –s. and h. Ralph (plaintiff) ; ibid. R. 233, m. 14 d.

[38] 'By an undated deed Thomas the Hermit of Stockport and Margaret daughter of Robert de Standleye conveyed one messuage and lands in Denton, certain lands in Reddish called Egecroft and other specified lands' ; Booker, *Didsbury*, 226. A William Stanley of Reddish in 1603 made Margaret his wife executrix and residuary legatee ; ibid. 227. The residence of the Stanleys was called Woodhall, and was in 1844 in possession of the Rev. William Fox's heirs ; ibid. 201. There was a suit about Woodhall in 1594 ; *Ducatus Lanc.* iii, 308.

Two members of the Stanley family seem to have taken opposite sides in the Civil War. Edward Stanley took part in the defence of Manchester in 1642, when the Earl of Derby besieged it, and died of wounds he received there. He had desired that his estate should be divided

warehouses and works. The London and North-Western Company's Manchester South Junction and Altrincham Railway [6] passes through the centre, with stations at Old Trafford, the cricket ground, and Stretford. The Bridgewater Canal also passes through the centre and north of the township, after crossing the Mersey from Cheshire by Barfoot Bridge.

In 1666 there were in Stretford 117 hearths to be taxed; the principal house was that of Sir Cecil Trafford with twenty-four.[7] A century ago it was famous as a fat pig market, some six hundred animals being killed weekly for Manchester.[8] There was a paper-mill at Old Trafford in 1765. Weaving was formerly one of the chief industries.

The wakes were held at the beginning of October.

A stone celt, Roman remains, and a hoard of Anglo-Saxon coins have been found.[9] The cross[10] was taken down about 1840; the stocks, which were near the cross, had been removed about 1825. The Great Stone—now inclosed by a railing—lies in Old Trafford beside the Chester road; it has two cavities.[11]

A local board was formed in 1868,[12] and its offices were built in 1888; it has become an urban district council of eighteen members, elected from six wards—Stretford, Longford, Trafford, Talbot, Cornbrook, and Clifford. There are a public hall, free libraries, and other institutions. There is a recreation-ground at Old Trafford. At Stretford are a cemetery, opened in 1885, and a sewage-farm. Gas-works were erected in 1852.

Stretford gives its name to one of the parliamentary divisions of the county.

John Holker, who established factories in France, was born at Stretford in 1719.[13] Edward Painter, pugilist, was also a native; 1784–1852.[14] A distinguished resident was John Eglington Bailey, the antiquary, author of a life of Thomas Fuller; he died there in 1888.[15]

An exhibition of art treasures held at Old Trafford in 1857 was opened by Queen Victoria. The Royal Jubilee Exhibition of 1887 was held there.

MANORS In this township there were anciently two manors, both held in the thegnage of the king in chief as of his manor of Salford. The principal was in 1212 *STRETFORD*, rated as one plough-land and held by Hamon de Mascy by the service of a judge;[16] the other was *TRAFFORD*, held by Henry de Trafford at a rent of 5*s*. yearly.[17] Under Mascy a moiety of the former was held by Hugh de Stretford, who performed the service of the judge; and a fourth part was held by the above-named Henry de Trafford, who paid 4*s*. a year.[18] About 1250 another Hamon de Mascy gave the whole of Stretford to his daughter Margery,[19] who afterwards granted Stretford to Richard de Trafford.[20] The moiety of the manor held by Hugh de Stretford in 1212 does not occur subsequently in the records.[21] The Trafford family thus acquired the whole of Stretford and Trafford, and the two manors have descended together. The principal residence remained at the latter place until about 1720, when Trafford Park in Whittleswick was chosen.[22] Manor courts continued to be held until 1872.[23]

MASCY. *Quarterly gules and argent in the second quarter a mullet sable.*

The pedigree of the lords can be traced at least to the early part of the 12th century. Hamon de Mascy before 1190 gave Wolfetnote and his heirs to Ralph son of Randulf and to Robert his son for 4 marks.[25] This was afterwards confirmed to Robert son of Ralph.[26] A further grant was made to Henry

---

[6] Opened in 1849. The Great Central Company is a part-owner of the line.

[7] Subs. R. bdle. 250, no. 9; John Falkner's house had eleven hearths, Edmund Trafford's and Robert Owen's six each.

[8] Baines, *Lancs. Dir.* 1825, ii, 680.

[9] *Lancs. and Ches. Antiq. Soc.* iii, 269; x, 251.

[10] The pedestal is now in the churchyard.

[11] Crofton, op. cit. iii, 44–9, with photographs. See also Harland and Wilkinson, *Traditions of Lancs.* 53.

[12] *Lond. Gaz.* 7 Apr. 1868.

[13] Crofton, op. cit. iii, 158–63. Holker was a Jacobite and became lieutenant in the unfortunate Manchester Regiment of 1745. He escaped from prison, and found a refuge in France, where, with the encouragement of the government, he introduced various manufactures. He was ennobled in 1775, and died in 1786. There are biographies of him in *Dict. Nat. Biog.*; *Lancs. and Ches. Antiq. Soc.* ix, 147; *Pal. Note Bk.* iv, 47, &c.

[14] *Dict. Nat. Biog.*

[15] Crofton, op. cit. iii, 153, 154; there is a portrait at the beginning of vol. i. A list of his writings, compiled by Mr. E. Axon, is in *Lancs. and Ches. Antiq. Soc.* vi, 129.

[16] *Lancs. Inq. and Extents* (Rec. Soc. Lancs. and Ches.), i. 72. Land in Lancashire which had been Hamon de Mascy's was in the king's hands in 1187; Farrer, *Lancs. Pipe R.* 64.

[17] *Lancs. Inq. and Extents,* i, 70. The payment of 5*s*. for his land in Trafford is

recorded in a roll of 1226 as due from Robert son of Ralph de Trafford (ibid. 138), but the entry must have been copied from an old roll, as it will be seen that Robert was dead in 1205.

[18] Ibid. i, 72. A large collection of Trafford charters will be found in the Raines MSS. (Chet. Lib.), xxv; some of them are printed by Crofton, op. cit. iii, 234, &c. Among others are two which show how the Traffords became possessed of the two oxgangs held in 1212. Hamon de Mascy granted to Robert son of Ralph an oxgang of land in Stretford, viz. an eighth part of the land of the vill, at a rent of 2*s*.; Hugh and Henry de Stretford were witnesses; op. cit. iii, 234. The same or a later Hamon granted to Henry son of Robert de Trafford an oxgang of his demesne in Stretford, formerly held by William son of Robert, at a rent of 2*s*.; ibid. This charter mentions that the service of a judge due from the vill was discharged by another.

The deeds quoted below as 'De Trafford deeds' have been taken from the originals.

[19] *Final Conc.*(Rec. Soc. Lancs. and Ches.), i, 154, quoting Trafford muniments.

[20] Margery daughter of Hamon de Mascy about 1260 granted to Richard de Trafford the whole vill of Stretford with all its appurtenances in freemen and villeinages, at a rent of 1*d*.; Crofton, op. cit. iii, 237. The seal is described. Then Hamon de Mascy released to Richard all his claim in the whole vill of Stretford,

son of Robert of an oxgang of Hamon de Mascy's demesne in Ashley, previously held by Uctred, it being a fourth part of the whole vill.[37] Henry, surnamed 'de Stratford,' agreed in 1205 to pay 40*s.* as relief for the half plough-land he held in Trafford.[28] In 1212, as above shown, he held Trafford of the king and a fourth of Stretford of Hamon de Mascy. He died in 1221, when his son and heir Richard paid 20*s.* for relief of the land held of the king.[29]

Apart from his acquisition of Stretford little is known of Richard de Trafford,[30] whose son Henry in 1278 agreed to a partition of the family estates, taking as his share eight oxgangs of land, &c., in Stretford, Chorlton-upon-Medlock, and Withington.[31] Six years later Henry obtained a charter of free warren for his manors of Trafford and Stretford.[32] He was succeeded by his son Henry before 1292,

in which year the younger Henry had a dispute with his brother Richard.[33] Henry de Trafford in 1302 contributed to the aid as holding part of a knight's fee in Harwood near Bolton,[34] and five years afterwards he made a settlement of the manor of Clifton.[35] In the Parliament of 1312 he was a knight of the shire.[36] In 1324 Henry de Trafford had the king's leave to settle his manors of Trafford and Stretford upon Henry son of John son of Henry and his heirs ;[37] and in the following year accordingly this was done.[38] In 1334 Sir Henry de Trafford acquired John Grelley's lands in Chorlton-upon-Medlock.[39]

Soon after this probably he was succeeded by his grandson Henry, also a knight,[40] who died between 1373[41] and 1376, leaving a son Henry under age.[41] The younger Henry died in 1395, holding the manor of Trafford and vill of Stretford, together with two-

---

[27] De Trafford D. no. 142.

[28] *Lancs. Pipe R.* 203, 215. The relief paid was comparatively high.

Henry son of Robert son of Ralph de Trafford received lands in Chorlton-upon-Medlock and in Withington ; De Trafford D. no. 122, 310. He had a dispute with Hamon de Mascy regarding Adam son of William de Stretford, and Hamon agreed that Adam was a free man ; Crofton, op. cit. iii, 235. Henry de Stretford or de Trafford was perhaps a younger son of Robert de Trafford. William son of Robert has already been named and a Richard de Trafford was witness to a charter which must be dated between 1200 and 1204 ; *Hulton Ped.* 3.

There is frequent confusion between Stretford, Stratford, Stafford, and Trafford.

[29] *Fine R. Excerpts* (Rec. Com.), i, 75. Avice widow of Henry de 'Stretford' was of the king's gift in 1222–6. She paid 20*d.* yearly—the amount is a third of the 5*s.* due from Trafford—and her land was worth 3*s.* clear ; *Lancs. Inq. and Extents,* i, 129.

[30] About 1250 he attested a charter respecting Audenshaw ; *Lancs. Pipe R.* 333. In 1255–6 he gave the king 1 mark for a writ ; Orig. 40 Hen. III, m. 8. He obtained a grant of lands in Withington ; De Trafford D. no. 129.

To Richard son of Robert de Stretford he granted an eighth part of the vill of Stretford, that part namely, which Robert the father had held, at a rent of 6*s.* The second best pig was to be rendered for pannage, and corn was to be ground at Trafford Mill to the twentieth measure ; Crofton, op. cit. iii, 237.

[31] *Final Conc.* (Rec. Soc. Lancs. and Ches.), i, 154. This portion had been the dower of Christiana then wife of William de Hacking, but was 'of the inheritance' of Henry de Trafford. It is presumed that Christiana was the widow of Richard de Trafford. The other lands, &c., went to the Chadderton family.

[32] Chart. R. 12 Edw. I (no. 77), m. 4, no. 24. From Richard son of Jordan de Stretford a surrender of his claim to lands held of Henry de Trafford was obtained by the latter ; Crofton, op. cit. iii, 238. Avice widow of Nicholas de Stretford and daughter of Jordan de Stretford in 1292 released her claim on the same to Henry son of Henry de Trafford ; ibid. iii, 241.

[33] The dispute concerned lands, &c., in Clifton, Crompton, and Edgeworth ; Assize R. 408, m. 3 d.; *Final Conc.* i, 170. Lora widow of Henry de Trafford had

called Henry son of Henry to warrant her. Lora appears as plaintiff in 1305 ; Assize R. 1306, m. 20 d.

In 1292 Henry had also to defend his title to the manor of Stretford against Hamon de Mascy, Loreta, his father's widow, then holding a third part and himself the remainder. The plaintiff was non-suited ; Assize R. 408, m. 36. Henry also defeated a claim to a tenement in Stretford put forward by two sisters— Alice wife of Thomas son of Richard (or Roger) de Manchester, and Avice wife of Henry de Openshaw ; ibid. m. 32, 36 d. As grandson of Richard de Trafford he claimed the manor of Chadderton ; ibid. m. 40 d, 47 d.

[34] *Lancs. Inq. and Extents,* i, 312.

[35] *Final Conc.* i, 210 ; the remainders were to his sons Henry (a minor), Richard, Robert, Ralph, and Thomas. These would be the younger sons. The manor of Clifton does not appear again among the Trafford estates.

[36] Pink and Beaven, *Parl. Rep. of Lancs.* 15.

[37] Inq. a.q.d. 17 Edw. II, no. 92. The jurors found that the manors named were held of the king by the service of 5*s.* yearly, and suit at the county court from three weeks to three weeks, and were worth 20 marks clear. Henry de Trafford also held twelve messuages, 260 acres of land, and 30 acres of meadow in Withington of Nicholas de Longford by the service of 1*d.* yearly, and worth 60*s.* clear ; the land and meadow were of no value, because in waste among the heath ; another 40 acres were held by a rent of 12*d.*

In 1324 Henry de Trafford held half a plough-land in Trafford by the service of 5*s.* yearly ; Dods. MSS. cxxxi, fol. 38.

[38] *Final Conc.* ii, 60. Henry de Trafford and Margaret his wife were plaintiffs ; the remainders, after Henry the plaintiffs, were to the elder Henry's sons—Richard, Robert, Thomas, Henry, Geoffrey, and Henry. See also the remainders in a fine respecting lands in Withington in 1323 ; ibid. ii, 54. These younger sons appear to be the Traffords of Prestwich of 1350 ; ibid. ii, 128. There are a number of deeds relating to them among the De Trafford muniments ; in some the father is called Sir Henry, e.g. in one of 1343 by which John son of John the Marshal gave his lands in Manchester to Geoffrey son of Sir Henry de Trafford ; no. 9.

A number of Traffords were killed at Liverpool in 1345 together with Adam de Lever, viz. Geoffrey son of Sir Henry de Trafford ; Richard de Trafford, son of

Sir John the elder, and John and Robert his brothers ; also Richard brother of Henry de Trafford ; Coram Reg. R. 348, m. 22.

[39] De Trafford D. no. 124.

[40] In 1353 Sir Henry de Trafford came into court and proffered letters patent dated 12 June 1343, by which the king ordered that he should not be put on assizes, juries, &c. all his life ; Assize R. 435, m. 17. The same protection, which had been granted at the request of the famous soldier Walter de Mauney, had in 1346 excused him from the obligation of receiving knighthood ; Q.R. Mem. R. 121, m. 142 d. He had therefore served in the French wars.

Henry de Trafford and John de Ashton in 1343 pleaded guilty to retaining people with them who went against the king's peace ; Assize R. 430, m. 29. They and others had in 1341 assembled at Leigh and prevented John de Tyldesley, &c. from entering the church until they agreed to a *dies amoris* with a view to settlement of disputes ; ibid. m. 17. In 1346 Henry de Trafford was found to hold the manor of Trafford in socage by a rent of 5*s.*, paying double as relief, and performing suit of county and wapentake ; Add. MS. 32103, fol. 146. Stretford is not separately named.

In 1359 and again in 1369 Sir Henry de Trafford purchased lands in Manchester from John Grelley ; De Trafford D. no. 15, 18, 19. In the former year he made a feoffment of lands in Crompton, Ancoats, Beswick, and Chorlton to Thomas de Trafford and William Saunpete, chaplain, until his return from the king's service beyond the sea. The remainders were to John de Trafford, Henry son of Robert de Trafford, and John son of Thomas de Trafford ; Court of Wards and Liveries, box 13A/FD12.

Licence for his oratory at Trafford was in 1368 granted to Sir Henry ; Lich. Epis. Reg. Stretton, v, fol. 20.

[41] In Dec. 1373 Sir Henry released to John son of Nicholas de Trafford his right to lands in Ancoats ; De Trafford D. no. 84.

[42] At Easter 1376 Henry de Torbock claimed the custody of lands in Turton until the coming of age of Henry son and heir of Sir Henry de Trafford ; De Banco R. 462, m. 89 ; 463, m. 67. Henry de Trafford had a licence for an oratory at Trafford for two years from 1387 ; Lich. Epis. Reg. vi, fol. 123. He came of age in or before 1389 ; De Trafford D. no. 125, 28.

thirds of a third part of the manor of Edgeworth, and leaving a son and heir Henry, six years of age.[43] This son died in 1408, the manors going to his brother Edmund,[44] known as the Alchemist, from his having procured a licence from the king in 1446 authorizing him to transmute metals.[45] Sir Edmund, at Eccles in 1411, married Alice daughter and co-heir of Sir William Venables of Bollin, and thus

TRAFFORD of Trafford. *Argent a griffin segreant gules.*

acquired a considerable estate in Cheshire, which descended in the Trafford family for many generations.[46] Sir Edmund died in 1458[47] leaving a son Sir John,[48] who was regularly succeeded by five generations of Edmunds.[49] In the latter half of the 16th century the fortunes of the family began to decline; several estates were sold,[50] and Sir Edmund the fourth, having conformed to the Established religion, appears to have attempted, and with some success, to acquire fresh wealth by an active prosecution of the recusants.[51] As sheriff he was specially zealous against them. He also arranged the marriage of his son Edmund with Margaret daughter and co-heir of John Booth of

[43] *Lancs. Inq. p.m.* (Chet. Soc.), i, 63. For the dower of Elizabeth widow of Henry de Trafford and afterwards wife of Ralph de Staveley, see Pal. of Lanc. Chan. Misc. 1/8, m. 21, 22.

[44] Lancs. Rec. Inq. p.m. no. 21, taken in 1414. By this it was found that Henry son of Henry son of Sir Henry de Trafford died on 20 Feb. 1407–8, seised of the manor of Trafford and two-thirds of the vill, held of the king as of his duchy of Lancaster in socage by the service of 5s. yearly, and worth £20 per annum clear; also two-thirds of three parts of the hamlet of Chorlton-upon-Medlock ('Chollerton'), held of Thomas La Warre; lands in Hulme in Barton, Blackrod, and Edgeworth. Edmund the heir was of full age in 1414. His custody during minority had been granted to Sir Ralph de Staveley. See also *Dep. Keeper's Rep.* xxxiii, App. 11. Further inquisitions were made in 1417, after the death of Margery, grandmother of Edmund; ibid. 13; *Lancs. Inq. p.m.* (Chet. Soc.), i, 127; and in 1421 after the death of Agnes widow of the last Henry; Towneley MS. DD, no. 1505.

[45] The licence was granted on 7 April 1446, to Sir Edmund Trafford and Sir Thomas Ashton; Rymer, *Foedera*, Syllabus, ii, 676; Crofton, *Stretford*, iii, 112.

Sir Edmund was knighted in 1426 for his conduct at the battle of Verneuil; Metcalfe, *Bk. of Knights*, 1. In 1431 he was one of the jurors for Salford-shire; *Feud. Aids*, iii, 95. In a plea of 1445 he was described as the son and heir of Henry, brother of Joan, mother of Thomas Booth, father of Alice wife of Thomas Duncalf; Pal. of Lanc. Plea R. 8, m. 23.

[46] See Ormerod, *Ches.* (ed. Helsby), iii, 589, &c. The Cheshire inquisitions there printed give the descent as follows : Sir Edmund died 24 Jan. 1457–8, leaving a son John, aged 25; Sir John died 11 Jan. 1488–9, leaving a son Edmund, aged 34; Sir Edmund died in 1513, leaving a son Edmund aged 28; Sir Edmund died in 1533, leaving a son also named Edmund, aged 26. These may be compared with the Lancashire inquisitions.

[47] Writs of *Diem clausit extr.* were issued in 1460 and 1462; *Dep. Keeper's Rep.* xxvii, App. 177, 176.

[48] Sir John Trafford and Edmund his son, in conjunction with Hugh Scholes, the priest, in 1468 made a lease for ninety-six years of certain chantry lands in Manchester for 15s. 6d. net; De Trafford D. no. 51. Sir John died 20 Jan. 1488–9 holding the manor of Trafford, the vill of Stretford, and two parts of the third part of the manor of Edgeworth; the service for Trafford was unknown; Sir Edmund, the son and heir, was thirty-

six years of age; D p.m. iii, 85.

A pedigree draw t ates the cla'm to th Saddleworth, purcha the first Sir Henry d fault of he'rs it cam Henry, who granted Piers and John, another son, Thoma co], fro th l s to his grandson Hen and Liv. box 13A/F

[49] (i) Sir Edmund knight at the creatio Duke of York in 14 25. He died in A manor of Trafford o of 5s.; its clear val also held twenty mes of th h ' f the service of a pai annual value was £

Barton,[52] and though the son afterwards disinherited the children of this marriage, the Trafford share of the Barton estates has descended like Trafford to the issue of a second marriage—with Mildred daughter of Thomas Cecil, first Earl of Exeter.[53]

Cecil Trafford, the eldest son of this union, was made a knight at Hoghton Tower in 1617.[54] He was at first, like his grandfather, a Protestant and a persecutor, but afterwards, about 1632, embraced the faith he had attempted to destroy.[55] In 1638, accordingly, the king seized a third of his estates and granted them on lease to farmers.[56] Siding with the king on the outbreak of the Civil War, he was seized and imprisoned by the other party and his estates were sequestered.[57] His sons appear to have gone abroad, as they are mentioned as present at Rome and Douay.[58] In 1653 Sir Cecil begged leave to contract under the Recusants Act for the sequestered two-thirds of his estates.[59]

Sir Cecil died in 1672,[60] his eldest son Edmund[61] died twenty years later, and was followed by a brother Humphrey, who was accused of participation in the

rigorously; *Cal. S.P. Dom.* 1547–80, p. 656.

The rhetorical account of his persecution of the Allens in 1584 in Bridgewater's *Concertatio* reads thus: 'The furious hate of this inhuman wretch was all the more fiercely stirred by the fact that he saw offered to him such a prospect of increasing his slender means out of the property of Catholics and of adorning his house with various articles of furniture filched from their houses. For though as far as his own fortune went he could scarcely be called a gentleman, still with other people's gold, no matter how wrongfully come by, he might rightly be called and accounted a knight'; Gillow, *Haydock Papers*, 31. This may be balanced by the equally rhetorical eulogium of his chaplain, William Massie, who in 1586 addressed him as 'a principal protector of God's truth and a great countenance and credit to the preachers thereof in those quarters,' who had 'hunted out and unkenneled those sly and subtle foxes the Jesuits and Seminary priests out of their cells and caves to the uttermost of his power, with the great illwill of many both open and private enemies to the prince and the church.' He also says that Sir Edmund had 'maintained still his house with great hospitality, in no point diminishing the glory of his worthy predecessors, but rather adding to it'; quoted by Crofton, op. cit. iii, 123. His portrait is given ibid. 129.

[53] Ibid. iii, 131–3, 265–72; the marriage led to many disputes and appears to have been unhappy. The parties separated before 1592.

[53] This apparently unjust disinheriting of the elder children was naturally resented, and in 1620 the Earl of Exeter wrote to the Council stating that he feared the machinations of the elder brothers against Sir Cecil, and begging that they might be ordered to abstain from violence, and that a competent guard might be placed in the chief manor-house; *Cal. S.P. Dom.* 1619–23, p. 146. A settlement of the manors was made in 1622 by Sir Cecil Trafford, acting with Edmund, John, and Richard Trafford; Pal. of Lanc. Feet of F. bdle. 100, no. 22.

[54] Metcalfe, op. cit. 171.

[55] Crofton, op. cit. iii, 136–7. Hollin-

worth states that rector of Ashton the College, havin ministered the Lo it was feared) som drink in Salford, morning in the Bridge, no one there; Dr. But Cambridge, hange afterwards; and s

rated by the John Rylands Library in Manchester, founded by his widow.[69]

From a survey of the tithes made in 1649 it appears that there were in Stretford Manor twenty-four whole seats, or holdings. The tithe corn in 1643 had filled three bays and the greater part of a fourth; it was mostly oats and barley.[70]

The land tax returns of 1796 show that John Trafford was then the principal landowner, he paying more than one-third of the tax; the remainder of the land seems to have been much divided.[71]

CHURCH The earliest record of the chapel of Stretford is in a lease of 1413, in which land is described as lying next to the chapel.[72] Rather more than a century later a chantry was founded in it by Sir Edmund Trafford, for the souls of his ancestors.[73] At the confiscation in 1547–8 the rental of the chantry was only 44s.; the chapel had a chalice and two vestments.[74] Service appears to have been maintained in this chapel even after the Elizabethan changes, for in 1563 William Hodgkinson was 'curate of Stretford,'[75] and seems to have remained there until 1586; he was in 1581 censured for keeping an alehouse.[76] The names of many curates are on record,[77] but except during the Commonwealth period there was no adequate provision for them, there being neither residence nor endowment.[78] At the beginning of the 18th century the 'settled maintenance' was only 11s. 2d.,[79] but

some further endowments and contributions were secured, the chapel was rebuilt in 1718,[80] and from about that time the succession of curates and rectors appears to be unbroken. In 1842 the present church of St. Matthew was consecrated;[81] it was enlarged in 1861. A district had been assigned in 1839.[82] The Dean and Canons of Manchester present to the benefice.

The following is a list of the recent curates and incumbents[83] :—

1716	Samuel Bolton, M.A. (Brasenose College, Oxf.)
1717	Roger Masterson
1718	Robert Armitstead, B.A. (Magdalen Hall, Oxf.)
1721	John Jackson, M.A.
1741	John Baldwin, M.A.
1747	John Baxter,[84] B.A.
1766	William Stopford,[85] B.A. (Brasenose College, Oxf.)
1778	Thomas Seddon [86]
1796	Thomas Gaskell
1818	Robinson Elsdale,[87] D.D. (Corpus Christi College, Oxf.)
1850	Joseph Clarke,[88] M.A. (St. John's College, Camb.)
1860	William Edward Brendon
1864	Thomas Daniel Cox Morse [89]

---

[69] Crofton, op. cit. 164–6; a portrait is given. John Rylands was born at St. Helens in 1801, began business in Manchester in 1823, and died in 1888. He was a Congregationalist in religion. There is a notice of him in *Dict. Nat. Biog.*

[70] Crofton, op. cit. 193–6.

[71] Land tax returns at Preston.

[72] Quoted in Raines, *Chantries* (Chet. Soc.), i, 55.

[73] The only endowment was a tenement at Whitehall in Budworth, Cheshire, and the chantry priest in 1547 could produce no deeds. There were long suits concerning the lands from 1554 onwards; Duchy of Lanc. Misc. Bks. xxiii, 72 d, and Crofton, *Stretford*, i, 51–5. From the depositions it appears that the land had been purchased from Thomas Hardware by Edmund Trafford, father of the Sir Edmund Trafford living in 1560, i.e. by the Sir Edmund who held the Trafford estates from 1513 to 1533. This chantry was probably founded soon after 1530, for a witness stated that her husband, who had been tenant, had 'twenty years past' (i.e. in 1540) been told that the chantry priest had become his landlord. This chantry is not named in the *Valor Eccl.* of 1535.

Two cantarists are known:

c. 1540, Christopher Rainshaw; Crofton, op. cit.; *Clergy List* (Rec. Soc. Lancs. and Ches.), 11, 'paid by Edmund Trafford and others at Stretford.'

c. 1547, Charles Gee, whose name also appears in the Visitation lists of 1548 and 1554.

[74] Raines, *Chantries*, i, 55, 56. The 'ornaments' were sold for 10d.; ibid. ii, 277.

[75] Visit. List at Chest.

[76] Crofton, op. cit. i, 60; he is described as 'aged 40'—i.e. forty or more—in 1586, so that he must have been quite young in 1563. A William Hodgkinson obtained a schoolmaster's licence for Middlewich or elsewhere in the diocese in 1576; and later in the year the same

or another of the n
Roger H dg
nant's Acct Bk Ch

SALFORD

1868 Dudley Hart, M.A. (T.C.D.)
1903 James Peter Rountree, M.A. (T.C.D.)

St. Bride's, Old Trafford, consecrated in 1878, is in the patronage of trustees ;[90] All Saints, 1885, is in the Bishop of Manchester's gift. At Old Trafford there are also St. Thomas's, the chapel of the Blind Asylum,[91] and St. Hilda's, consecrated in 1904, with the districts of St. Cuthbert and St. John, not yet having permanent churches ; the Crown and the Bishop of Manchester present alternately to these benefices ; and also to the new district of St. Peter, Stretford.

There was in 1718 only a private school, without endowment. Soon afterwards the township shared in the benefaction of Ann Hinde.[92]

The Wesleyan Methodists and the Primitive Methodists each have churches at Stretford and Old Trafford ; and the Independent Methodists have one at the former place.[93] The Baptists also have a church at Stretford. The Congregationalists have churches at Stretford and Old Trafford[94] ; in the latter part of the township there is also a Welsh Congregational chapel.

The Unitarian Free church, begun in Moss Side in 1887, has from 1901 had its place of worship within Stretford township.

Although from the time of Sir Cecil Trafford, the chief resident family, as well as some minor ones, professed the ancient faith,[95] no chapel was erected in the township[96] until 1859, when a temporary one was opened. This was followed by St. Anne's in 1863 ; it was consecrated in 1867.[97] St. Alphonsus's, Brooks' Bar, was opened in 1904.[98]

HULME

Overholm and Noranholm, 1226 ; Hulm, 1310.

The township of Hulme is bounded on the north, west, and south, in the main, by the Medlock, Irwell, and Cornbrook respectively. It has an area of 477¾ acres[1] and is wholly urban. There was a population of 66,916 in 1901.

The principal thoroughfare is the Chester Road, starting at Knott Mill and proceeding south-west to Stretford.[2] It is on the line of the old Roman road to Chester. Almost parallel to it are City Road, from Gaythorn to Stretford, and Stretford Road from Ardwick to Stretford. Across these runs Jackson

MANOR The early descent of *HULME* is obscured by the number of places of this name in South Manchester and Eccles, and by its being included either in Salford or in Manchester. It seems clear that Jordan, Dean of Manchester, in the 12th century held it of the manor of Salford in thegnage by a rent of 5s.,[4] and that in 1212 Henry de Chetham held it by the same service, it being assessed as four oxgangs of land.[5] The same tenure is alleged in the later inquisitions touching the manor. On the other hand Hulme is included within the boundary of the manor of Manchester in the survey of 1320,[6] at which time Robert de Ashton held a moiety of the manor of Hulme by Alport by a rent of 5s. at the four terms, payable to the lord of Manchester.[7] It seems possible, therefore, that the Grelleys had secured the

[90] For district see *Lond. Gaz.* 17 May 1879. It was an offshoot of St. Margaret's, Whalley Range, a school church having been built in 1863 ; Crofton, op. cit. iii, 49.

[91] For district see *Lond. Gaz.* 13 Aug. 1858 ; and Crofton, op. cit. iii, 62. The gift of the chapel to the Bishop of Manchester was decided to be a breach of the trusts, but the order creating a district does not appear to have been rescinded.

[92] Gastrell, *Notitia*, ii, 96; above p. 201.

[93] The Wesleyans held services in Stretford as early as 1814, and then or soon afterwards used a tent set up once a week. In spite of the opposition of Sir Thomas de Trafford, who refused to sell any land, a site was secured and a chapel built in 1844. The present church was built in 1862.

[94] The first Congregational chapel, built in 1840, was the outcome of open-air preaching, begun as early as 1825. The present church was built in1861. Chorlton

mesne lordship of the manor, but that in course of time this mesne lordship was, as in many similar cases, forgotten, and the immediate tenants were considered to hold directly of the honour of Lancaster, paying their rent at Salford manor-house. Another explanation is that one moiety became absorbed in the lordship of Manchester, the other moiety being that afterwards known as the manor of Hulme, held of Salford.

Whatever may be the solution of this difficulty,[8] the actual possessors adopted the surname of Hulme[9] and were succeeded early in the 14th century by the Rossendales,[10] and these by a branch of the Prestwich family, who also held lands in Oldham, perhaps a portion of the Hulme inheritance.[11] Of the Prestwich family little is known[12] until the 16th century, when Ralph son of Ellis Prestwich entailed the lands. Edmund, his son and heir, being without issue, gave them 'by deed and fine' to his cousin Edmund son of Edmund Prestwich deceased.[13] The elder Ed-

mund died on 27 November 1577, holding the manor of Hulme and extensive lands in Manchester and Oldham ; Hulme was held of the queen as of her manor of Salford in socage by the ancient rent of 5s., and its clear annual value was £10.[14] His successor, the younger Edmund Prestwich, died in 1598 holding the manor as before, and leaving as heir his son Edmund, then twenty-one years of age.[15] The last-named Edmund died at Hulme in February 1628–9, holding the family estates, and leaving a son and heir Thomas, aged twenty-eight.[16]

Thomas Prestwich, who was educated at Oxford,[17] compounded for the two-thirds of his estate liable to sequestration for recusancy in

Prestwich of Hulme. *Gules a mermaid proper crined or holding a glass and comb of the last.*

[8] The whole of Hulme may have been held half of Salford and half of Manchester ; but the Prestwich inquisitions do not support this, though it is clear that if there were such moieties this family held both in the 15th century.

[9] Geoffrey de Hulme appears to have been the possessor about 1300 ; *Lancs. Inq. and Extents,* i, 301.

[10] In 1310 Adam de Rossendale and Margery his wife settled the manor of Hulme near Manchester, with remainders to their children in succession—Geoffrey, John, Robert, and Cecily ; *Final Conc.* (Rec. Soc. Lancs. and Ches.), ii, 5.

Geoffrey de Hulme about 1324 held a plough-land in Hulme by the service of 6s. a year ; John La Warre held a plough-land in Hulme by the service of 5s. a year ; *Dods MSS.* cxxxi, fol. 38, 38b.

[11] Cecily de Hulme in 1346 paid to Salford the rent of 5s. due for half a plough-land in Hulme ; *Add. MS.* 32103, fol. 146b.

Alice widow of John son of Geoffrey de Hulme in the same year demanded dower against Cecily widow of John de Prestwich in two-thirds of nine messuages, 100 acres of land, &c., in Oldham and in two-thirds of the manor of Hulme by Manchester ; also against Margaret widow of John son of Adam de Rossendale in the remaining third of the estate in Oldham and Hulme. The defence, which the jury accepted, was that John de Hulme had never been seised in fee, so that no dower was due to Alice ; De Banco R. 346, m. 286 d. It seems clear from this case and the fine of 1310 that John de Rossendale succeeded to Hulme, and dying without issue his sister Cecily became the heir. Geoffrey de Hulme (in possession in 1324) was apparently the eldest son of Adam de Rossendale.

From another suit, four years later, it appears that John's widow Margaret afterwards married a Richard de Vernon, for Ralph de Prestwich—presumably the son and heir of Cecily—proceeded against Richard de Vernon and Margaret his wife for waste in the latter's dower lands ; De Banco R. 364, m. 89.

[12] A writ of *Diem clausit extr.* for a Nicholas de Prestwich was issued in 1377 ; *Dep. Keeper's Rep.* xxxii, App. 350 ; see also *Mamecestre,* ii, 267. It is not stated that he was of Hulme.

In 1440 Ralph Prestwich made a feoffment of the manor of Hulme and of various messuages and lands in Manchester, Crompton, and Oldham ; *Final Conc.* iii, 105 ; see also *Pal. of Lanc.* Plea R. 3, m. 14b ; 5, m. 3, 8. Ralph held half a plough-land in Hulme near Manchester in 1445–6 of the king as duke, in socage, rendering 5s. yearly ; the relief due was 5s. ; *Duchy of Lanc.* Knights' Fees, 2/20.

Ellis Prestwich in 1473 held the manor of Hulme of the lord of Manchester by knight's service and 5s. rent ; also burgages in Manchester by a rent of 29d. ; *Mamecestre,* iii, 482–7. An Edmund Prestwich, holding land in Manchester, occurs in the same rental ; ibid. 485. Ellis Prestwich made a feoffment of lands in Crumpsall in 1478 ; De Trafford D. no. 89. He received a general pardon in 1487, so that he may have been a Yorkist ; *Dep. Keeper's Rep.* xl, App. 541. The writ of *Diem clausit extr.* after his death was issued 9 June 1501 ; Towneley MS. CC (Chet. Lib.), no. 707.

Nicholas and Ralph Prestwich in 1506 made a feoffment of the manor of Hulme, with a mill, messuages, and lands in Manchester, Salford, Hulme, and other places ; *Final Conc.* iii, 162. Ralph son of Ellis Prestwich is named in a writ of 1526 ; *Pal. of Lanc.* Writs Proton. The arms only were recorded at the herald's visitation in 1533.

[13] *Visit.* of 1613 (Chet. Soc.), 41 ; it appears that Edmund the beneficiary was son of Edmund son of Richard Prestwich, a younger brother of Ralph. A pedigree was recorded in the *Visit.* of 1567 (Chet. Soc.), 6, by Edmund son of Ralph.

The fine referred to is that of 1566, by which Edmund Prestwich settled the manor of Hulme, with its appurtenances and messuages, water-mill, dovecote, land, pasture, &c., in Hulme, Withenshaw, Manchester, Salford, Crumpsall, Oldham, and Crompton ; *Pal. of Lanc.* Feet of F. bdle. 28, m. 190. The uses are stated in his inquisition.

[14] *Duchy of Lanc.* Inq. p.m. xii, 4. The indenture defining the uses of the fine of 1566 is recited in full, as well as Edmund's will. Fearing lest his 'ancient inheritance at his decease might be scattered and dispersed to the utter decay of hospitality at his said house of Hulme,'

he settled his property upon Edmund Prestwich the younger, son of Edmund Prestwich deceased, and his heirs male, with remainder to Ralph Prestwich and his heirs male. By his will his wife Isabel was to hold Hulme, residing there and maintaining due hospitality, holding also the manor of Northall *alias* Bracebridge and lands at Canwick in Lincolnshire, paying £6 13s. 4d. a year to Edmund Prestwich the younger and £4 to Ralph Prestwich. His messuage of Withenshaw in Hulme he gave to his servant Gilbert Wilkinson for life. Bareyshaw in Oldham and Broadbent in Sholver are also named in the will, by which £40 was given to the building or repair of Crossferry Bridge. The lands in Withenshaw (though described as in Hulme) were held of Nicholas Longford in socage by a rent of 3s. 4d. ; the messuages and lands in Manchester were held of Lord La Warre by a rent of 12s., and those in Salford of the queen by a rent of 12s. 4d. The next of kin and heirs were—James Ashton, son and heir of Anne sister of Edmund Prestwich ; Alexander Reddish, son and heir of John late son and heir of Alice, another sister ; Anne Ashton, daughter and one of the heirs of Cecily, another sister ; and Isabel wife of John Gridlow, daughter and heir of Eleanor, the remaining sister.

[15] *Duchy of Lanc.* Inq. p.m. xvii, 27. By his will Edmund the father left to his son and heir his 'chain of gold and all the glass in every window in the hall, parlour, and chambers belonging to Hulme Hall, and also all the wainscot and ceiling standing in every place of the said hall, chambers, and parlours,' on condition that leases made to the younger sons should be allowed. The younger sons were Ralph, Ellis, John, and Thomas ; Piccope, *Wills* (Chet. Soc.), iii, 103–5.

A settlement of the manor of Hulme, &c., was made by Edmund Prestwich in 1625 ; *Pal. of Lanc.* Feet of F. bdle. 107, no. 3.

[16] *Duchy of Lanc.* Inq. p.m. xxvii, 74. An abstract of his will is printed in *Manch. Ct. Leet Rec.* iii, 152. There is a notice of John Prestwich, B.D., a younger son of Edmund's, in *Pal. Note Bk.* ii, 181, 225. He left his books to Manchester.

[17] Foster, *Alumni Oxon.*; M.A. 1629. He was also of Gray's Inn.

1632, his annual fine being £6 13s. 4d.[18] He zealously espoused the king's side during the Civil War ; was a commissioner of array in 1642 ; fought in the wars with varying fortune, being made a baronet in 1644, and a knight afterwards on the field of battle.[19] He compounded for his estates in 1647,[20] but his exertions in the king's cause resulted in the ruin of his house,[21] and in 1660 Hulme was sold to Sir Edward Mosley of Hough End in Withington.[22] Passing to the Mosleys of Ancoats,[23] the Hulme estate descended to Lady Bland, and was sold by her son Sir John Bland in 1751 to George Lloyd.[24] In 1764 a portion was purchased by the Duke of Bridgewater.[25]

Hulme Hall stood on a rise of red sandstone rock overlooking the River Irwell just below where it is joined by the Medlock, and about half a mile above Ordsall. It is described by Aikin in 1795 as 'an old half-timbered house,' and from the evidence of sketches and drawings made while the building was still standing seems to have been a good specimen of the domestic timber architecture of the county.[26] It was of two stories and built round a quadrangle, but no plan has been preserved showing the disposition and arrangements of its various parts. The river front facing north-west appears to have been the most picturesque side of the house, presenting an irregular line of building, one of its three gables containing ' an oriel window with a projecting story above.'[27] The approach was by an avenue of fine elm trees, and the entrance seems to have been by an archway under a tower on the south-east side of the quadrangle, on one side of which the building was only one-storied. The timber work to the quadrangle is said to have been more ornate than that in the front of the building, but some parts of the house appear to have been of brick covered with plaster. It is not easy to reconcile the various views of the hall taken by different people at different times, or any of them with the block plan of the hall as shown in Green's map of Manchester (1794). In the 18th century the gardens of Hulme Hall 'were celebrated for their beauty, and decorated with various works of art and antiquity, among which were several Roman altars and other remains of the former domination of that warlike race, which had been discovered from time to time in the immediate neighbourhood.'[28] The portion of the hall facing the gardens, consisting of two or three gables of two stories with the porch on the extreme right, is described early in the 19th century as containing ' a staircase of large dimensions and massy appearance. It is composed of ancient oak, which age had turned to a dark brown or black colour. The upper rooms are panelled and have large fireplaces with chimneypieces and twisted pillars in a grotesque style. The interior is more perfect, and the exterior more decayed, than the other parts of the hall.'[29] The hall was 'fast falling into decay' in 1807 (Britton), and was then let out in tenements to poor families. In one of the rooms was a series of 16th-century oak panels sculptured with carved heads and figures, but these were removed to Worsley Old Hall about 1833 (or before), and are now in the new hall there.[30] Hulme Hall was pulled down about 1840 to give place to buildings and works in connexion with the Bridgewater Canal, and murky smoke begrimed workshops and mills now cover the site.

It is said that in front of the hall, at the river side, was a red sandstone rock called Fisherman's Rock, in the face of which was a cave known as Robbers' Cave.[30a]

In 1787 the chief proprietors were George Lloyd, the Duke of Bridgewater, and William Egerton, together paying four-fifths of the land-tax ; Thomas Bullard or Bullock also had a fair estate.[31]

The increase of the population as Manchester expanded from the end of the 18th century has led to the erection of a number of places of worship. In connexion with the Established Church, St. George's, built in 1826–7, was consecrated in 1828 ;[32] Holy Trinity, 1843 ;[33] St. Mark's, 1852 ;[34] St. Paul's,

---

[18] Lucas's 'Warton' (MS.) from Thoresby.

[19] G.E.C. Complete Baronetage, ii, 222. In 1642 he endeavoured to secure the stock of powder in Manchester, and afterwards took part in the siege of the town ; Civil War Tracts (Chet. Soc.), 15, 51. He was taken prisoner at the defeat of the Royalists near Ormskirk in 1644, being then described as Colonel Sir Thomas Prestwick ; ibid. 204. See also War in Lancs. (Chet. Soc.), 92.

[20] Cal. of Com. for Compounding, ii, 1443. In 1646 he desired to compound for his 'delinquency,' on the Truro articles. He was an officer under Lord Hopton. The fine was £925, reduced in 1649 to £443.

[21] Sir Thomas is traditionally said to have been encouraged in his expenditure for the king by his mother, who assured him of a treasure she had hidden ; but she died without revealing the place of deposit, which was never found. Sir Thomas died at the beginning of 1674.

[22] A settlement of the manor, with lands, &c., in Hulme and Manchester, was made in 1657 by Thomas Prestwich the elder and Mary his wife, Thomas Prestwich the younger and Mary his wife, Nicholas Mosley, Fabian Phillips, and Edward Percival ; Pal. of Lanc. Feet of F. bdle. 160, m. 171. The sale to Sir Edward Mosley was immediately confirmed by an Act of Parliament in 1661 ; 13 Chas. II, cap. 2 (private).

[23] Under the will of Sir Edward Mosley his cousin Edward, a younger son of Oswald Mosley of Ancoats, acquired his estates, Hulme on the subsequent partition being retained by him ; Mosley Fam. Mem. 25, 29. See further in the accounts of Ancoats and Withington. For fines concerning it see Pal. of Lanc. Feet of F. bdle. 204, m. 66 ; 213, m. 84.

Sir John Bland in 1747 held the manors of Heaton Norris and Hulme, with lands, &c., in Hulme, Rusholme, Fallowfield, Burnage, Birch Hall-houses, Chorlton, and Heaton Norris ; Com. Pleas Recov. R. Mich. 21 Geo. II, m. 85.

[24] A pedigree of the Lloyds, who continue to hold a large portion of the Prestwich estates, is given in Crofton's Old Moss Side, 38.

[25] Raines in Notitia Cestr. ii, 68. It was the Duke of Bridgewater who was in 1779 liable for the ancient 5s. rent to Salford ; Duchy of Lanc. Rentals 14/25.

[26] See Lancs. and Ches. Antiq. Soc. xiv, 194. There is a lithographed drawing of the hall in James's Views, 1825, and an engraving in Britton's Beauties of Lancs.

[27] Pal. Note Bk. i, 201.

[28] Mosley Fam. Mem. 32.

[29] Notes by R. Milne-Redhead to his drawings of Hulme Hall.

1857 ;[35] St. Mary's[36] and St. John Baptist's,[37] both in 1858 ; St. Philip's, 1860 ;[38] St. Michael's, 1864 ;[39] St. Gabriel's[40] and St. Stephen's,[41] both in 1869. The incumbents, who are styled rectors, are appointed in five cases by bodies of trustees ; the Crown and the Bishop of Manchester nominate alternately to St. Mark's, the bishop alone to St. John's, the Dean and Canons of Manchester to St. George's and Holy Trinity, and Earl Egerton of Tatton to St. Mary's. St. Michael's and St. Philip's have mission rooms.

A Methodist chapel existed in Hulme in 1842. The Wesleyans had chapels in Radnor Street and George Street. The Methodist New Connexion has one church, and the United Free Church two ; the Primitive Methodists also have one. The Baptists have a church in York Street with a mission chapel. The Welsh Baptists formerly had one. The Congregationalist church in Chorlton Road, Stretford, has three dependencies in Hulme, their principal church is Zion in Stretford Road, and there are two others.[42]

The Salvation Army has two stations. The Church of United Friends has a meeting place ; the Catholic Apostolic Church (Irvingite) also has one. The Unitarians have a mission to the poor.

The Roman Catholic Church of St. Wilfrid was opened in 1842. The large convent and school of Our Lady of Loreto is in this township.

ASHTON-UNDER-LYNE

Eston, 1212 ; Ashton, 1277 ; Aston, 1278 ; Asshton, Asheton, Assheton, 1292 ; Ashton-under-Lyme, 1307 ; Assheton-under-Lyme, 1345. Lyne, for Lyme or Lime, seems to be modern.

This single-township parish[1] occupies the southeastern corner of the county, and has an area of 9,494 acres. The surface is hilly, particularly in the east ; a long ridge, attaining a height of 1,000 ft., stretches from north to south near the eastern border, various spurs shooting out to the west. These spurs are separated from each other by the Medlock and its tributaries, and by other streams flowing into the River Tame, which forms the eastern and southern boundary of the parish.[2] There are numerous bridges over this river. The Millstone Grit series occurs in the valley of the Tame and northward to Lees. Westward the Lower and Upper Coal Measures follow in sequence until on the western side of the parish the Lower Red Sandstone of the Permian Rocks occurs at Audenshaw and extends towards Droylsden and the Manchester Waterworks.

The population was thus returned in 1901 : Ashton Town, 43,890 ; Audenshaw, 7,216 ; Little Moss, 595 ; Woodhouses, 832—8,643 ; Knott Lanes, including Alt, 1,037 ; Bardsley, 2,194 ; Crossbank, 1,077; Lees, 3,621 ; Waterloo (with Taunton), 3,858— 11,787 ; Hartshead (with Hazelhurst), 745 ; Hurst, 7,145 ; Mossley, 13,452 ; Stalybridge, 27,673— 49,015 ; making a total of 113,335 ; but some places outside Lancashire are herein included.

The town of Ashton stands on an eminence overhanging the Tame, near the centre of the southern boundary, and having Stalybridge[3] immediately to the east. From Ashton itself the principal roads branch out, to Oldham on the north, Manchester on the west,

[35] The district was formed in 1858 ; *Lond. Gaz.* 13 Aug.

[36] For district see ibid. 2 Dec. 1859.

[37] Ibid.

[38] A district was assigned to it in 1861 ; ibid. 22 Nov.

[39] For district see ibid. 30 Aug. 1864.

[40] Ibid. 10 Aug. 1869.

[41] Ibid. 20 May, 1870.

[42] A cottage meeting begun in 1812, followed by Sunday-school and temperance work, led to the building of a small chapel in 1817 in Jackson's Lane. This, the original of Zion Chapel, was enlarged four years later, but the church was dissolved for a time. Regular preaching was re-

viz. (i) Ashton Town, 1,373½ acres, bounded on the east by Cock Brook, and on the west by Ashton Moss, with the hamlets or suburbs of Chamber Hills, Oversteads, Lees Fields, Charlestown, Ryecroft, Moss Side, and Guide Bridge ; (ii) Audenshaw, 2,589½ acres, in the west, containing, beside Audenshaw proper with North Street, Hooley Hill, High Ash, Shepley, Little Moss, Waterhouses, Woodhouses, Sunderland, Medlock Vale, and Buckley Hill ; (iii) Knott Lanes, on the north, 2,417 acres, with Wood Park, Cross Bank, Alt Edge, Taunton, Waterloo, Bardsley, Lees or Hey, Mill Bottom, Birks, Rhodes Hill, Lanehead, High Knolls, Alt, and Alt Hill ; (iv) Hartshead, on the east, 3,114 acres, with Stalybridge, Mossley, Hurst and Higher Hurst, Smallshaw, Greenhurst, Hazelhurst, Heyrod, Luzley, Souracre, and Ridge Hill. In 1894,

Stalybridge being added to Cheshire, the remainder of the parish of Ashton and a divided into the existing townships of Ashton-under-Lyne, Audenshaw, Little

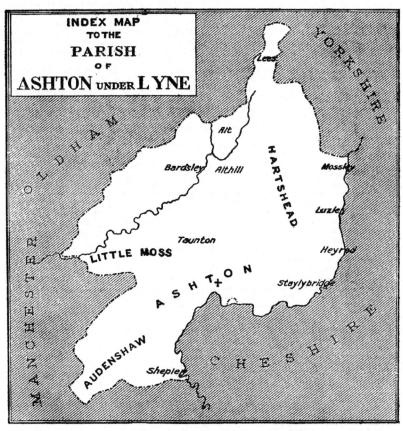

INDEX MAP
TO THE
PARISH
OF
ASHTON UNDER LYNE

(ed. 1868), i, 430. The document is printed in full in Jas. Butterworth's *Ashton*, 155–65.

  Much the same are the hamlets recorded in the hearth-tax return of 1666. There were 538 hearths liable, of which in Ashton proper the houses of Richard Hurst and Nicholas Walker had six each, of Rector

Ellison, five ; at Audenshaw — Robert Ashton, ten, and John Sandford, six ; at Little Moss—William Bell, eight ; and at Woodhouses—Samuel Jenkinson, seven. No other dwelling had as many as six hearths ; Subs. R. bdle. 250, no. 9.

  ⁵ For an account of Lees see *Oldham*

Notes and Gleanings, ii, 5, 14, 24 ; also ibid. i, 78.
  ⁶ *Lond. Gaz.* 3 July 1874.
  ⁷ Ibid. 19 Apr. 1861 ; district extended by 37 & 38 Vict. cap. 1.
  ⁸ *Lond. Gaz.* 30 Sept. 1859 ; the district was called Lees with Crossbank.

were formerly paid.[9] On Hartshead Pike was a conical pillar, built 1...d St. surmounted by a hart's head ; it fell down about 1820, but was partly rebuilt in 1863 to commemorate the marriage of King Edward VII and Queen Alexandra.[10] Near Lees was a noted chalybeate spring called Lees Spa ; there are other similar ones in the parish. In the bed of the Medlock are the so-called Druidical basins.

The public buildings include a mechanics' institute founded in 1825, clubs, and a theatre. The infirmary was built in 1859–60, and a children's hospital in 1893 ; a nurses' home has been added.

A Volunteer regiment was raised in 1803.[11] Ashton is the headquarters of the 3rd V. B. Manchester Regiment ; the drill hall was built in 1887. There are barracks at Hurst, built in 1843.

There are two weekly newspapers and an evening daily paper.

The market cross was taken down in 1829.[12]

The ceremony of 'riding the Black Lad,' still to some extent kept up, was performed on Easter Monday ; the effigy of a knight in black armour was paraded through the streets on horseback in derision, afterwards hung up on the old market cross and used as a target, being finally plunged in a stagnant pool. There are contradictory accounts of the origin and intention of the ceremony.[13] The 'gyst ale' was another Ashton custom.[14] The annual wake, formerly kept on the third Sunday in September, is now held on the Sunday next after 15 August.

In Ashton Moss red fir trees used to be dug up, and split up for light for the poor ; large oaks were also found.

Copper tokens were issued in Ashton in the middle of the 17th century.[15]

A cotton mill was established at Stalybridge in 1776,[16] and the manufacture rapidly grew under the favourable conditions of easy water carriage and abundant coal supply. The modern industries of the district, in addition to this staple trade, include hatmaking, brewing, and silk-weaving ; there are also iron foundries, engineering works, machine factories, and collieries. At Ashton Moss are market gardens. Audenshaw has cotton factories and engineering works, and some hat factories ; Hurst also has great cotton mills and some hat-making, together with collieries ; at Lees, again, are cotton mills, as also at Mossley. Stalybridge has much the same industries as Ashton

itself ; also nail-making, and some woollen manufacture.[17]

The agricultural land is now apportioned thus : arable land, 173 acres ; permanent grass, 5,574 ; woods and plantations, nil.[18]

The history of the place, apart from its modern manufacturing progress, has been quite uneventful save for the political and industrial riots which have broken out from time to time. To the 'fifteenth' Ashton paid £2 14s. out of £41 14s. 4d. charged on the hundred of Salford, and to the county lay of 1624 it paid £5 16s. out of £100.[19]

In addition to some of the lords of the manor and one or two of the rectors, the local worthies include John Chetham, psalmodist, who died in 1746 ; William Quarmby of Hurst, a poet, who died in 1872 ; Thomas Earnshaw, watchmaker, 1749–1829 ;[20] James Butterworth, the topographer, born in 1771 at a place called Pitses ;[21] the Rev. John Louis Petit, artist, 1801–68 ;[22] Evan Leigh, inventor and manufacturer of cotton-spinning machinery, 1811–76[23] ; and John Dean Blythe, miscellaneous writer, 1842–69.[24]

The above were natives of Ashton. Joseph Rayner Stephens, brother of George Stephens the runic archaeologist, at first a Methodist preacher, caused a schism in the body at Ashton as mentioned later, and as an agitator and journalist exercised great influence in the town and district for many years from 1840 onwards. He died in 1879.[24a]

ASHTON MANOR — Originally ASHTON appears to have been rated as three plough-lands, of which two became part of the estates of the lords of Penwortham, and the third, together with the advowson of the church, was attached to the barony of Manchester.[25] The former portion, Ashton proper, is probably the two plough-lands held by one Warin in 1086, by grant of Roger of Poitou.[26] It also was granted to the lords of Manchester, and in 1212 Robert Grelley held the two plough-lands and should render 20s. or a goshawk ;[27] but Albert Grelley, the father, or perhaps the grandfather of Robert, had given to Roger son of Orm ' the whole land of Ashton, with all its appurtenances,' with other lands, just as the said Roger had held them of Albert's father, at the rent of 20s. or a hawk.[28] This Roger was the ancestor of the Kirkbys of Kirkby Ireleth, and the lordship of Ashton descended in this family till the 17th century.

[9] Lancs. and Ches. Antiq. Soc. xv, 195.
[10] Ibid. xv, 35. There is a view of the old tower in Aikin's Country Round Manchester, 211 ; the writer (p. 231) describes the Pike as ' a favourite and well-known object for the surrounding country, which is seen at a considerable distance, and in general has been supposed to be a sea mark. It is situated on very high ground betwixt Oldham and Mossley, from whence the traveller has a most delightful view of the surrounding country. We have ascertained from good authority that it was formerly used as a beacon, and there are others in the neighbourhood to answer it.'
[11] Local Gleanings Lancs. and Ches. ii,206.
[12] For this and the crosses at Hurst and Mossley see Lancs. and Ches. Antiq. Soc. xxii, 118–23.
[13] W. E. A. Axon, Black Knight of Ashton.

	Arable Acres	Grass Acres
Ashton . .	.	190
Knott Lanes . .	.	1,407
,, ,, . .	.	224

Hulme Hall : The Courtyard in 1843

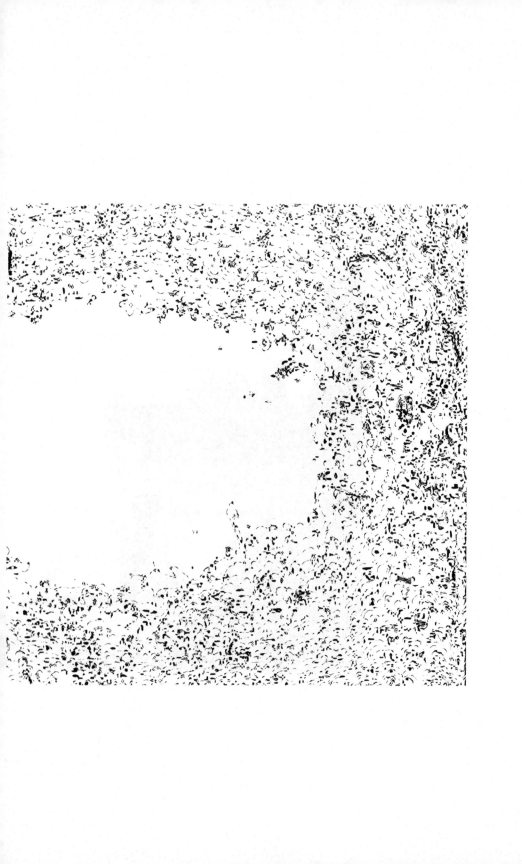

In the reign of Henry II William de Kirkby granted Ashton to one Orm, probably a relative, who thus became the immediate lord, and whose descendants assumed the local surname.[29] A later Orm de Ashton, who is described as the 'son of Roger' in a fine of 1195,[30] was living in 1201.[31] He was succeeded by his son Thomas,[32] and Robert de Ashton occurs in 1254,[33] but the descent in the absence of evidence cannot be made out quite clearly. In 1274 Thomas de Ashton defended his title to the manor of Ashton against John de Kirkby,[34] and in 1284 an agreement was made between them by which Thomas's right was acknowledged, a rent of 1d. being due from him.[35] It is perhaps the same Thomas who occurs a number of times to 1307,[36] while in 1320 John de Ashton

KIRKBY of Kirkby.
Argent two bars gules, on a canton of the second a cross patonce or.

mullet

[29] From a plea of 1276 ; De Banc. R. 15, m. 4.

[30] *Final Conc.* (Rec. Soc. Lancs. and Ches.), iii, 172. Roger (de Burton) and Orm his brother are called sons of Roger son of Orm. Their mother was a daughter and co-heir of Richard de Lancaster. William de Kirkby was son of Roger son of Orm son of Ailward ; his father was the grantee of Ashton from Albert Grelley.

[31] *Lancs. Pipe R.* 116, 153. Orm de Ashton granted part of his land in Ashton to Robert son of Simon de Statlee (Staley) ; the boundaries mention Hurst and Greenlache ; Dods. MSS. xxxix, fol. 121b. Orm son of Roger gave land called Mugehale to Cockersand Abbey ; *Chartul.* i, 214. As Medlock and Sunderland are named in the bounds, the charter must refer to this township, though entered in the section relating to Ashton in Preston.

[32] Thomas son of Orm de Ashton made to Richard de Byron a grant of a moiety of the land between the Reed Brook and Stony Brook, the Medlock and the bounds of Werneth, at a rent of 12d. a year ; Byron Chart. (Towneley MS.), 7/19.
Some early charters are preserved by Dodsworth, loc. cit. Thomas de Ashton gave to Ralph son of William Ruffus of Staley all his land of Souracre, in the Olerene hey, the Helm rode, and the Otford bottom, which lands had formerly been held by Richard Ruffus (Roo) ; he also granted land within the bounds of Loseley (Luzley), the meres beginning at the Bicestal (Bestal).

[33] *Lancs. Inq. and Extents*, i, 193. Robert de Ashton released to Robert de Byron the services due from Greenhurst and Sunderland, viz. 18d. a year from each ; Byron Chart. 9/22. William son of Thomas de Ashton released to Sir Richard de Byron all claim in the land called Greenhurst, as contained in the charter of his brother Robert ; ibid. n. 8/20. It is possible that William and Robert were the sons of the later Thomas de Ashton, but they may have been grandsons of Orm.
Robert de Ashton granted to Ralph Ruffus de Staley part of his land within the fee of Ashton lying between the Bicestal and the Water Walsyke ; to which

charter William son of Olibern de Ashton was a witness ; Dods. *ut supra*. Richard le Roo and Sir Henry de Trafford were defendants in 1351 ; John de Heghgren, the plaintiff, did not prosecute ; Duchy of Lanc. Assize R. 1, m. 5.

[34] De Banc. R. 11, m. 3 ; 15, m. 4 (printed in *Lancs. Pipe R.* 405) ; 21, m. 8 d. ; 27, m. 29 ; 28, m. 24 d. Six oxgangs of land and the advowson of the church were excepted from the claim for the manor. The oxgangs were perhaps in the hands of free tenants, while the advowson belonged to the lord of Manchester.

[35] *Final Conc.* i, 162 ; the dispute had therefore occupied ten years.
Thomas de Ashton was a juror in 1282, when he was said to owe the rent of a sor goshawk annually as one of the free foreign tenants of Manchester ; he also did suit for Parbold, Dalton, and Wrightington ; *Lancs. Inq. and Extents*, i, 244, 246, 248.

[36] Thomas de Ashton in 1292 was defendant to claims made by Richard de les Lees of Ashton for a right of way and for common of pasture ; Assize R. 408, m. 21. At the same time inquiry was made whether or not Adam son of Simon the Serjeant of Ashton had held a messuage and lands, which should descend to his son John, a minor ; Thomas de Ashton held them, alleging a grant by Adam, made long before his death ; ibid. m. 34 d.
Henry de Ashton recovered a messuage and land against Gervase de Ashton, who claimed as brother and heir of William de Ashton. It was shown that William had made the grant to Henry while under age, but had given a release when twenty-three ; ibid. m. 11 d.
Thomas de Ashton and Cecily his wife in 1305 made a feoffment of a messuage and land in Ashton ; *Final Conc.* i, 206 ; De Banc. R. 162, m. 200 d.
A settlement of the manor was made in 1307, Thomas de Ashton granting it to John son of Thomas de Ashton, a minor, with remainders to Robert the brother of John ; to William son of Adam Banastre ; to Alexander brother of Thomas for life ; and to Robert brother of Richard de Ashton for life ; *Final Conc.* i, 212.

Ashton his successor,[44] prominent in the French wars of Henry V, and Seneschal of Bayeux in 1416.[45] In 1413 Sir John obtained a release of the service due from the manor. After reciting that he held it of Sir Richard de Kirkby by the rent of 1 d., and that Sir Richard held it of Thomas La Warre, lord of Manchester, by the rent of 22 s. and a hawk or 40 s., which services Sir John de Ashton had to render on behalf of Sir Richard, the feoffees of Thomas La Warre granted that Sir John, Sir Richard, and their heirs should be free from the said service after the death of Thomas.[45a] This Sir John died in 1428, holding the manor of Ashton of Robert de Ogle (in right of his wife Isabel, granddaughter and heir of Sir Richard Kirkby), and other manors and lands. Thomas, his son and heir, then twenty-five years of age,[46] came to be known as 'the Alchemist'; [47] he left a son John,[48] made a knight in 1460.[49] Sir John died in 1484, holding the manor of Ashton, with the advowson of the church, lands in Manchester, Oldham, and Wardle ; and the manor of Alt. Sir Thomas, his son and heir, was sixty years of age in 1507, when the inquisition was taken.[50]

In 1513 Sir Thomas Ashton made a feoffment of his manors of Ashton and Alt, and his lands and rents there and in Oldham, Hundersfield, and Manchester,

for the fulfilment of his will ; and died a year later, on 21 July 1514, leaving as heirs George Booth, son

BOOTH. *Argent three boars' heads erect and erased sable.*

HOGHTON. *Sable three bars argent.*

of his daughter Margaret, who had been the wife of Sir William Booth, and his other daughters Elizabeth Ashton, and Alice wife of Richard Hoghton, all of full age.[51] In accordance with Sir Thomas's will the estate was held for the use of the three heirs, a division being sought in 1537.[52] Elizabeth Ashton died on 31 December 1553, without issue,[53] so that afterwards the manor and lands were held equally by the Booths[54] and Hoghtons.[55] Before the close of the 16th century, however, the whole had come into the possession of the former family,[56] and descended

---

[44] Sir John de Ashton and John his son occur in 1391–2 ; Dods. MSS. xxxix, fol. 121 b.

The king in 1401 granted to his dear bachelor John de Ashton the wardship of all the lands of Richard de Byron, deceased, with annuities to Robert, Piers, and Nicholas de Ashton ; Lancs. Inq. p.m. (Chet. Soc.), i, 65.

Sir John de Ashton was knight of the shire in 1411 and 1413; Pink and Beaven, op. cit. 47, 49.

[45] See the notice in the Dict. Nat. Biog.; Sir H. Nicolas, Agincourt, 359 ; Norman R. in Dep. Keeper's Rep. xli, xliv. A letter of his is printed by Ellis, Original Letters (Ser. 2), i, 72.

[45a] Manch. Corp. D. See also Lancs. Inq. p.m. (Chet. Soc.), ii, 19 ; Dep. Keeper's Rep. xxxiii, App. 28.

[46] Lancs. Inq. p.m. (Chet. Soc.) ii, 22 ; the value of the manor is given as £40 a year. The service is not stated. Sir John de Ashton had purchased the advowson of the church from Thomas La Warre ; ibid. ii, 18. See also Dep. Keeper's Rep. xxxiii, App. 30.

Sir John's younger son, Roger, was the ancestor of the Ashtons of Middleton, Great Lever, and Downham.

[47] He was a partner with Sir Edmund Trafford in the licence to transmute metals, granted in 1446 ; see the account of Stretford ; also Dict. Nat. Biog. He was in 1442 exempted from serving on assizes, &c. ; Dep. Keeper's Rep. xl, App. 537.

[48] The descent is given thus in a document which may be dated about 1510, relating to the manor of Manchester, of which Sir John Ashton appears to have been a trustee in 1413 : Sir John—s. Thomas—s. John—s. Thomas ; Pal. of Lanc. Sessional P. Hen. VIII, bdle. 4.

[49] At the battle of Northampton ; Metcalfe, Bk. of Knights, 2.

Sir John Ashton in 1471 complained that Ambrose Baguley of Manchester had trespassed on his turbary at Ashton ; Pal. of Lanc. Plea R. 38, m. 2 d. He was knight of the shire in 1472 ; Pink and Beaven, op. cit. 57. In the following

year he was return manors of Ashton, the other Moston) chester, by the rent iii, 483. 'Alt' may

[50] Lancs. Inq. p.m. 138.

to George Harry Grey, seventh Earl of Stamford and Warrington, who died in 1883.[37] Under his will, it is stated, the Lancashire estates are to pass to his wife's grand-niece, Katherine Sarah, wife of Sir Henry Foley Lambert, baronet.[38] Trustees are in possession.

Ashton Old Hall stood on the south side of the church on elevated ground about 200 yds. north of the River Tame and overlooking its valley. Dr. Aikin described it in 1795[39] as a building of great antiquity, and attributed its erection to about the year 1483, but there seems to have been no particular reason for his assigning this date to the structure.

Adjoining to it (he wrote) is an edifice which has the appearance of a prison, and till of late years has been used as such. It is a strong rather small building with two round towers overgrown with ivy, called the dungeons. The prison is now occupied by different poor families. It has two courtyards, an inner and an outer, with strong walls. Over the outer gate was a square room ascended to from the inside by a flight of stone steps and very ancient. It has always gone by the name of the Gaoler's Chapel . . . [but] was taken down in 1793. The house to the inner court is still standing, and in tolerable repair. . . . The front of the old hall adjoining the prison overlooking the gardens and the River Tame [has] a beautiful prospect. On this side of the building are strong parts of immense thickness with numbers of loopholes.[40]

The main building was repaired and modernized in 1838 for the occasional residence of the Earl of Stamford, thereby no doubt losing a good deal of its ancient appearance. By the middle of the last century it was L-shaped on plan, but an earlier plan of the

GREY, Earl of Stamford. *Barry of six argent and azure.*

town published in 1824 shows it possessing a short east wing running northward from the south-

ASHTON-UNDER-LYNE OLD HALL

east corner. This, however, must have disappeared before 1862, when an account of the building was written by John Higson, a local antiquary.[61] The long west wing overlooking the valley had then two small bays and projecting chimney-shafts in its west front, but was covered with rough-cast coloured black. On its east side the greater part was also rough-cast, but a portion at the south end near the 'dungeons' was of timber and plaster. The roofs were covered with stone slates. The east inner elevation had doors and windows with semicircular heads, and over the door was an escutcheon with the arms, crest, and supporters of the Earl of Stamford, all this work being probably part of the 1838 reconstruction. Before that date the hall had long been divided into several tenements with separate entrances, having passed into non-resident possession as far back as the 16th century, at which time probably a floor was introduced into the great hall. A portion of the

George Latham had recently inclosed divers parcels of waste on the moor called 'Odenshawe,' and had alleged that John Hunt was joint lord of the wastes and commons of the manor. The other 'wastes' were Luzley Moor, Mossley, and Little Moss. Robert Lees, a defendant, said that he was tenant to Richard Shaw-cross (in right of Katherine Shawcross, his wife, widow of Richard Hunt, grandfather of John), and had inclosed no waste grounds ; Duchy of Lanc. Plead. Eliz. clxxix, B 7.

In 1606 a settlement of the manor and advowson was made by Sir George Booth and Katherine his wife ; Pal. of. Lanc. Feet of F. bdle. 70, no. 23. A similar settlement was made in 1648 by Sir George Booth and George Booth ; ibid. bdle. 143, m. 5. George Lord Delamere and Elizabeth his wife were in possession in 1671 ; ibid. bdle. 186, m. 12. For later recoveries, &c., see Pal. of Lanc. Plea R. 464 (1696), m. 6 ; August Assizes, 37 Geo. III (1797), R. 9.

[37] The pedigree of the Booths and their successors is thus given in Ormerod's *Ches.* (ed. Helsby), i, 523–35 : Sir William Booth of Dunham (d. 1519) married Margaret daughter and coheir of Sir Thomas Ashton of Ashton-under-Lyne —s. George, d. 1531 —s. George, d. 1543 —s. Sir William, d. 1579 —s. Sir George, baronet (1611), d. 1652 —s. William, d. 1636 —s. Sir George, cr. Lord Delamere (1661), d. 1684 —s. Henry, cr. Earl of Warrington (1690), d. 1693 —s. George, d. 1758 —da. Mary (d. 1772), married Harry Grey, fourth Earl of Stamford —s. George Harry, cr. Earl of Warrington (1796), d. 1819 —s. George Harry, d. 1845 —s. George Harry Booth, Lord Grey of Groby (1832), d. 1835 —s. George Harry, d. 1883, s.p. The heir male, who succeeded as eighth Earl of Stamford, was Harry Grey, descended from a younger son of Mary Booth and the fourth Earl thus : John Grey, d. 1802 —s. Harry, d. 1860 —s. Harry, eighth earl, d. 1890, who has been

343

roof in 1862 is said to have had shaped braces forming quatrefoils in the spaces between the principals and purlins, showing that it was originally intended to be seen. The rooms, however, had been so much modernized that every trace of antiquity had been removed or concealed, though in the second story there were mullioned and transomed windows with diamond glazing.[62]

The south wing was thought by Higson to be not older than about 1500, or probably later. It had three square-headed windows on each floor of two trefoiled lights, and was flanked at each end by a round tower standing a little in advance of the main wall, and rising considerably higher than the roof. The walls of the towers were about 2 ft. 6 in. thick at the bottom, and the interior was square to the height of two stories, above which it finished off as a circular tower. The roofs were of stone with a central finial, and the towers had evidently served the purpose of garderobes.

At this time there was no trace of the two courtyards mentioned by Aikin. 'The gaoler's chapel was probably an offshoot or irregular continuation to the dungeon wing and some old buildings since removed,[63] but then seeming to form a third side, and probably there had been a fourth, rendering the building quadrangular.'[64]

Still later the front of the south wing appears to have had new and longer windows of three lights inserted, those on the first floor having pointed heads. The building, whose original appearance had long been marred not only by alterations to the structure, but by the change in its surroundings, was pulled down in 1890 by the Manchester, Sheffield, and Lincolnshire Railway Company, who had purchased it prior to extensions and improvements of the Park Parade Station. With so little trustworthy evidence to go upon, it is difficult to assign any date to the erection of the hall or to convey any but a vague idea of its plan and disposition. Mr. Higson inclined to about the year 1480 for the west wing, with portions, perhaps, a little older, but there was some work belonging apparently to alterations in the 17th century. A Gallows Meadow adjoined the hall.

The manor mills were closed in 1884, and have since been removed.

The manor of *ALT* has been mentioned above as part of the holding of the lords of Ashton. The tenure is uncertain, it being sometimes stated to be held of the barony of Manchester,[65] but more usually of the king as Duke of Lancaster as of his manor of Salford.[66] It seems at one time to have been held by a local family,[67] and there is no record of its acquisition by the Ashtons.[68] It disappears from notice as a manor in the 16th century.

The custom roll of the manor of Ashton for 1422 has been printed.[69] The lord gave a dinner to his tenants and their wives on Yule day, the tenants at will making regulated 'presents' to him at the same time. A tenant was to plough one or two days, according as he had half a plough or a plough; to harrow one day, to cart ten loads of turf from Doneam Moss, 'shear' four days in harvest, and cart corn for one day; at death each paid a 'principal,' i.e., the best beast he had after the due of holy kirk. The tenants were to grind at the lord's mill to the sixteenth measure; if they bought corn they should 'muller' to the Love sucken, i.e. to the twenty-fourth measure.[70] The names of the tenants at will, with their services and rents, follow: John of the Edge farmed both corn mills at 16s. 4d., 'the lord to hold up the mills at his costs, as it has been customed.' The 'gyst ale' of the town of Ashton amounted to 20s. in all; the tolls of fairs and markets 2 marks;[71] the courts and fines, 40s. There were a few tenants for life, but the list of free tenants is a long one. The tenants at will took their farms, &c., from Martinmas to Martinmas, and were bound to leave everything in as good condition as they found it. The free tenants took part in the business of the hallmote and assisted in preserving order. By an agreement made in 1379–80 the tenants' swine, if ringed, were allowed to range over the demesne from the end of harvest until sowing-time.

A manor court is still held every six months, its jurisdiction extending over the whole parish.

In the absence of records no account can be given of the descent of the various free tenancies in Audenshaw,[72]

[62] Glover, op. cit. quoting Higson.

[63] The wing shown on the plan of 1824.

[64] Glover, op. cit. quoting Higson.

[65] Hawise widow of Robert Grelley in 1295 claimed dower in one virgate in Alt against Thomas de Ashton; De Banco R. 110, m. 119 d. In the Manchester Survey of 1320 it is stated that John de Ashton held Alt by a rent of 2s.; *Mamecestre*, ii, 290.

[66] This is the more usual account. In the survey of the Earl of Lancaster's lands in 1346 John de Ashton was said to hold half an oxgang in Alt in socage; Add. MS. 32103, fol. 146. In 1429 the rent to the king as duke was given as 10d.; *Lancs. Inq. p.m.* (Chet. Soc.), ii, 22. Later still the holding was called one oxgang; ibid. ii, 137. In 1514 the rent was again stated as 10d. and the clear value of the manor was 20 marks; Duchy of Lanc. Inq. p.m. iv, 80.

[67] Alban de Alt occurs about 1200; *Lancs. Pipe R.* 330. Eva de 'Halt' was of the king's gift in 1222–6, and was to be married; her land was worth 12d.; *Lancs. Inq. and Extents,* i, 130. Thomas son of William de Alt in 1276 claimed a

free tenement in Paldenley against Robert son of Robert de Tounton and Margery de Hache, but failed, because Paldenley was not a town or borough, but only a place in the field of Ashton; Assize R. 405, m. 1. In 1292 Richard son of Robert de Turton unsuccessfully claimed one tenement in Alt against Margery daughter of Robert de Alt and Richard son of Robert de Tong, and another (by writ *de consanguinitate*) against Thomas de Ashton; Assize R. 408, m. 32, 30 d. Adam son of Ellis de Alt acted for Thomas de Ashton in 1307; *Final Conc.* i, 212.

[68] Sir John Ashton who died in 1428 had assigned Alt as dower to his wife Margaret at the door of the church on the day he married her; *Lancs. Inq. p.m.* (Chet. Soc.), ii, 22. In 1507 a later Sir John had held Alt 'as Hugh de More of Alston and Richard the son of Robert Spymne had held it'; ibid. ii, 138.

[69] Chetham Soc. lxxiv, 93–116.

[70] Ibid. 95, 109, 112.

[71] The charter for the markets and fairs does not seem to have been preserved, but it is stated that an exemplification was granted to Sir George Booth

Alt, Asps, Alston [73] lands, Bardsley,[74] Beckington Field,[75] Heyrod,[76] Hurst,[77] Knolls,[78] Light Birches,[79] Lees,[80] Mossley,[81] Palden,[82] Rasbotham,[83] Rougheyes,[84] Rhodesfield,[85] Shepley,[86] Sherwind,[87] Sunderland,[88] Taunton or Tongton,[89] Three Houses,[90] Waterhouses,[91] Woodhouses,[92] and Williamfield.[93] The Hospitallers [94] and the priory of Lenton [95] had lands in the township.

a note in the account of Moston township, as held by the Hydes of Denton. Edmund Ashton (of Chadderton) was farmer of the Mostons' Audenshaw lands in 1480, George Moston giving him an acquitance for £4 9s. 10d., one year's rent ; Raines D. (Chet. Lib.), bdle. 3, no. 45. In 1514 Margery widow of Thomas Lidyard and sister and heir of George Moston, granted to her son Edward Lidyard lands in Audenshaw and Warwickshire ; D. Enr. Com. Pleas, Mich. 35 Hen. VIII.

73 The Rental shows that in 1422 Alston lands (or Ashton lands) were divided among Peter Trafford (11. 8d.), the heirs of Adam Mossley (10d.), and the heirs of Richard Dene (11.), at varying rents.

74 Richard son of John Bardsley rendered a rose yearly for Bardsley, and paid 9d. for Old Alt, 2s. for Asps, and 5d. for part of Hurst ; Rental of 1422. For a case concerning the Bardsley family see Pal. of Lanc. Plea R. 82 (1496), m. 1.

75 Richard Hunt in 1422 paid 4s. for his portion ; Rental. An account of this family will be found under the township of Manchester ; they appear to have belonged to Audenshaw originally. See also Final Conc. ii, 148, 158, for acquisitions in Ashton in 1355 and 1358. Richard Hunt in 1559 purchased messuages, &c., in Ashton (probably in Audenshaw) from Sir Robert Worsley ; Pal. of Lanc. Feet of F. bdle. 21, m. 49 ; 22, m. 5 ; see also Ducatus Lanc. (Rec. Com.), i, 136. It will be seen below that the Hunts held land of the Hospitallers.

76 It was held in 1422 by John de Heyrod at a total rent of 7s. 2d. ; Rental. Agnes daughter of William son of Richard de Heyrod (Heighroide) was in 1359 claimant of lands in Heyrod ; Duchy of Lanc. Assize R. 7, m. 3 d. A John de Heyrod was plaintiff in 1372 against John son of Cecily de Hulton ; De Banco R. 445, m. 28.

77 The principal tenants in 1422 were Nicholas de Hurst, paying 3s., and Thomas de Staley, paying 1s. 6d. ; Rental. Nicholas Hurst and Lucy his wife had a messuage in Ashton and Hurst in 1578 ; Pal. of Lanc. Feet of F. bdle. 40, m. 42. See further in Local Glean. Lancs. and Ches. ii, 280.

78 In 1302 Margery wife of Roger de Barlow and Alice her sister, daughters of Richard de Knolls, were heirs to messuages and lands in Ashton. Agnes (apparently the widow of Richard), then wife of Richard de Limepithurst, and Joan widow of Adam de Knolls, had dower. Gilbert son of Adam son of Thomas de Alt was called to warrant ; De Banco R. 141, m. 75 d. 53 d. Adam Wilson paid 12¾d. in 1422, and the heirs of Robert Lees 2s. 6d. ; Rental.

79 Adam Tetlow paid 12d. rent in 1422 ; Rental. This family is further noticed under Oldham. Lawrence Tetlow made a settlement of six messuages, &c., in Ashton in 1551 ; Pal. of Lanc. Feet of F. bdle. 14, m. 178. He died in 1582 holding three messuages, &c., in Ashton of the queen in socage by a rent

of 5d. yearly ; Duchy of Lanc. Inq. p.m. xiv, 56. John Tetlow, who died in 1598, held messuages, &c., in Ashton of Richard Hoghton and George Booth in socage at 4d. rent ; ibid. xvii, n. 15.

80 Thomas Lees and Adam Lees were free tenants in 1422, the former paying 6d. rent and the latter 10d. ; Rental. About 1555 a messuage and lands in Lees were in dispute between Robert Lees the elder and Robert Lees the younger ; Ducatus Lanc. i, 300 ; also ibid. iii, 363.

81 Henry son of William de Mossley (Moslegh) in 1309 claimed land in Ashton ; De Banco R. 174, m. 197 d. Richard de Mossley (Moselegh) in 1319 gave to William son of William de Mossley, Emma his wife, and their issue male, two messuages, 100 acres of land, &c., in Ashton ; Final Conc. ii, 30.

82 Paldenwood seems to have been improved and divided among several tenants before 1422 ; Rental.

83 Robert Rasbotham paid 5d. a year in 1422 ; Rental.

84 Peter Worsley paid 2s. a year in 1422 ; Rental.

85 John Knolls paid 3s. 5d. in 1422 ; he also paid a like rent for Reedy Lee ; Rental.

86 Thomas de Shepley contributed to the subsidy of 1332 ; Exch. Lay Subs. (Rec. Soc. Lancs. and Ches.), 32. John del Heyrod and Maud his wife in 1335 claimed land in Shepley against Thomas de Shepley and others ; De Banco R. 303, m. 83. Peter Shepley paid 3s. 7d. in all for his tenement in 1422 ; Rental.

87 Peter Trafford in 1422 paid 6d. for this ; Rental.

88 At present the name is often spelt Cinderland. In 1422 it was held by Richard Byron, paying 6d., and the heirs of Thomas de Hatfield, paying 2s.; Rental. Stephen de Bredbury gave to Robert de Byron all his land in Sunderland, a pair of white gloves to be rendered at St. Martin, and 2s. to the chief lords ; Byron Chartul. no. 19/7. In 1473 a William Heaton paid 12s. to the lord of Manchester for the manor of Sunderland ; Mamecestre, iii, 479. This may be a different place.

89 This estate was long held by the Claydens of Clayden in Manchester. Richard son of William del Ridges in 1315 claimed four messuages, two oxgangs of land, &c., in Ashton against Richard son of Richard de Clayden ; De Banco R. 231, m. 92 d. In 1422 Thomas Clayden was tenant, paying 3s. 6d. rent in all ; Rental. In some pleadings in 1511 it was stated that Sir Thomas Ashton had only recently caused a leet to be kept in the manor, and on Richard son of Richard Clayden of Taunton refusing to appear, had fined him and distrained on default. Richard stated that he did not live within the manor of Ashton, he and his ancestors having done suit to the king's leet wapentake and sheriff's tourn at Salford. It appeared, however, that his lands in Taunton were held of Sir Thomas Ashton by a rent of 3s. 4d. ; Duchy of Lanc. Plead. Hen. VIII, iii, C 1. Robert Clayden died in 1579 holding six mes-

suages, &c., in Tongton and Middlewood in Ashton of Thomas Hoghton in socage by 3s. 6d. rent ; Duchy of Lanc. Inq. p.m. xiv, 84, 12. Bridget, one of his daughters, held them at her death in 1588, leaving three sisters as heirs ; ibid. xv, 28. Taunton was afterwards held by a family named Chadwick, who recorded a pedigree in 1664 ; Dugdale, Visit. 74.

90 Thomas Staveley (or Staley) held this in 1422, at a rent of 1s. ; he also held Bestal at 1d. ; Rental. Some charters relating to this have been given in a previous note.

91 Henry de Waterhouses contributed to the subsidy of 1332 ; Exch. Lay Subs. 32. John Moss of Waterhouses occurs in 1616 ; Manch. Free Lib. D. no. 77.

92 Richard Byron held in 1422 at a rent of 1s. ; Rental. Some of the grants to the Byrons have been recited above. Richard de Byron died in 1397, holding ten messuages, 60 acres of land, and 20 acres of meadow in the Woodhouses of the Duke of Lancaster ; Lancs. Inq. p.m. (Chet. Soc.), i, 65. Sir John Byron died in 1489, holding what appears to be the same estate, but the tenure was said to be of Sir Thomas Ashton in socage by a rent of 12d. (agreeing with the Rental) or of 4d. ; Duchy of Lanc. Inq. p.m. iii, 48, 70

The freeholders in 1600 [96] were Miles Ashton of Heyrod,[97] Robert Ashton of Shepley,[98] Randle Hulton of Sunderland,[99] and Richard Shalcross of Limehurst.[100] A few other names can be gathered from the fines and inquisitions.[101] At Alt Hill in the 18th century were seated the Pickfords, ancestors of the Radcliffes of Royton.[102]

BOROUGHS

With the growth of the town on the introduction of the cotton manufacture, the manorial government soon became inadequate, and in 1827 and 1828 Police Acts were obtained for the regulation of *ASHTON*.[103] The market, which had fallen into decay, was revived in 1828, Saturday being the day chosen. A market place was in 1829 presented to the town by the lord of the manor; a covered market was built on the site in 1867, and was enlarged in 1881.[104] This is now open daily. The old fairs were replaced by others on 3 March, 29 April, 25 July, and 21 November. There was a local tradition that Ashton had been a borough,[104a] and though the election of a mayor had become obsolete a revival was made in 1831. In the following year, under the Reform Act, Ashton—the parliamentary borough consisting merely of the divi-

[96] *Misc.* (Rec. Soc. Lancs. and Ches.), i, 247-8.

[97] Miles died in 1612, holding the capital messuage called the Heyrod, with lands, &c., of Sir George Booth, in socage by 6s. 8d. rent. His heir was his grandson John Ashton (son of John); *Lancs. Inq. p.m.* (Rec. Soc. Lancs. and Ches.), i, 239. Maurice Ashton had in 1571 made a settlement of messuages in Heyrod, Harley, &c.; Pal. of Lanc. Feet of F. bdle. 33, —— 30. Miles Ashton (son of Maurice, according to the pedigree) made a similar settlement in 1583; ibid. bdle. 45, m. 115.

A pedigree was recorded in 1613; *Visit.* (Chet. Soc.), 14. A later one of 1664 shows that the family had been scattered; Dugdale, *Visit.* (Chet. Soc.), 13. Heyrod was 'afterwards in the possession of John Duckenfield of Duckenfield, esq. and was held by Sir Charles Duckenfield, bart. in 1750. It is now [1849] the property of Ralph Ousey, esq.'; Raines, in *Notitia Cestr.* ii, 5.

[98] The Ashtons of Shepley recorded a pedigree in 1664, tracing their descent from a Geoffrey son of Thomas Ashton, who married the heiress of Shepley; Dugdale, *Visit.* 16. Geoffrey Ashton and Margery his wife in 1450 made a feoffment of three messuages, 60 acres of land, &c., in Ashton; *Final Conc.* iii, 117. Geoffrey Ashton in 1467 complained that a bull of his had been seized by John, Richard, William, and Thomas Shepley of Withington; Pal. of Lanc. Writs Proton. (6 Edw. IV, C); see also Writs of Assize (bdle. 8), 6 Edw. IV.

The estate descended in the Ashton family till 1713, when Samuel Assheton sold it to John Shepley of Stockport, grocer. In 1675 Robert Assheton of Shepley, John his son, and Thomas his grandson, mortgaged the Great Ridings, part of the demesne lands near Shepley bridge; Manch. Free Lib. D. no. 104. 'It is now (1854) vested in Edward Lowe Sidebotham, esq., as heir of the late Mr. John Lowe, a successful calico printer, its intermediate possessor'; Booker, *Denton* (Chet. Soc.), 137. It has since descended to Mr. Edward John Side-

botham, of Erlesdene, Bowdon, the present owner.

[99] John Hulton (or Hilton), of Sunderland, occurs frequently in the time of James I; *Lancs. Inq. p.m.* (Rec. Soc. Lancs. and Ches.), i, 234; iii, 334.

[100] The nature of the Shallcross or Shawcross tenure has been stated above.

[101] George Chadderton of Nuthurst had lands in Ashton in 1552; Pal. of Lanc. Feet of F. bdle. 14, m. 121. Robert Chadderton of Bradshaw in Alkrington had a messuage and lands in Audenshaw in 1639; Towneley MS. C 8, 13 (Chet. Lib.), 248.

John Carrington had messuages, &c., in Audenshaw in 1573; Pal. of Lanc. Feet of F. bdle. 35, m. 30.

The Reddishes of Reddish had lands in Audenshaw, held of the heirs of Sir Thomas Ashton in socage by a rent of 18d.; Duchy of Lanc. Inq. p.m. v, 48; xi, 60. In 1613 the rent was stated to be 2s. 10d.; *Lancs. Inq. p.m.* (Rec. Soc. Lancs. and Ches.), i, 253.

Joseph Taylor died in 1610 holding Hartshead of the lord of Manchester by the rent of a rose; his heir was his daughter Mary, a few months old; ibid. ii, 120.

Richard Hartley, who died in 1620, held a messuage and lands in Ashton of the lord of Manchester; ibid. ii, 189. See also *Lancs. and Ches. Rec.* (Rec. Soc. Lancs. and Ches.), ii, 242.

Ralph Sandiford died at Hull in 1620 holding several messuages with lands, &c., in Ashton, of the lord of Manchester in socage by the rent of a rose and the fraction of a penny; John, his son and heir, was twenty-two years of age; *Lancs. Inq. p.m.* ii, 194. For this family see further in the account of Nuthurst in Moston. Their estate was called the High Ashes; Dugdale, *Visit.* 253.

The landowners contributing to the subsidy of 1622 were :—Robert Ashton, John Ashton, Randle Hulton, Thomas Newton, William Walker, John Sandford, and Thomas Chetham; *Misc.* (Rec. Soc. Lancs. and Ches.), i, 155.

A large amount of information as to the different estates in Ashton will be

ASHTON-UNDER-LYNE PARISH CHURCH: GLASS IN SOUTH-WEST WINDOW OF SOUTH AISLE

ASHTON-UNDER-LYNE PARISH CHURCH: GLASS IN MIDDLE WINDOW OF SOUTH AISLE

the mace, mayor's chain and badge, and silver loving-cup.[110]

STALYBRIDGE, chiefly in Cheshire, though taking its name from a former hamlet in Ashton, obtained a Police Act in 1830,[111] and was incorporated in 1857. The boundaries were extended in 1881 to include Millbrook in Stayley and Heyrod in Ashton. It has a council composed of mayor, eight aldermen, and twenty-four councillors. The whole was included in Cheshire in 1898.[112]

MOSSLEY,[113] formed from the three counties of Lancaster, York, and Chester, has since 1888 been included in Lancashire for administrative purposes. A local board was formed in 1864,[114] and a charter of incorporation was granted in 1885 ; the council consists of mayor, six aldermen, and eighteen councillors.

15th century (c. 1460–70). It appears a small portion of the glass belonging

CHURCH The church of *ST. MICHAEL* is at the present day of greater historical than architectural interest. The site is ancient; the church stands at the east end of the town in what was formerly a picturesque situation on rising ground on the north side of the River Tame, and consists of chancel with north vestry, nave with north and south aisles, south porch, and west tower. The present church is entirely modern, but is the direct descendant of a building which appears to have been erected at the beginning of the 15th century (c. 1413), and which was repaired and enlarged about a hundred years later, in the lifetime of Sir Thomas Ashton (died 1514), when a new tower was built. In January 1791 this tower was struck by lightning and great damage was done, necessitating a general repair of the structure in the following year. In 1817 the tower was taken down and a new one erected (1818), and soon after the whole of the north side of the church was rebuilt as at present. Whilst the work was in progress (March 1821) a fire occurred, doing much damage to the original building, which was only partially repaired, the south side continuing in a more or less ruinous state till 1840, when a general rebuilding began, and in the course of a few years the whole fabric underwent a complete restoration and reconstruction, assuming its present aspect (1840–4). The work is of a very elaborate description, with rich ornamentation in wood and plaster, and is a good specimen of the florid Gothic of the period. The east end of the chancel was rebuilt in 1883, and three years later the tower, which was in a dangerous state, was pulled down and a new one built (1886–8). The new tower, the total height of which is 139 ft. 6 in., is 19 ft. higher than the former one, and 3 ft. longer from east to west.

The arcade is of seven bays with a clearstory, and there are side galleries and one at the west

[110] These particulars have been taken principally from the corporation's *Manual* and the *Lancs. Directory.*

[111] Stat. 9 Geo. IV, cap. 26. The town hall is in Lancashire.

[112] Loc. Govt. Bd. Order, P. 1416.

[113] Mossley was thus described by Dr. Aikin in 1795 : 'A considerable village, with upwards of 100 houses, many of them large and well built, chiefly of stone. It is about three miles from Ashton, in the high road to Huddersfield, with a large chapel in the gift of or under the rector of Ashton' ; *Country round Manchester*, 231.

Two fairs were established in 1824, on 21 June and the last Monday in October ; Baines, *Lancs. Directory*, ii, 667.

The Mechanics' Institute was built in 1858, and the town hall in 1862.

[114] *Lond. Gaz.* 26 Feb. 1864.

[115] Glynne visited the church in 1858, and describes the interior as 'expensively fitted up,' but 'heavy, though not without grandeur.' *Notes on the Churches of Lancs.* Dodsworth records that in his time there was on the tower the name Alexander Hyll, with a butcher's cleaver and the five of spades. The story was that Hyll, playing cards, swore that if the five of spades was turned up he would build a foot of the steeple, and it did so ; J. E. Bailey, quoting Dods. MSS. clv, fol. 116.

[116] See J. Paul Rylands, 'Lancs. Church Notes and Trickings of Arms,' *Trans. Hist. Soc.* xlii.

[117] Ibid.

[118] There is a detailed description of the windows, with photographs, by the Rev. G. A. Pugh, M.A., rector, in the *Trans. Antiq. Soc.* xx, 'The old glass windows of Ashton-under-Lyne Parish Church.'

[119] See *Ashton Customs R.* (Chet. Soc.), 112–15.

[120] The only other churches in Lancashire possessing twelve bells are St. Nicholas, Liverpool, and St. Mary, Oldham.

[121] *Brief Hist. Sketch of Ashton-under-Lyne Parish Ch.* (1888), loc. cit.

The plate consists of two patens of 1735, inscribed 'The gift of Emmanuel Smith, late of Taunton, gentleman, to the Parish Church of Ashtor; July 25th 1735;' two embossed chalices of 1753, inscribed with the names of the churchwardens and the date 6 October 1753, and bearing the marks of William Shaw and William Priest; a large paten of 1755, 'The gift of Edmund Harrop, yeoman, late of this Town Deceas'd to the Church of Ashton under Line 1755,' with the same makers' marks; two large flagons of 1764, one inscribed 'Mrs. Tabitha Smith daughter of Emanuel Smith, gent, formerly of Taunton, in the Parish of Ashton underline, gave £20 towards this Flaggon A.D. 1764.'; and a modern chalice, paten and flagon presented by Emma Hulme, June 1893.

The registers of baptisms and marriages begin in 1594 and those of burials in 1596, with blanks as follows: baptisms from 1641 to 7 December 1655 inclusive; marriages from 1641 to November 1653, and from April 1661 to 1668; burials from 1641 to 3 October 1653.

The accounts of the churchwardens begin with those for 1639 (the first leaves are torn out), and continue uninterruptedly till the end of 1657, when a break of twenty-six years occurs, the next accounts being those presented 1 April 1684.[122]

The church of St. Michael is *ADVOWSON* in Domesday Book recorded to have shared with the parish church of Manchester an ancient endowment of one ploughland.[123] On the formation of the manor of Ashton the advowson of the church was reserved, and was granted with that of Manchester to the Grelleys.[124] As late as 1304, however, the rector of Manchester claimed to present on the ground that Ashton was merely a chapelry belonging to his church.[125] A century later the reversion of the patronage was transferred by Thomas La Warre to Sir John Ashton and his heirs,[126] and the advowson has since that time descended with the manor of Ashton.[127] The trustees of the late Earl of Stamford are now the patrons. The value of the benefice was reckoned as 20 marks or £20 in 1282,[128] but the Taxation of 1291 did not allow it to exceed £10,[129] and fifty years later the ninth of sheaves, wool, &c., was only £5 15s. 6d.[130] In 1535 the value was recorded as £26 13s. 4d.,[131] and by 1650 it had risen to £113 6s. 8d.[132] At present the rector's income is recorded as £730.[133]

The following is a list of rectors:—

Instituted	Name	Patron	Cause of Vacancy
c. 1262	Clement [134]	Thomas Grelley	—
oc. 1282	William de Gringley [135]	—	—
oc. 1292	William [136]	—	—
16 Mar. 1305–6	Nicholas de Ardern [137]	Thomas Grelley	—
4 April 1308	Adam de Leighton de Ardern [138]	" "	—
26 June 1322	Simon de Cranesley [139]	John La Warre	d. Adam de Ardern
12 June 1331	Ralph de Benningholme [140]	—	exch. S. de Cranesley

[122] *Brief Hist. Sketch of Ashton-under-Lyne Parish Ch.* (1888), loc. cit.

[123] *V.C.H. Lancs.* i, 287. It does not appear that the rector of Ashton has ever had any share of the revenue derived from Newton.

[124] In 1277 Robert Grelley, as grandson and heir of Thomas Grelley, lord of Manchester, claimed the advowson against Peter Grelley, his uncle, who claimed by a grant from Thomas. It was proved that although Peter had actually presented to the church, he did so in the lifetime and in the name of Thomas Grelley, who died in 1262, and his claim was therefore rejected; De Banco R. 20, m. 25 d.; 23, m. 2 d.

At the same time the manor of Ashton was in dispute between John de Kirkby and Thomas de Ashton, but the advowson of the church was expressly excluded.

[125] Thomas son of Robert Grelley was the plaintiff and Otho de Grandison defendant in the suit; De Banco R. 149, m. 50; 151, m. 71. The advowson of Ashton was included in settlements made by the Warres of Manchester; see *Final Conc.* ii, 4, 157.

[126] In 1403 Thomas La Warre, then rector as well as lord of Manchester, in conjunction with his trustees settled a rood of land in the Smith's Field in Manchester, abutting on the Irk, together with the advowson of the church of Ashton, on the said Thomas for life, with reversion to Sir John Ashton and his heirs; Manch. Corporation D. See also *Lancs. Inq. p.m.* (Chet. Soc.), ii, 18.

[127] From the account of the manor it

Ashton-under-Lyne Parish Church : Glass in South-east Window of South Aisle

Instituted	Name	Patron	Cause of Vacancy
? July 1332 .	Gregory de Newton [141]	——	exch. R. de Benning-holme
18 Jan. 1351–2 .	Thomas de Rodeston [142]	Joan La Warre . . .	d. Gregory de Newton
oc. 1356 . . .	Thomas de Wyk [143]	——	——
12 May 1362 .	Thomas son of Thomas de Wyk [144] .	Roger La Warre . . .	——
13 Oct. 1372 .	Thomas La Warre [145]	Lewis de Clifford . . .	d. T. de Wyk
1 Nov. 1373 .	John de Marchford [146]	John La Warre . · .	res. T. La Warre
18 May 1374 .	Henry de Nettleworth [147]	——	exch. J. de Marchford
c. 1400 . . .	John Huntingdon [148]	——	——
22 Nov. 1424 .	James Skellington [149] . . .	T. La Warre	
12 June 1425 .	John Huntingdon [150]	„ „ .	
16 Nov. 1458 .	Lawrence Ashton [151]	Sir Thomas Ashton . .	
31 May 1486 .	Gervase Ashton [152]	Thomas Ashton . .	
	Edward Molyneux [153]		
2 Oct. 1535 .	William Thomson [154]	A. Radcliffe, &c. .	
11 Aug. 1554 .	William Rogerson [155]	Sir T. Stanley	
12 June 1557 .	Hugh Griffith, D. Decr. [156] .	King and Queen . .	
29 Jan. 1563–4 .	Robert Braboner [157] . . .	T. Hoghton . .	
—— 1605 . .	Robert Parker, M.A. [158]	Exors. G. Parker . .	
15 Mar. 1618–19	Henry Fairfax, D.D. [159]	Sir T. Fairfax . .	
c. 1646 . . .	John Harrison, B.A. [160] . . .	Parliament	——

[141] Ibid. ii, fol. 108 ; the new rector had been vicar of Blyth in the diocese of York, and there had been an interchange of letters between the archbishop and the Bishop of Lichfield as to the purity of motive for this exchange.

[142] Ibid. ii, fol. 129 ; a chaplain. In the previous October leave had been granted to him to attend the obsequies (insistere obsequiis) of Sir Thomas de Holland for two years ; ibid.

[143] Ibid. ii, fol. 15 ; leave of absence for two years. Ibid. v, fol. 3b ; licence to him to attend the obsequies of Sir Roger La Warre for two years from Dec. 1360. He was rector of Manchester also.

[144] Ibid. iv. fol. 80 ; the benefice had been vacant since 16 March. To Thomas de Wyk the younger leave of absence was granted as follows : 1363—two years to attend the studium generale ; ibid. v, fol. 8. 1365—two years 'in a fit and reputable place' ; ibid. v, fol. 9b. 1366—one year ; ibid. v, fol. 15b. 1370-1—two years ; ibid. v, fol. 24b. (At the same time the other Thomas de Wyk, rector of Manchester, obtained leave of absence also.) It will be seen that this rector was little resident.

[145] Ibid. iv, fol. 86 ; in the first tonsure. The rectory had become vacant on 14 July at 'Skrerkynton,' dioc. Lincoln. For Thomas La Warre see the account of Manchester Church.

[146] Ibid. iv, fol. 86b.

[147] Ibid. iv, fol. 87 ; the new rector had been rector of Wakerley, dioc. Linc. In 1379 he had a year's leave of absence ; ibid. v, fol. 32b ; also three years' leave in 1384 ; ibid. v, fol. 36b. 'William rector of Ashton' occurs in like manner in 1389-90, but he may have been rector of Ashton-on-Mersey ; ibid. vi, fol. 125b.

[148] He is said to have begun the re-building of Ashton Church in 1413. For his life see Raines, Wardens of Manch. (Chet. Soc.), 16–23, and the account of Manchester Church, of which he was warden from 1422 to 1458, when he died. In 1420 John Huntingdon, B.Can.Law, rector of Ashton, obtained the papal dispensation to hold another benefice ; Cal. Papal Letters, vii, 143.

[149] Baines, Lancs. (ed. Croston), ii, 317,

from the Lichfield registers. Mr. Earwaker's note gives the name as 'Ikelyngton.'

[150] Croston and Earwaker, from Lichfield registers.

[151] Lich. Epis. Reg. xi, fol. 43b ; a chaplain. According to an inscription formerly in the windows this rector continued the building of the church.

[152] Ibid. xii, fol. 120b ; a clerk. He also took part in the erection of the church, which was completed by Sir Thomas Ashton. Rector Gervase was living in 1513 ; Duchy of Lanc. Inq. p.m. iv, 80.

Instituted	Name	Patron	Cause of Vacancy
25 Sept. 1662 14 Jan. 1662–3 }	Thomas Ellison, M.A. [161] . . .	Lord Delamere . . .	ejec. J. Harrison
3 May 1700 .	John Simon de la Heuze	Earl of Warrington . .	d. T. Ellison
3 Mar. 1726–7.	John Penny, M.A. [162]	„ „	d. J. S. de la Heuze
9 Sept. 1758 .	Sir George Booth [163]	T. Hunt	d. J. Penny
1 Dec. 1797 .	Oswald Leycester, M.A. [164] . . .	Earl of Stamford and War rington	d. Sir G. Booth
5 Apr. 1799 .	Hon. Anchitel Grey, M.A. [165] . .	„ „	res. O. Leycester
7 May 1810 .	John Hutchinson, B.A. [166]	„ „	res. A. Grey
16 May 1816 — May 1829 }	George Chetwode, M.A. [167] . . .	„ „	res. J. Hutchinson
31 Dec. 1870 .	Thomas (Thompson) Eager, M.A. [168]	„ „ . . .	d. G. Chetwode
13 Feb. 1893 .	George Augustus Pugh, M.A. [169] .	The Stamford Trustees .	d. T. Eager
1909 .	Frederick Robert Chapman Hulton, M.A. „	„	d. O. A. Pugh

The rectors do not call for special notice. There does not seem to have been any chantry or chapel of ease in the parish before the Reformation, but the list of 'ornaments' existing in 1552 names three altars as fully equipped.[170] In 1542 the rector had two assistant clergymen, one paid by himself and the other by Sir Richard Ashton.[171] In 1554 there was one curate, who remained till 1565, though 'decrepit' in 1563 ;[172] and a new curate occurs in the Visitation list of 1565. In 1559 it was presented that the rector did 'no service in the church,' nor did he distribute to the poor as former parsons had done.[173] There was probably no curate as a rule, unless when the rector was non-resident,[174] and the recommendation of the surveyors of 1650 that a new parish should be formed in the northern half of Ashton was not carried out.[175]

presented to the benefice ; Commonwealth Ch. Surv. 21. He was a member of the Manchester classis from its formation in 1646. He signed the 'Harmonious Consent' of 1648 as 'pastor' of Ashton. On the other hand he paid his firstfruits on 2 April 1653, and exhibited a presentation to the rectory, made by Sir George Booth, as late as October 1655 ; Plund. Mins. Accts. (Rec. Soc. Lancs. and Ches.), ii, 95. He was a Royalist, and joined in the abortive rising of 1659. He was ejected for Nonconformity in 1662, and died in 1669. There is an account of him in Dict. Nat. Biog.
[161] Thomas Ellison (Wadham Coll., Oxford, B.A. 1665 ; Pemb. Coll., Camb., M.A. 1668) was proposed for Presbyterian ordination in 1660 ; Manch. Classis (Chet. Soc.), iii, 347. His nomination to Ashton was intended to be favourable to the expelled rector ; Newcome's Diary (Chet. Soc.), 184. He appears to have been buried in Dukinfield Nonconformist chapel, the register giving the date as 26 Feb. 1699–1700.
[162] Of Christ Church, Oxford ; M.A. 1707 ; Foster, Alumni.
[163] The patron was the devisee under the will of George Earl of Warrington, a cousin of the new rector. The rector was created a baronet in 1790.
[164] King's College, Cambridge, M.A. 1777, rector of Stoke-upon-Terne 1806. For pedigree see Ormerod, Ches. (ed. Helsby), i, 507.
[165] Third son of the patron. He was educated at Trinity College, Cambridge, M.A. 1797 ; and became prebendary of Durham in 1809, and rector of Thornton in Craven in 1812.
[166] He was a 'warming pan,' and on resigning the rectory became curate to his

successor. He was afterwards first incumbent of the new church of St. Peter, 1824.
[167] M.A., Brasenose College, Oxford. He was nephew of the patron, and perpetual curate of Chilton, Bucks, from 1829, a second institution to Ashton being necessary. He scarcely ever visited Ashton, though drawing a large income from it.
[168] M.A., T.C.D., 1840. He was a native of county Derry and had been incumbent of Audenshaw ; honorary canon of Manchester, 1884.
[169] Of Jesus College, Oxford, M.A. 1876. Vicar of Swindon, Staffs., 1882.
[170] Ch. Goods (Chet. Soc.), 16. The church seems to have been well furnished; among other things there were 'a pair of organs,' a banner of green silk, and a holy-water stock of brass. There were then four churchwardens, and this continued to be the rule ; one was chosen by the lord of the manor, another by the rector, and the others by the parishioners ; Gastrell, Notitia, ii, 5.
[171] Clergy List of 1541–2 (Rec. Soc. Lancs. and Ches.), 13.
[172] Visitation lists in Chester Diocesan registry.
[173] Ch. Goods, 17, quoting S.P. Dom. Eliz. x, 293.
[174] A 'lecturer,' Mr. Peabody, occurs in 1622 ; Misc. (Rec. Soc. Lancs. and Ches.), i, 66.
[175] Commonw. Ch. Surv. 22. The proposed bounds were thus described : To begin at the division where Lancashire, Yorkshire, and Cheshire meet in Mossley hamlet ; following the brook between Lancashire and Yorkshire as far as the beginning of Oldham at Watergate Mill, then along the boundary between Oldham and Ashton to the Park, thence to Alt

case.
[186] Patrons, five trustees. A district was assigned in 1866 ; Lond. Gaz. 12 June.
[187] Patrons, five trustees. A district was assigned in 1879 ; Lond. Gaz. 14 Feb.

ASHTON-UNDER-LYNE PARISH CHURCH : GLASS IN WEST WINDOW OF NORTH AISLE

including St. James's and St. Matthew's at Leesfield, and St. Augustine's at Mossley.

The Wesleyan Methodists had a chapel in Ashton in 1782 ; [188] now they have churches in Ashton, Mossley, Woodhouses, and Audenshaw. The New Connexion had a chapel as early as 1798 ; they have now four churches in Ashton,[189] and others in Hurst, Lees, Mossley, and Audenshaw. The Primitive Methodists are represented in Ashton, Hurst, Lees, Bardsley, and Mossley.[190] The Independent Methodists have a church in Ashton.[191]

There is a Strict Baptist chapel in Ashton ; also a Baptist church.[192]

The Nonconformists of 1662 and later were able to worship at Denton and Dukinfield ; the latter congregation is now Unitarian. In 1816 the Congregationalists took the old Methodist chapel in Harrop's Yard, it being difficult for Nonconformists to obtain land from the Earl of Stamford ; and they built and opened a new chapel in 1817. This first Albion Chapel was followed by a second in 1835 ; and has now been replaced by a third, on another site, opened in 1894.[193] There are now three Congregational churches in Ashton itself, and another in Mossley.[193a]

---

[188] John Wesley preached there on 4 April 1782 ; Wesley's *Works* (ed. 1829), iv, 224.

[189] The first chapel was in Harrop's Yard ; a view is given in Nightingale's *Lancs. Nonconf.* v, 298. A removal was made to that in Stamford Street in 1799 ; Butterworth, op. cit. One chapel at Mossley was built in 1823 and rebuilt in 1835 ; and a second in 1824 ; Edwin Butterworth, *Ashton*, 135. A chapel in Stalybridge, opened in 1802, was removed to Dukinfield in 1832 ; ibid. 150.

[190] 'The Primitive Methodists, commonly called Ranters, have a place for religious worship in Church Street' ; Jas. Butterworth, *Ashton* (1822), 83.

[191] The Independent Methodists occur as early as 1818 ; a chapel at Charlestown was built in 1838, under the following circumstances :—' "The Stephensites" originated in the secession of the Rev. J. R. Stephens from the Wesleyan Methodists. The admirers of this singularly distinguished personage erected in 1837 a large but plain building for worship in Charleston, which is calculated to accommodate 1,100 persons' ; Edwin Butterworth, *Ashton*, 68. They had also a chapel at Mossley and another at Rassbottom, Stalybridge, called Mount Zion.

[192] It originated about 1836 ; E. Butterworth, op. cit. 68. There was formerly another at Mossley ; ibid. 136. The General Baptists had a chapel in Rassbottom in 1819, removed to Cross Street, Stalybridge, in 1828 ; ibid. 151.

On the early troubles of the Baptist congregation at Stalybridge, which divided into Arminian and Calvinistic, see A. Taylor, *Engl. General Baptists*, 394.

[193] Nightingale, op. cit. v, 299–303.

[193a] Ryecroft was founded in 1848, the chapel being built in 1853 ; from this the school-chapel at Hooley Hill has sprung ; ibid. v, 306–8. Work at Mossley originated in 1838, but Abney Church there was not built till 1854–5 : ibid. v, 322.

[194] Edwin Butterworth, op. cit. 67 ; the room was the old Methodist chapel in Harrop's Yard.

In 18
of the place
anti Catholic
a notorious
large crucifix
and windows
priest, Fr. J.
tain compens

Infirmary has an endowment of £1,325 a year, to which is added £414, the gift of Samuel Oldham.[201] The educational endowments amount to £557,[202] and the above-named Samuel Oldham gave £193 a year to the park.[203] There are two small church endowments.[204] For the new township of Mossley an inquiry was held in the year 1899.[205]

ECCLES

| BARTON | PENDLETON | CLIFTON |
| WORSLEY | PENDLEBURY | |

The ancient parish of Eccles measures about 7 miles across, from the Irwell south-west to the Glazebrook, and has an area of 22,004 acres. The position of the church, from which the parish takes its name, was fairly central for the portion of the district habitable in former times, while the great area of moss land in the west was still unreclaimed, being close to the boundary between Pendleton, Pendlebury, and Clifton on the east, and the large areas of Worsley and Barton on the west. The general slope of the surface is from north to south, the highest land, about 300 ft. above sea level, being in the stretch of higher ground between Worsley and Kearsley.

The parish was anciently divided into three 'quarters'—Barton, Worsley, and Pendleton, assessed for the county lay of 1624 at £3 19s. 8¼d., £2 18s. 3d., and £3 5s. 4¾d. respectively, when the hundred paid £100.[1] For the 'fifteenth' the townships paid as follows:—Barton, including Farnworth, £1 12s.; Worsley, £1 11s.; Pendleton, 13s. 6d.; Pendlebury, 5s.; Clifton, 7s., or £3 18s. 6d. out of £41 14s. 4d. for the hundred.[2]

Though the parish is of great extent, and lies near Manchester and Bolton, its particular history has been uneventful. There was a skirmish at Woolden in the Civil War, and in 1745 the Young Pretender's army passed through in its advance and retreat. The

geological formation of the southern and central part of the parish consists of the New Red Sandstone, the northern part of the Permian Rocks and Coal Measures. Coal mines have been worked from the 16th century, and perhaps earlier. In the 18th century the Worsley navigation schemes led to a great development of mines, and later of manufactures, and Eccles and Pendleton have shared in the growth of Manchester trade. The following is the apportionment of agricultural land within the ancient parish : Arable land, 7,587 acres ; permanent grass, 5,914 ; woods and plantations, 716.[3]

Chat Moss remained waste until the beginning of the last century.[4] Defoe, who passed it on the way from Warrington to Manchester early in the 18th century, has given a description of it. It stretched along the road for 5 or 6 miles, the surface looked black and dirty, and it was 'indeed frightful to think of, for it would bear neither horse nor man, unless in an exceeding dry season, and then so as not to be travelled over with safety.' The land was entirely waste, 'except for the poor cottagers' fuel, and the quantity used for that was very small.'[5] Leland and Camden tell of a great eruption of the moss in the time of Henry VIII.[6] The carrying of the Liverpool and Manchester Railway over Chat Moss in 1830 was considered a great triumph of engineering.[7] The

---

for coals and clothing at Christmas time for the poor of Audenshaw. He desired it to be considered an ecclesiastical charity.

Thomas Turner Broadbent in 1896 bequeathed the residue of his estate, after the expiry of certain interests still [1899] existing, to the foundation of a convalescent hospital.

[201] Full details of these endowments are given in the *Rep.* of 1899, pp. 15–19.

[202] John Newton, 1731, £3 rent-charge on an estate called The Crime in Ashton, for teaching six poor children.

John Walker, 1755, £6 8s. 4d., for buying books and teaching the Catechism.

Edward Wright, 1882, £2 17s., for Bibles for the children attending the parish church schools.

George Heginbottom, 1879, £40 exhibition, at Owens College, tenable for three years.

Titus Tetlow, 1890, £212 17s. 4d., exhibitions, &c., for Ashton-under-Lyne Mechanics' Institution.

Samuel Broadbent, 1891, £3, for the Woodhouses British Schools.

Helen Swallow, 5s. 9d., for the Sunday School.

Froghall School, 1824, £23 3s. 3d.; the school was discontinued in 1840, and the income is paid to Hey Church of England Schools and to Austerlands School in Saddleworth.

Edward Hobson, 1764, £266 10s. 3d.,

for Audenshaw (British) School, and for exhibitions.

[203] *Rep.* 16.

[204] For St. John the Baptist's, Hey, £11 11s. 8d.; for a Bible woman, St. James's, Ashton, £2 18s. 4d.

[205] The report was published in 1900. Mossley, from its composite formation, has a share in some charities of Ashton-under-Lyne, Mottram in Longdendale, and Rochdale.

[1] Gregson, *Fragments* (ed. Harland), 22; the third quarter's contribution was divided thus : Pendleton, £1 16s. 9½d.; Pendlebury, 10s. 2½d.; Clifton, 18s. 4¾d.

[2] Ibid. 18. For other assessments see *Manch. Sess.* (Rec. Soc. Lancs. and Ches.), i, 13—House of Correction, 1616 ; and 60—ox. lay, 1618.

[3] The details given are :—

	Arable Acres	Grass Acres	Wood, &c. Acres
	•		210
•	•		
•	•		

Hist. of Lancs. (ed.
[5] *Tour Through*

210

35

whole has now been reclaimed.[8] The corporation of Manchester has a sewage farm there.

Dr. Aikin says of Eccles in 1795 :—

the *Telegraph.*

The agriculture of the parish is chiefly confined to grazing, and would be more materially benefited by draining ; but the tax upon brick, a most essential article in this process, has been a very great hindrance to it. The use of lime—imported from Wales, and brought by the inland navigations to the neighbour-hood of our collieries—has become very general in the improve-ment of the meadow and pasture lands . . . The advance of population in the parish of Eccles [the effect of the great demand for hands in our manufactures] has been attended with a due care respecting public worship and the religious education of children. . . . The excellent institutions of Sunday schools were early patronised in Eccles parish, and continue to receive the steady and liberal support of the parishioners. There are now, it is calculated, near one thousand children regularly taught in these schools, and with very considerable improvement.[9]

Eccles gives a name to one of the parliamentary divisions of the county formed of this parish and Flixton ; it returns one member.

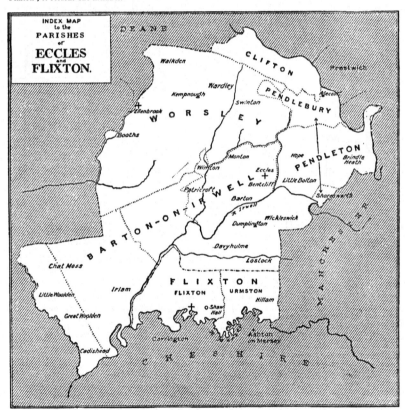

INDEX MAP to the PARISHES of ECCLES and FLIXTON.

Where it was softest, branches, brushwood, and hurdles (twigs and heath twisted and plaited in frames) were laid down to form a foundation, and the whole was covered with sand and gravel two to three feet thick as occasion required. Upon

this, as it became compacted, were laid the wooden sleepers for the rails, and the road over the moss is now not inferior to that on any part of the line.' The writer goes on to speak of the efforts then being made to reclaim the moss.

[8] The moss abounded with vipers ; *Manch. Guardian N. and Q.* no. 480. For the Woollen Ringing pits on the moss, see ibid. no. 848.

[9] *Country Round Mancl.* 218–21.

The earliest parts of the building are the responds of the arch to the south transept in St. Katherine's Chapel, which are of 14th-century date, and may belong to the year 1368, when the chapel was founded. These form the only remaining fragment of a church which probably consisted of a chancel with north chapel and nave with south aisle, to which this chantry was added. Owing to the rebuilding of 1862–3 at the east end evidence of the extent of this early church is wanting, but both the chancel and nave seem to have been of the same length as at present, though of less width. The east wall of the north chapel, however, appears to have been standing up to 1861 in a line with the east wall of the chancel, and contained a good 14th-century window, of which the present window in the same position is said to

aisle was added or reconstructed. The Jesus altar stood here. This aisle was lighted at its west end by a three-light window with cinquefoiled heads under a four-centred arch, the remains of which may still be seen blocked up on the outside. Later in the same century, probably about 1450, when William and Lawrence Booth founded (or refounded) a second chantry of St. Katherine, the south aisle seems to have been rebuilt further southward. The evidence of the old plinth, now restored, showed it to be a later addition, and it is likely that the entrance to St. Katherine's Chapel was at this time taken down and reconstructed in its present position. That the south aisle is earlier in date than the 16th-century rebuilding, which brought the church to its present shape, is shown by the windows, whose jambs are moulded, in contrast with the plain cham-

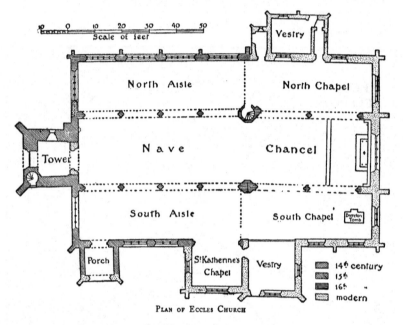

PLAN OF ECCLES CHURCH

be a copy.[10] Whether this earlier church had a north aisle it is impossible to say, and its south aisle was most likely narrower than the present one, though there is nothing actually to show that the arch to the south transept is not in its original position. If it is, the aisle must have been of almost equal width to the nave, which is unlikely. There was probably a west tower to the 14th-century church, but no positive evidence of this remains, successive rebuildings and restorations making it almost impossible to say whether the lower portion of the present tower is older than the upper part. Whatever the original western termination may have been, however, the tower was built, or rebuilt, centring with the nave, probably in the beginning of the 15th century, and at the same time, or shortly afterwards, the north

fered jambs of the later work, and by the generally better and more careful detail as shown in the hood-moulds to the windows and in the buttresses, which had cusped panelled fronts. In the rebuilding of this wall much, if not all, of the old detail has been lost, the middle buttress having disappeared, and the diagonal one at the south-west having been renewed.

The south aisle of the chancel, if it did not exist before, must have been built some time in the 15th century, and is probably the 'new chapel' which was built by Sir Geoffrey Massey, who died in 1457, having founded a chantry at the Trinity altar there in 1453. The old views of the church show the south chancel aisle with a three-light 15th-century window similar to that in the west end of the north aisle, together

[10] See Owen MSS. Manch. Reference Library.

with a priest's door with a pointed head and hood-mould in the south-west corner.

It is possible that the south arcade of the nave was rebuilt at the same time as the south aisle was enlarged, but this would mean that the work then executed was taken down within forty or fifty years. It is more likely that the original north and south arcade stood till the beginning of the 16th century, when the great rebuilding of the church commenced.[10a] The south arcade was the first to be taken down, and was reconstructed with a lofty clearstory on the same line. The north arcade was afterwards pushed out 5 ft. to the north, bringing the north aisle wall flush with the wall of the north chapel of the chancel, and throwing the tower out of centre with the nave. Whether there had been a chancel arch before this date it is impossible to say, but the chancel seems to have been reconstructed without one at this time or shortly after, and similarly widened to the north. The evidence of this was much more plain before the rebuilding of 1862–3 by the way in which the roof of the old chancel cut into that of the north chapel.[11] The axis of the chancel is twisted about 18 in. to the south, but whether this took place during the 16th-century rebuilding, or was so originally, there is nothing to show, and the south arcade of the chancel may be on the exact line of the former one. The only fixed point in the church through the various rebuildings seems to be the south pier between the chancel and nave, though this of course was only built in its present form in the 16th-century reconstruction. The arches and piers of the chancel are similar to those of the nave, but the arches are much wider and higher, leaving no space for the clearstory like that of the nave, unless the roof were taken very much higher. But the unfinished end of the nave roof as shown in old views of the church seems to suggest that it was intended to carry it on over the chancel, the two octagonal turrets alone marking the division of nave and chancel on the outside.

The building as finished in the first part of the 16th century remained more or less intact until 1801 when the taking down of the east end was begun prior to reconstruction. Many alterations, however, took place in the interior between these two dates, the first in 1595, when new pews and forms were set up. At this date, too, there were 'repairs to the church,' which probably included the insertion of much of the window tracery. In 1713 the church was 'beautified,' and in 1715 the vestry, which had been in the south aisle of the chancel, was removed to the west end under the tower. In 1717 a west gallery was ordered to be erected, and at the same time or shortly after the building was again thoroughly repaired. The roof was releaded in 1719. In 1770 north and south galleries were ordered to be erected, and in 1790 the south porch was restored. A gallery

was erected at the east end of the nave in 1803 excluding any view of the chancel, but this was removed in 1862. The other galleries still remain. There were further repairs in 1832, 1846, 1854, and 1856, the nave roof being repaired and the lead recast, new roofs constructed to the aisles, and the old flagged floor relaid.[11a] In 1862–3 the east end was entirely rebuilt and a small clearstory of three triangular-shaped lights added to the chancel walls. The work comprised the reconstruction of the chancel with its north and south aisles, the addition of a vestry on the north, and an organ chamber on the south, and the rebuilding of St. Katherine's Chapel, which had long been destroyed.[12] Three large circular 18th-century windows, formerly lighting the south gallery, were built up at this time, but their position may still be seen from the inside. The organ, formerly in the west gallery, was transferred to the chamber on the south side of the south chancel aisle and remained there till 1890, when a new one was erected on screens in the first and second bay on each side of the chancel, and the organ chamber turned into a vestry. At the same time the vestry on the north was converted to its present use. The organ chamber seems to have been erected prior to the rebuilding of St. Katherine's Chapel, as its west wall was built as an outside wall, as may be seen by the diagonal buttress and the blocked-up windows on that side. St. Katherine's Chapel, which is supposed to be on the site of the original chantry chapel, now forms a south transept.

The church is built of friable red sandstone, which had decayed so badly that an almost complete refacing of the old part became necessary in 1907. The work was completed in 1908, and very little of the exterior detail is now left. The interior was, till 1875, covered with an accumulated coat of limewash, but was then stripped and all its stonework cleaned. Externally the walls of the nave and aisles have battlemented parapets and the roofs are covered with lead. The aisles have lean-to roofs with a straight parapet on their west end. The walls of the chancel, south chapel and aisle, and transept also terminate in battlements, and the vestry has a stepped gable on the south side. The roofs of the chancel and chancel aisles are covered with slates, but those of the vestry and transept are leaded. The south aisle of the chancel has a lean-to roof, but the roof of the north aisle retains its original gable form.

The chancel is 43 ft. long by 23 ft. 6 in. wide and has north and south arcades of two bays with centre pier and east and west responds. The arches are 16 ft. 6 in. wide, and there is a piece of straight wall at the east end 4 ft. long. The columns and arches are similar to those in the nave, but the capitals are slightly different. The first bay from the west on each side is filled with a modern screen with an organ over and a similar screen partly fills the eastern bay.

10a Robert Langley of Agecroft in 1525 bequeathed £6 13s. 4d. to the building of the parish church of Our Lady of Eccles, to be paid as the work went on ; Wills (Rec. Soc. Lancs. and Ches.), 62.

11 See Owen MSS.

11a An account printed in the Manch. Advertiser, 24 Oct. 1846, gives a melancholy description of the state to which the building had been reduced ; for example : 'Over the chancel is a huge, unsightly gallery, in which the people turn their

backs to the altar, and above this, in the place of the ancient rood screen, is a representation of the royal arms' ; the gallery had lately been erected ' by the lay rector, Sir John Heathcote, of Longton Hall, Staffs., who had sold the pews to different holders.' There were still ' some very rude massive oaken benches in the nave' which remained in their primitive condition, but surrounded by high pews ; and ' near the door of the south porch was a very ancient alms box having three dis-

tinct locks.' On a board was painted the information that ' This church was beautified in the year 1713.' Baines (Lancs. iii, 115) states that the ancient gates leading to the chancel remained until 1803 ; this was the year in which the chancel gallery was erected.

12 Old views of the south side of the church show the arch to St. Katherine's Chapel as an external feature, the lower part built up and the upper part used as a window.

The east window is a modern traceried one of five lights in the style of the 15th century and belongs with the clearstory and roof to the 1862–3 rebuilding. The fittings are all modern and are of no particular interest. The chancel arch is a modern insertion of two chamfered orders springing high up from shafts corbelled out from the large octagonal piers which separate the nave from the chancel. The pier on the south side is 4 ft. 6 in. in diameter with a respond on its east and west faces and is built solid. That on the north side is bigger and contains a staircase leading to the roof, entered from the north aisle. On the outside these piers are carried up above the roof and are finished with pyramidal stone roofs and finials. The north aisle of the chancel, which is 17 ft. 6 in. wide, retains no ancient features, but has a copy of the five-light 14th-century window with reticulated tracery already mentioned at its east end. It has two three-light windows on the north side and a door to the strong room, with an outer door in the north-west corner to the west of the old vestry. The south aisle of the chancel, which is 16 ft. wide, has a three-light window at the east end and two three-light windows on the south side. The old organ chamber (present vestry) is built out to the south at its west end and is separated from it by a screen. The aisle contains a monument to Richard Brereton and his wife, described below.

The nave measures 60 ft. in length and 23 ft. 3 in. in width and is of four bays with north and south arcades having octagonal shafts 2 ft. 6 in. in diameter, their longer sides measuring 18 in. and the shorter 5 in., set diagonally. The longer sides have a hollow moulding stopping under the capitals, which are of a plain block character with upper and two lower fillets, and are carved with plain shields, three on each face. The capitals of the easternmost pier of the north arcade and of the east respond are slightly different, having only the upper and lower round fillet and two shields on each face. The arches are pointed and of two plain chamfered orders. On each side there are four pointed five-light clearstory windows of very poor detail. The jambs and heads are chamfered and there is no external hood-mould, while the tracery is straight and without cuspings. The sills of the windows on the inside are more than 2 ft. above the crown of the nave arcade, but they were formerly much lower, as may be seen by a straight joint at each side. In the recent restoration it was found that the jambs of the windows were continued below the present sills, these having been probably inserted at the time that the galleries were built, when the roofs of the aisles were raised in order to get head room. Two courses of masonry between the crowns of the nave arches and the sills of the windows above mark the former level of the clearstory. On the east wall of the tower the line of the 14th-century steep-pitched roof may still be seen, together with the places where the purlins were housed into the wall. The roof of the nave is of flat pitch and probably retains a good deal of the original 16th-century timber, but it was repaired in 1846 and the decayed pieces replaced. The north-east diagonal buttress of the tower, the lower part of which has been cut away, is now an internal feature, together with

the string-course marking the upper or belfry stage, with the lower part of a small window above. The tower arch is of two chamfered orders, the outer one of which is stopped at the springing, and is filled in behind the west gallery with a modern wood seven-light traceried window. Under the gallery a modern doorway has been inserted. The west walls of the north and south aisles are not bonded in with the tower,[12a] and it is possible that an extension of the nave westward or a rebuilding of the tower was contemplated by the 16th-century builders.

The two east piers of the north arcade and the east pier and east respond of the south arcade have canopied niches in the sides facing south-west (towards the entrance). The niches are empty, but show conclusively that the piers are of pre-Reformation date.[13] They are 3 ft. 6 in. high, and the shelf, which has a plain shield under, is 5 ft. 3 in. from the ground. The niche on the east respond of the south aisle, opposite St. Katherine's Chapel, has carved on either side a hammer and pincers together with a small cogged wheel, possibly with reference to St. Katherine.[13a] The west pier of the north aisle has a stone bracket about 6 ft. 6 in. from the ground.

The west and south galleries are in line with the centre of the piers, but the north gallery is set back about 6 ft. behind the arcade and rests on small iron pillars. The north and south galleries retain their 18th-century pews, and are approached from the west end of each aisle by staircases.

The 14th-century responds of the arch to the south transept have been already mentioned. The capitals are modern, but are probably copies of the originals, and the arch over is a four-centred one of two rounded orders. The chapel is modern and has a four-light window on the south and one of two lights on the west. The south aisle has two three-light windows with moulded jambs and hood-moulds, as before mentioned. The mullions and tracery, however, are of late date like those of the other windows of the church. In the upper lights portions of the tracery have been cut away as in other parts of the building. Each aisle has a five-light window at its west end, and the north aisle is lighted by four five-light windows along its north side, all of which have been renewed. The south porch appears originally to have been erected in the 15th century with the south aisle, but the front part was rebuilt in 1790, which date is carved upon it. The inner door is old, of thick oak and nail-studded. The outer iron gates were set up in 1809.

The tower is rather squat and of two stages, being divided about midway by a string-course. It has diagonal buttresses of four stages, moulded plinth, and embattled parapet with angle and intermediate pinnacles. There is a vice in the south-west corner, entered from the outside. Externally the tower is 20 ft. square, but the walls not being of equal thickness, its internal dimensions are 11 ft. by 12 ft. 6 in. The west doorway, which has a pointed arch, has been rebuilt, and above, separated from it by a string-course between the buttresses, is a three-light pointed window with hood-mould, which is said to have originally shown signs of well-designed cusping. This had been hacked off outside, but remained on the inside to

---

[12a] Information from Mr. Frank P. Oakley, the architect of the restoration.

[13] The canopy and ornament to the niche of the east pier of the north aisle have been hacked away.

[13a] St. Katherine with her wheel is the crest of Booth of Barton.

ECCLES CHURCH   SOUTH VIEW

the ringing chamber. The window, which was of
15th-century date has, however, been entirely reconstructed and the ancient detail lost. The lower stage
of the tower has a single-light window on the north
side, but on the south is quite plain except for the
door to the vice. The belfry stage has a three-light
square-headed stone louvred window on each face,
with a clock face below on the north, south, and west
sides.

The fittings, including the font and the pulpit, are
all modern, dating principally from 1862–3 and subsequent years. There are no traces of ancient ritual
arrangements. In 1856, when the old flagged floor
was relaid, two sepulchral slabs, one with a raised and
the other with an incised cross, were found near the
third column from the east on the south side of the
nave at a depth of 2 ft. 6 in. These slabs now stand
in the west porch under the tower at each side of the
inner doorway.[14]

The monument of Richard Brereton and his wife
was erected by the latter in 1600 and stands at the
east end of the south aisle of the chancel, but is not
in its original position. It is an altar tomb with
recumbent figures, the man being in armour with
helmet by his side and the lady in a ruff and with an
enormous headdress. There is a figure of a child
on a bracket on the south side of the tomb, around
which runs the inscription.

Besides the Brereton monument there is an old
brass to the Dauntesey family on the south side of the
chancel arch, and a painted wooden shield emblazoned
with the arms of George Legh (d. 1674) at the west
end of the north aisle.[15]

There is no ancient stained glass.

There is a ring of eight bells. Four are mentioned
in the inventory of Edward VI, but these were removed in 1709 and a new ring of six substituted.
One of these bearing the inscription ' Prosperity to
this church' still remains amongst the present ring.
The tenor has the inscription : ' I to the church the
living call and to the grave do summon all.' The
curfew is still rung every night.

The plate consists of two chalices of 1618, with
the date inscribed on each below the rim ; a paten of

---

[14] They are described in John Harland's
Eccles Church Notes, 1864. In the Owen
MSS. details are given of two other stones
each bearing a cross and sword, one of
which was found serving as a lintel of a
doorway in the north wall of the aisle of
the chancel, and the other on the spot
once covered by St. Katherine's chantry.
Owen also states that there were ' several
of this kind lying about.' Heywood,
Eccles Church (1907).

[15] Heywood, op. cit. 26.

[16] The entries 1563–1632 have been
printed by the Lancs. Par. Reg. Soc.

[17] In or before 1180 Albert Grelley presented William the Clerk to a fourth part
of the church of Eccles for life ; *Whalley
Coucher* (Chet. Soc.), i, 40. William's
father Haisolf and his brother Matthew
had previously held it ; the grant was
made ' in pure and perpetual alms for the
souls of the grantor's father and mother
and for himself, his wife and children,' so
that William was not in the position of
the modern lay impropriator, but would
be obliged to pray and fulfil the church
services in return. Though the lord of
Manchester presented at this vacancy he
probably did so as the guardian of the heir

on

would have to be employed for mass and other rites,[19] the clerks themselves no doubt taking their share in those services for which holy orders were not necessary.

That 'the clerks of Eccles church' were a regularly established body is shown by the grant of rights of common in the manor of Barton made by Gilbert de Notton and Edith his wife.[20] 'G. and H., W. and T., clerks of Eccles,' as holding the rectory, sanctioned the opening of a chapel at Worsley before 1233.[21] The initials no doubt stand for Geoffrey de Byron, Hugh, William, and Thomas. Hugh and Thomas must therefore have divided the fourth part of the rectory between them. The former was son of Ellis de Worsley, and was probably married, as his daughter Ellen inherited his property.[22] Thomas seems to have been the only priest, and unmarried. He may be identified with the 'Master T. de Eccles' who attested a grant by Gilbert de Notton and Edith his wife.[23]

The prohibition of hereditary succession to benefices and the requirement that those who held a benefice which a priest should serve must within a limited time be advanced to the priesthood put an end to the customary arrangements at Eccles. In 1234 Gilbert de Barton granted to his lord, John de Lacy, Earl of Lincoln, the advowson of the church of Eccles,[24] and Lacy at once conferred it upon Stanlaw Abbey.[25]

Some of the clerks who held the rectory seem to have been induced to resign, or were perhaps otherwise provided for;[26] episcopal and papal ratifications were obtained,[27] and a vicarage duly ordained.[28]

From this time until the suppression of Whalley, the rectory remained in the possession of the monks. In 1291 the revenues were taxed as £20 a year,[29] and in 1341 the ninth of the sheaves, &c., was found to be £15 7s.[30] In 1534 the gross value was returned as £57 2s.,[31] but about 1540, after the rectory had come into the king's hands, the net revenue from the glebe and tithe was found to be £104.[32] A division now was made; the tithes and other revenues of the rectory were leased out and afterwards sold,[33] but the advowson was retained by the Crown and presentations are now made by the Lord Chancellor. An independent vicarage was created in the chapelry of Deane, thus increasing the royal patronage.

The vicarage of Eccles was formally constituted in 1277; a competent dwelling-house was ordered to be provided, the land occupied by the de facto vicar was secured, and a pension of 16 marks assigned to him from the revenues of the church.[34] This pension continued to be paid by the monks of Whalley,[35] and then by the Crown, but on the sale of the rectory it was increased to £16 13s. 4d., which is still paid.[36] The

---

grant to John was in pure alms, and subject to an annual rent of a pound of incense, payable to the church of Eccles; *Whalley Couch.* i, 43.

Geoffrey de Byron also was married.

[19] David and Thomas, 'chaplains' of Eccles, are mentioned in grants before 1220; ibid. 47. Thomas was probably the 'clerk' who had a portion of the rectory. David, the priest of Eccles, attested a Lever charter; Add. MS. 32103, no 207.

[20] *Whalley Couch.* i, 47.

[21] Lord Ellesmere's D. no. 129.

[22] Ibid. no. 232–33.

[23] *Whalley Couch.* i, 47.

[24] Ibid. 63. The grant included all the liberties, &c., belonging to the advowson of the church in woods, meadows, roads, waters, &c.; also 10 acres in Barton adjoining Hennesden, between the 'great street' and moss by the boundaries of Pendlebury. It excluded Gilbert de Barton's hey of Bolesnape and allowed his right to make fisheries, mills, &c., as he might find it convenient. The consideration for this grant was an acquittance of a bond for 250 marks due to Aaron the Jew of York. Gilbert had previously granted or confirmed his grandfather's gift of free common to the clerks of Eccles and their men; ibid. 45.

[25] Ibid. 36. The witnesses are the same as those to Gilbert de Barton's charter, Roger de Notton being one. The grants mention the chapels of Eccles, perhaps those at Deane and Ellenbrook.

[26] The release by Thomas the chaplain to William the Clerk has been recorded above. Hugh the Clerk of Eccles, 'of his own free will,' resigned his 'portion' in the church of Eccles and its chapels in Apr. 1235, in full chapter at Warrington; ibid. 48. Hugh was no doubt the 'H. tunc persona de Eccles' of another deed; ibid. 42. After this it would appear that only William the Clerk remained.

[27] John de Lacy having intimated that he had given the advowson of Eccles and certain lands there to Stanlaw, Bishop Alexander de Stavenby in Dec. 1234 ratified the grant; the prior and convent of Coventry and the gave their consent i Alexande IV tions in 1255 and la [28] The pope, in s priation of the recto

Commonwealth surveyors in 1650 found the tithes of Eccles to be worth about £170; they had been sequestered by the authorities for the 'delinquency' of the impropriator, who had been accustomed to pay £18 a year to the vicar. They recommended that Ellenbrook Chapel should have a parish assigned to it,

that a new church should be built at Irlam, and that some re-arrangement of the other boundaries should be made.[36a] With the growth of Manchester the value of the glebe increased, and the income of the vicarage, which in 1718 was under £46,[37] has now become £700.[38]

The following is a list of the vicars :—

Instituted	Name	Patron	Cause of Vacancy
oc. 1277 . .	Roger [39]	———	———
oc. 1284 . .	John [40]	———	———
oc. 1294 . . .	William the Parker [41] . . .	———	———
oc. 1310–15 . .	Simon [42]	———	———
25 July 1320 . .	Adam de Blackburn [43] . . .	Abbot of Whalley . . .	———
31 Oct. 1349 .	John de Mulnegate [44] . . .	,,	d. A. de Blackburn
10 June 1372 .	Robert de Monton [45]	,,	d. J. de Mulnegate
oc. 1383 . . .	John de Craunton [46] . . .	———	———
oc. 1402 . . .	John de York [47] . . .	———	———
———	John de Moreland . .		
8 Feb. 1412–13 .	Richard Ewood [48]	———	res. J. de Moreland
5 Nov. 1456 .	Robert Lawe [49]	Abbot of Whalley . . .	d. R. Ewood
12 Apl. 1471 . .	Christopher Whitehead [50]	,,	res. R. Lawe
1474 . .	Thomas Wright [51]	Bishop of Lichfield . .	———
8 Mar. 1504–5 .	Thomas Holgate [52]	Abbot of Whalley . . .	d. T. Wright
oc. 1534–54 . .	Thomas Crane [53]	———	———
——— 1557 } 20 June 1559 } .	Edward Pendleton, B. Gram.[54] . .	The Crown	res. T. Crane

[36a] *Commonw. Ch. Surv.*(Rec. Soc. Lancs. and Ches.), 13.
A terrier of 1663 is printed in *Eccles Ch. Notes*, 49 ; it gives details of the lands held by the vicar, the vicarage house and outbuildings, and the cottages built upon the land. The same volume contains, among other interesting records, a case and opinion concerning certain fir trees in the churchyard which the vicar had cut down and sold (ibid. 35) ; an account of the pews in the church in 1595 (24) ; and the galleries erected in 1717 and 1769–71 (59).
[37] *Notitia Cestr.* ii, 46. The glebe land, 14 acres, let for £21, and surplice fees amounted to £6. Warden Wroe of Manchester had stated the value as £80 in 1706. 'In the terrier of 1705 it is stated that the vicar has no tithes, nor are there any estates in the parish tithe free ; neither has the vicar mortuaries, oblations, obventions, or herbage. He has liberty of a little common called the Warth, lying at the river side of the Irwell, and a property in the waste with the other charterers, together with the herbage of the churchyard.'
There were six wardens and six assistants; two wardens were nominated by the Duke of Bridgewater, two by Mr. Trafford, one by the vicar, and one was appointed alternately for Clifton and Pendlebury, the outgoing warden nominating.
[38] *Manch. Dioc. Cal.*
[39] He attested a number of the local charters, including three of the year 1277; *Whalley Couch.* iii, 906, 910, 913. As this was the date of the ordination of the vicarage, it may be assumed that Roger was the first vicar. Among the tenants when John de Barton sold his manors to Robert Grelley were 'Roger de Eccles, chaplain, William de Eccles, clerk' ; so that Roger may have been the officiating priest before becoming vicar ; De Trafford D. no. 202.
[40] *Whalley Couch.* iii, 912.
[41] *Cal. Pat.* 1292–1301, p. 120.
[42] He attested a Worsley charter ; El-

lesmere D. no. 237 one, 1315–16· Harl 181.
[43] Lich. Epis. R benefice had been v

Instituted	Name	Patron	
7 Dec. 1576	Thomas Williamson, M.A.[55]	The Crown	
20 May 1606	John White, D.D.[56]		;
9 Jan. 1610–11	John Jones, D.D.[57]		
?1659	Edmund Jones, B.A.[58]	—	
19 Nov. 1662	Robert Hartley, M.A.[59]	The Crown	
25 July 1671	Thomas Usherwood[60]		
24 Aug. 1678	Thomas Hall, M.A.[61]		
10 Jan. 1721–2	Thomas Chaddock, B.A.[62]		
8 Jan. 1724–5	Thomas Bell		
27 Nov. 1725	William Crooke[63]		
27 July 1726	Thomas Vaughan, M A.[64]		
9 Mar. 1747–8	Benjamin Nicholls, M.A[65]		d. T. Vaughan
3 June 1765	Cudworth Poole[66]		d. B. Nicholls
27 Dec. 1768	John Crookhall, B.A.[67]		d. C. Poole
31 Oct. 1792	John Clowes, M.A[68]		d. J. Crookhall
9 Apl. 1818	Thomas Blackburne, M.A.[69]		d. J. Clowes
8 Apl. 1837	William Marsden, B.D.[70]		res. T. Blackburne

(Chet. Soc.), 247 ; and graduated at Oxford, B. Gram. in 1547–8 ; Foster, *Alumni.* Anthony Wood calls him 'the famous schoolmaster of Manchester'; *Athenae* (ed. 1691), i, 700. He was presented by Philip and Mary to the vicarage of Eccles in 1557 and made one of the fellows of Manchester when it was restored. He conformed to the Elizabethan changes and was instituted to Eccles a second time in 1559 ; he married, retained his charges at Manchester and Eccles, and died in 1576. His will is printed in *Chantries,* 249.

[55] *Manch. Fellows,* 80–3. He was made fellow of the church of Manchester in 1578 ; he was also vicar of Childwall for a brief time, 1589. In 1590 he was described as 'a preacher,' but 'insufficient'; S.P. Dom. Eliz. xxxi, 47. He was a member of the Ecclesiastical Commission for the North, which conducted a vigorous persecution of recusants in the last quarter of the 16th century. A Thomas Williamson, born in Westmorland and educated at Sedbergh, entered St. John's Coll. Cambridge in 1567 ; B. Wilson, *Sedbergh Reg.* 61.

[56] Son of Peter White, vicar of St. Neots, Hunts. ; educated at Gonville and Caius Coll. Cambridge ; Venn, *Admissions,* 61. He was a chaplain to King James, had a benefice in Suffolk, was a fellow of Manchester 1606 ; *Manch. Fellows,* 104–8 ; *Dict. Nat. Biog.* At Eccles he showed himself a Puritan, and was presented for not wearing the surplice in 1608, but in 1609 he and the curate 'sometimes' wore it ; Visit. P. at Chester. About 1610 he was reported to be 'a preacher'; *Hist. MSS. Com. Rep.* xiv, App. iv, 12. He was brother of Dr. Francis White, successively Bishop of Carlisle, Norwich, and Ely (1626–38), who printed his works, including the *Way to the True Church* (issued in 1608) in 1624.

[57] From this time the institutions have been taken from the Institution books, P.R.O., as printed in *Lancs. and Ches. Antiq. Notes ;* there were no payments of first-fruits.

Mr. Jones contributed to the ship money and other exactions of Charles I from the clergy, though in 1639 he was described as 'poor'; *Misc.* (Rec. Soc. Lancs. and Ches.), i, 123, &c. He was a Puritan. In 1622 it was reported that he gave the communion to those who sat; and though nobody stood at the creed or bowed at the name of Jesus, no presentments were made at the visitation ; Papers

at Chester Dioc. Reg. He adopted Presbyterianism when established by law, and signed the 'Harmonious Consent' of 1648. In 1650 he was assisted by his son Edmund Jones ; *Commonw. Ch. Surv.* 13. He was still 'minister of Eccles' in April 1659 ; *Plund. Mins. Accts.* (Rec. Soc. Lancs. and Ches.), ii, 312. He is called D.D. by Piccope (xvi, 35) ; note by Dr. W. A. Shaw. His son John matriculated at Oxford (Brasenose) in 1626, being sixteen years of age ; M.A. 1631 ; Foster, *Alumni.*

[58] Edmund Jones, son of the preceding vicar, entered St. John's Coll. Cambridge as a sizar in 1645, being twenty-one years of age ; *Admissions,* i, 73. In *Manch. Classis* (Chet. Soc.) his ordination is recorded, 123, 131, 132. He was ejected from Eccles in 1662 for nonconformity, but continued to minister in the district until his death. He is mentioned in Oliver Heywood's *Diaries,* i, 197 ; iii, 81. 'Good Mr. Jones of Eccles walked out, was tolerably well though he had been distempered, went to bed at nine o'clock, was dead before twelve ; 2 May 1674'; ibid. iii, 137. He is also mentioned frequently in Henry Newcome's *Diary* and *Autobiog.* (Chet. Soc.), being described as 'a true-hearted, serious man, and a faithful minister.'

[59] He entered Brasenose Coll. Oxford, in 1650, being described as 'plebeian'; M.A. 1655 ; Foster, *Alumni.* He was nominated as vicar 25 Sept. 1662 ; Pat. 14 Chas. II, pt. 19, no. 143. He is mentioned in Newcome's *Diary,* 153.

[60] The name is also spelt Isherwood. He was of Christ's Coll. Cambridge, and was ordained in 1654 to the charge of Blackrod ; *Bury Classis* (Chet. Soc.), 237. Of his death Oliver Heywood records : 'I could not but reflect on my old schoolfellow, Mr. Thomas Isherwood, vicar of Eccles, that had been drinking with some gentlemen, returning home fell off his horse, was drowned in a ditch that scarce covered all his head'; *Diaries,* iii, 331.

[61] Also fellow of the Collegiate Church, Manchester, 1688 ; educated at Corpus Christi Coll. Cambridge ; M.A. 1688 ; *Manch. Fellows,* 192. He was 'conformable' in 1689 ; *Hist. MSS. Com. Rep.* xiv, App. iv, 229.

[62] He was of Brasenose Coll. Oxford ; B.A. 1692 ; and had been licensed to Ellenbrook in 1709.

[63] Mentioned in a petition by John Bridge of Eccles, printed in *Eccles Ch. Notes,* 33. A William Crooke was pre-

bendary of Chichester from 1727 to 1753; Le Neve, *Fasti,* i, 273, 276. One of these names matriculated at Oxford in 1716 ; another or the same was M.A. at Cambridge, 1724.

[64] Educated at Brasenose Coll. Oxford ; B.A. 1712 ; and St. Catharine's, Cambridge ; M.A. 1719 ; vicar of Pawlett, Somerset, 1723–6 ; Foster, *Alumni.* A letter of his, dated Edingdale, 1727, to the parish clerk shows him to have been non-resident, for the vicarage was let ; he remarks, 'I suppose the surplice fees rise high this sickly time' ; *Eccles Ch. Notes,* 34.

[65] Probably the Benj. Nicholls who matriculated at Jesus Coll. Oxford, in 1734 ; M.A. 1740. He is supposed to have attracted favourable notice in high quarters by a vehement sermon against the rebels of 1745. He lived twenty miles from the church, which he seldom visited, performing duty there not above two or three days a year ; *Eccles Ch. Notes,* 36.

[66] Cudworth and Edward Poole, aged eighteen and seventeen respectively, sons of Edward Poole of Woolden, but born at Newhall in Cheshire, entered St. John's Coll. Cambridge, in 1734 ; *Admissions,* iii, 75. Cudworth Poole died at Woolden, 8 Nov. 1768.

[67] Probably the John son of James Crookhall of Clifton, who matriculated at Queen's Coll. Oxford, in 1743 ; B.A. 1747 ; Foster, *Alumni.* In 1789, having fallen into debt, his benefice was sequestered for a time ; *Eccles Ch. Notes,* 39. He was also rector of Woodchurch in Cheshire from 1747 to 1792. His will (1788) is in the Manchester Reference Library ; note by Mr. E. Axon.

[68] Educated at Trin. Coll. Cambridge ; M.A. 1774. He died at the vicarage 28 Mar. 1818 ; he was also incumbent of Trinity Church, Salford. He had a son, the Rev. Thomas Clowes, who lived at Eccles.

[69] Son of John Blackburne of Orford ; educated at Brasenose Coll. Oxford ; M.A. 1815 ; Foster, *Alumni.* He was also rector of Crofton, Yorks, 1817, and on being presented to the rectory of Prestwich in 1836, he resigned Eccles.

[70] Educated at Brasenose Coll. Oxford ; M.A. 1796 ; B.D. 1811 ; incumbent of St. Michael's, Angel Meadow, Manchester. He died 15 Feb. 1861, and was buried at Chelmorton ; there is a monument to him in Eccles Church. His son, John Howard Marsden, fellow of St. John's Coll. Cambridge, became a canon of Manchester. Foster, *Alumni ; Manch. School Reg.* (Chet. Soc.).

Instituted	Name	Patron	Cause of Vacancy
Feb. 1861 . .	James Pelham Pitcairn, M.A.[71] . .	The Crown	d. W. Marsden
— — 1893 . .	Hon. Arthur Temple Lyttelton, M.A.[72]	,	d. J. P. Pitcairn
— — 1899 . .	Frederic D'Austini Cremer, M.A[73] .		prom. A. T. Lyttelton

Before the Reformation the regular staff consisted of the vicar, who was bound to reside, and three chantry priests ; there were, however, others residing in the parish, and at the visitation of 1548 seven names were recorded, while six appeared in 1554. The old priests dying out, there were only four at the visitation of 1563 ; viz. Edward Pendleton, the conforming vicar, who had also to attend to the school at Manchester ; his curate ; George Wirrall, the survivor of the chantry priests ; and John Pilsworth, chaplain of the Lady Brereton of Tatton. Two years later the curate had disappeared, his place being taken by ' a reader ' ; George Wirrall still survived, but the chaplain had no mention.[74] The parish church and the chapel at Ellenbrook were probably served for some time by the vicar and a licensed reader. In 1592 it was stated that the vicar, Thomas Williamson, did not wear the surplice, and the warden was enjoined to offer it to him 'so often as he shall hap to minister the sacraments.' Two men were presented for abusing one another in time of divine service, and giving bad words to ' the reader.'[75]

It was not long before things improved somewhat, for in 1610 the vicar and the incumbent of Ellenbrook were both ' preachers.'[76] In 1650 the parish church had two ministers, but Ellenbrook, which was not endowed, had sometimes 'a preaching minister'

[71] Educated at Jesus Coll. Cambridge ; M.A. 1851 ; rector of St. John's, Longsight, 1850–61. It was during his time that Eccles Church was restored.

[72] Son of the fourth Lord Lyttelton ; educated at Trinity Coll. Cambridge ; M.A. 1877 ; master of Selwyn Coll. 1882–93 ; Hulsean Lecturer, 1891. He published a volume of sermons and contributed to Lux Mundi. In 1898 he was made suffragan Bishop of Winchester, with the title of Bishop of Southampton. He died in 1903.

[73] Educated at Wadham Coll. Oxford ; M.A. 1873 ; vicar of Upholland, 1881 ; rector of Keighley, 1888.

[74] From the visitation lists at the Chest. Dioc. Reg.
The church ornaments, &c., existing in 1552 are recorded in Ch. Gds. (Chet. Soc.), 20.

[75] Lancs. and Ches. Antiq. Soc. v, 61–2. At the same time a number of non-communicants were admonished and the churchwardens were ordered to levy the 12d. fine for non-attendance at church, which had not been done. Two parishioners were censured for killing a pig ' at time of divine service upon the Sabbath day.'

[76] Hist. MSS. Com. Rep. xiv, App. iv, 12. The vicar of Eccles and the curate or lecturer of Ellenbrook appear somewhat later in the list of clerical contributors referred to above ; Misc. (Rec. Soc. Lancs. and Ches.), i, 54, 66, &c.

[77] Commonw. Ch. Surv. 13, 14.

[78] The visitation list of 1691 shows the vicar and the Ellenbrook curate to have been the only clergy ; the latter was also master of the school.

[79] Raines, Lancs. Chant. (Chet. Soc.), i, 129 ; the ornaments were a chalice,

of York 1452 to 1464, secured in 1460 the appropriation of Beetham rectory to the new chantry or college of Jesus and the Blessed Virgin Mary, for which the Jesus Chapel was built on the north side of the chancel. A house of residence adjoined for the use of the chaplains.[83] At the time of the Suppression the clear revenue was £20 1s. 8d., out of which the two chaplains or 'fellows' received each 10 marks, the 'conduct' or assistant priest had 7 marks, and 20s. was given in alms. The incumbents were bound to celebrate mass daily in the chapel and 'maintain the choir' at divine service, and all three, 'by the occasion of the large circuit of the said parish and the vicar thereof not [being] able to minister to all the same' were 'enforced often and many times to minister sacraments to the parishioners.'[84] Jesus Chapel was acquired by the Traffords, and Trinity Chapel by the lords of Worsley, as representatives of the founders.[85]

There was an ancient schoolhouse in the church-yard.[85ª] The schoolmaster of Eccles formerly claimed a small sum from each newly-married couple ; if refused, the boys took the bride's garter. The custom having become a nuisance, the churchwardens abolished it, levying 4d. or 6d. at each marriage, to be paid to the schoolmaster of Eccles.[87]

A place in the churchyard was known as Scots' Hole, the tradition being that a number of rebels had been buried there after execution.[88]

Near the church is a spring called the Lady's well.[88ª]

CHARITIES The ancient charities of Eccles were but small.[89] There was in 1828 a Poor's stock of about £60 ; and James Bradshaw of Croft's Bank had in 1800 left a rent-charge of £12 a year for education in that hamlet, while a school had been founded at Roe Green in Worsley as early as 1710.[90] The more recent charitable endowments are chiefly educational or ecclesiastical.[91]

---

appropriation was consequently nullified. Paul II in 1466 confirmed the appropriations of Slaidburn and Beetham to the respective chantries ; and both chantries benefited under the will of Archbishop Booth ; Test. Ebor. (Surtees Soc.), ii, 266.

[83] Chant. 134–8 ; from Lich. Epis. Reg. x, fol. 95–105. The royal licence was granted 1 Dec. 1460. The statutes were similar to those of St. Katherine's chantry. The chapel in 1548 seems to have been suitably furnished, though there was only one chalice ; the mansion-house had a garden, croft, and orchard adjoining ; a rent of 3s. 4d. was paid for it to the vicar of Eccles ; Chant. 138, 139.

The following names of cantarists occur : On 5 June 1460 John Badsworth and Thomas Shipton, priests, were appointed to the new foundation ; Lich. Epis. Reg. xii, fol. 98. In 1466, Badsworth having resigned, Peter Halstead succeeded ; ibid. fol. 102b. Halstead died two years afterwards, and was followed by James Bruche ; ibid. fol. 104. In 1474 Charles Prestwich was appointed, on the resignation of Bruche ; ibid. fol. 109. These refer to 'the first chaplaincy.' In 1475 Ralph Derwynd was promoted from St. Katherine's to be second chaplain at the Jesus chantry in place of John Worthington, resigned ; ibid. fol. 109b. Edmund Beswick followed, and in 1497, on his resigning, William Cramp succeeded ; ibid. xiii, fol. 230b. In July 1534, Thurstan Cocker having died, George Bowker succeeded him ; ibid. xiii–xiv, fol. 34. A year or so later Thomas and George Bowker were the fellows or chaplains ; Valor Eccl. v, 227. George Bowker resigned in 1539, and was followed by Roger Okell ; Lich. Epis. Reg. xiii–xiv, fol. 37b.

Okell was celebrating at the Suppression, being then aged fifty-two. His fellow-priest was George Wirrall, aged forty-six, who had paid firstfruits in 1538 on appointment to succeed Thomas Bowker, deceased ; Lancs. and Ches. Rec. (Rec. Soc. Lancs. and Ches.), ii, 408 ; Church Papers at Chest. Richard Hyde, a scholar of Cambridge, aged twenty-two, was their assistant ; Chant. 131, 137. Roger Okell was buried at Middleton, 5 Nov. 1565 ; Ch. Gds. 21. In 1556–7 Roger Okell and George Wirrall, clerks, complained that Thomas Fleetwood had disturbed them in possession of a mansion-house by Eccles Church ; Ducatus Lanc. (Rec. Com.), i, 287.

[84] Chant. loc. cit.

[85] A made in Gilbert 1567 · D

[86] Non of the sc

[87] Pal Lancs. a

[88] Loc

[88ª] La

[89] A Bishop G 11, 53.

[90] The of 1826

SALFORD

BARTON

Barton, 1195 ; there is no variation to record.

Barton, usually called Barton-upon-Irwell to distinguish it from other places of the name, has a length of 7 miles from the north-eastern end, at which the parish church of Eccles is situated, to the Glazebrook, which forms the south-western boundary. The greater part of it lies on the northern side of the Irwell, but there is on the south bank a considerable area, forming the modern township of Davyhulme. The Manchester Ship Canal, opened in 1894, has replaced the Irwell for the existing boundaries. The central and southern parts of the township lie upon the pebble beds of the New Red Sandstone ; Trafford Park, Barton, Patricroft, and Monton on the Upper Mottled Beds and Winton on the Permian rocks and Coal Measures. Round the parish church the town of Eccles has grown up, and is now a borough ; the limits include the village of Barton, a mile to the south-west, with the hamlets of Peel Green and Patricroft to the west, and Winton,[1] Monton, and Chorlton Fold on the northern boundary. Ellesmere Park is in the north-east corner.

The greater part of the area to the south-west of Barton village was formerly part of Chat Moss, but on the bank of the Irwell, about a mile north of its junction with the Mersey, the village of Irwellham, now Irlam, managed to exist ; and in the south-west corner, between the Mersey and Glazebrook, was Cadishead, with Great and Little Woolden to the north-west on the banks of the Glazebrook. Barton Moss and Irlam are the names of the modern townships which have resulted from the subdivision of the ancient Barton. The village of Irlam includes Higher and Lower Irlam and Jenny's Green.

The Davyhulme portion was crossed from east to west by a small brook, a tributary of the Irwell, the confluence marking the boundary between Barton and Flixton. Hulme or Davyhulme proper, and Moorside are on the south side of this brook, with Calderbank to the west, and Lostock in the eastern corner. On the north bank of the brook Bent Lanes occupied an area formed by a bend of the Irwell, now almost obliterated by the canal ; Crofts Bank, Wilderspool, Dumplington, and Bromyhurst, going northwards, occupy the centre, and Trafford Park, formerly Wickleswick or Whittleswick, lies in the north-eastern portion, between Stretford and Eccles Church.

school; Monton recreation ground; Trinity Wesleyan Chapel at Peel Green, Patricroft ; Sarah Anne Tetlow's benefaction to St. Catherine's, Barton, church and school ; endowment of St. Mary's, Davyhulme ; the school at Davyhulme, founded 1792 ; Greaves' School, Irlam, founded 1834 ; Irlam Church charity ; Taylor's charity for Cadishead Wesleyan school ; Allotment land, Cadishead. For Pendlebury, the Greaves' Free School and St. Augustine's National School ; endowment of St. John's Church ; parish club room and mission room at St. Augustine's.

[1] In Winton are Kitepool (formerly Kidpool) and Cleaveley.

[2] Made up as follows :—Barton, 1,108 acres ; Eccles, 400½ ; Monton, 434½ ; Winton, 319½ ; Newhall, 85¾ ; Foxhill, 729½ ; Boysnope, 416¾ ; Higher Irlam, 1,288 ; Lower Irlam, 1,129½ ; Cadishead, 2,111 ; Davyhulme, 706¾ ; Croft, 285¾ ;

Lostock, 423½ ; Bromyhurst, 115½ ; Dumplington, 359½ ; Whittleswick, 708¾.

The census report of 1901 gives the details of the new townships thus : Eccles, 2,057 ; Barton Moss, including 21 acres of an unnamed area, 1,489 ; Irlam, 4,620 ; and Davyhulme, 2,658, the total being 10,824. These areas include 40, 40, 81, and 81 acres of inland water respectively.

[3] The Manchester Ship Canal has been adopted as the boundary in Irlam, as more convenient than the old course of the Irwell ; Local Govt. Bd. Order, 34989 (30 Sept. 1896). By the Salford Corporation Act, 1892, modifications were made of the Barton and Pendleton areas.

[4] It was used for passenger boats down to 1860. The *Manch. Dir.* of 1800 thus describes the route : 'The aqueduct which passes the navigable river Irwell at Barton Bridge is astonishingly grand. It begins upwards of 200 yds. from the river, which

runs in a valley ; over the river itself it is conveyed by a stone bridge of great strength and thickness, consisting of three arches, the centre one of which is 63 ft. wide and 38 ft. above the surface of the water, admitting the largest barges navigating the Irwell with masts standing. The spectator is here gratified with the extraordinary sight, never before beheld in this country, of one vessel of burden sailing over another.' The fares from Manchester to Worsley were 1s. and 6d. and 1s. 6d. and 9d. return. There is a view of the bridge in Aikin's *Country round Manch.* 113.

[5] *Manch. Guardian N. and Q.* no. 361, 1292, where it is stated that bull-baiting ceased in 1834, and bear-baiting soon afterwards ; no. 974, 1101, refer to a picture of the Wakes. See also E. Axon, *Bygone Lancs.* 175. The Wakes continued to be held, but on private ground.

The close of the marling time was formerly marked by a 'guising.'[6]

A company of volunteers was raised at Eccles in 1797.[7]

For local government Barton, Eccles, Winton, and Monton obtained a local board in 1854.[8] In 1892 this area was constituted a municipal borough. The remainder of the ancient township of Barton was at the same time divided into three: Barton Moss, including Foxhill and Boysnope; Irlam, including Cadishead; and Davyhulme, including all to the south-east of the Manchester Ship Canal. Minor changes of boundaries were made in 1896. Irlam since 1894 has had an urban district council of twelve members; the other new townships have parish councils.

The Eccles Town Hall, built in 1881, is on the site of the old cock-pit.

At Patricroft are a hospital and a home for children. There also is the workhouse; the new building was opened in 1894. Newlands cemetery was formed in 1879. The Salford Corporation has a sanatorium in Eccles New Road.

The inclosure award for Cadishead Moss, with plan, is at Preston.

The shaft of a Saxon cross was found near Eccles Church in making the Ship Canal.[9] A later cross was at Barton Old Hall.[10] During the cutting of the Ship Canal a canoe and a hollowed log were discovered.[11] A causeway has been traced, probably mediaeval.

The hearth tax return of 1666 shows that Barton proper had 101 hearths liable; the principal houses were those of George Legh, with fourteen; Thomas Sorocold, thirteen, and John Barlow, six. Davyhulme had seventy-eight, no house having more than four hearths; Irlam thirty-seven, Mr. Lathom's, with six, being the largest dwelling; Cadishead, twenty-eight, Thomas Holcroft having eleven; Eccles and Monton eighty-two, John Valentine's house having eleven, and Thomas Minshull's eight.[12]

There are a large number of interesting field names, among them the following: Lower Irlam—Eaves, Morley Croft, Bosses, Poos, Sparth, Summerley (in strips); Jenny Green—Balshaw Fields; Boysnope—Stocky Dole, Parr Round Field, Pipers Field; Foxhill—Wall Congre, Hare Horn Meadow; New Hall—Stick Ings, Patch Ings, Broad Eyes, Street, Bagoletine, How Lane Head; Barton Village—Neckars, Scythy Field, Hoasefield, Acker Meadow; Barton Lane—Crossfields; Barton Bridge—Laster, Warth, Boatfield; Dumplington—Wall Congre, Stopes, Warcock Hill; Bromyhurst—Shoe Broad, Orkot, Cockleney (Great, Old, Greens); Bent Lanes—Shoe Broad; Davyhulme—Alder Forest; Croft's Bank—Cercicile, White Laches, Knows Corn Hill.

Dr. John Hewitt, born at Eccles in 1614, became chaplain to Charles I, and was executed in 1658 for taking part in a plot for the restoration of Charles II.[13] Richard Martinscroft, mathematician, 1586–1667, is said to have been a native of Eccles.[14] Barton Booth, a tragedian, is said to have been born at Barton in 1681.[15] William Tong, Presbyterian divine, was born at Eccles or Worsley in 1662; he ministered in London till his death in 1727.[16] John Johnson, Baptist minister, was born at Lostock in 1706; he died in 1791.[17] William Hill, a writer on mnemonics, who died in 1881, was another notability.[18] Joseph Wolstenholme, a mathematician of distinction, fellow of St. John's College, Cambridge, and professor at the Indian Engineering College, Cooper's Hill, was born at Eccles in 1829. He died in 1891.[19]

Under the lords of Manchester the *MANORS* great manor or fee of *BARTON* was held by a family using the local surname. In its full extent the fee extended over the greater part of the parishes of Eccles and Deane, and as the family held also the manor of Worsley with Hulton of the king in thegnage, the only townships exempt from their lordship were Pendlebury, Pendleton, and Clifton in the east, and Rumworth and Horwich in the north.[20] Originally the Barton fee appears to have been accounted as that of two knights, but, probably by division among co-heirs, a knight's fee and a half only was held in 1212 by Gilbert de Notton in right of his wife, Edith daughter of Matthew son of Leysing de Barton.[21] Of Edith's father and grandfather nothing is certainly known.[22] She

[6] The *Hist. of Eccles and Barton's Guising War*, printed about 1778, is noticed in Fishwick's *Lancs. Lib.* 13.

[7] *Local Glean. Lancs. and Ches.* i, 251.

[8] *Lond. Gaz.* 7 July 1854. The local board was constituted the Burial Board in 1877.

[9] Now in the Museum, Manchester University.

[10] *Lancs. and Ches. Antiq. Soc.* xi, 120. For these and other crosses see also ibid. xxii, 105–8.

[11] *V.C.H. Lancs.* i, 248–51.

[12] *Subs. R.* bdle. 250, no. 9.

[13] An elaborate account of Dr. Hewitt, with portrait and list of works, was given by Mr. J. P. Earwaker in *Local Glean. Lancs. and Ches.* i, 267, &c.

[14] Gillow, *Bibl. Dict. of Engl. Cath.* iv, 494; *Pal. Note Bk.* i, 124. Martinscroft is not a local name.

[15] He died in 1733. See *Dict. Nat. Biog.*

[16] *Dict. Nat. Biog.*

[17] Ibid.

[18] Gillow, op. cit. iii, 310.

[19] *Dict. Nat. Biog.*

[20] The lords of Manchester retained some portions in their own hands, e.g. Snydale in Westhoughton.

was one of four daughters and co-heirs, and by her first husband, known as Augustine de Barton,[23] she had a son John, who died young, and a daughter Cecily, who married William, a son of Gilbert de Notton by a former wife,[24] and carried to him the manor of Barton, and also in right of her father that of Breightmet.

Gilbert, the eldest son of William and Cecily, was a minor in 1220 at the death of his grandmother

[23] *Lancs. Inq. and Extents*, i, 137, 301. He was also known as Augustine de Breightmet, which place in 1212 was held by William de Notton; ibid. 71. See Ormerod, *Ches.* (ed. Helsby), i, 422, citing the Mobberley charters.

[24] *Whalley Couch.* ii, 521; Edith, lady of Barton, with the assent of her husband Gilbert de Notton, for their salvation and that of her son John and her daughter, wife of William de Notton, granted half of Cadishead to Stanlaw Abbey. Edith and her husband were in other ways benefactors of this abbey; ibid. i, 46, &c. The son John had seisin of a moiety of Mobberley as heir to his father; Ormerod, *Ches.* i, 411. William de Notton and Cecily his wife about 1200 confirmed a grant to Mobberley which had been made by Cecily's uncle Patrick with the assent of her father; ibid. i, 422.

[25] In October 1220 the sheriff was directed to put Robert Grelley in seisin of the fee of one knight and a half in Barton, because the heir of Edith, formerly wife of Gilbert de Notton, viz. the son of Edith's daughter, was under age, and his wardship belonged to Robert; *Rot. Lit. Claus.* (Rec. Com.), 438.

In 1222 Gilbert, described as *nepos et heres* of Edith de Barton, had livery of 32 oxgangs of land in Barton and Worsley and the members; Fine R. 6 Hen. III, m. 7.

[26] He sold the advowson of Eccles before 1234 to John de Lacy, because of an acquittance to Aaron the Jew of York which Lacy had made; *Whalley Couch.* i, 41. Aaron son of Joseus the Jew of York refeoffed Sir Gilbert de Barton of the manor of Barton, with remainder to John son of Sir Gilbert, and to Agnes the daughter; Dods. MSS. clxix, fol. 154b. Geoffrey de Chetham assigned to Sir Thomas Grelley the land and rent demised to him by Aaron, to hold until 205 marks should be paid to Sir Thomas, either by the grantor or by Gilbert de Barton; ibid. fol. 153b.

[27] To Thomas Grelley he sold at different times all his right in Westwood, 3 oxgangs of land held by Agnes widow of Geoffrey de Worsley and by Adam de Bowdon, 3 oxgangs of land held by Adam and Thomas de Hulme, 20 oxgangs of land held by Adam son of Wronow de Wardley, an orchard called the Imp Yard, and other lands; De Trafford D. no. 188–97. To one of these deeds (194) is appended the seal of Gilbert de Notton, showing a pile; to another (195) Gilbert de Barton's own seal, paly of four.

Gilbert de Barton in 1235 granted to Richard de Bracebridge 3 oxgangs of land in Brinsop in return for a release of all claims on the Barton fee; *Final Conc.* (Rec. Soc. Lancs. and Ches.) i, 62. In 1241 for a similar release he sold 4 oxgangs of land in Heaton to Richard son of Christiana de Allerton—probably Richard de Hulton; ibid. i, 88.

[28] In 1242 Gilbert de Barton held a knight's fee and a half of Thomas Grelley,

and Thomas held of and he in chief of *and Extents*, i, 153 Grelley claimed from customs and services fee of a knight and all gangs of land wher half a knight's fee; at the court of Ma weeks to three week a year as sake fee a bert undertook to d not to grant, sell, the said tenement in without the licence or his hei s, *Final C*

It is evident from that the Abbot of Co houghton as one oxg the fortieth part of the original fee of Ba gangs or ten plough-l part had been alie possibly, as above a land in Aspull, one i Brockholes. Of th gangs may have be that seventeen oxga for the s rvi e of h

...

her daughter and heir Loretta by marriage with John del Booth, about 1292, carried it into a family which, as Booth of Barton, retained it for 300 years.

John de Barton, the son of Gilbert, retained lands in the township which his descendants enjoyed for some generations; occasionally they laid a claim to the manor.[32]

By 1282 the manor was in the hands of the lord of Manchester, and it was surveyed with the estates of Robert Grelley, who died in that year.[33] In 1320–2 Barton proper seems to have reckoned as half a knight's fee, or eight oxgangs of land.[34]

Of the Booth family only a brief sketch can be given. Loretta, the heiress of Barton, was perhaps still unmarried in June 1292;[35] but about this time, if not earlier, John del Booth or Booths married her.[36] He was succeeded by his son Robert;[37] in or before 1343 Robert was followed by his son Thomas del Booth,[38] who died, apparently by violence,[39] in 1368, having directed his body to be buried before the altar of St. Katherine in Eccles Church.[40] His eldest son John succeeded, and lived until September 1422; he had a numerous

Booth of Barton.
Argent three boars' heads erect and erased sable langued gules.

---

next year demanded two-thirds, or two-thirds of a moiety, against Robert Grelley; De Banco R. 7, m. 21; 13, m. 3; 17, m. 25d. Cecily, the widow of Gilbert de Barton, had the other third; ibid. R. 33, m. 48; see De Trafford D. no. 199, 200.

Agnes may have married, secondly, Alexander le Mey of Bromyhurst; Alexander and his wife Agnes in 1277 granted to the former's son Alexander a messuage and two parts of an oxgang of land in Barton, to be held of the heirs of Agnes; *Final Conc.* i, 152. If so, she was living, a widow, in 1292; Assize R. 408, m. 32, 3 d. The Mey family long continued to hold lands in Barton.

[32] John de Barton was engaged in various suits regarding the manor in 1278 and 1279; De Banco R. 27, m. 39 d, 43 d.; 30, m. 48.

Thomas del Booth and Gilbert de Barton, with his sons Hugh, Edmund, and John, were implicated in a seizure of cattle and assault at Barton in 1345; De Banco R. 344, m. 21. Gilbert de Barton was a defendant in 1353; Assize R. 435, m. 4. In the following year John son of Gilbert son of John de Barton claimed certain lands in Barton which his father Gilbert had demised to Robert de Hulme and his heirs; Duchy of Lanc. Assize R. 3, m. 3. In 1361 he claimed two-thirds of the manor of Barton against Roger La Warre, Eleanor his wife, Thomas del Booth, and Ellen his wife; Assize R. 440, m. 1.

In 1360 John de Barton and Robert his son granted Thomas del Booth an acre by the Pool Brook near the Pool Bridge, to strengthen Thomas's mill race and enlarge the mill pool; De Trafford D. no. 224. In 1363 John de Barton, in conjunction with Denise his wife and Robert his son, enfeoffed Thomas del Booth and Ellen his wife of all their lands in Barton, between Eccles and Irlam and between Newham and Davyhulme, for an annuity of 20s.; ibid. no. 225. Releases were afterwards given by Alice and Margaret sisters of Robert de Barton, and by Edmund, a son of Gilbert de Barton; ibid. no. 227, 228.

In 1388 Maud, widow of Robert son of John de Barton, released to John del Booth her rights, including her dower in Boysnope, for a rent of 30s.; ibid. no. 232, 233. In 1404 Thomas de Barton allowed John del Booth and his heirs to bear his arms—three boars' heads sable; Dods. MSS. cxlix, fol. 160b.; Ormerod, *Ches.* (ed. Helsby) i, 524; while in 1423 Thomas son of Gilbert de Barton, perhaps the same person, gave a release to Thomas del Booth of all his right in the manor of Barton, and in all messuages, lands and tenements, rents and services in the vill;

De Tra
gard to t
arms, it
the coat
Booths;
De Traff

[33] *Lan*
were 40
26s. 8d
meadow
fishery y
pannage
were val
38s. 8d
ants 17s
a year, b
by the wi

[34] *Ma*
of Barto
worth 40
lord grou

offspring, of whom Sir Thomas, the eldest son, succeeded him ; Sir Robert married Douce daughter and co-heir of Sir William Venables of Bollin in Cheshire, and became ancestor of the Booths of Dunham Massey, Earls of Warrington ; Roger, a third son, was ancestor of the Booths of Mollington ; William and Lawrence, other sons, became respectively Archbishop of York and Bishop of Durham.[41] John del Booth died seised of the manor of Barton, with various messuages and lands in Barton and Manchester, all held of Thomas La Warre in socage by the service of 1d. yearly, and worth £60 a year. Thomas his son and heir was over forty years of age.[42]

The new lord of Barton, who became a knight, was succeeded by his son Thomas [43] and his grandson Robert. The last-named left a son and heir, Sir John Booth,[44] slain at Flodden in 1513 ;[45] his son and heir John, then about twenty-three years of age, died in December 1526, leaving as heir an infant son John,[46] who died in 1552,[47] and whose son John, then ten years of age, died in 1576, leaving four daughters as co-heirs—Margaret, who in 1564 was contracted to marry Edmund Trafford ; Anne, who

for some reason passed over by the husband, the manor of Barton and the estate there being bestowed upon Cecil, his son by a second marriage ; it has descended like Stretford.[60] Courts leet and baron continued to be held until about 1872.[61]

The vill of Eccles[62] is named in 13th-century charters ; it appears to have been largely in the hands of the monks of Whalley, being a rectory manor.[63] Possibly *MONKS' HALL*, standing on higher ground a quarter of a mile to the north-west of the church, took its name from them.[64] In 1632 Christopher Anderton of Lostock, as impropriator of the rectory, sold Monks' Hall to Ellis Hey.[64a] The Hey family were of some continuance in the neighbourhood, and a pedigree was recorded in 1664.[64b] In the Civil War they experienced the displeasure of the Parliamentary authorities for aiding the king's forces.[65] After the Restoration the hall became the place of worship for a Nonconformist congregation.[56]

By the end of the 17th century it had been acquired by the Willises of Halsnead near Prescot.[66a] Monks' Hall was described in 1836 as a 'venerable wood and plaster fabric now a farm-house.' Of this timber building, however, only a portion remains at the back of the present house, and a picturesque black and white half-timber end facing the garden on the east side has been spoiled by the insertion of a large bay window on the ground floor. A stone wing, now entirely modernized, has been added, probably in the 17th century, in front of the old timber building ; it is covered with rough-cast, and has little or nothing to distinguish it from an ordinary modern villa, except that the roofs are covered with stone slates. The building has long ceased to be used as a farm-house, and is now a private residence.[57] A stone with the inscription, 'Mrs. Helen Willis, relict of Martin Willis, gent. deceased, me aedificavit,'[58] is said to have been in the older part of the

MONKS' HALL

[60] The manor of Barton has been regularly included in the records of Trafford estates ; see *Lancs. Inq. p.m.* (Rec. Soc. Lancs. and Ches.), iii, 329 ; Pal. of Lanc. Feet of F. bdle. 80, no. 4 ; 100, no. 22 ; 282, no. 99.

[61] Information of Messrs. Taylor, Kirkman & Co.

[62] There is no variation in the spelling of the name calling for notice, except Heckeles, 1278.

[63] *Whalley Couch.* i, 42. William de Eccles released 8 acres belonging to the church of Eccles in exchange for half an oxgang of the church land, formerly held for life. To John his brother the same William granted 16 acres in the vill of Eccles ; ibid. i, 43. Monithorns was adjacent to Eccles and to Monton, and was granted by Gilbert de Barton to the monks in pure alms ; a pit at Sevenlows was one of the boundaries ; ibid. i, 50, 49. Iorwerth son of Morgan de Barton and Agnes his wife released all their claim to Monithorns in consideration of a payment of 6s. ; ibid. iii, 921. Iorwerth de Barton

ley ; *Couch.* iv, 1238. Roger Hey in 1541 contributed to the subsidy 'for goods' ; *Misc.* (Rec. Soc. Lancs. and Ches.), i, 140. In 1552 Thomas Hey and Isabel his wife had a suit with Robert Edge, Margaret his wife, Thurstan Woodward and Ellen his wife, respecting a house, &c., at Eccles ; *Ducatus Lanc.* i, 255.

[64a] Ellis Hey of Monks' Hall was, about 1647, stated to be 'very old and infirm, and too much in debt to compound' ; but later he or the trustees of his infant grandson and heir paid a fine of £309 for his 'delinquency in assisting the forces raised against the Parliament' ; *Cal. of Com. for Compounding*, iii, 1923 ; *Royalist Comp. Papers*, iii, 221.

[56] Nightingale, *Lancs. Nonconf.* v, 3.

[66a] Raines, in Gastrell's *Notitia*, ii, 53.

[67] Canon Raines (loc. cit.) says that when it was a farm-house the public had the privilege of a passage way through the building.

[68] She married Willis in 1681.

house or in a barn adjoining, but no trace of it can now be found.

Opposite the hall was formerly an orchard, the remains of which existed until recently, where, in August 1864, while laying a new street, an earthen vessel was discovered containing about 6,000 silver pennies, chiefly of the reigns of Henry I, II, and III, several of John, and a few of William I of Scotland. The coins were claimed as treasure trove by the Duchy of Lancaster, but selections were presented to the British Museum and to several museums in Lancashire.[59]

BENTCLIFFE was another mansion-house in Eccles, lying to the south-east of the church, on the border of Pendleton ; it was for a long period the residence of the Valentine family, who died out in the 18th century. They were originally of Flixton.[60] Richard Valentine died in July 1556, leaving a son Thomas, only three years of age. The capital messuage of Bentcliffe was held of the heir of William the Clerk in socage by rendering a pound of incense to the church of Eccles, this rent identifying it with the estate granted by William the Clerk to his brother John about 1250.[61] Land in Barton was held of the heir of

VALENTINE of Bentcliffe. *Argent a bend sable between six cinqfoils gules.*

Agnes daughter of Gilbert de Barton by the rent of a gillyflower, and messuages, &c., in Little Houghton and Haslehurst in Worsley of the lord of Worsley, by a pair of white gloves or 1*d.* yearly.[62]

Thomas Valentine was succeeded by his son John and grandson John.[63] The younger John's estate was sequestered by the Parliamentary authorities, because when he was high constable of the hundred of Salford in 1644, Prince Rupert, advancing into

[59] Mr. John Harland prevented the coins from being dispersed in the first instance.

[60] From the Vawdrey deeds it appears that Thomas Valentine, living in 1476 and 1487, had sons John, George, and Geoffrey. Jo n, who was dead in 1508, had sons Johnhand Thomas, of whom the latter survived. Thomas Valentine of Bentcliffe, son of John Valentine, and his mother Joan Langtree, widow, in 1516 made a feoffment of messuages, lands, &c., in Eccles, Barton, Little Houghton, Worsley, and Bedford. In 1536 he granted all his lands in Eccles, Barton, and Worsley, to his bastard sons John and Richard for life, with remainder to his right heirs. It is probable that this was the Thomas Valentine of Bentcliffe—the place is also called Bencliffe and Beancliffe—whose will (dated 1550) is printed by Piccope, *Wills* (Chet. Soc.), ii, 134, his son Richard being the chief beneficiary.

[61] *Whalley Couch.* i, 43.

[62] Duchy of Lanc. Inq. p.m. x, 31.

[63] Thomas Valentine was buried at Eccles 21 Apr. 1614, and his son John 30 Mar. 1625. For the latter, see Duchy of Lanc. Inq. p.m. xxv, 18. John his son and heir was born in 1611.

[64] Vawdrey D. *Cal. of Com. for Compounding,* iv, 2725. He recorded a pedigree in 1664, giving his age as fifty-five ; Dugdale, *Visit.* 320. He died early in 1681, and his son Thomas was buried a week after his father. Richard Valentine, the son and heir, was born in 1675, and appointed sheriff of the county in 1713. He died two years later, and by his will (1714) left Bentcliffe to 'Thomas Valentine, clerk, formerly of Dublin College, his kinsman.' This Thomas is believed to have been the son of Francis Valentine of Manchester, younger brother of Richard's father. Thomas Valentine lived at Frankford in Kilglass, co. Sligo, and 'in 1766 (1763) devised the estate to Samuel, eldest son of John Valentine of Boston in New England, by a settlement of 1751,' and the hall and 50 acres of land were sold about the year 1792 to a Mr. Partington'; Piccope, *Wills,* loc. cit. Samuel Valentine of Bentcliffe paid a duchy rent of 32*s.* 7*d.* in 1779 ; Duchy of Lanc. Rentals, 14/25.

This account of the Valentines is taken partly from the late Mr. Earwaker's notes on the family, compiled from the Eccles registers, wills at Chester, and other sources.

[65] 26 May 1892.

[66] 4 Aug. 1894.

[67] The library was established in 1904, and the present building erected in 1908. Information of Mr. C. J. Mellor, librarian.

[68] The tramways are worked by Salford Corporation.

[69] A full description of the boundaries is given in the council's *Year-book,* com-

abbots appears to have been quite uneventful.[72] After the suppression[73] it was in 1540 granted to Sir Alexander Radcliffe of Ordsall.[74] In 1612 it was sold to Roger Downes of Wardley.[75] The Slack is an ancient name in the locality.[76]

WINTON[77] gave a name to the chief residents.[78] This family seems to have been succeeded by the Wydales or Wedalls, who continued here till the 16th century.[79] *NEWHAM*, apparently represented by the more recent Newhall, was in the neighbourhood.[80] *BOYSNOPE*, anciently Boylesnape, is several times mentioned in the charters.[81] The name has practically become obsolete, but there is a Boysnope Wharf on the Ship Canal.

of 10d., with free common on her lands in Swinton, Little Houghton, and Monton ; *Whalley Couch.* iii, 894. William the Clerk sold all his right to Geoffrey de Byron for 13 marks ; ibid. 891. Gilbert de Barton granted land as an appurtenance of Monton to Geoffrey, the bounds beginning at Gildenhaleford, following the hedge of Eccles as far as the monks' gate, across Westslack to the brook by Torthalen, and along the brook to Caldebrook and up this to Denebrook ; ibid. 880. Richard de Monton son of Hugh the Clerk, and Ellen the daughter of Geoffrey de Byron, granted to Geoffrey son of Geoffrey de Byron lands of his mother in Monton, the rents being, to Cockersand 12d. and to Richard de Worsley 16d. ; ibid. 893. Geoffrey de Worsley granted an oxgang of land in Monton, previously held by Adam de Kenyon, to Richard son of Geoffrey de Byron, and this seems to have come to the younger Geoffrey as heir of his brother Richard ; *Whalley Couch.* iii, 897 ; Assize R. 404, m. 7.

The two Geoffreys de Byron had various lawsuits respecting their properties in Barton and Worsley from 1250 onwards ; Cur. Reg. R. 162, m. 3 d. ; 171, m. 8 d. ; 178, m. 13 d. ; Assize R. 1235, m. 11 d. Geoffrey the son finally granted his manor of Monton, with lands in Swinton, to the monks of Stanlaw ; *Whalley Couch.* iii, 877. It was alleged that he was of unsound mind at the time, having been paralysed ; and the monks had to refute this charge, and thought it prudent to procure releases and quitclaims from all those who could in any way allege a title to the lands included in the grant : Edmund Earl of Lancaster, Richard son of Geoffrey de Worsley, Henry de Worsley, Isabel daughter of Geoffrey de Byron and sister of the grantor, and Ellen another daughter of the elder Geoffrey ; ibid. 882–900.

At the grange of Monton in 1291 the monks were found to hold 2 plough-lands worth 30s. a year, assized rents of 33s., and profit of store cattle, 26s. 8d. ; ibid. i, 335.

[72] In 1292 Agnes widow of Richard de Monton made a claim for dower in an oxgang of land in Monton, but on the abbot showing that she had lived in adultery with Elias de Whittleswick and then with William le Norreys, and had never been reconciled to her husband, her claim was refused ; Assize R. 408, m. 1 d. Henry son and heir of Richard de Worsley in 1296 granted to Geoffrey son of Thomas son of Litcock de Salford the rents due to him from the monks of Whalley, viz. 2s. 8d. in Monton, 2s. 3d. in Swinton, and 3s. in Little Houghton ; Ellesmere D. no. 218.

In 1465 Ottiwell Worsley, Rose his wife, and Rowland the son, granted to Robert Lawe, vicar of Eccles, and John Reddish of the Monks' Hall, the elder, the lands called Monton, Monton Hey, the mill, the Westwood, Huntington Clough, &c., held of the Abbot and Convent of Whalley for a term of years, at the rent of £9 10s. 8d. ; 6s. was due to the king Ellesmer

[73] The that time been hel the paris o epair Swinton and the a lord of W a so had shaw. without officers ;

[74] Pat Duchy o

[75] In manor o and land Downes cliffe wit his wife, of F. bd 1612 Sir wife wer m. 31. after the ley, Mon but the held of Duch

IRLAM[82] was early divided among several tenants.[83] From one family, which adopted the local surname,[84] the Hultons of Hulton acquired a holding[85] which descended to the Farnworth stock, and apparently to an Irlam branch.[86] The surname Irlam is found in the district down to the 18th century.[87] About the 16th century the Lathoms of Irlam appear; they were the principal local family for about two centuries, holding, according to one inquisition, a third part of the manor, and they had another estate at Hawthorn, near Wilmslow, on the Cheshire side of the Mersey.[88] At the end of the 18th century Irlam Hall was owned by John Greaves, a wealthy merchant, partner with Sir Robert Peel as a banker, and it descended in his family till 1866.[89] Baines noted in 1836 that the hall was used as a farm-house, and was of Elizabeth's time, containing a principal beam of massive size, the largest, probably, in the county.

CADISHEAD[90] was in the 12th century held of the king by serjeanty of carpentry, one Edwin being

---

[82] Irwulham (1292); 'Irlam *alias* Irwellham' (1680).

[83] In 1322 Irlam, like Newham, Winton, and Monton, was a hamlet of Barton, in the possession of the lord of Manchester; *Mamecestre*, ii, 379.

[84] Dolfin de Irlam about 1190 granted his part of the land between the crooked oak and the stub at the head of Wulpitcroft, and his part of the wood between Elmtree Pool and Elbrook, to the canons of Cockersand; Simon, the brother of Dolfin, and John de Hulme concurred; *Cockersand Chartul.* (Chet. Soc.), ii, 719–21. About 1245 Henry, Abbot of Cockersand, granted this land to Geoffrey de Irlam and his heirs at a rent of 16*d*.; a mark of silver was to be paid at death in lieu of relief, and half a mark at the death of a wife; ibid. 722. In 1461 Richard del Booth held land in Irlam at a rent of 16*d*.; ibid. iv, 1238.

William son of Avice de Irlam granted to Adam son of William de Irlam certain lands upon the 'Ruedis' between the high road and the marsh, at the rent of a pair of white gloves or 1*d*.; De Trafford D. no. 259. In 1292 inquiry was made if William son of Avice de Irlam, uncle of William son of Cecily de Irlam, had been seised of a messuage and land then tenanted by Adam de Didsbury and Margery his wife; Adam stating that he held by grant of Cecily sister and heir of the former William. The charter was alleged to be a forgery, but a verdict was given for Adam; Assize R. 408, m. 5 d.

[85] Adam de Irlam (see last note) was defendant in suits respecting lands in 1278 and 1279, the plaintiffs being Richard and Ralph de Irlam; De Banco R. 23, m. 53; 24, m. 4; 28, m. 33. Agnes widow of Adam in 1301 released to Richard de Hulton the elder all her right in her husband's lands; De Trafford D. no. 262; while Thomas, the son of Adam, had in 1298 leased all his lands in Irlam for six years to William de Hulton, excepting the dower lands of his mother Agnes; Dods. MSS. cxlix, fol. 162*b*.

Richard son of John de Irlam granted to Richard de Hulton part of his land on 'Ruyedishe' in Irlam; ibid. fol. 162. To William son of John de Irlam, Richard son of Richard the Harper released all his claim upon Plumtree Butt, Thomas son of Richard de Irlam being a witness; De Trafford D. no. 263, 266. In 1317 William son of William son of John de Irlam granted all his lands in Irlam to Richard de Hulton; ibid. no. 265.

[86] Richard de Hulton in 1306 gave his son Adam lands in Irlam and Sharples and the mill pool of Flixton, with the service of John son of William de Hulton from all lands in Irlam; Dods. MSS. cxlix, fol. 162.

In 1324 Margaret widow of Adam de Pendlebury claimed as dower the third part of a plough-land in Irlam; Richard de Hulton was defendant, and charged Margaret with adultery, but she alleged that she had been reconciled to her husband; De Banco R. 248, m. 154 d.

Richard de Hulton in 1325 gave to Robert son of Adam de Hulton, for life, all his lands in the hamlet of Irlam in the vill of Barton, excepting those which he had acquired from Adam del Birches of Didsbury; Robert and his tenants were to grind their corn at Richard's mill at Flixton to the twentieth measure; De Trafford D. no. 264. The grandson, Richard de Hulton, made a similar grant in 1331 (ibid. no. 267), and in 1334 gave to John son of Henry de Hulton [of Farnworth] his purparty of the waste of Irlam, then held for life by Robert son of John de Hulton; John de Hulton and his tenants were to grind at the Flixton mill, without giving multure, being 'hopper free' for ever. William son of Ellen de Irlam, one of the tenants, paid an arrow as rent; ibid. no. 270–2. Adam de Hulton granted his lands in Irlam to his son Robert in 1340, with remainder to another son, Adam; ibid. no. 269. The Booths of Barton acquired lands from Cecily daughter of David de Hulton in 1350 from John de Barton in 1362, and from Henry son of John de Hulton of Irlam in 1425; ibid. no. 273–5. In the last grant the 'Ferry houses' are mentioned; in 1360 there lived William del Ferry of Irlam; Assize R. 451, m. 3. Adam son of Adam de Hulton in 1368 sold his lands in Irlam to Thomas del Booth; Dods. MSS. cxlix, fol. 163.

The Hultons of Farnworth continued to hold land in Irlam in socage of the lords of Manchester; *Lancs. Inq. p.m.* (Chet. Soc.), ii, 6. The Booths of Barton and Asshaws of Shaw were also landowners in the 16th century, as appears by the Cal. of Inquisitions p.m. In 1563 John Booth acquired from Richard Dutton messuages and lands in Irlam, and a free fishery in the Irwell; Pal. of Lanc. Feet of F. bdle. 25, m. 269.

[87] Richard de Irlam and Alice his wife and Thomas (son of Richard) and Maud his wife were plaintiffs in 1360; Duchy of Lanc. Assize R. 8, m. 13. William Irlam occurs in 1472; Agecroft D. no. 345. In 1580 John Johnson *alias* Irlam and Edmund Hey were deforciants in a fine respecting property in Irlam, Humphrey Barlow and Ellis Hey being the plaintiffs; Pal. of Lanc. Feet of F. bdle. 42, m. 181. Thomas Irlam and Isabel his wife in 1584 sold land to Humphrey Barlow; ibid. bdle. 46, m. 98. Thomas Irlam of Barton in 1631 paid £10 on declining knighthood; *Misc.* (Rec. Soc. Lancs. and Ches.), i, 215. Frances Irlam of Pendleton in 1717 registered an estate as a 'papist'; *Engl. Cath. Nonjurors*, 153.

[88] Pedigrees are given in Dugdale's *Visit.* 175; Earwaker, *East Ches.* i, 133; and Baines, *Lancs.* (ed. Croston), iii, 272. The origin of this branch of the Lathom family and of its interest in Irlam has not been ascertained, but they

the tenant. Afterwards Sweyn had it, and in 1212 it was held in thegnage by Gilbert de Notton, in right of his wife Edith de Barton, by a rent of 4s.[91] In 1222 there were two under-tenants, Geoffrey de Dutton and Alexander de Cadishead, each apparently paying 2s. yearly.[92] Before this date Edith de Barton had granted to the monks of Stanlaw the land which Alexander held of her, they paying the king the customary rent of 2s.[93] Afterwards 'the land of Cadishead' was granted to the monks by William de Ferrers, with the assent of Agnes his wife, at a rent of 6s. 8d. a year;[94] this rent he released about 1240, after the death of his son's wife Sibyl, and the monks held in frankalmoign.[95] In the sheriff's compotus of 1348 the 4s. thegnage rent was still found charged against the Abbot of Whalley, but on the abbot's producing the second charter of William de Ferrers, showing that he held in alms, the 4s. was deleted. WOOLDEN appears as Vulueden in 1299. In 1331

John son of John de Woolden made an agreement with Adam son of Thomas de Holcroft respecting land by the Glazebrook.[96] On the suppression of the abbey, Cadishead, with Great and Little Woolden, was granted to Sir Thomas Holcroft,[97] but appears to have been transferred by him to the Holcrofts of Holcroft. Like Holcroft Hall it was in 1619 in the possession of Ralph Calveley of Saighton, near Chester, being held of the king in chief by the fortieth part of a knight's fee.[98] In the 18th century it was held by the Poole family,[99] and was afterwards sold to the Bridgewater Trustees.

DAVYHULME[100] was a portion of the original Barton fee. It gave the surname of Hulme to a family, or probably two distinct families, who held lands of the Bartons and their successors in title, the lords of Manchester.[101] But little is known of them, though they continued to hold lands here till the 18th century.[102] Inquisitions were taken in 1600 and

[91] Lancs. Inq. and Extents, i, 66. The jury did not know how the land had been alienated from the king's service. The land is called 'one oxgang.' Edwin the carpenter had held it 'by the service of making carpentry in the king's castle of West Derby'; ibid. 133. If Sweyn was the son of Leysing (see above) the King Henry who granted Cadishead to Edwin was probably Henry I.

[92] Ibid. i, 133. That each paid 2s. is inferred from the rent of 4s. due from the whole of Cadishead (ibid. 137), and from Edith de Barton's charter to Stanlaw, in which it is stated that Alexander held a moiety.

[93] Whalley Couch. ii, 521.

[94] Ibid. 519. The 6s. 8d. would include the 2s. due from the moiety the monks already held; how they acquired the other moiety is not apparent, unless it had in some way escheated to William de Ferrers, who thereupon granted it to them at an increased rent.

[95] Ibid. 520. William de Ferrers died in 1247; his son William had by Margaret, his second wife, a son Robert, born in 1241, so that Sibyl, the first wife, must have died earlier than that year.

At Cadishead in 1291 the monks were said to hold two plough-lands worth 40s. a year; they had 40s. also from the profits of the store cattle; ibid. i, 335. About 1540 the tenants at will, nine in number, paid £7 0s. 7d. a year; ibid. iv, 1240.

[96] Kuerden MSS. iv, G. 5.

[97] Pat. 31 Hen. VIII, pt. 5; Lancs. and Ches. Rec. (Rec. Soc. Lancs. and Ches.), ii, 382. For subsequent disputes see Ducatus Lanc. iii, 95, 129, &c.

[98] Lancs. Inq. p.m. (Rec. Soc. Lancs. and Ches.), ii, 260. He seems to have held it as trustee of Dame Alice Fitton, the daughter and heir of Sir John Holcroft of Holcroft. His son John succeeded him, and was tenant at his death in 1634, when Charles I granted Great and Little Woolden and Cadishead to Sir Kenelm Digby; Pat. 9 Chas. I, pt. 5; Cal. S.P. Dom. 1631-3, p. 41. The jury in 1634 found that John Calveley was a bastard; Lancs. and Ches. Rec. (Rec. Soc. Lancs. and Ches.), ii, 346.

Edward Calveley died in 1636 possessed of the Cadishead lands; his son and heir John was then seventeen years of age; Duchy of Lanc. Inq. p.m. xxviii, 75. John Calveley's lands were sequestered by the Parliamentary authorities, but the Holcrofts appear about 1652 to have tried

to regai Soc. La Ca . Exc las g've The Ho of the'r 1652 an Pal. of 77 , bdl was own Great W ton ; Ba [99] Th suages, head and upon Ed

1641.[143] They acquired the adjacent manor of Urmston.[144] The hall was purchased by William Allen, banker, of Manchester, who became bankrupt in 1788, when Davyhulme was sold to Henry Norris, a Manchester merchant, who died in 1819. His daughter Mary conveyed it in marriage in 1809 to Robert Josias Jackson Harris, of Uley, Gloucestershire, who adopted the surname of Norreys, and died in 1844; their son Robert Henry Norreys resided in the hall till his death in 1887. The hall was

afterwards demolished and the grounds are used as golf links.[145] The house was entirely of brick, the only signs of antiquity being some old beams, perhaps belonging to a former house. In front of the house was a sundial made at Manchester in 1809. Other families formerly connected with Davyhulme were the Byroms of Salford[146] and the Bents.[147]

BROMYHURST became the seat of a branch of the Barton family,[148] and of another surnamed Mey, who also were known as 'de Bromyhurst.'[149] In

In 1317–18 Robert son of Thomas de Hulme had released to Sir John La Warre his claim on the soil and common of pasture of all the waste in Barton; Dods. MSS. cxlix, fol. 156b. As late as July and Michaelmas 1354 Margery widow of Robert son of Thomas de Hulme, then wife of Henry de Bolton, was defendant in a plea concerning land which Gilbert de Barton had granted to Robert de Hulme and his heirs, and which John de Barton sought to recover; Duchy of Lanc. Assize R. 3, m. 2, 3.

The Thomas son of Thomas de Hulme already mentioned made an exchange of land in Davyhulme, and on the Holt, and on the Hill, in 1313; De Trafford D. no. 254. 'Magote' widow of Thomas son of Thomas de Hulme occurs in 1324; C. of Wards, Deeds, and Evidences, box 153, no. 5.

Margaret widow of Thomas de Hulme the younger in 1347 received from the trustee lands in Flixton, the remainders being to John son of Thomas, and then to Thomas's brother; De Trafford D. no. 113. Margaret widow of Thomas de Hulme, and John and Adam his sons, were defendants in a Barton case in 1354; Duchy of Lanc. Assize R. 3, m. 1.

John son of Thomas de Hulme was a defendant in 1356 and later; Duchy of Lanc. Assize R. 5, m. 10 d.; 7, m. 3 d.; 8 m. 5, 12. In 1361 he claimed land in Barton as kinsman of Robert de Hulme; Assize R. 441, m. 3. Two years later he made a feoffment of all his lands in Barton, with common of turbary in Urmston, and the reversion of the dower of his mother Margaret; De Trafford D. no. 226.

In 1356, while still a minor, William son of another John de Hulme complained that Thomas del Booth, to whom his custody had been granted by Sir Roger La Warre, had made waste in his estate, consisting of fifteen messuages, 100 acres of land, &c., in Barton; messuages and granges had been pulled down, and twelve apple trees, worth 6s. 8d. each, had been cut down and sold; Duchy of Lanc. Assize R. 5, m. 28. William de Hulme in 1383 granted an annuity of 40s. to John de Cholmondeley and Agnes his wife, charged upon his lands in Hulme within the vill of Barton; De Trafford D. no. 255. William de Hulme—probably there were two persons—attested deeds in 1389 and 1430; ibid. no. 285, 257. In Jan. 1477–8, John, son and heir of Alice widow of William Hulme, made a feoffment of his lands in Hulme, Manchester, and elsewhere in the county, Alice releasing her right in the same. Hugh Hulme, chaplain, son of John Hulme, was one of the trustees; C. of Wards, Deeds, and Evidences, box 153, no. 9.

A writ for an inquisition after the death of James Hulme of Davyhulme was issued on 5 Apr. 1434; Dep. Keeper's Rep. xxxiii, App. 34. A deed of 1435

mentions James Hu his son William, w Alice, M scy of T rington Museum. dentures of James H and Clemence daugh cliffe of Ordsal ar Earwaker's notes.

In 149 m s charterers of Sir Joh at Warrington; Do 165 James Hulm made a feoffment of twelve burgages, 50 in Davyhulme, M 1528; Pal of Lanc m 145 In 1559 a recently died, and Jam heir, and of full a Rec. i, 47. In or befo n Manchester to 97. James Hulme waste called Lostoc Ducatus Lanc iii 14

[148] Robert son of at Newhall in West leaving a daughter

1322 the lord of Manchester had 120 acres of wood or moor there.[110]

DUMPLINGTON, which formerly included the modern hamlet of Crofts Bank, was with Cockney· in Bromyhurst in 1225 demised by Sir Robert Grelley to Cecily daughter of Iorwerth de Hulton[111] for six years. Four years afterwards Siegrith de Dumplington released to Robert Grelley her right in 40 acres in Dumplington.[112] John son of Thomas de Booth held the place in 1401.[113] The lords of Manchester had a wood in Lostock.[114]

WHITTLESWICK[115] was from an early date regarded as a manor,[116] being held by the Pendlebury

family.[117]   From Roger de Pendlebury it passed to his son Ellis,[118] and then to a younger son William, who enfeoffed Adam de Prestwich.[119]   Henry, the son of Adam, had a daughter Katherine, who married John son of Robert de Bold.   Their son Geoffrey forfeited his lands for treason, having taken part in the Hotspur rebellion of 1403 ; [120] but Whittleswick was afterwards restored, and Agnes daughter of Nicholas son of Geoffrey de Bold had livery in 1442–3.   She married Hugh, a son of Sir Geoffrey Massey,[121] and the manor continued in their family for nearly two centuries,[122] descending to Dorothy daughter of Thomas Massey and wife of Thomas Liversage of

m. 4 d.   Avina, widow of John the son of Wasce, claimed 6 acres in Barton against Alexander son of Alexander the Mey in 1292, but it was shown that Agnes, widow of Alexander the father, was in possession of a portion ; Assize R. 408, m. 3 d.; see also m. 32, 54. Nine years later, Alexander the Mey proceeded against Gilbert de Bromyhurst and others concerning a tenement in Barton ; ibid. 1321, m. 9 ; 418, m. 12 d.

Some of the Mey charters have been preserved.   Alexander the son gave a quitclaim respecting Westwood in 1281 ; Whalley Couch. iii, 914. Alexander the Mey of Bromyhurst granted to Robert son of Matthew de Birches lands in Saltey meadows and White-ridding ; the seal had a fleur-de-lis with the legend s' ALEXANDR : D' : BROMIRVRST ; De Trafford D. no. 212. Alexander the Mey (Meych) gave his son Hugh a moiety of the whole sixth part of the vills of Bromyhurst and Dumplington, a rent of 6d. being due to the chief lords ; De Trafford D. no. 224.

[110] Mamecestre, ii, 370.

[111] De Trafford D. no. 109; the grant was made 'in the year in which Richard the king's brother was made Earl of Cornwall.' Cecily paid 6 marks and was to pay an annual rent of 4s. 6d. Twenty-four acres in Dumplington and 4 acres in Kokenay were among the lands held in 1253 by Jordan de Hulton, in which Amery widow of Robert de Hulton claimed dower ; Final Conc. i, 151. Gilbert de Barton son of William de Notton granted the land of Cockney, between Waspool and Cockney Pool, to Peter de Dumplington his servant ; Dods. MSS. cxlix, fol. 154.

[112] Final Conc. i, 56.

[113] De Trafford D. no. 247 ; by this Ralph de Walkden released his right in Dumplington and in Heaton Norris to John de Booth, having already enfeoffed John of his lands there.

An account of Dumplington, with plan and many details, is given in Lancs. and Ches. Antiq. Soc. xxiv, 21.

[114] Gilbert de Barton granted Sir Thomas Grelley all his wood in Lostock ; Dods. MSS. cxlix, fol. 163b. In 1322 the wood of Lostock was valued with that in Cuerdley ; the lord of Manchester had also 20 acres of pasture in Lostock, in which all the tenants of the lord of Barton had common of pasture except during six weeks in the time of pannage, and the lord and tenants of Urmston had a similar right, 2s. a year rent being paid ; Lancs. Inq. and Extents, ii, 57.

[115] Quicleswic, Quyclisweke, xiii cent.; Whikleswyk, 1287 ; Quyclesweke, 1389 ; Whicleweeke, 1632.

[116] There is an article on the descent of

the man 24. It w tenants other c cestre, i' transfer Grelleys There is connexio

[117] A John de oxgang pair of Pendleb and Rob De Tra A el the Cle bury of the only Pendleb no. 27 Whittle

Wheelock, who in 1632 sold it to Sir Cecil Trafford.[132] It has since descended like Stretford, and was till recently the chief residence of the Trafford family, taking the name of Trafford Park from them. They appear to have resided here from the beginning of the 18th century.[133]

Trafford Hall was originally erected in the middle of the 16th century, but the modern classic building was built in 1762 by John Trafford, who is said to have removed the front of the older building for this purpose. The brick gabled wing on the north-west is supposed to belong to the original house, but is probably a later refacing and rebuilding. In James's view (1825) the four lower gables next to the house only are shown, the building farther north apparently having been erected since that date. The 18th-century mansion is a plain stuccoed two-story classic building with four engaged columns and pediment in the front or south elevation. A modern stuccoed wing runs northward on the east side of the house, parallel with the brick wing already mentioned. The house is now used as the head quarters of the Manchester Golf Club.

The Barton landowners contributing to the subsidy of 1622 were—Thomas Charnock, George Legh, Katherine Brereton, Dorothy Liversage, Ralph Ainsworth, — Hope, Richard Worsley, John Valentine, Edmund Lathom, James Crompton, and John Bent.[135]

The Sorocolds of Barton recorded a pedigree in 1665.[136]

The land tax returns of 1797 preserved at Preston provide a long list of landowners, arranged under these divisions :—Barton with Winton, Eccles, Monton, and Swinton ; farther side of water, including Urmston and Davyhulme ; Irlam and Cadishead. The principal estates were those of the Duke of Bridgewater, John Trafford, — Willis, — Lee, William Turner, John Page, Henry Norris, and Robert Barker.[137]

The parish church has been described above. In recent times a number of new churches have been consecrated to the service of the established religion. At Eccles, St. Andrew's was built in 1879,[138] and at Barton, St. Catherine's, built in 1843,[139] was enlarged in 1893 ; the patronage of these churches is vested in

---

Thomas Massey, father of the Thomas who died in 1590, had granted a third of the manor as dower to Dorothy, widow of his elder brother John, and she was still living at Elton in Cheshire ; Thomas the son assigned to Katherine widow of Thomas a third part of his two-thirds of the manor, and she was living at Whittleswick ; Thomas himself married Jane daughter of Thomas Lancaster, and she too was living at Whittleswick when the inquisition was taken, 28 Sept. 1591. Dorothy, the daughter and heir, was nine months old ; Duchy of Lanc. Inq. p.m. xv, 31. A later inquisition is extant (xvii, 85), the jurors altering the finding by stating that Adam de Prestwich died at Barton, Henry being his son and heir, and that Whittleswick was held of the queen by the tenth part of a knight's fee.

In 1500 William Massey of Whittleswick, being seventy years of age, was excused from serving on assizes ; Towneley MS. CC (Chet. Lib.), no. 689.

Thomas, father of the last Thomas Massey, died at the end of 1576, his son

being then a minor ; *Manch. Ct. Leet Rec.* i, 184. For his will see *Wills* (Chet. Soc., new ser.), i, 222.

Jane, the widow of the son, afterwards married William Moreton of Moreton in Cheshire.

[133] The deeds are printed (from Raines MS. xxv.) in H. T. Crofton's *Stretford* (Chet. Soc.), iii, 272, &c. See also *Pal. of Lanc.* Feet of F. bdle. 121, no. 15. The manor is mentioned in later Trafford settlements ; e.g. 1654 and 1718 ; ibid. bdles. 156, m. 194 ; 282, m. 99.

For the Liversages see Ormerod, *Chet.* (ed. Helsby), iii, 121. Dorothy afterwards married Thomas Balgay of Hope in Derbyshire ; *Journ. of Derbys. Arch. Soc.* vi, 23.

[134] *Lancs. and Ches. Antiq. Soc.* vi, 228.

[135] *Misc.* (Rec. Soc. Lancs. and Ches.), i, 153.

[136] Dugdale, *Visit.* 276.

[137] Land tax returns.

[138] For district assigned see *Lond. Gaz.* 25 May 1880.

[139] Ibid. 1 Mar. 1867 ; see also *End. Char. Rep.* for Eccles, 1904, p. 23.

18th century, and before 1800 Unitarianism was 'boldly preached.'[139]

Roman Catholics[140] have All Saints' Church, Barton; the mission was founded in 1798, having before been served from Trafford Park, and the present church was erected in 1868;[141] also St. Mary's school chapel at Eccles, opened in 1879, and St. Theresa's, Irlam, which became a separate mission in 1900. An iron church, St. Anthony's, was opened at Trafford Park in 1904. In 1827 the old chapel at the Park was pulled down and rebuilt in Dumplington; but it does not appear to have remained long in use.

WORSLEY

Werkesleia, 1195; Wyrkedele, 1212; Whurkedeleye, c. 1220; Worketley, 1254; Worcotesley, Workedesle, 1276; Wrkesley, Wrkedeley, Workedeley, 1292; Wyrkeslegh, Workesley, 1301; Worsley, 1444; 'Workdisley alias Workesley alias Worseley,' 1581.

The ancient township of Worsley measures 4½ miles from east to west, the breadth varying from 1 mile to 4 miles; the area is 6,928 acres.[1] Land 300 ft. and more in height divides it from Clifton and Kearsley; the slope in general is towards the south. Ellenbrook in the west divides it from Tyldesley and Astley, while another brook, rising near the boundary of Clifton and flowing south to the Irwell, divides Worsley proper from Swinton on the east. Swinton has now grown into a small town, lying on the road from Manchester to Wigan; to the north and northeast are Newton and Hope Mill; to the south-east Deans and Lightbown Green; to the south Moorside, Sindsley, Broad Oak, and Dales Brow; Little Hou hton, in the same quarter, has now disappeared from the maps; Drywood and Westwood occupy the south-west corner. The Worsley or western section of the township has Worsley Hall almost in the centre; to the west lie Booths Hall, part of Boothstown, Ellenbrook Chapel and Parr Fold; Walkden, now a town, and Linnyshaw occupy the north-west corner. Kempnough Hall, Daubhole, and Whittle Brook lie to the north of Worsley Hall; Hazelhurst, Roe Green, and Wardley are in the eastern portion. The southern half of this part of the township—the 100-ft. level being roughly the boundary—was formerly within Chat Moss, so that it has no ancient houses. To the south of the Bridgewater Canal and to the south-east of Hazelhurst, the Geological Formation consists mainly of the Pebble Beds of the New Red Sandstone. North of Boothstown and Winton the Coal Measures are everywhere in evidence. An intervening band of the Permian Rocks extends from Monton to Astley. In 1901 the population of Worsley was 12,462, and of Swinton 18,512.

The chief road is that from Manchester to Wigan, through Swinton, Wardley, and Walkden, along or near the track of a Roman road. From this a road branches off to go west through Worsley to Boothstown and Astley, and this has southerly branches from Swinton and Worsley to Eccles. There are numerous cross roads, including one from Worsley to Walkden. The Lancashire and Yorkshire Company's railway from Manchester to Hindley runs west through the northern part of the township, with three stations — Swinton, Moorside and Wardley, and Walkden. The London and North Western Company's line from Manchester and Eccles to Wigan, begun in 1861, has stations at Worsley and Ellenbrook; from it the Bolton line branches off at Rose Green, with a station at Walkden. There is also a single-line branch from Eccles to Clifton through Swinton. Down to 1860 passengers were taken from Worsley to Manchester by the canal.

In 1666 the hearth-tax returns show that Wardley Hall was the largest residence, having nineteen hearths; Worsley Hall and Booths had seventeen each. The total number of hearths in the township was 276, of which Worsley proper had 191.[2]

A century ago the collieries and the Duke of Bridgewater's canal were the notable features of the township, but the spinning and manufacture of cotton were also actively pursued. The same industries continue, the latter advancing. The south-west portion is agricultural.

In 1826 an archery society was established at Worsley.

Queen Victoria visited Worsley Hall in 1851 and 1857, and King Edward VII in 1869 when Prince of Wales.

At Worsley is a monument to the first Earl of Ellesmere, an octagonal shaft 132 ft. high. At Walkden an 'Eleanor cross' stands as a memorial to his countess. The Bridgewater Estate Offices are at Walkden. At Swinton is the Manchester Industrial School.

At Daubhole is a great boulder known as the Giant's Stone, the legend being that it was thrown from Rivington Pike by a giant.

A local board for Swinton and Pendlebury was formed in 1867.[3] The district was afterwards extended to include part of Barton township.[4] Since 1894 it has been governed by an urban district council of fifteen members. The remainder of Worsley, except a small part in the borough of Eccles, has also an urban council of fifteen members.

The lords of the manors have in many cases been men of distinction, as will be seen by the following record of them. Another 'worthy' of the place was Christopher Walton, 1809–77, of Wesleyan training, but ultimately a mystic or theosopher; his collections are in Dr. Williams's Library, London.[4a]

The earliest record of WORSLEY MANORS is in the Pipe Roll of 1195–6 in the claim of one Hugh Putrell to a fourth part of the fee of two knights in Barton and Worsley.[5] Worsley, as half a plough-land, was held of the king

---

[139] Nightingale, op. cit. v, 1–10; reference is made to a history of the chapel by the Rev. Thomas Elford Poynting, minister for thirty-one years until his death in 1878. For endowment, &c., see End. Char. Rep. Eccles, 1904, pp. 18–21.

[140] A list of recusants in the parish of Eccles in 1588 is given in Hist. MSS. Com. Rep. xiv, App. iv, 582.

[141] It was built by Sir Humphrey de Trafford.

[1] Made up thus: Higher Worsley, 1,362½ acres; Lower Worsley, 3,319½; Boothstown, 1,120—5,802; Swinton, 634½; Little Houghton, 491½—1,126.

The Census Rep. of 1901 gives the area of Worsley as 5,412 acres, including 70 of inland water; and Swinton, 1,346, including 10 of inland water. Part of Pendlebury has been included with Swinton.

[2] Subs. R. Lancs. bdle. 250, no. 9.
[3] Lond. Gaz. 26 Mar. 1867.
[4] 42 & 43 Vict. cap. 43.
[4a] Dict. Nat. Biog.
[5] Farrer, Lancs. Pipe R. 94.

by the Barton family in thegnage,[6] and of them by a family which took the local name. The earliest known member of it is Richard de Worsley, who in 1203 was defending his right to twenty acres of wood in Worsley,[7] and as Richard son of Elias in 1206 gave a mark for a writ.[8] Six years later he held a plough-land of Gilbert de Notton and his wife Edith de Barton, half of the land being in Worsley.[9] It appears that Hugh Putrell had granted 'to Richard son of Elias de Worsley the manors of Worsley and Hulton, i.e. half a plough-land in Worsley, which was the whole of Worsley, and half a plough-land in Hulton, rendering for all services 10s. for Worsley

and 6s. 8d. for Hulton,' these being the rents paid by Hugh to the king or chief lord.[9a] The mesne lordships were very quickly ignored, and the Worsleys were said to hold directly of the Earls or Dukes of Lancaster. Richard was a benefactor to the canons of Cockersand,[10] and two other of his charters have been preserved.[11]

His son Geoffrey succeeded and was in possession in 1254;[12] he died before 1268, leaving a widow Agnes.[13] His son and heir Richard de Worsley made several grants and acquisitions of land,[14] and was still living in 1292.[15] He had many children, including Richard, who seems to have died about the same time

---

[6] *Lancs. Inq. and Extents* (Rec. Soc. Lancs. and Ches.), i, 65. The whole 14 oxgangs so held may have been —Worsley 4, Swinton, 4 (or 3), Monton 2 (or 3), and Hulton 4. This, however, makes Monton a thegnage estate, though situated in Barton, which was held by knight's service.

[7] Curia Reg. R. 26; the plaintiff was Eda (or Edith) daughter of Matthew. The writ was found to require amendment, because her husband, Gilbert de Notton, was not named in it; and then because she had sisters, likewise not mentioned in it.

[8] *Lancs. Pipe R.* 216. Nothing is known of Elias the father of Richard. The legendary founder of the Worsley family was an Elias the Giant, who lived in the time of the Conqueror, became a Crusader, 'fought many duels, combats, &c., for the love of our Saviour Jesus Christ and obtained many victories,' and died and was buried at Rhodes; Harland and Wilkinson, *Lancs. Legends*, 78.

[9] *Lancs. Inq. and Extents*, loc. cit.

[9a] Abstract among the Ellesmere deeds. Another deed shows that Lescelina, a sister of Edith de Barton and co-heir, gave to the same Richard a moiety of Swinton and Little Houghton; ibid.

Hugh de Nowell (*sic*) in 1324 is said to have held in Worsley and Hulton six oxgangs by the service of 20s. a year; this should perhaps have been amended to 'the assign of Hugh Putrell' and 'six oxgangs and half a plough-land'; Dods. MSS. cxxxi, fol. 37b. About the same time the receiver of the forfeited estates and offices of Sir Robert de Holland rendered account of '20s. of farm of land of Hugh de *Menill*, which William de Nevill and Gerard de Camvile formerly held in Worsley and Hulton'; L.T.R. Enr. Accts. Misc. No. 14, m. 76d. For William and Gerard see *Lancs. Inq. and Extents*, i, 62, 65; they represented the heirs of Adam son of Sweyn in 1212.

In the sheriff's compotus of 1348 the rent of Henry de Worsley for 'the manor of Worsley' was returned as 13s. 4d.— that for Hulton being 6s. 8d., as above— so that the moiety of Swinton paid 3s. 4d.; the whole thegnage rent was 20s. The remainder of the 26s. payable by the Bartons in 1212 was contributed at the later date by the Abbot of Whalley for his tenement in Monton. In an extent made about 1445 it is recorded that Sir Geoffrey Massey held the manor of Worsley for half a plough-land in socage, rendering 13s. 4d.; the additional oxgang in Swinton was not reckoned, though the rent was paid; Duchy of Lanc. Knights' Fees, 2/20.

[10] *Cockersand Chart.* (Chet. Soc.), ii, 717. The bounds were Scaithlache, Millbrook,

Cartlache, Modibrook, Stanwall Syke, by Stanwall to Wolfpit Greaves, and by Peveril's Gate to the starting-point.

[11] To Thomas de Fleckenhow, chaplain, one of the rectors of Eccles, he leased 14½ acres in Wardley for twenty years, beginning in Nov. 1218, at a rent of 4s., with one pig, 'if the said Thomas or his men dwelling on the said land shall have pigs fattened on the mastfall of the said villa' of Wardley and Worsley; Lord Ellesmere's D. no. 133. R. de Maidstone, Archdeacon of Chester, was a witness. In 1219 he came to an agreement with Richard de Hulton as to the six oxgangs in Hulton pertaining to Worsley; *Final Conc.* (Rec. Soc. Lancs. and Ches.), i. 41.

As Richard son of Elias de Worsley he granted to Hugh the clerk, otherwise Hugh de Monton, his brother, the whole land of Hazelhurst and other land beside the brook flowing from Wardley Spring; Ellesmere D. no. 232. Half of Hazelhurst was afterwards given by Hugh's daughter Ellen, in her widowhood, to John son of Robert de Shoresworth, who had married her daughter Margery; ibid. no. 233. The whole appears to have been afterwards acquired by the Worsley family from Richard son of Hugh de Monton, Ellen de Hazelhurst herself (in 1276), Margery de Hazelhurst, and William son of Alice daughter of Ellen de Hazelhurst; ibid. no. 234–7. Hugh the clerk had been a benefactor of Cockersand; *Chart.* ii, 718.

Richard de Worsley took part in the inquiry as to the advowson of Flixton; *Lancs. Pipe R.* 355.

[12] In that year he was one of the jury to inquire into certain trespasses on Thomas Grelley's parks; *Lancs. Inq. and Extents*, i, 193. He occurs also in the Assize Roll of 1246 (R. 404, m. 7). He made grants in Hulton; Ellesmere D. no. 40, 45.

To his daughter Isabel, wife of Richard de Bolton, Geoffrey gave in free marriage certain land in Holeclough, with easements in Worsley, Mokenis excepted, the rent being a pair of white gloves; Ellesmere D. no. 115. This land Richard de Hulton in 1289 granted to his son Henry; ibid. no. 141.

[13] The lands which Richard de Worsley and Hugh the clerk had granted to Cockersand were by Abbot Roger given to Geoffrey son of Richard de Worsley at a rent of 2s., half a mark being payable at the death of himself, his wife, or heirs; ibid. uo. 139. In 1268 Richard de Worsley was in possession, so that Geoffrey had died before this year; *Cockersand Chart.* ii, 718.

Agnes widow of Geoffrey de Worsley released to the Abbot of Stanlaw all claim

as his father;[16] Henry, who succeeded, and held Worsley for about ten years, dying in or before 1304;[17] and Jordan, who had Wardley. Henry de Worsley was twice married, and left two sons, Richard and Robert; the latter, by the second wife,[18] had a share of the manor, known as Booths, assigned to him in 1323, so that in future, out of the free rent, he and his heirs were to pay 2s. to the chief lord, leaving 18s. to be paid by the lord of Worsley.[19] Richard, who was living in 1332,[20] was succeeded by his son Henry, dead in 1350;[21] and Henry in turn was followed by his grandson Sir Geoffrey de Worsley, son of Geoffrey.[22]

Sir Geoffrey de Worsley, who fought in the French wars, married Mary daughter of Sir Thomas de Felton, about 1376; but a divorce was procured in 1381, and Mary retired to a nunnery.[23] Thereon Sir Geoffrey married Isabel daughter and eventual heir of Sir Thomas de Lathom, but died shortly afterwards leaving a daughter by her named Elizabeth, only one year old. His former wife then left her convent, asserting that she had only entered it by compulsion, and as she also established the validity of her marriage, the infant daughter of Sir Geoffrey lost the inheritance as illegitimate, the manors of Worsley and Hulton passing into the hands of Alice sister of Sir Geoffrey and wife of Sir John Massey.[24]

[16] Richard son of Richard de Worsley attested a grant made to his father in 1293; Ellesmere D. no. 143. He had been defendant to a claim made in 1292, but it was shown that his brother Henry was in possession of the lands in dispute; Assize R. 408, m. 72 d.

[17] Henry may have been the eldest son; he describes himself as 'son and heir of Richard formerly lord of Worsley,' in a charter of 1296; Ellesmere D. no. 218. His first wife Joan was dead in 1293, when he granted a pound of wax for the service of the high altar of Eccles Church for her soul and the souls of his father, ancestors, &c.; Whalley Coucher, iii, 923. He then married Margaret, who survived him (1304) and became the wife of Robert son of Richard de Radcliffe in or before 1305; De Banco R. 149, m. 41; 153, m. 315 d.

In 1292 Henry de Worsley made a grant to Adam de Lever and his tenants in Farnworth of certain easements in Worsley by Walkden Brook; Ellesmere D. no. 142. He granted lands in Worsley to his brother Jordan, with remainder, in default of issue to the latter, to his own children by Margaret his wife; no. 130.

In another grant to Jordan he mentions his uncles John and Geoffrey; no. 131. He made yet another in 1299; and a little later Olive de Bolton released all her claim in these lands; no. 146, 148.

For a Roger de Worsley, indicted in 1299, see Lancs. Inq. and Extents, i, 305.

[18] In 1299 Henry son of Richard de Worsley granted to Robert his son land in Worsley called Mokenis, the bounds beginning at Acornsyke, where it was met by the fall of Kronkysker, between Worsley and Astley; along the fall to Blackbrook, thence by the bounds of Astley and Irlam, across the moss to Ringand Pits, and thence going down to the Meadowyard; Ellesmere D. no. 147. This was perhaps the grant confirmed in 1301; Final Conc. i, 193. In 1322 Margaret, formerly wife of Henry, sold and released to Robert her son all her goods in Worsley, movable and immovable, for £40 sterling which he had paid her; Ellesmere D. no. 140.

[19] Ibid. no. 162.

[20] In 1295 Maud, Margaret, and Ellen, daughters and heirs of Robert son of John son of Meuric de Hulton, released to Richard son of Henry lord of Worsley and Margaret his wife all claim on the lands which their father had held of Richard de Worsley according to the charter in possession of the above-mentioned Richard and Margaret; Ellesmere D. no. 145. In 1299 Richard had a grant of land in Worsley from his father (Final Conc. i, 187); though Henry the father was still living at the time the sons Richard and Robert (see preceding note) were in

the guardian Margaret, th mentioned in 52, 218. I Salford, as tr and the othe Worsley to remainder t Final Conc. i Jordan de 1305 granted house in Wo In 1307 Ric garet his fath &c. outside side by the demesne land under-tenan Worsley and Three days la Robert de R l d t R'h in Manches

WORSLEY of Worsley.
Argent a chief gules.

MASSEY of Tatton.
Quarterly gules and argent.

ton with their appurtenances, as also his lands in Salford and Manchester; the feoffees were to settle the same upon him and his issue, with remainder to his sister Alice, wife of Sir John Massey of Tatton; ibid. no. 121. Two years later the feoffees regranted the manors to Sir Geoffrey and Mary his wife, daughter of Sir Thomas de Felton; no. 167, also no. 122, and *Final Conc.* iii, 4. A further feoffment and fine were made in July and Aug. 1381; Ellesmere D. no. 169, and *Final Conc.* iii, 12. The proceedings for divorce had already begun at Chester. It was stated that in 1374, in the chapel of Sir Thomas de Felton's mansion-house in Candlewick Street in London, his daughter had married Sir Thomas Breton, and that in 1376 in the parish church at Leamington she had married Sir Geoffrey de Worsley, her former husband not dying till Nov. or Dec. 1380, in Aquitaine. On this account the second marriage was declared null; Ellesmere D. no. 268.

For the subsequent proceedings see Sir Peter Leycester's account in Ormerod's *Ches.* (ed. Helsby), i, 441. The above-cited record of 1401 merely states that Geoffrey had married Mary de Felton, by whom he had no issue, and then, during her life, had taken to wife Isabel daughter of Sir Thomas de Lathom, by whom he had a daughter Elizabeth; Ellesmere D. no. 203. In 1401 John de Stanley and (the same) Isabel his wife released to John Massey and Alice his wife all their interest in the manors of Worsley and Hulton; no. 175.

In 1376 the sheriff was ordered to arrest Sir Geoffrey to answer for 6,000 marks he had acknowledged due to Sir John Massey and others. Not finding him, the sheriff took a full account of his possessions. The manor of Worsley had a house with hall, chamber, chapel, kitchen, &c.; there were a *forcellettum* called the Peel, a water-mill, and various lands, messuages, and wood, &c. The free rents amounted to 60s. 8d.; a profit in Worsley, for digging and selling sea-coals, was worth 15s. a year. Among the out-goings were 18s. a year paid to the Duke of Lancaster for the tenements in Worsley, and 5 marks a year from Hulton to 'one Anabel, who was the wife of John Comyn'—no doubt Anabel mother of Sir Geoffrey. The sheriff handed all manors, &c., to the petitioning creditors; De Banco R. 462, m. 98 d.

The story of the refeoffment of Sir Geoffrey in his manor of Worsley is told in *Dep. Keeper's Rep.* xxxvi, App. 540. After that he went abroad, it is stated, and died there fully seised.

He died on the Thursday before Easter (30 Mar.) 1385, his daughter and heir

Elizabeth being about a year old. The manor of Worsley was held in socage by a rent of 13s. 4d., worth 40 marks clear; the manor of Hulton, three parts of the vill, also in socage, by a rent of 6s. 7d., and worth 12 marks; tenements in Salford in free burgage by a rent of 12d. for each burgage, and worth 40s.; Ellesmere D. no. 172 (a copy), and *Lancs. Inq. p.m.* (Chet. Soc.), i, 23, 46. Elizabeth was regarded as heiress of the Lathoms in 1389, and was then five years of age; ibid. i, 35. It appears that a life interest in the manor of Worsley had been secured to her; ibid. i, 118. She proved her age and had livery of her lands in 1401; *Dep. Keeper's Rep.* xxxiii, App. 2. She was born at Worsley on the Friday after St. Matthew, 1383, and baptized at Eccles by John de Craunton, vicar, her godparents being Thomas de Worsley and Emma de Hindley; Towneley MS. DD, no. 1499. The widow, Isabel de Lathom, had married Sir John de Stanley before the end of 1385; *Parl. R.* iii, 204, 205.

[23] Ormerod, *Ches.* i, 441.

[24] Alice daughter of Geoffrey de Worsley was wife of Sir John Massey in 1372; Raines MSS. xxxviii, 238.

Immediately after the death of Sir Geoffrey de Worsley his trustee, Richard de Worsley, chaplain, granted to Alice the manors of Worsley and Hulton; Ellesmere D. no. 171. Yet about three years later, when in the chapel at Deane, he was induced or compelled, as he afterwards confessed, to enfeoff Robert de Worsley or his representatives of the manors; *Dep. Keeper's Rep.* xxxvi, App. 540.

[27] Ibid. App. 329.

[26] Ibid. 332. In 1373 Sir John Massey had had an annuity of 50 marks from Edward the Black Prince, he to serve the prince at all times, and during war with an esquire; this was confirmed in 1377 by Richard as Prince of Wales; ibid. 329.

[29] Ibid. 333; Ormerod, *Ches.* i, 442, where his and other Massey inquisitions are printed.

[30] *Dep. Keeper's Rep.* xxxvi, App. 334; a grant to Alice, the widow, of a third of Sir John's possessions forfeited by the rebellion of himself and his son. In 1401 Sir John Massey of Tatton, Alice his wife, and Thomas, Geoffrey, and Richard their sons, had joined in a grant to Elizabeth wife of Arthur de Worsley, dispossessed daughter of Sir Geoffrey; Ellesmere D. no. 177, 178.

[31] *Dep. Keeper's Rep.* xxxvii, App. 516; Thomas Massey had died on 24 Aug. 1420, and Geoffrey his brother and heir was thirty years of age. A statement of the descent, drawn up at this time, will be found in *Dep. Keeper's Rep.* xxxiii, App. 29. [32] Ibid. xxxvii, 517

his nephew William son of Richard Massey.[34] William died eleven years later ;[35] his son and heir Sir Geoffrey[36] left an only child Joan, who by her first husband, William Stanley,[37] also left an only daughter Joan, heiress of Worsley, aged eighteen at her mother's death in 1511.[38]

By John Ashton, her first husband, who died in 1513, Joan Stanley, the daughter, had no issue ; but by her second, Sir Richard Brereton, a younger son of Sir Randle Brereton of Malpas, she had two sons and a daughter.[39] The eldest, Richard, died without issue, before his parents ;[40] the second, Geoffrey, died in 1565, leaving an only son Richard, who at his grandfather's death in 1570 succeeded to Worsley.[41] He married Dorothy daughter of Sir Richard Egerton, of Ridley in Cheshire, but their only child Richard died in infancy. It was no doubt by Dorothy's influence that the Worsley manors were

then granted by will to her father's illegitimate son, Sir Thomas Egerton, a distinguished lawyer, who rose to be Lord Chancellor, and was created Viscount Brackley in 1616.[42] Richard Brereton died in 1598; his widow Dorothy afterwards married Sir Peter Legh of Lyme, and dying in 1639 was buried at Eccles with her former husband.[43]

Shortly after Lord Brackley's death in 1617 his son John was created Earl of Bridgewater ;[44] he succeeded to Worsley in 1639, as above, and died ten years afterwards,[45] being succeeded in turn by two namesakes, the second and third earls, who died in 1686 and 1701 respectively. Scrope, the son of the third earl, was created Duke of Bridgewater in 1720. He died in 1745, leaving three children—John, second duke, who survived his father but three years ; Francis third duke, the great canal-maker, who died in 1803' and Louisa, who married the first Marquis of Stafford

[34] In 1452 William Massey son and heir of Richard, brother of Sir Geoffrey Massey, released his claim to manors, lands, services, &c. in Worsley, Hulton, Salford, Manchester, Tatton, Ollerton, Leigh, Northwich, Knutsford, and Rostherne, then in the hands of his uncle's feoffees ; Ellesmere D. no. 187, 262.

[35] Ormerod, loc. cit.

[36] Sir John Boteler in July 1457 received 6 marks from Sir Geoffrey Massey towards the maintenance of Geoffrey son and heir of William Massey, who had married Isabel daughter of Sir John ; Ellesmere D. no. 275. In 1466 William Massey of Worsley and Geoffrey his son and heir, leased to Henry Buckley land in Nether Acres at the south end of Manchester at a rent of 2s. ; ibid. no. 125. As Sir Geoffrey Massey of Worsley, he made a lease of Hulton Hey in 1484 ; no. 71. Sir Geoffrey is frequently named in the Chester Recognizance Rolls from 1475 to 1489 ; Dep. Keeper's Rep. xxxvii, App. 526-8.

Sir Geoffrey died 28 Sept. 1496, and his daughter and heir Joan, widow (1499) of William Stanley, was then twenty-four years of age. The manor of Worsley was found to be held of the king as Duke of Lancaster by knight's service and the yearly rent of 10s. ; Duchy of Lanc. Inq. p.m. iii, 68.

[37] The marriage took place in or before 1480, for in a charter of that year the remainders are to Joan daughter of Sir Geoffrey Massey and her issue by William son and heir apparent of Sir William Stanley ; Ellesmere D. no. 190. This Sir William was the brother of the first Earl of Derby, afterwards executed for high treason, all his lands being forfeited. A further settlement was made in 1488 ; ibid. no. 191.

Joan was left a widow in or before 1499 ; she married Sir Edward Pickering shortly afterwards, and after his death about 1503 she married Sir John Brereton, who was living in 1510 ; Ellesmere D. no. 211, 280, 284. There was a recovery of the manors of Worsley and Hulton in 1501, Sir Edward Pickering and Joan his wife being tenants ; Towneley's MS. CC (Chet. Lib.), no. 705. Sir John Brereton and Dame Joan his wife were defendants in a case relating to the Massey chantry at Eccles in 1510 ; Duchy Plead. (Rec. Soc. Lancs. and Ches.), i, 49.

[38] Duchy of Lanc. Inq. p.m. iv, 95 (now illegible). An old abstract states that Dame Joan with William Pickering

held the
with lan
pair of s
in the s
The val
held lan
Wigan,
worth.
her daug

[39] Orm
[40] An
widow,
Brereton,
and heir
22, m. 1
to 'the
b

and whose son was the first beneficiary under the Bridgewater trust. On the death of the third duke the title of Earl of Bridgewater and part of the family estates passed to a cousin, Lieut.-General John William Egerton, seventh earl,[46] who died without issue in 1823, and was succeeded by his brother, the Rev. Francis William, eighth earl, originator of the Bridgewater Treatises. On his death without issue in 1829 the earldom expired.[47]

The second Earl of Bridgewater divided the Worsley and Tatton estates between two of his younger sons, Sir William and Thomas. The latter became ancestor of the Egertons of Tatton, but the former leaving no sons, Worsley reverted to the main line of the family. Sir William's widow married Hugh, Lord Willoughby of Parham, and they lived at Worsley Hall, though not happily.[48]

Scrope, first Duke of Bridgewater, devised a navigation system for Worsley, but it was not carried out.[49] His son Francis, the third duke, on breaking off his match with Elizabeth widow of the fourth Duke of Hamilton, devoted himself to carrying out his father's plans. He lived at the Brick Hall in Worsley, now pulled down, and limiting his personal expenses to £400 a year, employed the remainder of his income in canal-making. He obtained Acts of Parliament in 1758 and 1759 for the construction of a canal from his collieries in Worsley and Farnworth to Salford and to Hollinfare. Starting from the underground colliery workings, the canal reached the surface near the centre of Worsley,[50] and was carried, without locks, by a circuitous route and by the famous aqueduct over the Irwell, to Castleford in the south of Manchester. The engineer was the celebrated James Brindley; John Gilbert, the duke's agent, also took an active part in the work. The subterranean canal extends nearly 6 miles in a straight line, its terminus being near Deane Church, 550 ft. below the surface of the ground; it has numerous branches intended to serve the collieries; and though no longer used for carrying coal, it is useful in draining the workings. Before the first canal was finished the duke, in 1761, obtained an Act for the construction of a more important one from Manchester to Runcorn, at which point a descent is made to the Mersey by a series of locks. By these undertakings the duke, who took the keenest personal interest in the works, rendered important help to the rapidly growing commerce and manufactures of the Manchester district, and enormously enriched himself. By his will he left his estates in Lancashire and Cheshire, and at Brackley, with Bridgewater House, London, its art treasures and valuable library, on trusts for the benefit of his nephew the Marquis of Stafford, afterwards Duke of Sutherland, with remainder to his second son, Francis Leveson-Gower, and his issue; he directed that in case Lord Francis or his issue should succeed to the marquisate of Stafford, the Bridgewater estates should pass to the next in succession. The trust came to an end in 1903, but in 1872 the canals had been transferred to a company, and were purchased in 1887 by the Manchester Ship Canal.[51]

Lord Francis in 1833, in accordance with the duke's will, took the surname and arms of Egerton, on succeeding his father as the beneficiary of the trust. He determined to reside at Worsley, conceiving, as he said, that 'his possessions imposed duties upon him as binding as his rights.' He found it 'a God-forgotten place; its inhabitants were much addicted to drink and rude sports, their morals being deplorably low. The whole district was in a state of religious and educational destitution; there was no one to see to the spiritual wants of the people, and teaching was all but nullity itself.' The women working in the coal-mines were at once withdrawn, and helped to maintain themselves till they could find more suitable occupation. Churches and schools were built; a lending library instituted; the cottages of labourers and artisans repaired and rebuilt; and Lord Francis and his wife afforded a suitable example of life. He built Worsley Hall, rebuilt Bridgewater House, and added to its literary and artistic collections, and also made his mark in literature; nor did he neglect public duties, serving the state in Parliament and in office. He was created Earl of Ellesmere in 1846, refusing the offer to revive the earldom of Bridgewater.[52] Dying in 1857 he was succeeded by his son George Granville Francis, who only lived till 1862, being followed by his son Francis Charles Granville, born in 1847, the third earl, who in 1903, on the close of the trust, became not only the beneficiary, but the owner of the estates in Worsley and elsewhere.

At the beginning of last century courts baron were

[46] Son of John Egerton, successively Bishop of Bangor, Lichfield, and Durham, who died in 1787, and who was son of Henry Egerton, brother of the first Duke of Bridgewater, and Bishop of Hereford 1724–46. By the will of the third duke he had the family estates in Herts., Bucks. and Salop. By the will of the seventh earl's will these have become the possession of Earl Brownlow; G.E.C. Complete Peerage.

The Duchy rents of 18s. for Worsley and 2s. for Booths were paid in 1779; Duchy of Lanc. Rentals, bdle. 14, no. 25.

[47] He gave his collection of manuscripts, known as the Egerton MSS., to the British Museum. See Dict. Nat. Biog.

[48] Sir William Egerton was made a Knight of the Bath at the coronation of Charles II in 1661. The grant of Worsley to him in tail male was made in 1674; Ellesmere D. He died in 1691 and was buried at Hemel Hempstead. His wife was Honora, sister of Thomas Lord Leigh of Stoneley; their only son died young, while of four daughters one married; Collins, Peerage. For Lady Honora and her second husband see Hist. MSS. Com. Rep. xiv, App. iv, 417–21.

Sir William's daughter Honora married Thomas Arden Bagot of Pipe Hall, Staffs., whose descendants own land in Worsley and Hulton.

[49] The Irwell and Mersey Navigation was begun by Act of Parliament in 1720 (7 Geo. I, cap. 15); it effected improvements in the waterway between Manchester and Warrington. In 1737 the Duke of Bridgewater procured an Act (10 Geo. II, cap. 9) for making Worsley Brook navigable from Worsley Mill to the River Irwell.

Two settlements of the Worsley manors by Scrope, Earl and Duke of Bridgewater, are recorded—in 1703 and 1739; Pal. of Lanc. Feet of F. bdle. 250, m. 17; Plea R. 549, m. 6.

[50] In the formation of the canal this order was no doubt reversed, the canal being driven in underground till a seam was reached; the coal was then worked and carried away by the canal, the mines and canals progressing together; note by Mr. Holme.

[51] From an account in the Times of 25 Aug. 1903, derived from one in the Quarterly Rev. of Mar. 1844, by the Earl of Ellesmere.

A pamphlet describing the Bridgewater Navigation was published in 1766, with later editions in 1769 and 1779; it contains a map of the canals and gives an abstract of the Act of Parliament. There are early notices of the canals by A. Young, Six Months' Tour (1770), iii, 251, and Aikin, Manchester (1795), 112–16; see also Dict. Nat. Biog. and Smiles, Engineers. For a note on the portraits of the duke, see Pal. Note Bk. ii, 130.

[52] From a Guide to Worsley (Eccles, 1870): also G.E.C. Complete Peerage, and Dict. Nat. Biog. The earl was the first president of the Camden Society, and wrote a Guide to Northern Archaeology.

One of his sons, the Hon. Algernon Egerton, M.P., resided at Worsley Old Hall, and was superintendent of the Bridgewater Trust for many years. After his death in 1891 a memorial fund of £1,100 was raised, the interest of which is given in exhibitions or scholarships to pupil teachers proceeding to college.

held at Easter and Michaelmas.[58] They continued to be held regularly until 1856, but only two have been held since, in 1877 and 1888. Some court rolls are extant for the end of the 16th and beginning of the 17th centuries; the regular series begins in 1722.[54]

Worsley Hall is a large house built in 1840–6 by Lord Francis Egerton as above stated, Edward Blore being the architect. It stands on high ground looking southward over Chat Moss, and is a spacious stone building of florid Gothic style, with a skyline which from the lower ground is very imposing. It replaces Brick Hall, which was pulled down in 1845.

Worsley Old Hall, which was abandoned as the residence of the lord of the manor when the 18th-century house was built, yet stands in the park to the north of the modern mansion. It is a picturesque low two-storied building, partly of wood and plaster, and partly of brick, but has been so much altered that it has now little or no architectural interest. It makes a very charming picture, however, with its level lawns, ivy-covered walls, and contrast of colour in black and white work, red-brick chimneys, and grey-slated roofs. The house was originally built round three sides of a quadrangle, the fourth, facing north, being open; but the courtyard has now been almost entirely built over, and the interior of the building so much altered that little or nothing of the original disposition of the plan remains. There is nothing to indicate the date of the building, but it would not appear to be older than the 17th century. Parts of an older structure, however, are possibly incorporated in it, some of the roof-beams and principals in the south and south-east parts of the house appearing to be of earlier date. The cellars under the central portion of the house, however, are vaulted in brick, and are certainly not earlier than the 17th century. The principal front faces south, and is of timber and plaster, with gables at the ends, and two brick chimney stacks breaking the long line of the outside wall and roof. The timber work is of simple construction, being composed almost entirely of uprights and diagonal bracings, two quatrefoils near the garden entrance being the only enrichments. The timber construction is continued round the gable at the east side. The hall is said to have been moated, but no signs of a moat now remain. The three sides of the original courtyard are set at slightly different angles. In modern times a corridor was set along the side of the courtyard, connecting the two ends of the old wings, but this has disappeared in subsequent alterations. The courtyard was first encroached on at the east side by the erection of a wide entrance-hall, the principal

entrance to the house being on the north side. The quadrangle was by this means reduced to a space of about 34 ft. square, and this was almost entirely covered in 1905 by the erection of a billiard-room. The north entrance front of the house is entirely modern; it carries out the picturesque half-timber character of the garden front, but the black and white work is chiefly paint and plaster. About the middle of the last century (after 1855) a new west wing was added alongside the old one, with a timber gable at each end. This was originally of one story, but was afterwards raised. Further alterations took place in 1891, when the morning-room in the east wing was extended and a new bay added on three sides of the house, and in 1906 a further addition was made by the erection of a small north-west wing. There was formerly a bell turret over the west wing, but this has disappeared.

For a long time before the new Hall was built, Worsley Old Hall was divided into tenements, and it was not till the Hon. Algernon Egerton came to live there in 1855 and the house was entirely renovated, that it was again used as a residence. At the end of the 18th century when the Duke of Bridgewater was constructing his canal, James Brindley, the engineer, lived for some time at Worsley Old Hall, where the duke often consulted with him. The hall is now the residence of Viscount Brackley.

The carved oak panels which were brought from Hulme Hall, Manchester, at the time of its demolition, to Worsley Old Hall, have been removed to the new mansion and are now in Lady Ellesmere's sitting-room. They consist of a series of spirited grotesques, allegorical subjects, and ornamental devices, and are apparently 16th-century work.[55]

The formation of the estate or manor of BOOTHS in 1323 has been narrated.[56] Robert son of Henry de Worsley, the original grantee, was succeeded by his son William,[57] and the latter by Robert de Worsley his son,[58] who died 28 March 1402, seised of 'the manor of Booths,' which was held of the king as Duke of Lancaster in socage and by the yearly rent of 2s.; it was worth 20 marks. His son and heir Arthur was then of full age.[59] As already stated, the father had planned the reunion of the whole manor through the marriage of Arthur with Elizabeth daughter and heiress of Sir Geoffrey de Worsley, but was balked by the success of the Masseys in proving her illegitimate.

Arthur Worsley was stated to have been an idiot from his birth. He was entrusted to the guardianship of John Booth of Barton, who in 1414 was

---

[58] Baines, Lancs. (ed. 1836), iii, 145.

[54] Information of Mr. Strachan Holme. In 1877 the bounds were perambulated. The officers of the manor used to be the moss reeves, moor drivers, burley men, afferrers, constables, and pinfold keepers.

[55] They are engraved in Baines, Hist. of Lancs. (1st ed.), iii, 144.

[56] Final Conc. i, 193; also Ellesmere D. no. 147, 162, quoted above.

[57] In 1350 Agnes widow of Robert de Worsley claimed her dower in twenty-one messuages and various lands in Worsley and Heaton Norris. William son of Robert, in defending, denied Agnes's marriage, but she averred that it took place on the Wednesday after 29 Aug. 1346, at the door of St. Mary's Church, Deane;

De Banco R. 363, m. 78 d. William son of Robert de Worsley occurs again in 1353; Assize R. 435, m. 9 d. William de Worsley had licence for his oratory in 1360, 1362, and 1366; Lich. Epis. Reg. v, fol. 4, 8, 15.

[58] Robert de Worsley and Isabel his wife in 1376 claimed dower in certain lands in Blackrod; Isabel was the widow of John de Worthington; De Banco R. 462, m. 235. Robert had licence for his oratory in the manor of Booths in 1378; Lich. Epis. Reg. v, fol. 31b. In 1401 Robert son of William de Worsley had a release from the Masseys of all claim to Booths and Stanistreet; Ellesmere D. (Black Bk.). Robert de Worsley was knight of the shire in 1386 and 1391;

Pink and Beaven, Parl. Repre. of Lancs. 43–4. He complained that in order to ruin him the Masseys and others had accused him of treason in 1387, so that he had been imprisoned for some time in the Tower; Parl. R. iii, 445.

[59] Towneley MS. DD, no. 1448; an inquisition taken at Manchester on 3 Oct. 1402. The writ had been issued 6 Aug. 1402; Dep. Keeper's Rep. xxxiii, App. 2, where the date seems to be 1401. In the inquiry as to the sanity of Arthur de Worsley, however, Robert's death is said to have happened on Easter Sunday, 1403; and it is recorded that he held the Rakes in Heaton Norris, in addition to 'certain lands and tenements called the Booths' in Worsley.

accused of having caused waste in the possessions in his charge ;[60] the guardianship had been transferred to John Stanley.[61] Arthur did not long survive, dying in December 1415, and leaving as heir his son Geoffrey, then about six years of age.[62] Geoffrey appears to have been succeeded by a brother named Robert.[63] About 1460 Robert Worsley was in possession, he and his son Robert, with other gentlemen and yeomen, being accused of complicity in the death of Robert Derbyshire ;[64] and at the same time he charged William Massey, Sir Geoffrey Massey, and others, with the death of William Worsley his brother.[65] Robert Worsley the son is probably the Robert Worsley who died at the beginning of 1497, leaving a son and heir of the same name, thirty years of age. His possessions are described as the manor of Booths, held of the manor of Worsley ; also messuages, land, and pasture called the Rakes in Heaton Norris, held of the king as Duke of Lancaster. The services were unknown.[66]

Robert Worsley recorded a pedigree in 1533 ; it

---

[60] The first inquiry as to Arthur's sanity was made in Sept. 1413, and the next at Bolton a year later ; Duchy of Lanc. Inq. p.m. i, 24, 24a, 24b. Richard Worsley had had the custody of the lands for two years from the death of Robert ; then John Booth of Barton the elder had had it for eight years—see the grant to him dated 18 Dec. 1403 in *Dep. Keeper's Rep.* xl, App. 531—and had caused waste by felling and carrying away eighty oaks, worth 6s. 8d. each, in a certain wood called Mokena, parcel of the tenements in Worsley ; also forty saplings in the Rakes, and forty more in Winlehurst in Worsley ; he had also damaged the hall and chapel at the Rakes and the 'manor place' of the Booths.

[61] The grant to John Stanley was made on 20 Nov. 1413, shortly after the former inquiry ; *Lancs. Inq. p.m.* (Chet. Soc.), i, 118 ; but see *Dep. Keeper's Rep.* xxxiii, App. 11, for a renewal of the grant to Booth.

[62] *Lancs. Inq.* loc. cit. ; Pal. of Lanc. Plea R. 2, m. 24b. Besides the Booths and the Rakes he had held the manor of Worsley, except the site and certain lands, for the life of his wife Elizabeth. There seems to have been a further inquiry in 1417 ; *Dep. Keeper's Rep.* xxxiii, App. 14.

[63] In 1432 Robert son of Arthur Worsley and Edmund Worsley granted to feoffees lands in Withington, Heaton Norris, Urmston, Barton, Ashton under Lyne, and Stanistreet in Worsley ; Ellesmere D. no. 26.

[64] Pal. of Lanc. Plea R. 28, m. 9d. The other defendants included Hamlet and William Atherton of Bickerstaffe.

[65] Ibid. The other defendants were Thomas Tyldesley, Richard Prestall, Nicholas Massey, Gilbert Parr, and John son of William Massey the elder. Another William Worsley, Dean of St. Paul's, 1479–99, is supposed to have been of the Booths family ; *Dict. Nat. Biog.*

[66] Duchy of Lanc. Inq. p.m. iii, 50.

[67] *Visit.* of 1533 (Chet. Soc.), 81.

[68] Duchy of Lanc. Inq. p.m. vii, 5 ; a settlement of 1524 is recited.

[69] See the account of Upholland. Thurstan Tyldesley says in his will (1547) : 'Notwithstanding that my son-in-law Sir Robert Worsley knight is married to Margaret Beetham, his wife yet living, yet I remit and pardon to him

£7 10s., upon co yearly unto my da £5 or more for he absence from him, he take his said and entreat her Piccope, *Wills* (Ch bigamous union m counts for the thre in the pedigrees.

Deer were kept *Duchy Plead.* (Rec. Sir Robert Wo

Bridgewater Trustees, the Earl of Ellesmere being the present owner.[74]

WARDLEY, the possession of Jordan de Worsley in the first half of the 14th century, has been mentioned above. Jordan held part of Wardley of the Hospitallers by a rent of 8d.;[75] he had other lands in Wardley and Worsley, held of the lord of Worsley.[76] He left an only daughter Margaret as his heir; she was a minor and in ward to Richard de Worsley. In November 1330 a number of the neighbours carried her off from Richard's house and married her to Thurstan son of Richard de Tyldesley.[77] She was still living in 1401, when in conjunction with her son Thomas she made a settlement with the Masseys regarding her estate in Worsley.[78] This descended to another Thomas Tyldesley, who died in 1495,[79] leaving as his heir a son Thurstan. By his first wife Thurstan, who died in 1554,[80] had a son Thomas,[81] succeeded two years later by his son Thurstan,[82] who died in 1582, having between 1562 and 1568 sold Wardley and other lands in Worsley to William and Gilbert Sherington.[83] This family did not hold them long, selling to Roger Downes, who was living at Wardley in 1609.[84] He had various public employments[85] and was twice married. The eldest son by the first marriage having died before his father,[86] the heir at the latter's death in 1638 was found to be Francis Downes, eldest son by the second wife.[87] Francis also seems to have died without

---

[daughter of John Tipping of Manchester']; Raines in Gastrell's *Notitia*, ii, 51. In a recovery of the manor of Booths in 1799, Samuel Clowes the elder and Samuel Clowes the younger were vouchees; Pal. of Lanc. Aug. Assizes, 39 Geo. III, R. 6.

[74] Samuel Clowes in 1810 sold the manor of Booths and the estate there to Robert Haldane Bradshaw of Worsley, the first superintendent under the Duke of Bridgewater's will. He contracted to sell his properties in the neighbourhood to the first Earl of Ellesmere, and his executors carried the contract out in 1836. The trustees of the Earls of Ellesmere held the estate till 1900, when it was sold to the Bridgewater Trustees; in 1903 it was transferred, with the other properties, to the Earl of Ellesmere.

[75] The prior of the Hospitallers called upon Gilbert de Barton to warrant him in 1246; Assize R. 404, m. 13. Wardley (Wordelegh) is named among the Hospitallers' lands in 1292; *Plac. de Quo War.* (Rec. Com.), 375. In 1329 the prior alleged that Richard de Worsley (4 acres), Jordan de 'Worleye' (20 acres), and Ellen daughter of Adam de Worleye (2 acres) had withheld their due services; De Banco R. 279, m. 180 d; 280, m. 294 d.

About 1540 the Hospitallers' tenants were Thurstan Tyldesley, who paid 8d. rent, and Richard Holland (of Denton), who had Little Wardley and paid 4d.; Kuerden MSS. v, fol. 84.

[76] A grant has been quoted in a previous note; see also *Final Conc.* i, 190, 202, for lands in Worsley and Hindley. In 1301 Richard son of Roger de Worsley demanded common of pasture in 300 acres of wood and 100 acres of moor which Henry lord of Worsley had approved from the waste; Jordan brother of Henry was the tenant. It was shown that plaintiff had sufficient pasture, and the verdict was against him; Assize R. 321, m. 8.

[77] Assize R. 430, m. 16; in one place Thurstan is called 'son of Henry de Tyldesley'; Henry was the father of Richard. Thurstan occurs in 1357; *Final Conc.* ii, 151. He had a licence for an oratory at Wardley in 1361; Lich. Epis. Reg. v, fol. 6.

[78] *Final Concs.* iii, 62; *Dep. Keeper's Rep.* xxxiii, App. 2. Wills of Thomas Tyldesley of Eccles and of St. Giles, Cripplegate, 1410, are in P.C.C.

The succession from this point is not clear. Hugh de Tyldesley held Wardley of the Hospitallers in 1420; Ellesmere D, no. 184. James de Tyldesley of Worsley occurs in 1444; Pal. of Lanc. Plea R. 6, m. 1b; Thomas Tyldesley,

senior, a 28, m. 9 desley in church o brook ·

In 147 Wardley Thomas Richard

[79]

[80] Du He held water-m q (pitallers) annual held lan Warring ton, W Westwo the quee

ʔ

issue,[86] the heir being his brother John, who took sides with the king in the Civil War and died in 1648,[89] leaving by his wife Penelope, a daughter of Sir Cecil Trafford, two children—Roger, born about the year named, and Penelope.[90] The son, after a short and dissipated career in London—Lord Rochester was one of his companions—died from a wound received in a brawl with the watch,[91] and his sister inherited the estate. By her husband Richard Savage, fourth Earl Rivers,[92] she had a daughter and heir Elizabeth, who in turn left a daughter and heir Penelope by her husband James Barry, fourth Earl of Barrymore.[93] Penelope married General James Cholmondeley, but was divorced for adultery, and died childless in 1786.[94] Wardley was sold by her in 1760 to Francis Duke of Bridgewater, and now forms part of the Earl of Ellesmere's estate in Worsley.[94a]

Wardley Hall is a quadrangular building of great interest, which, though very much restored, yet preserves many of its ancient features and retains to a great extent its original arrangement of plan. The house is situated about a mile north of Worsley village, and stands on high ground at the head of a wooded hollow. Its immediate surroundings are yet of a rural character, though the workings of collieries have entirely changed the aspect of the district around.

The house was formerly surrounded by a moat, but of this only a portion remains on the west side, where it has been formed into a small lake, adding greatly to the picturesqueness of the building.

The date of the first house is not known, but the oldest part of the present structure, containing the great hall, may belong to the end of the 15th or first half of the 16th century. The building has been so much altered and restored in the course of the 19th century, however, that it is very difficult to affix a date definitely to any portion of it. At the beginning of the last century it was in a very dilapidated condition, and some repairs were effected about 1811.

WARDLEY HALL : THE GATEWAY

Parliaments of 1625 ; Pink and Beaven, op. cit. 224.

The will of Roger Downes, dated 1637 and proved in 1638, mentions his brother Francis as married, his sons Francis and John, and his daughter Jane, then wife of Ralph Sneade ; his cousin Bessie Halliwell ; and John Preston and Arthur Alburgh, who had married his sisters.

In his later years Roger Downes appears to have been reconciled to the Roman church, and his sons adhered to the same faith. John Downes, the younger son, stayed a week in the English College at Rome in 1638 ; Foley, *Rec. S.J.* vi, 616.

[88] A settlement by Francis Downes in 1642 is mentioned in Exch. of Pleas, Cal. of D. enrolled, L. 124.

Francis died 5 Mar. 1648, and his wife Elizabeth 9 Mar., John following in May; *The Month*, xcviii, 379, &c. (from information of Mr. Joseph Gillow).

A further repair appears to have taken place about 1849; and in 1894, the hall having fallen into decay, a further and more complete restoration was carried out. For about twenty years before this time the house was unoccupied, with the exception of the east wing, which had been made into three cottages, tenanted by colliers. During that period it had only been so far repaired as to be kept weather-proof, and had suffered some damage from the coal-workings beneath it. The only two living-rooms were those now called the boudoir and the dining-room ; the lower part of the hall was a washhouse, and its upper part divided into several rooms, and the minstrels' gallery used as a dovecote. The principal entrance to the house from the courtyard had been built up and a later one made on the west side near to the staircase bay. Other rooms were used as places for firewood

right up to the walls on this side, if this view is to be taken as correct. The ground is now levelled right up to the building. The elevation on this side is of brick, and is about 60 ft. in length, standing in front of the rest of the house. The roof, which was formerly lower on the east side of the gatehouse, is now of uniform height and pitch with overhanging eaves and a plaster cove. The appearance of the house on this side, relieved only by the central gateway with its single gable and two tall chimney-stacks, is plain and uninteresting, the end gables of the two side wings of the quadrangle standing too far back to enter into the composition of the north front. To the west of the gatehouse, the recess formed by the junction of the north and west wings is now occupied by a low one-story addition erected in 1895–6.

The courtyard is of irregular shape, none of its

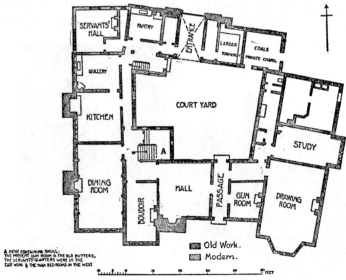

PLAN OF WARDLEY HALL

and rubbish, and the whole structure had been most cruelly mutilated. The work aimed at restoring as much of the building as possible to something like its former state, and reconstructing the remainder.

The house is of two stories throughout, and the entrance is under a gatehouse on the north side of the quadrangle. Immediately opposite, and occupying the whole of the south side of the courtyard, is the great hall. The family apartments were no doubt originally in the west wing, and the servants' rooms in the east wing. The west wing now contains the dining-room, kitchen, and offices, while the east wing, which has been successively used as cottages and stables, was converted into a drawing-room and study in 1903.

The gatehouse was formerly approached over a bridge, and is so shown in Philips's view of the house made about 1822,[95] the moat at that time coming

sides being square with the others, and measures about 45 ft. by 35 ft., the greater length being from west to east. The east and west wings, which converge slightly to the south, are said to follow the lines of two streams which fed the moat.[96] All the outside elevations, with the exception of the central portion of the south front, which is of timber, are of brick with stone dressings and with timber in some of the gables, and all the windows are new, both in the brick and timber portions of the house. Three sides of the courtyard are of timber on a stone base, the north or gatehouse side only being of brick. The roofs are covered with stone slates.

The entrance to the house by the courtyard is by the door at the north end of the passage behind the screen. The passage is still retained and on the side opposite the hall has its two doors to the east wing.

[95] Henry Taylor, *Old Halls in Lancs. and Ches.* 47.   [96] Ibid.

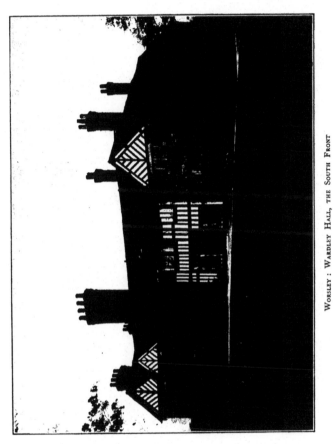

Worsley : Wardley Hall, the South Front

This part of the house has been entirely modernized, what was probably the buttery being now a gun-room, and the passage to the kitchen now leading to a modern drawing-room and study. The great hall, originally about 40 ft. long by 21 ft.,[97] was, at a comparatively early date, divided into two by a wall about 12 ft. from its west end. A floor appears to have been inserted at the same time, and the staircase in the south-west corner of the courtyard built. The appearance of the open timber-roofed hall may, however, still be realized in the upper room, the whole extent of the original roof having been exposed in the last restoration. The roof is divided by two principals into three bays, and is of a plain king-post type with curved and moulded pieces underneath the tie beam. It has a flat wooden ceiling with moulded ribs at the level of the tie beams. The arrangement

WARDLEY HALL : COURTYARD FROM NORTH-EAST

of the great hall followed the usual type. The screens were at the east end, with a gallery over, and the room was lit on the north side by a range of windows to the courtyard. On the opposite side was the ingle-nook and a window to the garden. Beyond the fireplace at the west end to the right of the high table was the bay window with a projection and width of about 10 ft. All these arrangements may still be seen, but the greater part of the dais end of the hall together with the bay window is now a separate room (boudoir), and the masonry fireplace is a restoration. The fireplace in the upper hall, however, has its old stone arch reinstated after having been repaired. Both these fireplaces were discovered and opened up in 1895–6. At the north-west end of the hall is the staircase occupying a projecting bay in the south-west angle of the courtyard, and beyond this a corridor giving access to the rooms in the western wing. These

of uniform character. At the same time a new stair-case bay and entrance were added in the north-west corner of the courtyard. In the original plan there was a smaller projecting bay in the south-east corner of the courtyard with a small gable facing north, forming a kind of balancing feature to the large gable of the staircase bay, but in the reconstruction this feature has been merged into the general arrangement of the east side of the house by the rebuilding and advancing of the east side of the quadrangle to the line of the former angle-projection and the continuing of the little gable as a second and smaller roof along the whole length of the east wing. The courtyard is paved with stone sets.

Over the gatehouse was formerly the date 1625, which though usually taken to indicate some alteration or addition to the building, probably refers to the year of the erection of the gatehouse, or at any rate

97 40 ft. including the screen, 34 ft. without.

to its facing in brick. There may have been a wooden building on the site before, but the timber front to the gatehouse shown in old drawings of Wardley Hall, which was so characteristic a feature of the house in the view from the north, was not timber at all, but only a painted plaster covering in front of the brick-work. The old brick walls have now been restored to their original appearance. The other brick eleva-tions are, perhaps, more rebuildings than restora-tions, and have no special interest. The room east of the gatehouse upstairs is said to have been a chapel, but there appears to be no documentary evidence for this, and the building itself at the present time offers none. The position, however, would be a convenient and likely one for the purpose, and a former tenant of the hall is stated to have said that he formerly saw evidences of the apartment having been a chapel.[98]

In an inventory of goods in Wardley Hall dated 10 July 1638, the following rooms and places are mentioned :—[98a]

'The little parler, the old yeaman's chamber, newe flored chambers, buttery chamber, maydon's chamber, gatehouse chamb', mattdd chamber, garden chamber, steare head chamber, yellowe chamber, corner cham-ber, inner corner chamber, chamber over hall, chappell chamber, cookes chamber, masters' cham-ber, inner chamber, chamber over pantry, greate parlor, grounde parlor, the hall, servantes chamb', oxe house chamber, garner chamb', mylne, stable chamber, brewhouse, back house, dry larder, wett lar-der, dryhouse, cheese chamber, kytchein, Mr. Milling-ton's clossett, storehouse, washe house, buttery and sellor, mylne.'

A peculiar interest has long been attached to the house on account of a human skull being kept there. The superstition is that if the skull is moved from its place great storms will follow, to the damage of the dwelling.

The skull is in a niche in the wall on the staircase landing, carefully protected by glass and a wooden outer door. Concerning it there are several legends and traditions, but it is now supposed to be that of the Ven. Ambrose Barlow, who served the private chapel at Wardley along with other places in South Lanca-shire, but was arrested on Easter Sunday, 1641, and executed in the September following at Lancaster. After his execution it is thought that his head may have been secured by Mr. Francis Downes, and pre-served by him at Wardley Hall.[99] The story of the skull being that of the last Roger Downes (died 1676) has been disproved.

The Hollands of Denton held another part of the Hospitallers' lands in Wardley by a rent of 4d.[100]

Another ancient estate in Worsley was *KEMP-NOUGH*,[101] granted early in the 13th century by Richard de Worsley to Roger his brother (or son) at a rent of 2s.[102] Richard son of Roger appears fre-quently as a witness to local charters and in other ways during the second part of the 13th century.[103] Probably he was the father of Robert the Clerk of Worsley, whose grandson Richard in 1346 made a settlement of his lands in Worsley upon his son Robert, with remainder to his daughter Ellen.[104] The last-named seems to have succeeded. She married Richard de Parr, and in 1408 a further settlement was made, Oliver being their eldest son.[105] Oliver married Emma daughter and heir of Margery, widow of Henry Tootill ; she had lands in Tyldesley, which descended to their son and grandson, each named Richard.[106] The estate descended to John Parr, who in 1560 made a settlement.[107] His heir was his daughter Anne, whose marriage with Nicholas Starkie carried Kempnough into this family,[108] and their descendants, the Starkies of Huntroyde, retained possession until 1876, when it was sold to the Bridge-water trustees.[109]

[98] Taylor, op. cit. 68 n.
[98a] Printed in H.V. Hart-Davis's *Hist. of Wardley Hall, Lancashire* (1908), 120–35.
[99] An authoritative account will be found in Hart-Davis's and Holme's *Wardley Hall*, 153. See also Harland and Wilkinson, *Lancs. Legends*, 65–73 ; *Lancs. and Ches. Antiq. Soc.* i, 31–8 ; xvi, 143 ; *Month*, xcviii, 379.
[100] Kuerden MSS. v, fol. 84 ; *Lancs. Inq. p.m.* (Rec. Soc. Lancs. and Ches.), ii, 146.
[101] Kempenhalgh and other variations of spelling occur.
[102] Towneley MS. DD, no. 948. The bounds began at Peverelsgate, went by Haysbrook to Holclough across to Hankechirche, by Hulteley Brook to Millbrook, along this to Scaythelache, and so to the starting point. The grantor must have been Richard son of Elias de Worsley, for Roger de Worsley made a grant of land in Swinton in 1231 ; Elles-mere D. no. 215.
Richard de Worsley gave to Roger his son an oxgang and a half in Swinton ; *Whalley Couch.* iii, 904. As *filio* im-proves the pedigree, seeing that Roger's son Richard lived till the end of the cen-tury, *fratri* may be an error in transcrip-tion. Cecily de Rivington was Roger's widow ; ibid. 905.
[108] In 1278 he claimed the common of pasture pertaining to 80 acres of arable land in Worsley against Richard son of Geoffrey de Worsley, Agnes widow of Geoffrey, and many others, in virtue of a

WORSLEY : WARDLEY HALL, FROM THE SOUTH-WEST

PENDLEBURY : AGECROFT HALL, NORTH-EAST ANGLE OF COURTYARD, C. 1875

SALFORD

Kempnough Hall is a small black and white timbered building on a stone base, much renewed with brickwork, and said to have been almost entirely rebuilt in comparatively recent times. Much of the old timber work has been preserved, though the greater part of the 'timber' front is paint on plaster. The house is a two-story building with a slightly projecting gabled wing at each end, and is now divided into three cottages. It lies, surrounded by trees, about half a mile north-east of Worsley, near to Roe Green, but presents no remarkable features. The roofs are covered with stone slates and the chimneys are of brick. Two gates, with piers, which in the early part of the 19th century stood in front of the house have now disappeared. There is a large stone

WORSLEY : KEMPNOUGH HALL

[110] *Plac. de Quo War.* (Rec. Com.), 375.

Gilbert de Barton gave to William de Swinton two parts of the land which Ellis son of Godwin de Swinton held of the Hospitallers, in exchange for an oxgang in Chadderton ; Ellesmere D. Roger de Worsley granted to Richard son of Geoffrey de Byron half of Swinton—being all he held—except 12 acres given to the Hospitallers ; *Whalley Couch.* iii, 905. There are other allusions to the Hospitallers' holding ; ibid. 929, 934. The prior of the Hospitallers in 1329 made a claim against Elota the widow and Richard the son of Alexander de Swinton ; De Banco R. 297, m. 180 d.

In 1325 it was found that Joan wife of William de Multon held, among other properties, the third part of an estate at Swinton, which her former husband, William de Holland, had held of the Hospitallers by a rent of 12 d. a year ; Inq. p.m. 19 Edw. II, n. 96.

About 1540 the Hospitallers' tenants were Thomas Holland, paying 5¼ d., William Chapman, for half of Little Scholecroft, 7 d., and James Eckersall, 2½ d.; Kuerden MSS. v, fol. 84.

[111] *Whalley Couch.* iii, 877–936 ; see further in the account of Monton in Barton. In 1331 Richard Hunewyn granted to the abbey all his lands in Swinton in Worsley, his eldest daughter Alice confirming it ; ibid. 926–28.

Paulinus de Halghton granted to Cecily daughter of Iorwerth de Hulton the third part of the vill of Little Houghton ; ibid. i, 59 ; this seems to have been given to the abbey ; ibid. i, 55. An oxgang and a half in Little Houghton was among the lands of Robert and Jordan de Hulton in 1253 ; *Final Conc.* i, 151. Geoffrey de Byron gave half the vill to his brother John, who gave it to the monks ; *Whalley Couch.* 57, 58 ; see also iii, 901.

The abbey lands were largely derived from the benefactions of Geoffrey de Byron, who in 1275 accused Richard de Worsley of a burglary at Swinton ; Coram Rege R. 15, m. 12 d. A year or two later Geoffrey and the abbot were defendants in claims made by the Smith family ; Assize R. 1238, fol. 31, 31 *b* ; 1239, fol. 39. Later the abbot had disputes with the Boltons. In 1292 he recovered damages from Adam de Rossendale and others, who had cut and felled timber without licence, for the use of Ellen de Bolton, but Ellen herself was acquitted ; and at the same time Richard de Bolton, Richard son of Roger de Worsley, and others, were non-suited in a claim against the abbot for eight messuages, two mills, land, &c. ; ibid. 408, m. 102 d., 100, 101, 23 d. More interesting was the claim by Olive de Bolton for common of pasture in 100 acres of moor and heath as belonging to her free tenement, formerly held by Richard de Worsley. The jury found that John de Worsley (probably of Little Houghton), who had enfeoffed Olive, had in the time of Geoffrey de Byron, lord of Swinton, been accustomed to common in the pasture. After Geoffrey had granted his lands to the abbot the latter refused common until John impleaded him in the king's court. It was accordingly ordered that Olive should recover seisin and damages of half a mark ; ibid. m. 17.

Grants to and from Henry de Worsley and Olive de Bolton are among the Ellesmere D. no. 148 (dated 1300), 256. In 1327 Henry son of Richard de Bolton granted his land in Holclough heys in Worsley to his son John, who granted the same to Richard de Worsley ; ibid. no. 163, 164.

[112] Pat. 32 Hen. VIII, pt. 4. The grant included Swinton, Little Houghton,

Swinton [113] and Stanistreet [114] were other estates or portions of Worsley named in the ancient deeds. Westwood also was among the lands of Whalley Abbey.[114a] Little Houghton gave a surname to a resident family.[115] This estate seems to have passed by descent or purchase to the Valentines of Bentcliffe in Barton.[115a]

WALKDEN, down to the 15th century, appears to have had a wider meaning than at present, spreading into Farnworth and Little Hulton.[116] It also gave a surname to a local family.[117] Northdene in Worsley—probably 'the Deans' in Swinton, north of Little Houghton—was another estate.[118]

Many of the neighbouring landowners, as appears from the inquisitions, held estates also in Worsley and

Swinton.[119] Until the end of the 17th century all the farms in the district were held on life leases; somewhat earlier it was customary for the leases to contain a provision that the tenants should rear one or more hunting dogs for the lord.

The principal landowner in 1786 was the Duke of Bridgewater, owning apparently over half the land; Samuel Clowes had a large estate at Booths, and the smaller owners included the Rev. Walter Bagot, James Hilton, and — Starkie.[120]

In 1686 an agreement was made as to the inclosure of Swinton Moor and Hodge Common in the parish of Eccles.[121] Walkden Moor, a great part of which is or was in Little Hulton, was inclosed about 1765.[121a]

Westlakes, Kitpool, Westwood, and Marland (or Moorland).

Generally speaking, there was little disputation during the tenure of the monks. After the Dissolution a long quarrel was waged between the Sheringtons, as representing the Tyldesleys, and others. A precept to keep the peace with Thurstan Tyldesley of Wardley was issued in 1566 to Sir William Radcliffe, Edward Holland, Thomas Valentine, Robert Chapman, and others ; Agecroft D. Many references will be found in the *Ducatus Lanc.* Richard Brereton of Tatton, son of Geoffrey son of Joan Brereton, as lord of Worsley, in 1581 claimed the waste grounds called Swinton Moor and Walkden Moor, and the moss called Pendleton hey. Gilbert Sherington then held the last-named ground, and Sir John Radcliffe claimed Swinton Moor as representing Whalley Abbey ; John Gawen occupied an inclosure from the moor as tenant of Gilbert Sherington ; and John Derbyshire had a barn in the Stanistreet ; Duchy of Lanc. Plead. Eliz. cxv, B 4. Ten years later Gilbert Sherington claimed an inheritance in Swinton Moor as part of his manor of Swinton. He stated that the moor on the east extended to Hendene Brook, dividing Swinton from Pendlebury, and on the west to a brook near Wardley wall ; and that parcels of it had been improved by Geoffrey de Byron in the time of Edward I, by the Abbot of Whalley about 1460–80, and by Thurstan Tyldesley, Thomas his son, and Thurstan his grandson, more recently. A witness stated that the tenants of Roe Green had had common of pasture on Swinton Moor. The moor included Pendleton (or Pelton) hey and moss and the White Moss ; ibid. clv, S 9. In 1594 Richard Brereton complained of the inclosures of Gilbert Sherington adjoining Linnyshaw Moss at the head of a mere called Howclough ; ibid. clxii, B 9.

For a plan of Worsley and Linnyshaw see *Lancs. and Ches. Rec.* (Rec. Soc. Lancs. and Ches.), i, 24.

[113] *Whalley Couch.* iii, 889, 916, 917, 921. It is now within the borough of Eccles.

[114] Ibid. iii, 886.

[114a] Ibid. iii, 907–15.

[115] Paulinus de Halghton has been mentioned ; he is also called 'de Barton' in a grant by his widow Beatrice ; ibid. i, 55. Thomas son of Robert de Halghton in 1276 released to the Abbot of Stanlaw all his right in the new inclosures of the Hope in Swinton made by Geoffrey de Byron ; ibid. iii, 921.

John de Halghton was one of the de-

fendants in a Worsley R. 1321, m. 8 Rob Halghton was a defen Duchy of Lanc. A Nine years later the took pro 'ng Halghton for waste · m. 201 Robert de made a settlement of of Little Halghton a in favour of himself a with remainders grandson Robert son deeds among the El From another of th that this estate had be by Richard, lord of Richard son of G John · John son of

---

The chapel of *ELLENBROOK*[122]

CHURCH owes its foundation to the lords of Worsley, and has remained to the present day a donative in their gift. The Abbot of Stanlaw, as rector of Eccles, between 1272 and 1295, granted his licence to Richard de Worsley to have a free chantry in his chapel of Worsley, provided that no loss was caused to the mother church, to which 6d. was to be paid yearly as oblations.[123] There is no continuous record of the chapel's existence, but in 1549 Sir Richard Brereton complained that his son Richard, among other lawless deeds, had recently taken a chalice from his chapel in the manor of Worsley, which chalice the inhabitants had purchased for use in divine service.[124] The fate of the chapel in the Reformation period is uncertain, but as the lords of Worsley appear to have conformed to the Elizabethan system without difficulty, service was probably continued in it with but little interruption. Dame Dorothy Legh in 1638 left the interest of £50 for its maintenance, and other small gifts were made ;[125] but in 1650 it was found that there was no certain income, and that it sometimes had a preaching minister and sometimes not.[126]

In 1677 the Bishop of Chester made an order as to the payment of seat rents, the endowment of the chapel not exceeding £20 a year.[127] Lord Willoughby, on coming to live at Worsley about 1693, appears to have had a design to use this as a Nonconformist place of worship ; he locked out the curate in charge and put a Mr. Cheney in as preacher, but was defeated by the feoffees, headed by Roger Kenyon, and the bishop.[128] In 1719 Bishop Gastrell found the income to be £23 6s. 3d., of which £17 was the rent or value of the house and ground attached to the chapel.[129] Though it was a donative the curates appear at times to have been licensed to it by the

bishop.[130] The following are the names of some of them :—[131]

oc.

oc. [133]

oc.

[136]

oc.

oc.

? [140]

oc.

---

[122] The dedication is now given as St. Mary the Virgin.

[123] Ellesmere D. no. 127. The chaplain to be provided was to be presented to the abbot at Eccles and swear fidelity and obedience to the abbot and the church, and thus receive the ministry of the chapel.

[124] Duchy of Lanc. Plead. Edw. VI, xxv, B, 15. Though the chapel is called Sir Richard's the gift of a chalice by the people is evidence that it was not a private chapel at Worsley Hall.

[125] *End. Char. Rep.* Eccles, 1904, pp. 6, 34 ; Dame Legh in 1638 gave £400 for charitable uses to trustees, one of whom in 1654 deposed that 'her intention was that it should go for the maintenance of a minister at the chapel of "Ellenborough," so that the bishop should have no hand in the putting in, placing or displacing of the minister there . . . and for so long time as the Lord Bridgewater should suffer the chapel to stand.'

[126] *Commonw. Ch. Surv.* 140. It appears that £40 a year had in 1646 been ordered to be paid to the minister at Ellenbrook out of Christopher Anderton's sequestered tithes, but the order had to be renewed in 1650 ; *Plund. Mins. Accts.* (Rec. Soc. Lancs. and Ches.), i, 88, 252.

[127] *Hist. MSS. Com. Rep.* xiv, App. iv, 104.

[128] Ibid. 275, 289, 290 ('Perhaps if you told my Lord Bridgewater of the Lord

Walkden is the church of St. Paul, opened in 1838, and rebuilt in 1848 ; the Earl of Ellesmere is patron.[149] St. John the Baptist's, Little Hulton, is also within Walkden, at Hill Top ; it was built in 1874 ; the Bishop of Manchester is patron.[150]

There are Wesleyan chapels at Worsley, first built in 1801, and at Boothstown ; also at Swinton and Walkden. The Primitive Methodists have two chapels at Swinton and one at Walkden. At Swinton there is also a Methodist Free Church. The Independent Methodists have a chapel at Roe Green,[151] and another at Swinton.

The Congregationalists have two churches at Swinton ; also one at Sindsley Mount and another at Walkden.[152]

At Swinton is a Unitarian Free Church.[153]

The Swedenborgians built a church at Worsley in 1849.

At Swinton is the Roman Catholic church of St. Mary of the Immaculate Conception, opened in 1859.

PENDLETON

Penelton, 1199 ; Pennelton, 1212 ; Penilton, 1236 ; Penhulton, 1331 ; Penulton, 1356, contracted into Pelton ; Pendleton, c. 1600.

This township measures about 2½ miles from the Irwell on the east to Gilda Brook on the west ; the area is 2,253⅜ acres.[1] From a ridge of higher land which juts into the centre from the north-west the ground slopes away to the north-east, east, and south. The greatest height is 230 ft. above sea level. The population in 1901 was 66,574.

The great road from Manchester to Bolton, with a branch to Wigan, crosses the township in a north-west direction. From it several other roads branch off ; one goes west to Eccles, others north-east to Broughton, and from these a road runs north-west to Agecroft in Pendlebury. The Lancashire and Yorkshire Company's railways from Manchester to Bolton and to Hindley pass through, the former having a station at Pendleton, and to Hindley pass through, the former having a station at Pendleton, and the latter at Broad Street, Pendleton, and at Irlams-o'-th'-Height.[2] The two lines effect a junction on the south-east border of the township. The London and North-Western Company's Manchester and Liverpool line crosses the southern part of the township, and has two stations—Seedley and Weaste. The Manchester and Bolton Canal goes along by the side of the former railway. From Hope Hall to Pendleton a band of

the Permian Rocks divides the New Red Sandstone to the south from the Coal Measures on the north. A fault almost on the line of the Manchester and Bolton Canal has left the New Red Sandstone in evidence on the eastern side.

The supposed camp at Hyle Wood, in the northern bend of the Irwell, has been found to be a natural hill. The Roman road from Manchester to Wigan passed through Weaste and Hope. There was formerly a cross on Pendleton Green.[3]

In 1666 there were 138 hearths liable to the tax ; the largest house was that of John Hollinpriest, with nine, but there were several with five hearths each.[4] The Pendleton morris dancers occur in 1792.[5]

In 1833 there were cotton mills, with dyeing, printing, and bleaching establishments, also a flax mill upon an improved principle ; others of the people were employed in silk manufacture and others in the neighbouring collieries. Most of these industries still remain in the township. The Spence Alum Works were removed to Newton Heath in 1857 in consequence of a law suit.

A large portion of the surface is covered with dwelling-houses and factories. Pendleton being a suburb of Salford, the whole township was taken into the borough in 1852 ; a small part was added to Eccles in 1891. The township is divided into six wards—St. Thomas's, St. Paul's, Charlestown, Hope, Seedley, and Weaste. Charleston and Douglas Green occupy the northern corner, Irlams-o'-th'-Height the north-west ; Paddington lies on the eastern border, Little Bolton to the south-west, Weaste in the south, and Wallness on the north-east. Chaseley and Seedley lie between Pendleton and Weaste ; and Hope Hall and Buile Hill to the west. Brindle Heath, formerly Brindlache, lies on the western edge of the urban part of Pendleton proper.

Pendleton Town Hall was built in 1868. A Mechanics' Institution was founded in 1856. A small library was established in 1829,[6] but does not seem to have continued. A branch of the Salford library was opened in 1878 at Pendleton, another branch at Weaste in 1894, and a third at Irlams-o'-th'-Height in 1901. A reading room was opened at Charlestown in 1894.[6a]

A park at Buile Hill has been acquired by the corporation.[7] The mansion-house there was in 1906 converted into a natural history museum. The David Lewis recreation-ground lies on the eastern side of the township, bordering on the Irwell. The new Manchester Race-course is a little distance to the

---

[149] An Anglican Sunday School was opened as early as 1784, but after thirty years fell into the hands of the Wesleyans. St. Paul's Chapel was a foretaste of the great public benefactions of the first Earl of Ellesmere. An Act was passed in 1840 to enable the Bridgewater Trustees to endow it, and it was consecrated in 1841. There is a churchyard. For district see *Lond. Gaz.* 28 July 1863, and 20 Feb. 1877.

[150] For district, ibid. 20 Feb. 1877.

[151] A manufacturer named Richard Clarke turned part of his house into a small chapel ; when the Independent Methodist chapel was built it absorbed the congregation already formed there ; information of Mr. Holme.

[152] A Congregational chapel was built in 1824 in Hilton Lane, Worsley, but it

failed about 1840. Preaching at Swinton began about 1825, from Pendlebury, and Trinity Church, built in 1882, represents the old congregation of Pendlebury. The church in Worsley Road began in 1861 through the efforts of some men of a local mill ; the building was raised in 1870 ; Nightingale, *Lancs. Nonconf.* v, 20–4.

[153] Built 1825 (or 1829) ; rebuilt 1857.

[1] 2,430, including 50 of inland water ; *Census Rep.* 1901. In 1883 a part of Pendlebury was brought within Pendleton ; Loc. Govt. Bd. Order 14672.

[2] The village so named is partly in this township and partly in Pendlebury. It took its name from one Irlam, who kept the Packhorse Inn there ; *Manch. Guardian N. and Q.* no. 392 ; *Pal. Note Bk.* ii, 174.

[3] *Lancs. and Ches. Antiq. Soc.* xxii, 104.

[4] Subs. R. Lancs. bdle. 250, no. 9.

[5] W. Axon, *Manch. Annals*, 119.

[6] Lewis, *Gaz.* (ed. 1833).

[6a] Information of Mr. B. H. Mullen, librarian.

[7] Bewle Hill is named in the *Salf. Portmote Rec* (i, 13), in 1598. On 25 Dec. 1695 Alice widow of Leftwich Oldfield leased to Edward Birch of Pendleton, whitster, a close called the Bule-hill containing 2 acres. Alice Oldfield was daughter of Richard Haworth of Manchester; Morley, *Bolton Hist. Glean.* i, 347. On 4 Jan. 1717–18 Edward Byrom of Pendleton leased to William Gregory of Pendleton, whitster, a field called the Bulehill, late in the holding of Edward Birch. Note by Mr. Crofton.

north of it.[8] There are other recreation-grounds. Claremont is the Manchester seat of Sir Arthur Percival Heywood, bart.

The worthies of Pendleton include Peter Gooden, Roman Catholic controversial writer, who died 1695 ; Felix John Vaughan Seddon, orientalist, 1798–1865 ; George Bradshaw, who published the railway guides, 1801–53 ;[9] Robert Cotton Mather, a missionary in India, 1808–77. Notices of them will be found in the *Dictionary of National Biography*.

PENDLETON was originally included MANOR in the royal manor of Salford. King John in 1199 gave it to Iorwerth de Hulton in exchange for Broughton and Kersal on the Manchester side of the Irwell, which, while Count of Mortain, he had bestowed on Iorwerth.[10] It was assessed as four oxgangs of land, and held by the service of a sixth part of a knight's fee.[11] It remained for about fifty years in the Hultons' possession ;[12] but was in 1251 exchanged for Ordsall in Salford and

part of Flixton.[13] Robert de Ferrers ten years later granted Pendleton to the priory of St. Thomas the Martyr, Stafford.[14] The right of the prior was called in question in 1292,[15] but was soon afterwards allowed,[16] and the house retained possession until the Dissolution.[17]

Pendleton, as part of the priory estates, was in 1539 granted to Rowland Lee, Bishop of Lichfield.[18] On his death his property was divided among his four nephews, and the priory site, together with the manor of Pendleton, went to Bryan Fowler,[19] whose descendants enjoyed it down to the beginning of the 18th century. The family, who adhered to the old religion, do not seem to have resided at Pendleton, nor is there much sign of their connexion with the place. Walter Fowler, the great-grandson of Bryan, took the king's side in the Civil War, and the 'well affected inhabitants of Stafford' complained of him to the Parliament 'not only as a Papist, but a malignant, because he took up arms for the king and abused and

---

[8] It was opened in 1902. Races had been held on the same ground from 1847 to 1868. Mr. J. L. Purcell FitzGerald, the landowner, refused to renew the lease on moral grounds ; 'he took a warm interest in the evangelization of the masses' ; W. Axon, *Annals of Manch.* 372.

[9] On the origin of the *Guide* in 1839 see *N. and Q.* (Ser. 6), xi, 16.

[10] *Chart. R.* (Rec. Com.), 27 ; the gift was of 'the vill of Pendleton and all its appurtenances' to be held 'by the service of the sixth part of one knight.' See also Farrer, *Lancs. Pipe R.* 112, 115, &c.

[11] *Lancs. Inq. and Extents* (Rec. Soc. Lancs. and Ches.), i, 65.

[12] In 1218 Richard de Hulton had not paid the 20 marks relief on succeeding his father Iorwerth at Pendleton ; *Rot. Lit. Claus.* (Rec. Com.), i, 380. To Eccles Church he gave a piece of land in Pendleton, on the west side of the road to Pendlebury, as a site for the tithe-barn; no one was to dwell in it ; *Whalley Couch.* (Chet. Soc.), i, 52.

In 1236 Richard de Hulton, and in 1242 the heirs of Richard de Hulton, held the sixth part of a fee in Pendleton ; *Lancs. Inq. and Extents*, i, 144, 153. It is noteworthy that in 1256 the Hultons' estate was described as a plough-land and half a plough-land only, as recorded in 1212 ; *Final Conc.* (Rec. Soc. Lancs. and Ches.), i, 122. As late as 1302 Richard de Hulton was recorded as holding the sixth part of a fee in Pendleton, but this is a duplication (in error) of his tenement in Ordsall and Flixton, which is also given ; *Lancs. Inq. and Extents*, i, 314.

[13] William de Ferrers, Earl of Derby, granted to David de Hulton his land in Flixton and manor of Ordsall in 1251 ; Gregson, *Fragments* (ed. Harland), 347.

[14] The grant in frankalmoign was made in Dec. 1261 ; it included the manor of Swineshurst and of the Walneys (now Wallness) by Salford, with the mill on the Irwell, &c., the town of Pendleton with all the villeins holding the villeinage of the town, their chattels, and sequel ; Phillips MS. 7899, printed in *Staff. Coll.* viii.

The bounds of the waste of the New Hall by Saltfield and of Pendleton about the same time were as follows :—From Wallness Pool to Broad Oak Snape, fol-

lowing the lache to Wetsnape, by the Rowe Lache to Saltfield Clow as far as Wolfhays meanigate ; thence by the high road [? to Eccles] to Little Leyhead and thence to Gildenaver Ford [Gilda Brook] and so by Tippesbrook [Folly Brook] to Bispeslowe [? Irlams-o'-th'-Height], thence by the Black Lache to Alwine Mere and Redford, and by the syke under Pendlebury Park to the Irwell, and down this to the starting-point ; *Coll. Topog. et Gen.* i, 248.

In 1284 the king granted the Prior and convent of St. Thomas free warren in their demesne lands of Swineshurst; *Chart. R.* 77, m. 6, no. 45. For a further licence see *Cal. Pat.* 1292–1301, p. 146.

There is a brief notice of St. Thomas's Priory in Dugdale, *Mon.* vi, 471. Some charters and notes will be found in *Staff. Coll.* (Wm. Salt Soc.), viii, 125–201, referred to above.

[15] *Plac. de Quo War.* (Rec. Com.), 386. The estate was eighteen messuages, twelve oxgangs (i.e. a plough-land and a half) and 120 acres of land, a toft, and a mill, held by the sixth part of a knight's fee. Master John de Craven was in possession. It was asserted that the grant to the priory had been made without the king's licence. The sheriff took possession, and returned the annual value as £18 13s. 4d. ; ibid. 228.

[16] The king confirmed the grant of Robert de Ferrers in Aug. 1295 ; *Cal. Pat.* 1292–1301, p. 146.

A curious claim was made in 1292. Agnes widow of David de Hulton claimed dower in Pendleton, on the ground that the tenements in Flixton and Ordsall which William de Ferrers had given her in exchange for Pendleton were not of equal value. The jury agreed, finding Pendleton the more valuable by £6 a year, and averred that Agnes should retain her dower in Flixton and have a further 40s. a year from Pendleton ; Assize R. 408, m. 39. This claim appears as early as 1285 ; De Banco R. 59, m. 31. Possibly there were other suits, for in 1302 she surrendered her right in return for an annuity of 44s., to be paid by the prior out of Pendleton ; *Staff. Coll.* viii.

In 1324 account was given of 15s. of the farm of eight oxgangs of land which Sir Robert de Holland had in farm of the prior of St. Thomas, among Sir Robert's

other forfeited lands ; L.T.R. Enr. Accts. Misc. no. 14, m. 76 d. (2).

[17] Maud de Worsley in 1332 granted to the prior her interest in lands, &c., in Pendleton, Newhall, Woodhouses, Wallness, and Swineshurst ; *Staff. Coll.* viii. Henry, Earl of Lancaster, in 1339 gave the prior 12 acres of heath in Salford and Pendleton as recompense for the priory's common of pasture on the heath ; Duchy of Lanc. Anct. D. L, 2084. To the aid levied 1346–55 the Prior of St. Thomas contributed 6s. 8d. for the sixth part of a knight's fee, held in free alms ; *Feud. Aids*, iii, 91. In the survey of 1346 a rent of 11¾d. was charged for one ploughland held by the prior ; this reappears in an extent made a century later, the prior stating that he held in frankalmoign and not in socage ; Add. MS. 32103, fol. 146 ; Duchy of Lanc. Knights' fees, 2/20. In 1525 the prior demised lands in Pendleton to Ottiwell Wirrall for a term ; *Staff. Coll.* viii.

[18] Pat. 31 Hen. VIII, pt. vi ; see *L. and P.* xiv (2), 156.

[19] The account of the Fowlers is in the main taken from Gillow, *St. Thomas's Priory*, where a pedigree of the family is given, 147–57.

Bishop Lee (see *Dict. Nat. Biog.*) died in 1543. His sister Isabel had married Roger Fowler of Broomhill, Norfolk, and the four nephews were Rowland of Broomhill, Bryan, William of Harnage Grange, Shropshire, and James of Pendeford, Staffordshire.

Bryan Fowler in 1547 took action against Robert Shaw, the king's farmer, respecting Brindlache and other lands in Pendleton ; *Ducatus Lanc.* (Rec. Com.), ii, 93. He was frequently presented for recusancy, and died in 1587. By his wife Jane, daughter and heir of John Hanmer of Bettisfield, he had a son Walter, who died in 1621, leaving a son Edward, father of the Walter Fowler named in the text.

Inquisitions are extant taken after the death of Bryan Fowler, whose son Walter was thirty-six years of age in 1588 ; and of Walter Fowler, who died in 1621, leaving a son and heir Edward, aged thirty. The tenure of Pendleton is not stated ; Chan. Inq. p.m. ii, 216, 393. Edward Fowler died in Nov. 1623, holding the manor of Pendleton, and leaving a son and heir Walter, only three years old ; ibid. (Ser. ii), vol. 404, no. 126.

cruelly ill-treated the adherents to Parliament ; yet he was sequestered only as a recusant, and he undervalued his estate, which was worth £1,500 a year.'[20] His lands in the counties of Stafford, Lancaster, Chester, Derby, and Flint were declared forfeit and sold for the benefit of the Navy.[21] As in other cases, however, they were recovered,[22] and he was succeeded by his sons Walter and William. The latter, the last male representative of the family, died in 1717. By his first will, dated 1712, he left his estates to his niece Katherine, wife of John Betham, who took the name of Fowler, and as a 'papist' registered his estate in 1717, Pendleton being included.[23] He left as heir an only daughter Katherine, who in 1726 married Thomas Belasyse, fourth Viscount Fauconberg.[24]

William Fowler had, however, secretly made a second will in 1715, by which a nephew, Thomas Grove, son of the testator's elder sister Dorothy, became entitled to a moiety of the estate. This will was at first overlooked,[25] but brought forward in 1729, and, after a suit in Chancery, and an appeal to the House of Lords, was established ; Rebecca, the

daughter and heir of Thomas Grove, being in 1733 declared co-heir.[26] She had married Richard Fitz-Gerald, an Irish barrister.[27] 'Dying sine prole, he bequeathed the manor of Pendleton . . . and certain other Fowler estates in Staffordshire, to his relatives the FitzGeralds, who still retain possession.'[28] The present representative of the family is Mr. Gerald Purcell FitzGerald, of the Island, Waterford, who owns a considerable estate in the township.

The HOPE in Pendleton appears to be the estate of two oxgangs of land held by Ellis de Pendlebury in 1212 by Iorwerth de Hulton by a rent of 4s.[29] It was afterwards held by the Radcliffes, who succeeded the Hultons at Ordsall, but by the greatly increased service of £4 2s.[30] It seems to have been acquired by a branch of the Bradshaw family.[31] In the 18th century it was purchased by Daniel Bayley of Manchester, whose son succeeded him ; but it was again sold on the latter's death in 1802.[32]

BRINDLACHE, a name represented by Brindle Heath, was leased and then purchased by the Langleys of Agecroft.[33] Windlehey descended with this

---

[20] Cal. of Com. for Compounding, iii, 1891–6. Among other complaints against him was one that he, 'being admitted tenant to his own estate, put the tenants to rack rents "to screw up the fifths."' In 1654 there was granted the discharge from sequestration of lands in Pendleton Pool, Eccles Parish, bought by John Wildman. In 1651 Constance wife of Walter Fowler had been allowed her fifth of her husband's sequestrated estate ; ibid. v, 3289.
[21] Index of Royalists (Index Soc.), 30.
[22] A pedigree was recorded in 1663 ; Staffs. Coll. (Wm. Salt Soc.), v (2), 134–7. Walter Fowler died in 1684, and his son Walter about 1695.
[23] Estcourt and Payne, Engl. Cath. Nonjurors, 115. Katherine, who died in 1725, was the daughter of William Fowler's younger sister Magdalen, whose husband's name was Cassey.
[24] In a fine of 1733, after the decision of the lawsuit narrated in the text, the deforciants of the manor of Pendleton alias Pendleton Pool, and lands there, were Thomas, Viscount Fauconberg, and Katherine his wife ; Pal. of Lanc. Feet of F. bdle. 307, m. 130.
[25] The will remained in the custody of the lawyer who drew it up, Christopher Ward of Stafford. After his death it was discovered by his son Edward, who communicated with Lord Aston, the principal Fowler trustee, and he in turn laid it before Richard FitzGerald, who saw that Rebecca Grove would be entitled to a moiety of the estate at her father's death, and married her ; Gillow, op. cit. 73, quoting Clifford's Par. of Tixall, 39.
[26] The father had died during the progress of the suit.
It is said to have been disgust at the result of the suit that led Lord Fauconberg to sell his Lancashire estates and renounce his religion ; but Smithills had been sold earlier ; he conformed to the Established Church in 1737, being rewarded with an earldom. He is said to have returned to the Roman communion on his death-bed, 1774.
[27] He was the eldest son of Colonel Nicholas FitzGerald, who was slain at the battle of the Boyne, fighting for Jas. II. In a fine relating to the moiety of

Pendleto and Reb Pal of L
[28] Gill
[29] Lan also Pipe
[30] Am Robert d of Hope, 62s. 2d. no. 14, of Ordsa

estate.[34] A branch of the Holland family was seated at Newhall in Pendleton.[35]

In 1423 Robert Orrell and Margaret his wife made a settlement of their estate in Salford, Pendleton, and Pendlebury.[36]

LITTLE BOLTON, held by William de Bolton in 1200, was assessed as six oxgangs of land, and held of the king in chief in fee farm by a rent of 18s.[37] The Boltons were about 1350 succeeded by the Gawen family, who continued to hold the whole or part for about two centuries.[38] The more recent history is uncertain. The Valentines of Bentcliffe acquired two-thirds;[39] and the Goodens or Gooldens, a recusant family, were seated here in the 16th and 17th centuries.[40]

Act of Resumption of 1464, a £10 annuity was secured to Thomas Langley, granted by letters patent on farms in Pendleton and pastures called Brindlache and Windlehey; *Rolls of Parl.* v, 247.

In 1539 Henry VIII gave a lease of Brindlache and Windlehey to Robert Langley at 42s. rent, but six years afterwards he sold the land for £42; Agecroft D. no. 111, 112, 116, 117. For a complaint against Robert Langley in 1546 respecting this land see *Duchy Plead.* (Rec. Soc. Lancs. and Ches.), ii, 214.

[34] By settlements of 1561 Brindlache and Windlehey, with a slight exception, were to descend to Anne daughter of Robert Langley of Agecroft, with remainder to another daughter, Margaret wife of John Reddish; Agecroft D. no. 132, 129.

In 1623 it was found that William Dauntesey of Agecroft held Windlehey of the king by a rent of 12d.; *Lancs. Inq. p.m.* (Rec. Soc. Lancs. and Ches.), iii, 349.

[35] The origin of this branch of the Holland family is unknown.

In 1534 the Prior of St. Thomas's leased to Otho son of George Holland of Eccles land in Pendleton; the term was eighty years, but renewable up to 240 years; Clowes D. (recited in a deed of 1719). Otho Holland contributed, 'for goods,' to the subsidy of 1541; *Misc.* (Rec. Soc. Lancs. and Ches.), i, 141. In 1597 Otho Holland of Newhall was contracted to marry Katherine daughter of George Linne of Southwick, Notts.; Clowes D.

Otho Holland died in 1620 seised of Garthall Houses in Pendleton, with land attached, held of the king as of his manor of Salford by a rent of 4d. His heir was his son George, not quite of age; *Lancs. Inq. p.m.* (Rec. Soc. Lancs. and Ches.), ii, 218.

In 1699 Sir Edward Coke of Langford leased Drinkwater's tenement in Pendleton to Otho Holland, who agreed, among other things, 'to plant yearly during the term in some part of. the premises four good plants of oak, ash, or elm, and eight more boughs of poplar, and to do his best to preserve them from spoil'; Manch. Free Lib. D. no. 109. Alice widow and executrix of Otho Holland was party to a deed in 1715 providing for the issue of his daughters—Mary wife of Robert Cooke; Elizabeth wife of John Fletcher; and Alice wife of Robert Philips; ibid. no. 111.

In later times what was called the Old Hall was a residence built about 1760, and in the possession of the Barrow family; while the New Hall, pulled down in 1872, was a farm-house, built in 1640 on the site, as it is supposed, of an older house.

[36] *Final Conc.* iii, 89.

[37] King John while Count of Mortain made a grant of this estate to William son of Adam, and confirmed it in 1201, after he had come to the throne; *Chart. R.* 90b; *Lancs. Pipe R.* 132. In 1212 William de Bolton was dead, and his heir was

in ward of the k one oxgang only; i, 71. The wardsh de Pendlebury in (Rec. Com.), 25 Cockersand Willi ton granted the T Bolton, the bound ley) syke, the carr clough, Brendoak ditch, and Bradley including quittan pigs, were also all ii, 703

Richard son o curs in 1241; *Fi* another Richard Bolton in thegnag a year; Dods. About the same t granted to his so which Richard th gether with half the hamlet of B dleton, his capita near the Pool b Vawdrey D. In to his son Henry let of L'ttle Bolto

In 1332 Hen Bolton w s pla'n

WEASTE, i.e. the Waste, is mentioned in the year 1570.[41]

Humphrey Booth of Salford,[42] Roger Downes of Wardley,[43] and Richard Pendleton,[44] held lands in the township in the time of Charles I. In 1784 the principal landowners were John FitzGerald, John Gore Booth, and Thomas Butterworth Bayley ; Miss Byrom, Thomas Chorlton of Weaste, — Valentine, — Calvert, and many others had smaller shares.[45]

The Duchy of Lancaster has an estate in Pendleton ; the rents in 1858 amounted to over £1,000.[46]

In 1444 there was a serious affray at Pendleton, several men being killed.[47]

A chantry chapel was founded in Pendleton about 1220, but nothing further seems known of it.[48]

A considerable number of churches have been erected in modern times, to accommodate the growing population. In connexion with the Established Church the first St. Thomas's, at Brindle Heath, was acquired in 1776 and the second was built on the present site in 1831 ;[49] the old building is used as a chapel of ease, and called St. Anne's ; the Vicar of Eccles is patron of this. The Crown and the Bishop of Manchester present alternately to St. Paul's, Paddington, built in 1856.[50] St. George's, Charlestown, was built in 1858 ;[51] St. James's, Hope, in 1861 ;[52] St. Luke's, Weaste, in 1865 ;[53] St. Barnabas's and St. Ambrose's, both in 1887. The Bishop of Manchester collates to St. George's and St. Barnabas's ; St. James's and St. Luke's are in the gift of trustees.

The Wesleyans are said to have been the first possessors of old St. Thomas's, built about 1760 ; they now have a church dating from 1814, and four others more recently built. The United Free Methodists have three churches, the Primitive Methodists and the New Connexion two each, and the Independent Methodists one.

The Congregationalists had a preaching station at Irlams-o'-th'-Height about 1825, but no permanent church followed at that time. At Charlestown a Sunday school was begun in 1829, and next year public services were held, a church being formed in 1836 ; a place of worship in Broad Street was built in 1847–9. At Charlestown itself a church was built in 1864, and a school chapel at Seedley ten years later.[54] At Weaste is the Lightbowne memorial church.

The Baptists have a chapel here. The Society of Friends have also a meeting-place.

At Seedley Grove is a place of worship of the Presbyterian Church of England, founded in 1871.

The Swedenborgians have a temple called New Jerusalem in Broad Street.

The Roman Catholic Church of the Mother of God and St. James, Seedley, was built in 1875 ; the mission began in 1858. All Souls', Weaste, was opened in 1892. In 1898 the Dominicans took over the struggling mission of St. Charles in the north of the township, and have built the church of St. Sebastian.

---

died seised of various lands in Little Bolton held of the king as of his manor of Salford in socage by a rent of 31. 4d. ; also of lands in Monton and Winton ; *Lancs. Inq. p.m.* (Rec. Soc. Lancs. and Ches.), ii, 209. Edmund his son and heir, then twenty-two years of age, died a year after his father, leaving as heir his daughter Ellen, eighteen months old ; his widow Ellen was living at Little Bolton ; ibid. ii, 242. By virtue of a settlement recited in the inquisition the estate passed to Thomas Gooden, younger brother of Edmund, with remainders to Richard, John, and Peter Gooden. Thomas Gooden contributed as a landowner to the subsidy of 1622 ; *Misc.* (Rec. Soc. Lancs. and Ches.), i, 154. In 1631 he paid £10 as composition for declining knighthood ; ibid. i, 215.

Thomas Gooden, a recusant and delinquent, was in 1651 suspected of having borne arms for the king, and his estate was sequestrated by the Parliament ; whereupon he petitioned. His brother John had been wounded by some of Prince Rupert's men. Another man altogether, Lieut. Gooden, had taken part in the defence of Lathom house ; *Cal. of Com. for Compounding*, iv, 2723, 3160 ; *Royalist Comp. Papers* (Rec. Soc. Lancs. and Ches.), iii, 81, 86. Thomas Gooden of Little Bolton, Edmund his son (of Trafford), and Thomas Gooden of Pendlebury occur in a deed of 1664. Richard Gooden of Pendlebury, as a 'papist,' registered an estate in Manchester in 1717 ; Estcourt and Payne, *Engl. Cath. Nonjurors*, 153. See also *Hist. MSS. Com. Rep.* xiv, App. iv, 110.

In 1738 Thomas Gooden had lands in Pendleton in the Old Hall (now the New Hall) and Walness ; he was the grandnephew of Thomas Gooden of Pendleton; Piccope MSS. (Chet. Lib.), iii, 262, from Roll 12 of Geo. II at Preston. At the

expiry of a lease of the Old Hall in 1774 the tenant was of the same name ; *Manch. Guardian N. and Q.* no. 1123. Three years later Little Bolton Hall was sold by Dorothy sister and heir of Thomas Gooden and wife of Albert Hodshon of Leighton, to Thomas Worsley ; Dorothy had two daughters—Mary wife of Ralph Standish of Standish, and Anne ; the former had a portion of £2,000 ; ibid. iii, 342, 344, from Roll 15 of Geo. II. In the same volume (p. 236) is the will of Richard Gooden of Pendlebury, 1728 ; he had lands in Barton, Tottington, Pendlebury, and Stretford ; Richard and other sons are named.

In 1741 Thomas Starky of Preston sold to Thomas Worsley the capital messuage called Little Bolton Hall ; ibid. iii, 344, from Roll 15 of Geo. II. Samuel Worsley paid a rent of 9l. 11d. to the duchy for Little Bolton in 1779 ; Duchy of Lanc. Rentals, 14/25.

[41] John Gawen of Worsley and Robert Barlow of Little Bolton were under bond in 1570 to allow Thomas Tyldesley and Margery his wife to occupy the mansion-house called the Waste in Little Bolton lately held by Ralph Malbon, former husband of Margery ; John Gawen, however, repudiated his liability ; Vawdrey D.

Kuerden (iii, P 3) has preserved a grant by William Benastre to Roger del Wood and Isabel his wife, of Salefield under Pendleton and adjoining Little Bolton.

[42] Duchy of Lanc. Inq. p.m. xxvii, 44 ; messuages and lands in Pendleton, Pendlebury, Little Bolton, &c., held of the king as of his manor of Salford.

[43] Ibid. xxvii, 54.

[44] Ibid. xxix, 52 ; 4 acres held of the king as of his manor of Salford in socage.

[45] Land Tax Returns at Preston.

[46] House of Commons Return, 5, 6. The report also gives particulars of a number of sales of land.

PENDLEBURY

Penelbiri, 1201 ; Pennilbure, 1212 ; Pennebire, 1226 ; Pennesbyry, 1278 ; Penilburi, 1300 ; Penulbury, 1332 ; Penhulbury, 1358 ; Pendulbury, 1561; Pendlebury, 1567.

Lying on the west bank of the Irwell between Clifton and Pendleton, but with a detached part—the ancient Shoresworth— to the south of Pendleton, this township has an area of 1,030½ acres.[1] The town proper lies in the north-west part of the district, while Agecroft Hall stands apart upon the Irwell in the north-east corner. The surface of the land slopes generally from west to east, from nearly 300 ft. to about 120 ft. above the ordnance datum. The population in 1901 was 8,493.

The principal road is that from Manchester to Bolton, from which the ancient Wigan road parts company near the southern boundary ; a cross road leads through Agecroft by a bridge over the Irwell to Prestwich, and near the bridge another road from Manchester joins it. The Lancashire and Yorkshire Company's line from Manchester to Bolton runs north-westward, and that from Manchester to Hindley also crosses the township, and has two stations— Irlams-o'-th'-Height and Pendlebury. The former nearly follows the line of a fault which brings up the Coal Measures to the west, leaving the New Red Sandstone in evidence to the east. The Manchester and Bolton Canal runs along the easterly side of the former line, between it and the River Irwell.

There were thirty-five hearths liable to the tax in 1666. Agecroft Hall was the only large house, having eleven hearths.[2]

The manufacture and printing of cottons have long been the principal industries.

Pendlebury was joined with Swinton in 1875 to form a local board district ; it is now governed by the Swinton and Pendlebury Urban District Council.[3] The Public Hall was built in 1870. The detached portion of the township was, with Pendleton, included in the borough of Salford in 1852. One of the Salford cemeteries is at Agecroft and another at New Barns. The great children's hospital on the south-west side was erected in 1873.

An ancient Campfield exists in the detached part of Pendlebury near Salford ; and a neolithic hammer axe was found at Mode Wheel in the excavations for the Manchester Ship Canal.[4]

The manors of *PENDLEBURY* and *SHORESWORTH* were in 1212 held of the king in chief in thegnage by a rent of 12s.[5] The tenant was Ellis son of Robert de Pendlebury, to whom King John had granted Pendlebury while he was Count of Mortain, confirming or renewing the grant when he obtained the throne.[6] Ellis was also master serjeant of the wapentake of Salford, and this office, like the manor, was to descend to his heirs.[7] Ellis was a benefactor of Cockersand Abbey.[8] He died in or about 1216, and his son Adam succeeded him in his manors and serjeanty.[9] But little is known of him, and his son Roger appears to have been in possession in 1246 and 1254.[10] He also was a benefactor of Cockersand.[11] At this stage of the descent there is some difficulty. In 1274 Ellis son of Roger came to a violent death,[12] and Amabel, as widow of Ellis son of Roger the Clerk, claimed dower in various lands against Roger de Pendlebury.[13] Again, a short time afterwards, Amabel having received her dower, she and Roger de Pendlebury had to defend a suit brought by one Adam de Pendlebury, who satisfied the jury of his title to the manor.[14]

Ellis had a brother William and daughters Maud, Lettice, and Beatrice. Maud married Adam son of Alexander de Pilkington, and had a daughter Cecily.[15]

MANORS

[1] This includes the detached part, now included in Pendleton. The census report of 1901 gives only 866 acres, including 36 of inland water, for the reduced township.

[2] Subs. R. Lancs. bdle. 250, no. 9.

[3] See Worsley.

[4] *Lancs. and Ches. Antiq. Soc.* x, 251.

[5] *Lancs. Inq. and Extents* (Rec. Soc. Lancs. and Ches.), i, 68. Pendlebury was assessed as one plough-land, and Shoresworth as an oxgang ; the separate rent of the former was 10s.

[6] *Chart. R.* (Rec. Com.), 26. This grant is among the Agecroft D. (no. 1). It concerns Pendlebury only, one ploughland ' in free thegnage by the free service of 10s. yearly.' Ellis de Pendlebury's other lands, as shown by the survey of 1212, were Shoresworth (1 oxgang), Hope in Pendleton (2 oxgangs), and Snydale in Westhoughton (? 1 oxgang) ; *Lancs. Inq. and Extents,* i, 68, 65, 58. He also had lands in Westhoughton, which went to Thomas, a younger son. Robert de Pendlebury, probably the father of Ellis, raised a dyke in Westhoughton ; *Cockersand Chart.* (Chet. Soc.), ii, 679.

[7] *Chart. R.* 27. Ellis is mentioned in the Pipe Rolls down to 1208 ; Farrer, *Lancs. Pipe R.* 151, 232, &c.

[8] *Cockersand Chartul.* ii, 688—grant of Priestcroft in Westhoughton.

[9] Ellis de Pendlebury and Adam his son were witnesses to a grant by Gilbert de Notton and Edith his wife ; *Whalley Couch.* (Chet. Soc.), i, 47. Adam de Pendlebury is named in 1216 ; *Rot. Lit. Claus.* (Rec. Com.), 251. He succeeded his father as serjeant of Salfordshire in 1218 (ibid. 366) ; but this office had been lost by 1222 ; *Lancs. Inq. and Extents,* i, 133. In October 1219 the king ordered livery to Adam, who had done homage, of the lands his father Ellis had held, viz., a plough-land in Pendlebury and the fourth part of an oxgang in Shoresworth ; *Fine R. Excerpts,* i, 38. 'The farm of the land of Adam de Pendlebury in Pendlebury,' 10s., occurs in 1226, but Adam may have been dead ; *Lancs. Inq. and Extents,* i, 137.

[10] Roger is mentioned in Assize R. 404, m. 1 ; *Lancs. Inq. and Extents,* i, 193 ; *Cockersand Chartul.* ii, 676. He granted land in Westhoughton to Richard son of Geoffrey de Byron, held about 1244 by Geoffrey and by Thomas, brothers of Richard ; *Whalley Couch.* i, 66, 62.

[11] He gave all his land in Westhoughton; *Cockersand Chartul.* ii, 677.

[12] *Cal. Close,* 1272-9, p. 97.

[13] De Banco R. 5, m. 102. It seems probable that Roger the Clerk was Roger the son of Adam de Pendlebury, while the defendant Roger was a trustee for the daughters of Ellis. Amabel's claim was for the third part of 11 oxgangs, 16 acres of land, two-thirds of an oxgang, the half of two mills, and two-thirds of one mill with appurtenances in Pendlebury, Pendleton, Whittleswick, and Halliwell. At the same time she sought dower in 26 acres in Clifton, the holder being Alice daughter of William the Clerk of Eccles. Roger de Pendlebury granted Whittleswick to his son Ellis, and the latter regranted it to his father ; De Trafford D. no. 276, 278. This Roger seems to be the 'clerk' of Amabel's plea. The Clerks of Eccles appear here as in Whittleswick.

Among the Holland of Denton deeds are some further illustrations of the pedigree. Thus William son of Roger de Pendlebury made a grant in Sharples of lands which should come to him after the death of his brother Ellis's daughter Maud; Harl. MS. 2112, fol. 145b/181b. Lettice and Beatrice, other daughters, also occur ; ibid. fols. 160b/196b, 145b/181b.

[14] Assize R. 1238 (6 Edw. I), m. 31 d. It was ordered that Amabel should receive equivalent land for dower from Roger. Drailesden, the Mill ridding, and half of a mill were excepted from the disseisin by Roger.

[15] From pleas relating to Whittleswick, cited by Mr. Bird in the *Ancestor,* pt. iv, 211, it appears that Maud daughter and heir of Ellis recovered land, &c., there in 1284 ; Assize R. 1265, m. 21 d. She was dead in 1291, when William de Pendlebury, as uncle and heir, claimed it from Adam de Pilkington, who said he had an estate for life because his wife Maud had borne him a daughter Cecily. William asserted that the child was stillborn, but the jury found that she lived a short time and was baptized ; Assize R. 1294, m. 8 d.

The manor was sold before 1300 to Adam de Prestwich.[16]

The new lord of Pendlebury married Alice de Woolley daughter of Richard son of Master Henry de Pontefract,[17] the eventual heir being a daughter Alice, wife of Jordan de Tetlow. Her heir also proved to be a daughter, Joan, who married Richard de Langley,[18] and the manor descended regularly in this family until the end of the 16th century. Joan de Langley died in or before 1374, and her son and heir Roger being a minor the sheriff took possession of the manors. Roger himself died in 1393, holding the manor of Pendlebury as one plough-land by a rent of 16s., and a messuage called Agecroft, the family seat, by a rent of 6s. 8d. Again the heir was a minor, Roger's son Robert being fifteen years of age, but already married to Katherine daughter of Sir William de Atherton.[19]

Robert Langley died in April 1447, seised of the manors of Pendlebury and Prestwich, and

LANGLEY of Agecroft.
Argent a cockatrice sable beaked or.

various other lands ; Thomas Langley his son and heir was then forty years of age.[20] Another son, Ralph, was rector of Prestwich and warden of Manchester. There was a third son, John.[21] Thomas had a son John, who succeeded him [22] in the manors and died in 1496, leaving a son and heir Robert about forty years old.[23] Dying in 1527, holding the manor of Pendlebury in socage by a rent of 16s. yearly, besides other manors and lands, he was succeeded by his grandson Robert son of Thomas Langley, the last of the male line in possession.[24] Robert was made a knight in 1547,[25] and died 19 September 1561, leaving four daughters as co-heirs.[26] On the division of the estates, Agecroft and lands in Pendlebury became the portion of Anne,[27] who married William Dauntesey, springing from a Wiltshire family.[28] The ' manor ' of Pendlebury also was claimed by the Daunteseys for some time,[29] but was afterwards said to be held with Prestwich, descend-

received the Crimbles, Anesley, the Lumns, &c.

Robert de Langley proved his age in 1403. John de Langton stated that Robert was born at Huntingdon on 6 June 1379, and baptized at Eccles by Robert de Monton, Robert de Worsley and Ellen Gawen being sponsors ; he remembered because he was present in the church at the obit of Robert Johnson ; Towneley's MS. DD, no. 1466.

In 1416 Robert de Langley leased to Piers de Holland for life lands called the Wete Park in Agecroft, which Piers thereupon leased to Robert for eighty years ; Agecroft D. no. 70–1.

[20] Dep. Keeper's Rep. xxxix, App. 541. Pendlebury was held in socage as 1 ploughland by a rent of 10s., and the residue of the manor by a rent of 6s. 8d. Margaret, the widow of Roger, was still living and in possession of Tetlow, which would revert to Katherine, the widow of Robert. Thomas Langley, the son, was in 1412 contracted to marry Margaret daughter of Sir John Ashton ; Piers and James, brothers of Thomas, are mentioned ; Agecroft D. no. 60. Thomas and Margaret were married in 1419 ; ibid. no. 74.

[21] Thomas and John Langley were living in 1470, when the latter was defendant in an Alkrington case, in which the fine of 1313, with pedigree, was recited ; Pal. of Lanc. Plea R. 37, m. 12 d. ; also R. 55, m. 7, where John Langley is called the son of Robert.

[22] Thomas Langley died 20 Jan. 1471–2, seised of the manors of Pendlebury and Prestwich, the advowson of Prestwich Church, and of various lands. The tenure of Pendlebury is stated exactly as in the preceding inquisition. John Langley, his son and heir, was forty-two years of age, and had married Maud daughter of James Radcliffe ; Agecroft D. no. 80, 81.

In 1475 John Langley enfeoffed Ralph Langley, warden of Manchester, of all his manors, &c. ; Thomas son of John was one of the attorneys to deliver seisin ; ibid. no. 82.

[23] The inquisition (taken in 21 Hen. VII) after the death of John Langley, who is stated to have died in Aug. 1496, is given in a plea of 1511 ; Pal. of Lanc. R. 112, m. 4 ; printed in Lancs. Inq. p.m. (Chet. Soc.), ii, 145. Robert the son is said to have been fifty years of age and more at the time of the inquisition. He and his wife Eleanor daughter of William Radcliffe of Ordsall, recovered the disputed lands. Robert Langley received a general pardon from Henry VII in 1486, and an annuity of 10 marks for services rendered and to be rendered ; Agecroft D. no. 88, 89.

[24] The first part of the inquisition is torn off, but Robert Langley's will, dated 22 Feb. 1524–5, and proved 1 Apr. 1528, is printed in Wills (Rec. Soc. Lancs. and Ches.), 62. He desired to be buried in the new chapel on the south side of St. Mary's, Prestwich, and left legacies to

his younger sons Ed
his grandson and h
sisters ; also money
The executors were
late rector of Prestw
then rector, and his
bequests to Robert
appertaining unto th
wit, a chalice, a mas
for a priest to say
portatile, with o her
the altar.' The will
Robert L gl y, d
in Piccope's Wills (C

Thomas, the fathe
1504 been contrac
daughter of William
hall, and they we
when various lands i
vill of Pendleton' an
apart for Cecily ; Ag

The possessions
1528 'ncl ded the
wich (with the advo
Pendlebury, and Al
and lands in Tetlow
ton, Oldham, Mi
and S f d Th

v·

ing in the Coke family[30] until about 1780, when it was sold to Peter Drinkwater of Irwell House, Prestwich.[31]

William Dauntesey of Agecroft, who died in 1622,[32] was succeeded by a son[33] and a grandson, also named William. The last-named, a minor at his father's death in 1637, was succeeded by his brother John, who, dying about 1693,[34] was succeeded in turn by his sons William and Christopher.[35] The latter of these married Mary daughter of Sir Edward Chisenhale or Chisnall, and had several children.[36] Edward, the eldest son, was subject to fits of lunacy, and his younger brother Christopher had the management of the estates, and succeeded.[37] He left a son John, in holy orders, who resided at Agecroft[38] till his death in 1811, and bequeathed his estate to cousins, the Hulls of Chorley.[39] John son of Richard Hull had but a short enjoyment of Agecroft, dying in 1813, when he was followed by his brother-in-law, the Rev. Richard Buck, who had married Margaret Hull, and their son Robert succeeded.[40] His younger brother, John Buck, the next owner, took the name

DAUNTESEY of Agecroft. *Per fesse dancetty or and gules a lion rampant seizing upon a wyvern erect counterchanged, a bordure engrailed ermine.*

of Dauntesey in 1867,[40a] and was followed by his sister Katherine Dauntesey Foxton, who died in 1878, when Agecroft Hall passed to Robert Brown, grandson of Thomas Hull. Mr. Brown took the name of Dauntesey on succeeding. Dying in 1905 he was succeeded by his brother, Captain William Thomas Slater Hull, who also adopted the surname of Dauntesey.[40b]

Agecroft Hall stands on slightly rising ground on the west side of the Irwell valley, where the river flows southwards towards Manchester between the high ground of Kersal and Prestwich on the east and north, and Irlams-o'-th'-Height and Pendlebury on the west. The surroundings of the house are now greatly altered from what originally obtained, the colliery workings of the neighbourhood and the immediate proximity of railway and canal having almost entirely destroyed the former picturesqueness of the scenery. The hall, however, yet stands in grounds which preserve to the building something of its original country aspect, though the trees have suffered much damage from the smoke and fumes of the surrounding district.

The house is a very interesting example of timber construction standing on a low stone base with portions in brick, built round a central courtyard. The ground on the west side of the building falls precipitously, the walls standing close to the edge of the cliff. The three remaining sides are said to have been

---

[30] The manor of Pendlebury was in 1630 counted as the inheritance of Sarah Coke, who died in 1623–4 ; Duchy of Lanc. Inq. p.m. xxvi, no. 53 ; see also Pal. of Lanc. Feet of F. bdle. 179, m. 92; 217, m. 20.

[31] Baines, *Lancs.* (ed. 1870), i, 599.

[32] *Lancs. Inq. p.m.* (Rec. Soc. Lancs. and Ches.), iii, 349. The rent of 8s. is half of the old composite rent for Pendlebury. William Dauntesey died 19 May 1622, his wife Anne having died in 1618 ; William, the son and heir, was over forty years of age. He had entered Oriel College, Oxford, in 1590, giving his age as nineteen ; Foster, *Alumni.*

In 1613 a settlement was made on the marriage of William son and heir apparent of William Dauntesey and Anne his wife with Katherine daughter of Lawrence Crompton, late of Breightmet, and Alice his wife ; Roger Downes of Wardley was the principal trustee ; Agecroft D. no. 143. The subsequent fine is recited in the Inq. p.m. In 1624 William Dauntesey acknowledged the receipt of the goods due to his wife from Lawrence Crompton her brother ; Agecroft D. no. 147.

[33] William Dauntesey II paid £10 in 1631 as a composition on refusing knighthood ; *Misc.* (Rec. Soc. Lancs. and Ches.), i, 215. He died 2 Jan. 1636–7, his son and heir William being about fifteen years of age ; Duchy of Lanc. Inq. p.m. xxviii, no. 78. In 1634 he had made a settlement of Agecroft Hall and the rest of the estate, eight children being named : William, John, Mary, Anne, Elizabeth, Sarah, Alice, and Katherine. A third part having been assigned to his wife Katherine, another third given to his son William for his maintenance, and provision for the other children was to be made from the rest ; Agecroft D. no. 152. His will, dated the day of his death, mentions the £500 bequest from Sir John Dauntesey of Bishop's Lavington, a kinsman ; ibid.

no. 153, 317   Se
Soc. Lancs. and Che
T

PENDLEBURY : AGECROFT HALL, FROM THE SOUTH-EAST

protected by a moat, but there is no trace of this, and the position of the house, being not far from the River Irwell on the east side, does not make the probability of the moat having existed very great.[41]

The Lancashire and Yorkshire Railway from Bolton to Manchester and the Bury Canal both pass close to the house on the north side.[41a]

The entrance to the court is on the east side, and the great hall is at the south end of the west wing, with the former kitchen and scullery at its north end. The chief living rooms are in the south wing, and the north and east wings were occupied by the offices and servants' quarters. The building appears to be of two main dates, but has been very much modernized both inside and out in the middle of the last century, considerable repairs and alterations having taken place

AGECROFT HALL

there about the year 1865-7. There have also been subsequent additions and alterations, the last having taken place in 1894 after a fire which destroyed the roof of the greater portion of the east and south wings.

The house was probably begun at the end of the reign of Henry VII, or the beginning of that of Henry VIII, and much of the carving under the bay windows on the east side is very Gothic in detail, and of excellent design. The south wing and the greater part of the west wing appear to have

[41] A small pond in the grounds to the south-east of the house is sometimes said to be the remains of the moat, but there seems to be no good evidence of this. The course of the Irwell is stated to have been formerly much nearer to the hall, forming a natural protection on that side.

[41a] When the line of railway was first projected between Manchester and Bolton, Agecroft Hall narrowly escaped destruction, the owner, Mr. Buck, offering the most uncompromising opposition; a slight diversion in the contemplated route of the line was made, and the hall preserved intact. See Booker, *Prestwich*, 201.

elevation, which is 101 ft. in length, had formerly only one chimney at the junction of the old and later work of the two wings, but a modern brick chimney added in the north end has had the effect of breaking the straight line where most needed, and giving a balance to the original elevation which it formerly lacked. The windows are for the most part slightly projecting wooden bays carried on carved brackets, the carving along the west wing being mostly original, but in the south side modern copies. Over the entrance archway is a small oriel, the corbel beneath it richly carved with Gothic tracery in a series of radiating panels springing from a shaft which rises from a small blank shield on the crown of the four-centred entrance archway. The projecting sills of the other first-floor windows exhibit equally good carved tracery, and one has the figure of a hart couchant, a fine piece of work.[41b]

The entrance to the court on the east side is under a plain timber arch, 10 ft. 6 in. wide, the old oak door and wicket still being in position. An inner wall, however, has been built, blocking the open way to the court ; the present entrance therefore now only leads into the corridor which runs along the east side of the courtyard. Originally this corridor, which runs round the court on the east and south sides, was an open one carried on wood posts resting on stone bases, but the greater part of it is now inclosed. Its original appearance, however, can still be gathered from the north-east corner of the courtyard, where a length of about 20 ft. still remains as built, forming a very picturesque feature of the inner elevation. The old stone and wood posts are still in position the full length of the east side, the later wall being merely filled in between them, and continue for a distance of about 12 ft. along the south side, opposite the junction of the dining and drawing-rooms. The open corridor may indeed only have extended this far, and the dining-room (which is said to have been the ancient chapel) may belong to the earlier portion of the building. Its present condition is so entirely modern as to make it impossible to say whether this is so or not. The dining-room and drawing-room, however, are clearly of different dates, the division between them consisting of two walls side by side with a small space between, and their floors on different levels. Probably the rebuilding of the south wing was begun from this point westward at some time in the 17th century, and the old chapel converted to its later use at some subsequent date.

The courtyard is of irregular shape, and measures 43 ft. 6 in. across at its widest part from west to east, and 52 ft. from south to north. It presents a great contrast to the outer elevations of the house, the skyline being broken on the west side by three gables, two over the hall and one over the projecting bay formed by the old kitchen. The timber framing of the bay preserves something of the plainness of the garden fronts, but the vertical lines give place to diagonal tracings, and the upper story projects on brackets and a plaster cove. The gables over the hall, however, are richly ornamented with quatrefoil panels, and a panelled cove runs the full length of the hall, at the first-floor line, at a higher level than those of the old kitchen bay line, the lower portion of the wall being

occupied by a long continuous window of fifteen lights on a moulded stone base 3 ft. 6 in. high. The gables are without barge-boards or hip-knobs, being quite plain, with overhanging slates. The only two gables in the building with barge-boards are shown at the ends of the south and east wings facing east and north, which have both been constructed in late years. The north side of the court preserves its old black and white wood and plaster construction, but in the west and south the elevations have been a good deal modernized, though in harmony with the old work, and much of the 'half-timber work' is paint or plaster. The east corridor runs right through the building to an outer door on the north side, and the south corridor leads direct to the great hall. A modern butler's pantry has been added in the south-east corner of the courtyard.

The rooms in the north and east wings, which are 9 ft. 6 in. high, are for the most part unimportant, being still used as the servants' part of the house, the present kitchen being immediately to the north of the entrance. North of the kitchen is a small staircase leading to the upper floor with good 17th-century flat pierced balusters. Another small staircase in the west wing north of the hall also preserves some 17th-century detail, but the main staircase in the south wing is modern. Internally the whole of the south wing is so much modernized as to be of little architectural interest ; it contains the library, drawing-room, and dining-room, with the principal entrance and staircase. In the east window of the dining-room, which, like the oak panelling and other fittings, is modern, is preserved some ancient glass, some of which was formerly in other parts of the house. The initials R.L. (Ralph Langley) occur in several of the lights, either in a lozenge or circle, and sometimes with the Langley crest (a cockatrice). The centre light bears the Royal Arms (France and England) encircled by a garter, and surmounted by a crown, and in other lights are the badge of Edmund of Langley, Duke of York (a falcon in a closed fetter lock), a lion's head erazed gules collared and lined or, a red and a white rose with stalks entwined, and a crown and initials H.E. for Henry VII and Elizabeth of York, and a daisy (root and flower) with the head of a greyhound over. The Langley crest also occurs twice by itself. The drawing-room preserves its original square-framed oak panelling on three sides, and over the north door are four full-length figures and four heads, said to be emblematic of peace and war, originally part of the pulpit in the private chapel.[42] On either side of the same door are carved panels, some with tracery, and others with a variety of linen pattern. The library, which is wholly modernized, has also some fragments of heraldic glass in the window, one showing part of a shield argent, two hunting horns gules, stringed or. The staircase window preserves some old diamond quarries, five of which bear the initials R.L., while on another is scratched the name of William Dauntesey, and the date ' June y° 12, 1645.'

The great hall is 14 ft. in height, and has a flat panelled ceiling divided into four bays by three wide oak beams, and with intermediate moulded ribs. It measures 29 ft. in length and 23 ft. 6 in. in width,

[41b] This has made Booker (*Prestwich*, 200) suppose that the figure is the badge of Richard II, and makes him think the work may date back to the reign of that monarch. But, as he himself allows, the animal has no collar and chain, and there is nothing in the rest of the work to suggest such an early date.

[42] Booker, *Prestwich*, 198.

and is lighted on the east side by the continuous ranges of mullioned and transomed windows already referred to, and has three similar lights in the return to the lobby at the end of the corridor in the southeast corner. In each of the top lights are the initials R.L. with an interlacing pattern between, surmounted by the cockatrice, and in the lower middle light are the arms of Dauntesey with helm, crest, mantling, and scrolls. The walls are mostly panelled to a height of 6 ft. 6 in. The hall appears to have always had a flat ceiling, and there are no signs now of either dais or gallery. The position of the screens is marked by the vestibule and passage on the north side, and the kitchen and pantry have now been made into a sitting-room and smoke-room. Neither of these rooms retains anything of its original appearance except the great twelve-light kitchen window overlooking the courtyard, which occupies the whole of the east side of the room. The fireplace opening, now modernized, is 10 ft. wide, the wall above carried by a beam 12 in. square at a height of 5 ft. 8 in. from the floor.

On the first floor corridors run round the inner sides of the north, east, and south wings, opening to a series of rooms which have little architectural interest. In the south wing the bedroom over the drawing-room, known as the 'panelled room,' preserves its original square oak wainscot mouldings worked in the solid, and contains a fine oak bedstead. Other rooms also contain good oak furniture, though much has been taken away, the house being at present (1910) unoccupied. The rooms in the east range exhibit their timber construction throughout, and their ceilings, together with those on the south side of the house, partly follow the rake of the roof. A small room at the west end of the north wing has a good 17th-century angle fireplace with plaster ornaments and egg-and-dart moulding.

The upper corridors on the east and south appear to have been originally open to the court and carried on posts, forming a kind of upper gallery. A portion of what appears to have been external quatrefoil panelling is still in position on the inner wall at the east end of the south corridor. The appearance of the courtyard as originally erected must have been ex-

ceedingly picturesque, and in marked contrast to the plain work of the outside elevations.

The house contains a valuable collection of paintings, including a so-called portrait of Jane Shore, attributed to Holbein.[42a]

In a deed dated 26 June 1694, and an inventory of the same year,[42b] the following rooms and places at Agecroft Hall are mentioned :—' The great parlor and chamber over it, the hall, the dyneinge roome, the chappell, the chappell chamber, the farther chappell chamber, the greene chamber, the porter's warde, the kitchen, the buttery, the seller and chamber over it, the seller and brewhouse and the chambers over them, the great barn commonly called the new barn, the stable, the garden and orchard behind the garden.'

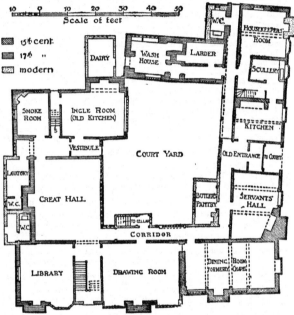

PLAN OF AGECROFT HALL

An old painting of the house preserved at Agecroft shows a long building, either a stable or barn, standing at right angles to the east side of the house at the north end, apparently meant to be some distance away, with a stone wall and gate-piers along the east front. This building is said to have stood until the construction of the railway. The present stables and outbuildings are on the north side of the house, and are all modern.

SHORESWORTH,[43] though the name has long been forgotten, was the detached part of Pendlebury. In 1212 it was held as one oxgang of land by Ellis de Pendlebury in thegnage by a rent of 2s., and of

42a Booker, op. cit. 199.
42b Lancs. and Ches. Antiq. Soc. iv, 214.
43 Chadeswrthe, 1212 ; Shoresworth, 1241 ; Scheresworth, 1276 ; Shorswrth,

1292. A deed quoted in the account of Little Bolton in Pendleton describes land in that hamlet as situate between Shores-

worth Brook and the Millbrook. A century ago three fields were still known as Shoolsworth.

him it was held by the same service by his nephews, or grandsons, Richard, Adam, Henry, and Robert.[44] From these descended one or more families taking the local surname, but no detailed account can be given of them.[45] Early in the 14th century the Radcliffes of Ordsall acquired it, and held possession for several generations.[46] The place-name occurs as late as 1590 in the inquisition after the death of Sir John Radcliffe, who held ' 20 acres of land, &c. in Showersworth in the town of Pendlebury,' but it was then included with Ordsall so far as the service was concerned.[47] On the alienation of the Radcliffe estates in the 17th century it was obtained by Humphrey Chetham,[48] and descended through the Chethams of Smedley and Castleton to Samuel Clowes, who owned it about 1800.

The principal landowners in 1798 were the Rev. John Dauntesey, Thomas William Coke, and Samuel Clowes, whose lands together paid three-fourths of the tax.[49]

A monument to Joseph Goodier of Mode Wheel, Pendlebury, who died in 1854, is in Eccles Church.

In connexion with the Established Church, St. John the Evangelist's, Irlams-o'-th'-Height, was built in 1842 ; the patronage is vested in five trustees.[50] The Bishop of Manchester is patron of Christ Church, built in 1859,[51] and of St. Augustine's, built in 1874 ;[52] the latter has a mission hall—St. Matthew's.

The Wesleyan Methodists have two churches in Pendlebury ; the United Free Methodists also have two, and the Primitive Methodists one.

The Congregationalists began preaching on Sundays in 1819, the population of the place having at that time an evil reputation for profligacy. The first chapel was built in 1821, and a somewhat larger one four years later. The congregation declined, but in 1832 a fresh start was made, and in 1882 a new church was built in Swinton, the old building being used for a school.[53]

A Swedenborgian church was erected at Pendlebury in 1852.

CLIFTON

Clifton, 1184 ; Cliffton, 1278.

This township stretches along the Irwell for some two miles and a half, having a breadth south-westward from the river of three-quarters of a mile. Its area is 1,194½ acres.[1] The highest land, over 300 ft. above sea level, lies at the western end, near the Worsley boundary, and is moss land. The population in 1901 numbered 2,944. The main road from Manchester to Bolton passes through the township, and along it the village of Clifton has sprung up. The Lancashire and Yorkshire Company's railway between the same places also runs through it near the Irwell, and has two stations near the east and west ends, named Clifton and Dixon Fold. Worsley Fold is a hamlet to the east of Clifton village. The Manchester and Bolton Canal passes through part of Clifton, crossing the Irwell. A strip of the New Red Sandstone formation is traceable up to Ringley. All the rest of the township lies upon the Coal Measures.

There are several collieries in the township.

There were in 1666 forty-nine hearths liable to the tax. The largest dwellings were those of Elizabeth Holland and Daniel Gaskell, with six hearths each.[2]

The township is now governed by a parish council.

An urn or 'incense cup' with ashes, &c. was discovered here.[2a]

Robert Ainsworth, the lexicographer, was born at Woodgate in 1660. He kept a school at Bolton, but removed to London, teaching at Bethnal Green and Hackney. His *Latin Dictionary* was published in 1736 ; and he wrote some smaller works. He died in 1743 and was buried at Poplar.[3]

MANOR The earliest record of *CLIFTON* by name is that in the Pipe Roll of 1183–4, the sheriff giving account of 8s., the issues of Clifton, which had belonged to Hugh Putrell, outlawed ;[4] in the following half-year 4s. was received.[5] Hugh was probably pardoned, for a few years later Richard, 'the heir of Clifton,' son of Hugh the Hunter, made grants to Cockersand Abbey.[6] 'The heir of Richard de Clifton' paid half a mark to the scutage in 1205–6.[7] He was probably the Robert de Clifton who in 1212 held four oxgangs in Clifton of the king in chief by a rent of 8s. ; at this time Roger Gernet held three of the oxgangs of Robert by

[44] *Lancs. Inq. and Extents,* i, 68. Ellis de Pendlebury had a brother Richard (*Cockersand Chartul.* ii, 725), and these may have been his four sons. By 1219 one of the parts into which it was divided seems to have escheated to the Pendleburys ; *Fine R. Excerpts,* i, 38.

[45] Hugh de Shoresworth in 1241, as tenant of the fourth part of an oxgang of land there, had his title recognized, but agreed to pay Richard son of William de Bolton 2s. a year ; *Final Conc.* i, 80. It was probably the latter who, as Richard son of William, at the same time acquired an annual rent of 1s. from Richard son of Robert, the holder of another fourth part; ibid. i, 87. In 1276 Hugh son of Alexander the Mey claimed a messuage and acre of land from Hugh son of Adam de Shoresworth ; De Banco R. 13, m. 32. In 1292 Avina widow of Roger son of Loueote was non-suited in her claim against Adam the Smith and Isabel his wife for a tenement in Shoresworth ; Assize R. 408, m. 44. Margery widow of John de Shoresworth occurs in 1292 ; De Banco R. 92, m. 113 ; Assize R. 408, m. 72 d.

Others of the family will be found mentioned in the accounts of neighbouring townships. The most notable is the Margaret de Shoresworth who married Henry de Worsley, and was mother of Thurstan de Holland, ancestor of the Denton family ; see *Lancs. Inq. p.m.* (Chet. Soc.), i, 150.

[46] The particulars of the acquisition are not known. Richard de Hulton was in 1324 returned as paying 7s. 7d. (?) for an oxgang of land in Shoresworth ; Duchy of Lanc. Rent. and Surv. 379, m. 13 ; but John de Radcliffe the elder, of Ordsall, appears to have held the oxgang in Shoresworth by the old service of 2s. about the same time ; Dods. MSS. cxxxi, fol. 38. The Hulton and Radcliffe estates in Pendlebury in 1316 and 1337 respectively may have relation to Shoresworth ; *Final Conc.* ii, 23, 103. Henry, Earl of Lancaster, in 1341 demanded from John de Radcliffe a messuage, &c. in Pendlebury which Robert de Shoresworth had held of him and which ought to revert to the earl ; De Banco R. 328, m. 123.

In 1380 Richard de Radcliffe was found to have held Shoresworth by 2s. rent. There were a messuage and 60 acres of land, worth 60s., and 2 acres of meadow worth 4s. ; *Lancs. Inq. p.m.* (Chet. Soc.), i, 8. In 1422 it was called a

' manor,' and again in 1498 ; ibid. i, 148; ii, 124.

[47] Duchy of Lanc. Inq. p.m. xv, no. 45.

[48] Humphrey Chetham (Chet. Soc.), 114, 247 ; Sholsworth otherwise Suzeworth.

[49] Land tax returns at Preston.

[50] See *End. Char. Rep.* for Eccles, 1904, p. 46.

[51] For district ibid. *Lond. Gaz.* 15 Oct. 1861.

[52] For district ibid. 20 Oct. 1874 ; *End. Char. Rep.* 44–7. This church is considered one of the finest works of the late G. F. Bodley, the architect.

[53] Nightingale, *Lancs. Nonconf.* v, 16–21.

[1] 1,267 acres, including 45 of inland water, and 72 of an unnamed area ; *Census Rep.* 1901.

[2] Subs. R. Lancs. bdle. 250, no. 9.

[2a] *V.C.H. Lancs.* i, 252.

[3] See account in *Dict. Nat. Biog.*

[4] Farrer, *Lancs. Pipe R.* 52. For Hugh Putrell or Pultrell see further in the account of Worsley. [5] Ibid. 54.

[6] *Cockersand Chartul.* (Chet. Soc.), ii, 724. By one charter he gave 2 acres of the demesne, with a toft sufficient for building houses. By another he gave 3 acres adjoining Asseley Ford.

[7] *Lancs. Pipe R.* 205.

8s., thus discharging the service due from the whole.[8] Hugh son of Robert was in possession in 1246,[9] and seems to have left a family of daughters—Ellen, Alice, and Margery being named in 1276-8.[10]

About this time the manor passed to the Traffords, apparently by Alice's marriage,[11] and descended in this family for half a century or more.[12] In 1346 William son of Thurstan de Holland and Roger son of Richard de Tyldesley held one plough-land in Clifton by a rent of 8s.[13] Shortly afterwards William de Holland had possession of the whole.[14] He was succeeded by his son Otes,[15] and by another Otes living about 1440.[16] This last had a son and heir William,

who died in 1498, and his son Ralph being childless Clifton passed to a cousin, William Holland son of Thomas son of Otes.[17] The new lord, or perhaps another William, died in 1521 or 1522,[18] leaving, among others, sons named Thomas and John. The elder's heir was his daughter Eleanor,[19] who married Ralph Slade, and retained the manor till her death in 1613.[20] It then went to John Holland's grandson Thomas,[21] whose estates were sequestered by the Parliamentary authorities during the Civil War for his own delinquency and that of his son William, who had served with the king's forces at Lathom and elsewhere.[22]

[8] Lancs. Inq. and Extents (Rec. Soc. Lancs. and Ches.), i, 69. The rent of 8s. continued to be paid for Clifton (ibid. 138, 301), but later the vill was assessed as one plough-land.

Of the Gernet holding nothing further appears, but there may have been a connexion by marriage with the Masseys (ibid. 119), so that Henry son of Hamlet joined as defendant in a Clifton suit of 1278 mentioned below, may represent the Roger Gernet of 1212.

[9] David son and heir of Richard de Hulton recovered from him 4 acres in Clifton ; Assize R. 404, m. 13.

[10] Alice widow of Hugh de Clifton claimed dower in 1277 against Henry de Trafford and Alice daughter of Hugh ; she also made claims against Robert son of Beatrice, and Ellen and Margery daughters of Hugh de Clifton ; De Banco R. 21, m. 18, 82 d. In the former case Robert de Brumscales and Maud his wife were called to warrant, and Margery and Cecily, Maud's sisters, were also summoned.

Alice daughter of Hugh de Clifton was prosecuting a suit in 1292 ; Assize R. 408, m. 32, 44. She granted to Alice daughter of William the Clerk of Eccles the house and grange, with adjoining land, formerly held by Diota, Hugh's mother, at the rent of a pair of white gloves ; Ellesmere D. no. 223. Alice daughter of William the Clerk was defendant in a Clifton plea in 1274 ; De Banco R. 5, m. 102.

[11] See the preceding note. Alice de Eccles complained in 1278 that she had been disseised of her common of pasture in Clifton by Henry de Strafford (Trafford) and Henry son of Hamlet. The former Henry stated in reply that Clifton was of his fee and demesne and that he approved for himself what he liked, by the Provision of Merton. The jury found that Alice had a several tenement, and that by Henry's improvement she had lost free entry and egress ; she therefore recovered and damages of 12d. were allowed ; Assize R. 1238, m. 32 ; 1239, m. 37.

Henry de Trafford in 1280 purchased land in Clifton from Hugh the Mey and Alice his wife ; Final Conc. (Rec. Soc. Lancs. and Ches.), i, 157.

[12] In 1292 Richard son of Henry de Trafford claimed lands in Crompton, Edgeworth, Quarlton, and Clifton against his brother Henry, and against Lora his father's widow ; Assize R. 408, m. 5, 36. The settlement effected did not touch Clifton ; Final Conc. i, 170. It seems to have been the younger Henry who was the husband of Alice.

In 1307 the manor of Clifton was by Henry de Trafford settled upon his sons in succession—Henry, Richard, Robert,

Ralph, and Thomas ; ibid. i, 210. These were probably younger sons.

In 1324 Henry de Trafford held a plough-land in Clifton by the yearly service of 8s. ; Dods. MSS. cxxxi, fol. 38. This Henry died about ten years later.

In 1338 the fine of the township for the goods of Henry son of Henry de Trafford, a fugitive, was 40d. ; Coram Rege R. 312, m. 50.

[13] Add. MS. 32103, fol. 146 ; they obtained it by marrying respectively Margery and Cecily, daughters and co-heirs of Henry de Trafford, i.e. Henry son of Henry.

[14] In 1353 William de Holland prosecuted William Bridde for cutting down his trees at Clifton ; Assize R. 435, m. 11. In the following year Thurstan and William de Holland were plaintiffs ; Duchy of Lanc. Assize R. 3, m. vi.

[15] Thurstan de Holland, the father of William, seems to have been the ancestor of the Denton family. William de Holland was son of Alice de Pusshe ; he and his son Otes are mentioned in 1368 ; Final Conc. ii, 165, 174. Otes son of William de Holland occurs in 1397 ; Towneley's MS. CC (Chet. Lib.), no. 854.

[16] Extent of 1445-6 ; Duchy of Lanc. Knights' fees, 2/20. He held one plough-land in socage, rendering 8s. yearly.

Ralph son of Otes Holland of Clifton was with others charged with trespassing in the wood of Sir John Pilkington in 1444, and taking three hawks, worth £20 ; Pal. of Lanc. Plea R. 6, m. 5b.

[17] Lancs. Inq. p.m. (Chet. Soc.), ii, 134-7 ; Dep. Keeper's Rep. xxxix, App. 539. The succession is stated also in Pal. of Lanc. Plea R. 119, m. 11.

[18] Duchy of Lanc. Inq. p.m. v, 49. He was seised of the manor of Clifton with its appurtenances, and of lands in Clifton, Manchester, Swinton, Leyland, and Farington, and in 1517 made a settlement, providing for the dower of Alice his wife and for his younger children. Thomas the heir was sixteen years of age at the taking of the inquisition, the date of which is uncertain—'Saturday after Low Sunday, 14 Hen. VIII.'.

An agreement respecting the marriage of their children was made in 1517 between William Holland of Clifton and Robert Langley of Agecroft ; Agecroft D. no. 97.

At the Court of Clifton held in 1514 the bounds were thus described : Beginning at the Fennes stock at the end of Redford hedge and at the end of Cheping clough, and so following up Nordenbrook unto amends the Tynde oak, and so up the Fether snape as the water falls from the head, and so in again unto the [Qwab] head, and from thence unto the Black dyke, following this to the Butted

The Holland family do not appear to have been able to overcome their losses. The manor was sold a number of times.[23] It afterwards came into possession of the Heathcotes, Captain Justinian Heathcote Edwards-Heathcote being the lord of it.[24] The hall was sold to Lawrence Gaskell in 1652, and was his family's chief residence for some generations. It has descended regularly to the present owner, the Rt. Hon. Charles G. Milnes Gaskell of Thornes House, near Wakefield.[25] About 1800 Ellis

GASKELL. *Gules a saltire vair between two annulets in pale and as many lions passant in fesse or.*

Lever, but the marriage had not taken place. Besides the mansion reservation was made of certain liberties for digging for coal and cannel, and carrying away from the mines there open.

As to the delinquency nothing is stated about the father's share, but William Holland had stayed some days in the garrison at Lathom House, and was one of the foot company under Captain Rawstorne ; he had asked for a place of command. He had also been seen in a troop of horse at Wigan, when that town was kept by the Earl of Derby against the Parliament.

[23] In 1671 Humphrey Trafford and Elizabeth his wife made a settlement of the manor of Clifton and various lands, &c., there and in Manchester, Pendlebury, and Leyland ; Pal. of Lanc. Feet of F. bdle. 186, m. 138. The wife was the daughter and heir of William Holland of Clifton, but her children did not sur-

vive ; Stretford Chapel (Chet. Soc.), ii, 142. The estate appears to have been mortgaged to James Butler and others about 1685 and eventually sold ; Pal. of Lanc. Feet of F. bdle. 215, m. 57 ; Exch. Deps. (Rec. Soc. Lancs. and Ches.), 73, 75, 76. In 1731 and 1743 it was the property of Tobias Britland ; Pal. of Lanc. Feet of F. bdle. 305, m. 112 ; 331, m. 4. He died in 1750 and ordered his estates to be sold for the benefit of his daughters ; Earwaker, East Ches. ii, 148.

In 1687 Holland paid 6s. and Daniel Gaskell 2s. 3d. to the bailiff of the wapentake for Clifton.

In 1777 Richard Edensor and Richard Ireland paid the Duchy 5s. 11¾d. for the manor of Clifton, while James Gaskell paid 2s. 6d. for Clifton Hall ; Duchy of Lanc. Rentals, 14/25. The total is rather more than the old rent of 8s.

[24] For pedigree see Burke, Landed Gentry.

Fletcher, coal proprietor, acquired an estate in Clifton ; he was succeeded by his son Jacob, whose daughter, Mrs. Wynne Corrie, is the present owner.[26] In 1786 Sir John Heathcote owned nearly two-thirds of Clifton, Daniel Gaskell having the remainder.[27]

Clifton Hall stands close to the Clifton railway station and is a red brick house of plain 18th-century type. During its occupation as a private asylum in the 19th century it underwent considerable alterations. About 1825 Benjamin Heywood, one of the founders of Heywood's Bank, lived here.

St. Anne's was built in 1874 for the Established Church ; Mrs. Wynne Corrie is patron.[28] It has a mission chapel—St. Thomas's.

[25] Information of Mr. Milnes Gaskell. For pedigrees of the family see Foster's Yorkshire Ped. and Burke, Landed Gentry, Gaskell of Thornes House ; also Lancs. and Ches. Antiq. Soc. iii, 170, and Baker, Mem. of a Dissenting Chapel, 69, from which it appears that the Gaskells were worshippers at Cross Street Chapel, Manchester. There is a short notice of the family in Booker's Prestwich, 225.

[26] Ellis Fletcher was living at Clifton House in 1824. He died in 1834. His eldest son Jacob entered Brasenose College, Oxford, in 1807, aged 16 ; Foster, Alumni ; see also Manch. School Reg. (Chet. Soc.), ii, 22, 23. For Jacob's daughter and heir, now Mrs. Wynne Corrie, see Burke, Family Rec. 181, and the account of Little Hulton.

[27] Land tax returns at Preston.

[28] For district assigned see Lond. Gaz. 5 Feb. 1865.

Lightning Source UK Ltd.
Milton Keynes UK
UKOW06f1917171217
314644UK00006B/172/P